International Directory of

COMPANY
HISTORIES

International Directory of
COMPANY
HISTORIES

VOLUME 92

Editor

Tina Grant

ST. JAMES PRESS
A part of Gale, Cengage Learning

Detroit • New York • San Francisco • New Haven, Conn • Waterville, Maine • London

LIBRARY OF CONGRESS CATALOG NUMBER 89-190943
ISBN-13: 978-1-55862-613-3
ISBN-10: 1-55862-613-1

This title is also available as an e-book
ISBN-13: 978-1-4144-2976-2   ISBN-10: 1-4144-2976-2
Contact your Gale, a part of Cengage Learning sales representative for ordering information.

BRITISH LIBRARY CATALOGUING IN PUBLICATION DATA
International directory of company histories, Vol. 92
Tina Grant
33.87409

Printed in the United States of America
1 2 3 4 5 6 7 12 11 10 09 08

Contents

Preface

The St. James Press series *The International Directory of Company Histories* (*IDCH*) is intended for reference use by students, business people, librarians, historians, economists, investors, job candidates, and others who seek to learn more about the historical development of the world's most important companies. To date, *IDCH* has covered over 9,000 companies in 92 volumes.

INCLUSION CRITERIA

Most companies chosen for inclusion in *IDCH* have achieved a minimum of US$25 million in annual sales and are leading influences in their industries or geographical locations. Companies may be publicly held, private, or nonprofit. State-owned companies that are important in their industries and that may operate much like public or private companies also are included. Wholly owned subsidiaries and divisions are profiled if they meet the requirements for inclusion. Entries on companies that have had major changes since they were last profiled may be selected for updating.

The *IDCH* series highlights 25% private and nonprofit companies, and features updated entries on approximately 35 companies per volume.

ENTRY FORMAT

Each entry begins with the company's legal name; the address of its headquarters; its telephone, toll-free, and fax numbers; and its web site. A statement of public, private, state, or parent ownership follows. A company with a legal name in both English and the language of its headquarters country is listed by the English name, with the native-language name in parentheses.

The company's founding or earliest incorporation date, the number of employees, and the most recent available sales figures follow. Sales figures are given in local currencies with equivalents in U.S. dollars. For some private companies, sales figures are estimates and indicated by the abbreviation *est.* The entry lists the exchanges on which the company's stock is traded and its ticker symbol, as well as the company's NAIC codes.

Entries generally contain a *Company Perspectives* box which provides a short summary of the company's mission, goals, and ideals; a *Key Dates* box highlighting milestones in the company's history; lists of *Principal Subsidiaries, Principal Divisions, Principal Operating Units, Principal Competitors*; and articles for *Further Reading*.

American spelling is used throughout *IDCH*, and the word "billion" is used in its U.S. sense of one thousand million.

SOURCES

Entries have been compiled from publicly accessible sources both in print and on the Internet such as general and academic periodicals, books, and annual reports, as well as material supplied by the companies themselves.

CUMULATIVE INDEXES

IDCH contains three indexes: the **Index to Companies**, which provides an alphabetical index to companies discussed in the text as well as to companies profiled, the **Index to Industries**, which allows researchers to locate companies by their principal industry, and the **Geographic Index**, which lists companies alphabetically by the country of their headquarters. The indexes are cumulative and specific instructions for using them are found immediately preceding each index.

SUGGESTIONS WELCOME

Comments and suggestions from users of *IDCH* on any aspect of the product as well as suggestions for companies to be included or updated are cordially invited. Please write:

The Editor
International Directory of Company Histories
St. James Press
Gale, Cengage Learning
27500 Drake Rd.
Farmington Hills, Michigan 48331-3535

St. James Press does not endorse any of the companies or products mentioned in this series. Companies appearing in the *International Directory of Company Histories* were selected without reference to their wishes and have in no way endorsed their entries.

Notes on Contributors

Gerald E. Brennan
Writer and musician based in Germany.

M. L. Cohen
Novelist, business writer, and researcher living in Paris.

Ed Dinger
Writer and editor based in Bronx, New York.

Paul R. Greenland
Illinois-based writer and researcher; author of two books and former senior editor of a national business magazine; contributor to *The Encyclopedia of Chicago History, The Encyclopedia of Religion*, and the *Encyclopedia of American Industries*.

Robert Halasz
Former editor in chief of *World Progress* and *Funk & Wagnalls New Encyclopedia Yearbook*; author, *The U.S. Marines* (Millbrook Press, 1993).

Evelyn Hauser
Researcher, writer and marketing specialist based in Germany.

Frederick C. Ingram
Writer based in South Carolina.

Micah L. Issit
Philadelphia-based writer, historian, ecologist and humorist.

Carrie Rothburd
Writer and editor specializing in corporate profiles, academic texts, and academic journal articles.

Daniel Thurs
Writer and researcher specializing in issues related to science and technology.

Frank Uhle
Ann Arbor-based writer; movie projectionist, disc jockey, and staff member of *Psychotronic Video* magazine.

Ellen D. Wernick
Florida-based writer and editor.

A. Woodward
Wisconsin-based writer.

List of Abbreviations

¥ Japanese yen
£ United Kingdom pound
$ United States dollar

A

AB Aktiebolag (Finland, Sweden)
AB Oy Aktiebolag Osakeyhtiot (Finland)
A.E. Anonimos Eteria (Greece)
AED Emirati dirham
AG Aktiengesellschaft (Austria, Germany, Switzerland, Liechtenstein)
aG auf Gegenseitigkeit (Austria, Germany)
A.m.b.a. Andelsselskab med begraenset ansvar (Denmark)
A.O. Anonim Ortaklari/Ortakligi (Turkey)
ApS Amparteselskab (Denmark)
ARS Argentine peso
A.S. Anonim Sirketi (Turkey)
A/S Aksjeselskap (Norway)
A/S Aktieselskab (Denmark, Sweden)
Ay Avoinyhtio (Finland)
ATS Austrian shilling
AUD Australian dollar
ApS Amparteselskab (Denmark)
Ay Avoinyhtio (Finland)

B

B.A. Buttengewone Aansprakeiijkheid (Netherlands)
BEF Belgian franc

BHD Bahraini dinar
Bhd. Berhad (Malaysia, Brunei)
BRL Brazilian real
B.V. Besloten Vennootschap (Belgium, Netherlands)

C

C.A. Compania Anonima (Ecuador, Venezuela)
CAD Canadian dollar
C. de R.L. Compania de Responsabilidad Limitada (Spain)
CEO Chief Executive Officer
CFO Chief Financial Officer
CHF Swiss franc
Cia. Companhia (Brazil, Portugal)
Cia. Compania (Latin America (except Brazil), Spain)
Cia. Compagnia (Italy)
Cie. Compagnie (Belgium, France, Luxembourg, Netherlands)
CIO Chief Information Officer
CLP Chilean peso
CNY Chinese yuan
Co. Company
COO Chief Operating Officer
Coop. Cooperative
COP Colombian peso
Corp. Corporation
C. por A. Compania por Acciones (Dominican Republic)
CPT Cuideachta Phoibi Theoranta (Republic of Ireland)

CRL Companhia a Responsabilidao Limitida (Portugal, Spain)
C.V. Commanditaire Vennootschap (Netherlands, Belgium)
CZK Czech koruna

D

D&B Dunn & Bradstreet
DEM German deutsche mark
Div. Division (United States)
DKK Danish krone
DZD Algerian dinar

E

EC Exempt Company (Arab countries)
Edms. Bpk. Eiendoms Beperk (South Africa)
EEK Estonian Kroon
eG eingetragene Genossenschaft (Germany)
EGMBH Eingetragene Genossenschaft mit beschraenkter Haftung (Austria, Germany)
EGP Egyptian pound
Ek For Ekonomisk Forening (Sweden)
EP Empresa Portuguesa (Portugal)
E.P.E. Etema Pemorismenis Evthynis (Greece)
ESOP Employee Stock Options and Ownership
ESP Spanish peseta
Et(s). Etablissement(s) (Belgium,

France, Luxembourg)
eV eingetragener Verein (Germany)
EUR euro

F
FIM Finnish markka
FRF French franc

G
G.I.E. Groupement d'Interet Economique (France)
gGmbH gemeinnutzige Gesellschaft mit beschraenkter Haftung (Austria, Germany, Switzerland)
G.I.E. Groupement d'Interet Economique (France)
GmbH Gesellschaft mit beschraenkter Haftung (Austria, Germany, Switzerland)
GRD Greek drachma
GWA Gewerbte Amt (Austria, Germany)

H
HB Handelsbolag (Sweden)
HF Hlutafelag (Iceland)
HKD Hong Kong dollar
HUF Hungarian forint

I
IDR Indonesian rupiah
IEP Irish pound
ILS new Israeli shekel
Inc. Incorporated (United States, Canada)
INR Indian rupee
IPO Initial Public Offering
I/S Interesentselskap (Norway)
I/S Interessentselskab (Denmark)
ISK Icelandic krona
ITL Italian lira

J
JMD Jamaican dollar
JOD Jordanian dinar

K
KB Kommanditbolag (Sweden)
KES Kenyan schilling
Kft Korlatolt Felelossegu Tarsasag (Hungary)
KG Kommanditgesellschaft (Austria, Germany, Switzerland)
KGaA Kommanditgesellschaft auf Aktien (Austria, Germany, Switzerland)
KK Kabushiki Kaisha (Japan)
KPW North Korean won
KRW South Korean won
K/S Kommanditselskab (Denmark)
K/S Kommandittselskap (Norway)
KWD Kuwaiti dinar
Ky Kommandiitiyhtio (Finland)

L
LBO Leveraged Buyout
Lda. Limitada (Spain)
L.L.C. Limited Liability Company (Arab countries, Egypt, Greece, United States)
L.L.P. Limited Partnership (United States)
L.P. Limited Partnership (Canada, South Africa, United Kingdom, United States)
Ltd. Limited
Ltda. Limitada (Brazil, Portugal)
Ltee. Limitee (Canada, France)
LUF Luxembourg franc

M
mbH mit beschraenkter Haftung (Austria, Germany)
Mij. Maatschappij (Netherlands)
MUR Mauritian rupee
MXN Mexican peso
MYR Malaysian ringgit

N
N.A. National Association (United States)
NGN Nigerian naira
NLG Netherlands guilder
NOK Norwegian krone
N.V. Naamloze Vennootschap (Belgium, Netherlands)
NZD New Zealand dollar

O
OAO Otkrytoe Aktsionernoe Obshchestve (Russia)
OHG Offene Handelsgesellschaft (Austria, Germany, Switzerland)
OMR Omani rial
OOO Obschestvo s Ogranichennoi Otvetstvennostiu (Russia)
OOUR Osnova Organizacija Udruzenog Rada (Yugoslavia)

Oy Osakeyhtî (Finland)

P
P.C. Private Corp. (United States)
PEN Peruvian Nuevo Sol
PHP Philippine peso
PKR Pakistani rupee
P/L Part Lag (Norway)
PLC Public Limited Co. (United Kingdom, Ireland)
P.L.L.C. Professional Limited Liability Corporation (United States)
PLN Polish zloty
P.T. Perusahaan/Perseroan Terbatas (Indonesia)
PTE Portuguese escudo
Pte. Private (Singapore)
Pty. Proprietary (Australia, South Africa, United Kingdom)
Pvt. Private (India, Zimbabwe)
PVBA Personen Vennootschap met Beperkte Aansprakelijkheid (Belgium)

Q
QAR Qatar riyal

R
REIT Real Estate Investment Trust
RMB Chinese renminbi
Rt Reszvenytarsasag (Hungary)
RUB Russian ruble

S
S.A. Société Anonyme (Arab countries, Belgium, France, Jordan, Luxembourg, Switzerland)
S.A. Sociedad Anónima (Latin America [except Brazil], Spain, Mexico)
S.A. Sociedades Anônimas (Brazil, Portugal)
SAA Societe Anonyme Arabienne (Arab countries)
S.A.C. Sociedad Anonima Comercial (Latin America [except Brazil])
S.A.C.I. Sociedad Anonima Comercial e Industrial (Latin America [except Brazil])
S.A.C.I.y.F. Sociedad Anonima Comercial e Industrial y Financiera (Latin America [except Brazil])

S.A. de C.V. Sociedad Anonima de Capital Variable Mexico)

SAK Societe Anonyme Kuweitienne (Arab countries)

SAL Societe Anonyme Libanaise (Arab countries)

SAO Societe Anonyme Omanienne (Arab countries)

SAQ Societe Anonyme Qatarienne (Arab countries)

SAR Saudi riyal

S.A.R.L. Sociedade Anonima de Responsabilidade Limitada (Brazil, Portugal)

S.A.R.L. Société à Responsabilité Limitée (France, Belgium, Luxembourg)

S.A.S. Societá in Accomandita Semplice (Italy)

S.A.S. Societe Anonyme Syrienne (Arab countries)

S.C. Societe en Commandite (Belgium, France, Luxembourg)

S.C.A. Societe Cooperativa Agricole (France, Italy, Luxembourg)

S.C.I. Sociedad Cooperativa Ilimitada (Spain)

S.C.L. Sociedad Cooperativa Limitada (Spain)

S.C.R.L. Societe Cooperative a Responsabilite Limitee (Belgium)

Sdn. Bhd. Sendirian Berhad (Malaysia)

SEK Swedish krona

SGD Singapore dollar

Sdn. Bhd. Sendirian Berhad (Malaysia)

S.L. Sociedad Limitada (Latin America (except Brazil), Portugal, Spain)

S/L Salgslag (Norway)

S.N.C. Société en Nom Collectif (France)

Soc. Sociedad (Latin America (except Brazil), Spain)

Soc. Sociedade (Brazil, Portugal)

Soc. Societa (Italy)

S.p.A. Società per Azioni (Italy)

Sp. z.o.o. Spólka z ograniczona odpowiedzialnoscia (Poland)

S.R.L. Sociedad de Responsabilidad Limitada (Spain, Mexico, Latin America [except Brazil])

S.R.L. Società a Responsabilità Limitata (Italy)

S.R.O. Spolecnost s Rucenim Omezenym (Czechoslovakia

S.S.K. Sherkate Sahami Khass (Iran)

Ste. Societe (France, Belgium, Luxembourg, Switzerland)

Ste. Cve. Societe Cooperative(Belgium)

S.V. Samemwerkende Vennootschap (Belgium)

S.Z.R.L. Societe Zairoise a Responsabilite Limitee (Zaire)

T

THB Thai baht

TND Tunisian dinar

TRL Turkish lira

TWD new Taiwan dollar

U

U.A. Uitgesloten Aansporakeiijkheid (Netherlands)

u.p.a. utan personligt ansvar (Sweden)

V

VAG Verein der Arbeitgeber (Austria, Germany)

VEB Venezuelan bolivar

VERTR Vertriebs (Austria, Germany)

VND Vietnamese dong

V.O.f. Vennootschap onder firma (Netherlands)

VVAG Versicherungsverein auf Gegenseitigkeit (Austria, Germany)

W–Z

WA Wettelika Aansprakalikhaed (Netherlands)

WLL With Limited Liability (Bahrain, Kuwait, Qatar, Saudi Arabia)

YK Yugen Kaisha (Japan)

ZAO Zakrytoe Aktsionernoe Obshchestve (Russia)

ZAR South African rand

ZMK Zambian kwacha

ZWD Zimbabwean dollar

Ajegroup S.A.

Avenida La Paz Lt. 30
Lima, 15
Peru
Telephone: (51 1) 371-1812
Web site: http://www.ajegroup.com

Private Corporation
Founded: 1988 as Industrias Añaños
Employees: not available
Sales: $800 million (2006 est.)
NAIC: 311411 Frozen Fruit, Juice, and Vegetable Processing; 312111 Soft Drink Manufacturers; 312112 Bottled Water Manufacturing; 312120 Breweries

■ ■ ■

Ajegroup S.A., a Peruvian-based beverage company, produces, markets, and sells, through its subsidiaries, carbonated soft drinks, fruit juices, beer, and water. In only 20 years Ajegroup has made its mark, challenging the Coca-Cola Co. and PepsiCo, Inc., throughout Latin America. By offering beverages similar to but lower priced than those marketed by the two giants, Ajegroup, best known for its Kola Real and Big Cola soft drinks, has won the allegiance of millions of thirsty customers from Peru north to Mexico. The company has also established an Asian presence and has entered the beer business in Peru.

PRODUCING AND SELLING SOFT DRINKS CHEAPLY: 1988–98

Eduardo Añaños and his wife, Mirta Jerí de Añaños, had fled their family farm in southern Peru by 1988, taking refuge from the Maoist group Sendero Luminoso (Shining Path) in the nearby city of Ayacucho. The insurgents were slowly strangling the economy of this Andean highland community by such means as hijacking Coca-Cola trucks. Sensing an opportunity, the couple and their five sons entered the soda business, borrowing $30,000 on their property. Jorge, the eldest son and an agricultural engineer, developed the formula for the main ingredients of the cola drink, which was sold in recycled beer bottles with the labels hand pasted. Another account credits another son, Carlos, a chemist, with developing the "secret formula." The product, Kola Real, proved a hit with the townspeople.

Four of the five brothers soon decided the business could be taken elsewhere. They opened a second plant in Huancayo in 1991 and a third in Bagua in 1993. Industrias Añaños, as the business was then called, next entered northern Peru at Chiclayo, Trujillo, Tumbes, and Piura, and in 1994 opened its first plant on the Pacific coast, at Sullana, near the northern border, from which it exported into Ecuador. In 1997 the company entered Lima, gaining attention by selling its soft drinks as low as half the price of the leading brands. In Peru these were not Coke and Pepsi, but Coke and Inca Kola, which formed an alliance in 1999. By late 2001 Kola Real had about 10 percent of the Peruvian market for soft drinks and sales of about $30 million a year.

KEY DATES

1988: Eduardo Añaños and his wife begin making soft drinks in Ayacucho, Peru.
1994: Industrias Añaños has plants in eight cities.
1997: The company enters Lima, Peru's capital, underselling name brand soft drinks.
1999: Industrias Añaños opens its first plant outside Peru, in Venezuela.
2002: The company begins operations in Mexico.
2005: The company, now called Ajegroup, has 15 plants in various Latin American countries.
2006: Ajegroup enters Asia with a plant in Thailand.
2007: The company's Peruvian subsidiary introduces Ajegroup's first beer; Ajegroup has 22 production plants in 13 countries.

The two big brands were facing a challenge in the form of what became known in Latin America as B-brands: soft drinks—not necessarily colas—produced and sold inexpensively by smaller companies. Their production costs were much lower because they did not have to pay royalties to (usually foreign based) brand owners. Putting the product in plastic rather than glass bottles also kept costs low. When these receptacles became available in the 1990s they not only proved to be a less expensive option than glass but also could be made larger in size to achieve economy of scale. Marketing was minimal in comparison with the brand leaders. These savings were passed on to the consumer; in Peru, Industrias Añaños and two other B-brand companies were, in 2001, selling half-liter bottles of their beverages to supermarkets and convenience stores at more than 40 percent below the price of the leading brands.

Starting out on a shoestring, the Añaños family members were neither inclined to spread their money around or go into debt. They obtained capital for expansion not from banks but from their suppliers and their own profits. In their business model, the key was the distribution system. Thirty-to-fifty-ton trucks owned by independent contractors carried the products in cases from the bottling plant to distribution centers, where smaller vehicles were loaded for delivery to the company's numerous points of sale. These, too, were operated by independent contractors who provided their own vehicles, often small pickups, and, given the realities of the Peruvian economy, were easy to find and easy to hire. Salesmen as well as deliverymen, they worked on commission, paid for the cases they carried, and could not return the ones that they did not sell.

Plant locations were likely to be in rundown industrial parks where sites were vacant and rents were low. Advertising was so limited that for some time the marketing personnel consisted of two sign painters putting up wall murals with the Kola Real logo. When Industrias Añaños finally began advertising on television, it hired poorly paid freelancers who were said to have produced inferior quality commercials. Executives and managers, too, received salaries much below industry standards. Furthermore, the company was not interested in sponsoring big attractions such as soccer's America Cup, but rather only a few small local events.

EXPANDING NORTHWARD: 1999–2004

Industrias Añaños made its first move outside Peru in 1999, when it spent $4 million to open in Valencia, Venezuela, with a plant capable of turning out 30 million liters a year. By 2003 this investment had reached $12 million to $15 million. The company was distributing Kola Real and a second brand, Big Cola, in all of Venezuela, and had reached 12 percent market share, its original objective. Ángel Añaños, the company's president, told Lucien O. Chauvin of *Beverage World,* "We are not interested in being market leaders. Our goal is to establish a solid share and maintain that." Ecuador was the next country to house an Añaños plant, in Michala. By 2003, however, the company was nearing completion of a $3 million bottling plant in Guayaquil, the country's largest city. Kola Real and another Añaños brand, Sabor de Oro, said to look and taste somewhat like Inca Kola, had by then carved out an 8 percent market share. According to the company's figures in 2004, its market share had reached 17 and 12 percent, respectively, in these two countries. In Peru, where Kola Real was available in five flavors, it claimed 19 percent.

The Añaños family had its eyes on a much bigger prize, Mexico, by far the largest Spanish-American country and a market for soft drinks second only to the United States. Even the poorest Mexican families directed an average of 7.3 percent of their spending to carbonated beverages, according to a 2005 survey. Carlos and Arturo Añaños were sent in 2002 to oversee the operation, which was based in a new plant in an industrial park outside Puebla, less than two hours by motor vehicle from Mexico City. They began with a single product, Big Cola in an economy sized 2.6-liter bottle. Created by their brother Ángel, a chemical engineer, Big Cola's syrup had a less citric flavor than Kola Real and ingredients, including unrefined brown sugar, intended to make it intermediate in sweetness between Pepsi and Coke.

Once again, costs were kept low, with very few people at the no-frills corporate headquarters and not much in the way of advertising. Some 600 trucks were leased to haul Big Cola from the Puebla-area plant to 24 distribution centers, from which 800 freelance sales personnel labored to distribute the product to 100,000 points of sale ranging from supermarkets to tiny country stores and tortilla stands. Within two years the company, by that time renamed Ajegroup (combining the prefixes of Añaños and Jerí), had won about 5 percent of the Mexican soft drink market through its Ajemex subsidiary. It was offering Big Cola and First, a grapefruit flavored soda, in three sizes, including a 3.3-liter jumbo bottle. Pepsi Cola had been forced to cut its prices by 15 percent, and some of Coca-Cola's 16 bottlers, which dominated the industry in Mexico, had followed suit.

Coca-Cola did not take this incursion lying down. Some of its salespeople threatened to stop deliveries to retailers who had Big Cola on their shelves. A federal commission ruled that some of Coke's practices, such as exclusive contracts, were illegally designed to stem competition, and in 2005 it fined 15 Coke bottlers and distributors nearly $15 million. The Coca-Cola company then turned to inducements, such as offering proprietors free life insurance policies, cooking oil, refrigerators, and cases of Coke if they would reject Big Cola. Most of its salespeople were monitoring the retailers' nearly million Coke display coolers to make sure they did not stock rival brands.

In the midst of this heated competition, a valve in the Puebla plant failed, resulting in the emission of dangerous quantities of carbon dioxide. Suspecting sabotage, executives of Ajemex created a "crisis manual" for supervisors and vendors to counter unforeseen events. The firm's strategy for opening operations in a small community was to arrive unannounced and sign up retailers before the competition could adopt countermeasures. In stores, many times the competition no longer was about which brand sold more but which truck arrived first to sell.

MORE COUNTRIES, MORE PRODUCTS: 2005–07

In late 2005 Mexico was accounting for almost half of Ajegroup's sales. Ajemex's 3,000 delivery people were offering nine different products to 310,000 points of sale, including Big Country, a juice line; Mega First in

lemon, orange, and apple as well as grapefruit flavors; and Free World and Free World Light, flavored bottled water lightly carbonated and fortified with vitamins, antioxidants, and minerals. The company had five production plants covering every part of the country. Big Cola was believed to have won 10 percent of the market for carbonated beverages. Seventy percent of sales came from small stores, 20 percent from supermarkets, and the rest from dance halls, festivals, and large scale events.

By the end of 2005 Ajegroup subsidiaries had implanted themselves throughout Central America. Ajegroup had 15 plants, 98 distribution centers, and 720,000 points of sale in Latin America.

Then, in 2006, the group entered an Asian country, Thailand, where its affiliate, Ajethai, recorded sales of perhaps $50 million in its first year of producing Big Cola in Bangkok. Cambodia, Laos, and Vietnam were neighboring countries being explored for expansion by the parent company, as well as the area's giant, China. Colombia became, in 2007, the next Latin American country to receive Ajegroup's products.

In Peru, Ajeper held about one-fifth of the soft drink market. Its Cielo brand of bottled water, also marketed in Mexico, Venezuela, and Ecuador, accounted for 40 percent of a market which was enhanced when the government, at the beginning of 2007, dropped the 17 percent selective tax it had imposed on products in this sector. Other products included First and Sporade, a drink introduced in 2004, similar to Gatorade, but selling for only half the price. In 2007 Chip Fruit, a drink made of concentrated citrus juices that was being marketed in Ecuador, was introduced. Later in the year, Ajeper launched the parent company's first beer, named Franca, on a $35 million initial investment. The company, which unveiled roadway billboards featuring a noted Peruvian chef touting the product, was expecting to win a 12 to 15 percent market share during 2008.

In Mexico, Ajemex had been planning to introduce a beer named Big Chela since 2005 but had been dissuaded by Mexico's Congress, which passed a law giving favorable tax treatment to beer in returnable bottles. Companies entering the business and thus challenging the nation's two big brewers, Grupo Modelo, S.A. de C.V., and Fomento Económico México, S.A. de C.V. (Femsa), would either have to pay a higher tax or add investment in bottle distribution, collection systems, and delivery vehicles to their start-up expenses.

Ajegroup was producing beverages in 13 countries in 2007 and had 22 production plants worldwide. Big

Cola had annual production of 3.1 billion liters, of which Mexico alone accounted for 2.5 billion.

Robert Halasz

PRINCIPAL SUBSIDIARIES

Ajecuador (Ecuador); Ajecen (Costa Rica); Ajemaya (Guatemala); Ajemex (Mexico); Ajeper (Peru); Ajethai (Thailand); Ajeven (Venezuela).

PRINCIPAL COMPETITORS

Corporación José R. Lindley S.A.; Fomento Económico México, S.A. de C.V.; Grupo Gemex S.A.; Peru Beverage Limited S.R.L; Pepsi Bottling Group, Inc.; Unión de Cervecerías Peruanas Backus y Johnston S.A.A.

FURTHER READING

Aldunate Montes, Felipe, "El fenómeno Añaños," *AméricaEconomía,* June 18–July 8, 2004, pp. 22–25.

Aspin, Chris, "Big Cola, Soon Big Chela to Mix in Mexican Market," *Banderas News,* November 2005.

"The Big War," *Expansión,* September 18, 2007.

Castillo Mireles, Ricardo, "In Mexico, Big Cola Is the Real Thing," *Logistics Today,* March 2004, p. 9.

Celis Estrada, Dario, "Tiempo de negocios," *Reforma,* May 4, 2004, p. 4.

Chauvin, Lucien O., "Cinderella Story in Peru," *Beverage World,* March 15, 2003, p. 67.

———, "Hydro Power," *Beverage World,* March 15, 2007, p. 4.

"Cola down Mexico Way," *Economist,* October 13, 2003, pp. 69–70.

Howard, Rebecca, and Robert Kozak, "Bubbling Economy Boosts Competition in Peru's Beer Market," *Dow Jones International News,* October 24, 2007.

Luhnow, David, and Chad Terhune, "A Low-Budget Cola Shakes Up Markets South of the Border," *Wall Street Journal,* October 27, 2003, pp. A1, A18.

"Soft Drinks and JR Lindley—Inca Cola the Rise of Non-global Brands," *Latin American Economic and Business Report,* March 20, 2001.

Apple & Eve L.L.C.

2 Seaview Boulevard
Port Washington, New York 11050
U.S.A.
Telephone: (516) 621-1122
Web site: http://www.appleandeve.com

Private Company
Incorporated: 1975
Employees: 65
Sales: $200 million (2006 est.)
NAIC: 311421 Fruit and Vegetable Canning

∎∎∎

Apple & Eve L.L.C. is a Port Washington, New York–based company specializing in 100 percent juice and organic juice products. Well established in the Northeast where it is among the top juice brands, Apple & Eve is extending its reach nationally following the 2005 acquisition of Wisconsin's Northland Cranberries, Inc. The company made its mark selling unfiltered 100 percent apple juice, but also offers natural cranberry juice and cranberry juice blended with other juices, including apple, raspberry, grape, peach mango, wild berries, and pomegranate. A "lite" line offers cranberry juice and cranberry blends with reduced calories and carbohydrates. Apple & Eve organic juices include apple, peach mango, a cranberry-blueberry blend, lemonade, Strawberry Mango Passion, pomegranate, and fruit punch. The company offers four Tropicals juice blends primarily aimed at the Hispanic market: Mango Passion, Strawberry Passion Mango, Pineapple Orange Banana, and Orange Tangerine. In addition, Apple & Eve offers juice boxes for children, larger On the Go pouches for older children and adults, and a line of Sesame Street licensed juice boxes and 64-ounce bottles. Through its Northland Cranberries subsidiary, the company also sells Northland branded cranberry juice blends as well as juice bearing the Seneca label. Products are sold through a wide variety of channels, including supermarkets, health food stores, warehouse clubs, mass retailers, retailers, and schools.

FOUNDER STARTS AS NATURAL-FOODS DISTRIBUTOR: 1972

Apple & Eve was founded by Gordon Crane, a self-described long-haired hippie who, after graduating from the University of Rhode Island in 1972, started a natural foods distribution company. In an interview with *Beverage Industry,* he explained that he was "interested in macrobiotics and natural foods and changing the world." Setting up shop in the basement of his parents' home in Bayside, Queens, New York, he leased a truck and began delivering granola and the like to stores in Manhattan. Most consumers did not share his passion for natural foods, however, so after a couple of years of trying to make the business work, and living at home, Crane decided to return to school, gaining admission to the law school at Hofstra University. However, before classes began he found a product that had much greater commercial potential: pure unfiltered natural apple juice. In 1975, with less than $3,000 in seed money, he formed a company to market the juice, relying on a processor who made the product on a contract basis. Crane called the company Apple & Eve, and with designer Lily Hou developed the brand's distinctive logo featuring an apple with a bite taken out, an image that would undergo few changes over the ensuing decades.

Crane began pitching his apple juice at local farmers' markets but by the time he landed his first major order from a retailer he had begun law school. At this stage, Crane viewed Apple & Eve as a way to pay for law school, and to help out, his mother filled in while he was attending classes. Crane earned his law degree in 1978 and passed the bar but would never practice. Instead, growing Apple & Eve became his career. In the same year that he graduated from Hofstra, Apple & Eve cracked the $1 million mark in annual sales to New York City bodegas and a Midwestern supermarket chain, Cincinnati-based Kroger's Supermarkets.

Running the business was a family affair. Crane's mother became his full-time assistant and secretary, while older brother Alan headed sales and younger brother Cary joined the company as well, after completing a marketing degree at the University of Buffalo. In addition to serving as the company's president, Gordon Crane acted as its buyer, paying visits to apple growers throughout the Northeast and as far south as Georgia. As the business grew, it commandeered every room in the house, with the exception of his parents' bedroom. The young company moved into offices in Great Neck, New York, and began hiring nonfamily members, including a full-time apple buyer, who would also acquire fruit on the spot market.

With the company's apple juice product established in New York City and some other markets, Crane displayed a willingness to take chances, deciding to tackle the cranberry market and the giant that dominated the category, Ocean Spray, by offering a 100 percent cranberry juice product, as opposed to Ocean Spray's beverage line offering 5 percent juice. He approached a New Jersey juice processor, Clement Pappas

& Co., Inc., a longtime canner that had decided to limit its focus to juice, and a co-packing deal was forged to bottle the United States' first line of 100 percent juice Cranberry Blends, introduced in 1978. The relationship with Clement Pappas proved to be a good one for both parties, who would grow in concert with one another over the ensuing years.

FIRST ASEPTIC BOXES OFFERED: 1982

Apple & Eve enjoyed strong growth into the 1980s, spreading the distribution of its products all along the East Coast and as far west as Chicago, represented in almost every retail channel, including grocery stores, natural foods stores, and drug stores. The company also began to sell to club stores. One club store Crane visited suggested that Apple & Eve consider offering 100 percent juice in an aseptic pack. As he recalled for *Beverage Industry,* "I left there and said, 'I don't know how we're going to do it, but we're going to do it.' And I came back here and we figured out a way to do it. It's that kind of 'just get it done' attitude that we've established here." Thus, in 1982 Apple & Eve became the first juice company in the United States to offer "Brik Pak" aseptic juice boxes, beating the rest of the market by several months. Aseptic juice boxes relied on a flash pasteurization process and did not require refrigeration until opened. Their rectangular shape took up less space than bottles, making them less expensive to ship and allowing retailers to stock more of them. At the end of 1982, Apple & Eve, which employed ten people, recorded sales in the neighborhood of $10 million.

Apple & Eve toyed with the idea of offering pure juice from fresh vegetables but elected to remain focused on fruit juices. The rest of the 1980s were somewhat challenging for the company, as sales increased at a modest pace, about 3 to 5 percent each year, reaching $20 million by the end of the decade. It had to contend with greater apple juice competition in the Northeast, supplied by a number of large multinational companies entering the market, but Apple & Eve persevered and by the early 1990s found itself the number three brand in the key New York City market, trailing the Mott's and Red Cheek labels but performing better than a score of other branded apple juices. The key to the company's success was its long-standing reputation for quality.

During the 1980s Apple & Eve had to contend with beverage terminology that confused the public and hurt the company's effort to promote its 100 percent juices. "Many consumers were under the impression that the juice drink they were buying was all juice," Gordon Crane told *Long Island Business News* in 1994. "They had no idea—and no way of finding out—what

KEY DATES

1975: Gordon Crane founds Apple & Eve.
1978: Company introduces cranberry juice product.
1982: Apple & Eve becomes first company to sell aseptic juice boxes.
1992: Nothin' But Juice line launched.
1999: Licensed Sesame Street juice introduced.
2003: Organic juice line launched.
2005: Northland Cranberries, Inc., acquired.

percentage of juice the product contained." The U.S. Food and Drug Administration felt no urgent need to strengthen labeling regulations that would disclose juice percentages in diluted juice, so in 1987 Apple & Eve took the lead and recruited other juice companies to form "The Coalition of Responsible Juice Companies," which began lobbying Congress for a Percentage Juice Declaration Regulation. Their efforts were to pay off in 1994 with the passage of the Nutrition Labeling and Education Act.

The Cranes realized that the key to the company's success lay with children, more specifically offering healthful products that could be marketed to mothers. In 1992 Apple & Eve introduced a children-oriented product line of pure 100 percent fruit juices sold under the "Nothin' But Juice" banner, aimed at 8- to 12-year-olds. Later in the 1990s the company signed a licensing deal with Sesame Workshop, producer of the popular television program *Sesame Street,* to develop a line of juice boxes featuring Muppet characters for younger children, first introduced in 1999.

Although Sesame Workshop had done countless licensing deals for toys and other products, this was the first time it had licensed its characters to a food company. The company was clearly pleased with Apple & Eve's commitment to a 100 percent natural product. Head of Sesame Street licensing June Archer told the *New York Times,* "I've never had the feeling that Gordon [Crane] struck a deal only for short-term benefits. When he started working with us, he was willing to invest in new flavors, new packaging and new distribution channels. Gordon has been very willing to invest in our brand and be innovative on behalf of it." As a result, according to the *Times,* "Apple & Eve has become the beverage of choice among the preschool set." In order to gain the same edge with grade school children, Apple & Eve exchanged the juice box associated with the younger set for a "power pouch," emblazoned with brighter graphics that were more appealing to 7- to 12-year-olds.

Apple & Eve did not ignore teens or adults, of course. In 1992 Apple & Eve introduced its first non-juice product, a honey-sweetened entry in the flourishing iced tea category. In 1995 the company launched its "Made in the Shade" product line, which included its iced tea drinks as well as lemonade, and tropical-flavored fruit juice drinks. Keeping up with consumer preferences, Apple & Eve turned to green tea–based beverages in 1998 with its Tribal Tonics line of four varieties, including Mental Refresher, Energy Elixir, Immune Boon, and Herbal Slimmer. As part of its marketing effort, and in keeping with the tribal theme, the company pledged to donate 5 percent of all profits from the drinks to indigenous people around the world.

A major goal of the single-serve product was to create a beachhead in the convenience store channel for Apple & Eve. However, the decision not to use the Apple & Eve brand, which the company had been nurturing for a quarter-century, proved unwise. The Tribal Tonics line lingered for a few years before being pulled. "We launched a new brand name in a channel we didn't have much experience in," Crane said, conducting a postmortem for *Long Island Business News* in 2005. "So we started with two strikes. We had no consumer equity, because no one knew what Tribal Tonics was."

Tribal Tonics was a rare misstep for Apple & Eve. At the start of the new century sales were growing at a fast clip and the small company's ability to adapt quickly to a changing marketplace gave it an important edge. Apple & Eve was able to conceive, develop, and launch a new product in four to six weeks, a task that took at least several months for much larger rivals.

In 2000 the company introduced Cranberry Juice & More as well as the first Multi-Vitamin fortified 100 percent juice Cranberry Blend. A new single-serve line was unveiled in 2002, and the following year Apple & Eve introduced its line of Organically Certified 100 percent juice, an example of the company reacting to developing demands.

The company had always maintained strong ties to natural foods channels, and in the new century recognized that organics were becoming more mainstream. Producing a line of organic juices was in keeping with the Apple & Eve brand promise, but more than that, the company recognized that the supermarket channel would be receptive to the new line, as well as Whole Foods and other natural food stores. In 2004 Apple & Eve began selling Light Cranberry Blends and Cranberry Wild Berry, and offering multipacks. The company looked to tap into the growing Hispanic market by introducing its Tropicals line of Caribbean-flavored juice drinks, available in 64-ounce containers at the supermarket instead of the single-serve drinks sold in bodegas and elsewhere. In 2005 the company entered the water business as well, introducing a line of water flavored with natural juice called WaterFruits, which was sold to Long Island schools.

NORTHLAND ACQUIRED: 2005

In the early years of the new century, Apple & Eve topped the $100 million mark in annual sales and continued to grow. For 30 years the company had relied on organic growth but that changed in 2005 when Apple & Eve seized the opportunity to acquire a rival in the 100 percent cranberry juice market, Wisconsin-based Northland Cranberries, Inc., paying $10.8 million for the business. Northland was started in 1987 as a cranberry supplier to Ocean Spray but in 1993 struck out on its own to become an independent cranberry marketing company. The company became involved in the juice business in 1996, taking on Ocean Spray in the main category and Apple & Eve in the 100 percent juice market. Northland soon became the second largest cranberry juice brand in the country but it was a distant second to Ocean Spray. In order to grow the business the company took on considerable debt, about $65 million, acquiring the juice division of Seneca Foods Corporation and Minot Food Packers, Inc., a cranberry processor. By 2001 the company was on the verge of bankruptcy; a Florida merchant bank took control and a number of assets were sold off. Although available at an attractive price, Northland remained a valuable property, especially to Apple & Eve, which in addition to the Northland brand picked up Treesweet, Awake, and Northland's license to the Seneca juice brand. Even of more importance was Apple & Eve's ability to take advantage of Northland's distribution network, which would in effect allow Apple & Eve to create a national footprint.

With the addition of Northland and its growing lines of branded products, Apple & Eve was able to increase sales beyond the $200 million mark in 2006. New products in the wings included the Awake energy juice line and the Fizz Ed line of sparkling juices. To help grow the company further through internal means and acquisitions if suitable opportunities arose, Apple & Eve received an investment in October 2007 from ClearLight Partners, a California-based private equity firm. Although the amount of the investment was not specified, ClearLight typically made investments of $10 million to $50 million.

Ed Dinger

PRINCIPAL SUBSIDIARIES

Northland Cranberries, Inc.

PRINCIPAL COMPETITORS

Mott's LLP; Ocean Spray Cranberries, Inc.; Tropicana Products, Inc.

FURTHER READING

Demery, Paul, "Apple & Eve Goes Up Against Giants," *Long Island Business News,* June 15, 1992, p. 1.

Jabbonsky, Larry, "Purity of Essence," *Beverage World,* March 1992, p. 98.

Markus, Stuart, "Port Washington–Based Apple & Eve Maintains Low Profile but Survives Against Big Brands," *Long Island Business News,* August 24, 2001.

Reich-Hale, David, "Long Island–Based Juice Company, Apple & Eve Completes First Acquisition," *Long Island Business News,* October 28, 2005.

Strugatch, Warren, "Apple & Eve: Breaking Out of Its Northeast Niche," *New York Times,* June 23, 2002.

Theodore, Sarah, "Core Values," *Beverage Industry,* April 2005, p. 25.

Tuthill, Mary, "Young Firm's Sales: $1 Million Per Capita," *Nation's Business,* September 1982, p. 90.

The Arthur C. Clarke Foundation

———■———

P.O. Box 42307
Washington, D.C. 20015-0907
U.S.A.
Telephone: (301) 879-1613
Web site: http://www.clarkefoundation.com

Not-for-Profit Corporation
Founded: 1983
Employees: not available
Total Assets: not available
NAIC: 813319 Other Social Advocacy Organizations

■ ■ ■

Nominally based in Washington, D.C., the Arthur C. Clarke Foundation (ACCF) is an international not-for-profit organization dedicated to promoting the contributions and interests of science fiction writer and futurist Sir Arthur C. Clarke, who was knighted in 1998. The ACCF seeks to support the use of satellite and other forms of communication, make contributions to the world through the use of technology, recognize achievements in the field of communications and information, and provide scholarships, fellowships, and travel grants.

The organization sponsors lectures and educational seminars and forums, museum exhibitions, practical training programs aimed at young people (such as teaching them how to build communication systems), as well as occasional publications, including books, brochures, and research reports. Through subsidiary Clarke Institute for Telecommunications and Information (CITI), the organization works with research organiza-

tions, universities, and governmental agencies to pursue the betterment of the world through science, technology, and information systems. For example, CITI is involved with partners in Project Warn to use communications and information technology systems to warn of pending natural or manmade disasters.

Another project, the Global Services Trust Fund, works with the Global University System to help persuade world leaders to make new low-cost communications technology available to remote populations to deliver education and healthcare. In a similar vein, the Millennium Village Project in conjunction with the Solar Electric Light Fund seeks to use modern technology to solve some of the problems found in rural and remote parts of the world. Working with George Washington University, ACCF is involved in the Space Safety Study, to investigate ways of making current and future space travel safe.

ARTHUR CHARLES CLARKE: ENGLAND BORN, 1917

Arthur Charles Clarke was born in 1917 in Minehead, a seaside town in Somerset, England. Growing up in a farming family he developed a keen interest in science, in particular space, as well as science fiction, especially the works of H. G. Wells and Olaf Stapledon. In 1936 he moved to London where he joined the British Interplanetary Society and began to write science fiction, earning his living as an assistant auditor.

By this time the seeds of war were being sown in Europe and after England and France went to war against Nazi Germany and its allies, Clarke in 1941 joined the Royal Air Force (RAF). His service would prove to be a turning point in his life. Assigned to work with the new ground radar system that provided a crucial edge to the British, Clarke became a radar instructor and a technical officer in charge of a new "talk-down" system, a rudimentary form of air traffic control.

This experience with radar inspired him to postulate a system for global radio communications by way of "rocket stations" that orbited at the same rate as Earth, thus keeping them in place above the same portion of the planet. Clarke laid out the idea in a technical paper titled "Extra-terrestrial Relays," published by a British magazine, *Wireless World*. Clarke did not patent the idea, losing out on countless royalties for the satellite communication systems that were to develop some 20 years later. He also envisioned onboard astronauts and space walks under the assumption that burned-out radio tubes would have to be replaced. His vision for the future would become more immediate just a few years later with the invention of the transistor, which eliminated the need for space handymen to service satellites and set the stage for the space age.

After his discharge from the RAF, Clarke earned degrees in physics and applied mathematics from King's College in London, graduating with honors in 1948. By this time he had also begun enjoying success with his science fiction. His first short story, "Rescue Party," appeared in *Astounding Science* in May 1946.

Clarke's science fiction mostly concerned space exploration and the discovery of intelligent life in the universe. Not only did he seek to popularize scientific ideas through fiction; he also wrote nonfiction for a general audience, such as *The Exploration of Space*, published in 1951, in which he predicted how space exploration programs were likely to proceed.

He solidified his reputation as a futurist in 1962 with the publication of *Profiles of the Future*. While some of his predictions seem amusing half a century later—cars traveling on jets of compressed air and conveyer-belt highways—others retained interest, such as his prediction that robots and computers would become our companions.

He would pursue this idea further with film director Stanley Kubrick, as the two men began work in 1964 on the screenplay of *2001: A Space Odyssey*, based on Clarke's 1951 short story "The Sentinel." Simultaneously Clarke, working in his adopted home of Sri Lanka, wrote a novel from the *2001* story, which was published three months after the hit film's release, answering many of the questions that puzzled moviegoers. Regardless, the audience was captivated by the spaceship's computer, HAL 9000, who took over the mission to investigate the origins of radio signals being emitted from a black monolith discovered on the moon. The film also solidified Clarke's reputation as a writer and futurist. He would also gain further public attention on television, coanchoring CBS television coverage of three Apollo missions with Walter Cronkite and hosting popular investigative programs, including "Arthur C. Clarke's Mysterious World," "World of Strange Powers," and "Mysterious Universe."

FOUNDATION TAKES SHAPE: 1982

The Arthur C. Clarke Foundation was established in 1983, growing out of the United Nations' General Assembly's proclaiming 1983 World Communications Year. The purpose was to stimulate the growth of communications infrastructures around the world in order to bring advances in communications and other areas such as education, health care, and banking that would benefit from improved communications. The president of the United States, Ronald Reagan, announced his own proclamation in support of the resolution. The U.S. effort was headed by Dr. Joseph N. Pelton, who took the opportunity of World Communications Year to issue a press release at the White House announcing the creation of the Arthur C. Clarke Foundation (ACCF) of the United States, a 501c3 educational organization, the goal of which was to enhance Clarke's legacy, the embodiment of the very goals of World Communications Year.

Pelton was a well-regarded scientist in his own right. Born in Tulsa, Oklahoma, in 1943, the son of a tool design engineer, he earned a PhD from Georgetown University in 1971. At the same time, he began his career with the global satellite organizations, COMSAT and INTELSAT, where he was well aware of Clarke's contribution to the field of satellite communications.

KEY DATES

1983: Arthur C. Clarke Foundation established.
1986: First foundation-sponsored lecture delivered.
1995: Separate Arthur C. Clarke Foundation of the United Kingdom started.
1999: Clarke Institute for Telecommunications and Information (CITI) founded.
2004: U.S. and U.K. foundations and CITI are consolidated.
2005: Project Warn is launched following an Asian tsunami.

Like Clarke, Pelton was also a prolific writer, authoring two-dozen books as well as hundreds of articles and editorials about satellites, telecommunications, and the future impact of technology on society. In addition to founding ACCF, Pelton was the founding president of the Society of Satellite Professionals International.

Pelton was instrumental in organizing the first board meeting of the ACCF, held at INTELSAT's Washington, D.C., headquarters. The first chairman of the foundation was Dr. John McLucas, former administrator of the Federal Aviation Administration and former secretary of the Air Force. Pelton became the organization's vice chairman. When Clarke came to the United States in September 1983 for the World Communications Year celebrations he served as honorary chairman of ACCF. Clarke was also featured at one of the foundation's first symposiums held at George Washington University in 1983.

The ACCF also worked with the government of Sri Lanka, where Clarke had made his home since 1956, and established a relationship with the University of Moratuwa in Sri Lanka. The school played host to the Arthur C. Clarke lectures sponsored by the foundation every year or so. In 1986, at the first lecture, ACCF's chairman, Dr. McLucas, addressed the subject "Technology and Development." A year later, Dr. John R. Pierce of Stanford University, creator of the Telstar and the Echo satellite projects, spoke on "Space Enough for All." In 1990, after a gap of three years, Dr. Harold Rosen, a Hughes Aircraft Company senior scientist and developer of many of the early communication satellites, delivered a lecture on "Space Communications." In 1992 Dr. Joseph V. Charyk, the founder of Comsat Corporation, discussed "The Global Market of Information Satellites," and in 1994 former head of the Indian space program and former minister in the Indian government Dr. Yash Pal spoke.

In 1995 Clarke returned to George Washington University where he was again featured in a communications symposium. In that same year his brother Fred established the Arthur C. Clarke Foundation of the United Kingdom and in 1997 launched a web site to preserve the archives of Arthur C. Clarke as well as to provide a time line of communications and computing technology and track advances in four areas: communications, futures, space, and the oceans. Although the U.S. foundation and U.K. organization fostered similar aims, they operated separately for several years.

In 1996 the Arthur C. Clarke lecture, "Satellites: First Choice for the New Millennium," was delivered via videoconference by former director general and CEO of INTELSAT, Irving Goldstein. The final lecture of the 1990s was delivered at the University of Moratuwa by Dr. Olof Lundburg, founder and former director general of Inmarsat. At the start of the new century, the Clarke lectures would leave Sri Lanka for Washington, D.C. In 2000 Pelton spoke about "The Next Billion Years and the Significance of the Emerging Global Brain." Then, in 2004, Norman Augustine, former chairman and CEO of Lockheed Martin Corporation, delivered the lecture, "From Kitty Hawk to Mars, or 'How Could I Have Lived for Two-Thirds of the Aerospace Age.'"

CITI FOUNDED: 1999

In 1999 the groundwork was laid for a new ACCF unit, the Clarke Institute for Telecommunications and Information (CITI), at an organizing conference held at INTELSAT's headquarters in Washington, D.C. A founders' conference was then sponsored in February 2000 by INTELSAT; Phillips International, Inc., the *Satellite News* publisher; SatLink Communications Corp.; Trex Communications Corp.; as well as the Arthur C. Clarke Foundation of the United Kingdom and the Arthur C. Clarke Institute for Modern Technologies based in Sri Lanka. Both Clarke and Walter Cronkite made video addresses to the conference. In addition to linking the U.S., U.K., and Sri Lanka Clarke foundations, CITI served as a "virtual" research organization and an "electronic institute," dedicated to interdisciplinary work in communications, networking, and the future. In practice, CITI's purpose was to bring together governmental agencies, universities, and research organizations to pursue the common goal of improving world conditions through the use of communications, technology, and science. For example, in 2003 CITI worked with NASA and other organizations to present the Space Education Workshop at George Washington University.

Because of the popularity of Kubrick's *2001: A Space Odyssey*, it was natural that 2001 would be an important year for ACCF, highlighted by the "2001: A Space Odyssey" symposium held at the Smithsonian National Air and Space Museum. Also in 2001 the ACCF presented its first lifetime achievement award at the Smithsonian, given to Santiago Astrain, INTELSAT's first CEO and a key player in bringing to life Clarke's vision of geostationary satellites. A year later the Smithsonian played host to an ACCF symposium with astronaut Gene Cernan and science fiction writer Ben Bova.

In January 2003 Dr. McLucas died and was replaced as ACCF's chairman by Tedson Meyers, a Washington, D.C., telecommunications attorney. Meyers established a strategic planning group to consider future endeavors of the foundation. One of the main objectives to develop from this effort was the creation of a permanent home for the Arthur C. Clarke Center. In addition, the various Clarke organizations were brought under one roof, ACCF. In 2004 the U.K. foundation and CITI were merged into ACCF and the different web sites consolidated into a single Internet location.

The revamped foundation launched a new project in 2005, Project Warn, which grew out of the tsunami that devastated parts of South Asia, including the destruction of the Clarke underwater research facility in Hikkaduwa on the southwestern coast of Sri Lanka. The foundation coordinated the development of a satellite database system to spread education materials and warnings of pending disasters, as well as working on the improvement of ways to coordinate relief efforts and the creation of a GPS propagation measurement program that had the potential of providing almost immediate detection of earthquakes and volcanic eruptions. The year 2005 was also noteworthy because it marked the 60th anniversary of Clarke's paper that outlined the geosynchronous system for satellite communications.

Arthur Clarke turned 90 in 2007. Although confined to a wheelchair in Sri Lanka he continued to write and remained active in the work of the foundation that bore his name. By now, after discussions with a number of U.S. entities, the search for a permanent Arthur C. Clarke Center to celebrate Clarke's accomplishments centered on the University of Nevada–Las Vegas. The next step in the actual creation of such a center involved the formation of "Friends of Arthur C. Clarke," an organization spearheaded by the school and the foundation to build interest in the project within the Las Vegas business community and among potential donors around the world.

Ed Dinger

PRINCIPAL DIVISIONS

Clarke Institute for Telecommunications and Information.

FURTHER READING

Blackman, S. James, "The World Keeps Up with Arthur Clarke," http://www.space.com/peopleinterviews/arthur_clarke-991216.html, December 16, 1999.

"Founders Conference for New Arthur C. Clarke Institute for Feb. 5," *Satellite News*, January 17, 2000.

McGookin, Stephen, "Futurologist Looks Back," *Financial Times*, June 30, 1997, p. 17.

Pelton, Joseph N., "40 Years of Satellite Communications—Past, Present and Especially the Future," *Space News*, March 21, 2005.

Schelmetic, Tracey E., "Welcome to the 21st Century," *Customer Interaction Solutions*, January 2001, p. 50.

Artsana SpA

Via S Catelli 1
Grandate, I-22070
Italy
Telephone: (39 031) 382111
Fax: (39 031) 382800
Web site: http://www.artsana.it

Private Company
Incorporated: 1946
Employees: 7,200
Sales: EUR 1.2 billion ($1.4 billion) (2005)
NAIC: 322291 Sanitary Paper Product Manufacturing;
326299 All Other Rubber Product Manufacturing;
339112 Surgical and Medical Instrument
Manufacturing

∎∎∎

Artsana SpA is the holding company for a diversified group of companies involved in the production, marketing, and distribution of hypodermic needles, thermometers, and other medical and paramedical products; children's strollers, accessories, and toys; prenatal and postnatal maternity and infant goods; and condoms, sanitary napkins, and incontinence products, among others.

Artsana's Health Products division is most widely known for its flagship brand, Pic Indolor, which pioneered the development of painless syringes and boasts more than 1,000 items in its product line. Other health division products include Control condoms; the Dr. Marcus line of over-the-counter medicines; the You brand of sanitary napkins; and the Plantas line of orthopedic products.

The company's Baby Products division encompasses the Chicco line of strollers, car seats, cribs and high chairs, toys, games, and early developmental products, as well as clothing, shoes, and diapers. In Italy, Artsana also operates nearly 300 Chicco retail shops. The company also produces a full range of baby and children's toys and products for the supermarket and third-party retail sector under the Neo Baby brand. The company's Prénatal retail network focuses on the maternity and postnatal markets, offering clothing, toys, and toiletries for women and young children, and is the largest such specialist in Europe. Prénatal stores operate in Italy, Spain, Portugal, France, Greece, Mexico, Cyprus, Russia, the Netherlands, and elsewhere.

Artsana's third major business is its Cosmetics & Beauty division, which includes Lycia deodorants; Korff cosmetics; Momma Donna pre- and postnatal beauty and hygiene products; and Infinite Dolcezze, part of the Chicco brand family, which produces pediatric cosmetics and hygiene products. Artsana maintains much of its manufacturing in Italy, with 11 factories, primarily in the region around the company's Como home base. The company also operates production facilities in Romania and Spain, and sales, marketing, and distribution subsidiaries throughout Europe, as well as in the United States and Hong Kong. A private company, Artsana remains controlled by the founding Catelli family, with Michele Catelli serving as the company's chief executive. In 2006, Artsana's revenues topped EUR 1.2 billion ($1.7 billion).

COMPANY PERSPECTIVES

The company's mission is to look after the family and its members, from babies to old folk, treating them all as people and not merely as consumers. With reciprocal respect of values and dignity. Listening to their problems and providing straightforward, effective and innovative solutions.

THERMOMETER SALES IN POSTWAR ITALY

Artsana was founded by Pietro Catelli in Como in 1946. Catelli was born in 1920 in the small village of Moneolimpino, located near the Italian city of Como and the Swiss border. When Catelli was 17, he took a job working for a small Swiss manufacturer of thermometers and syringes. Catelli soon convinced his employer to give him a job as a salesman. His sales territory spanned the region between Como and Reko. However, as Catelli noted in an interview published by *P.M. Communications,* the sales job was made more difficult because the products "were not as good quality as I might have liked."

Catelli served in the Italian army during World War II and returned to the Como region in 1946. One of Catelli's older sisters had died during the war, and Catelli was able to take out a mortgage on her house, raising ITL 500,000 in order to start his own business, which he called Artsana. Catelli used his networking experience in pharmaceutical sales to import thermometers from Eastern Germany. At that time, thermometers, like most other goods, were scarce in Italy. Catelli started out his new career with only a bicycle for making his sales rounds. Soon, however, his sales volume had risen sufficiently to allow him to buy a scooter.

The start of the Cold War cut off Catelli's thermometer supply. Rather than contract with another manufacturer, Catelli decided to launch his own production operations, opening his first manufacturing plant in the Como region. Drawing on his experience working in Switzerland, where more advanced products were available, Catelli focused on bringing product innovations to Italy. He became one of the first in Italy to begin developing so-called painless hypodermic needles. He also recognized the importance of design in sales; his thermometers featured distinctive blue-colored mercury. Catelli's product stood out among the others, including those of such rival Italian brands as Atto and Icco.

Catelli married in the mid-1950s, and his wife joined him in building the business, which rapidly expanded its range of medical and health products through the 1950s. The company also expanded its production capacity, adding the first of a series of new factories in Italy's Lombard region. The Catellis' first child, Enrico, was born in 1958. Catelli gave his son the nickname Chicco, the name of a pharmacist he had met while making sales calls on bicycle years before. The birth of his first child provided Catelli with the inspiration for the launch of the company's second main product category. The company began developing its own range of strollers, cribs, cradles, and other childcare products and named the new division Chicco.

The Chicco brand caught on quickly in Italy, where it soon became nearly synonymous with the children's market. The Chicco line continued to grow, later becoming a well-known brand of toys and games. At the same time, the Catellis recognized an opportunity to extend the Chicco brand into retail operations, and the company opened its first Chicco store in Italy. Over the coming years, the company expanded the Chicco store network throughout Italy. By 2005 the company's retail segment had grown to include nearly 300 Chicco stores.

INTERNATIONAL EXPANSION IN THE EIGHTIES

Artsana's level of success with Chicco was realized in its health products operations as well. In the late 1950s, the company launched a research and development effort to produce a new generation of painless syringes. By 1960, the company had introduced a new product line called Pic Indolor ("painless" in Italian). The new type of syringe achieved rapid success in Italy's healthcare communities. Before long, Pic Indolor had become a prominent, internationally recognized brand name, representing more than 1,000 products.

The company also launched a new line of footcare products, under the Plantas brand. Introduced in 1969, the Plantas line grew to include orthopedic footwear by the early 1980s. The company broadened the scope of operations when it began producing hygiene products, including the Lycia brand of feminine hygiene products, as well as deodorant, hair removal products, cleansing tissues, and other items.

The company's success allowed it to begin thinking about international expansion. For its first foreign endeavor, Artsana chose Greece, rolling out its brands there to great success. After that, the company rapidly began developing a sales and marketing presence throughout Europe, starting with Belgium, France, and Spain. By the early 1980s, the company had entered the Americas, and it founded its U.S. subsidiary in 1983.

KEY DATES

1946: Pietro Catelli founds Artsana as a thermometer sales company, then launches production of thermometers, syringes, and other medical supplies.

1958: Company begins production of childcare products under Chicco brand.

1969: Plantas brand of footcare products is introduced.

1979: Lycia brand of feminine hygiene and beauty products debut.

1989: Launch of Momma Donna maternity products.

1996: Stake in the Prénatal chain of retail pre- and postnatal stores is acquired.

2006: Prénatal acquisition is completed through purchase of Prénatal operation in the Netherlands.

For the U.S. launch of its Chicco brand, the company focused on introducing products that filled niches left vacant by its rivals, while also positioning itself as an upscale European company. The company captured a strong share of the "umbrella" stroller category, which became highly popular among young urban professionals at the start of the 1990s, before being eclipsed by the even trendier jogging stroller. The Chicco brand also led the company into the South American market, where it also opened a number of Chicco retail stores, many of which were based in Venezuela.

By the early 1990s, Artsana had spotted another new growth opportunity. The retail sector in Italy, as well as elsewhere in Europe, had over the years seen a small number of large-scale supermarket groups grow to dominate the sector. Artsana recognized the potential for success in developing a new brand of childcare products and toys specifically for that supermarket and hypermarket channel. In 1991 it launched the Neo Baby line of baby bottles, with dishes and silverware, cribs and playpens, carriers, and high chairs in an initial product range that included nearly 80 products in all. In 1993, the Neo Baby line was expanded to include toys as well. Over the next decade, Artsana continued to refine the Neo Baby concept, adding thermometers and similar products in 1997 and expanding the range in 2000 to include some products, such as car seats, for older children.

MULTIPLE PRODUCT LINES FOR THE NEW CENTURY

Artsana's Momma Donna line, established in 1989, focused specifically on the maternity market, offering pre- and postnatal corsets, stockings, and other items. Momma Donna was soon expanded to include creams, infant feeding products, breast pumps, and related accessories, as well as a line of cosmetics developed specifically for expectant mothers.

The growth of the maternity market in the mid-1990s prompted Artsana to keep its focus on these operations. In 1996, the company launched the first in its line of infant creams and cosmetics, which it called Infinite Dolcezze and placed under the Chicco product group. The launch of Infinite Dolcezze became part of a wider move into the cosmetics sector in general as Artsana acquired the Korff cosmetics in 1995. That purchase allowed Artsana to begin marketing a full range of cosmetics, skin care, suncare, hair care, and makeup products. By then, the company had come under direction of Catelli's three sons, led by Michele Catelli who served as the group's chief executive officer.

The mid-1990s also marked Artsana's move into the international retail sector. In 1996, the company acquired Prénatal SpA, which operated one of Europe's leading specialist retail chain stores focused on the maternity and children's wear markets. Prénatal had been founded in 1963, with a first store in Milan, followed soon after by a store in Spain. By the mid-1970s, the brand was operating 74 stores throughout Italy and had begun a wider European expansion. In 1985, France's La Redoute, a mail retailer and mail-order sales company, took control of Prénatal and continued its expansion, introducing the stores to Portugal and Greece, then bringing it across the Atlantic, with a first store in Mexico in 1995. Under Artsana, Prénatal continued to build new markets, adding stores in Argentina in 1999, in France in 2001, Cyprus in 2003, and Russia in 2006.

In 2006, Artsana reached an agreement to acquire the Prénatal operations in the Netherlands, which had not been part of the initial acquisition. In this way, Artsana gained full control over what, in the meantime, had become the leading European specialist retailer in its segment. Pietro Catelli died that same year. He had built Artsana into a major diversified group with successful operations worldwide.

M. L. Cohen

PRINCIPAL SUBSIDIARIES

Artsana Sud SpA; Caben Ltd (Hong Kong); Chicco Argentina S.A.; Chicco Austria GmbH; Chicco Babyausstattung Gmbh (Germany); Chicco Do Brasil Ltda.; Chicco Española S.A. (Spain); Chicco Tekstil Sanayi (Turkey); Chicco U.S.A. Inc.; Chicco UK Ltd; Co-Graf SpA; Farsana Portugal; Manifattura Jonica S.R.L.; N.V. Pharsana S.A. (Belgium); Pharsana S.A. (Switzerland); Prénatal Aebe (Greece); Prénatal Argentina S.A.; Prénatal GmbH & MBK Gmbh (Germany); Prénatal Lda (Portugal); Prénatal Mexico SA de CV; Prénatal S.A. (Spain); Puericulture de France S.A.; S.C. Grigioverde Company S.R.L.; S.C. Grigioverde Company S.R.L. (Romania); Tecnilatex S.A.

PRINCIPAL DIVISIONS

Health Products; Baby Products; Cosmetics & Beauty; Prénatal.

PRINCIPAL COMPETITORS

Ansell Ltd.; Avent Holdings Ltd.; SMOBY; Little Tikes Inc.; Jumbo S.A.

FURTHER READING

"Artsana Industria Group," *Medical Device Technology,* November 2002, p. 56.

"Artsana Launches St. John's Wort Plus DHA," *Nutraceuticals International,* February 1999.

"Chicco: After the Disappearance of Pietro Catelli, the Three Children at the Top of Society," *Fashion Magazine.it,* January 23, 2006.

Godbody, Jerry, "Chicco's Strollers Have Heavy Italian Accent," *Adweek's Marketing Week,* September 10, 1990, p. 20.

"Interview with President and Founder Cavaliere Pietro Catelli," *P.M. Communications* for the *Daily Telegraph,* http://www.pmcomm.com.

"Italy: Health Care Equipment & Supplies," *Datamonitor Industry Market Research,* June 15, 2007.

Simkins, John, "Artsana Buys French Business," *Financial Times,* January 23, 1996, p. 26.

"Venezuela: Chicco Looks to Franchising," *South American Business Information,* November 9, 2001.

Belleville Shoe Manufacturing Company

---

100 Premier Drive
Belleville, Illinois 62220-3423
U.S.A.
Telephone: (618) 233-5600
Toll Free: (800) 376-6978
Fax: (618) 257-1112
Web site: http://www.bellevilleshoe.com

Private Company
Incorporated: 1904
Employees: 700
Sales: $40.50 million (2006 est.)
NAIC: 316213 Men's Footwear (Except Athletic)
Manufacturing

■ ■ ■

Belleville Shoe Manufacturing Company is the leading supplier of boots to the U.S. armed forces. Government contracts account for most of its business, but its products are also available online. Established in 1904, the family-controlled company has provided military footwear since World War I. Its two plants in Illinois and Arkansas together produce more than a million pairs of boots per year.

ORIGINS

Belleville Shoe Manufacturing Company began operations in 1904 in Belleville, a southern Illinois town near St. Louis, Missouri. Among the founders was William Weidmann, a veteran of one of the earliest National Guard units of Illinois. Others were local businessmen Adolph Knobeloch, H. E. Leunig, J. B. Reis, and James Rentchler.

The company was originally located at East B Street and Douglas Avenue, once the site of farm-equipment manufacturer Rentchler Agricultural Works. Around 1909 it moved to a new building at Walnut and East Main in downtown Belleville that would be its home for more than 75 years. The Jordan Shoe Company had previously stood on the spot until it was razed by fire.

Belleville Shoe first concentrated on dress shoes for men and boys. During the Great Depression, Belleville shipped footwear to Chicago for use in poverty relief efforts.

Belleville Shoe began its long relationship with the U.S. military in 1917. In World War II, it was one of a handful of boot suppliers to receive the government's E Award for excellence. It made thousands of pairs of shoes and boots during the war; one of many contract awards quotes a price of $3.625 each for 25,000 leather-soled shoes.

The company made a variety of athletic shoes in the postwar years, including the Rawlings brand shoes favored by baseball great Stan Musial. In 1952, Homer Weidmann succeeded founder William Weidmann as company president.

RENEWED FOCUS ON THE BOOT

The company's focus eventually shifted back to the military. While the rest of the U.S. footwear industry would be almost entirely outsourced to Asia in the com-

COMPANY PERSPECTIVES

Belleville Shoe has become an industry leader in research and development of new boot technologies by reinvesting heavily in cutting-edge, computer driven equipment. It has pursued an expanding market share aggressively and is now the country's largest supplier of military boots.

ing decades, the armed forces were under a mandate to buy from U.S. suppliers, offering a protected niche. Nevertheless, the number of domestic competitors had shrunk from dozens during World War II to just a handful.

Meanwhile, military footwear was evolving. Jungle boots of the Vietnam War incorporated breathable nylon uppers and steel plates to protect against traps. The standard Army boot underwent another major redesign in the 1980s. Crafted of water-resistant leather, it featured details such as improved eyelets and a cleaner-tracking sole. Three other manufacturers besides Belleville Shoe were contracted to produce it, together making more than one million pairs per year.

Eric R. Weidmann became company president in 1982, the fourth generation of the family in charge. In 1986 Belleville Shoe moved its Illinois plant from Main Street to a new 112,000-square-foot facility in the Belle Valley Industrial Village on the southeastern side of town. The new plant cost $2.5 million, much of it financed with low-interest government loans.

By the end of the 1980s, the company's military boot sales were worth about $25 million annually. It employed about 350 people. However, the end of the Cold War was accompanied by a sharp falloff in business in 1990. Layoffs followed for more than 100 employees. Belleville Shoe was hit particularly hard, as it then focused exclusively on making boots for the military, which was deferring contracts in order to reduce a 2.5-million-pair surplus in its inventory.

Within months, however, the Pentagon was sending Belleville new orders for hot weather boots to replenish stocks used in the Gulf War. This included new desert footwear similar to the suede and nylon tropical boots used in Vietnam, but tan colored. The boots also lacked protective metal plates, since they became too hot in the desert.

Demand was so urgent that the plant began operating three shifts seven days a week. Recently laid off workers were brought back to work, and a few dozen new ones were hired. Employment peaked to 385 during the Gulf War, but more layoffs followed the end of hostilities.

NEW TECHNOLOGIES

By this time, the innovation-driven outdoor recreation industry had surpassed traditional military suppliers in terms of materials and design for many products, such as tents and clothing. Boots were another item due for an upgrade. Borrowing concepts from athletic footwear and commercial hiking boots and sneakers, Belleville introduced military models that were much more comfortable than their predecessors.

Belleville was one of two companies chosen to update the Marine Corps' traditional black leather boots in 1997. Its new TLS-700 design featured a breathable Gore-Tex layer, woven nylon uppers, and a cushioned midsole similar to those in athletic shoes. In 1999 the TLS-700 boot and an insulated winter version called the TLS-770 were approved by the Air Force for flight crews.

Branding was another civilian style innovation. In 1997 the company began stamping its military footwear with the Belleville name, helping it become something of a generic term for boots.

Belleville also updated its working methods, installing computerized machinery and drafting systems. In 1998, the company tried its hand at direct sales via a new web site. Products were available for purchase by civilians, albeit at higher prices than through military contracts.

Revenues for the privately owned company were reportedly $25 million in 1999. Belleville Shoe then employed about 250 people making about 400,000 pairs of boots a year. Sales rose to $30 million in 2000.

BELLEVILLE SOUTH OPENS IN 2002

Business received a big boost in the military buildup that followed the September 11, 2001, terrorist attacks against the United States. The company was soon expanding its Illinois plant at a cost of $1 million and looking for additional capacity elsewhere.

In 2002 Belleville Shoe took over the DeWitt Footwear Co. plant in Arkansas. Belleville leased the facility, dubbed Belleville South, from owner Munro & Co., with plans eventually to buy it. Originally opened in the early 1960s, the DeWitt factory had previously been owned by two other shoe companies and had

<table>
<tr><td colspan="2" align="center">KEY DATES
■</td></tr>
<tr><td>1904:</td><td>Belleville Shoe established in southern Illinois.</td></tr>
<tr><td>1909:</td><td>Company moves to new building in downtown Belleville.</td></tr>
<tr><td>1917:</td><td>Belleville Shoe begins making military footwear.</td></tr>
<tr><td>1945:</td><td>Company is one of a handful of boot suppliers to receive the "E" Award for wartime excellence.</td></tr>
<tr><td>1986:</td><td>Illinois operations moved to new $2.5 million plant in Belle Valley industrial park.</td></tr>
<tr><td>1997:</td><td>Belleville brand begins appearing on the outside of military boots.</td></tr>
<tr><td>2002:</td><td>DeWitt, Arkansas, shoe factory acquired.</td></tr>
</table>

manufactured civilian work boots, children's shoes, and other leather footwear.

Demand continued to grow during the war in Iraq. By 2003, the company employed 1,300 people, split evenly between its Illinois and Arkansas facilities. Belleville Shoe began subcontracting some work to its Ohio-based rival Rocky Shoes & Boots, Inc., which had a plant in Puerto Rico.

Government contracting nevertheless remained a highly cyclical business. In August 2005, more than 250 Belleville Shoe employees were laid off following the end of a couple of large Army and Marine Corps contracts.

Belleville Shoe continued to further the evolution of the boot. Toward the end of 2006, the company introduced a handful of models specifically sized for women's feet. At this time its two plants in Illinois and Arkansas together were making more than a million pairs of boots per year.

Frederick C. Ingram

PRINCIPAL OPERATING UNITS

Belleville Shoe Manufacturing Company; Belleville Shoe South, Inc.

PRINCIPAL COMPETITORS

Wellco Enterprises, Inc.; McRae Industries, Inc.; Altama Delta Corporation; Weinbrenner Shoe Company; Cove Shoe Company.

FURTHER READING

"Army Boots Being Made with Renewed Vigor," *Bloomington (Ill.) Pantagraph*, January 28, 1991, p. D2.

"Belleville Company Robbed," *Edwardsville (Ill.) Intelligencer*, December 24, 1942, p. 2.

Bohn, Gary, "Foot Soldiers," *St. Louis Post-Dispatch*, February 13, 1991, p. 1E.

Bowen, Jennifer A., "Belleville, Ill., Maker of Shoes, Army Boots Begins Round of Layoffs," *Belleville News-Democrat*, July 1, 2005.

Bryant, Tim, "Belleville Shoe, Union Reach Tentative Contract Agreement," *St. Louis Post-Dispatch*, April 4, 1994, p. 1B.

Burson, Marion, "Plan to Ease Seasonal Layoffs in Shoe Industry Put Forward," *Lowell (Mass.) Sun*, April 17, 1952, p. 7.

Buss, Will, "Shoe Company Has Deep Roots in Belleville, Ill.," *Belleville News-Democrat*, October 21, 2004.

Dalin, Shera, "Belleville Shoe Bets Boots on Military Sales," *St. Louis Post-Dispatch*, July 24, 2000, p. 5.

"Dies at Belleville," *Harrisburg (Ill.) Daily Register*, September 13, 1948, p. 4.

Donald, Leroy, "'Bellevilles' Revive Idled Plant, Reboot DeWitt Economy," *Arkansas Democrat Gazette*, November 7, 2004, p. 70.

Gansmann, Beth, "Belleville Shoe Manufacturing Plans $1 Million Expansion Project in Illinois," *Belleville News-Democrat*, April 4, 2002.

Goodman, Adam, "Belleville Shoe Plans to Lay Off 203," *St. Louis Post-Dispatch*, June 2, 1990, p. 8C.

———, "Boot Workers Return; Gulf Crisis Boots Belleville Shoe Co.," *St. Louis Post-Dispatch*, November 15, 1990, p. 1B.

———, "Company Had Borrowed Heavily to Build New Plant," *St. Louis Post-Dispatch*, June 18, 1990, p. 12.

———, "Getting the Boot: Manufacturers Pay the Price of Peace," *St. Louis Post-Dispatch*, June 18, 1990, p. 12.

Goodrich, Robert, "Air Force Will Buy Belleville Boots; Approval May Boost New Orders, Jobs," *St. Louis Post-Dispatch*, June 11, 1999, p. C2.

———, "Booty GI Shipments Are Stepped Up," *St. Louis Post-Dispatch*, January 31, 1991, p. 10A.

———, "Foundry Area Is Historic; Turn-of-the-Century Neighborhood Named for Title in Belleville," *St. Louis Post-Dispatch*, Illinois Sec., March 9, 1994, p. 1.

"Gulf Victory Means Boot for Shoemakers," *Chicago Sun-Times*, March 21, 1991, p. 50.

Manning, Margie, "Belleville Shoe Jumps into Direct Sales on the Internet," *St. Louis Business Journal*, October 5, 1998, p. 36.

Merrion, Paul, "Small Biz Sees Threat in Prison-Made Goods," *Crain's Chicago Business*, August 6, 1990, p. 44.

Minton, Mark, "Arkansas Shoemaker Reopens DeWitt Factory," *Knight-Ridder/Tribune Business News*, May 21, 2002.

Niquette, Mark, "Nelsonville, Ohio, Company to Make Shoes for Military," *Knight-Ridder/Tribune Business News*, March 11, 2004.

Paulk, Michael, "Shoe Manufacturer Reopens in DeWitt," *Memphis Business Journal*, May 24, 2002.

Perry, Tony, "Marines Go Sole Searching," *Stars and Stripes,* November 30, 1998, pp. 1–2.

Picht, Randolph, "Defense-Industry Doldrums," *Stars and Stripes,* December 19, 1989, pp. 14–15.

Pierce, Rick, "Belleville Company Develops New Boot for Marines," *St. Louis Post-Dispatch,* October 10, 1998, p. 14.

Ramey, Joanna, "Desert Warfare–Firms Fight over Growing Military Boot Contracts," *Footwear News,* May 5, 2003, p. 1.

Scripps Howard News Service, "'Waffle-Stompers' Give Old Army Footwear the Boot," *Elyria (Ohio) Chronicle-Telegram,* March 7, 1986, p. E7.

Van den Berg, David, "Belleville, Ill., Shoe Manufacturing Has Rise in Demand for Military Footwear," *Knight-Ridder/Tribune Business News,* October 2, 2001.

Bernstein-Rein

4600 Madison, Suite 1500
Kansas City, Missouri 64112
U.S.A.
Telephone: (816) 756-0640
Toll Free: (800) 571-6246
Fax: (816) 531-5708
Web site: http://www.bernstein-rein.com

Private Company
Incorporated: 1964 as Bernstein, Rein & Boasberg, Inc.
Employees: 351 (2007)
Gross Billings: $564 million (2006 est.)
NAIC: 541810 Advertising Agencies

■ ■ ■

Bernstein-Rein is one of the 40 largest advertising agencies in the United States and among the ten largest independently owned ones. The Kansas City, Missouri–based firm produces ads for brands such as Hostess snacks, NetZero, Classmates.com, Sunbeam, and Mr. Coffee, and its best-known efforts include McDonald's Happy Meal, H&R Block's Rapid Refund, and Wal-Mart's "Real People" ads. Bernstein-Rein's services include general creative work, direct marketing, interactive ads, database work, and account planning. Founders Bob Bernstein and Skip Rein remain involved with the firm more than 40 years after it was started.

EARLY YEARS

Bernstein-Rein dates its beginnings to May 1964, when Robert A. "Bob" Bernstein, Irwin D. "Skip" Rein, and

Howard T. Boasberg founded Bernstein, Rein & Boasberg, Inc. (BRB), in Kansas City, Missouri. Kansas City native Bernstein had been working for the city's largest advertising agency, Potts-Woodbury, and after meeting young ad man Skip Rein they decided to found their own agency along with eight-year industry veteran Boasberg, who would serve as director of client services and public relations. A start-up loan of $2,500 was negotiated with some difficulty by company president Bernstein, but within six months the firm was doing so well that the loan was paid down and plans for a second loan were scrapped.

The agency's clients were mainly local at first, but in 1967 BRB won an assignment to perform regional work for McDonald's. The entrepreneurial Bernstein also founded a side business called Specialty Promotions around this time, and in 1969 he proposed the arch-shaped "Sippy Dipper" straw to the hamburger chain, which requested 33 million of them within 90 days. Bernstein scrambled to find manufacturers of the item, but the straw generated a sizable profit, which he subsequently used to buy a Las Vegas radio station.

By the early 1970s BRB was producing for Milgram's grocery stores a series of folksy ads, which in 1974 caught the attention of Sam Walton, the owner of a growing Arkansas-based retail chain called Wal-Mart, who had no advertising agency of record. He drove to Kansas City to ask about hiring the actress who played "Janie from Milgram's" in the ads, but Bernstein informed him that she was under contract and could not work for Walton. After Walton left, Bernstein called his accountant to check on Wal-Mart's finances, and when he learned that the firm had nearly 75 stores and

COMPANY PERSPECTIVES

Bernstein-Rein understands that real enduring strength comes from being true to who you are. As an independent marketing communications agency rooted in the heartland, it's uniquely positioned to deliver that authenticity and connection to real consumers. Established in 1964, Bernstein-Rein continues to build some of the world's best-known brands, turn them into household names and inspire consumers to act.

sales of $350 million, he decided to drive to the retailer's headquarters in Bentonville, Arkansas, to seek its business. BRB was soon asked to produce test commercials for spot markets, but the campaign, which featured unpretentious-looking actors reading a list of store specials, was expanded before the results of the testing were even known, and the firm subsequently became Wal-Mart's official ad agency.

HAPPY MEAL CREATED FOR MCDONALD'S IN 1976

BRB scored again in 1976, after McDonald's asked the agency to help it attract more children. When Bernstein observed his 10-year-old-son Steve reading a cereal box at breakfast, he was inspired to create a boxed burger-fries-drink-dessert-toy package that had games and cartoons printed on the side. Dubbed the Happy Meal, it became one of the burger chain's most successful offerings after its national launch in 1979. Entrepreneur Bernstein also patented the packaging.

In 1981 Howard T. Boasberg left BRB to found The Boasberg Company, which would grow to become one of the 50 largest independently owned public relations firms in the United States. After the departure of Boasberg, the company changed its name to Bernstein-Rein Advertising, Inc.

During these years the firm's client list continued to grow, in the mid-1980s adding well-known companies like H&R Block, Sterling Drug, and D-Con Co. Bernstein-Rein had satellite offices in Spokane, Washington, and Portland, Oregon, and employed more than 100.

In 1985 Wal-Mart asked the firm to revise its ads, which had changed little over the preceding decade. With sales of more than $8 billion, it was the number one general merchandise retailer in the United States,

and this higher profile brought it unwanted attention for the number of foreign-made products it carried as American workers saw increasing numbers of jobs exported to Asia and Mexico. In Bernstein-Rein's "Buy American" ad campaign, which used real company employees and customers, the retail giant pledged to support American manufacturers.

By 1986 the firm had advertising billings of $70 million and gross income of $7.6 million. Slightly more than two-thirds of ad dollars went for spot television ads, with radio accounting for 13 percent, newspapers 8 percent, magazines 5 percent, and outdoor ads 3 percent.

As Wal-Mart's rapid growth continued, its management decided one ad agency was not enough, and in 1987 GSD&M of Austin, Texas, was tapped to share the work. Bernstein-Rein would focus on retail branding, while its new partner would handle the realm of people and product.

BLOCKBUSTER ADDED IN 1988

In 1988 the company won the account of a small but rapidly growing video store chain, Blockbuster Entertainment Corp., which had $4 million in billings. Two years later Bob Bernstein founded a company called Serendipity Entertainment to operate franchised Blockbuster stores, and although it struggled at first to turn a profit, Serendipity would eventually become the largest Blockbuster franchisee in the United States, with nearly 100 outlets.

During the late 1980s and early 1990s criticism of Wal-Mart's corporate practices was rising steadily, and in 1992 a *Dateline NBC* exposé revealed that the percentage of imported goods it sold had grown since the "Buy American" campaign began, while some products labeled in stores as American had actually been produced overseas. The retailer, whose founder Sam Walton had died earlier in the year, quickly de-emphasized the tagline and later replaced it with Bernstein-Rein's "smiley face" campaign, which focused on low prices.

Although it had created the popular "Make It a Blockbuster Night" ads, in December 1993 Bernstein-Rein lost the video-store firm's account and closed a 24-employee office in Fort Lauderdale, Florida, that had been opened to service it. Important new clients were being added, however, including meat products producer Farmland Foods, clothing retailer Edison Bros., and, in the spring of 1995, the $15 million account of Shoney's Restaurants, which had 915 outlets in the Southeast, Midwest, and Northeast. Bernstein-Rein subsequently gave up working for three large McDonald's franchisee groups in the Midwest to avoid a

KEY DATES

1964: Bernstein, Rein, and Boasberg ad agency founded in Kansas City, Missouri.

1967: Firm begins doing work for McDonald's.

1974: Sam Walton hires agency to develop ads for his 75-store Wal-Mart chain.

1976: Bob Bernstein creates Happy Meal for McDonald's.

1981: Howard Boasberg leaves; firm shortens name to Bernstein-Rein Advertising.

1988: Agency begins producing ads for Blockbuster.

1998: Insight Marketing Communications, Inc., acquired.

1999: Impact Direct Marketing purchased; Blockbuster drops firm.

2006: Wal-Mart account lost; agency rebrands itself as Bernstein-Rein.

2007: Steve Bernstein named president of company.

conflict of interest. The firm also took on Bayer Animal Health, maker of pet care products, and Beauty Brands, a salon/spa/retail chain founded by Bob Bernstein and his son David that would open more than four dozen outlets in 11 states over the next decade.

In the fall of 1996 Bernstein-Rein was again chosen by Blockbuster, this time splitting its $150 million account with Young & Rubicam. Duties included planning and buying ads for the chain's music stores and marketing to children. That year also saw the loss of H&R Block, which was followed in 1997 by the departure of Shoney's. Bernstein-Rein's billings topped $260 million, and the firm was Kansas City's largest ad agency.

Freed up by the loss of Shoney's, in 1998 the agency was again hired to create ads for two Midwest McDonald's operator groups, which represented about 250 restaurants. During the year the firm also won the accounts of NationsRent, a heavy equipment firm backed by former Blockbuster owner H. Wayne Huizenga, and Thrifty Car Rental, which had 1,200 outlets and ad billings of $10 million.

ACQUISITIONS BOOST OFFERINGS IN 1998 AND 1999

In 1998 Bernstein-Rein bought Insight Marketing Communications, Inc., which used databases to help advertisers target customers, and in February 1999 it acquired Impact Direct Marketing. The latter would give it stronger capabilities in an area where it had previously relied on subcontractors or in-house staff.

In March 1999 the firm again lost the Blockbuster account after Wherehouse Entertainment, which had its own in-house ad agency, bought the video chain. In June a new $17 million campaign was launched for Kansas City-based Russell Stover, which was introducing its first single-serving candy bar line. During the year Bernstein-Rein also won the retail and investor services accounts of Commerce Bancshares, for which it had created commercial banking ads. In 1999 billings grew to $340 million and gross revenues increased to $40 million.

In 2002 the firm won the account of United Online, owner of web-based reunion facilitator Classmates.com and Internet service providers Juno and NetZero, for which it had done account planning work starting in 2000. Bernstein-Rein also established an account planning department and a marketing unit called the Brand Relationship Group during the year, the latter of which would work with clients such as Wal-Mart and Thrifty as well as targeting companies with smaller promotional budgets that made fewer media buys. In addition to assisting its commercial clients, the firm was performing thousands of hours of work per year on a pro bono basis for such organizations as the Kansas City Zoo and the United Way.

In 2000 Bob Bernstein had sold the Las Vegas radio station he owned and the 32 acres it was on, and four years later he took the profits to invest in a $116 million Kansas City development project called the West Edge, which would eventually house the agency's offices (as well as those of Beauty Brands and Serendipity Entertainment), a boutique hotel, restaurants, retail outlets, an auditorium, parking, and the Advertising Icon Museum, headed by former partner Howard Boasberg. The latter would feature Bernstein's growing collection of ad icons like Tony the Tiger and the Jolly Green Giant, many of which had been acquired from another collector in 2003. Bernstein later also added a nearby apartment building which he converted to condominiums.

LOSS OF WAL-MART IN 2006

With 3,800 stores and sales of $300 billion, by 2006 Wal-Mart was the largest retailer in the world. Recently outpaced in sales growth by rivals like Target, the Arkansas-based company began laying plans to reach more upscale customers and in August announced it would look for a new advertising agency. Although partner GSD&M was allowed to compete in the agency "shootout," Bernstein-Rein was told not to submit a proposal. It was a great blow to the firm, which according to some estimates had derived half of its 2005 billings of $553 million from Wal-Mart. Some employees were reportedly relieved no longer to represent the controversial company, however, and the agency was also freed to seek new accounts in previously conflicting categories such as electronics, auto parts, drugs, groceries, shoes, and jewelry. Bernstein-Rein continued to perform work for the retailer through the end of the year, for which it posted billings of $564 million and revenues of $60 million.

By mid-2007 the agency had replaced about 70 percent of its Wal-Mart work, with new accounts including video-game-maker Ubisoft; the Hostess Snack Cakes brands of Interstate Bakeries Corp.; phone carrier SunCom Wireless; premium vodka importer Stiletto Brands; and the Sunbeam, Crock-Pot, and Mr. Coffee brands of Jarden Consumer Solutions. Although massive layoffs had initially been feared, just four of the firm's 350 workers had left through attrition and 30 job listings were posted on the company web site. While annual billings were expected to shrink because of Wal-Mart's dependence on expensive TV ads, gross revenues were projected to rise slightly.

In May 2007 the firm named Steve Bernstein to the title of president. He had been with the company his father helped found since 1992, most recently serving as chief operating officer. Bob Bernstein would remain chairman and CEO, with Skip Rein continuing as vice-chairman. Bernstein's other son David, and daughter Susan, also worked for the firm. A few months earlier its name had been shortened to Bernstein-Rein, and it had introduced a new logo.

As the agency continued to reshape itself post–Wal-Mart, it launched two new analytical tools, MediaMetrix and Brand Humanity Quotient. The former measured ways consumers used media, while the latter examined relationships they had with brands. The firm was also preparing for the planned 2008 move to Bernstein's West Edge complex.

Now in its fifth decade, Bernstein-Rein was adapting to the challenge posed by the loss of top client Wal-Mart by burnishing its image and broadening its list of clients. Still the top ad agency in Kansas City, the firm represented a mix of local and national firms that included familiar brands such as Mr. Coffee, Hostess snacks, and Thrifty Car Rental.

Frank Uhle

PRINCIPAL OPERATING UNITS
Bernstein-Rein Yellow Pages; B-R Method.

PRINCIPAL COMPETITORS
Barkley; VML, Inc.; Valentine-Radford Communications, Inc.; Nicholson Kovac, Inc.; Kuhn & Wittenborn, Inc.; McCann Worldgroup; Ogilvy & Mather Worldwide; Draft FCB Group; Leo Burnett Worldwide, Inc.; JWT; Young & Rubicam Brands.

FURTHER READING
Baar, Aaron, "Bernstein Buys Impact Direct," *Adweek Midwest Edition,* February 8, 1999, p. 2.

———, "Bernstein-Rein Boosts Research with Planning Arm," *Adweek Midwest Edition,* May 27, 2002, p. 4.

———, "Bernstein-Rein Consolidates Below-the-Line Work," *Adweek Midwest Edition,* September 2, 2002, p. 5.

———, "Bernstein-Rein Names President," *Adweek,* May 30, 2007.

Baar, Aaron, and Glen Fest, "Bernstein-Rein Gets Thrifty," *Adweek Southeast,* October 12, 1998, p. 84.

Barton, Eric, "Life Without Wal-Mart," *Kansas City (Mo.) Pitch,* December 7, 2006.

Creamer, Matthew, "Bernstein Puts Smiley Face on a Life Without Wal-Mart," *Advertising Age,* August 14, 2006, p. 1.

Galvez-Searle, Dixon, "Agency of the Year: Bernstein-Rein," *Screen,* January 27, 2006.

———, "Business Is Pleasure," *Screen,* January 11, 2007.

———, "A Life in the Business: Bob Bernstein to Receive Lifetime Achievement Award at *Screen*'s Fourth Annual Star Awards," *Screen,* August 31, 2006.

Grenz, Chris, "Agency Looks for Gains in Wal-Mart Loss," *Kansas City Business Journal,* August 18, 2006.

———, "Bernstein Bounces Back from Wal-Mart," *Kansas City Business Journal,* February 17, 2007.

Lee, Kate, "A Conversation with … Bob Bernstein," *Greater Kansas City Business,* June 2003, pp. 10–13.

Martin, Ellen Rooney, "Bernstein-Rein's Connections Regain Blockbuster Account," *Adweek Midwest Edition,* October 7, 1996, p. 4.

Menninger, Bonar, "Bernstein-Rein Ranks Among Nation's Top 100 Ad Agencies," *Kansas City Business Journal,* June 18, 1999.

Osterman, Jim, and Steve Krajewski, "W-Mart Savvy at Bernstein Wins Shoney's," *Adweek Southeast Edition,* May 15, 1995, p. 4.

Sechter, Sheridan, "Bob Bernstein: The Man with the Midas Touch," *Flourish,* September/October 2006.

Sedensky, Matt, "Still Making Kids Happy, 25 Years Later," *Associated Press Newswires,* August 13, 2004.

Smith, Joyce, "Bernstein Finds Fun in Every Challenge," *Kansas City Star,* June 22, 2006.

Biffa plc

——■——

Coronation Road
Cressex Industrial Estate
High Wycombe, HP12 3TZ
United Kingdom
Telephone: (44 01494) 521 221
Fax: (44 01494) 463 368
Web site: http://www.biffa.co.uk

Public Company
Incorporated: 2006
Employees: 5,147
Sales: £742.7 million ($1.5 billion) (2007)
Stock Exchanges: London
Ticker Symbol: BIFF
NAIC: 562111 Solid Waste Collection

■ ■ ■

Biffa plc is the United Kingdom's leading integrated waste management company, with operations that include waste collection services, landfill operations, the collection and disposal of hazardous and other specialty waste, and renewable power generation. Biffa helped pioneer waste collection services for the industrial and corporate sectors, and with more than 75,000 industrial and commercial customers, Biffa remains the leading player in this sector.

Biffa also provides services directly to residential communities, maintaining contracts with 20 local authorities and serving more than two million private households across the country with its own fleet of 1,500 vehicles. As part of the country's Private Finance Initiative (PFI), Biffa has been awarded two fully integrated waste management contracts (including treatment and recycling) with the city councils of Isle of Wight and Leicester.

The company's Waste Collection division accounted for nearly 54 percent of the group's revenues of nearly £743 million ($1.5 billion) in 2007. Biffa's next largest business is its Landfill division, which operates 37 landfills sites as well as 19 transfer stations and 15 waste sorting and recycling sites. In 2007, Biffa's Landfill division processed more than 7.5 million tons of waste, and these operations generated more than 38 percent of the company's total sales.

An increasingly important area of Biffa's operations is its Special Waste division, which collects, treats, recycles, and disposes of hazardous solids and liquids for the industrial and commercial sectors. This division, which contributed nearly 6 percent to the group's revenues, operates from 20 sites throughout the United Kingdom and includes three special liquid treatments facilities, as well as its own fleet of 80 vehicles.

Biffa's final division is its Power Generation division, which produces electricity based on gas emissions, principally methane, produced at its landfills. The company is one of the major generators of landfill gas-based power, considered a renewable energy source, with an installed capacity of 109 megawatts. Formerly part of water services group Severn Trent, Biffa was spun off as an independent company in October 2006 and listed on the London Stock Exchange.

CLINKER CARRIER IN 1919

Biffa began as a small collection service launched by Richard Henry Biffa in the village of Wembley in 1919. The Biffa family name had achieved some prominence in that village in the previous century, as one Baptiste Biffa, a building contractor and restaurateur, was said to have owned much of Wembley village by the late 1880s. Richard Henry Biffa, who was born in 1882, went into the business of collecting the ash and clinker produced as waste at coal-fired power stations, which remained a primary source of power in the United Kingdom until well past the mid-20th century. Clinker, ash, and other coal residues were at the time used by the construction industry for paving roads, as well as for manufacturing breeze blocks, which were used for constructing the interior walls of houses. Biffa's business quickly graduated from using dust carts to operating its first truck. With the savings from other family members, Biffa soon added a second truck.

Before long, Biffa had expanded his business into the greater London area and was joined in the enterprise by son Richard Frank Biffa. In the years leading up to and during World War II, the company's clinker collection played a significant role in the construction of the airfields serving the British military effort. The reconstruction of London during the postwar period provided Biffa's business with a new boost. Into the 1950s, the company began its first expansion, adding

the excavation of sand and gravel to its clinker collection operations. The company also extended its collection operations beyond clinker and coal waste, launching its first general waste collection services. In 1958, a new generation of the Biffa family joined the company as Richard Biffa, Jr., came aboard.

The younger Biffa recognized a new opportunity for the company: the general waste collection market. While waste collection for private individuals remained the province of the local governments, the industrial and corporate market increasingly turned toward private contractors. Under the newly organized Biffa Ltd. the company launched its own waste collection operation in 1960 and began building up its client list from the London area's industrial and commercial sector.

WASTE COLLECTION FOCUS IN THE EIGHTIES

Soon after creating the division, Biffa Jr. hit upon the formula that was to enable the company to grow into one of the sector's leaders. Biffa introduced a new waste collection concept to the U.K. market—the use of container systems for hauling trash and waste. The new service quickly gained popularity, and as a result, Biffa expanded its services across England. By the end of the 1960s, the company's annual profits had grown to a respectable £100,000. This profitability also brought the company to the attention of the fast-growing conglomerate British Electric Traction (BET). In 1971, BET reached an agreement to acquire the Biffa waste disposal and construction materials group in a deal worth more than £750,000.

As part of BET, Biffa joined the subsidiaries of the Reclamations & Disposals unit, alongside Re-Chem International. Richard Biffa later joined the management at Re-Chem and then led a management buyout of that company in 1985. In the meantime, Biffa grew strong under BET, tripling its profits by the end of the 1970s. By the early 1980s, environmental issues surrounding waste disposal, particularly of hazardous wastes, had led to increasing legislation in the sector. The regulation of the sector, and the demand for ever-increasing technological investments to meet legislation, forced a consolidation of the market.

Biffa was able to play a role in leading the initial phase of consolidation. The company completed a series of acquisitions through the 1980s, starting with the 1982 purchase of the waste control division of the Hoveringham Group for £2.65 million. That deal added seven new depots to Biffa's operations, strengthening its presence especially in the Midlands and Home Counties regions. The purchase also placed Biffa in the top three

KEY DATES

1919: Richard Henry Biffa founds business in Wembley collecting clinker from coal-based power plants.

1960: Richard Henry, Jr., grandson of the founder, leads Biffa into waste collection and disposal sector.

1971: British Electric Traction (BET) acquires Biffa for £754,000.

1991: BET sells Biffa to Severn Trent for £212 million.

2000: Biffa acquires UK Waste for £380 million, taking the lead in the country's waste management sector.

2006: Severn Trent spins Biffa off in a public offering on the London Stock Exchange.

among Britain's waste disposal sector.

Biffa prospered as a privatization of the waste collection and disposal industry was carried out under the Thatcher administration during the 1980s. Through the decade, Biffa's landfill operations also grew strongly, and by the end of the decade the company was operating 26 landfill sites in Britain. The company also made its first international move, adding four landfill sites and a waste collection and disposal subsidiary in Belgium. By the end of the decade, Biffa had become a significant profit source for BET, generating nearly £14 million in operating profit, on sales of £90 million, by the early 1990s.

While Biffa continued to grow strongly, however, BET found itself struggling to carry its debt load into the 1990s. Hard hit by the international recession at the start of the decade, BET conducted a strategic review of its operations. In 1991, the conglomerate announced its decision to sell off its waste management division. In May of that year, the company announced that it had sold Biffa to Severn Trent plc for £212 million. That company, the former Severn Trent Water Authority, had been formed in 1989 as part of the privatization of Britain's water utilities.

Birmingham-based Severn Trent, which retained its monopoly over water services in its region, remained under regulatory control of the British government. The acquisition of Biffa, therefore, formed an important part of Severn Trent's efforts to develop its nonregulated operations as well.

Severn Trent financed the Biffa acquisition through the use of high-interest-bearing Eurobonds. With inter-est payments topping £24 million per year, the financing package initially depressed Biffa's earning picture, ruling out immediate acquisitions. Nonetheless, Biffa itself remained financially strong and focused on building its operations through organic expansion, backed by a small number of regional acquisitions. The company's landfill operations grew especially strongly during the decade, and by the 2000s Biffa landfills comprised more than 73 million cubic meters at 37 sites. These landfill operations, which were far less labor intensive than the group's waste disposal business, also represented a significant source of profits.

INDEPENDENT IN 2006

Biffa returned to acquisitions in the late 1990s. The company entered Scotland in 1998, buying the Paterson waste collection operation, one of the largest independent groups in that region. Also that year, the company acquired two landfills in Swindow and Salsbury. Biffa completed a £23 million spending spree that year with the purchase of a landfill and recycling operation in Canford, near Bournemouth. Significantly, this acquisition provided Biffa with a 50 percent share of a power generation plant, which produced electricity using gases generated by the decomposition of matter in the landfill. That area became a small but important operation for Biffa as the alarming acceleration of global warming conditions brought about a new urgency for the development of environmentally sound power sources in the new century.

Biffa recognized the growing importance of the waste industry's role in the larger effort to reduce fossil fuel emissions, as the company invested in expanding its recycling capacity. Biffa also began working directly with companies in various industries to develop custom recycling and disposal programs in order to reclaim a maximum amount of materials. In 1999, for example, the company launched the Bottleback program in partnership with the Brewers and Licensed Retailers Association, generating more than 300,000 tons of recycled glass each year.

Biffa rose to the top of its industry in 2000 when Severn Trent announced its purchase of UK Waste, the British branch of U.S. giant Waste Management Inc., for £380 million. The purchase added 26 new collection depots, six paper recycling facilities, and eight landfills to Biffa's operations, giving it the leadership spot in the United Kingdom. The UK Waste acquisition came as part of a wider effort by Severn Trent to transform itself into a dual-focus business, balancing its regulated water business with nonregulated waste operations. By 2000, Severn Trent had succeeded in boosting its nonregulated operations to 50 percent of its total.

Biffa grew again in 2003, as Severn Trent backed a new large-scale acquisition, paying £141 million for Hales, part of the RMC cement group. The Hales purchase strengthened Biffa's presence in the London and East Anglia markets, adding eight landfill sites as well as regional operations in Birmingham, Manchester, Leeds, and Newscastle. The completion of the Hales acquisition boosted Biffa's market share to 12 percent of the total U.K. market, solidifying its leadership position. By the midpoint of the first decade of the 2000s, Biffa alone accounted for more than one-third of Severn Trent's total sales of £1.2 billion.

The arrival of a new management team at Severn Trent, led by CEO Colin Matthews, prompted a strategic review of Biffa's business in 2005. Severn Trent concluded that it had not been able to realize the hoped-for synergies between its water and waste collection operations. At the same time, the increasing sophistication and importance of the waste management industry had raised the profile of the sector in the investment community. In 2006, therefore, Severn Trent announced its decision to de-merge its Biffa arm in a public offering on the London Stock Exchange. That offer was completed in October 2006, following the sale of Biffa's Belgian arm to Veolia. The offering valued Biffa at £1 billion. As an independent company, Biffa faced the promise of ever-stricter recycling standards, but it had positioned itself as a leader in what had become one of the United Kingdom's, and the world's, most vital industries in the new century.

M. L. Cohen

PRINCIPAL SUBSIDIARIES

Biffa (UK) Ltd.; Biffa Corporate Holdings Ltd.; Biffa Holdings Ltd.; Biffa UK Group Ltd.; Biffa UK Holdings Ltd.; Biffa Waste Ltd.; Biffa Waste Management Ltd.; Biffa Waste Services Ltd.; Poplars Resource Management Company Ltd.; Reclamation & Disposal Ltd.; UK Waste Management Holdings Ltd.; UK Waste Management Ltd.

PRINCIPAL DIVISIONS

Waste Collection; Power Generation; Landfill; Special Waste.

PRINCIPAL COMPETITORS

Service Management International Ltd.; Exel plc; Group 4 Securicor plc; Thiess Proprietary Ltd.; SITA Holdings UK Ltd.; Veolia ES Cleanaway (UK) Ltd.; Shanks Group plc.

FURTHER READING

"BET to Cut Costs and May Sell Biffa," *Times* (London), February 19, 1991.

"Biffa Cleaning Up," *Birmingham Post,* October 2, 2007, p. 20.

"Biffa Takes a Bashing," *Investors Chronicle,* June 12, 2007.

"Biffa Ties Up Pounds 141m Deal," *Birmingham Evening Mail,* June 20, 2003, p. 26.

Bream, Rebecca, "Fund Managers Lined Up to Make Rubbish Collection," *Financial Times,* October 10, 2006, p. 23.

Essen, Yvette, "Biffa's Worth Putting in the Storage Bin Ready for Turnaround," *Daily Telegraph,* October 2, 2007.

"'Go It Alone' Biffa Thrives," *Birmingham Mail,* June 12, 2007, p. 34.

Harvey, Fiona, "Severn Trent Sells Biffa's Belgium Arm for Euros 45m," *Financial Times,* May 13, 2006, p. 18.

———, "Waste Companies Turning Muck into Money," *Financial Times,* April 11, 2006, p. 23.

Hume, Neil, and Robert Orr, "Shanks and Biffa Are Tipped for Waste Industry Consolidation," *Financial Times,* April 18, 2007, p. 40.

"Organic Growth Boosts Biffa," *Birmingham Post,* December 7, 2006, p. 21.

"Severn Trent Pays Pounds 212m for Biffa Waste Business," *Times* (London), May 14, 1991.

Bronner Brothers Inc.

———— ■ ————

2141 Powers Ferry Road
Marietta, Georgia 30067
U.S.A.
Telephone: (770) 988-0015
Toll Free: (800) 241-6151
Fax: (770) 953-0848
Web site: http://www.bronnerbros.com

Private Company
Incorporated: 1964 as Bronner Brothers Wholesale
    Beauty and Drug Supply Co., Inc.
Employees: 300
Sales: $30 million (2006 est.)
NAIC: 325620 Toilet Preparation Manufacturing;
    325611 Soap and Other Detergent Manufacturing;
    511120 Periodical Publishers; 541690 Other
    Scientific and Technical Consulting Services;
    541990 All Other Professional, Scientific, and
    Technical Services; 721110 Hotels (except Casino
    Hotels) and Motels; 812990 All Other Personal
    Services

■ ■ ■

Bronner Brothers Inc. operates one of the country's
leading black hair and beauty products businesses.
Facilities include two manufacturing plants, two retail
stores, a distribution center, and a headquarters in a
suburb of Atlanta. It is unique for remaining a rare
independent, black-owned company in the $5 billion
ethnic hair care industry, which has come to be increasingly dominated by multinational corporations. "Where

there's hair, there's hope," says one of the company's
early mottos.

A focal point of the business is a long-running
series of annual trade shows that draw tens of thousands
of people and hundreds of exhibitors. Probably Bronner's oldest brand is an oil-based hair conditioner called
SuperGro; the company also sells the African Royale,
Nu Expressions, and Pump It Up brands and various
products proudly displaying the company's "BB"
initials. The family has many other outside interests as
diverse as magazine publishing, motels, health food, and
worship centers. CEO Bernard Bronner, son of
company founder Dr. Nathaniel H. Bronner, Sr., once
said he would like to be involved in 100 companies.

ORIGINS

Dr. Nathaniel Hawthorne Bronner, Sr., set out to enter
the beauty supply business in 1947. He was joined by
two of his ten siblings: Arthur Edward Bronner, Sr., and
Emma Bronner. Art Bronner left a dry cleaning business
he had started in Cleveland, Ohio, after the war in
order to help out his brother.

The Bronners had grown up on a farm in Kelly, a
town in rural East Georgia, and led a hardscrabble existence picking crops until they left to work in nearby
Atlanta, the largest city in the South. This was where
they set up their new enterprise.

Dr. Bronner developed an entrepreneurial mind-set
at an early age. While still a teenager, he delivered
newspapers during the Great Depression, walking past
destitute souls on a daily basis. He was later inspired by

a sign he saw at the Apex Beauty Parlor, where his sister was studying cosmetology, which touted the recession-proof nature of the beauty business. World War II arrived before he could set out on his own.

Bronner attended Morehouse College, writing a paper on the black cosmetics industry for one of his classes. According to one account, Bronner launched his career by selling Sister C.J. Walker products door-to-door. This brand was named after the famous African American entrepreneur who had created a hair care products empire in the early part of the 20th century.

Deciding to cut out the middleman, Bronner acquired the formula for a hair care product called SuperGro. Another early Bronner Bros. product was "BB Hair Food," the initials referring to the company name. Bronner soon added a handful of other products and extended his sales pitch to salons. National supermarket and drugstore chains began carrying the goods in the 1960s.

GROWING ALONG WITH THE INDUSTRY

Bronner Brothers Wholesale Beauty and Drug Supply Co., Inc., was incorporated in Georgia on January 3, 1964. The name was shortened to Bronner Bros., Inc., in January 1994, a month after it merged with Bronner Brothers Manufacturing Company. Another entity, Bronner Brothers Beauty and Drug Stores, Inc., was also incorporated in 1964 and dissolved in 1992.

Annual revenues were just $500,000 in the early 1980s. Discount retailing goliath Wal-Mart Stores, Inc., began carrying Bronner Bros. products around 1984, helping spur a huge growth in sales. Twenty years later, Bernard Bronner called Wal-Mart his most reliable and

"most loved" customer, crediting the chain with helping Bronner Bros. learn how to control costs.

Annual revenues of $15 million in 1986 earned Bronner Bros. a spot among the *Black Enterprise Magazine* listing of the country's 100 largest black-owned businesses. By this time, there were two manufacturing plants, two warehouses, and four shops. In the mid-1980s the entire black hair care product industry was then estimated to be worth as much as $1 billion, and the growing market had caught the attention of consumer goods giants since the 1970s.

FAMOUS TRADE SHOWS

The Bronners had been putting on their famous trade shows from the very beginning. The first was held at Atlanta's Butler Street YMCA, where Emma Bronner taught cosmetology. Events moved to progressively larger venues through the years as attendance swelled. In 1967, Atlanta's Hyatt Regency Hotel began a 20-year run of hosting the shows. They were eventually moved to the Georgia World Congress Center.

The main hair show was drawing 40,000 attendees and 300 exhibitors by the mid-1990s. In 1996 it was held in Orlando, Florida, to make room for the Olympics. The company remained committed to its Atlanta base, although it considered the prospect of moving the smaller winter show to another city for the sake of variety.

SIDE VENTURES

The Bronner family diversified into magazine publishing with the launch of nationally distributed *Upscale* in 1989. They may have seen a logical connection between its glossy pages and the glamour-driven beauty products business. The magazine was a separate venture from the Bronner Bros. hair care company.

In July 1991 the Bronners acquired a small-scale tourist attraction in a tiny Alabama town near the Florida border. The Cottonwood Hot Springs Spa and Motel featured mineral baths and dated back to the 1920s. Family members continued to get involved in many other side ventures. By 2004, the Bronners were trying their hand at the movie business.

SECOND GENERATION

Company founder Nathaniel Bronner, Sr., passed away in July 1993 at the age of 79. He left behind a company selling some four-dozen items, which were distributed in eight countries. There were 200 employees.

Bernard Bronner, previously head of the company's manufacturing operations, succeeded his father as

KEY DATES

1947: Bronner Brothers launch beauty products business and annual trade show.
1967: Trade show moved to Atlanta's new Hyatt Regency Hotel.
1989: *Upscale* magazine launched.
1991: Alabama's Cottonwood Hot Springs Spa and Motel acquired.
1993: Bernard Bronner succeeds his father as president and CEO.
1994: Company buys new $2 million headquarters building.
2007: Annual revenues are about $30 million.

president and CEO. His own brothers, Charles, James, and Nathaniel Bronner, Jr., were also active in company management. Cofounder Arthur Bronner, Sr., died in 2006.

"Always own the roof that's over your head" was among the aphorisms passed down to the Bronner children. The company heeded this advice when a new three-story headquarters building was purchased in 1994. The company bought it for $2 million from MONY Insurance Co. It kept its factory at 600 Bronner Brothers Way. There were also three more manufacturing facilities, one of them leased.

By the time of the company's sixtieth anniversary in 2007, revenues were about $30 million a year. This represented a small slice of what had grown to a $5 billion industry. Most of Bronner Bros.'s black-owned competitors had long since sold out to multinational conglomerates like Procter & Gamble and L'Oréal, the latter of which Nathaniel Bronner, Jr., called "a Microsoft of the haircare industry."

Frederick C. Ingram

PRINCIPAL OPERATING UNITS

Bronner Bros. Beauty Products; Upscale Magazine; Cottonwood Hot Springs Spa and Motel; Bronner Bros. International Beauty and Trade Shows; Word of Faith Family Worship Center; Ark of Salvation Worship Center.

PRINCIPAL COMPETITORS

Revlon Inc.; L'Oréal USA, Inc.; The Procter & Gamble Company; Dudley Products, Inc.; Luster Products, Inc.

FURTHER READING

Adamy, Janet, "Word War Erupts Among Firms," *Knight-Ridder/Tribune Business News: Detroit Free Press,* May 29, 1998.

Barry, Tom, "All in the Family," *Atlanta Business Chronicle,* October 15, 2004.

Bennett, Tom, "Nathaniel Bronner Sr., Was Founder of Black Hair-Care Products Firm," *Atlanta Constitution,* July 20, 1993, p. D4.

"Bronner Bros. Beauty and Trade Show Draws 30,000 to Atlanta Luxury Hotels," *Jet,* September 16, 1985, p. 10.

Carmichael, Rodney, "Bernard Bronner; President/CEO, Bronner Bros., Upscale, Rainforest Films: The Formula," *Rolling Out,* May 13, 2004, p. 8.

Crabb, Cheryl, "Black Convention Boom," *Atlanta Business Chronicle,* August 8, 1997, pp. 1Af.

Dugas, Christine, and Kenneth Dreyfack, "A Gaffe at Revlon Has the Black Community Seething," *Business Week,* February 9, 1987, p. 36.

Evertz, Mary, "Hair, Apparent: Bronner Bros. Mid-Summer International Hair Show Battle Royale '98," *St. Petersburg Times,* August 7, 1998, p. 1D.

Ezell, Hank, "Family-Owned Bronner Brothers Among Honorees," *Atlanta Journal and Constitution,* May 28, 1992, p. D7.

Farhi, Paul, "Hair Care Battle Lines Drawn in Black, White," *Washington Post,* December 27, 1993, p. A1.

Hocker, Cliff, "Bad Hair Days—African American Firms Losing Control of the Ethnic Haircare Industry," *Black Enterprise,* November 2000.

"Homegrown Hair-Care Company Marks Milestone," *Atlanta Business Chronicle,* May 25, 2007.

Jones, Adam, "Bernard Bronner; Creator of Upscale Magazine/CEO of Bronner Bros., Inc.," *Rolling Out,* February 15, 2007.

Lambert, Bruce, "N.H. Bronner, 79, Atlantan Who Led Cosmetics Company," *New York Times,* July 21, 1993, p. B18.

Lawlor, Julia, "The Crowded Road to Riches; By the Time 'Forbes' Names the 400 Richest Next Weekend, Thousands More People in the USA Will Be Worth a Million," *Chicago Daily Herald,* USA Weekend Sec., October 2, 1988.

McGee, Sherri A., "Beauty-Show Manager," *Essence,* October 2004, p. 120.

Poole, Shelia M., "Bronner Brothers Inc. Moving to New Offices," *Atlanta Constitution,* June 24, 1994, p. G2.

———, "Hair-Care Patriarch Opens Alabama Spa; Making Room for Children," *Atlanta Journal and Constitution,* October 11, 1991, p. D1.

———, "Hair Products Company Stages Its 52nd Annual Show in Atlanta," *Knight-Ridder/Tribune Business News,* August 15, 1999.

———, "Hair Today, Hair Tomorrow—Event in Atlanta for 50th Year," *Atlanta Journal/Atlanta Constitution,* August 16, 1997, p. D2.

———, "Smaller of Two Events Featuring Ethnic Hair Products May Leave Atlanta," *Knight-Ridder/Tribune Business News,* August 3, 2000.

Powell, Kay, "Arthur Bronner Sr., 89, Hair Products Executive," *Atlanta Journal-Constitution,* May 15, 2006.

Reid, S. A., "Bronner Bros. Hair Show: 60 Years, No Bad Hair Days," *Atlanta Journal-Constitution,* August 18, 2007, p. C1.

Welch, Mary, "Brushing Up on Black Hair-Care History with Bronner Brothers," *Atlanta Business Chronicle,* April 27, 1987, p. 12A.

Burberry Group plc

18–22 Haymarket
London, SW1Y 4DQ
United Kingdom
Telephone: (44 20) 7968 0000
Fax: (44 20) 7318 2950
Web site: http://www.burberryplc.com

Public Company
Founded: 1856
Employees: 4,651
Sales: £850.3 million ($1.76 billion) (2007)
Stock Exchanges: London
Ticker Symbol: BRBY
NAIC: 315230 Women's and Girls' Cut and Sew Apparel Manufacturing; 315220 Men's and Boys' Cut and Sew Apparel Manufacturing; 448140 Family Clothing Stores

■ ■ ■

Burberry Group plc is a designer, manufacturer, and distributor of luxury and casual men's and women's apparel and accessories. It operates its own retail stores around the world and also distributes its products through concessions and wholesale customers and third-party licenses. The Burberry name is virtually synonymous with the tan gabardine raincoat pioneered by the company more than 150 years ago, and outwear continues to be the company's foundation. An icon of classic clothing, Burberry builds on its traditions to appeal to a younger generation of fashion-conscious customers.

19TH-CENTURY ORIGINS

Founder Thomas Burberry was born in 1835 and apprenticed in the drapery trade, establishing his own drapery business in Basingstoke, Hampshire, in 1856. A sportsman, Burberry was dissatisfied with the then-popular rubberized mackintosh raincoat, which was heavy, restricting, and stifling, and thus unsuitable for extended outings. Inspired by country folk's loose smocks, Burberry designed a tightly woven fabric made from water-repellent linen or cotton yarn. Although sturdy and tear-resistant, this "Burberry-proofed" cloth was lightweight and allowed air to circulate, making it considerably more comfortable than the heavy mackintosh. The tailor trademarked his cloth "Gabardine," a Shakespearean term that referred to shelter from inclement weather. Burberry developed five different weights of gabardine: Airylight, Double-Weave, Karoo, Wait-a-bit, and Tropical. He even patented Burberry-proofed linings made from silk and wool.

Burberry was a shrewd marketer, employing trademarking and advertising to great benefit. Illustrated advertisements touting the clothing "designed by sportsmen for sportsmen" drew customers to Burberry's retail outlet, which was established in London's Haymarket section in 1891. Having used a variety of labels to distinguish its garments from imitations, the company registered the Equestrian Knight trademark in 1909. Also employed in the corporate logo, this trademark image represents several Burberry ideals. The armor signified the protection afforded by the outerwear, the "Chivalry of Knighthood" reflected the company's own standards of integrity, and the Latin adverb *prorsum* ("forward") referred to Burberry's innovative fabrics and styles.

Although the gabardine name was used under exclusive trademark by Burberry until 1917, Britain's King Edward, one of the first members of the royal family to don the gabardine coat, has been credited with popularizing the Burberry name by requesting the garment by name. Burberry garments have enjoyed a loyal following among royalty and celebrities around the world ever since. The company's clientele has included Winston Churchill, Gary Cooper, Joan Crawford, Humphrey Bogart, George Bernard Shaw, Al Jolson, Peter Falk, Ronald Reagan, George Bush, Norman Schwarzkopf, and Paul Newman. The company also boasts warrants (endorsements of quality) from Her Majesty Queen Elizabeth II and H.R.H. The Prince of Wales. Considered a rite of passage by some commoners, a Burberry coat was a prerequisite to a first job interview.

NEW PRODUCTS FOR A NEW CENTURY

By the turn of the century, Burberry offered an extensive line of outerwear for both men and women. The company designed hats, jackets, pants, and gaiters especially for hunting, fishing, golf, tennis, skiing, archery, and mountaineering. The garments' time- and weather-tested reputation for durability helped make them the gear of choice for adventurers of the late 19th and early 20th century. Balloonists and early aviators wore specially made Burberry garments that let neither wind nor rain penetrate. Captain Roald Amundsen, Captain R. F. Scott, and Sir Ernest Shackleton wore Burberry clothing and took shelter in Burberry tents on their expeditions to the South Pole in the 1910s.

Burberry established its first foreign outlet in Paris in 1910 and soon had retail establishments in the United States and South America. It exported its first shipment of raincoats to Japan in 1915. It was World War I, however, that brought widespread acclamation and fame to Burberry. First worn by high-ranking generals during the turn of the century Boer War in South Africa, the Burberry coat soon was adopted as standard issue for all British officers. With the addition of epaulets and other military trappings, the garments came to be known as Trench Coats, so named for their ubiquity and durability through trench warfare. One Royal Flying Corps veteran wrote a testimonial noting, "During the War, I crashed in the (English) Channel when wearing a Burberry trench coat and had to discard it. It was returned to me a week later, having been in the sea for five days. I have worn it ever since and it is still going strong." The company estimated that 500,000 Burberrys were worn and, perhaps more important, brought home, by veterans.

Rainwear became so important to Burberry that the company soon whittled its lines down to little more than trench coats and tailored menswear for much of the 20th century. The notoriously conservative manufacturer stuck primarily to its well-known raincoats until the 1960s, when a fluke led Burberry to capitalize on the garments' trademark tan, black, red, and white plaid lining. It all started with a window display at the company's Paris store. The shop's manager spiced up her arrangement of trench coats by turning up the hem of one coat to show off its checked lining, then repeated the check on an array of umbrellas.

The clamor for the umbrellas was so immediate and compelling that Burberry's made and quickly sold hundreds. This experiment eventually led to the introduction of the cashmere scarf, also a perennial bestseller. By the 1990s, Burberry offered six different umbrella models and scarves in eight color schemes. This turning point in the company's merchandising scheme notwithstanding, rainwear remained Burberry's single largest line into the late 1970s and early 1980s, and menswear continued to dominate.

EMPHASIS ON EXPORTS AND WOMEN'S AND CHILDREN'S APPAREL: 1980–96

Burberry's export business increased dramatically during the 1980s, fueled primarily by Japanese and American craving for prestigious designer goods. By mid-decade, exports constituted two-thirds of the British company's sales, with more than one-fourth of exports headed to Japan and another 15 percent sold in the United States. By 1996, Burberry had accumulated a record six Queen's Awards for Export Achievement and ranked among Great Britain's leading clothing exporters.

KEY DATES

1856: Thomas Burberry establishes his first shop.
1891: Burberry begins selling clothing under the Burberry name in London's Haymarket section.
1909: The firm registers the Equestrian Knight trademark.
1915: Burberry ships its raincoats to Japan.
1966: The firm becomes a wholly owned subsidiary of Great Universal Stores (GUS).
1994: The company begins using well-known model Christy Turlington in its ad campaigns.
1997: Rose Marie Bravo is hired as CEO.
2000: Burberry breaks ground on a new flagship store in London.
2002: Company goes public.
2005: Parent GUS plc demerges Burberry.
2006: Company celebrates its 150th anniversary.

Overseas sales continued to grow by double-digit percentages in the early 1990s.

Realizing that "A fine tradition is not in itself sufficient today," Burberry sought to broaden its appeal to a younger, more fashion-conscious female clientele. Acknowledging that "The first thing people think of when they hear Burberry is a man's trench coat," U.S. Managing Director Barry Goldsmith asserted in a 1994 *WWD* article, "That's the image we're up against." One result was the Thomas Burberry collection, first introduced in Great Britain in 1988 and extended to the United States two years later.

The new merchandise was priced 15 percent to 30 percent less than Burberry's designer lines, bringing a blouse down to $90 versus the normal $150 to $225, for example. Yet it was not just the price tags that set this "bridge line" apart from the brand's more traditional garb. The collection emphasized more casual sportswear, as opposed to career wear. Updated Classics included youthful plaid mini kilts, jumpers, and snug "jean fit" slacks. U.S. advertising executive David Lipman called the line and its model, Christy Turlington, "modernly relevant, yet classically beautiful." At the upper end of the scale, Burberry launched a personal tailoring service for the ladies. The company's women's division grew 30 percent from 1994 to early 1996.

Although it continued to manufacture 90 percent of its merchandise in British factories, Burberry also started licensing its name, plaid, and knight logo to other manufacturers. By the mid-1990s, the Burberry name added panache to handbags and belts, throw pillows and boxer shorts, cookies and crackers, and fragrances and liquor. Childrenswear, stuffed toys, watches, handbags, golf bags, and even a cobranded Visa credit card sported the Burberry check.

Burberry's efforts at product and geographic diversification appeared to be paying off in the mid-1990s. Sales (including a small sister subsidiary called Scotch House) increased by more than one-third, from £200.9 million in fiscal 1994 (ended March 31) to £267.8 million in 1996. Net income before taxes grew twice as fast, from £41.1 million to £70 million, during the same period.

STRENGTHENING THE BURBERRY BRAND

Despite diversification efforts, it became clear to company management that the Burberry brand did not have the spark it once claimed. In 1997, Rose Marie Bravo was selected CEO of Burberry. Her expertise in brand management fit in with company plans to strengthen the Burberry brand throughout the United States and Europe. Bravo began focusing on product and design development and hired creative director Roberto Menichetti to lead this initiative.

While the company focused on positioning itself among leaders in the fashion industry, it began facing problems caused by its overdependence on Asian customers. Sales decreased by 7 percent in 1998 and profits tumbled in its retail and wholesale sectors due to the Asian economic crisis. As a major exporter, Burberry also was hurt by the strength of the British pound. The company also began to slow down its shipments to the Asian gray market—a market in which its products were sold cheaply or reimported back to Europe and sold at a discount—and shut down three production facilities in the United Kingdom. Whereas this decision hurt the firm's profits in 1998, management felt it would, in the long run, protect the Burberry image.

In 1999, the company profits continued to falter. Sales decreased by 19 percent as the firm battled its Asian-related problems. Amidst its financial struggles, however, the company continued to focus on brand development and aggressive marketing. Under the leadership of Bravo, Burberry was once again reemerging as an international luxury brand. The company launched its Prorsum collections in 1999, a new designer line that was part of Bravo's strategy. According to a June 1999 *Daily News Record* article, the launch was, "The latest step in the Bravo-directed makeover of the brand. Over the last 18 months, she's trimmed its distribution, cut the number of licensees, and ramped up marketing and advertising. The goal is to turn the Burberry name into a brand as hip as Gucci, Louis Vuitton, or Prada."

UPS AND DOWNS IN THE NEW MILLENNIUM

As Burberry entered the new millennium, its financial results improved dramatically. The Asian market recovered, its European and American markets grew, and its new brand strategy began to pay off. Trading profits increased 103 percent over the previous year and sales rose by 11 percent. The company also closed unprofitable stores and opened new stores in Las Vegas, Nevada, and in Tokyo. Burberry also opened a new three-floor flagship store in London that was 16,000 square feet in size and featured new product lines including lingerie and swimwear. A new licensing agreement was signed with Mitsui in Japan, securing a greater share of profits from that region, and the firm acquired its Spain-based licensee; Spain was the firm's second largest market after Japan.

In 2001, Menichetti left the company. The new creative director was 30-year-old Christopher Bailey, a designer from Gucci, who reportedly bought his first Burberry trench coat at a flea market when he was 13 years old. While Menichetti had been responsible only for the Burberry Prorsum line, Bailey would be in charge of all of the company's product design.

In May 2002, GUS plc (Great Universal Stores), Burberry's parent, announced it was selling 22 percent of Burberry stock through an initial public offering (IPO). GUS did not consider the company one of its core businesses, and in light of Burberry's successes, it considered an IPO much more lucrative than selling the firm. That transaction went ahead in July, despite a worldwide market slump resulting from accounting irregularities at several U.S. companies along with the drying up of travel and tourism following the terrorist attack on New York in 2001.

Burberry took several steps to expand sales. It added accessories, including handbags, introduced a line of children's clothing, and offered custom-made trench coats at 30 percent above regular retail prices. The company also bought several of its Asian distributors, thus gaining control of product supply. It also opened new retail stores, including two more flagship locations, in Barcelona, and New York. Noticeable among amenities was the private club area for male customers in the New York store's penthouse.

NEW CHALLENGES: 2003–05

In less than 12 months, however, Burberry's had sales slowed significantly. In addition to fewer tourists because of the SARS virus and fears of terrorism, it appeared that the Burberry brand had become overexposed. This was painfully obvious as television screens in Britain showed riots led by football hooligans wearing caps and jackets sporting the Burberry check. At one point, the London police even had a special Burberry task force.

Burberry had become a luxury brand, but like many other luxury brands, it was facing major challenges. These high-fashion companies needed to attract new, younger customers to remain profitable within a worldwide luxury retail market estimated to be worth more than $160 billion in 2004. They had to avoid damaging their brands' prestige (and image) in the process, however, and they had to deal with knockoff products. They needed to find a balance between exclusivity and accessibility, between innovation and tradition.

Despite the problems in 2003 and 2004, Bravo and Bailey did succeed in establishing that balance. They kept the plaid alive, but playfully toned it down, offering, for example, swim trunks with the check only inside on the crotch. The company also continued its strong movement into accessories and continued revamping the designs of its lines. Add to these factors a hip marketing campaign, and Burberry became a trendy fashion house. During Bravo's tenure as CEO, between 1997 and 2006, sales exploded from $460 million to $1.3 billion.

In May 2005, GUS announced it would demerge, or spin off, Burberry, transferring its 66 percent share in the company directly to GUS shareholders. That action was worth nearly $2 billion. In October, Bravo announced she would be stepping down when her contract expired in July 2006, and the company named Angela Ahrendts of Liz Claiborne Inc. to be CEO. Bravo remained with Burberry as vice-chairman, a newly created position, until 2007. As this was happening, Christopher Bailey was named Britain's designer of the year.

The company celebrated its 150th anniversary by launching the Icons collection, which incorporated iconic company design elements, such as D-rings, with flourishes such as quilted linings to the classic Burberry look. The collection included handbags (priced at $2,000), shoes, boots, and silk pajamas, as well as its mainstay, outerwear. At the same time, lower-end products, costing less than $50, were less available.

Ahrendts also took aim at the company's less glamorous operations, such as sourcing, production, and delivery, to get products into stores more quickly. In line with those efforts was the company's five-year Project Atlas plan to redesign the company's business processes. Sales for the 2006–07 fiscal year rose 14 percent, with growth across all regions, sales channels, and product lines. Moreover, for the first time, retail became the company's largest distribution channel, over wholesale and licensing.

Burberry's future depended to a great extent on maintaining its customer base, on predicting what products these customers would want, and on the continuing demand for luxury goods. In the meantime, Ahrendts and her team were introducing product lines customers could use every hour of the day, including jewelry and footwear, opening or overhauling stores, presenting new store formats, and moving into under-penetrated markets, including North America and China. The company also sold its headquarters building and began overhauling a former government building in central London. The new headquarters, which would bring all the company's operations under one roof, was expected to open in late 2008.

April Dougal Gasbarre
Updated, Christina M. Stansell; Ellen Wernick

PRINCIPAL COMPETITORS

House of Fraser plc; Polo Ralph Lauren Corporation.

FURTHER READING

Board, Laura, "GUS Prices Burberry IPO," *Daily Deal,* June 25, 2002.

"Brand Health Check: Burberry—Does Burberry Need to Rebuild Its Exclusivity?" *Marketing,* June 12, 2003, p. 17.

Brunelli, Richard, "Burberry, Back in Fashion," *Adweek Online,* October 1, 2007.

"Burberry Gains Independence," *WWD,* May 26, 2005, p. 3.

"Burberrys Goes Casual," *WWD,* December 21, 1993, p. 8.

"Burberry: Mining the Past to Seize the Future," *Business Week,* August 6, 2007, p. 58.

Burberrys of London: An Elementary History of a Great Tradition, London: Burberry Ltd., 1987.

"Burberry's Women's Lines Thriving," *WWD,* May 15, 1996, p. 7.

Colavita, Courtney, "Christopher's Check Point," *Daily News Record,* June 19, 2006.

Collier, Andrew, "Burberry Toasts Its History with Museum Exhibit," *WWD,* February 14, 1989, p. 10.

Conti, Samantha, "Bravo Departs Burberry," *WWD,* June 21, 2007, p. 3.

———, "Burberry Net Up Slightly," *WWD,* May 25, 2007, p. 2.

———, "Burberry Rolls On as New CEO Steps In," *Daily News Record,* July 17, 2006, p. 12.

———, "Burberry's Bonanza: Luxe Brand Eyes Growth as Earnings Climb 75%," *WWD,* May 25, 2004, p. 1.

———, "Checklist for Ahrendts: Burberry CEO in Drive to Hone Brand's Image," *WWD,* May 23, 2007, p. 1.

Emert, Carol, "Plaid in Dispute Concerning Sale of Burberry's Items," *Daily News Record,* August 8, 1995, p. 5.

Fallon, James, "Bravo on Burberry's Luxe New Digs: 'A Big Strategic Move,'" *Daily News Record,* August 23, 2000, p. 1.

———, "Prorsum from Burberry: More Revolution than Evolution," *Daily News Record,* June 21, 1999, p. 5.

"Findings: Burberry Bags It …," *WWD,* July 2, 2007, p. 12.

Gray, Robert, "A Green and Pleasant Brand," *Marketing,* July 20, 1995, pp. 22–23.

Gray, Robert, and Arthur Friedman, "Finally, Some Sunshine for Rainwear," *WWD,* April 16, 1996, pp. 7–8.

Gumbel, Peter, "Burberry's New Boss Doesn't Wear Plaid," *Fortune,* October 15, 2007, p. 124.

Gumbel, Peter, and Eugenia Levenson, "Mass vs. Class," *Fortune,* September 17, 2007, p. 5.

Heller, Richard, "A British Gucci," *Forbes,* April 3, 2000, p. 84.

Hobday, Nicola, "Burberry IPO Bottoms Out," *Daily Deal,* July 12, 2002.

Horyn, Cathy, "Tea and Sympathy," *New York Times Magazine,* May 12, 2006, p. 141.

Kapner, Suzanne, "Acquisitions and New Clothing Give a Lift to Burberry's Profits," *New York Times,* November 20, 2002, p. W1.

Norton, Kate, "Burberry, Plain in Check, Is Hot Again," *Business Week Online,* April 17, 2007.

Pogoda, Dianne M., "Tipping the Sales," *WWD,* May 4, 1994, pp. 8–9.

Porter, Janet, "Burberrys Weathers Dollar Fall," *Journal of Commerce and Commercial,* February 26, 1987, pp. 1A, 6A.

Ritson, Mark, "Burberry Boss Needs Poetry Lessons," *Marketing,* July 12, 2006, p. 19.

Rubin, Courtney, "The Rainmaker," *People Weekly,* October 9, 2006, p. 125.

The Story of the Trenchcoat, London: Burberry of London, 1993.

"Stretching the Plaid," *Economist,* February 3, 2001, p. 7.

Underwood, Elaine, "Check-ing Out," *Brandweek,* December 11, 1995, p. 32.

Werdigier, Julia, "Goodbye to Burberry," *New York Times,* June 24, 2007, p. BU2.

Woolcock, Keith, "The Great Universal Mystery," *Management Today,* November 1994, pp. 48–52.

Cantor Fitzgerald, L.P.

499 Park Avenue
New York, New York 10022
U.S.A.
Telephone: (212) 938-5000
Fax: (212) 829-5280
Web site: http://www.cantor.com

Private Company
Incorporated: 1945 as B.G. Cantor & Co., Inc.
Employees: 3,000 (est.)
Sales: $265 million (2004 est.)
NAIC: 523120 Securities Brokerage; 523130 Commodity Contracts Dealing

■ ■ ■

Best known to the general public as the firm that survived the terrorists attacks of September 11, 2001, when 658 of its employees were killed in the upper floors of the World Trade Center towers, Cantor Fitzgerald, L.P., continues to maintain its headquarters in New York City and remains an important global financial services company. Since the early 1970s Cantor has been an important dealer in the secondary market for U.S. government bonds. The firm also deals in global equities, fixed income products, and derivatives; provides brokerage services; and is involved in investment banking and asset management. Long known for its high-tech capabilities, Cantor operates an electronic U.S. Treasury futures exchange and offers electronic trading of sovereign debt, while Cantor Gaming lends its expertise to online gaming and mobile gaming concerns.

In addition to its New York headquarters, Cantor maintains about a dozen other offices in North America, as well as offices in London, Paris, Zürich, Milan, and Hong Kong.

FOUNDER BORN 1916

Cantor Fitzgerald's founder, Bernard "Bernie" Gerald Cantor, was born in 1916 and raised in a family of modest means in the Bronx, New York, where as a teen he occasionally worked as a vendor at Yankee Stadium, selling peanuts, popcorn, and hot dogs. Even then he kept an eye out for an edge, later claiming to have worked only Sunday doubleheaders because the time between games allowed him to sell more of his goods. After graduating from high school, Cantor enrolled at New York University (NYU) in 1935 to study law but switched his focus to finance after spotting a lawyer he knew working construction for the Works Project Administration, created during the Great Depression to provide employment opportunities. Cantor soon switched to night classes so he could work days as a junior analyst for the Wall Street firm of Brown, Young & Co. He never completed his degree at NYU, leaving in 1937 to become a stockbroker. Cantor's career was interrupted by a stint in the military during World War II. He served as a paratrooper in the South Pacific, an episode that he would refuse to discuss for the rest of his life.

After the war Cantor founded his own investment banking and general brokerage firm, B.G. Cantor & Co., Inc., in 1945. At the time, the brokerage business was dominated by the Irish. In 1947 Cantor, who was

Jewish, brought in a partner, John J. Fitzgerald, an insurance company president, who took a 10 percent stake in the firm and lent his name to the company letterhead, which read Cantor, Fitzgerald & Co. Other partners included Jack J. Bernstein, Louis G. Behr, and Ernest Butt. Fitzgerald remained a partner until his death in 1964, but there was never a doubt as to who was the driving force in the firm.

Cantor became involved in the entertainment field. In 1949 the firm served as the underwriter for Hotelvision, Inc., a Long Island City–based company that developed a master control system allowing hotels to deliver television signals to a large number of rooms via coaxial cable. In the 1950s a Beverly Hills office was opened and Bernie Cantor soon gained a reputation as the stockbroker to the stars, especially adept at creating elaborate tax strategies, employing shelters, straddles, and other elaborate schemes. His clients included Kirk Douglas, Clint Eastwood, Zsa Zsa Gabor, and Eli Wallach. In the 1960s Bernie Cantor also lent his talents to the conglomerate builders of the time, such as Meshulam Riklis, a pioneer in the art of leveraged buyouts.

TURN TO BOND MARKET: 1972

Cantor experienced a turning point in 1972 when the firm transformed itself into a broker of government securities. While equities, other than the top 50 stocks, were not faring well, Bernie Cantor recognized that there was less competition in the government bond market, a field that was also less regulated. Moreover, he spotted an edge, a struggling company called Telerate, which listed interest rates for commercial paper (essentially company IOU's) on computer terminals. The company had been founded in 1969 by a young college dropout, Neil S. Hirsch, who had taken a job as a clerk at a Merrill Lynch brokerage office. Here he became familiar with electronic stock quote monitors and soon realized that prices for other money market instruments

had to be gathered by calling a number of participating firms. He launched Telerate to streamline and computerize this process. Although Hirsch was able to secure several dozen customers, he was soon in need of more money to grow the business and about to sell stock in the company to the public when Bernie Cantor intervened, initially paying $500,000 for a 25 percent stake and eventually buying control of the operation for $3 million.

Cantor was one of five major brokers that served as middlemen in the market for Treasury bonds, notes, and bills, selling these instruments to dealers, who then sold them to investors. Because of its unique position, Cantor was one of just a handful of firms with inside information about the interest rates the government planned to offer when it borrowed money, information that was guarded closely. U.S. Treasury securities comprised the world's largest debt market, thus driving the price of all other money market instruments. Thus, Cantor possessed extremely valuable information that impacted investors of all stripes, and through Telerate the firm had a way to deliver that information for a fee.

According to *Financial World*, by broadcasting live bids and offers for government securities over the network, Bernie Cantor gave birth to what became known as "screen brokerage," part of the changes that "broke the old-boy network in government bonds." Aside from giving birth to computerized trading, "Cantor broke from tradition by dealing not only with primary dealers but with the largest institutions as well. … He would broker trades for smaller lots than dealers were accustomed to, and for much smaller commissions, resulting in narrower spreads. … It led to greater volume overall, helping to set the stage for the roaring 1980s." Cantor sold Telerate for $100 million in 1981, reaping a considerable profit, and continued to make money from the service by arranging an exclusive deal to provide pricing information. It was also in 1981 that Bernie Cantor moved the firm into some of the top floors of the World Trade Center, receiving an attractive 25-year lease because most tenants did not wish to be located so high up. It was a time of explosive growth for the firm, which benefited from the Reagan administration's rapid accumulation of debt through the issuance of 30-year bonds, escalating interest rates, and an international demand for the bonds. Cantor drastically cuts its fees but more than made up the difference by increasing its volume of business. Moreover, Cantor prospered by offering a variety of other fixed-income products, including mortgage-backed securities and foreign issues, such as Eurobonds and French government securities.

```
┌─────────────────────────────────────────┐
│                                           │
│            KEY DATES                      │
│          ──────■──────                    │
│                                           │
│  1945:  Bernie Cantor forms B.G. Cantor & Co.,│
│         Inc.                              │
│  1947:  Name changed to Cantor, Fitzgerald & Co.│
│  1972:  Telerate acquired.                │
│  1981:  Firm moves into World Trade Center.│
│  1992:  Firm converted to partnership.    │
│  1996:  Bernie Cantor dies.               │
│  2001:  Terrorist attacks on World Trade Center claim│
│         lives of 658 Cantor employees.    │
│                                           │
└─────────────────────────────────────────┘
```

While Bernie Cantor was forging a reputation in Hollywood and on Wall Street, and growing quite wealthy, he was also becoming well known in art circles as a major collector, especially of the works of the sculptor Rodin. He first took notice of Rodin in 1945 while paying a visit to the Metropolitan Museum of Art, where he was fascinated by Rodin's "Hand of God." In 1947 he came across another version of the work in a Madison Avenue gallery and bought it. Over the next several years he turned his attention to paintings, most noticeably works by Kandinsky, but in the mid-1950s his interest in Rodin was rekindled after he bought "The Kiss." He became virtually obsessed with the sculptor. By 1968 he owned 84 Rodin sculptures, but that amount would pale in comparison to the hundreds of pieces he would buy in the next few years. He and his wife, Iris, either individually or through the foundation they created, lent out or gave away more than 450 Rodin sculptures while maintaining a private collection that numbered about 300. The couple also donated considerable sums of money to the Metropolitan Museum as well as to the Brooklyn Museum, which was located three blocks from where Iris grew up.

Bernie Cantor would share his love of Rodin with his protégé and the man he groomed to succeed him one day, Howard Lutnick, whose mother was a sculptor, painter, and college professor. His father taught history at Queens College. Raised on Long Island, Lutnick suffered the loss of his mother to leukemia in 1978 when he was a senior in high school. Then, after Lutnick enrolled at Haverford College a year later, his father died during a chemotherapy session. A year after earning a degree in economics from Haverford, Lutnick came to work at Cantor as a trainee. "For about 18 months," reported the *New York Times*, "Mr. Lutnick moved from one sector of the firm to anther, learning the ropes and gathering information. The last stop of his orientation tour was a desk in the corner of Mr. Cantor's office,

where the boss frequently interrogated the young man about what he found in his travels around the firm." Often what Lutnick shared was something being kept from Bernie Cantor, who wasted little time in castigating the executive responsible. Lutnick told the *Times*, "I was aggressively lectured by every executive who walked out of his office. But hey, my theory was that the guy whose name was on the door was the one who mattered."

Bernie Cantor took a liking to Lutnick and assigned him the task of managing his personal investments, as well as those of some of his friends. Lutnick made the most of the opportunity, bringing in outside clients that became the foundation for a new division, Investment Strategies Group, which moved aggressively in the retail sector of the Treasury market, selling directly to a wide range of customers from regional banks to wealthy individuals. By the time Lutnick was 29, in December 1990, Bernie Cantor named him his second in command and designated successor after the firm's president and a chief rival, James Avena, had tried to fire Lutnick that summer. A year later Lutnick was named president of Cantor Fitzgerald.

The question of who should succeed Bernie Cantor was hardly an academic question. In the late 1980s he broke his hip, and then his kidneys began to fail, leading to regular dialysis and a slow decline in his health. Although he wanted to leave Lutnick in charge, Bernie Cantor's original intention was to give ownership to his charitable foundation. However, he changed course, and because of tax reasons changed the firm from a corporation to a partnership in 1992. Soon 75 employees were named limited partners and allowed to buy stakes in the firm, and a succession plan was put in place that called for Lutnick and Cantor's wife Iris to serve as co-managing general partners. While he would exercise day-to-day control, she retained veto power over major decisions.

WORLD TRADE CENTER BOMBED: 1993

Although Bernie Cantor spent most of his time in Los Angeles, he remained in constant contact with Lutnick in New York, as the firm faced a host of new challenges in the early 1990s, including increased competition from other inter-dealer brokers and the U.S. government's decision to reduce the number of new 30-year bond issues in favor of more short-term securities. The firm also had to contend with a completely unexpected problem. On February 26, 1993, a car bomb was detonated by terrorists in the parking garage below the North Tower of the World Trade Center, killing six people and injuring more than 1,000. Without a workable backup plan to rely on, Cantor was temporarily put out of business. "Perhaps even more damaging than the lost revenue," opined *Industrial Investor,* "Cantor's week-long absence showed that the market could get by without it."

By 1994 Bernie Cantor was legally blind due to retinal bleeding. In 1995 Lutnick and two other partners offered to buy the firm but Cantor refused. His condition worsened considerably at the start of 1996, forcing him to go on life support and prompting Lutnick to activate a five-person incapacity committee, three members of which then voted to hand over control to Lutnick because of Cantor's condition. Also a committee member, Iris Cantor abstained, as did a fifth member. She was furious over the move, which she maintained was premature and disrespectful to her husband and amounted to little more than a "palace coup," in the words of one of her advisers. The matter soon turned into a court battle, with the firm seeking to enforce the succession plan and Iris Cantor countersuing to have Lutnick evicted from his office. A day after the trial began in Delaware Chancery Court in May 1996, the two sides reached a settlement agreement that called for the Cantors' stake in the partnership to be reduced to 20 percent, and Lutnick solidified his position as the new head of the firm. Some bitterness remained, however, and after Bernie Cantor died in July 1996 Lutnick was barred from the funeral. Iris Cantor would also continue to spar with the firm over other issues in the years to come.

A major effort in the second half of the 1990s to keep Cantor at the forefront was the development of the eSpeed system to conduct electronic trading. It was first used internally in early 1996, but it was not until March 1999 that the trading platform was fully operational and ready for outside use. By the end of the year Cantor spun off eSpeed in a $220 million initial public offering of stock while retaining control of the business. In 2000 eSpeed and Cantor and a number of energy companies formed TradeSpark, L.P., which used the eSpeed platform to create an electronic energy trading marketplace. In February 2001 eSpeed enjoyed another important achievement when it signed a software solutions agreement with Federal Home Loan Bank.

THE EVENTS OF 9/11

The successes as well as the challenges of doing business in a new century were soon rendered meaningless for Cantor Fitzgerald when, on the morning of September 11, 2001, a pair of airliners commandeered by terrorists were rammed into the twin towers of the World Trade Center. Cantor employees, who normally arrived at work early, had little chance, their escape from the tow-

ers cut off by the wreckage on the floors beneath them. When the towers crumbled to the ground, 658 Cantor employees were among the dead, about one in every four victims of the attack, three in ten of the Cantor workforce. Some key people in the firm were spared by chance, including Lutnick, who was delayed getting to work in order to accompany his son to the first day of kindergarten. He was only able to reach the World Trade Center site in time to witness the collapse of the towers.

Cantor and the survivors set themselves to the grim task of accounting for their living and their missing, presumably dead, colleagues, while setting up shop in temporary quarters and getting eSpeed back on line to allow the bond market to resume trading just two days later. After the experience of the 1993 bombing, the firm had established a backup center some 23 miles from the World Trade Center, and here employees worked around the clock to restore the computer systems. Lutnick was hailed a hero for his crisis management and pledge to look after the family members of perished employees, and then vilified when he made September 15 the last date for lost employees' paychecks, a move that outraged families, but one that he said he had to make in order to prove to bank regulators that the firm was determined to survive. In time, as the firm indeed recovered, the rancor dissipated as Lutnick and Cantor made good on its pledge to take care of surviving family members, dividing among them one-quarter of the firm's profits for five years and extending ten years of healthcare. Financial advice was also provided and regular town hall meetings were arranged for families and employees.

UP FROM THE ASHES

After three years of rebuilding, Cantor resumed growing its business. In addition to its core bond business, Cantor enjoyed strong growth from its stock trading division, which was fortunate to have a large number of key employees working at locations outside of New York City. On the other hand, eSpeed had to contend with more competition and experienced some ups and downs. In 2007, Cantor made plans to spin off its brokerage unit, BGC Partners, in a public stock offering. After fielding criticism from eSpeed investors, however, the firm decided to combine eSpeed and BGC to create a new publicly traded company called BGC Partners, Inc., a deal to be engineered by eSpeed issuing about 134 million shares to acquire BGC. Cantor looked to new opportunities as well. In 2007 it formed Cantor Entertainment, a Los Angeles–based unit to provide information, marketing, advisory, and financial services to the entertainment industry. The firm also ran the Hollywood Stock Exchange, a virtual market that allowed traders to bet on movie box-office performance. In addition, Cantor was becoming involved in property and equity derivatives.

Ed Dinger

PRINCIPAL SUBSIDIARIES

BGC Partners Inc.

PRINCIPAL COMPETITORS

GFI Group, Inc.; ICAP plc; Tullett Prebon plc.

FURTHER READING

Atlas, Riva D., "Firm That Was Hit Hard on 9/11 Grows Anew," *New York Times,* September 10, 2004, p. C4.

Davis, Ann, and Aaron Lucchetti, "'New' Cantor Fitzgerald Now Looks to Compete," *Wall Street Journal,* September 10, 2004, p. C1.

Davis, Stephen, "Where Was Cantor Fitzgerald?" *Institutional Investor,* April 1993, p. 21.

Esterow, Milton, "Ex-Stadium Vendor Is Giving a Rodin to Museum," *New York Times,* May 13, 1968.

Gordon, Meryl, "Howard Lutnick's Second Life," *New York,* December 10, 2001.

Henriques, Diana B., "With Partners Like These, Who Needs Rivals?" *New York Times,* April 28, 1996, p. 3.

Henriques, Diana B., and Jennifer Lee, "Flinty Bond Trader Leads His Firm Out of the Rubble," *New York Times,* September 15, 2001, p. A10.

Hiday, Jeffrey L., "Accord Reached in Cantor Fitzgerald Case," *Wall Street Journal,* May 8, 1996, p. C29.

Jaffe, Thomas, "Getting Between the Wall and the Wallpaper," *Forbes,* October 20, 1997, p. 66.

Pace, Eric, "B. Gerald Cantor, Philanthropist and Owner of Rodin Collections, Is Dead at 79," *New York Times,* July 6, 1996.

Taub, Stephen, "Life After Bernie," *Financial World,* November 22, 1994, p. 64.

"To Hell and Back," *Economist,* August 11, 2007, p. 60.

Cardone Industries Inc.

———————————— ■ ————————————

5501 Whitaker Avenue
Philadelphia, Pennsylvania 19124-1799
U.S.A.
Telephone: (215) 912-3000
Fax: (215) 912-3700
Web site: http://www.cardone.com

Private Company
Incorporated: 1970 as A-1 Remanufacturing
Employees: 4,200
Sales: $373.3 million (2007)
NAIC: 336322 Motor Vehicle Electronic and Electronic Equipment Manufacturing; 336340 Motor Vehicle Brake System Manufacturing; 336350 Motor Vehicle Transmission and Power Train Parts Manufacturing; 336330 Motor Vehicle Steering and Components; 493110 General Warehousing and Storage; 336399 All Other Vehicle Parts Manufacturing

■ ■ ■

Cardone Industries Inc. is one of the largest international auto parts distributors and is the largest privately owned automotive supplier in the world. Although Cardone Industries specializes in remanufactured auto parts, the company produces 37 product lines including a series of new parts and electrical tools. Cardone was founded and is currently headquartered in Philadelphia, Pennsylvania, and, since 1970, the company has expanded to operate 21 plants in seven divisions, with facilities in Chicago, Los Angeles, Canada, Mexico, and Belgium. Primary control of the company is divided among the family of Michael Cardone, Jr., son of the company's founder, and his wife Jacquie Cardone. In 2007, Cardone industries employed 18 members of the Cardone family representing three generations and offered all employees stock ownership on an annual basis as part of the company's benefits package.

FOUNDING AND EXPANSION

The Cardone family's interest in auto mechanics and parts may be traced to Michael Cardone, Sr., and his brothers, sons of Italian immigrants living in northern Pennsylvania. Not eager to join his father in the coal mines, Michael Cardone moved to the Philadelphia area when he was 18 and found work as a garage mechanic. In that city, he and his brothers eventually started an automotive parts supply business called Cardo Automotive Products Company in the basement of their grandmother's North Philadelphia home. The Cardone family realized success in the remanufacturing field, which had gained ground since the Great Depression had made it prohibitively expensive to obtain new parts.

In 1970, Michael Cardone, Sr., decided to start a new business with his son, Michael Cardone, Jr., who had graduated from Oral Roberts University. Together they founded A-1 Remanufacturing Inc., which had a workforce of six and focused on the remanufacture of windshield wiper motors. At first the company was based in a small storefront in North Philadelphia. Cardone, Sr., and his wife Frances Cardone shared ownership with Michael, Jr., and his wife Jacquie Cardone.

COMPANY PERSPECTIVES

Cardone Industries is dedicated to creating and maintaining a proactive, holistic work environment. Cardone supports the life success of its diverse employee population with a full-time staff of seven industrial chaplains to assist employees and their families. We believe the quality of our products and services is the most important issue to our customers; therefore quality is the foundation of our corporate culture. Values: We Value Our People, We Value Our Work, We Value Our Witness, We Value Our Word.

As the company expanded in the 1970s, Cardone, Sr.'s brothers joined the business. Anthony Cardone, Sr., served as warehouse manager while Nicholas Cardone served as facilities manager and Daniel Cardone served as quality-assurance manager. Cardone's products, bolstered by the know-how, work ethic, and energy of those who produced them, were highly successful in the competitive auto parts market and from 1970 to 1978 Cardone's staff grew from six to over 250 employees. In addition, between 1974 and 1978, the company opened nine new plants. In 1974, Cardone Industries was honored with the Automotive Services Industries Association's Remanufacturer of the Year award, which the company received again in 1987. In addition, in 1982 Michael Cardone, Jr., was awarded the Young Leadership Award from the Automotive Hall of Fame.

The Cardone family cited their religious convictions as a key element that defined their business ethics and the success of the company. Michael Cardone, Sr., was involved in founding several Pentecostal Christian worship centers in and around the Philadelphia area. In 1979, Cardone Industries began bringing a chaplain into their manufacturing centers to conduct voluntary prayer services and, by 1985, the company employed eight full-time chaplains. Cardone often hired bilingual chaplains to serve the needs of the company's multiethnic staff, which included employees from India, Haiti, Cambodia, Laos, Korea, and Italy.

In 1986, a Hindu immigrant who had been an employee of Cardone Industries for over eight years claimed he had been fired from his job for refusing to convert to Pentecostal Christianity. In June, a small group of former employees, most representing the Service Employees International Union (SEIU), staged a protest at the company's Rising Sun plant claiming they had also been victims of religious persecution. When questioned by the media, management and several non-Christian employees refuted the allegations, claiming that the company never forced any of its employees to attend religious services. Management further claimed that independent arbiters were brought in to evaluate the situation and determined that there was no pattern of persecution.

In 1988, Cardone, Jr., became acting president of the company, although Cardone, Sr., remained involved in company operations until his death in 1994, at which time Cardone, Jr., and his wife assumed ownership. After his death, Michael Cardone, Sr., was inducted into the Automotive Hall of Fame, in recognition for his pioneering work in the remanufacturing process.

GROWTH AND EMPLOYEE OWNERSHIP

In 1994, Cardone Industries purchased 1.4 million square feet of warehouse and manufacturing space formerly belonging to Sears, Roebuck and Company, which closed its last Philadelphia location in 1993. Cardone Industries received $5 million in public funds from the City of Philadelphia, based on estimates that the expansion would create 400 to 500 jobs for Pennsylvania residents. Cardone Industries received $2 million from the Pennsylvania Industrial Development Authority, $2 million from the Economic Development Partnership, $500,000 from the state's Machinery and Equipment Loan Fund, and $500,000 from the Philadelphia Industrial Development Corporation.

By 1995, Cardone had become the largest family-owned automotive supply company in the United States and was still experiencing rapid growth. In 1998, Cardone Industries instituted an employee ownership program, under which each employee who remained with the company for at least one year was given shares in the company on an annual basis. According to corporate releases, the employee ownership program was intended to foster a sense of personal investment and responsibility and thereby increase cohesion among the company's full time staff of over 4,000 employees.

Cardone Industries became a third-generation family business when Michael Cardone III joined the company full time in 1998 as a participant in the company's management training program. Cardone III had a long history of working with the company in various positions and graduated with an MBA from the Garvin School of International Management. Cardone, Jr.'s son-in-law Dan McClave also began working for the company in the 1990s and eventually became head of the company's international division, headquartered in Louviere, Belgium. Cardone III transferred to the company's Chicago plant in 2005 as head of operations.

KEY DATES

1970: Cardone Industries is founded by Michael Cardone, Sr.
1988: Michael Cardone, Jr., becomes president.
1998: Company is opened to employee ownership.
1999: Web site with online sales and service debuts.
2000: Company wins the Wharton Family Business of the Year Award.
2004: Cardone forms business alliance with Delphi Corporation.
2006: Private placement is conducted to raise $50 million in order to prevent downsizing.
2007: Company is awarded the Governors Award for Environmental Excellence.

Cardone Industries launched a comprehensive Internet marketing system in 1999, along with a new web site, at cardone.com, which provided 24-hour shopping, tech support, and product information. Cardone Industries' web site also provided industry news, manufacturing bulletins and instructions on how to install and use the company's products. Cardone later added a unique online feature, known as the CARDONE WebCat system, which allowed customers to access the company's catalog by searching for parts by application, part number, or product line.

CARDONE INDUSTRIES IN THE 21ST CENTURY

In 2000, Cardone Industries became the first automotive company to win the Wharton Family Business of the Year Award, given by Philadelphia's Wharton Business School. Cardone Industries was selected from among over 1,200 nominated companies and nine finalists from the large business (over 250 employees) category. Businesses were judged on multigenerational involvement and on their contributions to the industry and to the families of their employees. In 2000, Cardone was the largest provider of manufacturing jobs in Philadelphia and drew a majority of its employees from local communities near the company's manufacturing facilities.

Cardone Industries received certification for having achieved ISO 9001: 2000 status, a set of quality guidelines established by the International Organization of Standardization (ISO), which judges companies on their ability to monitor quality in manufacturing, service, and production. Among other requirements,

ISO 9001 certification requires that companies have developed a plan to monitor all divisions and company process areas for quality assurance purposes.

According to Cardone Industries, remanufacturing was an inherently environmentally friendly process that conserved over 80 percent of the energy and materials required to manufacture new parts. In addition, remanufacturing resulted in an estimated reduction of 28 million tons of carbon dioxide per year. Cardone received ISO 14001 certification, a measure of the company's commitment to environmentally friendly operations, which required that the company take an active role in reducing the environmental impact of the manufacturing process. In 2003, Cardone Industries became the first automotive parts manufacturer to achieve TS-16949 certification, also awarded by the ISO, to recognize the company's commitment to reducing waste produced during the supply process.

In 2004, Cardone's primary product line, known as A1 Cardone, consisted of six divisions and over 37 products. Although the company maintained its focus on remanufactured parts, in 2004 Cardone launched Cardone Select, a series of all new parts that were manufactured with attention to the most common failings associated with each part. Cardone Select operated in four divisions with five product lines including axles, wiper motors, starters, alternators, and water pumps. Cardone also provided three product lines under the title of Cardone Service Plus tools, which included caliper brackets, power steering filters, and a reprogrammer that allowed users to reprogram a car's computer components.

In 2004, Cardone Industries formed a business partnership with Delphi Corporation to cooperate in manufacturing and promoting remanufactured electronics for the international market. The larger Delphi Corporation, a public company headquartered in Troy, Michigan, was a national leader in automotive part manufacturing that focused on aftermarket customers. Through the business alliance, Cardone Industries benefited from Delphi Corporation's engineering and manufacturing expertise while Delphi benefited from Cardone Industries' experience with the remanufacturing process. Under the terms of the alliance, Cardone Industries remanufactured a variety of parts for Delphi Corporation, which was responsible for marketing and providing customer service and support for the joint products. Both companies hoped that the alliance would help them to compete in the growing remanufacturing market, which was estimated in 2005 at over $53 million in annual sales.

COMPETING IN A DECLINING MARKET

Although Cardone Industries grew extensively during the 1980s, declining profits in the 1990s and 2000s (which affected the entire U.S. auto industry and was closely linked to competition from foreign manufacturing companies) posed a significant problem for the company. Cardone's partner corporation, Delphi, suffered $2 billion in losses in 2006. In order to avoid downsizing, Cardone Industries initiated a private placement offering in 2006, which was intended to raise approximately $50 million in revenues to be reinvested in growth.

As the U.S. auto market continued to suffer competition from the Chinese import market, which provided less expensive parts due to low labor and manufacturing costs, the company considered outsourcing labor. In 2005, Cardone relocated several of the company's less profitable divisions to Mexico in an effort to save on production costs. While Michael Cardone, Jr., expressed reluctance to reduce the company's focus on local hiring practices, he maintained that reduced profits and increased competition left the company with few alternatives.

In an effort to control losses, Michael Cardone, Jr., petitioned the City of Philadelphia to allow Cardone to claim tax-free status for the company's manufacturing plants. With a corporate tax rate of over 9 percent, Cardone Industries' annual tax expenditures represented a significant loss of profit and tax-free status would have allowed the company to reinvest significant amounts of revenues each year. However, in 2006, Philadelphia officials refused to grant tax-free status to Cardone Industries unless the company moved to designated tax zones in South Philadelphia, a move that Cardone officials claimed was not cost effective.

Price cuts to Cardone Industries' products ensued, in order to keep customers in the face of intense competition, and these price cuts eroded profits. In 2005, Cardone cut the costs of drive axles by 60 percent while also cutting the price of water pumps by 22 percent. Although the lower cost appealed to U.S. customers, reduced revenues made it difficult for Cardone to conduct business according to its traditional model, which included providing relatively high wages ($7–15 per hour) and benefits packages to all employees.

In response to the challenging climate, Cardone Industries focused on its role as an environmentally friendly type of business. It was honored in 2007 to receive the Governor's Award for Environmental Excellence, an annual award given by the Pennsylvania Department of Environmental Protection to companies displaying a commitment to improving the environmental impact of their manufacturing or operational processes.

Micah L. Issitt

PRINCIPAL SUBSIDIARIES

Tridonex Inc.

PRINCIPAL COMPETITORS

Champion Parts, Inc.; Johnson Controls, Inc.; Motorcar Parts of America, Inc.; Enova Systems, Inc.; Huf North America Automotive Parts Manufacturing, Corporation; Delphi Corporation; Sense Technologies, Inc.; Yazaki North America, Inc.; Keihin Indiana Precision Technology, Inc.; S-Y Systems Technologies America LLC.

FURTHER READING

Bizouati, Yael, "Delphi-Linked CARDONE Launches $50M Placement," *Private Placement Letter,* July 10, 2006.

"Cardone," *Automotive Marketing,* December 1992, p. 48.

"Cardone Awarded 2007 Governor's Award for Environmental Excellence," *Aftermarket News Service,* April 11, 2007.

"CARDONE Leads the Way in Remanufacturing Innovations," *Aftermarket Business,* April 2000, p. 97.

"CARDONE's New Web Site Helps Inspire Sales and Installation," *Aftermarket Business,* February 1999, p. 16.

"Delphi-Linked Cardone Does Private Placement," *Investment Dealers' Digest,* July 10, 2006.

"Family Tradition and Experience Combined," *Aftermarket Business,* January 2005, p. 46.

Fernandez, Bob, "A Fight to Survive," *Philadelphia Inquirer,* March 26, 2006.

———, "Large Auto Firms Faring Badly vs. China," *Philadelphia Inquirer,* March 26, 2006.

Halbfinger, David M., "1,600 Jobs Are Planned for Old Sears Site," *Philadelphia Business Journal,* July 8, 1994, p. 1.

Kasper, Vince, "Baptism or Fire? Hindu Says He Was Ousted by NE Firm Because He Wouldn't Convert to Pentacostalism," *Philadelphia Daily News,* June 24, 1986, p. 4.

Mathis, Mike, "A Family That Doesn't Fear the Dirty Work," *Philadelphia Business Journal,* June 9, 2000, p. 16.

Rubin, Daniel, "Michael Cardone, 78," *Philadelphia Inquirer,* October 22, 1994, p. D8.

Salinas, Gilberto, "New Matamoros Maquiladora That Remanufactures Autoparts Creates 50 Jobs," *Brownsville (Tex.) Herald,* August 10, 2004.

Schaffer, Michael D., and Martha Woodall, "A Job Fight over Religion," *Philadelphia Inquirer,* June 25, 1986, p. B1.

Shutovich, Christina A., "Cardone Named Finalist in Wharton Family Business of the Year," *Aftermarket Business,* August 1999, p. 15.

Willins, Michael, "Business Union Adds to Delphi, Cardone Portfolio," *Aftermarket Business,* December 2003, p. 10.

Carrols Restaurant Group, Inc.

———■———

968 James Street
Syracuse, New York 13203
U.S.A.
Telephone: (315) 424-0513
Fax: (315) 475-9616

Public Company
Incorporated: 1996 as Carrols Holdings Corporation
Employees: 16,400
Sales: $751.4 million
Stock Exchanges: NASDAQ
Ticker Symbol: TAST
NAIC: 722211 Limited Service Restaurants

■ ■ ■

Listed on the NASDAQ, Carrols Restaurant Group, Inc., is a Syracuse, New York–based operator of three fast-food restaurant chains. It is the United States' largest Burger King franchisee, owning and operating about 330 units in a dozen states in the Northeast, Mid-Atlantic, and Midwest. Carrols also owns a pair of Hispanic restaurant brands: Pollo Tropical and Taco Cabana. The company owns and operates 70 Florida units of Pollo Tropical and has another 20 franchised units, mostly located in Puerto Rico. The Miami-based chain offers Caribbean-inspired fare, including grilled chicken marinated in tropical fruit juices, and such side dishes as fried sweet bananas, fried yucca, black beans and rice, as well as desserts, including Caribbean Crème Cake and caramel custard. Carrols owns and operates about 140 Taco Cabana restaurants in Texas, Oklahoma, and New Mexico and has franchised a handful of units. The San Antonio–based chain offers Tex-Mex and Mexican dishes.

FOUNDER OPENS FIRST RESTAURANT: 1961

Herbert N. Slotnick, the son of a longtime theater owner, founded Carrols Restaurant Group in Syracuse. After serving in the Army during World War II, he opened a drive-in movie theater with his father. While building a chain of drive-ins he became acquainted with the fast-food business through the theaters' concession stands. By the early 1960s he decided to branch into restaurants, interested in franchising the fast-growing McDonald's concept. Unable to secure a commitment from McDonald's for more than one or two restaurants, Slotnick turned his attention to a new competitor in the hamburger field, Carrols Drive-In, a chain developed by Chicago-based Tastee Freez Industries, Inc. Tastee Freez awarded him an upstate New York franchise that allowed him five years to open 40 restaurants. To build his first unit, the 36-year-old Slotnick had to bring his father with him to the bank to back a $100,000 loan that had been originally declined. "What do you think of this guy," his father told the bank president, Thomas W. Higgins, according to the *Syracuse Herald American*, "he wants to go into the hamburger business." Only because of the elder Slotnick did Higgins approve the loan, never thinking Herb Slotnick's burger joint would amount to much. "But he was full of zip and vinegar," Higgins recalled later. Slotnick formed Carrols Drive-In Restaurants of New York and opened his first unit in

Syracuse on Erie Boulevard in June 1961. The second followed in North Syracuse in 1962.

Slotnick then picked up the pace, opening his allotted 40 restaurants in just two and a half years. He expanded his franchise agreement, so that by 1966 he was operating 49 restaurants, emerging as Carrols' largest franchise group. At the same time, he grew the drive-in theater chain, owned by Slotnick Enterprises, to about 150 units.

Slotnick had hardly exhausted his supply of zip and vinegar, however. His goal was to build a national restaurant chain. To achieve this end he acquired Carrols from Tastee Freez in 1968, which he combined with Slotnick Enterprises to form Carrols Development Corporation. To raise funds for expansion, Slotnick took the company public, its shares trading on the American Stock Exchange. By this stage there were 110 Carrols restaurants in the chain, generating $25 million in annual revenues.

CONVERSION TO BURGER KING COMPLETED: 1978

As a regional operator, Carrols faced stiff competition from national chains, in particular McDonald's and Burger King. Lacking the resources of its larger rivals, the chain began to lag behind and in 1974 began to lose money. As the losses mounted, reaching $4.3 million in 1976, the stock price fell as well, dipping to $1 per share. In order to survive, Slotnick decided in 1976 to become a Burger King franchisee, and he began to convert Carrols restaurants into Burger Kings. The impact was immediate and dramatic, as sales soared at the new Burger Kings. "It was the same meat, same mustard and same management," Slotnick told the *Syracuse Herald American.* "But, it was the name—Burger King." Within 15 months Slotnick opened 60 Burger Kings and by 1978 all of the 121 Carrols units had been closed.

While Carrols Development was making the transition to Burger King, it also began divesting theaters, the result of pressure from the U.S. Department of Justice, which contended that because the company's 13

theaters in the Syracuse and Utica markets controlled 86 percent of all movie box-office revenue it was restraining trade. Instead of selling some of these upstate New York units, the company began gradually to divest all of its 106 theaters. The last were sold in 1983, the same year that the company shortened its name to Carrols Corp., and the stock gained a listing on the New York Stock Exchange, followed by a stock offering that netted $13 million.

Although exiting the theater business, Slotnick was not content with simply building a Burger King chain, which by 1981 totaled 85 units spread across seven northeastern states. In 1980 the company dabbled in the retail personal computer business on a test basis by acquiring a pair of Philadelphia, Pennsylvania, stores from Computer Systems Unlimited. Three more units operating as Omnifax Computers Stores were added, but little more than a year later, Carrols decided to sell the business after it failed to meet expectations. Carrols sought to achieve diversity by focusing on food service ventures. It launched a distribution operation to provide Burger King units with foodstuffs, paper products, and other supplies, and developed shopping mall food court concepts that served such fare as Philadelphia-style cheesesteaks and gyros. In 1983 Carrols acquired Jo-Ann's Nut House, Inc., which included the Jo-Ann's Nut House and Chez Chocolate concepts. All told, Carrols picked up 137 nut and chocolate shops in regional shopping malls along the East Coast as well as along the northern border, from Maine to Minnesota. Over the next three years approximately 50 units were added, some through franchising, but by 1985 the shops were losing money. When losses continued to mount in 1986, Carrols decided to sell the business.

All was not well with the company's core Burger King operation, either. The second largest Burger King franchisee with 122 units, Carrols made news in 1984 when Slotnick expressed disappointment in the performance of Burger King's new salad bars, an attempt to satisfy more health-conscious customers. While the salad bars produced a modest profit, they were labor intensive and produced a great deal of waste, elevating food costs. Another problem for Carrols was that many of its Burger Kings were formerly Carrols Drive-In units, which had been established in small towns that were no longer experiencing growth. Hence Carrols' same-store sales lagged behind national averages. The company expressed an interest in adding another restaurant concept, possibly involving pizza or perhaps a healthful-foods chain, but none were found. The company began losing money again, suffering a net loss of $3.4 million in 1985.

```
┌─────────────────────────────────────────────┐
│                                             │
│              KEY DATES                      │
│                   ■                         │
│  ─────────────────────────────────────────  │
│                                             │
│  1961:  Herbert N. Slotnick opens first Carrols │
│         Drive-In franchised restaurant.     │
│  1968:  Slotnick acquires Carrols trademark.│
│  1969:  Carrols Development Corporation taken │
│         public.                             │
│  1976:  Slotnick begins converting Carrols units to │
│         Burger King.                        │
│  1986:  Slotnick leaves; company taken private in │
│         leveraged buyout.                   │
│  1996:  Atlantic Restaurants, Inc., acquires controlling │
│         interest.                           │
│  1998:  Pollo Tropical, Inc., acquired.     │
│  2000:  Taco Cabana, Inc., acquired.        │
│  2006:  Carrols taken public.               │
│                                             │
└─────────────────────────────────────────────┘
```

SLOTNICK SELLS OUT: 1986

Slotnick decided to leave the company and began the process to find a suitable owner. With help from an investment banking firm, Carrols screened about 40 companies before deciding in 1986 to accept a $135 million leveraged buyout offer engineered by senior executives, led by President David J. Connor and backed by the investment house of Morgan Ventures III, which took the company private. Alan Vituli, a Morgan Ventures principal, replaced Slotnick as chairman of the board. From his stock, stock options, and other benefits, Slotnick walked away from the company with nearly $26 million.

Carrols enjoyed some early success in its return as a public company. Sales reached the $200 million mark in 1987, but dipped to around $190 million a year later and continued to fall. Moreover, the buyout left the company saddled with debt, the interest payments on bonds resulting in continued annual net losses despite the inherent profitability of the restaurants. In 1992 the company was on its way to losing $2.3 million on sales of $156.1 million from 177 Burger Kings located in ten states when Connor resigned in the fall of that year. Vituli stepped in as chief executive and the company began implementing a plan to establish firmer footing. Part of the focus was on expansion. A move in this direction was the October 1992 acquisition of ten Burger King restaurants in Michigan from the Cain Restaurant Company. More importantly, Carrols restructured its debt through an affiliate of Citicorp Venture Capital Ltd., World Subordinated Debt Partners, L.P. The refinancing was accomplished through

the issuance of $110 million in 11.5 percent senior notes that required only interest payments until maturing in 2003. In addition, Carrols received a $25 million revolving credit line to fund expansion and provide some financial flexibility.

In May 1993 Vituli turned over day-to-day control of Carrols to a new president, Daniel T. Accordino, who despite being only 42 years old had spent half of his life working for Carrols. He had been studying English and French at Notre Dame University in hopes of becoming a college professor but ran out of money in 1972, whereupon he took a job as a junior assistant manager for a Carrols eatery. He soon realized that he could quickly move up the ranks and discarded his academic aspirations for a career in the restaurant field. Within two years Accordino was a district supervisor overseeing eight Burger Kings. His story was hardly unusual for the Carrols organization, which boasted many long-term employees who like Accordino climbed steadily up the corporate ladder. It was this seasoned management team that attracted investors in the company under Accordino's leadership during the mid-1990s.

In April 1996, Atlantic Restaurants, Inc., affiliated with Stamford, Connecticut–based Dilmun Investments, acquired virtually all of Carrols' stock for $86.5 million. A year later Atlantic Restaurants sold a 44 percent stake in the company to Chicago-based Madison Dearborn Capital Partners. Atlantic kept a 44 percent stake for itself and provided Carrols' senior management with a 12 percent interest, awarded through newly issued shares of stock. By then Carrols had grown its Burger King holdings to 230 units and an infusion of cash from Madison Dearborn helped to fuel further expansion. At the same time, a deal was struck to acquire 24 Burger King units in North Carolina and South Carolina for $21 million from Omega Services, Inc. Later in 1997, Carrols added 63 units in western New York and northern Kentucky, bringing the total number of units at the end of the year to 338. Revenues in 1997 approached $300 million, resulting in a net profit of $2.16 million.

In order to avoid being overly dependent on Burger King, Carrols also kept an eye out for new restaurant concepts. In early 1995 it signed a franchise agreement with Pollo Tropical, Inc., operator of Caribbean influenced restaurants. Vituli was very familiar with Pollo Tropical, having become aware of the Miami-based chain while making visits to Burger King's headquarters in that city. He was invited to serve on its board of directors after Pollo Tropical went public in 1993. The chain had been founded ten years earlier by CEO Larry L. Harris and his brother, and had enjoyed success with company-owned units in Florida and some franchise operations in the Caribbean, Central America, and South America. The effort to take the concept north to Atlanta, Chicago, and New York in 1995 did not fare as well, leading to retrenchment. Harris attempted to take Pollo Tropical private but Carrols outbid him. In June 1998 Carrols acquired Pollo Tropical, Inc., paying $90.2 million for the 55-unit chain.

INTO THE 21ST CENTURY

Carrols continued to build on its Burger King holdings in 1998, and by year's end was operating 382 restaurants in 14 states. The company shed some poorly performing units, trimming its holdings to about 350 in 2000. With the addition of Pollo Tropical, Carrols was able to grow revenues to $456.5 million while netting $1.1 million in 1999. The company also remained interested in further diversification, both in terms of cuisine and geography. It turned its attention to the Mexican quick-serve category, in particular San Antonio–based Taco Cabana, Inc. The chain was launched in 1978, a pioneer in the Mexican patio café concept, and began expanding throughout the Southwest. Taco Cabana looked to enter new markets in the mid-1990s, and it was at this time that Carrols signed a franchise agreement. When Taco Cabana began experiencing difficulties, Carrols held off on opening units. Taco Cabana, which had gone public, continued to grow, but as the stock market soured in 2000 the company saw its stock price tumble. In the fall of 2000 Carrols stepped in to acquire the 126-unit chain for $152 million. Taco Cabana was happy to be taken private, while Carrols believed that the chain complemented Pollo Tropical, giving the company a strong presence in an emerging restaurant category, quick-casual Latin.

As early as its 1993 refinancing, Vituli indicated that at some point Carrols was likely to become a public company again. In June 2004 Carrols announced plans to make a $475 million initial public offering of Enhanced Yield Securities, which combined common stock with senior subordinated debt. Due to poor market conditions the offering was scrapped in late October, but the company revisited the idea in 2006. In December the company made an initial public offering of common stock priced at $13 a share, netting around $70 million. In order to fund further expansion, in March 2007 the company took advantage of favorable interest rates to arrange a new $185 million credit facility, which was used to pay off old debt and provide working capital.

Ed Dinger

PRINCIPAL SUBSIDIARIES

Pollo Tropical, Inc.; Taco Cabana, Inc.

PRINCIPAL COMPETITORS

Chipotle Mexican Grill, Inc.; McDonald's Corporation; Wendy's International, Inc.; YUM!

FURTHER READING

Billmyer, Steven, "Syracuse's Own 'Burger King,'" *Syracuse Herald American,* December 21, 1986, p. A1.

Doran, Elizabeth, "Building a Burger Kingdom," *Syracuse (N. Y.) Post Standard,* May 8, 1993, p. B8.

Jeffrey, Don, "Carrols 'Dissatisfied' with BK Salad Bar," *Nation's Restaurant News,* August 13, 1984, p. 6.

Liddle, Alan, "Carrols Corp. Revises LBO Debt to Fuel Fast BK System," *Nation's Restaurant News,* August 30, 1993, p. 15.

Rubinstein, Ed, "Carrols Corp.," *Nation's Restaurant News,* January 1998, p. 50.

Teichgraeber, Tara, "Valley Taco Cabana Shops Acquired by Carrols Corp.," *Business Journal—Serving Phoenix & the Valley of the Sun,* October 13, 2000, p. 5.

Clement Pappas & Company, Inc.

10 North Parsonage Road
Seabrook, New Jersey 08302-0550
U.S.A.
Telephone: (856) 455-1000
Fax: (856) 455-8746
Web site: http://www.clementpappas.com

Private Company
Incorporated: 1942
Employees: 793
Sales: $300 million (2006 est.)
NAIC: 311421 Fruit and Vegetable Canning

■ ■ ■

Clement Pappas & Company, Inc., is a family-owned-and-operated juice bottler and cranberry sauce producer based in Seabrook, New Jersey. Juices include apple, grape, grapefruit, orange, lemon/lime, pineapple, prune, and tomato. The company also offers cranberry juice cocktail and blends, blueberry juice cocktail and blends, grapefruit juice cocktail and blends, cocktail mixers, iced tea, lemonade, and sports drinks. A wide variety of organic juices and drinks are also produced. About 90 percent of the company's business comes from the bottling of store brands. The company's own brands include Ruby Kist and Crofter's Organic, sold through retail channels, including supermarkets, discounters, drug stores, dollar stores, specialty food stores, and natural organic stores. Clement Pappas also exports its products and serves foodservice customers, including restaurants, bars, and hotels. The company's 600,000-square-foot Seabrook plant operates two juice bottling lines and a cranberry sauce line. In order to serve customers on a national basis Clement Pappas also operates plants in Mountain Home, North Carolina; Springdale, Arkansas; and Ontario, California. The company is headed by the sons of its founder, and several top leadership positions are held by third-generation members of the Pappas family.

FOUNDER, EARLY 20TH-CENTURY IMMIGRANT

The company bears the name of its founder, Clement Dimitri Pappas. He was born around the dawn of the 20th century in the small Greek farming village of Kaporelli. The son of a shoemaker, Clement learned the shoemaker's trade, but like his two elder brothers, Christopher and James Pappas, decided that a better life could be made in America. His brothers had made the move when he was a teenager. To pay for his passage, he traveled to Athens to find work and saved his money. In 1914, at the age of 14, he was able to join his brothers in New Jersey, where they had settled. He found work at Princeton University in the dining halls. After three years he and his brothers relocated to Mobile, Alabama, to work in a cannery. Here they saved their money and learned the canning business. They returned to New Jersey in 1921, settling in Cologne, New Jersey, close to Atlantic City, and began raising tomatoes and other vegetables, which they soon began to can.

The Pappas brothers phased out farming to concentrate on a seasonal canning operation for locally grown fruits and vegetables. They took on a partner,

John Gilles, and launched Pappas Brothers and Gilles in 1925. In the early 1930s the company became pioneers in the commercial production of cranberries.

Clement Pappas struck out on his own in 1942, splitting with his brothers, who according to company sources were contemplating retirement and a return to their native Greece. The younger Pappas, who had become an American citizen in 1923, was more interested in expanding the business than in slowing down. He sold out his interest in Pappas and Gilles and formed the Clement Pappas Company in 1942 by acquiring and renaming the Mayhew and Husted canning factory in Cedarville, New Jersey. According to the *Cranberry Connection*, Christopher and James Pappas would remain in the United States, but they too would split. As a result, for the next 20 years there were three New Jersey canning companies bearing the Pappas name competing against one another.

In addition to tomatoes and cranberry sauce, Clement Pappas focused on the canning of locally grown blueberries, peaches, asparagus, and vegetables. The company enjoyed steady growth, leading to plant expansions and modernization efforts. The companies run by his brothers did not fare as well, however, and in time they went out of business.

CLEMENT PAPPAS DIES: 1966

When Clement Pappas's health began to fail suddenly in the mid-1960s, his eldest son, Dean C. Pappas, was thrust into a leadership role. A graduate of Dickinson College, he was just 22 years old at the time. His father died in January 1966, and he had to wait three years for his brother, Peter C. Pappas, to graduate from Boston University and join him to help run the company. In time, Dean would become chairman and co-CEO with Peter, who would also hold the title of president.

The young management team had to contend with a shifting landscape. Because of the rise of large and efficient Midwestern and California competitors, Clement Pappas was forced to drop its dependency on local crops. Moreover, seasonal processing was no longer vi-

able, requiring the company to find a way to become a year-round operation. The brothers used juice bottling as a way to achieve that end, starting in 1970 when the company began offering cranberry and tomato juice in glass bottles. Clement Pappas was still working at a competitive disadvantage, especially with California firms that had access to growers benefiting from longer growing seasons and more favorable weather. The family decided to focus all of its efforts on juice and cranberry sauce. In 1977 the tomato canning business, once the mainstay of the company, was sold off.

Soon after the shift to juice production, Clement Pappas forged a beneficial relationship with a young upstate New York juice company, Apple & Eve LLC, which started out producing unfiltered natural apple juice in 1975. It then approached Clement Pappas and a co-packing arrangement was reached to bottle the United States' first 100 percent juice cranberry blends. It was a mutually beneficial relationship, spurring growth for both companies.

The Clement Pappas juice bottling plant in Cedarville, New Jersey, soon outgrew its capacity. In 1983 the company bought the Seabrook Foods plant located nearby in Seabrook, New Jersey. The new plant was upgraded with state-of-the-art bottling and food processing equipment, including a pair of Standard-Knapp case packers that were able to safely handle glass bottles. More importantly, the packers could accommodate 200 bottles per minute, a major improvement over the previous bottle speed of less than 100 bottles per minute, allowing the plant to keep up with the company's growing sales. Eventually, Clement Pappas also moved its corporate headquarters to the Seabrook site. In the early 1990s Clement Pappas began to switch from glass bottles to plastic containers, a move that once again required new case packing equipment from Standard-Knapp in order to keep up with the company's steadily expanding business.

The reasons for strong sales increases were manifold. Peter Pappas told the *Cranberry Connection*, "We achieved this growth by constantly adding new products and packaging to meet customers needs." In order to better serve these customers the company looked to add new regional plants. "As our customers have become national, they wanted us to supply them nationally," Dean Pappas explained to *PL Buyer*. "We wanted to be close to their distribution centers and service them better so that's why we've invested in facilities elsewhere." The Seabrook plant was well located, positioned to serve about 70 million customers within a 350-mile radius that encompassed such major markets

KEY DATES

1942: Clement N. Pappas forms canning company.
1966: Following the death of Pappas, sons begin to take over business.
1970: Clement Pappas begins bottling juice.
1983: Seabrook, New Jersey, plant acquired.
1998: Springdale, Arkansas, plant acquired.
2001: Mountain Home, North Carolina, plant acquired.
2004: Ontario, California, plant opens.

as Boston, New York, Philadelphia, and Washington, D.C.

The first strategically located regional plant and distribution center to be added came in September 1998 with the acquisition of Ozark Valley Products and its cranberry and grape processing facility in Springdale, Arkansas. Built by Welch's Foods, Inc., in the 1920s after it began growing grapes in the area, the plant was phased out in the early 1990s. One of Clement Pappas's executives, Vice-President of Operations Michael P. Strickland, was from the area and had previously worked at the plant. He rounded up some investors and formed Ozark Valley Products in 1992 to keep the plant open. It produced grape juice and other products under its own label, but mostly operated as a co-packer. One of its customers was Clement Pappas. Hence, the 1998 acquisition of the Springdale business was not surprising given the connections between the two companies. As a result, Clement Pappas was well positioned to serve its customers in the southwestern United States.

NORTH CAROLINA PLANT ACQUIRED: 2001

The next regional plant was added in 2001 when Clement Pappas acquired the Mountain Home, North Carolina, manufacturing plant along with its cranberry sauce business for $13.3 million from Northland Cranberries, Inc. Northland had acquired the plant in late 1998 from Seneca Foods Corporation. The 220,000-square-foot facility possessed juice processing capabilities and four bottling and canning lines. The deal not only provided Clement Pappas with distribution coverage in the mid-Atlantic and southeastern United States, but also brought with it a contract manufacturing agreement to produce Northland products at the plant.

Clement Pappas looked to add a western operation to complete a national footprint. In 2003 it reached an agreement to acquire Corona, California–based Hi Country Foods, but backed out of that deal. Instead, it bought the organic juice business of Ontario, California–based Crofters Foods. The company's entry into the organic juice business proved profitable. The segment soon enjoyed an annual growth rate of 20 to 25 percent, higher than sales from regular juice products. Initially a Southern California juice company packed the Crofters products on a contract basis while Clement Pappas scouted for a site on which to build a manufacturing plant and distribution center to handle all of its juice and cranberry sauce product lines.

In 2004 the company opened a new plant in Ontario, California. In addition to Crofters organic juices, Clement Pappas launched its own organic label, Grown Right, which also enjoyed strong growth. Organics still accounted for only about 5 percent of the company's business by the end of 2005, but given rising consumer interest the category was expected to make even greater contributions in the future. In addition, Clement Pappas developed the Ruby Kist low-calorie line of fruit juice, fruit drinks, and cranberry sauces. Instead of high fructose corn syrup, these products relied on Splenda artificial sweetener. As a result, an eight-ounce drink that would typically contain 120 calories was reduced to around 35 calories. Also in the 2000s, Clement Pappas unveiled a new line of one-liter cocktail mixers, available in lime juice and grenadine. In 2007 the company completed an asset acquisition with Baltimore, Maryland–based HR Nicholson Company, picking up processing equipment to produce aseptic juice boxes in addition to bottles and cans. The new packaging allowed Clement Pappas to expand its food service business to include schools, healthcare facilities, and other institutional customers.

The new century also brought greater responsibility to a third generation of the Pappas family. The eldest of the group, Clement Pappas, son of Peter Pappas, studied engineering in college and then worked as a consultant for a major accounting firm before joining the family business. He played a key role in establishing the Ontario plant and managing it. The second eldest, Dean Pappas's son Dimitri, earned a law degree and worked for a Philadelphia law firm for two years. In 2005 he became the corporate counsel for Clement Pappas. Peter's other son, Edward, decided to pursue a master's degree in food science. In addition, Dean's daughter, Eleni, held a master's in foods management and worked for a major food brokerage firm. Hence, Clement Pappas appeared to be amply stocked with current and potential executives, leaving it well positioned to remain a family-run company for the foreseeable future.

Ed Dinger

PRINCIPAL OPERATING UNITS

Crofter's Organic; Grown Right; Ruby Kist.

PRINCIPAL COMPETITORS

Dole Food Company, Inc.; Ocean Spray Cranberries, Inc.; Tropicana Products, Inc.

FURTHER READING

Behar, Hank, "Family Values," *Beverage World,* November 15, 2005, p. 26.

"Juice Maker Packs a Punch," *Packaging Digest,* September 2006, p. 48.

Pappas, Peter, "Clement Pappas & Co., Inc.: A Three Generation Commitment," *Cranberry Connection,* December 2005, p. 1.

"Squeezing the Profits Out of Fruit," *NJBIZ,* August 21, 2006.

Theodore, Sarah, "An Old Friendship," *PL Buyer,* March 2005.

Colliers International Property Consultants Inc.

50 Milk Street, 20th Floor
Boston, Massachusetts 02109
U.S.A.
Telephone: (617) 722-0221
Fax: (617) 722-0224
Web site: http://www.colliers.com

Private Company
Incorporated: 1976
Employees: 1,120
Sales: $1.2 billion (2006)
NAIC: 531210 Offices of Real Estate Agents and Brokers

∎∎∎

Maintaining its headquarters in Boston, Massachusetts, Colliers International Property Consultants Inc. is one of the world's largest commercial real estate organizations, with almost 675 million square feet under management. The private company operates through a network of independently owned affiliates, which altogether maintain about 270 offices in some 60 countries spanning six continents and employing more than 10,000 people. Nearly half of the offices are located in the United States, about one-third in Europe, Africa, and the Middle East, and the rest in Greater Asia.

Colliers offers a wide range of services to building owners and investors, as well as tenants. These include transactional services (representing both owners and tenants in acquisition, leasing, and financing); development and property management services; valuation and appraisal; asset management; realty tax services; and corporate consultancy (helping companies to best meet their space needs).

Colliers practice groups include Hotels, Life Sciences, Law Firms, Investment Services, Multimodal Services (Shipping and Transportation); Advanced Technology (serving the unique needs of high technology companies, such as cleanroom buildings); and Not for Profit, serving nonprofit organizations, whether community-based or national in scope. Each of the affiliated firms is a shareholder in Colliers International, and each of the parent company's regional managers is in turn an owner of a Colliers firm.

In order for a real estate company to join the organization, it must rank among the top three independent firms in its local market. Although independently owned, member firms freely share information and collaborate with one another while maintaining an entrepreneurial attitude, which is a key aspect of the company culture. As a result, the individual firms avoid the pressures experienced by publicly traded companies and retain the flexibility to make deals to accommodate clients, thereby leading to long-term relationships with those clients.

COMPANY FORMED IN AUSTRALIA: 1976

Collier International was created when three independent Australian real estate firms joined forces in 1976. The new company took the Collier name to honor the recently deceased Ronald Collier, who had been an employer and mentor to several of the new partners. A British-born chartered surveyor, Ronald Collier had moved to Australia and played a key role in establishing that country's real estate investment industry. In 1957 he traveled to London and convinced the venerable real estate firm of Jones Lang Wootton that Australia was a ripe market, arguing that although people there owned real estate, there was not as of yet a property investment culture.

A year later Collier founded the firm's Australian operation, Collier Jones Lang Wootton, opening offices in Sydney and Melbourne to buy and sell commercial real estate as well as to offer management services. Within a few years Collier Jones was thriving, employing more than 20 partners, many of whom would team up to create Colliers International and all of whom owed Ronald Collier a debt of gratitude.

One of Colliers International's cofounders, and its eventual chairman, was Robert McCuaig. He too was born in Great Britain, where he made his start in real estate in London while attending college, serving as a clerk for a firm involved in property valuation, taxation, and town planning. He was about to embark on a two-year national service stint in the navy after graduation when national service was canceled by the British government.

McCuaig decided to take advantage of the opportunity and pay a visit to Australia. He arrived in 1961, loved the country, and soon decided to stay. His path then crossed with Ronald Collier, who hired the young man and became his mentor. In 1967 McCuaig launched his own firm in Sydney called Robert McCuaig & Company. The following year he and David Collier became partners, creating McCuaig & Collier in Sydney. Also in 1968 another of the three firms that would create Colliers International was formed in the city of Adelaide, Collier Duncan & Cook. A year later the final founding firm, Glynn Lynch & McHarg, took shape in Melbourne.

Colliers was officially formed in October 1976, albeit without "International" in its name. The firm opened offices in Brisbane, Canberra, and Perth, and then was forced, in effect, to venture beyond the Australian borders. One of the firm's most important

clients, Qantas, needed help as it spread internationally and hired Jones Lang Wootton to serve as a joint agent with Colliers, which had been the exclusive agent for Qantas. "That put the fear of bejesus into us," McCuaig told the *Australian* in a 2003 article. "We need to go international. The only options were to go cap in hand to one of the big London firms, or do it ourselves." The firm elected to go it alone. In 1978 Colliers International took shape entering the Hong Kong market through the merger with Tony Petty & Associates. The New Zealand market was also added through the formation of Collier Fletcher. In 1970 Singapore coverage was added when Collier Goh & Tan was formed.

LONDON CALLING: 1980

The 1980s brought further expansion. Colliers International bolstered its coverage in Southeast Asia in 1980 when Collier Jordan Kee & Jafaar was established in Malaysia. Also that year Colliers International invaded London and the United Kingdom through the creation of Colliers Edwards Bigwood & Barclay. The firm then became involved in North America. In 1981 Canada was brought within the purview of Colliers International when Macaulay Nicolls Maitland, which had been founded in Vancouver in 1898, was brought into the fold. Four years later Macaulay Nicolls merged with another large regional commercial real estate agency, Toronto-based Leasco Realty Inc. The resulting company operated under the name Colliers Macaulay Nicolls Inc., and was based in Vancouver with additional offices in Toronto, Edmonton, Calgary, and Seattle. It was the largest member of the Colliers International alliance.

Colliers International eyed the most important real estate market in the world, the United States. In 1985 Colliers International merged with Boston-based American Realty Services Group (ARSG) and the combined operation made Boston its home under the Colliers name. In addition, Colliers International USA was formed to act as the United States' arm of the corporate parent. ARSG had been formed in 1983 as a network of 22 independent commercial real estate brokerage firms that covered many of the major real estate markets across the United States.

Playing a key role in the organization's founding was the Boston member Leggat McCall & Werner. ARSG's primary purpose was to coordinate referrals on real estate information for its member-owners. In keeping with this mandate, the organization developed the Index of Office Starts, which tabulated 16 years of historical data, from 1966 to 1982, on office building growth to create an index for the U.S. office market. This informa-

KEY DATES

1976: Company formed in Australia.
1978: Company expands to Hong Kong.
1981: Macaulay Nicolls Maitland of Canada becomes part of the Colliers network.
1985: Headquarters are moved to Boston following merger with American Realty Services Group.
1991: Colliers Jardine is formed in Asia.
2001: Revenues top $1 billion mark.
2002: Colliers Macaulay Nicolls acquires Colliers Jardine and becomes CMN International.
2004: FirstService Corporation acquires majority control of CMN International.

tion could then be used to help forecast future vacancy rates.

Colliers International expanded its footprint in Asia in 1986 by becoming partners with Jardine Matheson Holdings Ltd. of Hong Kong, which had been originally established as a trading company in Canton, China, in 1832 by Scots William Jardine and James Matheson. The firm made its mark by exporting tea to England and helping to establish Hong Kong, which soon became a British colony. Over the years it had also become involved in real estate activities throughout Asia.

As Colliers International grew, it had to contend with affiliated companies spread over a wide area. To improve communications between the disparate units, the parent company connected everyone electronically in 1989. This move contributed greatly to the firm's ability to make deals on a global scale. Also in 1989 Colliers International's Australian unit assumed direct ownership of the New Zealand operation. The following year the company reached an agreement to merge its property services interests with those of a Jardine Matheson real estate unit, Jardine Pacific, which had interests in Hong Kong, Taiwan, Singapore, and Thailand. After the transaction was completed in 1991, the resulting operation took the name Colliers Jardine. Jardine Pacific assumed a half-interest in the company, with Colliers International Ltd. of Australia owning the other half and providing Colliers Jardine with its new chief executive officer. The immediate goal was to expand into Indonesia.

While the Jardine Matheson transaction was being developed in 1990, Colliers International was branching out from the United Kingdom to open offices across continental Europe. Because of the demise of the Soviet Union and the deterioration of the Eastern Bloc, Colliers International moved into Eastern Europe as well, importing seasoned personnel to develop talent in these growing new markets. In the mid-1990s, Colliers International looked to other emerging markets, opening offices in South America and South Africa.

COMPANY RESTRUCTURED: 1997

The largest of the Collier network continued to be Vancouver-based Colliers Macaulay Nicolls. In keeping with this reality, Colliers International was restructured in 1997 so that Colliers Macaulay Nicolls was afforded a half-interest in Colliers Jardine. As a result, Colliers Macaulay Nicolls found itself courted by Insignia Financial Group, which in 1998 made an unsuccessful bid to acquire the company in an effort to establish a global network of commercial property advisers.

Through the rest of the 1990s the network of Colliers International firms continued to expand the types of services they offered to clients, in effect creating a one-stop resource that made Colliers International a valuable partner for major corporations. Expanded services, for example, led to Colliers International being named the sole real estate services provider in North America for BF Goodrich, a manufacturer of aircraft systems and services with more than 14 million square feet of office and industrial property. Colliers International was charged with providing strategic planning and management services as well as property disposal.

Colliers International also grew the North American business by opening new offices in such markets as Las Vegas, Salt Lake City, and Honolulu. Worldwide revenues topped $750 million in 1998. By the end of the decade real estate firms were added to the network from around the world, including Colombia, the Caspian region, Montenegro, and Serbia.

Colliers International exceeded the $1 billion mark in annual revenues in 2001, ranking second in the industry. At the same time, the firm had the fourth largest amount of property under management and employed the third highest number of people. Growth continued in the new century with the opening of new offices and the expansion of the firm's Corporate Solutions platform by forming a dedicated team of professionals split between the New York and Los Angeles offices.

In 2002 Colliers Macaulay Nicolls acquired the remaining half-interest in Colliers Jardine, allowing the largest member of Colliers International to provide better service to its global customers. Colliers Macaulay Nicolls assumed the name CMN International Inc. In

2004 it would receive a new owner when a Canadian-based property services company, FirstService Corporation, acquired a 70 percent interest. The remaining 30 percent was divided among senior management, active brokers, and employees.

In 2006 and 2007 Colliers International continued to grow its network around the world to cater to the needs of its clients. Offices were added in Finland, Israel, and Spain. In Australia, PRDnationwide was acquired to make Colliers International the leading real estate services provider in Australasia. In the United States, in the meantime, offices were added in Wilmington, Delaware, and Columbus, Ohio. The firm covered all of the major and secondary U.S. cities and was looking to some smaller markets as well, but only if it served clients' needs and was not a matter of expansion for expansion sake.

Ed Dinger

PRINCIPAL SUBSIDIARIES

Colliers International USA; Colliers International Europe, Middle East, and Africa; Colliers International Asia Pacific; Colliers International Latin America; Colliers International Canada.

PRINCIPAL COMPETITORS

CB Richard Ellis Group, Inc.; Grubb & Ellis Company; Trammell Crow Company.

FURTHER READING

"Colliers, C&W Ally with Ohio-Based Companies," *National Real Estate Investor,* May 1999, p. 8.

"Colliers, Jardine Lines Merge," *Wall Street Journal,* December 7, 1990, p. 7E.

"FirstService Corp. Acquires 70% Interest in CMN International," *Daily Journal of Commerce, Portland,* December 13, 2004.

Foong, Keat, "WEB Profile: Colliers International," *Multi-Housing News,* March 11, 2007.

Manning, Paddy, "Co-Founder Looks Beyond Real Estate," *Australian,* November 27, 2003.

Roberts, Jane, and Rachel Frampton, "Insignia Deal Looms," *Estate Gazette,* September 19, 1998, p. 55.

Yudis, Anthony Y., "A New Guide to the Office Market: ARSG Creates Office Market Index," *Boston Globe,* May 29, 1983.

Cooperativa Nacional de Productores de Leche S.A. (Conaprole)

Magallanes 1871
Montevideo,
Uruguay
Telephone: (598 2) 924 7171
Fax: (598 2) 924 6672
Web site: http://www.conaprole.com.uy

Cooperative
Incorporated: 1935
Employees: 2,750
Sales: $297 million (2006)
NAIC: 311511 Fluid Milk Manufacturing; 311512 Creamery Butter Manufacturing; 311513 Cheese Manufacturing

■ ■ ■

Cooperativa Nacional de Productores de Leche S.A., or Conaprole, is the largest exporter of milk and dairy products in the Latin American region, and the largest private-sector company in Uruguay. Formed in the 1930s as a government-backed effort to stabilize and modernize Uruguay's dairy industry, Conaprole enjoyed near-monopoly status in that market for much of its history. The arrival of large, multinational groups into the South American market has forced Conaprole to adapt, particularly by developing its export operations. The cooperative company is one of the largest suppliers of milk and dairy products to Mexico, Brazil, and Argentina, where it also operates production subsidiaries.

Other major markets for the company include Venezuela, the United States, Russia, Japan, the United Arab Emirates, Cuba, Chile, and Korea. Altogether, the company exports to more than 50 countries worldwide. Altogether, exports represent 60 percent of Conaprole's total revenues, which topped $397 million in 2006. Conaprole operates seven production plants throughout Uruguay. The company processes more than 2.7 million liters of fresh milk each day, producing fresh milk, UHT (ultra-high temperature) milk, butter, cream, yogurt and other fresh dairy products, cheeses and powdered milk, as well as snacks and other food products. Conaprole is led by Chairman Jorge Panizza Torrens and Managing Director Ruben R. Nunez-Hernandez.

BIRTH OF A DAIRY COOPERATIVE IN 1936

Cooperativa Nacional de Productores de Leche S.A., or Conaprole, was created in 1936 as part of the Uruguay government's effort to restructure the country's dairy industry. The majority of the population was concentrated around the capital city of Montevideo, with little access to refrigeration. Producers, especially those in outlying regions, faced a great deal of uncertainty in selling their dairy production, especially given the lack of industrialization in the dairy industry. In the meantime, the Uruguayan dairy market had become heavily fragmented, with five major players competing for a share of the tiny market. The country's small population, and the relatively low consumption of milk, meant that these firms remained too small to invest in more modern production methods. For the government, the situation also raised a number of health

COMPANY PERSPECTIVES

Our vision of a natural world. Conaprole has always promoted a development policy that takes into account the nature care. Based on this fact, Montevideo local government and Conaprole agreed to promote an Environment Protection Programme, which not only had educational aims, but also contributed to reduce environmental problems. Besides, the use of grass and legume prairies to feed the cattle, in addition to the highest quality pastures, protects the soils allowing its natural and long-term exploitation. The use of winter crops as oat, ryegrass, wheat, and summer crops as sorghum has been promoted. The cultivation of corn to be kept in silos was introduced; corn was previously used only for winter-feeding in most of the dairy farms. Hay prairies have been incorporated with the aim of serving as fodder reserves in bales or using the new rolling technology. All the efforts regarding the crops have a common purpose: to provide cattle with a natural feeding throughout the year, keeping the environmental care in mind.

concerns, both in terms of hygiene, and the nutritional importance of dairy products.

In order to address these concerns, the Uruguayan government passed legislation at the end of 1935 that set up the government as the central purchasing authority for the dairy industry in the country. In this way, the state guaranteed the purchase of all milk production by the country's farmers. The country's five major dairy cooperatives were then merged together to form a single cooperative, Conaprole. Formalized in June 1936, the new organization included dairy farmers and producers, as well as representatives of both the state and local Montevideo governments.

Conaprole quickly reorganized the existing operations of its members, starting with two factories in Montevideo. The first of these, Plant 1, was then dedicated to milk deliveries made by truck, while Plant 2, located adjacent to the central railway station, received rail-based delivery. Conaprole also led the effort to improve the group's packaging and dairy quality. Into the 1930s, milk had traditionally been delivered to consumers in paper containers coated with paraffin wax. However, these presented a major inconvenience in that the paraffin easily became dislodged from the paper during transport, contaminating the milk. Soon after its

creation, Conaprole made the decision to invest in new bottling technology. Supplying milk in glass bottles had the added benefit of permitting pasteurization, thereby increasing the safety of the country's milk supply. At the same time, the decision to switch to glass bottles helped stimulate growth at another state-run operation, the Fábrica Nacional de Vidrios (National Glass Factory). Conaprole's bottled milk quickly became a national fixture, until the glass bottles were phased out in favor of new plastic bags, introduced in 1980.

GROWING FOCUS ON EXPORTS

Over the decades, Conaprole had expanded its range of products beyond fresh milk. The company took over the production of butter from another company, Cole SA., in the 1930s. Conaprole also launched production of cheese, ice cream, yogurt, powdered milk, and later UHT milk, which provided a shelf life of up to three months. Conaprole also developed a number of support operations, such as the operation of ice cream carts. The company also became one of the first in South America to begin developing its own dairy brands. Conaprole's efforts successfully boosted the consumption of dairy products in Uruguay, and by the end of the century, Uruguay claimed the highest per-capita milk consumption in the Americas region, and the third highest in the world.

At the same time, the cooperative became an important source of technical and financial assistance to Uruguay's farmers. As a single body dominating the country's dairy sector for most of the 20th century, Conaprole was able to develop environmentally sound agricultural policies. In the early 1980s, for example, the company introduced pasturing techniques imported from New Zealand, and developed new wheat crops, as well as sorghum as a summer crop. The company also developed a network of corn silos, allowing farmers to stock corn year-round. Nonetheless, the company encouraged pasture feeding, both as an environmental measure, and as a means of lowering costs.

While farmers benefited from these technical developments, Conaprole also continued to play a major role in stimulating growth in other areas. During the 1980s, Conaprole adopted the policy of contracting out for part of its technical services needs. For this, the company turned to local companies, helping to stimulate the growth of Uruguay's information technology (IT) and other technical sectors. In this way, the country later emerged as one of the South American region's IT centers, as well as a major player in the fast-growing call center industry in the region in the 21st century.

KEY DATES

1936: Founding of Cooperativa Nacional de Productores de Leche S.A.(Conaprole) in order to consolidate dairy processing in Uruguay.

1970s: Conaprole begins exports, starting with Brazil and Argentina.

1980: Launches new plastic packaging, replacing bottled milk.

1999: Forms distribution partnership with Bongrain of France, and opens dairy processing plant in Brazil.

2003: Launches distribution joint venture in Mexico with Ireland's Glanbia.

2007: First exports of butter to Qatar.

In the meantime, Conaprole's strong organization had permitted it to increase its production, particularly starting from the mid-1970s. As a result, Conaprole began targeting expansion into the export market. For this, the company initially turned toward its larger neighbors, especially Brazil and Argentina. Conaprole quickly gained significant shares in both markets, in part because of its prior experience in developing its own branded dairy products lines. By the end of the 1980s, Conaprole's exports had expanded throughout South America, while the company had also become a major supplier to such far-flung markets as South Korea, Japan, and Russia. The company continued adding to its production network, adding a number of factories outside of Montevideo, including in Rincón del Pino, Mercedes, Villa Rodriguez, San Carlos, and Florida. In 1983, the company also acquired additional milk pasteurization capacity when it merged with another cooperative group, Industria Lacteos Regionales, or INLAR, founded in 1974 in the department of Rivera.

By the late 1990s, exports had become the largest part of the group's business, accounting for 60 percent of its total revenues. The company supported its move into the international market by achieving a wide range of industrial certification for most of its plants, including ISO 9001, HAACP, LATU Systems, Brazil's INMETRO, and OQS IQNet. Also in the 1990s, the creation of the Mercosur market among Brazil, Argentina, Paraguay, and Uruguay, opened up new perspectives for the company, particularly in the rapidly expanding Brazilian market. During the 1990s, Conaprole's long-life milk became its strongest export product, backed by the cooperative's brand marketing efforts.

The Mercosur agreements also exposed Conaprole to new competition at home. While Conaprole had enjoyed near monopoly status in Uruguay, the other Mercosur markets had long featured the presence of many of the global dairy leaders, including Parmalat, Nestlé, Bongrain, and others. The creation of the Mercosur provided these companies with an opening into Uruguay, and by the end of the decade, Parmalat had begun to build a significant presence in the market. In response, Conaprole was forced to raise its purchasing price for its farmer members. Nonetheless, the company soon saw its share of the domestic milk market drop to just 80 percent of total production, and then to just 70 percent by 2005.

RENEWING GROWTH IN THE NEW CENTURY

Conaprole found itself in difficulty at the end of the 1990s. The signing of the North American Free Trade Agreement temporarily froze the company out of those markets, especially Mexico, which had become increasingly important to its export business in the late 1990s. Worse for the company, however, was its reliance on the Brazilian and Argentinean markets, as these economies crashed at the end of the decade. Faced with severe cash flow problems at the end of the decade, Conaprole's future as an independent cooperative appeared in doubt. A number of suitors, including Parmalat, Unilever, and Argentina's Exxel Group, lined up to buy out the company. Before agreeing to a purchase, however, Conaprole hired the McKinsey consultant group to help it review its options.

With McKinsey's help, Conaprole was able to put into place a new five-year business strategy for the new century. Part of that effort included developing a range of partnerships with multinational dairy groups, as a means of defending its domestic operations, while also boosting its export business. In 1999, the group found its first partner in France's Bongrain, the world's leading cheese producer. The company also restructured its processing operations, opening a new state-of-the-art factory, and shutting down two of its older facilities. In the process, the company eliminated more than 1,000 jobs—more than one-third of its workforce. The restructuring effort enabled the company to pay off a loan granted by the World Bank, which then lent Conaprole another $30 million for further investment. Conaprole did not accept all of McKinsey's advice: the consultancy had proposed that Conaprole split itself up into four separate companies—along the lines of its fresh milk; yogurt and desserts; cheese; and commodity dairy products. The cooperative's members refused that plan, however.

Conaprole signed a new partnership agreement in 2001 with Howald & Krieg SA, which marketed the Alpa dairy brand in Uruguay. The agreement called for cooperation at the industrial level, in order to share technology and develop new products, as well as to work together on building their exports. At the same time, the company had launched its own cross-border moves. The company opened a dairy factory in São Paulo, Brazil, at the end of 1999, in order to ensure direct access to that country. In 2000, the company targeted further penetration of Argentina, signing distribution deals with Molinos Rio de la Plata of Argentina, and Brazil's Sadia group.

Conaprole's fortunes appeared to shine again in the early 2000s, as the cooperative was able to resume exports to Mexico. The reopening of that market, and subsequently, the U.S. market, proved good timing for the company, as both the Argentinean and Brazilian markets softened. By 2003, Conaprole's earlier efforts at cost efficiency helped position it as an important supplier to the Argentinean supermarket sector. In that year, too, the company formed a joint venture with Ireland's Glanbia, creating a dairy ingredient distribution company, Conabia, based in Mexico.

In Uruguay, Conaprole continued to restructure its production operations. In 2004, it opened a new factory in Montevideo, which regrouped production from the company's smaller plants in the area into a single, state-of-the-art facility.

Conaprole found itself faced with growing competition at home in the middle of the first decade of the new century. In particular, the company faced an assault by global dairy behemoth Danone. That company had gained a rapidly growing share in the Uruguayan market, in large part by sourcing its milk from Argentina, where government subsidiaries allowed Danone to purchase milk at prices some 30 percent below those paid by Conaprole at home.

While protesting those subsidies, Conaprole continued building up its own export business. By 2007, the company had developed exports to more than 50 countries worldwide. In October 2007, the list grew to include Qatar, where Conaprole completed its first shipment of 50 tons of butter. Since its founding in 1936, Conaprole had grown to become the largest dairy products exporter in Latin America, and Uruguay's single largest private-sector company.

M. L. Cohen

PRINCIPAL COMPETITORS

Lala Torreon S.A. de C.V.; Lala Monterrey S.A. de C.V.; Grupo Industrial Lala S.A. de C.V.; INDULAC; Olvebra Industrial S.A.; Unifoods S.A. de C.V.; Leche Pascual S.A.

FURTHER READING

"Conaprole and Shefa Sign Partnership," *South American Business Information,* November 2, 2001, p. 1.

"Conaprole Dairy Eyes Mexican Market," *Dairy Markets,* April 11, 2002, p. 14.

"Conaprole Firms Position in Dairy Market," *South American Business Information,* December 18, 2000.

"Conaprole in Mexican Long-Life Milk Supply Deal," *Dairy Markets,* August 1, 2002, p. 10.

"Conaprole Readies Plant at Montevideo," *South American Business Information,* December 5, 2003.

"Conaprole Sets Up Subsidiary in Buenos Aires," *South American Business Information,* July 5, 2000.

"Conaprole to Beat US $100 Mil in Exports," *South American Business Information,* September 10, 2004.

"Conaprole to See Parmalat Assets for Acquisition," *South American Business Information,* June 4, 2004.

"Conaprole to Sell Industrial Ice Cream in Argentina," *Dairy Markets,* January 10, 2002, p. 11.

Dirven, Martine, "Dairy Clusters in Latin America in the Context of Globalization," *International Food and Agribusiness Management Review,* March 4, 2001, p. 300.

"Glanbia Agrees to Mexican Venture," *Irish Times,* February 18, 2003, p. 21.

"Glanbia in Latin American Joint Venture," *Dairy Industries International,* March 2003, p. 6.

"Several Companies Interested in Alliance with Conaprole," *Dairy Markets,* May 27, 1999, p. 4.

Corinthian Colleges, Inc.

6 Hutton Center Drive, Suite 400
Santa Ana, California 92707
U.S.A.
Telephone: (714) 427-3000
Toll Free: (800) 611-2101
Fax: (714) 427-3013
Web site: http://www.cci.edu

Public Company
Incorporated: 1995 as Corinthian Schools, Inc.
Employees: 9,500
Sales: $933.2 million (2007)
Stock Exchanges: NASDAQ
Ticker Symbol: COCO
NAIC: 611310 Colleges, Universities, and Professional
Schools

■ ■ ■

Corinthian Colleges, Inc., is one of the largest companies in the United States involved in for-profit, postsecondary education. Corinthian's schools offer diploma programs and associate, bachelor, and master degrees in occupation fields including healthcare, criminal justice, information technology, business, construction, and transportation technology and maintenance. In 2007, the company's network included 94 colleges in 24 states and 32 schools in seven Canadian provinces, with a total enrollment of approximately 62,000 students. Approximately 73 percent of Corinthian students are female, 70 percent are over the age of 21, and about 50 percent are minorities.

ORIGINS

Corinthian Colleges was founded in February 1995. The five founders—David Moore, Paul St. Pierre, Frank Mc-Cord, Dennis Devereux, and Lloyd Holland—were executives at National Education Centers, Inc. (NECI), a for-profit operator of vocational schools based in Irvine, California. The plan of the five founders was simple: to acquire schools that were fundamentally sound and with good reputations but which for one reason or another were performing below their potential.

Between June and December 1996 the group effected a management buyout of NECI, acquiring 16 colleges and uniting them in a new company called Corinthian Schools, Inc. At the time NECI schools were experiencing difficult times and the company was on the verge of shutting down many of its campuses. However, within barely nine months of acquiring the NECI colleges, the new owners effected a financial turnaround. The formerly ailing schools had enrollments that were near capacity, and they began turning a profit ahead of the schedule the founders had set for themselves.

One change Corinthian made was to tighten the focus of the academic programs at the colleges. Before the takeover, students could choose from a full junior college curriculum, including aviation science. Under Corinthian they offered only allied health and computer technology programs, skills much in demand among employers. Securing jobs for its graduates was a prime concern for Corinthian from the beginning. The company's goal was to place 70 percent of its students in jobs within three months of graduation. Each of its colleges employed a full-time placement officer to track

COMPANY PERSPECTIVES

Corinthian changes lives. We empower individuals with skills to achieve their career goals, build their self-worth, and improve the performance of organizations. We do so with integrity. We play by the rules. We are responsive to our customers. We respect the individual. We excel in all that we do. We are committed to innovation. We are transforming education to become the world's leading provider of learning solutions.

each graduate's progress monthly until he or she found a job, as well as for the first three months of his or her employment. Corinthian also offered lifetime employment placement services to its graduates.

Corinthian more than doubled its size in October 1996, when it acquired 18 colleges from Phillips Colleges Inc. Based in Gulfport, Mississippi, Phillips was one of the nation's largest private companies involved in postsecondary education. Phillips' decision to sell was related to an audit that revealed sizable student loan violations and left Phillips $107 million in debt to its students, banks, and the federal government. As a result of the loan irregularities, $3.7 million in Phillips' federally guaranteed student loans were frozen by the U.S. Department of Education, rendering its schools essentially inoperable.

The sale to Corinthian was made as part of the final settlement with the government, and a portion of the $30 million received from Corinthian went toward government penalties. The acquisition made Corinthian Colleges at the time the largest private, postsecondary school operator in the United States. Among the schools acquired were two of the oldest private business colleges in the country, Duffs Business Institute in Pittsburgh and Blair College in Colorado Springs.

The purchase broadened Corinthian's presence throughout the nation, adding the eight schools of Florida Metropolitan University, along with other campuses in New York, Washington, Nevada, Utah, Oregon, and Missouri. It also gave Corinthian an additional academic focus. Phillips colleges taught business and computer technology courses, along with court reporting, video production, hotel management, and the like. Moreover, they granted bachelor's and master's degrees.

As a further consequence of the acquisition, Corinthian underwent a complete corporate restructuring, organizing its schools into two corporate divisions. The schools acquired from Phillips were made part of Rhodes Colleges, Inc., under the corporate umbrella of Corinthian Colleges, Inc. Corinthian Schools also became a corporate division. Rhodes included primarily degree-granting business colleges, while Corinthian Schools were diploma-granting schools that taught allied health and computer technology primarily.

GOING PUBLIC

For the first three years of its existence, Corinthian was privately owned by the five partners who had founded it. In July 1998, however, they made the decision to go public, in order to repay the sizable debt incurred with the Phillips Colleges acquisition. By that time, the company had 35 colleges in 16 states with a total student enrollment of about 14,000. An initial public offering (IPO) was held in February 1999. Corinthian had hoped the stock would garner $16 to $18 a share. It sold 2.7 million shares at $18 each, raising approximately $49 million. Those shares accounted for about 30 percent of the firm's total stock, the rest remaining in the hands of company management.

Wall Street reacted favorably to the offering; Corinthian was attractive to investors for a variety of reasons. First, Corinthian's career-oriented schools were seen as the wave of the future. They were highly attractive to students looking for practical knowledge that would lead to secure job prospects. Second, because students enrolled for a year at a time and committed to paying a full year's tuition at the beginning of a school year, income was highly predictable. Moreover, profits for such businesses tended to come in at a healthy average of 15 percent.

In March 1999, Corinthian announced that it had received a license from the state of Virginia, as well as national accreditation from the Accrediting Council of Independent Colleges and Schools, for a Kee Business College, which Corinthian opened in Chesapeake, Virginia, on March 25, 1999. Corinthian already operated one Kee campus in Newport News, Virginia. The school offered various allied health programs of eight to ten month duration. In early April of the same year, the company announced the opening of a Houston, Texas, campus of its National Institute of Technology.

In late April 1999, Corinthian made public gains in both enrollment and earnings. Earnings were above previously publicized expectations, and the company's student population was up nearly 14.5 percent over the previous spring. As a result, Corinthian shares, which had fallen by 29 percent earlier, recovered. They first reached $16.38, and a day later climbed to $19 a share.

KEY DATES

1995: Company is founded as Corinthian Schools and acquires 16 colleges from National Education Centers, Inc.
1996: 18 colleges are acquired from Phillips Colleges and company is renamed Corinthian Colleges.
1998: Company goes public.
2000: Significant growth is realized through acquisitions.
2003: Company goes international with acquisition of CDI Education Corporation in Canada.
2005: Company exits the corporate training field.
2007: The 28 Corinthian brands are consolidated into six.

The stock had gone as high as $19.75 before the decline began. At the end of the fiscal year in June, when Corinthian announced its results for the year, it looked as if the confidence of Wall Street analysts at the time of the IPO had been well-founded. Corinthian's revenues for 1999 had increased nearly 30 percent over 1998, up from $106.5 million to an all-time high of $133 million. That represented a four-year increase in revenues of over 400 percent, from the 1996 figure of $31.5 million. Those gains were accounted for by the rise in enrollment, together with an average 9.7 percent increase in each student's tuition. "Our performance exceeded even our own high internal expectations," said Corinthian CEO and President David Moore in a press release.

During this time, Corinthian announced that it was developing a new Information Technology (IT) curriculum for its schools. The first phase was the introduction of a Computer Network Administration program. Students in the program could take courses toward an 18- to 24-month associate's degree at the National Institute of Technology campus in Southfield, Michigan, or a 12- to 15-month diploma at Corinthian campuses in Colorado Springs, Orlando, or Tampa. A second phase of the IT curriculum, the Microsoft Office User Specialist (MOUS) program, was initiated later the same year. Programs in Internet Engineering, Programming, and Corporate Training were being developed at the same time.

Corinthian also undertook a partnership with Embark.com, a web site that provided information and services on higher education. Corinthian's presence on Embark.com would enable prospective students and guidance counselors to access information on schools and to apply to Corinthian electronically through Embark's Enrollment Services Systems. Embark.com boasted over one million hits monthly, which Corinthian believed would translate to much higher visibility for its schools, while at the same time lower administrative costs.

GROWTH BY ACQUISITION

Corinthian made significant additions to its roster of schools in the early 2000s. Final approval from the state of Texas enabled the company to open its new National Institute of Technology school in Houston in 2000. At the same time it completed a deal to purchase the Harbor Medical College, an allied health school in Torrance, California. In April the company acquired the three campuses of the Georgia Medical Institute in Atlanta. That school had some 830 students and annual net revenues of $6 million.

In May 2000 Corinthian finalized a lease agreement that enabled it to open a new branch campus of the Florida Metropolitan University (FMU) in Jacksonville, Florida. FMU was one of the first campuses at which students could study in Corinthian's Internet distance learning program. In June 2000 Corinthian purchased all the assets of the Academy of Business Inc. from owner The Tesseract Group. Tesseract, a company in Phoenix that ran private and charter schools, had lost some $14 million over the previous two years. It was faced with the prospect of posting a $700,000 bond with Arizona education authorities in order to renew the license of the school (which operated under the name Academy of Business College) as well as to cover by cash or a letter of credit half of the $1.7 million in federal funds the business school received in 1999. Corinthian did not disclose the amount of the deal that gave the company its first foothold in the Phoenix area.

By the summer of 2000 Corinthian was operating 46 schools in 18 states with a total enrollment of approximately 20,000 students. New acquisitions were the backbone of Corinthian's growth strategy. According to the company's head, David Moore, it evaluated some 50 potential acquisition targets every year and seriously considered about ten of those. The company made huge financial strides in fiscal year 2000. In August 2000 it announced that revenues rose 28 percent from 1999 levels to $170.7 million. Company earnings more than tripled, from $4.5 million in 1999 to $15.4 million the following year.

In July 2000, anticipating the good results, Credit Suisse First Boston upped its 18-month price target for

Corinthian stock from $35 to $40 a share. Wall Street did not seem to be paying attention at first; by July Corinthian stock was at just over $23 a share and that was down from a high of $27.25. It jumped again following the announcement of the yearly results in August, however, and reached $55 a share by early September. Stock prices dropped again later in the month, by nearly 20 percent when the company announced that its executives and some major institutional investors would release about three million of their own shares for public trading in a secondary stock offering.

STOCK FLUCTUATIONS AMID CONTINUED GROWTH

The stock was offered to the market in October 2000 for $50 a share. Just a day later the shares had risen to $54. In November, Corinthian's stock was strong again. Its value had increased fourfold since the spring, reaching $65.63 per share. The company's board of directors announced that a two-for-one split of Corinthian common stock would take place in mid-December. After the split, the company had some 23 million shares available for trading.

Beginning in October 2000, Corinthian made more substantial additions to its portfolio of schools. First it acquired four colleges from Educorp, Inc. Located in Los Angeles, Whittier, Ontario, and Long Beach, California, the schools had about 1,400 students enrolled primarily in allied health programs. Just days after the Educorp acquisition, Corinthian purchased the two campuses of the California Training Academy. The information technology and business schools added about 500 students to Corinthian's total student body. Later, in January 2001, the company opened a branch campus in Rancho Cucamonga, California.

By the start of 2001, Corinthian had record numbers of students in Internet-based distance learning courses. 1,276 students were enrolled 28 different courses offered via 11 Corinthian campuses. The company planned to add 18 courses and five additional campuses, as well as the possibility of earning associate's and bachelor's degrees online by the middle of 2001. Moreover, at the beginning of February the company purchased the Grand Rapids Educational Center Inc. for approximately $3.1 million. The acquisition included three Michigan campuses in Grand Rapids, Kalamazoo, and Merrillville, with about 460 students altogether. Corinthian planned to merge its campus in Wyoming, Michigan, into the Grand Rapids campus. Early in 2001, the company announced plans to open new schools in Dearborn, Michigan, and one in Skokie Illinois. The Skokie campus would be Corinthian's first in the Chicago area.

The competitive job market operating from during this time was a boon to for-profit postsecondary institutions. Working adults wanted the skills to advance within their career or new skills to enter a better paying field. The for-profit sector, including Corinthian, was responsive to the employment needs of the local market. The schools quickly developed appropriate courses, for fields such as information technology in the 1990s and healthcare in the 2000s.

More courses led to more students, which generated internal growth. In fiscal 2001, Corinthian implemented 75 new programs. In 2002, it added 22 new and/or adapted programs. However, growth by acquisition continued to be the company's primary model. By August 2002, Corinthian operated 55 colleges in 20 states. Two months later, its network had grown to 64 campuses in 21 states, serving 34,000 students.

INTERNATIONAL EXPANSION

In 2003, the company went international, acquiring a 90 percent stake in CDI Education Corporation, a Canadian company, for about $32 million. This acquisition, along with that of Learning Tree University the same year, provided an entry into corporate training. By December 2003, enrollment stood at 59,502, up 49 percent over the previous year. Seventeen percent of this growth was on a same-school basis.

A major attraction for students was the company's flexible class schedule. Schools operated year-round, with classes offered on weekends and at night as well as during the day. Students could usually complete their program of study more quickly than they could at either a public community college or a private nonprofit college.

In November 2004, the company separated the roles of chairman and CEO, with Jack Massimino taking the CEO role from founder David Moore. By 2005, Corinthian was operating 94 schools in the United States and 34 in Canada. However, the company appeared to have some difficulty integrating its many campuses efficiently and effectively. In September, the company sold the corporate training component of its Canadian operations for about $16 million. This, along with the sale of Learning Tree University in 2004, took Corinthian out of the corporate education field.

Between its fiscal years 2002 and 2005, Corinthian's annual revenues grew 200 percent, jumping from $310 million to $949 million. Most of the company's revenues (some 80 percent) came from federal financial aid programs that provided students with grants or relatively low interest loans. The rest of student tuition fees come from private loans arranged by Corinthian.

However, by 2005, net income had begun to slip as enrollment dropped. Causes for the decline included the closing of the New Orleans school following Hurricane Katrina as well as publicity regarding federal regulatory issues and lawsuits regarding misrepresentation of its programs. The California attorney general's office was investigating possible rules violation in calculating its students' job-placement rates in that state. Florida's attorney general also was looking into advertising and marketing practices at FMU. In December 2006, Terry Hartshorn assumed the role of chairman, from founder David Moore.

2007 AND BEYOND

In fiscal 2007, for a second year, growth continued to be relatively flat as Corinthian moved from an acquisition model to internal growth model. One effort in this shift was to consolidate its 28 brands down to six, each in its own division. This move was expected to increase name recognition and attract more students while lowering marketing costs.

The CDI division, located in Canada, offered diploma programs for entry-level positions in healthcare, business, and technology. The CSi division, which included Everest College and Everest Institute, offered diploma courses for entry-level healthcare occupations including medical assistant, pharmacy technician, medical insurance billing and coding, and dental assistant. The FMU division, with ten campuses in Florida, offered associate, bachelor and master degree programs in business, accounting, criminal justice, paralegal, and healthcare. It also offered diploma programs in healthcare occupations. The TSi division offered both diploma and degree programs in healthcare, business, criminal justice, and computer technology. WyoTech division, with seven campuses, offered college-level education in the automotive, diesel, motorcycle, watercraft, HVAC, and plumbing fields. Finally, Corinthian's Online Learning division consisted of campuses that offered online classes full time.

Despite rising interest rates that made it more expensive for students to finance their education, for-profit schools continued to be a booming industry, with a national enrollment of some two million students. Although the company faced various challenges, Corinthian Colleges appeared to be taking action to attract more students, and the demand for its services continued to be strong.

Gerald E. Brennan
Updated, Ellen D. Wernick

PRINCIPAL DIVISIONS

CDI; FMU; TSi; CSi; WyoTech; Online Learning.

PRINCIPAL COMPETITORS

ITT Educational Services Inc.; Apollo Group, Inc.; DeVry Inc.

FURTHER READING

Blumenstyk, Goldie, "The Chronicle Index of For-Profit Higher Education," *Chronicle of Higher Education,* August 17, 2007.

Blumenstyk, Goldie, and Elizabeth F. Farrell, "For-Profit High Education, Buying Binge Heats Up," *Chronicle of Higher Education,* July 11, 2003.

"Corinthian Colleges' Income Nearly Doubles; Revenue Up 32%," *Los Angeles Times,* August 31, 2000, p. C3.

"Corinthian Colleges Raises $48.6 Million in Stock Sale," *Los Angeles Times,* February 5, 1999, p. C6.

Dessoff, Alan L. "Private Lessons," *Techniques: Making Education & Career Connections,* October 1996, p. 29.

Earnest, Leslie, "Corinthian Colleges Gets Off to Good Start on Initial Offering," *Los Angeles Times,* February 6, 1999, p. C1.

Edwards, Bob, "For-Profit Colleges Growing Quickly Due to Focus on Vocational Education," *National Public Radio, Morning Edition,* broadcast transcript, October 23, 2003.

Florian, Ellen, "Jobless Pick Up Tickets at Trade School," *Fortune,* November 25, 2002, p. 40.

Galvin, Andrew, "Corinthian to Pay $6.5 Million to Settle Allegations of False Advertising," *Orange County Register,* August 1, 2007.

Huettel, Steve, "Calif. Firm Buys Tampa College," *Tampa Tribune,* October 18, 1996, p. 1.

Jaffe, Michael, "Why Corinthian Tops the Class," *Business Week Online,* March 23, 2004.

Kelleher, James B., "Santa Ana, Calif.-based Vocational School Operator Performs Well," *Orange County Register,* July 1, 2000.

Kroll, Lisa, "One Tough Lesson Plan," *Forbes,* October 28, 2002, p. 238.

Marcial, Gene, "An Educated Bet on Corinthian," *Business Week Online,* June 10, 2003.

"Revenue Flat, Enrollment Growth Slows at Corinthian Colleges in 06," *Educational Marketer,* October 9, 2006, p. 5.

Ruffins, Paul, "The Secrets Behind Their Success," *Diverse: Issues in Higher Education,* August 23, 2007, p. 34.

"Tesseract Sells Business College," *Arizona Republic,* May 5, 2000, p. D7.

Wasley, Paula, "Fla. Investigates Corinthian Colleges," *Chronicle of Higher Education,* December 2, 2005.

Womack, Brian, "Fastest Growing Companies," *Orange County Business Journal,* October 24, 2005, p. 35.

Young, Todd, "Corinthian Colleges, Inc.," *Morningstar Analyst Report,* August 2007.

Corporación José R. Lindley S.A.

Jirón Cajamarca 371
Lima, 25
Peru
Telephone: (51 01) 481-2070
Toll Free: (in Peru) 0-800-1-4000
Fax: (51 01) 481-3266
Web site: http://www.incakola.com.pe

Public Company
Incorporated: 1928 as José R. Lindley e Hijos S.A.
Employees: 2,424
Sales: $300.4 million (2006)
Stock Exchanges: Lima
Ticker Symbol: CORJRI1
NAIC: 311411 Frozen Fruit, Juice, and Vegetable Processing; 312111 Soft Drink Manufacturing; 312112 Bottled Water Manufacturing

■ ■ ■

Corporación José R. Lindley S.A. (Lindley) is the Peruvian beverage company that produces, bottles, markets, and distributes Inca Kola, a bubble gum flavored soft drink so beloved in its native land that Lindley brought mighty Coca-Cola to heel. As a result of a joint-venture agreement, Coca-Cola now owns nearly half of Lindley and allows it to bottle, market, and distribute its products in Peru, while Coca-Cola does the same for Inca Kola and allied beverages outside Peru. In addition to Inca Kola, Lindley offers other soft drinks, fruit drinks, bottled water, and an energy drink.

THE COMPANY THAT GAVE PERU INCA KOLA

Joseph R. Lindley and his wife, an English couple, arrived in Lima in 1910 and established a plant to manufacture carbonated soft drinks. At first the small business, Fábrica de Aguas Gasificadas Santa Rosa, turned out some ten brands of handmade beverages under names such as Orange Squash, Lemon Squash, Champagne Cola, and Cola (or Kola) Rosada at the rate of one bottle per minute. In 1918 the enterprise acquired a semiautomatic machine. It was incorporated in 1928 as José R. Lindley e Hijos S.A. In 1935, on the occasion of the 400th anniversary of Lima's founding, Lindley introduced what was to become its most noted product, Inca Kola. Over the next 25 years, the business continued to modernize and add to its productive capacity. The Inca Kola bottle came to bear a logo with the image of an Inca Indian in high relief. In 1956, Isaac Lindley, the founders' youngest son, decided on the construction of a new, larger plant. It was designed so that the administrative offices would look like small family apartments that could be sold as housing if the venture failed.

In 1962 Lindley introduced a line of Bimbo cola soft drinks in strawberry, pineapple, lemon-lime, mandarin orange, and apple flavors. Bimbo and the company's several other soft drinks, as well as mineral water and fruit juices, were supplemental to Inca Kola, which although said to be originally a beverage of the lower classes, became the soft drink leader in Peru during the 1960s and 1970s. Although of little importance earlier, it came to the fore with the spread of television in Peru, striking a chord with viewers by means of com-

COMPANY PERSPECTIVES

Our mission: To satisfy our customers whenever they consume beverages, creating value in a sustained matter for our shareholders: Efficiently producing and distributing beverages of the highest quality and safety; advancing the development and welfare of our personnel; furthering the development of our suppliers, distributors, and clients; strengthening the ties with the community, in our role as responsible citizens.

mercials with the slogan, "Inca Kola, the drink of national flavor."

Flavored by a combination of 13 indigenous fruits (and either *hierbaluisa,* a native plant, or lemon verbena, a herb introduced from Europe) according to a formula that the company will not reveal, Inca Kola has a very sweet, bland taste that many people have compared to bubble gum. Others have compared the flavor to lemon-lime, pineapple, banana, or strawberry. The artificial golden-greenish color, adopted to resemble Inca gold, tends to put off the uninitiated because of its association with urine. Both Peruvians and foreigners have struggled to explain its appeal. National sentiment is one obvious reason. "I drink it because it makes me feel Peruvian," a man told Calvin Sims of the *New York Times.* "I tell [my daughter], 'This is our drink, not something invented overseas. It is named for your ancestors, the great Inca warriors.'"

In a sociologically oriented magazine article, Marco Avilés and Daniel Titinger stressed Inca Kola's appeal as a dining accessory and supposed aid to digestion rather than a thirst quencher. "We have made of Inca Kola a gastronomical flag whose nationality enters by the mouth," they concluded. Many Peruvians believe that Inca Kola is the perfect accompaniment to distinctively native dishes such as ceviche (sliced marinated raw fish) and *ají de gallina* (shredded chicken in a sauce that includes nuts and chili). For others, it stands not only for national pride and the pleasures of the table but for conviviality with family and friends around the table.

Inca Kola entered the United States in Miami in 1981. Distributed by Continental Food and Beverage, Inc., it soon expanded to New York City and California. In 1985 Continental began bottling it in Paterson, New Jersey. The beverage could soon be found in Chicago, Washington, D.C., and other cities with large concentrations of people from South and Central America. In Chicago, Inca Kola also found customers among Polish immigrants; the color apparently reminded them of a popular soft drink in Poland.

FIGHTING COCA-COLA TO A DRAW: 1992–99

During the 1980s Inca Kola found it difficult to deal with a national economic crisis that included runaway inflation and the rise of a terrorist insurgent movement called Shining Path. A 17 percent selective consumption tax, in addition to the 18 percent general value-added sales tax, kept soft drink consumption well below Peru's neighbors. Despite the golden brew's slogan in that period, "The Flavor That Unites Peru," Coca-Cola forged to the front among carbonated soft drinks, just as it had almost everywhere else in the world. In 1992, however, the Lindley family, which still controlled 72 percent of the eponymous enterprise, began a counterattack. It turned over day-to-day management to a new management team more oriented toward marketing, raised $9 million in capital, and consolidated its subsidiaries into the parent company.

One of the new team's priorities was to improve Inca Kola's image among young, affluent Peruvians, who saw the typical customer, according to studies commissioned by the company, as a fat and unfriendly middle-aged woman. A $5 million advertising campaign in 1995 included television commercials showing youths drinking Inca Kola while they played tennis, skateboarded, frolicked on Lima's beaches, and ate dishes identified with Peru. The campaign continued with promotions at rock concerts and sporting events, and giveaways at supermarket chains in return for bottle caps.

Lindley also negotiated deals with many restaurants, such as the Bembos hamburger chain in Lima, that obliged them to serve only Inca Kola and other company-owned beverages; introduced a highly successful diet version of Inca Kola; and repackaged its Bimbo line. One of its signal successes was to force McDonald's, Inc., because of customer demand, to break its contract in Peru to serve Coca-Cola soft drinks exclusively. In addition, Lindley increased its distribution to Lima's better neighborhoods and began offering the large disposable bottles that had begun to comprise nearly one-third of all sales. After several years of losing money, the company earned a small profit in 1995.

Soon even Harvard University Business School and the University of Oxford were taking notice, citing Inca Kola as a case study, because Lindley's fizzy golden drink had done what seemed unheard of for a local company—captured the lead from Coca-Cola in Lima,

KEY DATES

1910: J. R. Lindley and his wife arrive in Peru and establish a soft drink plant there.

1935: Lindley introduces its most notable product, the soft drink Inca Kola.

1981: Inca Kola enters the United States in Miami.

1992: Lindley begins a seven-year battle to revive sagging Inca Kola.

1999: The Lindley interests form a joint venture with the Coca-Cola Co.

2004: Lindley acquires and absorbs the largest bottling company in Peru.

home to one-third of Peru's population. Coke disputed the finding; Pepsi Cola was running a distant third. In 1996 the enterprise introduced a totally automatic and computerized German-made bottling production line, filling an average of 1,000 containers per minute. Inca Kola also had a presence abroad, with bottling plants in neighboring Ecuador and Bolivia. The product reached Tokyo in 1991, shipped by Continental from Los Angeles with a Japanese label. In the United States, it was available in at least 18 states by 1999, including Publix Super Markets stores in Florida and Georgia. Inca Kola was also being sold in France and Spain, and later in Canada.

Lindley underwent corporate restructuring in 1997. While bottling in Lima and other operations remained under Corporación José R. Lindley, control of the company's brands was spun off into Corporación Inca Kola Perú S.R.L. The reorganization was intended to increase efficiency and cut costs, but the debt load incurred in its expansion had taken a heavy toll, and Lindley lost almost $5 million in 1999. The company conceded that it was looking for a foreign strategic partner, and it found one—none other than the Coca-Cola Co., which acquired half of Inca Kola Perú and one-fifth of José R. Lindley for an undisclosed sum believed to have been about $200 million. Johnny Lindley Taboada, a grandson of the founder and chairman of José R. Lindley, became chairman of the joint venture between Coke and Inca Kola.

Coca-Cola's decision was seen as a preemptive measure to keep beverage conglomerates in Chile and Venezuela that were acting as bottlers for PepsiCo, Inc., from pursuing their own plans to acquire a piece of Lindley. In addition to the cash collected, the Lindley interests won the right, through franchise contracts, to

have their products distributed by the powerful Coca-Cola networks in Europe, Japan, and North America. Similarly, Lindley began distributing Coca-Cola products through a system of franchise contracts.

LINDLEY IN THE 21ST CENTURY

The irony of a relatively small national enterprise bringing gargantuan Coca-Cola to the bargaining table was not lost on Peruvians, particularly when Coke's chairman of the board arrived in Lima and resolutely quaffed the golden brew with a smile on his lips. Lindley's infusion of funds allowed it to modernize its support system for the 40 distribution centers and 180 route sales representatives delivering its products to Peru's retailers. By 2001 the paper based system of taking and fulfilling orders had been replaced by portable terminals that collected and transmitted data. In this way, the small stores, operated with little capital, that formed the backbone of Lindley's clientele could place their orders and be restocked without the prior delays. Moreover, the sales representatives could collect and pass on to the company critical market information that they previously had usually been unable to convey because of time restraints.

This merger was not, however, to the liking of Embotelladora Latinomericana S.A. (Elsa), a firm that had been bottling Inca Kola since 1973. It surrendered its contract in 2000, claiming that, following the merger with Coke, Inca Kola had increased the price of its concentrates six fold. In 2004, Lindley purchased two-thirds of Embotelladora Latinoamericana for $215 million, following this with a tender offer to public shareholders and absorbing the company in 2005 without making it a subsidiary. This bottling company, the largest in Peru, had been majority-owned by a Chilean group and 45 percent owned by Coca-Cola. Lindley thus became the bottler as well as marketer and distributor of Coca-Cola and its allied beverages in Peru as well as those of Inca Kola. However, the Coke-Inca Kola alliance suffered from differences regarding marketing, as Lindley's director general acknowledged in a 2004 interview published in *El Comercio,* Peru's most prestigious newspaper. He described Inca Kola as "the brand related to meals, to the home, to Peru; Coca-Cola is the brand related to youth, to good moments, to sport. Our task is to manage the two so that they grow together, each in its own orbit."

The Coke-Inca Kola alliance dominated the sale of soft drinks in Peru during the first decade of the 21st century, although pressed by lower priced cola drinks such as Ajeper S.A.'s Kola Real. Lindley claimed 59 percent of the market for carbonated soft drinks in 2005, with 23 percent held by principal Inca Kola brands and 22 percent by Coca-Cola brands. Lindley also claimed 44 percent of the fruit juice market, 25 percent of the bottled water market, and 15 percent of "isotonics" (sports drinks). Abroad, however, the national drink did not seem to be doing well, except in Ecuador and northern Chile. Avilés and Titinger noted that its vogue seemed not to stretch beyond the confines of the erstwhile Inca empire, while some other Peruvians hinted darkly that the contemporary Atlanta empire had bought into Lindley only with the intention of ruining its onetime rival. However, Continental, which had continued to run Inca Kola as a business unit within Coca-Cola, had a network of independent ethnically owned distributors especially active on the East and West coasts. Inca Kola was also sponsoring soccer teams in Miami and offering scholarships to Hispanic students in New York City.

By 2007 Peru Beverage Limitada S.R.L., which represented Coca-Cola's investment, held 38.5 percent of Corporación José R. Lindley, while Lindley family members held 59 percent.

In 2007 Lindley had 8 production plants, 49 distribution centers, and 240,000 customers. It was producing Inca Kola in both regular and light (diet) no-calorie versions and Kola Inglesia, a version aimed at youth. Lindley was also producing and marketing San Luis bottled water; Powerade, an energy drink; and Frugos, a fruit drink available in five versions. Inca Kola was available in sizes ranging from a half liter to 2¼ liters, and Kola Inglesa in sizes up to three liters. Lindley was also producing, distributing and marketing Coca-Cola's beverages, including allied ones, in Peru, such as Fanta, Sprite, Crush, Canada Dry, and three kinds of Dasani bottled water. Lindley lost money in 2004 and 2005 but made a small profit in the first nine months of 2006 and a larger one in the same period in 2007.

With the increasing consolidation of the beverage companies in South America, some observers and speculators believed that Lindley would be acquired by London-based SABMiller plc, the world's second largest beer brewer, which had in 2005 purchased Peru's lead-ing brewer, UCP Backus y Johnston S.A.A. SABMiller was also one of Coca-Cola's five principal bottlers.

Robert Halasz

PRINCIPAL COMPETITOR

Ajeper S.A.

FURTHER READING

Avilés, Marco, and Daniel Titinger, "El imperio de la Inca," *Letras Libres,* December 2005, pp. 42–48.

Chauvin, Lucien O., "Inca Kola Bids for Bottler," *Daily Deal,* December 12, 2003.

Eden, Ruper, "Cuerpo a cuerpo," *AméricaEconomía,* January 1998, p. 39.

Emling, Shelley, "Peruvian Soft Drink Gives Coke a Run for Its Money," *Atlanta Journal-Constitution,* March 31, 1998, p. C5.

"Empresa José R. Lindley destaca crecimiento de marca Inca Kola," *El Comercio,* August 16, 2004.

Ferro, Raúl, "Derrota *amarilla,*" *AméricaEconomía,* March 25, 1999, p. 25.

Fuhrman, Elizabeth, "Inca Kola: *Bebida de las masas,*" *Beverage World,* October 2007, p. 40.

Holligan, Jane, "Class Action," *Business Latin America,* November 30, 1998, p. 3.

Lizardi, Susana, "Peru's 'Golden Kola' Goes out to War," *Frontline Solutions,* February 2001, p. 16.

Mandel-Campbell, Andrea, "Peruvian Pop Takes Fizz out of Cola Giants," *Marketing Magazine,* September 4, 1995, p. 5.

"Matrimonio arreglado?" *Semana Económica 1066,* April 15, 2007, p. 18.

Seward, Christopher, "Coca-Cola Buys into Inca Kola," *Atlanta Journal-Constitution,* February 24, 1999, p. D1.

Sims, Calvin, "Peru's Pride That Refreshes: Kola of a Local Color," *New York Times,* December 26, 1995, p. A4.

"Softdrinks and JR Lindley—Inca Cola and the Rise of Non-global Brands," *Latin American Economic and Business Report,* March 20, 2001.

Stinson, Douglass, "Inca Kola," *Advertising Age International,* December 1996, p. 18.

Cowen Group, Inc.

1221 Avenue of the Americas
New York, New York 10020
U.S.A.
Telephone: (646) 562-1000
Toll Free: (800) 221-5616
Fax: (646) 562-1861
Web site: http://www.cowen.com

Public Company
Incorporated: 2006
Employees: 537
Sales: $345 million (2006)
Stock Exchanges: NASDAQ
Ticker Symbol: COWN
NAIC: 523110 Investment Banking and Securities
Dealing

■ ■ ■

Cowen Group, Inc., is a NASDAQ-listed financial services company in New York City. The boutique's investment banking units are involved in mergers and acquisitions, securities underwriting, private equity placements, and leveraged buyouts. Cowen focuses on small to midsized companies in several industries: aerospace and defense, alternative energy, consumer, healthcare, technology, and telecommunications. In addition, the firm offers research services in these fields, and serves institutional customers by acting as a market maker for NASDAQ stocks within its range of expertise, about 850 securities in all, and by providing list block trading services that cover all sectors of the S&P 500.

Cowen also acts as a market maker for more than 200 convertible and preferred securities for institutional customers. The firm maintains offices in Boston, Chicago, Cleveland, Denver, and San Francisco, as well as London and Geneva.

WORLD WAR I-ERA ORIGINS

Cowen Group was founded in 1918 as Cowen & Co. by brothers Harry G. Cowen and Arthur Cowen, Sr., who set up shop as a bond brokerage at 120 Broadway in the Wall Street district of New York City. Harry, the older of the two, graduated from Columbia University in 1902 and three years later received a law degree from the school. Arthur also earned a degree from Columbia, graduating in 1909. Four years after the establishment of Cowen & Co., their younger brother, Edwin A. Cowen, was brought into the fold through a merger with the firm Adler, Cowen Company. During the 1920s the firm gained a seat on the New York Stock Exchange and began providing clearing and execution services, specializing in industry stocks, such as Armco Steel Corporation, for which Arthur Cowen was the point person.

Cowen & Co. moved to 54 Pine Street in 1933. Despite the Great Depression, the firm never lost money during these years. In the 1940s it did a good deal of business acting as a specialist in railroad bonds. In February 1945 Edwin Cowen was injured when his chauffeur ignored a Long Branch, New Jersey, grade crossing guard waving a pair of red lanterns, and his automobile was struck by a Pennsylvania Railroad express train. Suffering from severe shock, Cowen was taken to an area hospital but his injuries were not life

COMPANY PERSPECTIVES

Nearly 90 years of successful growth through bull and bear markets is a testament to the recognition that our principal product is knowledge, and meeting the demands of our clients is our first order of business. We are convinced that the fundamental tenets that served us so well in the past century—uncompromising service, time-honored ethics, and a dedication to helping investors capitalize on change—will serve us well in this century.

threatening. He would actually outlive both of his brothers. Harry died of a heart attack in 1957 at the age of 74, while Arthur died in New York Hospital in 1963, reaching the age of 76.

By the time the first generation passed away, Arthur Cowen, Jr., had taken charge of the firm. He joined the firm in 1933 after graduating from Wesleyan University, and saw Cowen & Co. prosper during the post–World War II economic boom. Its headquarters were moved to 45 Wall Street during the 1960s, when the firm established a research and institutional sales unit. By the 1970s, however, the tide was turning. According to a 1986 *Forbes* profile, "Cowen & Co.'s capital was a minuscule $5.7 million, and a good part of it was borrowed. 'In the first half of 1974 business was so slow we lost money for the first time, including the Depression years,' recalls Cowen. ... Adds comanaging partner Joseph Cohen: 'We were headed for trouble.'" Although well into his 60s Cowen decided the time had come for drastic changes at Cowen & Co.

First, Cowen ended the tradition of bringing in family members of the partners, including his own. "Having family continue to run brokerage firms has been the downfall of more brokerage firms than you can imagine," he told *Forbes*. It was at this time that he promoted Cohen, now in his mid-30s, who had joined the firm in the late 1960s as his research assistant. According to *Forbes*, Cohen was "an analyst with an intellectual bent (his graduate thesis at Columbia University analyzed the impact of taxation on England during the Industrial Revolution)." In addition, Cowen hired an engineer and operations specialist to modernize the back office operations while he and Cohen mapped out a strategy to expand and diversify the firm. To improve margins costs were also trimmed, the partners' dining room among the first casualties.

G.S. GRUMMAN ASSOCIATES ACQUIRED: 1976

Cowen & Co. abandoned the industry stocks that had so long been its focus, eliminating the specialist trading business that Cowen himself had headed for more than 25 years, and pursued more profitable investments, primarily through the acquisition of other brokerages that brought with them additional branch offices. A step in this direction had been taken in 1970 when Cowen acquired the firm of Greene & Ladd, a move that brought the firm into the retail securities business. In 1976 Cohen learned that Boston-based G.S. Grumman Associates, a research-oriented stock brokerage, was on the block. Founded in 1964, Grumman was small but well respected for its coverage of the computer, pharmaceutical, and aerospace industries. Grumman decided to join forces with Cowen in part because of its desire to become part of a full-service firm and, as Arthur Cowen told *Forbes*, "We told them we want to make money together and we want to have fun." Cowen then added to its retail business through the 1977 acquisition of Hardy & Company. All told, during the 1970s Cowen added six offices across the United States and relocated its headquarters to One Battery Park Plaza in Lower Manhattan.

Cowen expanded internationally in the 1980s, adding offices in London, Paris, Geneva, and Tokyo. In addition, another domestic office was opened in San Francisco. By 1986 the changes made a decade earlier were bearing considerable fruit. With 150,000 clients, the firm's capital approached $100 million, the bulk of which belonged to the firm's 26 partners instead of to lenders, as had been the case in 1974. Moreover, with pretax returns on capital averaging 50 percent to 60 percent since the late 1970s, the partners were clearly prospering. In the past ten years Cowen's institutional brokerage business had grown from a mere $1.5 million to the neighborhood of $24 million. The firm looked to expand its retail business further in 1986 by acquiring Chicago-based Freehling & Company, while at the same time launching an investment-banking unit. It was also in 1986 that its ties to the Cowen family were severed when in April of that year Arthur Cowen died of a heart attack at the age of 75, literally working at the firm until the day that he died. Cohen succeeded him as chairman and chief executive.

Cowen expanded its investment banking business at the start of the 1990s. In 1990 Cowen helped companies raise $200 million through five initial public offerings (IPOs) of stock plus secondary offerings. This amount would pale in comparison to the unit's business just five years later, when in 1995 it would be involved in more than 75 transactions worth $5 billion. In a

```
┌─────────────────────────────────────────────┐
│                                             │
│              KEY DATES                       │
│            ──────────■──────────             │
│                                             │
│  1918: Harry Cowen and Arthur Cowen, Sr., start │
│        firm.                                │
│  1922: Third Cowen brother, Edwin, joins firm. │
│  1933: Arthur Cowen, Jr., joins firm.       │
│  1963: Arthur Cowen, Sr., dies.             │
│  1976: G.S. Grumman Associates acquired.    │
│  1986: Freehling & Company acquired.        │
│  1995: Media and entertainment unit added.  │
│  1998: Firm sold to Société Générale.       │
│  2000: Retail business sold to Lehman Brothers. │
│  2006: Firm spun off as Cowen Group, Inc.   │
│                                             │
└─────────────────────────────────────────────┘
```

third of these deals, Cowen was the lead manager. A major reason for this success was that an area of the firm's expertise, technology, had become extremely popular with Wall Street. At the start of the 1990s Cowen had bolstered it abilities in this area by adding telecommunications coverage. It was also during this period that Cowen launched its convertible sales and trading unit to provide an even greater level of service to its clients. In 1995 the firm added a fourth group to its research unit by then covering media and entertainment stocks. To head this unit the firm lured away a top executive from Merrill Lynch, Harold Vogel. In addition to growing its investment-banking unit, which between 1994 and 1995 almost doubled its number of bankers to 42, Cowen emphasized its asset management business. In less than three years the amount of assets under management had increased from $1.65 billion to $4.1 billion by the spring of 1995. Cowen's geographic footprint also grew through the opening of a Toronto office.

FIRM SOLD: 1998

In the late 1990s firms like Cowen became hot commodities for commercial banks and others looking to increase their investment banking capabilities. Some of Cowen's chief competitors specializing in technology and healthcare investment banking were snapped up by major banks in 1996 and 1997, including Alex Brown; Robertson, Stephens, Inc.; and Montgomery Securities. Putting itself up for sale became a highly attractive option for several reasons. First, the prices being paid for such firms were extremely high, about four times book value. With an estimated book value of its assets at $150 million, Cowen was looking to command a sales price between $500 million and $600 million. Moreover, a combination with a large bank provided access to more

capital to help grow the firm, and the parent firm's range of services could help in the recruitment of new clients. Cowen hired an investment bank, Lazard Freres & Company, to review its options, which in addition to a sale included an IPO of stock or an infusion of outside capital. The high sale prices were too tempting, however, and in February 1998 Cowen agreed to be sold for $540 million to the U.S. investment bank set up by one of France's largest banks, Société Générale.

Once government owned, the Paris-based Société Générale was privatized in 1987. To avoid becoming pigeonholed as a large regional European bank, it looked to establish operations in the world's major financial centers, a decision that naturally brought it to New York. To head this effort, Société Générale in 1996 hired an American investment banker, Curtis R. Welling, who had 20 years of experience working on Wall Street. Unlike the approach of other foreign banks becoming involved in the U.S. securities business, Société Générale elected to focus on smaller companies involved in select industries. This niche strategy won over Welling when he was recruited for the post and it made Cowen a highly desirable acquisition target. With its addition, Société Générale was able to underwrite U.S. securities for the first time.

After the sale, Cowen was renamed SG Cowen Securities Corporation, and Cohen became the firm's chairman while Welling took over as president and CEO. The integration of the acquisition did not go smoothly, however. *American Banker* reported in December 1999, "Some executives say the commercial bank's strategy in dealing with Cowen's general partners alienated some of the original staff members after the deal was completed. Early on, the banking company suffered departures of senior executives, and some say it was slow to attract top-tier talent." Both Cohen and Welling would leave the firm, with the reins turned over to Kim S. Fennebresque, who came to the firm from USB shortly after the merger to head the mergers and acquisitions unit. In November 1999 Fennebresque succeeded Welling and was eventually named chairman as well. To complicate matters, just as the acquisition was being completed Société Générale shied away from its strategy of building a global investment banking franchise. According to a 1999 *American Banker* article, "The company altered that plan, analysts say, because of losses in fixed-income resulting from the 1998 emerging-market crisis and a lengthy but unsuccessful bid this summer to merge with the French investment bank Paribas." All of this uncertainty combined to hurt SW Cowen's performance. In particular, the firm experienced significant erosion in its technology and healthcare investment banking activities.

In 2000 SG Cowen elected to focus on its core businesses of investment banking and research. As a result the firm's retail business was sold to Lehman Brothers. SG Cowen was not completely opposed to expansion, however. It soon added a new sector to cover the consumer industry, creating a complete team of analysts, traders, and bankers to be involved in this growth area. The firm enjoyed some good success in its sectors in the early years of the decade, but when in mid-decade investment bank IPOs began to do well, Société Générale took the opportunity to sell off SG Cowen in a public stock offering.

In July 2006 the stock offering was completed, all of the proceeds going to Société Générale. Subsequently the underwriters partially exercised an option to purchase more shares, so that the amount of money Société Générale received from the sale of stock was about $175 million. The bank also received a cash distribution from Cowen of approximately $180 million. Nevertheless, Cowen, which had been incorporated in Delaware as Cowen Group, Inc., possessed more than $200 million in capital and was well positioned to grow its business as its management saw fit, to add new sectors to cover, new products to offer, and new clients to serve. Later in 2006 Cowen formed a leveraged finance group to become active in the leveraged and structured finance areas. Then, early in 2007, the firm formed a new Alternative Energy Group.

Ed Dinger

PRINCIPAL SUBSIDIARIES

Cowen and Company, LLC; Cowen International Limited.

PRINCIPAL COMPETITORS

Greenhill & Co. Inc.; KBW, Inc.; Stifel Financial Corp.

FURTHER READING

"Arthur Cowen Sr., Broker, Founded Company in '18," *New York Times,* August 27, 1963.

"Broker Hurt by Train," *New York Times,* February 14, 1945.

"Cowen & Company in Deal to Acquire G.S. Grumman," *New York Times,* February 24, 1976.

"Cowen Is Latest I-Bank to Test IPO Water," *Investment Dealers' Digest,* April 3, 2006.

"Harry G. Cowen," *New York Times,* February 22, 1957.

Mandaro, Laura, "Cowen Merger, Two Years Later, Still a Struggle," *American Banker,* December 7, 1999, p. 1.

Pratt, Tom, "Cowen Beefs Up in Banking but Pace Remained Measured," *Investment Dealers' Digest,* May 15, 1995, p. 9.

Rudnitsky, Howard, "'I Like to Sleep at Night.' (Cowen and Cos. Has Nearly $100 Million in Capital and Has No Plans to Go Public or Merge)," *Forbes,* March 24, 1986, p. 50.

Tarquinio, J. Alex, "For Société Générale, 'Niche' Needn't Mean Small," *American Banker,* June 9, 1998, p. 9.

Truell, Peter, "French Bank to Buy Cowen for $540 Million," *New York Times,* February 23, 1998.

CulinArt, Inc.

---

175 Sunnyside Boulevard
Plainview, New York 11803
U.S.A.
Telephone: (516) 437-2700
Fax: (516) 437-6680
Web site: http://www.culinartinc.com

Private Company
Incorporated: 1970 as Business Food Services, Inc.
Employees: 800
Sales: $125 million (2007 est.)
NAIC: 722110 Full-Service Restaurants; 454210 Vending Machine Operators

■ ■ ■

CulinArt, Inc., is the largest private caterer in the northeast United States. It also has a California office. The company counts more than 100 clients among corporate cafeterias, educational facilities, museums, and recreational venues. Once a bulk producer of cafeteria foods, the company changed course in the mid-1980s to focus on "boutique on-site dining services," landing corporate foodservice contracts with big law firms, the New York Mercantile Exchange, and others. This led growth to explode; at one point revenues were doubling every five years. The company eventually added colleges and private schools to the mix.

COMMISSARY ORIGINS

CulinArt, Inc., began in 1969 with a business founded in Long Island City, New York, by Joseph Pacifico. Business Food Services, Inc., was incorporated in September 1970, its generic name fitting the mundane mission of shipping cafeteria stew. For its first decade and a half, the company operated as a commissary contractor, supplying other businesses without any onsite operations of its own.

In 1984 Pacifico hired hotel dining veteran Thomas Eich to help raise the company's capacity for higher-end cuisine. Eich persuaded Pacifico that the commissary business had little prospect for growth. The transition to onsite food service began in 1986 when the first cafeteria was opened.

Results were soon apparent. A 1987 *New York Times* review of museum cafés credited Business Food Services with elevating the cuisine, particularly the salad bar, at the newly renovated Brooklyn Museum. This contract marked the beginning of the company's involvement in the leisure segment. In 1998, *Nation's Restaurant News* reported great success from the company's new strategy of providing regional cuisine styles to match the themes of traveling exhibits.

NEW MARKETS, NEW NAME

In 1991 Brooklyn's Pratt Institution became the company's first client in higher education. Four years later, Business Food Services bought La Cart, a caterer to private schools. In 1999 the company landed a challenging contract with New York's Keiko Academy boarding school requiring a mixed menu of American and authentic Japanese dishes.

The company was renamed CulinArt, Inc., in 1994, the new appellation reflecting its culinary aspirations. A

COMPANY PERSPECTIVES

Our culinary capabilities and profit and loss accountability enable us to focus more attention on large population accounts within sophisticated facilities. Our success lies in our ability not merely to adapt but to continually revitalize and transform our services, pioneering the cutting-edge and unconventional. Restaurant-style retail dining programs are our mantra. Our distinction lies in tailored boutique on-site services and our strength stems from a balance of expert talent with the ingenuity of food services' generation next.

period of rapid expansion followed. The 1995 acquisition of Corporate Food Management brought CulinArt into Connecticut.

Thomas Eich succeeded Pacifico as company president in 1999, while Pacifico took the titles of chairman and chief executive officer. Revenues were $52 million in 1999 and grew more than 50 percent the next year to $81 million.

Around this time, the company began looking to the recreation and leisure market for growth opportunities. Amusement parks such as Playland in Rye, New York, became venues for trying out franchised food concepts such as Burger King and Nathan's Famous Hot Dogs. CulinArt won a ten-year contract for most of the concessions there in 1999 and then lobbied for the business of the nearby Maritime Museum in Norwalk, Connecticut, as a rainy day counterpart, an official told *Food Service Director*. Part of CulinArt's involvement included developing its own marketing materials to pitch these facilities to event organizers.

In the corporate market, CulinArt was aiming to capitalize on the industry consolidation that left a few behemoths in control, noted *Nation's Restaurant News*. It hoped to provide superior service to customers who felt a lack of individualized attention from the big national firms. This was typified in the account of Cadwalader, Wickersham & Taft, a large New York law firm that in June 2000 was wooed away from the national foodservice giants.

A couple of smaller companies were acquired in the spring of 2000. InnerSystems of Long Island added seven new clients worth about $5 million a year. CulinArt also bought Norwalk, Connecticut–based Food 1st Restaurant Corp., which had been formed in 1993 and

brought 15 new corporate accounts to the table. CulinArt's geographic range was steadily increasing; it broke into the Boston market in 2000.

UPSCALE ACQUISITION

CulinArt's capabilities grew increasingly more sophisticated. In 2001 the company merged with Philip Stone Caterers, a specialist in upscale events. The deal added about $6 million to annual revenues, and included a kosher outfit named Regal Caterers. CulinArt also picked up a handful of local corporate accounts.

At the same time, the vibrant New York dining scene was giving many of CulinArt's corporate customers a taste for exotic cuisines, an official told *Nation's Restaurant News*. CulinArt introduced dishes such as Indonesian rice bowls under its Rijsttafel banner. It also developed a specifically health-conscious menu. Catering to corporate customers who wanted their greens delivered with more safety precautions than the industry standard "sneeze guard," CulinArt began converting salad bars from self-service to a made-to-order concept dubbed "Spinning Salads" (known on college campuses as "Great Caesars").

Revenues were up slightly in 2002 to $89 million, according to a long feature on the company in *Food Management*. CulinArt then had 1,400 employees. CulinArt had developed expertise in working in the cramped quarters of corporate facilities, noted *Nation's Restaurant News*. Half of CulinArt's roughly 100 accounts were in the corporate world, according to *Restaurants & Institutions*.

The company took over concessions at Manhattan's Bryant Park in 2003, replacing the individually owned kiosks there with corporate brands like Starbucks and its own concepts. CulinArt also opened its first West Virginia account during the year, signing up to serve the Clay Center, a new art and science museum.

CulinArt continued to serve up new ideas for its educational accounts. *Food Management* noticed its thriving new appetizer/side dish program at a New York law school. The company was on top of trends such as mini hamburgers and other retro fare, while maintaining a range of options for vegetarians.

On the technical side, CulinArt was one of the first catering companies to try out radio frequency identification (RFID) tags. A program with American Express helped speed its time-strapped customers through the lines at the New York Mercantile Exchange. The company was introducing different types of cashless programs at other sites as well.

Annual revenues were more than $125 million by 2007. The company had more than 120 accounts, and

KEY DATES

1969: Joseph Pacifico launches contract commissary business in Long Island City, New York.

1984: Thomas Eich hired to guide company to finer dining.

1994: Company renamed CulinArt, Inc.

1999: Eich succeeds Pacifico as company president; revenues are more than $50 million.

2001: CulinArt merges with Philip Stone Caterers, a specialist in upscale events.

2007: Revenues exceed $125 million.

had established an outpost on the West Coast via a new office in California.

Frederick C. Ingram

PRINCIPAL SUBSIDIARIES

Robbins Wolfe, Inc.; Philip Stone Caterers, Inc.; Regal Caterers, Inc.

PRINCIPAL DIVISIONS

Philip Stone Caterers/Regal Caterers; Leisure.

PRINCIPAL COMPETITORS

Sodexho Marriott Services; Aramark Corp.; Compass Group North America; Boston Culinary Group; Whitsons Food Services Corp.; Lackmann Culinary Services, Inc.

FURTHER READING

Barbieri, Kelly, "CulinArt Expands Menu As It Begins Fifth Season at Rye Playland," *Amusement Business,* June 23, 2003, p. 7.

Berta, Dina, "Food Banks Cook Up Job Opportunities Along with Hot Meals," *Nation's Restaurant News,* January 8, 2001, p. 14.

Buzalka, Mike, "Balancing Art & Commerce at CulinArt," *Food Management,* September 2003, pp. 48–56.

Clement, Jaci, "CulinArt Beefs Up," *Long Island Business News,* March 17, 2000, p. 22A.

Cohen, Joyce, "CulinArt Has Big Plans for N.Y.'s Playland Park," *Amusement Business,* August 2, 1999, p. 4.

Crow, Kelly, "Neighborhood Report: Bryant Park; Executive In-Baskets Meant for a Park Picnic," *New York Times,* Sec. 14, City Weekly, June 30, 2002, p. 5.

"CulinArt Embraces Cashless Systems," *Food Management,* February 1, 2005, p. 20.

"CulinArt Exec's Goal: Establishing Opportunities," *Food Service Director,* October 15, 2000, p. 26.

"CulinArt Expands Menu Diversity with Healthful, Economic Programs," *Nation's Restaurant News,* March 26, 2001, p. 20.

"CulinArt's Acquisitions: Gaining Best Practices," *Food Service Director,* January 15, 2001, p. 26.

"CulinArt Steps Up Event Catering," *Foodservice Director,* January 15, 2002, p. 24.

"CulinArt Uses Its Noodle," *Food Management,* November 1, 1999, p. 16.

Ferris, Marc, "Have Fun, Break Even," *New York Times,* June 15, 2003, Sec. 14WC, p. 3.

Friedland, Ann, "Appetizers with Attitude," *Food Management,* October 1, 2004, p. 42.

———, "Reinventing Salad," *Food Management,* July 1, 2004, p. 48.

Frumkin, Paul, "N.Y.C. Operator Upgrades Alfresco Fare at Bryant Park Kiosks," *Nation's Restaurant News,* July 8, 2002, p. 8.

King, Paul, "The Brooklyn Museum Combines an Afternoon of Art and Lunch," *Nation's Restaurant News,* October 26, 1998.

———, "CulinArt: Strategy of Offering Personalized Service," *Nation's Restaurant News,* July 6, 1998, p. 18.

———, "Smaller Players Serve Up Big Gains," *Nation's Restaurant News,* June 18, 2001, p. 47.

Lang, Joan, "Options at Every Station: New York Law Firm Is Vegetarian-Friendly," *Food Service Director,* August 15, 2001, p. 102.

———, "Training Day: CulinArt's Ongoing Approach to Culinary Training Doesn't Miss a Beat," *Food Service Director,* April 15, 2004, p. 64.

Markus, Stuart, "Philip Stone Caterers Merges with CulinArt," *Long Island Business News,* August 31, 2001, p. 6A.

"New Café a First for Workers; Firm Places Custom Meal Prep Front-and-Center," *Foodservice Director,* January 15, 2005, pp. 1, 5.

O'Brien, Tim, "Brand Names Help Boost Food Biz at Playland Park by 10%," *Amusement Business,* February 21, 2000, p. 15.

———, "CulinArt Gets 10-Year Contract for Playland Park in Rye, N.Y.," *Amusement Business,* May 10, 1999, p. 31.

———, "Food, Drink and Monet the Mix in Brooklyn," *Amusement Business,* September 13, 1999, p. 29.

Perlik, Allison, "Business Partners; To Sell B&I Self-Ops on Their Services, Contractors Must Assure Them That Standards Will Not Be Compromised," *Restaurants & Institutions,* October 1, 2004, p. 52.

Pristin, Terry, "Bryant Park Agency Replaces Kiosk Operators," *New York Times,* February 22, 2002, p. B3.

Schumer, Fran R., "Salad and Seurat: Sampling the Fare at the Museums," *New York Times,* April 22, 1987.

"Seeking Southern Comfort: CulinArt Looks Beyond Northeast for Expansion Opportunities," *Food Service Director,* October 15, 2004, p. 18.

"Squeezing Money Out of Tight Spaces," *Nation's Restaurant News,* February 16, 2004, p. 28.

"Within CulinArt's Growth Strategy: Caterers Add to Capabilities," *Food Service Director,* October 15, 2001, p. 28.

Wolson, Shelley, "CulinArt's Edward Leonard: Chef Parlays Passion into Top-Level Foodsvc. for Clients," *Food Service Director,* April 15, 2001, p. 108.

Delta Air Lines, Inc.

1030 Delta Boulevard
Atlanta, Georgia 30320
U.S.A.
Telephone: (404) 715-2600
Toll Free: (866) 715-2170
Fax: (404) 715-5042
Web site: http://www.delta.com

Public Company
Incorporated: 1934 as Delta Air Corporation
Employees: 51,300
Sales: $17.17 billion (2006)
Stock Exchanges: New York
Ticker Symbol: DAL
NAIC: 481111 Scheduled Passenger Air Transportation; 481112 Scheduled Freight Air Transportation; 481219 Other Nonscheduled Air Transportation

■ ■ ■

Delta Air Lines, Inc., is the third largest air carrier in the United States and the largest U.S. carrier serving Europe. Its route network serves 317 destinations in 55 countries. Its domestic network operates around a hub system at airports in Atlanta, Cincinnati, New York, and Salt Lake City. The Delta Shuttle serves business travelers flying between New York City, Boston, and Washington, D.C. Delta emerged from Chapter 11 bankruptcy protection in May 2007, after only 19 months of reorganization.

FROM CROP DUSTING TO PASSENGER TRANSPORT

The history of Delta may be traced to 1924, when Collet Everman Woolman and an associate joined in a conversation with some Louisiana farmers who were concerned about the threat to their crops from boll weevils. Woolman knew that calcium arsenate would kill the insects, but the problem was how to effectively apply the chemical. Having learned to fly the boxy "flying jennys" during World War I, Woolman considered dropping the chemical from an airplane. He engineered a hopper for the chemical and later perfected the system, and then began selling his services to farmers throughout the region. As a result, the world's first crop dusting service, named Huff Daland Dusters, was born.

In 1925 Woolman left the agricultural extension service to take charge of the duster's entomological work. In 1928 the crop dusting operation broke away from its parent company to become Delta Air Service. Woolman continued his crop dusting business across the South and expanded into Mexico and South America. The company began to diversify by securing airmail contracts, and in 1929 inaugurated passenger service between Dallas and Jackson, Mississippi. Later, routes to Atlanta and Charleston were added.

Delta began its climb to prominence when the U.S. government awarded it an airmail contract in 1930, remaining in business even during a temporary but costly suspension in the airmail contract system in 1934. By 1941, the company, called Delta Air Corporation by that time, would be awarded three more airmail contracts. During World War II, Delta, under contract

COMPANY PERSPECTIVES

We intend to be the airline of choice for customers by continuing to improve the customer experience on the ground and in the air. Our business strategy touches all facets of our operations—the destinations we will serve, the way we will serve our customers, and the fleet we will operate—in order to earn customer preference and continue to improve revenue performance. At the same time, we intend to remain focused on maintaining the competitive cost structure we have obtained from our reorganization to improve our financial position and pursue long-term stability as a standalone carrier.

to the War Department, devoted itself to the allied war effort by transporting troops and supplies. Delta returned to civilian service in 1945 and entered an age of growth and competition never before seen in the airline industry.

THE GROWTH OF AIR TRAVEL AFTER WORLD WAR II

On May 1, 1953, Delta merged with Chicago and Southern Airlines and continued to prosper as a major regional trunk carrier through the 1950s and 1960s. In June 1967 Delta merged with Delaware Airlines and officially adopted the name Delta Air Lines.

Delta's exposure to the northeast part of the country increased with the acquisition of Northeast Airlines on August 1, 1972. In July 1976 Delta purchased Storer Leasing, a move that added several jets to the existing fleet of about 200. Recognizing the value of high technology, Delta formed two computerized marketing subsidiaries, Epsilon Trading Corporation in 1981 and Datas Inc. in 1982, to coordinate and sell more passenger seats on all Delta flights.

Delta's consistent growth could be partially attributed to its successful transition of leadership. In the early days of commercial air transport airlines were run by individuals who would be better described as aviation pioneers first and as businessmen second. At American, Eastern, Pan Am, TWA, and Delta, these men established what could be described as almost dictatorial operations, retaining their posts as long as possible. Many of these leaders were majority stockholders who categorically refused to share their power or prepare successors to operate the company after them. For many

airline companies, when the chairman did eventually die, there was a difficult period of readjustment to the new management.

The departure of Delta's Woolman, however, was not surrounded by difficulties. He suffered a heart attack in his late 60s and was forced to relinquish some of his duties to Delta's board members. As Woolman's health deteriorated the board members gradually assumed more of his duties until his death at age 76. Although Woolman's absence was deeply felt at Delta, business continued as usual, and the airline was able to make a smooth transition to a more modern, corporate style of collective management. Under the new consensus-style management, Delta quickly became recognized for having one of the best planning and management teams in the airline industry. The company also earned a reputation for being on very good terms with its employees, treating its workers as family. By maintaining pay and benefits above the unionized competition, Delta was able to keep the majority of its employees non-unionized.

Although the company did not invent it, Delta was the first airline to widely employ the so-called hub and spoke system, in which a number of flights are scheduled to land at a hub airport within approximately 30 minutes, enabling passengers to make connections for final destinations conveniently and quickly. By the early 1990s the "big push," as it was called, was occurring about ten times a day at the Atlanta hub. Delta was also operating hubs at Dallas–Fort Worth, Boston, Memphis, and Cincinnati.

On the whole, Delta's management style remained conservative throughout the 1970s. While it boasted one of the most modern jetliner fleets in domestic service, the company developed a reputation for purchasing new planes only after they had been proven, often in a costly way, at other airlines. This "wait-and-see" policy saved the company a large amount of money. Only after competing airlines had used the Lockheed 1011 for several years did Delta purchase the plane, and Delta began replacing its fleet of Boeing 727s with the 757, 767, and MD-88 in the late 1980s, later than most, with the intention of using these technologically advanced and fuel efficient planes for at least 20 years. This 15-year strategy for flight equipment and support facility planning was typical of Delta. According to the vice-chairman and chief financial officer at the time, Robert Oppenlander, "Success is based on the long term maintenance of a technical edge, which is cost efficiency."

Delta also became known for having the most conservative balance sheet in the industry. With a debt-equity ratio that was consistently below one to one

KEY DATES

1924: Huff Daland Dusters, a crop dusting operation, is founded.

1929: Now known as Delta Air Service, the company inaugurates passenger flights between Dallas and Jackson, Mississippi.

1953: Delta merges with Chicago and Southern Airlines.

1967: Delta merges with Delaware Airlines, becomes Delta Air Lines.

1972: Delta acquires Northeast Airlines.

1986: Delta acquires Western Air Lines.

1994: Delta's Leadership 7.5 program is launched, seeking to dramatically restructure and streamline operations.

2000: Total number of passengers carried during the year reaches an all-time high of 120 million.

2004: Gerald Grinstein becomes CEO.

2005: Company files for Chapter 11 protection.

2007: Delta emerges from bankruptcy.

(meaning that their debts were usually outweighed by their net worth), the company was able to do most of its financing internally. This conservative approach was aptly summed up in a statement by the late chairman W. T. Beebe: "We don't squander our money on things like goofy advertising."

A NEW BUSINESS STRATEGY

In the 1980s, however, Delta assumed a more aggressive corporate personality, as its commitment to internal growth became increasingly threatened by a general trend in the industry toward external growth. Throughout the 1980s, Delta became relatively smaller, as companies such as TWA, Texas Air, and Northwest expanded through mergers. In order to remain competitive, in 1986 Delta announced its intention to take over the Los Angeles–based Jet America; however, the $18.7 million deal never materialized. Later that year Delta went ahead with the $680 million purchase of another air carrier based in Los Angeles: Western Air Lines. As Delta's Chief Executive Officer David Garrett explained, "For a merger to be worthwhile, two plus two has to equal seven." Enlarged by Western's hubs in Los Angeles and Salt Lake City, Delta management was able to make that kind of math work, in spite of initial difficulties integrating Western's unionized workforce into Delta's system.

In 1987 Ronald W. Allen, who rose through the ranks of Delta's personnel administration department, was named the airline's CEO. An aggressive and outgoing business person, Allen proved willing to make larger and riskier investments. Shortly after taking office, for example, he negotiated a $15 million dollar deal for Delta to become the official airline of Walt Disney World.

In the late 1980s and early 1990s, recession, rising fuel prices, and war in the Middle East all contributed to declining passenger traffic and inflated costs. Thanks in part to its financially solvent status, Delta weathered the industry troubles comparatively well, despite a 1991 operating loss of $450 million. Small, financially weak, and regional airlines were hardest hit by the trouble; Delta was one of the prime beneficiaries of the failure in January 1991 of Eastern Airlines, which like Delta had a significant portion of its routes in the southeastern United States. After Eastern's demise, Delta flew over 80 percent of traffic out of Atlanta.

In 1991 Delta made a major move toward becoming an international player by purchasing a $1.7 billion package of assets from Pan Am, outbidding chief rivals American and United. The package, which included the assumption of $668 million of liabilities, gave Delta a hub in Frankfurt, Germany, dozens of European routes, including flights from Miami and Detroit to London, a New York shuttle route, and 21 Airbus A310s. As with the purchase of Western, the deal was viewed by some in the industry as a departure from Delta's traditionally conservative business stance, and possibly too costly a purchase. Delta management, however, termed it a necessary stop in a consolidating purchase-or-be-purchased airline market: "We think it is a very conservative move," Allen told *Fortune* magazine, adding, "To have missed this opportunity would have been the risky course."

Delta appeared to have adapted well to the expansion-oriented market. Whereas Delta fliers used to joke that, although you might not know whether you would go to heaven or hell when you died, you would definitely have to change planes in Atlanta, the airline's customers could fly to Europe via its Frankfurt hub, or to Latin America via Miami. As it adapted to the aggressive and expanding modern market, Delta strove to maintain its policies of good labor relations and attention to service. Delta's employees were still among the highest paid in the industry and, like founder C. E. Woolman, Allen sometimes rode on Delta flights to interact with passengers. Indeed, *Forbes* magazine queried in a 1988 headline: "Is Delta too nice for its own good?" At the time, however, its emphasis on people seemed not to have hurt the company any.

RECORD PROFITS, NEW PROBLEMS

By 1992 it became clear that the financing agreement with Pan Am had come at a bad time for Delta. The general economic recession and continued high fuel prices, combined with the weight of Pan Am's heavy debt load, resulted in net losses of $506 million for fiscal year 1991. In an effort to lower costs, Delta was forced to reduce its workforce by 5 percent, in addition to implementing wage freezes and salary cuts. At the same time, the company was eager to integrate Pan Am's extensive European routes into its system, hoping to restore itself to profitability by improving its position as an international carrier. However, the lingering effects of the recession, as well as the Gulf War, had precipitated an overall decline in commercial air travel. To counteract this trend, Delta announced reductions of 45 percent on transatlantic fares at the onset of the summer 1992 season, resulting in record traffic of 8,511,966 passengers in August. In April 1993, in an effort to increase its share of transpacific air traffic, Delta launched new nonstop flights between Los Angeles and Hong Kong.

Initially, the stronger emphasis on overseas routes paid off for the company, leading to profits of $60.4 million in the first quarter of fiscal 1993, compared to a net loss of $125.2 million for the first quarter of the previous year. Inspired by this success, Delta strove to further expand its international presence by entering into code-sharing agreements with a number of foreign carriers in 1994, including Virgin Atlantic, Vietnam Airlines, and AeroMexico. Code sharing allowed an airline to purchase tickets from its rivals and resell them to its own customers, providing greater scheduling flexibility and control over prices. While some considered the practice deceptive, it had become prevalent throughout the airline industry by the mid-1990s, with the number of code-sharing partnerships reaching 389 by 1996. For its part, Delta established 14 such contracts with other airlines between 1992 and 1996.

Another wave of heavy losses in the first three months of 1994 forced the company to undertake a more drastic cost cutting scheme, and in April Delta launched its Leadership 7.5 program, a restructuring initiative designed to streamline operations. The goal was implied in the program's name; Delta hoped to reduce the cost of flying to 7.5 cents per mile, per seat, with an overall aim to cut operating expenses by $2 billion over a three year span. The reorganization called for a reduction of 20 percent of the company's workforce, a realignment of its domestic route system, and a discontinuation of some of its less profitable European routes. These drastic measures brought quick results, and the

company was able to claim a net profit of $251 million for the fourth quarter of fiscal 1995.

Delta's impressive financial comeback was not without costs to its reputation as a "family corporation." The reduction of the company's customer service team resulted in a significant increase in passenger complaints, and by 1997 Delta dropped to last place in on-time rankings among the ten leading U.S. airlines. The decline in customer service was hardly unique to Delta. Overall, the annual number of airline passengers in the United States jumped to 640 million in 1999, compared to 453 million in 1991, with the ratio of seats filled reaching an all-time high of 71.3 percent. Overcrowding, frequent delays, and poor service resulted in a substantial increase in the numbers of complaints lodged with the U.S. Department of Transportation in 1999, prompting Congress to consider legislation that would impose stricter regulations on the airlines' business practices.

ALLIANCES, LABOR PROBLEMS, AND TERRORISM

Delta took steps to make it easier for flyers to use its network to get to more places. In 1999, it acquired the remaining 80 percent of the stock in Atlantic Southeast Airlines, making that company a wholly owned subsidiary. The following year, Delta purchased Comair for approximately $2.3 billion. Both of these operators were already partners in the Delta Connection program. In June 2000, Delta and its partners AeroMexico, Air France, and Korean Air launched SkyTeam, an alliance to provide more flights and easier connections for their customers while filling more seats. By 2007, SkyTeam would become the second largest airline alliance, with 14 partners from four continents.

The expiration of the Delta pilots' contract in May 2000 was followed by several months of unproductive negotiations. When the impasse dragged into December, the pilots retaliated by refusing voluntary overtime during one of the airline's busiest seasons, forcing Delta to cancel 3,500 flights over the course of the month. The new year brought little relief, and another 1,700 cancellations followed in the first ten days of January 2001. While the company enjoyed net profits of $897 million in 2000 and saw its total number of passengers reach an all-time high of 120 million, it was clear Delta still faced several unresolved issues, both with customer service and labor.

Then the industry was profoundly affected by the terrorist attacks of September 11, 2001, on the United States. All flights were temporarily suspended, and when they resumed people stayed away in droves. As national fear surrounding flying ebbed, the heightened security still created inconveniences in the form of long lines and delays. All major airlines struggled during this time, and because Delta had a healthy balance sheet, it could (and did) keep borrowing money to stay afloat, despite losses of $1.6 billion that year.

COST-CUTTING EFFORTS

Even before the acts of terrorism, the company had been looking for ways to reduce costs. Despite its net profits, the company was carrying $10.5 billion in debt as of January 1, 2001. Delta laid off some 13,000 employees and began to shift the makeup of its fleet from three-engine planes to two-engine planes, which were less expensive to operate. Still, debt and losses mounted at Delta.

In 2004, CEO Leo Mullin resigned, and Gerald Grinstein, a Delta board member and former president of Western Airlines, came out of retirement to assume that position at age 71. To avoid bankruptcy, Grinstein cut jobs, increased flights, closed Delta's hub at Dallas–Fort Worth, and changed the fare structure. To try to save the airline, Delta pilots, the only unionized Delta workers, agreed to pay cuts of 32.5 percent across the board as well as to changes in work rules. To compete with budget airlines, such as JetBlue and Southwest, which were attracting customers with their low fares, Delta launched its own budget carrier, called Song. Delta also sold its share in the Worldspan reservation system. Still, losses amounted to $5.2 billion in 2004.

In August 2005, the company sold its Atlantic Southeast Airlines subsidiary to SkyWest Airlines for $425 million. The following month, it announced more personnel cuts along with cuts in domestic flights and expanded international flights to Europe and Latin America. These efforts could not, however, offset the effects of increasing fuel prices and high labor costs as a legacy carrier. On September 14, 2005, with $20.5 billion in debt, Delta (and its wholly owned subsidiaries) filed for bankruptcy protection under Chapter 11. By that time, U.S. Airways had declared bankruptcy twice, United Airlines had been in bankruptcy for nearly three years, and Northwest Airlines had just filed for Chapter 11 protection.

BANKRUPTCY REORGANIZATION

The company secured a $2 billion financing package from its creditors that allowed it to keep flying during the reorganization. In 2006, the pilots accepted a contract that cut their pay more and terminated their pension plan. Grinstein cut the workforce from 70,000

to 47,000 and cut all salaries, including his own. He also capped executive perks, eliminated bonuses, and promised nonexecutive employees that they would share in stock incentives available after exiting Chapter 11.

In addition to reducing labor costs, Delta folded the operations of Song, "right-sized" its planes, and expanded its international routes. It shifted wide-body planes that had lots of empty seats on routes between Atlanta and South Florida to its international routes and expanded international business. By 2007, the company's international flights represented 39 percent of Delta's business, up from 20 percent before the bankruptcy.

At the end of 2006, U.S. Airways made an $8.7 billion bid for Delta, which Grinstein and the creditors refused. U.S. Air then upped its bid to $10 billion, which was also refused. For the year, Delta showed its first operating profit since 2000, in the amount of $58 million. In addition, J.D. Power and Associates ranked Delta second in overall customer satisfaction for the year.

2007 AND BEYOND

Delta emerged from bankruptcy on May 30, 2007, as an independent airline. Grinstein had moved the company through a successful reorganization process in only 19 months. As promised, more than 39,000 nonexecutive employees received stock incentives and raises. In August, the board announced that Richard Anderson, former CEO of Northwest Airlines, would replace Grinstein. Then, in November, published reports indicated Delta was discussing a merger with United Airlines. Delta quickly denied those reports.

Delta had a reconstituted fleet, lower labor costs, fewer domestic flights, and an expanded international network that would include China as of March 2008. It was also facing high fuel costs, an aging fleet that would need replacing, and intense competition domestically and for Atlantic flights. As evidenced by reported talks with United, and speculation that Delta might join with CEO Anderson's former employer Northwest Airlines, Delta would need to contend with the continuing issue of consolidation in the airline industry.

John Simley
Updated, James Poniewozik; Stephen Meyer; Ellen Wernick

PRINCIPAL SUBSIDIARIES

Comair Holdings, Inc.; Delta AirElite Business Jets; Delta Connection Academy; DAL Global Services; Delta Technology, Inc.

PRINCIPAL COMPETITORS

AMR Corporation; UAL Corporation; Southwest Air Lines Company; Jet Blue Airways; Continental Airlines, Inc.; NWACO:USA.

FURTHER READING

Banks, Howard, "Is Delta Too Nice for Its Own Good?" *Forbes,* November 28, 1988.

Brelis, Matthew, "For Airlines, Forecast Is Still a Gloomy One," *Boston Globe,* January 20, 2001.

Foust, Dean, and Justin Bachman, "A Surprising New Pilot for Delta," *Business Week,* September 3, 2007, p. 44.

Harrington, Jeff, "Sky-High Frustration," *St. Petersburg Times,* February 27, 2000.

Helyar, John, "Delta's Chapter 11 Dogfight," *Fortune,* December 12, 2005, p. 61.

Ho, Rodney, "A Closer World: Airlines Extend Their Reach by Selling Tickets on Each Other's Flights," *Atlanta Journal and the Atlanta Constitution,* March 19, 1996.

Huettel, Steve, "Delta Seeks a Steady Course," *Tampa Tribune,* April 7, 1997.

Jonas, David, "Mullin Retiring, Grinstein Rising," *Business Travel News,* December 8, 2003, p. 3.

Laibich, Kenneth, "Delta Aims for a Higher Altitude," *Fortune,* December 16, 1991.

Lewis, David W., and Wesley Philips Newton, *Delta: The History of an Airline,* Athens: University of Georgia Press, 1973.

———, "The Delta-C & S Merger: A Case Study in Airline Consolidation and Federal Regulation," *Business History Review* (Boston), 1979.

Lipton, Joshua, "Delta Has a New CEO and, Maybe a New Partner," *Forbes.com,* August 23, 2007.

Maxon, Terry, "Burdened by Expense of Pan Am Move, Delta Air Lines Adjusts to Lean Times," *Journal of Commerce,* August 19, 1992.

Nelson, Brian, "Delta Air Lines," Analyst Note, *Morningstar,* October 16, 2007.

Newman, Rick, "Delta Takes Flight," *U.S. News & World Report,* May 28, 2007, p. EE2.

Reed, Dan, "Delta's Dawn: New Delta Executives Redefining Airline's Once-Stodgy Image, Boosting Bottom Line," *Fort Worth Star-Telegram,* January 24, 1999.

"A Safe Landing," *Economist,* May 5, 2007, p. 84.

Tatge, Mark, "Out of the Woods," *Forbes.com,* May 12, 2007.

Thurston, Scott, "Delta Joining Dogfight over Latin America," *Atlanta Journal and the Atlanta Constitution,* April 5, 1998.

———, "High Expectations: With Profits Back, Delta Focusing on Image and Service," *Atlanta Journal and the Atlanta Constitution,* March 9, 1997.

———, "New CEO Gives Delta a Brisk Shake," *Atlanta Journal and the Atlanta Constitution,* December 28, 1997.

Dietz and Watson, Inc.

———— ■ ————

5701 Tacony Street
Philadelphia, Pennsylvania 19135
U.S.A.
Telephone: (215) 839-9000
Toll Free: (800) 333-1974
Fax: (215) 831-1044
Web site: http://www.dietzandwatson.com

Private Company
Incorporated: 1939
Employees: 6,457
Sales: $260.5 million (2006 est.)
NAIC: 311611 Animal (Except Poultry) Slaughtering;
    311612 Meat Processed from Carcasses

■ ■ ■

Dietz and Watson, Inc., is one of the world's largest meat processing and export companies, specializing in providing products for delis and supermarkets. Dietz and Watson offers a wide variety of products including premium deli meats, healthful and low-sodium meats, artisan cheeses, and deli condiments. The company's products are produced in compliance with federal regulations to prevent animal cruelty and in accordance with the federal requirements to qualify as organic meat products. Headquartered in Philadelphia, Pennsylvania, Dietz and Watson's products are sold in 38 states and are shipped internationally.

A PHILADELPHIA FAMILY BUSINESS: 1939–75

Dietz and Watson, Inc., was founded by Gottlieb F. Dietz, a German sausage maker who immigrated to the United States in 1921, fleeing the economic collapse in Germany that followed World War I. Dietz found employment with a number of meatpacking companies in the northeastern United States until he was able to raise sufficient capital to go into business for himself. In 1939, Dietz purchased the financially ailing Watson Meat Company, in Philadelphia, Pennsylvania, and opened a small meat production business, combining his name with that of former owner Walter Watson, who remained with the company as a sales manager.

Dietz and Watson started out as a local distributor, supplying neighborhood delis and markets in the Philadelphia area. Gottlieb Dietz died in 1964, leaving control of the company to his daughter Ruth Eni, who assumed the role of president. When Eni took control of the company, Dietz and Watson had become the largest deli meat purveyor in Philadelphia and employed a staff of more than 100 full-time employees producing more than 100 pounds of meat per week from their Vine Street production facility.

In 1972, the Pennsylvania state government transferred responsibility for inspecting meat-processing facilities to the federal government. When Dietz and Watson's Vine Street facility was inspected in 1972, the company was found to be in violation of several of the newly established sanitation guidelines. In an effort to comply with federal guidelines, Dietz and Watson conducted an overhaul of the sanitation systems. During a subsequent inspection, the plant's sanitation procedures and worker conduct had improved significantly to satisfy federal guidelines. As a consequence of the switch from state to federal jurisdiction, meat production companies that passed federal

COMPANY PERSPECTIVES

The founder's primary goal was to create the most flavorful, highest quality meat delicacies in the marketplace. His mantra "Quality Above All Else" is perpetuated by the third generation of Dietz's family, and the company has established itself as the benchmark for quality and innovation for the industry. Our mission is always both perfection and originality. This is how we prepare wholesome, nutritious and uniquely premium meats. And, our Master cheese makers create our hand-churned, small batch cheeses with the same commitment to quality above all.

regulations were permitted to market their products in other states. Over the next decade, Dietz and Watson grew an average of 10 to 12 percent annually and expanded into neighboring states and eventually nationwide.

In the late 1960s, the city of Philadelphia informed Dietz and Watson that the company would eventually need to vacate its Vine Street location to make way for expansion of the Federal Interstate Highway System. In preparation for the move, Dietz and Watson purchased, in 1969, a former slaughterhouse located at the intersection of 3rd Street and Girard Avenue, in the Kensington neighborhood of Philadelphia. In 1972, after neighborhood residents learned that Dietz and Watson would occupy the former slaughterhouse, members of the Olde Kensington Redevelopment Corporation (OKRC) argued that disruptive odors from the plant would interfere with housing developments scheduled for the neighborhood. Although Dietz and Watson representatives argued that the plant's operations would not produce odors similar to those that emanated from the former slaughterhouse, neighborhood residents were staunchly opposed to the move and from 1972 to 1973 took their case to the courts to prevent Dietz and Watson from occupying the building. Dietz and Watson eventually abandoned the project and, when the Vine Street building was condemned in 1975, relocated to a former slaughterhouse located on Tacony Street.

ENTERING THE HEALTH FOOD AND INTERNATIONAL MARKETS: 1975–91

The American food market changed significantly after 1975 as new medical information led to increased concern about the relationship between diet and health. Studies conducted around the country suggested that the average American consumed unhealthy levels of fat and sodium, contributing to a number of health issues including heart disease and diabetes. In addition, an increasing number of consumers became concerned about the potentially harmful effects of consuming hormones and other chemicals fed to farm animals before slaughter.

Dietz and Watson was an early pioneer in the healthful deli meat market and in requiring humane and chemical-free farming practices. In 1979, Dietz and Watson introduced their Gourmet Lite product line, consisting of a sodium-free turkey breast and reduced sodium ham. Although healthful food alternatives would not become standard in many grocery store chains until the 1990s, Dietz and Watson invested heavily in the 1970s and 1980s in marketing their meat products as healthier alternatives to standard deli selections. Dietz and Watson's 1970s advertising campaigns also highlighted the company's commitment to complying with federal regulations regarding the humane treatment of animals at the company's farms and stressed that no animals were treated with hormones or growth stimulants. In 1985, Dietz and Watson expanded their healthful product line with low-salt salami, bologna, beef, and franks. In 1987, the company introduced a low-fat, low-sodium roast beef product.

In 1989 Dietz and Watson took the first step toward marketing their products to an international audience, when the company began shipping small quantities of deli meat (under 500 pounds annually) to Japanese delis. By 1991, Dietz and Watson's Japanese market had risen to over 4,000 pounds per year. While the Japanese deli market was not among Dietz and Watson's principal revenue sources, the company's experiments with the Asian market helped to refine marketing strategies and to prepare for future ventures into international sales.

INDUSTRY EXPANSION AND SAFETY CONCERNS: 1995–2003

Throughout the 1980s and 1990s, Dietz and Watson established their standing as one of a small group of top-tier deli meat providers. In 1995, Dietz and Watson was listed by *National Provisioner* as one of the top 125 meat and poultry processors in the nation with over $60 million in sales recorded for 1994. The company's top competitors, Lincoln Provision, Robzens, and Strauss Veal, recorded similar profit margins reflecting overall growth in the deli meat industry.

In September 1995, Dietz and Watson was cited by the U.S. Environmental Protection Agency for violating

KEY DATES

1939: Dietz and Watson founded by German sausage maker Gottlieb Dietz.

1964: Ownership of the company passes to Dietz's daughter Ruth Eni and husband Louis Eni, Sr.

1972: Meat production companies that pass federal regulations are permitted to market their products in other states.

1975: Company relocates to Tacony Street in Philadelphia.

1979: Company begins marketing reduced-salt products for the health food market.

1989: Company begins marketing deli meat to the international market.

1999: Plant opens in Baltimore, Maryland.

2004: Controlling interest in Corfu, New York, cheese manufacturer purchased.

2005: Deli condiments product line introduced.

2007: Distribution center opens in New Jersey.

federal regulations by failing to report the use of environmentally hazardous chemicals at the company's processing plants. The case was settled in 1996, when Dietz and Watson agreed to pay fines of $28,000 and to complete an overhaul of their production process to reduce solid and liquid waste. Dietz and Watson agreed to complete comprehensive pollution-control reforms, estimated at $428,000, which included reducing grease and oil effluent by 50 percent and solid waste by 25 percent. To complete the rehabilitated waste control system, the company installed new waste collection systems in each of their facilities and also installed a new pumping station and a treatment system for wastewater.

Dietz and Watson's healthful marketing strategy culminated in the establishment in 1996 of the company's Dedicated to Your Healthier Lifestyle campaign and a Healthier Lifestyle label being placed on more than 50 of the company's products. As the market for healthful and organic food grew, Dietz and Watson responded by increasing their focus and promotion on products that met or exceeded U.S. Department of Agriculture (USDA) and American Heart Association guidelines for healthier dietary choices.

In an effort to assuage public concern and prevent costly safety issues, in 1998 Dietz and Watson introduced the Puratherm Food Safety System, a combination of employee training and sanitation guidelines, which were designed to exceed government standards. In implementing the Puratherm System, Dietz and Watson formed a number of new positions in the company for individuals to supervise sanitation, waste removal, and food testing at various stages in the manufacturing process. Dietz and Watson's increased focus on contamination safety accompanied the USDA's development of more stringent inspection guidelines to combat contamination by *Listeria monocytogenes,* a common bacteria found in improperly preserved or stored meat products. Dietz and Watson's Puratherm System became one of the company's chief marketing campaigns in the 1990s as concern over meat contamination reached a peak in the United States.

In 1999, Dietz and Watson purchased the Parks Sausage Company in Baltimore, Maryland, in order to renovate the facility and build a new poultry processing plant. The Parks Sausage Company declared bankruptcy in 1996 but was reestablished with aid from private investors. The company continued to fare poorly and was again threatened by foreclosure when Dietz and Watson proposed purchasing the plant and investing $6.4 million to refurbish the facilities, while retaining a portion of the company's former employees.

Dietz and Watson requested $750,000 in loans from the city of Baltimore to complete renovations on the Parks plant on the basis that the new facility would provide employment to Baltimore residents. With the aid of state loans, renovations were completed in 1999 and the plant opened with a full-time staff of 148 employees.

Dietz and Watson's Baltimore expansion was fueled by growth in the deli meat industry as a whole. By 2000, over 97 percent of grocery stores operated a deli, as opposed to 89 percent in 1997. Industry estimates conducted by Chicago's Fresh Look Marketing Group indicated that, in 2000, deli meat was a $5 million industry.

In 2001, the USDA recorded over 95 recalls of contaminated meat products, which prompted the USDA Food Inspection Division to initiate more stringent inspection and safety guidelines. Although Dietz and Watson was not subject to product recalls, in 2003 the company expanded their Puratherm system to include a heat-treatment process, wherein finished meat products were exposed to high temperatures for a brief period prior to packaging. Dietz and Watson representatives claimed that the heat-treatment process eliminated most forms of harmful bacteria and exceeded federally mandated safety guidelines. In 2003, Dietz and Watson completed a comprehensive overhaul of their sanitation systems, which included purchasing new sanitation equipment for each of the company's processing locations.

EXPANSION IN THE NATIONAL MARKET: 2004–07

In 2004, Dietz and Watson purchased Yancey's Fancy Inc., a cheese maker located in Corfu, New York. Yancey's Fancy, founded in 1947 as Kutter's Cheese Factory, was the largest cheese manufacturer on the East Coast in 2004, and produced over 25 varieties of standard and specialty cheeses. Dietz and Watson maintained the company's management structure and retained the services of company President John Yancey, who was a third-generation member of the founding Kutter family. To further the company's move toward full-service deli production, Dietz and Watson introduced Deli Compliments in 2005, a product line that included a variety of sauces, horseradishes, and pickles to be sold at delis and supermarkets that carried Dietz and Watson meat products.

In 2006, Dietz and Watson expanded their Baltimore operation by purchasing several parcels of property peripheral to the poultry processing facility. The Baltimore Development Corporation lent the company $400,000 to complete its expansion, based on the company's goal of providing additional employment to Baltimore residents. In 2006, Dietz and Watson's Baltimore operations processed over one million pounds of poultry on a weekly basis.

Dietz and Watson distributed their products directly to many delis and markets in the Northeast but also sold a majority of their products to distribution companies, like Applegate Farms based in New Jersey, which then sold Dietz and Watson products to supermarket chains. By 2006, Applegate Farms was one of Dietz and Watson's largest customers, accounting for approximately half of the company's equipment budget in 2006. According to data released by Applegate Farms, the American market for natural meat increased to over $150 million in annual sales in 2006. Since 2005, several deli meat industry leaders, including Illinois' Oscar Mayer (a division of Kraft Foods), began competing in the natural food market, by introducing preservative-free deli meat alternatives to their standard product options.

In 2007, Dietz and Watson opened a distribution center in Delanco Township of southern New Jersey. Although the company maintained its processing facilities in Philadelphia, Baltimore, and Corfu, New York, the Delanco location, with a staff of at least 100 full-time employees, would consolidate distribution to various supermarkets across the nation. The Burlington County Board of Freeholders approved a $2 million loan for the expansion, and approval by the New Jersey Economic Development Authority was expected in March 2007.

In August 2007, Dietz and Watson was still a private, family-owned company with Ruth Eni serving as chairman of the company, while management and operational supervision passed to Eni's children and stepchildren. Louis Eni, Jr., served as chief executive officer, daughter-in-law Sandy Eni served as chief financial officer, daughter Cindy Yingling (formerly Cindy Eni) worked as finance manager, and son Chris Eni served as chief operations officer.

Micah L. Issitt

PRINCIPAL SUBSIDIARIES

Yancey's Fancy, Inc.

PRINCIPAL COMPETITORS

Lincoln Provision, Inc.; Robzens, Inc.; Strauss Veal, Inc.

FURTHER READING

Brubaker, Harold, "Area Processors' Costly Effort—Keeping Meat Safe for the Table," *Philadelphia Inquirer,* January 5, 2005, p. C1.

———, "Dietz and Watson Begins Burlco Move," *Philadelphia Inquirer,* March 1, 2007, p. C3.

———, "Philadelphia Meat Processing Plant Workers Insist on Cleanliness," *Philadelphia Inquirer,* December 9, 2002, Bus. Sec.

"Dietz & Watson," *National Provisioner,* April 1998.

Kridler, Kara, "Baltimore Development Corp. Ties Dietz & Watson Loan to Jobs," *Baltimore Daily Record,* May 18, 2006.

Lin, Jennifer, "Some City Firms Find the Recipe for Successful Exports to Japan," *Philadelphia Inquirer,* May 6, 1991, p. D8.

Mellgren, James, "Dietz & Watson Acquires Yancey's Fancy, Inc." *Gourmet Retailer,* May 2004, p. 26.

Petrak, Lynn, "Deli Case in Point," *National Provisioner,* November 2000, pp. 65–70.

Smyth, Jack, "City Units Study Plan for Kensington Plant," *Philadelphia Evening Bulletin,* December 3, 1972.

———, "Group Battles Reopening of Old Meat Plant," *Philadelphia Evening Bulletin,* January 14, 1973.

———, "Meat Plant Plan Opposed in Kensington," *Philadelphia Evening Bulletin,* December 28, 1972.

"Top 125 Meat & Poultry Processors," *National Provisioner,* May 1995.

Van Allen, Peter, "Dietz & Watson Adds Safety Steps: Processed Meat Purveyor Builds Defenses in Wake of Competitor's Listeria Problems," *Philadelphia Business Journal,* April 25, 2003, p. 1.

Dominick & Dominick
LLC

150 East 52nd Street, Suite 3
New York, New York 10022-6017
U.S.A.
Telephone: (212) 558-8800
Toll Free: (800) 221-2869
Fax: (212) 797-5268
Web site: http://www.dominickanddominick.com

Private Company
Founded: 1870 as Dominick & Dickerman
Employees: 100
Sales: $251 million (2000)
NAIC: 523120 Securities Brokerage

■ ■ ■

Dominick & Dominick LLC is one of Wall Street's most respected private full-service brokerage firms. Not only was it one of the New York Stock Exchange's early members, it supplied the Exchange with one of its presidents. By not offering proprietary products, the firm is unburdened by conflicts of interest, allowing it to take a fair-broker approach to providing clients with investment advice.

Dominick & Dominick offers wealth management services for affluent families; alternative investment advice (such as for hedge funds, private equity placements, and structured notes); fixed income investment solutions to help clients meet their cash flow and liquidity needs and tax objectives; investment banking and corporate finance services, providing corporate clients with financial and strategic advice; equity and debt

capital markets (serving both the issuers and purchasers of stock); and research, (making available to clients the work of various independent research firms, such as Argus Research Company, Credit Suisse Research, High Tech Strategist, Wall Street Source, and Webster Bank Morning Note). In addition to its New York City headquarters, Dominick & Dominick maintains offices in Atlanta, Miami, and Basel, Switzerland.

1870 ORIGINS

The company was founded on June 15, 1870, as Dominick & Dickerman by William Gayer Dominick and Watson Bradley Dickerman. Born in Chicago, Dominick moved to New York as a child. In 1869 at the age of 25 he purchased a membership in the New York Stock Exchange. Here he met Connecticut-born Dickerman, who was one year younger, and they decided to go into business together, forming their own stock brokerage firm. Two of Dominick's brothers, George and Bayard Dominick, also became Exchange members and partners in the firm.

Dominick & Dickerman prospered and in 1889 opened it first branch office, located in Cincinnati, where the firm was only one of two Exchange members. A year later Dickerman left the firm when he was elected president of the New York Stock Exchange. He had failed in an earlier bid in 1883, despite being the head of a ticket put forward by the regular Nominating Committee, losing out to an independent ticket. He would serve as president from 1890 to 1892, then return to the firm. His cofounder, William Dominick, died from typhoid fever in 1895. Dickerman would

COMPANY PERSPECTIVES

We focus on creating proprietary solutions rather than selling proprietary products or dictating to our advisors what to sell to their customers. We seek to provide intelligent investment vehicles that match our clients needs rather than serve some internal firm need.

retire in 1909 and devote the rest of his life to his great passion, the breeding of trotter racehorses. In 1884 he had purchased land in New Rochelle, New York, to establish Hillanddale Farm, which would grow into a 500-acre estate and one of the America's most respected and prolific stables. He passed away at the age of 77 in 1923.

Dominick & Dickerman changed its name in 1899 to Dominick & Dominick, and several new partners were added, including Milnor B. Dominick, Andrew V. Stout, J. A. Barnard, and Bernon S. Prentice. By this time George Dominick had left the firm but other family members would also join Dominick & Dominick, including Darius Dominick and Bayard Dominick, Jr.

The firm was not always adverse to offering proprietary products. In the 1920 Dominick & Dominick launched a closed-end fund, which raised some $10 million through the sale of 200,000 shares. Despite the stock market crash of 1929, and a crash almost as serious in 1937, the fund was able to hang on. It even gained a listing on the New York Stock Exchange in 1959 as Dominick Fund, Inc., before being merged with the Putnam Fund in 1973.

A. ISELIN & CO. IS ACQUIRED: 1936

In 1936 Dominick & Dominick expanded through acquisition, merging with A. Iselin & Co., one of Wall Street's oldest firms. Several months earlier the patriarch of the firm, Adrian Iselin, died at the age of 89. He had joined the firm, which his father formed, as a 22-year-old in 1868. At the time of the merger, Dominick & Dominick had 13 partners, including Gayer G. Dominick (senior partner since 1926), Bayard Dominick, and Gardener Dominick. It next picked up several partners from Iselin & Co., as well as Iselin Securities Corporation, which brought with it an office in Paris, and the Iselin Corporation of Canada with its office in Montreal. Because Dominick & Dominick already

maintained a London office, the London office of Iselin Securities was closed.

Other European offices would be opened as well, and Dominick & Dominick soon had a presence in all of the major cities in Europe. A major war, however, that would sweep up Europe and the rest of the world was on the horizon, and within a few years the United States would be drawn into the conflict as well. A large number of the firm's employees and partners either answered the call to military service or were drafted, forcing Gayer Dominick to return to oversee the firm for nearly five years, a period during which the firm was content to just keep its doors opened. Gayer Dominick had been with the firm since 1909 after graduating from Yale University. In 1935 he was elected a governor of the New York Stock Exchange and helped to hire the first paid president of the Exchange, at the behest of the new Securities and Exchange Commission (SEC). He then left the family firm in 1938 to enter public service, working for the Office of Price Administration in the Roosevelt administration.

After World War II came to an end and following a brief economic recession as the United States reverted to a peace-time footing, the economy enjoyed a long period of growth. Dominick & Dominick benefited from the country's prosperity. Some of the firm's most notable transactions during the postwar years involved Yonkers, New York–based Alexander Smith Carpet Company and Canada's Great Plains Oil. In the late 1950s Dominick & Dominick was also part of a banking syndicate that managed the initial public offering (IPO) of stock issued by Arvida Corporation, which was formed in Florida in 1958 to sell the real estate holdings of Arthur Vining Davis. The IPO gained attention because of objections raised by the SEC to the way the managers had announced the stock sale before filing a registration statement with the SEC, a violation of the law.

Dominick & Dominick dropped its partnership status in 1964 and was reorganized as a corporation. The 1960s also saw the firm spread its operation across the country, taking advantage of a bull market to build up a domestic retail brokerage business. In 1962 an office in Chicago was opened. Dominick & Dominick gained a major presence in New England in 1966 by acquiring the firm of Townsend, Dabney, Tyson. Not only did the firm pick up a large Boston office but another 15 offices throughout the Northeast. About 30 additional branch offices across the United States were opened by the end of the 1960s.

In 1970 Dominick & Dominick pursued a merger with Clark, Dodge & Co., Inc., a similar size firm, but called it off, electing instead to continue a program of

KEY DATES

1870: Firm founded as Dominick & Dickerman.
1899: Name is changed to Dominick & Dominick.
1936: A. Iselin & Co. is acquired.
1964: Company incorporated.
1973: Dominick begins to sell off some branch offices.
2003: Michael Campbell is named CEO.
2004: Miami office opens.
2007: Atlanta office opens.

opening new offices and pursuing the acquisition of smaller firms. This plan was also eventually terminated, however, as the stock market began to experience one of the worst bear markets in a generation, and Dominick & Dominick found that it had stretched itself far too thin.

Strapped for cash the firm sold four of its five seats on the New York Stock Exchange and one of two seats on the American Stock Exchange. It also sold a significant stake in the business for $7.25 million to an investment group led by Pierce National Life Insurance Company, which was in turn controlled by Houston banker Joe L. Allbritton. While the infusion of capital was welcome, Dominick & Dominick still found itself in a difficult position and decided to exit the domestic retail brokerage business and to sell the bulk of its branch offices.

The firm's chairman and chief executive, Peter M. Kennedy, explained to the *New York Times* that "a national retail structure is not right for a firm of our size. We either had to be bigger or smaller." He added, "We are not going out of business. We are just changing the nature of our business." Dominick & Dominick retained a modest retail business but mostly chose to focus on core strengths, including institutional business, money management, corporate finance, municipal bonds, and its international business. It was also in 1973 the Dominick Fund, which had about $55 million in assets, was taken over by Putnam Fund.

Over the next 20 years, Dominick & Dominick continued to shrink in size, closing offices in order to devote its resources to more profitable areas, such as research. It also became involved in the fixed income area, making corporate and municipal bonds, Eurobonds, and Treasury Notes available to its clients, and launched managed futures programs to participate in the global currency markets. The firm also did a

healthy business providing clearing services to more than 100 NASD (National Association of Securities Dealers) firms; its Dominick & Dominick Advisors unit provided investment and portfolio management services to high net worth investors and institutions in the United States, Europe, and Asia.

NEW LEADERSHIP IN 2003

By the start of the new century, Dominick & Dominick was no longer content with modest aspirations and sought a spark to revitalize the venerable firm. In October 2003 the firm brought in a new president and CEO, hiring 58-year-old Michael J. Campbell, a former Marine who had 30 years of experience in the industry, including a 25-year tenure with Donaldson, Lufkin & Jenrette (DLJ) and a stint with Credit Suisse/First Boston after Credit Suisse acquired DLJ. With DLJ Campbell played a key role in building the high net worth individuals and midsized institutional investor brokerage business, increasing it from 75 advisers to a network of more than 500 investment professionals. During his time at Credit Suisse Campbell managed the private client group.

Having received a significant stake in the firm, Campbell quickly assembled an experienced senior management team, comprised of several DLJ colleagues, and developed a plan to rebuild Dominick & Dominick, establishing a long-term goal of opening five branch offices staffed by some 200 account executives. He also relocated the firm's main offices from lower Manhattan to midtown, taking over space in 150 East 52nd Street. In addition, Campbell wasted little time in recruiting new brokers. A mere week after taking the helm, Campbell added Walter and Matthews Schulz, a father and son team he lured away from Credit Suisse.

Dominick & Dominick's first branch office to open under Campbell's watch came in the fall of 2004 when an operation in Miami was opened to focus on wealthy Latin Americans. Although not technically an acquisition, the firm was taking over the Miami office of Pennsylvania-based First Security Investments, which had been opened by another one of Campbell's former DLJ colleagues, Alain O'Hayon, who stayed on to manage the office. Campbell was very familiar with the potential of a Miami operation, having built up an office in the city for DLJ from just two brokers to more than 70.

Campbell also looked to add new services offerings. In 2006 Dominick & Dominick launched a new equity derivatives advisory group, which he hoped could develop synergies with the firm's existing institutional and high-net-worth client base. A year later, another regional office was added in Atlanta. Again, Campbell knew the market, having opened a private client office there for DLJ a dozen years earlier, and he hired one of that operation's brokers to serve as branch manager. There was every reason to expect that the energy and changes that Campbell had brought to Dominick & Dominick were just a down payment on what was to come.

Ed Dinger

PRINCIPAL SUBSIDIARIES

Dominick & Dominick Advisors.

PRINCIPAL COMPETITORS

Moors and Cabot Inc.; Stifel, Nicolaus & Co., Inc.; ThinkEquity Partners LLC.

FURTHER READING

Allan, John H., "Two Wall Street Firms Undergo Changes," *New York Times,* February 22, 1973.

"Anniversary Celebrated: Dominick & Dominick, Brokers, Observe Fiftieth Year in Business," *New York Times,* June 15, 1920.

"Dominick Branches Sold to Other Firms," *New York Times,* August 8, 1973.

"Gayer Dominick, Broker, 74, Dies," *New York Times,* August 19, 1961.

"Iselin Firm to End, Joining Dominicks," *New York Times,* June 17, 1936.

Vartan, Vartanig G., "Dominick to Quit Retail Brokerage," *New York Times,* July 31, 1973.

"William Gayer Dominick," *New York Times,* September 1, 1895.

Drinker, Biddle and Reath L.L.P.

—■—

1 Logan Square
18th and Cherry Streets
Philadelphia, Pennsylvania 19103-6996
U.S.A.
Telephone: (215) 988-2700
Fax: (215) 988-2757
Web site: http://www.drinkerbiddle.com

Private Company
Founded: 1849
Employees: 1,500
Sales: $129.9 million (2006)
NAIC: 541110 Offices of Lawyers

■ ■ ■

Drinker, Biddle and Reath LLC, is a leading national law firm with ten offices located in eight states. The firm's practice is organized into three major areas of focus: business and finance, personal and fiduciary law, and litigation. Subgroups include communications law, corporate and securities, intellectual property, real estate, and bankruptcy. Headquartered in Philadelphia, Pennsylvania, Drinker Biddle has a long history of involvement in Philadelphia's growth and expansion, having served as a representative for a number of the city's largest corporations and institutions. Drinker Biddle is a privately owned firm and currently employs over 1,500 employees including more than 650 lawyers and 69 partners.

FOUNDATIONS: 1849–1920

The firm that would become Drinker Biddle was founded in 1849 by Kentucky-based lawyer John Christian Bullitt. Over the course of his career, Bullitt became one of the most prominent private lawyers in Philadelphia and also took a personal interest in civic development and local government. Known later as the "Father of Greater Philadelphia," Bullitt founded the city's first country club, golf course, and the first skyscraper, the Bullitt building at the corner of South 4th Street. Bullitt also helped to found Benjamin Franklin Expressway and the Fourth Street National Bank. For his contributions to Philadelphia, Bullitt was honored with a statue of his likeness by artist John J. Boyle, placed in front of Philadelphia City Hall in 1907.

Bullitt was a specialist in corporate law and established his firm as a leader in mergers and acquisitions. Bullitt played a historic role in the formation of the dominant brokerage firm J.P. Morgan Co. (then Drexel, Morgan & Co.), when Bullitt acted as counsel for the merger of Drexel & Co. with competitor Morgan, Dabney & Co. In 1911 Bullitt's firm also became the legal representative for Brown Brothers Harriman and Co., which remained one of the nation's leading investment firms into the 21st century.

In 1863, Bullitt asked young legal scholar Samuel Dickson to join the firm as his legal partner. Dickson helped Bullitt to develop a professional relationship with the University of Pennsylvania and he served on the university's board of trustees until his death in 1915. After Bullitt's death in 1902 and the untimely death of

COMPANY PERSPECTIVES

Our rich 150-year practice history is marked by service to the public and to the bar, with an extraordinary tradition in leadership of legal ethics. Our prominence today combines a comprehensive range of traditional legal practices with significant national roles in such practices as class action defense, corporate and securities, government relations, health law, intellectual property, insurance, investment management, private equity, bankruptcy, environmental, education and communications. We remain committed to our long tradition of handling pro bono work and taking on unpopular causes.

third partner Richard C. Dale, Dickson became the senior partner and reorganized the firm as Dickson, Beitler and McCouch. Over the course of his career, Dickson became known as a leader in the Philadelphia legal community and served as chancellor of the Law Association of Philadelphia for over a decade.

Henry S. Drinker, Jr., joined the firm in 1904, shortly after his graduation from the University of Pennsylvania. Drinker began his association with the company as an unpaid associate before being asked to join the firm full time and then becoming a partner in 1918. Drinker was also nationally recognized as an expert musicologist and published translations of Bach and Mozart, as well as a number of scholarly works in academic journals. Drinker took over for Dickson as chief counsel for the University of Pennsylvania in 1927, by which time he was the chief partner in the firm. In 1931, Drinker became an associate trustee and member of the University of Pennsylvania's Board of Fine Arts.

Drinker and Biddle was one of the first law firms in the Philadelphia area to open its doors to female and minority lawyers. Ada M. Lutz was the firm's first female lawyer and served with the firm for over a year before leaving to pursue a private practice in the Philadelphia area.

GROWTH AND EXPANSION:
1920–90

Charles J. Biddle joined the firm in 1924, working as an associate under Henry Drinker's tutelage. Prior to joining the firm, Biddle earned international distinction for his military service during World War I, when he served as a major for the Lafayette Escadrille squadron in

France. Biddle was awarded the Legion of Honor and the *Croix de Guerre* from the French government and was also honored with the American Distinguished Service Cross from the U.S. government. Drinker published, in 1919, a book documenting his experience as a pilot during the war.

Before joining the firm, Biddle worked as a partner in his father's law firm. Biddle's decision to join Drinker's firm was significant as it was the first "lateral partnership" arrangement for the firm. Biddle brought a significant roster of clients including the Philadelphia Saving Fund Society (PSFS), which later became one of the firm's most prominent clients. Biddle became a partner in 1925 and was later promoted to senior partner. In 1932, the firm changed its name to Drinker, Biddle & Reath. Biddle helped take the firm in a new direction when he was named counsel for Merck, Sharp and Dohme in a prominent case involving federal regulations over price fixing. Merck was the first of numerous pharmaceutical clients represented by the firm over its history.

In 1940, when President Franklin Roosevelt asked Philadelphia financier Averell Harriman to rebuild the Cramp Shipyards, Harriman asked Drinker and Biddle partner Thomas Reath to oversee the project. Reath, who joined the firm in 1919, led the efforts to negotiate against the shipyard's $1 million tax lien and succeeded in allowing the shipyards to reopen in 1941, shortly before the Japanese attack at Pearl Harbor.

Lewis H. Van Dusen, who became one of the firm's leading partners in the 1940s and 1950s, joined Drinker Biddle in 1935 as an associate. Van Dusen served in World War II as a lieutenant colonel in the U.S. Army and was awarded numerous decorations, including the Purple Heart and the Bronze Star. In the 1950s, Van Dusen was asked to return to the army to serve as a representative to NATO.

During the early 1950s, Van Dusen began taking the leading management role as Henry Drinker neared retirement. Although the firm did not name an official chairman until the 1980s, Van Dusen was acknowledged as the leading partner until the 1960s. During this time, Van Dusen helped organize the formation of the South Eastern Pennsylvania Transportation Association (SEPTA) and served as the first general counsel for the company. Van Dusen organized the firm's first group of managing partners to determine profit distribution and develop strategies for growth. Van Dusen also became a leader in the Philadelphia legal community and served as chairman of the American Bar Association's (ABA) standing committee on ethics and professional responsibility. Van Dusen later received the Michael Franck Award, the highest honor bestowed by the ABA.

KEY DATES

1849: Firm founded by John C. Bullitt.
1863: Bullitt oversees the merger of Drexel, Morgan & Co.
1904: Henry Drinker joins firm.
1919: Thomas J. Reath joins the firm.
1924: Charles J. Biddle joins firm.
1927: Drinker becomes counsel for University of Pennsylvania.
1971: Amy Davis becomes first woman partner of the firm.
1979: Melvyn Breaux becomes firm's first African American partner.
1999: Drinker Biddle merges with Shanley and Fisher PC.
2001: Drinker Biddle merges with Seidel, Gonda, Lavorgna and Monaco.
2003: An office in Wilmington, Delaware, is opened.
2005: The tenth office, in Chicago, Illinois, opens.
2007: Firm merges with Chicago-based Gardner, Carton & Douglas LLC.

In the 1960s, Henry W. Sawyer, a partner with the firm, represented on behalf of the American Civil Liberties Union several clients who had been called before the House Un-American Activities Committee and the Senate Internal Security Committee for suspected communist association. The controversial decision drew criticism for the firm from some conservative members of the Philadelphia legal and governmental community. In the mid-1960s, Biddle also led the firm into a prominent civil rights issue when he represented seven African American students who had been barred entrance from Girard College. The case played a role in the state's decision to force desegregation of the college.

During the 1970s, as the staff of Drinker Biddle grew, the firm also achieved milestones in racial and gender integration. Amy Davis became the firm's first female partner, after joining the firm in 1971. The firm's second female partner, Kathryn H. Levering, joined in 1976 as an associate and eventually became the first female to serve as a managing partner for the firm. Drinker Biddle's first African American associate, Melvin Breaux, joined the firm in 1970 and became a partner in 1979.

FIRM EXPANDS THROUGH LATERAL ACQUISITIONS: 1999–2004

Although Drinker Biddle experienced modest growth during the 1980s and 1990s, in the 21st century the firm began growing exponentially with a number of lateral acquisitions that elevated the firm to national prominence. Much of the firm's growth occurred under the management of executive chairman Jim Sweet, who was elected in 1999 to serve a four-year term.

In late 1999, Drinker Biddle merged with Shanley and Fisher PC, a New Jersey litigation firm started by Bernard Shanley in 1930. Shanley was well known in the East Coast legal community and had served as deputy chief of staff for President Dwight D. Eisenhower in the 1950s. As a result of the merger, the firm received a number of prominent clients and added 111 lawyers to its permanent staff. In addition, Drinker Biddle's legal services were expanded through Shanley and Fisher's expertise in litigation.

Drinker Biddle expanded their intellectual property (IP) division in 2001 with the acquisition of Philadelphia IP firm Seidel, Gonda, Lavorgna and Monaco, which increased Drinker Biddle's IP staff to 27 specialists. In addition, Drinker Biddle hired ten litigators away from competing firm Stradley, Ronon, Stevens & Young. The personnel acquisition brought Drinker Biddle a number of high-profile clients including Allstate Life Insurance Co., CNA Life Insurance, ACE Insurance, State Farm Life Insurance, and Penn National.

In late 2001, Drinker Biddle expanded its operations to the West Coast through a merger with San Francisco–based firm Preuss Shanagher Zvoleff & Zimmer LLP and shortly thereafter opened a new Los Angeles location with several former Preuss Shanagher employees. With additional personnel acquisitions from other West Coast firms, Drinker Biddle increased its staff by 35 lawyers. The West Coast expansion was largely focused on increasing the firm's ability to handle pharmaceutical litigation cases and more than doubled the firm's specialists in key market areas. At the end of 2001, Chairman Jim Sweet announced that the firm had grown by more than 40 percent since 1999.

Sweet's term as chairman marked the greatest single period of expansion in the firm's history with the acquisition of over 200 lawyers and new offices in Wilmington, Delaware; San Francisco; and Los Angeles. The firm's California expansion allowed Drinker Biddle to bring in a number of high profile clients including Hewlett-Packard and Cingular. Drinker Biddle also made its first appearance in the *American Lawyer's Magazine* annual survey of the 100 most profitable firms. In 1999, Drinker Biddle placed 163rd in the magazine's rankings, which calculates profits per partner. In 2003, the company was ranked 83rd in the magazine's rankings, with an increase in revenues of more than $470,000 per lawyer.

BECOMING A MODERN LEGAL GIANT

In 2005, Sweet decided to step down as managing chairman, despite his reelection the previous year. Associate Alfred Putnam was selected to serve as Sweet's replacement, while the management structure of the firm was reorganized. Under the new structure, part of the managerial duties given to the chairman were vested in the newly created office of executive partner, thereby reducing managerial duties for both individuals and allowing the executive staff time to maintain legal work. Partner Andrew Kassner, who served as assistant to Sweet, was elevated to executive partner.

Drinker Biddle's criminal defense department suffered in 2005 when Michael Holston and two other partners decided to leave the firm for a position with competing Philadelphia firm Morgan Lewis & Bockius. Holston's decision to leave Drinker Biddle was facilitated by his long personal and professional acquaintance with Jack Dodds, the head of Morgan Lewis' criminal defense practice. Holston and Dodds worked together in the U.S. Attorney's Office before both men returned to private practice. In addition, 11 associates left with Holston to join Morgan Lewis' newly invigorated criminal department.

In 2005, Drinker Biddle opened a seven-attorney office in Chicago, Illinois, to expand the firm's product liability practice. The office was headed by two partners acquired from the firm of Kelly Drye & Warren, John Dames and David Sudzus, who had been working with members of Drinker Biddle on cases involving shared pharmaceutical clients. Putnam said that the motivation to open the new office was the acquisition of Sudzus and Dames, rather than a desire to move into Chicago specifically.

In 2006, Drinker Biddle and Chicago-based firm Gardner Carton & Douglas formalized a merger agreement approved by the managing partners of both firms and set to take effect on January 1, 2007. The firm maintained the name Drinker Biddle, except in Illinois and Wisconsin, where the firm would be known as Drinker Biddle Gardner Carton until 2008, in order to maintain continuity for the firm's clients. With the expansion, the newly invigorated firm had a list of 651 lawyers stationed in 12 offices across the country. Drinker Biddle concluded its 2006 fiscal year with an announcement that the firm had achieved over 10 percent growth during 2006, with revenues rising from $223 million in 2005 to $246 million in 2006.

In 2007, Drinker Biddle became one of several national law firms using Internet video programs to promote the company. Partner Audrey Talley, who headed the firm's hiring practices department in 2007, was part of the project to place a video on the company's hiring page taking perspective associates through the hiring practices of the company and introducing the company's employment benefits. In Talley's opinion, using web-based videos was the company's way of keeping current with trends and recognizing the development of technology and the Internet in bolstering the job market. In an interview for the *Legal Intelligencer*, Talley said that using videos was the "wave of the present."

Micah L. Issitt

PRINCIPAL COMPETITORS

Blank Rome LLP; Morgan, Lewis and Bockius LLP.

FURTHER READING

"At Drinker Biddle & Reath, Success Is Sweet," *Legal Intelligencer,* March 29, 2004.

Blumenthal, Jeff, "Drinker Biddle Elevates, Loses Holston," *Legal Intelligencer,* March 14, 2005.

———, "Drinker Biddle Opens New 7-Attorney Office in Chicago," *Legal Intelligencer,* April 5, 2005.

———, "Van Dusen, 93, Dies; Was Longtime Leader at Drinker Biddle," *Legal Intelligencer,* November 17, 2004.

"Charles J. Biddle Dies: Lawyer, World War Ace," *Evening Bulletin,* March 23, 1972.

"Drinker Biddle to Merge with Gardner," *Recorder,* November 14, 2006.

Feiler, Jeremy, "Drinker IP Lawyer," *Philadelphia Business Journal,* August 31, 2001.

———, "Intellectual Property Lawyers Still in High Demand," *Philadelphia Business Journal,* February 16, 2001, p. B9.

———, "Soon-to-Be Chancellor Working to Raise the Bar," *Philadelphia Business Journal,* January 5, 2001.

———, "Stradley Insurance Litigators Jump Ship," *Philadelphia Business Journal,* June 29, 2007.

———, "Two Big Phila. Firms Gain Through Mergers," *Philadelphia Business Journal,* November 1, 2007.

Fried, Jennifer, "Second Chance," *American Lawyer,* May 2003.

"Offices Leased to Law Firm," *Evening Bulletin,* January 22, 1957.

Passarella, Gina, "Ex-N.J. Chief Justice Joins Drinker Biddle," *Legal Intelligencer,* December 12, 2006.

———, "Firms Reach Out to YouTube Generation with Web Videos," *Recorder,* September 28, 2007.

"Samuel Dickson Dead; Widely Known Railroad Lawyer Who Had Practiced 57 Years," *New York Times,* May 29, 1915, p. 11.

"Thomas Reath Sr. Dies; Corporate Law Expert," *Evening Bulletin,* February 6, 1975.

"Worked to Open Girard College to All Races," *Evening Bulletin,* July 10, 1966.

Yingling, Bill, "Drinker Biddle May Move to One Logan," *Philadelphia Business Journal,* October 25, 1996.

Book and Journal Manufacturing Since 1893

Edwards Brothers, Inc.

2500 South State Street
P.O. Box 1007
Ann Arbor, Michigan 48106
U.S.A.
Telephone: (734) 769-1000
Fax: (734) 769-4756
Web site: http://www.edwardsbrothers.com

Private Company
Incorporated: 1893
Employees: 750
Sales: $78 million (2006 est.)
NAIC: 323117 Books Printing

■ ■ ■

Edwards Brothers, Inc., is a leading printer of short and medium run books and journals. The Michigan-based firm's output largely consists of academic, medical, technical, and other special-interest titles, typically printed in quantities of less than 15,000. The company also offers ultra-short runs via seven Digital Book Centers, five of which are located at customer distribution sites. Owned and managed by the fourth generation of its founding family, Edwards Brothers has printing plants in Michigan and North Carolina and sales offices in Boston, Chicago, New York, Washington, D.C., and San Diego.

BEGINNINGS

Edwards Brothers was founded in 1893 by Thomas and Daniel Edwards, students at the University of Michigan

Law School in Ann Arbor. To help pay for tuition, they began mimeographing copies of their lecture notes and selling them to fellow students. The venture proved so popular that the brothers decided to take turns alternately running the business for a year and attending class. After graduating in 1899 both moved to Washington, D.C., to practice law, and brother John J. Edwards, known as J. J., took over the operation. Over the next 20 years he expanded it to provide lecture notes for schools around the Midwest.

In 1920 J. J. Edwards' son John William "J. W." Edwards moved to Ann Arbor to run the firm when his father became ill, and after J. J.'s death two years later J. W. began to broaden its offerings again. He came to focus on selling copies of lecture notes to science professors in Michigan, Indiana, and Ohio, who were contacted through purchased mailing lists. Printed in editions of several hundred or less, the notes were used in their classes, and occasionally as the basis for published textbooks.

By the late 1920s the firm employed 60, and its growth had enabled the purchase of German-made offset printing presses, which produced higher-quality copies than mimeograph machines. Company head J. W. Edwards was spending considerable time on the road as a salesman.

STOCK OFFERING IN 1930

In 1929 Edwards Brothers built a new printing plant in Ann Arbor, but just after it began operations the stock market crashed and sales dropped off. In 1930 the firm was incorporated and stock was sold to bring in new

COMPANY PERSPECTIVES

Edwards Brothers is a complete book and journal manufacturer, specializing in short and medium runs for publishers, authors, scholarly societies, industrial firms, colleges, universities, and other customers. With more than 750 employees and sales offices in 8 cities producing sales of nearly $80 million per year, Edwards Brothers is truly a leader in its industry.

Edwards Brothers, Inc., has prospered through good times and endured the challenges of difficult times, never losing sight of the principles that have built a reputation for quality, service, and excellence for over 100 years. This tradition continues to grow even stronger in Edwards Brothers' second century.

capital and help it stay afloat. Through careful management the company was able to turn a profit during the Great Depression years, and even expand.

In the 1930s a subsidiary called J.W. Edwards Publishers, Inc., was formed to handle other work, with much business coming from the University of Michigan. This unit's sales took off during World War II when it was called on to reprint German technical books and journals that were not otherwise available in the United States.

After the war sales continued to grow and the firm upgraded its plant with new presses, binding equipment, cameras, and typewriters. J.W. Edwards Publishers also undertook a number of major projects that included printing the *Library of Congress Catalog,* the *National Union Catalog,* and the complete works of Bach, Beethoven, Mozart, and Brahms.

In 1949 the company started a profit-sharing program for its employees, and in 1950 J. W. Edwards' son Joseph, who had earned a business administration degree after serving as a bomber pilot during the war, was named president. His father would hold the title of board chair. In 1954 Joseph's younger brother Martin received his MBA from the University of Michigan and began working for the company, although he took two years off to serve in the army in Germany. Another of J. W. Edwards' four sons, William, also worked for the firm briefly in the 1950s.

In 1954 the company began construction of a new, larger printing plant, and two years later sales topped $2 million for the first time. The first of several expansions was completed in 1959 and the firm also upgraded its

technical capabilities with additions like a case binding line in the 1960s. During these years Edwards Brothers' offerings were broadened from academic titles to a more diverse range of books printed for several hundred different publishers. This new business was brought in by a network of sales offices that were opened in cities such as New York, Washington, D.C., Chicago, Boston, San Francisco, and Atlanta. In 1973 the firm completed the fourth major expansion of its plant, which stood at 196,000 square feet in size.

NORTH CAROLINA FACILITY ADDED IN 1979

In 1979 Martin Edwards was named president and older brother Joseph took the title of chairman. During the year Edwards Brothers bought a Raleigh, North Carolina, firm called The Graphic Press to boost its prepress, press, and soft bindery capacity and to put it closer to more clients. Renamed Edwards Brothers Carolina, it endured several difficult years and changes in management before moving in 1983 to nearby Lillington to facilitate expansion. A second plant was later added there which boosted production space to more than 100,000 square feet.

By 1985 Edwards Brothers employed 550 and had annual sales of $31 million, with net income of $1.7 million. In 1986 Joseph Edwards retired and the firm returned to private ownership when it bought back shares owned by his family and that of brother Samuel Edwards, as well as those of about 75 smaller investors. Company president Martin Edwards and his family held a 27 percent stake.

In 1989 the firm began examining ways to cut spending on medical costs, and in 1991 it started paying for healthcare directly to local providers, rather than through an insurer. Several other area firms subsequently joined it to form the South Central Michigan Health Alliance, Inc., which claimed savings of 20 percent or more over traditional insurers.

In 1993 Edwards Brothers celebrated its 100th birthday. The firm was Michigan's largest printing company, with 750 employees at its three plants in Michigan and North Carolina, and nine sales offices around the United States. The firm printed half a million books and journals per week, which primarily consisted of scientific, technical, and medical textbooks, along with 185 professional journals. Most were printed in short and medium runs of a few thousand copies, with the best-selling title being a book for cardiologists that had sold 1.5 million copies over 20 years. Although sales had slowed of late as specialized information resources began shifting to computer formats, the ongo-

KEY DATES

1893: Thomas and Daniel Edwards begin selling lecture notes at University of Michigan.

1899: J. J. Edwards takes over business, begins expanding to other schools.

1922: J. W. Edwards assumes control, targets science professors in Midwest.

1929: New printing plant opens in Ann Arbor, Michigan.

1930: Firm incorporated; stock sold to keep it afloat.

1950: Joseph Edwards named president.

1954: Construction of new Ann Arbor plant begins.

1979: Raleigh, North Carolina, printing company acquired.

1983: North Carolina operations moved to Lillington to facilitate expansion.

1986: Martin Edwards named president; firm buys back stock, goes private.

1997: First Digital Book Center opened at North Carolina plant.

1998: Martin Edwards' son John named president of firm.

2000: Company opens Digital Book Center at Rowman & Littlefield warehouse.

2001: Hutchinson, Kansas, printing company acquired.

2005: Kansas plant closed; Digital Book Center opened in England.

ing growth of scientific literature had helped the firm's annual sales grow to $57 million, nearly double the amount of eight years before. Paper prices were rising rapidly, however, and the firm was forced to pass the cost on to customers, some of whom cut back on their orders.

FIRST DIGITAL BOOK CENTER OPENED IN 1997

Seeking to remain competitive as digital technology impacted the printing industry, especially the specialized world of short run and academic titles, in 1997 Edwards Brothers opened its first Digital Book Center at the Lillington plant to print runs of 50 to 200 books, or fewer, on a large-format Xerox machine. Although typically printed from a scanned copy of an out-of-print title or a computer file, the firm strove to give such works the same quality as traditional books, offering both soft and hardbound covers.

In 1998 John J. Edwards was named company president, while his father Martin Edwards remained CEO and chairman. Two siblings, James and Laura, were also involved with the firm. In 1999 James and John Edwards founded a publishing company called Ann Arbor Media Group to reprint public domain titles whose copyrights had lapsed. Based at Edwards Brothers' headquarters in Ann Arbor, it used ten "leased" employees of the firm, and over the next several years added sports and children's imprints and cut distribution deals with Amazon.com and regional superstore chain Meijer.

In 2000 Edwards Brothers opened a new Digital Book Center at the Blue Ridge Summit, Pennsylvania, distribution warehouse of longtime client Rowman & Littlefield, which would be staffed by two company employees. During its first year short run digital books generated $1 million in sales from out-of-print titles that would otherwise have been lost. Several years later the firm trademarked the phrase "Life of Title" for this program.

In 2000 Edwards Brothers also added an interactive web site where customers could check the status of their printing jobs. The firm began to implement lean manufacturing techniques, which cut inventory and waste and sped up processing time. For 2000 it reported sales of more than $77 million.

HUTCHINSON, KANSAS, PLANT ACQUIRED IN 2001

In 2001 Edwards Brothers acquired a 50,000-square-foot printing plant in Hutchinson, Kansas, from Equifax, which had recently bought its owner, city directory publisher R.L. Polk and Co. The operation was named Wolverine Printing and Publishing and continued producing the very short run directories, which were later taken over by Nebraska-based InfoUSA. During the year the firm also took work printing two best-selling *Harry Potter* titles. With the fourth volume in J. K. Rowling's popular series soon due out, Edwards Brothers accepted a $500,000 order to print 200,000 copies each of the second and third entries in the series, splitting the work between Ann Arbor and Lillington. In late 2001 another Digital Book Center was also launched at the University of Chicago Press.

During 2001 Edwards Brothers won the first of several awards in trade group Printing Industries of America's "Best Workplace in America" competition, while chairman Martin Edwards was inducted into the

Printing Impressions/Rochester Institute of Technology Printing Industry Hall of Fame, one of four individuals so honored each year. He had ceded the title of CEO to his son John.

In 2002 the firm began a $12 million, multiyear technical upgrade program, and the next year it partnered with MIT Press to add a new Digital Book Center in Ann Arbor. A total of 1,750 out-of-print titles would eventually be made available in "Print-on-Demand" form, shipped directly to customers within 48 hours of an order being received, and priced comparable to an edition published in larger quantities. While digitally printed books accounted for less than 10 percent of Edwards Brothers' revenues, they made up more than 10 percent of the total titles offered.

In 2003 the firm also printed 500,000 copies of *Harry Potter and the Order of the Phoenix,* the latest installment in the series to date. To keep its contents secret per author Rowling's request, employees were required to sign a confidentiality agreement and completed copies were shipped weekly to publisher Scholastic Books.

In 2004 the firm printed 426,000 copies of another top-selling title, H. G. Bissinger's *Friday Night Lights,* which topped the *New York Times* bestseller list when a movie version boosted interest. A Digital Book Center was also added at the National Academies Press warehouse in Landover, Maryland, during the year.

KANSAS PLANT CLOSED IN 2005

In August 2005 Edwards Brothers announced that its 42-employee Hutchinson, Kansas, plant would close by year's end, after the InfoUSA directory-printing work that accounted for the bulk of its business was lost. Equipment would be moved to the firm's Michigan and North Carolina facilities. During the year the company also opened a Digital Book Center in Plymouth, England, in partnership with Rowman & Littlefield affiliate National Book Network International. Two Edwards Brothers employees would run the small operation, which was established to save the time and expense of shipping books from the United States.

In early 2006 the firm's Ann Arbor plant suffered a flood that caused $500,000 worth of damage after a water pipe burst. In August, company chairman Martin Edwards died at age 74, just a few months after his wife Rosalie's death. Sales for the year topped $78 million.

In the spring of 2007 a fifth remote Digital Book Center was opened at a Houghton-Mifflin Co. facility in Geneva, Illinois, and in the fall the firm won approval from the city of Ann Arbor to seek a tax abatement from the State of Michigan to help it pay for a new $2 million printing press and power station. Edwards Brothers officials complained about the city's high tax rate and cost of living, which made it difficult to attract and retain entry-level workers, and city officials were concerned about losing the plant's 450 jobs in the midst of a severe downturn in Michigan's economy. Although demand was becoming more seasonal, with greater peaks and valleys in output, the firm had added more than 40 positions in Ann Arbor, and it had also invested $6 million in a Heidelberg cover press there, as well as new Kolbus binding equipment for North Carolina and other machinery for its digital printing operations.

Now in its second century of business, Edwards Brothers, Inc., was branching out from short and medium run technical, medical, and scientific books and journals to take on extremely limited digital runs of obscure titles as well as the occasional bestseller. With the fourth generation of its founding family at the helm, a dedicated workforce, and many well-established client relationships, the firm looked toward many further years of success.

Frank Uhle

PRINCIPAL SUBSIDIARIES

J.W. Edwards Publishers, Inc.; Edwards Brothers Carolina; Digitalbookcenter.com; Edwards Brothers UK, Ltd. (United Kingdom).

PRINCIPAL COMPETITORS

The Sheridan Group, Inc.; Malloy, Inc.; McNaughton & Gunn; R.R. Donnelley & Sons Co.; Quebecor World, Inc.; Cenveo, Inc.; Courier Corp.; Quad/Graphics, Inc.; The Maple-Vail Book Manufacturing Group; IBT Global; Lightning Source, Inc.

FURTHER READING

Bauer, Chris, "Speaking Volumes," *Printing Impressions,* April 2003, p. 24.

Cagle, Eric, "2001 Hall of Fame: Martin Edwards: Enriching a Tradition," *Printing Impressions,* September 2001, p. 30.

Chandler, Michelle, "Success Is Tie That Binds Area Book Printers," *Detroit Free Press,* February 7, 1985.

Child, Charles, "Leveraged Buyouts Popular, but They're Not Without Risk," *Crain's Detroit Business,* March 17, 1986, p. 4.

"Edwards Brothers: Partnering for Life," *American Printer,* August 2002, p. 114.

"Edwards to Open Digital Short-Run Center," *Publishers Weekly,* March 3, 1997, p. 18.

Green, Chris, "Publishing Plant Slated to Close by End of Year," *Hutchinson News,* August 16, 2005.

Hoffman, Bryce G., "Ann Arbor Media Book Business Booms; Edwards Brothers Make Old Family Strategy Pay Off," *Ann Arbor News,* July 6, 2004, p. C1.

Milliot, Jim, "MIT Press, Edwards Brothers in POD Deal," *Publishers Weekly,* May 19, 2003, p. 22.

———, "University Presses Embark on Digital Initiative," *Publishers Weekly,* November 5, 2001, p. 10.

O'Brien, Katherine, "Short Story: A Digital Book Printing Update," *American Printer,* November 2006, p. 18.

O'Donnell, Catherine, "Local Book Printing Industry Adapts to Rough Economy," *Ann Arbor News,* March 7, 2004.

Raphael, Steve, "Firms Buy Health Care Direct," *Crain's Detroit Business,* April 6, 1992, p. 3.

Rode, Jenny, "Printer's Growth Prompts Investment," *Ann Arbor News,* August 2, 2007.

Rohan, Barry, "Bound and Determined, Edwards Bros. Family Keeps Presses Running at Printing Company," *Detroit Free Press,* August 4, 1993.

"Rowman & Littlefield Begins On-Demand Printing Onsite," *Publishers Weekly,* July 10, 2000, p. 9.

Eka Chemicals AB

Lilla Bommen 1
Göteborg,
Sweden
Telephone: (46 31) 58 70 00
Fax: (46 31) 15 62 12
Web site: http://www.eka.com

Subsidiary of Akzo Nobel
Incorporated: 1895 as Elektrokemiska Aktiebolaget; 1986 as Eka Nobel; 1994 as Eka Chemicals
Employees: 2,856
Sales: EUR 963 million ($1.2 billion) (2006)
NAIC: 325131 Inorganic Dye and Pigment Manufacturing; 325998 All Other Miscellaneous Chemical Product Manufacturing

■ ■ ■

Eka Chemicals AB is one of the world's leading producers of organic and inorganic chemicals for the pulp and paper industries. The company groups its products into three main categories. Bleaching Chemicals, which accounts for 53 percent of the company's sales, include chlorine dioxide, hydrogen peroxide, sodium chlorate, as well as sodium hydroxide and other extraction agents; chelating agents, dissolving chemicals, surfactants, and the like. The company is the world's leading producer of sodium chlorate, with an annual production capacity of nearly 900,000 tons. Eka also ranks in the global top five hydrogen peroxide producers, with total annual production capacity of nearly 240,000 tons.

The company's Paper Chemicals group accounts for 30 percent of its revenues. Eka produces chemicals for the full range of pulp and paper industry applications, including retention, dewatering, coating, cross-linking, lubrication, emulsions, tissue additives, wet strength products, fluff pulp additives, microbiological control, and defoamers. The third Eka product is Specialty Chemicals, adding 16 percent to the group's revenues. This category includes the company's Kromasil branded, silica-based color separation products, used for the production of chromatographic paper for such applications as insulin level testing, and the like.

The Specialty Chemicals group includes the production of Bindzil silicas, fine chemicals including chemically pure alkali, the Expancel brand of microspheres, used for the production of footwear, tennis balls, ink, explosives, paper and carton, artificial corks, and many other products. Another important product category in this division is its Purate process technology for the production of chlorine dioxide, used as a water treatment and disinfectant. The Specialty Chemicals group also includes the company's Permascand subsidiary, which produces activated titanium anodes and electrolyze cells. Eka Chemicals, based in Sweden, has production facilities in 18 countries, including Norway, Finland, France, Germany, the United States, Canada, Brazil, Chile, China, and Australia. Eka Chemicals is the largest company in Akzo Nobel's Chemicals Group. In 2006, Eka posted revenues of EUR 963 million ($1.2 billion). Jan Svaerd serves as president of Eka Chemicals.

COMPANY PERSPECTIVES

Our vision: To be the preferred supplier of bleaching and performance chemicals to the worldwide pulp and paper industry. We will be the most valuable partner for pulp and paper industry customers globally, through being the most cost-efficient supplier of pulp and paper chemicals, through close cooperation in developing products and processes in the technological frontline, and through close industry presence; To develop other businesses that support and contribute to our overall performance. By also developing and applying our products and technology to applications outside the pulp and paper industry, we will develop our overall performance and improve cost efficiency; To grow the business by being recognized for our innovative use of our unique knowledge of chemistry to improve our customers' products and processes. We will develop our partnership with customers by extending our offerings to improve performance in larger parts of the value chain. We will improve our customers' competitiveness by developing and applying our unique and combined knowledge of chemistry, the cellulose fiber, pulp and paper production, as well as industrial IT.

NOBEL COMPANY IN 1895

Eka Chemicals was founded as Elektrokemiska Aktiebolaget in 1895. The company originated as part of the vast group of chemicals and manufacturing companies founded by Alfred Nobel in the late 19th century. Nobel, who had registered more than 350 patents, continued to develop new business interests right up until his death in 1896. Eka proved to be one of the last of the companies founded by Nobel, set up in partnership with C. W. Collander, with Nobel's close friend Rudolf Liljequist serving as the company's first managing director. Liljequist had started his career as a civil engineering; among his designs was the Forth Railway Bridge, built in Scotland in the 1880s. Liljequist and Nobel became friends and business partners, and, following Nobel's death, Liljequist became one of the executors of Nobel's famous will, which established the basis of the famed Nobel Prize awards. Eka initial's base was in Bengtfors, in Sweden, where it began producing chlorine and alkali, among other products. The company later came under the direction of Liljequist's son, Åke.

Eka grew into one of Sweden's major chemicals groups. By 1924, the company had moved to larger facilities in Bohus, near Göteborg. That site was to remain the company's headquarters into the 21st century. It was also to remain the company's sole production base until the beginning of the 1980s. The company quickly ramped up its production capacity, and by 1927 boasted a total output of 3,000 tons. At the same time, the Bohus-based company began expanding its range of products, adding water glass in 1927, and then launching a range of new chemicals in the 1930s, such as hydrochloric acid, ferric chloride, and, especially, hydrogen peroxide, used as a bleaching agent for the paper industry. Sweden's large forestry industry had in the meantime given rise to one of the world's major pulp and paper industries. Eka's operations turned increasingly toward support of that industry as the century went on. The company also became an important producer of specialty chemicals during World War II, producing such products as consumer-grade metasilicate, among others.

In 1951, Eka was acquired by Iggesunds Bruk, one of the country's top forestry products groups, which later became part of the Holmen group of companies. Under its new owners, Eka expanded its range of production again, to include ammonia, in 1956. The company later acquired the license to a new hydrogen peroxide production process, developed in the Soviet Union, in 1968. The new technology played a part in Eka's later growth into one of the world's top producers of hydrogen peroxide. The following year, the company debuted its newly developed single-vessel process (SVP), used for the production of chlorine dioxide, another important bleaching agent used by the paper industry.

The beginning of the 1970s marked the first stirrings of environmental controls on the paper and paper chemicals market. Eka reacted early, launching the first of a long series of environmental protection initiatives in 1972. In that year, also, the company built a new state-of-the-art chlorine-alkali plant, which enabled it to address some of the environmental concerns of its own chemicals production. The increasing criticism of the negative ecological effects of much of the production process involved in the pulp, paper, and carton industries encouraged Eka to invest heavily in research and development initiatives. In 1975, for example, the company teamed up with Rockhammar in Sweden to develop a new hydrogen peroxide based bleaching process, for use with chemi-thermo-mechanical pulp.

INTERNATIONAL GROUP IN 1990

Eka's production of metasilicate provided the basis for the company's first expansion beyond Sweden. In 1980,

KEY DATES

1895: Alfred Nobel founds Elektrokemiska Aktiebolaget (Eka) to produce chlorine and alkali.

1924: Eka establishes new production facilities and headquarters in Bohus, Sweden.

1951: Forestry group Iggesunds Bruk acquires Eka, which begins to focus on paper and pulp chemicals production.

1986: Nobel Industries acquires Eka, which becomes Eka Nobel.

1994: Akzo and Nobel merge, becoming Akzo Nobel; Eka Chemicals becomes largest part of Akzo Nobel's Chemicals Group.

2000: U.S.-based Hopton Technologies acquired, boosting paper coatings chemicals business.

2007: Brazilian operations expand, with new agreement to build $50 million chemicals island in Tres Lagoas.

the company added its first factory outside of Sweden, with a metasilicate production facility in Maastricht, in the Netherlands. Three years later, the company added a subsidiary in Finland as well. This era also marked the company's increasing focus on its paper and pulp chemicals production. The company's long-standing expertise in silicate production played a role in the group's increasing paper chemicals focus. During the 1980s, Eka developed a new retention system based on the use of silica particles, which provided a breakthrough in the creation of new retention and dewatering systems for the wet end of the paper production process. Also in the 1980s, Eka launched a research and development program, which resulted in new microparticle technology that enabled the creation of new paper grades, while increasing the efficiency and reducing the environmental impact of paper production systems.

At the same time, however, Eka had set out to conquer more of the worldwide market. This effort coincided with sale of Eka by Iggesunds Bruk in 1986. The company's new parent, Nobel Industries, enabled it to come full circle, in a sense, and provided it with new resources for its international growth. In particular, the company, renamed as Eka Nobel, targeted expansion into the North American market, where it developed especially strong operations in the production of sodium chlorate. By the middle of the first decade of the 21st century, the company had emerged as the world's lead-

ing producer of sodium chlorate, with total production nearing one million tons. The group's North American operations accounted for more than half of its total sodium chlorate production.

A major boost to the company's international growth came in 1990, when Eka Nobel merged its operations with the paper chemical divisions of Albright & Wilson, Alby Klorat, and Stora Kemi. Following the completion of the merger, Eka Nobel emerged as one of the world's leading paper chemicals specialists, with operations spanning 14 countries. The group added another market the following year, when it started up a hydrogen peroxide manufacturing subsidiary in Venezuela.

By then, the paper industry had almost completely phased out the use of chlorine as a bleaching agent. Eka had helped play a role in this development, in part through the launch of its Lignox bleaching system. Based on the use of hydrogen peroxide, the Lignox system became widely adopted throughout the global papermaking industry, forming the foundation of subsequent generations of totally chlorine free (TCF) paper bleaching processes.

LEADING AKZO NOBEL'S CHEMICALS GROUP IN THE NEW CENTURY

The early 1990s witnessed a massive consolidation of the global chemicals industry, resulting in the creation of many of the world's largest corporations. In order to remain competitive, Nobel Industries was forced to seek a partner of its own, and for that the company turned to Dutch chemicals giant Akzo. The two companies formalized their merger in 1994, becoming Akzo Nobel. Eka Chemicals absorbed Akzo's own paper and pulp chemicals operations, becoming the largest company within the newly restructured Chemicals Group. By 1996, Eka had been refocused almost entirely on the paper chemicals market. As part of that process, Akzo Nobel transferred Eka's production of chlorine-alkali, the use of which by then had been more or less eliminated from the pulp and paper industry, to its Akzo Nobel Base Chemicals subsidiary.

In the meantime, Eka had relaunched its international expansion. The company added new chemicals factories in Brazil and Finland in 1995, then in Thailand and Indonesia in 1996. Further plants were added in Taiwan in 1997; in that year, also, the acquisition of Enso Paperikemia added new factories in Finland, as well as new expertise in paper coating chemicals. Through the end of the decade, the company added new sodium chlorate factories in Norway and

Chile. In 1999, the company entered South Korea through the acquisition of Dongsung Chemical Industrial's paper chemicals operations, including a factory in Kunsan. That acquisition also gave Eka a 70 percent stake in a joint venture in China. The company increased its presence in the Chinese mainland the following year, when it completed construction of a $10 million chemicals plant in Suzhou.

Eka had also continued to expand its range of chemicals. The company launched new bleaching agents based on paracetic acid in 1995, and sodium percarbonate in 1998. The purchase of U.S.-based Hopton Technologies in 2000 helped boost the company's growing paper coatings business as well. At the same time, Eka had continued to develop more environmentally friendly bleaching techniques, focusing on the use of hydrogen peroxide, resulting in the introduction of its HP-A bleaching system. In 2002, the company bought a chlorine dioxide plant operated by paper producer Korsnas, in Gävle, Sweden, then converted its operations to the new HP-A technology.

Into the middle of the decade, Eka turned its focus more and more to a rapidly growing trend within the global pulp and paper industry—the outsourcing of on-site chemicals production. In 2001, for example, Eka had taken over the production of chlorine dioxide at two pulp mills in Sweden. Over the next several years, the company developed a number of new outsourcing contracts, including an agreement in 2003 to construct a $50 million chemicals island for the Veracel pulp mill in Bahia, Brazil. That agreement positioned Eka as the sole supplier for all of the Veracel mill's chemicals requirements, with production launched in 2005.

Among the most successful of Eka's chemicals outsourcing operations was its production of chlorine dioxide. For this the company developed technology that enabled the remote monitoring of its client-based chlorine dioxide plants. By 2005, the company had taken over chlorine dioxide production at 15 pulp and paper mills. Many of these contracts included Eka's agreement to construct its own production facilities, such as a $15 million chlorine dioxide plant based at the Mucuri pulp mill in Bahia, Brazil. That factory tripled the company's chlorine dioxide production in Bahia. Eka also continued to build up its own global network of chemicals factories. The company added a new facility in Guangzhou, China, in 2006. By 2007, the company's Brazilian operations expanded again, with an agreement to build a $50 million chemicals island for a new pulp mill being constructed by Votorantim Celulose and Papel in Tres Lagoas. With its own revenues

nearing EUR 1 billion ($1.4 billion), Eka Chemicals had become one of the world's leading specialists in paper chemicals production.

M. L. Cohen

PRINCIPAL SUBSIDIARIES

Akzo Nobel Chemicals GmbH (Germany); Eka Chemicals Pty Ltd. (Australia); Eka Chemicals (Guangzhou) Co., Ltd. (China); Eka Chemicals Pty Ltd. (South Africa); Eka Chemicals (Suzhou) Co. Ltd. (China); Eka Chemicals Co., Ltd. (Taiwan); Eka Chemicals Ltd. (Thailand); Eka Chemicals Austria GesmbH; Eka Chemicals Canada, Inc.; Eka Chemicals de Venezuela C.A.; Eka Chemicals do Brasil S.A.; Eka Chemicals Ibérica S.A. (Spain); Eka Chemicals, Inc. (United States); Eka Chemicals K.K. (Japan); Eka Chemicals Korea Co., Ltd.; Eka Chemicals Ltd. (United Kingdom); Eka Chemicals Oy (Finland); Eka Chemicals Portugal, Lda.; Eka Chemicals Rana A/S (Norway); Expancel; Expancel (Germany); Expancel Vietnam; Permascand AB; PT Eka Chemicals Indonesia; Z.I. du Bec (France); Eka PolymerLatex (50%); Eka Chile S.A. (50%); EkO Peroxide LLC (50%).

PRINCIPAL COMPETITORS

Hercules Inc.; Hexion Specialty Chemicals Inc.

FURTHER READING

"Akzo to Build Chlorine Dioxide Plant in Brazil," *Chemical Week*, June 21, 2006, p. 6.

Bains, Elizabeth, "Eka Seals Brazil Deal to Supply Pulp Mill," *ICIS Chemical Business*, May 28, 2007.

D'Amico, Esther, "Eka to Restructure North American Business," *Chemical Week*, November 5, 2003, p. 28.

"Eka Acquires Hopton," *Chemical Week*, September 27, 2000, p. 41.

"Eka Chemicals Expands in China," *Chemical Week*, November 29, 2006, p. 34.

"Eka Chemicals to Build Paper Chemicals Plant," *Chemical Market Reporter*, December 15, 2003, p. 2.

Gordon, Michael, "Eka Invests in New Technology," *ECN European Chemical News*, February 16, 2004, p. 26.

Sim, Peck Hwee, "Eka and OCI Chemicals in Hydrogen Peroxide Alliance," *Chemical Week*, November 15, 2006, p. 9.

Walsh, Kerri, "Akzo Nobel Invests in Brazil," *Chemical Week*, May 30, 2007, p. 13.

Établissements Jacquot
and Cie S.A.S.

21 rue Beauregard
Troyes, F-10000
France
Telephone: (33 03) 25 82 51 89
Fax: (33 03) 25 75 36 85
Web site: http://www.jacquot.fr

70% Owned Subsidiary of Cemoi S.A.
Incorporated: 1920 as Établissements Veuve Jacquot et Fils
Employees: 600
Sales: EUR 132 million ($170 million) (2006)
NAIC: 311320 Chocolate and Confectionery Manufacturing from Cacao Beans

■ ■ ■

Établissements Jacquot and Cie S.A.S. is one of France's major producers of chocolate. The Troyes-based company, founded in the early part of the 20th century, specializes in supplying seasonal and festive chocolates primarily for the two major chocolate-buying seasons of Easter and Christmas. The majority of the company's sales of EUR 132 million are generated during these two holiday periods.

Jacquot's product range is grouped into four primary categories: hollow aluminum-wrapped figures (Easter eggs, bunnies, Santa Claus figures, and the like); solid decorated figures (in themes similar to the hollow variety); Advent calendars (milk chocolate and other confections in cardboard frames) and specialties and gift boxes (filled chocolates, cherry liqueurs, pralines, and

eggs, as well as the higher-end Alibi line, created in partnership with Philippe Urraca in 2002).

Nearly all of Jacquot's sales are made through the large distribution outlets, supplying supermarkets and hypermarkets with its own branded production. The company also produces private-label products for the supermarket groups as well as for discount labels. Jacquot's production takes place at its main Troyes facilities as well as at three other factories in France. The company's total production capacity tops 20,000 tons per year. France represents Jacquot's major market, with more than 75 percent of the company's total revenues generated in its home country. Facing bankruptcy in 2007, Jacquot agreed to be acquired by French chocolate giant Cemoi S.A., which bought nearly 70 percent of Jacquot through a EUR 17 million recapitalization deal. Members of the founding Jacquot family, including Paul, Philippe, and Pierre-Pascal Jacquot, remained active in the company's management following the buyout.

SWEET SHOP AT THE TURN OF THE 20TH CENTURY

Jacquot grew from a small pastry and sweet shop operated by Jules Jacquot in Bar-sur-Aube in the early years of the 20th century. There, Jacquot developed his own recipes for sweets, cakes, cookies, sugar-covered almonds, ice cream, and chocolate. The shop remained a small one during his lifetime. Upon his death in 1914, his widow, Pauline, took over the pastry shop and by the end of the decade was engaged in more large-scale production. Jacquot was joined in the enterprise by her

COMPANY PERSPECTIVES

The company beats to the rhythm of Easter and Christmas and offers consumers a constantly new and wide collection of chocolate, combining quality, authenticity, creativity and fantasy for the delight of children and adults!

sons Paul, Henri, and Marcel. By 1920, the increase in sales of the Jacquot family's chocolate and other confectionery items prompted Jacquot to establish a new company, which she called Établissements Veuve Jacquot et Fils.

The company grew quickly and by 1923 was successful enough to build its own factory on the rue Beauregard in the city of Troyes. That site was to remain the center of the company's operations into the next century. Jacquot's expansion over the next decades was stimulated by the expansion of the chocolate market itself. The arrival of new quantities of cocoa beans, especially following the development of cocoa plantations in much of French-controlled and/or influenced Africa, helped establish the confection as a popular consumer item. In France, chocolate became a popular gift item, particularly in the holiday seasons surrounding Easter and Christmas, as well as to mark other dates on the Catholic calendar.

The company's leadership was handed over to Jacquot's sons following World War II. Under the new generation, Jacquot expanded to become one of the most well-known names in the highly competitive chocolate industry. The company's growth also stimulated the steady expansion of its main Troyes production facility. The emergence of the large-scale distribution sector in the 1960s and especially in the 1970s provided a new source of growth for the company.

The smaller number of major supermarket companies that came to dominate the French retail grocery sector also had a dramatic impact on the country's food production sector. Like a number of other chocolate producers, such as Cemoi located in the south of France, Jacquot ensured its own growth by teaming up with the large-scale distributors. In addition to placing its own products on supermarket shelves, the company also began producing chocolates for the supermarkets' own private labels, as well as for other, private-label chocolates. The French chocolate industry's reputation as being among the world's finest producers

of chocolates also helped Jacquot build its own exports to international markets.

SEASONAL SPECIALIST IN THE EIGHTIES

The rising influence of the large-scale supermarket and hypermarket groups in France in the 1980s continued to have a major impact on the chocolate market. The supermarket sector came to account for a major percentage of everyday chocolate purchases, with chocolate bar selection dominated by a handful of larger brands, including Nestlé, Lindt & Sprungli, and Cemoi. Intense competition came too from another fast-growing branch of the chocolate industry, as such brands as Ferrero, Kinder, Roche, and Pyrénéens came to dominate the retail confectionery segment.

Jacquot's survival during this period came through its decision in the mid-1980s to abandon its more diversified product range. Instead, the company decided to focus its production and marketing efforts solely on the seasonal chocolates sector. The company had long enjoyed a leading position in the French market for seasonal chocolates, and the group's chocolates remained a popular gift choice among consumers especially during the Easter and Christmas seasons. Traditionally, these two periods of the year made up the bulk of French chocolate buying.

In order to cement its position, the company invested heavily in new production technologies especially in hollow-molding machinery and foil-wrapping equipment. The company also developed new lines of decorated, molded chocolates, and gift packs of filled chocolates. Backing these investments was a significant advertising effort. As a result, the company soon outgrew its existing production facilities and by 1990 had added a new, larger factory in the Ecrevolles industrial zone of Troyes. The company continued to expand that site with several new buildings into the mid-1990s.

NEW OWNERS FOR A NEW CENTURY

Jacquot's decision to specialize on the holiday market gave new impulse to the group's export sales as well. By the early 2000s, the company's chocolates were available in more than 70 countries and were especially popular in North America and Japan, as well as in other European markets. By the turn of the century, Jacquot's exports accounted for approximately one-fourth of its total revenues of more than EUR 120 million. Yet France remained the company's primary market, taking

KEY DATES

1900s: Jules Jacquot operates a pastry and confectionery shop in Bar-sur-Aube, France.

1920: Jacquot's widow, Pauline Jacqot, creates Établissements Veuve Jacquot et Fils, launching large-scale production of chocolate and confectionery items.

1980s: Company refocuses as a specialty seasonal chocolates producer.

1996: Construction of second production site in Troyes is completed.

2002: Higher-end Alibi chocolate line debuts.

2007: On verge of bankruptcy, Jacquot sells majority stake to Cemoi S.A.

up 75 percent of its total production. By then, too, the company had achieved a supermarket penetration rate of more than 90 percent.

The increasing domination of the French chocolate market by larger and multinational companies sent Jacquot on its own expansion drive. The company added new production facilities, as well as new brands, including Ferton, based in Fère-Champenoise, in the Marne region near Paris; Mosser, based in Molsheim, in the Haut-Rhin region near the German border; and Roches Blanches, at Beaurepaire in the Isère region.

Jacquot also attempted to capitalize on the trend toward cross-marketing within the confectionery industry in the late 1990s. As such, the company acquired the licenses for a number of popular characters, including the Marsupilami comic book characters, the cartoon character Franklin, and the perennial French children's favorite Barbapapa, among others. Jacquot began developing its own lines of chocolates and confectionery based on these licenses. Into the 2000s, Jacquot also attempted to expand its range into the higher-end categories. For this, the company teamed up with noted chef Philippe Urraca to launch the Alibi line of fine chocolates.

Despite Jacquot's expansion efforts, the group remained outpaced by the consolidation of the chocolate sector. Worse for the company, the sudden and dramatic increases in the price of its two primary raw materials, milk and cocoa, left the company struggling financially. With cocoa prices rising by more than 25 percent and milk prices skyrocketing by 75 percent in 2007, Jacquot ran out of steam. By July 2007, following a difficult Easter season and with the all-important Christmas

season still a ways away, the family-owned company stood on the brink of bankruptcy.

The company was saved, however, with the arrival of Perpignan-based Cemoi S.A., which became majority shareholder in Jacquot. Cemoi, which traced its history as far back as the early 19th century, had been expanding rapidly particularly through a vertical integration effort that had transformed it into one of the cocoa and chocolate industry leaders. While Cemoi took majority control of Jacquot, with nearly 70 percent of its shares, the Jacquot family represented by Paul, Philippe, and Pierre-Pascal Jacquot remained active managers of the company, as well as shareholders. At the same time, the Swiss-based Barry chocolate group, Jacquot's primary chocolate supplier, also held a minority stake in the company.

The presence of two rivals among the company's shareholders led to tensions in October 2007, when Cemoi balked at new price increases imposed by Barry on its supplies to Jacquot. As a result, Barry stopped its deliveries to Jacquot, which was forced to temporarily suspend production, just ahead of the Christmas season. Cemoi attempted to take Barry to court over the matter; its efforts were quickly frustrated, however, when the courts refused to hear the case and ordered Cemoi to uphold the conditions of Jacquot's purchasing contracts.

Despite this setback, Cemoi, which produced more than 200,000 tons of chocolate per year, appeared a good match for Jacquot. While both companies were primarily active in the supermarket sector, their product focus remained highly distinctive, with Jacquot's own focus on the seasonal market complementing Cemoi's own line of proprietary-brand, private-label, and discount-label chocolates. The backing of its new and powerful shareholder ensured Jacquot of the financial backing it needed as it turned toward the new century.

M. L. Cohen

PRINCIPAL SUBSIDIARIES

Ferton S.A.; Mosser S.A.; Roches Blanches S.A.

PRINCIPAL COMPETITORS

Nestlé Suisse S.A.; ADM Cocoa B.V.; Cadbury Schweppes plc; Orkla ASA; Ferrero International S.A.; Cargill B.V.; Barry Callebaut AG; Mars (UK) Ltd.; Koninklijke Wessanen N.V.; Tiger Brands Ltd.

FURTHER READING

Ambrosi, Pascal, "Cemoi Sauve Jacquot du Dépôt de Bilan," *Capital*, July 2, 2007.

"French Chocolates Inspired by Pastries," *Professional Candy Buyer,* May–June 2004, p. 102.

Locurcio, Laurent, "Chocolats Jacquot: à Paques, C'est Déjà Noël," *Mercure,* April 2007.

Magee, Patricia L., "Push-Button Bon Bons Bring Success to Jacquot," *Candy Industry,* April 1988, p. 36.

"Merci pour Vos Chocolates!" *Le Journal du Conseil Général,* Winter 2001.

Finisar Corporation

---------■---------

1389 Moffett Park Drive
Sunnyvale, California 94089-1134
U.S.A.
Telephone: (408) 548-1000
Fax: (408) 541-6138
Web site: http://www.finisar.com

Public Company
Incorporated: 1987
Employees: 4,200
Sales: $364.3 million (2006)
Stock Exchanges: NASDAQ
Ticker Symbol: FNSR
NAIC: 334413 Semiconductor and Related Device Manufacturing

■ ■ ■

Finisar Corporation is a leading provider of fiber-optic subsystems, which make high-speed communications possible over different kinds of computer networks, including local area networks (LANs), storage area networks (SANs), and metropolitan area networks (MANs). In addition, the company offers test systems that are used to monitor and maintain network performance. From its headquarters in Sunnyvale, California, Finisar's 4,200 employees serve clients such as Cisco and EMC from sales and support sites throughout the world. In addition, the company's operations include manufacturing and development sites in China, Malaysia, Singapore, and Texas.

GETTING STARTED: 1987–99

Finisar was cofounded on April 17, 1987, in Sunnyvale, California, by Jerry S. Rawls and Dr. Frank Levinson. As president and CEO, it was Rawls who was responsible for shaping the company during its formative years. In the December 1, 2003, issue of *MSI,* Rawls elaborated on the ingredients that were used to create a successful culture, explaining: "When we started the company, we cast several principles in stone. We were going to take great care of our customers, deliver truly innovative products, and hire really good people. We believe that if you do those three things consistently, success will follow."

Born in Texas on July 31, 1944, Rawls earned a BSME degree from Texas Tech University, followed by a master's degree in industrial administration from Purdue University's Krannert Graduate School of Management. Prior to cofounding Finisar, Rawls started his career with Raychem Corp. in 1968, where he held marketing and sales positions before becoming general manager of the company's Aerospace Products Division, and later the general manager of its Interconnection Systems Division.

In an August 23, 2000, *CNBC/Dow Jones Business Video,* Rawls explained that Finisar's product offerings, which include devices such as transceivers, transmitters, and receivers, "convert electricity into optics, into light, and light into electricity. And the signals are transmitted at a billion bits per second or faster, or known in the industry as a gigabit per second."

During the early 1990s, Finisar was among several industry players (including IBM and Hewlett-Packard) working to develop components that were capable of supporting high-speed data communications in the gigabit-per-second (Gbps) range. Such components allowed information to travel faster than existing components, which then operated at a speed of 100 megabits per second (Mbps).

Early on, Finisar claimed a number of industry firsts with transceivers—devices on computer networks that can both transmit and receive data. For example, in 1992 the company was first to market with 1.25 Gbps transceivers for multimode fiber. In 1994 Finisar struck an agreement with the Fiber Optic Products Group of Chicago-based Methode Electronics, resulting in a second supplier for optical components and furthering expansion into Asia and Europe.

In the March 1994 issue of *Optical Materials & Engineering News,* Methode Executive Vice-President James McGinley described Finisar's "groundbreaking approach to laser physics," which he said allowed "networking equipment manufacturers to build network adapters with 100 times more bandwidth than existing copper wire solutions at comparable costs."

Product breakthroughs continued at Finisar into the late 1990s. The company unveiled transceivers offering digital diagnostic capabilities in 1996. The following year, it introduced a transceiver using a vertical cavity surface emitting laser. This type of laser, called VCSEL for short, supports high-speed data transmission in the 1-to-10-gigabit range.

By 1999 Finisar's customer base had grown to include the likes of Sun Microsystems, 3Com, IBM, and EMC. Unlike many technology start-ups, Finisar was actually profitable. Midway through the year, the company's revenues reached $13.9 million, and earnings totaled $1.3 million.

Finisar ended the decade with a highly successful initial public offering (IPO). Held on November 12, 1999, the IPO saw Finisar's stock quadruple in value, closing at almost $86.88 per share and boosting the company's market capitalization past the $4 billion mark. Finisar reincorporated in the state of Delaware at this time.

WHEELING AND DEALING: 2000–02

While it faced heavy competition from the likes of Agilent and IBM in the market for optical components, Finisar began the new millennium with a strong hold on the market for test systems. Things were going well, as the company celebrated 12 consecutive years of profitability in 2000. In April of that year, a secondary stock offering allowed Finisar to raise another $300 million in cash. By this time Finisar's stock had garnered the attention of institutional investors, who held about 36 percent of its shares. The burgeoning growth of Internet-related firms presented the company with what seemed to be endless opportunity.

In a June 19, 2000, *Business Wire* release, Jerry Rawls remarked: "We're one of the arms merchants to the e-commerce world in that as all these sites build their physical infrastructure, they have to have storage; they have to have switches; and they have to have networks. All of that is connected with optics. Our optical systems and our test systems are all employed in the development and the building of these networks. Yes, the Web is very much a part of our future."

Finisar initiated an acquisition spree during the latter part of 2000. In October, the company acquired Princeton, New Jersey–based optical component manufacturer Sensors Unlimited, Inc., in a deal worth approximately $700 million. The following month, Finisar agreed to acquire three California-based optical companies for a total of $363 million in stock, with a goal of bolstering its staff of engineers.

The company snapped up El Monte, California–based laser diode maker Demeter Technologies for $165 million; Fremont, California–based passive optical component developer Transwave Fiber, Inc., for $90 million; and San Jose, California–based monitoring software developer Shomiti Systems, Inc., for $108 million. When the buys were completed, Finisar had added 66 new professionals to its engineering staff, which already exceeded the 100 mark.

A departure from the acquisition path occurred in February 2001, when San Jose, California–based ONI Systems Corp. acquired Finisar's Opticity product line for $30 million in cash and $20 million in stock. However, the departure was a brief one. Acquisition activity resumed that very month when Finisar announced plans to acquire thermoelectric cooler firm Marlow Industries, Inc., for $30 million in cash and

KEY DATES

1987: Finisar is cofounded in Sunnyvale, California, by Jerry S. Rawls and Dr. Frank Levinson.
1999: Finisar makes its initial public offering in November, and the company reincorporates in Delaware.
2000: A secondary stock offering generates $300 million in cash.
2006: President and CEO Jerry Rawls assumes the additional role of chairman, succeeding cofounder and Chief Technical Officer Dr. Frank Levinson.

$260 million in stock. However, the deal was tabled in June in the wake of tough times in the telecommunications market. Finisar completed one additional deal in 2001 when it acquired Medusa Technologies, Inc., in March for approximately $7 million in cash.

In 2002 Finisar continued to achieve new product breakthroughs. According to the company, it was first to market with several new transceiver models that year, including the 1000Base-T GBIC transceiver, the DWDM GBIC transceiver, and the XFP transceiver.

These developments came in the midst of more acquisitions. In February, the company acquired the assets of Munich, Germany–based AIFOtec GmbH for $2.3 million. In addition, 30 former AIFOtec employees were added to Finisar's staff. Three months later, Finisar acquired New Focus, Inc.'s, passive optical component product line for $12.8 million, and added about 30 New Focus workers to its employee base, which totaled 1,200.

GLOBAL ENTERPRISE: 2003–07

In 2003 Finisar began putting more emphasis on international expansion. Helping to guide the company's global strategy was President and Chief Operating Officer Dick Woodrow, who helped forge an arrangement with distributor Macnica I&C Co. to push Finisar products in the Japanese market.

New offerings in 2003 included Finisar's next-generation Xgig system, which it called the "industry's first distributed, scalable, analysis platform for SANs and LANs." The company enhanced its ability to produce such products with new performance management software at all of its manufacturing facilities. Camstar's InSite system, installed at Finisar's facilities in the

United States, Singapore, and Malaysia, allowed for better management of, and faster changes to, detailed manufacturing process.

Finally, in 2003 CEO Jerry Rawls honored Purdue University's Krannert School of Management, where he graduated in 1968, with a $10 million gift. The funds were applied toward a new $35 million building for the business school, which was named Jerry S. Rawls Hall. Several years earlier, in 2000, Rawls had donated $25 million to Texas Tech University, where he graduated in 1967.

New product breakthroughs continued in 2004, and included the release of Finisar's RoHS/lead-free 4G Fibre Channel SFP transceiver. In March of that year, the company gave up approximately $75 million in cash and $1.2 million in common stock to acquire Honeywell International, Inc.'s, VCSEL Optical Products arm.

The Honeywell transaction was followed by two other deals. In August, Finisar acquired Data Transit Corp.'s assets for $500,000 in cash and a $16.3 million promissory note. However, a more significant deal had started brewing four months before, when Finisar agreed to acquire Infineon Technologies AG's optics business. The $245 million stock deal, which would have given Infineon a 38 percent stake in Finisar, was significant for several reasons. It included about 450 new patents for Finisar, as well as 1,200 additional employees. In addition, it would have allowed Finisar to enter new markets, because about 40 percent of Infineon's sales were tied to areas where Finisar had no presence.

In early 2005, problems developed in relation to the pending acquisition of Infineon's optics arm. The German company canceled the deal on January 10, in the midst of legal delays and waning interest among Finisar's board. However, the two companies came to new terms on January 25. A mere sliver of the original deal, the final deal involved Finisar acquiring the portion of Infineon's optics business that pertained to optical transceiver and transponders for $48 million in stock (34 million shares). Completed on January 31, the transaction gave Infineon a 13 percent interest in Finisar.

Acquisitions continued at a rapid pace throughout the remainder of 2005. The network testing and monitoring firm I-TECH Corp. was acquired on April 8 for approximately $12 million in stock. Following the deal, I-TECH continued operations as a Finisar subsidiary. The following month, Scotts Valley, California–based InterSAN, Inc., was acquired for $8.8 million in stock. Finally, Milpitas, California–based Big Bear Networks, Inc., was acquired on November 15 for $1.9 million in cash.

A number of other notable developments occurred in 2005. In April Finisar sued DirecTV Group, Inc., for infringing upon technology that subscribers used to access content from the satellite provider, including electronic program guides. Around this time, Finisar revealed it had invested $50 million in the expansion of its Ipoh plant, located in Malaysia's Perak state. The investment was related to the Infineon deal, as some production at Infineon operations in the Czech Republic and Germany was moved to the Malaysia facility.

Finisar kicked off 2006 by electing Jerry Rawls as chairman. Rawls, who retained his role as president and CEO, succeeded cofounder and Chief Technical Officer Dr. Frank Levinson, who had resigned to pursue other technical and philanthropic interests. Midyear, the company celebrated victory in its lawsuit against DirecTV. Following a two week trial in U.S. District Court, a jury ruled in favor of the company, ordering DirecTV to pay Finisar $78.9 million in damages.

There were other things to celebrate at Finisar in 2006. That year, the company boosted VCSEL production via a plant expansion in Allen, Texas. In addition, the firm's Advanced Optical Division celebrated the production of its 50 millionth VCSEL. New offerings for the year included Bus Doctor, a product that was used to perform analysis on consumer electronics.

As of late 2007, Finisar was focused on helping the telecommunications industry upgrade its infrastructure. Its capabilities in this market area were strengthened by the acquisition of two companies that brought more telecommunications strength to Finisar's product lines. Announced in March, the acquisitions included South Plainfield, New Jersey–based Kodeos Communications, Inc., and Wilmington, Massachusetts–based AZNA

LLC. The Kodeos deal was made for $7 million in cash, while the AZNA acquisition had a total value of approximately $19.7 million.

Paul R. Greenland

PRINCIPAL SUBSIDIARIES

Finisar Sales, Inc.; Finisar Shanghai, Inc. (China); Finisar Singapore Pte. Ltd. (Singapore); Finisar Hong Kong Ltd. (Hong Kong); Finisar Japan Ltd. (KK) (Japan); Finisar Malaysia Sdn Bhd. (Malaysia); Inter-SAN, Inc.

PRINCIPAL COMPETITORS

Avago Technologies Ltd.; JDS Uniphase Corporation; Opnext, Inc.

FURTHER READING

"Chairman of Finisar Ponders Fiber's Future," *Electronic Engineering Times,* October 16, 2006.

"Finisar Agreement with Methode," *Optical Materials & Engineering News,* March 1994.

"Finisar, CEO—Interview," *CNBC/Dow Jones Business Video,* August 23, 2000.

"Finisar Corporation Names Jerry Rawls Chairman," *Internet Wire,* January 5, 2006.

"Finisar's CEO Jerry Rawls Talks to the *Wall Street Transcript,*" *Business Wire,* June 19, 2000.

"Finisar Wins Patent Infringement Claim against DirecTV," *TELEVISION A.M.,* June 27, 2006.

"How Finisar CEO Jerry Rawls Forges a Culture of Success," *MSI,* December 1, 2003.

"IPO Report: Finisar Quadruples on Opening Day," *CBS MarketWatch,* November 12, 1999.

Flatiron Construction Corporation

10090 I-25 Frontage Road
Longmont, Colorado 80504
U.S.A.
Telephone: (303) 485-4050
Fax: (303) 485-3922
Web site: http://flatironcorp.com

Private Company
Incorporated: 1947 as Flatiron Structures
Employees: 743
Sales: $116.6 million (2007 est.)
NAIC: 237990 Other Heavy and Civil Engineering
Construction

■ ■ ■

Flatiron Construction Corporation, which operates as part of Dutch construction giant Royal BAM, is one of the largest bridge builders in the United States. Flatiron provides design and construction services for transportation and heavy civil projects. Its experience includes major highways, traditional and specialty bridges, toll roads, tunnels, and rail transit projects throughout the United States. The company operates two major subsidiaries, Flatiron Constructors, Inc., and FCI Constructors. Flatiron Constructors provides design/build, construction management, and specialized construction services for transportation projects. This subsidiary is a leading player in bridge projects, including cable-stayed, precast segmental, and suspension bridges. Its services include piling, complex lifting and erecting, deep and large-diameter foundations, tunnel-

ing, and marine construction. FCI Constructors, Inc., focuses on projects throughout California and the western U.S. market. It operates both a northern and southern division. Flatiron Construction Company has worked on such projects as California's Carquinez Strait Bridge and the San Francisco/Oakland Bay Bridge. In 2004, the company changed its name back to Flatiron Construction Corporation from HBG Constructors, Inc., reflecting the firm's pride in its history. In 2007, Hochtief Aktiengesellschaft, Germany's largest construction company, agreed to acquire Flatiron from the Royal BAM Group.

BEGINNINGS TO BUYOUT

Founded in 1947, Flatiron was named after the unique rock formations in the foothills of Boulder, Colorado. The company quietly grew from a small construction company in a sparsely populated region approximately 40 miles west of Denver to a nationally recognized firm in the transportation industry. Formerly known as Flatiron Structures, the firm grew into national prominence by allowing its local management considerable autonomy and control. This independence at the local level produced an environment conducive to seizing opportunities and looking for new ways of delivering a project. The company was bought out in 1993 by the Hollandsche Beton Group (HBG), a construction and dredging group that worked on infrastructure projects worldwide. Among its diversified operations, HBG also provided engineering, mechanical, and electrical contracting; consulting; and property development services. Its U.S. holdings operated under the group HGB Constructors, which comprised FCI Constructors

Flatiron Construction Corp. is a family of companies specializing in transportation and heavy civil construction projects both on a national scale and in local districts in North America. Our experience encompasses major bridge and highway projects, toll roads, light and heavy rail transit, tunnels, and other infrastructure projects. Flatiron is consistently ranked among the top bridge and highway builders in North America.

and HBG Flatiron. In addition to working in the Netherlands and the United States, the firm operated in the United Kingdom, Germany, and Belgium.

While under new ownership, HBG Flatiron's work ranged from the Central Artery projects in Boston to the Benicia-Martinez Bridge Seismic Retrofit on the West Coast. In a joint venture, the firm also worked on building the Carquinez Strait Bridge in the greater San Francisco Bay Area. In August 1997, Flatiron also won a $46.6 million contract to build a new four-lane bridge across the Kennebec River between the towns of Bath and Woolwich, Maine, replacing the old Carlton Bridge. Flatiron beat out the competition not only on price, but also on design.

COMPANY PROSPERS WITH
FEDERAL FUNDING IN U.S.
INFRASTRUCTURE

In 2000, HBG refused an unwelcome acquisition bid from Netherlands-based Royal Bos Kalis Westminster N.V. that also would have included Flatiron. The bid came after failed merger talks between the two Dutch firms. To defeat such takeover attempts, HBG had formed an independent foundation two years earlier that could exercise an option to acquire shares from HBG. In this attempt, the foundation acquired enough shares to give it 50 percent voting rights. In principle, HBG supported consolidation in the dredging business. After prolonged discussions, however, HBG decided against merging with Bos Kalis, keeping its options open for other deals.

The hostile bid came amid golden times for companies in the United States working in heavy construction, with upturns in federal and private sector spending for highways, bridges, airports, pipelines, waterworks, and rail. In 1999 alone, the top 400 contractors working in heavy construction, including Flatiron, earned about $27.2 billion in revenue, 13.1 percent more than the previous year. The federal government was the biggest contributor to this gain. The boost in funding stemmed mostly from the 1998 $217 billion, six-year Transportation Equity Act for the 21st Century, which provided federal aid for highway and mass transit projects. Lawmakers also appropriated billion of dollars in aid for water projects and airport construction. Further, despite the 2001 and 2002 stock market tumble and the economic downturn, total domestic revenue for the top 400 contractors slipped only 2.9 percent in 2002. Nevertheless, heavy construction and highway markets earned double digit increases, with the transportation market alone contributing $24.4 billion in revenue for heavy contractors, a 25 percent increase over 2001.

In 2002, as Flatiron benefited from the boost in these transportation projects in the U.S. market, it became a group company of the Netherlands-based Royal BAM Group, after Royal Bam acquired the HBG Group. Headquartered in the Netherlands, the Royal BAM Group was a diversified construction company ranking among the world's largest construction firms. With a global workforce of over 30,000, its annual revenues exceeded $8.8 billion in 2003. In 2004, HBG Constructors, Inc., and HBG Flatiron, Inc., changed their names to Flatiron Construction Corporation and Flatiron Constructors, Inc., respectively. FCI Constructors, Inc., Northern Division, and FCI Constructors Inc., Southern Division, continued to operate under those same names.

With its continued success and under new ownership, Flatiron won new major contracts in 2005. Among these were two multimillion-dollar contracts awarded by the Florida Department of Transportation—a $191 million contract to rebuild a portion of the State Roadway 60/Memorial Highway in Tampa and a $243 million project to construct two parallel bridges along Interstate 10 across Escambia Bay in Pensacola. After four years of construction, Flatiron, in a joint venture with Tidewater Skanska, also completed a new $541 million cable-stayed bridge over the Cooper River in Charleston, South Carolina. The new 1,546-foot bridge connected historic downtown Charleston with Mt. Pleasant.

In 2006, the company's contracts included such projects as constructing a new $76.5 million bridge connecting Madeira Beach and Treasure Island in Florida, which Flatiron began in January. In March 2006, FCI Constructors, Flatiron's California subsidiary, was commissioned by the state of California to build a $420 million Mid-City/Exposition Light Rail in Los Angeles, California. The project involved building 9.6 miles of

KEY DATES

1947: Company is founded.
1993: Company is acquired by Netherlands-based Hollandsche Beton Group (HBG).
2002: Company becomes part of Royal BAM Group, after Royal BAM acquires the HBG Group.
2004: HBG Constructors, Inc., and HBG Flatiron, Inc., change their names to Flatiron Construction Corp. and Flatiron Constructors, Inc., respectively.
2007: Hochtief AG of Germany buys Flatiron from Royal BAM Group.

new light rail transit from downtown Los Angeles to Culver City, as well as constructing 11 passenger stations, three park-and-ride lots, bicycle lanes, and one cut-and-cover tunnel near the University of Southern California.

In May 2006, Flatiron received a $348 million contract from the Louisiana Department of Transportation and Development to construct a new cable-stayed bridge across the Mississippi River. Leading a construction team that also included Granite Construction and Parsons Transportation Group, Flatiron was to build a new bridge, called the John James Audubon Bridge, to replace a ferry system. The bridge would connect St. Francisville and New Roads just north of Baton Rouge, Louisiana. The main cable-stayed span was to stretch 1,583 feet across the Mississippi River to become the longest cable-stayed bridge in North America.

In July 2006, Flatiron's California subsidiary also was awarded two contracts totaling $131 million. The largest contract consisted of a $91 million California Department of Transportation project to improve the I-238/I-560 highways in San Leandro and Hayward, California. The company also won a $40 million contract to widen I-15 in San Diego, California.

Following the tragic collapse of the Interstate 35-W bridge into the Mississippi River during the height of a Minneapolis rush hour on August 1, 2007, the Minnesota Department of Transportation chose Flatiron to lead the rebuilding of the bridge. The $234 million project represented Flatiron's first major project in Minnesota. Although Flatiron's proposal was the most expensive in the bidding contest, state officials said other factors were involved, such as bridge design, aesthetics, and improvements to surrounding roadways.

COMPANY ACQUIRED BY GERMAN CONSTRUCTION GIANT

Also at the end of August 2007, the parent company of Flatiron, the Netherlands-based Royal BAM Group, one of Europe's largest construction companies, announced that it was on the verge of selling the Longmont, Colorado–based bridge builder. In 2006, Flatiron and its almost 1,700 strong workforce generated revenues of more than $496 million and ranked among the top ten vendors in the U.S. transportation market. The company had gained attention through its work on such projects as constructing significant portions of the $1 billion San Francisco/Oakland Bay Bridge and the repair of two Florida bridges damaged by Hurricane Ivan in 2004. In September 2007, Hochtief Akiengesellschaft, Germany's largest construction company, publicized that it was taking over Flatiron Construction Company from the Royal BAM Group for $240 million. The acquisition would give Hochtief a bridge builder to add to its commercial property operations in North America and would be folded into its Turner unit, the number one general builder in the U.S. market. According to Hochtief, the acquisition would give its Turner subsidiary a presence in the field of civil engineering and enable it to profit from future federal and private multibillion-dollar investment programs in infrastructure improvements. It also would allow Hochtief to position itself in the developing U.S. market for public-private partnerships at an early stage.

Bruce P. Montgomery

PRINCIPAL DIVISIONS

Flatiron Constructors, Inc.; Flatiron Constructors, Inc., Intermountain; FCI Constructors, Inc., Southern Division; FCI Constructors, Inc., Northern Division.

PRINCIPAL COMPETITORS

Peter Kiewit Sons'; Skanska USA Civil; Walsh Group.

FURTHER READING

Angelo, William J., "All Contenders Are Shortlisted for $1.6 Billion Denver Project," *ENR,* August 7, 2000.

"Flatiron to Design and Build New Calgary Ring Road As Part of Public-Private Partnership," *Canada NewsWire,* February 23, 2007.

"Flatiron Wins $131 Million Contracts," *Boulder County Business Report,* September 15–28, 2006.

"Germany: U.S. Deal by Builder," *New York Times,* September 26, 2007.

Hampton, Tudor, "Design Process Advances for New Minneapolis Bridge," *ENR,* August 27, 2007.

Hewitt, Rich, "DOT Selects Team to Build New Bridge; Cianbro, Reed & Reed to Erect Overpass," *Bangor Daily News,* November 13, 2003.

"Hochtief AG," *Wall Street Journal Europe,* September 26, 2007.

Ichniowski, Tom, "Engineers Swarm on U.S. Bridges to Check for Flaws," *ENR,* August 20, 2007.

Langston, Carter, "North Carolina's Knightdale Bypass," *Southeast Construction,* February 2005.

Leib, Jeffrey, "Bechtel Pulls Bid on I-25, Light-Rail Job," *Denver Post,* November 2, 2000.

———, "Plan Rings Eastern Springs in Toll Roads," *Denver Post,* July 31, 2006.

Llia, Tony, "Hoover Dam Bridge Bids More Costly than Expected," *Las Vegas Business Press,* October 11, 2004.

Vuong, Andy, "Parent Firm Mum on Potential Buyer for Flatiron Construction; Royal BAM Says the Sale Is Expected to Close Next Month for Its Longmont Subsidiary," *Denver Post,* August 30, 2007.

Francotyp-Postalia Holding AG

Triftweg 21-26
Birkenwerder, 16547
Germany
Telephone: (49 3303) 525 777
Fax: (49 3303) 53 70 77 77
Web site: http://www.francotyp.com

Public Company
Founded: 1923
Employees: 939
Sales: EUR 143.1 million ($187.93 million) (2006)
Stock Exchanges: Frankfurt
Ticker Symbol: FPH
NAIC: 333313 Office Machinery Manufacturing

■ ■ ■

Francotyp-Postalia Holding AG is the parent company of the Francotyp-Postalia Gruppe (FP). FP's main activities are the development, manufacture, marketing, and servicing of franking and letter insertion equipment for businesses with small to medium mailroom volumes. These activities are performed by FP's Mailroom group, which accounts for the lion's share of FP revenues and employees. The second corporate group is Mailstream, which was established in November 2006 to offer new services to public and private organizations with large mail volume.

Two subsidiaries form the core of Mailstream, Iab-Internet Access GmbH and Freesort GmbH. Both companies provide hybrid mail handling services based in electronic and Internet technologies. FP has subsidiaries throughout the world, including the United States, the United Kingdom, Canada, the Netherlands, Austria, Italy, and Singapore. FP is the leading producer of franking equipment in Germany, with 45 percent of the total market. It has an 18 percent share of the European market and about 4 percent of the U.S. market where it has been active since about 1996.

INDUSTRY BACKGROUND AND COMPANY ORIGINS

The franking machine, also known as a postage meter, was first invented by Erich Komusin in Germany in 1921. Its development was hastened by the crippling period of inflation that struck Germany in 1923, during which prices changed literally by the hour. As a result, the German post office began issuing stamps without a printed value. When one was purchased, the postal clerk would write the then-current rate on the stamp by hand. The time was ripe for a machine that could print postage with various, easily changeable prices. Komusin's invention, unfortunately, was not adjustable—it could print only a specific, predetermined value denomination.

It was not until 1922 that a prototype of a franking machine that could change the value was developed by the Anker-Werke, a company in Bielefeld, Germany, which applied to the German government's postal administration, the Reichspostverwaltung, for authorization to produce and market it. Coincidentally, a Berlin firm, Bafra, was seeking certification for a similar postage meter that it had developed as a counterpart to a letter-sealing machine that it already had on the market.

The German postal authorities hesitated to authorize a single company to produce and sell the new franking machines. Anker and Bafra were forced to work out an agreement to produce and market postage meters jointly, and in July 1923 a new company was founded, Postfreistempler GmbH, Bielefeld—the name is loosely translatable as Postal Franker—by three firms, Anker, Bafra, and Uhrenfabrik Furtwängler, a clock and watch maker that would bow out of Postfreistempler just four years later.

Postfreistempler put two postage meters into production, presumably the two machines that Anker and Bafra had each developed on their own earlier. The Francotyp A was produced at Anker's facilities in Bielefeld, and the Francotyp B was manufactured in Bafra's factory in Berlin. Two years after its founding Postfreistempler GmbH took the name of its two products, Francotyp. By 1925, realizing the cost savings that franking machines offered, Germany's largest companies, including publishers Mosse and Ulstein, and manufacturers Siemens and AEG, had begun using Francotyp postage meters. In addition, Francotyp's innovative "value strip" system for calculating postage was extremely popular with customers. It enabled users to add postage to the franker themselves, and hence it was no longer necessary to take the heavy meter to the post office have it added.

COUNTRYWIDE EXPANSION

By 1927, Francotyp had customers throughout the young German republic and it set its sights on foreign markets in Europe. It was already selling its equipment in Austria and Belgium. Early on it became evident that selling postage meters abroad possessed an inherent difficulty that most other products did not have: Before it could market a franking machine in another country, the equipment first had to be submitted for testing and approval to national postal authorities. Francotyp was often also required to establish a domestic branch office in countries targeted for exports. Fortunately, Anker-Werke had been doing export business for some years and had already established branches abroad. Francotyp used these branches to establish its foreign contracts more quickly. One of the first export deals the firm acquired of was the sale of 12 postal meters to the National Bank of Russia.

By the end of the 1920s Francotyp had become Europe's leading producer of franking machines. One reason was its technical innovations. In 1929, for example, it introduced the Model C, a compact, hand-operated postage meter that was ideal for smaller businesses. One year later it brought out the first electrical franker, the Model Cm. By 1930, according to official statistics, there were more than 30,000 postage meters in use in Germany, and most of them had been made by Francotyp. There were other companies, however, and competition was sometimes cutthroat. In 1931 Francotyp won a suit for patent violation against Erich Komusin, who had invented the first postage meter. As a result Francotyp took over all of Komusin's maintenance and repair contracts.

A new company entered the market in Germany in 1934. Telefonbau- und Normalzeit (T&N), working with Erich Komusin, began producing and selling the Komusina, a franking machine that could print the meter tag, cut and moisten it, stick it on the envelope, and cancel it. T&N founded a company, Freistempler GmbH, in 1938 to take over its postage meter production. At the time there were five German-made postage meters being sold in Germany, four made by Francotyp, and the Komusina. Within a year, however, Freistempler had developed a revolutionary new product, the Postalia D2, the smallest postage meter in the world, with a correspondingly low price. Attempts were made to market it as the Volksfreistempler—the people's postage meter, reminiscent of the Volkswagen that Adolf Hitler had ordered into production around the same time in Germany. The D2 would not really take off until the 1950s, however, but then in a big way; by 1991, when it went out of production, more than a half million had been sold.

WORLD WAR II AND ITS AFTERMATH

The years of World War II were difficult for both Francotyp and Freistempler. The former was required by the Nazi government to change its production lines over for the manufacture of goods for the war. Freistempler had to transfer its production D2 lines to sites in France. When the war had ended, many of the facilities of both Francotyp and Freistempler had been either destroyed or

KEY DATES

1923: Postfreistempler GmbH, Bielefeld is founded.

1925: Postfreistempler is renamed Francotyp GmbH.

1929: Francotyp hand-operated machine Model C is introduced.

1938: Freistempler GmbH is founded by Telefon- und Normalzeit (T&N); Freistempler transfers its D2 production to France.

1949: Production of Francotyp Model Cc is launched.

1960: Freistempler becomes the first foreign manufacturer of postage meters to be certified by the U.S. Post Office.

1969: Anker-Werke acquires Freistempler GmbH shares held by T&N.

1972: Francotyp GmbH, Bafra Maschinen GmbH, and Okafold Briefkuviertermaschinen GmbH merge to form Francotyp GmbH.

1973: Freistempler GmbH is renamed Postalia GmbH.

1977: Bergmann AG acquires both Francotyp GmbH and Postalia GmbH.

1983: Holding company Francotyp-Postalia GmbH, Berlin/Offenbach is founded.

1989: Acquisition of Francotyp-Postalia by Gebr. Röchling KG of Mannheim.

1990: The first completely electronic franking machine with thermotransfer printing is introduced.

1991: Company and brands are reorganized under banner FP, Francotyp-Postalia.

1994: Production, R&D and company administration in Germany are centralized in Birkenwerder near Berlin.

1995: Company is acquired by Quadriga Capital.

1996: Company is reorganized as Francotyp-Postalia AG & Co.

1997: FP-Direkt is founded.

2006: Company goes public.

badly damaged in air raids and artillery bombardments, or dismantled and confiscated by the Allied occupation forces. The Allies banned postage meters altogether from the end of the war in May 1945 until the end of the following July. They were finally permitted again on the condition that the swastika and all other signs of the Nazi regime had been completely removed from the meter's imprint.

Production was resumed in the first postwar years, but very slowly and using mainly leftover parts. At the start of the 1950s, however, both Francotyp and Freistempler reasserted themselves as leaders in their market. In 1949 Francotyp's solid research and development work began paying dividends once again. It brought the Francotyp Cc onto the market, a desktop-sized postage meter that was a hit with customers, eventually selling more than 100,000 units. In the meantime Freistempler was making advances of its own. In 1950 it put its Postalia D2 franker back into production. The new model was powered by an electric motor and featured a modular component system. The 1960s witnessed similar advances in both firms. In 1960 Francotyp launched another new product, the A 9000, a fully automated postage metering system designed for the needs of large firms. That same year, Postalia became the first foreign postage meter to be certified by the U.S. Post Office. Three years later it celebrated its 25th anniversary and could look back on the remarkable progress it had made since the end of the war. Between 1949 and 1963 it had built a base of 50 foreign customers. During the previous decade Postalia's revenues had increased by 700 percent.

The 1970s were a period of radical structural reorganization at both Francotyp and Freistempler, that would eventually lead to their merger. In 1969 Anker-Werke acquired Freistempler from T&N, with the result that Anker (one of the major shareholders in Francotyp) was producing and distributing both the Francotyp and Postalia postage meters. However, under Anker the two companies remained separate and their product lines were marketed and sold completely independently of one another. Meanwhile big changes were in progress at Francotyp. It had been working closely with Okafold Briefkuvertiermaschinen GmbH, a firm that produced an office mail system that inserted letters in envelopes and sealed them. In 1971 Francotyp introduced the Cm 1000, a high-performance franking machine that could be integrated as a component of Okafold's mail management systems.

One year later, Francotyp, Okafold, and Bafra Maschinen GmbH merged their operations into a single company named Francotyp. Six years later Bergmann AG, a member of the Siemens group of companies, acquired both Francotyp and Postalia—as Freistempler had been known since 1973—and the two firms were placed in a new holding company called Francotyp-Postalia GmbH, Berlin/Offenbach.

NEW OWNERSHIP AND CONSOLIDATION

In 1989 Bergmann was itself purchased, and ownership of Francotyp-Postalia passed into the hands of Gebr. Röchling KG, Mannheim, a manufacturer of plastics with $6.1 billion in annual revenues and one of Germany's 50 largest companies. In 1991 the company created a uniform Francotyp-Postalia FP brand, and Francotyp GmbH and Postalia GmbH formally merged in 1993. That same year all company facilities in Offenbach and Berlin were relocated to a single, newly built, central location in Birkenwerder, a suburb of Berlin. The company was converted to an *Aktiengesellschaft*, a share company, in 1996.

The mid-1990s were a period of sudden financial growth for Francotyp-Postalia, thanks largely to a bonanza created by the German government. In summer 1993, nearly three years after the country had been reunified, the German Post Office announced the introduction of a brand-new system of standardized postal codes for the entire country. Owners of postage meters (in Germany postage meters are almost always sold rather than leased to customers) were notified that their meters had to be able to print the new codes as well as other new information no later than January 1, 1997. After that date, post offices would refuse to accept metered mail that did not conform to the new standards.

Postal customers protested so vociferously that postal authorities pushed back the deadline by a year and a half. But FP called the new regulations "a gift from heaven." Some 65 percent of the firm's domestic German customers (and FP controlled almost 70 percent of the entire German market for postage meters) had Francotyp-Postalia retool equipment their meters to conform to the system. As a result, the firm reported all-time record revenue increases for its 1993 business year; when uncompleted orders were taken into account, it was an increase of some 48 percent to DEM 211 million.

To avert the downturn that was certain to occur after customers had modified their old franking systems, FP set its sights on strengthening its presence in foreign countries. A major step was taken in 1996 when FP launched its M-series of mailing equipment in the Untied States. It also expanded into new postal technologies. FP, together with Microsoft, Compaq, and AT&T Ventures, became partners as the company E-Stamps, which was developing electronic stamp technology that would enable customers to purchase stamps via the Internet and print them out themselves. In addition, FP bought shares in two firms that were developing secure printing technologies.

GOING PUBLIC

In the early 2000s, the gigantic Röchling conglomerate began experiencing financial difficulties and made a strategic decision to refocus its operations on core competencies, the production of high-quality, technical plastics. One result of that decision was that Francotyp-Postalia was put on the sales block. In April 2005 it was acquired for an undisclosed amount by Quadriga Capital, a German venture capital firm. One and a half years later, in November 2006, with assistance from the Commerzbank and the British securities firm Cazenove, plans were finalized for an initial public offering (IPO) of Francotyp-Postalia stock on the Frankfurt stock exchange. The IPO brought the company a net gain of approximately EUR 147 million.

FP used the funds to pay for the acquisition of two German technology firms, Iab of Berlin and Freesort of Dusseldorf, for EUR 7.5 million and EUR 20 million, respectively. The acquisitions signaled FP's entrance into the area of so-called hybrid mail. In this type of system, companies whose business is mail intensive, for example, banking or insurance, outsource the administration of their mail processing to a contractor such as Iab. Iab then sends the mail electronically to another contractor, in this case Freesort, which prints mail and inserts it into envelopes, then meters and sorts it. FP did not offer its shareholders a dividend in 2007, informing them it intended to reinvest all profits in the company operations. It also told stockholders, however, that it anticipated revenue growth of approximately 10 percent in the coming fiscal year.

Gerald E. Brennan

PRINCIPAL SUBSIDIARIES

FP-Konzern; Francotyp-Postalia GmbH; Francotyp-Postalia Vertrieb und Service; FP Direkt Vertriebs GmbH; FP International GmbH; FP Hanse GmbH; Iab—Internet Access GmbH (51.1%); Freesort GmbH; Francotyp-Postalia N.V. (Belgium; 99.97%); Francotyp-Postalia (Österreich) Ges.m.b.H. (Austria); Ruys Handelsverenigung B.V. (Netherlands); Italiana Audion s.r.l.; Francotyp-Postalia Ltd. (United Kingdom); Francotyp-Postalia Inc. (United States); Francotyp-Postalia Canada Inc.; FP/GPS Assembly Pte. Ltd. Singapore (55%).

PRINCIPAL DIVISIONS

Mailroom; Mailstream.

PRINCIPAL COMPETITORS

Pitney Bowes Inc.; Neopost S.A.; Hasler, Inc.

FURTHER READING

"Francotyp-Postalia erfreut Altaktionäre," *Börsen-Zeitung,* November 16, 2006, p. 10.

"Francotyp Postalia erreicht Rekordergebnis," *Frankfurter Allgemeine Zeitung,* May 17, 1994, p. 22.

"Francotyp-Postalia wieder auf Wachstumskurs," *Frankfurter Allgemeine Zeitung,* September 3, 1998, p. 24.

"Francotyp-Postalia will zurück zu den Wurzeln," *Welt am Sonntag,* December 29, 2002.

Geatern. Heute. Morgen, Birkenwerder: Francotyp-Postalia AG & Co, 1998.

"Geglückter Börsenstart für Francotyp-Postalia," *Frankfurter Allgemeine Zeitung,* December 1, 2006, p. 23.

Gericke, Ulli, "Francotyp addressiert höhere Marge," *Börsen-Zeitung,* February 17, 2007, p. 13.

Himmelbauer, Leo, "Quadriga Capital kauft Francotyp-Gruppe," *Wirtschaftsblatt,* March 10, 2005, p. 17.

"Neue Postleitzahlen waren 1993 'ein Geschenk des Himmels,'" *Frankfurter Allgemeine Zeitung,* December 9, 1993, p. 23.

"Postalia-Greenshoe findet Interessenten," *Börsen-Zeitung,* December 30, 2006, p. 15.

Frisch's Restaurants, Inc.

2800 Gilbert Avenue
Cincinnati, Ohio 45206-1206
U.S.A.
Telephone: (513) 961-2660
Fax: (513) 559-5160
Web site: http://www.frischs.com

Public Company
Incorporated: 1947
Employees: 9,000
Sales: $289.93 million (2007)
Stock Exchanges: American
Ticker Symbol: FRS
NAIC: 722110 Full-Service Restaurants; 722212 Cafeterias

■ ■ ■

Frisch's Restaurants, Inc., an Ohio corporation engaged in the foodservice business, is probably best known for its midwestern chain of Frisch's Big Boy restaurants. Frisch's operates a total of 87 family-style restaurants—in Ohio, Kentucky, and Indiana—under the Big Boy name, while another 28 are licensed to outside operators. The company also operates 34 Golden Corral grill buffet restaurants and plans to expand that chain. In 2007, CEO Craig Maier was at the helm of the company, while his sister Karen Maier served as vice-president of marketing. After launching a restructuring in the late 1990s, Frisch's sold many of its noncore holdings, such as a horse farm, a stake in the Cincinnati Reds, and a couple of hotels.

EARLY 20TH-CENTURY BEGINNINGS

The history of Frisch's Restaurants may be traced to 1905, when Samuel Frisch opened a small restaurant on Freeman Avenue in Cincinnati, Ohio. The venture lasted only five years; when Frisch was earning just enough money to support his growing family, in 1910, he was also ready to find something more profitable. Frisch moved his wife and ten children to the Cincinnati suburb of Norwood to begin a new career in the grocery business. However, he soon returned to the service side of the food industry, opening a café in Norwood. Business was good, and by 1915 Frisch was ready to try a larger operation.

Frisch constructed a new restaurant in Norwood, known as Frisch's Stag Lunch, and this became one of the town's most popular gathering places. By the early 1920s, Frisch's Stag Lunch had moved into a larger building, and Frisch had been joined in the business by three sons, Dave, Irving, and Reuben. Sam Frisch died in 1923, and his son Dave, then only 20 years old, took over the restaurant. The Frisch brothers would continue to work together at Frisch's Stag Lunch for several years.

DAVE FRISCH VENTURES OUT

In 1932, Dave Frisch sold his interest in the Stag Lunch to his brothers and opened his own restaurant, Frisch's Café, also in Norwood. The new venture was quickly successful, garnering a loyal customer base, particularly among the local autoworkers who lunched there. Soon Frisch opened another location. However, in the aftermath of the Great Depression, he was forced into bankruptcy and closed both restaurants in 1938.

Fortunately, Frisch soon received some much-needed moral and financial support in the form of investor Fred Cornuelle, a local businessman. With Cornuelle's backing, Frisch again opened a restaurant in Norwood called the Mainliner, one of the first year-round drive-in restaurants in the Cincinnati area. The Mainliner was so successful that Frisch and Cornuelle were able to construct a second Frisch's restaurant in 1944. Located in Cincinnati, the new restaurant was designed to recall the historic Mt. Vernon home of George Washington.

At an industry convention in California in 1946, Frisch met Bob Wian, who introduced Frisch to the Big Boy, a double-decked hamburger made of two thin patties that cooked faster than one larger patty. Frisch secured Wian's permission to adopt the concept and began offering the Big Boy at his restaurant in Cincinnati. However, he personalized the sandwich by dressing it with a specially formulated tartar sauce rather than the Thousand Island sauce that Wian used. The recipe was unique to Frisch's and became a big hit with Frisch's customers.

Shortly after their initial meeting, Frisch and Wian entered a franchise agreement under which Frisch would become the exclusive franchiser of Frisch's Big Boy restaurants in Ohio, Kentucky, Indiana, and Florida. Frisch incorporated his business in 1947 and the following year opened his first Big Boy restaurant in Cincinnati. During the same time period, Frisch's new son-in-law, Jack Maier, began working at the Mainliner.

The double-decked Big Boy hamburgers, served at drive-in restaurants, were an instant hit. Over the following three decades Frisch's business grew steadily. The Big Boy concept was becoming immensely popular throughout the Midwest and South, with other restaurateurs establishing Big Boy chains of their own and generations growing up recognizing the front entrance statue of the chubby Big Boy character with jet-black hair and checkered overalls. New Frisch's Big Boy restaurants were constructed and franchised at a rapid pace.

PUBLIC IN 1960

Frisch's went public in 1960, its common stock selling for $12.75 a share on the over-the-counter market. By 1961, the Frisch's chain had expanded to 140 locations, including franchises, which offered Big Boy hamburgers, Brawny Lad steak sandwiches, and Buddie Boy ham and cheese sandwiches. In 1966, Frisch opened a more formal restaurant in the Cincinnati area, called Annette's, after his wife.

In the late 1960s, the Big Boy concept was acquired by the Marriott Corporation, and most of its franchisers enjoyed remarkable growth. Another industry-wide trend among the Big Boy owners was to enter the hotel business as a complement to the restaurant holdings. In 1967, Frisch's entered the lodging business with the opening of Quality Hotel Central in Norwood, across the street from the original Stag Lunch. Five years later, a second hotel was built in Covington, Kentucky, featuring a revolving restaurant on its top floor.

Dave Frisch died in 1970 leaving behind a company with $30 million in annual sales. Jack Maier, who had by this time had been with the company for 23 years and had worked his way up to become executive vice-president, was named president and chairman.

CONTINUED GROWTH

Under Maier, the company experienced another period of remarkable growth, expanding its Big Boy holdings to Texas, Oklahoma, and Kansas through the purchase of the Kip's Big Boy franchise. Frisch's also entered the fast-foods market during this time, adding another Marriot Corp. franchise to its holdings, Roy Rogers Roast Beef restaurants. With the economic slowdown of the early 1980s and subsequent high interest rates, Frisch slowed its expansion plans somewhat. However, by 1986, the company owned 105 Big Boy restaurants, 19 Roy Rogers restaurants, and three Prime 'n Wine restaurants. In 1987, it acquired the rights to develop Big Boys in parts of Georgia and Tennessee in addition to the rights already secured in Florida, Indiana, Kentucky, Ohio, Oklahoma, Texas, and parts of Kansas.

In 1989, Craig Maier was tapped as president and CEO of Frisch's. His father remained chairman until his death in 2005. The younger Maier had started with the business as a manager trainee at a restaurant; he had gone on to own and operate a franchise in New

KEY DATES

1905: Samuel Frisch opens a restaurant in Cincinnati.

1921: Frisch manages a chain of three restaurants and his sons join the business.

1946: Dave Frisch is introduced to the Big Boy double-decked hamburger.

1947: Frisch's Restaurants is incorporated.

1960: Company goes public.

1970: Upon Dave Frisch's death, son-in-law Jack Maier is named president and chairman.

1989: Jack Maier's son, Craig, is named president and CEO.

1998: Company begins divesting its noncore assets in order to refocus on restaurants, begins operating Golden Corral locations under license.

2006: Sales reach a record $292 million.

Richmond, Ohio, before being named a divisional vice-president for both Frisch's and Kip's Big Boys. During the period from 1989 to 1991, under Craig Maier's leadership, Frisch's sold or reorganized company-operated restaurants in Florida, Oklahoma, and Texas, preferring to focus on Ohio and neighboring states for restaurant expansion. Moreover, Frisch's began phasing out its fast-food holdings. In 1990, when Marriott Corp. sold Roy Rogers to Hardee's, all but one of Frisch's Cincinnati area Roy Rogers outlets was converted to a Hardee's restaurant. By midyear, Frisch's had reduced its Hardee's restaurants to seven. The company continued to operate 101 Big Boys, two Prime 'n Wine restaurants, and two Quality Hotels.

As it reduced some foodservice holdings, Frisch's also began to diversify, acquiring stakes in a wide variety of businesses, including a horse farm in Kentucky and a stake in the major league baseball team the Cincinnati Reds. In the meantime, critics alleged, the company took on a debt burden and neglected its restaurants.

RESTRUCTURING

Between 1993 and 1996, Frisch's opened 30 restaurants in Ohio and in neighboring states. During this time, however, the company experienced a huge decline in net income, which management attributed to increased labor costs and overly rapid growth.

In 1996, two nonmanagement investors, calling themselves Wolverine Partners, launched a proxy fight to gain themselves and two other nonmanagement investors seats on the board of directors of Frisch's Family Restaurants. Their goal, according to industry analysts, was to break the hold of the Maier family on the chain, which they claimed was dragging down the company's profitability. In the ensuing battle, stock prices dropped below their 1960 initial public offering price, and Jerry L. Ruyan and Barry S. Nussbaum, together owning an 8 percent stake in the chain, drafted a management plan that required Frisch's to pay off its debts through the sale of its nonrestaurant assets. The Wolverine Partners claimed that the immediate sale of those holdings could generate $20 million to $30 million, which could then be used to eliminate Frisch's long-term debt (approximately $20 million), invest in restaurant improvements, and buy back stock. Wolverine also proposed revamping the company's board of directors, giving the majority voice to nonmanagement directors and requiring the entire eight-member board to be reelected annually.

Frisch's management maintained that many of the changes proposed by Wolverine Partners had already been considered by the company. Restaurant improvements, a computer system in particular, had been slow in development; the Cincinnati Reds investment was once profitable and could become so again; the farm and hotels operated at a profit and would be sold upon receipt of a suitable offer. Management was also not receptive to the board restructuring recommendations. Moreover, the Maier family alleged, the goal of the Wolverine Partners was only to realize short-term gains on their investments.

Frisch's management firmly held that the loss of profitability over the previous few years was due to overzealous expansion in a competitive environment. The company had opened 30 restaurants, primarily in Indianapolis and in Columbus, Ohio, which overextended their management resources. Frisch's also pointed out that it had indeed been receptive to selling its peripheral assets, and had done so with the Hardee's and Prime 'n Wine chains.

Nussbaum and Ruyan were elected to Frisch's board in 1996 for two-year positions (although shareholders would vote to replace them at the company's 1998 annual meeting). During their tenure, the company sold its horse farm, 15 underperforming Big Boy restaurants in Indiana, and its 6.6 percent share of the Cincinnati Reds baseball team. Moreover, Frisch's reached a development agreement with Golden Corral Restaurants to operate more than 20 of the casual steak-buffet restaurants in Cincinnati, Dayton, and Louisville. Golden Corral gave Frisch's the opportunity to expand without extending outside its geographic parameters.

During this time, Frisch's also began installing point-of-sale computer systems for its 88 Big Boy restaurants, thereby finally introducing computerized workstations at the drive-thru windows, carryout counters, and dining areas. At the end of 1999, the company's board of directors announced the approval of an additional repurchase of up to 200,000 shares of its common shares. This approval supplemented a previous authorization in 1998 to purchase up to 500,000 shares.

Frisch's performed strongly as it closed out the 1990s, with reports of record sales. On March 14, 2000, Frisch's announced that its board had voted to divest the company's Clarion Riverview Hotel and the Quality Central Hotel. This decision, Maier asserted, was consistent with earlier declarations made by the company to maintain focus on Frisch's core restaurant business.

RENEWED FOCUS ON RESTAURANTS

The two money-losing hotels were sold within several years. Radisson acquired the riverfront hotel for $12 million in November 2000. One of Frisch's managers bought the Quality Hotel for about $4 million a few months later. Frisch's thus began the new century with a streamlined operation.

Management was also more or less free of the annoying burden of its two dissident shareholders according to some analysts. By January 2000 they had sold most of their shares back to the company. Within months, the company's share price began a steady climb from about $10 that would see it triple within a few years.

Frisch's was able to tidy up another business issue, acquiring ownership of the Big Boy trademark rights it had been leasing. These were first acquired by Liggett Restaurant Enterprises following the bankruptcy of Elias Bros. Restaurants Inc. Liggett sold the rights to Ohio, Kentucky, Indiana, and some of Tennessee Big Boy's outlets to Frisch's while buying Frisch's rights to the name in other states (Florida, Kansas, Texas and Oklahoma). The deal assured Frisch's future access to the Big Boy name in its core areas.

Frisch's had expected the most growth from its Golden Corral concept, but this proved elusive. In 2001 it committed to add 41 new restaurants over the next six years. (One of these had to be torn down and rebuilt before it could open, due to structural problems from building on spongy soil.) Nevertheless, same-store sales stalled at Golden Corral while increasing slightly at the Big Boy sites. The stagnant steak-house growth was attributed to intense competitions due to the dense spacing of the restaurants.

The company had its reasons for banking on Golden Corral, for which it was the largest franchisee. Golden Corral restaurants each did an average of $3 million a year, about one-third more than the Big Boy locations. In 2006 the company signed another franchising deal, bringing the total of planned Golden Corral locations to 61 by 2011. There were 26 Golden Corrals by mid-2004, and 89 company-owned Big Boy restaurants.

Frisch's made minor changes to the Big Boy chain. It experimented with smaller stores for secondary markets. Some underperforming restaurants were closed. The end of the last downtown Cincinnati location, a popular gathering place for nearly 20 years, made front page news. The downtown restaurants were less profitable, however, since they did not have space for the lunch and breakfast buffets that had proved so popular at other locations.

Freed from its unprofitable side ventures, Frisch's enjoyed several years of record financial performance. Sales exceeded $260 million in fiscal 2004 as profits hit the $10 million mark. However, only a life insurance payout related to the death of chairman Jack Maier kept net income from slipping the next year. Daniel Geeding, formerly dean of the business school at Xavier University, was named chairman following Maier's death in February 2005.

The company noted it had been profitable since going public in 1960 and boasted a string of more than 160 consecutive quarterly dividend payments. Long undervalued by Wall Street due to the company's relatively small size and small number of investors, Frisch's shares made an impressive climb over several years, rising to $38 in 2007. Revenues slipped a bit to about $290 million while profits were flat at about $9 million. There were some increases in food costs as well as a jump in the minimum wage in Ohio. By this time, it was clear the Golden Corral concept did not have the Midas touch management expected. Same-store sales there had been on the way down for three years, while the Big Boy sites managed to hold relatively steady.

Ana Garcia Schulz
Updated, Frederick C. Ingram

PRINCIPAL SUBSIDIARIES

Frisch Kentucky LLC; Frisch Indiana, Inc.; Frisch Ohio, Inc.; Frisch Pennsylvania, Inc.; Frisch West Virginia, Inc.

PRINCIPAL OPERATING UNITS

Big Boy; Golden Corral.

PRINCIPAL COMPETITORS

Bob Evans Farms, Inc.; CBRL Group, Inc.; Perkins & Marie Callender's Inc.; The Steak n Shake Company; Ryan's Restaurant Group Inc.; Buffets, Inc.

FURTHER READING

Bohman, Jim, "Golden Corral Expanding," *Dayton Daily News,* December 1, 2001, p. 1E.

"CEO/Company Interview: Donald H. Walker; Frisch's Restaurants, Inc.," *Wall Street Transcript,* January 1, 2001.

Cook, Tony, "Frisch's Exits Downtown," *Cincinnati Post,* November 13, 2004, p. A1.

Coolidge, Alexander, "Frisch's to Open 21 More Golden Corrals," *Cincinnati Post,* July 26, 2004, p. B7.

———, "Frisch's Upbeat Despite Problems," *Cincinnati Post,* October 5, 2004, p. C6.

———, "Warning Signs," *Cincinnati Post,* July 30, 2005, p. B8.

Driehaus, Bob, "Frisch's Buys Rights to Big Boys," *Cincinnati Post,* January 10, 2001, p. 8B.

———, "Frisch's Predicts Profits; Expansion Planned for Restaurant Chain," *Cincinnati Post,* April 6, 2000, p. 8B.

———, "Frisch's Sells Hotel in Norwood," *Cincinnati Post,* May 15, 2001, p. 6B.

———, "Frisch's Strategy Pays Off in Profits," *Cincinnati Post,* July 16, 2001, p. 7B.

———, "Frisch's Will Sell Hotels, End Drain," *Cincinnati Post,* March 16, 2000, p. 6B.

"Ex-XU Dean Takes Reins at Frisch's," *Cincinnati Post,* March 17, 2005, p. 8B.

Fasig, Lisa Biank, "Big Boy Still Golden at Frisch's Meeting," *Business Courier of Cincinnati,* October 1, 2007.

———, "Diners, Shareholders Hunger for Frisch's but Wall St. Isn't Biting," *Business Courier of Cincinnati,* October 6, 2003.

———, "Frisch's Chairman Dies at Age 79," *Business Courier of Cincinnati,* February 4, 2005.

———, "Frisch's Serves Up Something Hot: Stock Price," *Business Courier of Cincinnati,* May 4, 2007.

———, "Frisch's Still Has Taste for Buffet Chain," *Business Courier of Cincinnati,* August 26, 2005.

Fisher, Mark, "Frisch's Big Boy; Frisch's Restaurant Gives Glimpse into Dayton's Delicious History," *Dayton Daily News,* June 29, 2007, Go! Sec., p. 27.

Frazier, Mya, "Frisch's Buys Critics' Stock," *Business Courier of Cincinnati,* January 17, 2000.

"Frisch's Buys Liggett Trademarks," *Dayton Business Journal,* January 9, 2001.

"Frisch's Restaurants, Inc.," *Cincinnati Business Courier,* September 7, 1987, p. 25.

Hamstra, Mark, "Frisch's Eyes Expansion, Inks Golden Corral Pact," *Nation's Restaurant News,* January 19, 1998, p.1.

———, "Investors Launch Proxy Fight at Frisch's Family," *Nation's Restaurant News,* September 30, 1996, p. 3.

Hayes, Jack, "Frisch's New Deal for Golden Corral Franchise Growth Sparks Race with Metro Corral Group," *Nation's Restaurant News,* August 9, 2004, pp. 4, 50.

———, "Profits Plus Reds' Stake Sale Puts Frisch's on 'Golden' Trail," *Nation's Restaurant News,* February 1, 1999, p. 11.

Lawley, Lauren, "Frisch's Hopes Riding High with Golden Corral," *Business Courier Serving Cincinnati–Northern Kentucky,* December 18, 1998, p. 30.

Littman, Margaret, "What's Your Fantasy, Big Boy?" *Chain Leader,* November 2000, pp. 30–31.

May, Lucy, "More Employees Having to Earn Pay Hikes Through Performance, Not Base Increases," *Business Courier Serving Cincinnati–Northern Kentucky,* November 24, 2006, pp. 1f.

Milstead, David, "Big Boy Faces Big Challenges," *Cincinnati Business Courier,* April 17, 1995, p. 1.

Monk, Dan, "Frisch's Banking Smaller Is Better with Big Boys," *Dayton Business Journal,* November 27, 2000.

———, "Frisch's: Some Assets for Sale," *Cincinnati Business Courier,* August 19, 1996, p.1.

Rosencrans, Joyce, "Old Recipe Kept Fresh at Frisch's," *Cincinnati Post,* November 22, 2006, p. B3.

Schaber, Greg, "Roy Rogers Restaurant Chain Ready to Ride Off into Sunset," *Cincinnati Business Courier,* August 5, 1991, p. 4.

Schor, Adam, "Frisch's New Strategy: Add New Stores, Franchise," *Cincinnati Business Courier,* September 7, 1987, p. 1.

Zuber, Amy, "Frisch's Seeks to Nix 2," *Nation's Restaurant News,* September 7, 1998, p. 1.

Furmanite Corporation

2435 North Central Expressway
Richardson, Texas 75080
U.S.A.
Telephone: (972) 699-4000
Fax: (972) 644-3524
Web site: http://www.furmanite.com

Public Company
Incorporated: 1953 as Kaneb Pipe Line Company
Employees: 1,647
Sales: $246.6 million (2006)
Stock Exchanges: New York
Ticker Symbol: FRM
NAIC: 236220 Commercial and Institutional Building
   Construction

■ ■ ■

Listed on the New York Stock Exchange and based in Richardson, Texas, Furmanite Corporation is a technical services company serving customers worldwide involved in offshore drilling, pipelines, refineries and power generation, chemical and petrochemical production, steel mills, automakers, pulp and paper mills, food and beverage processors, semiconductor manufacturers, pharmaceutical companies, and U.S. governmental agencies.

Furmanite offers a wide variety of industrial repair services, including concrete repair; leak detection and repair; leak sealing; valve care and repair; a full range of bolting services, from design to tightening; pipeline intervention; passive fire protection; and tank roof repair. The company also offers maintenance services to prevent pipeline leaks, maintain the integrity of pressurized systems, and maintain the effectiveness of valves. Furmanite's eCompliance service leverages the power of the Internet and wireless data collection technology to help companies ensure they comply with all government regulations. In addition, Furmanite offers a number of associated products, including absorbency products used to clean up leaks and spills, fire protection products, shims to prevent wave damage to offshore drilling components, jointing compound, tube plugs, and valve and flange covers. The company maintains 40 offices spread across five continents.

COMPANY ORIGINS: 1953

The history of the present-day Furmanite may be traced through that of the Kaneb Pipe Line Company in Houston, Texas, which was founded by Herbert E. Fisher. Born in Mobile, Alabama, in 1911, Fisher was raised in Tulsa, Oklahoma, and earned a degree from the University of Oklahoma in 1932, at which point he went to work for the Tulsa-based Stanolind Pipe Line Company. He then struck out on his own in 1951, establishing Pipe Line Technologists Inc., a Houston engineering company that would grow into a global business.

Two years later he launched his own pipeline, Kaneb, which started out with 250 miles of eight- and ten-inch pipe along the Kansas-Oklahoma border, stretching from Arkansas City and Wichita, Kansas, to Fairmont, Nebraska; hence, the company name was created by fusing "Ka" for Kansas and "neb" for Nebraska.

COMPANY PERSPECTIVES

Furmanite's single mission and business goal is to Maximize Asset Uptime for customers. Specifically, everything Furmanite does directly relates to keeping an asset up, productive and profitable; be it a pipeline, a plant, or personnel. Whether it's new product development or expansion into new markets, Furmanite is always focused on ways to improve customers' business, thereby creating and solidifying long-term business partnerships.

Kaneb soon expanded into Nebraska, Iowa, and North and South Dakota. Taken public Kaneb would gain a listing on the American Stock Exchange, and by the end of the 1960s the system spanned 1,250 miles, mostly concentrated in southeast Kansas where it was connected to eight refineries, and Oklahoma where it served another 14 refineries.

In the late 1960s Kaneb contracted with a Texas-based computer data management company, Agency Records Control, Inc. (ARC), to process its operating and financial data. The firm mostly provided record-keeping services to independent insurance agencies. After working with ARC for nearly three years, Kaneb acquired the company in July 1969, the first step in an effort to diversify the company beyond pipeline hauling.

A year later Kaneb added another special service to its portfolio: land clearing. In March 1970 it acquired a pair of North Carolina companies, Appalachian Contracting Co. and Phillips & Jordan, Inc., which provided land clearing and earth moving services for pipeline construction companies, electric utilities, telephone companies, and the Army Corps of Engineers. Kaneb's next step was to become involved in coal production and marketing, achieved through the acquisition of Stansbury & Co., Inc. Other coal companies were added in 1973 (Interstate Coal Co., Inc.; Leeco, Inc.; and Mountain Clay, Inc.) along with a number of coal leases. Also, in 1972, Fisher brought Pipe Line Technologists into the fold, and later in the decade Kaneb became involved in oil and gas exploration through the acquisition of Houston's Weaver Oil & Gas Corporation, and added offshore and land drill contracting services through the acquisition of Diamond M. Co. and Wels Drilling & Service, Inc.

With the contributions of these new businesses. Kaneb experienced a sharp rise in revenues in the early 1970s. Sales of $12 million in 1969 grew to more than $100 million in 1974, while net income during this time increased from $2.1 million to $12 million. During this period the company also changed its name to Kaneb Services, Inc., reflecting its expanded scope, and graduated from the American Stock Exchange to the New York Stock Exchange.

In the early 1980s Kaneb beefed up its coal and exploration businesses while also adding some uranium interests and acquiring a few savings and loan companies, including World Savings Association in 1980 and Parker Square Savings & Loans Association and Wharton County Savings & Loan Association in 1981. As a result of this extended acquisition spree, Kaneb was able to increase revenues to well over $500 million. It accumulated considerable debt, however, along the way. Servicing that debt began to take its toll on earnings, prompting management to divest some assets in order to lessen the burden.

In 1982 ARC was sold to the Fireman's Fund Insurance Companies for $52.5 million. Three years later a Canadian oil and gas subsidiary was sold for more than $2.2 million. Although Kaneb was unsuccessful in its bid to divest Diamond M. in early 1985, later in the year it was able to sell its coal operations to Transco Energy Company, fetching $234 million in cash while eliminating $7 million in debt. All told, Kaneb was able to reduce its debt by about $160 million, one-quarter of the total amount. Given that the energy sector was suffering from an international slump, the relief was greatly needed.

FISHER RETIRES: 1981

Herbert Fisher retired as Kaneb's chairman in 1981; he remained a director until his death four years later at the age of 74. The company's chief executive officer, James R. Whatley, took over the chairmanship as well. Kaneb also added a new position in 1981, chief operating officer, which was awarded to 49-year-old Michael D. Shoup, who later became president and CEO.

Shoup would become embroiled in a company controversy during his tenure. A lawsuit filed in 1986 by a terminated officer of the company, Roger C. Sims, charged the company with having him fired after he refused to certify fraudulent tax returns and failed to approve Shoup's and another senior vice-president's personal expenditures. Some of these expenses allegedly included improper use of the corporate jet, which Sims maintained the executives used on one occasion to fly to Dallas with their wives for the Cotton Bowl, and Shoup used on another occasion to fly to Austin to lobby officials about a personal financial matter.

After Kaneb hired a law firm to investigate Sims' charges, Shoup resigned. He then received a compensa-

KEY DATES

1953: Herbert Fisher founds Kaneb Pipe Line Company in Houston.
1969: Company begins to diversify.
1981: Fisher retires.
1986: John R. Barnes named CEO; headquarters moved to Dallas area.
1991: Furmanite plc is acquired.
2001: Pipeline assets spun off, company renamed Xanser Corporation.
2007: Name changed to Furmanite Corporation.

tion package valued at more than $550,000, sparking outrage at the company's annual shareholders meeting, which had been postponed once because of the matter. There were some calls for the entire board to resign and for the company to be sold. Much of the anger resulted from the difficult financial situation that Kaneb was facing due to falling oil and gas prices.

Whatley, who took over as CEO on an interim basis, tried to placate shareholders by pointing this out. According to the *Wall Street Journal,* he told them somewhat facetiously, "I think we could join together and request an audience with the king of Saudi (Arabia) and straighten these things out." Sims' suit made its way through the courts until December 1989 when he prevailed, and a jury awarded him $32.4 million in actual and punitive damages plus interest.

Kaneb's board did not step down, but it did bring in a new chief executive in October 1986, John R. Barnes, the former president of Stanton Oil Company and Dorchester Gas Corporation. During his four years at the helm at Dorchester, Barnes increased revenues to $1.5 billion, a major improvement over the $50 million the company generated when he joined it in 1976 as vice-president of corporate development.

TURNAROUND ATTEMPTS

Barnes quickly set himself to the task of turning around Kaneb, which barely had enough assets to satisfy creditors if it were liquidated. At first he and his new management team from Dallas lived out of suitcases in Houston for several months before relocating the company's headquarters to Richardson, Texas, near Dallas. His first step in the resurrection of Kaneb was to sell the offshore drilling units, followed by the divestiture of one-third of the company's interest in Kaneb Pipeline Partners Ltd., which housed the

company's pipeline assets, a move that garnered $100 million. He then merged the Kaneb Metering Corporation subsidiary with its chief rival, NDE Environmental Corporation, receiving $13 million in stock and a pair of seats on the NDE board. Moreover, Barnes declared a moratorium on dividends and debt payments in order to renegotiate the terms of the company's debt. As a result of these steps, he was able to eliminate about $500 million in debt.

With Kaneb's finances in much better shape and some cash at his disposal, Barnes looked for a new source of revenues. "I want a balanced portfolio of service businesses," he told the *Dallas Business Journal,* adding, "I don't believe in putting all the eggs in one basket no matter how good one is." In March 1991 he found a new basket, acquiring Furmanite plc for $66 million in cash and stock. Based in Kendal, England, Furmanite, a specialized industrial services company, produced nearly $100 million in annual sales.

The balance sheet showed steady improvement in the early 1990s, increasing from $176.7 million in 1992 to more than $212 million in 1995. Net income improved from a loss of $7.2 million in 1992 to $3.5 million in 1995. Furmanite was doing especially well. In 1996 the unit enjoyed a 31 percent increase in operating income due to internal expansion. Kaneb also increased its international service offering by forming an alliance from Framatome Technologies, Inc., subsidiary of France's Framatome S.A., which offered proprietary diagnostic technologies to industrial markets and was particularly well positioned to serve the Gulf Coast region. Revenues increased to $228.9 million in 1996 and net income grew to more than $6.5 million.

Furmanite's Asia-Pacific business was strengthened in 1997 by acquiring a licensee in Australia, but a downturn in that region's economy as well as in the United Kingdom soon provided Furmanite with difficult business conditions. Barnes efforts to spread the risk through diversity paid dividends, as Kaneb was able to shift the focus of its services operations to find alternate sources of revenue. As a result, the company was able to retain the financial wherewithal to take advantage of acquisition opportunities as the arose. In 1998 Kaneb's pipeline business was bolstered by the addition of terminals in Chicago, Vancouver, and Linden, New Jersey, as well as tankage at Savannah, Georgia, and Stockton, California.

Wall Street did not appreciate Kaneb's diversity, however, refusing to take into account the underlying value of the company's assets, at least in the opinion of management. Thus, in 2000 the company announced a plan to spin off the pipeline, terminals, and product marketing businesses as a new company, Kaneb Services.

The technology and technical services assets would remain but Kaneb Services would take a new name, Xanser Corporation, which would consist of Furmanite and an information technology service subsidiary called Xtria. These changes took effect in August 2001.

Following the split, Xanser struggled, mostly due to the performance of some of the information technology units. Furmanite, on the other hand, delivered excellent result. In 2001 revenues totaled $144.7 million, resulting in new income of $25.7 million. A year later, however, sales dipped to $131.4 million and the company reported a $47.5 million net loss. Sales improved to $135.7 million in 2003 but Xanser lost a further $13.1 million. The company returned to profitability in 2004 but whatever improvements exhibited by Xtria were short lived, as in 2005 the subsidiary turned in another poor performance to overshadow Furmanite's contribution. To grow Furmanite further, Xanser acquired Flowserve USA Inc. for $18.8 million. Not only did the Flowserve assets provide a good geographic fit, they added complementary business lines, including pressurized online repair services and general valve repair services.

Company revenues totaled $246.4 million in 2006, a significant improvement over the $153.9 million recorded the prior year. A net loss resulted in both years, $0.43 million in 2006 and $3.4 million in 2006. In 2007 Xtria's operations were combined with those of Furmanite. Because the company was operating as a single unit, the decision was made to scrap the Xanser name and to build upon that of Furmanite. Following shareholder approval, the company changed its name to Furmanite Corporation in May 2007.

Ed Dinger

PRINCIPAL SUBSIDIARIES

Furmanite Equipment Leasing Company LLC; Furmanite Worldwide, Inc.; Furmanite America Inc.; Xtria LLC.

PRINCIPAL COMPETITORS

Perini Corporation; Forest City Enterprises, Inc.; Matrix Service Company.

FURTHER READING

Campanella, Frank W., "Acquisitions Spur Swift Growth in Operations at Kaneb Pipe Line," *Barron's,* October 19, 1970, p. 29.

Crown, Judith, "Kaneb Services Moving Headquarters from Sugar Land to Dallas," *Houston Chronicle,* June 6, 1987.

Green, Wayne E., and Amy Dockser Marcus, "Fired Executive Gets Huge Jury Award," *Wall Street Journal,* December 5, 1989, p. 1.

Hill, Dee, "Kaneb Chief Revamps an Oil Industry Dinosaur," *Dallas Business Journal,* August 30, 1991, p. 1.

Hussey, Allan F., "Growing Stake in Coal Fuels Sharp Gains at Kaneb Services," *Barron's,* June 28, 1976, p. 29.

"Services Set for Herbert E. Fisher, 74," *Houston Chronicle,* June 28, 1985.

"Slimmed Down: Kaneb Services Sees Profits Again After Reshaping Its Business," *Barron's,* July 29, 1985, p. 39.

Solis, Dianna, "Kaneb Officers Face Hostile Questioning at Annual Meeting," *Wall Street Journal,* August 13, 1986, p. 1.

———, "Kaneb Services, Directors Are Sued by Major Holder," *Wall Street Journal,* May 8, 1986, p. 1.

"Transco to Acquire Kaneb Coal Unit for $238 Million," *Wall Street Journal,* May 23, 1985, p. 1.

Getrag Corporate Group

———■———

Hermann-Hagenmeyer-Strasse
Untergruppenbach, D-74199
Germany
Telephone: (49 7131) 644-40
Fax: (49 7131) 644-3805
Web site: http://www.getrag.de

Private Company
Incorporated: 1935 as Getriebe- und Zahnradfabrik Hermann Hagenmeyer AG
Employees: 10,500
Sales: EUR 2.4 billion ($3 billion) (2006)
NAIC: 336350 Motor Vehicle Transmission and Power Train Parts Manufacturing

■ ■ ■

Getrag Corporate Group is an independent supplier of manual and automatic transmissions and other components to large carmakers, such as BMW, Porsche, Ford, General Motors, Chrysler, Daimler, Volkswagen, Fiat, Ferrari, Renault, Nissan, Mitsubishi, and Toyota. Headquartered in Untergruppenbach, Germany, the company has additional manufacturing plants in Italy, Sweden, the United Kingdom, the United States, India, and China. In addition to transmissions, the company supplies spiral bevel gear sets, driveline systems, axles, and other components to various car manufacturers. Getrag also produces diesel engine timing gears and special transmissions for heavy commercial vehicle makers Cummins and Caterpillar in the United States and for the Indian market, and motorcycle transmissions for Harley-Davidson.

Getrag Ford Transmissions, a joint venture between Getrag and Ford Motor Company, accounts for roughly 45 percent of the group's total sales. Headquartered in Cologne, Getrag Ford Transmissions manufactures manual transmissions for Ford and Mazda in the United Kingdom and France, and manual transmissions, power take off units, rear drive units, and chassis parts for Ford and Volvo in Sweden. Getrag is privately owned and headed by Tobias Hagenmeyer, the son of Hermann Hagenmeyer, who founded the company in 1935.

INITIAL SUCCESS WITH MOTORCYCLE AND PASSENGER CAR TRANSMISSIONS

Before he became an entrepreneur, Hermann Hagenmeyer worked as a commercial clerk for Nürnberger Treuhand-Gesellschaft in Nuremberg, Germany. One day, riding the train from Stuttgart to Nuremberg, Hagenmeyer reviewed the financial statements of a company in Ludwigsburg, a manufacturer of transmissions for motorcycles a few miles north of Stuttgart. As he looked through the paperwork, Hagenmeyer suddenly felt an impulse to buy this company. His parents, successful entrepreneurs who owned a brewery in Schweinfurt, as well as his uncle, an industry insider and shareholder in FAG Kugelfischer, a Schweinfurt-based manufacturer of ball and roller bearings, tried in vain to talk Hagenmeyer out of his idea. The company did not have a particularly good reputation, nor did Hagenmeyer have any experience in the area of machining.

COMPANY PERSPECTIVES

Our success and the growth we have enjoyed over the last few years are founded on three basic values that go to the core of our being: Precision. Passion. Partnership. Precision not only cements the good reputation of our transmissions and drivetrain components, but is internalized in our global organization and sets the benchmark for the reliability that our customers have come to expect in every area. Passion is what drives each and every one of us to constantly strive for better solutions, push the boundaries of what is feasible and deliver genuine excitement to our customers and partners. Partnership stands for the high standards of our relationships with customers, suppliers and associates as well as the cooperation between the individual companies in our organization. For us, partnership means constantly enhancing and maintaining trustful and professional relationships both in what we think and in what we do. It is our goal to live out these basic values day by day with all the people in our organization.

Nonetheless, using money he had inherited, the 21-year-old went ahead and acquired Pfeiffer-Getriebewerke in Ludwigsburg, a company with some 80 employees.

Shortly after the acquisition he moved the company to new premises in Ludwigsburg and renamed it Getriebe- und Zahnradfabrik Hermann Hagenmeyer AG, or Getrag for short, on May 1, 1935. In the beginning, the company manufactured primarily moped and motorcycle transmissions, putting out almost 5,000 of them per year. Customers for the three-gear manual shift transmissions, delivered in a complete housing and ready to be flange-mounted to the engine, included many renowned motorcycle makers of the time, such as Victoria, DKW, NSU, and Zündapp. In addition, Getrag manufactured components such as gear wheels and gear shafts and, for a limited time, even food processors.

The early death of his first wife in 1940 was a tremendous loss for Hermann Hagenmeyer, who subsequently moved to Austria. That same year he took over a second gear wheel manufacturer in Vienna, which was renamed Zahnradwerk Hagenmeyer and employed up to 1,000 workers during World War II. After the war, however, the company was expropriated by the Austrian government, which compensated and rehabilitated Hagenmeyer years later.

In 1951 Getrag, which by then employed more than 800 people, was transformed into a limited liability company. In the 1950s the company expanded its product range to four-gear manual shift transmissions for automobiles. Due to Hermann Hagenmeyer's close connections to Ferdinand "Ferry" Porsche, the famous auto designer, and to other motorcycle and auto manufacturers, Getrag received orders from Hans Glas GmbH and from Bayerische Motoren Werke AG (BMW). Later in the decade, Getrag took on part of BMW's transmission manufacturing. In the mid-1950s Getrag added transmissions for heavy commercial vehicles and agricultural machinery to its line of products. As a result, during the postwar economic boom Getrag's sales rose by 250 percent, from about 10 million marks in 1951 to over 25 million marks in 1959. During the same period, the number of employees climbed to more than 1,100. Together with Hans Glas, Getrag developed its first automated four-gear inline transmission for the Glas 1700, a middle-class sedan. A masterpiece of engineering, the innovation was too far ahead of its time, however, and flopped commercially.

SUBSTANTIAL GROWTH IN GERMANY BEFORE AND AFTER OIL CRISIS

The 1960s and 1970s were a time of dynamic expansion for Getrag. By the late 1950s it became clear that the site in Ludwigsburg was not sufficient to contain the company's future growth. After weighing the pros and cons of different locations, a new production plant was built in Oberstenfeld, about 30 miles north of Stuttgart, in 1960. Starting out with 200 employees, the new subsidiary became a competence center for lathe jobs and for manufacturing parts for clutches. By the end of the decade the company's business volume had again outgrown its production capacity. Hermann Hagenmeyer acquired a new site in Rosenberg, a small town with roughly 2,000 inhabitants in northern Baden-Württemberg, where a third factory was set up in 1970. However, to ensure that he would find enough qualified employees, the company founder announced to the members of Rosenberg's city council that he was inviting everyone to a public meeting at a local restaurant, but that he would attend only if at least 100 people interested in working for his company signed up beforehand on a list for job interviews. The list was compiled and the first employees were hired on the spot. Getrag's Rosenberg plant carried out lathe jobs and manufactured parts for clutches. Over the following decades the factory's capacity was constantly expanded.

In 1974 Hagenmeyer took over PAV Präzisions-Apparatebau-Vaduz AG in Vaduz, Liechtenstein. For

KEY DATES

1935: Getriebe- und Zahnradfabrik Hermann Hagenmeyer AG is founded.

1951: Getrag is transformed into a limited liability company.

1960: The company builds a new production plant in Oberstenfeld.

1970: A third factory is set up in Rosenberg.

1975: Fortuna-Werke in Stuttgart and Audi NSU in Neuenstein are taken over.

1981: FZ Fränkisches Zahnradwerk in Bad Windsheim is founded.

1982: Tobias Hagenmeyer becomes Getrag president and CEO after his father's death.

1983: Getrag Gears of North America is established in the United States.

1991: The company opens a sales office in Nagoya, Japan.

1995: Engineering center Getrag Innovations GmbH is founded; Getrag Precision Gear Company is established in South Carolina.

1996: A production subsidiary is set up in Italy.

1999: The company starts a joint venture in India.

2000: Dana Corporation acquires a 30 percent stake in Getrag.

2001: Getrag and Ford set up the joint venture Getrag Ford Transmissions.

2004: Getrag All Wheel Drive AB is established in Sweden.

2007: A joint venture with Jiangling Motors Company Group begins operations in China; the Hagenmeyer family buys back the 30 percent stake in Getrag from Dana Corporation.

Hagenmeyer, who was deeply affected by his experiences during and after World War II, this was no coincidence, but a security measure. In case of an emergency, according to his plan, he and his family could escape to Liechtenstein, a neutral country in times of a war. However, the company was later sold.

While the world powers immersed themselves in a cold instead of a "hot" war, a different kind of crisis situation was the cause for major changes at Getrag in the mid-1970s. The first oil price shock of 1973 caused a deep recession in many parts of the world, and subsequently resulted in a severe crisis in the German automobile industry. Volkswagen announced the closure of several production plants and put some of them up for sale. Hagenmeyer received an offer to take over the transmission manufacturing plant of Volkswagen's struggling subsidiary Audi NSU. The same offer was made to Getrag's longtime customer BMW, which was pondering the idea of setting up its own production line for transmissions.

In hopes that Getrag could win Volkswagen as a new major customer, Hagenmeyer agreed to employ the plant's workforce of 468 with the same benefits they had received, although Volkswagen promised to purchase the plant's output only for two years. After the state and federal governments had agreed to support the transaction financially, the deal was finalized by December 1975 and the company renamed ZWN Zahnradwerk Neuenstein GmbH & Co.

Volkswagen did not immediately become a major new customer for Getrag. However, with orders from other automakers, ZWN enjoyed significant growth after the takeover by Getrag. In the beginning, the new subsidiary produced transmissions and steering mechanisms for the Audi 100; transmissions and rear axles for the VW LT; transmissions for the Audi-NSU RO 80; and replacement parts for Audi-NSU. In addition, the subsidiary assembled chassis and door components.

Also in 1975 Hagenmeyer acquired Fortuna-Werke in Stuttgart-Bad Cannstadt, a struggling manufacturer of spindles used by machine tool manufacturers and in milling, grinding, boring, and engraving operations, with 800 employees. Because of the additional business, Getrag's annual sales, which had tripled during the 1960s, doubled again between 1970 and 1975. By that time, roughly 1,900 employees worked at the company's various subsidiaries. In 1980, Getrag's growing business again reached the company's capacity limits, and Hagenmeyer decided to set up another subsidiary, FZ Fränkisches Zahnradwerk, for the production of transmission parts, in Bad Winsheim, Bavaria, in 1981. However, the company founder was not able to witness the opening of the brand-new plant in June 1982. He passed away two months beforehand.

INTERNATIONAL EXPANSION AND REORGANIZATION AFTER GENERATION CHANGE IN 1982

After the company founder's death, his son Tobias Hagenmeyer, who had joined the company as an authorized signatory in 1977, became Getrag's president and CEO in 1982. Under his leadership the company expanded abroad and underwent a reorganization process during the following two decades.

International expansion began in 1981 with the establishment of a joint venture, the Lamont and Getrag Gear Company, Inc., in Norristown, Pennsylvania, for the production of timing gears for Consolidated Diesel Co., BMW, and Ford. Two years later the company set up Getrag Gears of North America, an engineering subsidiary, in Sterling Heights, Michigan. In 1986 a new transmission plant was built in Newton, North Carolina, to which the production of timing gears was moved from Pennsylvania.

In the mid-1990s the company further strengthened its foothold in the United States when Getrag Precision Gear Company, a joint venture with U.S. heavy-duty vehicle manufacturer Cummins, was established in Charleston, South Carolina. Starting out with a staff of 126, the factory manufactured timing gears for heavy-duty diesel engines and special transmissions. In 1996 the plant became a fully owned Getrag subsidiary and continued to grow—as did Getrag's other ventures in the United States.

In the second half of the 1980s Getrag was reorganized under a new management team that consisted of four members, headed by Tobias Hagenmeyer. A new vision that defined the company's strategic focus was developed in 1989 and implemented in the 1990s. Based on a list of convictions that stressed open and respectful work relationships and emphasized the importance of mutual understanding and trust, it declared the company's aim of remaining an independent and innovative partner for the world's automakers. In 1994 an advisory board consisting of five members was put into place. Four years later ZWN Zahnradwerk Neuenstein and FZ Fränkisches Zahnradwerk were merged with Getrag Getriebe- und Zahnradfabrik Hermann Hagenmeyer GmbH & Cie.

Internationalization continued throughout the 1990s, when the company expanded its activities to southern and eastern Europe and to Asia. In 1991 Getrag opened a sales office in Nagoya, Japan, and eventually won Mazda Motor Corporation, Nissan Motor Co., and Toyota Motor Corporation as new customers. Five years later a production subsidiary was set up in Modugno, in southern Italy, after Getrag had secured a major long-term contract for the serial production of gearboxes for the Opel models Astra and Vectra from General Motors' European division. Additional contracts were won from MG Rover Group and Fiat S.p.A. which contributed to the substantial growth in sales generated by the new subsidiary. In 1999 Getrag together with the Indian firm Hi-Tech established a joint venture named Getrag HiTech Gears for the production of timing gears for heavy diesel engines in Bhiwadi, India. Along with Getrag's international growth, the company invested in additional production capacity in Germany. One of the larger projects was the serial mass production of the transmission-type 220 for longtime customer BMW. At the end of the 20th century, with nine production plants and three engineering centers, Getrag's workforce of about 4,700 generated approximately EUR 750 million in sales.

DYNAMIC GROWTH WITH NEW PARTNERS

The beginning of the new century also marked an important milestone for Getrag's future. Around that time Tobias Hagenmeyer was approached by Ford Motor Company, which was planning to outsource the manufacturing of manual transmissions for the European market and looking for a contractor to take on the task. This was an extraordinary opportunity for Getrag and in spring 2000 the partners agreed to set up a joint venture. The cash needed to finance the project came just in time from Dana Corporation, a major U.S. supplier of auto parts such as axle and chassis parts, with Ford being their biggest customer. The Toledo, Ohio–based company had shown an interest in acquiring Getrag, because the two companies' product lines complemented each other very well and because Dana was hoping to boost its own sluggish business in Europe. After it was clear that Getrag was not for sale, Dana agreed to form a strategic partnership with Getrag in 2000 based on an equity arrangement. A stake of 30 percent in Getrag GmbH & Cie KG was acquired by Dana. Dana also bought a 49 percent share in Getrag's U.S. subsidiary Getrag Corporation. Getrag in turn used the cash derived from the deal to finance the estimated EUR 225 million investment in the 50-50 joint venture with Ford. Getrag Ford Transmissions was established in February 2001, headquartered in Cologne, Germany, and managed by Getrag.

The deal with Ford, which included an initial annual production volume of 1.6 million manual gear boxes, catapulted Getrag into the first league of global auto suppliers. The new subsidiary with over 3,000 employees at manufacturing sites in Cologne; Bordeaux, France; and Halewood, United Kingdom, more than doubled Getrag's revenues almost immediately. Getrag's first major project with Dana went through in 2004 when the two companies established a joint venture with Volvo Car Corporation, the Swedish automaker owned by Ford, to establish a competence center for the growing all-wheel-drive market. After acquiring a 60 percent share in the all-wheel-drive assembly plant in Köping, Sweden, from Volvo, the venture was named Getrag All Wheel Drive AB and in its first year, with a staff of about 1,000 employees, supplied power takeoff units, front and rear axles, and other components worth $240 million to Volvo, Ford, and Fiat.

NEW TECHNOLOGIES PAVE THE WAY TO FURTHER EXPANSION

In the mid-1990s Getrag began to invest in additional engineering capacities. By that time, concerns about the connection between the progressing worldwide motorization and global climate change significantly gained in importance in the public arena. Nongovernmental organizations, politicians, and environmentally conscious consumers demanded automakers cut down carbon dioxide emissions and improve the fuel economy of their vehicles. This trend was an opportunity for suppliers to offer innovative solutions to carmakers. A new research and development subsidiary, Getrag Innovations GmbH, was founded in 1995 to develop innovative future technologies for vehicle transmissions. One of the new subsidiary's first projects was the development of turbo-transmissions for fuel cell drives. In 1996 Getrag pioneered sequential automated gearboxes for the BMW M3—another one of the company's early innovations. In 2002 Getrag founded Getrag Driveline Systems, an engineering and software development center for integrated transmission, safety, actuator, and all-wheel-drive (AWD) systems.

A major element of Getrag's strategic partnerships with its new U.S. partners, Dana and Ford, was the joint development of innovative future technologies and designs. In connection with the AWD joint venture with Dana and Volvo in Sweden, Getrag Ford Transmissions took the lead in the development of transmissions for new Volvo models by setting up Getrag Ford Transmissions Sweden AB in Göteborg. Another promising technology was automated manual transmissions (AMT), a new kind of automatic transmission based on manual transmission technologies. Traditionally, European car buyers preferred manual transmissions to the automatic gearboxes used in U.S. cars because of the lower price, better fuel economy, and faster acceleration. AMTs combined these advantages with the convenience of automated gear shifting and were hailed by industry forecasters as a promising growth market in Europe and Asia. In 2002 Getrag teamed up with Dana subsidiary FTE Automotive to work on several AMT projects.

Banking on the trend that a growing number of carmakers would outsource more of their parts manufacturing to outside suppliers, Getrag as well as Getrag Ford Transmissions invested heavily in additional research and development capacities for the development of new transmission technologies. In May 2002 Getrag opened a brand-new innovation center staffed with 450 engineers at its new headquarters in Unter-gruppenbach near Heilbronn, where the company had moved in 2001 to make space for additional production facilities in Ludwigsburg.

Only 17 months later Getrag Ford's Transmission Innovation Center with over 500 employees opened in Cologne. One of Getrag Ford's first major projects was the development of their own version of dual-clutch transmissions (DCTs), a technology pioneered by Volkswagen. DCTs consist of two clutches that alternate when gears are shifted. As a result, the power is not interrupted as it is in conventional manual transmissions, which quickens shifts, increases performance and saves fuel, between 6 and 10 percent compared with common automatic transmissions using torque converters. Drivers still have the choice to switch between automatic and manual operation.

In December 2004 Getrag Ford announced plans to set up a manufacturing subsidiary for DCTs in Kechnec, eastern Slovakia, near the Hungarian border. The new subsidiary, Getrag Ford Transmissions Slovakia, a EUR 300 million investment with a capacity of 200,000 units per year, was to begin operations in mid-2007. In 2006 Getrag and Dana began development work on electronically controlled driveline components for axles, transaxles, and power-transfer units. In the same year Getrag started a joint research and development project with German auto supplier Bosch for developing hybrid drive systems and electric drive systems with DCTs. Getrag engineers were also working on flexible modular hybrid drives, electric drives for fuel cell–powered vehicles.

REORGANIZATION AND NEW JOINT VENTURES IN CHINA AND THE UNITED STATES

To revive the company's slowing business in Germany and to secure future competitiveness and profitability, Getrag reorganized its German business operations. Focusing on core competencies, the company sold non-core operations. In 2003 Getrag sold Fortuna's spindle business, the last remaining division of Fortuna-Werke, to the Swiss Fischer AG. A few years later the company sold its synchronizer systems subsidiary with 400 employees in Oberstenfeld to Bavarian auto component supplier Hoerbiger Antriebstechnik Holding AG.

At the remaining locations in Germany Getrag streamlined capacities for component production, introduced a centralized logistics system, and planned to reduce its workforce by about 400. However, in 2005 Getrag changed its plans and decided to manufacture DCTs for the European market in Germany instead of Slovakia, after the company's German workers agreed to significant cuts on their future pay checks and benefits packages and to make Saturday a regular workday. In mid-2006 the company reorganized its worldwide business under the umbrella of Getrag Group, which together with Getrag Ford Transmissions, formed the Getrag Corporate Group. In March 2007 the company announced that the Hagenmeyer family bought back the 30 percent stake in Getrag from Dana Corporation after Dana had filed for Chapter 11 bankruptcy.

Despite the long-term threats of increasing steel prices and emerging low-cost competitors in Eastern Europe and Asia, Getrag's prospects seemed to look bright for the near future. In January 2007 the company signed a contract for a new joint venture with Jiangling Motors Company Group, a Chinese manufacturer of vans, light trucks, and sport-utility vehicles. With over 2,000 employees at three locations, Getrag (Jiangxi) Transmission Co. Ltd., in which Getrag held 67 percent, planned to put out half a million manual transmissions and three times as many transmission components a year for the Chinese market.

In September 2007, longtime member of Getrag's executive management board Dieter Schlenkermann predicted that by 2010 five automakers would build the company's new Powershift DCTs into their vehicles and that by 2014 Getrag would sell two million of them per year. One of Getrag's new customers was Chrysler LLC, which in mid-2007 started building a $530 million manufacturing plant for DCTs for minivans in Tipton County, Indiana. The joint venture, in which Getrag held 85 percent, was the first time Chrysler awarded a large contract for transmissions, which are considered core components, to an outside supplier. Production was scheduled to begin in June 2009—just in time to equip Chrysler's 2010 models.

Evelyn Hauser

PRINCIPAL SUBSIDIARIES

Getrag Getriebe- und Zahnradfabrik Hermann Hagenmeyer GmbH & Cie KG (Germany); Getrag Ford Transmissions GmbH (Germany; 50%); Getrag Driveline Systems GmbH; Getrag Corporation (United States); Getrag Transmissions Corporation (United States); Getrag Precision Gear Company LLC (United States); Getrag Innovations GmbH; Getrag S.p.A. (Italy); Getrag All Wheel Drive AB (Sweden); Getrag Ford Transmissions Sweden AB (Sweden); Getrag Ford Transmissions Slovakia s.r.o.; Getrag (Jiangxi) Transmission Co. Ltd. (China; 67%); Getrag HiTech Gears (India) Pvt. Ltd.

PRINCIPAL COMPETITORS

ZF Friedrichshafen AG; Graziano Transmissioni S.p.A.; CARRARO S.p.A.; Punch Powertrain NV; Prodrive; GKN plc; Valeo SA; Aisin Seiki Co., Ltd.; MAN-Trans L.L.C.

FURTHER READING

"AWD Partnership," *Ward's Auto World,* February 1, 2004.

"Chapter 5: Key Events. Getrag Company Profile," *just-auto.com,* December 2004.

Chew, Edmund, "Dana Counts on Link with Getrag," *Automotive News,* April 22, 2002, p. 17.

———, "Dana Suppliers Lead Work on Automated Transmissions," *Automotive News,* June 3, 2002, p. 24D.

———, "Getrag Plans to Double Gearbox Output," *Automotive News,* December 21, 1998, p. 24.

Gedenkfeier zum 20. Todestag von Hermann Hagenmeyer, Untergruppenbach, Germany: Getrag, 2002, 22 p.

"Germany: Bosch and Getrag Develop Hybrid Systems," *just-auto.com,* June 2, 2006.

Lewin, Tony, "Getrag's Dual-Clutch Transmissions to Take Off; Unit on 2008 Volvo Signals Wider Use on Ford Models," *Automotive News Europe,* September 17, 2007, p. 1.

Marsh, Peter, "Into Top Gear with Outsourcing: Manufacturing Partnerships Can Transform an Engineer's Competitive Position," *Financial Times,* May 20, 2002, p. 13.

Palmen, Nick, "Putting Power on the Road—GETRAG," *Automotive Industries,* May 2005, p. 18.

"US: Dana and Getrag to Collaborate on Driveline Components," *just-auto.com,* January 12, 2006.

Wernle, Bradford, "Chrysler Bets Big on Dual-Clutch Transmissions," *Automotive News,* July 2, 2007, p. 37.

———, "Ford, Getrag Create JV in Manual Transmissions," *Automotive News Europe,* February 12, 2001, p. 17.

———, "Ford Joins the Shift to Dual-Clutch Gearboxes," *Automotive News Europe,* September 5, 2005, p. 1.

"World Leading Transmission Producer Sets up Joint Venture in China," *Xinhua Economic News,* January 16, 2006.

Wrigley, Al, "Ford or Chrysler May Get Getrag Transmission," *American Metal Market,* January 30, 1984, p. 8.

GraceKennedy Ltd.

—■—

P.O. Box 86
73 Harbour Street
Kingston,
Jamaica
Telephone: (876) 922 3440 9
Fax: (876) 948 3073
Web site: http://www.gracekennedy.com

Public Company
Incorporated: 1922 as Grace, Kennedy and Company
Employees: 1,672
Sales: JMD 36.09 billion ($523 million) (2006)
Stock Exchanges: Jamaica Barbados Trinidad & Tobago
Ticker Symbol: GKC
NAIC: 311422 Specialty Canning; 524210 Insurance Agencies and Brokerages; 551112 Offices of Other Holding Companies

■ ■ ■

GraceKennedy Ltd. is one of Jamaica's largest and most diversified companies, with holdings spanning the food processing and canning, supermarket and other retail sectors, and banking and insurance industries. Kingston-based GraceKennedy is structured into two primary divisions: GK Foods and GK Investments.

GK Foods represents the company's food processing and canning operations, with a range of more than 75 products, including basic foods, as well as prepared foods such as ketchup and other sauces, cereals and the like, under the Grace brand. GK Foods also oversees the company's chain of Hi-Lo supermarkets, as well as the company's international trade subsidiaries throughout the Caribbean and in the United States, Canada, and the United Kingdom. In 2006, the company acquired its first international production unit, WT Foods, an ethnic foods producer based in the United Kingdom, as part of its goal of establishing itself as a globally operating company by 2020.

Helping to finance that strategy is GraceKennedy's GK Investments wing. This division represents the company's operations in banking, finance, and insurance, through subsidiaries including Allied Insurance Brokers Ltd., a general insurance provider; First Global banking, financial services, and insurance group; GraceKennedy Remittance Services, which serves as a Western Union agent in Jamaica and elsewhere in the Caribbean; and the company's 30 percent stake in the Trident Insurance group, acquired in 2007. GK Investments also includes Hardware & Lumber Ltd., one of Jamaica's largest retail hardware chains; a Nissan car dealership; and a subsidiary providing catering to airplanes. GraceKennedy is listed on the Jamaica, Barbados, and Trinidad & Tobago stock exchanges and is led by Chairman and CEO Douglas Orane. In 2006, GraceKennedy posted revenues of more than JMD 36 billion ($523 million).

W.R. GRACE OFFSHOOT IN 1922

GraceKennedy stemmed from the small Jamaican outpost of W.R. Grace & Company, serving as the U.S. giant's import office in Kingston, with branches in Montego Bay and St. Ann's Bay. W.R. Grace had expanded aggressively in the post–World War I

COMPANY PERSPECTIVES

Our mission continues to be to satisfy the unmet needs of Caribbean people wherever we live in the world with the right skills, necessary tools and shared vision.

economic boom. A dip in the economy at the end of 1921, however, led the New York company to decide to trim its operations. When the company launched preparations to shut down the Jamaican operations, two of its employees, John J. Grace and Jamaican native Fred Kennedy, stepped in to buy out the company, including its Kingston and Montego Bay offices. The St. Ann's Bay office was subsequently shut down. The partners then invited James Moss-Solomon, also a native of Jamaica, to join the company.

Grace, Kennedy and Company, as the new business was called, initially served purely as an importer of food items into Jamaica. However, from the start, the company nurtured further ambitions, and its founding charter included provisions for the entry into manufacturing and other sectors. In order to ensure its warehousing capacity, the company formed a joint venture with another local importer in order to build a wharf in Kingston, later known as Grace Wharf. That structure was completed in 1924.

Over the next decade, the company built up its list of imported items, acquiring contracts with more than 30 foreign manufacturers to serve as Jamaican agents for such items as rice, salted and pickled fish, flour, and tonic, as well as silk and even steel safes. Food imports remained the company's primary focus, backed by its acquisition in 1928 of its first ship, a converted schooner called *Admiral Beatty*, which served to transport salt from Pigeon Island. The increase in the company's operations led to an expansion of Grace Wharf, with the acquisition of a neighboring wharf in 1928 and construction of an extension in 1931.

Into the 1930s, Grace, Kennedy and Co. had begun to display an interest beyond the import business. The company acquired a soap manufacturing business in 1935, and also launched a company producing cigarettes during the decade. While neither business lasted for very long within Grace, Kennedy and Co., they pointed the way to the company's future development as one of Jamaica's most important conglomerates. Important early operations through World War II included an extension of the group's shipping operations, as well as

an entry into the insurance sector. In the meantime, the company had been joined by two additional important members of its staff, Luis Fred Kennedy, son of the cofounder, who died in the mid-1930s, and Carlton Alexander, a relative of James Moss-Solomon. Both men later served as chairmen of the company and were especially responsible for its expansion in the years following World War II.

A GROWING CONGLOMERATE

Grace, Kennedy and Co. thrived despite perennially difficult economic, political, and trade conditions in Jamaica. The company's importance as a flour supplier enabled it to weather the import quotas and rationing applied during World War II. Ongoing trade disputes also disrupted the company's operations throughout the period. However, Grace, Kennedy and Co. continued to seek new areas for its operations, developing import interests in the agricultural supply and pharmaceutical goods sectors by the end of the 1940s. Following the devastation of Hurricane Charlie in 1951, Grace, Kennedy and Co. became a major importer of hardware supplies into Jamaica. Importantly, during this period the company, which originally supplied the country's wholesale sector, began dealing directly with retailers. This would lead the company to launch its cash and carry operations in the early 1960s.

Grace, Kennedy and Co. also established its first international office in the 1950s, opening a subsidiary in Montreal, Canada, in 1952. The Canadian operation not only served as a new source of goods for import into Jamaica, but also represented Grace, Kennedy and Co.'s first effort to develop export operations of Jamaican goods for the international market. Indeed, the upheavals in Jamaica had led to the massive migration of its population to the United Kingdom, the United States, and Canada. Demand for products from Jamaica represented a new opportunity for Grace, Kennedy and Co. The company nonetheless continued to focus on its import business, which grew in 1960 through the company's first acquisition, of Cecil de Cordova & Co., Ltd., which served as importer and distributor of such brands as Del Monte and Haig Whisky.

The 1960s represented an era of significant growth for Grace, Kennedy and Co., by that time under the leadership of Luis Fred Kennedy. The company, which had begun marketing a range of goods under the Grace label since the 1950s, moved to take control of its own production in the mid-1960s. For this, the company founded a new subsidiary, National Processors, which began producing cosmetics and other nonfood items, mostly under license for other brands. At the same time, however, the company began negotiations to acquire

KEY DATES

1922: John Grace and Fred Kennedy buy out W.R. Grace & Company's import business in Jamaica.

1951: Import and distribution of hardware goods is begun.

1967: Food canning and production operations begin.

1986: Company goes public on Jamaican stock exchange.

1999: Stock is listed on Barbados and Trinidad & Tobago Stock Exchanges.

2005: Company introduces a new logo and identity as GraceKennedy Ltd.

2006: WT Foods in the United Kingdom is acquired and becomes GK Foods and GK Investments divisions.

Jamaica Canners, a deal finally completed in 1972. By then, Grace, Kennedy and Co. had also acquired Western Meat Packers, Ltd., adding its meat slaughtering and packing operations. At the same time, Grace, Kennedy and Co. had also built up interests in dairy, through its share in the Dairy Industries (Jamaica) Ltd. partnership formed with the New Zealand Dairy Board and others; and in fruit and vegetable canning, through Harbour Cold Stores Ltd. The company continued to build up its food processing operations. By the early 1990s the company, which had initially imported everything its sold, boasted that more than 60 percent of the products it sold in Jamaica came from its own factories and canning facilities.

The move into fruits and vegetables came in part to support the group's growing overseas operations. By 1958, Grace, Kennedy and Co. had made its first move into Europe, opening a subsidiary in Rotterdam that year. That business grew quickly, importing goods through the company's Jamaican and Canadian operations. Similarly, in 1962, the company expanded into the United Kingdom, launching its subsidiary there in time to supply a fruit and vegetable market suffering from poor harvests due to a long spell of cold weather. At the same time, the company also found a ready market of immigrants from the West Indies and the Caribbean for its own products. Neighboring markets, including Barbados and Trinidad & Tobago, were also important markets for the company. By the beginning

of the 1980s, the company had added a subsidiary in the United States as well.

Back at home, Grace, Kennedy and Co. had made its first entry into the retail sector, after taking over the Sheffields retail hardware group in 1967. The company also began building up its financial wing, buying George & Branday, Ltd., which, in addition to significant import and export operations, also operated insurance and shipping agencies. Acquired by Grace, Kennedy and Co. in 1964, the George & Branday operations provided the basis for Grace, Kennedy and Co.'s expansion into general insurance, banking, and other financial services.

GLOBAL FOCUS FOR THE NEW CENTURY

The group's focus remained for the time being on its import and growing wholesale distribution operations. The company's cash-and-carry operations grew particularly strongly in the 1970s after Jamaica's wholesale sector—long controlled by ethnic Chinese—collapsed amid new political and economic upheavals during the decade. Grace, Kennedy and Co. moved to fill the gap, opening five cash-and-carry centers by the end of the decade. However, this division faced a number of problems at the beginning of the 1980s, with an outbreak of gang warfare, violent political clashes, the development of a parallel market, and the rapidly growing competition from the so-called "higglers." Originally a type of itinerant salesmen, the higglers had grown into a potent alternative force in the country's economy, particularly in the development of black market import, wholesale, and retail circuits. By 1982, the company was forced to sell its cash-and-carry stores and exit the sector. In order to counter the growing impact of the higglers and the parallel market on its own wholesale distribution businesses, the company acquired one of Jamaica's leading supermarket chains, Hi-Lo Food Stores, from Neal & Massey Ltd., in a deal completed in 1984.

Grace, Kennedy and Co. had also been hard hit by the economic policies of the radical left-wing government under the People's National Party (PNP), which had nationalized much of the food import market, with disastrous consequences. The period also saw a rapid increase in migration from the country. While many of the country's smaller food importers collapsed under the PNP regime, Grace, Kennedy and Co.'s larger size allowed it to remain in business. Nonetheless, the company, like the rest of the country, struggled to generate the foreign currency necessary to its continued business.

The growing numbers of the Jamaican expatriate community provided Grace, Kennedy and Co. with an important source of foreign revenues. Into the early 1980s, the company began building up its export operations, creating a dedicated Export Department during the decade. Things began to take off for the company in 1983, when it gained a contract to supply a number of its Grace-branded products to a small Canadian supermarket group, Nob Hill Farms. This contract then led to a new supply agreement in 1984 to the far larger Loblaws group, which agreed to stock some 24 Grace products on its shelves. Another breakthrough came in 1985, when U.K. supermarket giant Tesco agreed to stock six Grace products in its stores. By the end of the decade, the company's export operations had enabled Grace, Kennedy and Co. to generate more than 30 percent of its own foreign exchange needs. A new source of much-needed foreign currency came in 1991, when the company set up Grace Remittance Services, which then became the agent for Western Union in Jamaica and elsewhere in the Caribbean.

As the Jamaican economy continued to reel from crisis to crisis through the 1990s, Grace, Kennedy and Co. sought new avenues to ensure its future. The company had gone public in 1986, listing on the Jamaican stock exchange, in part to solve succession issues as Carlton Alexander, then the head of the company, planned his retirement. At the time of the listing, the company appointed Douglas Orane and E. G. Muschett as comanaging directors. Orane later took over as the company's chairman and CEO.

By 1995, the company had set out a new long-term strategy, called 2020 Vision, mapping out the company's growth plans into the next century. Under this plan, the company sought a new transformation, from a Jamaica-focused company to a globally active trading concern. The company began to expand its network of international subsidiaries, and by the early years of the new century counted some 60 subsidiaries operating throughout the Caribbean, as well as in the United Kingdom, and North and Central America. Fueling this expansion was the company's decision to add its listing to the Barbados and Trinidad & Tobago stock exchanges, becoming the first Jamaican company to do so on both exchanges.

Grace, Kennedy and Co.'s transformation appeared well underway in 2005, as it reached the halfway point of the 2020 Vision strategy. By then, the company had more than tripled its revenues, topping JMD 33 billion ($470 million). Equally important was the surge in the company's market value, which grew approximately 1,500 percent, nearing JMD 21 billion by the middle of the first decade of the new century. During this time the company launched a new corporate identity, shortening its name to GraceKennedy Ltd. and introducing a new logo.

The company's rising fortunes allowed it to put into place the next phase of its strategy. In 2006, the company made its first acquisition outside of the Caribbean, buying the United Kingdom's WT Foods and its three subsidiaries, the production unit Enco Products, and importers and distributors Chadha Oriental Foods and Funnybones. That company, which specialized in the production of ethnic foods, was expected to add more than $100 million to the group's sales of more than $500 million that year. In this way, GraceKennedy had expanded its portfolio to include many of the leading ethnic food brands, including Pickapeppa, Excelsior Crackers, DG Sodas, Mighty Malt, Dunn's River, Enco Flavourings, DG Ginger Beer, and Encona. Following the WT Foods acquisition, Grace, Kennedy and Co. put into place its new structure, based on its GK Foods division, while placing its growing insurance, banking, and other interests into the GK Investments division. GraceKennedy appeared well on its way to achieving its vision of becoming a global trading company by 2020.

M. L. Cohen

PRINCIPAL SUBSIDIARIES

GK Foods & Services Ltd.; Grace Food Processors Ltd.; Grace Foods International Ltd.; GraceKennedy (Belize) Ltd.; GraceKennedy (Ontario), Inc.; GraceKennedy (United Kingdom), Inc.; GraceKennedy (United States), Inc.; WT Foods (United Kingdom); Allied Insurance Brokers Ltd.; EC Global Insurance Company Ltd.; Fidelity Motors Ltd.; First Global Bank Ltd.; First Global Insurance Consultants Ltd.; First Global Leasing Ltd.; Hardware & Lumber Ltd.; Jamaica International Ins. Co. Ltd.; ONE1 Financial Ltd.; Signia Financial Group; Trident Insurance Co. Ltd.

PRINCIPAL DIVISIONS

GK Foods; GK Investments.

PRINCIPAL COMPETITORS

Wray and Nephew Group Ltd.; Life of Jamaica Ltd.; Bank of Jamaica; NCB Jamaica Ltd.; Musson (Jamaica) Ltd.; Gorstew Ltd.; Alkali Group of Cos.; Eastern Banana Estates Ltd.; Jamaica Producers Group Ltd.; Neal and Massy (Jamaica) Ltd.

FURTHER READING

"Colour, Fun and Ambition," *Grocer*, March 30, 2002, p. 40.

Dey, Sudipto, "Jamaican GraceKennedy Sews Up Alliance for Ready-to-Eat Foray," *Economic Times*, August 15, 2007.

Echevarria, Vito, "Jamaica's Grace Foods Sells Indirectly to Al-import," *CubaNews,* October 2004, p. 6.

"GraceKennedy Launches New Grace Caribbean Traditions Frozen Meals," *CNW Group,* July 31, 2007.

"Grace, Kennedy Listed on Barbados Stock Exchange," *Caribbean Update,* November 1999.

"Grace Kennedy Seeks Agencies for UK Push," *Marketing,* July 27, 2005, p. 5.

Hall, Douglas, *Grace, Kennedy & Company Limited: A Story of Jamaican Enterprise 1922 to 1992,* Kingston: GraceKennedy, n.d.

Mercer, Tenisha, "Southfield, Troy Firms Cook Up Look for Jamaican Food Biz," *Crain's Detroit Business,* March 8, 1999, p. 20.

"Tropical Rhythms Plans 'Caribbean' Roll-Out Ads," *Marketing,* April 28, 2004, p. 4.

Harris Interactive Inc.

60 Corporate Woods
Rochester, New York 14623-1457
U.S.A.
Telephone: (585) 272-8400
Toll Free: (800) 866-7655
Fax: (585) 272-8680
Web site: http://www.harrisinteractive.com

Public Company
Founded: 1956 as Louis Harris and Associates
Employees: 1,300
Sales: $211.80 million (2007)
Stock Exchanges: NASDAQ
Ticker Symbol: HPOL
NAIC: 541611 Administrative Management and General Management Consulting Services; 541613 Marketing Consulting Services; 541910 Marketing Research and Public Opinion Polling

∎ ∎ ∎

Harris Interactive Inc. is one of the world's fastest-growing market research companies, and a pioneer in online research. After Louis Harris and Associates was purchased in 1996 by a Rochester, New York, market research company—Gordon S. Black Corporation—it de-emphasized the telephone as a primary means to conduct its surveys, opting instead for the Internet. After being briefly known as Harris Black International, the combined company changed its name to Harris Interactive in 1998 to reflect better its changing business and focus. Although the transition led to losses to the bottom line, the company returned to profitability three years after going public in 1999. A series of major acquisitions in 2004 and 2005 was accompanied by a substantial but temporary dip in earnings. Most of the firm's revenues are drawn from commercial clients, but it continues to conduct the Harris Poll, which has tracked public opinion on political and societal issues for decades. Internet-based projects have come to account for about 60 percent of revenues. While the company has made a number of acquisitions overseas, three-quarters of revenues come from North America.

PUBLIC OPINION POLLING COMES OF AGE IN THE 20TH CENTURY

Political polls in the 1800s were conducted by newspapers and magazines by means of a straw vote. Ballots were printed within the publication, and readers then mailed in or hand delivered their votes. This method was susceptible to ballot box stuffing, however; in fact, the practice was actually encouraged by the publishers, who were more interested in greater sales than greater accuracy. To offset this obvious defect, the idea of the "sample" was developed to create a random group of votes from which to derive more accurate results. Early pollsters then tried to achieve a cross-section of voters by creating quotas of respondents—for example, people of differing incomes. This intuitive concept eventually led to the scientific polling methods pioneered by George Gallup in the 1930s. During the 1932 presidential election, he upstaged the best-known straw poll of the day—sponsored by the *Literary Digest*—and ushered in the modern age of public

COMPANY PERSPECTIVES

In an increasingly chaotic and competitive world, Harris Interactive can provide clarity and confidence. We believe that market research helps our clients understand the drivers of decision making and can strengthen enterprise equity. By focusing on the full spectrum of the dynamics involved in making choices—and especially why those are made—we can help our clients make better choices too. Providing clients with this accurate knowledge will help them achieve measurable and enduring performance improvements. We study people. Specifically, why people make the decisions they do and how our clients can best influence those decisions.

opinion polling, as well as the image of the pollster as a wizard.

One of Gallup's early rivals was Elmo Roper, who drifted into market research after failing in the jewelry business. His attempts to sell stock to other jewelers involved conducting some market research, and in 1934 he and two partners started their own market research firm and began printing the results of its surveys in *Fortune* magazine. Questions about the 1936 presidential election were also asked, resulting in an accurate prediction that helped Roper to launch his own marketing firm. Several years later he looked for someone to write up his material. He hired a young World War II veteran named Louis Harris.

Born in 1921, Harris joined the Navy soon after graduating from the University of North Carolina at Chapel Hill. After World War II, he went to work for the American Veterans Committee and in 1947 met Roper, who at the time was conducting research on veterans. Roper offered Harris a job writing his radio spots, as well as his regular column on veterans. Harris turned down the offer, however, because he did not want to write for someone else. Roper hired him anyway, putting him to work instead on commercial projects. Following the 1948 presidential election, though, when the polls inaccurately predicted that Harry S. Truman would be defeated by Thomas Dewey (which led to many years of public distrust of pollsters), Roper put Harris in charge of political polling.

In 1954 Harris published a seminal book on political polling, *Is There a Republican Majority? Political Trends, 1952–1956.* He argued that polls were more important in explaining elections than predicting them. Having established his own reputation, and becoming dissatisfied with a meager partnership offer from Roper, Harris left in 1956 to form his own company, Louis Harris and Associates, in New York City. He took with him three major clients, which infuriated Roper. For the rest of his life, Roper would condemn his former protégé as a "crook." In his defense, Harris insisted that it was the clients themselves who convinced him to break away from Roper.

KENNEDY'S 1960 PRESIDENTIAL CAMPAIGN MAKES LOUIS HARRIS THE TOP POLITICAL POLLSTER

Harris served on a number of political campaigns, but it was his work for John F. Kennedy in the presidential election of 1960 that elevated him to a stature close to that of Gallup. Until then, no presidential candidate had ever hired a personal pollster. Although valuable to the campaign, especially given the wafer-thin margin of victory, Harris made a number of mistakes that have since been glossed over. Kennedy himself noted that "a pollster's desire to please a client and influence strategy sometimes unintentionally colored his analyses." Moreover, his opponent Richard M. Nixon had a pollster of his own, Claude Robinson. If Nixon had prevailed in 1960, Robinson would have likely eclipsed Harris in reputation.

Considered the top in his field but exhausted after working on more than 240 campaigns, Harris decided to discontinue private political polling and challenge Gallup and his long-running syndicated newspaper column, "America Speaks." Indeed, if Harris were to publish national public opinion polls, he had to give up private political work, to avoid any appearance of a conflict of interest. The Harris Poll began running in newspapers in 1963. Over the years to come, he provided political polling for two of the three major television networks, as well as for *Newsweek, Time, Life, Business Week,* the Associated Press (AP), and National Public Radio (NPR). At the same time, his firm also began to attract lucrative commercial work.

In 1969 Harris sold his company to a brokerage firm, Donaldson, Lufkin & Jenrette, staying on as the head of the polling organization. Louis Harris and Associates was then sold in 1975 to the Gannett newspaper chain, with Harris agreeing to serve as chief executive officer of the new subsidiary. The focus of his work was very much commercial by that point. He created the Harris Perspective, a public opinion service that cost subscribers—mainly corporations—$25,000 a year.

<table>
<tr><td colspan="2">

KEY DATES
■

</td></tr>
<tr><td>1956:</td><td>Louis Harris and Associates founded in New York City.</td></tr>
<tr><td>1963:</td><td>Syndicated Harris Poll is launched.</td></tr>
<tr><td>1969:</td><td>Harris acquired by Donaldson, Lufkin & Jenrette, Inc.</td></tr>
<tr><td>1975:</td><td>Harris is sold to Gannett Corporation.</td></tr>
<tr><td>1992:</td><td>Louis Harris leaves company.</td></tr>
<tr><td>1996:</td><td>Gordon S. Black acquires Louis Harris and Associates to become Harris Black International.</td></tr>
<tr><td>1999:</td><td>Company changes name to Harris Interactive Inc., goes public.</td></tr>
<tr><td>2002:</td><td>Revenues are $100 million.</td></tr>
<tr><td>2004:</td><td>Harris buys former Reagan pollster Richard Wirthlin's firm for $41.8 million.</td></tr>
<tr><td>2005:</td><td>Revenues are nearly $200 million.</td></tr>
</table>

FOUNDER LEAVES COMPANY

By the early 1990s, Louis Harris and Associates was generating approximately $7 million in annual revenues. In January 1992, at the age of 71, Harris announced that he had decided to leave the firm that bore his name in order to start a new public opinion and market research company that would concentrate on international issues. He and Gannett management maintained that his departure was amicable and, in fact, they hoped to work together on future projects. They also agreed to share the Harris name.

While his former company retained the Harris Poll, Harris was still able to publish his new works as "surveys by Louis Harris." Meanwhile, taking over for Harris as the CEO of his old company was Humphrey Taylor. Taylor's U.K. polling firm had been acquired by Harris in 1970, at which point Taylor took charge of the company's expanding international business. He moved to New York in 1976 and had become president of Harris in 1981.

Although considered a prestigious acquisition some 20 years earlier, Louis Harris and Associates was just a small part of Gannett's media empire by the mid-1990s. Even Gannett's flagship publication, *USA Today,* relied on the Gallup Organization for its polling. The syndicated weekly Harris Poll was relegated to medium and smaller-sized newspapers. Roughly half of the company's work was in the public policy field, providing research in health care, aging, education, and race relations. Only 3 percent of revenues were derived from

political polling. The company also engaged in strategic research for commercial clients such as banks, insurers, and telecommunications companies. Overall, Gannett was disappointed in the financial performance of Harris and no longer felt that the company fit in with its future plans.

GORDON S. BLACK CORPORATION BUYS HARRIS IN 1996

In 1994 Gannett sold the Harris European subsidiaries located in London and Paris. Then in 1996, the company sold Louis Harris & Associates itself to the market research firm Gordon S. Black Corporation for an undisclosed amount. Analysts estimated the cost to be between $14 and $20 million. The plan was to operate separately under a holding company, Harris Black International. The CEO and chairman of the company, Gordon Black, had earned a doctorate in political science from Stanford University, and had then begun teaching political science at the University of Rochester in 1968. He was soon doing consulting work on the side, with his first assignment coming in 1969 when he was hired by a group of local Republican officials to determine their chances of being unseated from office. When Black's study indicated that they would lose, his results were readily dismissed. Every one of the officials, however, was subsequently voted out.

Black's first major client was Xerox Corporation, which commissioned a study from him in 1973. That job would lead to others, and several years later, in 1978, Xerox would save Black from bankruptcy. While working on a project for the city of Troy, New York, Black was caught up in a political imbroglio that resulted in the city refusing to pay his bill and leaving him responsible for $35,000 in expenses. With the young professor on the edge of financial ruin, Xerox asked him to bid on two projects for a total of $80,000. The company also paid Black up-front, allowing him to pay off his debt. Years later, he would learn that the Xerox management knew of his difficulties. Their unsolicited help earned Black's lifelong loyalty.

Although a tenured professor, Black resigned from his teaching post in 1978 to run his company full-time. Within a few years he was generating $1.5 million in annual revenues and serving other well-known clients such as Eastman Kodak and Gannett. By the time he bought Louis Harris and Associates from Gannett, his firm was posting $12 million in annual revenues, which ironically was double what his better-known acquisition was producing.

NEW FOCUS ON INTERNET POLLING

Black began to recognize the possibilities of using the Internet for market research in the late 1980s when his company began working for the Media Advertising Partnership for a Drug Free America. Rather than contact a set number of households for their study, Black's people conducted interviews in central locations around the country, such as shopping malls, and then used a non-probability model to account for differences in the population to arrive at their data. They found that the results matched perfectly with those obtained by telephone interviews. Black became convinced that they could perform projectable research if they had a large enough database. Later work done for *Business Week* on Internet penetration revealed how rapidly the population was getting online and how the demographics were converging with the general population.

Moreover, an increasing number of people were refusing to participate in telephone or in-person surveys. When receiving surveys via e-mail, however, participants could respond at their own pace and convenience. The Internet also allowed pollsters to conduct surveys at a much faster pace than could be done using traditional methods. Aside from speed, the Internet held the promise of lower costs and the ability to reach desired pools of people. Web capabilities also allowed marketers to test out ad concepts or movie trailers.

Black was convinced that the Internet was going to revolutionize polling, and felt that if his company failed to embrace the new technology it would only be a matter of time before it simply failed to exist. In January 1998 his management team met and decided to change the direction of the company. At a time when Harris Black was worth just $18 million, it began looking for $15 million in funding in order to buy the necessary hardware and establish a large enough polling panel of respondents. The Chicago venture capital firm of Brinson Partners, Inc., provided $14.7 million in funding, and Black signed a deal with MatchLogic, Inc., a company also looking to develop a database for advertising. They agreed to co-finance a 5 million-name database for $15 million.

By July 1998 Harris Black had developed a panel of 700,000 online respondents, but the company had yet to generate any revenues using its new capabilities. Customers were cautious, and internally at Harris Black there were signs of discontent. Nevertheless, Black and his chief financial officer, David Clemm, pressed on. In 1999 the company finally began to generate Internet revenues. Also in that year, Black changed the name of the company to Harris Interactive to reflect better the changing nature of its business.

GOING PUBLIC IN 1999

In December 1999 Black took Harris Interactive public. The company offered 5.8 million shares of common stock, initially priced at $14 per share, and raised $81.2 million. By this point, the size of its online panel had surpassed 4 million. The company also entered into a significant alliance with the advertising agency of Young & Rubicam, which invested in Harris Interactive as part of the deal between them.

In 2000 the company focused more on international business, signing an agreement with Blauw Research of the Netherlands to expand its panel of European respondents. This move was followed by a deal with Le Vote, a Honduran firm, to expand its presence in Latin America; and also by a deal with MASMI Research, a Russian company, to expand into Russia and Eastern Europe. By July 2000, Harris Interactive had more than 6.5 million online panelists in its database. It had also increased its Internet-based clients from 261 to 363 over the previous quarter.

As was expected, however, the transition to an Internet-based business was expensive. Revenues, which jumped to $37.3 million in 1999, a 34.2 percent increase over the previous year, simply could not match the transition costs. The company posted a loss of $1.9 million in fiscal 1998, followed by a loss of $8.8 million in 1999, and $20.9 million in 2000. During those three years, Harris Interactive spent almost $13 million to develop its Internet panel and approximately $21.6 million on infrastructure. As a result of these high losses, the company soon began instituting some cost saving measures.

In the summer of 2000, Harris Interactive faced a major problem in how it conducted its business: a large number of its e-mail surveys were blocked by efforts to prevent "spamming" (unsolicited mass e-mailings), affecting approximately 2.7 million of its 6.6 million panelists. Harris Interactive quickly filed suit, contending that a nonprofit organization, Mail Abuse Prevention System, had wrongfully identified Harris as a "spammer," a matter they alleged was instigated by an executive of a competing research firm, Incon Research, Inc. Named in the suit were America Online, Microsoft, and a dozen Internet companies that Harris Interactive accused of blocking e-mail to its users. By October the company had dropped its suit after agreements had restored connections to 98 percent of its panelists.

In November 2000, Harris Interactive put its methods to the test by predicting national election results, which according to Black was the industry's gold standard. Harris correctly predicted 36 out of the 38 states it polled for the presidential race, as well as 27 senatorial and 7 governors' races. It was the only organization correctly to forecast the nationwide presidential race as a dead heat, estimating 47.4 percent of the popular vote for Al Gore and 47.2 percent for George W. Bush. While telephone polling methods had produced results that were generally within normal sampling error, Harris Interactive's online model, according to Black, "succeeded on a scale that cannot be explained by luck, statistical accident or any false claim about what we do."

Harris Interactive cut 12 percent of its workforce, about 70 workers, in response to a slowing U.S. economy in 2001. Nevertheless, the company hoped to return to profitability within the first year or two of the new millennium. The company had a significant amount of cash and securities in hand—some $60 million—so that it was well positioned to ride out both a downturn in the economy and the completion of its transition to an Internet-based business.

RAPID EXPANSION

Harris Interactive was becoming one of the fastest-growing companies in a fast-growing industry. Revenues were $60 million in fiscal 2001 as the loss narrowed from $5.9 million to $4.5 million. The company started posting a profit in 2002, when revenues were $100 million. By 2005 they were nearly $200 million, with three-quarters of the total coming from the United States. The United Kingdom accounted for most of the remainder. The company had broadened its range of online services, adding studies to track brand awareness, customer satisfaction, and market trends. More than half of total revenues were coming from the Internet business.

Much mergers and acquisitions activity lay behind the growth of Harris. In 2001 the company combined with Total Research Corporation of Princeton, New Jersey, swelling the ranks to 1,000 employees. The transaction was valued at $56 million. During the year, Harris also added another U.S. market research company, Connecticut-based Yankelovich Partners, Inc., in addition to making some purchases overseas.

The United Kingdom's Market Research Solutions, Ltd. (MRSL), was one of the firms acquired in 2001. A part of AC Nielsen until 1993, the business had revenues of about $9 million a year and operated through two divisions, Magenta and IQ+. Based in Oxford, MRSL also had branches in London and Wales.

The March 2004 purchase of Novatris S.A. added a French online research pioneer. It had 20 employees and revenues of about $3 million a year. Three years later, Harris paid EUR 9 million ($12 million) for Media-Transfer AG Netresearch & Consulting, a German firm

with annual sales of $6 million. Although both Media-Transfer and Novatris were relatively small, they provided a toehold in a vast market. Many of Harris Interactive's largest competitors were based in Europe.

Harris outsourced most of its telephone survey operations to Canada by 2004. In August 2007, the company acquired Ottawa-based Decima Research. Decima dated to 1979 and had annual revenues of CAD 30 million.

Harris Interactive built a business in Japan, including the 2001 acquisition of Tokyo's M&A Create Limited. However, this was sold to management within a few years. In 2007 Harris added MarketShare, based in Hong Kong and Singapore. With revenues of $2.6 million, MarketShare was a tiny player in another vast market.

By this time, there were only a dozen or so market research firms that were larger than Harris. The company continued to look for acquisition opportunities. It also operated in partnership with the Harris Interactive Global Network, which grew to more than 20 members in 2005, adding research firms in Israel, El Salvador, and Serbia. The network was active across most of the world. A Kenyan affiliate joined in 2007.

WIRTHLIN ACQUISITION

Harris had made a particularly important buy in 2004 when it acquired WirthlinWorldwide of Reston, Virginia, for $41.8 million. The business had been founded by Richard Wirthlin, a political pollster who had helped Ronald Reagan put his finger on the emotional pulse of America. Wirthlin later employed such "values research" techniques in the service of the milk and plastics industries.

In addition to about 300 clients, Wirthlin Worldwide brought with it a concept known as the Advanced Strategy Lab (ASL). Developed in the late 1990s, this brought together up to two-dozen participants at fixed or mobile settings with the possibility of connecting over the Internet to other groups. Harris brought the ASL idea to Europe in 2007.

CHANGES AT THE TOP

Gordon S. Black stepped down as executive chairman at the end of 2004. He was succeeded in the position by Robert E. Knapp, who had joined the company as CEO at the beginning of the year. Knapp resigned after a few months at the top spot, however, and was replaced by George Bell as chairman. The company promoted president and chief operating officer Gregory T. Novak to CEO in September 2005.

Ed Dinger
Updated, Frederick C. Ingram

PRINCIPAL SUBSIDIARIES

Decima, Inc.; Decima Research, Inc. (Canada); GSBC Ohio Corporation; Harris Interactive Asia Ltd. (Hong Kong); Harris Interactive Asia LLC; Harris Interactive International, Inc.; Harris Interactive U.K. Ltd.; HI U.K. Holdings Ltd.; Louis Harris & Associates, Inc.; MarketShare Limited (Hong Kong); MarketShare Pte Ltd. (Singapore); MediaTransfer AG Netresearch & Consulting (Germany); Novatris S.A. (France); Opinion Search, Inc. (Canada); Opinion Search, Inc.; Romtec U.K. Ltd.; Teligen U.K. Ltd.; The Wirthlin Group International LLC; Wirthlin Europe Ltd. (United Kingdom); Wirthlin U.K. Ltd.; Wirthlin Worldwide LLC; 2144798 Ontario Inc. (Canada).

PRINCIPAL DIVISIONS

Automotive and Transportation; Consumer Packaged Goods; Emerging and General Markets; Financial Services; Public Affairs and Policy; Healthcare and Pharmaceutical; Technology and Telecom; Brand & Strategy Research; Loyalty Research; Marketing Communications (Advertising) Research.

PRINCIPAL OPERATING UNITS

Harris Interactive North America; Harris Interactive Europe; Harris Interactive Service Bureau; Harris Poll Online.

PRINCIPAL COMPETITORS

Arbitron, Inc.; GfK AG; GreenfieldOnline, Inc.; IMS Health, Inc.; Intage, Inc.; Ipsos; NationalResearch Corp.; Taylor Nelson Sofres plc; YouGov plc.

FURTHER READING

"American Firm Buys Pollster Decima Research; $20 Million Merger Will Give Harris/Decima Largest Online Panel in Canada, Companies Say," *Toronto Star*, August 17, 2007, p. A19.

Ball, Jeffrey, "The Oil Industry Calls On an Image Expert," *Wall Street Journal*, November 9, 2006, pp. B1f.

Cauley, Leslie, "Polling Put to Court Test; Verizon Sues Yellow Book After Harris Changes Rules," *USA Today*, September 27, 2004, p. B9.

Dickinson, Mike, "Forging a New Direction for His Industry," *Rochester Business Journal*, February 25, 2000.

Farhi, Paul, "Gannett Sells Harris Survey Research Firm," *Washington Post*, February 13, 1996, p. D2.

"Firm Links Up with U.S. Polling Giant," *Nation* (Kenya), June 21, 2007.

Flynn, Laurie J., "Harris Files Suit Against AOL over Blocking of E-Mail," *New York Times*, August 3, 2000, p. C7.

"Gannett to Sell Its Polling Unit to Competitor," *New York Times*, February 13, 1996, p. D8.

"Gordon S. Black Corp.: Market-Research Company Buys Gannett Polling Firm," *Wall Street Journal*, February 13, 1996, p. B7.

"Harris Interactive Inc.," *Marketing News*, September 15, 2006, pp. SH31f.

"Harris Interactive Inc. (HPOL)," *Wall Street Transcript*, November 6, 2006.

Harris Interactive, Inc., "Why Should We Believe the Polls? Commentary by Humphrey Taylor, Chairman of The Harris Poll," *PR Newswire*, October 29, 2004.

"Harris Interactive Launches Advanced Strategy Lab in Europe," *Wireless News*, July 1, 2007.

"Harris Interactive Uses Election 2000 to Prove Its Online MR Efficacy and Accuracy," *Research Business Report*, November 2000.

Haughney, Christine, "Pollster Samples Larger Offices," *Crain's New York Business*, September 6, 2004, p. 22.

Krauss, Michael, "Research and the Web: Eyeballs or Smiles?" *Marketing News*, December 7, 1998, p. 18.

Lipke, David J., "You've Got Surveys," *American Demographics*, November 2000, pp. 42–45.

"Louis Harris Leaves Firm He Started to Begin Other," *Wall Street Journal*, January 10, 1992, p. B4.

"Magnetic Poll Pulls Through; 17: Harris Interactive Inc.," *Crain's New York Business*, November 26, 2001, p. 23.

Moore, David W., *The Superpollsters*, New York: Four Walls Eight Windows, 1992.

Nasar, Sylvia, "Louis Harris Forms New Polling Company," *New York Times*, January 15, 1992, p. D2.

Sandlund, Chris, "A History on Its Side; Harris Interactive Inc.," *Crain's New York Business*, November 27, 2000, p. 64.

Stone, Mary, "Harris Interactive Lands Patent," *Rochester Business Journal*, March 12, 2007.

———, "Units Take Harris Interactive Name," *Rochester Business Journal*, September 5, 2007.

Tomasula, Dean, "MAPS, Harris Settle Spam Dispute," *DM News*, August 27, 2001, pp. 2f.

Wheeler, Michael, *Lies, Damn Lies, and Statistics*, New York: Liveright, 1976.

The Harris Soup Company (Harry's Fresh Foods)

17711 Northeast Riverside Parkway
Portland, Oregon 97230
U.S.A.
Telephone: (503) 257-7687
Toll Free: (800) 257-7363
Fax: (503) 257-7363
Web site: http://www.harrysfresh.com

Wholly Owned Subsidiary of Basic American Foods
Incorporated: 1984
Employees: 225
Sales: $105 million (2007 est.)
NAIC: 311422 Specialty Canning

■ ■ ■

The Harris Soup Company, a subsidiary of Basic American Foods since August 2007, is best known for its Harry's Fresh Foods brands of fresh and prepared foods. The culinary-school trained chefs at Harry's Fresh Foods make a wide variety of ready-to-eat foods, including soups, sauces, entrées, gravies, and desserts, in small batches for retail and food service operations. Customers include ski resorts, hospitals, chain restaurants, colleges, hotels, cafés, and delicatessens. The company prides itself on creating outstanding recipes that it produces on a large scale—more than 160,000 pounds of food each day in an 80,000-square-foot plant; however, in order not to lose product integrity, foods are prepared step-by-step and cooked in 55-gallon kettles. They are then packaged and sealed at high temperatures and rapidly cooled in a 100-foot-long ice-water tank. Products are shipped to Canada, Mexico, Taiwan, and throughout the United States under the Harry's brand name at some independent grocers and under private label at most grocery chains.

ORIGINS IN THE RESTAURANT BUSINESS: 1978–84

In 1984, Rod Harris was the owner and operator of the Hilltop Pub and Harry's Mustache in Oregon City, Oregon. Harris had served in the U.S. Coast Guard from 1971 to 1975 as a cook. There, he had learned to cook for large numbers of people. He had also learned an important lesson: "It takes the best ingredients to make good food," as he explained in a 2001 *Oregonian* article. Harry's Mustache, which opened in 1977 and owed its name to Harris' Coast Guard nickname, had begun as a thriving business, but the 1980s timber recession and tighter drunk-driving laws had taken a vast toll, and in 1984, Harris was down to his last $5,000 dollars. In a last-ditch effort, Harris turned to the sideline business that he had begun in 1978: making and selling clam chowder in 15-gallon stock pots for sale to restaurants. "The worst day of my life," he recalled in a 1997 *Oregonian* article, the day on which he decided to close his restaurant, "turned out to the best thing that ever happened to me ... I figured the worst I could do was go completely broke and work for somebody else. I never thought I'd find myself a food manufacturer." Thus began Harry's Fresh Foods in 1984.

BECOMING A HOT FILL, QUICK CHILL PRODUCER

The company focused on providing top-quality food made with ingredients without preservatives or artificial colors or flavors. Items were cooked in 55-gallon kettles (instead of the 400-gallon kettles used by competitors) to provide better texture and to allow chefs close quality control. Individual portions of each batch of food so prepared were sealed in plastic bags or tubs and chilled in a cold water bath. The company quickly moved from its original clam chowder to casseroles and puddings until, by 2001, it had about 200 active recipes with a 45- to 60-day shelf life in its catalog. If a particular customer wanted a special item, Harry's would also create a proprietary recipe.

Harry's business was a success and experienced an average annual growth rate of 25 percent from inception through the late 1990s, thanks to the growing trend toward home meal replacements. By 1990, the company had revenues of $1 million. Working in a 32,000-square-foot complex in northeast Portland, Oregon, the company's 142 employees chopped, mixed, cooked, packaged, and chilled as much as 80,000 pounds of food a day, which it then shipped out to regional customers. Company chef and culinary Vice-President Ron Hendren, who joined the company in 1990, traveled to various regions throughout the United States and abroad to taste local cuisines and incorporate aspects of these into Harry's ever-evolving menu of possibilities. Harris' wife, Linda, was the company's chief operating officer. Hendren's wife, Lori, was administrative vice-president.

GROWTH FROM A SMALL TO A MIDSIZED COMPANY

As Harry's grew from a small to a midsized company, Harris had to change the way he did business. In the beginning, he hired family and friends, but soon his company needed professional managers and staff. In 1999, the company opened a restaurant in northeast Portland called Harry's Fresh Deli, which showcased the company's products to an audience of about 300 customers per day. Beginning in 2001, with the company's growth approaching 30 percent annually, and the company's 175 employees working two shifts, Harry's kitchen was at its limit. Harris granted company stock to his senior managers to reduce turnover as he began to look at possibilities for national expansion. He also purchased about eight acres in Portland on which to start construction of a new 80,000-square-foot factory.

The new $15 million corporate plant housed production, refrigeration, storage, and corporate offices under one roof. At its center was a 20,000-square-foot room with 24 stainless steel kettles, which were stirred by chefs. Rolling carts with measured ingredients were moved from prep rooms to the kitchen. The kettles had scales for measuring ingredients. This entire building was completed in 2003 and contained three 40-degree water baths called the Willamette, the Columbia, and the Sandy, after local rivers.

The new plant made it possible to prepare a wider range of items—among them risottos and polentas. "Our quality is more consistent," said Hendren in a 2003 *Oregonian* article, "because we can cook faster, hotter and cool faster." That year the company employed 200 plus employees, among them two dozen chefs; prepared 25 million pounds of food products annually, or 110,000 to 120,000 pounds of food a day; and shipped to an international market that included Taiwan, where Harry's home-style macaroni and cheese was the hit from among its 660 recipes.

THE SHANSBY GROUP BUYS IN: 2003

From 1993 to 2003, company sales increased about 30 percent a year to $35 million. From 2002 to 2003, they increased 40 percent to an annual high of $41 million. In a move to eliminate debt, reward original investors, and position the company to become a stronger, national brand, in 2003 Harris sold a 42 percent share of his company to an investment group, the Shansby Group, which since 1987 had been buying midsized entrepreneurial businesses to build and resell. The Shansby Group's prior investments included Spic and Span, Cutex, Compound W, Denorex, and New Skin brands. Run by Gary Shansby, the Shansby Group had decided to focus on convenience, premium, refrigerated, and high-end foods; its goal for Harry's was to triple revenue from $35 million in 2002 in five years or less.

KEY DATES

1977: Rod Harris opens Harry's Mustache in Oregon City, Oregon.

1978: Rod Harris begins a small business making and selling clam chowder.

1984: Harris begins Harry's Fresh Foods.

1999: The company opens a restaurant in northeast Portland called Harry's Fresh Deli.

2003: Harry's moves into its new corporate plant in Portland; the Shansby Group invests in a 42 percent share of the company.

2007: Basic American Foods of Walnut Creek, California, acquires Harry's Fresh Foods.

Harris' goal in the deal was to cash out part of his ownership without losing control of the company. Helped along in its growth by the increased popularity of soup, Harry's had prepared 25 millions pounds in 2004 and 40 million in 2005. Revenues increased from $40 million in 2003 to $50 million in 2004 and $60 million in 2005. In fact, the growing success of premium soup was noticed by other soup manufacturers and suppliers, including traditional national brand companies, such as Campbell's, which acquired Stockpot, Inc., a fresh refrigerated soup competitor in 1998. However, many grocers still preferred to offer Harry's. Bashas', for example, which was successful in selling Harry's branded products, began to offer the same in a private label line in 2005.

When Harry's first started out, it did about 80 percent food service and 20 percent retail, but by 2005, those figures had reversed. Capitalizing on consumers' growing interest in convenience and in quality foods, which had transformed the supermarket deli into a destination for ready-to-cook and ready-to-eat items, Harry's responded in late 2005 by adding a new line of single-serve certified organic soups. It also committed to using local ingredients when available. Although the market for organic food was then still small—2.5 percent of total food sales—retail sales for organic products were growing at a rate of 15 to 20 percent per year.

By 2005, just two years after moving into its new facility, Harry's had outgrown it. Named Portland's Top Vendor of the Year in the perishable food category by Food Services of America in 2004 and 2005, the company began a multiyear, $3.5 million expansion plan. The plan created 35 new positions, adding to the slightly more than 225 already employed; included multiple new kettles; a new fill and packaging line; and an enlargement of the chill system. Postexpansion, the company would be able to prepare 60 million pounds of product per year.

Harry's had reached production levels of one million pounds of fresh food each week by 2006. While clam chowder still remained a top seller, the company sought to find new ideas for recipes and new ways of getting people involved. The 2006 "Stir the Pot with Harry!" contest for home chefs offered as a reward inclusion in the spring line of offerings. Also in 2006, Harry's partnered with the Oregon Food Bank to organize a Stone Soup giveaway for the holiday season. "It's Stone Soup—hold the stones, please," explained Harris in a 2006 *Oregonian* article, describing a vegetable minestrone with pasta made with ingredients donated by suppliers and sold to customers at Fred Meyer and Albertson's to raise money for the Oregon Food Bank.

ACQUISITION BY BASIC AMERICAN FOODS: 2007 AND BEYOND

Long-awaited change came to the company in 2007 when Basic American Foods of Walnut Creek, California, one of the world's leading suppliers of convenience food products, acquired Harry's Fresh Foods. Harris would continue as president and chief executive officer for three to five years, and the company's current management, operations, and staffing remained intact. Production and operations also continued to be housed at Harry's Portland facilities with marketing and sales support from Basic American Foods. In 2001 in an *Oregonian* article, Harris had said, "You can't be sure about the future. You just have to be determined." In a 2007 *Oregonian* article he projected that "[t]hese guys have the strength, interest, and capacity to take Harry's Fresh Foods national." As for the past, he summed it up thus: "This ends 30 years of entrepreneurship for me. It's been great going the distance."

Carrie Rothburd

PRINCIPAL COMPETITORS

Campbell's Soup Company.

FURTHER READING

Brinckman, Jonathan, "Harry's Fresh Foods Bought by Equity Fund," *Oregonian*, July 21, 2007, p. E1.

———, "Inside Oregon Business: A Weekly Look at Businesses' Strategic Decisions: A Matter of Taste," *Oregonian,* March 11, 2004, p. B1.

Gatty, Bob, "Preferred Stock," *Supermarket Grocery Business,* September 15, 2005, p. 64.

"Harry's Fresh Boosts Capacity," *Portland Business Journal,* July 8, 2005.

Leeson, Fred, "Harry's Is Stirring Up Big Interest with Small Kettles," *Oregonian,* November 23, 1997, p. B4.

Perry, Sara, "Pleasing Soup Lovers One Kettle at a Time," *Oregonian,* May 21, 2006, p. 4.

Rojas-Burke, Joe, "Organics Outgrow Local Farms," *Oregonian,* July 8, 2006, p. A1.

Trevison, Catherine, "Harry's Fresh Foods Bets on Growth," *Oregonian,* December 13, 2001, p. 1.

———, "A Hotter, Faster Kitchen," *Oregonian,* February 14, 2003, p. D3.

Hayel Saeed Anam Group of Cos.

P.O. Box 5302
Anam Building, Al Mugama Street
Taiz,
Republic of Yemen
Telephone: (967 04) 215171
Fax: (967 04) 212334
Web site: http://www.hsagroup.com

Private Company
Incorporated: 1938 as Hayel Saeed Anam & Brothers
Employees: 10,500
Sales: $32 billion (2007 est.)
NAIC: 424410 General Line Grocery Merchant Wholesalers; 311511 Fluid Milk Manufacturing; 311821 Cookie and Cracker Manufacturing; 312221 Cigarette Manufacturing

■ ■ ■

Hayel Saeed Anam Group of Cos. is the largest private-sector company in Yemen, and reportedly controls as much as 60 percent of that country's economy. The Hayel Saeed Anam Group operates as a holding company across a broad spectrum of industries, including domestic and international trade, shipping, import/export, wholesale and retail; services, including insurance, maritime logistics and support; real estate and hotel operations; and manufacturing, ranging from biscuits, sugar, dairy products, and other foods, to plastics, sponges, and other household goods, plastic bags, pipes, houses, and corrugated cartons.

The group's flagship operation is its Hayel Saeed Anam & Co. trade subsidiary, which markets and distributes the group's own products, as well as those of a number of international companies, including Kraft, Unilever, Nutricia, Nestlé, and British American Tobacco. Other trade subsidiaries include Middle East Trading Co.; National Trading Co.; United Marketing Co.; Al-Saeed Trading Co.; Artex Trading Co., which distributes household appliances and consumer electronics goods; and Widyan Trading Company, acting as a Yemen-based distributor for China's Jotun, Chinese Beijing Baxian, and Chinese Yuchen companies, among others. The company's oldest manufacturing business—and the first in Yemen—is Yemen Company for Industry & Commerce (YCIC), which produces cakes, cookies, biscuits, and confectionery.

Another important part of the group's manufacturing wing is National Company for Sponge & Plastic Industry Ltd. (NCSPI), which oversees the group's plastics manufacturing business. Hayel Saeed Anam has also expanded internationally. The company operates National Biscuits & Confectionery Co. and National Food Industries Co. in Saudi Arabia; Arma Food Industries and Hi-Pack Company for Packaging in Egypt; Cepac, a producer of corrugated carton, in the United Kingdom; palm oil producer Pacific Oils & Fats Industry in Malaysia; and several factories in Indonesia producing soaps, dairy products, yarn, and other products. Many of the company's domestic operations have also been established with foreign partners, including an oil refinery in partnership with Reliance of India, expected to begin operation by 2010.

Founded in 1938 by Hayel Saeed Anam, the company remains privately owned and controlled by the Saeed family, under the leadership of the founder's nephew and group chairman, Ali Mohammed Saeed. Nearly all of the company's management appears to be comprised of members of the Hayel Saeed family. The company's total revenues are estimated at US$32 billion per year.

FOUNDING A YEMENI EMPIRE IN 1938

Born in the village of Qaradh in 1902, Hayel Saeed Anam's early years were marked by the extreme poverty of what was then Northern Yemen. As a boy, Saeed worked in his father's weaving business, and often accompanied his father on his journeys to the Khadeer and Al-Rahidar markets. In the early 1920s, however, Northern Yemen, which had formerly been under the control of the Ottoman Empire, had been placed under the oppressive rule of Imam Yahya Hameed al-Deen, who instituted a new series of higher taxes. The new tax system meant the Saeed family's weaving business could no longer support the extended family. In 1923, Saeed left Yemen for France, where he found work aboard a ship in Marseille, and spent time traveling to various ports. Later, Saeed found work in an oil factory, where he remained for six years. In the early 1930s, however, Saeed decided to return to Yemen, opening a small leather goods shop in Aden.

By the end of the decade, Saeed had begun to look beyond retail sales, and in 1938 established a new business for the import and distribution of food and grocery items. Saeed's brothers, who had also worked for a time in France, joined him in the business, which was called Hayel Saeed Anam & Brothers. The family's French experience enabled them to secure a trade partnership with a French businessman, ensuring a steady supply of goods during the war years.

Through the 1940s, Saeed's business became an important focus for the Yemeni import sector. Toward the end of that decade, Saeed decided to expand beyond the Aden region into Northern Yemen. The company's first move was to Hedidah in 1947. The murder of the imam during the coup d'état in 1948 introduced a new, less oppressive era for the region, and Saeed, joined by his son Ahmed and nephew Ali Mohammed, began extending his business to other towns, including Mokha and Sana'a. In 1952, the company took on a new name, Hayel Saeed Anam & Co.

Saeed's thriving import business led to the development of warehousing operations; the company also put its own wheat mill into service. By the end of the decade, the Saeeds had also launched their first foreign operations, under Ahmed Saeed. For this the family formed a second trading company, Middle East Shipping Company. That company's initial focus was on Somalia, before extending elsewhere in the region.

YEMEN'S FIRST PRIVATELY OWNED MANUFACTURER IN 1970

Throughout its modern history, Yemen had remained divided into Northern and Southern Yemen, while the strategic Aden port region had been under British colonial control. In the mid-1960s, the United Kingdom was forced to exit Yemen. Aden came under control of a new government, which began nationalizing the region's economy. The Saeed family was then forced to abandon their holdings in Aden, and regroup their business interests in Taiz, in Northern Yemen, in 1969. By 1970, the company had established a new trading arm, Middle East Trading Company (METCO).

The move nonetheless led to new opportunities for Saeed. Northern Yemen at the time benefited from large-scale economic, political, and military support from Saudi Arabia, Egypt, and the western powers, opposed to the increasingly Marxist-oriented government in Southern Yemen. The influx of aid enabled Northern Yemen to launch a drive toward modernizing its infrastructure especially toward developing a degree of industrial independence. Saeed recognized the potential for developing the family's own industrial interests, and in 1970 built the region's first privately owned manufacturing operation, Yemeni Company for Industry and Commerce (YCIC). For this, Saeed found a German partner, which supplied the technology and

KEY DATES

1932: Hayel Saeed Anam opens retail shop in Aden.

1938: Operations are extended to include import and trade, founding Hayel Saeed Anam & Brothers.

1947: Operations in Northern Yemen are added.

1952: Main trading operation, Hayel Saeed Anam & Co., is launched.

1970: Saeed opens Northern Yemen's first privately owned manufacturing plant, Yemeni Company for Industry and Commerce (YCIC), to produce biscuits.

1977: First foreign subsidiary, Longulf, a trading operation, is created in the United Kingdom.

1987: First foreign manufacturing operation, National Biscuits & Confectionery Co. Ltd. (NBCC), opens in Saudi Arabia.

1990: Following death of Hayel Saeed Anam, nephew Ali Mohammed Saeed becomes company chairman.

1999: Cepac packaging arm in the United Kingdom is launched.

2007: Joint venture is formed with India's Reliance to build $532 million refinery complex in Yemen.

equipment. YCIC was launched with a single production line and just 120 employees. Over the next decade, the company grew into Yemen's largest producer of biscuits, cookies, cakes, and confections, with 15 production lines and more than 1,500 employees.

The Saeed family benefited again following the military takeover of Northern Yemen in 1974. The new government instituted a technocrat-based government in order to speed up the country's economic modernization effort. The Saeeds emerged as an important part of that effort. In 1974, the family founded its second manufacturing company, National Company for Sponge & Plastic Industry (NCSPI), which began producing household sponges. NCSPI experienced strong growth, building up a wider list of plastic-based products.

The Saeed family empire grew again in 1976, with the founding of Yemen Company for Ghee & Soap Industry (YCGSI). That company at first focused on producing vegetable-based ghee, a clarified shortening that was an essential cooking ingredient in Yemeni cuisine, as well as margarine and vegetable oils. YCGSI then expanded, as its name indicated, into the produc-

tion of soap, starting in 1982, and then detergents in 1984.

By then, the Saeed group had completed a number of new expansion efforts. The company boosted its international position with the creation of Longulf, in the United Kingdom, in 1977. Longulf focused on supplying materials, machinery, and equipment for Saeed's manufacturing operations, as well as other manufacturers in the region. Saeed added a mineral water operation, Arwa Mineral Water Co., in 1978. The company also extended its trading arm with the creation of National Trading Company (Natco), which focused on consumer goods, electronics, pharmaceuticals, home appliances, and other goods.

INTERNATIONAL PRODUCTION NETWORK FOR THE NEW CENTURY

Saeed continued to add to its array of manufacturing operations in the 1980s. The company entered the packaging market in 1983, creating General Industries and Packages Co. (Genpack). The following year, the family founded Arabia Felix Industries in order to produce pesticides and insecticides. In that same year, Saeed launched United Industries Co. (UIC), which began producing cigarettes for the local market. UIC later expanded its reach into Iraq and to a number of markets in Africa.

Toward the end of the 1980s, the Saeed group targeted further expansion beyond Yemen. The company launched its first foreign manufacturing operation in 1987, creating National Biscuits & Confectionery Co. Ltd. (NBCC) in Saudi Arabia, which became the largest producer of chips and biscuits in the Middle East. Next, Saeed entered Malaysia, establishing Pacific Inter-Link, focused on export operations. In 1992, Saeed entered Egypt as well, forming Arma Food Industries, in partnership with Malaysia's Filda, in Cairo. At home, the company extended its packaging capacity with the creation of Yemen Company for Packaging Material Industry (YCPMI), which added the production of polyethylene preforms and plastic closures. The company also formed a joint venture with Shell, Mobil, and Nagi Engineering & Trading to found the country's first lubricants factory, Yemen Lubricants Manufacturing Company, in 1993. In the meantime, the Saeed group also sought to develop export markets for its own production, and formed a new trading company, Al-Saeed Trading Co., for this purpose in 1994. By then, Ali Mohammed Saeed had taken over as chairman of the company, following Hayel Saeed Anam's death in 1990.

By then, too, the discovery of vast oil and natural gas deposits in Yemen had provided the final impetus toward the country's long sought after unification. The country's new political stability, coupled with its new-found wealth, provided still more opportunities for the Saeed group's growth, both at home and abroad. The new purchasing power led the company to develop a distribution wing for home appliances and consumer electronics and other goods, Artex Trading Company, founded in 1994. Two years later, the company added a new import arm, Widyan Trading Company, which focused especially on introducing Chinese consumer and construction goods into Yemen. In 1998, the group inaugurated its first production operations in southern Yemen, the Hadramout Industrial Complex.

Toward the dawn of the new century, much of the Saeed group's growth occurred on an international level. The group invested in corrugated cartons, setting up subsidiaries including Hi-Pack, in Egypt in 1997, and Cepac, in England, in 1999. By then, the group had targeted the Indonesia market for its largest foreign investment. Starting in 1999, the company bought or established six factories there, adding the production of soap, milk powder and other dairy products, and yarn, among other products.

At the same time, Yemen's growing wealth had inspired a number of other projects for the Saeed group into the middle of the first decade of the new century. The company began construction of a cement plant, with a daily capacity of 4,000 tons, in 2004. In 2006, the company formed a joint venture with China's Jotun Paints to build a 17,000-square-meter paint factory in Aden. In that year, also, the Saeed group led an investment consortium in the launch of a US$100 million sugar refinery, to be built in the Aden Free Zone. By 2007, the Saeed group had entered the refinery market, forming a US$532 million joint venture with India's Reliance to build a refinery in Yemen. That complex was expected to be operational by 2010. With sales estimated at more than US$32 billion per year, the Saeed group had grown into Yemen's largest corporation. Indeed, the company claimed to represent as much as two-thirds of that country's economic activity.

M. L. Cohen

PRINCIPAL SUBSIDIARIES

Al-Alam Industrial Company; Al-Saeed Company for Manufacturing Concrete &Contracting; Al-Saeed Trading Co. Ltd.; Arabia-Felix Industries Ltd; Arma Food Industries (Egypt); Artex Trading Company Ltd.; Arwa Mineral Water Company Ltd.; Cepac (United Kingdom); General Industries and Packages Company; Hadramout Industrial Complex; Hi-Pack Company for Packaging (Egypt); Longulf (United Kingdom); Middle East Shipping Co. Ltd; National Biscuits & Confectionery Co. Ltd. (Saudi Arabia); National Company for Sponge & Plastic Industry Ltd.; National Dairy & Food Company; National Food Industries Company Ltd. (Saudi Arabia); National Products Marketing Co.; National Trading Company Ltd ; Pacific Inter-Link Sdn Bhd (Malaysia); Pacific Oils & Fats Industry S/B (Malaysia); Pt Oleochem Soap Industry (Indonesia); Pt Pacific Texindo Industry (Indonesia); United Industries Company Ltd.; United Insurance Company; United Marketing Company; Widyan Trading Company Ltd.; Yemen Company for Flour Mills & Silos; Yemen Company for Ghee & Soap Industry; Yemen Company for Industry & Commerce Ltd.; Yemen Company for Packaging Material Industry; Yemen Lubricants Manufacturing Company Ltd.

PRINCIPAL COMPETITORS

Shaher Trading Company Ltd.; Thabet Group of Cos.; National Tobacco and Matches Co.; Yemen Company for Industry and Commercial Ltd.; Mareb Yemen Insurance Co.; Yemen Insurance and Reinsurance Co.; Adhban Trading Corp.; Agricultural Cooperative Co.; General Industries and Packages Co.; National Drug Co.; El Aghil Group of Cos.; United Industries Co.; Middle East Trading Co.

FURTHER READING

Al-Saqqaf, Imad, "Hael Saeed Ana'am Group of Companies," *Yemen Times,* January 7, 2002.

———, "A Story of a Blessed Yemeni Man," *Yemen Times,* November 11, 2004.

Brunton, Daniel, "New Kids on the Block!" *International Paper Board Industry,* June 2000, p. 24.

"Hayel Saeed Anam," *MEED Middle East Economic Digest,* April 7, 2000, p. 34.

"HSA to Rope in RIL for Retail Venture in Yemen," *Economic Times,* February 16, 2007.

"Jotun Yemen Paints Unveils New Factory," *Coatings World,* May 2006, p. 12.

Nadim Issa, Zawya, "DJ Yemen-Based Group to Build $100M Sugar Refinery," *FWN Financial News,* August 22, 2006.

"New Cement Plant Planned," *MEED Middle East Economic Digest,* January 9, 2004, p. 21.

"Sugar Refinery Planned," *MEED Middle East Economic Digest,* September 22, 2006, p. 27.

"Yemeni Investor Builds a Textile Factory in Indonesia," *AsiaPulse News,* July 25, 2000.

"Yemen's HAS Builds Six Factories in Indonesia," *AsiaPulse News,* August 4, 2000.

Herbalife Ltd.

P.O. Box 309GT
Ugland House, South Church Street
Grand Cayman, 90067
Cayman Islands
Telephone: (310) 410-9600
Toll Free: (866) 617-4273
Fax: (310) 216-5169
Web site: http://www.herbalife.com

Public Company
Incorporated: 1979
Employees: 3,644
Sales: $1.88 billion (2006)
Stock Exchanges: New York
Ticker Symbol: HLF
NAIC: 454390 Other Direct Selling Establishments;
325412 Pharmaceutical Preparation Manufacturing

■ ■ ■

Herbalife Ltd. is a holding company that operates through Herbalife International, Inc. This global multilevel marketing company produces and distributes a broad spectrum of more than 120 herb- and botanicals-based weight management and dieting products, cosmetics, and general health and nutrition products. Its goods are sold through a worldwide network of over one million independent distributors in 63 countries. Herbalife products, sold under a variety of brand names, include ShapeWorks meal replacement program, Niteworks nutritional supplement, Liftoff energy drink, and Radiant C and Skin Activator cosmetic products. Herbalife has thrived despite negative claims against its marketing schemes, product ingredients, and distribution methods.

AMERICAN SUCCESS STORY BEGINNING IN 1980

Master salesman Mark Hughes began Herbalife in a Beverly Hills warehouse in 1980, selling the new company's dieting aids from his car. Hughes, whose parents were divorced soon after his birth in 1956, was raised in Lynwood, California, outside of Hollywood. By ninth grade, Hughes had dropped out of high school. He became involved in drug use and by the age of 16 was sent to the Cedu School, a private residential home for emotionally disturbed and troubled teenagers. It was there that Hughes developed a knack for salesmanship, rehabilitating himself by selling door-to-door raffle tickets in support of the school. By the end of his tenure, Hughes had joined the school's staff.

Another turning point for Hughes came at the age of 18, when his mother died due to an overdose of diet pills. As Hughes would tell it, according to *Inc.* magazine: "My mom was always going out and trying some kind of funny fad diet as I was growing up. Eventually, she went to a doctor to get some help, and he prescribed ... a form of speed, or amphetamine. ... After several years of using it, she ended up having to eat sleeping pills for her to sleep at night. After several years of doing that, her body basically began to deteriorate." The death of his mother stimulated Hughes' interest in herbs and botanicals, the use of which had become popular during the 1960s. Hughes set out to develop a dieting program based on herbal and botanical products that would enable people to lose weight safely.

Before founding Herbalife, Hughes the salesman received another kind of training when, in 1976, he began selling the Slender Now diet plan from multilevel marketer Seyforth Laboratories. Hughes quickly rose to become one of the pyramid's top earners. When that operation collapsed, Hughes joined another multilevel marketer, selling Golden Youth diet products and exercise equipment. By 1979, however, Hughes, then 23 years old, decided to form his own company.

Together with Richard Marconi, former manufacturer of the Slender Now products, Hughes developed the first Herbalife line of diet aids. Marconi, who claimed to hold a Ph.D. in nutrition, would later admit that his doctorate was a mail-order certificate from a correspondence school. Nevertheless, Marconi would remain an officer at D&F Industries, Inc., which would continue to manufacture much of the Herbalife line throughout the company's history. Also joining Hughes in the new venture was Lawrence Thompson, formerly of Golden Youth, and earlier, Bestline Products, which in 1973 was fined $1.5 million for violating California's pyramid scheme laws. At both Bestline and Golden Youth, Thompson worked with Larry Stephen Huff, later to become a Herbalife distributor, who was involved in what *Forbes* labeled the "father of all pyramid schemes," Holiday Magic, Inc., a multilevel marketer charged by the Securities and Exchange Commission (SEC) in 1973 with defrauding its distributors of $250 million.

The Herbalife plan involved limiting meals to one per day and supplementing the diet with protein powders and a regimen of as many as 20 pills per day. According to the company, Herbalife was an instant success, selling $23,000 in its first month and $2 million by the end of its first year. Hughes, described by *Inc.* as "a honey-tongued spellbinder" and "a tanned and blow-dried California swashbuckler," and by *Forbes* as a "firebrand preacher," brought multilevel marketing to a new height, by taking the Herbalife message to

television. Booking two- to three-hour slots on cable television, including the USA Cable Network, Herbalife was an early purveyor of the so-called infomercial. The Herbalife television programs, led by Hughes himself, were, as described by *Forbes,* "full of inspiring testimonials from common people and resemble[d] old-style revival meetings in their fervor." At the same time, Herbalife published its own magazine, *Herbalife Journal,* equally filled with testimonials, for which the company reportedly paid $200 each, from distributor success stories to weight-loss victories of Herbalife customers. Within a short time, the Herbalife slogan, "Lose Weight Now—Ask Me How," began appearing on buttons and bumper stickers everywhere.

LEGAL CHALLENGES: 1984–86

Herbalife grew rapidly. By 1985, the company appeared on *Inc.* magazine's list of fastest-growing private companies. That magazine labeled Herbalife's five-year growth "from $386,000 to $423 million, an increase of more than 100,000 percent, [as] by far the highest growth rate in the history of *Inc.* 500 listings." In that year, the company claimed more than 700,000 distributors in the United States, Canada, the United Kingdom, and Australia, bringing annual (gross) revenues of nearly $500 million. Yet, as early as January 1981, the U.S. Food and Drug Administration (FDA) began receiving complaints of nausea, diarrhea, headaches, and constipation, which were attributed to the use of Herbalife products. Herbalife distributors reportedly were instructed to assure customers that these side effects were the result of the body purging itself of toxins. By 1982, when the company published that year's edition of the *Herbalife Official Career Book*—a guide given to distributors that contained a full product list and descriptions of the uses and benefits for each product, as well as advice on building their Herbalife sales—the FDA took action against the company.

Among the complaints leveled against the company were a number directed toward the claims Herbalife made for its products in the *Career Book*. The Herbal-Aloe drink, for example, was said to help treat kidney, stomach, and bowel "ulcerations"; and Herbalife Formula #2 was said to be a treatment for 75 conditions ranging from age spots to bursitis to cancer, herpes, and impotence. In the summer of 1982, the FDA sent Herbalife a "Notice of Adverse Findings" requiring the company to remove the mandrake and poke root ingredients—both considered unsafe for food use—of Slim and Trim Formula #2, while also finding questionable the existence of "food-grade" linseed oil in the products. In response, Herbalife removed the mandrake and poke root and promised to modify the product claims found in the 1982 *Career Book*.

KEY DATES

1980: Mark Hughes establishes Herbalife and begins selling diet aids out of the trunk of his car.

1982: The FDA sends a "Notice of Adverse Findings" to the company.

1985: Herbalife is labeled one of the fastest-growing companies in the United States by *Inc.* magazine amid negative publicity.

1986: The company officially takes on the name Herbalife International and goes public.

1988: The company continues aggressive international expansion into Japan, Spain, New Zealand, Israel, and Mexico.

1991: With the help of international business, sales reach $191 million.

1993: Sales reach $700 million.

1995: The company introduces a line of personal care products.

1997: The firm again becomes subject to negative publicity when Clint Fallow, a former distributor, files suit against Herbalife.

1999: Hughes attempts to take the firm private.

2000: The buyout attempt falls short and, in May, Hughes dies unexpectedly.

2002: Investor group takes company private.

2004: Company goes public as Herbalife Ltd.

Herbalife was well into its surging growth—and Hughes was riding high himself, purchasing for $7 million the former Bel-Air mansion of singer Kenny Rogers, and marrying Angela Mack, a former Swedish beauty queen—when the FDA released a "Talk Paper" on its complaints against Herbalife to the press and public in August 1984. The company's troubles increased several months later when Canada's Department of Justice filed 24 criminal charges for false medical claims and misleading advertising practices against Herbalife. In December of that year, Hughes went on the attack, filing a suit against both the FDA and the U.S. Secretary of Health and Human Services, accusing them of "grossly exceeding their authority by issuing false and defamatory statements and by engaging in a corrupt trial-by-publicity campaign against the company." In a press release, Hughes said: "[We're] not about to stand around and let this agency or anyone else issue blatant lies about us or our products, or to lie down and roll over while they take pot shots at us. In the five years we've been in business, literally billions of portions of Herbalife products have been consumed by millions of people. And we have never been sued or subjected to any formal proceedings by the FDA." In the same press release, Hughes also suggested that the FDA "attack" on Herbalife was inspired by legislation pending in Congress that sought to regulate the rapidly expanding dietary supplement market.

Although Hughes would withdraw the lawsuit the following year, Herbalife began to suffer from the negative publicity surrounding not only its products, but also its marketing tactics. After a still-strong first quarter, the company ended 1985 with only $250 million in retail sales. In March 1985, Herbalife itself was charged in a civil suit brought against it by the California attorney general, the California Department of Health, and the FDA. That suit, which included Hughes as a defendant, charged Herbalife with making false product claims, misleading consumers, and with operating an illegal endless-chain scheme. At the same time, both the U.S. Senate and U.S. House began investigations into the company, during which the investigating subcommittees pursued allegations that Herbalife products had been responsible for as many as five deaths. While the civil suit was based in California, the Washington investigations brought the negative publicity surrounding the company nationwide.

With sales stalling, the company cut its workforce—which had reached approximately 2,000 people—laying off 270 in April 1985, and nearly 600 more the following month. Herbalife distributors were also hard hit, leaving many with unsalable inventories of Herbalife products and many others seeing their income drop to nothing overnight. Sales dropped even more precipitously the following year. Despite repeated vows to fight the charges against his company, Hughes reached an out-of-court settlement with the California attorney general's office. Under terms of the settlement, Herbalife paid $850,000 in civil penalties, investigation costs, and attorneys' fees. Herbalife also agreed to discontinue two of its products, Tang Quei Plus and K-8, at FDA insistence that, although the products posed no safety risks, the claims made for them by the company would require them to be considered as drugs under the Food, Drug and Cosmetic Act. In addition, the company agreed to make further changes to its *Career Book,* including dropping claims for its Cell-U-Loss product as a natural eliminator of cellulite. By the end of 1986, Herbalife posted a $3 million loss.

OVERSEAS AND BACK AGAIN: 1986–95

Herbalife's domestic sales were at a standstill, so Hughes took the company overseas to expand its international markets. To finance the expansion, the company went public in December 1986, merging with a public Utah-based shell company, which allowed the company to go public much faster than if it had been required to file an initial public offering. Hughes became chairman of the new company, called Herbalife International, taking 14.8 million of 16.8 million shares of outstanding common stock. The remaining two million shares went to newly named director and executive vice-president, Lawrence Thompson.

By 1988, Herbalife had moved into Japan, Spain, New Zealand, and Israel, and soon added Mexico as well. The company's aggressive expansion forced it to take a loss of nearly $7 million that year, but international sales built quickly, raising worldwide sales to $191 million in 1991. Meanwhile, domestic sales continued their slide, reaching a low of $42 million that year. At the same time, critics of the company pointed to an emerging pattern: that in many of the countries Herbalife entered, sales would surge initially, then plunge, often in the face of government scrutiny.

Nonetheless, Herbalife continued to grow strongly through the first half of the 1990s. Retail sales doubled to $405 million in 1992 and jumped again to nearly $700 million in 1993. Although 80 percent of sales still came from international markets, Herbalife's U.S. sales began to climb, reaching $85 million. Buoyed by this growth, Herbalife filed for a secondary offering of five million shares in 1993.

The company came under attack again, however. An Herbalife program introduced in 1992 called Wealth Building—in which newly recruited distributors could achieve supervisor status, with an immediate discount of 50 percent, if they made a first purchase of $500—was seen as skirting the edge of an illegal endless-chain scheme. The company's newly introduced Thermojetics Program of products also was criticized by the FDA and others for containing the Chinese herb *ma huang,* which contains ephedrine. In response to a Canadian threat to ban Thermojetics, the company agreed to reformulate the product. Despite this publicity, sales of Thermojetics were credited with raising Herbalife's retail sales still higher, to $884 million in 1994 and to $923 million in 1995, for net earnings of $46 million and $19.7 million, respectively.

The company's international operations also were faced with problems. In France, claims that a group of Herbalife's distributors were part of an unpopular religious group led to falling sales in that region. In 1995, the firm suspended the sale of Thermojetics Instant Herbal Beverage in Germany after receiving complaints from government agencies about the product. The suspension led to a sharp increase in product returns and distributor resignations as well as a decline in sales of related products.

The firm continued to thrive, however, despite the conflicts in which it was involved. In 1994, the company began developing a new line titled Personal Care, which focused on health awareness. The products were launched in 1995 and included the Skin Survival Kit, Parfum Vitessence fragrances, and Nature's Mirror, a line of facial products. Herbalife also entered the catalog sales market in 1994 and developed "The Art of Promotion" catalog that was used by distributors and complemented existing product lines.

GROWTH AND CONTINUED PROBLEMS: 1996–2000

The company entered the mid-1990s focused on international expansion as well as continuing its growth in existing markets. By 1996, Herbalife was operating in 32 countries and international sales accounted for more than 70 percent of total sales; sales in the United States, however, declined by 16.2 percent to $279.6 million. The firm also began restructuring its European distribution system. It closed four warehouse facilities, leaving five in operation, and established new sales centers for distributor meetings. The company also opened a main sales office in the United Kingdom that could process telephone orders from European distributors.

The firm came under fire once again in 1997 when Clint Fallow, a former distributor, filed suit against Herbalife claiming that the firm withheld earned income. The suit, which Fallow detailed on a public web site, garnered negative attention and was the first of many filed against the company by disgruntled distributors.

Nevertheless, the company forged ahead, securing $54.7 million in net income in 1997, a 22.2 percent increase over the previous year. By 1998, the firm had expanded into Turkey, Botswana, Lesotho, Namibia, Swaziland, and Indonesia. The next year, Hughes set plans in motion to take the company private in a $17 per share buyout plan after claiming that Wall Street was undervaluing his firm. Although the Herbalife board approved the offer, many shareholders claimed that the offer was not fair and filed suit against the firm.

Herbalife continued to battle problems into the new century. The use of ephedrine in its products raised issues as the FDA linked heart attacks and strokes and even death to its use. Herbalife was one of the first companies to eliminate ephedra from its products. Then in April, Hughes abandoned his buyout efforts when he was unable to raise enough capital to fund the deal. The firm settled the suit with shareholders and its stock price faltered, trading around $10 per share after the announcement; in spring 1998 the stock had traded at $27 per share.

The company was again faced with hardship when in May 2000, Hughes died accidentally of a legal combination of alcohol and the antidepressant Doxepin. For the first time in five years, sales declined and the firm recorded a 35.1 percent decrease in net income over the previous year.

AFTER MARK HUGHES: 2000–03

The company moved forward as it had done in the past when faced with adversity. It entered new markets, including Morocco, and recruited more distributors. However, it was involved in pending litigation regarding ephedra-related lawsuits, and Hughes' ex-wife was demanding diversification of the $244 million family trust. The trust held 57 percent of Herbalife's voting stock; Hughes' young son was the sole beneficiary. Shortly after Hughes' death, the trustees rejected an unsolicited purchase offer of $172 million for the trust's shares.

In 2002, the company accepted an offer of $695 million from an investor group that included two equity firms, Whitney & Company and Golden Gate Capital, Inc. Sales for that year were $1.1 billion, with net income of $23 million. Within a year, the now-private company had a new parent, Cayman Islands–based WH Holdings Ltd., and a new management team in place, headed by CEO Michael O. Johnson, a former Walt Disney executive.

The company was carrying a lot of debt from the buyout. To get back to its earlier sales and profit numbers, Johnson implemented cost-cutting measures and introduced Niteworks, a heart-healthy product, and ShapeWorks, an enhancement of Herbalife's longtime diet program, Formula #1. He also began buying TV and radio time in selected markets for traditional commercials for ShapeWorks.

"Scientific-based" had become a critical and more common characteristic of weight-loss products, and nutrition supplements such as Herbalife and its competitors sought to reassure those customers who, after the ephedra findings, were still leery about ingredients or had questions as to whether the products would actually do what the ads said. Herbalife helped to establish the Mark Hughes Cellular and Molecular Nutrition Lab at the University of California–Los Angeles, and initiated a scientific advisory board to review product development efforts.

GROWTH AND PUBLIC OWNERSHIP (AGAIN): 2004–06

In 2004, WH Holdings Ltd. changed its name to Herbalife Ltd., and took Herbalife public. The company raised $203 million at its initial public offering in December. According to articles in the *Daily Deal,* the money was used to pay down debt and to pay a cash dividend to the investor group of at least $109.3 million. The investors had already received $221 million in a stock buyback earlier in the year, and the price of $14 a share put a valuation of $734 million on their 52.4 million shares of stock. With the dividend and stock buyback, the value of the initial $176 million investment by Whitney and Golden Gate Capital had grown to $1.06 billion. Revenue for 2004 came in at $1.3 billion, with net income of $24 million.

By this time, Herbalife was operating in over 60 markets, with 35,000 distributors. China lifted a ban on door-to-door marketing that had been in effect since 1988, and in March 2005, Herbalife received a license there to operate direct sales businesses in selected cities. In August, the company's stock price was $28 and revenues were up. Sales were particularly strong in Mexico, with triple-digit growth, and in Brazil. Part of the reason for that growth may have come from Herbalife's strategy of building what the company called "customer clubs" in emerging markets. These clubs met daily and products were tailored to lower-income customers. Sales were also improving in the United States, likely in response to the country's obesity problem. New products that year included Liftoff, an energy drink, and the skin care line NouriFusion.

2007 AND BEYOND

Herbalife had a shaky start in 2007, as sales growth was slower in Mexico than expected and stock prices fell in January. In February, Whitney & Company, the largest shareholder, made a $2.7 billion cash takeover bid at $38 per share, which the board rejected as too low, although it remained open to a higher offer. The following month, the company announced it had signed a $25 million jersey sponsorship deal with the Los Angeles Galaxy soccer team. China expanded Herbalife's license to cover one whole province. In November, the stock price was around $39 per share.

Herbalife successfully recovered from the death of Mark Hughes. It was poised to capitalize in the coming years on the growing concern in the United States about obesity as well as continued interest in healthy living. With 82 percent of revenues coming from overseas, the company remained very dependent on its international distributors network and on eliminating any issues that might harm recruitment.

M. L. Cohen
Updated, Christina M. Stansell; Ellen Wernick

PRINCIPAL COMPETITORS

Alticor, Inc.; GNC, Inc.; Nature's Sunshine Products; Nu Skin Enterprises, Inc.; WeightWatchers International, Inc.

FURTHER READING

Barker, Robert, "Suppress Your Appetite for Herbalife," *Business Week,* December 20, 2004, p. 109.

Barrett, Amy, "A Wonder Offer from Herbalife," *Business Week,* September 13, 1993, p. 34.

Bartiromo, Maria, "Herbalife—CEO Interview," *CNBC/Dow Jones Business Video,* August 4, 2005.

Belgum, Deborah, "Herbalife Stock Ailing After Unsuccessful Buyout Effort," *Los Angeles Business Journal,* April 24, 2000, p. 42.

Carey, David, "PE Firms Feast on Herbalife," *Daily Deal,* November 17, 2004.

Cole, Benjamin Mark, "Herbalife Plans Share Offering of $101 Million," *Los Angeles Business Journal,* August 23, 1993, p. 1.

Darmiento, Laurence, "New Herbalife CEO Seeks Return to Glory Days," *San Diego Business Journal,* November 24, 2003, p. 9.

Day, Kathleen, "Herbalife Lays off 573, Blames Slowing Sales," *Los Angeles Times,* May 29, 1985, p. D1.

DeSanto, Lauren, "Herbalife, Ltd.," Analyst Report, *Morningstar, Inc.,* August 13, 2007.

Evans, David, "Herbalife Faced Struggle After Death of Founder Mark Hughes," *MLM Watch,* August 11, 2000.

Evans, Heidi, "Agencies Sue Herbalife, Alleging False Claims," *Los Angeles Times,* March 7, 1985, p. D1.

Farrell, Andrew, "Herbalife Halts Sale Talks," Forbes.com, April 9, 2007.

Gorham, John, "Till Death Do Us Part?" *Forbes,* August 20, 2001, p. 44.

Hartman, Curtis, "Unbridled Growth," *Inc.,* December 1985, p. 100.

"Herbalife: Down Mexico Way," *Business Week Online,* January 8, 2007, p. 1.

"Herbalife Founder Dies," *Los Angeles Business Journal,* May 29, 2000, p. 49.

"Herbalife Ltd.," *China Business Review,* July/August 2007, p. 40.

"Herbalife Nixes $172MM Offer from Rbid.com," *Chemical Market Reporter,* October 2, 2000, p. 14.

Hiestand, Jesse, "There Is Herbalife After Disney," *Hollywood Reporter,* April 4, 2003, p. 5.

"It's a Wonderful Herbalife," *Business Week,* November 1, 1999, p. 166.

Kravetz, Stacy, "Bitter Herb Distributor Hopes," *Wall Street Journal,* November 12, 1997.

Lambert, Phineas, "IPO Roundup," *Daily Deal,* December 17, 2004.

Linden, Dana Wechsler, and William Stern, "Betcherlife Herbalife," *Forbes,* March 15, 1993, p. 46.

Lubove, Seth, "But Where Are the Directors' Yachts?" *Forbes,* October 20, 1997, p. 43.

Paris, Ellen, "Herbalife, Anyone?" *Forbes,* February 25, 1985, p. 46.

Pomerantz, Dorothy, "Supplemental Income," *Forbes,* October 4, 2004, p. 116.

"Private Equity Firms to Buy Herbalife for $685 Million," *New York Times,* April 11, 2002, p. C4.

"Self-Healing," *Forbes,* November 17, 1986, p. 14.

Shiver, Jube, Jr., "Herbalife Says All Queries into Tactics Now Resolved," *Los Angeles Times,* October 17, 1996, p. D4.

Svetich, Kim, "Herbalife Seeking to Rebuild Its Domestic Market," *California Business,* February 1990, p. 18.

"Today in Business a Bid for Herbalife," *New York Times,* February 3, 2007, p. C2.

Whitaker, Barbara, "Charismatic Leader Left an Image Problem and Other Issues," *New York Times,* June 23, 2000, p. C1.

Yoshihashi, Pauline, "The Questions on Herbalife," *New York Times,* April 5, 1985, p. D1.

HickoryTech Corporation

221 East Hickory Street
Mankato, Minnesota 56002-3248
U.S.A.
Telephone: (507) 387-3355
Fax: (507) 625-9191
Web site: http://www.hickorytech.com

Public Company
Incorporated: 1898 as Mankato Citizens Telephone
    Company
Employees: 400
Sales: $132.9 million
Stock Exchanges: NASDAQ
Ticker Symbol: HTCO
NAIC: 517110 Wired Telecommunications Carriers

■ ■ ■

HickoryTech Corporation is a Mankato, Minnesota–based provider of communications products and services, offered via a regional fiber network. According to the company, it is organized into two main arms. From facilities in Iowa and Minnesota, HickoryTech's Telecom Sector serves both business and residential customers with a host of services, from local and long-distance phone service to high-speed Internet and digital television. This portion of HickoryTech also develops customer management systems and billing solutions for telecommunications providers.

Meanwhile, HickoryTech's Enventis Sector offers Internet protocol-based services to business customers in five states, including voice, data, and network solutions.

Called IP for short, Internet protocol is the communications protocol or method that is used for transmitting information between computers on the Internet.

ORIGINS AS A LOCAL PHONE COMPANY

Named after the street in front of its corporate headquarters, HickoryTech's deepest roots stretch back to 1898, when the company's Mankato Citizens Telephone Co. (MCTC) subsidiary was established to provide local phone service to residents in and around Mankato, Minnesota. MCTC's business grew throughout the 20th century, resulting in the formation of subsidiaries named National Independent Billing, Inc. (NIBI), and Mid-Communications.

It was this growth that resulted in the formation of Hickory Tech in 1985, to serve as a holding company for MCTC and the other two businesses, and to provide a framework for creating a full-service communications company. While telephone service accounted for 75 percent of Hickory Tech's revenues in 1985, this would quickly changes as the firm branched out into other service areas.

By 1989 Hickory Tech was a $30 million company, according to *Corporate Report-Minnesota,* which described it as a "cash cow." Shares of the company's stock were hard to find, and it was not uncommon for brokers to scan the obituary section of the local paper in an effort to find deceased shareholders. The publication explained: "One Mankato broker says that when a few shares are located—usually put up for sale by a church or other nonprofit that acquired them as a donation from an estate—the broker in the office who found the shares gets to funnel most of them to favored clients. The rest are parceled out among the other brokers in increments as small as 10 shares."

By this time, Paul Stevens served as Hickory Tech's CEO. *Corporate Report-Minnesota* explained that, under Stevens' watch, the company was tight-lipped when it came to disclosing information to the press and investment communities. Financial information was disclosed only to shareholders. As for the reason, theories ranged from a desire to ward off a potential takeover to a simple desire to reduce interest in the company's stock, which was reportedly funneled to company directors whenever possible.

RAPID GROWTH: 1990–99

A period of rapid growth began in 1990, as Hickory Tech poured millions of dollars into its infrastructure and began acquiring other firms. In August, the company's Information and Communications Services, Inc. (ICSI), subsidiary acquired a controlling interest in communications equipment firm Digital Techniques, Inc., for $900,000. Two months later, ICSI was involved in another deal, acquiring a business telecommunications systems firm named Collins Communication Systems Co. in a $1.3 million deal.

In 1991 Hickory Tech's Computoservice, Inc., subsidiary acquired an 80 percent stake in Quest Data Systems, Inc., in a deal worth $146,638. Additionally, a $1.8 million deal garnered Hickory Tech full ownership of its National Independent Billing, Inc., business, in which it already had a 50 percent stake.

Growth continued throughout the early 1990s, with ICSI acquiring the assets of communications systems provider Coastcom Business Enterprises, Inc., for $300,000. In addition, a $1 million cash deal secured Hickory Tech a satellite television programming license for seven counties in its home state.

In 1993, Robert D. Alton, Jr., was named as Hickory Tech's president and CEO. Under his leadership, the company began to improve the profitability

and financial performance of the many businesses it was acquiring. By 1994, Hickory Tech's earnings had grown to $9.1 million on revenues of $58.2 million. This was an increase of 10 percent over the previous year.

Acquisitions continued as Hickory Tech headed into the mid-1990s. In April 1994, the company entered the Amana, Iowa, market by acquiring Amana Society, Inc.'s, telecommunications business, Amana Colonies Telephone Co., for $6.5 million. Although it served a mere 1,200 subscribers, the acquisition allowed Hickory Tech to secure Amana Refrigeration as a customer, which was a heavy user of telecommunications services.

Hickory Tech's biggest acquisition to that time came in mid-1995, when in a $232 million deal with U S West, the company agreed to acquire 82 rural telephone exchanges. A $48 million investment garnered the company whole ownership of 14 of these exchanges (15,500 access lines) in the Iowa and Minnesota markets. Along with other investors, Des Moines, Iowa–based Alpine Communications partnered with Hickory Tech to establish a new company called Tritech Communications to acquire 63 of the exchanges (35,000 access lines), which Hickory agreed to manage. Alpine itself acquired whole ownership of the remaining five exchanges in Iowa (9,600 access lines).

With Alton at the helm, some notable changes were made at Hickory Tech. Although the company became more open about sharing information with the media, its stock was still hard to come by, remaining mostly in the hands of Mankato-area residents. Alton sought to change this. On March 23, 1995, Hickory Tech began trading on the NASDAQ National Market under the symbol HTCO.

In a March 24, 1995, *Business Wire* release, Alton commented: "The listing on NASDAQ is a step towards our goal of widening the distribution of our stock. We have businesses in four states and would like to see the ownership of the company reflect the diversification the business has achieved. In addition to increased market visibility, NASDAQ offers Hickory Tech the advantage of multiple market makers that compete to offer the best bid and ask prices, as opposed to a single specialist setting a price."

However, by mid-1996 the NASDAQ listing had resulted in many shareholders selling their stock, but not many share purchases. Investors who had paid as little as $1 a share sold Hickory Tech's stock in blocks as large as 25,000 shares, causing the share price to fall from a high of almost $35 to $25.

By April 1996, shares of Hickory were trading at $28. At that time Hickory Tech, which had almost no

KEY DATES

1898: Mankato Citizens Telephone Co. (MCTC) is established to provide local phone service to residents in and around Mankato, Minnesota.

1985: Hickory Tech Corporation is formed to serve as a holding company for the Mankato Citizens Telephone Company and its subsidiaries.

1998: The company enters the wireless business.

2000: Subsidiaries are organized under a new brand name: HickoryTech; efforts begin to offer bundled services, such as phone, Internet, and cable television.

2003: HickoryTech exits wireless communications in December, selling its Minnesota Southern Wireless Co. to Western Wireless Corporation.

debt, announced a plan to buy back up to 500,000 shares for $15 million in an effort to increase demand. By the year's end, the company had repurchased 331,000 (6.5 percent) of its outstanding shares. Pleased with this progress, the board approved a plan to continue the buyback effort until April 1997.

In the spring of 1997, the company's $35.3 million deal with U.S. West Communications, Inc., to obtain 11 rural telephone exchanges in Iowa was approved by the Federal Communications Commission. Midway through the year, Hickory Tech generated about $7.2 million in cash via the sale of its DirecTV distribution rights in seven Minnesota counties to Kansas City, Missouri–based Golden Sky Systems, Inc. Growth continued in the later part of the year with the acquisition of Brooklyn Park, Minnesota–based Datacomm Products in October, which was made a division of Hickory Tech's Collins Communications Systems Co. business. For the year, sales reached $76 million.

As part of its competitive local service operations, Hickory Tech formed a new subsidiary named Crystal Communications in early 1998. A $40 million cash deal allowed the company to enter the wireless business that year, via the acquisition of Rochester, New York–based Frontier Corporations's cellular assets in southern Minnesota, which served a population of 230,000 people. Midway through the year, the company announced a three-for-one stock split. Following splits in 1987, 1988, and 1990, the split increased the number of Hickory Tech shares from about 4.54 million to 13.63 million,

and was meant to encourage higher trading volume. Hickory Tech rounded out the year by selling Digital Techniques, Inc., to Troy Holdings International and an employee group named DTI Holdings, Inc.

More developments occurred in the company's wireless business in 1999. In June, Hickory Tech struck a $41.5 million deal with Massachusetts-based McElroy Electronics Corporation to acquire a cellular territory that included some 200,000 people in the Minneapolis–Saint Paul area.

ALL BUNDLED UP: 2000–07

Hickory Tech began the new millennium by organizing all of its various subsidiaries under a new brand name: HickoryTech. In a May 15, 2000, *PR Newswire* release, CEO Robert Alton elaborated on the development, commenting: "With the realignment and name change announced today, HickoryTech will be able to provide our customers with local telephone, long-distance, wireless, and Internet services under a single brand. In the future, our customers can expect to receive all those services on a single monthly bill and will be able to call a single point-of-contact for all of their customer service needs. We will also be able to service all of our customers' voice and data system needs under that same brand."

During the early years of the new century, HickoryTech began taking steps to provide bundled services, such as phone, Internet, and cable television, to its customers via one line and on one bill. By mid-2001 the company was laying fiber-optic cable in the Minnesota communities of St. Peter, Faribault, and Waseca, and also in Waukee, Iowa. In order to determine if cable television would work as part of its business model, St. Peter was selected as a test site, where HickoryTech sought to secure more than half of the town's 3,400 homes as customers.

It was around this time that Bellevue, Washington–based Western Wireless Corporation acquired 238,000 shares of HickoryTech. The purchase followed a $14.7 million purchase of nearly 1 million shares the previous year and gave Western an 8.75 percent ownership interest in HickoryTech, paving the way for a possible merger or partnership of some kind in the future.

The company also continued building its wireless business in 2001. As part of a larger, $100 million deal in which McLeodUSA, Inc., agreed to sell its personal communications services (PCS) licenses in South Dakota, Nebraska, Minnesota, Illinois, and Iowa, to four different buyers, HickoryTech acquired two of the licenses in June 2001 for $11.1 million in cash.

A final major development in 2001 occurred in August when HickoryTech sold Amana Colonies

Telephone Company in a $6.5 million deal with South Slope Cooperative Telephone Company, Inc.

The following year, HickoryTech's market value reached about $200 million. As telecommunications industry giants saw the bottom fall out of their stock, HickoryTech's shares remained steady, trading around $15 per share. In July, John Duffy succeeded Robert Alton as CEO. Alton remained as chairman until January 1, 2003, when he was succeeded in that role by Myrita P. Craig.

A major strategic decision was made in 2003, when HickoryTech announced plans to exit the wireless communications business. In December, the company sold Minnesota Southern Wireless Company, its wireless arm, to Western Wireless Corporation (WWC). The terms of the deal called for WWC to give up approximately 1 million shares of HickoryTech stock it held, which the company retired, along with about $16.25 million in cash.

Commenting on the decision in a September 19, 2003, *Fair Disclosure Wire* report, HickoryTech CEO John Duffy said: "From a technological perspective it's clear that we were going to have to make a major investment in our technology and from a competitive perspective as you remember originally wireless companies shared their networks as partners they paid roaming fees to each other and now there's many duplicate investments and there's been large carrier coalitions have been formed and our existing growing partners are compatible only with our current technology that we have in place and not with a new technology required to support future growth."

In 2004 HickoryTech's revenues reached $90.5 million, and the company generated earnings of $7.6 million. In December of the following year, HickoryTech acquired Enventis Telecom in a $35.5 million cash deal with Duluth, Minnesota–based ALLETE, Inc. The acquisition allowed HickoryTech to boost its sales by 47 percent and expand its business into new geographic areas. Within its home state, HickoryTech's reach expanded from the south-central region to include most of Minnesota. Following the deal, the company also began serving customers in Wisconsin, North Dakota, and South Dakota.

In June 2006, John Finke succeeded John Duffy as HickoryTech's president and CEO. Finke was elected chairman of a state trade association named the Minnesota Telecom Alliance in March of the following year.

In 2007 Hickory continued to introduce new services to its customer base, including digital television in its hometown of Mankato, Minnesota, and also in

Janesville, Minnesota. The rollout expanded the company's so-called triple-play offerings of high-speed DSL Internet, local/long-distance phone, and digital TV to ten communities.

In August 2007, HickoryTech introduced a new home monitoring service that allowed customers to track remotely a range of conditions in their home (such as temperature changes, water leakage, lighting, and window/door activity) using wireless phones and broadband Internet connections. The service was one more example of how HickoryTech had continued to expand beyond its origins as a local phone company some 110 years before.

Paul R. Greenland

PRINCIPAL SUBSIDIARIES

Cable Network, Inc.; Collins Communications Systems Company; Crystal Communications, Inc.; Heartland Telecommunications Company of Iowa, Inc.; Mankato Citizens Telephone Company; Mid-Communications, Inc.; National Independent Billing, Inc.

PRINCIPAL COMPETITORS

AT&T, Inc.; Hector Communications Corporation; McLeodUSA, Inc.

FURTHER READING

Alexander, Steve, "Hickory Tech Expands Its Reach with Enventis Buy," *Star Tribune,* November 10, 2005.

Beran, George, "Minnesota's Hickory Tech to Buy 82 Northern Plains Telephone Exchanges," *Knight-Ridder/Tribune Business News,* June 15, 1995.

Burcum, Jill P., and Jane E. Brissett, "A New Tone for Hickory Tech," *Corporate Report-Minnesota,* May 1995.

"HickoryTech Announces Agreement to Sell Wireless Properties—Final," *Fair Disclosure Wire,* September 19, 2003.

"Hickory Tech Corp. Begins Trading on Nasdaq," *Business Wire,* March 24, 1995.

"Hickory Tech Corporation Announces Purchase of US West Telephone Exchanges," *Business Wire,* June 15, 1995.

"Hickory Tech Corporation Announces Stock Split," *Business Wire,* July 20, 1998.

"Minnesota Telecom Company HickoryTech Announces Subsidiary Name Changes to Reflect Future Integration Initiatives," *PR Newswire,* May 15, 2000.

Schafer, Lee, "Hickory Tech Stock: They'd Take It with Them if They Could," *Corporate Report-Minnesota,* July 1989.

Spear, Joe, "Calling All Shareholders," *Corporate Report-Minnesota,* June 1996.

InFocus Corporation

27500 Southwest Parkway Avenue
Wilsonville, Oregon 97070-8238
U.S.A.
Telephone: (503) 685-8888
Toll Free: (800) 294-6400
Fax: (503) 685-8887
Web site: http://www.infocus.com

Public Company
Incorporated: 1986
Employees: 456
Sales: $374.8 million (2006)
Stock Exchanges: NASDAQ
Ticker Symbol: INFS
NAIC: 334119 Other Computer Peripheral Equipment
    Manufacturing

■ ■ ■

Based in Wilsonville, Oregon, InFocus Corporation is a leading player in the digital projection industry. The company manufactures digital projectors and related products and services for both home and business use. According to InFocus, the company holds a commanding lead in the market for its products, and is considered to be a pioneer within its industry. Over the years, In Focus has been recognized for a number of product breakthroughs, including the first data/video projector, the first flat-panel overhead display, and the first hand-held data/video projector to weigh less than two pounds.

PROJECTION PIONEER: 1986–89

InFocus's origins date back to 1986, when the company was formed by a 21-year Navy veteran and electronic engineer named Steve Hix and his partner Paul Gulick. Hix and Gulick had both worked for Planar Systems Inc., a company that the former had played a hand in establishing with a band of colleagues who split from Tektronix Inc.

When their prototype projection device was well-received at a trade show, it inspired the partners to bring such a product to market. Hix, who still held a stake in Planar, approached the company about developing it. However, Planar was already developing an electroluminescent flat-panel display.

After deciding to develop information display systems on their own, In Focus Systems Inc. was established. Hix put several hundred thousand dollars of his own money into the new business, and a Portland, Oregon, land developer named Nick Bunick contributed $500,000. Steve's brother, Al Hix, quite Planar to work for In Focus in February 1986, and Gulick followed suit two months later.

The company, then based Tualatin, Oregon, found early success when it unveiled its first product in March 1987. Called PC Viewer, the device consisted of a black-and-white liquid crystal display (LCD) panel that, when used in tandem with a standard overhead projector, allowed users to magnify, illuminate, and project digital content from a personal computer (PC) for group viewing.

Education was a key market for PC Viewer, because donations from Apple Computer had helped to make

COMPANY PERSPECTIVES

Nearly twenty years of experience and engineering breakthroughs are at work here, constantly improving what you see in the marketplace, and delivering immersive audio visual impact in home entertainment, business and education environments. Being the inventor and leader is simply a great bonus of making the presentation of ideas, information, and entertainment a vivid, unforgettable experience, and we believe our product contributions set the standard for what a big picture experience should be like.

computers more pervasive in schools. However, there also was great demand in the business sector, and by early 1988 the product was being sold at more than 250 audiovisual stores nationwide.

Three different versions of PC Viewer were offered, ranging in price from $895 to $2,795 apiece. One version included a memory chip that allowed the device to save memory from the computer and display it independently, giving the company an edge over competitors, none of whom offered such a feature. A color version of the PC Viewer, dubbed the 480C and costing a hefty $4,995, was introduced in 1989. To develop the new product, which was an industry first, InFocus teamed with Kyoto, Japan–based Kyocera.

While PC Viewer was a success, the company was not without challenges during its formative years, according to *Business Journal-Portland*. A scant two months before the market rollout of PC Viewer, the Eastman Kodak Company unveiled a similar device. In Focus lost $267,000 in 1986, and one of the five dealers that sold PC Viewer went bankrupt in 1987.

Despite these difficulties, several things turned out to be in the company's favor. Kodak actually helped In Focus by spending a fortune on advertising for its new product, because it generated overall awareness of the emerging computer projection segment. Additionally, In Focus had an edge over noteworthy competitors, such as Japan's Sharp Corporation, because it was able to roll out new products faster.

Conditions improved quickly, with sales reaching $3.7 million during the first half of 1988, a sizable increase from $700,000 for the same period in 1987. Profits for the year were roughly $12 million. The company ended the 1980s by securing $3.5 million of venture capital, which it earmarked for promoting new

products and ramping up its research and development efforts.

INITIAL GROWTH: 1990–99

The infusion of venture capital at In Focus during the late 1980s helped support a number of new products that were unveiled in 1990, including the company's LiteShow II presentation system for Macintosh computers, and the Color LCD Flat-Panel Monitor, available for both Macs and PCs. The latter introduction was part of a key strategic move at In Focus, as the company revealed plans to enter the computer display market and sell monitors for use with computers, as well as medical devices and other types of equipment.

Beyond new products, several key developments unfolded at In Focus during 1990. By midyear the company was in the midst of a legal battle with competitor Computer Accessories, which it sued for alleged patent infringement. In Focus charged that after exploring a possible joint venture with Computer Accessories, the company stole trade secrets for its stacked-panel technology that were used to produce its Proxima Versacolor display. In July, Computer Associates countersued, seeking $20 million in punitive damages.

After hiring Fujitsu America executive Eystein Thordarsen as president and chief operating officer in October, In Focus made an initial public offering that raised $24 million the following month. By this time, the company's employee base had grown to include 100 workers.

In 1990, In Focus rolled out the LitePro, describing it as "the first fully enclosed digital projector." In addition to its own light source, the projector included a digital image device, as well as ports for accepting input from multimedia devices. The following year, the company announced that Compaq had signed an agreement to license its display technology for possible future use.

An important leadership change occurred in 1992. That year, the company named John Harker as president and CEO. He took the helm at a time of several new product breakthroughs. These included the TVT6000, which was the first digital projector to display both video and data content, as well as the PanelBook, a device considered to be the industry's first digital, 16-bit color overhead panel.

In 1993 In Focus established Motif, a joint venture with Motorola. The new enterprise was focused on developing economically-priced LCDs. A new subsidiary named In Focus Services Inc. was acquired in 1994. That same year, the subsidiary acquired Genigraphics

1986: In Focus Systems Inc. is formed by Steve Hix and Paul Gulick.
1987: The company unveils its first product, called PC Viewer.
1990: In Focus makes its initial public offering, raising $24 million.
1995: Cofounder Paul Gulick leaves In Focus.
2000: The company changes its name from In Focus Systems Inc. to InFocus Corporation.

Services Corporation, an imaging services provider, for approximately $1.5 million. In Focus also bolstered its research and development arm by striking up an alliance with office furniture manufacturer Steelcase.

Cofounder Paul Gulick departed from In Focus in 1995. That year, the company introduced the LitePro 580—the first portable projector. Additionally, In Focus expanded beyond its traditional niche when its Motif venture began licensing In Focus technology to other companies for use in devices such as wireless phones and handheld games.

In 1996 In Focus unveiled the LP610, which was the first digital projector to use digital light processing (DLP), a technology created by Texas Instruments that uses as many as 1 million small mirrors to produce a deeper, wider array of colors. The following year, In Focus introduced a new high-resolution projector named the LitePro 730. Priced at approximately $12,000, the unit was idea for displaying fine detail required in fields such as architecture and electronic design.

Although it held a position of market leadership within the projection industry, In Focus was facing stiff competition from Asian competitors in 1998. This led the company to implement a restructuring initiative aimed at lowering costs and increasing efficiency. As part of the plan, headed by Chairman, President, and CEO John Harker, Genigraphics Corporation was sold to business partner Boxlight Corporation. In addition, the company trimmed its workforce by 7 percent.

In addition to the restructuring effort, In Focus made a number of key strategic moves in the late 1990s in order to maintain its leadership position. To create better access to suppliers in Asia, an office was established in Singapore in 1998. The following year, Shanghai General Electronics began producing In Focus

projectors for the Chinese market, and the company began supplying its projectors to the likes of Toshiba.

In Focus moved into the consumer electronics market in 1999. That year, the company partnered with Sunnyvale, California–based Faroudja Inc. to offer the LS700, an LCD projector for home theater use. Priced at almost $13,000, the projector was certainly aimed at a limited market segment. However, the emerging home theater niche was preparing for explosive growth, and the product gave In Focus a foothold on the future.

BROADER FOCUS IN 2000

As the new millennium dawned, major developments unfolded at In Focus. In early 2000, the organization bolstered its European business via the acquisition of Norwegian competitor Proxima ASA. Then, on June 14, the company changed its name from In Focus Systems Inc. to InFocus Corporation.

InFocus' European business became even stronger in 2001, when the company acquired distributors in Sweden, Germany, and Russia. That year, Flextronics began manufacturing about half of the company's production. In addition, InFocus introduced the Hummingbird, a projector weighing less than three pounds.

After testing the home theater market a few years earlier, InFocus proceeded to introduce more offerings for this industry segment during the early 2000s. In 2002 the company unveiled a line of digital projectors for the home entertainment market under the ScreenPlay brand name. The first product in the series was the SP110 projector, which was quickly followed by the high-definition ScreenPlay 7200.

InFocus also rolled out its X-series digital projector line in 2002. The product grouping was aimed at business users who also liked to use their projectors at home for entertainment purposes. It included the X1, an affordably priced projector costing an unprecedented $999.

Product innovations continued as the company headed into the middle of the first decade of the 2000s. In 2003 InFocus introduced an ultra-portable, high-resolution projector called the LP120. Weighing less than two pounds, the unit pushed limits in the areas of performance and size, and remained a leading product four years later.

While the LP120 was a huge success, a new lineup of thin-display projection and LCD products that InFocus developed for the home entertainment sector did not fare as well. Marketed under the company's ThinDisplay and ScreenPlay nameplates starting in 2003, competitive price pressure prompted InFocus to pull the plug on these projection products in late 2005 and exit the thin display category altogether.

The middle years of the first decade of the 2000s brought leadership changes to InFocus. In 2004 President Kyle Ranson assumed the additional role of CEO. He succeeded John Harker, who continued to serve the company as chairman until September of the following year and resigned from InFocus' board of directors shortly thereafter.

A new brand identity was introduced at InFocus in 2006, which supported a new line of projectors for the business, education, and home sectors. Despite this development, 2006 was a difficult year for the company. Although it remained debt-free, sales fell nearly 30 percent that year, to $374.8 million, and losses totaled almost $62 million. Subsequently, InFocus' workforce was scaled back more than 17 percent. In October, the company hired Banc of America Securities to explore a potential sale. InFocus's third largest shareholder, Caxton International Ltd., formally laid blame for the poor performance on the company's board, and called for a change.

Following the challenges of 2006, more leadership changes occurred at InFocus. In 2007 Kyle Ranson stepped down as CEO and was succeeded by Bob O'Malley, who had served as Tech Data's senior vice-president of marketing. He led InFocus in a market consisting of approximately 40 competitors, about 12 of which held about 80 percent of all projection equipment sales. Supported by its pioneer status, InFocus remained an industry leader approaching the 21st century's second decade.

Paul R. Greenland

PRINCIPAL SUBSIDIARIES

InFocus Benelux BV; InFocus Systems Asia Pte Ltd.; InFocus (Shanghai) Co. Ltd.; Motif Inc. (50%); InFocus AS; ASK AS; InFocus Norge AS; InFocus GmbH; InFocus SARL; InFocus Sweden AB; InFocus AG; InFocus International BV; InFocus International (Cayman) Ltd.; South Mountain Technologies Ltd. (50%); South Mountain Technologies (USA) Inc. (50%); South Mountain Technologies (Norway) AS (50%); Shenzhen South Mountain Technologies Ltd. (50%).

PRINCIPAL COMPETITORS

NEC Corporation; Seiko Epson Corporation; Sony Corporation.

FURTHER READING

"InFocus Invites Bids," *Mergers & Acquisitions Report,* October 23, 2006.
"In Focus Systems Announces Corporate Restructuring," *Business Wire,* July 14, 1998.
"In Focus Systems Will Take Stock Public," *Business Journal-Portland,* November 19, 1990.
McMillan, Dan, "In Focus Projects Itself into Consumer Niche," *Business Journal-Portland,* January 1, 1999.
Wilkerson, Jan, "In Focus Attracts $3.5 Million in Venture Capital," *Business Journal-Portland,* January 2, 1989.
———, "Tualatin Start-Up's Products Project Bright Future," *Business Journal-Portland,* September 19, 1988.

Interpool, Inc.

211 College Road East
Princeton, New Jersey 08540
U.S.A.
Telephone: (609) 452-8900
Fax: (609) 452-8211
Web site: http://www.interpool.com

Private Company
Incorporated: 1988
Employees: 254
Sales: $374.2 million (2006 est.)
NAIC: 488390 Other Support Activities for Water
   Transportation

■ ■ ■

Interpool, Inc., is a Princeton, New Jersey–based private company involved in the leasing of intermodal dry cargo containers, chassis, and related equipment. The company maintains a fleet of more than 800,000 twenty-foot equivalent units (TEUs, the industry standard unit of measurement). Because they are intermodal, the containers can be transported by ships, trains, and trucks. Interpool's chassis fleet, totaling almost 210,000 units, is used to shuttle containers between ships and trains. In addition, the company offers chassis management services under the PoolState name, providing customers with such information as usage patterns and fleet efficiencies through an Internet-based report generator. Interpool's slate of more than 600 customers includes most of the top two-dozen international container shipping lines as well as the largest North American railroads.

POSTWAR EFFORTS TO STANDARDIZE CONTAINERS

The drive to create standardized cargo containers did not begin in earnest until the late 1950s when ships specifically intended to transport containers were first built. Until that time cargo on ships was stored in conventional bulk break vessels. To complete its journey the cargo then had to be unloaded from the ship and reloaded to train cars or truck trailers at considerable time and expense. The obvious way to make the process more efficient was to make use of intermodal containers that could be stored in a ship's hold as well as hauled by train or truck without the need to touch the cargo within. In order to achieve that end, there would have to be a worldwide consensus on the standard dimensions and features of these containers. Internationally the task was taken up by the International Organization for Standardization (ISO), and for the United States, the American National Standards Institute (ANSI) participated.

Coming to an agreement proved difficult, however. Size was only one consideration. There was also the question of whether to employ the metric system that most of the world used for measurements, or the imperial system, based on feet and inches. Because the United States and Australia both used the imperial system and contained large land masses, as well as the United States' importance in world trade, the participants eventually agreed to use the imperial system. They then established a 20-by-40-foot configuration for the standard intermodal container. Originally they settled on the height at eight feet, but this was soon changed to eight feet, six inches, because truck trailers were at that height and the extra six inches made no difference in how ships stacked the containers in their holds. A more contentious issue involved the design rights to corner fittings. In the end the standardization committees created a new design that became the standard and was made available to manufacturers around the world at no royalty. It was not until 1966 that a final agreement was reached on the standard intermodal container.

INTERPOOL FORMED: 1968

Interpool was formed in 1968 by four engineers involved in the standardization effort, most notably Warren Lewis Serenbetz and his protégé Martin Tuchman. Serenbetz, the elder of the two, was born in New York City in 1924 and earned a bachelor of science and a master's degree from Columbia University, completing his education in 1949. After stints with an engineering firm and a farm equipment manufacturer, Serenbetz joined Railway Express Agency, Inc. (REA), in 1953 and became involved in the shipping business. In 1958 he began his work on intermodal container standardization. Serenbetz became Tuchman's boss at REA in 1962 after Tuchman, a Brooklyn native, graduated from the New Jersey Institute of Technology with a bachelor of science in mechanical engineering degree. He joined Serenbetz and other REA colleagues in their work with the American National Standards Institute. During the same time he returned to school, earning a master's of business administration from Seton Hall University in 1968, a business education that he put to use when he, Serenbetz, and two other engineers formed the Interpool subsidiary for REA, taking advantage of the new standards to provide containers to shippers. Derived from "international container pool," the company name was chosen because "it just had a nice ring to it," Tuchman explained to the *New York Times.*

REA was a natural candidate to enter the container business. The company's origins dated to World War I,

when in 1918 the U.S. government assumed temporary control of the nation's railroads. As part of this effort, the major express carriers—Adams & Company; American Express Company; Southern Express Company; and Wells, Fargo & Company—were brought together in a new entity called the American Railway Express Company. When the war came to an end, the railroads returned to their previous ownership but American Railway Express remained intact. A decade later, in December 1928, 86 railways formed Railway Express Agency, Inc., and a year later bought out American Railway Express. Handling all of the railroads' domestic express shipping business, the company thrived through World War II, but express volume fell off significantly in the 1950s, due in large measure to the railroads' perception that express service was too expensive to operate. To meet changing conditions, in 1959 REA renegotiated its contract with the railroads, and was permitted to use any available mode of transportation. The company dabbled with containers but with little success, and in the 1960s it began to post losses. By the time it backed the creation of Interpool, REA was in difficult straits and unable to provide much funding to the fledgling operation. "We formed it on a shoestring," Tuchman recalled in a 1988 *New York Times* interview. REA was sold to its management team in 1969, and despite a new name, REA Express, it continued to struggle, unable to compete adequately against the U.S. Postal Service and United Parcel Service.

Serenbetz served as Interpool's first chief executive officer with Tuchman acting as his chief lieutenant. In the beginning the company maintained its headquarters in New York City. It was not long before the company had a new owner, Canada's Steadman Industries, Ltd., which assumed control at the start of 1969. Steadman played a key role in making intermodal containers a success by pioneering the development of the handling equipment needed to move the containers between modes of transportation. Interpool had a fleet of 5,000 containers at this point, second among independents to Containers Service, Inc., and its fleet of 5,861 containers. Interpool was also looking to expand its customer base beyond ships, railroads, and trains. It began designing 20-foot containers to be leased to airlines through a unit to be called Airpool.

While the idea of using containers that were interchangeable between air and surface modes of transportation was attractive enough to land agreements with three major airlines—American, Trans World, and United—Airpool never panned out and Interpool focused all of its attention on the 40-foot containers. In time Steadman was merged with Interpool and the company was taken public in 1972 under the Interpool

KEY DATES

1968: Interpool founded as unit of Railway Express Agency, Inc.
1969: Steadman Industries, Ltd., acquires Interpool.
1972: Interpool is taken public.
1978: Thyssen-Bornemisza acquires company.
1988: Founders buy back Interpool.
1993: Company again taken public.
2007: Fortress Investment Group acquires Interpool.

name, its shares listed on both the American Stock Exchange and the Toronto Stock Exchange.

Standardized containers were embraced by shippers for obvious reasons. According to *Transportation & Distribution,* for example, "Using containers, a conventional round-trip voyage from the United States to Australia dropped from 120 days to 70 days." The savings in both time and cost led to explosive growth in the use of containers, which Interpool took advantage of. Revenues increased from $18.7 million in fiscal 1973 to more than $31 million in fiscal 1974, while net income improved from $2.6 million to $4.8 million. The container fleet in the meantime grew to 58,000 TEUs, and would have increased further if manufacturers had not been so overwhelmed with orders. Interpool simply was not willing to pay the higher prices that the manufacturers were demanding.

COMPANY ACQUIRED: 1978

Revenues topped $47 million in fiscal 1977 and net income improved to $7.6 million. A few months later, in June 1978, the company was acquired by Thyssen-Bornemisza N.V., a Dutch industrial holding company. Interpool continued to be run by Serenbetz and Tuchman, however. In 1986, they, along with Raoul J. Witteveen and two other Interpool executives, formed a chassis leasing company called Trac Lease, Inc. The three men then acquired Interpool from Thyssen in 1988. Tuchman took over as chairman and CEO, while Serenbetz became a member of the board of directors. The company's headquarters was also moved to Princeton, New Jersey, where Tuchman had settled because he split much of his time between New York and Philadelphia.

Although they shared the same management, Interpool and Trac Lease were run separately for several years. Trac Lease acquired 25,000 chassis owned by Interpool, giving it a total of 35,000 units. Interpool was free to focus on its container fleet of 100,000 units. Trac Lease

was combined with Interpool in 1993 when Interpool paid $22.9 million to Sequa Capital Corp. for its half-interest in the business. Trac Lease then became a wholly owned subsidiary in 1996.

Also in 1993 Interpool completed an initial public offering of stock and secured a listing on the New York Stock Exchange. At the end of the year 1993 (the fiscal year and calendar year now coinciding), Interpool recorded revenues of $79.5 million and net income of $20 million. As the economy improved following a recession during the early 1990s, revenues increased at a steady clip, reaching $127.9 million in 1995, while net income rose to $29.5 million. To fuel further growth Interpool invested about $167 million for new equipment in 1996, so that by the end of the year its container fleet increased 25 percent to 301,000 TEUs and the number of chassis units grew 6 percent to 57,000. The capital improvements were funded by $200 million in new financing the company received. The additional containers and chassis helped Interpool to increase revenues to $147.1 million and net income to $38.1 million in 1996. Because of the company's strong performance the company engineered a three-for-two stock split in March 1997, a move that increased the number of shares available for trading by 50 percent. In short order, the price of the split stock increased to its 1993 offering price.

During the remainder of the 1990s, Interpool continued to expand its fleet. The company invested $260 million in capital equipment in both 1997 and 1998, increasing the container fleet to 500,000 TEUs. In 1999 another 75,000 TEUs were added. Moreover, in 1998 Interpool acquired a 50 percent stake in Container Applications International, Inc. (CAI), which focused on the short-term leasing business while Interpool specialized in long-term leases. As a result of this strategic relationship with CAI, Interpool was in a position to offer customers a full range of leasing options. By the end of the decade Interpool and CAI's combined fleet boasted more than 850,000 TEUs. Trac Lease, in the meantime, enjoyed strong growth as well, increasing the number of chassis to 90,000 by the end of 1999. Also, in 1997 the subsidiary began offering chassis pool management services, taking advantage of proprietary software to help steamship lines maintain appropriate levels of chassis pools. Almost immediately Trac Lease became the largest administrator of marine shipping chassis in the United States.

Interpool bolstered its position in the chassis leasing market in 2000 with the $681 million purchase of the North American intermodal division of Transamerica Leasing, Inc., a deal that added 70,000 chassis and also brought with it containers and trailers. Furthermore, Interpool increased the number of locations from which it could serve its customers. To help pay for the Transamerica acquisition, Interpool in early 2001 sold its intermodal trailers and domestic rail containers, noncore assets, to TIP Intermodal Services for about $345 million.

With enlarged container and chassis fleets and utilization rates in the high 90 percent range, Interpool increased sales to $242.3 million in 2000 and more than $305 million in 2001, while net income grew from $42.6 million to $46.2 million. These record results were achieved despite difficult conditions for the transportation and financial services industries.

Reported revenues continued to increase, but concerns arose regarding the company's accounting methods, prompting an investigation by Interpool's outside counsel, which then found that some transactions authorized by the company's president and chief operating officer, Raoul Witteveen, improperly inflated earnings during one quarter in 2001. Witteveen resigned and a formal investigation was launched by the Securities and Exchange Commission. The company's chief financial officer also resigned, albeit for unrelated reasons, according to the company. Interpool's stock was hard hit by these developments, and Interpool was almost delisted by the New York Stock Exchange as it struggled to restate earlier financial returns as well as file its 2002 annual report. The company also had to contend with the downgrading of its debt.

Over the next few years, Interpool repaired its relationship with investors, helped in no small measure by the posting of a record profit, $106.6 million, on revenues of $374.2 million in 2006. In 2007 Tuchman attempted to take the company private, offering $24 a share, but Interpool's board of directors formed a special committee that then decided to solicit competing bids. Private equity firm Fortress Investment Group outbid Tuchman, offering $27.10 per share, and following shareholder approval in July 2007 it acquired Interpool. Including the assumption of debt, the price amounted to $2.4 billion.

Ed Dinger

PRINCIPAL SUBSIDIARIES

Interpool Ltd.; Trac Lease, Inc.; Container Applications International, Inc. (50%).

PRINCIPAL COMPETITORS

Flexi-Van Leasing, Inc.

FURTHER READING

Boyd, John D., "A Mighty Fortress," *Traffic World,* July 2, 2007, p. 1.

"Containers Pool Looks to Air Age," *New York Times,* April 14, 1969

Cuff, Daniel F., "Leasing Official Regains a Company He Started," *New York Times,* March 25, 1988, p. D4.

Drury, George H., "Railway Express Agency," *Trains Magazine,* June 5, 2006.

Perone, Joseph R., "NYSE Moves to Delist Interpool," *Newark (N.J.) Star-Ledger,* December 30, 2003, p. 23.

Weissman, Dan, "Thinking Outside the Box," *Newark (N.J.) Star-Ledger,* June 16, 1999, p. 29.

Zuckerman, Amy, "Standards and Containerization: A Model for World Trade," *Transportation & Distribution,* December 1997, p. 88.

Intevac, Inc.

———————————————————— ▪ ————————————————————

3560 Bassett Street
Santa Clara, California 95054
U.S.A.
Telephone: (408) 986-9888
Fax: (408) 727-5739
Web site: http://www.intevac.com

Public Company
Incorporated: 1991
Employees: 362
Sales: $260 million (2006)
Stock Exchanges: NASDAQ
Ticker Symbol: IVAC
NAIC: 333298 All Other Industrial Machinery
 Manufacturing

■ ■ ■

Intevac, Inc., is a NASDAQ-listed company based in Santa Clara, California, comprised of subsidiaries split between two business units: Equipment and Imaging. The Equipment division produces sputtering equipment used by hard disk drive manufacturers to deposit thin films onto the magnetic disks to store digital data for computers and other electronic devices, including MP3 players, digital video recorders, and video-game consoles.

Intevac equipment is responsible for about 60 percent of the world's annual production of thin-film disks, serving such customers as Seagate Technology LLC, Hitachi Global Storage Technology, and Komag Inc. Intevac also manufactures sputtering systems to produce flat panel displays. Intevac's Imaging unit develops and manufactures extreme low-light-level cameras and military targeting equipment. Commercial markets include medical imaging, physical and life science research, pharmaceutical, petroleum, and machine vision.

In addition to its 180,000-square-foot Santa Clara headquarters and manufacturing facility, Intevac maintains imaging manufacturing plants in Fremont, California, and Laramie, Wyoming, as well as a manufacturing and customer support operation in Singapore. Intevac also maintains sales and customer support offices in the United States, Singapore, Malaysia, Korea, China, and Japan.

COMPANY FOUNDED: 1991

Intevac was founded in 1991 by Norman H. Pond. Born in 1938, Pond earned a degree in physics from the University of Missouri at Rolla, followed by a master's degree in physics from the University of California at Los Angeles while working as a project manager at Hughes Aircraft Company. He then went to work for GT&E Sylvania for a three-year stint before joining Teledyne Inc., a diversified electronics company where he held a number of posts, including group executive. In 1984 he joined Palo Alto, California–based Varian Associates Inc., which was involved in the manufacturer of semiconductor, communication, medical, and defense products. Pond served as president of the company's electron device group, and after four years he was named president and chief operating offices of the entire company. According to the *Business Journal,* Pond "left the company on less-than-friendly terms in January

1990. Back then, most of the financial community, along with Mr. Pond himself, felt he was heir apparent to Varian's chairmanship, then held by Thomas Sege. When the company settled on J. Tracy O'Rourke, Mr. Pond resigned."

A short time after taking the helm at Varian, O'Rourke decided to focus Varian efforts by selling off five business and eight product lines involved in chip making and defense electronics, two areas that were struggling. Well familiar with these operations, Pond sensed an opportunity. Despite difficult economic conditions at the time, he was able to use his connections in 1990 to raise funds from Kairer Aerospace and Electronics Corporation as well as venture capital from the investment firm of Dougery, Wilder & Howard. In February 1991 Pond formed Intevac and acquired three Varian divisions: Santa Clara–based Vacuum Systems Division, maker of disk-sputtering equipment, and Molecular Beam Epitaxy Equipment, maker of molecular-beam equipment for designing and producing advanced materials; and Palo Alto–based Electro Optical Sensors, which developed and manufactured night-vision goggles. After Pond cobbled together Intevac from Varian "leftovers," according to the *Business Journal*, "few people thought much of it. 'No one gave them a snowball's chance in hell,' said Mark Geenen, president of TrendFocus Inc., a market research firm in Palo Alto." Skepticism was understandable given the stiff competition Intevac faced, in particular giants in the disk drive equipment field: Ulvac, Japan Ltd., Leybold AG, and Anelva Corp.

Despite its doubters, Intevac wasted little time in becoming a profitable concern and paying off the debt taken on to acquired the Varian assets. A major help were contracts from the U.S. Army for night-vision gear that relied on gallium arsenide technology rather than standard electronics. Nevertheless, Pond elected to focus on disk-sputtering equipment and a new area, rapid thermal procession, used to produce flat panel displays. The molecular-beam unit was sold to Chorus Corp. for a 20 percent stake in Chorus in October 1992, and then in May 1995 the night-vision operation was sold to Litton Systems Inc. for about $7.5 million in cash. Later in

1995 Intevac sold its interest in Chorus for about $3 million.

Intevac's disk-sputtering unit was launched in 1982 by Varian to address limitations with the in-line disk-sputtering systems used by thin-film disk manufacturers to deposit magnetic media on disks. Information could then be recorded on the media. Instead, Varian took a similar approach to that used by single wafer processing machines used by semiconductor manufacturers, creating a single disk, multiple chamber static sputtering system, eliminating excess movement between the disk being coated and the sputtering source, thus providing greater control and disk uniformity. This static sputtering system that Intevac refined attracted the attention of disk manufacturers who began to purchase the new systems.

Aside from the disk-sputtering business, Intevac also elected to pursue the rapid thermal processing (RTP) business, entering the field in 1994 by acquiring assets from Aktis Corporation and some patents from Baccarat Electronics, Inc. RTP was a semiconductor manufacturing process that Intevac employed to create a system for the production of flat panel displays, the work conducted under the auspices of the U.S. military. Although Intevac had sold its night-vision business to Litton, it retained assets in the area of photocathodes, which were combined with the RTP business to create the company's Advanced Technology Division.

IPO COMPLETED: 1995

Enjoying the benefits of increased disk drive sales to its disk-sputtering business, Intevac turned to the equity markets in 1995. An initial public offering (IPO) of stock managed by Robertson, Stephens & Company, L.P., and Hambrecht & Quist LLC was completed in November 1995, raising about $12 million. The company had higher hopes, however. Originally looking to sell 2.8 million shares at $8.50 each, an offering that could have fetched $25 million, Intevac had to settle for 2 million shares at $6 each.

The money raised from the IPO was earmarked for acquisitions and to finance growth. Less than two months later, in January 1992, Intevac paid $1 million in cash and $2 million in notes to acquire Cathode Technology Corporation (CTC), a company that developed sputter source technology for computer hard disk drive production, essentially sweeping the disk to create a uniform surface for sputtering and resulting in disks with increased performance. CTC technology was incorporated into Intevac's sputter system. Then, in May 1996, Intevac spent $3.7 million to acquired San Jose Technology Corporation, adding technology that

KEY DATES

1991: Norman Pond founds Intevac by acquiring former Varian units.
1995: Company is taken public.
1996: Cathode Technology Corporation is acquired.
2000: RPC Technologies is divested.
2004: Secondary stock offering is completed.
2007: DeltaNu and Creative Display Systems acquired.

followed disk sputtering, the lubrication of thin-film drives.

Intevac enjoyed a steady increase in revenues during the mid-1990s. Sales totaled $20.5 million in 1994, grew to $42.9 million in 1995, again doubled the following year to $88.2 million, and improved to $133.2 million in 1997. Net income during this period improved from $1.4 million in 1994 to $12.5 million in 1997. Disk-sputtering equipment was by far the company's largest business. As its technology became accepted, Intevac broadened the customer base and increased market share. At the same time the company looked to improve its position in the flat panel display equipment market, establishing a joint venture in Japan in 1997 that operated as a separate division. Intevac also continued to develop its proprietary technology in negative affinition photocathodes with backing from the U.S. military, making advances in the design of technology that could detect and identify military vehicles from long distances. Also, in late 1997 Intevac acquired RPC Technologies, Inc., a maker of electron beam processing equipment.

In the second half of 1997 the data storage industry entered a downturn that continued in 1998, brought about high inventory levels of disk drives and the adoption of just-in-time inventory practices by disk drive and computer manufacturers. More importantly the entire disk drive industry had made some serious miscalculations. While correct in projecting that the demand for storage capacity was going to experience strong growth, the industry failed to take into account changes in technology that resulted in higher capacity disk drives that were able to absorb this increased demand. Hence, the demand for the drives was actually flat and disk manufacturers, which had been ramping up production, suddenly stopped adding capacity and no longer needed new Intevac sputtering machines. As a result, Intevec's revenues decreased 28 percent to $96 million in 1998 while net income totaled only

$400,000. Matters grew even worse in 1999 when revenues dropped a further 55 percent to just $43 million, leading to a net loss of $10 million. In response, Intevac cut its workforce in half and shut down its electron beam product line, closing the RPC Technologies operation in Hayward, California, in early 2000 and later selling some of its assets to Quemex Technology. Intevac did not abandon its disk drive business, which remained the core unit, and also continued to invest in its photonics business and flat panel display activities.

Difficult times continued for Intevac as it entered the new century. Sales continued to erode, dropping another 16 percent to $36 million, resulting in a net loss of $12 million in 2000. The year also brought a new CEO, Dr. Ajit Rode, but he lasted little more than a year at the helm, and in October 2001 Pond once again added the CEO responsibilities while continuing to serve as Intevac's chairman. Revenues picked up in 2001, due to newly developed flat panel display deposition and thermal processing equipment, as well as new photonics contracts. Nevertheless, the company suffered a net loss of $16.9 million in 2001, resulting in further cuts in head count.

NEW CEO: 2002

In early 2002 a new president and CEO was installed, Kevin Fairbairn, a 25-year industry veteran who had previously served as general manager of the Plasma Enhanced Chemical Vapor Deposition Business unit of Applied Materials Inc., and held a similar position with the Conductor Etch Organization, leading a group that topped $1 billion in sales. The new management team focused on the company's imaging technology while preparing to take advantage of an expected rebound in the demand for hard disk drive manufacturing equipment. In November 2002 Intevac completed the sale of its thermal processing equipment business to San Jose–based Photon Dynamics for $20 million plus the assumption of some liabilities. The money helped Intevac to make a significant reduction in debt, which in turn lowered the company's cost structure. The sale also resulted in Intevac reporting net earnings of $9 million in 2002 on revenues of $34 million.

Revenues improved slightly in 2003 to $36 million and the company posted a net loss of $12.2 million. However, the worst was over and having weathered the storm, Intevac was ready for better times, as evidenced by a significant increase in orders for sputtering equipment in late 2003. Moreover, Intevac introduced its next generation magnetic media sputtering system, Intevac 200 Lean, which began to gain significant market penetration in 2004. Intevac's revenues almost doubled to $70 million in 2004 and the net loss was reduced to $4.3 million. In addition, the company was able to raise $42 million from a secondary stock offering in 2004, helping the company to end the year with no debt and $50 million in cash and investments on the balance sheet. Intevac also positioned itself for further growth with the introduction in late 2004 of the Night Vista Camera, a day/night video camera that used the company's extreme low-light CMOS-based sensor. As a result of these advances, Intevac enjoyed a 97 percent increase in revenues to $137 million in 2005, leading to a return to profitability, the company recording earnings of $16 million. In order to bolster its business in Asia, the company opened a field office in Shenzhen in the People's Republic of China in late 2005 and made plans to launch an operation in Thailand in 2006 to provide further manufacturing and engineering services.

In 2006 sales increased another 89 percent to a record $260 million, resulting in record earnings of $46.7 million. Moreover, the company ended the year with an order backlog of $125 million, providing a springboard for even better results in 2007. Taking advantage of its regained prosperity, Intevac completed a pair of acquisitions in 2007. The company picked up DeltaNu LLC, a Wyoming developer of small spectroscopy instruments, and Carlsbad, California–based Creative Display Systems LLD, maker of high-

performance micro-display products for both commercial and military use.

Ed Dinger

PRINCIPAL SUBSIDIARIES

Lotus Technologies, Inc.; IRPC, Inc.; DeltaNu Inc.; Intevac Asia Pte. Ltd.

PRINCIPAL COMPETITORS

Aviza Technologies, Inc.; ULVAC Inc.; OC Oerlikon Corporation AG.

FURTHER READING

Goldman, James, S., "Intevac Arises from Varian's Restructuring," *Business Journal Serving San Jose & Silicon Valley,* April 13, 1992, p. 1.

Hostetler, Michele, "Former Varian Executive Proves His Critics Wrong," *Business Journal Serving San Jose & Silicon Valley,* October 16, 1995, p. 1, 34.

"Intevac, Inc.," *Spectroscopy,* December 2005, p. 34.

"Intevac Names Kevin Fairbairn as New President and Chief Officer," *Data Storage News,* January 27, 2002.

Jacques Whitford

---

3 Spectacle Lake Drive
Dartmouth, Nova Scotia B3B 1W8
Canada
Telephone: (902) 468-7777
Fax: (902) 468-9009
Web site: http://www.jacqueswhitford.com

Private Company
Incorporated: 1972
Employees: 1,600
Sales: $100 million (2006 est.)
NAIC: 541330 Engineering Services

■ ■ ■

Based in Nova Scotia, Canada, Jacques Whitford is an environmental science and engineering firm providing a wide variety of consulting services in North America, the Caribbean, South America, the Middle East, Russia, China, and Southeast Asia. All told, the company operates in more than 85 countries, served by a network of more than 45 offices in Canada and the United States, as well as outposts in the United Arab Emirates and Qatar. Clients come from the ranks of oil and gas companies, real estate companies, government agencies, mining operations, agricultural concerns, fisheries, forestry companies, paper mills, water suppliers, manufacturers in a broad range of industries, transportation entities, and insurance firms.

Services offered by Jacques Whitford include environmental audits and site assessments, environmental impact studies, environmental planning,
remediation, water resource management, air quality monitoring, sold waste management, and terrestrial and marine biological resources surveys and analysis. Jacques Whitford is 100 percent employee-owned, with about one-third of the staff owning shares. Shareholders are selected by a group of senior colleagues. In addition, the company provides a profit-sharing plan.

COMPANY FOUNDED: 1972

Jacques Whitford was founded in 1972 by Hector J. Jacques and Michael S. Whitford. Jacques was born in Goa, a former Portuguese colony located on the west coast of India that became part of India in 1961. He came from a well-to-do family. His uncle built CMM Group, a pharmaceutical manufacturer and trading firm into one of the largest companies on the island nation of Gao and also served as a mentor to Jacques. The young man studied geotechnical engineering at the Indian Institute of Technology in Bombay and immigrated to Canada to enter a master's degree program at the Technical University of Nova Scotia, primarily because of a scholarship offer. After graduating in 1967 with a degree in soil mechanics and foundation engineering, he remained in the area, taking a position in the geotechnical department of Warnock Hersey International Ltd., a national engineering firm that was involved in the construction of the A. Murray MacKay Bridge, an innovative bridge that connected the Halifax peninsula to Dartmouth, where the firm maintained a office to which Jacques was assigned. One of his colleagues was Michael Whitford.

Jacques became the head of his division, but after nearly five years with the firm, Warnock Hersey was

In 1972, Hector Jacques and Mike Whitford became the original Jacques Whitford team with a simple promise: to understand your business better than anyone in our industry, and deliver customized, value-added solutions that meet your needs.

acquired by a larger international firm and a non-engineer was put in charge. Jacques had always believed that being part of a larger firm would be advantageous on a number of levels, but he was disenchanted with Warnock Hersey. He told *Atlantic Oil & Gas Magazine,* "This company was at odds with the fundamental vision that I always had, right from the very, very start, that people are the number one driving force in business."

Moreover, the company was poorly run, adding to his frustration. Although Jacques told *Canadian Business,* "I had no compelling zeal to set up my own firm," he and Whitford decided to strike out on their and form a partnership to provide site-consulting services. With C$5,000 in seed money they spent three months setting up shop in the basement of the CHNS building in Halifax with a single telephone, opening their doors for business in June 1972. The partners were far from certain, however, about their prospects for success.

Jacques recalled in a company-written profile, "In those early days it was all about survival. I remember even saying to Michael that I would buy my own desk and my own stapler and that he should do the same. That way, if things didn't work out, we could each go our own way without having to divvy up the assets." His fears proved unnecessary. Within the week the fledgling firm turned profitable, landing its first major project, the Micmac Mall in Dartmouth, Atlantic Canada's largest shopping center. In the first week, the firm signed ten clients, and within a month it signed a second major contract, the Mabou Bridge in Cape Breton. In the first eight months Jacques Whitford recorded revenues of $89,000 CAD.

Jacques Whitford did well in its original field of expertise, involved in bridges and almost every office tower project in downtown Halifax, including Purdry's Wharf and the Sheraton Hotel, the World Trade and Convention Centre, and the CIBC and TD bank buildings. The goal at this stage was to become the largest engineering firm of its type in the Atlantic Provinces, a task that the partners estimated would require six years of effort. Instead, they hit the mark in just two years. By 1980 the company was operating in all four of Canada's Atlantic Provinces. Jacques Whitford set its sights on establishing a national footprint. It also looked to become diversified, growing into a multidisciplinary engineering firm that was not only dependent on any one sector but could also tackle complex projects that required the service of engineers with different areas of expertise.

MOBIL OIL CONTRACT SIGNED: 1980

In the late 1970s Jacques became interested in the oil and gas industry, which at the time was beginning to emerge offshore in the Atlantic Provinces. "Maybe it is the spirit I have or the kind of drive I have," Jacques told *Atlantic Oil & Gas Magazine,* "but I said there is no way I am going to be sitting 100 miles from where all the action is going to take place and not get my fingers in the pot."

Hence, in 1979 he forged a strategic relationship and joint venture with Houston, Texas–based McClelland Geosciences to provide geotechnical services to the oil and gas companies who were beginning to operate off Canada's Atlantic coast. Although Jacques Whitford was told that it could not hope to complete against multinational consulting firms, Jacques Whitford was able to firmly established itself in this field in 1980 when Mobil Oil became its first major client. According to *U.S. Business Review,* "The Mobil contract gave Jacques Whitford the leverage and name recognition to expand its services to oil and gas projects first throughout Canada and ultimately around the world. The business also gained ground thanks to the increasing environmental awareness of the late 1970s and early 1980s."

Jacques Whitford began offering environmental consulting services to offshore oil and gas companies in 1985. In order to provide the kind of information clients needed to complete their Environmental Impact Reviews, the firm was forced to broaden its capabilities through the hiring of new people. The company's commitment to hiring highly trained people (about four out of five members of the professional staff held master's or doctorate degrees) spurred even greater growth. To help retain these employees, as well as to spur productivity, the company kept bureaucracy to a minimum. Further incentive came when the company became completely employee owned. This deep and dedicated talent pool helped Jacques Whitford to further its efforts at diversification, allowing the firm to move into new fields as the market dictated. As a result, the company was able to expand its reach to include such areas as hydrogeology and waste-management systems. In time, half of

KEY DATES

1972: Hector Jacques and Michael Whitford found engineering firm.
1980: Contract signed with Mobil Oil.
1985: Environmental services are offered to oil and gas clients.
1992: First office in the United States is opened.
1993: Office in Russia opens.
2002: Hector Jacques retires as CEO.
2005: Company acquires AXYS Environmental Consulting Ltd.
2007: North American Wetland Engineering LLC and EcoCheck, Inc., are acquired.

its revenues would come from environmental projects. Jacques Whitford's capabilities also came to the notice of the Canadian government, which hired the firm to serve a national consultant on the Canadian Green Plan, a comprehensive environmental policy initiative that was launched in the late 1980s.

It was the experience gained through work on all of the major projects on the Scotian Shelf and Grand Banks that led to contracts elsewhere. Jacques Whitford also benefited from the 1989 merger of McClelland Geosciences with Fugro Consultants International, creating the world's largest offshore geotechnical firm. The joint venture between Jacques Whitford and Fugro was then able to take advantage of the scope of international Fugro's operations.

VANCOUVER OFFICES OPENS: 1997

Jacques Whitford continued to add offices as it expanded its capabilities and developed its client base. An office was opened in the nation's capital, Ottawa, in 1988. A Toronto office was added in 1991, which was followed one year later by a branch in Calgary. Also in 1992 Jacques Whitford looked to the south, opening its first office in the United States. The opening of the firm's first overseas office occurred in 1993 when a Russian branch debuted. Finally, in 1997 Jacques Whitford opened an office in Vancouver, giving the firm coast-to-coast coverage in Canada. By this time the firm employed more than 500 people working in about two dozen offices located in Canada, the United States, and Russia, as well as in Argentina, China, and Trinidad. For the past 25 years the firm had enjoyed an annual growth rate of about 17 percent, so that revenues were in the

$65 million CAD range, half of which came from environmental work.

In the mid-1990s, Jacques, who was in his early 50s, announced that he planned to quit his job as chief executive officer by the time he was 55. As much as he admired his uncle, who continued to run the family business at the age of 89, Jacques reportedly desired to have more time to serve on the boards of start-up companies, where he could pass on the wisdom he had gained in that area. He also wanted to pursue some public service work; he already sat on the board of the Victoria General Hospital, for example.

Jacques stayed on longer than anticipated, finally retiring from the firm in 2002, after 30 years as CEO. He did not leave entirely, however, as he retained the post of chairman. Taking over as chief executive, just the second in the history of Jacques Whitford, was Robert (Bob) Youden, who took over in 2003. Youden held a commerce degree from Dalhousie University. After serving as corporate controller at Bow Valley Offshore Drilling and chief financial officer at Schwartz Inc., Youden began a 17-year career at J.D. Irving Ltd., where he held several senior-level executive positions. He eventually became vice-president of transportation there, responsible for the running of six subsidiaries.

With Youden at the helm, Jacques Whitford continued to enjoy steady growth. In April 2005 the company acquired AXYS Environmental Consulting Ltd., a major environmental specialist in western and northern Canada that was also employee-owned and had a similar history to Jacques Whitford. AXYS had been founded in 1974 in Sidney, British Columbia.

In April 2007 Jacques Whitford reshaped its operation by selling a Boston-based subsidiary, iTAG-PARCEL LLC, developer of a web-based methods to produce and deliver environmental site assessments, property condition assessments, and other types of due diligence reports used to complete real estate transactions. The business was sold to Environmental Inc. A short while later, Jacques Whitford made a pair of acquisitions, picking up North American Wetland Engineering, LLC (NAWE), and its subsidiary EcoCheck, Inc. NAWE was a young company, founded in 1997 to focus on wetland technology, and it had launched EcoCheck in 2002 to provide management services for wetlands' wastewater treatment systems.

Although Jacques Whitford continued to grow its business, it strove to remain true to its core corporate values and gained regular recognition as a good place to work. In 2006, it garnered three accolades; it was named among the top 100 employers by *Maclean's*, as one of the *Financial Post*'s Ten Best Companies to Work For, and as one of the top-ten family-friendly employers by *Today's Parent* magazine. In 2006 the company allied itself with the Carbonfund.org to reduce its carbon footprint by purchasing carbon offsets and instituting conservation measures to make its operation carbon neutral, part of the effort to reduce gas emissions to reverse global warming.

Ed Dinger

PRINCIPAL SUBSIDIARIES

Jacques Whitford Company Inc.; Jacques Whitford AXYS; Jacques Whitford NAWE; Jacques Whitford EcoCheck.

PRINCIPAL COMPETITORS

Golder Associates Ltd.; Gartner Lee Ltd.; Malcolm Pirnie, Inc.

FURTHER READING

Berman, David, "Engineered for Success," *Canadian Business,* December 1996, p. 112.

"Diverse Service," *US Business Review,* January 2006, p. 101.

"Hector Jacques Pioneers the Power of People," *Atlantic Oil & Gas Magazine,* October 2006.

Martin, Robert, "From a Standing Start: Hector Jacques and His Partner Have Built a Huge National Engineering Firm from the Ground Up," *Halifax (Canada) Daily News,* September 25, 1996, p. 24.

McLeod, John, "Celebrating a 25-Year Success Story," *Halifax (Canada) Daily News,* June 3, 1997, p. 21.

Jenny Craig, Inc.

———— ■ ————

5770 Fleet Street
Carlsbad, California 92008
U.S.A.
Telephone: (760) 696-4000
Toll Free: (800) 597-5366
Fax: (760) 696-4009
Web site: http://www.jennycraig.com

Wholly Owned Subsidiary of Nestlé S.A.
Incorporated: 1983
Employees: 3,400
Sales: $462 million (2005)
NAIC: 812191 Diet and Weight Reducing Centers; 311999 All Other Miscellaneous Food Manufacturing; 812990 All Other Personal Services

■ ■ ■

Jenny Craig, Inc., headquartered in Carlsbad, California, operates approximately 650 company-owned and franchised weight loss centers with locations in the United States, Canada, Australia, New Zealand, and Puerto Rico. Through these centers as well its Direct Consultant telephone service, Jenny Craig markets a meal plan that includes preprepared foods and provides individual diet counseling/motivational services to its clients. In July 2006, following several years of losses, Jenny Craig was acquired by Nestlé S.A. for approximately $600 million. Under Nestlé, in its Nestlé Nutrition division, Jenny Craig but continuing to operate as a separate entity.

COMPANY ORIGINS

Cofounder Jenny Craig developed an interest in the fitness industry in the 1960s through her efforts to lose weight following a pregnancy. She operated a gym in her hometown of New Orleans before joining the staff at the Body Contour fitness center in 1970. Body Contour was headed by Sid Craig, who maintained a 50 percent interest in the company. Jenny and Sid married in 1979, and together they helped turn the struggling company into a thriving business that was reporting $35 million in sales by 1982.

That year, the Craigs sold Body Contour to a subsidiary of Nutri/System Inc. With the $3.5 million they made from the sale, the Craigs formed Jenny Craig, Inc., in 1983. Initially barred from entering the U.S. diet industry by a noncompetition clause, the company opened its first weight loss center in Australia. By 1985, 69 Jenny Craig Weight Loss Centers were in operation in Australia, and the company became one of the biggest players in that country's diet industry. That year, the Craigs returned to the United States, opening 13 centers in the Los Angeles area, which were soon followed by six additional facilities in Chicago.

U.S. EXPANSION IN THE EARLY YEARS

By 1987, the company had established 46 centers in the United States and 114 in foreign countries; of these 160 units, 45 were franchised operations. Seeking capital from outside investors, the Craigs considered taking their company public but were discouraged by a weak market for initial public offerings. Instead, Michael Ten-

COMPANY PERSPECTIVES

In response to the needs of today's hectic, fast-paced world, Jenny Craig, Inc., offers a comprehensive weight management program that takes a practical, non-dieting approach to losing weight to help clients develop a healthy relationship with food, build an active lifestyle, and create a more balanced approach to living.

nenbaum, vice-chairman of investment banking at Bear Stearns Companies, Inc., stepped in. Tennenbaum brought together a group of investors that included his partners at Bear Stearns, the New York Life Insurance Co., and TA Associates, an investment and venture capital firm, among others. Together they invested $50 million in Jenny Craig, and two bank loans contributed another $50 million to the company's recapitalization. The successful expansion left the Craig family with a $108 million dividend.

Marketing was integral to Jenny Craig's success. In the early 1990s, 10 percent of sales went into commercial advertising each year, and franchises were required to spend the higher of 10 percent of sales or $1,000 a week on advertising for their centers. The company's television campaigns featured celebrities, such as actors Elliott Gould and Susan Ruttan, who had achieved success with the Jenny Craig program. Moreover, ads provided a toll-free number that automatically connected callers to the center nearest to them. In 1991, the company also began a direct-mail campaign based on its extensive database of two million current and former clients.

The Jenny Craig program was designed by its staff of registered dieticians and psychologists and approved by an advisory board consisting of health and nutrition research experts. The three principal tenets of the program were behavior education, proper nutrition, and exercise. Central to the program was Jenny's Cuisine, portion- and calorie-controlled foods that participants were required to purchase. Jenny's Cuisine was created by suppliers in compliance with standards set by a board of dieticians; suppliers included Overhill Farms, Magic Pantry Foods, Truitt Bros., Campbell Soup Company, Carnation, and Vitex Foods. The program made available 60 different breakfast, lunch, dinner, dessert, and snack food items, including apple cinnamon oatmeal, teriyaki beef, and chocolate mousse. Menus were updated to include microwaveable entrees and canned

foods in 1986. The company's gross revenues from food sales increased from 60 percent in 1986 to 91 percent in 1993.

Another important part of the Jenny Craig program was its twice-weekly meetings. New clients met with a counselor, who would monitor their progress and sell them installments of Jenny's Cuisine. At subsequent group meetings, participants attended classes covering subjects such as "dining out," "asserting yourself," and "dieting as a team." In 1989, videocassette programs were introduced into counseling classes to ensure consistency at all centers. After viewing videocassettes, participants engaged in discussion facilitated by their counselor.

A PUBLIC OFFERING AND A CHALLENGING MARKETPLACE

In 1991, under improved market conditions, Jenny Craig was taken public, issuing 3.5 million shares at $21 per share. The offering generated $73.5 million in capital, which was used to satisfy the company's bank loans and its debt to the investment group. During this time, the Craigs sold another 1.65 million of their own shares for $36 million, and the banks and investors garnered $11.5 million for the 550,000 shares they sold. As a result, the Craigs retained 59 percent of the company, while banks and investors controlled 20 percent and the public claimed 29 percent.

Sid Craig's expectations for company revenues to grow by 15 to 20 percent a year through expansion proved unrealistic. After a period of remarkable growth in the weight loss industry as a whole during the 1980s, public attention focused on the potential health risks involved in dieting during the early 1990s, and enrollment at diet centers dropped. In 1990, Jenny Craig and its rival Nutri/System Inc. were named as defendants in a class action lawsuit alleging that weight loss programs, like those promoted by the companies, had resulted in cases of gallbladder disease. Moreover, Jenny Craig was named in 11 other personal injury cases during this time. The disputes were settled, and the alleged link between gallbladder problems and the Jenny Craig program was never proven. However, the cases prompted a Federal Trade Commission (FTC) investigation into the validity of the claims for successful weight loss made by Jenny Craig and other companies in the diet industry.

The company soon terminated its operations in the United Kingdom, due to their lack of profitability, and, in 1992, a secondary offering of public stock was postponed indefinitely, due to weak market conditions and a decline in profits linked to a failed promotional

KEY DATES

1983: Sid and Jenny Craig form the company with the opening of its first weight loss center in Australia.

1985: The Craigs begin opening weight loss centers in the United States.

1991: The company is taken public.

2001: Following a decade of growth and decline, Jenny Craig sells its headquarters building, is delisted by the New York Stock Exchange, and begins trading over the counter.

2002: An investor group acquires the company in a deal valued at about $115 million; the company is taken private.

2004: Jenny Craig launches its customized delivery service, Jenny Direct, and the Jenny Craig YourStyle personalized weight management program.

2005: A television advertising campaign featuring actress Kirstie Alley debuts; Patricia Larchet advances into the CEO position.

2006: Jenny Craig is acquired by Nestlé S.A. for $600 million.

2007: Advertising campaign featuring Valerie Bertinelli results in record number of callers.

campaign. Nevertheless, Jenny Craig continued the expansion of its diet center chain, opening 89 new centers and repurchasing 41 franchises.

During 1993, the ongoing FTC investigations into the advertising and promotional practices of the diet industry generated more negative publicity. Specifically, the FTC questioned whether advertising was leading consumers to mistakenly believe that maintaining weight loss after finishing the diet program would be easy. Moreover, medical journals and newspapers reported that "yo-yo dieting"—the repeated gain and loss of weight—caused more health problems than simply remaining slightly overweight. Jenny Craig and four other major commercial weight loss companies—Weight Watchers, Nutri/System, Diet Center, and Physician's Weight Loss Center—petitioned for standard advertising rules for the industry, but the petition was rejected.

When Nutri/System reported severe financial setbacks in April 1993 and was forced to close its headquarters and 283 of its centers, Jenny Craig immediately began an advertising campaign offering Nutri/System clients the opportunity to continue their weight loss programs at Jenny Craig at no additional service fee. In its open letter to Nutri/System clients, Jenny Craig emphasized its financial strength as a "debt-free, $500 million New York Stock Exchange Company with ten years of proven success." However, neither Jenny Craig nor Weight Watchers International, which had launched a similar campaign, saw a significant increase in enrollments.

Increased competition in the industry, largely by "do-it-yourself" diet companies, also began to cut into Jenny Craig's market by emphasizing the high costs of membership in diet center programs. Typical Jenny Craig clients—women wanting to lose 30 or more pounds—could spend more than $1,000 as clients of Jenny Craig, paying an initial start-up fee and about $70 a week for meals. Other companies, such as Just Help Yourself, began offering self-administered diet plans, marketing themselves as less expensive, more convenient alternatives to diet centers.

Despite the shrinking market, the Craigs continued to expand. In 1993, Jenny Craig added 100 new centers and bought back 48 franchises, bringing its total outlets to 794. The company also introduced a program for those living in areas beyond the reach of its centers, allowing customers to order products by telephone and receive direct shipments.

Some shareholders disagreed with the company's expansion policy. Stock purchased at $21 per share in 1991 had sunk below $15 the following year. In October 1993, three shareholders filed a suit against the company, alleging that the expansion was designed to bolster sales figures, overshadowing the company's financial difficulties. While Jenny Craig's total revenues for the year ended June 30, 1993, were $490.5 million, up 6 percent from 1992, average revenues for each company-owned center had declined 10 percent from the previous year. Moreover, although the company's Southern California centers remained profitable, these outlets had experienced a 26 percent decline in revenues.

NEW LEADERSHIP AND CHALLENGES IN THE SECOND DECADE

When Ronald E. Gerevas, chief operating officer and president, departed unexpectedly in November 1993, Jenny Craig stock dropped to $11.75 a share. Gerevas's replacement, Albert J. DiMarco, left after just four months; William R. Lewis, a former business associate of DiMarco who had just been appointed chief financial officer the month before, left with DiMarco. By this time, confidence in the company was declining, and its stock was trading at about $6.25 per share, less than one-third of its original price. In April 1994, hoping that new management would help restore investor confidence, the company appointed C. Joseph LaBonté as president and CEO, and Ellen Destray was made chief operating officer. Sid Craig remained as the company's chairperson.

Jenny Craig introduced modifications to its original program in 1994. A wider variety of meetings were offered, and clients were allowed to choose the classes most pertinent to their lifestyle. The company's video programs also were updated and made available for home use. Perhaps most important, the program was modified to reflect current trends in popular psychology that suggested that overeating was a result of emotional distress. Accordingly, Jenny Craig encouraged clients to discover, address, and overcome individual emotional issues that might impede the success of their dieting. Nonetheless, the company continued to struggle with declining membership into the late 1990s.

The late 1990s brought new challenges for Jenny Craig, some in the form of litigation against the company both by consumer groups and the U.S. government. In May 1997, as a result of an earlier charge of deceptive advertising against the company, the FTC imposed restrictions requiring Jenny Craig to stipulate in its advertising: "For many dieters weight loss is temporary." Furthermore, testimonials of those who had been very successful under the plan had to be accompanied by a disclaimer: "This result is not typical. You may be less successful." In addition to these provisions, Jenny Craig was forced to publish the average weight loss its customers experienced and to provide scientific data supporting future claims.

Next, in September 1997 the U.S. Food and Drug Administration recalled a popular diet drug composed of either dexfenfluramine (sold as Redux) or fenfluramine and phentermine (fen-phen). Data indicated that fen-phen damaged the heart valves of some people who used the drug. This decision affected Jenny Craig, as the company had begun using physicians outside its organization to write prescriptions for fen-phen and had incorporated the drug into the weight loss program. Also during this time, the company faced litigation on the part of some former employees in Boston, men who alleged sex discrimination in the workplace.

In February 1999 Jenny Craig joined a coalition of weight loss organizations in issuing guidelines to give consumers regarding program effectiveness, safety, and costs. This effort, it was hoped, would forestall further efforts at regulating the weight loss industry. These full disclosure guidelines required weight loss organizations to give consumers information about the qualifications of their staffs, health risks associated with obesity, health risks of rapid weight loss, and the full costs of their program, including the price of the food.

The weight loss industry in general and Jenny Craig in particular experienced financial setbacks during this time. Net income between 1994 and 1998 was a roller-coaster ride for Jenny Craig, with postings of $36.7 million in 1994, to $11.7 million in 1995, a rebound of $22.9 million in 1996, and a decline to $2.12 million in 1998. The company reported that its membership rate had stalled, and its number of outlets had fallen to 675.

1999 AND BEYOND

Jenny Craig reacted to uneven profits on several fronts. On December 9, 1998, the company announced the appointment of a new president, Philip Voluck, who would continue to serve as chief operating officer, a position he had gained six months earlier, coming to the company with considerable experience at ex-rival Nutri/System. Founder Jenny Craig continued to serve as vice-chairman of the company, while her husband Sid Craig remained chairman and CEO. In March 1999 the company announced its plans to refocus its mission into one of self-improvement rather than weight loss. The new program included two new product lines: a new Advanced Nutrients line of food supplements, sold exclusively via the Internet, and a new Jenny Craig line of exercise equipment. At the same time, the company refocused its food program, and the resulting ABC program was simpler to use and gave clients more choices. Subsequent program variations included a less costly plan for clients, under which they were able to purchase supplements rather than meals.

Personal struggles also ensued for Jenny Craig herself. She had not appeared as company spokesperson since she had been injured in a car accident that resulted in a speech impediment. Craig's daughter, Denise, took over as company spokesperson as Craig sought medical treatment from one expert after another. Finally, three years later, a California surgeon reconstructed her jaw and placed her on a rigorous therapy program. No stranger to rigorous exercise routines, Jenny Craig reported success and hoped she could start the new century with fully restored ability to speak, a hope that was eventually realized. Similarly, Jenny Craig management hoped that its efforts to refocus the company's mission would help it withstand changes in the weight loss industry.

In its ongoing efforts to attract a diverse clientele and promote healthy lifestyles, in July 1999 Jenny Craig launched a new health and fitness show on television. Called *Jenny's Fit in 15,* the show aired on The Health Network, a new cable television network integrated with an Internet site. The half-hour daily program was geared toward women of all ages, ethnicities, and body types and combined 15 minutes of aerobic and toning exercise routines with interviews featuring women who had overcome adversity and worked to achieve health and happiness (much like cofounder Jenny Craig).

Still, net losses at the company continued to mount, and in November 1999 the company began restructuring efforts. First it announced the closing of 86 of its U.S. weight loss centers, eliminating 103 positions, including 26 at company headquarters. Also new management was brought in; Patricia A. Larchet was named president and chief operating officer. Larchet had served previously as general manager of Jenny Craig's Australian operations. She became only the second woman in the company's history to take on the position of president, after cofounder Jenny Craig herself. In another bold move, the company hired former White House intern Monica Lewinsky, known widely for her relationship with President Bill Clinton, as a commercial spokesperson in a $7.2 million advertising campaign. The company maintained that Lewinsky was hired because of her commitment to overcoming weight loss struggles, but some Jenny Craig franchises chose not to use the ads, claiming that the notorious former intern was not a role model who would appeal to many. By June 2000, the company dropped Lewinsky as its spokesperson for undisclosed reasons.

At the onset of the new century, Jenny Craig introduced new menu programs. In January 2000, a new low-carbohydrate menu option was introduced. In February, Jenny Craig ventured into the retail market for the first time when it collaborated with Balance Bar in the launch of a new nutrition bar. In April, the company initiated a new promotional campaign called It's Your Choice, through which it introduced new products and programs to fit different lifestyles, tastes, and budgets. At this time, a total of 660 Jenny Craig Centres were in operation, down from 767 from the year before; of these, the company owned 548 centers, and 112 were run by franchisees.

Losses mounted, however, for the second largest company in the weight-loss industry, and clearly some more radical shifts were in order. In 2001, Jenny Craig generated $16 million through the sale of its corporate headquarters building in La Jolla, California, to nearby National University. Still, given its lack of profitability, and its subpar equity and market capitalization, Jenny Craig was delisted from the New York Stock Exchange during this time and began trading over the counter.

Jenny Craig remained a highly recognized brand name, with a loyal customer base, and was therefore considered by some an attractive acquisition target. In January 2002, a group of investors that included the Craigs and was headed by ACI Capital Co., Inc., and MidOcean Capital Partners, Inc. (a spinoff of the Deutsche Bank's private equity arm), took Jenny Craig private in a leveraged buyout (LBO) valued at about $115 million. Sid Craig remained on the board but gave up his position as CEO, and he and Jenny Craig reduced the 67 percent stake in the company that they had founded nearly 20 years ago, retaining a minority interest of 20 percent.

Later that year, the company's headquarters were relocated to Carlsbad, California. At this point, Jenny Craig operated 652 company-owned and franchised centers and employed more than 3,000 workers worldwide. A new CEO, James P. Evans, who had served as CEO at the hotel chain Best Western International, was named to replace Sid Craig. The company then quickly set about improving its financial picture, upgrading its data platforms as well as its weight loss centers and enhancing the training available to its sales staff. The company celebrated its 20th anniversary in 2003, announcing itself as reinvigorated and ready to increase business in the coming years. It was inducted that year into the U.S. Small Business Administration's Hall of Fame.

In an age of increasing media focus on the so-called obesity problem, some analysts speculated that Jenny Craig's strength—its commitment to healthy eating and gradual weight loss with attendant counseling services—failed to match the public's demand for quick fixes. Without straying from its principles, Jenny Craig acknowledged the need for convenience and privacy by introducing a customized delivery service called Jenny Direct. Clients could have their food delivered to their homes and receive advice and encouragement via telephone consultations with trained staff.

In December 2004, Jenny Craig received a much-needed advertising boost when film and television actress Kirstie Alley joined the Jenny Craig program. Alley was set to star in a Showtime network television series called *Fat Actress,* which showcased Alley's struggles with weight along with her irreverent sense of humor. In one episode of the show, Alley receives a contract offer from Jenny Craig; in reality she had accepted that offer and introduced a greater and more diverse viewing audience to the Jenny Craig program. A high-profile campaign of television commercials and print ads for Jenny Craig starring Alley helped further fuel a turnaround for the company.

In 2005, veteran executive Patricia A. Larchet advanced into the CEO position. The following year, in June 2006, management announced that Nestlé S.A., a giant in the food industry, had agreed to acquire Jenny Craig for about $600 million. A company first and perhaps best known for chocolate products had chosen to add to its fold a company dedicated to weight management through healthy lifestyle choices. It was a better fit than it seemed, however, as Nestlé already owned the Lean Cuisine brand of frozen meals and had established a nutrition division, into which Jenny Craig would be incorporated. Nestlé enjoyed prominent and abundant shelf space in the country's supermarkets, and analysts predicted that sales of the Jenny Craig brand of prepackaged meals might again become available in stores. Nestlé planned to retain Jenny Craig's current management to continue running the chain of more than 600 weight loss centers from the company's Carlsbad, California, headquarters.

Meanwhile, the advertising campaign using actress Kirstie Alley had been wildly successful, nearly doubling the number of Jenny Craig clients. However, Alley's 75-pound weight loss meant that a new public success story was needed to promote the company's customized programs. In the spring of 2007, actress Valerie Bertinelli was signed to represent Jenny Craig, as her own efforts to lose weight were documented to inspire potential clients. The launch of the Bertinelli campaign reportedly garnered the greatest number of new callers to Jenny Craig in company history.

Elaine Belsito
Updated, Shannon and Terry Hughes; Robynn Montgomery

PRINCIPAL COMPETITORS

Nutri/System Inc.; Slim-Fast Foods Co.; Weight Watchers International Inc.

FURTHER READING

Allen, Mike, "Jenny Craig Trims Fat After $3.8 Million Loss," *San Diego Business Journal*, November 8, 1999, p. 34.

Barret, Amy, "How Can Jenny Craig Keep on Gaining?" *Business Week*, April 12, 1993, p. 52.

Berman, Phyllis, "Fat City," *Forbes*, February 17, 1992, pp. 72–73.

Bird, Laura, "Jenny Craig Kicks Off a Database Program," *Adweek's Marketing Week*, January 7, 1991, p. 8.

"Craigs Again Take Control of Jenny Craig," *San Diego Business Journal*, October 13, 1997, p. 47.

Goldman, Kevin, "Ads Dished Up for Nutri/System Dieters," *Wall Street Journal*, May 7, 1993, p. B8.

Harrison, Joan, "Weight Loss Firm Jenny Craig Is Considering a Sale," *Mergers & Acquisitions Journal*, July 2001, p. 27.

Holden, Benjamin A., "Financial Officer Quits Jenny Craig After Brief Tenure," *Wall Street Journal*, March 10, 1994, p. B10.

Hyten, Todd, "Ex-Jenny Craig Male Workers Allege Discrimination," *Boston Business Journal*, October 14, 1994, p. 5.

Leon, Hortense, "Doctors, Pharmacies Say Fen-Phen Recall No Problem," *South Florida Business Journal*, September 19, 1997, p. 5.

Lippert, Barbara, "The Weighting Game: Jenny Craig Calls on Candid Kirstie Alley for Fresh Approach," *Adweek*, January 10, 2005, p. 27.

———, "Weighty Matters," *Adweek*, January 10, 1994, p. 28.

Melton, Marissa, "Guaranteed: Lose 1 Pound in 90 Days," *U.S. News & World Report*, February 22, 1999, p. 67.

Pollack, Judann, "Fed Up with Promoting Diets, Weight-Loss Rivals Branch Out," *Advertising Age*, March 29, 1999, pp. 3–4.

Rundle, Rhonda L., "Jenny Craig Inc Delays Planned Stock Offering," *Wall Street Journal*, May 28, 1992, p. A8.

Saddler, Jeanne, "Three Diet Firms Settle False-Ad Case; Two Others Vow to Fight FTC Charges," *Wall Street Journal*, October 1993, p. B5.

Sorkin, Andrew Ross, "Nestlé to Buy Jenny Craig, Betting Diets Are on Rise," *New York Times*, June 19, 2006, p. C1.

Valeriano, Lourdes Lee, "Diet Programs Hope Broader Services Fatten Profits," *Wall Street Journal*, August 5, 1993, p. B4.

Warner, Melanie, "In Ads, 'Fat Actress' Label Seems Less Fitting," *New York Times*, September 12, 2005, p. C9.

Winter, Greg, "Jenny Craig Founders Are Selling Chain in $115 Million Deal," *New York Times*, January 29, 2002, p. C4.

JEPPESEN.

Jeppesen Sanderson, Inc.

55 Inverness Drive East
Englewood, Colorado 80112-5498
U.S.A.
Telephone: (303) 799-9090
Toll Free: (800) 621-5377
Fax: (303) 328-4153
Web site: http://www.jeppesen.com

*Wholly Owned Subsidiary of Boeing Commercial Aviation
    Services*
Incorporated: 1934 as Jeppesen Company
Employees: 3,000
Sales: $235 million (1999)
NAIC: 511990 All Other Publishers; 511210 Software
    Publishers; 54137 Surveying and Mapping (Except
    Geophysical) Services; 611512 Flight Training

∎ ∎ ∎

Jeppesen Sanderson, Inc., is the world's leading provider
of navigational charts and other aviation information. It
also provides training materials for pilots and mechanics
and serves the marine and rail markets. Launched with
the handwritten notes of an early mail pilot, the
company has evolved along with changing technology. A
unit of the Boeing Company, Jeppesen has offices at
several locations across the United States and in more
than a dozen foreign countries. Its products are a fixture
at most of the world's airlines and on 18,000 commercial ships; the company counts one million users
overall.

ORIGINS

Jeppesen Sanderson, Inc., holds a special place in aviation history, having manufactured products that opened
the way for instrument flying: clocks, compasses, and
other gauges to chart a plane's course when visible
outside cues such as landmarks and the horizon are
obscured by weather. Before Jeppesen's charts, pilots
typically consulted road maps, often following highways
or railways, and often had to land in fields to wait out
inclement weather.

The company counts as its founding date 1934,
when Captain Elrey Borge Jeppesen launched the business out of his Salt Lake City home. Born in Lake
Charles, Louisiana, to Danish immigrant parents,
"Captain Jepp" was infatuated by flying at an early age
and earned his wings on the barnstorming circuit,
eventually earning a pilot's license signed by Orville
Wright.

In 1930 Jeppesen started flying night airmail routes
to Cheyenne, Wyoming, and Oakland, California, for
Varney Airlines and then Boeing Air Transport. Travers-
ing hundreds of miles of desert and mountain ranges in
an underpowered airplane was an epic adventure, and
Jeppesen began taking note of terrain, obstacles, airfield
details, and other information relevant to navigating the
treacherous skies safely.

A number of Jeppesen's colleagues asked for copies
of his notes, which he started selling at $10 each. After
a merger of Jeppesen's previous employers formed
United Airlines, he continued to fly for United, marry-
ing a flight attendant there, Nadine, in 1936. She
helped him run his maps business as a sideline dubbed

COMPANY PERSPECTIVES

For more than 70 years, aviation professionals worldwide have relied on Jeppesen for the information they need to reach their destinations safely and successfully. It's a record of success we take great pride in, but also one that we never stop building upon. Our constant innovation and willingness to challenge the status quo has led to countless advancements in navigational information and data delivery, including an industry paradigm shift from analog to digital information. While our roots are in aviation, today we leverage our expertise to deliver innovative information solutions to air, sea and rail operators. We are an industry pioneer, a reliable partner for our customers, and the most trusted source of accurate and timely information for professionals on the ground, in the air and on the water.

Jeppesen & Company. The airline also became an early subscriber. Jeppesen kept his lucrative day job at United until the mid-1950s.

"Captain Jepp" went to great lengths to make his maps as detailed as possible, traveling the country and scaling obstacles such as mountains and towers with an altimeter so he could mark their precise height. He later hired artists to render detailed relief maps simulating a bird's eye view of terrain.

Jeppesen moved to Denver in 1941. The company supplied the U.S. Navy during World War II, and in 1945 signed up its first airline customer. Jeppesen grew to more than 100 employees by the mid-1950s. An office opened in Frankfurt, Germany, in 1957 to give the company a presence in the Eastern Hemisphere.

Jeppesen's charts became indispensable to most of the world's airlines; airline pilots could be seen carrying large leather briefcases full of them through terminals the world over. Although vital, reliance on the printed page had its drawbacks. A wide-ranging captain could spend a couple of hours each week simply replacing outdated maps for all his routes.

Los Angeles's Times-Mirror Publishing Co. acquired Jeppesen's business in 1961. Annual sales were reported at $3 to $5 million. In 1968, Times Mirror acquired Sanderson Films of Wichita, Kansas, a maker of aviation-related instructional materials. It was merged with Jeppesen six years later.

INTO THE DIGITAL AGE

Jeppesen involved itself early in the shift toward electronic distribution of information. Its NavData database entered service with National Airlines in 1973. By the early 1980s Jeppesen entered the emerging electronic flight calculator business with a product called the NavStar, produced in partnership with Texas Instruments. A more advanced model called the ProStar followed soon after. These types of products handled calculations previously made by the E6B flight computer, a kind of circular slide rule for determining the effect of wind on one's route.

Around 1996 Jeppesen began offering electronic versions of its maps, primarily for the general aviation market. This CD-ROM software, called JeppView, allowed users to print out maps for their planned trips. The company's top-of-the-line handheld electronic flight computer was then called the TechStar Pro.

Annual revenues had risen to $80 million by 1990, when the company employed more than 800 people. Some of the growth came through acquisitions. Lockheed Corporation's DataPlan unit, a maker of computerized flight planning systems for airlines, was acquired around 1989. International Aviation Publishers, a Casper, Wyoming, producer of maintenance training materials, was acquired from Hawks Industries in 1995. Jeppesen had a presence in Australasia by 1990 and added a China office in 1996. By this time the company had more than 1,000 employees.

Elrey Jeppesen passed away in 1996. The importance of his legacy was reflected in the naming of the main terminal at Denver International Airport after him, and a giant statue there of Jeppesen in his aviator gear. His wife Nadine had preceded him in death by a few months.

BOUGHT BY BOEING

Jeppesen had 1,400 employees in 1999 and revenues of $235 million. It claimed an 80 percent market share and was said to have profit margins of more than 25 percent. Printed charts remained a central part of the business; the company produced more than 2.5 billion of them per year.

Jeppesen changed hands after Chicago's Tribune media group acquired Times Mirror. It was bought by the Boeing Company in August 2000. The acquisition had nostalgic overtones; Elrey Jeppesen had flown one of the company's 40-B biplanes on his first mail routes for Boeing Air Transport. At the time of the purchase, the deal also made practical sense for Boeing, which was interested in growing its range of aviation services.

KEY DATES

1934: Mail pilot Elrey Jeppesen starts business selling navigation guides to colleagues.

1941: Jeppesen moves from Salt Lake City to Denver.

1961: Company acquired by Times Mirror Co.

1973: Jeppesen produces first electronic navigation database for airlines, NavData.

1974: Jeppesen merged with Sanderson Films.

1989: DataPlan flight planning software firm acquired from Lockheed Corporation.

2000: Jeppesen acquired by Boeing Company for $1.5 billion.

2005: Commercial marine business unit established.

2006: Jeppesen acquires Carmen Systems, entering railway market.

airlines, ship operators were sensitive to increasing fuel costs, and navigation software that could streamline their journeys could save a great deal of time and money.

In 2005 Jeppesen established a business unit devoted to the commercial marine market. It had begun producing recreational boating products after acquiring Portland, Oregon's Nobeltec brand four years earlier. In January 2007 Boeing bought certain operations of C-Map, an Italian producer of electronic maps for recreational boaters with U.S. offices in Massachusetts.

Another market segment was breached when Boeing Company acquired Sweden's Carmen Systems in 2006, folding the business into Jeppesen Sanderson. Carmen made resource optimization software for the aviation and railroad industries, the latter a new area for Jeppesen.

Frederick C. Ingram

At $1.5 billion, the price was handsome, but Jeppesen had one of the best-known names in the aviation community and the potential to expand into new markets. The deal attracted some grumbling from Europe, where a handful of airlines and aerospace firms had formed their own flight support companies. Jeppesen remained by far the dominant force in the industry. In 2003 Jeppesen became the first commercial entity to be cleared by the Federal Aviation Administration to distribute weather information and other alerts to pilots via the Internet.

Jeppesen was introducing "electronic flight bag" software designed to replace the hefty square satchels toted by airline pilots on every journey. The growing popularity of charts delivered electronically had halved the company's paper output in a few years to a little more than one billion printed charts in 2004.

The delivery of information in the digital realm opened new possibilities. Real-time weather and other data could be displayed on the same screen as the plane's position and course. Jeppesen was working on "synthetic vision," a system for displaying terrain, waypoints, and other relevant information in 3-D for use when visibility outside the cockpit was obscured.

DIVERSIFICATION DRIVE

The name Jeppesen was known to virtually everyone in the aviation business, but it was clear there were opportunities to apply the company's tools and methodologies to other market segments. Like the

PRINCIPAL DIVISIONS

Business and General Aviation Services; Commercial and Military Aviation; Jeppesen Marine; Jeppesen GmbH; Rail, Logistics, and Terminals; Global Navigation Data Services; Training, Jeppesen/Alteon.

PRINCIPAL COMPETITORS

CMC Electronics, Inc.; European Aeronautical Group; Lufthansa Systems Group GmbH; Rockwell Collins, Inc.

FURTHER READING

Backover, Andrew, "Boeing Bid Lands Area Mapmaker; Jeppesen Sanderson Sells for $1.5 Billion," *Denver Post,* August 16, 2000, p. C1.

Cheddar, Christina, "Boeing Sees Increased Focus on E-Business at Jeppesen," *Dow Jones News Service,* August 15, 2000.

Chuter, Andy, "Airbus Urges Europeans to Rival Boeing's Jeppesen Deal," *Flight International,* February 27, 2001, p. 7.

———, "Boeing Buys Jeppesen in Bid to Build Huge Services Unit," *Flight International,* August 22, 2000, p. 27.

George, Fred, "Introducing Jeppesen's Q-Service; Jeppesen Sanderson Has Produced an Alternative Chart Service in a Conveniently Updatable U.S.-Coverage Package That Challenges the NOS System," *Business & Commercial Aviation,* February 1988, pp. 73, 75–76.

Greim, Lisa, "Flying Brain; Jeppesen Sanderson Computer Debuts on Global Flight," *Rocky Mountain News,* May 7, 1997, p. 1B.

Griffin, Greg, "3-D Navigation Looks to Send Flight Charts Packing," *Denver Post,* August 27, 2004, p. C1.

Henderson, Danna K., "From Airways to Electrons; Jeppesen Is Expanding into Electronic Information and Document Management," *Air Transport World,* August 1, 1996, pp. 95f.

Hughes, David, "Cockpits Shed Paper: The Digital Revolution Is Eliminating a Lot of the Paperwork Cluttering the Cockpits of Business Jets and Airline Aircraft," *Aviation Week & Space Technology,* February 2, 2004, pp. 52ff.

Katok, Elena, William Tarantino, and Ralph Tiedeman, "Improving Performance and Flexibility at Jeppesen: The World's Leading Aviation-Information Company," *Interfaces,* January/February 2001, vol. 31, iss. 1, pp. 7ff.

Kelly, Emma, "Jeppesen Signs NASA Deal for Databases," *Flight International,* August 8, 2000.

Larson, George C., "Fifty Years of Jeppesen Sanderson," *Business & Commercial Aviation,* October 1984, pp. 43–45.

Lert, Peter, "Computer Wars! Jeppesen Strikes Back," *Air Progress,* September 1983, pp. 28, 63f.

"Maps Looking 'Just Like Earth' Now Produced by Cartographers," *Panama City (Fla.) News,* August 9, 1954, p. 8.

Smythe, Christie, "Boeing's Jeppesen Division Charts Future Course for C-Map," *Cape Cod Times* (Hyannis, Mass.), January 31, 2007.

Thomas, Robert McG., Jr., "Elrey B. Jeppesen, Pilots' Friend, Dies at 89," *New York Times,* November 28, 1996, p. D18.

Whitlock, Flint, and Terry L. Barnhart, *Capt. Jepp and the Little Black Book: How Barnstormer and Aviation Pioneer Elrey B. Jeppesen Made the Skies Safer for Everyone,* Superior, Wis.: Savage Press, 2007.

Wolk, Arthur Alan, "Point of Law: Who Is Ultimately Responsible?" *Business & Commercial Aviation,* October 1985, p. 102.

Yamanouchi, Kelly, "A Conversation with Mark Van Tine, President of Jeppesen Sanderson Inc., a Longtime Flight-Chart Company Based in Arapahoe County," *Denver Post,* May 22, 2005, p. K3.

The Kansas City Southern
Railway Company

—■—

427 West 12th Street
Kansas City, Missouri 64121
U.S.A.
Telephone: (816) 983-1303
Fax: (816) 983-1446
Web site: http://www.kcsouthern.com

Wholly Owned Subsidiary of Kansas City Southern
Incorporated: 1887 as Kansas City Suburban Belt
 Railway
Employees: 2,600
Sales: $537 million (2006 est.)
NAIC: 482111 Line-Haul Railroads

■ ■ ■

The Kansas City Southern Railway Company (KCSR), based in Kansas City, Missouri, is the primary operating unit of holding company Kansas City Southern, a public company that also operates Kansas City Southern de Mexico, S.A. de C.V. (KCSM), and the Texas Mexican Railway Company. Linked together they create a major north-south rail corridor for commerce between Mexico and the United States. The parent company also owns a half-interest in Panama Canal Railway Company as well as controlling other transportation subsidiaries. KCSR is comprised of 3,226 miles of tracks spread across ten states: Alabama, Arkansas, Illinois, Kansas, Louisiana, Mississippi, Missouri, Oklahoma, Tennessee, and Texas. The line hauls intermodal containers, motor vehicles, coal, and such general commodities as agricultural and mineral products, chemical and petroleum products, minerals, and forest products.

19TH-CENTURY ORIGINS

KCSR was founded in 1887 as Kansas City Suburban Belt Railway by Arthur Edward Stilwell. He was born in Rochester, New York, the grandson of one of the founders of the New York Central Railroad, Hamblin Stilwell, who was also involved in the founding of the Western Union Telegraph Company and the building of the Erie Canal. As a child, Arthur Stilwell was asked by one of his grandfather's friends, Commodore Vanderbilt, what he would do when he grew up, and he replied, "I'm going West to build a railroad!" He took a circuitous route to railway building, becoming a printer and then the publisher of advertising-supported railroad timetables before moving to Kansas City where he planned to realize his long-held dream. To raise the necessary capital he formed a trust to sell lots and houses on the installment plan, a venture that made him a fortune. In 1886 one of his shareholders, former Kansas City Mayor Edward Lowe Martin, told him of an option he held to build a belt line railroad intended to link all of the railroads that came into the city, but it was set to expire in two days. Stilwell was able to raise the money required to begin construction, the "belt line" was incorporated in 1887, and it began operations in 1890.

 Stilwell's grand scheme was to build a railroad that would extend south to a port in the Gulf of Mexico, thereby challenging the supremacy of the eastern railroads. Although he claimed to be the originator of

COMPANY PERSPECTIVES

Our Vision: To be a strong, independent transportation company that consistently delivers exceptional service to our customers, challenging careers to our employees and increasing value to our shareholders.

the idea, in truth the concept was apparent to anyone with a map. To his credit, however, he was the first to succeed. Even as the Kansas City belt line was being constructed, Stilwell began acquiring small lines and securing charters to the south of Kansas City. In 1893 he formed a company called the Kansas City, Pittsburg & Gulf Railroad Company (KCP&G) to consolidate these lines and extend them to Texas, where he terminated the line at the Gulf port city he built and named after himself, Port Arthur.

EMERGING FROM BANKRUPTCY
UNDER A NEW NAME: 1900

The 800-mile KCP&G was completed in 1897, funded in large part by Dutch investors. Kansas City became a major grain city because of the new railroad, which prospered immediately, but it quickly became apparent that it had been hastily constructed. Due to poor grading, a lack of ballast, and poorly built bridges, the KCP&G suffered regular derailments. Moreover, it lacked an adequate supply of locomotives and rolling stock. Stilwell was unable to arrange further financing and in April 1899 the KCP&G went into receivership. A year later the line was reorganized by eastern financiers and was renamed The Kansas City Southern Railway Company. Stilwell was also removed as president. He would go on to build another railroad, the Kansas City, Mexico & Orient, which was to connect Kansas City to the Pacific Ocean. Although never completed, it was eventually incorporated into the Atchison, Topeka and Santa Fe System.

After Stilwell's departure, KCSR soon enjoyed good fortune when in early 1901 oil was discovered near Port Arthur, establishing the Spindletop Oil Field and setting off an oil boom that provided a great deal of business for the railroad. Oil fields developed near the KCSR line in Louisiana and Arkansas, and refineries were built at Port Arthur and Shreveport, Louisiana. Lumber mills south of Shreveport and elsewhere provided a great deal of business as well. In 1939 KCSR expanded its scope by acquiring the Louisiana and Arkansas Railway Company, the addition of which allowed the line to reach Dallas and connected Kansas City to New Orleans. Soon luxury passenger service was provided between Kansas City and New Orleans on the famed Southern Belle, which was regularly used by Kansas City's favorite son, President Harry S. Truman.

In 1941 William Neal Deramus, Jr., was named president of KCSR. He had worked his way up from the bottom, dropping out of school after the eighth grade to take a job sweeping a station and tending the switch lamps. He then studied Morse code and became a telegraph operator and began learning the railroad business. In 1909, at the age of 21, he joined KCSR and began his steady rise through the ranks, playing a key role in keeping the line solvent during the Great Depression. Deramus became chairman of the board in 1945. Under his leadership a long-range improvement program was instituted and KCSR was able to increase freight and diversify into other areas at a time when other railroads were beginning to suffer. The company was also an important innovator, developing ways to control parts of the lines through microwave transmissions and computers to streamline accounting systems.

Deramus was succeeded as president in 1961 by his son, William Neal Deramus III. Although he held a law degree from Harvard University, he was very much a railroad man like his father. He started out working for the Wabash Railway and in 1949 became president of the Chicago Great Western, becoming the youngest person ever to head a Class I railroad. Despite his railroad pedigree, however, the younger Deramus recognized that given the rise of a national highway system and large truck fleets, the prospects for growth in the railroad industry were bleak, and he did not hesitate to seek opportunities outside of rail transportation. In 1962 he established Kansas City Southern Industries to serve as a holding company for KCSR and a variety of non-rail investments, including mutual funds, and radio and television stations.

KCSR was soon neglected. Following three years of losses, the line terminated passenger service in 1967. By 1973 the system was in dire condition and in need of major repairs. A new president, Thomas S. Carter, a civil engineer by training, was able to convince the parent company to invest $75 million to improve rail beds. He then used operating revenues, supplemented to a large degree by a 20-year contract to ship coal to Texas and Louisiana power plants, to make further improvements that helped to bring in more coal business. While the hauling of coal accounted for just 1 percent of the line's cargo in 1973, it grew to 20 percent in 1982 and 33.1 percent in 1991. Much of that increase in volume was due to the export of coal, a large amount of which went through Port Arthur.

KEY DATES

1887: Kansas City Suburban Belt Railway incorporated.
1900: Name changed to Kansas City Southern Railway Company.
1939: Louisiana and Arkansas Railway Company acquired.
1962: Kansas City Southern Industries becomes parent company.
1987: Bid to acquire Southern Pacific fails.
1994: MidSouth Rail Corporation acquired.
1996: Rights secured to operate Mexico's Northeast Railway.
2005: Mexico operation named Kansas City Southern de Mexico.

MIDSOUTH RAIL CORPORATION ACQUIRED: 1994

To grow the business Kansas City Southern Industries invested $500 million between 1987 and 1993 to buy new diesel locomotives and to upgrade track and facilities. KCSR also looked to expand through acquisitions. In 1987 it offered $2.6 billion for Southern Pacific Corp., about ten times larger in size, but the bid proved unsuccessful. The line enjoyed better luck in 1993 when it struck a deal to acquire MidSouth Rail Corporation for $200 million. The transaction was completed on the first day of 1994. The addition of 1,200 miles of track extended KCSR's territory to such areas as Meridian, Mississippi; Counce, Tennessee; and Tuscaloosa and Birmingham, Alabama. Moreover, KCSR obtained trackage rights into Gulfport, Mississippi, and was positioned to interchange with Norfolk Southern and CX, resulting in what would be called the Meridian Speedway, a major route linking the Southeast and Southwest.

By this point, KCSR's parent company was an unusual collection of railroad and financial asset management units. Kansas City Southern Industries decided to divest KCSR, which at the time was the 12th largest railroad in the United States. In 1994 an agreement was reached with Illinois Central Corporation to sell KCSR for $1.6 billion in stock plus the assumption of $929 million of debt, but just three months later the deal fell through due to Wall Street tepidness, and KCSR remained a part of Kansas City Southern Industries.

It was a time of consolidation in the railroad industry, which saw the creation of Burlington Northern-Santa Fe and Union Pacific-Southern Pacific, a pair of giant Class I railroads that in effect surrounded KCSR and threatened to choke off business. To meet the challenge KCSR brought in a new president and chief executive officer in May 1995, Michael R. Haverty, Santa Fe's former president. Like many of the men who preceded him in this office, Haverty hailed from a railroad family, the fourth generation to be involved in the industry. His great-grandfather began the association when as an Irish immigrant he began laying track for the Central Branch of the Union Pacific in 1860. Haverty began his own railroad career 102 years later, after becoming the first in his blue-collar family to graduate from college, serving as a brakeman on the Missouri Pacific. In 1967 he completed the line's management training program and three years later went to work for the Santa Fe, making his way through the executive ranks until becoming president and chief operating officer in 1989. In 1994, however, his relationship with Santa Fe chairman Rob Krebs soured and he left the company.

After taking over KCSR, Haverty was quick to begin a major transformation of the line, looking to take advantage of the North American Free Trade Agreement (NAFTA). It was ratified in 1993, eliminating trade restrictions between the United States, Mexico, and Canada, and promising to result in major changes to North American shipping. With the north-south orientation of most of its tracks, KCSR was uniquely situated to exploit the new business that was to develop. Moreover, Mexico decided to privatize its railways.

Haverty first acquired a 49 percent stake in the 157-mile Texas-Mexican Railway (operating from Corpus Christi, Texas, to the Mexico border), from Transportacion Maritima Mexicana S.A. de C.V. (TMM), careful not to acquire majority control in order to avoid the need for approval from the Surface Transportation Board. He then maneuvered to take advantage of the Union Pacific and Southern Pacific merger that was still facing approval, and ultimately secured trackage rights in Texas that would provide a key connection between KCSR and a Mexican railroad.

The first Mexican line to be privatized was Ferrocarril del Noreste (the Northeast Railway). In 1996 KCSR and TMM made a winning $1.4 billion bid to operate the Northeast Railway for 50 years, thus creating a rail corridor from Mexico through the heart of the American Midwest. It began business in June 1997 as

Transportacion Ferroviaria Mexicana S.A. de C.V. (TFM), and was an immediate success.

Also in his first two years at the helm of KCSR, Haverty acquired the 400-mile Gateway Western line, which connected Kansas City to St. Louis and provided haulage rights from Springfield, Illinois, to Chicago over Southern Pacific lines. KCSR gained access to Minneapolis and the upper Midwest through an alliance that bought Canadian Pacific's Chicago–Kansas City and St. Paul-Kansas City routes. Finally, KCSR took over the 47.6-mile Panama Railroad Co. (despite its modest length, the world's first transcontinental railroad when it was built in 1855), which would be operated in the Canal Zone by subsidiary Panama Canal Railway Co. This assemblage of lines was dubbed the "NAFTA Railroad" by KCSR.

Kansas City Southern Industries made plans to spin off KCSR in a public offering of stock in 1997, but like the earlier deal to sell the line, it too failed to materialize. Instead, the line continued to build its Mexican business, which benefited from automobile parts and grain from the Midwest shipped to Mexico. KCSR also looked to do business with the northern member of NAFTA, Canada. In 1998 it reached a 15-year marketing agreement with Canada National and Illinois Central that generated significant traffic with pharmaceutical and chemical companies.

KCSR's Mexico-U.S. rail corridor, while successful, proved difficult to operate through multiple ownership, especially because TMM was struggling. Thus, in the early years of the 21st century KCSR moved to bring all of the assets of the NAFTA Railroad under single ownership in order to improve operational efficiency. Negotiations were begun with TMM and in April 2003 KCSR announced that it had reached an agreement to acquire a controlling interest in TFM for $400 million in cash and stock. Union Pacific Railroad, still smarting over KCSR's maneuvers during its acquisition of Southern Pacific several years earlier that resulted in the winning of valuable trackage rights, did its best to stymie approval of the deal. Soon the rival lines were exchanging charges of intimidation in filings presented to the Surface Transportation Board. Complicating the matter further, in August 2003 TMM shareholders rejected the sale. Months of intense negotiation followed and it was not until July 2005 that KCSR finally completed the purchase of a controlling interest in TFM. The Mexican government still owned a 20 percent stake in the line, but it too was acquired later in the year. TFM was renamed in December 2005, becoming Kansas City Southern de Mexico.

KCSR was able to upgrade Kansas City Southern de Mexico, allowing the company to take advantage of the surge in intermodal traffic, the railroad industry's fastest-growing market, fueled by soaring imports. East-west railroads were congested with trailer and container traffic, allowing KCSR to pick up business, essentially serving as a release valve, directing traffic to Mexico's Pacific port of Lazaro Cardenas. Not only did congestion make Mexico a viable option, but less expensive, nonunion labor was also available. As a result, KCSR was well positioned to grow its Mexican business in the years to come.

In 2002 Kansas City Southern Industries shortened its name to Kansas City Southern. Haverty served as chairman and CEO as well as heading KCSR. In 2006 Arthur Schoener was named Kansas City Southern's president and chief operating officer and CEO of KCSR, allowing Haverty, who remained CEO and chairman of Kansas City Southern, to groom his likely successor. Schoener had started his railroad career with Missouri Pacific Railroad in 1968 and became an executive with Union Pacific after its acquisition of Missouri Pacific in 1982, staying with the company until 1997 when he left to form a transportation consulting firm. In October 2007 Kansas City Southern made further changes to its executive ranks. Scott E. Arvidson became KCSR's chief operating officer, Schoener's number two man and his possible successor at the helm of the railroad. Haverty, meanwhile, remained chairman and CEO of the parent company with Schoener continuing to wait in the wings.

Ed Dinger

PRINCIPAL SUBSIDIARIES

Kansas City Southern de Mexico, S.A. de C.V.; The Texas Mexican Railway Company; Panama Canal Railway Company; Meridian Speedway, LLC.

PRINCIPAL COMPETITORS

Burlington Northern Santa Fe Corporation; Canadian National Railway Company; Union Pacific Corporation.

FURTHER READING

Aguayo, Jose, "The Little Railroad That Hopes It Can," *Forbes*, April 21, 1997, p. 58.

Frailey, Fred W., "Mike's Big Railroad: Remember the Little Kansas City Southern?" *Trains Magazine*, August 2003, p. 28.

Gallagher, John, "Bridging a New Connection," *Traffic World*, July 31, 2006, p. 18.

———, "KCS Names Schoener President," *Traffic World*, June 26, 2006, p. 27.

Galloway, Jennifer, "A Sale and a Partnership Derailed," *Latin Finance,* December 2003, p. 28.

Glischinski, Steve, "Kansas City Southern Fights Back," *Trains Magazine,* June 1997, p. 60.

"KCS Takes Century-Old Vision into the Future," *International Railway Journal,* July 2005, p. 20.

Vantuono, William C., "Mike Haverty, Railroader of the Year," *Railway Age,* January 2001, p. 33.

Veenendaal, Augustus J., Jr., "The Kansas City Southern Railway and the Dutch Connection," *Business History Review,* Summer 1987, p. 291.

L.A. Darling Company

1401 Highway 49B North
Paragould, Arkansas 72450
U.S.A.
Telephone: (870) 239-9564
Toll Free: (800) 643-3499
Fax: (870) 239-6427
Web site: http://www.ladarling.com

Wholly Owned Subsidiary of The Marmon Group LLC
Incorporated: 1897 as Ideal Fixture Company
Employees: 1,150
Sales: $107.7 million (2007 est.)
NAIC: 337215 Showcase, Partition, Shelving, and Locker Manufacturing

■ ■ ■

L.A. Darling Company is a leading manufacturer of display fixtures for retail stores. The firm's offerings include metal, wire, and wood shelving units; racks; counters; checkout systems; and freestanding kiosks. Darling provides a complete range of services from design and manufacturing to installation. The Arkansas-based company's customers include Wal-Mart, Best Buy, and Famous Footwear, and its products are sold throughout North America and in many overseas markets.

BEGINNINGS

The L.A. Darling Company traces its roots to 1897, when the Ideal Fixture Company was founded in Cold-water, Michigan, to make store displays. In 1909 the firm opened a new plant in the nearby town of Bronson, and three years later Ideal Fixture was acquired by Lewis Archer Darling, who subsequently renamed it the L.A. Darling Co. Over time its stock also began trading on the over-the-counter market.

In 1937 Darling was reorganized, and during World War II the firm turned to production of items for the war effort. Between 1941 and 1946 a new plastics division doubled in size to turn out more than $1 million worth of displays per year, while its precision casting foundry also grew to produce more than $1 million worth of metal-based displays. After the war the company, headed by Trowbridge H. Stanley, undertook a substantial plant upgrade program, although it also endured a four-month strike in 1946.

By 1948 Darling was considered the largest manufacturer of metal store displays in the United States, and the largest manufacturer of plastic mannequins in the world, which were touted as stronger and lighter than the traditional papier-mâché and plaster ones. The firm had also refined the precision casting process to yield tolerances of less than two- to three-thousandths of an inch, good enough to eliminate much machining heretofore required, which brought new opportunities to produce items for other clients.

Darling was continually working on innovative new display products, and in 1949 it introduced a coin-operated device that could record a customer's order on audiotape. It enabled window shoppers to buy items when a store was closed, with the 25-cent charge (which was intended to discourage pranksters) refunded when the goods were paid for.

In the early 1950s the firm again began producing defense-related products such as parachute hardware and self-sealing fuel tank parts as the United States entered the Korean War. With department store construction slowing, the company was also branching out into dif-ferent types of civilian work, making parts for fans, refrigerators, amusement park rides, small cars, and boats.

In 1953 Darling introduced a new merchandising system called Vizusell, which had taken three years to develop. It was easy to assemble and install, relatively inexpensive to ship, and yielded significantly more display space than competing products. The firm was soon turning out large orders for such retailers as J.C. Penney, F.W. Woolworth, S.S. Kresge, and Montgomery Ward, the latter of which bought 15,800 units to upgrade its toy departments.

In 1956 Versatile Fittings, Ltd., of England licensed Vizusell to manufacture for European customers, and in 1960 the firm also licensed the system in the Far East. By this time Darling had introduced similar wall and panel systems for use in stores, residences, offices, and institutional settings. The company continued to make auto and other industrial parts in both plastic and metal, as well. In addition to its 150,000-square-foot metals plant in Bronson, Michigan, and plastics and foundry plants in Coldwater with a combined total of 130,000 square feet, the firm had five sales offices around the United States. For 1959 annual sales topped $11 million.

DARLING JOINS PRITZKER EMPIRE IN 1960

In 1960 the company purchased the Colson Corpora-tion for 125,000 shares of stock. Colson, a maker of casters, hand trucks, institutional housekeeping equip-ment, wheelchairs, and other products, was headed by Chicagoan Robert Pritzker, who with his brother Jay had bought it in 1953. Jay Pritzker was already serving

as a director of Darling when it purchased Colson, and after the deal closed Robert was named the firm's chairman.

In 1962 Robert Pritzker was appointed president of the firm, and it began buying shares in the Marmon-Herrington Co., Inc., a onetime auto manufacturer that now produced tractors, bus chassis, and transit vehicles. The company later acquired controlling interest of Marmon-Herrington.

In 1965 Darling added a manufacturing plant in Paragould, Arkansas, where a $1.4 million municipal bond was issued to finance construction. In 1968 the company moved its headquarters and all manufacturing operations from Michigan to Arkansas.

In the late 1960s the Pritzker brothers consolidated their business operations under the name The Marmon Group, which was publicly traded beginning in 1966 but five years later went private through a merger with the Pritzker-owned Bess Corporation. Darling, which had been used as a vehicle to help assemble their grow-ing roster of independently operated industrial firms, would henceforth be a subsidiary of its onetime acquisition.

CORNING, ARKANSAS, PLANT ADDED IN 1970

In 1970 Darling added a second Arkansas plant in the town of Corning, which like the Paragould plant would focus on making metal fixtures. During the 1970s and early 1980s operations were expanded to include an ad-ditional manufacturing facility in the town of Piggott that produced wood fixtures. In 1983 sales topped $40 million, and two years later a 125,000-square-foot warehouse and shipping facility was added in Pocahon-tas, Arkansas.

In 1988 Kent Toomey was named to head the firm. The former vice-president of operations for Dempster Dumpster and Fontaine Fifth Wheel soon instituted production changes that helped improve product quality.

In 1992 the firm's Colson subsidiary was renamed Darling Special Products, Inc. It employed 100 at a 130,000-square-foot plant in Caruthersville, Missouri, which made material handling and storage equipment for retailers, hotels, and industrial users, as well as metal custom merchandising systems.

By this time Darling had grown to employ 2,500 and utilized more than two million square feet of manufacturing space. It had sales offices around the United States that serviced accounts with such major retailers as Wal-Mart and Kmart. Products were also

KEY DATES

1897: Ideal Fixture Company founded in Coldwater, Michigan.

1909: Manufacturing plant opens in Bronson, Michigan.

1912: Lewis Archer Darling buys Ideal Fixture, later renames it L.A. Darling Co.

1948: Darling is considered the largest manufacturer of metal store displays in the United States and the largest manufacturer of plastic mannequins in the world.

1953: Vizusell display system introduced.

1960: Pritzker brothers take control of company.

1968: L.A. Darling moves headquarters and manufacturing from Michigan to Arkansas.

1970: Corning, Arkansas, plant opens.

1985: Warehouse and shipping facility added in Pocahontas, Arkansas.

1998: Famous Footwear display fixtures plant acquired in Sun Prairie, Wisconsin.

2001: Firm lays off 215 workers as battered U.S. economy impacts sales.

2006: Sun Prairie plant closes, jobs moved to Piggott, Arkansas, facility.

2007: Fixture refurbishment plant opens in Rock Hill, South Carolina.

exported to Canada, Mexico, Japan, China, Russia, Australia, Singapore, Taiwan, South America, and the United Kingdom.

In June 1995 the firm bought SignMaster Corporation of Jonesboro, Arkansas, a 48-year-old maker of exterior and interior signs for banks, retailers, and other customers, which employed 15. In January 1997 Darling purchased Eletrofrio SA of Brazil, a 51-year-old maker of electric store fixtures that included refrigerated cases, shelving systems and checkout equipment, and an international trading unit called Compass Ltda.

FAMOUS FOOTWEAR PLANT ACQUIRED IN 1998

In early 1998 Darling bought a Sun Prairie, Wisconsin, display fixtures manufacturing facility from shoe retailer Famous Footwear. The 182,000-square-foot plant employed 200 and would add approximately $20 million to the firm's annual revenues. During 1998 the company also spun off a small unit called Advanced

Pharmacy Concepts, which helped drugstore chains design and plan their stores. For the year sales topped $100 million, with 40 percent of the total coming from retailers like Kmart that were refurbishing their stores with new displays. By this time, Darling was also performing some manufacturing in Mexico and had an office in Quebec, Canada.

Over time the company's offerings had evolved to encompass a wide range of store display and warehousing systems including point-of-purchase displays, interactive kiosks, clothing racks, shelving, checkout equipment, counters, and showcases, while other products such as mannequins were no longer produced. Its services included design, manufacturing, and installation worldwide for major retailers in the general merchandise, drug, specialty, and department store categories. Darling was the third largest store fixture maker in North America.

In early 2001 the company bought Streater, Inc., from Spectrum International. The Minnesota-based firm made wood and metal fixtures and displays, which were largely sold via catalog. The U.S. economy was faltering, however, and in June Darling laid off 215 workers as store display orders fell. Early the next year bankrupt retail giant Kmart also won court approval to cancel a major order from the company.

In the fall of 2002 Darling announced that Thomas Weiss would succeed the retiring Evarts B. English as president. Weiss had been executive vice-president for global operations of Watlow Electric Manufacturing Co.

Compounding the effects of the U.S. economic downturn, the display fixtures market was also struggling with industry consolidation, customer bankruptcies, and raw materials price increases, at the same time that competition from Chinese manufacturers was growing. In July 2006 Darling announced that it would consolidate the manufacturing of wood store fixtures at its Piggott, Arkansas, facility, causing the loss of 100 jobs in Sun Prairie, Wisconsin. Downsizing had reduced the firm's total workforce to just over 1,100 from a high of 2,500 in the early 1990s.

In the spring of 2007 Darling opened a 181,500-square-foot plant in Rock Hill, South Carolina, to refurbish display fixtures, which employed 50. It would be the firm's first refurbishment facility, created because of retailers' interest in reusing fixtures due to the rising price of steel.

More than a century after its founding, the L.A. Darling Company had grown to become one of the top store display fixture makers in the United States, with a wide range of products and customers like Wal-Mart and Best Buy. Although it had grown smaller in recent years, the firm was working to adapt to a changing market with new ventures like a refurbishing operation.

Frank Uhle

PRINCIPAL SUBSIDIARIES

L.A. Darling Wood; L.A. Darling Specialty Metal; L.A. Darling SA de CV (Mexico).

PRINCIPAL COMPETITORS

Leggett & Platt Store Fixtures Group; Lozier Corp.; Madix, Inc.; Xiamen Yiree Display Fixtures Co.; Umdasch Shop Concept; Colony, Inc.; FFr Inc.; idX Corporation.

FURTHER READING

"Abreast of the Market," *Wall Street Journal,* August 23, 1948, p. 9.

"Abreast of the Market," *Wall Street Journal,* April 21, 1952, p. 17.

Adams, Barry, "Move to Leave 100 Sun Prairie Workers Jobless," *Wisconsin State Journal,* July 15, 2006.

Carlton, Rachel, "Riding the Wave of Change: U.S. Retail Fixture Companies Are Striving to Keep Pace Under Pressure from Inflation, Global Sourcing, and Declining Profit

Margins," *Display & Design Ideas,* July 1, 2004, p. 24.

Clifford, Dick, "Business Leader Credits Workers with Success of Company," *Associated Press Newswires,* November 3, 1997.

"Colson Equipment Is Changing Its Name," *Jonesboro Sun,* December 27, 1992.

"Darling Co. Holders Vote to Buy Colson for 125,000 Shares," *Wall Street Journal,* May 13, 1960, p. 4.

"Darling Fires 215 Workers," *Associated Press Newswires,* June 9, 2001.

"Gadget in Window Tells It to Santa," *New York Times,* December 14, 1949, p. 37.

Harris, Jim, "A Growing Fixture in Corning," *Arkansas Business,* September 28, 1992, p. 28.

"L.A. Darling Co.," *Wood & Wood Products,* April 1, 2001.

"L.A. Darling Displays Good Form As Sales and Profits Rise Sharply," *Barron's,* October 31, 1960, p. 26.

"L.A. Darling Purchases Another 47,000 Shares of Marmon-Herrington," *Wall Street Journal,* March 15, 1963, p. 32.

"L.A. Darling to Open Plant in Rock Hill, South Carolina," *US Fed News,* April 12, 2007.

Medina, Alison Embrey, "Staying Competitive," *Display & Design Ideas,* July 1, 2006.

"Sales of New Display Unit Point Up Favorable Outlook for L.A. Darling," *Barron's,* May 28, 1956, p. 26.

"SignMaster Sold to L.A. Darling," *Jonesboro Sun,* July 1, 1995, p. 1.

Lillian Vernon Corporation

2600 International Parkway
Virginia Beach, Virginia 23452
U.S.A.
Telephone: (757) 427-7700
Toll Free: (800) 901-9291
Fax: (757) 427-7819
Web site: http://www.lillianvernon.com

Private Company
Incorporated: 1951 as Vernon Specialties
Employees: 3,000
Sales: $175 million (2006 est.)
NAIC: 454110 Electronic Shopping and Mail-Order Houses

■ ■ ■

The Lillian Vernon Corporation is a leading national catalog and online retailer specializing in household, organizational, children's, and fashion accessory items. Personalizing these items for free has been one of the company's trademarks since the beginning. A pioneer in direct marketing and personalized merchandise, Lillian Vernon publishes three catalog titles: Lillian Vernon, Lilly's Kids, and The Big Sale Catalog. The catalogs have become a fixture in American popular culture.

BEGINNING AT HOME

Lillian Vernon Corporation was founded in 1951 under the name Vernon Specialties. The name was taken from the founder's adopted home in Mount Vernon, New York; her Jewish family had fled Nazi Germany in 1934 and emigrated to America in 1937. In 1951, Lilly Menasche Hochberg was recently married, pregnant, and looking for a business she could run from her kitchen table. Hochberg soon changed her first name to the more American-sounding "Lillian," and eventually became known as Lillian Vernon. She formally changed her name after a divorce in the 1990s.

Using part of the $2,000 she and her husband had received as wedding gifts, Vernon took out a $495 advertisement in *Seventeen* magazine offering monogrammed leather handbags and belts for $2.99 and $1.99 each. The leather goods were purchased from Vernon's father, Herman Menasche, who ran a small leather factory. The 24-karat gold monograms were purchased from a distributor and hand-applied on the goods by Vernon herself.

Vernon received $16,000 worth of orders from her first ad. She then used her profits to buy ads in other popular women's magazines. She took in $32,000 for the year; sales grew and, within a few years, the company landed several contracts to manufacture custom-designed products for major corporations, including Max Factor, Elizabeth Arden, Avon, and Revlon. In 1954, Vernon Specialties moved out of Vernon's kitchen and into three facilities in Mount Vernon in order to meet the growing demand for its products.

GROWING THE BUSINESS: 1956–70

Two years later, in 1956, Vernon Specialties mailed its first catalog to the 125,000 customers who had

---

responded to the company's magazine ads since 1951. The catalog had 16 pages of black-and-white photos offering items such as signet rings, combs, cuff links, and blazer buttons—all of which could be personalized through the company's free monogramming service.

In fact, the key to Vernon Specialties' early success in the mail-order business was its offer of free monogramming, which continued as one of the features that distinguished the company from its competitors into the mid-1990s. Within a few years of its debut, the catalog was expanded by Vernon to include products for the home. She personally chose every product featured in her catalogs and had an "uncanny knack" for judging the needs and desires of middle-class housewives. Based on her own experiences, she knew that housewives required well-built products at reasonable prices. Although products were bought from a variety of manufacturers, most were customized under the Lillian Vernon name. As proof of the quality of its products Lillian Vernon offered a 100 percent money-back guarantee, which stated, "customers can return a product even ten years after it has been purchased."

Vernon Specialties' catalog was quite successful in its first decade, and sales continued to increase. In 1965, the company changed its name to Lillian Vernon Corporation. Sales were given an added boost in 1968, when Lillian Vernon introduced personalized Christmas ornaments in its catalogs. This product line would grow so popular that within a few years, over 75 million ornaments would be sold.

MORE EXPLOSIVE GROWTH: 1970–84

Annual sales in 1970 hit $1 million. By 1984, the company had sales of $115 million. In 1978, as a response to the growing number of catalog customers interested in retailing Lillian Vernon products in their own stores, the company established its Provender wholesale division. Provender provided retailers with Lillian Vernon's own line of imported toiletries, fancy foods, and kitchen textiles, such as towels, aprons, and potholders. Around that time, the company also opened The New Company, a wholesale manufacturer of brass products headquartered in Providence, Rhode Island.

In 1982, sales jumped again when the company introduced its first sale catalog offering overstocked merchandise at prices up to 75 percent off the original retail prices. Due largely to the success of its sale catalogs, Lillian Vernon posted record revenues of $75 million in 1983. The following year, Lillian Vernon introduced a line of private-label, exclusively designed home organization products in its catalog, a line that grew to represent 25 percent of business within ten years. In 1985, the company streamlined its operations by incorporating its Provender division into the main wholesale division.

The mail-order industry grew by leaps and bounds in the 1980s, with the number of people ordering merchandise by phone or mail increasing 70 percent between 1982 and 1992. Small specialty catalogs like Lillian Vernon entered the market in full force, taking sales away from traditional mail-order giants like Sears and Montgomery Ward.

EXPANDING A PUBLIC COMPANY: 1987–89

By 1987, Lillian Vernon was mailing out 80 million catalogs a year. The company went public that year, becoming the first public listing on the American Stock Exchange of a firm founded by a woman. Proceeds for the initial offering of 1.9 million shares were used to construct a state-of-the-art National Distribution Center in Virginia Beach, Virginia. That year, net income totaled $4.4 million on revenues of $115.5 million. The following year, net income grew to $6.9 million on revenues of $126 million.

Expansion continued with the 1989 addition of a computer center at the company's National Distribution Center. That year, Laura Zambano was named to the position of senior vice-president, general merchandise manager, taking over many of the merchandising responsibilities from Vernon. Also that year, the company opened its first outlet store near its Virginia Beach distribution center. The company made an attempt to further diversify its product offerings by introducing a high-end home furnishings catalog, which ultimately was incorporated into the company's other catalogs.

SPECIALTY CATALOGS AND NEW SALES CHANNELS: 1990–95

In 1990, Lillian Vernon introduced the highly successful Lilly's Kids catalogs, specializing in toys, games, and

KEY DATES

1951: Lilly Hochberg starts a home-based mail-order business.

1954: Vernon Specialties moves out of Hochberg's home.

1956: First catalog mailed.

1965: Name changes to Lillian Vernon Corporation.

1982: Company introduces first sale catalog.

1987: Lillian Vernon lists on the American Stock Exchange.

1989: First outlet store opened.

1995: Lillian Vernon goes online.

1996: Lillian Vernon begins mailings to consumers in Japan.

1998: Lillian Vernon enters British market.

2001: Company celebrates its 50th anniversary.

2003: Ripplewood Holdings and ZelnickMedia acquire company, taking it private.

2004: Owners create Direct Holdings Worldwide, consisting of Lillian Vernon Corp. and Time Life, Inc.

2006: Sun Capital Partners buys company, moves headquarters to Virginia.

personalized gifts for children. Sales hit $162 million in 1991 with profits of $9.5 million. A new customer service center was opened in Virginia, as were two new outlet stores: one in a suburb of Washington, D.C., and the other in Williamsburg, Virginia.

Lillian Vernon was able to stay on top of the booming catalog industry by constantly introducing new products and by keeping prices reasonable. As the company entered its fourth decade, the average price of a product was $17 and the average customer order totaled $39. In 1992, the company declared its first quarterly dividend of $0.05 per share. That year, it also introduced its Christmas Memories catalog, specializing in Christmas ornaments and holiday decorations for the home. By 1992, Lillian Vernon was adding over 1,000 new products a year to its four catalogs and had three more outlet stores in Virginia and New York.

In 1993, Lillian Vernon launched its Welcome catalog, offering home organization products and decorative accessories for people who had recently moved to new homes. Net income for 1993 totaled $12.8 million on revenues of $196.3 million. Headquarters were moved from Mount Vernon to New Rochelle, New York.

Although the catalog and direct marketing industry boomed in the 1980s, cyclical downturns were inevitable. Company management regarded increased specialization and diversification of its catalogs as essential to success in the rapidly changing environment. In response to increased competition, Lillian Vernon began test-mailing its catalogs in Canada and also began investigating other foreign markets. The company offered products on television's QVC Shopping Network, and Vernon personally appeared on Joan Rivers' television shopping program in 1994. In another effort to keep on top of trends in the direct marketing industry, Lillian Vernon became one of 39 catalogs to be featured on *The Merchant,* one of the first CD-ROM shopping discs.

The company launched another specialized catalog in February 1995 offering cookware, cutlery, table accessories, gourmet gifts, and small electric appliances. Two months later, it launched a special section in its core catalog featuring luggage and travel accessories. The company began selling its products through the Prodigy online service and was also looking into further growth through acquisitions and expansion of its corporate gift, premium, incentive, and gift certificate markets.

The sudden departure of her son Fred Hochberg from the president's post in 1992 made Lillian Vernon reevaluate her plans for the company. A French company offered to buy it in 1994, and the next spring, a New York–based investment group, Freeman Spogli & Co., offered $190 million for three-quarters of it. To sweeten the deal, both Vernon and her son David Hochberg were to keep their executive positions for five years; they would also control one-quarter of the company's equity.

Although the Lillian Vernon Corporation posted record revenues of $222.2 million for the fiscal year, a postal rate hike was announced in January and the company had seen paper costs rise 50 percent in the preceding 12 months. Freeman Spogli reportedly ran into problems with its financing due to the tough environment; the cataloger did have numerous competitors, after all. When Vernon and Hochberg would not consent to lower the agreed-upon price, the deal was called off.

Also in the spring of 1995, the gourmet Lillian Vernon's Kitchen catalog debuted. It was more organized and more brand-oriented than the company's main catalog. The company also began to make its products available over the Internet via an America Online store.

President Stephen Marks left the company in May 1995. His replacement, Howard Goldberg, was not named until the end of March 1996. Goldberg had formerly been in charge of the Macy's catalog.

MORE CATALOGS: 1994–2000

In the fiscal year ending February 1996, Lillian Vernon mailed 179 million catalogs to 18 million people. This garnered nearly five million orders. Revenues rose slightly to $238.2 million, although profits were halved due to increased costs. There were more auspicious developments in the rest of the year. HarperCollins published Vernon's autobiography, *An Eye for Winners*, and paper prices came down.

At the time, Lillian Vernon was producing a new catalog every couple of weeks. It began mailings in Japan and expanded its National Distribution Center in Virginia by 335,000 square feet. A new seasonal telemarketing center opened in New Rochelle, New York. The company also test marketed a membership-based buyer's club.

The Lillian Vernon catalog had long included garden-related products when the company launched its first dedicated gardening catalog in March 1998. With more upscale offerings than the core catalogs, it proved instantly profitable. In the fall of 1998, Lillian Vernon began mailing to U.K. consumers in cooperation with Great Universal Stores PLC.

In August 1998, corporate headquarters moved to a seven-acre site in Rye, Westchester County, New York. The company began buying back its stock, which lost almost 20 percent of its value in one year, in October 1998. After takeover rumors had caused it to rise in the mid-1990s, investors doubted the company's prospects, even though it managed to stay virtually free of long-term debt. One believer in Lillian Vernon the woman was fashionable Manhattan hairstylist Paolo Martino, who married her in 1998.

As Vernon noted in an interview, buyers had become more affluent in the previous decades. More could purchase luxuries like Wedgwood china, for example. They still appreciated bargains, however. The annual clearance sale for the Virginia Beach distribution center became something of a tourist attraction, visited by about 16,000 shoppers. The event grossed half a million dollars in four days.

Employment at Lillian Vernon swelled from 600 to 4,000 in the weeks before Christmas. The company faced increased competition for workers at its Virginia Beach call center due to the opening of other, similar businesses in the area. A new online catalog debuted in December 1998. At the time, Lillian Vernon managed 16 outlet stores and eight catalogs.

Lillian Vernon launched the Neat Ideas catalog in the fall of 1999, featuring kitchenware, a category that accounted for 15 percent of the company's total sales. (Lillian Vernon's Kitchen had been dropped by then.)

Lillian Vernon acquired the Rue de France catalog in 2000 and launched a new web site. Revenues for the fiscal year slipped from $255.2 million to $241.8 million as the mailing list was trimmed somewhat to reduce costs; profits doubled to $6.3 million.

As Lillian Vernon prepared to celebrate its 50th anniversary in 2001, the company was publishing seven catalog titles: Lillian Vernon, Lilly's Kids, Personalized Gift, Lillian Vernon Gardening, Christmas Memories, Neat Ideas, and Favorites. It had added seasonal call centers in Las Vegas, Nevada, and New Rochelle, New York, and was debuting 3,000 unique products a year.

NEW OWNERS TAKE COMPANY PRIVATE

However, in the early 2000s, the company faced significant challenges. The catalog retail environment had grown increasingly competitive, with many clothing and home furnishing retailers expanding their catalogs to include household and gift items similar to those offered by Lillian Vernon. The company also had to contend with the impact of the September 11, 2001, terrorist attacks against the United States, as well as the move by customers from catalogs to online shopping. A study of catalog use found that over a 3-month period in early 2002, usage dropped to 32 percent compared to 42 percent in 2000. Over the same period, online shopping more than doubled, from 10 percent to 24 percent. Even though Lillian Vernon's web site was accounting for 15 percent of annual sales, the company found it more difficult to differentiate its goods from those offered by thousands of other catalogs and web sites.

The company found itself with falling sales and increasing losses, even after reducing catalog circulation and laying off employees in 2001. In 2002, Vernon stepped down as CEO, although she remained chairman of the board. That same year, the company's web site was named one of the "Top 25 Retail Web Sites," and the company began exploring licensing of the Lillian Vernon name. However, sales continued to drop, declining by 9 percent in fiscal 2002, with losses of $9.1 million. Despite those financials, several companies expressed interest in buying Lillian Vernon, primarily because of the strength of the brand name.

In July 2003, Vernon and the board accepted an offer of $60 million in cash and turned the company over to the investment firm ZelnickMedia, which was backed by private equity fund Ripplewood Holdings LLC. Vernon, who owned about 5 percent of the new company, assumed the positions of nonexecutive chairman and corporate spokesperson. Strauss Zelnick was the head of ZelnickMedia. The former president of 20th Century

Fox and BMG Entertainment named himself chairman of Lillian Vernon, assumed the day-to-day management, and took the company private.

In December, ZelnickMedia bought Time Life, Inc., a direct marketer of books, music, and videos, from Time Warner's magazine division. Lillian Vernon's huge distribution center in Virginia Beach, Virginia, provided call center and distribution services to Time Life. In 2004, Zelnick created Direct Holdings Worldwide LLC, as the parent company of Lillian Vernon and Time Life, and moved headquarters from Rye to White Plains, New York.

Zelnick admitted there was little catalog experience in the new management when they took over Lillian Vernon. However, Zelnick told *Catalog Age,* "We see direct marketing as media," and envisioned opportunities in TV home shopping as well as on the Web. The new company established both a corporate gifts business and a home-party business and entered into licensing agreements. It also folded the Rue de France business, redesigned the Lillian Vernon catalog and the web site, and initiated a syndicated column by Lillian Vernon for Scripps Howard News Service. In 2003 it started outsourcing some of its ordering and customer service calls to Asia. It also offered free shipping and handling for orders over $40 and doubled the number of items available for personalization from 1,000 to 2,000. It also began charging for personalization services, and in 2005, it raised prices about 10 percent in total.

Zelnick's efforts failed to turn Lillian Vernon around, though the losses appeared to slow. By 2006, sales had fallen to around $180 million, down from $238 million for fiscal 2003, its last year as a public company.

2006 AND BEYOND

In May 2006, Direct Holdings Worldwide sold Lillian Vernon for a reported $10 million in cash to Sun Capital Partners, Inc., a private investment firm based in Florida. The new owners named Michael Muoio to be president and CEO, consolidated facilities by moving the company's headquarters from White Plains to Virginia Beach, and asked Vernon herself to take a more active role. "The company is going back to the essence of the brand through merchandising, pricing, and packaging," Muoio told *Multichannel Merchant* in November 2006.

Muoio came to Lillian Vernon from direct-market retailer Miles Kimball, which he had headed for 14 years. During his tenure there, annual revenues increased from $50 million to $200 million. At Lillian Vernon, he reinstituted free personalization services,

dropped prices by 10 percent, cut higher priced and slower-moving items, and began sharing more business information with employees to help them better understand the company's challenges and goals. In 2007, the company closed its call center in Manila, consolidating activities in Virginia Beach. Challenges continued. It lost the Time Life fulfillment business and had to deal with increased postal rates.

Fifty-six years after its establishment, Lillian Vernon Corporation continued to offer a wide range of merchandise, with an average price point of $14.98. Half of its business came from the Lilly's Kids catalog, and half of all items sold were personalized. The plans for building the brand included offering personalized products for pets. After a rocky period, the company appeared to be heading toward a healthier time.

Maura Troester
Updated, Frederick C. Ingram; Ellen Wernick

PRINCIPAL COMPETITORS

Collections Etc.

FURTHER READING

Belton, Beth, "Catalog Queen Has More up Her Sleeve," *USA Today,* November 29, 1996, p. B7.

Bryan, Marvin, "How a Refugee Created a Mail-Order Empire," *Profit,* March 2000, pp. 12–21.

Burney, Teresa, "The Matriarch of Mail Order," *St. Petersburg Times,* December 23, 1996, p. 8.

Byrne, Harlan S., "Lillian Vernon Corp.: Segmentation Builds Catalog Sales," *Barron's,* June 4, 1990, p. 58.

"Cause of Failed Lillian Vernon Sale Is Disputed," *Mergers & Acquisitions Report,* September 25, 1995, p. 11.

Coleman, Lisa, "I Went Out and Did It," *Forbes,* August 17, 1992, p. 102.

Del Franco, Mark, "Efficiencies Enable Lillian Vernon to Shut Manila Contact Center," *Direct,* March 22, 2007.

Dorich, Alan, "Something for Everyone: Lillian Vernon Corp. Has Positioned Itself at the 'High of the Low End,'" *Furniture and Interiors,* Summer 2007, p. 48.

"Entrepreneurs and Professional Managers," *Management Review,* February 1999, p. 13.

Fannin, Rebecca, "Opting Out: The Public Markets Look Better, but There Are Still Plenty of Reasons for CEOs to Take Their Companies Private," *Chief Executive* (U.S.), May 2004, p. 44.

Furman, Phyllis, "Exec Losses, Wrecked Deal Unhinge Lillian Vernon: Tough Catalog Industry Environment Hinders Efforts to Find a New Buyer," *Crain's New York Business,* September 25, 1995, p. 39.

Garbato-Stankevich, Debby, "Lillian Vernon's Kitchen Catalog Debuts," *HFN*, March 20, 1995, p. 41.

———, "Lilly's Red-Hot Love Affair," *HFD—The Weekly Home Furnishings Newspaper*, June 21, 1993, p. 52.

———, "Vernon, Suitor Ax Buyout Agreement," *HFN*, September 25, 1995, p. 49.

Gattuso, Greg, "Lillian Vernon Looks to the Future," *Direct Marketing*, August 1994, p. 33.

Goldbogen, Jessica, "Lillian Vernon's New Green Thumb," *HFN*, March 9, 1998, p. 26.

Kehoe, Ann-Margaret, "The Profits Are in the Mail," *HFN*, September 16, 1996, p. 57.

Lesonsky, Rieva, "Living Legend," *Entrepreneur*, June 2003, p. 12.

Levy, Richard H., "Lillian Vernon Bought by Ripplewood Holdings," *Direct*, May 1, 2003.

Lisovicz, Susan, and Bill Tucker, "Lillian Vernon, Founder & CEO," *Entrepreneurs Only* (television program), CNNfn, August 26, 1999.

Mason, Julie Cohen, "Lillian Vernon Focuses on Customers," *Management Review*, May 1993, p. 22.

Odell, Patricia, "Taking a Bow: Lillian Vernon to Step Down as CEO," *Direct*, April 2002, p. 1.

Oser, Kris, "Lillian's Way: Lillian Vernon Reflects on a Career in Catalogs," *Direct*, April 2002, p. 11.

Peltz, James F., "Lillian Vernon Still the Head of Catalog House," *Los Angeles Times*, June 26, 1995, p. D4.

Richards, Gregory, "Florida Company Buys Lillian Vernon," *Virginian-Pilot*, May 31, 2006, p. D1.

———, "In Need of Delivery," *Virginian-Pilot*, December 24, 2006, p. D1.

———, "Lillian Vernon to Lay Off 230 After Losing Business," *Virginian-Pilot*, March 30, 2007.

Simeone, Lisa, "Lillian Vernon Talks About Her Mail Order Business," *Weekend All Things Considered* (PBS radio interview), December 9, 2001.

Simon, Virginia, "A Marketing Maestro Orchestrates," *Target Marketing*, October 1992, p. 16.

Sinha, Vandana, "Catalog Retailer Lillian Vernon Expands Virginia Beach, Va. Clearance," *Norfolk Virginian-Pilot*, August 8, 1998.

———, "Seasonal Help Scarce at Virginia Beach, Va. Catalog Call Center," *Norfolk Virginian-Pilot*, December 22, 1998.

Thau, Barbara, "Lillian's Kitchen: Cataloger Taps E-Commerce, Innovative Products for Growth," *HFN*, August 9, 1999, p. 51.

Tierney, Jim, "New Life for Lillian," *Multichannel Merchant*, November 1, 2006.

Vernon, Lillian, *An Eye for Winners: How I Built One of America's Greatest Direct-Mail Businesses*, New York: Harper-Collins, 1996.

M. DuMont Schauberg GmbH & Co. KG

Neven DuMont Haus
Amsterdamer Strasse 192
Cologne, D-50735
Germany
Telephone: (49 0221) 22 40
Fax: (49 0221) 22 42 493
Web site: http://www.dumont.de

Private Company
Founded: 1802
Employees: 1,300
Sales: EUR 556.7 million ($734.99 million) (2006 est.)
NAIC: 511120 Periodical Publishers; 511130 Book
  Publishers

■ ■ ■

M. DuMont Schauberg GmbH & Co. KG (MDS) is Germany's fourth largest publisher of newspapers. Based in Cologne, the company dominates the local newspaper market, publishing all of the city's major newspapers, including *Kölner Stadt-Anzeiger, Kölnische Rundschau,* and the tabloid *EXPRESS.* In addition, MDS publishes the *Mitteldeutsche Zeitung,* a major daily in central-eastern Germany, and the *Frankfurter Rundschau,* a national daily based in Frankfurt am Main.

The firm has a 25 percent interest in the Israeli daily paper *Haaretz,* its sole foreign holding. The Du-Mont Literatur und Kunst Verlag is one of the most well-known and respected publishers of books on art for the educated public. Other areas in which MDS is active include ticket sales for special events, marketing,

advertising, market research services, and local advertising papers. The firm and its predecessor businesses have been in family hands since the early 17th century.

17TH-CENTURY ORIGINS

The history of the firm M. DuMont Schauberg extends back into 17th-century Cologne, Germany. In 1620 Bertram Hilden moved from the surrounding countryside to the city where he established a printing business that specialized in prayer books and *Festschriften*—publications, written for special occasions. His son, Peter, who took over the business in 1661, was named the official printer for the law and theology departments of the University of Cologne and three years later became the publisher of *Relationes extraordinariae* (Extraordinary News), a serious Cologne newspaper with correspondents throughout Western Europe and which was written in Latin for academics and the educated classes.

In 1736 the enterprise passed into the ownership of Gereon Arnold Schauberg, the husband of one of Bertram Hilden's great-granddaughters. Schauberg obtained an important contract from the influential Thurn und Taxis postal organization in 1763: the right to print the post office's official newspaper, *Kaiserlichen Reichs-Oberpostamtszeitung.* The Schauberg heirs had a contract to print the *Kölnische Zeitung* (*KZ;* the Cologne Newspaper), which in 1802 they were able to purchase outright. Three years later, a lawyer, Marcus DuMont, acquired the paper for 1,400 *Reichstaler* (the currency at the time). Around the same time, he married Katharine Schauberg, uniting the DuMont and Schauberg families.

The company regards 1802 as the date of its founding, although according to Kurt Weinhold's history of the firm, the first written record of the name M. DuMont Schauberg does not appear until 1811.

The *KZ* became the flagship of the M. DuMont Schauberg company and quickly developed into one of the most significant German-language newspapers of the 19th century. It was outspoken enough to be suppressed by Napoleon after the French occupied Cologne in 1809 and could be published again only in 1814 after Napoleon's defeat. By 1847 the paper had 62 employees, a subscription list of 9,500, and had moved to a larger headquarters on Breite Strasse in central Cologne. One year later, anti-monarchical revolutions swept across the European continent, including Germany. The *KZ* was one of the liberal voices supporting the aims of the revolutionaries. In just two months time, the paper's circulation jumped to 17,400 subscriptions.

The paper was technologically innovative. In 1833 it started printing on a König and Bauer rapid press. In 1849 it introduced its carrier pigeon service for the rapid transmission of stock prices from Paris and Brussels. Later that year, it became the first newspaper to print a news story that had been transmitted to its editors by so-called optical telegraph. The *KZ* also expanded the idea of what a newspaper was. In 1837, for instance, it became the very first German newspaper to introduce a feature section, with cultural news, book reviews, and the like. By 1860 the paper was so successful that advertising exceeded news and other editorial matter for the first time. Six years later it began printing two editions daily.

A new era began in 1871. Following the conclusion of three victorious wars against Denmark, Austria, and France, the German Reich was proclaimed. The center of the nation shifted to Berlin, where the imperial court was located, and the *KZ* sent a full-time correspondent to Berlin to cover the news of the capital. The paper, which by the time of the Reich had become a paper of national stature and significance in Germany, turned its attention back to its local Cologne advertising market in mid-November 1876 when it launched the *Kölner Stadt-Anzeiger.*

Half the size of the *KZ,* the *Stadt-Anzeiger* was at first merely a local advertising supplement. When subscribers in Cologne received the first edition (it came free with their copy of the *KZ*) they had something unheard of at the time, a paper whose entire front page was comprised of nothing but advertising. Stories were included occasionally, but only as filler. By 1890, however, the *Stadt-Anzeiger* had developed into a full-blown local paper for Cologne, independent of its big brother, the *KZ.*

DURING AND AFTER THE GREAT WAR

World War I affected the press in Germany like most wars always have before and since. In the first days of the fighting, with the public hungry for news, the *KZ*'s circulation jumped to 200,000. Soon content was limited, however, primarily to news from Germany only. The paper's few foreign correspondents were in neutral nations where it was often difficult to collect information, and the foreign news that did make it to the paper's editorial offices frequently fell victim to the scissors of the German government censors. In the United States, the firm encountered a different problem. Its reporter there was arrested and thrown in jail as a spy, a casualty of the anti-German hysteria. Problems did not end immediately with the cessation of conflict. After Germany's defeat, the Rhineland, including Cologne, was occupied by the French, who regularly banned the *KZ* for its outspoken advocacy of a return of German government to the region.

The hyperinflation of the early 1920s hit MDS papers hard. The price of a single copy of a newspaper in mid-1923 could skyrocket by the hour. For example, a monthly subscription to the *KZ,* which cost 3.30 reichsmarks in January 1918, rose to 42 reichsmarks in May 1922, then to 100 million reichsmarks in September 1923, before it peaked at 3.3 trillion reichsmarks in the first week of December 1923. Somehow the firm survived, and by 1927 the reputation of the *KZ* was approaching prewar levels. The paper had one of the largest staffs of editors, journalists, and freelancers of any paper in Germany. The *Kölner Stadt-Anzeiger,* on the other hand, had to make due with an extremely

KEY DATES

1620: Bertram Hilden sets up a printing business in Cologne, Germany.

1664: Hilden begins printing the *Relationes extraordinariae.*

1736: Operation is named publisher of *Kaiserlichen Reichs-Oberpostamtszeitung* by Thurn und Taxis.

1802: Acquisition is made of the *Kölnische Zeitung* by the Schauberg heirs, setting up the firm M. DuMont Schauberg.

1805: Marcus DuMont acquires *Kölnische Zeitung.*

1849: Company begins transmission of stock prices by carrier pigeon.

1871: First permanent correspondent to Berlin is sent.

1876: *Kölner Stadt-Anzeiger* is launched.

1906: Firm moves into new headquarters in Cologne.

1945: *Kölnische Zeitung* ceases publication during World War II.

1956: Book publishing company is founded.

1963: *EXPRESS* is founded.

1969: *EXPRESS* editions are launched in Bonn and Düsseldorf.

1985: New printing plant in Cologne-Niehl goes into operation.

1992: Founding of the Mitteldeutschen Druck- und Verlagshaus GmbH.

1998: Company relocates to new headquarters, Neven DuMont Haus, in Cologne-Niehl.

2004: Sells DuMont travel book publishing.

2006: Frankfurter Rundschau and Bundesanzeiger Verlag are acquired.

small staff; it did not even have a reporter covering the local Cologne beat.

PUBLISHING UNDER THE NAZIS

Throughout the latter 1920s MDS papers, with their liberal political viewpoints, were a target of Nazi propaganda. The attacks continued after Adolf Hitler came to power in 1933, but with a new intensity. The Nazi paper in Cologne, the *Westdeutscher Beobachter,* launched an all-out campaign in its pages to persuade readers to cancel their subscriptions to the *Kölner Stadt-Anzeiger.* Eventually the Nazi Party district leader in Cologne approached MDS's head, Dr. Kurt Neven Du-Mont, and told him that the party had decided it was unacceptable for the *Stadt-Anzeiger* to continue to exist alongside the *Beobachter* in Cologne, implying the MDS paper had to be either merged into the *Beobachter* or to cease publication. DuMont replied that without *Stadt-Anzeiger*'s financial support, the *KZ* would go out of business too, knowing full well that the Nazi government was interested in keeping the *KZ* going because of its high profile outside Germany. Faced with DuMont's threat, the party backed down, and the *Kölner Stadt-Anzeiger* was able to continue publication until the end of the war.

The *KZ*'s circulation dropped immediately following Hitler's ascension to power to about 65,000, but by 1936 it had bounced back to about 180,000. It continued to climb after the war began in 1939, in particular because of a decision of the army's propaganda office to send copies of the paper to soldiers in the field, a practice it continued until the end of the war. While some have viewed this as evidence that the *KZ* was toeing the government's propaganda line, MDS vociferously denies this allegation.

Critics also point to the fact that the head of the company Kurt Neven DuMont himself joined the Nazi Party in 1937. Company historians have written that the Wehrmacht propaganda office was stubbornly independent of the government's monolithic Propaganda Ministry, and that the army merely wanted its soldiers to have a real newspaper from the home front. Another factor that must to some extent have played a role was that a former editor of the *KZ* was on the staff of the army propaganda division when the decision was made.

REBUILDING FROM THE RUBBLE

By the end of the war Cologne and MDS lay literally in ruins. Its magnificent Breite Strasse headquarters in Cologne had been largely destroyed in an air raid and lay buried up to its second floor windows in rubble. Its staff, many of whom had lost their homes to the raids, had been scattered through the countryside around the city. In the final years of hostilities much of the *KZ*'s printing had been moved to Siegen in the mountains southwest of Cologne, while editing was done in a nearby hotel until Siegen itself was destroyed by bombs. Nonetheless, somehow the MDS papers managed to continue publication until the war ended in May 1945.

German daily newspapers were banned by the occupation forces after fighting stopped. The American army, however, which occupied Cologne in spring 1945, immediately recognized the importance of printing machinery for circulating official edicts and announcements and took over the few printing presses that were still operational in MDS's wrecked building. At the end of the 1940s the Allies lifted their ban, and Kurt Neven Schauberg resumed newspaper publication. He had decided in 1948 not to revive the *KZ*. The *Kölner Stadt-Anzeiger*, however, resumed publication in October 1949 with a run of 70,000 newspapers. In its first few years it focused almost completely on local news. By 1951 circulation had grown to 100,000, and two years later it stood at 160,000. In 1956 the entire layout of the *Stadt-Anzeiger* was overhauled and given a more modern look.

BOOK PUBLISHING BEGINS

The year 1956 also marked the beginning of book publishing for MDS. A line of art books was produced that would soon garner a worldwide reputation. Characterized by their high standards of typography and color reproduction as well as by the renowned art historians who contributed texts, DuMont's art titles covered the history of art from its beginnings in Mesopotamia to the modern day. The special imprints that were gradually introduced included the DuMont Dokumente series about significant historical and contemporary cultural, social, and political topics; DuMont Aktuell, which dealt with important problems in contemporary cultural life; and studio dumont, which presented the theoretical, literary, and artistic work of young authors who had never before been published. In total the publishing house released more than 400 titles in its first 13 years.

In the 1960s the *Kölner Stadt-Anzeiger* began to transform itself into a newspaper of national import such as the *KZ* had been before the war. Early in the decade its circulation reached 230,000, and the number of advertisements it ran annually topped the one million mark, the highest of all German newspapers. In May 1963 the *Stadt-Anzeiger* launched a new weekend supplement, *EXPRESS*, which primarily featured sports news and was issued three times every weekend.

Not long afterward, the Axel Springer Verlag, a major newspaper publisher based in Berlin, acquired the Düsseldorf tabloid *Mittag*. Springer announced plans to redesign the paper and launch it in Cologne. MDS responded immediately by completely changing its *EXPRESS* concept; in March 1964 the paper became a tabloid daily that covered all news, not only sports, although still with a focus on local and regional stories. MDS set itself the goal of achieving a circulation of 30,000 in order to fend off the Springer challenge. *EXPRESS* was so successful though that by 1969 its daily circulation had climbed to 300,000. As a result, in 1969 the company launched editions of *EXPRESS* in

Düsseldorf and Bonn, two other major cities in the Rhineland region.

In the late 1960s and the 1970s MDS took an outspokenly leftist position, supporting Chancellor Willy Brandt's social democratic programs, in particular his so-called *Ostpolitik*, his program of rapprochement with the government of the German Democratic Republic. In the 1980s the firm launched plans for a new printing center in the Cologne suburb of Niehl.

ACQUISITIONS AT THE END OF THE CENTURY

The fall of the Berlin Wall and the subsequent opening of the East German market to western companies brought a unique opportunity to MDS. In 1991 it acquired the *Freiheit*, the newspaper of the governing Socialist Unity Party in the East German city of Halle. The company changed the paper's name to *Mitteldeutsche Zeitung* (Central German Newspaper) and formed a subsidiary, Mitteldeutschen Druck- und Verlagshaus GmbH, to publish it. The new paper was launched in 1992. With a relatively large staff of some 150 editors and reporters, the paper quickly established itself as a valuable independent regional voice in the German state of Sachsen-Anhalt. In December 1999 the Norwegian newspaper publisher Schibsted launched a free daily newspaper *20 Minuten Köln* in Cologne.

German publishers MDS and Springer reacted vehemently to the threat, first asking the courts to ban the paper (any free newspaper, in fact) on antitrust grounds, claiming as well that such publications threatened the freedom of the press in Germany. Nonetheless, at the same time MDS launched its own free paper, *Kölner Morgen*, in retaliation. However, the paper ceased publication after barely a year and a half after Schibsted stopped publishing *20 Minuten Köln* and abandoned the German market completely.

By September 2000 MDS owned all three major papers in Cologne: *Kölner Stadt-Anzeiger, EXPRESS,* and the *Kölnische Rundschau,* which it had acquired in 1999. That year the German business magazine *Wirtschaftswoche* reported the MDS share of the total German newspaper market had gone up from 4 percent in 1997 to 4.4 percent in 2000. Despite its participation in the growing concentration of the German newspaper market, the firm entered an up-and-down period financially in the early 2000s. It slipped into the red for the first time in its postwar history in 2003, reporting a loss of some EUR 20.7 million, after turning a EUR 4.3 million profit one year earlier, but bounced back in 2004 with a profit of EUR 8.8 million, before showing a loss once again in 2005. By then the company could boast that it was the fourth largest German newspaper publisher, after Axel Springer, Holtzbrinck, and the Westdeutsche Allgemeine Zeitungsverlagsgesellschaft.

MDS broadened its portfolio of newspapers significantly in 2006. After failing in an attempt to acquire the *Berliner Zeitung,* a major Berlin daily, in July 2006 the company purchased the highly respected *Frankfurter Rundschau* from SPD-Medienholding DDVG for a reported EUR 35 million. The price was more symbolic, according to the *Frankfurter Allgemeine Zeitung,* which reported that in addition MDS had assumed all the *Frankfurter Rundschau*'s outstanding debts. The *Rundschau* was DuMont Schauberg's first truly national newspaper since the demise of the *Kölnische Zeitung* after World War II.

A more controversial acquisition took place around the same time when the company bought a 25 percent holding in the Israeli daily *Haaretz.* The controversy (it was primarily in Israel) concerned the appropriateness of selling part of a Jewish company to a German business whose earlier head had been a member of the Nazi Party. It seemed to pose no problem for *Haaretz* owner Amos Schocken, however, who had developed a close relationship with MDS head Kurt Neven DuMont. DuMont Schauberg paid approximately EUR 25 million for the share in the paper, which was the second largest media company in Israel, and also owned several other weekly newspapers and its own printing plant. Both *Haaretz* and DuMont Schauberg share a liberal viewpoint, and the German company expressly committed itself to the maintenance of *Haaretz*'s editorial independence.

The *Haaretz* deal was MDS's first foreign investment. In early 2007 the firm's executives stated that they would do everything necessary to increase the company's market share. Its head, Kurt Neven DuMont, announced his intention to acquire additional German newspaper properties and, if the opportunity presented itself, to enter the English-language newspaper market.

DuMont did not mention which, if any, particular properties the company was targeting.

Gerald E. Brennan

PRINCIPAL SUBSIDIARIES

M. DuMont Schauberg Expedition der Kölnischen Zeitung GmbH & Co. KG; Sagittarius Verwaltungs- und Beteiligungs GmbH & Co. KG; Mitteldeutsches Druck- und Verlagshaus GmbH & Co. KG; Druck- und Verlagshaus Frankfurt am Main GmbH; Rheinische Zeitungs-Zustellgesellschaft Köln mbH & Co. KG; DERTICKETSERVICE KT GmbH; WESTMAIL GmbH & Co. KG; West Mail Zustelldienst Köln/Bonn GmbH; DISKRET GmbH; Ha'aretz Daily Newspaper Ltd. (25%); K.I.Mediengesellschaft mbH; DUMONT Literatur und Kunst Verlag GmbH & Co. KG; delta Marktforschung.

PRINCIPAL COMPETITORS

Verlagsgruppe Georg von Holtzbrinck; Axel Springer Verlag AG; Westdeutsche Allgemeine Zeitungsverlagsgesellschaft.

FURTHER READING

Klawitter, Nils, "Klüngeln im Krieg," *Der Spiegel,* February 13, 2006, p. 77.

Kundnani, Hans, "A Deal That Confronts a Painful History," *Guardian,* October 30, 2006, p. 2.

Leske, Nicola, "Cologne Publisher Keen to Buy at Home and Abroad," *Reuters,* April 15, 2007.

Meier, Christian, "Alfred Neven DuMonts Reich," *Welt am Sonntag,* February 13, 2005.

Weinhold, Kurt, *Die Geschichte eines Zeitungshauses: 1620–1970,* Cologne: Verlag M. DuMont Schauberg, 1969.

"Wurzel in der Tradition—Die Gruppe M. DuMont Schauberg." *Frankfurter Rundschau,* July 19, 2006, p. 2.

Mackays Stores Group Ltd.

———————————————————————— ■ ————————————————————————

Caledonia House
Caledonia Street
Paisley, PA3 2JP
United Kingdom
Telephone: (44 0141) 887 9151
Fax: (44 0141) 887 8069
Web site: http://www.mackaysstores.co.uk

Private Company
Incorporated: 1834 as J. Mackays (Drapers) Ltd.; 1973 as
  Mackays Stores Group
Employees: 2,700
Sales: £159 million ($283.60 million) (2005)
NAIC: 448120 Women's Clothing Stores; 448110
  Men's Clothing Stores; 448130 Children's and
  Infants' Clothing Stores

■ ■ ■

Mackays Stores Group Ltd. is one of Scotland's oldest retailers and is a leading operator of clothing stores throughout the United Kingdom. The Paisley-based company operates more than 300 stores in Scotland, England, and Wales, and, since 2007, in Northern Ireland. Although many of the company's stores still bear the Mackays name—long one of the most well-known names in the United Kingdom's shopping districts—Mackays launched a rebranding of its network in the first decade of the 21st century. As part of that process, the company has rolled out a new store brand, M&Co. The new brand shifts the company's target market away from its traditional image as a discount family clothing supplier toward a more upscale, women's fashions format.

The company's stores feature a department store format, and include sections for ladies' wear and lingerie, as well as separate departments for plus, petite, and tall sizes. The company targets the younger girls' market with its Kylie brand, which is backed by a popular web site and ezine. Mackays stores also typically feature a large home-wares section, as well as men's and children's sections. Mackays' own clothing lines include more than 4,000 designs, most produced by the company's own design team. Mackays also operates a buying office in London. Mackays remains controlled by the McGeoch family, with chairman and CEO Iain McGeoch holding more than 90 percent of the company. In the middle of the first decade of the 21st century, Mackays stores generated revenues of more than £160 million ($300 million).

FROM PAWNBROKER TO CLOTHING SELLER AFTER WORLD WAR II

Mackays originated as a pawnbroker's shop in Paisley, Scotland, in 1834. Founded by the McGeoch family, the pawnbroker business grew into a string of shops by the end of the century, and later took on the name of J. Mackays (Drapers) Ltd. The movement toward the modern day Mackays retail group came in the years following World War II, when Neil McGeoch converted a number of the family's pawnshops into clothing stores. The first store, opened in Clydebank in 1953, proved a success and over the next decade the family converted its other stores to the clothing format.

COMPANY PERSPECTIVES

Mission statement: To offer customers an exciting shopping experience, offering high quality, value-for-money fashion for all the family.

The company's fortunes truly took off as the next generation of the family entered the business. Lennie McGeoch joined his father at the company in 1961, followed by younger brother Iain in 1965. The family continued to open new stores through the decade, focusing on the market in Scotland. By the end of the 1960s, Mackays boasted more than 50 stores in operation. The company then made its first move outside of Scotland, opening a store in London in 1970. As part of its move south, the company bought another retail clothing chain that year, Ghinns Ltd. Based in Peckham, London, Ghinns brought seven subsidiaries to Mackays, as well as a small shopfitting operation, Havelock Textiles (later Havelock Europa), created in 1963.

Neil McGeoch retired from the business in 1973, turning the company over to his two sons, who shared the managing directors positions. The brothers proved highly complementary, with Len McGeoch focused on the textiles side of the business, while Iain McGeoch oversaw the group's real estate side. The company soon distinguished itself by its choice of location. Rather than acquire sites in the country's major urban markets particularly in the highly competitive "High Street" shopping districts, Mackays targeted smaller, often rural markets largely ignored by competitors. Another strategic success for the company came from its adoption of a discount pricing policy. By maintaining its own design staff, and carefully selecting manufacturing partners, the company was able to build its reputation as a retailer of quality clothing at low prices.

Mackays continued to build up its store network through the 1970s, gradually expanding into a national clothing operation. The company also saw growing success from its Havelock shopfitting business, which was regrouped as a separate division in 1972. At first Havelock focused its operation on Mackays' own fast-growing string of retail stores. In 1974, however, the company made the decision to begin offering its shopfitting services to other retailers, and restructured Havelock as an independently operating subsidiary. Havelock quickly emerged as a leading player in that market, and by the early 1980s had outgrown its parent

company. Recognizing this, Mackays spun off Havelock as a publicly listed company in 1984, placing its shares on the London Stock Exchange's Unlisted Securities Market. Mackays held on to a 49 percent stake in the company until 1986, when Havelock was merged with Fife-based Store Design Ltd., becoming one of the U.K.'s top shopfitting specialists.

ENTERING AND RETREATING FROM THE UNITED STATES

By the mid-1980s, Mackays' U.K. operations had grown to more than 150 stores. Buoyed by this success, the company decided to cross the Atlantic and build up a new empire in the United States. Leading this effort was Len McGeoch himself, who moved to the United States and oversaw the acquisition of Apparel Affiliates, Inc., in 1986. Originally a clothing manufacturer focused on career women's clothing, that company had also built up a national network of 120 stores, operating under such names as Corner House, Paraphernalia, Para, and Parallel.

Soon after the takeover, Mackays shut down its U.S. manufacturing business, and instead began contracting out for the production of its clothing designs. The decision proved an unfortunate one for the company. By the end of the decade, as the workplace adopted an increasingly more casual clothing style, Apparel Affiliates suffered from the drop in demand. Furthermore, the group was hurt by the long lead times required by its manufacturing contracts, hurting the group's ability to respond to the shift in the market. By the end of the decade, Mackays' U.S. subsidiary had seen its network drop back to just 105 stores. Worse, the subsidiary had slipped into the red, posting a loss of nearly $6 million on sales of just over US$46 million. The company initially sought a buyer for the operation. However, faced with the prospect of waiting at least six months for a sale, the U.S. business instead declared bankruptcy.

Mackays had not fully abandoned its efforts to expand internationally, however. Into the 1990s, the company acquired licenses to operate Benetton shops in Australia, Scotland, and Ireland. However, Mackays failed to find a good fit with the Italian clothing chain, and eventually abandoned that business as well. Len McGeoch returned to Scotland, once again overseeing the main company's textiles operations. Mackays made one last attempt at international expansion, opening a store in Poland in 1996 and setting up a franchised children's clothing store format in China. Both operations were shut down by the end of the decade.

In the meantime, the McGeoch brothers had made moves to step back from the company's day-to-day

KEY DATES

1834: McGeoch family founds a pawnbroker business in Paisley, Scotland.

1953: Under Neil McGeoch, company begins converting pawnshops to clothing stores.

1970: Company acquires Ghinns Ltd., extending its retail clothing business in the London area.

1973: Len and Iain McGeoch take over company from their father and adopt low-priced retail clothing format under Mackays name.

1986: Company acquires Apparel Affiliates Inc., owner of 140 retail clothing stores in the United States.

1990: Apparel Affiliates is forced to declare bankruptcy, and Mackays exits United States.

1996: A store in Poland is opened.

2001: Iain McGeoch buys out his brother's share of the company.

2003: The Laroque store chain in Coventry is acquired; a new new upscale clothing format, M&Co, is launched.

2005: Company begins converting all 270 stores to M&Co format.

operation. In 1996, the brothers, who remained co-chairmen, turned over the managing director's job to a family outsider, James Pow. The move, which also involved the hiring of a new financial director, was seen as preparation for a public listing of the company. It also coincided with the headlines raised by Len McGeoch's divorce; his American-born wife succeeded in winning the largest divorce settlement made by a Scottish court. The divorce trial also provided a glimpse into the lifestyle of the extremely publicity shy McGeoch family.

Mackays' plans for a public listing seemed to be moving forward in 1998 when Len McGeoch announced his decision to retire, at first to Ireland, and later to Portugal in order to play golf. In addition, a dip in the company's profits into the second half of the decade, which came in part because of attempts to expand the group's clothing mix beyond the discount price range, forced the group to put the public listing on hold. The failure to go public also resulted in the abrupt departure of company CEO Pow that year. Into the end of the decade, the company refocused its product line around its core low-price strategy, trimming its store network back from a high of 270 stores at mid-

decade, and launching a revamping of its store brand. The improvement in profits then led the company to seek to sell the company outright. By 1999, the company was said to have approached the Close Brothers merchant banking group to help find a buyer for the business.

In the end, however, the McGeoch brothers decided to keep the company in the family. In 2001, Len McGeoch agreed to sell his stake in the business to his brother Iain McGeoch. The younger McGeoch then controlled more than 90 percent of the company, with his mother holding a 1 percent stake, and most of the remainder shared out to company employees. These included a new CEO, Paul Vann, who later boosted his stake in the company to more than 4 percent.

EXPANSIVE MOOD FOR THE NEW CENTURY

By then, Mackays had rebuilt its retail network to nearly 260 stores. However, as Vann promised to the *Scotsman*, the beginning of the century was expected to be "the start of a new dynamic era for Mackays. We have been one of Britain's best-kept secrets in many ways, but there is no doubt that we are second to none in our reputation as a value-for-money retailer." The upbeat Mackays sought to capitalize on that reputation, announcing plans to add 25 new stores and more each year.

The slump in the United Kingdom's economy that year created a glitch in the company's immediate plans, however, as its new store openings proceeded at a crawl. In 2003, the company appeared to have a found a new formula for expansion, when it acquired the Laroque chain of clothing stores. The acquisition of more than 20 retail stores provided Mackays with a presence in the Coventry area of the Midlands for the first time. It also gave the company a test market for a new store concept, M&Co.

With its new store format, Mackays sought to position itself on the upscale side of the clothing market. The lowering of European trade barriers with China had led to the inundation of the United Kingdom and the rest of Europe with that country's low-priced production. The flood of cheaply produced textiles encouraged the increasing adoption of department store–like hypermarket formats by the United Kingdom's major retailers, placing Mackays and other retailers under even greater pressure than before. In this light, Mackays' interest in a more upscale, women-oriented product mix could be seen as a defensive move. The development of the M&Co brand also allowed the company to rejuvenate its image, broadening its appeal into the younger, more modern consumer segment.

The success of the M&Co launch soon led the company to roll out the brand across the whole of its women's clothing lines. Mackays then added a number of other new brands, including Kylie, targeting the fast-growing trendy young girls' market, and Kidzunlimited for its children's clothing lines. Backing the reorientation of the group's branding and marketing strategy, Mackays beefed up its buying, merchandising, and sourcing operations. As Vann explained to the *Herald:* "You can't get away with producing fuddy-duddy clothes for the 35 to 50 age range any more. People are now prepared to buy what we offer at full price."

If the rest of the U.K. retail clothing sector remained in the doldrums through the first half of the decade, Mackays' own M&Co-driven fortunes remained buoyant. By the beginning of 2005, the company had converted 23 stores to the new format. The company, which instead of adding new stores had been streamlining its existing portfolio of locations, announced new plans to add up to 20 new stores that year.

The surprise departure of Paul Vann that year led the company to make a new about-face in its strategy, developed solely by Iain McGeoch as chairman and chief executive. While the company continued to seek new store sites, these amounted to just six or seven during the year. Instead, Mackays announced its decision to convert the whole of its retail chain to the increasingly successful M&Co format. By 2006, the company had converted more than half of its 270 stores to the new formula, a process largely completed by 2007. The company had also reinforced its M&Co sales with the launch backed by its own e-commerce enabled web site during the year.

By 2007, Mackays was preparing for new expansion. The company targeted a new market, Northern Ireland, opening its first store there in Belfast's Laharna Retail Park. Mackays also moved to larger headquarters that year, from Paisley to nearby Inchinnan. The nearly 175-year-old company appeared to have found a new life for the new century.

M. L. Cohen

PRINCIPAL DIVISIONS

M&Co.

PRINCIPAL COMPETITORS

NEXT plc; Arcadia Group Ltd.; Coats Holdings Ltd.; Burberry Group plc; New Look Group Ltd.; Top Shop/Top Man Ltd.; The Peacock Group plc; Monsoon plc; Ossian Retail Group Ltd.; H and M Hennes Ltd.; French Connection Group plc.

FURTHER READING

"Fashion Store First for Larne Retail Outlet," *Belfast Telegraph,* June 25, 2007.

Fields, Julia, "Mackays Adds 20 New Stores to Shopping List As Profits Rise," *Sunday Herald,* October 16, 2005.

Friedli, Douglas, "Mackays Chief Spends GBP 2m on Raising Stake," *Scotland on Sunday,* January 30, 2005, p. 1.

"Mackays Shake-up Paves Way to Market," *Sunday Times,* October 13, 1996, p. 2.

"Mackays Stores Profits Driven by M&Co and Fashionable Children," *Scotsman,* July 13, 2004, p. 23.

Nicholson, Mark, "Iain McGeoch Keeps Mackays in the Family," *Financial Times,* December 18, 2001, p. 27.

Rutherford, Hamish, "Mackays to Roll Out M&Co Rebranding Nationwide," *Scotsman,* July 22, 2006.

Smith, Stephen, "Exile for Store Boss After Divorce Payout," *Daily Mail,* April 8, 1997, p. 5.

Staples, John, "Tycoon Brothers Split Clothing Empire," *Scotsman,* December 18, 2001.

"Strategic Vision," *Personnel Today,* September 14, 2004, p. 32.

Marfin Popular Bank plc

P.O. Box 22032
Nicosia, CY-1598
Cyprus
Telephone: (357 22) 75 20 00
Fax: (357 22) 81 14 91
Web site: http://www.laiki.com

Public Company
Incorporated: 2006
Employees: 3,425
Total Assets: EUR 22.59 billion ($28 billion) (2006)
Stock Exchanges: Cyprus Athens
Ticker Symbol: CPB
NAIC: 522110 Commercial Banking; 523120 Securities
Brokerage; 524113 Direct Life Insurance Carriers

■ ■ ■

Marfin Popular Bank Public Co. Ltd. is the largest bank group in Cyprus and one of the largest in the Hellenic region. Formed through the merger of three banks: the Laiki Group of Cyprus, the Marfin Financial Group of Greece, and its subsidiary Egnatia Bank, Marfin Popular Bank operates from 114 branches in Cyprus and 144 branches in Greece. The bank has also followed the Greek and Cypriot diaspora, establishing a subsidiary in Australia, with ten branches, and in the United Kingdom, with five branches.

Marfin Popular's main focus is on developing its position as a major regional bank, as well as supporting the international operations of Greece's powerful shipping industry. Having failed in attempted takeovers of two other major Cypriot banks (Bank of Cyprus and Pireaus Bank) Marfin Popular has focused on building its growth through organic expansion and smaller acquisitions.

As such, the group has acquired majority control of Centrobanka in Serbia and has extended its operations into Romania, with eight branches. The company acquired Estonia's AS SBM Pank and Ukraine's Marine Transport Bank in 2007. Marfin Popular also operates a subsidiary in Guernsey, as well as representative offices in the United States, South Africa, Russia, and Canada. Marfin Popular is listed on the Cyprus and Athens stock exchanges and has total assets of more than EUR 22 billion ($28 billion). Dubai Financial Group, owned by the Dubai government, holds nearly 20 percent of Marfin Popular and expects to increase its stake to 30 percent during 2008.

MARITIME BANKING SPECIALIST IN 1998

While a major part of Marfin Popular Bank had operations dating back to the dawn of the 20th century, the driving forced behind the creation of the group (one of the largest in the Hellenic region) was a company created in the late 1990s as an investment holding company created by several Greek shipping companies. Marfin (the name stood for Maritime and Financial) was founded as Marfin Financial Services in Athens in 1998.

The company soon turned its focus toward acquisitions and in 2000 acquired Helleniki Securities S.A. The following year, Marfin entered the private banking sector

COMPANY PERSPECTIVES

Marfin Popular Bank plc was created by the merger of three Groups: Marfin Financial Group, Laiki Group and Egnatia Bank. The subsequent consolidation has created a major financial institution with a leading competitive advantage. New synergies will enable the group to accelerate its expansion in South-eastern Europe. And it is now able to offer even more competitive products and a higher quality of service while it continues to increase shareholder value.

for the first time, through its acquisition of Piraeus Prime Bank, the Greece-based subsidiary of Cyprus' Piraeus Bank. Backing Marfin's expansion was a listing on the Athens stock exchange. By 2005, more than 73 percent of the group's stock had been floated on the Athens exchange, while vice-chairman Andreas Vgenopoulos retained a 6.5 percent share, alongside a strategic investors group with 20.5 percent.

Marfin restructured its holdings in 2004, merging its Maritime and Financial Investments subsidiary with Comm Group and its Marfin Classic Close End Fund, to form the new Marfin Financial Group. In that year, the company's Marfin Helleniki Securities merged its business into that of the Investment Bank of Greece S.A., with Marfin retaining an 87 percent share of the newly enlarged securities operation.

Marfin completed a share capital increase in 2005, raising EUR 400 million for further expansion. The company quickly choose its next target and in 2005 reached an agreement to acquire a minority stake in Greece-based Egnatia Bank, gaining a 14 percent share.

Egnatia had been founded in Thessalonica in 1991 and had remained a small, local bank through most of that decade. In 1998, however, Egnatia began its extra-regional drive, winning the bid to buy out the Central Bank of Greece. That merger, completed in 1999, allowed Egnatia to take over Central Bank of Greece's listing on the Athens Stock Exchange, beginning in August of that year. By the end of 1999, Egnatia had largely completed the integration of its newly expanded operation, rolling out a new Globus-based software platform for the entire group. With the merger completed, Egnatia focused on its growth, building up its branch network to more than 100 locations across Greece. The bank also made its first inroads internationally with the acquisition of Bank BNP-Dresdner in Romania. The

company then renamed its new subsidiary as Egnatia Bank (Romania).

The early 2000s marked a significant transition period in the Hellenic banking sector. The emergence of most of Cyprus's largest banks as major players in the Greek banking market during the 1990s and into the 2000s had placed that country's banking groups under pressure to expand as well. Greek merger and acquisition rules, which required takeovers to be made on a 100 percent basis, made expansion in that market difficult. The more flexible regulations in Cyprus, coupled with its role as a major shipping and offshore banking market, made that country a more attractive destination for Marfin. At the same time, as Cyprus prepared for its entry into the Eurozone, slated for the beginning of 2008, its banking sector entered a consolidation phase.

The consolidation of the Cypriot market offered new expansion opportunities for Marfin, as well as for foreign investors seeking an entry into the region's banking sector. Nonetheless, with total assets of just EUR 1.6 billion ($1.98 billion), Marfin remained a tiny player in the region. In order to bulk up in preparation for its expansion plans, Marfin found a new strategic investor in Dubai Financial, part of the state-owned Dubai Investment Group. In 2006, Dubai Financial bought a 31.5 percent stake in Marfin. Backed by the deep pockets of its new major shareholder, Marfin quickly settled on its expansion target: Laiki Bank, the second largest banking institution in Cyprus.

MOVING TO CYPRUS IN 2006

Laiki Bank had been founded in 1901 in Limassol by three local lawyers and a wine merchant in order to establish that town's first Cypriot-owned bank. Laiki was among the first Cypriot banks to appear on the island (the first being Bank of Cyprus, which had been founded just two years earlier in Nicosia) as Cyprus remained a British protectorate at the turn of the century. Cyprus's growing importance as a strategic naval outpost for the British Empire enabled the bank, called the Popular Savings Bank of Limassol, to grow strongly over the next two decades.

By the early 1920s, Popular Bank had moved from its original premises, a private residence, into its own headquarters on Limassol's Athenon Street. After Great Britain had formally established colonial control over Cyprus, the island's economy had grown strongly, and by the beginning of the 1920s the Popular Savings Bank had expanded its initial mandate to include the full range of banking services. In 1924, the bank adopted a new name, Popular Bank of Limassol Ltd., and became

KEY DATES

1901: Founding of the Popular Savings Bank of Limassol in Cyprus.

1924: The bank expands to offer a full range of services and goes public on new Cyprus stock exchange as Popular Bank of Limassol.

1967: Bank expands across all of Cyprus and changes name to Cyprus Popular Bank.

1991: Egnatia Bank in Greece is created.

1998: Marfin Financial Services is formed in Athens.

2000: Cyprus Popular Bank changes its name to Laiki Group.

2006: Marfin acquires majority control of Egnatia Bank, then leads a three-way merger with Laiki Group, forming Marfin Popular Bank.

the first bank to list its shares on the newly created Cyprus stock exchange.

Popular Bank nonetheless remained focused on its local market throughout most of the next 40 years. The bank's decision to expand its operations across all of Cyprus came only following the island's independence from Britain in 1960. In 1967, the bank adopted a new strategy of national expansion and began adding branch offices throughout the country. At that time, the bank changed its name to Cyprus Popular Bank Ltd.

By 1968, the bank had opened its first branch in Nicosia. This was closely followed by the opening of branches in Famagusta in 1969, in Paphos and Larnaca in 1970, and in Kyrenia in 1973. Throughout that decade, despite the turmoil brought on by the scission of Cyprus into separate Greek and Turkish entities, Cyprus Popular continued to build its operations. The group expanded internationally, with the opening of a branch in London in 1974, and also expanded its range of operations, acquiring an insurance subsidiary, Labancor Ltd., in 1972. Backing the group's growth during this period was the introduction of a strategic shareholder, Hongkong Bank (later known as HSBC), which acquired more than 21 percent of Cyprus Popular's shares.

The start of the 1980s, however, marked Cyprus Popular Bank's emergence among the island state's banking leaders. In 1983, the bank acquired the operations of Grindlays Bank, then the country's third largest. Grindlays was also one of the oldest of the foreign-owned banks that had dominated the country's financial

markets since the British had placed it under its administration in the mid-19th century. Its acquisition by Cyprus Popular, therefore, proved highly significant, marking the coming of age of the country's financial sector.

Cyprus Popular added a new Cypriot branch in Lefkoteha in 1985. The bank also became one of the first to offer its own credit cards that year, starting with Visa. In 1987, the bank also became the first to roll out automated teller machines as well. In that year Cyprus Popular added its own American Express–backed credit card as well.

INTERNATIONAL GROWTH TARGETS

Cyprus Popular added new foreign operations in 1988, opening a representative office in Australia in order to cater to the needs of the large Greek diaspora population there. By the end of the decade, the bank had launched its own investment and assets management operation, Laiki Investments. This was followed by the creation of a factoring subsidiary, Laiki Factors, in 1991. The following year marked a new milestone in the group's history, as it opened its first branch in Greece, on Panepistimiou Street in Athens. This entry was quickly followed by a second Athens-based branch in 1993.

Through the rest of the decade, Cyprus Popular continued to follow both the Greek diaspora and the Greek and international shipping sectors, setting up representative offices in South Africa, Canada, and the United States. The bank also launched an entry into the Balkan and East European regions, adding offices in Yugoslavia and Russia. The bank would later face criticism for its actions in the former Yugoslavia, in particular its role in helping to finance wars waged by former Serbian strongman Slobodan Milosevic. The bank and its management were accused of illegally transferring billions of dollars from the former Yugoslavia into front company accounts in Nicosia. The resulting scandal led the bank to replace its chairman and much of its board of directors in order to salvage its tarnished reputation. The company then changed its name, to Laiki Group, in 2000.

In the meantime, the bank continued to expand its range of services and businesses. The company launched an Internet banking operation in 1998, followed by the creation of a call center–based subsidiary, Laiki Telebank, in 1999. In that, the group expanded its insurance operations through the acquisition of Interamerican and Philiki, both part of the Paneuropean Group of Insurance Companies. The company also launched an electronic banking service, Laiki eBank, for the Cyprus market in 2000.

Laiki rolled out full banking services to the Australian market in 2001, rapidly opening five branch offices to service the local Cypriot and Greek populations. The company extended its Laiki eBank operations to the Greek market that year. Laiki eBank was then launched in the United Kingdom and Australia in 2004.

The runup to Cyprus's adoption of the euro, along with an accompanying deregulation of the country's banking sector, forced Laiki to seek greater expansion. The need to achieve greater mass, as well as to establish itself as an international player, led Laiki to Serbia, where it bought that country's Centrobank in 2005. In that year as well Laiki added a Channel Islands banking subsidiary, setting up an office on Guernsey.

THE 2006 MERGER

By 2006, Laiki had come under the acquisitive eye of the Marfin group. Marfin had started to bulk up, buying up majority control of Egnatia Bank that year to become Greece's eighth largest bank. Marfin then reached an agreement with HSBC to buy out part of its more than 21 percent stake in Laiki. As part of that agreement, Marfin also acquired Laiki's operations in Greece. By the end of the year, Marfin had received permission from the Cyprus exchange authorities to launch a full takeover of Laiki Bank. The company then launched a three-way merger among itself, Egnatia Bank, and Laiki, creating Marfin Popular Bank. Following the merger, Dubai Finance's stake in the new company dipped below 18 percent; at the end of 2007, however, Dubai Finance indicated its intention to increase its holding to 30 percent during 2008.

With headquarters in Cyprus, the new bank group claimed to be Cyprus's largest within Cyprus itself, although Bank of Cyprus, based in Nicosia, remained the country's leading financial institution. Marfin Popular immediately sought to remedy that situation and in early 2007 launched dual takeover offers for both Bank of Cyprus and Pireaus Bank. In the end, after a takeover battle that lasted for several months, and which included rival takeover offers launched by Pireaus Bank against Marfin, the parties agreed to end all takeover attempts. The agreement included a three-year moratorium against any new takeover offers.

Instead, Marfin Popular targeted further expansion into a wider European market. For this, the bank targeted the international shipping market, seeking acquisitions that would enhance its profile in that sector. In preparation for its next growth phase, the company completed a EUR 5.2 billion capital increase, the largest ever placed on the Athens stock exchange. The company then moved to acquire a majority share in AS SBM Pank, in Estonia. The entry into Estonia was joined by expansion into Ukraine, through the purchase of that country's Marine Transport Bank for more than $137 million in March 2007. Marfin Popular had become a major player in the Hellenic banking market, and, with its strong focus on the international maritime sector, hoped to become a major banking presence in the new century.

M. L. Cohen

PRINCIPAL SUBSIDIARIES

AS SBM Pank (Estonia; 48%); Egnatia Bank (Romania) S.A. (86%); Egnatia Bank S.A. (Greece; 86%); Egnatia Finance S.A. (Greece; 61%); Investment Bank of Greece S.A. (87%); Laiki Bank (Australia) Ltd.; Laiki Bank (Guernsey) Ltd.; Laiki Bank (Hellas) S.A. (Greece); Laiki Bank a.d. (Serbia; 95%); Laiki Factoring S.A.; Laiki Insurance Ltd.; Laiki Investments E.P.E.Y. Public Company Ltd. (Cyprus; 57%); Laiki Leasing S.A. (Greece); Marfin Bank S.A. (Greece; 95%); Marfin Financial Group Holdings S.A. (Greece; 95%); MFG Capital Partners Ltd. (United Kingdom; 95%); Paneuropean Insurance Co Ltd.; The Cyprus Popular Bank (Finance) Ltd.

PRINCIPAL COMPETITORS

Bank of Cyprus Group; Mortgage Bank of Cyprus Ltd.; Hellenic Bank Public Company Ltd.; Alpha Bank Ltd.; National Bank of Greece (Cyprus) Ltd.; Emporiki Bank–Cyprus Ltd.; Universal Bank Public Ltd.; Cyprus Development Bank Public Company Ltd.; Arab Bank plc.

FURTHER READING

"Cyprus Laiki Bank to Buy Majority Share in Serbian Centrobanka," *Xinhua News Agency,* November 8, 2005.

"Dubai Stakes Claim on Marfin," *MEED Middle East Economic Digest,* March 24, 2006, p. 40.

Evans, John, "All-Out Turf War Hits Greece," *Retail Banker International,* February 24, 2007, p. 8.

Hadjipapas, Andreas, and Kerin Hope, "Laiki Chief Quits over Job Loss Fears," *Financial Times,* July 19, 2006, p. 26.

Hope, Kerin, "In Search of a Regional Role," *Financial Times,* December 19, 2006, p. 2.

———, "Marfin Continues Expansion," *Financial Times,* March 20, 2007, p. 17.

———, "Marfin to Raise Euros 5.2bn in Capital," *Financial Times,* March 30, 2007, p. 22.

Kontogiannis, Dimitris, "DFG Increases Stake in MPB," *Financial Times,* November 1, 2007, p. 16.

"Marfin Popular Bank Acquires Bank in Estonia," *Financial Mirror,* June 14, 2007.

Wagstyle, Stefan, and Kerin Hope, "Defiant Cyprus Bank That Helped Fund Two Wars," *Financial Times,* July 25, 2002, p. 6.

Mariella Burani Fashion Group

———■———

Via della Repubblica 86
Cavriago, I-42025
Italy
Telephone: (39 0522) 373131
Fax: (39 0522) 576922
Web site: http://www.mariellaburani.com

Public Company
Incorporated: 1999
Employees: 2,480
Sales: EUR 672.6 million ($758 million) (2006)
Stock Exchanges: Milan London AIM
Ticker Symbol: MBFG
NAIC: 315232 Women's and Girls' Cut and Sew Blouse and Shirt Manufacturing; 315292 Fur and Leather Apparel Manufacturing; 316214 Women's Footwear (Except Athletic) Manufacturing

■ ■ ■

Mariella Burani Fashion Group (MBFG) is one of Italy's fastest-growing designers, producers, and distributors of what the company calls "accessible luxury" clothing, leatherware, and accessories. Through an impressive string of acquisitions both in Italy and elsewhere in Europe, MBFG's revenues had soared by 500 percent since its initial public offering (IPO) in 2000, nearing EUR 675 million in 2006. The company operates four primary divisions: Apparel, Leather Goods, Digital Fashion, and Fashion Jewelry.

Apparel is the group's core business, generating 51 percent of its revenues primarily from its flagship Mari-

ella Burani brand family, as well as from René Lezard, Mila Schön, and others. These account for more than 90 percent of the group's apparel sales. The company also produces clothing under license for such labels as Mugler (Thierry Mugler), Anglomania (Vivienne Westwood), and Fuchsia (Emmanuel Ungaro).

MBFG's Leather Goods division, launched at the beginning of the 2000s, contributes 32 percent of the group's sales and is grouped under publicly listed subsidiary Antichi Pellettieri. The group's leather goods brand stable includes the Sebastian and Baldinini shoe brands; accessories through the Braccialini and Francesco Biasia brands; and, since 2006, a 51 percent stake in leather handbag and accessories group Coccinelle.

The company's small Digital Fashion division is a provider of software and web-hosting services to the fashion industry, including the operation of fashionweb.net for Italy's Chamber of Commerce. MBFG's Fashion Jewelry Division is its youngest, having been launched in 2007 following the acquisitions of 51 percent of Facco Corporation SpA, 50 percent of Rosato SpA, and 60 percent of Valente Gioiellieri SpA.

MBFG has long pursued a vertical integration strategy. In addition to producing most of its clothing, leather goods, and accessories and jewelry designs in its own factories, the company has built up its own international network of retail stores. These include more than 310 directly owned or franchised single-brand boutiques and nearly 2,000 multibrand stores and department stores. The company also distributes its brands to nearly 8,000 retailers throughout the world.

COMPANY PERSPECTIVES

Mariella Burani Fashion Group designs, produces and distributes accessible luxury apparel, handbags and accessories, footwear, and fashion jewelry collections worldwide under its own brands and under license for renowned international designers. The Group's mission is to strengthen its leadership in the fast-growth accessible luxury sector by extending its influence in emerging markets, expanding its distribution network, and further leveraging its brands.

Italy remains the company's single largest market, at 36 percent of sales, while the rest of Europe represents 52 percent of sales. The group is also present in North America, as well as in Japan and elsewhere in Asia. Mariella Burani Fashion Group remains controlled by the founding Burani family, with Giovanni Burani serving as its chairman and CEO. The company is listed on the Milan stock exchange, and, since 2007, on the London AIM exchange.

FROM BABY CLOTHES TO WOMEN'S FASHION IN 1970

MBFG had its roots as a small manufacturer of baby clothing, set up by Walter Burani in his hometown of Reggio Emilia, in the Emilia-Romagna region south of Milan. Founded in 1960, the Burani company's original name was Selene SpA. Burani's partner in the business was his wife, Mariella Burani, who took charge of the company's design operations. By 1970, the Buranis were ready to make the leap into the far larger market for women's fashions, launching their first collection that year.

Selene began narrowing its operations in the early 1980s, with a focus on the women's ready-to-wear market through most of that decade. By the end of the 1980s, the Mariella Burani label had grown into a small, but respected midlevel brand, building its reputation on Burani's highly feminine designs. An important factor in the group's growth during this period was its decision to develop its own retail distribution operations. The company's first store opened in Milan in 1986 under the Mariella Burani name. In 1988, the group decided to focus its retail expansion on opening single-brand boutiques. By the early 1990s, the company operated nearly 25 directly owned or franchised stores, primarily in Europe but also in Japan. The company made its entry into the United States in 1993, opening its first store in Beverly Hills, as a testing ground for a future launch in New York City.

Another factor in the company's growth through the 1990s was its decision, starting in 1988, to develop a portfolio of licensed designer labels. The company's focus on what it called the "accessible fashion" market (midlevel designer fashions) made it an important partner for a growing number of major design houses. The company secured a major contract, for example, when it gained the license for the Carisma and Carisma Rouge collections created by Valentino. Other successes included the global license for ready-to-wear and "comfortable size" collections created by Gai Mattiolo, awarded in 1996. The following year, the company extended its partnership with that design house, gaining the license for Gai Mattiolo's fashion jeans collection.

Walter Burani's sons, Giovanni and Andrea, took over the family business in 1999, while their mother remained in charge of the group's design operations. Under Giovanni's leadership, the company adopted a new strategy for the turn of the century. By then, the Italian clothing and fashion industries had come under new pressure, particularly from the growing numbers of imports from India and China. At the same time, the fashion industry was undergoing a rapid consolidation, led by such luxury behemoths as LVMH, which began buying up Italy's typically small, family-run clothing and textiles companies. In order to survive, the Buranis recognized that their company needed to adapt to the new marketplace.

GOING PUBLIC IN 2000

Selene launched an acquisition program designed to expand the group's manufacturing and design operations while increasing its geographic focus, and, importantly, diversify its range of products. The company's first major acquisition came in 1999, when it acquired Dimensione Moda, a knitwear company marketing under the Laura Casini brand.

In that year, too, the company acquired a 50 percent stake in Mila Schön. That design house, launched by the designer of the same name in 1958, had been acquired by Japan's Itochu in the mid-1980s, growing into a highly respected designer name in the Asian region. The purchase of Mila Schön not only gave Selene a second major label, it also added 20 new stores to the company's retail network, which by then included 21 directly owned stores and 54 franchised stores. During this time, the company changed its name to Mariella Burani Fashion Group. MBFG's early acquisitions into the end of the decade had helped the company boost its revenues from just $52 million in 1997 to $144 million by 1999.

KEY DATES

1960: Walter and Mariella Burani establish Selene SpA as a producer of baby clothing.
1970: Company expands into production of women's clothing.
1988: Licensed production operations, as well as retail distribution operations through Mariella Burani ready-to-wear collection, are launched.
1999: Mila Schön designer label is acquired, and company reincorporates as Mariella Burani Fashion Group (MBFG).
2000: Company goes public on Milan stock exchange; company launches aggressive acquisition strategy.
2002: New leather goods division is formed under subsidiary Antichi Pellettieri.
2006: Antichi Pellettieri goes public on Milan exchange.
2007: MBFG launches new IPO on London AIM exchange as well as a new Fashion Jewelry division.

The company continued to seek new licenses. In 2000, the company began a short-lived production and distribution agreement with Calvin Klein, in part to support a brief effort by the company to expand its U.S. profile. As it prepared for its public offering in 2000, MBFG's focus fell more sharply on building up its own portfolio of designer labels.

Acquisitions formed the heart of this new growth strategy as the company sought to position itself as a leader in the growing "accessible luxury" market, positioned between high-end houses such as Prada and Gucci, and traditional mid-market groups such as Benetton. Indeed, between 2000 and 2007, the company carried out more than 20 acquisitions. Most of these were for relatively small companies, which found themselves increasingly unable to compete by themselves in the highly competitive fashion market during this time. In 2000, for example, the company acquired a new knitwear label, Gabriella Frattini. MBFG's acquisition targets also served to support another component of its expansion strategy to diversify its operations into other luxury goods categories.

This led the company to enter the leather goods sector in 2000, with the purchases of two leather goods designers, Braccialini and DeiMutti. These acquisitions also strengthened the group's licensed production wing,

adding customers including Vivienne Westwood. By 2001, the company had completed four new acquisitions in the leather goods sector, including the footwear labels Baldinini, Mario Cerutti, and Mafra, and leather apparel group Enrico Mandelli. In that year, MBFG created a new subsidiary, Antichi Pellettieri, as a holding company for its leather goods operations.

"MINIATURE" FASHION HOLDING COMPANY IN THE 21ST CENTURY

By 2003, MBFG was well on its way to building what the *Financial Times* described as a "miniature fashion holding company," with total sales nearing EUR 275 million. With its new leather goods division growing strongly, the company targeted new areas of expansion. The company bought the Sahzà design house from GFT, adding its label as well as its network of 13 in-store boutiques. MBFG also branched out from its core women's wear operation through a joint venture producing and distributing men's and children's clothing with Stephen Fairchild.

In 2002, the company expanded its geographic base, buying a 50 percent stake in Germany's luxury clothing label René Lezard Mode GmbH. MBFG also expanded its retail holdings, buying the Revedi group, which gave the company 18 retail outlets, including its first stores in Switzerland. At the same time, the company increased its vertical integration, buying a Como-based producer of silk and jersey fabrics, ITM SpA, in a deal worth $10.7 million.

MBFG's next acquisition came in 2003, when it took on a 60 percent stake in the business of noted Italian leather handbag designer Francesco Biasia. In November of that year, the company had also purchased Le Trico Perugia SpA, a knitwear specialist, for EUR 5.4 million. By then, MBFG had also moved to raise fresh capital for expansion. The company sold a 33 percent stake in the family's holding company to Interbanca,and then sold 30 percent of Antichi Pellettieri to L Capital, an investment fund attached to the LVMH empire. That deal raised an addition EUR 110 million as the company continued its search for acquisition candidates. It also provided Antichi Pellettieri with agreements to begin manufacturing products for the LVMH group.

Retail operations represented another growth area for MBFG. By 2004, the company's operations included more than 150 boutiques. In that year, the company also launched a new multibrand boutique format, simply called Mariella Burani, in Pescara. The new format featured the full collection of the company's leather good brands. In another international expansion effort, the company acquired Don Gil GmbH, based in Austria, adding its 38 retail stores. MBFG opened a flagship Braccialini store in London, its first in the United Kingdom, and also turned its attention to the Eastern European markets, opening six stores in Russia and elsewhere. By the beginning of 2005, MBFG's retail operations had grown again, this time with the acquisition of Bernie's AG, a leading luxury goods retailer in Switzerland with 16 stores.

MBFG returned to the market in 2006, carrying out a public offering of Antichi Pellettieri on the Milan stock exchange. The listing raised another EUR 130 million for the company, which showed little sign of slowing down its expansion. Indeed, by 2007, MBFG itself returned to the market, placing 23 percent of its shares on the London Stock Exchange's AIM market, adding another EUR 130 million to its coffers. In the meantime, MBFG had completed several new acquisitions, including the purchase of 51 percent of Coccinelle SpA, a leading leather handbags and accessories producer with operations in Italy and Germany.

With both its apparel and leather goods divisions growing strongly, MBFG in 2007 launched a new division: Fashion Jewelry. For this, the company set about building a portfolio of luxury jewelry brand holdings, including 51 percent of Facco Corporation; 50 percent of Rosato SpA; 60 percent of Valente Gioliellieri SpA; and 51 percent in Calgaro SpA. At the same time, the company launched a fashion jewelry joint venture with Damas Jewellery. By then, the company's sales had risen past EUR 675 million, representing an increase of more than 500 percent since its IPO in 2000. For MBFG, the leading ranks of the accessible luxury segment appeared entirely accessible in the 21st century.

M. L. Cohen

PRINCIPAL SUBSIDIARIES

Antichi Pellettieri SpA; Baldinini SRL; Bernie's AG (Germany); Braccialini SRL; Coccinelle SpA; Coccinelle Store France S.A.; Coccinelle Store GmbH (Germany); Design & Licenses SpA; Don GIL GmbH (Germany); Enrico Mandelli SpA; Faccio Corporation (51%); Francesco Biasia SpA; Leather Apparel SRL; Longwave SRL; Mariella Burani Retail SRL; Mariella Fashion SL; René Lezard Mode GmbH (50%, Germany); Revedi SA (Switzerland); Revedi SpA; Sedoc.It SRL.

PRINCIPAL DIVISIONS

Apparel; Leather Goods; Digital Fashion; Fashion Jewelry.

PRINCIPAL COMPETITORS

Christian Dior S.A.; LVMH Moët Hennessy Louis Vuitton S.A.; Industria de Diseno Textil S.A.; DELTON AG; Coats Holdings Ltd.; Mango S.L.; Cortefiel S.A.; Devanlay S.A.; Alexon Group plc.

FURTHER READING

Braithwaite, Tom, "Burani Brings Italian Style to AIM and Raises Euros 130m," *Financial Times,* June 16, 2007, p. 18.

"Burani Developments," *WWD,* September 1, 2006, p. 2

"Burani Purchasing Stake in Baldinini," *WWD,* February 1, 2001, p. 11.

"Burgeoning Burani," *WWD,* November 19, 2003, p. 2.

Ilari, Alessandra, "Burani Group Acquires ITM for $10.7M," *WWD,* March 26, 2002, p. 7.

Kapner, Fred, "Burani Enters Big League," *Financial Times,* September 27, 2003, p. 9.

"Mariella Burani Raises EUR 130m in London IPO," *just-style. com,* June 15, 2007.

Sylvers, Eric, "Stretching to Survive, Italian Fashion Firm Grows from Its Roots," *International Herald Tribune,* February 17, 2007, p. 14.

Zargani, Luisa, "Burani Buys Two Leather Firms," *WWD,* November 6, 2000, p. 16.

——, "Burani IPO Will Kick off Expansion, Acquisitions," *WWD,* July 10, 2000, p. 11.

——, "Burani Net Skyrockets Thanks to Top Brands," *WWD,* April 1, 2004, p. 13.

——, "Burani Set to Sell Pellettieri Shares," *WWD,* May 23, 2006, p. 3.

The McClatchy Company

2100 Q Street
Sacramento, California 95816
U.S.A.
Telephone: (916) 321-1846
Fax: (916) 321-1964
Web site: http://www.mcclatchy.com

Public Company
Incorporated: 1930
Employees: 16,790
Sales: $1.67 billion (2006)
Stock Exchanges: New York
Ticker Symbol: MNI
NAIC: 511110 Newspaper Publishers

■ ■ ■

The McClatchy Company is one of the leading media companies in the United States, owning more than 30 daily newspapers and nearly 50 nondaily papers in markets all across the country. Some of McClatchy's largest properties are the *Miami Tribune,* the *Sacramento Bee,* the *Kansas City Star,* and the *Fort Worth Star-Telegram.* McClatchy also runs news-related web sites in its newspaper markets, run through its subsidiary McClatchy Interactive. The company made several major acquisitions in the 1990s and in the first decade of the 21st century, including its purchase of Knight-Ridder, Inc., in 2006. Although publicly traded, the bulk of McClatchy's stock remains in the hands of the McClatchy family.

MID-19TH-CENTURY FOUNDATIONS

The group's first and for many years only paper was the *Sacramento Bee,* founded in 1857 by James McClatchy. An Irish immigrant, McClatchy had served as a correspondent with Horace Greeley's *New York Tribune* during the early 19th century before heading west in 1849 to try his hand at gold mining. It was not long, however, before he reconsidered his first career and took a job with Sacramento's first newspaper, the *Placer Times.* In 1857, he was among the founders of the *Sacramento Bee* and became the paper's editor within its first year of operation. Over the course of his quarter-century at the helm, McClatchy used the *Bee* as a forum to support the causes of environmentalism and abolitionism, among other issues.

At his death in 1883, the patriarch willed joint ownership of the paper to his two sons. Charles Kenny (C. K.) became editor, while Valentine Stuart assumed the role of business manager. Throughout his more than 50 years at the helm, C. K. carried on his father's liberal-leaning causes, including environmentalism (editorials supported urban beautification through tree-planting, for example), steadfast support of First Amendment rights, and trust-busting. C. K. obtained exclusive ownership of the paper in 1923 and began grooming his son, Carlos, as his successor. Having graduated from Columbia University, Carlos established the family firm's two other "*Bees*" in the 1920s, founding the *Fresno Bee* in 1922 and acquiring the *Modesto Bee* (formerly the *Modesto News-Herald*) five years later. When Carlos died in 1933, C. K. turned to his youngest daughter, Eleanor, to assume the mantle of leadership.

DIVERSIFICATION INTO RADIO, TV, CABLE

Studying at Columbia University to be a playwright, Eleanor was living in New York in 1936 when her father died, leaving her in charge of the three-newspaper group. Over the course of her more than four decades as president and later CEO of the family business, Eleanor shepherded growth and diversification. Following the lead of her brother, Carlos, who had guided the company's first radio acquisition in 1925, she acquired 11 more radio stations throughout California by the mid-1960s. McClatchy obtained its first television-broadcasting license in Fresno in 1953, and added a Sacramento station a decade later. Sensing that cable television would siphon advertising dollars from newspapers, Eleanor bought into that industry in the late 1960s. The company also participated in a cellular telephone network joint venture. Eleanor even made a very early foray into electronic news delivery in 1937, when she launched a yearlong experiment into facsimile delivery of news and information. This experiment foreshadowed the company's Internet ventures by more than half a century.

DIVESTMENT OF ELECTRONIC MEDIA

Eleanor McClatchy passed the media company reins to her nephew, Carlos's son Charles Kenny (C. K.) McClatchy, two years before her death in 1980. C. K. had made his start in the family business in 1958 as a reporter for the *Sacramento Bee*. Characterized as a "maverick," he determined that the electronic properties were distracting management from the profitable and important core newspaper business. Over the course of the decade, the company shed its radio, broadcast television, and cable interests. It sold the television stations in 1980 and 1981, four radio stations in 1983, and its 96,000-subscriber cable system in 1986.

During this same time, McClatchy was investing the proceeds of its electronic media sales in newspapers, thereby expanding its geographic reach within California and throughout the Northwest. Acquired in 1979, the Gilroy, California, *Dispatch* and the Anchorage, Alaska, *Daily News* served their markets daily, while the *Morgan Hill Times* and *Clovis Independent,* both of California, appeared weekly. Two more California weeklies, the *Lincoln News Messenger* and the *Hollister Freelance,* were added in 1980 and 1981. After a five-year hiatus, McClatchy acquired the *Tacoma News Tribune,* a Washington daily, in 1986. With newsprint prices rising to record levels throughout the late 1980s, McClatchy also entered a venture with three other publishers to create a paper mill in Spokane, Washington, in 1987.

MCCLATCHY GOES PUBLIC IN 1988

Questions of succession—most significantly the lack of a successor within the McClatchy clan—presaged the 1987 decision to take the company public. C. K. reflected, in a 1988 *Advertising Age* article, that "I was worried about what could happen 15 to 20 years from now when you can't anticipate what might develop. If a few members of the family wanted to sell their stock ... they would not be in a position to break up the company." The seven heirs to the McClatchy fortune agreed to sell 10 percent of the media firm to the public, retaining a 90 percent stake in the form of preferred shares that enjoyed a 99 percent voting majority. C. K. himself retained a 53 percent voting interest.

Their plan for the initial public offering (IPO) proved ill timed, however. The family members had hoped to launch their stock in the fall of 1987, but the stock market crash that October shrank the share price from a hoped-for $20 to $23 down to less than $18 by the time of the IPO in February 1988. The offering raised $32.8 million, which was used to retire debt from previous acquisitions. Once noted for its secrecy—especially during Eleanor McClatchy's reign—the newspaper group threw open its books to reveal a recent history of dramatic growth in sales and net income. Under C. K.'s guidance, McClatchy's revenues had increased from $192 million in 1983 to $283.8 million in 1986, while net income multiplied from $6.9 million to over $45 million.

The period immediately following the IPO was not nearly as successful, however, as rising newsprint costs

KEY DATES

1857: James McClatchy establishes the *Sacramento Bee.*
1930: Company is incorporated.
1936: Leadership of the company passes to Eleanor McClatchy, the founder's granddaughter.
1953: Company acquires its first television broadcasting license.
1988: McClatchy goes public.
1997: Company acquires competitor Cowles Media.
2006: Company acquires Knight-Ridder, Inc.

ate into profits. While revenues increased by 46.7 percent, from $229.9 million in 1986 to $337.4 million in 1991, net income slid 47.5 percent, from $45.1 million to $23.7 million.

The company entered an important growth market with its 1988 acquisition of Senior Spectrum, publisher of ten tabloids distributed throughout California. Founded in 1973 in Sacramento, Senior Spectrum was by the end of 1991 America's largest chain of senior newspapers with editions in Las Vegas, Denver, Seattle, and Portland, Oregon, as well as California. McClatchy added to this high-potential area with the 1991 acquisition of three editions of *Senior World* published in Washington state.

C. K. McClatchy's concerns regarding his successor came to bear much sooner than anyone expected when he died in 1989 while jogging. His shares were distributed among relatives and top executives, thereby maintaining voting control in the family. (Shares sold to nonfamily members are automatically converted to Class A status.) He was succeeded as president and CEO by Erwin Potts, who had joined the company in 1975 as director of newspaper operations.

MAJOR ACQUISITIONS

In January 1990, McClatchy acquired six South Carolina newspapers (three dailies and three weeklies) for $74.1 million from the News & Observer Publishing Company, a Raleigh, North Carolina, media group. Five years later, McClatchy purchased the remainder of the group for $373 million in cash, stock, and assumed debt. The purchase included the daily *News & Observer,* six weeklies, the Nando.net online service, *Business North Carolina* magazine, and a commercial printer.

With an estimated two million hits per week, the one-year-old Nando.net was considered "one of the most successful online newspaper services in the industry." Its name was derived from the *News & Observer,* also known as the "N & O." By its third birthday in 1997, it was the third most widely read newspaper site on the World Wide Web, behind *USA Today* and the *Washington Post.* However, like many ostensibly successful Internet ventures, it continued to lose millions of dollars per year through 1997.

Potts guided a gradual succession program in the mid-1990s, advancing to chairman in 1995. Former *Fresno Bee* publisher Gary Pruitt became president of McClatchy at that time and succeeded Potts as CEO the following year. The year 1995 also saw the acquisition of the *Peninsula Gateway,* another Washington state weekly. McClatchy divested five other West Coast weeklies in the fall of 1996.

Then, in 1997, the company stunned the newspaper industry with the acquisition of Cowles Media and its flagship *Minneapolis Star Tribune,* Minnesota's largest daily. The $1.4 billion purchase vaulted McClatchy onto the industry's top-ten circulation list and brought to a close the story of one of America's last remaining independent newspaper publishers. Known among its readers and peers as the "*Strib,*" the Minneapolis paper was one of the nation's top dailies. Its circulation even topped that of the *Sacramento Bee,* and boosted McClatchy's total daily unit volume to about 1.4 million. The acquiring company planned to recoup some of its acquisition costs through the divestment of Cowles' magazine publishing interests. In fact, by the time the acquisition was finalized in March 1998, McClatchy had made arrangements to sell two subsidiaries to Primedia, Inc., thereby recovering $200 million of the purchase price.

Some analysts thought the deal was too pricey, and in fact the executives acknowledged that the merger might suppress earnings in the short term. Furthermore, McClatchy agreed to carry on the Cowles family's philanthropic endeavors at a cost of $3 million per year, and shouldered more than $1.3 billion in debt to finance the purchase. Investors registered their disapproval of the deal by sending McClatchy's stock down 14 percent on the day after the agreement was made public. In spite of the stock market reaction, CEO Gary Pruitt commended the purchase as "a rare opportunity for McClatchy to obtain a quality newspaper while adding geographic diversity in a premiere growth market." Moreover, Jon Fine of the online magazine *MediaCentral* asserted that "McClatchy acquisition history, going back to the '70s, has gone like this: They pay a high multiple, observers shake their heads and gasp in disbelief—and then McClatchy makes it work better than anyone had reckoned."

In fact, McClatchy's net income had risen substantially throughout this period of pricey acquisitions, increasing from less than $24 million in 1991 to a record $46.6 million by 1994 on sales of $368.1 million. Net declined to $33.6 million in 1995, and then rebounded to establish a new benchmark of $68.8 million on sales of $641.9 million in 1997.

CONTINUED EXPANSION

In 1999, company revenue passed the $1 billion mark for the first time in McClatchy's history. McClatchy was well positioned, with a firm foothold in California, the Northwest, the Southeast, and finally the Midwest, and the company weathered the economic downturn at the end of the 20th century with more ease than some of its competitors. The newspaper industry was in a slump in 2001, as a confluence of events (the end of the technology boom, the terrorist attacks of September 11, 2001, in New York and Washington) brought a halt to the widespread effervescence that had characterized the late 1990s. McClatchy sought to control costs and to make no nonessential hires, but the company was firm in not laying off news staff and in not cutting news coverage. CEO Pruitt believed that consistent management would see the company through both good times and bad, and that it was especially foolish to cut back news coverage at a time when consumers had more reasons than ever to find their news outside of newspapers.

In fact there was little change in the company's strategy between the 1990s and the early years of the 21st century. McClatchy continued to grow through acquisitions, making two notable purchases in the first decade. In December 2003, McClatchy announced that it had paid $40.5 million for the Merced (California) *Sun-Star* and a group of five affiliated nondaily newspapers. The deal was completed in early 2004. The newspaper group McClatchy bought had revenue of $12.6 million, and the papers were located in the rapidly growing Merced and Merced County area. The area was expected to gain population at a rate well above the national average, and new retailers had just started to arrive. With McClatchy's long ties to California newspapers, the Merced group seemed a good fit with the chain's other properties.

The biggest acquisition to date was McClatchy's purchase of Knight-Ridder, Inc., the nation's second largest newspaper chain, in 2006. Knight-Ridder, based in San Jose, California, owned the *Miami Herald*, the *Philadelphia Inquirer*, and the *Kansas City Star*, among other top papers, with a total combined newspaper circulation of 3.36 million copies. It was second only to Gannett Co. in the U.S. market, but it was beginning to struggle financially. Its big-city newspapers were not doing as well as they had, and as its stock price fell, the company's leading shareholders pressed the board to sell. McClatchy stepped up, and in 2006 finalized a deal worth about $4.1 billion. When the sale was completed, McClatchy found itself in the number-two position in the industry, as measured by circulation. McClatchy then quickly sold off a number of its new properties. It divested 12 Knight-Ridder papers that were in markets McClatchy perceived as not high growth.

Then in December 2006, McClatchy sold the *Minneapolis Star Tribune* for $530 million. The company had paid more than twice that for the Minnesota paper just seven years earlier. Although the *Star Tribune* was said to be profitable, McClatchy saw it as a drag on the chain's overall profit margin, and the paper was not performing as well as McClatchy's units in other parts of the country. The sale brought a significant tax advantage to McClatchy, but the low price tag and the suddenness of the sale shocked many in the industry. The year 2007 saw more trouble for the company. Advertising revenue fell off sharply as reversals in the housing market affected the number of real estate classifieds McClatchy papers ran. The housing downturn was particularly sharp in California, where McClatchy had many papers, and in Florida, home of McClatchy's *Miami Herald*. Once again, CEO Pruitt urged sound management and cost discipline, to see the newspaper chain through shifting economic conditions.

April D. Gasbarre
Updated, A. Woodward

PRINCIPAL SUBSIDIARIES

Miami Herald Media Co.; Beacon Journal Publishing Co.; News & Observer Publishing Co.; CareerBuilder, Inc.; Classified Ventures LLC; ShopLocal LLC; McClatchy Interactive.

PRINCIPAL COMPETITORS

Tribune Company; Gannett Company.

FURTHER READING

Beauchamp, Marc, "All in the Family," *Forbes*, May 2, 1988, pp. 37–38.

Bowen, Ezra, "From the Boneyard to No. 1," *Time*, August 4, 1986, p. 68.

Correa, Tracy, "McClatchy Company Buys California Newspapers from Pacific-Sierra Publishing," *Fresno Bee*, December 5, 2003.

Cuneo, Alice Z., "Maverick McClatchy Plays by Own Rules," *Advertising Age*, November 7, 1988, p. S10.

DiStefano, Joseph N., "Shareholders Approve Sale of Knight-Ridder," *Philadelphia Inquirer,* June 27, 2006.

"Eleanor McClatchy, 85, CEO for 42 Years, Dies," *Editor & Publisher,* October 25, 1980, p. 12.

Endicott, William, "McClatchy Buys Media Company for $1.4 Billion," *Fresno Bee,* November 14, 1997.

Fine, Jon, "The Cowles Media Sale: A Closer Look," http://www.mediacentral.com/Magazines/MediaCentral/Columns/Fine/19971118.htm.

Fitzgerald, Mark, "McClatchy Lands Big One," *Editor & Publisher,* May 27, 1995, pp. 14–15.

Fitzgerald, Mark, and Robert Neuwirth, "Twin City Slickers," *Editor & Publisher,* November 22, 1997, pp. 8–10.

Fost, Dan, "Senior Newspapers Gain Readers and Credibility," *American Demographics,* December 1991, p. 18.

Galarza, Pablo, "The Newspaper Is the Message," *Financial World,* November 7, 1995, pp. 38–39.

Gremillion, Jeff, "'Star Tribune' to McClatchy," *Mediaweek,* November 17, 1997, p. 8.

Hallinan, Joseph T., "Knight-Ridder's Top Investor Presses Publisher to Find Buyer," *Wall Street Journal,* November 2, 2005, p. C5.

Karnitschnig, Matthew, "MediaNews, Hearst to Purchase Four Newspapers from McClatchy," *Wall Street Journal,* April 27, 2006, p. A2.

"Knight-Ridder, Inc.: Investors Clear McClatchy Sale, Heralding End of the Publisher," *Wall Street Journal,* June 27, 2006, p. B14.

Langdell, Ted, "McClatchy Sells Off Its Cable Systems in Electronic Purge," *Business Journal-Sacramento,* December 1, 1986, p. 2.

Larson, Mark, "McClatchy Exec Draws Blast over Salary Raises," *Business Journal Serving Greater Sacramento,* May 27, 1991, p. 2.

———, "Record McClatchy Earnings Also Reward Top Brass," *Business Journal Serving Greater Sacramento,* April 9, 1990, p. 11.

"McClatchy August Ad Revenues Plunge 9.2%," *Editor & Publisher,* September 19, 2007.

"Primedia Pays $200M for Cowles Units," *Mediaweek,* January 12, 1998, p. 4.

Pruitt, Gary, "Newspaper Economics 2001: The McClatchy Way," *Nieman Reports,* Fall 2001, pp. 74–76.

Seelye, Katharine Q., "Equity Firm Buys Paper in Minnesota," *New York Times,* December 27, 2006, p. C1.

———, "White Knight Turns Pragmatist, and Newspapers Tremble Again," *New York Times,* February 12, 2007, p. C1.

Seelye, Katharine Q., and Andrew Ross Sorkin, "Newspaper Chain Agrees to a Sale for $4.5 Billion," *New York Times,* March 13, 2006, p. A1.

Serwer, Andrew E., "How Much Would You Pay for the Morning Newspaper?" *Fortune,* August 7, 1995, p. 32.

Strow, David, "Nando: A Hit on the Net," *Sacramento Business Journal,* August 1, 1997, p. 11.

McNaughton Apparel Group, Inc.

———■———

498 7th Avenue, 9th Floor
New York, New York 10018
U.S.A.
Telephone: (215) 785-4000
Toll Free: (800) 214-0552
Web site: http://www.jny.com

Wholly Owned Subsidiary of Jones Apparel Group, Inc.
Incorporated: 1993 as Norton McNaughton, Inc.
Employees: 525
Sales: $500 million (2006 est.)
NAIC: 315234 Women's and Girls' Cut and Sew Suit, Coat, Tailored Jacket, and Skirt Manufacturing; 315232 Women's and Girls' Cut and Sew Blouse and Shirt Manufacturing; 315999 Other Apparel Accessories and Other Apparel Manufacturing; 551112 Offices of Other Holding Companies

■ ■ ■

McNaughton Apparel Group, Inc., produces moderately priced women's apparel. It has traditionally been heavily dependent on the department store sales channel. In addition to the Norton McNaughton brand, whose products generally retail for $28 to $121, the firm also has a few other labels. McNaughton began a comprehensive restructuring in 1997, when it was an independent, publicly traded company. Following the prevailing industry trend, virtually all production was moved offshore to avoid significant capital expenditures and the fixed cost of managing a large workforce.

A unit of the giant Jones Apparel Group since 2001, McNaughton and its moderately priced sister labels suffered the economic downtown that afflicted the retail sector after the terrorist attacks against the United States on September 11, 2001. Relentless competition from better-known brands did not help. Peter Boneparth, the man who had led the restructuring at McNaughton, became CEO of Jones Apparel Group but resigned after a few years. By this time, the mood at Jones was one of scaling back: closing warehouses and making plans to sell off McNaughton's Erika label and other assets in the moderately priced segment.

THE EARLY YEARS: 1981–93

Sanford Greenberg, who later served as Norton's president and chairman, worked for Squire Fashions, Inc., a New York apparel firm, from 1960 to 1981. Then he joined forces with Jay Greenberg and Norton Sperling to buy out Squire; the company was renamed Norton McNaughton of Squire, Inc. The Norton McNaughton product line (Norton McNaughton, Norton McNaughton Petite, Maggie McNaughton, and Maggie McNaughton Petite) was introduced in 1981; it was marketed in miss, petite, and large sizes to department stores and national chains.

In July 1991 officers of the company formed NM Acquisition Corporation to acquire Norton McNaughton of Squire, Inc., in a leveraged buyout that led to the formation of Norton McNaughton, Inc., a holding company incorporated in January 1993. The company's net sales increased from $82.29 million in fiscal 1991 to $133.33 million in fiscal 1993, for a compound annual

COMPANY PERSPECTIVES

McNaughton designs, markets and contracts for the manufacture of a broad line of brand name, moderately-priced women's and juniors' career and casual clothing.

growth of 27.3 percent. During this period net income increased from $1.6 million to $3.33 million, for a compound annual growth rate of 44 percent.

The company's profitability in fiscal 1992 and 1993 was affected by the start-up and subsequent discontinuation of a dress division. Norton entered the dress market in early 1992 but soon realized that there were insufficient synergies in operating the dress and separates businesses. Norton discontinued the dress division's operations during the second quarter of fiscal 1993 and introduced two new products, the Pant-her and Modiano product lines. The Pant-her line, designed for women ranging in age from 40 to 70, featured traditional related separates in miss, petite, and large sizes. Norton McNaughton of Squire, Inc., now a Norton subsidiary, contracted to sell Pant-her products exclusively to May Company stores. Norton and May Company agreed to terminate their agreement effective March 1, 1998, but, at that time, May Company continued to buy Norton's other product lines.

In fiscal 1993 Norton's reproductions of popular designer fashions were produced by domestic and foreign contractors, thereby allowing the company to avoid significant capital expenditures and the fixed cost of managing a large production workforce. A substantial majority of Norton's products were made in the United States. Domestic contracts for manufacturing minimized excess inventory by giving the company maximum flexibility: Norton could defer production until initial orders were received and then make a closer adjustment to buying trends. In fiscal 1993 the company engaged the services of approximately 30 sewing and knitting contractors in the United States and two overseas master contractors in the Dominican Republic and the Far East. Norton did not have any long-term supply agreements with any of its sewing or knitting contractors. The company, however, did have long-term agreements for the exclusive services of its domestic cutting contractor, Roni-Linda Productions, Inc., and its domestic distribution contractor, Railroad Enterprises, Inc., for initial terms ending June 30, 2000 (distribution), and June 30, 2001 (cutting), respectively.

PUBLIC OFFERING IN 1994

Norton went public in 1994, trading on NASDAQ under the symbol NRTY. In January 1994 the company broadened its Modiano product to a full line of related separates targeted to national and regional retail chains. The Modiano line had silhouettes similar to those of the Norton McNaughton line but sold at slightly lower prices in such retail chains as Sears, Roebuck and Co. The company also established its own retail outlets, called Norty's, in which it sold end-of-stock, out-of-season, and other miscellaneous merchandise. Norton used these retail outlets to minimize sales to off-price retailers and as a means of liquidating excess inventory.

During 1995 and 1996 Norton presented four other product lines. The Lauren Alexandra line (June 1995), sold exclusively to Federated Department Stores, offered moderately priced career sportswear collections in miss and large sizes for women ranging in age from 25 to 60. The denim-driven casual Danielle Paige line and D.P.S. product lines (August 1996) consisted of moderately priced weekend wear: jumpers, sport dresses, pants, shirts, skirts, shorts, jackets, and leggings. These lines were sold to department stores, chains, and mass merchants. The Norton Studio product line (January 1996), also sold in department stores, consisted of women's career and casual knitwear collections and, as of spring 1997, included a large-size product division.

As always, Norton's design philosophy was to reproduce popular designer fashions at moderate prices. The company's design team was responsible for the creation, development, and coordination of product lines that interpreted and mirrored existing fashion trends in women's better apparel. The team also sought to enhance consumer appeal by combining functional fabrics in creative looks and color schemes to encourage the coordination of outfits—and the purchase of more than one garment. Rather than buying all of its printed fabrics, Norton's design staff started with "artwork" purchased from more than 25 art studios worldwide. Then, working with the art departments at mills and fabric suppliers, the company redesigned the artwork by altering colors, backgrounds, graphics, and shapes to have the printed fabrics appeal to the fashion tastes of its target retail consumers.

During fiscal 1995 and 1996, approximately 71 and 57 percent, respectively, of Norton's products were manufactured in the United States, mostly in the New York City metropolitan area. In fiscal 1996 the company engaged the services of nearly 60 sewing and knitting contractors in the United States and nine overseas master contractors in the Dominican Republic, Central America, the Far East, the Middle East, and Europe.

KEY DATES

1993: Norton McNaughton undergoes management buyout; Norton McNaughton, Inc., holding company formed.

1994: Initial public offering on NASDAQ.

1997: Investment banker Peter Boneparth hired to lead response to increasingly competitive market; Miss Erika casual apparel firm acquired.

1998: Company enters juniors market with acquisition of Jeri-Jo Knitwear, Inc.

1981: Sanford Greenberg leads buyout of Squire Fashions; firm renamed Norton McNaughton of Squire, Inc.

1999: Norton McNaughton renamed McNaughton Apparel Group.

2000: Distribution center established near Charleston, South Carolina.

2001: McNaughton acquired by Jones Apparel Group.

2007: After years of diminishing sales in its moderately priced segment, Jones closes distribution centers, announces plans to sell McNaughton's Erika label.

In fiscal 1995 net sales of $227.53 million reflected an increase of 34.9 percent from the net sales of $168.62 million in fiscal 1994. Norton's growth strategy, however, brought trouble. Foreign sourcing of products, as compared with domestic production, required a significant lead time ranging from four to eight months in the case of Dominican Republic and Central American sourced manufacturing and six to ten months in the case of Far Eastern, Middle Eastern, and European sourced manufacturing. Belated design changes forced postponements; shipments from abroad arrived late; competition increased for moderately priced women's apparel; and products entering the market too late in the fashion cycle were left on the shelves.

During fiscal 1996 approximately 43 percent of Norton's products were manufactured outside the United States. According to Yolanda Gault's story in the October 21, 1996, issue of *Crain's New York Business,* at this time there was an "industrywide malaise in moderate wear. Norton expanded too quickly in a weak market, introducing six divisions in under three years ... Norton—known for its nimble entrepreneurial culture—lost its fashion sense. Consumers stayed away,

leading to scads of markdowns, stinging losses and Wall Street's wrath." Compared with the net sales of fiscal 1995, net sales for fiscal 1996 decreased by $6.7 million, or 2.9 percent, to $220.82 million. Over and above the aforementioned problems, this drop also was attributable to a planned decrease in sales volume as Norton began to minimize the production of merchandise that it did not anticipate could be sold at a profit and, in response to competitive pressures from other moderately priced apparel wholesalers, granted customers a higher level of sales allowances.

ADJUSTMENT TO A CHANGING MARKET: 1997

In an effort to improve the profitability and position the company for future growth, in fiscal 1997 Norton implemented several strategic initiatives. These strategies included narrowing management's focus to the company's key divisions, Norton McNaughton and Norton Studio; making changes in pricing and product assortment; improving product sourcing; and significantly reducing overhead. Furthermore, to diversify its distribution channels, broaden its product offerings, increase its global product sourcing capability, and gain access to additional merchandising and managerial talent, the company adopted a special strategy for relevant acquisitions.

By early and timely attention to production planning, Norton aimed to offset the long lead time necessary for foreign sourced fabrics and manufacturing. For instance, the woven components of the Norton McNaughton and D.P.S. product lines were sourced primarily through import programs in China; a lead time of two to four months was needed to develop the required fabric. The time elapsed from the factory's fabric purchase commitment to the finished goods was generally an additional four to six months, thereby creating a total cycle time of six to ten months in the case of Far Eastern, Middle Eastern, African, and European sourced manufacturing. Norton also sourced a large portion of its woven products in countries of the Caribbean basin or in Mexico, making the most of favorable "807" customs regulations. In general, these regulations exempted from U.S. duties the products assembled abroad from U.S. components.

On May 6, 1997, Norton appointed Peter Boneparth, an investment banker whose previous firm had taken Norton public in 1994, as president and chief operating officer and director to succeed Norton Sterling, one of the company's cofounders. In a telephone interview reported by Anne D'Innocenzio in the May 7, 1997, issue of *Women's Wear Daily,* Boneparth noted that he would use his expertise in acquisitions "to play a hand in expanding Norton Mc-Naughton's sales." Future acquisitions, he predicted, would catapult sales, which had been hovering at around $220 million, to $500 million within three to five years. "We have $50 million in shareholders' equity. The whole industry is consolidating. We want to be the consolidator," he said.

Boneparth began his tenure by following through on many of the moves the company had begun making to get back on track. During the second quarter of fiscal 1997, Norton closed its 12 retail outlets because this division did not meet the company's profitability targets. A new merchandising strategy began to reduce excess inventory; excess merchandise could more cost-effectively be disposed of through discounters and other retailers. During the third quarter, Norton sold merchandise under its existing product lines to Sears and discontinued the Modiano product line, which had been produced for that company. A new pricing strategy, to be effective in August, was planned for the company's private-label line, which was "priced 15 percent above the traditional labels and 25 percent below such upper-moderates as Halston and Emma James," D'Innocenzio wrote in the May 14, 1997, issue of *Women's Wear Daily*. For instance, jackets were to retail from $68 to $72, compared with $80 to $90 in 1996.

On September 30, 1997, Norton acquired New York–based Miss Erika, Inc., a privately held firm established in 1968. Miss Erika manufactured moderately priced knit and woven separates, including knit tops and bottoms, sweaters, dresses and jackets, and more casual apparel, such as shorts, skirts, tank tops, and jumpers. The target customers were middle-income, budgeted-minded but fashionable women ranging in age from 15 to 50 years old. Miss Erika's merchandise was sold primarily under the Erika label and was distributed through regional chains, department stores, and specialty chains. Miss Erika contracted for the production of its garments through a network of purchasing agents located overseas. In addition to products sold under its brand names, Miss Erika worked with retail chains to develop product lines sold under the retailers' private labels.

Upon completion of the Erika acquisition, Norton President Boneparth commented, "This transaction highlights our strategy of acquiring companies that are accretive to earnings, have strong management teams in place, and broaden our existing channels of distribution," D'Innocenzio reported in "Norton McNaughton's New Mode" in the May 14, 1997, issue of *Women's Wear Daily*. This acquisition reduced sales seasonality, since Miss Erika's revenues were weighted toward the

first half of the year and Norton's sales were typically higher in the second half of the year. Norton also implemented other new distribution channels (for example, QVC and Sam's Warehouse Club) and began to sell to catalog firms, such as Chadwick's.

In addition, in the fourth quarter, Norton discontinued the Lauren Alexandra private-label line produced for Federated Department Stores and the Pant-her private-label product line sold to the May Department Stores Company. To further streamline operations, Norton reduced its workforce by close to 33 percent. Other cost-savings measures that were implemented included merchandising changes that enabled the company to produce fewer samples and reductions in executive compensation and ancillary expenses.

By October 30, the end of fiscal 1997, Norton's implementation of new strategies, discontinuation of unprofitable products and divisions, and acquisition of well-established, profitable Miss Erika boded well for the future but did not immediately show a profit. Net sales for the year decreased by 1 percent to $218.78 million, compared with net sales of $220.82 million in fiscal 1996. These decreases were offset in part by savings resulting from a significant downsizing of the company's work force through further centralization, by an increase in net sales of $10.2 million in the Norton Studio product line, an increase in net sales of $2.8 million in the D.P.S. product line and, following the September acquisition of Miss Erika, net sales of $10.4 million for Erika products.

TOWARD THE 21ST CENTURY: 1998 AND BEYOND

A more disciplined mode of operation in the fiercely competitive women's apparel business was reenergizing Norton's niche in its industry. President and Chief Operating Officer Peter Boneparth commented, "results for the first quarter of fiscal 1998 were in line with management's expectations. The company posted a 28.6 percent increase in net sales and a 26.7 percent increase in operating income over the same period" in 1997. Two significant acquisitions were completed during the third quarter of fiscal 1998: Jeri-Jo Knitwear, Inc., and Jamie Scott, Inc. Founded in 1975, New York–based Jeri-Jo/Jamie Scott designed, imported and marketed juniors' and misses' apparel. The companies retained their current management and operated together as Jeri-Jo Knitwear, Inc., a Norton subsidiary.

For the first nine months of fiscal 1998, Norton's net sales increased 59.5 percent to $227.59 million, compared with $142.7 million for the same period of the previous year. It is noteworthy that sales for the first nine months of fiscal 1998 were considerably higher than the $218.78 million net sales for all of fiscal 1997. When Peter Boneparth became Norton's president in 1997 he commented that within the next three to five years the company could reach annual sales of $500 million. As the 21st century drew near, it seemed that his expectations were within the realm of possibility.

NEW NAME IN 1999

The company was renamed McNaughton Apparel Group, Inc., in 1999, reflecting its status as an owner of multiple labels. McNaughton aimed to emerge on top of the wave of consolidation that was sweeping the industry; Boneparth was soon saying it could one day be a $1 billion business.

The renamed, restructured group operated in a markedly different manner than in its previous incarnations. Over three years, the workforce was reduced by more than half to 140 employees. Virtually all of its production had been moved offshore. The company did establish a distribution facility in the United States in 2000, feeling it could handle these previously subcontracted operations more efficiently in-house. The 300,000-square-foot warehouse, located near Charleston, South Carolina, was shuttered several years later, however.

Revenues were about $400 million in 1999. Mc-Naughton's stock price doubled as Boneparth's cost-cutting measures raised the company's bottom line, but was halved again before the end of the calendar year. A potential cause for concern was $125 million in debt added in its recent buying spree. McNaughton revenues reached $506.1 million in the 2000 fiscal year, up 24 percent. Profit of $27 million was more than three times the previous year's figure.

While some of McNaughton's major department store clients were struggling, it expected to benefit from an anticipated expansion at Kohl's. McNaughton then had little involvement with the world of budget retailers such as Wal-Mart and Target, although it was making progress into warehouse stores. It also planned to expand its range of product offerings by adding accessories.

ACQUIRED BY JONES IN 2001

Jones Apparel Group, Inc., of Bristol, Pennsylvania, acquired McNaughton in June 2001. The cash and stock deal was worth $275 million, plus $272 million in assumed debt. With annual sales of $4 billion, Jones was one of the giants of the industry, boasting such high-end labels as Nine West (women's shoes), Jones New York (classic women's clothing) and Anne Klein (women's designer clothing). It also produced several other upscale brands under license and then owned high-end retailer Barneys New York. Heavily invested in luxury lines, Jones valued McNaughton as a way to boost its sales of moderately priced garments at department stores such as Sears and Kohl's.

The retail environment in the United States became much more difficult after the September 11, 2001, terrorist attacks. The department stores upon which Mc-Naughton relied turned to steep discounts to keep goods moving. Over the next few years, sales slipped in the face of fierce competition from better-known brands such as those in the Liz Claiborne stable. Parent company Jones Apparel Group ultimately reported a $441 million goodwill impairment charge for 2006, much of it attributed to the McNaughton acquisition, which indicated it had not gotten its money's worth out of the purchase.

McNaughton CEO Peter Boneparth had become head of parent company Jones in 2002. He had the previous year succeeded Sanford Greenberg as chairman of McNaughton Apparel Group. However, he resigned from Jones Apparel Group in July 2007, a move that took many by surprise, as he had just led the company's hugely profitable sell-off of its Barneys New York unit.

A few months later, Jones announced it was closing the McNaughton distribution center near Charleston, South Carolina, plus a second warehouse it had built nearby. (Both were leased.) Losing money, Jones was planning to sell or close some of its moderately priced clothing lines, including McNaughton's Erika label.

Gloria A. Lemieux
Updated, Frederick C. Ingram

PRINCIPAL COMPETITORS

Kellwood Company; Liz Claiborne, Inc.

FURTHER READING

Anderson, Katie, "Jones Buys McNaughton for $572M," *New York Daily Deal,* April 16, 2001.

"CEO/Company Interview: Peter Boneparth; McNaughton Apparel Group, Inc.," *Wall Street Transcript,* March 20, 2000.

Curan, Catherine, "Clothier Measures Up; CEO Mending Mc-Naughton's Bottom Line," *Crain's New York Business,* September 25, 2000, p. 3.

D'Innocenzio, Anne, "Boneparth Appointed McNaughton President," *Women's Wear Daily,* May 7, 1997, pp. 1, 18.

———, "Norton McNaughton's New Mode," *Women's Wear Daily,* May 14, 1997.

Dodes, Rachel, and Joann S. Lublin, "Jones Apparel, Struggling to Adapt, Gets New CEO," *Wall Street Journal,* July 13, 2007, p. A2.

Fung, Shirley, "McNaughton's Cautious Comeback," *WWD,* October 25, 2000, p. 8.

Gault, Ylonda, "A Familiar Thread at Finity: McNaughton Vet Shelves Retirement to Foster Neglected Sportswear Firm," *Crain's New York Business,* April 27, 1998, Profiles Sec.

————, "Fashioning a Comeback: New Executive Peter Boneparth," *Crain's New York Business,* June 2, 1997, Profiles Sec.

————, "No Casual Fling at Norton: New Executive San Sommers," *Crain's New York Business,* October 21, 1996, Profiles Sec.

"Jones Apparel Cuts 300 Jobs by Closing SC Distribution Centers," *Associated Press Newswires,* October 19, 2007.

"Jones Apparel Swings to Loss on Charges," *Dow Jones Business News,* February 14, 2007.

McDermott, John P., "Buyout of Clothing Maker to Have No Effect on Charleston, S.C. Area Center," *Charleston Post and Courier,* April 17, 2001.

Parets, Robyn Taylor, "McNaughton Apparel Group: Holiday Slump Behind It, Designer Presses On," *Investor's Business Daily,* January 3, 2001, p. A8.

Young, Vicki M., and Scott Malone, "Jones Seeks an Edge in Moderate Market," *WWD,* April 17, 2001, p. 2.

Meidensha Corporation

—■—

36-2 Nihonbashi-Hakozakicho
Chuo-ku
Tokyo, 103-8515
Japan
Telephone: (81 03) 5641 7000
Fax: (81 03) 5641 7099
Web site: http://www.meidensha.co.jp

Public Company
Incorporated: 1897
Employees: 6,561
Sales: ¥183.75 billion ($1.64 billion) (2006)
Stock Exchanges: Tokyo
Ticker Symbol: 6508
NAIC: 335314 Relay and Industrial Control Manufacturing; 333613 Mechanical Power Transmission Equipment Manufacturing; 333999 All Other General Purpose Machinery Manufacturing; 335999 All Other Miscellaneous Electrical Equipment and Component Manufacturing

■ ■ ■

Meidensha Corporation is a world-leading producer of heavy machinery and equipment. The Tokyo-based company, part of the massive Sumitomo group of companies, develops and manufactures a wide range of products ranging from electric motors, generators, and transformers to forklifts and other handling equipment, and from construction and maintenance equipment to turnkey wind-power generation plants. Meidensha's engineering and manufacturing operations are grouped into three main divisions.

Social Infrastructure Systems targets the power, railway, and private sector markets; Information and Communications Systems develops equipment, components, machinery, and production systems for a variety of industries, including the semiconductor industry, while also overseeing the company's development of motors and automated guidance systems for forklifts and other handling equipment; and, finally, Engineering Systems provides heavy electric machinery maintenance services, builds utility plants, including wind farms, develops generators, switching devices, power converters, transformers and lightning and surge arrester, and many others.

The company also develops a range of water treatment and waste disposal systems. Other Meidensha businesses include business process outsourcing, medical and related services, and accounting services, primarily for other companies in the group. Meidensha operates from five primary facilities in Japan and also operates manufacturing and marketing subsidiaries in Thailand, China, the United States, Singapore, Indonesia, Malaysia, South Korea, and England. The company is listed on the Tokyo Stock Exchange, and in 2006 its revenues neared ¥184 billion ($1.65 billion).

ELECTRIC MOTOR PRODUCER IN 1897

The 19th century witnessed the arrival of industrialization to Japan, which had closed itself to foreign influence for more than two centuries. With the rise to

COMPANY PERSPECTIVES

Ever since its founding in 1897, Meidensha Corporation has been working on the relentless pursuit of new technology and product developments and witnessed steady growth. Our product offerings cover a wide area, such as generators, substation equipment, electronic equipment and information equipment. Our mission is not only to provide these products but also to recommend the best solutions on the basis of what a customer values best. In order to realize these best solutions, we engage in the supply of various products and provide related services such as engineering, facility management (including operation and maintenance), repair and product-life support.

power of the Meiji emperor in 1868, Japan launched its first efforts at modernization and industrialization. The period leading up to the turn of the century was marked by the formation of most of the country's major conglomerates, called *zaibatsu*.

The rapid embrace of industrial production techniques, driven by electrical power, was in part fueled by a national desire to achieve industrial independence. At the same time, the new Japanese government that came to power following the Sino-Japanese War in 1895 opened new opportunities for the creation of privately held businesses. Thus many new companies appeared at the turn of the century, either founded under the auspices of the *zaibatsu* or later absorbed by them.

Among these was Meidensha, founded by Hosui Shigemune in Kyobashi, Tokyo, in 1897. Shigemune's company focused on the production of electric motors and became an important industrial link in the fast-rising Sumitomo group.

The Sumitomo conglomerate had been one of Japan's richest for nearly three centuries when it turned toward industrialization in the late 19th century. Founded by Masatomo Sumitomo as a small Chinese medicine and book shop in Kyoto in 1630, the group had instead built its fortunes first by developing its own copper smelting technology, and later as one of the world's largest copper mining concerns. Copper provided the raw material for Sumitomo's decision, starting from 1897, to branch out into industrial production. In that year the company acquired its first copper works in Osaka and also founded a company to produce copper wire and cables. These products were es-

sential to the country's creation of its electrical power and telecommunications infrastructure. At the same time, copper wire was an extremely important material for the production of electric motors.

Meidensha grew steadily in the years leading up to World War I and by 1912 had moved to a larger factory in the Osaki district of Tokyo; the following year, the company set up a research facility in Tokyo as well. Meidensha went public in 1917, listing its shares on the Tokyo exchange, with Shigemune taking the role of president and chairman. By then, the highly nationalist Japanese government had launched a new industrialization program in an effort to achieve full independence from foreign imports.

These policies, coupled with the massive buildup of the country's military infrastructure in the 1930s, provided Meidensha with significant growth opportunities. Through the 1930s, the company continued to expand its industrial capacity, adding a factory in Nagoya in 1935, followed by factories in Shinagawa and in Nishino, in 1937 and 1939, respectively. At the same time, the company had begun to branch out from its core electric motor production. In 1930, for example, the company became the first in Japan to launch production of synthetic quartz crystals.

POSTWAR TECHNICAL PARTNERSHIPS

Sumitomo and the other *zaibatsu* also expanded rapidly in the buildup to World War II. During the war, the policies of the military government enabled the zaibatsu to gain still more dominance over the country's economy. By cooperating with the government, the *zaibatsu* completed a series of takeovers of smaller industrial companies. As such, during the war, Sumitomo's empire spanned nearly 150 companies. However, the postwar period brought major changes to Japan's industries, most notably with the forced breakup of the country's *zaibatsu*. The breakup of Sumitomo into its separate components created Sumitomo Metal Industries, which became the ultimate parent of Meidensha Corporation.

Meidensha played its own role in Japan's spectacular rise to industrial prominence in the second half of the 20th century. Technical partnerships formed a major part of the company's growth, as it teamed up with a number of foreign companies in order to acquire and develop new technological prowess. Among the company's first such partnerships was a technical license agreement reached in 1955 with Germany's AEG, for the production of transformers and other electrical power equipment. Similarly, in 1961, the company teamed up with ASEA, of Sweden, to build

KEY DATES

1897: Hosui Shigemune founds Meiden in Tokyo in order to manufacture electric motors.

1917: Meidensha lists stock on Tokyo Stock Exchange.

1966: First foreign subsidiary, in Thailand, is established.

1975: Sales and later manufacturing base are set up in Singapore.

1994: A dedicated sales and support subsidiary in Europe, based in London, is launched.

2000: A new Information and Data Communications division is set up in order to reduce reliance on heavy machinery and power generation sector.

2006: Opens 25,000 kilowatt (kW) wind-power plant in Akita as part of expansion into power generation sector, with plans to boost capacity to 300,000 kW by 2010.

asynchronous machines. Two years later, the company reached an agreement with RCA, in the United States, to begin producing transistors. These agreements enabled Meidensha to expand its industrial base, with the construction of a new factory in Numazu in 1961.

Other partnerships formed during the 1960s and 1970 displayed the wide range of Meidensha's interests. In 1969, for example, the company formed a new agreement with AEG to produce rectifiers and other control and processing equipment. At the same time, the group had developed a relationship with the United Kingdom's Sevcon, which permitted Meidensha to build expertise in manufacturing electrical motors and systems for forklifts and other handling equipment. This segment later became a major part of the group's business. In 1970, the group signed the first of a series of agreements with U.S. giant General Electric (GE), in order to produce temperature control systems. The company also took over the maintenance and service contracts for GE's installed systems in Japan. By the end of the decade, GE and Meidensha had completed several other partnership agreements, including the creation of a joint venture, Gemvac Co., in 1974.

INTERNATIONAL EXPANSION INTO THE 1990S

These technical partnerships, coupled with Meidensha's own long-standing research and development efforts, al-

lowed the company to develop increasingly sophisticated technologies, products, and systems. The group's developing industrial and technological clout also allowed Meidensha to compete on an international level, establishing the Meiden brand as a major name in the heavy machinery and equipment sectors. The company's first foray into the overseas market came in 1966, when the group established a subsidiary in Bangkok called Thai Meidensha Co.

The company next turned to the Singapore market, establishing a subsidiary there in 1975. By 1979, the company had also built a manufacturing presence in Singapore, building a factory to produce distribution transformers for the local electrical power sector. In that year, also, the company extended its synthetic quartz production to Singapore as well, with the creation of a new dedicated subsidiary there. The company later added a second international quartz operation, in Malaysia, in 1989.

Meidensha had also been developing its industrial presence in Japan. The company built a new factory in Ohta, in 1977, in order to produce rotary machines. The new facility allowed the company to shut down its aging Nishino factory in 1981.

Through the 1990s, Meidensha continued to develop its international network. The company established Meiden Engineering Indonesia in 1991, in a partnership with two local companies. Meiden's share of the new venture, which was set up to provide consultancy services in order to develop Meiden's marketing reach in Indonesia, was 70 percent. Two years later, the company entered mainland China, establishing Meiden Pacific (China) Ltd. in order to manufacture heavy machinery and electrical equipment, including power transformers, high voltage switch systems, variable speed motor drives and others for the fast-growing power utility and construction sectors, both on the mainland and in Hong Kong. Meidensha had also been building a sales presence in Europe, setting up an office in London. This was followed by an office in Frankfurt in 1991, established specifically to market the company's power inverters and automotive testing dynamometers in Germany as well as in the newly opening Eastern European markets. In 1994, Meidensha moved to set up a dedicated European subsidiary, based in the United Kingdom. The company also developed its operation in the United States, culminating in the creation of a dedicated U.S. sales and support subsidiary, Meiden America Inc.

Nonetheless, Japan remained Meidensha's principal market. At the same time, the company's focus had largely remained on its core electric motor and heavy machinery operations through the end of the century.

However, the ongoing recession in Japan, coupled with an expected slump in heavy machinery spending by Japan's power generation sector in that country, prompted Meidensha to take steps to diversify its product offerings. As part of its diversification effort, the company established a new Information and Data Communications division in 2000, which began developing and marketing data processing systems to local governments, as well as for the health and welfare markets, such as hospitals, nursing homes and the like. Also in 2000, the company teamed up with Sumitomo to form a distribution agreement with U.S.-based Capstone for that company's microturbine technology in Japan.

ENVIRONMENTAL SECTOR FOCUS IN THE 21ST CENTURY

At the same time, Meidensha launched a restructuring of its manufacturing operations. The company shifted much of its heavy machinery production to its factories in Thailand and Singapore, as a cost-cutting measure against the projected slowdown in the domestic market. Meidensha also formed two joint ventures with fellow Japanese industrial giants Hitachi and Fuji. The first, Japan AE Power Systems Corporation, took over the partners' production of transmission and distribution equipment in 2000. This was followed by the creation of a second joint venture, called Japan Motor & Generator Co. Ltd., which combined the three companies' production of high-voltage motors and mid-sized generators in 2001. In 2002, the company spun off its hoist and crane manufacturing subsidiary into a joint venture with Finland's KCI Konecranes International. The agreement gave KCI a 49 percent stake in the joint venture, with an option to boost its position past 65 percent. In that year also the company established a new factory, in Kofu, which took over as the group's engineering headquarters the following year.

Increasingly, Meidensha had begun developing operations in the environmental sector. The company initially began to develop systems for the water and wastewater treatment sector, developing a variety of equipment and systems, such as water-quality control systems and advanced battery and power storage equipment. The company also began acting as a sales agent for an imported wind-powered generator. In 2003, however, Meidensha decided to enter the market directly and announced its intention to begin developing turnkey wind-power plants for the Japanese market. The company's first plant, a small 3,000 kilowatt (kW) facility in the region of Chiba, came online by the end of that year. By 2006, the company had opened a larger 25,000 kW plant in Akita Prefecture. The company then announced plans to build and operate its own wind-power plants, while expanding its total output capacity to 300,000 kW by 2010.

Meidensha continued to expand its overseas operations as well, targeting an increase in foreign sales from nearly 13 percent in 2006 to 20 percent by 2008. In 2006, the company opened a new $13 million transformer factory in Singapore. This was followed by the company's announcement that its U.S. subsidiary would spend $17 million in order to build a new contract testing and engineering services facility in Michigan in 2007. In that year, too, Meidensha targeted an expanded presence in the Middle East, setting up an sales office in Dubai. After 110 years, Meidensha Corporation remained one of Japan's industrial success stories.

M. L. Cohen

PRINCIPAL SUBSIDIARIES

Dongguan Meiden Electrical Engineering Co., Ltd. (China); Meiden America, Inc.; Meiden Asia Pte. Ltd. (Singapore); Meiden Electric (Thailand) Ltd.; Meiden Electric Engineering Sdn. Bhd. (Malaysia); Meiden Europe Ltd. (UK); Meiden Hangzhou Drive Systems Co., Ltd. (China); Meiden Korea Co., Ltd.; Meiden Pacific (China) Ltd.; Meiden Power Solutions (Singapore) Pte. Ltd.; Meiden Shanghai Co., Ltd. (China); Meiden Singapore Pte. Ltd.; Meiden Zhengzhou Electric Co., Ltd. (China); P.T. Meiden Engineering Indonesia; Shanghai Meiden Semiconductor Co., Ltd. (China); Thai Meidensha Co., Ltd.

PRINCIPAL DIVISIONS

Social Infrastructure Systems; Engineering Systems; Information and Communications Systems.

PRINCIPAL COMPETITORS

Fujitsu Ltd.; Mitsubishi Electric Corporation; ABB Ltd.; Johnson Controls Inc.; Emerson; Mondragon Corporacion Cooperativa; Finmeccanica S.p.A.; Texas Instruments Inc.; Eaton Corporation; Fuji Electric Holdings Company Ltd.; Oki Electric Industry Company Ltd.; Fanuc Ltd.; Yaskawa Electric Corporation; SMC Corporation; LS Industrial Systems Company Ltd.

FURTHER READING

"Japan's Meidensha Eyes 10-Fold Increase in Wind Power Generation," *AsiaPulse News,* August 1, 2005.

"Japan's Meidensha to Build Wind-Powered Plants, Sell Electricity," *AsiaPulse News,* March 19, 2003.

"Japan's Meidensha to Expand Sales in Asia, U.S.," *AsiaPulse News,* May 19, 2004.

"Japan's Meidensha to Open Middle East Sales Office," *AsiaPulse News,* May 10, 2007.

"Japan's JV Begins Production of Advanced Lightning Arrester," *AsiaPulse News,* May 12, 2006.

"Meiden and Applied Materials Announce New System Remanufacturing Center in China," *Business Wire,* December 3, 2003.

Metal Management, Inc.

500 North Dearborn Street, Suite 405
Chicago, Illinois 60610
U.S.A.
Telephone: (312) 645-0700
Fax: (312) 645-0714
Web site: http://www.mtlm.com

Public Company
Incorporated: 1981 as General Parametrics Corporation
Employees: 1,829
Sales: $2.2 billion (2007)
Stock Exchanges: New York
Ticker Symbol: MM
NAIC: 423930 Recyclable Material Merchant Wholesalers

■ ■ ■

One of the largest full-service metal recyclers in the United States, Chicago-based Metal Management, Inc., operates about 50 recycling facilities in 16 states. The company collects scraps of ferrous metal, iron and steel, and nonferrous metals, including aluminum, brass, copper, nickel-based materials, titanium, and high-temperature alloys. Metal Management then processes the scrap to produce usable nonferrous metals and ferrous metal products, such as shredded, sheared, cold briquetted, and bundled scrap metal, as well as turnings, cast, and broken furnace iron.

The company's supplies of metal come from junkyards, railroads, demolition firms, steel plants, and manufacturers. Customers include mini steel mills,

foundries, and metal brokers. Each year the company sells about five million tons of ferrous scrap and nearly 500 million pounds of nonferrous scrap. Shipping out of ports in New Jersey and Connecticut, Metal Management exports products around the world to such countries as China, Indonesia, Korea, Malaysia, Taiwan, Turkey, and Mexico. Metal Management is a public company listed on the New York Stock Exchange.

CORPORATE LINEAGE DATES TO 1981

Although Metal Management took shape in the 1990s, the corporation that would be used to house its metal recycling assets was established in Berkeley, California, in 1981 as General Parametrics Corporation by Herbert B. Baskin, a researcher at IBM who in the 1960s developed the first computer scanner able to recognize ordinary typewriting. In the mid-1970s he went to work for Texas minicomputer manufacturer Datapoint where he developed a color graphics system. After growing wealthy from Datapoint stock he retired at the age of 47.

Less than two years later, however, he felt the need to return to work. With $100,000 of his own money and another $500,000 supplied by friends and others he launched General Parametrics to develop an electronic method of showing graphics without the use of photography, which would be ideal for producing corporate slide show presentations. At the time, such shows cost as much as $4,000 to produce because they required the services of a graphic artist. Baskin developed a slide presentation software package, Pic-

COMPANY PERSPECTIVES

The rationale for creating Metal Management was to enhance the quality, integrity and scope of services available to industrial scrap generators and consumers by pooling and consolidating the resources of many of the nation's premier scrap companies.

tureIt, that could be run on an IBM-compatible personal computer.

The company also developed hardware called VideoShow that allowed a computer monitor, television, or video project to display the presentation. For a time, General Parametrics was a high-flying company, going public in 1986, but in time its star would be eclipsed by Microsoft's Power Point and other slide show programs. By 1996 Baskin was ready to sell the company and he found willing buyers who had no interest in computer graphics. Rather, they wanted to consolidate the scrap metal industry in much the same fashion as Chicago's Waste Management had done with great acclaim in solid-waste collection. Hence, they called their company Metal Management.

The men behind Metal Management were investment banker T. Benjamin Jennings, attorney Gerard Jacobs, and Donald F. Moorehead, the chief executive officer of Dallas-based USA Waste Services Inc., the third largest player in the waste management industry and a mutual client of Jennings and Jacobs. The men knew firsthand about consolidation in the waste-management field. It was through USA Waste that they became interested in metal recycling after the company acquired a trash-hauling operation that brought with it Emco Recycling Corporation, a full-service Phoenix yard that included five feeder yards and generated about $70 million in revenues.

EMCO was itself a local result of consolidation, formed in 1993 in answer to a couple of difficult years in the scrap business. In 1993 a pair of family-owned Phoenix-area scrap yards, Empire Metals Inc. and Copperstate Metals Inc. merged to create EMCO. Later in the year it added a third metal recycler, Valley Steel and Supply Co. Moorehead, Jennings, and Jacobs recognized that what EMCO was doing on a small scale could be done nationally in a manner similar to what had taken place in waste management. They scouted around for a public company to acquire EMCO, and whose stock they could then use as currency to buy more recyclers and create an industry consolidator.

GENERAL PARAMETRICS SOLD: 1995

In 1995 the Jennings, Jacobs and Moorehead–led investment group bought out Baskin and his 27 percent stake in General Parametrics and began to exert their influence on the company. They then took steps to redirect General Parametrics into metal recycling. In April 1996 a $12.8 million acquisition of EMCO was negotiated and approved by General Parametrics shareholders, which also agreed to change the company name to Metal Management Inc. In addition, Jennings was named chairman of the board and chief development officer, his primary task to line up further acquisitions, Jacobs became president and chief executive officer, and Moorehead gained a seat on the board of directors. Shareholders also agreed to double the amount of common shares of stock to prepare for further acquisitions, and approved moving the refashioned company's headquarters to Chicago, where Jennings and Jacobs lived. General Parametric's printer business continued to operate out of Berkeley until it was sold in July of that year. A month later the Jacobs-Jennings-Moorehead group won complete control of Metal Management in a proxy fight.

In the final months of 1996 Metal Management lined up acquisitions that were completed in January 1997. They included the five companies that comprised California-based The MacLeod Group: California Metals Inc., Firma Inc., MacLeod Metals Inc., Firma Plastics, and Trojan Trading Inc. Together they generated about $35 million in annual sales. Also in early 1997 Metal Management completed the acquisition of HouTex Metals Company, Inc., which added another $20 million in annual sales and established a base from which Metal Management hoped to consolidate the south-central United States.

A spate of acquisition agreements followed in the rest of 1997, with some of them closing in 1998. In May 1997 Reserve Iron & Metal L.P., a Cleveland-based ferrous metal-breaking operation, was acquired. The following month Metal Management added Maumee, Ohio–based The Isaac Group of companies, which included Ferrex Trading Corporation; the Isaac Corporation; Paulding Recycling, Inc.; and Briquetting Corporation of America, Inc. Isaac Group produced about $175 million a year in sales, mostly from the sale of ferrous briquettes to steel minimills and integrated mills located in Chicago, Cleveland, Detroit, and Pittsburgh.

Much of the raw material came from cast-iron borings from car engine blocks produced by the likes of General Motors at their foundry operation. Proler Southwest, Inc., and sister company Proler Steelworks L.L.C. were added in August 1997. The former was a

KEY DATES

1981: General Parametrics Corporation formed as computer graphics company.

1986: General Parametrics is taken public.

1996: Name is changed to Metal Management, Inc., and focus shifts to recycling.

2000: Company declares Chapter 11 bankruptcy.

2001: Company emerges from bankruptcy protection.

2004: Daniel W. Dienst is named CEO.

2006: Company gains listing on New York Stock Exchange.

Houston ferrous scrap recycler that served area steelmakers as well as Mexican mills, while the latter operated a small steel scrap processing facility in Jackson, Mississippi. The most significant deal of 1997, first announced in March 1997 but not completed until the end of the year, was the $111 million cash and stock acquisition of Chicago-based Cozzi Iron & Metal Inc., which processed about 1.5 million tons of ferrous scrap per year. The deal also led to a restructuring of Metal Management's senior leadership ranks. Albert Cozzi became president and chief operating officer while his brother Frank was named vice-president. They also became directors of the corporation.

Several other deals negotiated in 1997 closed in early 1998. They included Hartford, Connecticut–based Aerospace Metals Inc., which recycled titanium and high-temperature nickel and cobalt alloy scraps from aircraft engine, airframe, and helicopter plants; Houston Compressed Steel Corporation, a processor and dismantler with two yards in Houston; and the half-interest in Salt River Recycling L.L.C., a Phoenix shredder not already acquired through the Cozzi deal. Four more deals were completed in February and March: Accurate Iron and Metal of Kankakee, Illinois; Arizona-based Ellis Metals Inc. with operations in Tucson and Casa Grande; and Superior Forge, Inc., a California aluminum scrap operation.

When fiscal 1998 came to a close on March 31, Metal Management had generated sales of $570 million and posted a net loss of $41.3 million. Revenues would grow to $805.3 million in fiscal 1999 as the company continued its acquisition spree despite a steady decline in the company's stock price, which fell from $30 a share in the fall of 1997 to slightly more than $2 a share a year later. "Seeming to have a 'spare no expense'

outlook," according to *American Metal Market,* Metal Management's "principals agreed in 1998 to lay out $46.4 million in cash for the purchase of M. Kimerling & Sons Inc., Birmingham, Ala., and another $105 million in cash for three East Coast operations, Naporano Iron & Metal Co. and Nimco Shredding Co., Newark, N.J., and Michael Schiavone & Sons Inc., North Haven, Conn." Metal Management was not the only industry consolidator in trouble; Canada's Philip Services Corp. put itself up for sale, but Metal Management was so strapped by that time that it had to pass on buying the business, unable to take advantage of the situation. Instead, management maintained that it would focus on developing synergies between its existing units.

FOUNDERS LEAVE

Matters only worsened, however, as low-cost steel imported from Eastern Europe, Asia, and South America crippled demand for recycled metal, the prices of which were cut in half in 1998. By the start of 1999 a new executive management committee, headed by Albert Cozzi, took charge and soon Jacobs resigned as president and CEO. "To the chagrin of shareholders," reported *American Metal Market,* "the company sold him a property—Superior Forge Inc., Huntington Beach, Calif.—for less than MTLM had paid for it in July 1997." Later in 1998 Jennings also left the company.

Cozzi became CEO and attempted a turnaround. Although in debt to the tune of $350 million, Metal Management was still willing to acquire Arizona-based National Metals Co. out of bankruptcy in October 1998. By the end of the year business conditions appeared to be improving. The worst of the economic crisis in Asia was over, creating more demand for metals in the region and causing recyclers to no longer dump surplus metals at rock-bottom prices in the United States. Metal Management was able to trim its net losses to $13.9 million on sales of $915.1 million in fiscal 2000, but as the U.S. economy lapsed into recession, fiscal 2001 proved far more difficult.

In November 2000 Metal Management sought Chapter 11 bankruptcy protection. To turn around the company, Daniel W. Dienst, a former investment banker, was hired. He recognized that the company had taken on too much debt, although it had bought a "bunch of the best businesses available at the time," he told *Recycling Today* in a 2005 profile. He maintained, "Metal Management in the late 1990s was a great thesis, but the execution was not there, and markets clearly did not cooperate."

Metal Management emerged from bankruptcy protection in June 2001 with a clean slate financially but still had to contend with a metals market that remained in one of the worst slumps in recent memory. The company lost another $6 million in sales of $464.8 million in fiscal 2002. However, the demand for scrap in export markets led to a surge in prices that significantly improved Metal Management's fortunes. Revenues jumped to $770 million in fiscal 2003, and the company recorded net earnings of $20.5 million. The price of Metal Management stock rose accordingly, from $2 a share when it emerged from Chapter 11 to around $20 in the autumn of 2003. The sector that was doing particularly well was stainless steel scrap. To take advantage of rising demand, Metal Management doubled the number of its facilities that handled stainless steel scrap, adding it to the Denver and Toledo facilities.

Revenues topped $1 billion in fiscal 2004 while net income increased to $51.4 million. Business continued to thrive in fiscal 2005 with sales improving to more then $1.7 billion and net income to $9.25 million. The company also focused on nonferrous metals and became involved in the port management industry through joint ventures. In 2005 it joined forces with Donjon Marine Inc. to create Port Albany Ventures LLC to provide stevedoring and marine services operations near the Port Albany Terminal on the Hudson River in upstate New York. It also formed Metal Management Nashville LLC with partner Houchens Industries Inc. to operate scrap metal facilities in Nashville and Bowling Green, Kentucky.

In the meantime, Albert and Frank Cozzi, along with another brother and their sister, left the company in early 2004, the result, according to *American Metal Market,* of a "boardroom coup." After joining the board of directors in June 2001, Dienst had become chairman in April 2003, and succeeded Albert Cozzi as CEO.

Ferrous selling price declined in fiscal 2006, leading to a dip in revenues for the year to $1.6 billion and net earnings to $60.3 million. Nevertheless, it remained a strong performance, one that allowed Metal Management to gain a listing on the New York Stock Exchange in 2006. The company also resumed external expansion, acquiring 20 southern scrap yards from Mississippi-based Morris Recycling Inc. at the cost of $25.8 million, as well as an East Chicago scrap yard from OmniSource Corp. of Fort Wayne, Indiana. In early 2007 the company acquired a scrap yard in The Bronx, New York. A short time later fiscal 2007 came to a close, producing record results: more than $2.2 billion in sales and $116.4 million in net income.

Ed Dinger

PRINCIPAL SUBSIDIARIES

CIM Trucking, Inc.; Metal Management Aerospace, Inc.; Metal Management Northeast, Inc.; Metal Management Proler Southwest Inc.; Metal Management West, Inc.

PRINCIPAL COMPETITORS

Schnitzer Steel Industries, Inc.; Appliance Recycling Centers of America; Environmental Energy Services Inc.

FURTHER READING

Androeli, Tom, "Chicago Firm Targets Larger Scrap Industry," *Waste News,* October 28, 1996, p. 20.

Browning, E. S., "Metal Management Moves to Buy Scrap Yards in a Step Toward Consolidation of the Industry," *Wall Street Journal,* January 12, 1998, p. 1.

Giblin, Paul, "Merger Results in Arizona's Largest metal Recycling Firm," *Business Journal—Serving Phoenix & the Valley of the Sun,* November 19, 1993, p. 21.

Marley, Michael, "Metal Management in Spree," *American Metal Market,* September 1, 1997, p. 1.

———, "Metal Management on Purchasing Path," *American Metal Market,* August 7, 1997, p. 7.

Murphy, H. Lee, "Metal Mgt. Back in the Scrap Yard," *Crain's Chicago Business,* October 2, 2006, p. 24.

———, "Metal Mgmt. Forging a Turnaround," *Crain's Chicago Business,* December 6, 1999, p. 49.

———, "Rival Takes Shine to Metal Recycler," *Crain's Chicago Business,* October 6, 2003, p. 4.

Taylor, Brian, "Giant Steps: Daniel Dienst Helps Guide Metal Management Inc. into Profitable Territory," *Recycling Today,* July 2005.

Tita, Bob, "Scrap Collector," *Crain's Chicago Business,* June 25, 2007, p. 4.

Uttal, Bro, "The Latest Word in Show and Tell," *Fortune,* May 14, 1984, p. 101.

Worden, Edward, "Metal Management Broadens Its Reach," *American Metal Market,* June 25, 1997, p. 1.

———, "Metal Management Seeks Relief in Ch. 11," *American Metal Market,* November 22, 2000, p. 7.

Miami Herald Media Company

One Herald Plaza
Miami, Florida 33132
U.S.A.
Telephone: (305) 350-2111
Toll Free: (800) 437-2535
Web site: http://www.Miami-Herald.com

Wholly Owned Subsidiary of the McClatchy Company
Founded: 1903 as *Miami Evening Record*
Employees: 1,600
Sales: not available
NAIC: 511110 Newspaper Publishers

■ ■ ■

The Miami Herald Media Company operates the *Miami Herald,* the leading daily newspaper in south Florida. It also operates the Spanish-language newspaper *El Nuevo Herald* for the Miami market and distributes the *Miami Herald International Edition* in major markets in Latin America and the Caribbean. The Miami Herald Media Co. also produces a variety of magazines, tourism guides, and niche publications in both Spanish and English, such as *Home & Design, Condo Living,* and *Travel Magazine.* The company runs an extensive news web site, www.Miami-Herald.com, and has partnerships with several Florida radio stations. The *Herald* owns an 800,000-square-foot plant, and maintains news bureaus in seven Florida cities as well as in Washington, D.C.; Bogota, Colombia; and Lima, Peru. The *Miami Herald* has been publishing since 1903, when Miami was a tiny frontier town. Its market is unique in the United States,

with 44 percent of the population identifying as Hispanic, more than three times the national average. The *Herald* was the flagship paper of the Knight-Ridder newspaper chain until 2006, when Knight-Ridder was bought by the McClatchy Company.

EARLY YEARS

The *Miami Herald* was established in 1903 as the *Miami Evening Record,* the venture of publisher A. L. LaSalle and editor Frank B. Stoneman. Miami was at that time still a newly established town, founded in 1895 by three families. Miami grew quite rapidly, so that by 1909, the population was 5,000. Miami was home to more than the *Evening Record.* The *Miami Metropolis* and the *Miami Morning News* predated the paper. Much of Miami and south Florida was owned by Henry M. Flagler, one of the town's founders and the president of Flagler System, a corporation that built and ran the Florida East Coast Railway, among other enterprises. Henry Flagler was a partner of John D. Rockefeller in Standard Oil, and was an enormously influential force in the Miami area. In 1907, LaSalle and Stoneman bought out one of their competitors, the *Miami Morning News,* and the paper changed its name to the *Miami News-Record.* To make the acquisition, the newspapermen borrowed from Flagler. At the same time, the other Miami paper, the *Metropolis,* came under the sway of a fiery new editor, Bobo Dean. Dean had been a strong supporter of Henry Flagler early in his career, but at the *Metropolis,* he put out story after story critical of the massive Flagler System. The *News-Record,* heavily in Flagler's debt, did not dare run the kind of taunting stories that the *Metropolis* put out. Made to look tame by its competitor's more daring brand of journalism, the *News-Record* foundered, and by 1910 was close to bankruptcy.

About to close its doors, the young newspaper looked around for a rescuer. An Indiana lawyer, Frank B. Shutts, had just moved to town to become the receiver for a failed Miami bank. Shutts was what would in business circles today be called a "turnaround artist," and LaSalle and Stoneman came to him, asking him to take their business under his wing. Shutts went to New York to seek out the elderly Henry Flagler, the *News-Record*'s largest creditor. Shutts recommended that Flagler buy out the paper and keep it in business. Flagler agreed, but only if Shutts would become publisher. This was not exactly what Shutts had had in mind. Nevertheless, he said yes. On December 1, 1910, the paper reorganized with Shutts as publisher and Stoneman as editor, taking the new name *Miami Herald*.

Shutts was not a journalist, and he favored a very staid, conservative type of newspaper. The early *Miami Herald* had a rather dull front page, eschewing bold headlines. It put out a daily paper six days a week, which ran to eight pages, and later added a slightly longer Sunday edition. In 1912, its circulation was 2,000. Circulation grew rapidly in the next decade, as Miami entered its boom years. By 1921, the *Herald*'s circulation stood at 9,350, while the population of Miami had grown to 30,000. The city expanded rapidly, and the *Herald* was filled with classified advertising. The *Herald* bought a new building in 1922, and then over the next few years ran its aging presses in continuous shifts as the paper grew at an astounding rate.

THE FLORIDA LAND BOOM

A huge speculative bubble in Florida real estate began to swell in 1923. Thousands of people poured into south Florida, and Miami's population grew from 45,000 in 1922 to 70,000 in 1923, and then to some 177,000 in 1925. Housing could not be built fast enough, while multistoried office buildings went up all over Miami's downtown. The *Miami Herald* was a major source of information for all the newcomers, and the paper was so short-staffed that virtually anyone who walked in the door was offered a job. For some months over 1925 and 1926, the *Miami Herald* was actually the largest

newspaper in the entire world, when measured in terms of lines of advertising. The *Herald* occupied three adjoining buildings by this time, and in 1925 built a fourth building to hold its mechanical plant. The paper's circulation reached 47,600 at its peak in 1927 and then dropped rapidly.

Thousands of speculators made massive paper profits by buying plots of Florida land with only a 10 percent down payment and then reselling them within hours or days as prices spiraled upward. Many acres that sold for extravagant prices were in the depths of the Everglades or were otherwise unreachable by road or rail. The boom ended in early 1926. A ship had capsized in Miami's harbor in January, and in the six weeks it took to reopen the port, the frenzy of real estate speculation had simmered down. In September 1926, a devastating hurricane hit Miami, killing hundreds, injuring hundreds more, and damaging thousands of homes and buildings. These events combined to slow Miami's wild growth. For a while, the *Herald* was unaffected, as it was still a vital source of news and information for the populace. However, circulation dropped year by year in the late 1920s, and finally sank to around 38,000 in 1934. By that time, the whole country was deep in the grip of the Great Depression.

SALE TO KNIGHT FAMILY IN 1937

Miami's economy was a little different than that of the nation as a whole. By 1937, with most of the country still stagnant and suffering, the Miami area was at the beginning of another growth spurt. Miami's potential as a retirement community was just being realized, and builders were putting up new hotels and houses. The *Herald* was doing well in terms of the amount of classified advertising it carried, and circulation was once again growing. Its presses were old and outdated, however, and the paper remained exceedingly stuffy and conservative, especially compared to a new competitor, the tabloid-style *Miami Tribune*. Frank Shutts was ready to retire as owner and publisher of the paper, but his position was difficult. Although he had a lavish lifestyle, he was deeply in debt. He had borrowed from various friends and business partners to keep the newspaper going, and he apparently did not really know the extent of his, or his newspaper's, debts.

Shutts wanted to escape the complications of the newspaper, and he gingerly offered the *Herald* to two Ohio newspapermen, James and John Knight. The Knight brothers had inherited the *Akron Beacon Journal* from their father in 1933, and had struggled over the next four years to get that paper out of debt. The Knights liked Miami, and they wanted the *Herald*, although not at Shutts' price. They eventually talked

KEY DATES

1903: Paper begins publication as *Miami Evening Record.*

1910: Paper reorganizes with Frank Shutts as publisher; renamed *Miami Herald.*

1926: *Herald* largest newspaper in the world in terms of lines of advertising at height of Florida land boom.

1937: Knight brothers buy *Herald* from Shutts.

1946: *Clipper* edition begins shipping to Latin America.

1960: Paper moves into new downtown landmark headquarters.

1974: Parent Knight Newspapers merges with Ridder Publications.

1976: *Herald* produces Spanish-language insert, *El Herald.*

1998: Alberto Ibarguen named *Herald*'s publisher.

2006: *Herald*'s parent Knight-Ridder acquired by McClatchy Company.

him down from $3 million to $2.25 million, and in October 1937, they closed the deal and became the *Miami Herald*'s new owners. Within two years, the paper had increased its circulation by 14,000. The Knights updated the paper's look with more lively type and formatting. The paper's rather stodgy outlook also changed under the Knights, as the new publishers were less conservative than Shutts had been. Founding editor Frank Stoneman died in 1941. Even under the new owners, he had continued to write somber and old-fashioned editorials. With his passing, the paper was in a new era altogether. The *Herald* moved into a new building that year.

WORLD WAR II AND POSTWAR YEARS

Miami became a center of military activity as the United States entered World War II. After the war, many of the military men and women who had been stationed in Miami or who had passed through decided to settle there. Miami's population came close to doubling between 1940 and 1950. The *Herald*'s circulation also doubled over that time period. Meanwhile, the *Herald*'s owners expanded their chain of newspapers. They not only ran the *Miami Herald* and the *Akron Beacon Journal*, but in 1940 also bought the *Detroit Free Press*, and four years later bought the *Chicago Daily News.*

Knight Newspapers, as the parent company was called, continued to make acquisitions in the 1950s and 1960s, buying papers in North Carolina, the *Tallahassee Democrat*, and in 1969 buying five daily papers, including the *Philadelphia Inquirer* and the *Boca Raton News.*

The *Miami Herald* was not neglected while the parent company was on its buying spree. In 1946, the *Herald* began shipping an international edition to cities in the Caribbean and in Central and South America. This was an English-language paper that was bought by readers with ties to the United States and all those who had an interest in U.S. business and politics. This edition was at first called the *Clipper*, because it was flown out on Pan American Airways planes known as "Clipper Ships." The *Clipper* started with a press run of 50 copies, and by 1967 had a circulation of some 11,000. Readership may have been significantly higher, since a single paper was said to pass through 20 or 30 hands. The *Herald* was in every way a leading international paper, with reporters stationed throughout the world, and a definitely cosmopolitan rather than provincial outlook.

The *Herald* invested in a new building, spending $30 million in 1960 for a landmark building named One Herald Plaza, which it continued to occupy into the 21st century. Circulation had climbed to 322,500 by 1963. Over the next ten years, circulation continued to increase, reaching 404,846 in 1973. The paper also grew in terms of the amount of advertising it carried, and in news coverage. In 1972 the *Herald* was the nation's leading newspaper as measured in terms of lines of news coverage, surpassing both the *New York Times* and the *Los Angeles Times.* The *Herald* was quite a bulky paper, with Sunday editions running from 400 to 500 pages and sometimes weighing as much as five pounds. With quantity came quality, too, as *Time* magazine listed the *Herald* as one of the ten best daily newspapers in the country in 1974. The *Herald* was also profitable. Its financial soundness allowed parent Knight Newspapers to buy more daily and community newspapers across the country. Knight went public in 1969, and its stock quickly sold out as investors flocked to it.

CHANGES IN THE TWO NEXT DECADES

By 1974, Knight Newspapers owned a string of 16 newspapers, with the *Miami Herald* among its most prominent properties. The parent company had revenue of $342 million that year. Knight announced it was merging with a West Coast newspaper chain, Ridder Publications, a Los Angeles–based firm with 19 newspapers and revenue of $166 million. The *Herald*'s parent was then renamed Knight-Ridder Newspapers, Inc. Headquarters remained in Miami. The late 1970s and 1980s proved more difficult times for the newspaper. The rising cost of newsprint meant the long and lavish *Herald* was increasingly expensive to produce. The paper's circulation, which had grown precipitously, held level through the 1980s, at around 407,000.

In some ways, the *Herald* was slow to adapt to the needs of Miami's Spanish-speaking population, and this caused some missteps. In 1976, the *Herald* started producing a Spanish-language insert to the paper, called *El Herald*. The *Herald*'s executive editor described *El Herald* as "a 'transitional' paper that would accustom Cubans to reading the English paper," according to a profile of the paper in the *New York Times* (March 5, 1987). This seemed like a wise move, since the Miami area was a magnet for Cuban and other Spanish-speaking immigrants. By the mid-1980s, over 40 percent of the area's population was Hispanic. The traditional pattern of immigration in the United States was typically toward assimilation, where the first generation might cling to their home language and customs, but their children and grandchildren would speak English and have more of a mainstream culture. If this had been true in Miami, then a transitional paper would have been what was needed. However, Miami's Cuban population in particular resisted assimilation, and instead founded a vibrant Spanish-speaking community that operated within and beside the now minority Anglo culture. The *Herald* in the 1980s looked very much like a paper of the old guard, with few Spanish-speaking reporters and no Hispanics on its board. By 1987, the Spanish-language insert still had only two reporters assigned to it. The *Herald* missed out on stories about the Hispanic community and had trouble covering Hispanic cultural events. The paper too was constantly at odds with the more right-wing politics of leaders of the Cuban community.

In the early 1980s, the *Herald* began moving into the towns north of Miami. The demographics in Palm Beach County and Broward County looked similar to the demographics of *Herald* subscribers. However, this move gained the paper little in circulation. In the late 1980s, the *Herald* changed direction again and began a conscious push to appeal to the Spanish-speaking community in Miami. One major move was to hire a Cuban American associate editor, Angel Castillo. However, the paper still found itself at times at odds with the Cuban population. The *Herald*'s publisher and two other Knight-Ridder executives received death threats in 1992 after angering the head of a leading Cuban exile group, the Cuban American National Foundation. In the *New York Times* 1987 profile of the *Herald,* the paper's circulation director lamented that no other "paper in the country has as complex a marketing problem as we do."

SHIFTING LEADERSHIP

The *Herald* throughout the 1990s continued to formulate new ways to deal with its changing readership and stagnant circulation. The newspaper cut jobs and closed down some news bureaus in the early 1990s. Its focus on news also shifted somewhat; part of a new strategic plan in 1995 was to concentrate on stories in nine subject areas that readers had identified as being of most interest to them. The readers' list was topped by local government, but did not include either national or international politics. This was particularly striking as the *Herald* had been considered a notable leader in these areas 20 years earlier.

In 1995, the *Herald*'s Spanish-language edition, then called *El Nuevo Herald,* got a new publisher, Alberto Ibarguen. Ibarguen became publisher of the *Miami Herald* itself three years later. Ibarguen was half-Cuban, half–Puerto Rican, and as such he was considered to have more insight into Miami's immigrant population than previous publishers. Ibarguen moved to differentiate *El Nuevo Herald* from the English-language paper, and to market a distinct version of the *Herald* for suburban readers. He also began planning new ways to get the *Herald* to readers in Latin America. Ibarguen came in at a difficult time. The paper's profit margin was slipping, circulation had fallen from 386,000 in 1995 to 350,000 in 1997, and $32 million in budget cuts a few years earlier had seemingly done little to halt these declines.

Ibarguen countered these problems by investing $120 million in new equipment and unveiling a colorful, updated new design for the paper. Ibarguen was also dedicated to courting Hispanic readers, whether they read the paper in English or in Spanish. The paper opened new news bureaus in Bogota, Colombia, and in Managua, Nicaragua. Although Hispanic readers were central to the *Herald*'s survival, the paper also gained ground with its suburban readers. It had long been number two in the northern suburbs to the *Fort Lauderdale Sun-Sentinel.* By the late 1990s, the difference in circulation between the *Herald* and the *Sun-Sentinel* had lessened. One other change in the late 1990s was the relocation of parent company Knight-Ridder from Miami to San Jose, California.

By 2003, the *Herald* had met its target as far as profit margin, reaching the 22 percent figure set by parent Knight-Ridder. The *Miami Herald* was said to be among the most profitable papers in the Knight-Ridder stable by the early 2000s. The *Herald* had also seen its circulation rise to about 392,000 in 2003. This figure was bolstered by the new strength of the Spanish-language edition, *El Nuevo Herald*.

The news business was anything but smooth, however, as new challenges rose up in the middle of the decade. In July 2005, a Miami politician distraught over coming media reports of a personal scandal committed suicide in the lobby of the *Herald*. The paper then fired a reporter who had illegally recorded a phone conversation with the politician just before his death. Colleagues of the deceased politician called for a boycott of the paper, while journalists across the country expressed outrage at the firing of the reporter. Shortly after, the *Herald* got a new publisher, Jesus Diaz. Then in 2006, parent company Knight-Ridder was acquired by the California-based McClatchy Company, another media conglomerate. Diaz lasted barely a year as the *Herald*'s publisher. After firing several reporters who had received payment for speaking on an anti-Castro radio network, Diaz hired the reporters back and handed in his resignation. Diaz complained that he could no longer control the *Herald*'s newsroom, and his post was taken by David Landsberg. Clearly, the paper's relations with the Cuban community remained turbulent, and the middle years of the first decade of the 21st century were not a peaceful time for the *Herald*. Meanwhile, new parent McClatchy seemed as concerned about costs as Knight-Ridder had been. The year 2007 saw a round of layoffs at the paper's call center, where customer complaints were handled.

A. Woodward

PRINCIPAL COMPETITORS

News & Sentinel Company Inc.

FURTHER READING

Barringer, Felicity, "*Miami Herald* Copes with Bilingualism, Staff Desertions, and an Energized Rival," *New York Times,* November 15, 1999, p. C1.

Bussey, Jane, "*Herald* Parent Makes 'Cost-Effective' Decision," *Miami Herald,* August 1, 2007.

Deogun, Nikhil, "Lawrence to Leave Post as Publisher of *Miami Herald*," *Wall Street Journal,* August 5, 1998, p. 1.

Glaberson, William, "The *Miami Herald*'s Ninefold Path to Reader Enlightenment Raises Some Journalists' Eyebrows," *New York Times,* October 23, 1995, p. D7.

Jaffe, Greg, "Publishing: At the *Miami Herald*," *Wall Street Journal,* September 21, 1998, p. B1.

Seelye, Katherine Q., "Miami Publisher Steps Down over Payments to Reporters," *New York Times,* October 4, 2006, p. A16.

Smiley, Nixon, *Knights of the Fourth Estate,* Miami: E.A. Seemann Publishing, 1974.

Villano, David, "Finding Its Footing," *Florida Trend,* May 2003, p. 18.

———, "Hope at the *Herald*," *Florida Trend,* July 1, 2006, p. 26.

The NASDAQ Stock Market, Inc.

1 Liberty Plaza
165 Broadway, 50th Floor
New York, New York 10006
U.S.A.
Telephone: (212) 401-8700
Fax: (212) 401-1024
Web site: http://www.NASDAQ.com

Public Company
Incorporated: 2000
Employees: 898
Sales: $1.7 billion (2006)
Stock Exchanges: NASDAQ
Ticker Symbol: NDAQ
NAIC: 523210 Securities and Commodity Exchanges

■ ■ ■

Based in New York City, The NASDAQ Stock Market, Inc., lists about 3,200 companies, including itself, making it the largest electronic stock market in the United States. Business is primarily divided between two segments: Issuer Services and Market Services. Issuer Services is responsible for listing securities, providing shareholder services, and the sale of financial products such as the QQQ and other exchange-traded funds (ETFs), and derivatives of NASDAQ indices, including the NASDAQ Biotechnology Index and the NASDAQ Composite Index. Further revenue is generated by the licensing and listing of third-party-sponsored ETFs and other structured products. The Market Services segment provides quotations, order execution, reporting, and other services to market participants. Quote and trade information is also packaged for sale to market participants and data vendors.

GREAT DEPRESSION BRINGS CHANGES

NASDAQ is an acronym for National Association of Securities Dealers Automated Quotations, a system created for the National Association of Securities Dealers (NASD), which was created in 1939 to bring some order to over-the-counter (OTC) stock transactions. In the early 1800s private banking houses literally sold securities over countertops, leading to the OTC term, and while essentially any tradable financial product could be acquired in this way, OTC became associated exclusively with stocks that were not listed on the New York Stock Exchange, the American Stock Exchange, or any of the regional stock exchanges. The exchanges were able to provide, to some extent at least, a check on the abuses of stock manipulators, but the same could not be said for the OTC market, which gained an especially unsavory reputation in the 1920s. Following the stock market crash of 1929 that ushered in the Great Depression, stock brokers were well aware that something needed to be done to reassure customers, and with the help of the Securities and Exchange Commission (SEC) new regulations were enacted that paved the way for a registered securities association with the power to police its members and transform the OTC market. To encourage brokers to join an association, a new law, the Maloney Act, passed in 1938 as an amendment to the Securities Exchange Act of 1934, allowed members to trade among themselves at wholesale prices and to

COMPANY PERSPECTIVES

NASDAQ is the largest electronic screen-based equity securities market in the United States, both in terms of number of listed companies and traded share volume. With approximately 3,200 listed companies, it is home to category-defining companies that are leaders across all areas of business including technology, retail, communications, financial services, transportation, media and biotechnology industries.

outsiders at retail prices. This incentive led to the creation of NASD, and within a year about 1,500 security dealers joined.

Because several thousand stocks were traded on the OTC market, many of them small and obscure, wholesalers had a difficult time determining the market for a vast number of stocks, unable to determine what they were selling for over the course of a day. To meet this need a private firm, the National Quotation Bureau, Inc., published what became known as the "sheets," which listed stock quotes received each day by subscribers. Some small contemporary stocks sold on the "pink sheet" are a legacy of this system. Regional sheets were differentiated by the color of the paper on which they were printed. The Eastern Section relied on pink paper, hence "pink sheets," while the Western Section used green paper and the Pacific Coast Section was simply white. Dissemination of the sheets was supposed to be limited to reputable wholesalers but well-connected traders were also able to secure copies. By the 1960s a new breed of stock underwriters were emerging whose willingness to use the sheets to manipulate stock prices began to raise concerns within both the SEC and NASD.

In 1963 the SEC issued to Congress the Special Study of the Securities Markets, which reported a great deal of problems in the OTC market and recommended that an automated quotation system be created to help check these abuses. At the urging of the SEC, NASD became more of a national organization instead of a collection of regional units. In 1966 it then formed an Automation Committee to determine the requirements for a national automated stock quotation system, and two years later bids were solicited to build the system. Winning the $15 million contract in December 1968 was Bunker Ramos Corporation, which offered to lease the system to NASD with an option to buy. Given that the system's estimated cost was $20 million at a time

when NASD's annual budget was less than $6 million, leasing was the only viable way to proceed. Moreover, Bunker Ramos was well qualified to perform the work. It was founded in 1928 as The Teleregister Corporation, its first product a stock quotation board system that served New York brokers. Later it developed the airline industry's first automated reservation system, the banking industry's first online teller terminal system, the first commercial voice response system, and the first CRT data terminal.

NASDAQ GOES LIVE: 1971

The system Bunker Ramos created for NASD relied on a pair of Univac 1108 mainframe computers housed in a Trumbull, Connecticut, facility. Through 30,000 miles of high-speed transmission lines, Trumbull was connected to regional computers located in New York City, Atlanta, Chicago, Dallas, and San Francisco, from which brokerage firms were connected. The system, known as NASDAQ, became operational on February 8, 1971, displaying quotes for more than 2,500 OTC stocks. It was an immediate hit with brokers, despite some growing pains. The system experienced occasional problems with faulty telephone lines, and it took some time to iron out human errors, such as dealers refusing to honor quotes they entered into the system, and attempts to move the market on a particular stock by increasing bids in the hope that a pack mentality would take over and drive the price even higher. In time, brokers learned to recognize such phony quotes, and the NASDAQ experienced no major abuses.

NASDAQ evolved its operation over the years, growing from a computer bulletin board service into an electronic stock market. In 1975 it weeded out the smaller OTC stocks, and it only displayed NASDAQ-listed stocks. To prevent abuses from market makers (who received a commission to bring together sellers and buyers at a fixed price), the NASDAQ in 1980 began displaying inside quotations, allowing brokers to see the best bid and best sell prices. As a result, the gap between these prices narrowed considerably, limiting opportunities for market makers to step in to buy stock for their own accounts and take advantage of wide spreads. These spreads were reduced further when the NASDAQ gained permission from the SEC to quote stock trading above $10 in 1/16ths of a dollar.

Other changes followed in the early 1980s. NASDAQ introduced its National Market System in 1982, later renamed NASDAQ National Market (NNM), an effort to put NASDAQ on a similar footing with the New York Stock Exchange. To achieve this end, only the most actively traded stocks gained entry, a mere 40 or so at the start. Smaller companies would be represented on

```
┌─────────────────────────────────────────────┐
│                                               │
│              KEY DATES                        │
│              ───■───                          │
│                                               │
│   1939:  National Association of Securities   │
│          Dealers (NASD) formed.               │
│   1971:  National Association of Securities   │
│          Dealers Automated Quotations         │
│          (NASDAQ) launched.                    │
│   1982:  NASDAQ National Market System        │
│          introduced.                           │
│   1997:  Abuses lead to new regulations.      │
│   2000:  NASDAQ splits from NASD.             │
│   2005:  NASDAQ gains NASDAQ listing.         │
│                                               │
└─────────────────────────────────────────────┘
```

the NASDAQ SmallCap Market. In addition to being limited to the top stocks, NNM sought to rival the New York Stock Exchange with the type of information it offered to brokers and investors, including real-time quotes. Instead of only being available at the end of the day, the price and volume of each trade was posted just 90 seconds after execution. Traders were also offered margin, allowing them to buy stocks on credit from brokers. NASDAQ implemented an automated trading system as well. Investors who were unable to reach a market maker by phone could place an order through SOES, NASDAQ's automated "small-order execution system." Participation was voluntary, however, and market makers did not have to complete the trade. This provision became controversial during the stock market crash of 1987, so-called Black Monday, when a number of dealers stopped answering their phones and refused to accept SOES orders, leaving investors desperate to sell with no way out of the market. Several months later the NASDAQ began to require market makers to accept trades at the prices they quoted up to 1,000 shares.

Mandatory participation in SOES led to a new form of abuse, however. SOES brokerages cropped up to provide self-service trading, giving so-called SOES bandits trading software and direct electronic access to the NASDAQ. These traders were able to take advantage of lag time in the system that created price gaps between the price of a stock posted by the lead dealer and the market makers that followed suit. Should the lead dealer, for example, increase the offering price of a stock while another dealer briefly maintained a lower price, SOES bandits were quick to place an SOES order to buy at the lower price and then place another mandatory SOES trade with another dealer at the higher price, thus pocketing the difference. To curb these practices, over the next few years changes were made to SOES: SOES firms were prevented from splitting large orders into increments of 1,000 to take

advantage of SOES rules, professional trading accounts (PTAs) were no longer allowed to place SOES orders, SOES trades were cut back to a maximum of 500 shares, and a limit was placed on the market maker's exposure to SOES orders in a trading day.

The NASDAQ was also rife with abuses from market makers in the early 1990s, leading to SEC charges in four general areas: tape painting, broadcasting fake quotes to deceive investors about the movement of the market; front running, using inside information about unannounced buy orders to purchase shares in order to quickly resell them; refusal to honor posted quotes, growing out of the fear that a large order reflected something a market maker did not know about a stock but could lead to unwarranted volatility in a stock; and delaying reported trades to drive up the price of a stock.

While these problems were coming to light in the system, NASDAQ enjoyed strong growth on a number of fronts. It became the home for many technology companies and began promoting itself through free media and television commercials that employed the slogan, "The Market for the Next 100 Years." In the early 1990s NASDAQ established a junk bond bulletin board, a system to automate all penny stock trades, and launched Portal, a system to trade debt and equity private placements. In 1993 it introduced three new indices to cover three important growth industry sectors: biotechnology, computers, and telecommunications. Share volume rose steadily, reaching an average of 317.4 million shares traded daily in the first quarter of 1994, for the first time eclipsing the New York Stock Exchange, which averaged 312.4 million shares during the same period. In July 1995 the NASDAQ composite stock index reached the 1,000-point mark for the first time.

In July 1996 the U.S. Justice Department charged two dozen NASDAQ securities firms with "fixing transactions costs." A month later the SEC announced the result of its own investigation focusing on the abuses of market makers, which grew out of laxity in NASD. In early 1997 the SEC imposed new rules to rein in market makers, primarily making their transactions more transparent to the public. At the end of the year, about 30 NASD firms reached a settlement on a class-action suit over price fixing, agreeing to pay $910 million in damages.

Despite the bad publicity received by dealers, the NASDAQ's reputation did not suffer much damage. NASDAQ continued to soar in the second half of the 1990s, fueled by the growth of high-technology stocks and the allure of anything associated with the Internet. In 1998 the NASDAQ joined forces with the American Stock Exchange, a longtime rival, to form the

NASDAQ-AMEX Market Group, the first of what the NASDAQ hoped would become a series of global market alliances. The idea was to create the "Market of Markets," taking advantage of the Internet to create a common platform for 24-hour-a-day trading, activity switching from one continent to the next as a new day dawned. A step taken to realize this goal was the creation of NASDAQ Japan in 2000. NASDAQ was not alone in its desire to leverage technology, however. In the late 1990s it began to face a new challenge from electronic communications networks (ECNs), equity trade-matching systems that brought buyers and sellers together, cutting out the middleman. ECNs had been around for decades, but had been mostly used by dealers to make private transactions in order to limit market repercussions. The new order-handling rules of 1997, however, gave all investors access to ECN trading, thus creating new competition for NASDAQ's trading systems. By the early 2000s ECNs would account for nearly half of all trading in NASDAQ-listed stocks, while NASDAQ executed about 22 percent.

NASDAQ SPLITS FROM NASD: 2000

The new century brought major changes to the NASDAQ. In 2000 it was separated from NASD, becoming an independent public company, accomplished in a two-phase private placement of securities that began in June 2000. A year later the restructuring was completed and NASDAQ became a public company. All told, NASDAQ raised about $1 billion in capital, money that could be used for upgrades and innovations to ward off the encroachment of ECNs, aid in its ongoing battle with the New York Stock Exchange, and allow it to pursue its global plans. However, at the same time that the NASDAQ was preparing to go public, it had to contend with a crash in April 2000, fueled by problems in high-technology stocks and the bursting of the Internet bubble. The market, which had just topped the 5,000 level, steadily lost value over the next year and a half, and to make matters worse, a number of companies abandoned the NASDAQ for the New York Stock Exchange. The terrorist attacks of September 11, 2001, against the United States only served to worsen a bad situation, so that ten days later the market bottomed out at 1,387. Little more than a year later the conditions of the bear market took its toll on NASDAQ Japan, which was forced to close its doors.

As the NASDAQ suffered an erosion in value, it took steps to better position itself for future growth. After splitting from NASD, it moved its headquarters from Washington, D.C., NASD's longtime home, to the Times Square area of New York City. Finding itself in a nebulous position, hardly an ECN yet not quite an exchange, the NASDAQ in November 2000 formally began the process with the SEC to become an exchange. To fend off the challenge of ECNs, the NASDAQ also launched, after three years of effort, its SuperMontage system, a significant upgrade over the previous trading system, providing brokers with much greater information about the depth of a market, and a truer picture about a share's supply and demand to help brokers in making decisions.

As part of its effort to rebuild its position, the NASDAQ completed a secondary offering of stock in February 2005, and gained a listing on its own exchange. More capital was raised through two later offerings, the money used in part to acquire one of its ECN rivals, Instinet, a transaction that helped to improve NASDAQ's technology platform. The NASDAQ also resumed the pursuit of its global aspirations. It bought a large interest in the London Stock Exchange and in September 2007 received permission to open an office in Beijing, China. The NASDAQ also sought to become involved in promising new businesses, in particular ETFs, open-ended mutual funds that often mimicked a stock market index (the S&P 500, for example) but could be traded throughout the course of the day. In July 2007 the NASDAQ unveiled its plan for the NASDAQ Exchange Traded Fund Market to accommodate both ETFs and index linked notes (ILNs), hybrid securities typically linked to stock indices, providing the benefits of both fixed income and equity securities. In light of these developments, the NASDAQ appeared to be well positioned to lay new claims to being "The Market for the Next 100 Years."

Ed Dinger

PRINCIPAL SUBSIDIARIES

NASDAQ Global Funds, Inc.; NASDAQ International Marketing Initiatives, Inc., NASDAQ International Limited; NASDAQ Technology Services, LLC.

PRINCIPAL COMPETITORS

American Stock Exchange LLC; New York Stock Exchange.

FURTHER READING

Armour, Lawrence A., "In Terms of Technology, It's an 'Idea Whose Time Has Come,'" *Barron's National Business and Financial Weekly,* February 28, 1972, p. 2.

————, "NASDAQ Has Opened a New Competitive Era on Wall Street," *Barron's National Business and Financial Weekly,* March 8, 1971, p. 3.

Ingebretsen, Mark, *NASDAQ: A History of the Market That Changed the World,* Roseville, Calif.: Prima Publishing, 2002.

McNamee, Mike, "A Magic Bullet for NASDAQ?" *Business Week,* September 30, 2002, p. 80.

Morgenson, Gretchen, "Fun and Games on NASDAQ," *Forbes,* August 16, 1993, p. 74.

"NASDAQ: Not Far Enough?" *Business Week,* January 17, 2000, p. 82.

Sales, Robert, "SuperMontage Showdown," *Wall Street & Technology,* July 2002, p. 22.

The Navigators Group, Inc.

---

1 Penn Plaza
New York, New York 10119
U.S.A.
Telephone: (212) 244-2333
Fax: (212) 244-4077
Web site: http://www.navg.com

Public Company
Incorporated: 1974 as New York Marine Managers Inc.
Employees: 275
Sales: $526.59 million (2006)
Stock Exchanges: NASDAQ
Ticker Symbol: NAVG
NAIC: 524126 Direct Property and Casualty Insurance
Carriers

∎ ∎ ∎

Based in New York City, The Navigators Group, Inc., is an international insurance holding company primarily involved in the writing of marine insurance. The company's main insurance subsidiary, Navigators Insurance Company, offers a full slate of ocean and inland marine insurance, providing hull and cargo coverage, war insurance, as well as energy insurance to cover offshore and onshore oil and gas operations. NIC Insurance Company, Navigators' specialty insurance unit, offers a wide variety of niche insurance products for such industries as contracting, manufacturing, real estate, and hospitality. Navigators' underwriting operations include Marine, Specialty Property-Casualty, and Professional

Liability (covering corporate directors and officers, lawyers, and others).

In addition, Navigators Underwriting Agency, Ltd., is a member of Lloyd's of London, the world's premiere marine insurance market. Navigators maintains domestic offices in Chicago, Houston, Seattle, San Francisco, and Corona, California; conducts business in the United Kingdom through offices in London, Manchester, and Bassingstoke; and operates internationally through an office in Antwerp, Belgium. Navigators is a public company listed on NASDAQ, 20 percent of its shares held by chairman and founder Terence N. Deeks and his family.

COMPANY FOUNDED: 1974

Born in London, Terence Deeks joined Lloyd's of London in 1957 and over the next decade rose through the ranks as a major insurance writer to become deputy marine underwriter. In the meantime he pursued an associate's degree from London's Chartered Insurance Institute, graduating in 1966. He then immigrated to the United States, employed by New York City–based General Reinsurance Corporation to start a marine department.

Deeks relocated to Houston in 1968 to establish and manage a marine department for Highlands Insurance Company. In 1974 he struck out on his own, returning to New York City to launch the Somerset Agencies to provide underwriting management services for marine, aviation, property insurance, and reinsurance companies. He also formed New York Marine Managers Inc., Navigators' predecessor. New York Marine operated a marine insurance pool, serving as a marine underwriting department for a group of property and casualty insurance companies.

New York Marine was an immediate success, and just one year after its launch, the firm opened an office in Houston to become involved in the Gulf of Mexico. Another regional office was opened in San Francisco in 1982. In that same year the business was reorganized as a Delaware corporation under the name Navigators Group, Inc. This set the stage for the creation of Navigators Insurance Company in 1983, permitting the firm to write insurance and become a risk-taking member of the pool it managed.

COMPANY TAKEN PUBLIC: 1986

Navigators went public in 1986. In an initial public offering of stock managed by Donaldson, Lufkin & Jenrette, the company raised $25 million, the money earmarked to increase the firm's insurance underwriting capacity. Some of that new business would be generated from a new office in Seattle, opened in 1987. A year later Navigators formed International Aviation Insurance Group, which began doing business at the start of 1989. This bid to launch a general aviation underwriting firm, primarily to cover U.S. jet fleets, evolved into NIC Insurance Company, which in addition to aviation and inland marine insurance added property insurance lines of specialty reinsurance. As a result, revenues of the parent company increased to $70.8 million in 1991 and two years later approached the $120 million mark. Net income during this period grew from $16 million to $21.6 million. Also in 1993 Navigators arranged to acquire the 50 percent stake it did not already own in the eight affiliated Somerset companies that provided underwriting management services for Navigators Insurance and other insurance companies. The transaction closed in June 1994.

Navigators' success was even more impressive in light of difficult market conditions that had been in place since the company was launched in the mid-1970s. Moreover, at the start of the 1990s marine and aviation direct insurers had to deal with escalating rates from reinsurers, which had taken considerable losses in

recent years and had increased their rates significantly. Direct insurers were forced to raise their rates but lacked leverage with shipowners and airlines because of excess supply of insurance that depressed rates. As a result, there was a shakeout in the industry. Navigators emerged as one of the survivors, and for the first time since its founding benefited from favorable market conditions that allowed it to raise rates and grow from a $50 million to a $100 million company in just five years.

Although Navigators was able to withstand losses caused by Hurricanes Andrew and Iniki in 1992 to maintain profits, the same could not be said for 1994. In January of that year a 6.7 magnitude earthquake, the Northridge Earthquake, struck northwest of Los Angeles, California, killing 72 people, injuring 11,000, and causing an estimated $12.5 billion in damage. Navigators was one of many insurance companies that suffered significant losses due to the earthquake. For the year, the firm posted a net loss of $20.5 million on revenues that dipped to $113.9 million.

It was a major setback for Navigators, which took steps to reduce its exposure to such domestic catastrophes and focus on becoming a true international specialty marine underwriter. In 1995 the firm withdrew completely from the property business and returned to profitability in 1996, recording earnings of $12.6 million on revenues of $113.7 million. The loss of property insurance premiums led to a decline in revenues to $102.8 million in 1996, but net income continued to rise, approaching $16.8 million. That number fell to $12.5 million on sales of $108.2 million in 1997. Due to increased competition in the aviation insurance field, Navigators withdrew from this segment as well in 1997, and Somerset Marine Aviation Property Managers, Inc., became an inactive subsidiary.

In the late 1990s Navigators took further steps to focus on its core marine insurance business. The Non Marine division was consolidated as four subsidiaries (Somerset Re Management, Inc.; Navigators Management Corporation; Somerset Casualty Agency, Inc.; and Somerset Property, Inc.) and merged into Somerset Marine, Inc. Moreover, Navigators decided to cease writing inland marine insurance, with the exception of onshore energy insurance. This move allowed Navigators to trim operating costs by closing inland marine offices in Atlanta, Chicago, and Dallas in 1997, and in Cranbury, New Jersey, in 1998. To increase its international business, in 1996 Navigators formed Somerset Asia in Sydney, Australia, and a Singapore subsidiary called Somerset Services Pte. Ltd. In early 1997 Somerset Asia began writing coverage on marine, onshore energy, engineering, and construction in China, Indonesia,

KEY DATES

1974: Terence Deeks founds New York Marine Managers Inc.
1982: Business reorganized as Navigators Group, Inc.
1986: Company taken public.
1998: Mander, Thomas & Cooper acquired.
1999: Anfield Insurance Services acquired.
2003: Stanley Galansky named CEO.
2005: Antwerp, Belgium, office opens.

Malaysia, Taiwan, Thailand, and Vietnam, while Somerset Services did loss prevention consulting work.

Also in late 1996 Navigators formed Somerset UK to offer marine, aviation, onshore energy, engineering, and construction coverage. Once authorization was received the unit began conducting business in October 1997. Three months later, in January 1998, Navigators acquired the Lloyd's of London underwriting agency, Mander, Thomas & Cooper (Underwriting Agencies) Ltd. (MTC), manager of Lloyd's Syndicate 1221, which possessed one of Lloyd's largest specialist marine portfolios. Navigators was well familiar with the syndicate because it was the largest participant, and as such had developed a long-term relationship with the MTC staff.

In addition to gaining entry into Lloyd's important market, the MTC acquisition provided Lloyd's worldwide licenses, creating a platform on which Navigators could build its international program. It also allowed Navigators to cut costs by relocating Somerset UK's accounting and support staff to the MTC offices, while the underwriters were assigned to Lloyd's underwriting floors.

Conditions in the marine insurance field were difficult in the mid- to late 1990s. Premium levels declined each year and because of increased competition, rates fell. By the end of the decade they were about 40 percent of their 1993 level. Having elected to focus on its marine line, which accounted for almost 90 percent of its business, Navigators saw net income fall to $11.5 million on revenues of $115.2 million in 1998. The company then posted a loss of $5.4 million in 1999 on revenues of $105.6 million, due in large measure to a $6.6 million write-off of uncollectible reinsurance.

Despite these disappointing results at the end of the decade, Navigators was able to position itself for the future, especially in its U.K. business. In 1999 it began writing engineering and construction, and onshore energy policies through its newly launched Robertson Consortium at Lloyd's, and later in the year Navigators established Pennine Underwriting Ltd., based in Manchester to provide cargo and engineering business for its Lloyd's Syndicate 1221. An office in Leeds would follow later. In order to become less dependent on marine insurance, in 1999 Navigators also acquired San Francisco–based Anfield Insurance Services, which specialized in construction liability insurance and provided a foundation for Navigators specialty lines.

Navigators returned to profitability in 2000 at a time when rival firms experienced continued losses. Despite difficult market conditions during much of the year, Navigators was able to grow revenues to more than $120 million and post earnings of $7 million. The company also moved its headquarters in 2000 from lower Manhattan to One Penn Plaza in Midtown.

NEW CEO: 2003

To help in growing the business, Navigators in 2001 implemented a new global branding strategy that called for all subsidiaries to operate under the Navigators name. At the same time, the company announced that Stanley A. Galanski joined the firm as executive vice-president and chief operating officer of the Group, as well as president and COO of the insurance companies. He was also Deeks' heir apparent. Galanski was a seasoned insurance executive. From 1980 to 1995 he held a variety positions with the Chubb Group of Insurance Companies. He then became president of New Hampshire Insurance company, and in 1997 was named president of XL Specialty Insurance Company. In May 2002 he would become Navigators' president, and succeeded Deeks as CEO in January 2003, while Deeks remained the firm's chairman.

Another development in 2001 was Navigators Management Company's opening of a midwestern regional office in suburban Chicago. In September 2001, the subsidiary also expanded into management and professional liability lines with the launch of the Navigators Pro division. The terrorist attacks that took place in that same month had worldwide repercussions, and the destruction of the World Trade Center had a direct impact on Navigators' balance sheet. The company incurred a $18 million gross loss, and a $4.5 million net loss after reinsurance and tax considerations. As a result the company lost $3.7 million to the bottom line. In the end, Navigators netted $3.7 million on revenues that improved to $171.2 million.

Navigators was able to take greater advantage of an improving underwriting environment in 2002 that resulted in escalating rate increases. Revenues soared to $252.7 million and net income improved to $16.4 million. Moreover, the amount of premiums the Group wrote increased from $278.2 million in 2001 to nearly $450 million in 2002. As rates continued to climb, Navigators continued to post record revenues, which topped $300 million in 2003. The company took advantage of this growth to make a secondary securities offering in October 2003, which netted $11 million. Earnings fell to $7.7 million in 2003 due to a write-off connected to asbestos liabilities incurred from policies written in the late 1970s and early 1980s, but soared to nearly $35 million on revenues of $343 million a year later. As a result, Navigators Insurance Company was the fourth largest U.S.-based ocean marine insurer and 14th largest in the world.

To help sustain growth, Navigators added a marine and energy product line to its London operation in 2004 and made plans to expand its international business by opening an office in Antwerp, Belgium, the Group's first continental European office, which began operations in 2005 by focusing on ocean marine coverage not available to the London market. Navigators also launched its Excess Casualty Division in 2005 to offer businesses with commercial umbrella and low level excess liability policies. To gain greater flexibility in its Lloyd's business, Navigators bought out the minority interest in Syndicate 1221.

Hurricanes Katrina and Rita hurt profits in 2005, when Navigators' net income fell to $23.6 million on revenues of $385.2 million. However, business from the new product lines and an increased contribution from Syndicate 1221 helped to fuel solid gains in 2006 that more than made up for the losses of the previous year. Revenues reached $526.6 million and net income totaled $72.6 million for the year. Moreover, the amount of gross written premiums approached the $1 billion mark.

Ed Dinger

PRINCIPAL SUBSIDIARIES

Navigators Insurance Company; NIC Insurance; Navigators Management Company, Inc.; Navigators Management (UK) Ltd.; Navigators NV.

PRINCIPAL COMPETITORS

Highlands Insurance Group, Inc.; CIGNA Property & Casualty Insurance Company; Insurance Co. of North America.

FURTHER READING

Bray, Julian, "Navigators Stages a Strong Recovery," *Lloyd's List International,* April 6, 1994.

"CEO Interview: The Navigators Group, Inc.," *Wall Street Transcript,* December 13, 1993.

"Navigators Group Says Asbestos Charge Will Impact Earnings," *A.M. Best Newswire,* February 13, 2004.

"Navigators Opens Marine Unit in Belgium," *A.M. Best Newswire,* January 18, 2005.

"New Aviation Subsidiary Formed by Navigator's Group," *Lloyd's List International,* December 14, 1988.

Network Equipment Technologies

Network Equipment Technologies Inc.

6900 Paseo Padre Parkway
Fremont, California 94555
U.S.A.
Telephone: (510) 713-7300
Fax: (510) 574-4000
Web site: http://www.net.com

Public Company
Incorporated: 1983
Employees: 238
Sales: $84.1 million (2007)
Stock Exchanges: New York Stock Exchange
Ticker Symbol: NWK
NAIC: 334119 Other Computer Peripheral Equipment
    Manufacturing

■ ■ ■

Fremont, California–based Network Equipment Technologies Inc. (NET) is a leading provider of voice and data communications equipment. An industry pioneer, in the first decade of the 21st century the company focused on developing so-called next-generation technology that supported the movement from more traditional platforms to ones based on Internet protocol (IP). IP is the communications protocol or method that is used for transmitting information between computers on the Internet. Voice over Internet protocol (VoIP), which allows voice communications via the Internet, is one example of the IP technology with which NET has been involved. NET's wide-ranging product lines are marketed under the NX Series

(network exchange) and VX Series (voice exchange) banners. Its NX platform includes the Promina product line, while the VX platform includes the Shout product line. The company's customer base includes leading corporations such as Microsoft and Reuters, as well as government and military organizations such as the U.S. Navy and Marines, as well as the North Atlantic Treaty Organization (NATO).

A SUCCESSFUL START: 1983–89

NET was established in 1983 by Bruce Smith, an engineer who earned an MBA from Harvard University. According to the February 6, 1989, issue of *Forbes,* while working as vice president of corporate development for Communications Satellite Corp. (Comsat), Smith generated a long memo to his employer outlining how telecommunications giant AT&T could potentially threaten Comsat's Satellite Business Systems (SBS) unit. At the time, SBS helped companies use satellite technology to bypass AT&T and save money on long-distance calls. At the heart of the threat were circuits of specially configured copper wire known as T1 lines, which were capable of handling 24 times the capacity of regular phone lines. Smith argued the day would come when AT&T would begin leasing T1 lines to business clients, allowing them to make long-distance calls for less. However, his remarks fell on deaf ears.

Competition from the likes of MCI and U.S. Sprint forced AT&T to begin leasing T1 lines in September 1983. This had a negative impact on Comsat's SBS business, which was eventually sold at a loss to MCI. Along with deregulation of the telecommunica-

COMPANY PERSPECTIVES

For nearly a quarter of a century, Network Equipment Technologies, Inc. (NET), has provided voice and data communications equipment for multi-service networks requiring high degrees of versatility, interoperability, security and performance.

tions industry, this situation led Smith to relinquish his post at Comsat and establish Network Equipment Technologies (NET) in Redwood City, California, with $25 million in venture capital from investors including Anderson & Eyre, Hambrecht & Quist, Merrill Lynch, Merrill Pickard, and Morgan Stanley & Co.

From the very start, NET's approach was to sell high-end telecommunications equipment to *Fortune* 1000 companies. The company began shipping actual products, some costing as much as $250,000, in September 1984. NET's first product was a multiplexer called the Integrated Digital Network Exchange (IDNX). Multiplexers are devices that route large amounts of voice and data to the right location on a network. Within two years, the company's employee base had grown to 250 people, who helped clients including American Airlines, Bank of America, Macy's of California, MCI Communications, Shearson Lehman Brothers Inc., MCI Communications, and Wells Fargo to build their own independent telecommunications networks.

NET's initial public offering took place in February 1987, generating $40 million. Of this amount, approximately $25 million was slated for capital needs and future expansion. Sales reached $47.4 million in 1987, up from $8.7 million the previous year, and the company generated its first profit ($5.1 million). By this time, NET had sold about 400 IDNX devices. Further progress was bolstered by a licensing agreement with International Business Machines Corp., which agreed to sell and service NET products.

In April 1988, NET agreed to merge with San Jose, California–based Excelan, Inc., a local area network (LAN) company. The $125 million deal, which called for Excelan to become a NET subsidiary, would have enabled the combined firms to compete with Novell, Inc., and 3Com Corp. However, when NET failed to increase its offer by an additional $35 million, Excelan shareholders pulled the plug on the merger in June.

Despite this setback, NET ended the decade on a high note when American Airlines chose the company to provide a new, private infrastructure for its Sabre reservation service, which then handled some 470,000 daily reservations. Sales soared to $136.7 million in 1989. In November, Bruce Smith hired Hewlett-Packard executive Daniel Warmenhoven to serve as president and chief operating officer.

DISASTER AND RECOVERY: 1990–99

Things took a turn for the worse at NET during the early 1990s, according to the July–August 1991 issue of *California Business*. In July 1990 the company's board asked Smith to resign as CEO, and NET's chief financial officer stepped down. Warmenhoven remained on board as president and CEO, guiding NET through one of the darkest periods in its history. The bad times resulted from a variety of factors, including major orders that failed to materialize, increased competition, and the effects of an economic recession that put the brakes on spending by top customers. In the wake of these setbacks, Warmenhoven attempted to turn the situation around with a restructuring plan that included a workforce reduction and expense cuts. Research and development spending doubled in 1990, as the company accelerated efforts to roll out new products.

Shortly after he was named chairman in January 1991, Warmenhoven trimmed 15 percent of the company's employee base. Positive developments eventually began to occur. One of NET's new products received a warm reception, and more than 75 new customers came on board. Backed by a new management team, Warmenhoven proceeded to guide the company into calmer seas. After losing $38.9 million on sales of $66.8 million in 1991, the company lost $14.5 million on sales of $102.6 million in 1992.

By 1993, NET was back in the black, netting $4.7 million on sales of $119.6 million. Warmenhoven left NET in late 1993, and former Harris Corporation executive John Arnold temporarily assumed the role of CEO. Joseph Francesconi, an executive from Sunnyvale, California–based Amdahl Corp., was hired as CEO in 1994. He continued to implement cost-saving measures at the company, including the elimination of redundant jobs, as well as unprofitable programs and divisions.

Conditions continued improving at NET into late 1994 as the company secured agreements related to new long-distance phone networks that were being constructed in Columbia and China. In addition, Federated Department Stores was added to NET's client roster. In early 1995, pharmaceutical giant Glaxo hired the company to help build a communications network in the United Kingdom. Finally, in August of the fol-

KEY DATES

1983: Network Equipment Technologies is established by former Communications Satellite Corp. executive Bruce Smith, with $25 million in venture capital funding.

1987: NET's initial public offering generates $40 million.

1997: Plans are made to relocate the company's headquarters to Fremont, California.

2000: The company's Federal Service Business is sold to CACI International, Inc.

lowing year, Hans A. Wolf succeeded John B. Arnold as company chairman, upon the latter's retirement.

After operating in Redwood City, California, for 15 years, in 1997 NET announced plans to relocate its headquarters to a 17.5-acre site in Fremont, California. The new campus in Ardenwood Corporate Park included a manufacturing facility, as well as two other buildings to house the company's offices and research and development arm. The buildings, which spanned a collective 280,000 square feet, surrounded an open-air amphitheater and were adjacent to acreage that would accommodate 200,000 square feet of additional space if further expansion was needed.

Heading into the late 1990s, NET experienced more leadership changes. Citing personal reasons, Joseph Francesconi announced his resignation in January 1999. He remained at the helm until the company was able to hire Hubert "Bert" Whyte as his successor in June. Prior to joining NET, Whyte served as president and CEO of Advanced Computer Communications, which he led through a $290 million acquisition by telecommunications giant Ericsson.

Like his two predecessors, Whyte continued to implement changes in an effort to reduce expenses. In July, a reorganization plan was unveiled that called for a 7 percent reduction of the company's employee base, as well as a reorganization of its sales and marketing departments. The plan, which Whyte claimed would make NET more market-focused, was spearheaded by a new top management team.

Heading into the latter part of 1999, NET bolstered efforts to grow its Asian business. In August the company inked three deals—with the Zhejiang Province PTA, the City of Chonging PTA, and the Province of Shandong PTA—pertaining to digital data networks in China. In November an alliance was formed with Toyo Communication Co. Ltd. to further expansion in Japan. Specifically, the two companies teamed up to create a Japanese interface for NET's Promina 800 and Promina 4000 products.

TOWARD AN IP FUTURE: 2000–07

NET kicked off the new millennium by acquiring San Jose, California–based FlowWise, Inc., in a $16 million cash deal. The addition of FlowWise complemented NET's offerings in the wide-area network realm by adding Internet protocol (IP) capabilities.

Following the FlowWise deal, the new millennium brought new changes at NET. In January the company trimmed 300 positions from its employee base as part of a continuing quest to lower costs. In addition, it announced plans to reorganize into two units, including one focused on broadband Internet equipment.

Revenues for 2000 fell to $225.7 million, down from $263.8 million in 1999, and the company recorded a $40.1 million net loss, which was worse than the $7.0 million loss it incurred the previous year. By this time NET had 25,000 of its systems in place with approximately 1,750 customers in 75 countries across the globe.

In May, NET acquired networking solutions provider Convergence Equipment Co. from Global Communication Technologies, Inc., in a $1.5 million cash deal that brought more IP technology to NET, in the form of an IP telephony platform. At this time, NET began doing business as net.com as part of a strategy focused on broadband technology. In addition, the company unveiled its Service Creation Manager (SCREAM) product line. According to a May 30, 2000, *PR Newswire* release, SCREAM was "based on open, non-proprietary architecture" and gave "service providers the tools they need to leverage broadband networks into competitive advantages."

NET ended 2000 with the divesture of its Federal Service Business to CACI International, Inc., which the company said was part of a service creation strategy. Commenting on the move in a December 6, 2000, *PR Newswire* release, Bert Whyte explained: "We are receiving strong endorsement that our message of service creation for service providers is beginning to be heard. The negative market reaction to those carriers focused exclusively on building bandwidth in lieu of developing value-added services for competitive differentiation is yet another indication that we are on the right track. In order to remain focused, it is incumbent upon us to direct all of our energy to delivering our product strategy, while ensuring that our strong government customer base is well served."

Difficult market conditions had a negative impact on NET's sales during the early years of the new century. Revenues fell to $145.7 million in 2001, and the company recorded a net loss of $19.4 million. However, the year was not without progress, as NET settled a trade secret misappropriation lawsuit it had filed against CoSine Communications, Inc., in late 2000. In addition, *Internet Telephony* recognized NET's SCREAM platform with its Product of the Year Award.

NET's focus on VoIP technology increased as the company headed into the middle of the decade. By 2003 the company had forged a co-marketing agreement with software provider Digiquant to develop a VoIP solution with advanced billing features for applications such as wholesale voice communications, calling cards, and electronic toll payment systems. In early 2005 NET announced that France's SCT Telecom had rolled out its SHOUTIP VoIP platform to small and midsized business customers. Several months later, NET revealed plans to further showcase the capabilities of Shout VoIP by joining the Microsoft Partner Solutions Center, a technical program aimed at testing new communications products and services.

In July 2005, another top-level leadership change occurred when President and CEO Bert Whyte was succeeded by C. Nicholas Keating, who had served on the company's board since 2001 and had worked as a NET vice-president from 1987 to 1993. A Fulbright Scholar to Mexico, Keating also served as president and CEO of IP Infusion, Inc., from 2000 to 2004.

Keating was at the helm of NET as the company forged a number of important alliances. These included the renewal of a strategic partnership with Singapore-based Datacraft in April 2006, which had allowed the company to make inroads in the Chinese market since 1994. In January 2007, NET also established a strategic co-marketing alliance with Lisle, Illinois–based Intrinsic Technologies to roll out unified communications and messaging systems that enabled employees to communicate regardless of the device or network involved.

In mid-2007 NET expanded an existing partnership with chipset developer Bay Microsystems to include the development of processing technology for high-speed networking. The partnership, dubbed a "strategic advance" by CEO Keating, was expected to bolster NET's ability to serve federal government clients in areas such as secure data transfer, real-time intelligence gathering, data backup and recovery, and business continuity.

Approaching the 21st century's second decade, NET seemed prepared to maintain its position in the constantly changing market for networking technology.

Paul R. Greenland

PRINCIPAL COMPETITORS

Alcatel-Lucent; Cisco Systems, Inc.; Nortel Networks Corporation.

FURTHER READING

Carlsen, Clifford, "Redwood City Firm Signs Pact with Big Blue," *San Francisco Business Times,* June 22, 1987.

Halstead, Richard, "High-Tech Phone Company Wants to Call Up Investors," *San Francisco Business Journal,* November 3, 1986.

Meeks, Fleming, "I Can Get It for You Wholesale," *Forbes,* February 6, 1989.

"NET Announces Broadband Product Strategy and New Identity—'net.com,'" *PR Newswire,* May 30, 2000.

"net.com Completes Divesture of Federal Service Business," *PR Newswire,* December 6, 2000.

"Network Equipment Technologies and Bay Microsystems Extend Collaboration," *Wireless News,* July 20, 2007.

"Network Equipment Technologies Changes Name to net.com," *Telecomworldwire,* June 1, 2000.

Rothman, Matt, "Cool in a Crisis; Anatomy of a Turnaround: Bringing NET Back from the Brink," *California Business,* July–August 1991.

Nippon Suisan Kaisha, Ltd.

Nippon Building
2-6-2 Otemachi
Chiyoda-Ku
Tokyo, 100-8686
Japan
Telephone: (81 3) 3244 7101
Fax: (81 3) 3244 7426
Web site: http://www.nissui.co.jp

Public Company
Incorporated: 1943
Employees: 7,764
Sales: ¥552.87 billion ($2.5 billion) (2006)
Stock Exchanges: Tokyo
Ticker Symbol: 1332
NAIC: 424460 Fish and Seafood Merchant Wholesalers

■ ■ ■

Nippon Suisan Kaisha, Ltd., also known as Nissui, is one of the world's leading fishing and seafood companies. In Japan, the world's largest fish market, Nissui holds the second position, trailing only the Maruha-Nichiro group. The company operates through two primary divisions: Marine Products (including fishing, fish farming, and fish purchasing) and Foods (including frozen and prepared seafood).

Marine Products are the company's historic core; the division represents the firms globally operating fishing fleet, as well as its growing fish-farming operations in Chile, the United States, Australia, and New Zealand.

This division continues to represent 42.4 percent of the company's sales.

In efforts to diversify, however, Nissui is also focusing on its Foods division. This division includes the company's production of frozen and shelf-stable processed seafood, including breaded fish and shrimp and the like. The Foods division includes the popular Nissui brand in Japan, and Gorton's, the leading processed seafood brand in the United States. In 2006, the Foods division accounted for more than 50 percent of Nissui's total revenues of ¥552.87 billion ($2.5 billion).

Other divisions include General Distribution, which supports the group's other division with freezing and cold storage operations, as well as specialized logistics; and Pharmaceuticals, especially seafood-derived substances for medical use and nutritional supplements. Japan remains the company's core market, accounting for 85 percent of its sales, but it has been building its presence in the United States, acquiring Georgia's King & Prince Seafood, and Gloucester, Massachusetts–based FW Bryce. The company also operates fishing and processing subsidiaries in Redmond, Washington, and in Alaska. Other Nissui subsidiaries are present in the Netherlands, Singapore, Spain, Thailand, Denmark, Canada, and Indonesia. Nissui is listed on the Tokyo Stock Exchange and is led by president and CEO Naoya Kakizoe.

FIRST TRAWLER IN 1908

Advances in fishing technology at the beginning of the 20th century launched the transformation of Japan's fishing industry from one based on small-scale, coastal fishermen into the world's largest, most sophisticated, and, some would say, most voracious fishing fleet. The development of stronger engines, netting machinery, and new communications devices in the years leading into World War I provided the setting for the creation of Japan's first large-scale fishing companies.

An important moment came in 1908, when Ichiro Tamura built Japan's first steel-frame trawling vessel. In 1911, Tamura created the Tamura Kisan Company and its Tamura Steamship Fishery Division, which began trawling operations in partnership with Kosuke Kunishi. This partnership would grow into the latter-day Nippon Suisan. However, Japan's entry into World War I, and the concentration of the nation's resources on the war effort, meant that the domestic fishing industry grew little during the war years.

Renamed Kyodo Gyogyo Kaisha, Ltd., the young fishery department made a fresh start in 1919. The success of its operations during the following ten years sparked a bolder venture. On April 6, 1929, the company sent a trawler far beyond Japanese waters to begin fishing operations in the Bering Sea. Six years later, another trawler was sent to Mexico's Gulf of California to begin shrimp fishing, and still another went to fish in Argentine waters. By 1937, the company, renamed Nippon Suisan Kaisha, Ltd., was the largest company in Japan involved in conducting trawler and factory-ship operations. On factory ships, marine products were processed and canned or packaged right on the ship and then transported directly to distribution centers to be sent to markets worldwide. Nissui, however, distributed most of its fresh seafood to large "coldchain" wholesale stores with vast refrigeration facilities to be sold in local markets.

In 1938, Nissui launched what was at the time the largest trawler in the world: the 980-ton *Suruga Maru*. The waters of the Pacific were already churning with Japanese naval maneuvers, however, in preparation for a massive war effort. To an even greater degree than World War I, World War II devastated domestic businesses, particularly fisheries, whose operations depended on venturing beyond the nation's borders. After Japan's defeat, the fisheries lost valuable island bases on four small islands in the Kurile chain north of Hokkaido, whose waters had afforded particularly rich harvests. (Although the waters were technically accessible to Japanese fishing boats, they found the new owners—the Soviets—less than hospitable.)

During nearly seven years of occupation by the Allied forces, profound changes were made in the structure of Japan's government, economy, and businesses. Free enterprise with firm government controls, plus some financial help from the United States, helped many struggling businesses—including Nissui—gain or regain a substantial portion of their markets. The company went public in 1949, listing its stock on the Tokyo exchange. In that year, too, Nissui relaunched its first processing operations, opening a canning plant in Hakodate. By the time the Treaty of San Francisco and the United States–Japan Security Treaty were signed in April 1952, ending the occupation, Nissui was ready to resume fishing operations in the northern seas.

POSTWAR EXPANSION

In that year, too, the company launched production of fish sausages, which became one of its bestsellers in Japan. By 1962, the company was ready to launch its processed foods operations on an industrial level and set up a new factory in Hachioji. Along with the rapid recovery of the Japanese economy, the fishing industry boomed, and by the end of the decade Nissui had extended trawling operations along the coasts of Africa, Australia, and New Zealand.

The largest trawler built in Japan in 1960 was Nissui's, at 2,500 tons. The company continued to build larger and larger vessels; by 1970 a 5,000-ton trawler and 21,700-ton factory ship had been added to Nissui's fleet. In 1967, the company began trawling operations off the east coast of North America.

The first outpost Nissui built after World War II was in Las Palmas, on the Canary Islands, off the west coast of Africa in 1962. The company also set up subsidiaries in North America, in Halifax, Canada, and, in 1974, in Seattle, Washington.

In order to broaden the company's line of marine products and reach new markets, Nissui began to enter into joint ventures with companies in foreign countries during the 1970s—the first four were in Indonesia, Spain, Chile, and Argentina. These joint ventures, cooperatives, and overseas trawling operations have added a variety of seafood from remote waters to the extensive array Nissui harvests in Japan's coastal waters. Nissui also cultivated large fish farms, oyster beds, and edible seaweed in Japanese waters. Seaweed gained in

KEY DATES

1908: Ichiro Tamura builds first steel-frame trawler in Japan then founds Tamura Kisan Company in 1911.

1949: Company goes public as Nippon Suisan Kaisha and launches canning operations.

1962: Industrial-scale production of processed foods begins under Nissui label at new factory in Hachiioji.

1974: Unisea subsidiary is established in the United States.

1988: Fish-farming business in Chile is acquired.

2001: As part of shift to branded foods operations, company acquires Gorton's and Blue Water companies from Unilever.

2005: A breaded shrimp business, King & Prince, based in the United States, is acquired.

2006: Company acquires FW Bryce in the United States and Nordic Seafood in Denmark, and opens new factory in Kashima, Japan.

importance with the growth in popularity of health foods and natural foods during the 1970s and 1980s.

In 1974, Nissui began sending large trawlers to the Antarctic seas to fish for krill, several varieties of small sea creatures rich in protein and highly marketable when harvested and processed into feed for livestock, poultry, and farmed fish. At that time, the market for krill was undeveloped because of the high cost of transporting krill from Antarctica. During the next decade, many companies tried fishing for krill, but most were unable to make it cost-effective. The problem was particularly acute during and after the OPEC oil embargo of 1973. Nissui, however, was one of the few fisheries other than Soviet fisheries to persevere and succeed in making money from krill.

In 1976 an international agreement extended the jurisdiction of each coastal nation by 200 miles into its bordering waters. Nissui, like other fisheries that routinely ventured into foreign waters, had to make major changes in the conduct of its business. One solution was to concentrate more on fishing on the open sea. Another was a quota system negotiated by the Japanese government with nations whose waters Japanese fishermen wanted to enter. Still another solution was to purchase seafood from the foreign fisheries entitled to fish within the 200-mile limit. Nonetheless, by the late 1980s (particularly after the United States

abolished the granting of fishing quotas to foreign vessels in the North Pacific Ocean) Nissui was forced to recognize the need to adapt in the face of the looming depletion of the world's oceans.

SHIFTING TO FOOD PROCESSING FOR THE NEW CENTURY

Nissui developed a twofold strategy, calling on the one hand to develop its own fish-farming operations, and, on the other, to expand its food processing business. This led the company to found a new subsidiary, called Great Land Seafood in Redmond, Washington, which began producing crab-flavored fish paste. In 1990, the company formed a joint venture with foods giant ConAgra to develop and market frozen foods for the Japanese market. Meanwhile, the company had also boosted its surimi production with the launch of a new, state-of-the-art processing vessel. The company also extended its seafood processing operations to Thailand, setting up the A&N Foods Company joint venture, and to South Korea, through another joint venture, Dongil Frozen Foods, from 1987.

Nissui's fish-farming efforts were also gaining speed. The company, which had established fishery bases in Chile in 1978 and Argentina in 1981, returned to the region to establish its first fish-farming operations. In 1988, the company acquired Chile-based Salmones Antártica, which specialized in the production of salmon and trout. Nissui's aquaculture operations also spread to the Southeast Asian region, notably in Indonesia, and then in mainland China. Into the 2000s, the company acquired a 50 percent stake in New Zealand's Sealord. The company also established a yellowfish farm in Japan in 2004. In 2006, the company acquired tuna-farming operations through its acquisition of Natakani Suisan.

Yet Nissui's major growth came through the development of its food processing operations. For this, the company focused on two primary markets: Japan, which remained the world's single-largest consumer of fish and seafood products, and the United States. The company's U.S. presence took a giant leap forward in 2001, when the company paid Unilever $175 million to acquire Gorton's, based in Massachusetts, the country's leading producer of branded frozen fish products. That purchase also gave the company control of the Blue Water brand, the second largest in Canada. The following year, the company acquired 25 percent of Alaska Ocean Seafood, and then turned to Peru, where it bought NAL Peru, which focused on fish meal and fish oil.

Nissui raised industry eyebrows through its purchase of breaded shrimp specialist King & Prince

Seafood, based in Georgia, in the United States. The acquisition, which cost nearly $150 million, gave the company stronger access to the country's restaurant sector. By 2006, the company had added to its U.S. presence through its purchase of Gloucester-based FW Bryce, a leading importer of frozen seafood to the United States.

By the end of that year, Nissui's Foods division had become its largest operation, accounting for more than 50 percent of its sales. Yet Nissui continued to invest in its Marine Products division. The company targeted expansion into Europe, opening a seafood laboratory in the Netherlands, and buying the Europacifico seafood marketing group in Spain. The company also acquired a stake in Nordic Seafood in Denmark in 2006. In Japan, Nissui launched a partnership with Kyowa Suisan and completed construction of a new factory in Kashima. By then, too, the company had built a new factory for its Chinese operations, in Qingdao. At the end of 2007, the company's Chilean subsidiary announced the launch of a local joint venture to market its production of fish fillets and processed foods there.

Nissui's vertical integration efforts had enabled it to transform itself from primarily a fishing company to an integrated marine products group. The company's research and development efforts had also enabled it to build its Pharmaceuticals division, notably with the launch of fish-derived EPA products in 2004. The company had also established strong specialized frozen foods logistics operations, regrouped under a new subsidiary in April 2007. Nissui appeared to have prepared itself for the challenges facing the international seafood industry in the 21st century.

M. L. Cohen

PRINCIPAL SUBSIDIARIES

Carry Net Co., Ltd.; Chilldy Co., Ltd.; Emdepes (Chile); Gorton's Inc. (United States); Hohsui Corporation; Kanesho Co., Ltd.; Kitakyushu Nissui Co., Ltd.; Kurose Suisan Co., Ltd; Kyowa Tecnos Co., Ltd; N.A.L. (Chile); Nippo Shokuhin Kogyo Co., Ltd; Nippon Cookery Co., Ltd; Nippon Suisan (U.S.A.),Inc.; Nish-

isho Co., Ltd; Nissui Engineering Co., Ltd; Nissui Marine Industries Co., Ltd; Nissui Pharmaceutical Co., Ltd; Nissui Shipping Corporation; Pesantar (Argentina); Pespasa (Argentina); Salmones Antártica S.A. (Chile); Seibu Reizo Shokuhin Co., Ltd; Teion Co., Ltd; Tobu Reizo Shokuhin Co., Ltd; Unisea,Inc. (United States); Yamatsu Suisan Co., Ltd.; Yokohama Trading Corporation.

PRINCIPAL DIVISIONS

Marine Products; Foods; General Distribution; Pharmaceuticals.

PRINCIPAL COMPETITORS

SYSCO Corporation; Marubeni Corporation; EDEKA ZENTRALE AG; Maruha Group Inc.; Marine Harvest; Pesca S.A.; Dagrofa A/S; Thai Union Manufacturing Company Ltd.; Brake Brothers Ltd.; Icelandic Group hf.

FURTHER READING

"Gorton's Enters into Merger with King & Prince Seafood," *Quick Frozen Foods International,* July 2005, p. 52.

Hedlund, Steven, "Nissui Buys FW Bryce," *Seafood Business,* May 2006, p. 6.

"Japan's Nippon Suisan Launches Grouper Cultivation in China," *AsiaPulse News,* October 8, 2003.

"Japan's Seafood Cos Stepping Up Overseas Sales," *AsiaPulse News,* October 11, 2007.

McNeill, David, and Michael McCarthy, "Canned! Food Firms Bail Out of Whaling," *Independent,* April 5, 2006, p. 3.

"Nippon Suisan Kaisha in Consortium to Expand Saury Fish Exports," *AsiaPulse News,* October 22, 2007.

"Nippon Suisan Raising Branded Stakes with Takeover of Gorton's, BlueWater," *Quick Frozen Foods International,* October 2001, p. 34.

"Nippon Suisan to Construct European Satellite Lab," *JCNN News Summaries,* June 11, 2007.

"Nippon Suisan to Expand Chilean Fish Farming Ops by 50 Pct.," *AsiaPulse News,* March 1, 2007.

Redmayne, Peter, "Nippon Suisan Gambles on Breading Shrimp," *Seafood Business,* August 2005, p. 16.

"Seafood Maker Nippons Suisan Sees 38.8% Profit Surge in FY 2006," *Kyodo News International,* May 16, 2007.

Wright, James, "NGOs Confront Gorton's over Parent Nissui's Whaling," *Seafood Business,* January 2006, p. 6.

Nissan Motor Company Ltd.

17-1 Ginza, 6-chome
Chuo-ku
Tokyo, 104-8023
Japan
Telephone: (81 813) 35435523
Fax: (81 813) 35440109
Web site: http://www.nissan-global.com

Public Company
Incorporated: 1933
Employees: 183,356
Sales: ¥10.46 trillion ($87.4 billion) (2006)
Stock Exchanges: Tokyo NASDAQ
Ticker Symbols: 7201; NSANY
NAIC: 336111 Automobile Manufacturing; 336112 Light Truck and Utility Vehicle Manufacturing; 551112 Offices of Other Holding Companies

■ ■ ■

Nissan Motor Co. Ltd. is one of the world's top automakers, selling nearly 3.5 million vehicles per year and boasting a market capitalization that places it fourth in the industry worldwide. The Tokyo-based company builds and markets a broad range of models that includes the Maxima, Infiniti, Versa, and Sentra automobiles, the Xterra sport-utility vehicle, and the Pathfinder truck.

The North American market is Nissan's largest, accounting for more than 31 percent of its vehicles sales, with Japan adding 21 percent, the Asian and Oceania regions accounting for 17 percent; and Latin American markets adding 8 percent. The company supports its global sales with manufacturing facilities in Japan, the United States, Taiwan, China, Thailand, Philippines, South Africa, Indonesia, Iran, Egypt and Kenya.

Faced with collapse at the end of the 1990s, Nissan's rebound was largely due to its global alliance with French automaker Renault, which acquired a 44 percent ownership stake in Nissan. The alliance's annual combined output topped six million vehicles in 2007. Part of the alliance's success has been its ability to share engines, transmissions and vehicle platforms across the two company's automotive models. The companies also have highly complementary operations, as Renault is especially strong in Europe. Architect of Nissan's transformation is Carlos Ghosn, who serves as CEO for both Renault and Nissan. In 2006, Nissan's sales reached ¥10.46 trillion ($87.4 billion).

EARLY HISTORY

In 1911 Masujiro Hashimoto, a U.S.-trained engineer, founded the Kwaishinsha Motor Car Works in Tokyo. Hashimoto dreamed of building the first Japanese automobile, but lacked the capital. In order for his dream to come true, he contacted three men—Kenjiro Den, Rokuro Auyama, and Keitaro Takeuchi—for financial support. To acknowledge their contribution to his project, Hashimoto named his car DAT, after their last initials. In Japanese, "dat" means "escaping rabbit" or "running very fast."

Debuting in 1914, the first DAT was marketed and sold as a ten horsepower runabout. Another version, referred to as "datson" or "son of dat," was a two-seater

COMPANY PERSPECTIVES

This is an exciting time. In pursuit of environmentally sustainable mobility, we are now engaged in a great race—one of the greatest engineering competitions in history. The outcome will deliver significant benefit to humanity. And within our industry it will distinguish the winners from the rest. Where will the solutions be found? Will it be it fuel-cells, electric cars, bio-fuels, advanced diesels, hybrids—or something not yet invented? No one knows. As yet there is no "silver bullet" and no winner in sight. Still, we are confident that effective solutions are within reach. But when a winner does emerge the decision will not be made by engineers. Consumer demand is the most powerful force for global environmental progress. And it is very democratic: by exercising their right to choose, every new car buyer in every country gets a vote. So consumers will dictate both the pace of change and its direction.

This poses a significant challenge. Since no one knows which solution will prevail, we must invest massively in R&D in pursuit of every viable alternative. Fortunately, Nissan is now ready to go the distance in this race.

sports car produced in 1918. One year later, Jitsuyo Jidosha Seizo Company, another Nissan predecessor, was founded in Osaka. Kwaishinsha and Jitsuyo Jidosha Seizo combined in 1926 to establish the Dat Jidosha Seizo Company. Five years later, the Tobata Imaon Company, an automotive parts manufacturer, purchased controlling interest in the company. Tobata Imaon's objective was to mass-produce products that would be competitive in quality and price with foreign automobiles.

In 1932, "Datson" became "Datsun," thus associating it with the ancient Japanese sun symbol. The manufacturing and sale of Datsun cars was taken over in 1933 by the Jidosha Seizo Company, Ltd., which was established in Yokohama that year through a joint venture between Nihon Sangyo Company and Tobata Imaon. In 1934 the company changed its name to Nissan Motor Co., Ltd., and one year later the operation of Nissan's first integrated automobile factory began in Yokohama under the technical guidance of American industrial engineers.

Datsun cars, however, were not selling as well as expected in Japan. Major U.S. automobile manufacturers, such as General Motors Corporation (GM) and the Ford Motor Company, had established assembly plants in Japan during this time. These companies dominated the automobile market in Japan for ten years, while foreign companies were discouraged from exporting to the United States by the Great Depression of 1929.

With the advent of World War II in 1941, Nissan's efforts were directed toward military production. During wartime, the Japanese government ordered the motor industry to halt production of passenger cars and, instead, to produce much needed trucks. Nissan also produced engines for airplanes and torpedo boats.

POSTWAR RECOVERY AND OVERSEAS EXPANSION

After World War II, the Japanese auto industry had to be completely recreated. Technical assistance contracts were established with foreign firms such as Renault, Hillman, and Willys-Overland. In 1952 Nissan reached a license agreement with the United Kingdom's Austin Motor Company Ltd. With American technical assistance and improved steel and parts from Japan, Nissan became capable of producing small, efficient cars, which later provided the company with a marketing advantage in the United States.

The U.S. market was growing, but gradually. Nonetheless, Nissan felt that Americans needed low-priced economy cars, perhaps as a second family car. Surveys of the U.S. auto industry encouraged Nissan to display its cars at the Imported Motor Car Show in Los Angeles. The exhibition was noticed by *Business Week*, but as an analyst wrote in 1957, "With over 50 foreign car makers already on sale here, the Japanese auto industry isn't likely to carve out a big slice of the U.S. market for itself."

Nissan considered this criticism as it struggled to improve domestic sales. Small-scale production resulted in high unit costs and high prices. In fact, a large percentage of Datsun cars were sold to Japanese taxi companies. However, Kawamata, the company's new and ambitious president, was determined to increase exports to the United States. Kawamata noted two principal reasons for his focus on exports: "Increased sales to the U.S.A. would give Nissan more prestige and credit in the domestic markets as well as other areas and a further price cut is possible through mass producing export cars."

By 1958 Nissan had contracted with two U.S. distributors, Woolverton Motors of North Hollywood, California, and Chester G. Luby of Forest Hills, New

KEY DATES

1911: Masujiro Hashimoto founds the Kwaishinsha Motor Car Works in Tokyo.

1914: Hashimoto introduces his first car, the DAT.

1918: The Datson model is first produced.

1932: The Datson brand is changed to Datsun.

1933: The manufacturing and sale of Datsun cars is taken over by the Jidosha Seizo Company, Ltd.

1934: Jidosha Seizo changes its name to Nissan Motor Co., Ltd.

1943: The company makes military trucks and engines for airplanes and torpedo boats.

1951: Nissan becomes a publicly traded company.

1952: Nissan enters into a license agreement with U.K.-based Austin Motor Company Ltd.

1958: Export of cars to the U.S. market begins.

1966: The company merges with Prince Motor Company Ltd.

1981: The company begins changing its name from Datsun to Nissan in the U.S. market.

1989: The Infiniti line of luxury automobiles is introduced.

1992: The company posts the first pretax loss in its history as a public company; Nissan introduces the Altima small luxury sedan and the Quest minivan, the latter a joint development with Ford Motor Company.

1999: Nissan and Renault S.A. enter into a global alliance, and a massive restructuring begins.

2000: Nissan returns to profitability; Renault raises stake to 44 percent, while Nissan acquires 15 percent of Renault.

2007: Nissan-Renault alliance is Japan's second largest automaker after Toyota.

York. Nevertheless, sales did not improve as quickly as Nissan had hoped. As a result, Nissan sent two representatives to the United States to help increase sales: Soichi Kawazoe, an engineer and former employee of GM and Ford; and Yutaka Katayama, an advertising and sales promotion executive. Each identified a need for the development of a new company to sell and service Datsuns in the United States. By 1960 Nissan Motor Corporation, based in Los Angeles, had 18 employees, 60 dealers, and a sales total of 1,640 cars and trucks. The success of the Datsun pickup truck in the U.S. market encouraged new dealerships.

Datsun assembly plants were built in Mexico and Peru during the 1960s. In 1966 Nissan merged with the Prince Motor Company Ltd.—gaining the Skyline and Gloria models—and two years later Datsun passenger cars began production in Australia. During 1969 cumulative vehicle exports reached one million units. This was a result of Katayama and Kawazoe's efforts to teach Japanese manufacturers to build automobiles comparable to U.S. cars. This meant developing mechanical similarities and engine capacities that could keep up with American traffic.

The introduction of the Datsun 240Z marked the debut of foreign sports cars in the U.S. market. Datsun began to receive good reviews from automotive publications in the United States, and sales began to improve. Also at this time, the first robotics were installed in Nissan factories to help increase production.

FROM ECONOMY CARS TO LUXURY SEDANS

In 1970, Japan launched its first satellite on a Nissan rocket. Only five years later, Nissan export sales reached $5 million. However, allegations surfaced that Nissan U.S.A. was "pressuring and restricting its dealers in various ways: requiring them to sell at list prices, limiting their ability to discount, enforcing territorial limitations," according to author John B. Rae. In 1973 Nissan U.S.A. agreed to abide by a decree issued from the U.S. Department of Justice that prohibited it from engaging in such activities.

The 1970s marked a slump in the Japanese auto industry as a result of the oil crisis. Gasoline prices started to increase, and then a number of other difficulties arose. U.S. President Richard Nixon devalued the dollar and announced an import surcharge: transportation prices went up and export control was lacking. To overcome these problems, Nissan U.S.A. brought in Chuck King, a 19-year veteran of the auto industry, to improve management, correct billing errors, and minimize transportation damages. As a result, sales continued to increase with the help of Nissan's latest model, the Datsun 210 "Honeybee," which was capable of traveling 41 miles on one gallon of gas.

In 1976 the company began the production of motorboats. During this time, the modification of the Datsun model to U.S. styling also began. Additions included sophisticated detailing, roof racks, and air conditioning. The new styling of the Datsun automobiles was highlighted with the introduction of the 1980 model 200SX.

During the 1980s Nissan established production facilities in Italy, Spain, West Germany, and the United

Kingdom. An aerospace cooperative agreement with Martin Marietta Corporation also was concluded, and the Nissan CUE-X and MID4 prototypes were introduced. In 1981, the company began the long and costly process of changing its name from Datsun to Nissan in the U.S. market.

The new generation of Nissan automobiles included high-performance luxury sedans. They featured electronic control, variable split four-wheel drive, four-wheel steering, an "intelligent" engine, and a satellite navigation system, as well as other technological innovations. Clearly, the management of Nissan had made a commitment to increase expenditures for research and development. In 1986 Nissan reported that the company's budget for research and development reached ¥170 billion, or 4.5 percent of net sales.

During the late 1980s, Nissan evaluated future consumer trends. From this analysis, Nissan predicted that consumers would prefer a car with high performance, high speed, innovative styling, and versatile options. All of these factors were taken into account to form "a clear image of the car in the environment in which it will be used," said Yukio Miyamori, a director of Nissan. Cultural differences also were considered in this evaluation. One result of this extensive market analysis was the company's 1989 introduction of its Infiniti line of luxury automobiles.

The use of robotics and computer-aided design and manufacturing reduced the time required for computations on aerodynamics, combustion, noise, and vibration characteristics, enabling Nissan to have an advantage in both the domestic and foreign markets. The strategy of Nissan's management during the late 1980s was to improve the company's productivity and thus increase future competitiveness.

STRUGGLES IN THE NINETIES

By the start of the next decade, however, Nissan's fortunes began to decline. Profits and sales dropped, quelling hopes that the 1990s would be as lucrative as the 1980s. Nissan was not alone in its backward tumble, however: each of the major Japanese carmakers suffered damaging blows as the decade began. The yen's value rose rapidly against the dollar, which crimped U.S. sales and created a substantial price disparity between Japanese and U.S. cars. At the same time, the United States' three largest automobile manufacturers showed a surprising resurgence during the early 1990s. According to some observers, Japanese manufacturers had grown complacent after recording prolific gains to surpass U.S. manufacturers. In the more cost-conscious 1990s, they allowed the price of their products to rise just as U.S.

manufacturers reduced costs, improved efficiency, and offered more innovative products.

In addition, the global recession that sent many national economies into a tailspin in the early 1990s caught Nissan with its resources thinly stretched as a result of its bid to unseat its largest Japanese rival, Toyota Motor Corporation. Toyota, much larger than Nissan and possessing deeper financial pockets, was better positioned to sustain the losses incurred from the global economic downturn. Consequently, Nissan entered its ninth decade of operation facing formidable obstacles.

The first financial decline came in 1991, when the company's consolidated operating profit plummeted 64.3 percent to ¥125 billion ($886 million). Six months later, Nissan registered its first pretax loss since becoming a publicly traded company in 1951—¥14.2 billion during the first half of 1992. The losses mounted in the next two years, growing to ¥108.1 billion in 1993 and ¥202.4 billion by 1994, or nearly $2 billion. To arrest the precipitous drop in company profits, Nissan's management introduced various cost-cutting measures—such as reducing its materials and manufacturing costs—which saved the company roughly $1.5 billion in 1993, with an additional $1.2 billion savings realized in 1994.

Nissan also became the first Japanese company to close a plant in Japan since World War II and cut nearly 12,000 workers in Japan, Spain, and the United States from its payroll. Nissan also was staggering under a debt load that reached as high as $32 billion and threatened to bankrupt the company. Only intervention from Nissan's lead lender, Industrial Bank of Japan, kept the company afloat.

There were some positive signs in the early 1990s to inspire hope for the future. Nissan's 1993 sales increased nearly 20 percent, vaulting the carmaker past Honda Motor Co., Ltd., to reclaim the number two ranking in import sales to the all-important U.S. market. Much of this gain was attributable to robust sales of the Nissan Altima, a replacement for its Stanza model, which was introduced in 1992 and marketed in the United States as a small luxury sedan priced under $13,000. To the joy of Nissan's management, however, the Altima typically was purchased with various options added on, giving the company an additional $2,000 to $3,000 per car. Nissan also was encouraged by strong sales of its Quest minivan, which was introduced in the United States in 1992 and had been developed jointly with Ford Motor, which marketed its own version, the Ford Windstar.

Nissan's losses continued through the fiscal year ending in March 1996, cumulating to $3.2 billion over a four-year span. The company's return to profitability in fiscal 1997 came about in part because of the cost-cutting program and in part from the yen's dramatic depreciation against the dollar. Despite the return to the black, Nissan remained a troubled company. From its 1972 peak of 34 percent, the company's share of the Japanese auto market had fallen to 20 percent by early 1997. Competition from the more financially stable Toyota and Honda played a factor in this decline, but Nissan also hurt itself by failing to keep pace with changing consumer tastes both in Japan and in overseas markets. For example, Nissan was behind its rivals in adding minivans and sport-utility vehicles to its product lineup, having for years dismissed these sectors as passing fads. Meanwhile, minivans, sport-utility vehicles, and station wagons accounted for half of all passenger car sales in Japan by early 1997, up from just more than 10 percent in 1990.

In the U.S. market, the Altima lost ground to two midsized rivals, the Honda Accord and the Toyota Camry, because Nissan's model was smaller and thus less desirable. In the luxury car sector, Toyota's Lexus line became the hot brand in the United States, triumphing over the Infiniti. Because of these and other factors, Nissan returned to the red for fiscal years 1998 and 1999. Although the losses were not as large as earlier in the decade, the company's continued sky-high debt load—which stood at $19.7 billion in late 1998—did not bode well for Nissan's future.

ALLIANCE BUILDING IN THE 21ST CENTURY

The late 1990s was a period of intense consolidation in the auto industry, stemming from rapid globalization, the increasing cost of developing ever more sophisticated vehicles, and worldwide automotive production overcapacity. The November 1998 merger of Daimler-Benz AG and Chrysler Corporation that formed DaimlerChrysler AG was the largest partnership created in this period, but there were a number of smaller mergers, acquisitions, and strategic alliances as well. Both Nissan and Renault S.A. of France were eagerly looking for a partner in order to compete in the 21st century. Nissan was rebuffed by both DaimlerChrysler and Ford and Renault was turned away by other Japanese automakers, before the two companies reached an agreement on a global alliance in March 1999. The combination of Nissan and Renault made strategic sense in that the companies' main sales territories and production locales were complementary. In vehicle sales, Nissan was strongest in Japan and other parts of Asia, the United States, Mexico, the Middle East, and South Africa, while Renault concentrated on Europe, Turkey, and South America. The production side followed a similar pattern. On a global basis, the two companies held just more than a nine percent market share, which would position the combination number four in the worldwide auto industry.

As part of the agreement, Renault pumped $5.4 billion into cash-hungry Nissan in exchange for a 37 percent stake in Nissan Motor and a 22.5 percent stake (later raised to 26 percent) in Nissan Diesel Motor Co., a heavy truck unit. Although it did not secure complete control of Nissan, Renault gained veto power over capital expenditures and installed Carlos Ghosn (rhymes with "bone") as Nissan's chief operating officer (he became president as well in 2000). The Brazilian-born Ghosn was an executive vice-president at Renault and had engineered a rapid turnaround there after joining the company in 1996. French newspapers tagged him with the nickname "le cost killer" because of his tenacious approach to cost cutting—his Renault restructuring slashed $3.5 billion in costs over a three-year period.

The capital injection from Renault quickly reduced Nissan's debt load to ¥1.4 trillion ($13 billion). Ghosn rapidly began implementing a massive restructuring of Nissan. Nonautomotive operations began to be divested, including mobile and car telephone operations and the aerospace division. Nissan's forklift unit was likely to be sold and Nissan Diesel was a candidate for sale as well, given that Nissan Motor had declared that making cars and light trucks was its core business. In early 2000 Nissan sold a stake it held in Fuji Heavy Industries Ltd. As for the automotive operations, Ghosn in October 1999 laid out a tough cost-containment program slated to be completed by 2002.

The program included: a 14 percent workforce reduction—representing 21,000 jobs, primarily in Japan—through attrition, early retirement, and noncore business spinoffs; the closure of five production plants in Japan in 2001 and 2002; the slashing of ¥1 trillion ($9.5 billion) in annual costs, including a 20 percent reduction in purchasing costs and a 20 percent cut in overhead, the latter to include the elimination of one-fifth of Japanese Nissan dealers; and a 50 percent reduction in debt, to ¥700 billion ($6.5 billion). Ghosn also began tackling the crucial need for a revitalization of Nissan's bland line of vehicles by substantially increasing capital spending, toward a goal of speeding new products to market four times faster than before. Although such a restructuring was by this time routine in the United States and becoming more commonplace in Europe, Ghosn's plan ran counter to many established business practices in Japan. The biggest question was whether Ghosn could implement the plan without resorting to large-scale layoffs in Japan, which would likely face fierce opposition from workers and labor unions and even from leaders of other Japanese firms. Perhaps to underscore the seriousness of his mission and his determination to turn Nissan around, Ghosn also announced that he would resign if Nissan was not profitable by March 2001.

Ghosn's restructuring had Nissan back in the black by the end of its 2000 fiscal year. The successful turnaround also led the two companies to deepen their relationship, as Renault boosted its stake in Nissan past 44 percent, while Nissan took a 15 percent stake in its French partner. Nissan launched a challenge for itself—to expand its vehicles sales by more than one million by the end of 2004. Again, Nissan met its goal, boosting its vehicle sales to 3.6 million by 2005. The company now became one of the world's fastest-growing carmakers, posting a surge in revenues from $50 million at the beginning of the decade to more than $87 million by 2006. Nissan's growth was all the more remarkable given the declining sales in the overall auto market into the mid-decade. The rescue of Nissan—and its more than 186,000 jobs—transformed Ghosn into an icon in Japan, and even inspired a comic book based on his success in saving the automaker.

A key component to Nissan's success, and the success of the Nissan-Renault alliance had been the companies' decision to develop their models based on common engine, transmission, and vehicle platforms. The decision represented significant cost-savings, while also enabled both companies to move ahead of competitors in vehicle design and technology. As part of the shared platform program, the two companies also began developing a network of shared production facilities, starting with a factory in Brazil opened in 2001.

In 2004, the two companies joined together to launch a new automotive company, Dacia, in Romania. That company launched its first vehicle, the Logan, a low-cost, no-frills concept developed especially to boost the alliance's sales in a developing market. The new vehicle soon became a bestseller for the companies. By 2007, the companies had announced the launch of construction of their latest common production facility, in India's Chennai region, expected to have a capacity of more than 400,000 vehicles per year. In the meantime, Nissan expanded its own production base, buying Egypt's Seoudi Group in 2004. The company also created an engine manufacturing joint venture with China's Dongfeng auto group, setting up a jointly owned factory in China in 2006.

Nissan's success was especially strong in the United States, where its new lineup, led by its high-end Infiniti line, helped that market become the company's largest by 2007. In support of its operations there, the company built a new factory in Canton, Mississippi, in 2003, enabling the company to begin domestic production of its highly popular Sentra line. Another important addition to the company's line came with the launch of a new-generation Versa for the 2007 model year.

The relationship between Nissan and Renault appeared strengthened in 2005, when Louis Schweitzer announced his decision to retire as head of Renault. Schweitzer wanted Ghosn to return to France to take over Renault's top spot. Nonetheless, as Ghosn told *Forbes:* "It was too early. I told him the only way it would work is if I was CEO of both companies." Renault, which by then had been struggling with its own declining sales agreed, and in April 2005, Ghosn took over as that company's CEO as well. By the end of 2007, Ghosn appeared to be working his restructuring magic at Renault. With combined vehicle sales expected to top 6.4 million by the end of that year, the company launched an effort to open its alliance to a third partner, approaching General Motors (in danger of losing its long-held global leadership position to Toyota) with an offer to join the alliance. While those talks fell through, Nissan-Renault remained interested in bringing a North America partner into the alliance. With Ghosn in command, Nissan had been transformed from a failing midsized Japanese automaker to an industry pacesetter.

Jeffrey L. Covell
Updated, David E. Salamie; M. L. Cohen

PRINCIPAL SUBSIDIARIES

Nissan Shatai Co. Ltd.; Aichi Machine Industry Co. Ltd.; JATCO Ltd.; Nissan Kohki Co. Ltd.; Calsonic Kansei Corporation; Nissan Network Holdings Corporation; Nissan Financial Services Co. Ltd.; Nissan Chuo Parts Sales Co. Ltd.; Nissan North America, Inc. (United States); Nissan Canada Inc.; Nissan Mexicana S.A. de C.V. (Mexico); Nissan Europe S.A.S. (France); Nissan International Holding B.V. (Netherlands); Nissan Motor Company (Australia) Pty. Ltd.; Nissan New Zealand Ltd.; Nissan Motor Company South Africa (Pty) Ltd.; Nissan Motor (China) Ltd.; Kinugawa Rubber Industrial Co., Ltd. (Japan; 20.28%); Renault (France; 15.42%).

PRINCIPAL COMPETITORS

Toyota Motor Corporation; General Motors Corporation; Ford Motor Company; Honda Motor Company Ltd.; Daimler AG; Chrysler LLC; Volkswagen AG; Peugeot Citroën Automobiles S.A.; Fiat S.p.A.; Hyundai Motor Company.

FURTHER READING

Armstrong, Larry, "Can Nissan Regain Its Youth?" *Business Week,* July 13, 1998, p. 132.

Beatty, Sally Goll, "Mixed Message: Nissan's Ad Campaign Was a Hit Everywhere but in the Showrooms," *Wall Street Journal,* April 8, 1997, pp. A1+.

Chang, C. S., *The Japanese Auto Industry and the U.S. Market,* New York: Praeger, 1981.

Chrysler, Mack, "Tackling a Big Turnaround: Nissan Chief Says Automaker's Suffering Is Solvable," *Ward's Auto World,* December 1998, p. 14.

Crate, James R., "Japan's Big Five Atone for Sins of Late '80s: Drive to Cut Costs Focuses on Proliferation of Parts," *Automotive News,* May 17, 1993, p. 19.

Diem, William, "The Renault Nissan Deal," *Ward's Auto World,* May 30, 1999.

"Dynamic Duo," *Business Week,* October 23, 2000, p. 26.

Edmondson, Gail, and Emily Thornton, "He Revved Up Renault. Will Nissan Be Next?" *Business Week* (international edition), April 12, 1999, p. 23.

Edmondson, Gail, et al., "Dangerous Liaison: It Could Take 10 Years for Renault-Nissan to Yield a Return," *Business Week* (international edition), March 29, 1999, p. 22.

Edmondson, Gail, and Ian Rowley, "Putting Ford in the Rearview Mirror," *Business Week,* February 12, 2007, p. 44.

Fulford, Benjamin, "Gambatte!" *Forbes,* June 22, 2002, p. 72.

Gross, Ken, "Doomed to Niches?" *Automotive Industries,* May 1992, p. 13.

———, "Learning from Mistakes," *Automotive Industries,* March 1994, p. 64.

Hall, Kenji, "A Letdown on the Lot," *Business Week,* November 21, 2005, p. 64.

Inaba, Yu, "Nissan Motor Company: Aiming for the Top Spot," *Tokyo Business Today,* December 1988, pp. 50+.

———, "Nissan's Management Revolution," *Tokyo Business Today,* October 1989, pp. 38+.

Johnson, Richard, "Nissan Loss Widens to Nearly $2 Billion," *Automotive News,* June 6, 1994, p. 6.

Maskery, Mary Ann, "Nissan Gets First Taste of Red Ink," *Automotive News,* November 9, 1992, p. 6.

Miller, Karen Lowry, and Larry Armstrong, "Will Nissan Get It Right This Time?" *Business Week,* April 20, 1992, p. 82.

Muller, Joann, "The Impatient Mr. Ghosn," *Forbes,* May 22, 2006.

"Nissan Earnings Dive 64.3 Percent," *Automotive News,* June 3, 1991, p. 4.

Rowley, Ian, "Potholes Ahead," *Business Week,* June 12, 2006, p. 42.

Sapsford, Jathon, "A Tuned-Up Nissan Takes on Its Rivals," *Wall Street Journal,* August 12, 1997, p. A10.

Shirouzu, Norihiko, "Nissan Calls Truck Unit Noncore, Possibly Signaling Eventual Sale," *Wall Street Journal,* February 18, 2000, p. A12.

———, "Nissan's Revival Relies on Operating Chief's Agility," *Wall Street Journal,* October 18, 1999, p. A37.

Simison, Robert L., "Nissan's Crisis Was Made in the U.S.A.," *Wall Street Journal,* November 25, 1998, p. B1.

Simison, Robert L., and Norihiko Shirouzu, "Nissan Unveils Tough Program to Cut Costs," *Asian Wall Street Journal,* October 19, 1999, p. 1.

Sobel, Robert, *Car Wars: The Untold Story,* New York: Dutton, 1984.

Strom, Stephanie, "Can Nissan Turn on a Centime: Trying to Revamp a Company and a Corporate Culture," *New York Times,* October 14, 1999, p. C1.

———, "No. 2 and Not Enjoying the Ride: Nissan Announces New Losses and Sweeping Changes," *New York Times,* May 21, 1998, p. D1.

Taylor, Alex, III, "The Man Who Vows to Change Japan Inc.," *Fortune,* December 20, 1999, p. 189.

Thornton, Emily, "Remaking Nissan," *Business Week* (international edition), November 15, 1999, p. 38.

Thornton, Emily, and Kathleen Kerwin, "Back in the Mud: Nissan's Makeover Hasn't Jump-Started Profits," *Business Week* (international edition), November 2, 1998, p. 26.

Thornton, Emily, and Larry Armstrong, "Nissan's Slow U-Turn: Its Recovery Is Far from Complete," *Business Week,* May 12, 1997, p. 54.

Thornton, Emily, et al., "A New Order at Nissan," *Business Week,* October 11, 1999, p. 54.

Updike, Edith, et al., "Japan Is Back," *Business Week,* February 19, 1996, p. 42.

Weinberg, Neil, "Member of the Pack," *Forbes,* May 19, 1997, p. 65.

Welch, David, "Nissan: The Squeaks Get Louder," *Business Week,* May 17, 2004, p. 44.

Woodruff, David, "Cultural Chasm: Renault Faces Hurdles in Bid to Turn Nissan Around," *Asian Wall Street Journal,* March 31, 1999, p. 1.

Nuplex Industries Ltd.

12 Industry Road
Penrose
Auckland, 1061
New Zealand
Telephone: (64 09) 579 2029
Fax: (64 09) 571 0542
Web site: http://www.nuplex.co.nz

Public Company
Incorporated: 1991
Employees: 450
Sales: NZD 1.46 billion ($992.5 million) (2006)
Stock Exchanges: New Zealand Australia
Ticker Symbol: NPX
NAIC: 325211 Plastics Material and Resin Manufacturing; 325212 Synthetic Rubber Manufacturing; 325520 Adhesive and Sealant Manufacturing

■ ■ ■

Nuplex Industries Ltd. is a leading producer of resins, polymers, and other materials used in the production of flooring, paints, inks, plastics, adhesives, and the like. The company also produces functional raw materials; plastics products including packaging, molding, and carpeting; flooring and other construction materials; and even food, nutritional, and pharmaceutical products. Nuplex's Resins division is its largest, accounting for 78 percent of the group's NZD 1.45 billion ($993 million) in sales in 2007.

This product category includes coating resins, adhesive resins, composite resins, and reinforcement process chemicals. Acquisitions have enabled the company to claim the lead in the Australasian region's resins market, as well as a major position in the global market. The companies acquisitions include Australian Chemical Holdings in 1998, Akzo Nobel Coating Resins in 2004, Multichem/Polychem in 2005, and Huntsman Chemical Company's composite resins operations in 2007, as well as a series of smaller acquisitions, including the purchase of a resins factory in China.

Nuplex's Specialties division includes its functional raw materials operations, as well as its other diversified businesses; it contributed 21 percent of group sales in 2007. Nuplex is listed on both the New Zealand and Australian Stock Exchanges. John Hirst is the company's managing director, while Fred Holland, who orchestrated most of the company's growth since the early 1980s, remains company chairman.

FLOORING MANUFACTURER IN 1952

The history of Nuplex may be traced to 1952 when Bill Campbell and friend Max Nairn established a business in Auckland to distribute a newly developed resin-based flooring system to the New Zealand market. These new materials could literally be poured out in order to lay seamless floors and once set offered greater flexibility and resistance to wear than concrete flooring. While the resin-based flooring was initially developed for the institutional sector, the floor coverings and tiles, available in a wide variety of colors and patterns and far less expensive than traditional wood flooring, made them extremely popular for residential markets as well.

Campbell and Nairn called the company Floor Tiles and Parquet NZ Ltd. By 1956, that company had launched its public offering, listing its shares on the New Zealand Stock Exchange. The company also set up a distribution subsidiary to specialize in the installation of the company's flooring products. In 1958, the company set up a small distribution unit in Australia, Vinylpave Products Pty. Ltd.

Campbell in the meantime had continued to focus on expanding the group's range of flooring products and had begun seeking licenses from manufacturers in the United States, Germany, and the United Kingdom. Campbell developed a strong relationship with one company in particular, Revertex (UK), part of a group of resins companies founded in Malaysia in the 1920s. The association, launched in 1957, deepened through the end of the decade, in large part because Revertex did not have any direct operations in the New Zealand and Australian region.

When the New Zealand government drafted new protectionist tariffs, severely restricting imports, Campbell recognized an opportunity to begin manufacturing resins. For this, he turned to Revertex, which supplied the technology in exchange for a 32 percent stake in Floor Tiles and Parquet NZ. Revertex then set up a subsidiary in New Zealand, and in 1967 Floor Tiles and Parquet NZ merged with Revertex NZ, forming Revertex Industries (NZ) Ltd. with Campbell as managing director and, later, company chairman.

Protectionism in New Zealand allowed Revertex NZ to operate profitably, despite the small scale of its manufacturing operations. However, the company faced an increasing number of competitors, leading to a highly fragmented market. By the end of the 1970s, there were more than a dozen resins producers in New Zealand, most of which were subsidiaries of foreign companies and focused on manufacturing and distributing the parent companies' products. Revertex NZ, however, had from the start sought to broaden its product range and the depth of its technology, seeking out new areas for expansion within the small New Zealand market. As such, the company developed a long list of technology agreements and licenses during the 1960s, adding such products as ink, adhesives, paints, and coatings. The expanded product list prompted Revertex NZ to build a new facility in 1971.

The company then launched production of high-temperature resins and branched out as a supplier of raw materials, such as alkyds for the paint industry and unsaturated polyesters used in fiberglass manufacture. The new facility also featured the company's own research and development center, which provided an important step in the company's development. Initially, Revertex sought to adapt existing products, materials, and technologies for the specific weather and UV conditions of the New Zealand market. In the process, however, Revertex also developed new applications for its flooring technologies, adapting them for use as wall coverings, ceilings, and for external applications, before succeeding in developing its own technologies.

FOREIGN OWNERSHIP IN THE EIGHTIES

Through the end of the 1960s, Revertex NZ's export business was largely limited to the Australian market, which had enacted similarly restrictive import policies. When the New Zealand government began taking down its trade barriers in the 1970s, Campbell, joined by future CEO and chairman Fred Holland, recognized that the company's future depended on its ability to establish itself beyond New Zealand. For this the company took advantage of a series of export incentives put into place by the New Zealand government and began developing markets in Hong Kong, Indonesia, Singapore, Thailand, and China through the 1970s.

Unlike many of its New Zealand counterparts, however, Revertex's international expansion carefully avoided a reliance on the government's export subsidies. Instead, while the company made use of the subsidies for the initial start-up phase of its foreign businesses, the new companies were expected to be profitable in their own right. Into the late 1970s, the company sought in particular to expand its operations in Australia and began exporting its resins to that market.

Revertex NZ's expansion plans were challenged, however, when Revertex UK was taken over by Monsanto in 1981. The New Zealand business was then put under control of Monsanto's Australian operations. Bill Campbell moved into the chairman's position, while Fred Holland took over as company CEO. While there were some benefits to its new ownership, Revertex NZ found its foreign growth opportunities limited. The company returned its attention to the New Zealand resins market, which, faced with new competition from foreign suppliers, was ripe for consolidation.

KEY DATES

1952: Bill Campbell and Max Nairn found Floor Tiles and Parquet NZ Ltd.

1956: Company goes public on New Zealand Stock Exchange.

1967: Revertex UK acquires majority control and changes company's name to Revertex NZ.

1981: Monsanto acquires control of company, which is placed under its Australian chemicals business.

1988: Consolidated Press Holdings (CPH) acquires control of the company.

1991: CPH sells company, which is now called Nuplex Industries.

1998: Nuplex acquires Australia Chemical Holdings (ACH), becoming region's largest resins group.

2005: Nuplex acquires Akzo Nobel Coating Resins division in the Netherlands, expanding operations to a global scale.

The company became determined to lead that consolidation; it had already made its first acquisition of the majority stake in Fletcher Chemicals Company, renamed Titan Chemicals, in 1976 and through the 1980s began buying many more of its rivals. In 1988, the company acquired the remainder of Titan Chemicals, as well as another rival, Giant Polymers. By the end of that decade, there were just four larger resins groups left in the country. Revertex, which benefited from the increasing economies of scale, had emerged as the market leader.

Revertex NZ's main factory was destroyed by fire in 1984. While that event adversely affected production and sales it also proved to have a beneficial side, as the company rebuilt the complex into a state-of-the-art manufacturing facility, which came on line in 1985. The following year, the company opened a newly expanded research and development center at the site as well.

Two years later, Revertex NZ found itself under new ownership when Monsanto sold the company, and its Australian parent, Chemplex, to the fast-growing Consolidated Press Holdings (CPH), owned by Australian media magnate Kerry Packer. Under its new owner's policies, Revertex NZ eliminated its debt load, building a sizable treasury. The company put that to use in 1990, when it acquired two more competitors, Lockfast Chemicals and Reese Chemicals. In that year, the

company also changed its name, becoming Nuplex Industries Ltd.

INDEPENDENCE IN THE NINETIES

Just one year later, CPH decided to sell Nuplex to a group of New Zealand–based investors. Independent for the first time in a decade, Nuplex was free to pursue its international expansion. The company naturally targeted Australia first and foremost, particularly as that market was only just at the beginning stages of consolidation. In 1993, Nuplex bought a small resin manufacturer, Frankston Manufacturing, based in Melbourne. That purchase provided the company with a production foothold in Australia and with a more solid position for the launch of its own products on the Australian market. In the meantime, the company carefully studied the Australian market, which, despite its proximity to New Zealand, retained its own distinct character.

In the meantime, Nuplex focused its domestic efforts on expanding its range of businesses. The company bought Stratos Gelcoat, a manufacturer of polyester resins, in 1992. Nuplex also built an extension to its main Penrose facility, expanding its capacity by 30 percent. In 1994, Nuplex built up its construction materials operations, buying two companies, Conspray and Dryvit, which specialized in external cladding and insulation systems. Similarly the group bought another construction materials business in 1996, Plaster Systems Ltd.

During this period, Nuplex attempted a wider diversification. The company entered the waste management industry in the mid-1990s, starting with the purchase of United Environmental. By 1997, the company had also added waste management operations in Australia as well. The company continued to build up a profitable waste management business into the 2000s before selling the division during a restructuring in 2006.

In the meantime, the company's patience in Australia had paid off. In 1998, Nuplex initiated talks with Australian Chemical Holdings (ACH). That company, which was twice the size of Nuplex, had very similar operations to the New Zealand company, with a similar product range. ACH had fallen into financial trouble in the late 1990s. Nuplex initially approached the company with an offer to buy out its small New Zealand operation. When ACH rejected that offer, Nuplex instead launched an offer to acquire the whole of ACH.

Nuplex's acquisition of ACH was remarkable in that it reversed an ongoing trend of Australian business buying up their New Zealand counterparts. It also established Nuplex as the leading resins manufacturer in the Australasian market and set the stage for the company's further expansion onto the global market.

GLOBAL GIANT IN THE 21ST CENTURY

John Hirst, who had joined the company in 1967, took over as CEO of the company in 1998 following Bill Campbell's retirement from the company. Fred Holland, who had built the company from a small concern posting sales of just NZD 25 million in the early 1980s to a regional powerhouse with revenues of more than NZD 400 million, took the chairman's seat.

In 2002, Nuplex entered a bidding war for Asia Pacific Specialty Chemicals, based in Melbourne. APS complemented Nuplex's core resins operations while adding broader expertise in specialty chemicals used in the construction, food, soap, rubber, and other industries. Nuplex succeeded in its bid, paying AUD 47 million. Nuplex then completed several smaller acquisitions in 2004, including that of Melbourne's Megachem, a producer of surfactants and esters, and another Australian company, Colour Dispersion Company, which produced color pigment dispersions. Nuplex also added its first production facility outside of Australia and New Zealand, when it bought a small resins factory in China, called Foshan Veeya Chemical Company. By the end of that year, the company's revenues had surpassed NZD 650 million.

Nuplex's revenues were set to double the following year, as the company took a place in the global market for the first time. This transformation began at the end of 2004, when the company reached an agreement with Akzo Nobel to acquire its Netherlands-based Coating Resins business for NZD 215 million. The purchase not only boosted Nuplex's sales past NZD 1.2 billion, but it also provided the company with an entry into the European and American markets for the first time.

Australia and New Zealand nonetheless remained the group's primary markets into the mid-decade, representing 44 percent and 14 percent of the company's revenues, respectively. Nuplex maintained its commitment to growth in the region, while continuing to drive the consolidation of the resins sector. Nuplex next acquired Multichem/Polychem, paying AUD 44 million at the end of 2005. In 2007, the company spotted a new growth opportunity in Australia, paying AUD 20.3 million for Huntsman Chemical Company. Nuplex had built its empire, literally from the floor up, to

become a major player in the global resins market in the 21st century.

M. L. Cohen

PRINCIPAL SUBSIDIARIES

Asia Pacific Specialty Chemicals Ltd.; Cong Ty Nuplex Resins (Vietnam); Multichem Pty Ltd.; Nuplex Finance Holdings Ltd.; Nuplex Industries (Aust) Pty Ltd. Manufacture; Nuplex Producao de Resinas Ltda (Brazil); Nuplex Resins (Foshan) Co. Ltd. (China); Nuplex Resins (Suzhou) Company Ltd. (China); Nuplex Resins BV (Netherlands); Nuplex Resins Ltd. (United Kingdom); Nuplex Resins LLC (United States); Octel Valvemaster Ltd. (50%); Plaster Systems Ltd.; PT Nuplex Raung Resins (Indonesia; 80%); Quaker Chemical (Australia) Pty Ltd. (49%); Synthese (Malaysia) Sdn bhd (62%); Synthese (Thailand) Company Ltd. (45%).

PRINCIPAL DIVISIONS

Resins; Composites; Paper; Construction Products; Specialty Products; Life Sciences.

PRINCIPAL COMPETITORS

China National Chemical Corporation; Honeywell Burdick and Jackson American Inc.; Sinopec Jinling Company; Sinopec Tianjin Petrochemical Company; SONATRACH; BASF AG; Dow Chemical Company; Vietnam National Chemical Corporation; DuPont Delaware Inc.; Toter Inc.; JFE Holdings Inc.; SABIC; GS-Caltex Corporation; Mitsubishi Chemical Corporation.

FURTHER READING

Forster, Christine, "Nuplex Cuts Profit Outlook Due to Weak Demand, High Costs," *Chemical Week,* April 27, 2005, p. 16.

———, "Two Bidders Vie to Acquire Australian Specialties Maker," *Chemical Week,* May 15, 2002, p. 15.

McCarthy, Ken, and Douglas Mabey, "Nuplex Industries Ltd. (Case History)" in *CANZ Research Programme,* Wellington, N.Z.: Victoria University, August 2001.

"Nuplex Buys Dispersions Maker," *Chemical Week,* March 10, 2004, p. 13.

"Nuplex Buys Surfactants Firm," *Chemical Week,* January 7, 2004, p. 13.

"Nuplex Completes China Acquisition," *Chemical Week,* July 14, 2004, p. 17.

"Resin Firm Sticks It Out as Costs Keep Rising," *New Zealand Herald,* February 23, 2007, p. 3.

"Transition of Akzo Nobel Resins to Nuplex Industries Complete," *Paint & Coatings Industry,* March 2005, p. 28.

Nutrexpa S.A.

Lepanto 410
Barcelona, E-08025
Spain
Telephone: (34 93) 290 02 90
Fax: (34 93) 290 03 42
Web site: http://www.nutrexpa.es

Private Company
Incorporated: 1940
Employees: 1,330
Sales: EUR 350 million ($500 million) (2007)
NAIC: 311320 Chocolate and Confectionery
Manufacturing from Cacao Beans; 551112 Offices
of Other Holding Companies

■ ■ ■

Nutrexpa S.A. is a leading Spanish food company focused primarily on chocolate- and cocoa-based drinks, snacks, and confections. The company's flagship brand is Cola Cao, which has been one of Spain's favorite cocoa drinks since the 1950s and is one of the top five most recognized brands in Spain. Cola Cao is also the company's most global brand, backed by manufacturing and marketing subsidiaries in Chile and China, a distribution subsidiary in Portugal, and the company's own export and international marketing operations.

Another top Nutrexpa brand is its Granja San Francisco Honey brand, produced by bees near the San Francisco monastery. Other brands in the company's portfolio include the popular Nocilla chocolate spread; La Piara, a leading producer of patés and other meat

products; Okey dairy drinks and products; Phoskitos children's snacks; La Cafetera confectionery; and Mesura corn starch and food additives. Nutrexpa remains a private company controlled by the highly secretive Ferrero family. Javier Ventura Ferrero controls most of the company's shares. In 2007, Nutrexpa sales were estimated at more than EUR 350 million ($500 million).

POST–CIVIL WAR FOOD COMPANY

Nutrexpa had its start in the aftermath of the Spanish civil war when José Ignacio Ferrero Cabanach and José Maria Ventura Mallofré founded a small food production company in the district of Gracia in Barcelona. The company's initial product line was comprised of basic processed cooking ingredients, including fish bouillon and yeast. It also developed its own brand, Gloria, which was used for marketing crème caramels and cocoa cream. Another early product, introduced in 1934, was Granja San Francisco Honey; this product became the company's first true success and would remain one of its flagship brands into the next century.

By 1946, Nutrexpa's interests had turned to chocolate, specifically to the production of chocolate drink mixes. In that year, the company launched the product that would put it on Spain's food map: Cola Cao. The powdered cocoa product, thinner than traditional Spanish chocolate drinks but still thicker than such chocolate mixes as Nestlé and Bosco, quickly became a Spanish favorite.

COMPANY PERSPECTIVES

The Nutrexpa Group's mission: grow organically through innovation; actively look for acquisitions to reach a competitive critical mass in the countries where we operate; to achieve profitability through a high level of competitiveness and excellence in every single component of the value chain.

It was only in the mid-1950s, however, that Cola Cao emerged as a truly national favorite. This development was partly the result of a radio advertising campaign launched in 1955. The campaign featured a song composed for the brand. Titled "Canción del Negrito," the song lyrics included the lines: "Yo soy aquel Negrito del Africa tropical/que cultivando cantaba la canción del Cola Cao." The song became a hit, vaulting Cola Cao to national recognition. The surge in demand for the product led the company to build a new factory in the Calle Lepanto district in Barcelona in 1957. Nutrexpa continued to back its new flagship product with strong advertising over the years; in fact, the company became one of the first in Spain to begin advertising on the television in 1962.

FIRST ACQUISITION IN 1964

With two strong brands among its product line, Nutrexpa sought further expansion in the 1960s. The company took out a major competitor in 1964 when it acquired Phoscao, a manufacturer of soluble cocoa powder and other chocolate-based products. In 1970, Nutrexpa extended its range of operations into the snack cakes and cookies sector with the purchase of Galletas Paja, a company based in the Girona-region town of Riudarenes. The move into snack cakes, combined with the company's control of the Phoscao brand, provided the basis for the launch of the company's popular snack cake line, Phoskitos. The company also launched its first exports during the decade.

Nutrexpa built a new production facility in 1979, in Parets del Vallès in Barcelona. This plant featured a new warehousing facility, which took over as the group's central distribution operation for the Spanish market. The new plant and warehouse also enabled Nutrexpa to begin seriously targeting the foreign market for the first time. In that year, the company also inaugurated a new International division, which began developing a marketing and distribution strategy for the global market. In the early 1980s, the company enjoyed

particular success in the Latin American market, and in 1981 Nutrexpa founded a dedicated subsidiary for the region, adding production and distribution facilities in Chile and later opening a factory in Ecuador as well. The Cola Cao brand became the group's international spearhead, accompanied by the Granja San Francisco Honey line. Portugal represented another important market for the company. Accordingly, in 1984, the company put into place a dedicated marketing and distribution subsidiary for that market.

Nutrexpa gained a new product line in 1985 when it acquired Dulces Unzue, a purchase that allowed the company to enter the confectionery sector for the first time. The Dulces Unzue acquisition also extended the company's production network, with a plant in Pamplona. By the end of the decade, Nutrexpa had added another product line to its growing holdings when it acquired Productos Selectos de Cerdo and its La Piara brand of patés, cold cuts and other meat- and fish-based spreads, hams, and delicatessen products in 1988. That company, founded in 1923, had initially targeted the youth market with iron-rich nutritional products, such as its Tapa Negra paté launched in 1974. Over the following decade, however, the company had expanded its range to include the full range of consumer segments. Under Nutrexpa, the company's product line was placed under the La Piara brand. In 1990, Nutrexpa expanded its meats production again with the acquisition of another Spanish company, Jamones Aneto. In another product extension, the company added infant formulas, under the Laboratorios Ordesa brand.

JOINT VENTURE IN CHINA IN 1991

The company's international operations received a new boost in the late 1980s when Nutrexpa became one of the first Spanish food companies to enter the slowly opening People's Republic of China. The company first began shipping its products to China in 1989. By 1991, Nutrexpa had reached a joint-venture agreement with state-owned Limind to build a factory in Tianjin. The new company became known as Tianjin Nutrexpa Food Company and set initial production targets at 2,000 tons per year. For the launch, the company adapted the name of its flagship Cola Cao brand for the local market, changing its name to Galoe Cao (or Gao Le Gao), which translated to "Grow Strong and Tall" in Chinese, a slogan shared by the Chinese Olympic team.

The joint venture proved a strong success for the company, and by the end of the 1990s it had achieved penetration on a national level. In 1999, Nutrexpa inaugurated a second and larger production facility in

KEY DATES

1940: José Ignacio Ferrero Cabanach and José Maria Ventura Mallofré found Nutrexpa as bouillon cube and yeast producer near Barcelona.

1946: The Cola Cao cocoa drink is introduced.

1955: A new ad campaign based on the song "Canción del Negrito" gives Cola Cao national recognition.

1970: Pastry and cookie production begin through acquisition of Galletas Paja.

1979: Nutrexpa International is created in order to develop export sales.

1981: Company's first foreign production subsidiary is created in Portugal.

1991: A joint venture production facility is established in Tianjin, China; company enters Eastern European markets, including Russia.

2002: Nocilla chocolate spread brand is acquired from Unilever.

2004: A partnership agreement is reached with Natraceuticals to develop functional food ingredients.

Tianjin in order to supply the Chinese market. The company by then had also expanded its product range there to include soluble powders, pastries, and cocoa creams. The company adapted its recipe for local tastes, adding new flavors in the new century including banana, vanilla, and strawberry in 2001, orange in 2004, and peach in 2005.

Not all of the group's expansion efforts met with equal success during the 1990s, however. The company attempted to launch its Cola Cao brand in Japan but was forced to withdraw from that market after only a few years. More promising for the company was its plans to enter the Eastern European market, particularly Russia, where it began marketing Cola Cao starting in 1992. The company launched a production subsidiary in Poland during this time. By the end of the decade, Nutrexpa had succeeded in building the brand into the top-selling instant-cocoa drink in Russia. In order to supply the growing demand for its products in that market, the company reached a production agreement with Moscow-based Inforum Prom to begin manufacturing Cola Cao in Russia. The agreement called for the construction of a new factory in Kasimov, in the Ryazan region.

FAMILY OWNED LEADER IN THE NEW CENTURY

In 1990, the company hired its first outside manager, Gianfranco Santoni, who came to the company from a position at Arthur Andersen. While the Ferrero family maintained ultimate control of the group's ownership, according to industry analysts the decision to hire professional management played an important role in Nutrexpa's ability not only to survive the difficult economic climate at the beginning of the 1990s but also to grow into a major food company distributing its products on a global basis.

Still, the family ownership did thwart some of Santoni's aspirations. In 1995, Nutrexpa was on the verge of acquiring rival food products group, Bimbo, then part of the Anheuser-Busch group. The acquisition would have doubled Nutrexpa in size, with sales of more than ESP 100 billion, and would have added a new line of pastas and bakery products. However, after the government refused to provide tax incentives to back the purchase, the Ferrero family quashed the acquisition.

The late 1990s brought a restructuring to Nutrexpa. A holding company structure was adopted with the primary subsidiary, Nutrexpa, overseeing the core Cola Cao and Granja San Francisco Honey operations. Also under the umbrella company was Laboratorios Ordesa, the infant formula operations, the La Piara meats company, and new acquisition Productos Ortiz breads, which was soon sold to rival Bimbo in 2001. Laboratorios Ordesa was eventually spun off as an independent company although the Ferrero family retained a majority stake in the sale.

Next Nutrexpa moved to boost its main cocoa operations, buying the Nocilla brand of cocoa-based products from Unilever plc's Spanish division in 2001. That acquisition was bolstered by another Unilever product family, the Mesura brand of sweeteners and corn starch and other food additives and ingredients. As part of this acquisition, the company took over a factory in Montmelo, in Barcelona. That facility continued to produce Maizena-branded corn starch and Starlux-brand bouillon cubes for Unilever. In the meantime, the addition of Nocilla gave Nutrexpa control of Spain's leading brand of chocolate spread, which boasted a share of nearly 70 percent of the Spanish market.

Nutrexpa continued to invest in its other operations as well. In 2003, the company inaugurated a new factory for its La Piara brand family. The company boasted that the Manlleu, Barcelona–based plant was the most modern paté production unit in Europe. At the same time, Nutrexpa's interests had increasingly turned toward extending its operations into the fast-growing healthful foods sector. As part of that effort, the company launched new fiber-enriched and fruit and cereal formulas of its Cola Cao brand. Nutrexpa also formed a partnership with another Spanish company, Natraceuticals, in order to develop new nutritional and functional foods compounds.

Nutrexpa remained committed to its family-owned status in the new century. At the beginning of 2007, however, the Ferrero family moved to restructure the company's ownership arrangement. As part of that effort, Javier Ventura Ferrero raised his share of the company to 50 percent, in an exchange with his brother, José Maria Ferrero, who then took full control of Laboratorios Ordesa. The other half of Nutrexpa remained controlled by Ferrero's cousins, led by Ignacio Ferrero Chloe. With internationally recognized brands including Cola Cao and Granja San Francisco Honey, Nutrexpa had become one of Spain's leading food groups, with sales estimated to be in excess of EUR 350 million ($500 million) for 2007.

M. L. Cohen

PRINCIPAL SUBSIDIARIES

Cola Cao Food (Tiajin) Co. Ltd. (China); Nutrexpa Chile S.A.; Nutrexpa Portugal.

PRINCIPAL COMPETITORS

Nestlé Espana S.A.; Natra S.A.; Cadbury Espana S.L.; Cantalou S.A.; Zahor S.A.; Lacasa S.A.; Nederland S.A.; Chocovic S.A.

FURTHER READING

Higgins, Kevin T., "Nutrexpa Turns Heads in Honey Package," *Food Engineering,* October 2004, p. 18.

"Javier Ventura Aumenta Su Poder en Nutrexpa y Controla ya un 50%," *Lalo Agustina,* January 25, 2007.

Labiano, Javier, "La Alimentacion Se Concentra," *Epoca,* August 30, 2002, p. 82.

Martinez, Felix, "La Multinacional Española Oculta Se Llama Cola Cao," *El Mundo,* July 7, 1997.

"Nutrexpa/Natraceuticals Functional Prod Deal," *Nutraceuticals International,* April 2004.

"Nutrexpa (Spain) to Produce Cola Cao Drink Range in Russia," *Inzhenernaia Gazeta,* May 29, 2001, p. 3.

"Nutrexpa to Acquire Nocilla and Mesura," *Expansion* (Spain), April 17, 2002.

"Unilever to Invest Two Million at Basque Factory," *Estrategia Empresarial,* June 30, 2004.

Oberto Sausage Company, Inc.

———————————— ■ ————————————

7060 South 238th Street
Kent, Washington 98032-2914
U.S.A.
Telephone: (253) 437-6100
Toll Free: (877) 453-7591
Fax: (253) 437-6153
Web site: http://www.oberto.com

Private Company
Incorporated: 1918
Employees: 500
Revenues: $83.2 million
NAIC: 311612 Meat Processed from Carcasses; 311919
    Other Snack Food Manufacturing

■ ■ ■

Oberto Sausage Company, Inc., makes more than 400 varieties of dried meat products, such as beef, pork, and turkey jerky, and sausage sticks, smoked dinner sausages, dry salami, kippered beef, and pickled sausages. Natural jerky accounts for more than 50 percent of the product line produced at its plants in Seattle, Washington, and Albany, Oregon. The company sells its products under the brand names Lowrey's Meat Snacks, Oh Boy! Oberto Beef Jerky and Classics, Pacific Gold Beef Jerky, and Smoke Craft. Oberto's products are distributed throughout the United States to supermarkets and club and convenience stores through a distribution alliance with Frito-Lay. The private company is owned by six adult members of the Oberto family.

A STRUGGLING FAMILY BUSINESS OVERCOMES THE ODDS

Constantino Oberto moved to the United States from Italy in 1918 and settled in Oakland, California, where he learned the art of making salamis. Within a year, he had relocated to Seattle, Washington, an area called "Garlic Gulch" after the Italian immigrants who lived there. He and an uncle set up the Oberto Sausage Company in a small shop there on South King Street. The men peddled the Italian sausages and salamis they made to the ethnic food stores that served Seattle's Italian community. Their business grew steadily, and they later relocated to a larger, 3,000-square-foot facility on South Dearborn Street and hired two employees.

Constantino was a good sausage maker and businessman; however, he had a tendency to gamble, and on more than one occasion gambled away his company's earnings. When he died unexpectedly in 1943, owing the business $10,000, leadership of the Oberto Sausage Company passed to Constantino's wife, Antoinette, and his 16-year-old son, Art. Friends urged the struggling family to sell the business, especially in light of the wartime scarcity of supplies. However, Art, who soon proved his talent as a natural-born salesman and entrepreneur, told his mother, "Don't worry; we can run it," as he recalled more than 50 years later in a 1998 *Oregonian* article.

While still a student at West Seattle High School, Art started up production at the family sausage factory each day before attending class, and then Antoinette ran the business during the day with two employees. When he first began to work at Oberto, Art was too young to

COMPANY PERSPECTIVES

As a trusted family owned and operated business, Oberto Sausage Company has created legions of loyal and happy customers. How? Through care, respect and pride. Care in listening to customer's needs. Respect for their employees. Pride in creating the best product possible. Oberto Sausage Company. It's a tradition of quality you can taste.

drive; later, he would load up the company's delivery truck after school to peddle Oberto salami, Italian sausage, cooked salami, and coppacola to customers. As demand for Oberto's products grew, the company hired more workers; by 1952, the Oberto Sausage Company had eight employees.

The Obertos spent almost nothing, putting all of their earnings back into the business. In 1953, after the shop on Dearborn was condemned, they began construction on a small, new factory on Rainier Avenue South. However, when the new building was only half-complete, they ran out of funds. Fortunately, they were able to borrow the money they needed to finish construction.

Art Oberto married Dorothy Vennetti in 1954. The couple moved into the basement apartment underneath Antoinette Oberto's house, which was adjacent to the sausage factory. In 1957, husband and wife became business partners by purchasing Antoinette's interest in the Oberto Sausage Company. For a while, Dorothy Oberto kept the company's books by hand and invited her kids' friends to the house on Sundays to help mix the spices that flavored the sausages. After growing to 20 employees, the Obertos purchased Baum's German Sausage Company in 1960, and extended their product offerings to include Polish and German sausages. Oberto specialty meats and sausages, including coppacola, pastrami, salami, linguica, and rulle pulsa (a Scandinavian lamb sausage), were by then distributed statewide to small delis and grocery stores. In the early 1960s, Oberto also began producing natural beef jerky, after being approached by Totem Foods, a tavern distributor, as a potential supplier, and added another 20 employees.

BECOMING THE LEADER IN THE NATURAL BEEF JERKY MARKET

A huge opportunity to expand production and distribution also came about indirectly in the 1960s. When a new government mandate required a federal inspection of the plant, the expenses involved almost put the company out of business; however, the process in the end paved the way to shipping products out of state. In 1967, Safeway became Oberto's first national supermarket chain customer. From the late 1960s through the early 1970s, the company grew larger each year, until product demand, an expanding product line, and a workforce of 80 employees contributed to its outgrowing the Rainier Avenue plant. In 1974, the Oberto Sausage Company purchased the Jilg's Sausage Plant and moved its operations to south Seattle.

In 1978, having once again almost doubled its workforce to 150 employees, the company opened a third production, packaging, and distribution facility in Kent, Washington. Within five years, sales were in excess of $20 million, the company employed 250 workers at its three production facilities, and the Oberto Sausage Company had emerged as a market leader in the natural beef jerky category.

By the early 1980s, Art and Dorothy were looking toward the future and their retirement, and, so, in 1983, they carefully selected a board of directors; Art Oberto resigned as company president at age 55 and became chairman of the board, although he remained actively involved in company publicity, continuing to dress in a white, red, and green suit and driving around in his "jerky mobile." Under the new company president, the Oberto Sausage Company expanded distribution of its products to the East Coast and to foreign markets such as Japan, where Oberto soon became a best-selling brand. As the company continued to grow, it expanded its Kent facility in 1989 to accommodate the need for increased production space.

The Obertos had four adult children by this time, but only one of them, Laura, had the desire to enter the family business. Laura's first job at the company began when she was five and she delivered the mail. At 14, she oversaw spice formulation, and at 16, began attending sales and marketing meetings. At 17, she began conducting Oberto interviews in place of her father. She then worked at the plant while earning a degree in finance at Seattle University. In 1991, after serving in a number of different capacities at Oberto, she became president of the company, working alongside her father. Laura took an aggressive approach toward company growth. "We've always grown at a double-digit rate, and, excepting one year, have always been profitable," she said in a 1995 *Snack Food* article. "But we've never been very aggressive. We had to become more aggressive in how we did things. We had to expect more." In 1994, Laura Oberto led the purchase of Curtice Burns Meat Snacks' Denver-based meat snacks business.

KEY DATES

1918: Constantino Oberto and his uncle found the Oberto Sausage Company.

1943: Art Oberto and his mother, Antoinette, assume charge of the Oberto Sausage Company.

1953: The company opens a plant on Rainier Avenue South in Seattle.

1957: Oberto and his new wife, Dorothy, purchase Antoinette's share of the company.

1960: Oberto purchases Baum's German Sausage Company.

1967: Safeway becomes Oberto's first national supermarket chain customer.

1974: The company moves its operations to south Seattle.

1978: The company opens a third production, packaging, and distribution facility in Kent, Washington.

1983: Art Oberto resigns as company president and becomes chairman of the board.

1991: Laura Oberto becomes president of the company.

1998: The company once again moves to larger facilities; Tom Campanile becomes president of the company as Laura Oberto moves to board member.

2000: Oberto partners with Frito-Lay to distribute its natural-style jerky products in both the United States and Canada.

2002: The company acquires Pacific Sun, Inc.

Oberto also leased Curtice Burns' Albany, Oregon, manufacturing facility and equipment to Oberto until February 1995, at which time it purchased these assets as well. In all, Oberto acquired a production facility, a distribution center, and 225 employees.

The Curtice Burns acquisition brought with it ownership of the Smokecraft, Denver Dan's, and Lowrey's meat snack brands and the addition of chopped and formed beef jerky products as well as microwaveable pork rinds. It doubled Oberto Sausage Company's capabilities by adding a fourth production facility. Following the purchase, Oberto's sales also doubled, and the company controlled 23.6 percent of the domestic meat snack market. Oberto Sausage Company became the nation's largest jerky manufacturer, and the second largest national meat snack company.

INCREASED COMPETITION LEADS TO INCREASED DIVERSIFICATION OF PRODUCT AND DISTRIBUTION

The acquisition occurred just as meat snacks were enjoying increased acceptance by the public as a healthful, protein-rich, low-fat snack, a desirable alternative to other snack foods. Along with other meat snack manufacturers, Oberto's began to experiment with new flavors and seasonings and to direct its advertising beyond its traditional male market to both women and children. Oberto chose to pitch its products to the exercise-minded and to mothers, for their nutritional content, their long shelf life, and their portability. As part of its more "healthful" approach, the company began producing turkey jerky and removing MSG from its items.

The company also began to look to broaden its distribution. Up until this time, 80 percent of all meat snack purchases had been impulse buys, and meat snacks were sold largely at places frequented mostly by men: bars, gas stations, auto parts stores, and sporting goods stores. In the mid-1990s, however, more and more companies began to distribute their dried meat products to supermarkets and drug chains. By 1995, 16 percent of meat snacks were sold in supermarkets and more than 30 percent of sales took place at vending machines, mass merchandisers, and other nontraditional outlets combined. Oberto's supermarket sales jumped 46 percent in 1995 while its overall market share went from 24 to 27 percent, and the company enjoyed revenues of $100 million. In 1998, it started shipping product to some General Nutrition Centers.

Laura Oberto also led the company in exploring foreign markets for its products, focusing primarily on Canada, Mexico, Japan, and Norway. By the mid-1990s, Oberto's exports were growing at a double-digit rate, according to company data. At the same time, the company's share of the domestic meat snack market increased to about 29 percent in 1997 with $25.1 million in meat snack sales. Total company sales reached $108 million. As a result, the company once again moved to larger facilities in 1998. Oberto's new, 100,000-square-foot headquarters and distribution facility went up adjacent to its Kent manufacturing plant. In 1998, with $118 million in overall revenue, Oberto had 800 workers and was the second largest producer of meat snacks in the country.

In 1998, Laura Oberto moved from president to Oberto board member as Tom Campanile transitioned from vice-president of operations to president. Campanile had many years of experience in the meat snack industry, and five years overseeing Oberto's manufacturing operation. Under his direction, Oberto launched efforts to ensure its ongoing leadership in a market grown increasingly competitive as the popularity of meat snacks increased. The company aligned with an international supplier of top quality beef to ensure its future meat supply and thus its ability to grow.

As part of its strategy to ensure solid growth and success, in 1999 Oberto launched its Snack Attack marketing campaign. This campaign focused on the healthful aspects of its products, which at the time commanded 21 percent of the meat snack market or $34 million annually. In 2000, it introduced "Grandma Oberto," who went on a series of wild outdoor adventures in its advertising. After Oberto partnered in 2000 with Frito-Lay, which became the company's distributor of its natural-style jerky products in both the United States and Canada, it began a $7 million radio campaign aimed at younger outdoor athletes. Sales for the year 2000 reached more than $125 million.

During the next several years, competition for control of the meat snacks market continued to be intense as the high-protein diet craze of the new century further fueled growth in the meat snack category, introducing a new group of consumers to portable, dried meat products. Meat snacks became America's fastest-growing salty snack food with stores dedicating sections, inline sets, and endcaps to the products that grew in sales more than double that of any other salty snack. Oberto again introduced new flavors and added new forms of meat snacks, including a softer jerky and bite-sized items, in a bid to gain consumers' attention. The company also acquired Pacific Sun, Inc., in 2002, a company that produced jerky products for Costco in California and other Southwest markets under the brand name Pacific Gold. Oberto also continued to focus on health to drive its meat snack sales as the American population continued to age.

For the next several years, Oberto's share of the meat snacks markets vacillated slightly as sales for meat snacks decreased slightly in the wake of the high-protein diet craze. In 2004, Oberto's meat snacks sales reached $70 million; in 2006, that number was down to about $66 million. Still, as the second largest producer of meat snacks and the manufacturer with the greatest supermarket sales, the company was committed to ensuring that Oberto remained a leading meat snacks company nationally and internationally. The goal was likely to be a challenging one, but one to which Oberto had already proved equal. As Art Oberto himself said in a 1998 *Oregonian* article, summing up his company's success, "Every move we made, we stuck our neck out. We were too stubborn to quit. We've never been happy with things being easy."

Carrie Rothburd

PRINCIPAL COMPETITORS

Bridgford Foods Corporation; Clemens Family Corporation; ConAgra Foods, Inc.; Goodmark Foods, Inc.; Lance Snacks; Jack Link's Snack Foods; Double B Foods, Inc.; Mitchell's Gourmet Foods, Inc.; Opa's Smoked Meats; Pioneer Snacks, Inc.; Weaver Meats.

FURTHER READING

"Hooking More Consumers: Meat Snacks," *Professional Candy Buyer,* November 1998, p. 50.

Kugiya, Hugo, "The Self-Made Man: Corporate America Does Not Have Much Room for Types Like Art Oberto, Candid in a Way That Frightens Most Managers," *Seattle Times,* January 11, 1998, p. 12.

Littman, Margaret, "A Meaty Issue," *Snack Food,* February 1995, p. 20.

Pacyniak, Bernard, "The Fire Behind the Smoke," *Snack Food,* March 1995, p. 22.

Parlin, Sandy, "Snacking on the Run: Hand-Held Meat Snacks Are Evolving to Meet New Taste Demands—and Satisfy an Ever-Expanding Consumer Taste," *National Provisioner,* November 2004, p. 40.

Ponder, Stephanie E., "A Work of Art," *Costco Connection,* February 2005, p. 4.

Onet S.A.

20 Traverse de Pomegues
Marseille, F-13414 Cedex 20
France
Telephone: (33 04) 91 23 22 21
Fax: (33 04) 91 23 22 91
Web site: http://www.groupeonet.com

Public Company
Incorporated: 1860 as Maison Format
Employees: 48,411
Sales: EUR 1.14 billion ($1.6 billion) (2006)
Stock Exchanges: Euronext Paris
Ticker Symbol: 3391
NAIC: 562111 Solid Waste Collection; 561320
   Temporary Help Services; 561612 Security Guards
   and Patrol Services

■ ■ ■

Onet S.A is a leading French services group. The Marseille-based company operates four main divisions: Cleaning Multiservices, Extreme Environment Technologies, Safety and Security, and Temporary Staff and Recruitment. Cleaning Multiservices remains the largest part of the company's operations, accounting for more than two-thirds of its annual sales of EUR 1.14 billion (US$1.6 billion) in 2006. This division operates through a network of 180 agencies and eight regional offices throughout France, and provides cleaning and maintenance service to the corporate, financial, industrial, and residential sectors. Through this division, Onet is also the leading cleaning services group in France; the company also provides cleaning services in Belgium, Switzerland, Italy, the United Kingdom, Luxembourg, and Spain.

Following the acquisition of France Présence in April 2007, Onet has extended its range of services to include home-based services, including cleaning, childcare, ironing, cooking, and services for the handicapped. Extreme Environment Technologies encompasses the company's nuclear power facility maintenance, decontamination, and risk protection services. This division has also developed a series of partnerships with such major industrial groups as Mitsubishi Heavy Industries, Nukem, Eiffage TP, Atomic Energy of Canada Ltd., and Kaefer Wanner.

Temporary Staff and Recruitment focuses on providing personnel for the logistics and airport services, construction, hotel and restaurants, and customer service sectors. This division also provides recruitment and training services for Onet's other operations, as well as for third parties. Onet's Safety and Security division provides a full range of personal, corporate, and industrial security services. In addition, Onet operates a wholesale division, which provides cleaning products and equipment for its own and other cleaning services. Founded in the mid-19th century, Onet is listed on the Euronext Paris Stock Exchange. Nonetheless, the founding Reinier family remains its majority shareholder, with approximately 90 percent of its shares.

PORT HANDLING SERVICES BY 1860

Onet was founded in the middle of the 19th century, as the construction of France's railroad system transformed the city of Marseille into one of the country's major ports. The arrival of the railroad introduced new employment opportunities, particularly for transporting goods to and from the holds of ships and the rail yard. The Format family were among those launching their own port handling businesses. While the original family business was most likely created in 1848, the formal beginning of the company dated from 1860, when Hippolyte Format took over from his father and created the Maison Format. The company was quite small, operating from a small shed of approximately six meters square. Through the end of the century, Maison Format developed a secondary business to provide cleaning services to the Marseille flour milling industry.

Maison Format remained a modest business into the early decades of the 20th century. In 1924, however, Hippolyte Format's grandson, Hippolyte Reinier, took over the family business and began its transformation into one of France's leading services companies. Reinier developed a strong relationship with the Société Nationale de Chemins de Fer (SNCF), the government-owned body that had become responsible for developing, operating, and maintaining the country's railroad system. Maison Format became an important partner for the SNCF, rolling out its handling services in railway stations and rail yards throughout much of southern France. By the 1930s, Maison Format had also begun its modernization, adding cranes, forklifts, and other mechanized vehicles and equipment to its operations.

The company had also continued to develop its cleaning services operations. These had taken on growing importance for the group in the years leading up to and during the World War II. It was especially in the aftermath of the war that the group's focus turned toward its cleaning services operations. By 1950, the company's cleaning business had grown to the extent that it created a dedicated subsidiary, called the Office Nouveau du Nettoyage, or ONET. That company was formally incorporated in 1959, controlled by Maison Format as the family holding company. As the next generation entered the company's operations, the group's shareholding was split between the two branches of the family, the Reinier and the Fabre families. The next generation, represented by Louis Reinier and Paul Fabre, took over as head of the company in 1978.

In the meantime, Maison Format had begun to diversify its businesses. The late 1960s witnessed new expansion for the group. France's decision to develop its nuclear power industry in order to reduce the country's reliance on imported fossil fuels provided a new opportunity for the company's development. By 1968, the company had introduced its first operations providing services specifically to the country's growing number of nuclear power installations. By then, too, Maison Format had taken its first steps beyond France, launching a subsidiary in Switzerland, where it targeted especially the provision of cleaning services to that country's banking and financial sectors.

Much of Maison Format's growth, especially beyond Marseille, had taken place through the creation of a number of locally based and operated subsidiaries. Into the 1970s, the main Marseille-based company began developing support operations for its subsidiaries. These included Formation Services, created in 1973, which provided employee training and recruitment services for the company's branches. In 1977, the company created another subsidiary, GIE Assistance Services, which became the central body of its internal support operations.

PUBLIC COMPANY IN 1987

The company expanded into Spain in 1986, creating a new subsidiary there, called Ganonet. In that year, also, the company restructured its operations, with Maison Format becoming the holding company for its operational subsidiaries. This restructuring was then completed in 1987, when the company changed its name to Onet SA and listed its shares on the Paris Bourse's Secondary Market. The public offering, of just over 10 percent of the shares, left the Reinier-Fabre families in firm control of the company, while providing capital for the group's further growth. In 1990, the two families regrouped their shareholdings under a new structure, Financiére Reinier.

The company's first new expansion effort came that same year, with the purchase of Groupe Buzzichelli, ac-

KEY DATES

1860: Hippolyte Format takes over his father's business providing port handling services in Marseille, creating Maison Format.

1924: Grandson Hippolyte Reinier takes over company.

1950: Office Nouveau du Nettoyage (ONET) is created to regroup cleaning services business.

1968: Onset of services to nuclear power industry.

1987: Company goes public on Paris Bourse's Secondary Market, changing name to Onet SA.

1992: Materials handling is divested to focus on cleaning and other services.

2001: Cleaning Multiservices concept is introduced across entire agency network.

2007: Multiservices concept is expanded into home care with acquisition of France Présence.

tive in the materials handling and industrial services sectors. Two years later, Onet entered Germany, through Sogedec Deutschland, which specialized in providing decontamination services. Sogedec represented the company's extension into the Italian market as well. Meanwhile, another company subsidiary, Ortec, focused on the industrial maintenance market, led Onet into the United Kingdom in 1990.

In that year, the company began the first of a series of organizational restructuring efforts, creating Onet Propreté as the main subsidiary for its cleaning services businesses. The restructuring continued through the following year, when the group reorganized its operations along dedicated branches. This effort resulted in the regrouping of the company's nuclear power operations into a single subsidiary, Onectra, which in turn created Sertec for its operations for Electricité de France; and another subsidiary, Sirad, which focused on the inspection, control, and security of nuclear power installations. In 1993, however, the company rebranded its nuclear power wing as Onet Nucléaire. At the completion of its restructuring, Onet had created a five-part organizational structure, for its Cleaning Services, Industrial Handling and Services, Nuclear, Security and Surveillance, and Temporary Employment branches.

Onet also continued adding to its operations. In 1991, the company acquired Alpes Méthodes Propreté, reinforcing its cleaning services in that region. The company also founded another cleaning and maintenance subsidiary that year, Isatec. Cleaning services also led the group into Belgium, through Intercleaner, and then, in 1994, into Luxembourg, with the creation of Onet Luxembourg that year. Onet also formed a dedicated cleaning services subsidiary in Italy in 1994, created as a joint venture with a local partner. The growth of the company's cleaning services by then had led the company to spin off its industrial maintenance operations, including its Ortec-Buzzichelli business, into a management buyout in 1992.

FRENCH CLEANING SERVICES LEADER IN THE NEW CENTURY

Through the 1990s, Onet completed a series of acquisitions in order to boost its increasingly diverse operations. The company's Security and Surveillance branch grew particularly strongly, notably through the purchases of Alarme Surveillance Protection, Audit Sécurité, Sécurité Écoute Permanent, SEP Gardiennage, and SEP Info Système et Applications Electroniques Industrielles in 1994. With the addition of Telem, in 1996, the company extended its security operations to become one of the leaders in the remote and video surveillance market as well. The company also boosted its nuclear branch, creating a new training subsidiary, Evolution Services, in 1997.

Onet strengthened its European profile in 1999 when it joined with Germany's Gegenbauerbosse and the United Kingdom's OCS to form Euroliance. The new operation was then able to claim control of some 10 percent of the European cleaning services market. The following year, the company stepped up its operations in the rail sector, buying Safen, which also boasted strong cleaning services operations. That same year, Onet expanded beyond French-speaking Switzerland with the purchase of Raidkal, based in Zürich. The company also created its Cleaning Multiservices concept, extending its operations beyond cleaning services to include a range of onsite and maintenance services. The Multiservices concept was then rolled out across all of the company's agency network the following year.

The beginning of the new century also saw a strengthening of the group's nuclear site services, which later formed the core of the Extreme Environment Technologies division. In 2000, the company launched the first of a series of partnerships with a number of major players in the nuclear power station construction industry, including Mitsubishi Heavy Industries in Japan, Eiffage in France, Nukem in Germany, ENS in the United States, Studvik in Sweden, and AECL in Canada.

Onet adopted a new divisional structure in 2002, creating four primary divisions, Cleaning Multiservices, Extreme Environment Technologies, Prevention and Security, and Temporary Employment and Recruitment, as well as a fifth division, dedicated to the group's operations in wholesale distribution of cleaning supplies and equipment. As part of its new restructuring, the company created four new operational subsidiaries.

Already the leading cleaning services group in France, Onet continued to seek new expansion opportunities into the middle of the decade. In 2005, for example, the company added GPI 2000 to its Prevention and Security division. In that year, also, the company purchased a 48 percent stake in temporary employment and recruitment specialist Axxis Conseil. The following year, the company expanded its operations in Belgium, acquiring Federal Cleaning. By the end of that year, Onet had passed the EUR 1 million mark for the first time.

Onet also continued to develop its Cleaning Multiservices concept. In April 2007, the company extended its range of services to the home care sector, buying France Présence. That purchase added expertise in the provision of a range of noncleaning services, including childcare, ironing, cooking, and services for the handicapped.

In October 2007, the group's shareholding structure was simplified in order to allow members of the Fabre branch to exit the company. As part of that process, Financière Reinier was dissolved, and the nearly 88 percent of shares held by the Fabre and Reinier families was transferred equally to two holding companies. The Reinier branch then bought out the shares of the Fabre branch. Both branches of the family could look back on more than 160 years of history and forward to a future as one of France's leading services companies.

M. L. Cohen

PRINCIPAL SUBSIDIARIES

Comex Nucléaire; Drome Service Nettoyage; Onectra; Onet (Suisse) SA; Onet Belgium; Onet Cleaning Europe; Onet Espana; Onet Europe; Onet Italia; Onet Laser Systems; Onet Luxembourg; Onet Nucléaire Rhone; Onet Services; Onet Services Industrie; Onet U.K.; Prodim Antilles; Rescousse; Telem Télésurveillance.

PRINCIPAL COMPETITORS

Service Management International Ltd.; SUEZ; RWE AG; Veolia Environnement; Vivendi S.A.; Waste Management, Inc.; ThyssenKrupp Services AG; ACS Actividades de Construccion y Servicios S.A.; Allied Waste Industries, Inc.; Fomento de Construcciones y Contratas S.A.; Exel PLC; Group 4 Securicor PLC; Outokumpu Oyj.

FURTHER READING

"Groupe Onet: Recomposition du Capital d'Onet," *Hugin,* October 24, 2007.

"Onet: L'Activité Annuelle Passe le Cap Symbolique du Milliard d'Euros," *Boursier.com,* February 15, 2006.

"Onet: La Famille Reinier Rachète la Part de la Famille Fabre à 136 Euros par Action," *Boursier.com,* September 6, 2007.

"Onet Se Lance Sur le Marché des Services à la Personne," *Les Echos,* April 27, 2007.

"Onet Veut Diversifier les Métiers de la Propreté," *Les Echos,* November 7, 2006.

Pelikan Holding AG

Chaltenbodenstrasse 8
Postfach 268
Schindellegi, 8834
Switzerland
Telephone: (41 044) 786 70 20
Fax: (41 044) 786 70 21
Web site: http://www.pelikan.de

Public Company
Founded: 1838
Employees: 979
Sales: CHF 211.34 million ($172.72 million) (2006)
Stock Exchanges: Zürich
Ticker Symbol: PEL
NAIC: 339941 Pen and Mechanical Pencil Manufacturing; 339942 Lead Pencil and Art Good Manufacturing

■ ■ ■

Pelikan Holding AG is a global group of companies based in Switzerland. Pelikan produces products in four broad ranges: writing instruments, especially fountain pens, ballpoint pens, and mechanical pencils; supplies for schools and schoolchildren, such as pens and pencils, drawing pads, folders, construction paper, and paint sets; office supplies, including markers, highlighters, stamp pads, glue and glue sticks, and correction supplies; and arts and crafts supplies such as paints, paper, and glue.

Pelikan Holding AG Group is organized into five geographical units: Europe, Latin America, Middle East/

Africa, Asia, and International Markets. Pelikan has 28 subsidiaries and affiliates, primarily in Europe, the Far East, and Latin America. These units are supported by four centralized departments: Product Development, Sourcing and Supply, Brand Management and Communication, and Group Corporate, Planning and Services. Pelikan Holding AG is owned by Pelikan International Corp. Bhd, a Malaysian company.

ORIGINS AS A PAINT AND INK FACTORY

The company that would eventually be named Pelikan was founded in 1832 by Carl Hornemann, a chemist from a family of artists and paint producers, who after his education began experimenting with formulas for paint, which he then produced in his father's small business. He eventually set up his own production site on a farm in the village of Gross-Munzel near Hannover and on April 28, 1838, he issued his first printed catalog of inks and paint. That date is the first date documented in the company's history, and Pelikan has since considered it the official date of the company's founding.

The company grew slowly, but it grew. One reason was Hornemann's marketing savvy. At a time when English and French paints had by far the best reputation for quality, Hornemann used not only the English language in his labels, but also the coat of arms of the Prince of Wales. In 1842 he decided to expand production and purchased a piece of land with two buildings and a half-acre yard. The new site also put him some 20 miles closer to customers in Hannover. Despite his

COMPANY PERSPECTIVES

In kindergarten, or at school; in the office or when you are enjoying your hobbies; or—the most refined form of personal communication—when writing with a high-class writing instrument, our innovative products are your trustworthy companions. With a company history going back nearly 170 years, Pelikan is one of the oldest registered trademarks in the world. From the past we gather strength for the future which we shall continue to form to your advantage.

English labels, however, Hornemann encountered quality problems in his paints, and it was a hand-to-mouth existence in the firm's early decades.

In 1863, with six men and eight women working production in the firm, in addition to a cabinetmaker and a clerk, Hornemann hired Günther Wagner as his plant manager. Wagner was a trained chemist who had worked earlier in a local Hannover chemicals plant. Over the course of the next eight years, Carl Hornemann would withdraw more and more from the day-to-day workings of his company, leaving its management to Wagner. In February 1871 he left it completely, selling the firm to Wagner for 25,000 thaler, the equivalent of about 75,000 gold marks.

Wagner gave the company his own name and set out to expand its business, acquiring customers in foreign countries such as Italy, Belgium, and Russia. It was an ideal time to grow. Germany had just won three wars, proclaimed its empire, and entered a period of prosperity and galloping industrial development. Wagner set his commercial sights on the Austrian Empire, a vast conglomerate of nations and peoples that included Czechs, Slovaks, Hungarians, Poles, Romanians, Slovenians, and Croatians. To gain access to Austria, his business first had to establish a presence on Austrian soil. Hence, in 1871 he built a factory just across the border in Eger, then a German-speaking area, now part of the Czech Republic. The plant was moved to the Austrian capital, Vienna, in 1879, to take advantage of the transportation links there.

It was also in the latter half of the 1870s that the Pelikan logo first entered the company's history. The bird appeared in the coat of arms of Wagner's family, and he adopted it for the logo of his firm. At that time, there was no official trademark protection; indeed there were no laws at all governing trademarks. Wagner registered it with German authorities in 1878 nonethe-

less, and when trademark rolls were finally introduced almost 20 years later in 1896, the pelican was officially registered as the emblem of Wagner's firm. It was one of Germany's very first registered trademarks.

The firm continued to grow through the 1880s. In 1881 a new building for production was built, and a horse and cart were purchased for deliveries. One of the new workers would turn out to be as significant for Günther Wagner as Wagner had been for Carl Hornemann. Fritz Beindorff entered the company as its sales representative for Austria, Italy, Belgium, Russia, and the Far East, and by 1888 he was managing Wagner's business and had married Wagner's oldest daughter. In 1894 he was named a full partner. In 1895 Wagner retired and Beindorff became the firm's sole owner. The company forged ahead under Beindorff's leadership. Facilities were further expanded. Office supplies were added to the product line. It launched one of its most successful products, its Pelikan 4011 India ink, in 1896. Around this time it introduced ink for fountain pens, which had been invented about fifteen years earlier in the United States. By the beginning of the 20th century the employee rolls had grown to 236 and annual revenues stood at one million gold marks. In 1906 another expansion took place, and a new factory was built in Hannover on Podbielskistrasse. When World War I broke out in 1914, the company had more than 1,000 workers and revenues of 4.4 million gold marks.

Pelikan survived the politically and economically turbulent 1920s in Germany. When the Depression hit at the end of the decade, it continued to introduce innovative products. It put a fountain pen of its own, the first in a long line of distinctive writing instruments, into production in 1929. The innovation was in its revolutionary piston mechanism, which delivered ink from the reservoir to the nib. Five years later, Pelikan brought out a less expensive fountain for the masses, the Rappen, that enjoyed great success. Around the same time it also developed a mechanical pencil as well as its first watercolor paint box, which would become the one most German schoolchildren continued to use over a half century later.

The name "Pelikan" was first used in the company's name in subsidiaries founded in the early 1930s— Günther Wagner Produits Pelikan S.A.R.L in France in 1931; and S.A. Günther Wagner, Prodotti Pelikan, Italy, and Günther Wagner Productos Pelikan S.A. in Spain, both in 1933. On the occasion of the company's 100th anniversary in 1938, on the eve of World War II, Pelikan had factories across the world, in Hannover, Vienna, Danzig, Milan, Barcelona, Bucharest, Sofia, Warsaw,

KEY DATES

1832: Carl Hornemann begins producing paint and inks.

1838: First printed catalog of inks and paint issued; official founding of company.

1871: Günther Wagner takes over the firm.

1878: Pelikan logo is developed and first registered with German authorities.

1895: Fritz Beindorff becomes firm's full owner.

1896: Pelikan logo is registered with newly formed patent authorities in Germany.

1929: Firm's first fountain pen is introduced.

1938: Company celebrates its 100th anniversary.

1950: Model 400 fountain pen is introduced.

1970: A 50 percent share in office supply manufacturer Rotring is acquired.

1978: Company is reorganized into an *Aktiengesellschaft* (share company) and name changed to Pelikan AG.

1982: Pelikan goes into insolvency.

1984: Swiss firm Metrogruppe becomes majority owner.

1986: Company goes public on Zürich exchange.

1989: Pelikan AG in Hannover is split into four separate companies.

1995: Glue and correction materials division is sold to Henkel KGaA; hardcopy division is sold to American firm Nu-kote.

1996: Malaysian firm Goodace SDN BHD takes over majority ownership from Metrogruppe.

2007: Delisted by Frankfurt and Düsseldorf stock exchanges.

Budapest, Zagreb, Buenos Aires, Rio de Janeiro, and Santiago de Chile, employing some 3,700 employees.

SHORTAGES IN WORLD WAR II AND A QUICK RECOVERY IN POSTWAR GERMANY

The years of World War II were difficult for Pelikan because of material shortages. Precious metals for the fountain pens in the high price range were extremely scarce, for example, as were steel and rubber. Fortunately the company's plants in Hannover survived the war with only slight damage. However, its subsidiaries abroad were seized by the foreign governments, some of which—Günther Wagner Buenos Aires, Argentina,

for instance—continued the manufacture of certain products under the Pelikan name.

Pelikan pushed forward toward economic recovery with the rest of Germany in the decades following World War II. It introduced two new items in its fountain pen line, both of which would go on to be mainstays. In 1950 the Model 400 hit the market. It soon became the most popular pen in the medium price range. Ten years later, the Pelikano, a fountain pen designed for schoolchildren, was introduced. Its special ergonomic design and a unique ink cartridge filling system soon made it one of the most popular fountain pens for schoolchildren. However, attempts to market the same cartridge system in a pen for adults flopped completely. It was not until the 1980s that the system was successfully marketed in a pen for adults.

In 1949 the German company incorporated "Pelikan" into its name as it had in its prewar subsidiaries, and became Günther Wagner Pelikan Werke Hannover. However, the name never seems to have been firmly established. Over the next 20 years the company was also known as Günther Wagner Hannover Pelikan Werke and also simply as Günther Wagner Pelikan Werke.

In 1970, Pelikan acquired a 50 percent stake in another German office supply manufacturer, Rotring. The partnership functioned well at first. The two companies purchased the American office supply producer Koh-I-Noor, Inc., of Bloomsbury, New Jersey, together, a venture that was so successful it strengthened the collaboration in Germany. However, when Pelikan slid into insolvency in 1982, it was required to sell to Rotring all of the shares it held.

By 1973 the Pelikan facilities on Podbielskistrasse had been completely built up; no further growth was possible there. As a result, the manufacture of writing instruments was moved to a new plant some 22 miles outside Hannover. In 1978, with a total value of approximately DEM 607.8 million, the company was completely reorganized. Its legal form was changed from a limited liability corporation to a share company (from a GmbH to an AG, in German terms), the shares were divided among the Beindorff family and over 40 other owners, and finally the name was changed to Pelikan AG. At the same time Pelikan made the decision to expand its product line well beyond its traditional areas of expertise, into games, hobby items, printers, photocopiers, projectors, data carriers, technical drawing equipment, and cosmetics. By the end of the decade, the firm had 46 subsidiaries and more than 12,000 employees.

CHANGES IN OWNERSHIP

Within just a very few years it was clear that Pelikan had badly overextended itself. In the years 1980 and 1981 the firm's technology division lost some DEM 120 million. In 1982 the acquisition of the Lumoprint photocopier company nudged it into insolvency. A reverse split of Pelikan stock, one for ten, took place and the company was taken over in 1984 by the Swiss firm Condorpart, a subsidiary of Metrogruppe. Over the next five years, Metrogruppe completely reorganized the Pelikan company. Its headquarters were transferred from Hannover to Zug, Switzerland. The production company, Pelikan AG, was placed in a holding company, Pelikan International, which in 1986 was renamed Pelikan Holding and listed on the Zürich stock exchange. In 1989, the operations in Hannover were split into four separate subsidiaries: PBS Servicegesellschaft mbH & Co. KG, Pelikan PBS-Produktionsgesellschaft mbH & Co. KG, Pelikan Internationale Handelsgesellschaft mbH & Co. KG, and Pelikan Vertriebsgesellschaft mbH & Co. KG-Geha Werke GmbH.

The early 1990s were a time of extreme uncertainty for Pelikan employees in the firm's old base in Hannover. The Swiss owners had plans to rationalize the entire company with a radical paring of products that had never been part of Pelikan's traditional range. It would be limited to office supplies and writing instruments. As part of the plan, an announcement was made of plans to shut down the three Pelikan facilities in Hannover and Voehrum, a move that would have led to the loss of some 1,860 jobs. The announcement set off a wave of protest in Hannover. There were mass demonstrations by workers and their families, expressions of support from the governing Social Democratic Party, and finally a ruling by the district labor court that the layoffs were illegal. In two countermoves in 1995, Pelikan sold its glue and correction materials division to Henkel KGaA. Around the same time a new division, Pelikan Hardcopy, which had been formed in 1994, was sold to the American company Nu-kote. Those two sales made it possible to prune some 300 from Pelikan's workforce. One year later the consolidation of two subsidiaries, Pelikan Vertriebsgesellschaft mbH & Co. KG and Internationale Handelsgesellschaft mbH & Co. KG, brought Pelikan's total workforce down to about 800.

In the mid-1990s Metrogruppe decided to divest itself completely of its Pelikan shares, however. In October 1996, it sold its 70 percent holdings to Goodace SDN BHD for approximately CHF 80 million. Goodace was a manufacturer and distributor of office supplies owned by the Malaysian Hooi Keat Loo. Loo's company had long ties to Pelikan—it had acquired Pelikan subsidiaries in Singapore, Malaysia, and Japan, and was acting as the firm's main distributor in Asia for the ten previous years. At the time of the takeover, Goodace said it would place particular emphasis on developing Pelikan's Asian markets, especially in India, Indonesia, and Thailand. Production, Goodace announced, would continue to be done in Hannover; the headquarters of Pelikan Holding AG would remain in Switzerland.

Two years later, however, it was clear that Pelikan had not yet turned the corner. Its net sales—except for a slight bump in 2000—continued to decline between 1996 and 2002 from CHF 230.2 million to CHF 183.5 million. The company's primary market continued, as always, to be Germany with CHF 97 million in sales, more than 50 percent of total international sales, although German sales were down some 10 percent from a year earlier. Furthermore, sales in the Far East, where growth had been actively targeted, were stagnating. Another trend in the early years of the 21st century was Pelikan's reacquisition of divisions it had divested in the 1990s. In 2000, for instance, the firm once again took over distribution to key accounts for Pelikan Hardcopy, the division it had sold to the American Nu-kote. Two years later, it bought back its former office supply division from Henkel KGaA.

Pelikan bounced back financially in 2003. From then until 2006 the company's sales grew steadily, reaching CHF 211.3 million, up nearly CHF 20 million since 2002. In October 2007 Pelikan shares were delisted by its two secondary stock exchanges, Frankfurt and Düsseldorf, for lack of activity. Pelikan continued to be traded on the exchange in Zürich, Switzerland. As 2007 ended Pelikan announced plans to take over all business activities of its former Hardcopy subsidiary. The move was described as a return to the company's roots.

Gerald E. Brennan

PRINCIPAL SUBSIDIARIES

Pelikan GmbH; Pelikan PBS-Produktionsgesellschaft mbH & Co. KG; Pelikan Vertriebsgesellschaft mbH & Co. KG; Pelikan Italia S.p.A. (Italy); Pelikan S.A. (Spain); Pelikan Faber-Castell (Schweiz) AG (Switzerland; 75%); Pelikan Benelux N.V./S.A.; Pelikan, Inc. (United States); Pelikan Asia Sdn. Bhd. (Malaysia); Pelikan Japan K.K. (25%); Pelikan Quartet PTY Ltd. (Australia; 40%).

PRINCIPAL COMPETITORS

Sheaffer Pen; Sanford L.P.; Aurora; A.T. Cross Pen Company; Caran D'Ache Pens of Switzerland; C. Josef

Lamy GmbH; Montblanc Simplo GmbH; Pilot Corporation of America; Visconti.

FURTHER READING

"Arbeitsgericht stoppt Kündigungswelle bei Pelikan," *Süddeutsche Zeitung,* September 23, 1994.

Bruce, Peter, "Drawing Strength from a Dynasty," *Financial Times,* April 18, 1986, p. 22.

Buchan, James, "Pelikan Insolvent and Seeks Debt Talks," *Financial Times,* February 20, 1982, p. 19.

Dittmer, Jürgen, and Martin Lehmann, *Pelikan Schreibgeräte/ Writing Instruments 1929–2004,* Aurich, Germany: Druckerei und Verlag Dunkmann, 2004.

"Die Hersteller von Bürobedarf Leiden unter Überkapazitäten," *Frankfurter Allgemeine Zeitung,* April 4, 2002, p. 16.

"In der Belegschaft regt sich Widerstand gegen die Werksschliessung," *Frankfurter Allgemeine Zeitung,* June 1994, p. 20.

"Pelikan Erwartet Cchwarze Null," *Börsen-Zeitung,* January 28, 1997, p. 6.

"Pelikan: Mit Glänzender Stahlfeder Weltweit Vertreten," *Peiner Wirtschaftspiegel,* No. 2, 2003.

"Der Pelikan Soll Wieder Fliegen," *Süddeutsche Zeitung,* November 15, 1994.

"Tausende Demonstrieren für Erhalt von Pelikan," *Frankfurter Allgemeine Zeitung,* June 6, 1994, p. 22.

"Which Came First at Pelikan—the Ink or the Nib?" http:// www.levenger.com/levenger/PenHistories.

Philadelphia Gas Works Company

1800 North Ninth Street
Philadelphia, Pennsylvania 19130
U.S.A.
Telephone: (215) 236-0500
Fax: (215) 684-6996
Web site: http://www.pgworks.com

Public Company
Incorporated: 1836 as Trustees of Gas Works
Employees: 1,767
Sales: $86.3 million (2005)
NAIC: 221210 Natural Gas Distribution

■ ■ ■

Philadelphia Gas Works Company is the largest municipally owned gas utility company in the United States and is also the nation's largest liquefied natural gas storage facility. The company manages over 6,000 miles of gas mains and serves more than 500,000 private and 19,000 industrial and commercial customers. Started in 1836, Philadelphia Gas Works is owned by the citizens of Philadelphia, managed and operated by the Philadelphia Facilities Management Corporation (a nonprofit corporation with members appointed by the mayor), and regulated by the Philadelphia Utility Commission.

19TH-CENTURY FOUNDING AND CONVERSION TO MUNICIPAL CONTROL

The foundation of a Philadelphia City gas company was first suggested by a citizen named James MacMurtrie,

who presented a plan to the Common Council of Philadelphia in December 1815. The issue was debated within the city council for the next 20 years with little progress until 1835, when engineer Samuel Merrick submitted a report detailing research on the development of gas power in the United States and Europe. Merrick's report convinced the city council to initiate plans for a municipal gas processing and distribution facility.

The City of Philadelphia designated a board of 12 individuals, known as the Trustees of Gas Works, to oversee construction of the city's first distribution station, later known as Philadelphia Gas Company and located on Market Street at the junction of the Schuylkill River. The board of trustees was composed by election, with six members elected by a special council and six elected by the general city council. Construction began in 1835 and the plant went into operation on February 8, 1836.

The founding of the gas works was funded by a combination of government loans and grants and by the sale of stock guaranteed by the city. Funds acquired for the operation and eventual expansion of gas service were placed in a trust and given to the Trustees of Gas Works as needed. Gas rapidly gained in popularity, driven by the high price of oil lighting. By 1840, a number of counties surrounding Philadelphia had constructed their own gas distribution facilities.

In July 1841, the City of Philadelphia bought the rights to the company from the various shareholders by replacing stock with interest-bearing bonds. The city was unable to claim full ownership over the company or to abolish the trusteeship until the bonds matured and/or expired, and the board of trustees therefore remained in place until 1885 although operation of the gas company was handled by city-appointed officials.

After taking managerial control, the city began expanding the gas company by incorporating peripheral distribution plants. The West Philadelphia Gas Company was incorporated in 1851 followed by the Manayunk Gas Company in 1853. In 1854, the city built Station A (the Point Breeze gas works) and in 1875 expanded again with Station B (the Richmond gas works). In 1887, the board of trustees was abolished and control of the gas works was formally transferred to the Bureau of Gas, which was part of the Department of Public Works.

The City of Philadelphia operated the gas works for over 60 years, during which time service expanded and the company began shifting from using coal gas to water gas. However, the city was unable to keep pace with the development of distribution technology, and the city's facilities were in need of rehabilitation. Between 1893 and 1897, the city suffered from financial losses at an average of $250,000 per year, and city officials decided that the gas company should be leased to a professional organization with the resources and knowledge to properly update the city's facilities. In 1897, the city entered into negotiations with the United Gas Improvement Company (UGI) to manage the city's gas services under the terms of an extended lease.

CONTRACTING WITH UGI

In November 1897, the city entered into a 30-year lease with the Philadelphia Gas Improvement Company, a division of UGI, for management and operation of the gas company. Under the lease, UGI was expected to supply all public buildings with gas, to provide for the addition of 300 street lamps each year and to spend a total of $15 million in improvements over the period of the lease.

The price of gas was established through debates between UGI and city councils at $1 per thousand cubic feet, of which the city was to receive part of the profits for the sale of gas on a graduated system. UGI's operations were immediately effective and the city received over $193,000 in revenues from the first year of operation. From 1897 to 1928, UGI paid over $61 million to the city and expended over $30 million to improve and enhance gas services, well in excess of the $15 million required by the lease.

Although UGI's management proved fruitful for the city, there were frequent debates over the price of gas, the function and development of the gas works, and other provisions of the lease. UGI's subsidiary, then called the Philadelphia Gas Works (PGW), was authorized for a ten-year renewal contract, effective in January 1928. Under the terms of the new lease, UGI's payment to the city was increased to $4.2 million annually. A new regulatory body, the Philadelphia Gas Commission, was created to represent the city's interests. Members of the Gas Commission were appointed by the city's government and empowered to approve or reject PGW's annual requests for rate changes.

During the 1920s and 1930s, UGI became one of the largest holding companies in the nation, with more than 38 gas and electric utility companies and ownership, or investment, in dozens of nonutility interests. Because of management strategies and broad interests, the company suffered little during the Great Depression in comparison to many of Philadelphia's corporations.

In 1935, the federal government passed the Public Utility Holding Company Act, an antimonopoly initiative that required companies managing gas and electricity to restrict ownership to smaller, regional interests. UGI challenged the act as unconstitutional and asked the courts to issue an injunction to prevent federal enforcement. The courts eventually ruled in favor of the federal government and UGI was forced to divest a number of its properties. In 1952, UGI reorganized its general structure from that of a holding company to a utility company serving Eastern Pennsylvania. That same year, UGI merged seven of its publicly owned utility companies, including PGW, into a single managerial unit.

During the 1950s, UGI began transitioning from manufactured gas to liquid natural gas. The company engaged in a campaign to boost natural gas sales across the country with Philadelphia as one of its largest gas markets. In 1969, UGI opened a liquid natural gas storage facility in the Philadelphia-area Richmond plant.

KEY DATES

1836: The utility is founded.

1841: Trustees of Gas Works comes under city ownership.

1854: Trustees is authorized to purchase all other gas provision companies in the city and county area.

1887: Operation of gas transferred to the Bureau of Gas under the Department of Public Works.

1897: United Gas Improvement Company is contracted by the city to manage gas distribution.

1927: Supervision of gas distribution transferred to the Philadelphia Gas Commission.

1951: City charter designates gas company as part of the Department of Public Property.

1963: Gas appliances in the city are converted to permit direct use of natural gas.

1972: Management is contracted to the Philadelphia Facilities Management Corporation.

2000: PGW comes under regulation of the five-member Pennsylvania Public Utilities Commission.

Philadelphia later became one of the largest liquid gas storage centers in the nation.

Although debates over service quality and gas prices repeated on an annual basis, the city continued working with UGI until 1972 and the relationship was widely considered to be functional and beneficial for both parties. Changes in the manufacture and distribution process were the major factors influencing the gas market from the 1928 lease until the 1970s. In the late 1960s, UGI's profits began to decline as a result of difficulty in ensuring customer payment and changes in the retail market.

A RETURN TO MUNICIPAL CONTROL: 1972–2000

During his second term in office, Philadelphia Mayor Frank Rizzo announced that he would cancel the city's contract with UGI thereby ending the 75-year partnership with the company. The decision came at the end of a poor fiscal period for the gas works, which had accrued substantial debt and had reported a $2.1 million loss for the 1972 fiscal period. Although PGW requested a rate increase earlier in the year, the request

was rejected by the Gas Commission, which PGW General Manager Edward Hubbard said would likely contribute to growing financial difficulties.

On December 31, 1972, control of PGW was transferred to the Philadelphia Facilities Management Corporation (PFMC), a nonprofit entity headed by a board of business executives appointed directly by the mayor. The company maintained over 90 percent of its employees, including General Manager Edward Hubbard and most of the senior staff. According to the contract, PFMC was required to maintain payment to the city in the amount of $15.5 million annually, the same sum paid under UGI management, while the city would be released from its annual management fee of $1 million, which UGI used to pay its top managers.

In 1977, the Gas Commission approved a controversial 16 percent rate increase despite protests from consumer groups that the increase exceeded the company's needs. By May 1980, it was announced that the company had accrued more than $40 million in unexpected profits, which many consumers felt validated the assertion that the 1977 rate increase was excessive. The budget surplus was linked by PGW officials to the number of residential conversions from oil to gas heating. Despite a brief period of surplus in the 1980s, by mid-decade the company's profits were again in decline. Customer nonpayment and insufficient revenues contributed to a gradual reduction in profitability during the late 1980s and throughout the 1990s. Some analysts have suggested that government mismanagement was the primary cause for the company's financial degradation and related the company's struggles to those suffered during the city's previous period of municipal management from the 1840s to the 1890s.

REGULATORY CONTROL PASSES TO THE PUBLIC UTILITIES COMMISSION: 2000–2005

Changes in Pennsylvania state law placed PGW under the regulation of the Public Utilities Commission (PUC) in July 2000, permanently dissolving the Gas Commission. The regulatory shift delayed PGW's plans to implement rate increases, expected to generate over $140 million in increased revenues. The Philadelphia City Council agreed in September to permit a city loan of $45 million to PGW as the company's financial situation was preventing payment to its employees and would potentially prevent the company from maintaining gas supplies. The loan was approved in October 2000 and the company's annual payment to the city was suspended until 2008 to allow time for repayment of the loan.

Although PGW's rate increases temporarily improved the company's profits, customer nonpayment remained a major threat to the company's stability. In November 2002, PGW began a program intended to aid low-income Philadelphia residents in paying their heating bills. The Low Income Home Energy Assistance Program (LIHEAP) was made available to residents with income levels under $28,000 and depending on the number of persons occupying the designated area. The program was also intended to aid the company by providing federal assistance to offset deficits from customer default.

In 2003, PGW engaged in a major collection campaign, which included removing services from over 10,000 customers who had persistently failed to make payments. According to company financial statements, nonpayment amounted to over $100 million in lost revenues for the company and was the most significant source of the company's financial difficulties. With assistance from the mayor and the PUC, PGW increased its collection percentage from 87 to 94 percent between 2003 and 2004, although increased revenues did little to offset the company's deficits. PGW press releases from 2005 revealed that more than half of the company's customers failed to pay their bills on time.

PGW FACES BUDGETARY CRISIS: 2006 AND BEYOND

In 2006, the PUC voted on PGW's proposed $1 billion budget for the 2007 operational year. The controversial budget was criticized for a provision requesting $500,000 in funds to pay bonuses to the company's management. The budget was put before a series of four PUC public hearings, during which social workers, legal experts, and customers were invited to share their input. The PUC eventually agreed to approve 25 percent of the company's requested rate increases, from $100 million annually to just over $25 million. PGW appealed the decision in 2007, saying that the approved increase would not allow the company to repay the city's 2000 loan of $45 million by 2008, by which time the company would be forced to resume paying the city an annual $18 million for ownership of the utility.

Financial statements, released in 2007, indicated that the company was faced with a large debt load, amounting to over $1.2 billion. In the wake of the company's continued difficulties, several mayoral candidates and city officials suggested selling the utility to a private management company. PGW management commented that the sale of the company might represent a long-term solution to the budgetary crisis but that immediate solutions needed to be pursued to prevent the company from defaulting on its loans.

Micah L. Issitt

PRINCIPAL COMPETITORS

TXU Energy Retail Company; Sprague Energy Corporation; UGI Energy Services Company.

FURTHER READING

"City Gas Works: A Marked Achievement Until Political Misuse Crept In," *Evening Bulletin,* August 4, 1921.

Davies, Dave, "Sell or Merge PGW—His Bill Calls for End of City Control," *Philadelphia Daily News,* January 23, 2007, p. 5.

Higginbotham, Stacey, "Philadelphia Looks to Help Bail Out Beleaguered Gas Works," *Bond Buyer,* September 26, 2000, p. 1.

Hoffman, David, "Philadelphia Gas Works Pushes Five-Year Financial Plan," *Bond Buyer,* August 16, 1999, p. 29.

———, "Philadelphia Ratings May Ride on PGW," *Bond Buyer,* January 26, 2000, p. 1.

Kruger, Daniel, "Philadelphia Mayoral Candidates Discuss Selling Gas Works," *Bond Buyer,* August 23, 1999, p. 38.

Lewis, William Draper, "The Lease of the Philadelphia Gas Works," *Quarterly Journal of Economics,* January 1898, pp. 209–24.

Lin, Jennifer, "Heating Aid Is Secured for Philadelphia Residents," *Philadelphia Inquirer,* December 27, 2006.

———, "Pa. Trims PGW's Rate-Hike Request," *Philadelphia Inquirer,* September 14, 2007, p. B1.

Lloyd, Jack, "PGW Brought Natural Gas to City 130 Years Ago," *Philadelphia Inquirer,* June 13, 1966.

McDonald, Mark, "Execs Bonuses Weigh Heavily on Vote for PGW's $1B Budget," *Philadelphia Daily News,* October 4, 2006, p. 11.

"Men and Things: Compound of Politics and Gas Caused Explosion in City Hall," *Evening Bulletin,* October 27, 1925.

"Men and Things: Conservative Philadelphia Hesitated for Years Before Using Gas," *Evening Bulletin,* October 22, 1925.

"Men and Things: Gas Works Period Under Cresson Was One of Good Service," *Evening Bulletin,* October 23, 1925.

"Men and Things: Revision of Lease of Gas Works from City," *Evening Bulletin,* March 5, 1937.

Olley, Christine, "PGW Boost Could Cost You $150+ — But Hike Likely Won't Happen This Winter," *Philadelphia Daily News,* December 23, 2006, p. 4.

"Phila. First in U.S. to Use Gas Light," *Evening Bulletin,* January 19, 1938.

"Phila. Gas Works Created by Council 125 Years Ago," *Evening Bulletin,* March 27, 1960, p. 3.

Sikora, Martin J., "... And No Price Increase Is Expected at PGW," *Philadelphia Inquirer,* December 3, 1972.

"Today We Remember: Our Gas Works Started in 1836," *Philadelphia Inquirer,* February 5, 1931.

"$245,000 Deficit Turned into Huge Asset for City," *Evening Bulletin,* August 7, 1944.

Urgo, Jacqueline L., "Planned Rate Hike by PGW Assailed at Last of 4 Hearings," *Philadelphia Inquirer,* April 10, 2007, p. B8.

Warner, Bob, "Users May Not Profit from PGW Windfall," *Philadelphia Daily News,* May 13, 1980.

Philadelphia
Media Holdings LLC

—■—

400 North Broad Street
Philadelphia, Pennsylvania 19130
U.S.A.
Telephone: (215) 854-2000
Fax: (215) 854-5954
Web site: http://www.pnionline.com

Private Company
Incorporated: 2006
Employees: 3,066
Sales: $180.1 million (2007 est.)
NAIC: 511110 Newspaper Publishers and Printing;
516110 Internet Publishing and Broadcasting

■ ■ ■

Philadelphia Media Holdings LLC is the parent company of the *Philadelphia Inquirer,* the *Philadelphia Daily News,* and the online accompaniment www.philly. com. Philadelphia Media Holdings (PMH) was formed in 2005 as a union of investors seeking to purchase local media assets from the McClatchy Company after Mc-Clatchy completed a major buyout of the Knight-Ridder Company in early 2006. During its first year of operation, PMH initiated measures to increase circulation and profitability, including reducing the budget and staff for both papers. As of 2007, the *Philadelphia Inquirer* was the eighth largest newspaper in the United States and revenues from all PMH assets totaled over $180 million annually.

HISTORY OF THE *PHILADELPHIA INQUIRER:* 1829–1969

The *Philadelphia Inquirer* was founded in June 1829, under the name *Pennsylvania Inquirer,* by John Norvell, a lawyer and former editor of the *Baltimore Whig,* and John R. Walker, a newspaper printer. In its own right, the *Inquirer* is the third-oldest printed paper in the nation; however, as a result of a merger with the *Philadelphia Public Ledger* in 1931, which itself merged with the *Pennsylvania Packet,* which began publication in 1771, the *Inquirer* holds claim to the oldest continuous newspaper lineage in the United States.

Jesper Harding, a Philadelphia native and publisher of religious materials, purchased the *Pennsylvania Inquirer* from Norvell and Walker several months after the newspaper began production. In the 1830s, Harding began publishing editorials against the presidency of Andrew Jackson, after Jackson began his attack against the Central Bank. The *Inquirer* was thereafter known for its editorial support of the opposing Whig Party. In the 1840s, Harding achieved another milestone for the *Inquirer* when he obtained the exclusive serial rights to publish several of the novels of Charles Dickens in the paper. Harding also published, in 1845, the Edgar Allan Poe poem, "The Raven."

Ownership of the *Inquirer* passed from Harding to his son William White Harding in 1855, while Jesper Harding went on to serve the federal government as Collector of Internal Revenue under President Abraham Lincoln. William Harding changed the paper's name to the *Philadelphia Inquirer* in 1860. Under the younger Harding's leadership, the *Inquirer* gained national fame

COMPANY PERSPECTIVES

■

Recognizing the rapidly changing environment of the communications industry, Philadelphia Media Holdings LLC and its subsidiaries, The Philadelphia Inquirer and Philadelphia Daily News, have moved to secure a leadership position among newspaper companies throughout the country. That means stretching the boundaries of how newspapers have traditionally defined themselves, reaching deeply into their core activities and developing new products to benefit their customers, both readers and advertisers. Already, The Inquirer and Daily News, together and separately, are testing new markets and delivering quality products to fit them.

for its coverage of the Civil War, when the paper was circulated to Union troops. In addition, Harding instated new distribution routes that significantly increased the paper's reach within the Philadelphia area.

In 1889, ownership passed to James Elverson, a British-born publisher and entrepreneur who was an avid supporter of the Republican Party. Elverson utilized the *Inquirer* to support and report on developments in politics and to organize Republican Party events. When Philadelphia hosted the Republican National Convention in 1900, Elverson had a sign constructed across Broad Street, the city's largest north-south thoroughfare, which contained over 2,000 lightbulbs spelling the message, "Philadelphia Inquirer: Largest Republican Circulation in the World."

Elverson was the first to add a Sunday edition to the *Inquirer,* which quickly became the paper's most popular publication. Ownership eventually passed to Elverson's son, James "Colonel" Elverson, Jr., whose innovations greatly increased the scope and influence of the paper. From 1900 to the 1920s, the *Inquirer* was known as the most prominent Republican publication in the nation and was often called the "Republican Bible."

After the death of Colonel Elverson the paper was passed to his sister Eleanor who sold the paper in 1930 to Cyrus Curtis, the publisher of the *Public Ledger,* for the sum of $10 million. Curtis' son, John Martin, assumed control after the death of his father in 1931 and merged the *Inquirer* with the *Public Ledger.* Martin was forced to sell the paper back to Eleanor Elverson when the merger failed to turn a profit. In 1936, Moses An-

nenberg purchased the *Inquirer* for a reported sum of $4 million and the assumption of $6.8 million in debt.

Moses Annenberg and his son Walter managed the paper together and invested heavily in increasing the paper's circulation and advertising revenues. The Annenbergs already owned a substantial media business with interests and ownership in newspapers, radio, and television, and used funds from their established media businesses to fund the expansion and rehabilitation of the *Inquirer.*

In 1939, Moses Annenberg was convicted for evading federal income taxes amounting to over $3.2 million and was sentenced to three years in prison. Annenberg died just over a month after his release from prison, and the business was inherited by his son. Walter Annenberg became famous on a national level for his investments and his interest in politics. Under his leadership, the *Inquirer* continued to expand, and in 1957 Annenberg purchased the *Philadelphia Daily News,* a tabloid-format paper that had come under financial strain and was thereby available at a reduced price.

Annenberg had a long history of involvement in national politics and in 1969 was asked to serve as ambassador to Britain under President Richard M. Nixon. Annenberg decided to sell both the *Inquirer* and the *Daily News* to John S. Knight, whose company, Knight Newspapers, Inc., had become one of the largest media ownership companies in the nation. The sale of both papers was completed in 1969 for a sum of $55 million.

HISTORY OF THE *PHILADELPHIA DAILY NEWS:* 1925–57

The *Philadelphia Daily News,* a tabloid-style newspaper focusing mainly on local news and sports, published its first issue in 1925, under owner and publisher Lee Ellmaker. Although Ellmaker is often credited as the newspaper's first owner, the Pennsylvania Historical Commission published, in 1937, a guide to the history of Philadelphia, which claims that William Scott Vare, a local construction industry leader and Republican Party politician, reportedly funded the establishment of the newspaper to aid in his 1925 election campaign for the U.S. Senate.

According to the Historical Commission, Ellmaker and Vare were friends and associates and Ellmaker served as general manager of the paper although he owned only a minority of the stock shares. After his election to the Senate, Vare sold stock in the *Daily News* to media mogul Bernard McFadden, who also published *Physical Culture* and *True Romance* magazines. McFadden sold his shares to Ellmaker in 1934, who was then the majority owner of the newspaper.

KEY DATES
■

1829: *Pennsylvania Inquirer* founded by John Norvell and John R. Walker; *Inquirer* purchased by Jesper Harding.

1860: Name changed to *Philadelphia Inquirer.*

1889: Ownership of *Inquirer* passes to James Elverson.

1925: *Philadelphia Daily News* started by William S. Vare and Lee Ellmaker.

1931: *Inquirer* merges with the *Public Ledger* to become the oldest paper chain in the United States.

1936: *Inquirer* sold to Moses Annenberg.

1940: *Daily News* sold to Matthew McCloskey.

1957: *Philadelphia Daily News* purchased by Walter Annenberg.

1969: *Daily News* and *Philadelphia Inquirer* sold to Knight Newspapers, Inc.

1972: Eugene Roberts hired as editor for the *Inquirer.*

1975: *Inquirer* receives its first Pulitzer Prize.

1995: Knight-Ridder launches www.philly.com.

2005: Philadelphia Media Holdings LLC incorporated by Brian Tierney and partners.

2006: *Inquirer* and *Daily News* sold to McClatchy Company; McClatchy sells *Inquirer* and *Daily News* to Philadelphia Media Holdings.

The *Daily News* had a long history of financial difficulty. Although the paper's circulation exceeded 200,000 in the 1930s, readership dropped during the 1940s and Ellmaker was faced with discontinuing publication or seeking loans to keep the paper in print. Ellmaker eventually decided to sell the *Daily News* to Matthew McCloskey, a construction industry contractor and a leading fund-raiser for the Philadelphia Democratic Party.

McCloskey tried to reverse the paper's financial collapse by reducing the budget and staff, after a series of negotiations with the unions. Although McCloskey had some minor success in increasing readership, the *Daily News* was still losing revenue and, in 1957, McCloskey sold the paper to Walter Annenberg, publisher of the *Inquirer.* In an effort to revitalize the paper, Annenberg transformed the *Daily News* into an afternoon edition format with an increasing focus on local news.

KNIGHT NEWSPAPERS OWNERSHIP: 1969–2006

After purchasing the *Inquirer* and the *Daily News,* Knight Newspapers, Inc., substantially altered the formats for both papers. The *Daily News* was returned to its initial morning publication format, while the *Inquirer* was shifted toward a more politically focused news format.

In 1972, Knight hired Eugene L. Roberts as executive editor for the *Inquirer.* Roberts had previously worked for the *New York Times* covering the civil rights movement as the paper's "Southern Correspondent," and later providing battlefield coverage during the Vietnam conflict. Under Roberts' leadership, the public perception of the *Inquirer* gradually improved and the paper's writers and editors were lauded by the journalism community for their efforts. In 1975, the newspaper received its first Pulitzer Prize, when writers Donald Bartlett and James Steele won the award for National Journalism. Between 1975 and 1990, writers at the *Inquirer* received a total of 18 Pulitzer Prizes. In 1982, when the *Evening Bulletin* ceased publication, the *Inquirer* and the *Daily News* were left as the sole daily newspapers in Philadelphia.

In 1974, Knight Newspapers merged with Ridder Publications to become Knight-Ridder, which was the largest newspaper publisher in the United States during the 1980s until it was surpassed by the Gannett Company, owner of *USA Today* magazine. While the acquisition and leadership of Roberts helped to elevate the *Inquirer,* the *Daily News* also gained recognition and won two Pulitzer Prizes in 1982 and 1992, for editorial writing and cartooning respectively. Despite its increased success, the *Daily News* continued to suffer from financial difficulties and it was often speculated that Knight-Ridder would abandon the paper.

During the 1990s, the national newspaper industry suffered from a decline in readership and subscriptions, partially linked to the advent and proliferation of Internet journalism. Knight-Ridder attempted to keep abreast of the trends by shifting to the online market. In 1993, Knight-Ridder began working with America Online to develop newspaper content for Internet readers and in 1995 they launched www.philly.com, a web site that gave readers access to the *Inquirer* and the *Daily News* through the World Wide Web. By the late 1990s, much of the content of both newspapers was available in online format.

By 2005, Knight-Ridder's profits had fallen to unacceptable levels and the company was considering selling off its media holdings. Although management was approached by several companies seeking to purchase portions of the company's assets, Knight-

Ridder preferred to sell the company as a single unit. In late 2005, it was announced that the company was negotiating an outright sale to the McClatchy Company. In June 2006, negotiations were concluded and McClatchy bought the company's assets for a combined sum of $6.5 billion, which included assuming over $1 billion in debt. At the conclusion of the sale, McClatchy operated 32 daily newspapers with a combined circulation of over three million.

PHILADELPHIA MEDIA HOLDINGS: 2006–07

Shortly after the announcement in 2005 of the impending sale to McClatchy, the company released an announcement that it would consider selling portions of the assets acquired from Knight-Ridder to interested companies. Brian Tierney, a public relations representative turned investor, began seeking partners to invest in purchasing the Philadelphia-area assets after the completion of the sale. In preparation for the bidding process, Tierney and partners formed Philadelphia Media Holdings LLC (PMH).

Following the completion of the June 2006 sale, McClatchy immediately resold twelve of its newspaper acquisitions. Tierney and partners at PMH acquired the *Inquirer, Daily News,* and the accompanying web site for a total of $562 million.

Among Tierney's co-investors were NutriSystem CEO Michael Hagan and Eastern Technology Fund, a King of Prussia, Pennsylvania–based investment group that owned technology and healthcare companies, and the Regional Carpenters' Union Pension Plan. Tierney took control of the papers as publisher and CEO and in November 2006 brought Mark Frisby from the *Courier-Post* in Camden, New Jersey, to serve as the company's executive vice-president.

A 2006 analysis by the Audit Bureau of Circulations reported that the circulation of the nation's newspapers had fallen by an average of 2.8 percent per year, while the circulation for the *Inquirer* had dropped by approximately 7.6 percent during the same period. Falling circulation posed a threat to PMH investments and forced Tierney and partners to initiate a broad strategy for company development.

Early in 2007, PMH announced that it would be reducing the staff at the *Philadelphia Inquirer* by 68 editorial employees. The employment cutbacks came at the end of strenuous negotiations with the Newspaper Guild of Greater Philadelphia. Employment reductions were part of a plan by PMH to increase the profitability of the newspapers, which also included curtailing sick pay and seniority benefits. According to official press releases, cutbacks would save approximately $6.8 million in annual expenditures.

In the wake of the 2007 layoffs, PMH came under criticism by organizations representing the city's African American journalists. According to the Philadelphia Association of Black Journalists, over 20 percent of persons removed from the *Inquirer* staff were African American, of the 11.3 percent of African Americans working on the *Inquirer* staff. Accusations of racial bias were lodged against PMH for the disproportionate representation of African Americans laid off during the company's restructuring.

In May 2007, Executive Vice-President Mark Frisby was asked to take over the helm as publisher of the *Philadelphia Daily News,* while Tierney remained publisher and CEO of the *Inquirer.* Frisby maintained his role as executive vice president of labor and production while focusing on increasing the circulation and relevance of the *Daily News.* The announcement of Frisby's appointment came along with announcements that the yearlong decline in circulation for both papers had begun to subside.

In June, Tierney organized a partnership with Monster Worldwide, Inc., the parent company of the national employment web site www.monster.com. In 2007, Monster Worldwide commanded over 50 percent of web-based employment searches. According to press releases, Philly.com received over two million unique visitors each month and was the fastest-growing portion of PMH. In order to capitalize on the web site's popularity, Tierney announced that the company would spend $20 million to improve the web service.

In August, PMH announced that it would be selling the historic Inquirer Building at the corner of Broad and Callowhill Streets. Tierney said that the sale was a result of a number of factors including the mismatch between the size of the building and the company's staff. Tierney said further that revenues from the sale would be reinvested in developing the company and paying down debt.

Micah L. Issitt

PRINCIPAL SUBSIDIARIES

Philadelphia Inquirer; Philadelphia Daily News; Philly.com.

PRINCIPAL COMPETITORS

Gannett Co., Inc.; Journal Register Company; South Jersey Publishing Company.

FURTHER READING

Campisi, Gloria, "Exec Exits Papers to Become Head of N.Y. Lottery," *Philadelphia Daily News,* September 19, 2007.

DiStefano, Joseph N., "Tech Fund Joins Group Buying Inquirer, Daily News," *Philadelphia Inquirer,* June 8, 2006.

Fernandez, Bob, "68 to Lose Jobs at Philadelphia Inquirer," *Philadelphia Inquirer,* January 2, 2007.

"Job Web Site Forms Venture with Two Philadelphia Papers," *New York Times,* July 26, 2007, p. C5.

Klein, Julia M., "Dark Days: Labor Loses More Ground in the Newsroom," *Columbia Journalism Review,* March/April 2007, pp. 16–17.

Lucey, Catherine, "Inquirer, News Building Up for Sale," *Philadelphia Daily News,* August 22, 2007.

———, "Mark Frisby Named People Paper Publisher," *Philadelphia Daily News,* May 24, 2007, p. 4.

Manly, Lorne, "Seeking to Cash In on the 'Hyperlocal,'" *New York Times,* December 31, 2006, p. 4.

Seelye, Katherine Q., and Andrew Ross Sorkin, "Newspaper Chain Agrees to a Sale for 4.5 Billion," *New York Times,* March 13, 2006.

Shapiro, Howard, "We're Still Here, and Still Asking Why," *Philadelphia Inquirer,* May 24, 2006, p. A14.

Steel, Emily, "Newspaper Circulations Slide More; Broad Decline May Hasten Move to Hone Web Focus; New York Tabloids Log Gains," *Wall Street Journal,* October 31, 2006, p. B2.

Steinberg, Brian, "Questions with … Brian P. Tierney," *Wall Street Journal,* November 29, 2006.

Toomer, Regan, "Philly Paper Demotes Stephen A. Smith," *New Pittsburgh Courier,* September 5, 2007, p. C5.

Washington, Rhodes E., "Layoffs Take Media in Wrong Direction," *Philadelphia Tribune,* January 16, 2007, p. 6A.

Plain Dealer Publishing Company

—■—

1801 Superior Avenue East
Cleveland, Ohio 44114
U.S.A.
Telephone: (216) 999-5000
Toll Free: (800) 362-0727
Fax: (216) 999-6354
Web site: http://www.plaind.com

Wholly Owned Subsidiary of Advance Publications Inc.
Incorporated: 1877
Employees: 900
Sales: $1.7 billion (2006)
NAIC: 511110 Newspaper Publishers

■ ■ ■

The Plain Dealer Publishing Company is the publisher of the *Cleveland Plain Dealer,* part of the Newhouse News Service group of some two dozen newspapers within the media conglomerate Advanced Publications Inc. With a circulation of more than 800,000, the *Plain Dealer* is ranked 20th on the list of largest U.S. daily newspapers and is the largest newspaper by circulation in the state of Ohio. The Sunday edition boasts a circulation of 1.1 million. The paper maintains news bureaus in Columbus, the state capital, as well as in Washington, D.C., where its reporters focus on Ohio's elected officials and matters that pertain to the state. The *Plain Dealer* also provides content to Cleveland. com, a web site owned by Advance Internet, another Newhouse venture that also runs a chain of suburban

weeklies, Sun Newspapers, which supply some content to the *Plain Dealer.*

MID-19TH-CENTURY ORIGINS

Although the *Plain Dealer* dates its founding to 1842, the newspaper could make a case for an earlier date. A predecessor publication, the weekly *Cleveland Advertiser,* published its first issue in January 1831. Five years later it became a daily but in time reverted to weekly status, as the floundering enterprise changed hands several times. On the brink of ruin, the *Advertiser* was in desperate need of new ownership by the end of 1841. Salvation arrived in form of two brothers, Admiral Nelson Gray and his brother, ten years younger, Joseph William (J. W.) Gray.

The brothers had arrived in Cleveland several years earlier to teach school, but J. W. quickly tired of the work, so he read for the law and became a practicing attorney in Michigan for a time before returning to Cleveland to indulge his passion for politics. A Democrat, he wrote partisan articles for the *Advertiser,* so that when the newspaper was forced to cease publication and be put up for sale he convinced his brother to become his partner in purchasing it. Thus, the elder brother handled the business aspects of the venture, while the younger Gray became editor. When the newspaper resumed publication in 1842, it did so under a new name: the *Plain Dealer.*

Although there is no official explanation for the name, J. W. Gray was possibly influenced by a short-lived New York weekly called the *Plain Dealer,* established in 1836 by William Leggett, who died three

---

COMPANY PERSPECTIVES

■

The Plain Dealer pays special attention to things medical with a five person health and science team. Other areas of interest: local government coverage, computer-assisted reporting, education and—reflecting Cleveland's preoccupation with athletics—sports, preps to pros.

---

years later. Given that Gray often paid tribute to Leggett in his writings, there is some reason to believe that he borrowed the name of Leggett's publication.

J. W. Gray possessed a combative, partisan spirit; he was a devout Democrat in what would become a Republican stronghold. Nevertheless, he found enough of a readership to encourage him to begin thinking about turning the weekly into a daily. He would do so, however, without his brother, who after 18 months of newspaper ownership sold out his share to J. W. Admiral Nelson Gray, more interested in business than picking political fights, went on to build a fortune in real estate and railroad enterprises. His younger brother, in the meantime, began publishing the *Plain Dealer* on a daily basis in April 1845, employing the grandiose motto: "Cleveland before any other town in the states; the state before any other state in the Union; and the Union against the world!"

Gray's loyalty to the Union as well as the Democratic Party would be tested in the years to come, as the issue of slavery divided the country and led to the rise of the Republican Party in the early 1850s. Gray became a supporter of Stephen A. Douglas, and the *Plain Dealer* endorsed him over Abraham Lincoln in the crucial election of 1860, but after Lincoln won the presidency, Gray supported the new administration and preservation of the Union at a time when southern states vowed to secede. By this time, however, Gray's health was failing, and he was able to devote only a limited amount of time to the publication. In 1856 he had been injured when his son's toy pistol sent part of a percussion cap into his right eye. He quickly lost sight in that eye, and the left was soon infected as well; gradually he succumbed to what was considered a form of paralysis affecting the brain.

Gray died in May 1862, and the *Plain Dealer* was taken over by the administrator of his estate, John S. Stephenson, who decided to try his hand as editor and publisher. While Gray had expressed a willingness to back Lincoln's effort to put down the rebellion in the

South, Stephenson became a staunch critic of the president. Lincoln never suffered from a shortage of critics, but after he won reelection in 1864, Union victory was within sight in 1865, and his popularity soared in the North, Stephenson toned down his remarks. His comments of the previous years were not so easily forgotten, however, and Gray's widow petitioned the courts to have Stephenson removed as administrator of her husband's estate. To end the matter, he resigned. With Stephenson gone, the *Plain Dealer* ceased publication in March 1865.

PLAIN DEALER PUBLISHING COMPANY FORMED: 1877

The newspaper resumed publication several weeks later under the editorship of new owner William M. Armstrong, a Tiffin, Ohio, newspaper publisher, who was also a Democrat. Armstrong had been more circumspect in his criticism of the war, however, and had thereby avoided alienating portions of the community. He was able to revive the newspaper, and while he sold a half-interest to William D. Morgan, which later went to Frederick W. Green, Armstrong ran the newspaper for 20 years. During this time he formed the Plain Dealer Publisher Company in 1877 to publish the newspaper as well as to conduct job printing and the publishing of books, pamphlets, and other documents. At the time the *Plain Dealer* was an evening daily, but to attract mail subscribers Stephenson also added a morning edition in 1872. That edition was soon shuttered, however.

OWNERSHIP CHANGES AND NEW FORMATS

In late 1884 Armstrong sold the Plain Dealer Publishing Company to a group of investors led by Liberty Emery Holden for $100,000. Under Holden's direction, the *Plain Dealer* reinstituted a morning edition in March 1885, following the acquisition of a morning paper, the *Cleveland Herald*, the assets of which Holden split with the *Cleveland Leader*. In essence, the *Plain Dealer* took over the *Herald*'s plant, equipment, and advertising contracts while the *Leader* acquired the circulation. Holden used the *Plain Dealer* to advocate his positions, in particular the cause of bimetallism, which would have put silver on an equal footing with gold as a monetary standard and could be coined without limit.

Holden had a vested interest in this heated question of the day because he was a silver producer. For the most part, however, he paid little attention to the day-to-day affairs of the newspaper, turning over editorial control to others after Armstrong retired in 1886. In addition to morning and evening editions, the *Plain*

Dealer soon launched a Sunday edition as well. In 1893 Holden took personal control of business, but by 1898, with the paper losing money each month, he decided the time had come to bring in a veteran newspaper man. He found such a man in Elbert Hall Baker, who would play a key role in making the *Plain Dealer* a success.

As the *Plain Dealer* entered the 20th century, the evening edition, which had been the foundation of the paper, did not perform as well as the other editions, partly because of a crowded field. A new company, the Meridian Printing Company, arose and began to consolidate the evening field. In July 1905 the Plain Dealer Publishing Company agreed to sell the evening paper to Meridian. Thus, the *Plain Dealer* became exclusively a morning and Sunday newspaper. The company would soon have a new, modern newspaper plant as well, precipitated by a fire in 1908 that destroyed the old plant.

Holden died in 1913 and ownership of Plain Dealer Publishing was placed in trust for his heirs. He did not live to witness one of the newspaper's greatest moments of triumph. Since its founding, the *Plain Dealer* had sparred with the rival *Cleveland Leader;* the two papers were opposed editorially and often challenged one another's circulation claims. Under Baker's leadership, however, the *Plain Dealer* outmaneuvered its bitter rival, whose business gradually withered. In August 1917 the Plain Dealer Publishing Company bought out the *Leader* for $750,000, leaving the *Plain Dealer* in the enviable position as Cleveland's only morning newspaper. Three years later Baker retired.

Plain Dealer Publishing remained in the hands of Holden's heirs. In 1932 they retained control but through a newly formed entity called Forest City Publishing Company. Forest City was incorporated in September of that year to consolidate Cleveland's newspaper field, acquiring both the *Plain Dealer's* morning and Sunday editions and the *Cleveland News* with its morning and Sunday editions. The Holden family held majority control of Forest City, and *Plain Dealer* management dominated the new company. Nevertheless, the *Plain Dealer* and *News* operated independently, maintaining their own staffs and printing in their own plants.

The *Plain Dealer* had been a staunchly Democratic paper for nearly a century when in 1940 it changed course and endorsed the Republican candidate for president, Wendell L. Willkie. Four years earlier the newspaper had reluctantly endorsed President Franklin Roosevelt, whom the editorial board considered more of a Socialist than a Democrat. While the *Plain Dealer* insisted that it remained a Democratic newspaper, claiming that it was Roosevelt who had forsaken the principles of the party, some maintained that it had become more Republican in orientation. Only in 1964 and 1992 did the newspaper endorse the Democratic candidate for president. (In 2004, in a somewhat controversial move, the newspaper's editorial board voted to endorse presidential candidate and Democrat John Kerry, but the publisher overturned the decision and declared that the paper would not endorse a candidate in that election.)

NEWHOUSE BUYS *PLAIN DEALER:* 1967

With no true competition in the morning, the *Plain Dealer* became somewhat staid during the postwar years. Finally, however, the Holden family began to shake things up. In 1960 Forest City sold the *News* to the *Cleveland Press,* the city and state's largest newspaper, and the *Plain Dealer* took over the *News* headquarters. Two years later, Thomas V. H. Vail, one of Holden's great-grandsons, took over as publisher and editor at the age of 36. He tried to reinvigorate the newspaper by hiring young reporters, resulting in a more aggressive approach to reporting.

As a result, the paper began to make significant increases in circulation, threatening the supremacy of the evening *Press,* whose circulation was about 380,000 by 1967. However, Vail often had his hands tied in the running the *Plain Dealer* because its ownership was divided among half a dozen trusts and their attendant bankers and lawyers, none of whom were "newspaper people." Instead they wanted to diversify. In addition to the newspaper, the Plain Dealer Publishing Company included a community TV antenna company, some lakeshore real estate, and the Art Gravure Corporation, a printer of Sunday supplements. In 1967 the conflict came to an end when publishing magnate Sam Newhouse added the *Plain Dealer* to his chain of 21 U.S. dailies, paying a record $54.2 million. Vail told *Time* magazine that he was more than pleased with the sale: "What we have now is a newspaperman committed to our program. His first interest is the paper and its future." The *Plain Dealer* became the largest newspaper in the Newhouse stable.

Vail stayed on as publisher and editor and was given a free hand to challenge the supremacy of the *Cleveland Press.* In 1968 the *Plain Dealer* surpassed the *Press* in circulation, becoming the largest newspaper in Ohio. It continued to grow while the *Press* fell further behind. Finally, in 1982 the *Press* went out of business leaving the *Plain Dealer* as Cleveland's only newspaper. In 1985 a grand jury was convened to investigate allegations that Advance Publications, the Newhouse subsidiary that assumed control of the newspaper chain, had conspired to drive the *Press* out of business and achieve a monopoly for the *Plain Dealer* in Cleveland. No charges were filed.

In 1991 Vail retired. He was replaced as publisher by Alex Machaskee. Shortly before Vail's departure, the newspaper began printing three "zoned" editions, for specific regions, to stimulate ad sales, a move that proved successful. Under Machaskee, the *Plain Dealer* took steps to open a new state-of-the-art printing plant and distribution center. About 90 acres of land was purchased in Brooklyn, Ohio, at the cost of $6.3 million in 1991. Three years later a new $200 million facility opened on the site. In 1997 Plain Dealer Publishing began buying up land near the site of its former printing operation. The company was then able to open Plain Dealer Plaza in the new century, housing the newspaper's editorial and administrative offices.

By the mid-1990s the *Plain Dealer*'s circulation was about 400,000 for the daily edition and 550,000 for the Sunday paper. The newspaper industry was undergoing some significant changes at this time; newspaper readership was on the decline when the Internet emerged to present new challenges. To adapt to changing environment, Plain Dealer Publishing formed Plain Dealer New Media in 1996 and launched a site called www.cleveland.com. Rather than simply post articles from the pages of the *Plain Dealer* online as most newspapers did, the new venture formed a separate news division for the Internet. In 1998 Advance acquired the Sun Newspapers

chain of 23 weekly newspaper serving suburban Cleveland, and editorial content from the weeklies was shared with the *Plain Dealer.*

The predicted demise of the newspaper did not materialize, and the *Plain Dealer* did realize increases in circulation. Not all was going well, however. The *Sunday Magazine,* published since the 1920s, experienced declining revenues. Because it was also expensive to produce, Plain Dealer Publishing elected to cease publication of the magazine in late 2005. That content was incorporated into the rest of the Sunday newspaper.

In 2006, a new publisher and president came to the *Plain Dealer:* Terrance C. Z. (Terry) Egger. Egger, who replaced the retiring Machaskee, had served as the publisher of the *St. Louis Post-Dispatch.* In May 2007 the *Plain Dealer* hired its first woman editor, 47-year-old Susan Goldberg, an industry veteran who left her post as executive editor and vice-president of the *San Jose Mercury News* to take the job in Cleveland. Egger and Goldberg were faced with several challenges as they settled into their new posts, among them cutting costs and bolstering readership in creative new ways.

Ed Dinger

PRINCIPAL DIVISIONS

Plain Dealer New Media.

PRINCIPAL COMPETITORS

The New York Times Company; Gannett Company Inc.

FURTHER READING

Booth, John, "Fit for Print: Next Plain Dealer Publisher to Face New Challenges in Changing Media Industry," *Crain's Cleveland Business,* January 23, 2006.

Cook, Bob, "PD Shuts News Staff Out of Online Venture," *Crain's Cleveland Business,* November 18, 1996, p. 2.

"A Cordial Welcome for Newhouse," *Time,* March 10, 1967.

Cunningham, Brent, "The Newhouse Way," *Columbia Journalism Review,* January/February 2000.

Mooney, Barbara, "Good News and Bad at PD," *Crain's Cleveland Business,* August 5, 1991, p. 1.

Roberts, Michael D., "News Maker: The Plain Dealer's New Publisher, Terry C. Z. Egger, Has His Work Cut Out for Him," *Inside Business,* November 1, 2006.

Shaw, Archer Hayes, *The Plain Dealer: One Hundred Years in Cleveland,* New York: A.A. Knopf, 1942, 399 p.

Reliable partners in innovation

Puratos S.A./NV

Industrialaan 25
Zone Maalbeek
Groot Bijgaarden, B-1702
Belgium
Telephone: (32 02) 481 44 44
Fax: (32 02) 466 25 81
Web site: http://www.puratos.com

Private Company
Incorporated: 1997
Employees: 4,500
Sales: EUR 750 million ($900 million) (2007 est.)
NAIC: 311822 Flour Mixes and Dough Manufacturing
from Purchased Flour

■ ■ ■

Puratos S.A./NV is a major producer of bakery ingredients and semifinished bakery, patisserie, chocolate, and confectionery products. The Groot Bijgaarden, Belgium–based company supports the global bakery industry through its complete range of bread improvers, including its flagship S500 and T500 lines. (Bread improver is a baking product similar in texture to flour and consisting of ascorbic acid, enzymes, and other ingredients that ensure the proper texture and volume of baked bread.) The company also produces enzymes, yeasts, sourdoughs, emulsifiers, milled flours, and flour mixes. Moreover, Puratos's bakery division produces semicooked, partially finished, and frozen breads for the industrial and wholesale markets.

Puratos is also widely known for its high-quality chocolate ingredients, a business conducted primarily through subsidiary Belcolade, the largest supplier of chocolate in Belgium. Belcolade produces a complete range of chocolate products, including coverture, coatings, fillings, and decorations, for the industrial and wholesale market. In fact, for that market, the company claims the global number two spot.

The third Puratos division, Patisserie, supplies fruit and cream fillings; mixes, including cake mixes, spongecake mixes, pudding, and cream mixes; glazes, icings, and fudges; and fats, greasing agents, margarines, and nondairy toppings to this market segment. Puratos's strong research and development division, which includes its network of 36 "innovation centers" around the world, enables the company to remain at the forefront of the global baked goods and foods industries. Puratos itself is a globally operating company, with more than 90 manufacturing and distribution subsidiaries and 4,500 employees in 53 countries around the world. The company has been controlled by the Van Belle family since the 1950s and claims sales of more than EUR 750 million ($900 million) in the early 2000s.

ORIGINS IN BRUSSELS IN 1919

Puratos originated in Brussels in the aftermath of World War I as a producer of food ingredients for the professional food sector. Founded in 1919, the company's first ingredients were mixes for ice cream and confectionery items. By the mid-1920s, however the company had entered into the bakery sector, following the launch of its first branded bread mix, Pura Malte, in 1923. The

COMPANY PERSPECTIVES

Our passion is to help bakers, patissiers and choco-latiers around the world be successful with their business. By working alongside them, we develop reliable, original and innovative ingredients, technologies and solutions. Our goal is to give our customers absolute peace of mind. Thanks to our global presence and understanding of different cultures, we also aim to be a source of creativity and new ideas. We work with our customers as partners every step of the way, so they can continue to offer the best to their clients. We want to be their reliable partners in innovation.

mix, featuring toasted wheat germ, became a popular item for the company, and would remain part of the company's catalog into the 21st century. The Pura Malte brand also served as the inspiration for the company's name.

The next major milestone for the company came during World War II, when Francois Van Belle and Pierre Demanet joined the company. The Van Belle family ultimately came to control the company and through its continued growth became one of the country's richest families. Part of that success came from the company's new commitment to research and development and product innovation in the postwar era. This led to the introduction of the company's first breakthrough product, a fat-based bread improver called S500. The new product played an important role in the increasing industrialization of the bread industry, enabling the large-scale production of bread, as well as increasing its shelf-life. Backed by the success of S500, the company rapidly expanded its sales throughout Europe. Into the mid-1950s, the company also launched a line of emulsifiers, necessary to restore the texture to bread lost to the industrialized baking process.

By the early 1960s, Puratos had begun to set up a network of distribution partners throughout Europe. Among these was a partnership created with a Fribourg, Switzerland–based distributor, which began importing T500 and other Puratos products for the Swiss market. By the early 1970s, the company had begun to set up its own internationally operating manufacturing and distribution network. As part of this effort, the company acquired several of its foreign distributors, starting with the Fribourg business in 1973. Puratos Schweiz AG, as the subsidiary was called, launched its own production of Puratos's products at a factory in Düdingen, in the

Fribourg region, before moving to new facilities in Domdidier, also in Fribourg, in 1978.

In the meantime, Puratos had been expanding its operations both in Belgium and globally. With rising demand from the domestic and international markets, the company founded a new factory and headquarters in Groot Bijgaarden, a suburb of Brussels, in 1968. The new facility also provided the group with expanded research and development (R&D) facilities, and the company's R&D effort soon led to its next breakthrough product.

In 1975, Puratos introduced its next generation bread improver, the S500. This product helped to revolutionize the bakery industry and set Puratos on course to becoming a globally operating company. Backed by strong international demand for its improvers, enzymes, bread mixes, sourdough starters, and other bakery products, Puratos continued to add new international subsidiaries. In 1981, for example, the company entered the U.S. market, establishing a headquarters in New Jersey. The company also entered Mexico, Brazil, Canada, and other markets in the Americas over the next decades. In Spain, the company teamed with a local partner to form T500 Puratos S.A., which quickly grew into a centerpiece of the company's total operations.

PRODUCT DIVERSIFICATION IN THE EIGHTIES

Into the early 1980s, Puratos sought its first expansion beyond the bakery sector. The company launched its own margarine subsidiary, Aristo, starting from 1980. By 1988, the company had added another new area of business—the production of chocolate. For this, the company became a cofounder of Belcolade, based in Erembodegm and dedicated to the production of Belgian chocolates. That company began developing a line of chocolate products for the industrial and professional sectors, such as chocolate drops. By 1993, the company had extended its main chocolate production into the chocolate- and nut-based fillings.

By then, too, Puratos had targeted another natural extension for its core ingredients and additives operations. In 1990, the company added a new division focused on products for the patisserie sector, starting with fruit-based fillings and other products. The company's patisserie product line later grew to include a complete range of ingredients, additives, mixes, toppings, and fillings, including cake and sponge-cake mixes; pudding, mousse, and custard mixes; cream and fruit fillings; and flavorings, glazes, and icings. Meanwhile, in the company's main bakery division, the

KEY DATES

1919: Founding of company in Brussels to produce mixes for ice cream and confectionery.
1923: Launch of Pura Malte brand bread mix.
1953: Launch of the T500 bread improver.
1973: First foreign subsidiary is created in Switzerland.
1975: Introduction of the S500 bread improver.
1980: Company establishes subsidiary in United States and launches margarine production.
1988: Cofounds chocolates subsidiary Belcolade.
1990: Production of patisserie ingredients is begun.
1997: Restructuring of international holdings, including T500 Puratos in Spain, creates Puratos Group.
2002: A new generation of bread improvers, Acti-Plus, is launched.

company launched new production operations in enzymes and sourdoughs.

A major stimulant to the company's growing line of products, and to sales as well, was the creation of its first Quality Center, constructed in 1984, which provided development services as well as customer support services. The company later rolled out a network of such support sites, which became known as Innovation Centers. By the early 2000s, the company operated 36 such centers. At the same time, Puratos continued to build its own internal R&D capacity. This effort was given a major boost in 1988 when Puratos founded its first dedicated R&D center.

Into the mid-1990s, Puratos began to rationalize its far-flung operations. A major step in the creation of a single, centralized corporation came in 1997, when Puratos acquired majority control of Spain's T500 Puratos S.A. By 1999, the company had taken full control of the Spanish business, which was then merged into the Belgium operations, creating the Puratos Group. By then, the company had gained a worldwide presence, with sales topping $500 million.

GLOBAL INGREDIENTS POWERHOUSE IN THE 21ST CENTURY

Puratos grew through acquisition as it approached the next century. In 1998, the company added whipped toppings to its lineup through the purchase of Cuore

Emiliano. In 2000, it bought Denmark's Vejle Marginefabrik from the Golden Vale group. The company's U.S. division also grew strongly, adding American Bakery Supply, based in San Francisco, California; Victory Foods in Houston, Texas; Deering Food Corporation in Tempe, Arizona; and an industrial chocolate factory owned by Lindt und Sprungli based in Kenosha, Wisconsin. The company completed its U.S. buying spree in 2001 when it bought the baked goods division of Seattle's Fisher Communications.

In Europe during this time, the company extended its operations into the semifinished products sector, buying more than 87 percent of publicly listed France's Boulangerie de l'Europe for EUR 11.23 million. The purchase gave the company an entry into the market for precooked frozen breads. The company subsequently acquired full control of that operation, which was then delisted from the Euronext stock exchange.

Continuing its commitment to innovation, Puratos introduced its new Acti-plus technology in 2002, then released its next generation of bread improvers, New Soft'r, based on that technology. In 2004 the company boosted its product line again with the industry's first cold-setting glaze, Sublimo. Sapore (Italian for "taste") was the brand name given to a new line of bread sours and aromas during this time.

Puratos restructured its operations in 2005, launching a new global corporate image initiative, placing all operations under the Puratos name with a modernized logo featuring a unicorn and the tagline "reliable partners in innovation." The company's network of Innovation Centers, which provided local testing services and training facilities in support of the company's products, was bolstered in 2007 with the opening of its latest and largest center, a EUR 10 million facility located near the company's headquarters. By the end of that year, Puratos had also reached a joint-venture agreement with Australia's Goodman Fielder to construct a factory for producing baking premixes for the Australian and New Zealand markets. The deal underscored Puratos's position as one of the global leaders in its industry in the 21st century.

M. L. Cohen

PRINCIPAL SUBSIDIARIES

Belcolade NV; Puratos Corporation (United States); Puratos De Mexico S.A. de C.V.; Puratos—Produtos e Artigos para a Industria Alimentar S.A. (Portugal); Puratos Schweiz AG; T500 Puratos S.A. (Spain).

PRINCIPAL DIVISIONS

Bakery; Patisserie; Chocolate; Research and Development.

PRINCIPAL COMPETITORS

General Mills Inc.; Orkla ASA; Henan Lingang Industrial and Trade Co.; Bunge Alimentos S.A.; Etablissements J Soufflet S.A.; Gruma SAB de C.V.; CJ Corporation; Tiger Brands Ltd.; George Weston Foods Ltd.; Pioneer Food Group Ltd.; Goodman Fielder Proprietary Ltd.; Vandemoortele S.A./NV.

FURTHER READING

"Creating a Single Market in South Eastern Europe," *Southeast Europe TV Exchanges,* January 10, 2003.

Malovany, Dan, "Strokes of Genius," *Snack Food & Wholesale Bakery,* July 2007, p. 52.

"Puratos Buys Boulangerie de l'Europe," *Les Echos,* February 20, 2001, p. 14.

"Puratos Buys US Chocolate Factory," *Milling & Baking News,* January 2, 2001, p. 10.

"Puratos Celebrate Big Five-O," *Food Trade Review,* August 2003, p. 487.

"Puratos Helps Sir Benfro Bakery to Awards Success," *Food Trade Review,* July 2004, p. 426.

"Puratos Launches New Corporate Identity," *Food Trade Review,* April 2005, p. 281.

"Real Belgian Chocolate from Puratos," *International Food Ingredients,* October–November 2004, p. 87.

Werner, Tom, "Puratos Purchases Former Nabisco Margarine Plant," *Philadelphia Business Journal,* September 23, 1994, p. 13B.

Redback Networks, Inc.

100 Headquarters Drive
San Jose, California 95134
U.S.A.
Telephone: (408) 750-5000
Fax: (408) 750-5599
Web site: http://www.redback.com

Wholly Owned Subsidiary of Telefonaktiebolaget LM Ericsson
Incorporated: 1996
Employees: 800
Sales: $153.3 million
NAIC: 334290 Other Communication Equipment Manufacturing; 423690 Other Electronic Parts and Equipment Merchant Wholesalers; 541990 All Other Professional, Scientific, and Technical Services

▪ ▪ ▪

From its headquarters in San Jose, California, Redback Networks, Inc., designs and markets networking technology that Internet service providers (ISPs) and telecommunications firms use to deliver and manage broadband Internet subscriptions and support popular online activities such as video and gaming.

Redback's portfolio of hardware and software products is marketed under the name SmartEdge, and is based on Internet protocol (IP) technology used on broadband or high-speed networks. IP is the communications protocol or method that is used for transmitting information between computers on the Internet. Toward the end of the 21st century's first decade, residential and business customers were relying on IP to receive multiple communication services, such as voice, data, and video, via the Internet, as opposed to purchasing them separately from different providers. This same trend allowed providers of multiple services to reap savings by consolidating separate service networks into one broadband-based network.

During the first decade of the 21st century, Redback's customer base consisted of approximately 500 service providers worldwide, including AT&T, BellSouth, British Telecom, Covad, France Telecom, China Netcom, China Telecom, Sprint, and Verizon.

FORMATIVE YEARS: 1996–2000

Redback was established in 1996 by former executives from Bay Networks and Cisco Systems. During its first three years the company, then based in Sunnyvale, California, received about $20 million in funding from firms like Sequoia Capital, Oaktree Capital Management, Mayfield, Lighthouse Capital Partners, Comdisco Ventures, and Accel Partners.

Dennis L. Barsema served as Redback's CEO during its formative years, beginning in 1997. After earning a management degree from Northern Illinois University in 1977, Barsema began his career as a salesman for Burroughs and later worked for Paradyne Corp. He eventually relocated to San Jose, California, to work for Centigram Corp. in 1996.

According to an article in the November 2000 issue of *Telecommunications,* Barsema explained that he was

COMPANY PERSPECTIVES

∎

Redback's hardware, software, and services are designed to create solutions that address the operational and technical challenges of building a next generation network that delivers consumer and business services.

"stone-broke" when he landed the job as Redback's top executive, with nothing to lose. "My greatest concern was picking the right people," he explained. "In a small emerging company, you don't get to make hiring mistakes for key positions. You have to put the right people into the right jobs."

Like many technology start-ups, Redback was not profitable during its early years. The company lost $142,000 in 1996, a figure that grew to $4.4 million the following year, and $9.9 million in 1998. However, Redback gained an edge on competitors like Cisco and Nortel Networks by being the first to market with subscriber management equipment. The company also offered products that were compatible with different brands of network equipment.

During the 1990s Redback offered products such as the Subscriber Management System 500, which small and midsized ISPs could use to manage up to 1,000 concurrent subscribers connecting via cable modem or digital subscriber line (DSL). DSL is a form of high-speed Internet connection that uses regular telephone lines. Larger ISPs and telephone carriers used products like the Subscriber Management System 1000, which consolidated high volumes of data traffic and lessened the load on backbone routers, the computers responsible for relaying data to the appropriate location on the Internet.

Redback ended the decade with several key developments, starting with an initial public offering (IPO) on May 18, 1999. The small IPO, involving only 2.5 million shares, was a huge success. Share prices rose from $23 to more than $84 by the day's end, and exceeded $90 a week later. After two months passed, the company announced a two-for-one stock split. By this time, Redback had shipped about 400 Subscriber Management Systems to some 80 customers, including the likes of Ameritech, Bell Atlantic, EarthLink, GTE, Qwest, SBC/Pacific Bell, and UUNet.

An authorized reseller program named PowerPartners was introduced in July, providing value-added resellers (VARs) with sales and technical tools for market-ing Redback products to ISPs. Participating VARs were grouped into either Solutions Partner or Expert Partner status, based on their ability to meet certain technical and service-related criteria.

On November 29, Redback agreed to acquire California-based Siara Systems, an optical networking company, in a $4.3 billion stock deal. Although Siara had not yet introduced actual products to the marketplace, the firm offered complementary technology that allowed Redback to offer a more comprehensive range of products and services. The deal increased the size of Redback's market by a factor of ten, and added 170 engineers to its workforce.

Redback began the 21st century in rapid growth mode. The company quickly outgrew its 45,000-square-foot facilities in Sunnyvale, despite an additional 95,000 square feet of leased space in San Jose. This led Redback to relocate its headquarters to a 96,710-square-foot building in San Jose's Corporate Technology Centre. By mid-2000, the company had announced plans to occupy a second 99,870-square-foot building, as well as a third 76,410-square-foot building.

A major leadership change occurred in 2000 when President and Chief Operating Officer Vivek Ragavan, who previously served as president and CEO of Siara Systems, succeeded Dennis Barsema as CEO. Barsema remained with Redback as vice chairman. Ragavan was at the helm when Redback announced the acquisition of Vancouver, British Columbia–based Abatis Systems in a $636 million stock deal. Abatis continued operations as a subsidiary of Redback.

At this time Redback was generating about 30 percent of its revenues from international operations, with Asia and Europe as especially strong markets. The company's Siara Systems acquisition bore fruit in the fourth quarter when it rolled out its SmartEdge optical product.

HARD TIMES: 2001–03

In June 2001, Redback announced plans to acquire the Fremont, California–based optical networking firm Merlin Systems, Inc., in a $57 million stock deal. Beyond that, the year was filled with numerous difficulties. A sluggish economy, which prompted capital spending cuts at many technology firms and telecommunications providers, put a clamp on Redback's growth.

Plans to hire up to 400 employees early in the year were replaced with a substantial workforce reduction. These challenges were exacerbated by the departure of CEO Vivek Ragavan to start-up competitor Atrica in May. Other challenges included a class-action lawsuit

October, Redback filed for Chapter 11 bankruptcy, and the company's stock fell below 30 cents a share.

KEY DATES

1996: Redback is established by former Bay Networks and Cisco Systems executives.
1999: The company makes its initial public offering on May 18.
2003: Saddled with $467 million in debt, Redback files for Chapter 11 bankruptcy.
2004: Redback emerges from bankruptcy.
2007: Ericsson acquires Redback for $1.9 billion.

A NEW BEGINNING: 2004–07

A new beginning occurred at Redback in January 2004, when the company emerged from bankruptcy after eliminating its debt and cutting annual expenses by $44 million. The company moved forward into the middle of the decade with $30 million in funding from Technology Crossover Ventures.

Redback soon began pursuing opportunities for growth in rural U.S. markets. In 2005, the company began focusing on helping rural telecommunications providers offer integrated voice, data, and video service to their customers. Redback's rural strategy received a major boost when its subscriber management system was approved by the U.S. Department of Agriculture's Rural Utilities Service (RUS), which made it eligible for inclusion in projects funded by the RUS.

In the April 11, 2005, issue of *Telephony*, Redback Chief Marketing Officer Marco Wanders explained: "The smaller and the rural carriers are starting to deploy new services because Internet access alone had limited revenue and opportunities for them. Expanding their service portfolio gives them a chance to get new customers on the network and also a chance to get more out of each customer. It makes the business more interesting."

In the fourth quarter of 2005, Redback recorded its first profit in five years, earning $300,000 on revenues of $48 million. Brighter times arrived as the company headed into 2006. Although it lost $2.6 million in the first quarter, the shortfall was 63 percent less than for the same period in 2005. Revenues increased to almost $58 million in the first quarter, an increase of 69 percent from the year before.

As conditions improved, Redback began to hire more engineering and sales personnel. A vote of confidence in the company was made when TCV Funds agreed to acquire 1.93 million shares of Redback's common stock for $42 million. TCV Funds was established by Technology Crossover Ventures, which had provided Redback with equity funding following its emergence from bankruptcy.

Improvement continued throughout the year. In the third quarter, sales reached $70.9 million, up 95 percent from the third quarter of 2005, and net income reached $9.1 million, as opposed to a $4.2 million loss the previous year. In an effort to cut costs, Redback announced plans to shift manufacturing from San Jose to Mexico. In addition, plans were also formed to relocate manufacturing for Asia, where the company was in

filed by Lucent employees who claimed they were misled by Redback's management to invest in the firm when they knew it was sailing in troubled waters. The company also faced a $54 million breach of contract lawsuit filed by Arrow Electronics.

From April to August 2001, Redback eliminated 17 percent of its workforce. In an effort to keep its best employees and reduce expenses, the firm offered a salary-for-stock plan that was expected to save $400,000 per quarter. Kevin DeNuccio, an executive from Cisco Systems, was hired as Redback's new president and CEO in August. As he took the helm, the road ahead was paved with more difficulties. In October, Redback's stock price dipped to $1.20 per share, down more than 99 percent from $169.81 only 13 months before, and from $190 in March 2000.

Redback suffered a loss of $187 million in 2002, on revenues of $125 million. At this time the company's workforce totaled approximately 600. While times were tough, Redback had developed a solid customer base that included all of the regional Bell operating companies (regional phone companies formed to provide local service when the federal government broke up AT&T's monopoly in 1983), as well as 17 of the leading 20 DSL networks. One positive development occurred when Nokia began working with Redback to help increase the company's sales and make inroads to more key customers. In May, Nokia acquired a 10 percent share of Redback, with an option to increase its stake to 20 percent.

Nevertheless, by 2003 Redback was saddled with a mountain of debt. The company proposed a plan to provide bondholders with 95 percent of its common stock, in an effort to wipe out some $467 million of debt. A day later, Redback lost Chief Information Officer Lars Rabbe, when he accepted the same position at Yahoo! Inc. When shareholders rejected the plan in heated competition with domestic players like Huawei, to a site in Malaysia.

A major development occurred in December 2006, when telecommunications equipment firm Ericsson announced plans to acquire Redback. Following the conclusion of the $1.9 billion deal in 2007, Redback became a subsidiary of Ericsson. The deal gave Redback capital to expand into areas like Internet protocol television (IPTV), the delivery of TV programming via the Internet.

Commenting on the acquisition in the December 20, 2006, issue of *Telephony*, Redback CEO Kevin DeNuccio explained: "This agreement is about accelerating market growth, integrating IP routing and mobility expertise and shaping the future of next generation networks. Video changes everything about networks today. We believe Redback now will have the global reach and financial resources to accelerate its own routing technology innovation and grow market share faster than our traditional routing competitors."

Consistent with DeNuccio's vision, in mid-2007 Redback unveiled the new SmartEdge 1200, which one analyst called the largest broadband remote-access server on the market. In the June 5, 2007, issue of *Network World*, DeNuccio said: "The primary [goal] was scale. We were trying to scale in two dimensions: We can deliver huge amounts of bandwidth for IPTV; the other dimension was to prepare for this broadband mobility where we have scaled the control plane eight times. You can put a half-million subscribers on this platform."

Heading into 2008, Redback enjoyed a customer base that included 15 of the world's leading telecom-munications companies, which used its SmartEdge platform to serve approximately 50 million subscribers. With support from parent Ericsson and product offerings needed to serve a burgeoning broadband market, Redback appeared to be in an excellent position for continued growth.

Paul R. Greenland

PRINCIPAL COMPETITORS

Alcatel-Lucent; Cisco Systems, Inc.; Juniper Networks, Inc.; Nortel Networks Corp.

FURTHER READING

Duffy, Jim, "Redback Looks to Redefine Edge Routing: Analyst Says Company's Device Largest Broadband Remote-Access Server on Market," *Network World*, June 5, 2007.

Mardesich, Jodi, "Redback Climbs Up on a Broadband Box: Ahead of Cisco," *Fortune*, July 19, 1999.

Medford, Cassimir, "How Leaders Lead; From Militaristic to Laissez Faire, Top Network Executives Favor Different Styles for Keeping Their Companies Operating Smoothly," *Network World*, April 24, 2000.

Nerney, Chris, "Network Supernovas Light Up the IPO Sky," *Network World*, July 12, 1999.

"Offline," *Telecommunications*, November 2000.

O'Shea, Dan, "Ericsson to Acquire Redback," *Telephony*, December 20, 2006.

Wilson, Carol, "Redback Launches Rural Initiative," *Telephony*, April 11, 2005.

Republic Services, Inc.

110 Southeast 6th Street, 28th Floor
Fort Lauderdale, Florida 33301
U.S.A.
Telephone: (954) 769-2400
Fax: (954) 769-2664
Web site: http://www.republicservices.com

Public Company
Incorporated: 1998
Employees: 13,000
Sales: $3 billion (2006)
Stock Exchanges: New York
Ticker Symbol: RSG
NAIC: 562219 Other Nonhazardous Waste Treatment
and Disposal

■ ■ ■

With its headquarters in Fort Lauderdale, Florida, Republic Services, Inc., is a New York Stock Exchange–listed waste management company. Comprised of about 140 hauling companies operating in 21 mostly Sun Belt states, Republic provides solid waste collection services for residential, municipal, commercial, and industrial customers. With annual revenues of more than $3 billion, Republic is the third largest player in its industry.

The company also operates more than 90 transfer stations, where waste is compacted for Republic collectors, as well as other private and municipal collectors, and transferred to trailers for relocation. Some of this waste makes its way to Republic's 59 landfills, located on more than 9,700 acres, or to the company's 33 recycling centers. In addition, Republic operates a Texas unit that converts yard waste and other materials into compost, mulch, and soil, which is then packaged and sold as landscape products.

SOLID WASTE DISPOSAL ACT OF 1965

Republic Services grew out of Republic Industries, Inc., one of several companies founded and nurtured by entrepreneur H. Wayne Huizenga, born in a Chicago suburb in 1938. His grandfather, a Dutch immigrant, had started a Chicago garbage hauling company in the 1890s, Huizenga & Sons, but Huizenga's father opted to become a home builder and moved the family to Fort Lauderdale, Florida, in the late 1930s.

Restless as a young man, Huizenga did not complete his college studies and after a stint in the military returned to South Florida in the early 1960s and bought a garbage truck along with a number of commercial customers in Pompano Beach, Florida. He added customers and bought more trucks, laying the foundation for a company called Southern Sanitation. Waste removal offered a great opportunity for the young man. The booming postwar economy led to a new consumer culture that created a host of new items (packaging, disposable products, and the like) that were thrown away and had to be collected.

Moreover, in 1965 the United States enacted the Solid Waste Disposal Act to impose heightened hygiene standards on the industry, increasing the cost of doing

COMPANY PERSPECTIVES

Republic Services will exceed its customers' highest expectations and provide a great place to work that fosters an entrepreneurial spirit for all members of the Republic Team. The Company will increase shareholder value by building its customer base through internal growth and strategic acquisitions.

business and leading to consolidation. To take advantage of this changing landscape, Huizenga joined forces with his wife's uncle, Dean L. Buntrock, who owned a Chicago hauling company called Ace Scavenger. In 1968 they merged their operations to form Waste Management Inc., a Chicago-based company that started out with operations in Florida, Illinois, and Wisconsin.

Huizenga harbored great ambitions for Waste Management. To fund expansion he took the company public in 1971. He was also not content to limit himself to hauling. By 1984 he built Waste Management into a $3 billion conglomerate, involved in the disposal of chemicals and toxic waste, while also operating internationally. Because he split his time between his home in Fort Lauderdale and Waste Management's headquarters in Chicago, however, Huizenga decided to resign and use the stock he had accumulated to pursue new business opportunities. One of them was video rental. In 1987 he and some partners took over a small chain of video rental stores operating under the Blockbuster Video name. Just as he had been a consolidator in the waste management business, Huizenga began buying up video stores in North America, creating another corporate giant.

A football and baseball player in his high school days, Huizenga next indulged his interest in sports. In 1989 he bought a stake in the Miami Dolphins of the National Football League as well as a 30 percent interest in Joe Robbie Stadium where they played. In addition, he created a bowl game to he hosted there, the Blockbuster Bowl, which enjoyed a successful debut in 1990. To get even more use out of the stadium, Huizenga landed an expansion franchise for Miami from Major League Baseball in 1991. Three years later Huizenga gained majority control of the Dolphins football team. He then acquired an expansion franchise from the National Hockey League, founding the Florida Panthers in Miami.

HUIZENGA ACQUIRES REPUBLIC WASTE INDUSTRIES: 1995

Huizenga became interested once again in the waste management field in 1994. The seed for the idea, according to *Waste Age*, was his brother-in-law Whit Hudson, who had worked with him at Waste Management and left in 1984 to start his own Florida waste company, Hudson Management Corporation, which by 1994 had grown to become the largest privately held waste company in the state. "Hudson asked Huizenga to join him in taking another crack at a national waste industry acquisition," reported *Waste Age*. Huizenga was interested in returning to his roots while also becoming involved in some new industries. In looking for a shell public company to hold the acquisitions he planned to make, he came across Atlanta-based, NASDAQ-listed Republic Waste Industries Inc. and in 1995 paid $27 million to seize control of the small waste hauler.

Republic Waste Industries actually got its start in Oklahoma City as an oil and gas exploration company in the 1980s, a particularly difficult time for the industry. After six years the NASDAQ-listed company was relegated to Pink Sheet status as a limited partnership that for three years invested in a line of automobile lubricants called Lubripac. Then in late 1989 a group of Houston investors became involved, and the company decided to turn its attention to the solid waste business. The corporate headquarters was moved to Houston in 1990 and a pair of landfills were acquired near Dallas. A year later, however, the company found itself in difficult financial straits. Canadian businessman Michael G. DeGroote, who had made his mark in trucking with Laidlaw International but had diversified into waste management in the late 1960s, would invest about $50 million in Republic through one of his companies. He then spent three years cleaning up Republic's financial situation before Huizenga decided to make it his new investment vehicle.

Republic's headquarters was moved to Fort Lauderdale, Hudson was installed as Republic's president, and his company was brought into the fold. With common stock at its disposal, Republic in the fall of 1995 acquired Southland Environmental Services Inc., provider of solid waste collection and recycling services in Northeast Florida. Several other acquisitions followed in short order to create the core for the company's waste management business in the Sun Belt states: Georgia-based United Waste Service Inc., Texas-based J.C. Duncan Company, North Carolina–based GDS, and South Carolina–based Fennel Container Corporation.

At the same time, Republic, which would be renamed Republic Industries, Inc., began taking steps to

KEY DATES

1995: H. Wayne Huizenga acquires Republic Waste Industries Inc., renaming it Republic Industries.

1998: Republic Industries spins off solid-waste disposal assets as Republic Services, Inc., in public offering.

1999: Remaining shares are distributed to Republic Industries' shareholders.

2002: Huizenga retires as chairman.

2006: Revenues top $3 billion.

2007: Company completes three-for-two stock split.

become involved in other industries. Huizenga expressed an interest in pursuing half-a-dozen areas, initially listing a pair of prospects: the home-security business and billboard advertising. Republic's first nonwaste management acquisition was Kertz Security Systems, which provided home security services to some 30,000 accounts in Florida.

Another target industry was used cars, which soon became a focal point of Republic Industries, especially after the company failed in its bid to acquire security giant ADT in 1996. Huizenga wanted to create a chain of used-car superstores under the AutoNation banner, the initial step taken in 1995 when he acquired Alamo Rent-a-Car Inc. Alamo's stock of older vehicles were meant to provide a stockpile for the superstores, the first of which opened in 1995. A year later he supplemented this supply by paying $600 million for National Car Rental Systems, a rental chain fleet of 100,000 vehicles.

In April 1996, the two rental companies were merged into Republic and AutoNation took shape. AutoNation's used-car business was so successful that Huizenga turned his attention to new cars and launched an acquisition spree of car dealerships, as well as several more car rental companies. The vision was to develop a one-stop-shop for vehicles, whether they were bought new or used, or rented.

REPUBLIC SERVICES SPUR OFF: 1998

With Republic Industry's auto business soaring, the home security business lost its appeal and those assets were divested in October 1997. The waste disposal division was also becoming a noncore activity, despite enjoying success on its own terms. Sales grew from $100 million to $1.1 billion in 1997. In 1998 Huizenga decided

to spin off a large portion of the business in an initial public offering (IPO) of stock in order to produce as much as $2 billion for Republic Industries, the money to fuel further expansion in the automotive retail and rental business.

Thus, in 1998, Republic Services, Inc., was formed to house the waste disposal operations of Republic Industries, and in July 1998 an IPO of stock was completed. Perhaps concerned that the new company was coming to the market in a hasty manner, not yet having assimilated its recent acquisitions, investor interest was tepid at best. Only able to command the lower end of its asking price, Republic Services raised $1.4 billion through the sale of 36.1 percent of the company. A year later, the rest of the company's shares were distributed to Republic Industries' shareholders.

At the time of the IPO, Republic Services was comprised of 96 collection companies operating in 24 states, making it the fourth largest company in the solid-waste industry. Huizenga indicated that he planned to step down as CEO, although he planned to retain the chairmanship and Whit Hudson would stay on as vice-chairman. In December 1998, his successor was appointed, 49-year-old James E. O'Connor, who had left Waste Management after a 22-year tenure, most recently heading the company's Southeast region. Prior to his time with Waste Management, O'Connor owned and operated his own solid-waste collection company in Indiana for four years. He would assume the chairmanship as well at Republic Services in 2002.

O'Connor took over a company that generated $1.37 billion in sales and net income of $177.6 million in 1998. Those numbers were poised to grow further in light of a pending agreement to buy a variety of assets from Waste Management for more than $500 million, including 136 commercial collect routes, 11 transfer stations, and 16 landfills. The deal also helped Republic to build up its footprint in four markets and allow it to enter 16 new markets, setting up the company for internal growth in these areas. In fact, it was much less expensive for Republic to grow internally rather than through acquisition.

"We can develop $1 of new revenues with $1 of capital," O'Connor explained to *Waste Age*. He explained, "If I acquire a company, I acquire $1 of revenues at a cost of $2 in capital. So our preferred investment will be growing the company internally." Another way to improve the balance sheet was through strategic trades. In 1999 Republic worked out a deal with Arizona-based Allied Waste Industries Inc. to exchange Republic operations in the Bronx and Pittsburgh for Allied operations in Indianapolis, and Winston-Salem, North Carolina. Both companies would have to divest some assets in 2000 in order to pass muster with the Justice Department to complete the deal.

All told, in 1999 Republic acquired 11 landfills and 11 transfer stations, helping to increase revenues to more than $1.8 billion for the year and net income approaching $400 million. The company also picked up a new investor, billionaire Bill Gates of Microsoft fame, who began buying up shares through his personal investment company, Cascade Investments. Over the next several years Gates would continue to buy shares, which continued to grow in price. By the summer of 2006 he emerged as Republic's largest shareholder, holding a 13 percent stake.

As the new century dawned, Republic continued to expand, so that between 1999 and 2000 it acquired more than 160 operations while continuing its internal growth. In 2001 the company sought to better assimilate these assets by standardizing its system, to grow beyond a decentralized group of collection companies. Republic hoped to better leverage its size, to improve its buying power to provide local units with trucks and other equipment at a less expensive price, thus allowing them to focus on growing their markets. Revenues improved from $2.1 billion in 2000 to $2.26 billion in 2001, while net income increased to $225.1 million in 2000 before receding to $211.6 million in 2001 as the U.S. economy retreated into recession.

The waste management industry may not have been recession proof, but it was certainly better able to cope than most industries. Revenues continued to grow, totaling $2.36 billion in 2002 and topping $2.5 billion in 2003. The number continued to grow until it exceed the $3 billion mark in 2006. Although Republic had to contend with rising fuel costs, it was also able to grow net income to $279.6 million in 2006. In the past five years the price of the company's stock doubled while the number of available shares decreased because of stock repurchases, prompting management to engineer a three-for-two split in March 2007, a move that made more shares available to the market, making the stock more attractive to both large and small investors. The company was on pace for another year of record results in 2007.

Ed Dinger

PRINCIPAL SUBSIDIARIES

Republic Disposal, Inc.; Republic Dumpco, Inc.; Republic Environmental Technologies, Inc.; Republic Services Financial LP; Republic Services Group LLC; Republic Services, Inc.

PRINCIPAL COMPETITORS

Waste Industries, Inc.; Waste Industries USA, Inc.; Waste Management, Inc.

FURTHER READING

"The Art of Trash," *US Business Review,* January 2006, p. 148.

Blackmon, Douglas A., "Republic Services Gets Mild Response in Public Offering," *Wall Street Journal,* July 2, 1998, p. 1.

Fickes, Michael, "The Place to Be," *Waste Age,* August 2002, p. 38.

Johnson, Jim, "Republic Hopes Split Will Lead to Investment," *Waste News,* February 19, 2007, p. 4.

Machan, Dyan, "Crime, Garbage—and Billboards," *Forbes,* November 20, 1995, p. 52.

McNamara, Victoria, "Landfill Sales Soar As New Regulations Take Effect," *Houston Business Journal,* May 21, 1990, p. 16.

Morse, Dan, "Republic Industries Intends to Spin Off Solid-Waste Unit to Boost Auto Division," *Wall Street Journal,* May 14, 1998, p. 1.

Serwer, Andrew E., "Huizenga's Third Act," *Fortune,* August 5, 1996, p. 73.

Walsh, Matt, "'Everything I've Ever Wanted to Do ... Rent Things,'" *Florida Trend,* March 1999, p. 38.

Wolpin, Bill, "Huizenga Plans Another Solid Waste Blockbuster," *World Wastes,* October 1995, p. 24.

Saur S.A.S.

———■———

1 av Eugene Freyssinet
Saint Quentin en Yvelines, F-78064
France
Telephone: (33 01) 30 60 22 60
Fax: (33 01) 30 60 27 89
Web site: http://www.saur.com

Private Company
Incorporated: 1933 as Société d'Aménagement Urbain et
    Rural
Employees: 12,400
Sales: EUR 1.4 billion (US$1.9 billion) (2006)
NAIC: 562998 All Other Miscellaneous Waste Manage-
    ment; 221310 Water Supply and Irrigation Systems;
    562111 Solid Waste Collection

■ ■ ■

Saur S.A.S. is France's third largest provider of water and wastewater services, and one of the country's leading providers of waste management services. Saur is also a leading engineering and construction firm specialized in water treatment plants. The company is also active internationally, particularly in Poland and Spain. Saur operates through four primary divisions. Saur France is the company's water and wastewater utility, with nearly 6,000 contracts covering more than 6,700 towns throughout France, serving a total population of more than 5.5 million people. This unit, the third largest in France after Suez's Ondeo and Veolia, contributed 64 percent of Saur's revenues of EUR 1.4 billion (US$1.9 billion) in 2006. Coved Waste Management is Saur's

waste management services arm, with more than 1,000 contracts throughout France providing coverage of more than five million people. This subsidiary generated 20 percent of the group's sales in 2006. Saur's engineering and construction operations fall under Stereau, which has operations in France, the United Kingdom, and Spain, and fulfills contracts through the world. This division produced 8 percent of group sales. Saur International governs the group's water services operations outside of France, chiefly in Poland and Spain, as well as holdings in Africa and elsewhere. Although Saur International generates just 7 percent of group sales, it extends the company's range of operations to some 29 million people throughout the world. Long operated as part of the Bouygues conglomerate, Saur has changed hands in the middle of the first decade of the 21st century, and since 2007 has become a privately held company owned by an investment consortium including Seche Environnement, AXA, and the Caisse des Depots et Consignations.

A THIRD FRENCH WATER SERVICES GROUP IN THE THIRTIES

France represented a dominant figure in the global water supply market at the start of the twenty-first century. Three of the world's leading water supply and treatment groups were French, led by Veolia (formerly Compagnie Générale des Eaux, or CGE), Suez (formerly Lyonnaise des Eaux), and Saur. Together these three groups accounted for some 40 percent of the world's supply of drinking water. Suez, through subsidiary Ondeo, while second-place in France, had claimed the lead on the global market, covering a population of more than 125 million. Veolia, spun off from Vivendi Universal, claimed the leading position in France, and second in the world, with more than 110 million customers. Saur remained the perennial third-place contender in France, while maintaining a place among the global top four with 29 million customers in its network.

Saur had been created in 1933 in part to provide a third alternative to the French water market, as well as to extend water treatment and distribution facilities to France's somewhat neglected rural sector. Until then, the country's water supply had been dominated by two companies created in the 19th century. The first of these, CGE, had been created following a law passed under Napoleon III in 1828, which placed water distribution under the responsibility of France's communities. The law, itself enacted in response to the outbreaks of cholera and other epidemics afflicting the country in the early 19th century, set into place the development of private-sector water services—an anomaly in a country with a long-standing history of state intervention at nearly every level of industry. By 1853, a group of shareholders, including members of Napoleon's family, joined together to found CGE. That company initially targeted larger urban markets, including Lyon, Nantes, and Paris, where it gained an extremely lucrative and long-term contract for the city's water distribution in 1860.

CGE faced its first serious rival in 1880, with the formation of the Société Lyonnaise des Eaux et d'Éclairage, created by the financial powerhouse Crédit Lyonnais. That company grew into CGE's only true competitor in France, leading to a situation where the two companies often joined together to share contracts for the country's major towns and cities. In Paris, for example, CGE eventually took control of the city's Right Bank, while Lyonnaise became the water supplier for the Left Bank.

As CGE and Lyonnaise divvied up the country's urban market, development of the rural sector's water distribution systems remained somewhat underdeveloped in the post–World War I era. As a result, an opening remained for the appearance of a third major contender for the French water distribution market. In 1933, therefore, a new company was created, called Société d'Aménagement Urbain et Rural (the Company for Urban and Rural Development), or Saur.

Saur's services to the rural areas allowed it to grow steadily over the next decades. In period following World War II, the French government nationalized the country's other utility sectors. The water distribution industry remained in the private sector, however, attracting the attention of investors. The growing financial resources permitted Saur to accelerate its growth, particularly after it began targeting urban markets in the 1950s and 1960s. The company succeeded in winning a number of important contracts, such as that for the city of Nimes.

JOINING THE BOUYGUES GROUP IN 1984

Saur had also started its diversification beyond water treatment and distribution during this time. In 1959, the company created a subsidiary dedicated to the engineering and construction of turnkey water treatment facilities. That subsidiary, Stereau, grew into the country's third largest water treatment plant specialist. Saur also became interested in developing its operation beyond the French metropolitan market, creating a subsidiary, Sodeci, to begin competing for contracts in France's outlying markets, such as Martinique and Reunion, as well as in a number of newly independent African markets, such as the Ivory Coast. By the end of the 1970s, Saur's operations had expanded to include Guinea, Mali, Zaire, Senegal, and Congo, among others. Into the early 1980s, the company expanded into other parts of the world, notably into Canada, starting from 1982. Meanwhile, in France, Saur had been expanding its range of operations, buying Luchaire Company's wastewater treatment division in 1979.

Saur also recognized the potential of another fast growing, and increasingly important, sector, waste collection and waste management. By 1984, the company had formed a dedicated subsidiary for the sector, called Coved. While lagging behind its rivals, notably the waste management subsidiaries of rivals CGE and Lyonnaise, Coved nonetheless developed its position as the third largest waste management group in France, serving a total base of more than five million customers.

Into the early 1980s, Saur itself remained a relatively small player compared to its larger rivals, CGE

KEY DATES

1933: Founding of Société d'Aménagement Urbain et Rural (Saur) to serve rural markets in France.

1959: Creation of engineering and construction subsidiary, Stereau, focused on water treatment plants.

1984: Launch of waste collection and treatment subsidiary, Coved; Bouygues group acquires majority control of Saur.

1994: Bouygues forms Saur International in partnership with Électricité de France.

2005: PAI Partners acquires Saur from Bouygues for EUR 1 million.

2007: Saur sold to consortium including Séché Environnement, CDC, and AXA for EUR 1.72 billion.

and Lyonnaise. However, those companies inadvertently helped the company gain a new major shareholder—subsequently launching Saur on a new expansion phase. At the time, French construction giant Bouygues had been developing its own diversification strategy in an effort to reduce its exposure to the heavily cyclical construction industry. The water distribution market became one of the primary targets of Bouygues, offering the opportunity not only for extremely stable revenue streams, but also the possibility for synergies with the group's construction and engineering operations. Bouygues at first targeted the acquisition of major shareholdings in the two largest water groups, yet failed to gain a significant stake in either CGE or Lyonnaise. Instead, in 1984, Bouygues turned to Saur, becoming its majority shareholder that year.

With the backing of Bouygues, Saur began a new expansion phase. The company grew rapidly, more than doubling its revenues by the end of the decade and expanding its range to more than five million customers across France. Saur, which remained positioned primarily in the rural market, was aided by the rapid growth of France's suburban market in the late 1980s and through the 1990s.

NEW OWNERS FOR A NEW CENTURY

As France's water grid reached completion, Saur increasingly targeted international growth. For this, the company willingly targeted expansion beyond the water

and waste management markets. In 1990, for example, the company created a new subsidiary in the Ivory Coast, called Compagnie Ivoirienne d'Électricité, which began competing for electricity distribution contracts in that market. Meanwhile, Saur became an early entrant into the newly privatized water distribution sector in the United Kingdom. In 1989, for example, the company launched a bid to acquire the Folkestone and District Water Company.

By the early 1990s, the company had succeeded in buying up four water authorities in England, as well as minority stakes in four others, for a total cost of BP 90 million. Saur also entered the United Kingdom's waste disposal sector at the same time, notably through the creation of two joint ventures, Stalwart Environmental Services and Cambrian Environmental Services, in partnership with Welsh Water in 1990. In 1993, Saur's U.K. arm created South East Water through the merger of three water authorities serving Mid-Sussex, Eastbourne, and West Kent. The company also sought further expansion on the Continent. In 1992, the company entered Poland, where it acquired a major stake in the company providing water and waste services to the city of Gdansk.

Saur's international profile was heightened in 1994 when Bouygues formed a joint venture with Électricité de France (EdF) to regroup parts of their international holdings into a new company, Saur International. As part of that deal, EdF acquired a direct stake in Saur. The newly formed Saur International grew to include electrical power generation operations in Guinea and Ivory Coast, as well as water distribution and treatment operations in Senegal.

In France, meanwhile, Saur consolidated its position as the number three player when it agreed to acquire CISE, the water and environmental services division of the Saint Gobain group in 1998. Following the integration of the CISE operations, the entire group was rebranded under the single Saur name. In the meantime, Saur continued to develop other markets, especially Spain, where it acquired control of Valencia-based Aguas de Valencia. The company had also raised its profile in the Polish market, gaining the water and waste contract for the city of Ruda Śląska in 1999.

By then, Bouygues, which had begun investing massively in the telecommunications sector, setting up France's third mobile phone network, was seeking an exit from its Saur shareholding. After initially searching to open Saur's shareholding to a partner, Bouygues made its first attempt to find an outright buyer in the early 2000s but, amid the uncertain financial climate of the period, proved unable to find a buyer.

Bouygues announced that it was putting Saur up for sale again in 2004. This time, the company received bids from some 15 potential buyers. Yet the company faced a major obstacle in the French government's reluctance to allow a foreign group to gain control of one of the country's top three water distribution companies. By the end of 2004, however, Bouygues had begun talks with French investment group PAI Partners, which ultimately led to the sale of Saur in 2005 for EUR 1 billion.

PAI's ownership of Saur proved only temporary, however. By the beginning of 2007, the investment group had announced that it was putting Saur up for sale again. At the time, the financial community was still recovering from the controversy caused when the French government had blocked the moves by foreign-held Enel to take control of the Suez group. With a number of foreign bidders, including Macquarie Bank of Australia, reportedly preparing bids in excess of EUR 2 billion for Saur, the French government moved to head off a new controversy. Instead, the government, through its Caisse des Depots et Consignations (CDC) unit, together with the investment management wing of the AXA insurance group, backed a takeover offer from Séché Environnement, a relatively minor waste treatment company, for a price of EUR 1.72 billion. With its ownership issues settled, Saur was able to focus again on its continued expansion. In 2006, for example, the company had entered the Middle Eastern market, joining a consortium for contracts in Saudi Arabia. One of France's and the world's top three water services groups, Saur was prepared to soar in the new century.

M. L. Cohen

PRINCIPAL SUBSIDIARIES

Aguas De Valencia (Spain); CISE Reunion; CISE Tp Nord-Ouest; Coved Waste Management; Gestagua (Spain); Harbin Saur Water Supply Company Co. Ltd (China); Idagua (Spain); Obras Sanitarias De Mendoza (Argentina); Rossa (Russia); Saur Eau & Assainissement; Saur Martinique; Saur Neptun Gdansk (Poland); Saur Polska (Poland); Stereau.

PRINCIPAL COMPETITORS

Suez; Veolia Environnement; Lyonnaise des Eaux France S.A.; Degremont S.A.S.; SADE Compagnie Generale de Travaux d'Hydraulique S.A.; Société des Eaux de Marseille S.A.; Société Eau et Force S.A.; Compagnie des Eaux et de l'Ozone S.C.A.; Compagnie des Eaux de Paris S.C.A.; Société de Distributions d'Eau Intercommunales S.A.; Société Française de Distribution d'Eau S.C.A.

FURTHER READING

"Bouygues May Seek Partner," *Financial Times,* November 17, 1998, p. 20.

Brierly, David, "French Bank on Further Stakes in English Water," *Sunday Times,* January 7, 1990.

Curtin, Matthew, "France-Based Bouygues Puts Water Services Unit up for Sale Again," *Sunday Business,* July 11, 2004.

"Le Fabuleux Destin des 'Trois Soeurs,'" *Convergences Revolutionaires,* November 10, 2005.

"French Win Water Work," *MEED Middle East Economic Digest,* April 14, 2006, p. 23.

"PAI Partners Acquired Saur Group," *Utility Week,* March 30, 2007.

"Saur Renews Water Management Contract in Valencia for 50 Years," *European Report,* April 10, 2002, p. 600.

"Saur Seeks Buyer for Its South East Water Arm," *Utility Week,* July 18, 2003, p. 4.

Strauss, Delphine, "French Team in Talks on Saur," *Financial Times,* March 20, 2007, p. 17.

Seattle Lighting Fixture Company

———■———

26 South Hanford Street
Seattle, Washington 98134
U.S.A.
Telephone: (206) 622-1962
Toll Free: (800) 689-1000
Fax: (206) 682-5939
Web site: http://www.seattlelighting.com

Wholly Owned Subsidiary of Dolan Northwest LLC
Incorporated: 1917
Employees: 300
Sales: $50 million (2005 est.)
NAIC: 442299 All Other Home Furnishings Stores

■ ■ ■

Seattle Lighting Fixture Company, a subsidiary of Dolan Northwest LLC, is a leading specialty wholesale and retail distributor of middle- and upper-end lighting products and ceiling fans in the Pacific Northwest. The company targets three primary markets: home builders, commercial customers, and retail customers. Seattle Lighting's six stores, one clearance outlet, and online shop called Destination Lighting offer products for indoor and outdoor lighting as well as furniture, hardware, and home décor. Parent company Dolan Northwest also does business as Builders Lighting in Idaho and Globe Lighting in the Portland area as well as in Bend, Oregon.

THE ROAD TO BECOMING A DOMINANT REGIONAL RETAILER

In 1916, the H. G. Behneman Co., an agency that sold consigned stock on commission for manufacturers, created a division called the Seattle Lighting Fixture Company to act as its dealer and distributor. After the company's president, H. G. Behneman, retired in 1917, Walter Funsinn and Joseph Schoemer headed the division as president and secretary/treasurer, respectively. H. G. Behneman Co. dissolved in 1919, but Seattle Lighting Fixture Co. remained, opting to focus on both manufacturing and selling lighting fixtures largely to electrical dealers. In 1925, Schoemer died, and Funsinn, along with former classmate C. B. MacDougall, who had joined the company in 1919, remained in charge of Seattle Lighting.

During the 1930s, despite a sharp drop in sales due to the Great Depression, Seattle Lighting expanded steadily through acquisitions. In 1930, it purchased Morel Foundry, which made castings for light fixtures, and in 1931, it bought San Francisco Lighting and Supply Company. Nemco Electric Company became a part of Seattle Lighting in 1939. The company built its last fixture in the 1930s and then transformed its fabrication facility in Seattle into its corporate offices and downtown Seattle showroom.

During the 1940s, the company underwent several internal changes: Tom Wimmer, who had started as a designer with Seattle Lighting in 1931, became general manager in 1946, the year in which MacDougall retired as president. Funsinn's son, William, joined the company in 1941, and after serving in World War II, returned to work for Seattle Lighting in 1944.

The next four decades were ones of steady growth on the West Coast for the company. In the 1960s and 1970s, the company opened additional branch stores in Bellevue, Lynnwood, Tacoma, and Seattle, Washington. In the mid-1980s, it added another store in Everett, Washington, and its design center branch in Seattle. A new warehouse facility came on board in 1976 and a new distribution center in 1987. The company also opened and closed stores in both San Francisco, California, and Vancouver, British Columbia. By 1989, the company had nine branch showrooms, almost 200 employees, and sales of $32.5 million, up from its 1971 totals of 21 employees and a little more than $1 million.

Throughout this period, the company changed ownership and leadership several times. Funsinn, who purchased stock in the company in 1961 when Mac-Dougall retired became vice-president that year. Later, in 1970, when Wimmer retired, Funsinn became president. He remained in that capacity with two junior partners, both active in opening new branches, until his retirement in 1989. Upon Funsinn's retirement in 1989, he and Seattle Lighting's other owners sold Seattle Lighting Fixture to the SLF Acquisition Group.

Seattle Lighting was then the dominant lighting showroom chain in the Seattle, Washington, area and a major force in the lighting industry in the Pacific Northwest. According to management, its focus on servicing three markets (retail, builder, and commercial) was largely responsible for its success. "As we all know," Bill Funsinn explained in a 1989 *HFD* article, "the economy fluctuates during the year and as one [market] is down, the others pick up. So it all evens out."

As a regional retailer, the company offered a flexible product mix; each of its eight branches offered slightly different items targeted to appeal to a local service base. This had come to be necessary as the Pacific Northwest began to draw people from other parts of the country,

and these people brought with them tastes shaped by their former surroundings. The company's 49,000-square-foot central distribution center was well known and used among designers and architects. "We try to run all of our interior design customers through there," explained Funsinn, adding, "Our other showrooms service builders and the retail market." To coordinate stock, all of the stores were online so that each could key in an order and ship it right out. The company also did a lot of advertising through local media to maintain its premier status; it ran print, radio, and television spots and had a banner at the Seattle Coliseum.

Then, when Phil Alexander took over as head of the company in 1989, the company began immediately to follow a course of acquisitions. In 1989, it acquired Village Lighting in Bellingham, Washington, and Brennan Lighting in North Seattle and Redmond, Washington. The following year, it bought Builders Lighting with stores in Vancouver, Washington, and Lake Oswego, Gresham, and Salem, Oregon. These acquisitions combined made Seattle Lighting one of the largest lighting chains in the country as well as the region.

DECREASED HOUSING STARTS AND SALES AMID INCREASED COMPETITION

Still, by the early 1990s, changes in the economy and home acquisitions led to challenges for Seattle Lighting. With consumer confidence in the economy low, 1991 sales started off more slowly than years past and then picked up dramatically toward the end of the year to reach close to $50 million. By 1992, the nationwide drop in home building and in real estate sales combined with the uncertain economy led to a trend among customers to buy energy-efficient fixtures with which to redecorate their surroundings. Seattle Lighting was among those few retailers to see a strong seasonal upswing in business that year.

Late in 1992, Seattle Lighting had 300 employees, 13 showrooms in Washington and Oregon, and revenues in the vicinity of $42 million. Hancock Park Investors (formerly SLF Acquisition Group) sold it to a publicly traded, but inactive Texas-based oil holding company, Alliance Well Service, Inc., an oil company out of Texas that belonged to a group of venture capitalists. As a wholly owned subsidiary of Alliance in 1993, the company sold off the assets of its Homestead Air Flow Systems division, distributor of ceiling fans nationwide, to Casablanca Fan Co. In 1995, it added a Builders Lighting store in Idaho.

Sales for Seattle Lighting continued to drop throughout the remainder of the early 1990s. Although

KEY DATES

1916: H. G. Behneman Company creates the Seattle Lighting Fixture Company as a division.

1919: H. G. Behneman dissolves, and Seattle Lighting becomes an independent company.

1931: The company purchases San Francisco Lighting and Supply Company.

1939: The company purchases Nemco Electric Company.

1978: The Dolan family opens Globe Lighting in Portland, Oregon.

1989: SLF Acquisition Corporation purchases Seattle Lighting.

1990: The company purchases Builders Lighting.

1992: Alliance Well Service, Inc., purchases Seattle Lighting.

1995: Alliance Northwest Industries (formerly Alliance Well Service) refinances the company.

1996: The company files for Chapter 11 bankruptcy protection; Dolan Northwest LLC purchases Seattle Lighting.

2006: Seattle Lighting introduces Internet sales at its Destination Lighting site.

still the largest lighting fixture distributor in Seattle, the company was plagued by the decline in housing starts and increased competition from giant hardware and building supply retailers, such as Eagle Hardware, Home Depot, and Lamps Plus. Revenues for 1995 totaled just under $40 million. In 1995, Alliance Northwest Industries (formerly Alliance Well Service) refinanced the company. However, a year later, under the direction of James Scarborough, who had become president and chief executive officer after Alexander, the chain wound up in bankruptcy court, citing liabilities of $12.3 million. Scarborough attributed the company's troubles to a 29 percent decline in single-family home starts in King County, Washington, for 1995.

Scarborough undertook a reorganization plan in early 1996 with the company. Then federal bankruptcy court approved the purchase of Seattle Lighting by Dolan Northwest, a limited liability company formed by the Dolan family, which did business as A-Boy Plumbing Supplies and Globe Lighting Supply of Portland, Oregon, for $1.25 million, including inventory. Globe was a 36-year-old company with three lighting and seven electrical and plumbing stores in Washington and

Oregon. Scarborough and the entire management team, except for the chief financial officer and the vice-president of sales, left the company. After the acquisition, Globe, led by managing member Dan Dolan, relocated Seattle Lighting's Seattle distribution center to a smaller facility. The Village Lighting store in Bellingham and the Builders Lighting store in Salem were both immediately sold; ten locations continued to operate as Seattle Lighting Fixture Company and Builders Lighting.

The Dolans had opened Globe Lighting in 1978 in southeast Portland with the goal of serving as a lighting store that offered fixtures for both builders and homeowners. Globe also had another division, Dolan Designs, that manufactured and imported exclusive lighting products for more than 350 stores nationwide. These products were added to Seattle Lighting Fixture's product mix. "Seattle Lighting is going from an investor-owned company to a company that knows lighting," announced Dolan in an *HFN* article in 1996. He noted: "We have got a lot of opportunities from our vendors, and we see a lot of opportunity for growth." Globe's sales had not dropped due to competition from Home Depot and other large chains in the early 1990s, and in 1995 it posted revenues of $22 million.

1996–2007: GROWTH AS A PART OF DOLAN NORTHWEST

The match between Seattle Lighting and Globe Lighting proved beneficial to both, and, in 1999, Seattle Lighting and sister chain, Builders Lighting in Idaho, added a Design Services Department. The company hired Al Thomas to start up the company's lighting design services by offering training sessions and lighting lab seminars to staff. "We didn't increase our locations, but … Seattle Lighting is doing more business now in nine stores than when it had 14 stores." Despite the arrival in the Pacific Northwest of a lighting superstore called World Lighting in 2000, Seattle Lighting remained unconcerned. "For our company, money's not the problem; it's a case of executing our strategy when we're having 30 to 40 percent in same-store sales," Patrick Dolan, one of the company's owners, announced in a 2000 *HFN* article.

According to David McKee, Seattle Lighting Fixture's chief operating officer, sales for Seattle Lighting doubled from 1996 to 2000. The company had five stores ranging from 7,000 to 17,000 square feet and an informational web site; it dominated the Puget Sound lighting market. By 2001, McKee wondered in a *Seattle Times* article about the renewed boom in home renovation and remodeling. "It's going to be interested to see where it goes down the road," he said, speaking of how

Seattle Lighting would stack up against the competition. Lighting was once again a profitable business, he noted, and the "stores continue to grow as they have for the past four or five years."

McKee attributed the company's success to its long history in the lighting business and its strong relationship with its homebuilder and retail customers. In addition, he said in a 2002 *Seattle Times* article, the company benefited from the fact that it marketed to contractors and homebuilders as well as specializing in retail sales. He stated: "We have a lot of things to count on when the economy deals [us] a blow on one side."

In 2002, Seattle Lighting further benefited when World Lighting shut down shop after less than two years in business and Seattle Lighting took over leases on two of its large 23,000-square-foot stores with 16,000 square feet of showroom space in Washington. The move increased Seattle Lighting's visibility and presence in Washington, doubled Seattle Lighting's showroom space in Bellevue, and allowed it to enter the Southcenter market. The three-unit World Lighting had positioned itself to compete with Seattle Lighting.

Between 2002 and 2007, Dolan Northwest acquired a 135,000-square-foot distribution center in Seattle and two distribution centers in Portland. In 2004, it opened an 11,500-square-foot Globe Lighting showroom in Portland in a new 23,500-square-foot building. The new showroom replaced Globe Lighting's original store in southeast Portland. The company also put a lot of resources into online sales, going live on its Destination Lighting site in 2006. Destination Lighting became Seattle Lighting's online brand, offering indoor and outdoor fixtures, home décor, and hardware. Overall, Dolan Northwest, focusing on selling to builders, homeowners, and commercial customers, had increased its sales by about a third in the first eight years of the new century. It looked forward to ongoing expansion.

Carrie Rothburd

PRINCIPAL COMPETITORS

Lamps Plus; Crescent Lighting.

FURTHER READING

Kim, Gina, "High-Wattage Competition—Seattle Lighting, Lamps Plus—Now Eagle Hardware Founder Flicks Switch on World Lighting," *Seattle Times,* March 20, 2001, p. C1.

Kim, Nancy J., "A-Boy Supply Purchases Troubled Seattle Lighting Chain," *Portland Business Journal,* June 14, 1996, p. 22.

Major, Brian, "Seattle Lighting and Fixture: A Radiant Regional Retailer," *HFD,* January 2, 1989, p. T11.

Meyer, Nancy, "Bright Prospects for Dallas Lighting Market; Attendees Hope to Repeat a Stellar Year by Searching for Illuminating Ideas," *HFN,* June 19, 2000, p. 34.

Vinluan, Frank, "World Lighting Stores to Go Dark in August," *Seattle Times,* June 18, 2002, p. C1.

Wilson, Warren, "Seattle Lighting Files for Chapter 11," *Seattle Post-Intelligencer,* March 22, 1996, p. B1.

Seattle Pacific Industries, Inc.

21216 72nd Avenue South
Kent, Washington 98032-1916
U.S.A.
Telephone: (206) 282-8889
Fax: (206) 298-2146
Web site: http://www.unionbay.com

Private Company
Incorporated: 1981 as Union Bay Sportswear
Employees: 315
Sales: $350 million (2006 est.)
NAIC: 315223 Men's and Boys' Cut and Sew Shirt (Except Work Shirt) Manufacturing; 315999 Other Apparel Accessories and Other Apparel Manufacturing

■ ■ ■

Privately owned Seattle Pacific Industries (SPI) is a designer and marketer of apparel. The company's primary brand is youth-oriented Unionbay, which has managed to remain fresh with customers since the early 1980s. Apparel for young men, target age 19, includes jeans, pants, T-shirts, fleece tops, sweaters, henleys, and shirts. Fashions for young women, target age 17, includes jeans, pants, capris, Bermudas, hoodies, tops, skirts, and jackets. Unionbay also offers similar products for boys and girls, and such licensed accessories as boots, handbags, watches, and eyewear. Other SPI brands include ReUnion Menswear for older males and upscale Sergio Valente jeans. SPI also owns Howe, the label of designer Jade Howe who describes the aesthetic of his premium sportswear line as "cowboy punk meets English country gentleman." In addition to its headquarters in Kent, Washington, SPI maintains offices in Seattle, New York, and Los Angeles.

COMPANY FOUNDED IN 1981

SPI was founded in 1981 by longtime apparel executive Richard Raymond Lentz and two Hong Kong–based partners, Tony Lau and Brian Leung. The son of a Naval officer and a Seattle native, Lentz made his mark in the apparel industry with the Brittania sportswear brand, which grew out of Shoenfeld Industries, a men's neckwear company. Lentz had joined Shoenfeld in 1968 as vice-president and spearheaded the development of the Brittania line, which was spun off in 1970 as a separate company. With Lentz as president over the next decade, Brittania thrived in Seattle. After he resigned, however, the company struggled, and just two years later filed for Chapter 11 bankruptcy protection. Lentz was planning to enjoy an early retirement after leaving Brittania and was vacationing in Hawaii when Lau and Leung telephoned to ask if he would be interested in starting a new sportswear company with them. The idea rekindled Lentz's enthusiasm, he flew to Hong Kong, and in short order the three men agreed with a handshake deal to go into business together.

Lentz in 1981 set up shop in Seattle, remodeling a former restaurant-disco—and adding a marina—on Union Lake, the location providing inspiration for the company's new name, Union Bay Sportswear. His partners remained in Hong Kong where manufacturing was to be done at a sister plant. Although the fashion

COMPANY PERSPECTIVES

UNIONBAY is all about thinking for yourself—without taking yourself too seriously. The cutting-edge designs of UNIONBAY appeal to teens who are style leaders, always a step ahead of the latest trends and a step outside the mainstream.

world was centered in New York and Los Angeles, Seattle was uniquely positioned to provide an edge to the city's apparel companies. Because the Port of Seattle was usually the first port of call from Hong Kong and other Asian countries, Union Bay could receive goods faster than companies located elsewhere and have them shipped and on store shelves sooner than rivals.

The moderately priced Union Bay sportswear line reflected a rugged Northwestern lifestyle that quickly caught on with younger males. Lentz then expanded the label to include a junior line. After two years sales volume reached $35 million. Building on this success, the company launched the ReUnion label, a "main-floor" men's line that was more conservative than Union Bay, essentially "casual Friday" clothing for businessmen; and Heet, intended as a pure fashion forward active line. In 1985 Union Bay looked to the high-price area by launching the Ary Cooper contemporary junior line. A higher-price misses' line of sportswear called Sync was added as well, and the company also grew through acquisition, purchasing the Breezin' line of skiwear and activewear.

SEATTLE PACIFIC NAME
ADOPTED: 1986

Because it had a growing stable of brands, Union Bay Sportswear in February 1986 changed its name to Seattle Pacific Industries. In explaining the move, Lentz told the press, "Each of our product divisions needs to be able to stand on its own merits without borrowing identity from our original line, Union Bay Sportswear. It doesn't make sense to present our sophisticated men's line as ReUnion, a division of Union Bay." In addition to the name change Lentz reorganized the company, giving virtual autonomy to the divisions, which would have their own executive vice-presidents, design teams, sales managers, and merchandisers. This arrangement instilled more of an entrepreneurial spirit and helped in the recruitment of top-notch talent. For example, Ernesto Aguirre, former Perry Ellis Men's Wear president, took over the young men's and men's division, and Pat

Buchanan, Bloomingdale's fashion coordinator of men's wear, was lured away to become vice president of merchandising for Sync. The creation of autonomous divisions provided an additional benefit as well. Lentz was able to keep closer tabs on the performance of each brand. Before the restructuring, Lentz told *WWD,* "everything was under one roof and one financial recording system, so we couldn't be specific. We couldn't see where we were going or what each division was doing individually."

In 1986 SPI had a sales volume of $200 million, generated through a dozen sales offices spread across the country, including New York City, where the space was doubled to 11,000 square feet to better meet demand. In addition, the company's warehouse in Kent, Washington, added 100,000 square feet. In 1987, the company launched a new line, Union Bay Children, and also refined its structure further. Six divisions were cut back to four: the active-oriented Heet and Breezin' divisions; ReUnion; the Sync and Ary Cooper women's sportswear lines; and the Union Bay young men's, juniors, and children's sportswear offerings.

Sales did not continue to grow as Lentz had anticipated, stalling at around the $200 million mark. In September 1989 Lentz left the company, selling his interest in the business to Leung and Lau. Other shareholders included Steve Ritchey, head of merchandise and design; Doug Sellin, in charge of finance and operations; and Gary Smalley, Heet's sales head. Leung stepped in for Lentz as president but he remained in Hong Kong and soon turned over the top post to Ritchey. Smalley became senior vice-president in charge of sales for the entire company.

SPI was clearly struggling when Ritchey took over. The company's ambitious expansion plans had resulted in excessive overhead and inventory. "We touched our knee to the turf," he told *Puget Sound Business Journal,* which reported: "Ritchey nursed the company back to health by dumping inventory, taking a huge markdown and paring down the organization. In a matter of months, the company's work force dropped from 550 to 220." One of his early moves was to eliminate the Sync line in its entirety.

Starting in 1990 the company began gradually to rebuild sales volume, due to many of the changes made to rekindle growth. The Heet line was folded into the Union Bay label and dissolved on the first day of 1990. It was in effect replaced by a new line of Russian-designed sportswear to be sold under the Soviet label through a license obtained from an Italian company, Manifatture Ittierre S.p.A. Heet offices in New York and Los Angeles represented the new line. The former head of the Heet division was also assigned the responsibility

KEY DATES

1981: Company founded as Union Bay Sportswear by Richard Lentz and Hong Kong partners.
1986: Company renamed Seattle Pacific Industries, Inc.
1989: Lentz leaves company.
1992: Sergio Valente label acquired.
1999: Company begins licensing.
2006: Howe acquired.

of overseeing Soviet. SPI held high hopes for the new line, the first major endeavor since the departure of Lentz. Smalley told *WWD,* "Soviet is a tangible expression of our renewed entrepreneurial spirit."

The Soviet-themed fashion line never lived up to expectations and was eventually dropped, as was the Ary Cooper label. SPI enjoyed better success in the early 1990s designing clothes related to snowboarding. The company's designers, who kept close tabs on the interests of its target demographic, recognized early on the increasing popularity of snowboarding. Seeing that snow boarders wore baggy pants on and off the slopes, they developed a line of 20-inch wide pants under the Union Bay label. The pants became an immediate hit, prompting the company to bring out wider shorts as well. To reinforce Union Bay's connection to the sport, the label sponsored the U.S. Open Snowboarding Championships through 1995, and then returned as a sponsor four years later.

Another success story for SPI in the early 1990s was women's sportswear. At the time of the 1989 shakeup at SPI, the women's business was too diffuse, divided between Sync, Ary Cooper, and then Soviet. A new vice-president was brought in to take charge of the unit, Mary Wiberding, who recognized that the business was really being run from a men's wear perspective and paying the consequences of such an approach. She focused on the Unionbay (now one word) junior line that retained its brand appeal, eschewing garments made from crepe, rayon, and twill to concentrate on denim, a material for which Unionbay had developed a strong reputation as an innovator. The junior line introduced new denim tops and bottoms, supplemented by knit and woven tops and outerwear. As a result of these changes, Wiberding grew junior sales from $19 million in her first year to about $90 million in 1995. SPI took other steps as well in the early 1990s to grow the business. In 1992 it acquired New York–based Englishtown Sportswear Ltd., which sold designer jeans under

the Sergio Valente label and the Never Legal line of oversized street-surf jeans and shorts.

By the mid-1990s SPI sales reached $225 million. To maintain momentum in the second half of the 1990s, the company looked to increase foreign sales by opening retail shops overseas, especially in Asia. The company also licensed its name for retail shops in the region. By 1997 there were about 180 stores (including stand-alone shops and shops-in-shops) in Asia, generating $75 to $80 million a year. These totals were on top of SPI's domestic business, which grew to $320 million in 1997 and $340 million in 1998. Licensing also became important to SPI in other ways. First, it became a licensee, obtaining the right to produce Nautica denim casual wear, the business handled by the new Nautica Marine Denim Co. division. More importantly, the company began exploring the possibility of licensing its own brands, in particular Unionbay, for an array of accessories.

LICENSING PROGRAM LAUNCHED: 1999

In 1999 SPI hired a vice-president of licensing, 20-year industry veteran Cathie Underwood, who was used to having companies turn to licensing as a last-ditch effort to keep a brand alive or milk it before its demise. SPI, on the other hand, had turned down licensing opportunities and bided its time. "SPI just wanted to wait until they could do it right," Underwood told *Brandweek* in 1999. "The company doesn't need to license; they are doing it as a brand enhancement." Her goal was to find long-term partners committed to producing quality merchandise that would reflect well on the Unionbay name. Because SPI offered a full line of apparel she focused on the licensing of accessories. In the fall of 2000 they would include belts, backpacks, handbags, eyewear, footwear, and small leather goods. New offerings in spring 2001 included sunglasses, hair accessories, fashion jewelry, legwear, headwear, and junior sleepwear and intimate apparel. An infant and toddler line was licensed in 2002. SPI awarded a license to Steven Madden Ltd. in 2003 to produce men's and boys' shoes under the Unionbay label, and in that same year an agreement was reached with Skyway Luggage Co. for a Unionbay line of luggage and casual travel bags aimed at younger travelers, SPI's ninth domestic license. After a couple of years, the company exited the headwear and sunglasses category.

Unionbay licensed accessories performed well, and helped SPI weather poor economic conditions in the early 2000s, allowing the company to maintain annual sales above the $300 million range (SPI stopped releasing sales figures after 2002). The company was also in a position to entertain expansion. In spring 2005 the Unionbay label introduced a new upscale line for juniors and young men. SPI turned to external means to grow the company as well. In September 2006 it acquired Howe, designer Jade Howe's five-year-old label reflecting a skate and street mentality that fit well with the Unionbay brand.

In 2007 SPI returned to the sunglasses and head-wear business, reaching three-year licenses with Colors in Optics Ltd. for Unionbay label sunglasses for young men and juniors, and with Koon Enterprises for juniors', young men's, boys', and girls' headwear. By that time licensing accounted for about 10 percent of Unionbay's total sales volume, but the company hoped to grow that amount to 25 percent. In order to achieve that mark, SPI was seeking licensees in such categories as fragrances, intimate apparel, swimwear, underwear, and outerwear.

Ed Dinger

PRINCIPAL COMPETITORS

Donna Karan International, Inc.; Levi Strauss & Co.; Perry Ellis International, Inc.; Williamson-Dickie Manufacturing Company.

FURTHER READING

Costin, Glynis, "Seattle Pacific's Richard Lentz: The Second Time Around," *WWD,* May 5, 1987, p. 10.

Ebenkamp, Becky, "Look for the Union Label," *Brandweek,* June 12, 2000, p. 50.

Fryer, Alex P., "Sea. Pacific Out to Create Garb That 'Right Side of Cool,'" *Puget Sound Business Journal,* June 25–29, 1995, p. 69.

"Lentz Leaves Seattle Pacific," *Daily News Record,* September 12, 1989, p. 8.

Lipke, David, "Seattle Pacific Acquires Howe," *Daily News Record,* October 16, 2006, p. 8.

Porter, Lynn, "Upscale Clothing Looks Sharp to Seattle Pacific," *Puget Sound Business Journal,* June 28, 2004.

Robinson, Sean, "Clothing Company Keeps Close Eye on Fashion," *Puget Sound Business Journal,* June 28, 1999.

Spector, Robert, "Calming Seattle Pacific's Waters," *Daily News Record,* November 28, 1988, p. 27.

———, "Unionbay's Denim Reunion," *WWD,* May 4, 1995, p. 13.

———, "Why Sportswear Makers Thrive in Seattle," *Daily News Record,* March 9, 1983, p. 38.

"Union Bay Sportswear Changes Name," *WWD,* February 6, 1986, p. 10.

Volk, David, "Out-Guessing the Youth Market," *Puget Sound Business Journal,* June 30, 1997.

Wilhelm, Steve, "Importer Surges: Apparel Firm's Unionbay Line Is Hot," *Puget Sound Business Journal,* February 3, 2003.

Seattle Seahawks, Inc.

11220 Northeast 53rd Street
Kirkland, Washington 98033
U.S.A.
Telephone: (425) 827-9777
Toll Free: (888) 653-4295
Fax: (425) 893-5066
Web site: http://www.seahawks.com

Private Company
Incorporated: 1972 as Seattle Professional Football, Inc.
Employees: 500
Sales: $158 million (2006 est.)
NAIC: 711211 Sports Teams and Clubs

■ ■ ■

Based in Kirkland, Washington, Seattle Seahawks, Inc., is the corporate parent of the Seattle Seahawks franchise of the National Football League (NFL). Playing in the West division of the National Football Conference (NFC), the Seahawks have enjoyed some success, playing in one Super Bowl, which it lost, in 2006. Off the field the team has fared. Under the ownership of billionaire Paul Allen, cofounder of Microsoft Corporation, the Seahawks have built one of football's best stadiums, Qwest Field, allowing the team to generate ancillary income from suites and other luxury options as well as lucrative corporate sponsorship deals. The value of the franchise has increased significantly, although according to *Forbes* magazine, it still ranks in the middle of the league and below the NFL club average.

THE NFL COMES TO SEATTLE: 1972

In the years following World War II professional sports teams, once relegated to the Northeast and Midwest, began looking to the growing cities on the West Coast that were becoming accessible through the rise of passenger air travel. While the relocation of baseball's Brooklyn Dodgers to Los Angeles and the New York Giants to San Francisco caused a stir in the late 1950s, the NFL was already established in each of those cities. In 1946 the Cleveland Rams moved to Los Angeles, and in that same year the San Francisco 49ers began play in the new All-America Football Conference and gained entrance to the NFL in 1950 following a merger of the two rival leagues.

Seattle residents were also eager to have big league sports teams as well, but an overabundance of rainy weather (on average 161 days a year) hindered their chances. By the late 1950s there was talk of building a domed stadium in order to attract sports teams to the Northwest. In the 1960s Seattle succeeded in landing an expansion franchise from the National Basketball Association (a team that became the Seattle Supersonics), and Major League Baseball (MLB) followed suit, resulting in the birth of the Pilots, which played just one season, 1969, before the MLB, dissatisfied with the small stadium, moved the team to Milwaukee and renamed it the Brewers.

In 1968 King County voters had passed a $40 million bond issue to build a domed stadium but the project was mired in delays as more than 100 potential

KEY DATES

1972: Seattle Professional Football, Inc., is formed.
1974: Seattle is awarded an NFL franchise.
1976: Seahawks play inaugural season.
1983: Team makes playoffs for the first time.
1988: Nordstrom family sells the team to Kenneth Behring.
1997: Paul Allen buys Seahawks.
2002: The new Seahawks Stadium (later renamed Qwest Field) opens.

sites were considered, protests were conducted, and a lawsuit against the county executive was filed. Should the city actually build the stadium, MLB essentially promised to bring another team to Seattle. In order to shepherd the stadium project and lure a professional football team to Seattle, a group of area businessmen formed Seattle Professional Football, Inc., in June 1972. While its spokesman was Herman Sarkowsky, president of the National Basketball Association's Portland Trailblazers, the major financial backer was Lloyd W. Nordstrom, a department store magnate. Other partners included David E. Skinner, Howard Wright, M. Lamont Bean, and Lynn P. Himmelman. Several months later, in November 1972, construction was begun on the Kingdome, which would seat 65,000 for football and 60,000 for baseball.

Working in favor of Seattle's effort to bring an NFL team to Seattle was the birth of a new professional football league in 1973, the World Football League (WFL), which as its name suggested was intent on taking American football to cities around the world. Just three years earlier the NFL had merged with another rival league, the American Football League, and was wary of being accused of antitrust practices if it placed teams in cities already occupied by the WFL. A veritable land grab resulted, as the NFL was eager to award expansion franchises in desirable cities before the WFL did. Tampa Bay was selected early on, leaving three other possible franchises to be rewarded. Seattle was one of the leading candidates, along with Memphis, Phoenix, and Honolulu, but the WFL beat the NFL to Memphis and Honolulu, leaving two cities for three slots. Because Phoenix was unable to provide a commitment for a new stadium, the NFL decided to grant only Seattle with an expansion franchise, which was awarded in June 1974 at the cost of $16 million.

FIRST SEASON: 1976

Seattle was experiencing its own financial problems, but the NFL was in a bind and willing to take its chances on the city. The Kingdome project was plagued with construction problems and inflation, and in December 1974 the contractor abandoned the project claiming he was unable to do the work for $40 million. A new contractor was hired several months later, and King County borrowed money to finish the project, which in the end cost $67 million and opened in March 1976. While the Kingdome had finally taken shape and appeared ready for the Seahawks' inaugural season of 1976, the ownership group tended to the other necessary groundwork.

In March a general manager was named: John Thompson, the former executive director of the NFL Management Council. A contest was also conducted to select a team name, resulting in more than 20,000 entries and 1,741 different names. The Seahawks, suggested by 151 participants, was selected in June 1975 along with the team colors of blue, silver, and green. In late July, season ticket applications were mailed. On the first day that applications were taken, the team received 24,168 season ticket requests. In less than a month the target of 59,000 season tickets was reached. Late in 1975 the Seahawks agreed to a long-term lease to play in the Kingdome.

Early in 1976 the club named its first head coach, Jack Patera, formerly the defensive line coach for the Minnesota Vikings. A short time later the team was stunned by the death of its owner, 65-year-old Lloyd Nordstrom, who died of a heart attack while on vacation in Mexico. The family trust, which held a 51 percent interest in the Seahawks, remained the official owner, with John Nordstrom in charge.

Both the Seahawks and its fellow newcomer to the NFL, the Tampa Bay Buccaneers, had to fill their coaching staffs and assemble their squads. Tampa Bay won a coin flip and was awarded the first pick in the 1975 college draft. The Seahawks would then make the first selection of 39 rounds in the March 1976 allocation draft of veteran players made available by NFL clubs, whose rosters were bursting due to the collapse of the WFL that sent players who had been under contract to the NFL back to their original clubs.

Despite paying $16 million to join the NFL, the Seahawks and Buccaneers were offered slim pickings from their fellow franchises from which to field a competitive team. It was no surprise that two teams struggled that first 1976 season. Seattle posted two wins and Tampa none. Seattle's first win was against Tampa Bay, with a final score of 13–10. They later beat Atlanta as well. Seattle played its first season in the NFC West division but was transferred to the AFC Western division the first following season, showing marked improvement there as its record included five wins and nine losses.

In 1978 the Seahawks had its first winning season, with a record of 9–7, and Patera was named NFL coach of the year. The Seahawks repeated their 9–7 performance the following year but again failed to make the playoffs, and the next several years saw them struggle. The club made the playoffs in 1983 under new head coach Chuck Knox and won a pair of playoff games before losing on the verge of a Super Bowl berth. The Seahawks returned to postseason play the following season as well, winning a game before bowing out. The team did not fare as well in 1987 and 1988, losing in the opening round of the playoffs.

Before the 1988 season, the Nordstrom family put the Seahawks up for sale. In August of that year Kenneth Behring and partner Ken Hofmann acquired the franchise for $80 million in cash and the assumption of $20 million in debt. Behring had grown wealthy building and selling houses in Florida and northern California, making the *Forbes* 400 list with an estimated fortune of $300 million. His tenure as the Seahawks' owner got off to a shaky start, serving as a harbinger of what was to come, when the man he hired as interim general manager, sports agent Michael Blatt, became involved in a scandal. Blatt was arrested and tried for paying two men to murder a former business associate, Laurence Carnegie, who was killed by an arrow shot from a crossbow. According to the prosecution, Blatt's motive was that he believed Carnegie had prevented him from becoming general manager on a full-time basis. The trial ultimately ended in a hung jury.

Under Behring's ownership, the Seahawks posted just one winning season, never made the playoffs, and in 1992 won just two games, the result, according to analysts, of poor draft picks and ill-advised trades. Not surprisingly, attendance begin to decline, dipping 27 percent during Behring's tenure. To make matters worse for Behring, his attempts to replicate his real estate success in King County were thwarted by local brokers and real estate agents as well as strict antidevelopment provisions in the area.

He eventually sold his interest in undeveloped land in King County, losing at least $5 million in the deal according to press accounts. Not happy with his time in Seattle, Behring looked to leave town with the Seahawks in 1995, hoping to relocate the team to Los Angeles, which was without an NFL team for the first time in 50 years following the departure of both the Rams, who left for St. Louis, and the Raiders, who were welcomed back to Oakland.

Not only was the NFL opposed to the move, Behring was locked into a contract with King County for the Kingdome that had ten years left to run. He maintained that engineering studies had shown the stadium to be unsafe and unable to withstand an earthquake; county officials sponsored their own study which concluded that the Kingdome was safe, and that all it required was about $15 million in cosmetic improvements. (In fact, Seattle would soon experience a significant earthquake; the Kingdome did not suffer any structural damage.) In February 1996 Behring tried to buy his way out, offering to pay King County $1 million a year for 20 years, a cheap price given the increase in value the franchise would have in Los Angeles. The proposal was rejected, and that same month King County received an injunction to keep the Seahawks in place.

PAUL ALLEN ACQUIRES SEAHAWKS: 1997

Paul Allen intervened, acquiring a 14-month option to buy the Seahawks for $194 million. Allen, who had grown wealthy from Microsoft Corporation, which he cofounded with Bill Gates, was raised in the Pacific Northwest and developed a passion for football as a youth when he attended University of Washington football games. The reason he took an option on the Seahawks rather than immediately buy it was to put pressure on the community to either renovate the Kingdome or, preferably, build a new football/soccer stadium and exhibition center, as well as a separate baseball park for the American League's Seattle Mariners. The matter of the new sports facilities was soon put to Washington State voters in the form of Referendum 48, which was passed in June 1997, the same month that Allen exercised his option and acquired the Seahawks.

In effect, the referendum created a public-private funding mechanism, the seven-member Public Stadium Authority. To manage construction and operate the new stadium and exhibition center through a 30-year master lease, Allen formed First & Goal Inc., which provided $130 million of the $430 million price tag. The public footed the rest. The exhibition center was completed in October 1999, and construction on the stadium portion of the project commenced a month later.

While the Seahawks waited for their new home to be completed, Allen took steps to rebuild the struggling franchise. A community outreach program was launched and an advertising campaign mounted, helping to increase corporate sponsorships that had fallen off and revive season ticket sale, which had dipped to an all-time low of 31,000, a far cry from the 65,000 season tickets the club sold in a matter of weeks 20 years earlier. That number rebounded to 58,000 in 1999 when the Seahawks played their last season in the King-dome and sold out every game. Aside from nostalgia for the Kingdome, Seahawks' fans were excited by the prospects of the team under the guidance of new head coach Mike Holmgren, who had a few years earlier won a Super Bowl with the Green Bay Packers.

A NEW STADIUM

While the Kingdome was dismantled and about half of it recycled for use in the new stadium, the Seahawks played two seasons at the University of Washington's Husky Stadium, where revenue opportunities were limited and the team had to split ticket sales, parking, and concession with the school, resulting in an estimated loss of $30 million for the team. The Sea-hawks were essentially marking time until they could move into their new home. In the meantime, the NFL underwent realignment and the Seahawks in 2001 were shuttled back to their original division, the NFC West.

Even before the opening kickoff of the first game, the team enjoyed the financial benefits of its new downtown stadium. Sponsorship revenue soared, almost all of the luxury suites were sold, and the team was able to charge high ticket prices. Moreover, the club received a windfall in the form of a onetime sale of charter seat licenses that ranged from $2,000 to $3,000, charged to season ticket buyers to lock-in premium seat locations. Seahawks Stadium, by all accounts, was one of the finest stadiums in all of football. It featured a plaza-styled en-tryway on the north end that could hold 5,000 people for festivals, open markets, and other events. The horseshoe shape of the stadium also opened onto the en-tryway to offer an unobstructed view of the Seattle skyline. The upper-deck seating was cantilevered over the lower deck, providing a more intimate view of the field. The 67,000-seat stadium also included a roof that covered 70 percent of the seats.

While the new stadium returned the Seahawks to profitability, the team was not able to completely sell all of its premium seats and initially had trouble finding a corporation to buy the naming rights to the stadium. Finally in the summer of 2004 the club reached a deal with Qwest Communications International to rename Seahawks Stadium as Qwest Field under the terms of a 15-year $80 million contract. What management struggled to complete, however, a winning team accomplished. At the end of the 2005 season the Sea-hawks went to the Super Bowl. Although losing the game to the Pittsburgh Steelers, the team's performance meant it was able to land a bevy of new corporate spon-sors in 2006. The team also made plans to move its headquarters from Kirkland to a 20-acre site Allen

owned on Lake Washington in Renton, where a new 120,000-square-foot complex with practice facility was to be opened in 2008.

In 2007 the Seahawks were able to sell the naming rights to the practice facility to Seattle-based Virginia Mason Medical Center. The team also had no trouble in 2007 selling all 80 memberships to its new luxury club area at Qwest Field, which also attracted the sponsorship of luxury carmaker Cadillac. In addition to seats to the game and reserved parking, the Cadillac Reserve Club provided food and beverage service for $5,000 per person for two preseason and eight regular season games. Members enjoyed high-end northwestern wines and dined on such fare as grilled wild Alaskan king salmon, watermelon skewers, and charred ahi.

Soon after the 2007 season began, *Forbes* published its annual rankings of major sports franchises. The Sea-hawks, following their Super Bowl run, increased in value 4 percent over the previous year, ranked 19th in the NFL, valued at $921 million, just less than the league average of $957 million.

Ed Dinger

PRINCIPAL COMPETITORS

Arizona Cardinals; Forty Niners, Ltd.; St. Louis Rams Football Company.

FURTHER READING

Baker, M. Sharon, "Allen Puts Ball in Community's Hands," *Puget Sound Business Journal*, April 26, 1996, p. 1.

———, "Seahawks Gain Ground with Marketing Efforts," *Puget Sound Business Journal*, September 18, 1998, p. 10.

Carroll, Bob, et al., *Total Football*, New York: HarperCollins, 1997.

Ernst, Steve, "Home-Field Advantage: Seahawks Already Reap-ing the Financial Benefits of New Stadium," *Puget Sound Business Journal*, July 22, 2002.

Lamm, Greg, "Qwest Would Spend $75 M for Stadium Nam-ing Rights," *Puget Sound Business Journal*, June 10, 2004.

Lindsey, Robert, "Dome Caps Seattle Efforts to Shows It's Big 'League,'" *New York Times*, August 10, 1975.

Meisner, Jeff, "More Sponsors Teaming Up with Seahawks," *Puget Sound Business Journal*, August 21, 2006.

———, "Seahawks 'Cadillac' Club Sold Out at $5K Per Year," *Puget Sound Business Journal*, August 17, 2007.

"Owners Picked for 2 New N.F.L. Clubs," *New York Times*, December 6, 1974.

Samuelson, James, "Clueless in Seattle," *Forbes*, November 4, 1996, p. 145.

Smith, Rob, "Multiple Options: Building Seahawks Stadium Was a Challenge for Architects and Engineers," *Puget Sound Business Journal,* July 22, 2002.

———, "Sustained Drive: Seahawks Stadium's Opening Culminates a Six-Year Effort," *Puget Sound Business Journal,* July 22, 2002.

Wallace, William N., "Expansion Tops Heavy N.F.L. Slate," *New York Times,* June 4, 1974.

Stephens Inc.

111 Center Street
Little Rock, Arkansas 72201
U.S.A.
Telephone: (501) 377-2000
Toll Free: (800) 643-9691
Fax: (501) 377-2666
Web site: http://www.stephens.com

Private Company
Incorporated: 1933 as W.R. Stephens Investment Company
Employees: 800
Sales: $1.8 billion (2005)
NAIC: 523120 Securities Brokerage

■ ■ ■

Based in Little Rock, Arkansas, Stephens Inc. is one of the country's largest investment banking firms based outside of New York City. For many years operating out of a single office, the privately owned, full service firm maintains about 20 branch offices across the United States, as well as in the United Kingdom, in London. Stephens serves high net worth individuals, offering wealth management services, as well as corporate clients, providing them with mergers and acquisitions advice, and public and private offerings of debt and equity securities.

Institutional investors are served by the firm's Equity Sales and Trading unit, offering advice as well as market making services. Stephens also underwrites bonds for state and local governments, colleges and universities, nonprofit corporations, public utilities, and others. In addition, Stephens operates internationally, its clients including public corporations, private companies, financial institutions, and state and local governments. Through Stephens Capital Partners, the firm invests in both private and public companies in such fields as oil and gas, technology, agriculture, publishing and media, healthcare, manufacturing, financial services, and retailing. Chairman, president, and chief executive officer Warren A. Stephens owns 100 percent of the business.

FAMILY BACKGROUND

Stephens Inc. was founded by Wilton Aubert Stephens, who later changed his name to Wilton Roberts Stephens but was known to everyone as Witt Stephens or simply as Mister Witt. Born in 1907 in Arkansas, Witt Stephens was the son of a hardscrabble farmer with a political bent who instilled in his children a desire to make money, telling them that while poverty was not something to be proud or ashamed of, it was, he recalled, "to be gotten shed of as soon as conveniently possible." As a youth, when he was not working on the family farm, Witt Stephens ran a shoeshine stand, picked cotton, worked in a sawmill, and developed sales skills by peddling peanuts.

In 1927, after high school, he became a novelty jewelry salesman, primarily of belt buckles, by answering an ad for the National Craft Company of Providence, Rhode Island, at the behest of his father. He also enrolled at the Citizen Military Training Corps, and was assigned to Fort Leavenworth, Kansas, where he was

COMPANY PERSPECTIVES

Our clients come first. It is this philosophy that ultimately enhances our reputation and profits. On the other side of every revenue-generating transaction there is a customer who must be dealt with fairly and with the highest of ethical standards. On the other side of every investment are partners, fellow shareholders and a management team who deserve the most candid reflection of our thoughts, opinions and advice. In dealing with these varied interests honestly and fairly, we will build trust in our judgment and integrity. This will forge relationships, the likes of which have been, and will continue to be, the cornerstone of our success. Extraordinary people create extraordinary companies, and we will make it our business to maintain relationships with as many extraordinary business people as is possible all over the world. From these relationships and from our commitment to minimization of missed opportunities will come the future revenue flow of Stephens Inc. This is our corporate definition of "rain making"—extensive relationships and no missed opportunities.

able to convince the paymaster to allow him to set up a desk with his belt buckle sample kit and order forms at the end of the pay line. Assuming he held an official position, a large number of the recruits received their pay and dutifully left a $1 dollar deposit for a $3.50 belt buckle, the same amount as his commission. As a result, Stephens made $2,600 in just two days, a performance that impressed National Craft, which named him regional sales manager. (Years later Witt Stephens would perform an even more impressive sales pitch after picking up a hitchhiker who then put a gun to his head in a robbery attempt. Stephens later told his son, "I really knew I could sell when I talked him out of killing me.")

Adding Bibles to his line of wares, Stephens, now based in Colorado, crisscrossed the Southwest until the Great Depression brought him home in 1932. By this time his father was serving in the state legislature and once again provided his son with sage advice. Because of the Depression, Arkansas bonds to build highway, schools, levees, and other improvements were in default and could be bought for as little as ten cents on the dollar. The elder Stephens was convinced that either the Roosevelt administration, or Arkansas itself once the

economy rebounded, would honor the bonds, and urged his son to become involved in the bond business.

Thus, Witt Stephens borrowed $1,500 from a pair of family friends and moved to Little Rock, Arkansas. After a three-month stint with a bond house, he struck out on his own and in 1933 formed W.R. Stephens Investment Company to buy and sell Arkansas highway bonds and generate fees by helping to refinance bond issues at lower interest rates. As his father had predicted, the bonds were eventually paid off at full value, netting his son a profit of $150,000, enough money that Witt Stephens pondered early retirement in the late 1930s. His father convinced him to stay active in business, however, and Witt Stephens began trading in a wide variety of fields, including bank stocks, farms, livestock, and automobiles.

JACK STEPHENS JOINS THE COMPANY: 1946

With his increasing wealth, Witt Stephens became active in Arkansas politics, using his financial contributions to gain influence for his business interests. In time the staunch Democrat would gain a reputation as a "king maker" in the state. He also spent some of his money to send his younger brother, Jackson T. Stephens, to Columbia Military Academy. After he graduated in 1941, Jack Stephens spent a year at the University of Arkansas before securing an appointment to the U.S. Naval Academy. After graduating in 1946 he was unable to take an officer's commission because of poor eyesight and returned to Arkansas to work with his brother, acquiring a half-interest in Stephens Inc.

By this time Witt Stephens was turning his attention to energy. In 1945 he acquired Arkansas Oklahoma Gas Company and renamed it Fort Smith Gas Corporation, which eventually took the name Arkansas Oklahoma Gas Corporation. Because it owned no gas reserves, Stephens Inc. paid $6.5 million for Oklahoma Producing Company in 1953. The transmission property was folded into Arkansas Oklahoma Gas, while the reserves were assigned to a new exploration company, Stephens Production Company, which would go on to develop natural gas reserves in Arkansas, Louisiana, Oklahoma, and Texas, as well as coal mining in Wyoming. In 1954 Stephens Inc. gained control of Arkansas Louisiana Gas Company (ArkLa) and succeeded in turning around the business. In 1956 Stephens Inc. elected to sell most of its stake in ArkLa rather than register as a utility holding company. Witt Stephens took over as president and chairman of the board at ArkLa, and his brother took charge of Stephens Inc. as chairman and CEO. Under Witt Stephens, ArkLa grew by acquisition of other utility companies

---

KEY DATES

1933: Witt Stephens founds firm.
1946: Jack Stephens joins brother's firm.
1956: Jack Stephens becomes chief executive.
1970: Stephens Inc. comanages the Wal-Mart initial public offering.
1986: Jack Stephens' son Warren becomes chief executive.
1991: Witt Stephens dies.
2005: Jack Stephens dies.
2006: Warren Stephens gains 100 percent control of Stephens Inc.

---

and diversified into such areas as chemicals, cement, fertilizer, plywood, and appliance manufacturing.

In the meantime, Jack Stephens transformed Stephens Inc. from an old-fashioned municipal bond house into a true investment banking house. The firm became more involved in the equity markets, expanding its bond trading department and developing a corporate finance practice. Stephens would be involved in all of the major stock offerings in the state, including the initial public offering of Wal-Mart in 1970. The firm would also manage secondary offerings from Wal-Mart over the next dozen years and stock offerings from another major Arkansas company, Tyson Foods. In addition, the firm offered brokerage services for institutions and wealthy individuals.

Under Jack Stephens, Stephens Inc. became the largest private investment bank outside of Wall Street by taking advantage of investment opportunities as they arose. In the late 1960s one of the firm's holdings, Union Life Insurance Company, was lobbying for a new mainframe computer, while another subsidiary, a computer leasing company, was always clamoring for more capital to buy computers to keep up with demand. Because Jack Stephens thought it made no sense to buy or lease computers that would be used for only a few hours each day, he decided to invest $3 million in three companies that provided data processing services, a far more economical approach than buying equipment. Although two of the investments did not pan out, one called Systematics did, despite some difficulty in the early years. Stephens had spent $400,000 to take a 49 percent stake in Systematics. In the early 1980s the company was taken public, and by 1990 that original investment was worth about $228 million when Systematics was acquired by Alltel Corporation in a $528 million stock swap. Systematics then became Alltel

Information Services and as such was sold to Fidelity National Financial Inc. for $1 billion in 1993.

NEW GENERATIONS TAKE THE LEAD

Witt Stephens retired from ArkLa in 1973 and returned to Stephens Inc. where, according to *Arkansas Business,* "he continued to sell bonds during the morning, chew on his cigars, entertain at lunch and then pen quaintly phrased missives before leaving for the day." The notes might be to friends, business acquaintances, or simply those who had done something that struck his fancy. Witt Stephens died of complications from a stroke in December 1991 at the age of 84. By that time, his son, Witt Stephens, Jr., was working for Stephens Inc., having joined the firm ten years earlier. A daughter, Elizabeth Stephens Campbell, also went to work for the firm in 1991.

Also employed by the firm was Jack's son, Warren A. Stephens, who had earned an undergraduate degree from Washington and Lee University and an M.B.A. from Wake Forest University. He managed the firm's capital markets group while being groomed by his father as his successor. In 1986 Jack Stephens, 62, stepped down as president and chief executive officer, turning over the reins to his 29-year-old son while retaining the chairmanship. Also that year the Tax Reform Act went into effect, prompting a change in structure for the Stephens family interests. Stephens Group was created, and Stephens Inc. became a subsidiary, capitalized with $100 million.

It was a period of transition for Stephens Inc., which harbored national and international aspirations that required a change in management structure and the hiring of a new breed of young professionals. Warren Stephens was more at home in this new world than his father and uncle. According to a 1988 *New York Times* profile, "The free-wheeling approach taken by Jack [Stephens] has been de-emphasized. ... Now Stephens Inc. is acting more like a conventional securities firm, concerned mainly with gaining clients and handling more investment banking deals."

Although the company was changing, so too was the financial services field, which in the 1990s became dominated by giant firms willing to pursue business anywhere, aided in no small measure by computer communications that eradicated regional differences. This spelled trouble for regional investment banking firms, even those with the reputation and clout of Stephens Inc. *American Banker* took stock of Stephens in 1998, noting that "since 1987 Stephens has slipped from 15th-largest in its business to the 80th spot."

In truth, the amount of capital in the firm was as much as the Stephens family wanted to list on the balance sheet, prompting one Wall Street executive to inform *American Banker,* "Stephens Inc. is the Stephenses' toy." The family fortune by the late 1990s was estimated at $3 billion, and holdings included Alltel, Donrey Media Group, trucking company J. B. Hunt Transport Services Inc., department store chain Dillard's Inc.; and nursing home operator Beverly Enterprises Inc. There was no disputing, however, that Stephens experienced a significant erosion in business in the early to mid-1990s. Warren Stephens admitted, "My inability to recognize what was happening hurt us. ... For a long time we weren't even in the game." To get back into the game, he "hired a new generation of investment bankers, analysts, and sales staff responsible for aggressively pursuing business with small and mid-size companies." Because the family owned all of the stock of Stephens Inc., however, the firm's efforts to hire talented executives was hindered by a lack of stock options to offer.

Stephens also took a hit to its reputation in the 1990s after a finance employee pleaded guilty to bribing a commissioner at Florida's Escambia County Utilities Authority. He was sent to prison, while Stephens was saddled with a $6 million fine from the Securities and Exchange Commission and had to contend with the taint of scandal despite having itself uncovered the wrongdoing and alerting the authorities. The firm was also banned from practicing municipal finance in Florida for five years, hurting business and leading to the departure of a number of staffers, including all three members of the Dallas office and five members of the New Orleans office.

With the public finance business struggling, Stephens looked to build up corporate finance and in the late 1990s showed some signs of improvement, especially in its mergers and acquisitions business. To focus more attention on this area, the firm also divested StephensLink, which it used to sell stocks to retail investors through commercial banks. Stephens also formed the Private Client Group in 1998 to serve high net worth clients.

In the early 2000s Stephens continued to expand its corporate finance and private client units, opening new offices in Nashville and beefing up other branch offices with new hires, many of whom were lured away from rival firms. In 2005 subsidiary Stephens Investment Management Group LLC established its first proprietary equity mutual fund, the Stephens Small Cap Growth Fund. It was followed a year later with another open-end mutual fund, the Stephens Mid Cap Growth Fund. In 2007 Stephens expanded its institutional equity trading business by opening trading desks in New York and Chicago.

In August 2005, Jack Stephens died at the age of 81. Several months later, in May 2006, the Stephens family reorganized their business interests. Warren Stephens acquired 100 percent of Stephens Inc. and its related financial services companies, while his cousins Witt and Elizabeth received the Stephens Group Inc. name. The two groups split ownership of the Stephens Group holding company, which was renamed SH Corporation. Moreover, Witt and Elizabeth formed a new company to pursue private equity investments. In a press release Warren Stephens maintained, "This reorganization is a natural evolution in almost all family businesses. It is not an end, but rather a new beginning." Where that would lead Stephens Inc. remained to be seen.

Ed Dinger

PRINCIPAL SUBSIDIARIES

Stephens Investment Management Group LLC; Stephens Capital Partners.

PRINCIPAL DIVISIONS

Private Client Group; Capital Markets; Public Finance; Research; Capital Management; Insurance Services.

PRINCIPAL OPERATING UNITS

Investment Banking; Equity Sales and Trading; Fixed Income Sales and Trading; Wealth Management.

PRINCIPAL COMPETITORS

Houlihan Lokey; Friedman, Billings, Ramsey Group, Inc.; Morgan Keegan & Co. Inc.

FURTHER READING

Albanese, Elizabeth, "Stephens Branches Out in Its Home Base of Arkansas and Beyond," *Bond Buyer,* May 21, 2002, p. 6.

Donald, Leroy, "Remembering Mister Witt," *Arkansas Business,* December 9, 1991, p. 1.

Eichenwald, Kurt, "W. R. Stephens, Political Leader and Arkansas Investor, Dies at 84," *New York Times,* December 4, 1991, p. D24.

Elstein, Aaron, "Stephens Remaking Itself for More Aggressive Era," *American Banker,* July 17, 1998, p. 24.

Ers, Lisa S., "Pledging to Fight Back: Scandals Cost Stephens More Than Money," *Bond Buyer,* September 30, 1999, p. 1.

Gilpin, Kenneth, and Aljean Harmetz, "Son Succeeds Father As Stephens President," *New York Times,* April 10, 1986, p. D2.

Hayes, Thomas C., "An Investment Banks' Big Shift," *New York Times,* January 1, 1988.

"Jackson T. 'Jack' Stephens," *Arkansas Business,* August 1, 2005, p. 15.

Moritz, Gwen, "Stephens Family Splitting Business," *Arkansas Business,* May 29, 2006, p. 10.

Moritz, Gwen, and Chip Taulbee, "Stephens Family Splitting Business," *Arkansas Business,* June 5, 2006.

Spillenger, Paul, "Stephens Ponders Its 'Culture,'" *Arkansas Business,* December 23, 1996, p 1.

Waldon, George, "Witt & Jack Stephens: Rural Charm and Urban Money," *Arkansas Business,* March 15, 2004, p. S10.

Walker, Wythe, Jr., "Stephens' Third Generation," *Arkansas Business,* January 7, 1991, p. 16.

Swedish Match AB

———————— ■ ————————

Rosenlundsgatan 36
Stockholm, SE-118 85
Sweden
Telephone: (46 8) 658 02 00
Fax: (46 8) 658 35 22
Web site: http://www.swedishmatch.com

Public Company
Founded: 1917 as The Swedish Match Company
Employees: 12,465
Sales: $1,886.4 million (2006 est.)
Stock Exchanges: Stockholm
Ticker Symbol: SWMA
NAIC: 312229 Other Tobacco Products Manufacturing;
424940 Tobacco and Tobacco Product Merchant
Wholesalers

■ ■ ■

Based in Stockholm, Swedish Match AB is a leading global manufacturer and distributor of well-known brands in five tobacco products: snuff/snus (moist snuff), chewing tobacco, cigars, pipe tobacco, and lights. It is the largest distributor of chewing tobacco in the United States, one of the largest producers of pipe tobacco and cigars in the world, and the only global producer of snuff. Among its brands are Macanudo, White Owl, and Garcia y Vega cigars; Red Man chewing tobacco; Timber Wolf, General, and Taxi snuff brands; Cricket lighters; and Swan matches and papers. Swedish Match sells products in more than 100 countries worldwide, with particularly strong markets in Europe and North America. It operates production units in 11 countries.

ORIGINS AND EARLY PLANS FOR GLOBAL DOMINANCE

Ivar Kreuger founded Swedish Match. Ivar Kreuger was an internationally renowned industrial magnate and a controversial figure who was regarded as a scoundrel by some. He was born in 1880 in Kalmar, a city in southern Sweden. His family owned and operated a match factory that his grandfather had started. The match industry was relatively young when the company was founded; matches had been produced commercially only since the early 1800s, but a large market had developed since matches were commonly used at that time to light kerosene lamps and gas stoves. By the late 1800s the Swedish match industry was employing 7,000 workers and producing about 40,000 tons of matches annually.

The early Swedish match industry was dependent on international suppliers and buyers. Aspen wood, for example, was supplied primarily by Russia. Chemicals such as potassium chlorate, phosphorus, and paraffin were purchased mostly from Great Britain and Germany. Similarly, Germany and England were the greatest export markets for Swedish matches. In fact, Sweden exported about 85 percent of the matches it produced. World War I disturbed the import and export dynamics because supplies were cut, and some countries imposed restrictive trade barriers. Nevertheless, by the time Ivar Kreuger entered the business, the foundation for his international empire had been established.

When Ivar Kreuger began his operations in the early 1910s, Sweden had assumed a global leadership role in the match industry. That lead was largely attributable to technological breakthroughs. In 1884 Gustaf Eric Pasch of the Swedish Royal Academy of Science invented the safety match. It utilized red phosphorus (instead of more toxic yellow phosphorus), which was applied to a striking surface rather than the match head. The result was a much safer match. Early matchmaking machines—what we now call lighters—had emerged as well.

Kreuger exhibited little interest in his family's enterprise as a young man. His business cunning and penchant for overseas adventure, however, were evident from an early age. As a boy Kreuger stole final term papers from the principal's office and sold copies to students for the equivalent of five cents apiece. After his schooling, in which he studied engineering, Ivar traveled the globe, taking jobs in South Africa, Canada, Germany, and the United States. His brother, meanwhile, operated the family's struggling match business. The match industry at the time suffered from the growing popularity of electric lighting. Only the increasing number of cigarette smokers, who were major purchasers of matches, prevented further damage to the industry.

Kreuger returned to Sweden when he was 28 years old. He and a fellow engineer, Paul Toll, started a real estate and construction company. Kreuger & Toll was successful, but Kreuger was soon sidetracked by opportunities related to the family business.

The Swedish match industry was highly consolidated by that time. One giant company, Jonkoping & Vulcan, controlled 75 percent of the market, and the Kreugers were one of a few small players still competing. Kreuger was intrigued by the challenge of overcoming Jonkoping's dominance. He also had greater designs—he believed that he could parlay Sweden's technological advantages into global dominance of the match industry.

CREATING AN INTERNATIONAL NETWORK

Kreuger's business savvy, although ethically questionable, was undeniable. During the early 1910s he managed to bring together most of the remaining Swedish match companies, including his family's, into a single organization called United Match Factories. Kreuger artificially inflated the value of United, making it look as though his company had much more capital than it actually possessed. He used that artificial value to back his takeover of Jonkoping in 1917, thus effectively establishing a monopoly in his home country. When World War I ended a year later, he shifted the focus of his newly formed holding company, The Swedish Match Company, to the European mainland.

During the 1920s Kreuger embarked on an aggressive acquisition campaign, striking deals and snapping up match factories all over Europe. Although his business acumen was revered at the time, his bid for industry dominance would later earn him a reputation for chicanery. For example, it was discovered that he sent secret agents to companies in which he had an interest. The undercover proxies made extremely low offers to buy the enterprises. Kreuger followed these agents in and offered a higher—though still low—price. The practice allowed him to snag new factories at deflated prices. In addition, he often secretly purchased interests in competitors in an effort to avoid national restrictions related to monopolies and foreign ownership.

By the late 1920s, the industrious Kreuger had amassed a huge match-manufacturing network. He controlled a significant share of the match business in Hungary, Yugoslavia, and other East European countries and acquired major stakes in leading British and U.S. match companies. Kreuger also built new factories in countries such as India. More importantly, Swedish Match effectively claimed control of the match industries in Norway, Denmark, Holland, Finland, and Switzerland. The company also diversified into other business areas during this time. By the end of the 1920s, in fact, Kreuger controlled a telecommunications company, a pulp and paper enterprise, and a mining company that owned the third largest gold deposit in the world.

Kreuger's empire churned out 2.8 million cases of matches annually by 1929, making up about 40 percent of total world match output. However, leadership in the match industry was only part of the Swedish Match story to that point, for Ivar Kreuger's international reputation grew significantly after the conclusion of World War I. Kreuger used part of his massive fortune

KEY DATES

1917: Ivar Kreuger establishes company and gains the match monopoly in Sweden.

1932: Kreuger commits suicide, leaving a financially troubled company; the Wallenberg family of Sweden takes over company.

1980: The company buys out the U.S. match manufacturer Universal Match.

1988: Swedish Match is acquired by Stora Kopparbergs Bergslags AB.

1990: Volvo buys Swedish Match.

1996: Volvo spins off Swedish Match through initial public offering.

1998: Lennart Sunden becomes president and CEO.

1999: Cigarette operations are divested.

2000: Company moves heavily into North American markets with purchase of 64 percent of General Cigar Holdings.

2001: Pipe tobacco operations in South Africa and dry snuff operations in Europe are acquired.

2004: Company receives U.S. Smokeless Tobacco Co. (USST) cigar business in claim settlement; Sven Hindrikes is appointed to replace Lennart Sunden.

2007: Cigars International, Inc., is acquired.

to make loans to needy national governments battered by the war. Although many of the loans were used to secure permission for Swedish Match to develop a monopoly in the borrower's country, many observers nevertheless viewed Kreuger's postwar lending to financially troubled governments as magnanimous. By 1930 Kreuger had doled out more than $350 million in loans to a dozen different countries.

In less than a decade, Kreuger had built one of the largest international companies ever created. His business acumen had achieved legendary status. Hundreds of millions of dollars flowed through his diverse holdings of companies, which were organized under four divisions: Swedish Match; Kreuger & Toll; International Match (New York); and Continental Investment (Liechtenstein). Kreuger's enviable reputation as a socially conscious business leader continued to grow, particularly after he made a celebrated $30 million loan to Germany to help that country pay war reparations. That move earned him the title of "the savior of Europe" from some politicians at the time.

COLLAPSE OF AN EMPIRE

Nevertheless, neither his success nor his reputation saved him. Kreuger shocked the global financial community when he shot and killed himself on March 12, 1932. His suicide in his Paris bachelor apartment capped the end of his two-year effort to keep his collapsing empire glued together. The previously hidden weaknesses of Kreuger's mammoth enterprise were exposed following the global financial meltdown spurred by stock market crashes around the world. As the value of his companies plunged, Kreuger's personal liabilities ballooned past the $250 million mark, and his companies were unable to meet their obligations. Kreuger took desperate measures, even going so far as to forge $142 million worth of Italian government bonds and promissory notes. Kreuger himself forged the signatures needed on the notes, but misspelled the names. The ruse failed, and Kreuger's reputation was damaged.

It was later discovered that Kreuger's dynasty was built partially on overvalued assets and deceptive accounting practices. Although his business acumen was undeniable, Kreuger had consistently engaged in questionable reporting practices in an effort to expand his holding company. "Throughout his bizarre career," wrote Robert Shaplen, author of the 1960 biography *Kreuger,* "Kreuger alone supplied the figures for the books of his various companies, and he mostly kept them in his head." Backing that assertion was Allen Churchill, who noted in *The Incredible Ivar Kreuger* that a former secretary of Kreuger's claimed that Kreuger once dictated the text of the annual reports for his four companies in a single afternoon: "I accounted for it by the fact that I had often been told that he was a genius," she explained.

To Kreuger's credit, he was a highly intelligent businessman and financier. Many of his defenders contend that, although his dealings may appear shady in retrospect, at the time many of his activities represented the norm. Shaplen's biography related the following excerpt from a statement made by Kreuger to Björn Prytz, a Swedish tycoon and diplomat: "In olden times, the princes and everyone would go to confession because it was the thing to do, whether they believed it or not. Today the world demands balance sheets, profit-and-loss statements once a year. But if you're really working on great ideas, you can't supply these on schedule and expose yourself to view. You've got to tell the public something, and so long as it's satisfied and continues to have faith in you, it's really not important what you confess."

PICKING UP THE PIECES AFTER KREUGER

Teams of attorneys, bankers, and accountants labored for four years sorting out Kreuger's affairs and divvying up the remains of his companies after his death. The Price, Waterhouse accounting firm finally calculated that Kreuger had inflated the earnings of his companies by more than $250 million between 1917 and 1932. Millions of dollars were never accounted for, and Ivar's brother, Tortsen, was sent to jail for 18 months. After his release, Tortsen spent much of the remainder of his life trying to prove that Ivar was murdered. Tortsen's story fell on deaf ears, and the company was wrested from Kreuger-family control.

The Wallenberg family of Sweden came to the rescue of Swedish Match. In an agreement that involved a transfer of $15 million from Stockholm to New York, Jacob Wallenberg was able to gain control of the injured enterprise. The company lost its monopoly contracts with foreign governments and was diminished in size and strength. Nevertheless, Kreuger had amassed massive holdings in the match industry that allowed Swedish Match to sustain its market leadership.

Following World War II and into the middle of the 20th century, Swedish Match tried to expand its match business. Swedish Match purchased the Cricket disposable cigarette-lighter division of Gillette in the mid-1980s, a purchase that, combined with its own Feudor and Poppell lighter brands, gave Swedish Match a hefty 15 percent of that global market. The company's entrance into the cigarette-lighter business illustrated how much Swedish Match had changed since Kreuger's reign. Indeed, in an effort to squelch competition from lighter manufacturers, Kreuger had succeeded in getting some countries to ban the use of lighters in public, and those laws lingered on the books for several years in a few nations.

DIVERSIFYING BEYOND MATCHES AND TOBACCO

By the late 1980s matches made up less than 25 percent of Swedish Match's global sales. Still, the company remained the largest manufacturer of matches in the world and continued to improve its position in the world market. In 1980, for example, Swedish Match bought out Universal Match, the largest producer of matches in the United States. In 1987 it acquired Britain's second largest match manufacturer, Wilkinson Sword. The latter purchase gave Swedish Match control of a leading 25 percent of world match markets. Going into the early 1990s, Swedish Match employed more than 25,000 workers globally and generated annual revenues of more than $17 million, about $250 million of which were attributable to U.S. sales.

The company also diversified into several other arenas. Swedish Match purchased Tarkett, making it the second largest manufacturer of floor coverings in the world by the late 1980s. Swedish Match also acquired cabinet makers Marbodal and HTH, and door maker Sweedor, which made it the biggest producer of doors in Sweden. Other acquisitions included forays into packaging material and razor-blade industries.

In 1988, Swedish Match was acquired by Stora Kopparbergs Bergslags AB, a diversified company and among the largest forestry companies in Europe. Stora reportedly paid SEK 5.9 billion for Swedish Match, in its efforts to enhance its line of raw materials with consumer products businesses. Stora's parentage was short-lived, however, as Swedish Match was sold to Volvo in 1990. Volvo held on to Swedish Match for only a few years before that company decided to jettison most of its nonautomotive subsidiaries. Volvo eventually spun Swedish Match off to its shareholders in 1996, in a deal worth SEK 10.1 billion.

PUBLIC COMPANY FOCUSES ON NICHE TOBACCO PRODUCTS

In 1998, leadership of the company passed to Lennart Sunden. The new CEO was known for his skill in marketing. He helped focus the company's long-term strategy on non-cigarette tobacco products and smoking accessories. Key products would be smokeless tobacco, cigars, matches, and lighters. Consequently in 1999 the company made one significant divestiture. In June, Swedish Match announced the sale of its entire cigarette division to Austria Tabak, for SEK 4.8 billion ($560 million). Swedish Match was Sweden's lone cigarette manufacturer at that time, where its brands made up almost half the market. It also had a large share of the Estonian cigarette market. Cigarettes were not a business the company could compete in globally. Cigars, however, were another matter.

At virtually the same time it was disposing of its cigarette operations, Swedish Match spent $200 million to buy the mass-market lines of the Virginia cigar manufacturer General Cigar Holdings, Inc. This purchase gave Swedish Match the well-known brands White Owl, Tiparillo, Tijuana Smalls, and Garcia y Vega. By that time, North America accounted for about one-fifth of Swedish Match's sales, and it hoped to use the General Cigar buy to help increase its U.S. sales, particularly in urban markets. A year later, Swedish Match made another offer to General Cigar, this time to purchase a 64 percent interest in the company. Swedish

Match's leading product in the U.S. market was chewing tobacco, where it marketed the venerable Red Man brand. In 2000, the company tried to buy the chewing tobacco brands of National Tobacco Company, including its Beech-Nut and Durango brands, but the Federal Trade Commission (FTC) stopped the sale on antitrust grounds.

Another key product in Swedish Match's stable of niche tobacco products was snuff. Snuff was a tobacco product that was used in Sweden as a passive way of absorbing nicotine. A thumbnail-sized portion of it sat in the mouth—it was not snorted or chewed. With the ascension of Lennart Sunden as CEO in 1998, the company began to change the way it presented snuff. It became not just another tobacco product but a smoking cessation aid. By 2000, Sweden had 900,000 snuff users, and according to Swedish Match, over half were former smokers. With smoking becoming less socially and medically acceptable, Swedish Match marketed its snuff as a neat, safe, effective way to enjoy tobacco while cutting down on or quitting cigarettes. The company began packaging snuff in premeasured packets something like a tea bag. The user placed the packet behind the upper lip and did not have to contend with spitting out unattractive tobacco juice or shreds. The product was referred to as moist snuff, or snus. The company saw a significant rise in its snuff sales with the new marketing campaign.

In other markets abroad, Swedish Match remained a strong seller. It dominated the cigar market in the Netherlands, where it had a host of established brands plus the new ones it bought from General Cigar. In England, the company found that, as cigarettes became more expensive, accessories for hand-rolling were a growing and profitable category. In 1999, it relaunched its Swan brand, with a line of papers, matches, lighters, and filters, aiming at younger smokers. These items had a profit margin of more than 40 percent, and the hand-rolling category was the fastest-growing segment of the entire tobacco products market in the United Kingdom.

COUNTERING THE ANTISMOKING ENVIRONMENT: 2001–03

Swedish Match continued to make acquisitions. In 2001, it purchased pipe tobacco operations in South Africa and dry snuff operations in Europe. However, during the first part of the decade, Swedish Match seemed to be spending much of its time in court, opposing efforts to curtail the sales of its products. In 2002, for example, the company was in court fighting the proposed U.K. ban on chewing tobacco, as well as the European Union ban on oral snuff. Meanwhile, across the Atlantic, Swedish Match brought an antitrust lawsuit against U.S. Smokeless Tobacco Co. (USST). Two years later, in 2004, to settle the claim, USST transferred its cigar operation (U.S. Cigar Sales, Inc.), which included Don Tomas, Astral, and Helix brands, to Swedish Match's North American subsidiary. Swedish Match North America, Inc., then sold the operation to another Swedish Match subsidiary, General Cigar Company.

The European Union ban on snus forced Swedish Match to market that product in Sweden (where the ban did not apply), Norway, South Africa, and the United States. In addition to introducing its snuff pouches to the United States, the company also lobbied the federal government to allow advertising that presented this product as a less risky alternative to cigarettes and a method to stop smoking. Despite the efforts of Swedish Match and USST Company, the FTC did not change the regulations.

NEW LEADERSHIP, NEW ACQUISITIONS

In 2004, Lennart Sunden was let go by the company, reportedly over a disagreement about Sunden's pension benefits. Sven Hindrikes, the company's executive vice-president and CFO replaced him as president and CEO.

In the United States, smoking restrictions, including statewide bans, were contributing to the continuing decline of cigarette consumption. However, sales of smokeless tobacco products (snuff, snus, and chewing tobacco) were growing at 8 percent a year. That significant growth caused the major tobacco companies to examine ways to take advantage of the trend. R.J. Reynolds Tobacco and Philip Morris test-marketed spitless products and, in 2006, Lorillard Tobacco Co. teamed up with Swedish Match North America to develop smokeless tobacco products for the U.S. market. The joint production agreement brought together the third largest tobacco manufacturer in the country and the third largest producer of moist snuff in the United States.

Mergers were another way for the major producers to gain market share—of cigars as well as smokeless products—and improve their bottom line. In 2006, Reynolds American, Inc., paid $3.5 billion for Conwood Sales, the country's number two smokeless producer, and maker of Kodiak, Grizzly, and Levi Garrett brands. In 2007, JT, formerly Japan Tobacco, merged with the United Kingdom's Gallagher Group. In the United Kingdom, Imperial Tobacco acquired Kentucky-based Commonwealth Brands and expected to complete its acquisition of Altadis (the Franco-Spanish tobacco company) early in 2008. The price for that purchase was reported to be $18.2 billion. Altria announced it was buying John Middleton, the Pennsylvania-based maker of cigars.

Swedish Match also used acquisitions to strengthen its cigar business. It gained new brands when it bought El Credito Cigars, a U.S. company, and two European premium cigar brands, Hajenius and Oud Kampen. Its purchase of direct marketer Cigars International gave the company access to additional ways to sell cigars to consumers, particularly through catalogs and the Internet.

2007 AND BEYOND

Swedish Match's brands had strong market positions and the company had a track record of developing successful new products in different markets. These ranged from upscale cigarette papers in the United Kingdom to aromatic cigars in Europe to menthol-flavored snus in a lavender-colored can to attract women users in Sweden.

The company's markets for snuff/snus and cigars were growing both in sales and in volume, even as demand for its other products declined. As more western countries implemented bans on smoking in public places and the sales of cigarettes continued to decline, demand for alternatives continued to grow. Emerging markets in Asia and South America offered additional markets for Swedish Match's products. The greatest challenge to the company's continued success could come from the mergers and consolidations in the tobacco industry.

Dave Mote
Updated, A. Woodward; Ellen Wernick

PRINCIPAL SUBSIDIARIES

Swedish Match North America, Inc.; General Cigar Holdings, Inc.; Cigars International Inc.

PRINCIPAL DIVISIONS

North Europe; North America; International.

PRINCIPAL COMPETITORS

USST, Inc.; Swisher International Group, Inc.; Conwood (owned by Reynolds American, Inc.); Gallaher Group (owned by Japan Tobacco); Altadis; North Atlantic Trading Company; Societe BIC S.A.

FURTHER READING

Abrose, Jules, "Swedish Match Again Strikes Out in New Directions," *International Management,* October 1987, pp. 87–90.

Anghelides, Bernard, "Swedish Match President Ousted," *World Tobacco,* May 2004, p. 13.

Beirne, Mike, "Puffed Up: Smokeless Has Air of Success," *Brandweek,* June 18, 2007, p. S59.

———, "Swedish Match to Turn Over a New Leaf," *Brandweek,* April 9, 2001, p. 14.

Croft, Martin, "Swedish Match Takes Government to Court over Ban on 'Oral Tobacco,'" *Marketing Week,* October 10, 2002, p. 6.

Fleenor, D. Gail, "Backup Plan," *National Petroleum News,* April 2006, p. 40.

"General Cigar in Acquisitive Mood," *World Tobacco,* July 2004, p. 8.

George, Nicholas, "Swedish Group Sells Cigarette Operations," *Financial Times,* June 1, 1999, p. 24.

Gutierrez, Carl, "Cigars Alright for Altria," *Forbes.com,* November 1, 2007.

Hassbring, Lars, *The International Development of the Swedish Match Company, 1917–1924,* Stockholm: Swedish Match Company, 1979.

"It's the Way to Go with RYO," *Grocer,* January 25, 2003, p. S14.

Kapstein, Jonathan, and Charles Gaffney, "Peter Wallenberg Is Rebuilding a Dynasty," *Business Week,* November 2, 1987, pp. 158–59.

Landler, Mark, and Andrew Martin, "Smokeless from Sweden," *New York Times,* October 3, 2007, p. C1.

Loeffelhyolz, Suzanne, "Global Report: Fore Products—Outside Looking In," *Financial World,* February 20, 1990, pp. 66–67.

"Lorillard, Swedish Match Announce Production Agreement," *National Petroleum News,* December 2006, p. 8.

Moskowitz, Milton, *The Global Marketplace,* New York: Macmillan, 1987.

Munro, Neil, "No Juice for Smokeless Tobacco," *National Journal,* June 14, 2003.

"Plenty of Fire in Smokeless Disputes," *World Tobacco,* July 2002, p. 9.

Ram, Vidya, "Imperial Tobacco Holds Ground," *Forbes.com,* October 30, 2007.

"Reduced Risk Claim for Snus," *World Tobacco,* January 2003, p. 8.

Ress, David, "Trying to Sell Europe on Snuff ... and Gearing Up to Host an EC Bash," *Business Week,* April 10, 2000, p. 4.

"Richmond, Va.-based Tobacco Business to Buy Four General Cigar Lines," *Knight-Ridder/Tribune Business News,* March 28, 1999.

"Setback for Swedish Match's EU Snus Ban Challenge," *World Tobacco,* September 2004, p. 3.

"Snuff, Puff and Paper Go to Euroland," *Euromoney,* October 1999, p. 86.

"Sunden Leaves Swedish Match," *Tobacco Retailer,* June 2004, p. 20.

"Swan's Offer Is Strikes Ahead," *Grocer,* July 8, 2000, p. S10.

"Swedish Match Finalizes Cigars International Acquisition," *Direct (Online Exclusive),* September 4, 2007.

"Swedish Match Remains Strong," *World Tobacco,* May 2000, p. 33.

"Swedish Mismatch," *Euromoney,* July 1995, pp. 111–12.

Wikander, Ulla, *Kreuger's Match Monopolies, 1925–1930,* Stockholm: Swedish Match Company, 1980.

Syntel, Inc.

525 East Big Beaver Road, Third Floor
Troy, Michigan 48083
U.S.A.
Telephone: (248) 619-2800
Fax: (248) 619-2888
Web site: http://www.syntelinc.com

Public Company
Incorporated: 1980 as Systems International, Inc.
Employees: 11,000
Sales: $270.23 million (2006)
Stock Exchanges: NASDAQ
Ticker Symbol: SYNT
NAIC: 541511 Custom Computer Programming Services

■ ■ ■

Syntel, Inc., is a leading information technology outsourcing firm. The company helps install and maintain software for clients, typically in partnership with more than 80 suppliers like Microsoft, Oracle, IBM, and Sun Microsystems; runs and maintains customers' web-based e-commerce sites; performs a variety of other business processes; and provides information technology staffing. Major clients include American Express, Chrysler, Humana, and State Street Bank. The bulk of Michigan-based Syntel's employees work at several large campuses in India, where it is aggressively expanding. Controlling interest in the publicly traded firm is owned by cofounders Bharat Desai and Neerja Sethi.

BEGINNINGS

Syntel was founded in Michigan in 1980 by Bharat Desai and his wife Neerja Sethi. Born in Mombasa, Kenya, Desai's family had moved to India when he was 11, and he later studied electrical engineering at the Indian Institute of Technology in Mumbai. After graduation he took a job with Tata Consultancy Services (TCS), which posted him to Detroit, Michigan, in 1976. There he met and married fellow TCS employee Sethi, and also enrolled in the University of Michigan Business School.

In 1980 the couple invested $2,000 to found an information technology staffing service based at their Troy, Michigan, apartment called Systems International (later condensed to Syntel). Sethi would keep her job with TCS while Desai ran the new business as he worked to complete his degree.

Much of Desai's efforts initially consisted of making cold calls to firms in the Detroit area, and although he began to win jobs from the likes of Blue Cross/Blue Shield of Michigan and General Motors, he grew frustrated with the amount of energy selling his services took. Vowing to retain any clients he won, he developed a strong focus on customer service that would earn his company a reputation for maintaining long-term business relationships.

By 1983 Syntel's annual sales topped $1 million, and over the next five years the company grew to employ about 70. Staffers worked at clients' facilities solving software problems, performing upgrades, and handling related projects.

Seeing the market for Syntel's services growing rapidly, in 1988 Desai, who had become a U.S. citizen,

COMPANY PERSPECTIVES

Syntel helps its Global 2000 customers remain at the forefront of their industries with innovative uses of technology to operate their businesses more efficiently. We deliver flexible, custom Information Technology and Business Process outsourcing solutions that improve quality and reduce costs. More than any other company, we explore, develop and adapt new, better ways to do this.

began actively to recruit new employees from other English-speaking countries such as India, Australia, New Zealand, and England. He found that these foreign workers were often better trained and had a better attitude than their American counterparts, who could afford to be picky because the demand for their services was so high.

GLOBAL DEVELOPMENT CENTER OPENED IN MUMBAI IN 1992

In 1992 Syntel opened its first Global Development Center in Mumbai, India, which would handle work in-house, rather than at a client's facility. The offshore location provided greater access to well-trained Indian workers whose average wage was less than in the United States, while the wide time difference allowed the firm to offer 24-hour service on projects in conjunction with its American operation, which significantly hastened their completion.

To link the two, Syntel leased a then-fast 9.5-kilobytes/second communications line for $500,000, a huge investment for the still-growing company. It took several weeks to establish a reliable connection, which caused concern among some customers. The new facility and its onsite work arrangement also upset some of Syntel's American employees, who saw the outsourcing operation as a competitor. For 1992, the company had revenues of $29.7 million and net income of $935,000.

By this time many of Syntel's state-side employees were in the country with visas granted under the H1-B program, which allowed foreign workers in specialized fields to come to the United States for up to six years. American computer technicians unhappy about the situation complained that such employees were paid less than the prevailing wage, and in 1992 the U.S. Department of Labor launched an inquiry into Syntel's employment practices, which three years later resulted in

a fine of $40,000 for paying below-market wages. Forty employees were also given $77,702 in back pay, and the company voluntarily withdrew from the H1-B visa process for three months and pledged $1 million to train American workers. Approximately half of Syntel's 1,200 U.S.-based employees were from India, while another 300 worked in Mumbai.

In 1995 the firm opened a second Global Development Center in Cary, North Carolina, which was near both clients and sources of trained employees. It was later followed by a third in Santa Fe, New Mexico. Smaller offices were also located in half a dozen other U.S. cities. The year 1996 saw Syntel awarded Q1 certification by Ford for its quality standards, and the company later received similar accreditation from Chrysler Corp.

INITIAL PUBLIC OFFERING IN 1997

Syntel had for some time been making plans for an initial public stock offering, and in August 1997 it raised $27.3 million by selling three million shares on the NASDAQ. The money was used in part to pay $7 million to Desai and Sethi to acquire Syntel Software Private Ltd. of India, as well as to provide $3.5 million to end the company's status as an S corporation. President and CEO Desai and Vice-President of Internal Affairs Sethi, who had previously owned all of the firm's stock, would retain 88 percent of the 25 million shares, with Syntel employees also becoming vested in the company. During the year the firm opened a new Global Development Center in Chennai, India, and offices in London, England, and Suntec City, Singapore.

To deal with the much-feared "Y2K" problem, where older software programs would not recognize dates past 1999, Syntel introduced a new service offering called Method2000. The firm also launched an eight-week Technical and Professional Development Training Program at its North Carolina and Detroit area facilities to meet its continuing need for new workers. After successful applicants completed the program, they were given another six to eight weeks of on-the-job mentoring.

Major clients at this time included IBM, Northwest Airlines, NationsBank, Dayton Hudson Corp., and the state of New Mexico. The company's top client was insurance firm AIG, which accounted for almost a third of revenues. Sales for 1997 topped $124 million, with net income reaching $10.2 million.

In January 1998 Syntel bought Waypointe Information Technologies, Inc., a Grand Rapids, Michigan–based firm with revenues of $10 million that specialized

KEY DATES

1980: Bharat Desai and Neerja Sethi found Systems International in Troy, Michigan.
1988: Firm begins recruiting workers from abroad.
1992: First Global Development Center (GDC) opened in Mumbai, India.
1997: Initial public offering on NASDAQ; Chennai, India, GDC opened.
1998: Waypointe Information Technologies, Inc., purchased.
1999: Acquisitions of IMG, Inc., and Metier, Inc., boost e-commerce offerings.
2000: Firm writes off $21.6 million related to underperforming Metier.
2002: Construction on Pune, India, GDC begins.
2007: With most operations located in India, employee count tops 11,000.

in enterprise resource planning. New clients for the year included Michigan-based Borders Group, Ryder System, and Blue Cross/Blue Shield of Georgia. Y2K work, which had comprised about 7 percent of the total in 1997, reached 18 percent in 1998. During the year the firm was ranked second on *Forbes* magazine's "Best Small Companies in America" list.

Although Syntel's stock had risen high in 1998, by early 1999 its price had fallen to under $10 as investors grew leery of companies that were targeting short-term Y2K projects. In March a 250,000-share buyback program was announced to help boost the price. Clients added during the year included Budget Rent a Car International, Humana, and Kemper Insurance Companies. The firm had begun partnering with firms like Microsoft, SAGA Software, and Siebel Systems to provide authorized support services. It would win a significant number of these arrangements from other software firms over the next few years.

ACQUISITIONS BOOST
E-COMMERCE OFFERINGS IN
1999

In August 1999 Syntel bought IMG, Inc., a technology consulting firm based in Beaverton, Oregon, that had annual revenues of $2 million. It would become part of the company's Enterprise Solutions Group, which provided e-commerce and data warehousing services.

This acquisition was followed in September by the purchase of Metier, Inc., of Los Angeles for $17.4 million and 300,000 shares of stock. Metier had annual revenues of $25 million and a similar lineup of services, with customers that included DreamWorks, Siemens, EarthLink Network, and the California Institute of Technology.

Syntel was using the slogan "The Architects of e" to herald its new focus on Internet business support, and during 2000 the company retrained 1,000 of its employees for e-commerce duties and shifted them from mainframe computer systems. This area, and software outsourcing services, accounted for more than three-fourths of revenues, while the staffing business continued to dwindle.

Taking a further plunge into the dot-com waters, in January 2000 Syntel formed a web incubator program to invest in or create new Internet businesses. Poor performance of the Metier subsidiary was dragging down the bottom line, however, and although revenues for the year grew to $164 million, net income fell from $21 million in 1999 to less than $8 million due to a $21.6 million pretax charge taken for impairment to goodwill from the acquisition. The firm later racked up additional losses from Metier (which was ultimately shuttered), and in 2002 settled a lawsuit with the unit's original shareholders, who had jumped ship six months after the sale to form a similar company of their own.

Meanwhile, Syntel was continuing to expand, announcing plans to develop a recently purchased 40-acre site near Pune, India, and opening new offices in Israel, Germany, Sweden, and Turkey. More than two-thirds of its 2,700 employees worked in India, with the chief operating officer, chief financial officer, and other executives based there, along with such units as payroll and legal affairs.

The Pune campus, which was expected to cost up to $100 million and employ as many as 9,000 when completed, was intended in part to raise Syntel's profile in India so that it could recruit workers, who often sought out better-known Indian-based information technology firms first. With high-speed connections making location relatively unimportant, the firm could also reap huge savings by paying its Indian workers $10 to 20 less per hour than the prevailing wage in the United States.

During the early 2000s Syntel continued to add major new clients such as GTE Data Services, Wells Fargo, HCA, Conseco, and GMAC. In 2001 the firm also wrote off $4.1 million related to failed web incubation investments.

CONSTRUCTION IN PUNE
BEGINS IN 2002

In November 2002 ground was broken on Syntel's new campus in Pune as the firm worked to shift most operations to India. The project, whose architect had studied similar sites run by Oracle, Microsoft, Cisco, and Sun, would eventually have 12 buildings and 2.1 million square feet of workspace. Top clients included American Express, AIG, Target Corp., and Verizon Wireless. In 2003 the firm's revenues grew to $179.5 million and its net income to $40.3 million.

In 2004 Syntel added to its Chennai operations by purchasing a 27.5-acre site for future development and leasing other space in the area. About 500 additional workers were hired there by year's end, which boosted the total to 1,300. The company employed more than 4,500 people worldwide. The firm's 130-plus clients were largely drawn from the financial services, healthcare, insurance, and retail sectors, and Syntel was also beginning to expand its offerings of business process services.

In early 2005 the company added a new program called SynTest, which could rapidly test software for defects, security, performance, and other critical issues. The firm was also working with a major bank on a joint venture called Syntel Solutions, of which it would own 49 percent. The new company would employ as many as 2,000 to provide investment reconciliation and management services to the bank.

EMPLOYEE COUNT TOPS 8,000 IN
2006

In 2006 the first phase of the new 40-acre Pune campus opened, which would employ 950, while Syntel also bought an additional 37 acres nearby and began looking at other Indian cities for future expansion. In December the firm appointed its chief operating officer, Keshav Murugesh, to the position of president, while Bharat Desai remained CEO and chairman. For 2006 sales jumped nearly 20 percent to $270.2 million, with net income growing to $50.9 million. More than 20 new clients were added, while another nine software support partnerships were formed, bringing the total to 80. The number of employees jumped 37 percent to 8,364 during the year.

At the start of 2007 Desai sold 3.55 million shares of Syntel stock for $98.3 million, which would leave him with about 45 percent of the total shares. Neerja Sethi owned another 25 percent, giving the couple a 70 percent stake.

By this time, Syntel's revenues were derived primarily from applications outsourcing work, with e-business, business process outsourcing, and staffing services making up the rest. Major business sectors served included financial services, which accounted for 45 percent of its revenues, as well as insurance healthcare, automotive, and retail making up the remainder.

In 2007 construction on the new Chennai campus was begun as the Pune campus expansion continued, with both projects expected to be completed in 2008. Each would include a large training center for new employees, who were increasingly being recruited through partnerships with universities. The two sites were capable of eventually housing as many as 35,000 workers, and Syntel was working toward a goal of 25,000 employees and $1 billion in revenues by 2010. About 90 percent of sales came from U.S. firms, and the company was also seeking to lower this to 70 percent and increase business in places like Europe, South Africa, and India, where it had recently signed its first client.

More than a quarter-century after its founding, Syntel, Inc., had grown into a major information technology outsourcing firm. As the company's dramatic expansion plans unfolded, its proven ability to adapt with the times, its interconnected offerings, and the continued involvement of its founders and primary shareholders all boded well for future success.

Frank Uhle

PRINCIPAL SUBSIDIARIES

Syntel Ltd. (India); Syntel Europe Ltd. (United Kingdom); Syntel Deutschland GmbH (Germany); Syntel (Singapore) Pte. Ltd. (Singapore); Syntel (Australia) Pty. Ltd. (Australia); Syntel Canada, Inc. (Canada); Syntel (Hong Kong) Ltd. (Hong Kong); Syntel (Mauritius) Ltd.; SkillBay LLC; Syntel Delaware LLC; Syntel Global Private Ltd. (India); Syntel International Private Ltd. (India); State Street Syntel Services (Mauritius) Ltd.; Syntel Sourcing Private Ltd. (India); Syntel Consulting, Inc.; Syntel Sterling BestShores Solutions Private Ltd. (India); Syntel Sterling BestShores (Mauritius) Ltd.; Syntel Worldwide (Mauritius) Ltd.

PRINCIPAL COMPETITORS

Cognizant Technology Solutions Corporation; Infosys Technologies Ltd.; Tata Consultancy Services Ltd.; Wipro Technologies; Accenture Ltd.; Electronic Data Systems Corporation; IBM Global Services; Keane, Inc.

FURTHER READING

Bennett, Jeff, "Troy, Mich.-based Computer Services Firm's Shares Drop As Off-Shoring Expands," *Detroit Free Press,* July 1, 2004.

Bonasia, J., "Syntel Rides the Services Wave with Expanded Offerings," *Investor's Business Daily,* January 22, 2003.

Bridgeforth, Arthur, Jr., "Syntel Launches IPO," *Crain's Detroit Business,* June 23, 1997, p. 2.

Dietderich, Andrew, "Sending Work Overseas Has Profits Rolling In for Syntel," *Crain's Detroit Business,* November 4, 2002, p. 4.

——, "Syntel's Profits Have Institutional Investors Tuned In; Stock's Rising," *Crain's Detroit Business,* February 10, 2003, p. 4.

——, "Troy-Based Syntel's New CFO, Five Other Execs to Work out of India," *Crain's Detroit Business,* May 16, 2005.

Gebeloff, Robert, "Labor 'Importers' on Notice—Syntel Fined $117,000," *Record* (N.J.), April 14, 1995, p. C1.

Ghosh, Rabin, "Syntel's Target by 2010: $1 Bn Revenues, $5 Bn Market Cap," *DNA (Daily News & Analysis),* November 17, 2007.

Grygo, Eugene, "Syntel Trims Red Tape Around Staffing Foreign Workers," *InfoWorld,* July 24, 2000.

Guha, Romit, "Syntel to Invest $75M to Expand India Operations," *Dow Jones International News,* August 23, 2007.

Henderson, Tom, "Diversifying, Offshore Moves Deliver Clients, Profits," *Crain's Detroit Business,* July 30, 2007, p. 11.

"Investors Snap Up IPO of 'Year 2000' Computer-Services Firm Syntel," *Dow Jones Online News,* August 12, 1997.

"IT Founder Cuts Stake," *Corporate Financing Week,* January 26, 2007.

Kapoor, Neha, "Syntel to Hike Presence, Manpower," *Hindu Business Line,* January 16, 2002.

Mathai, Palakunnathu G., "India's Software Firms Have Some Weaknesses; The Irony Is Delicious," *Business Standard,* March 24, 2004.

O'Brien, Chris, "Syntel's Year 2000 Training Camp," *Raleigh (N.C.) News & Observer,* January 7, 1998, p. D1.

Rajawat, K. Yatish, "US-Based Syntel Shifts Operations to India," *Economic Times,* July 16, 2002.

"Scripting a Success Story," *Financial Press,* July 18, 2004.

"Syntel Benefits from Offshore Move," *ComputerWire News,* February 20, 2002.

"Syntel Sets Up Software Centre in Chennai," *Hindu Business Line,* July 10, 1998.

"Syntel to Spread to Tier-2 Cities," *Business Standard,* November 8, 2005, p. 8.

Zachary, G. Pascal, "U.S. Reaches Pact with Software Firm over Payment of Foreign Professionals," *Wall Street Journal,* August 16, 1995, p. A3.

TALX

TALX Corporation

———■———

11432 Lackland Avenue
St. Louis, Missouri 63146
U.S.A.
Telephone: (314) 214-7000
Fax: (314) 214-7588
Web site: http://www.talx.com

Wholly Owned Subsidiary of Equifax Inc.
Incorporated: 1973
Employees: 1,827
Sales: $207.4 million (2006)
NAIC: 541512 Computer Systems Design Services

■ ■ ■

A leading human resources (HR) and payroll services company, TALX Corporation helps corporations automate and streamline the often mundane, inefficient, manual paperwork associated with hiring and maintaining a workforce. The company offers a wide range of services, including electronic on-boarding (automating new employee data collection), employment and income verification, I-9 management, paperless payment, tax credits and incentives, time tracking management, unemployment tax management, and W-2 management. According to TALX, in 2007 its base of approximately 9,000 customers included about 75 percent of the *Fortune* 500 companies.

BASEMENT BEGINNING: 1973–89

TALX got its start in 1973, when IBM's H. Richard Grodsky and four Monsanto Company employees established Interface Technology Inc. Operations commenced from a basement office, in which the company worked for about 18 months. Interface's first-year sales were well below the half-million-dollar mark. Eventually, the company got its first big break in the form of a $200,000 Small Business Administration loan that provided much needed capital. This funding allowed Interface to pioneer some of the first technology that enabled telephones to communicate with computers, according to the *St. Louis Business Journal.*

A major development occurred when MiTek Industries Inc., a manufacturer of industrial equipment, acquired Interface in 1983. By this time, the company had introduced one of its first products: a portable, handheld data entry device called the Model 740 Port-A-Store. At a cost of $333, the Model 740 allowed users to transmit data using touch-tone signals to the company's Total Entry System (TOES), or to another data collection system equipped for voice response. In addition, users were able to use the device to review data when it was not in online mode.

Interface Technology's sales totaled $3.2 million in 1984. The company's workforce included about 50 people by 1985, at which time an expansion effort was underway to increase the size of its 20,000-square-foot offices in St. Louis.

By 1985 Interface Technology had established a strong position in the emerging automatic touch-tone/voice response data collection systems industry. From Arby's Inc. to Xerox Corporation, the company was marketing its TOES to a host of major customers in several industries, according to an article by Gary Belsky

COMPANY PERSPECTIVES

From our roots as a software company, TALX has grown into a leading provider of payroll and HR services. Our client list includes over three-fourths of the *Fortune* 500 and over 9,000 clients altogether. Throughout our history, we have built our business around fulfilling our clients' needs with tools and services based on payroll and HR data.

in the April 22, 1985, issue of the *St. Louis Business Journal.*

During the mid-1980s, clients such as United Airlines discovered that the company's system was perfect for providing automated flight information to travelers. In addition, Upjohn and Bristol-Myers found the system well suited for use by the pharmaceutical industry, because drugs are organized according to a numbered ordering system. Likewise, cable companies used the technology for serving up pay-per-view movies to viewers. Anheuser-Busch found value in Interface Technology's system for the reporting of sales data, while Sun Oil used the technology to facilitate price inquiries.

William Canfield was named as Interface Technology's president in 1987. It was around this time that the company began to experience rapid growth. Interface Technology began focusing on large corporate human resources departments, which used its system to automate the process employees used to enroll in and make changes to benefit selections. In 1989 Interface Technology hired consultants from The Fortune Group to develop a new business plan and seek venture capital for future growth.

INITIAL GROWTH: 1990–99

Things kicked into high gear in 1990. After hovering around $2.5 million during much of the 1980s, Interface Technology's annual sales mushroomed to about $6.5 million, and its employee base grew to 70 workers. One contributing factor was the falling price of computer technology, which made voice response systems a viable option for more customers. This allowed Interface Technology to offer systems that once cost anywhere from $150,000 to $200,000 for $50,000 to $75,000.

Seventeen years after the company was established, the only founding employee that remained was Grodsky.

However, Marketing Vice-President Michael E. Smith, who had started a mere three months after Interface Technology was formed, still remained. In the August 27, 1990, issue of the *St. Louis Post-Dispatch,* Smith explained that despite its growth, the company's culture retained a family feel that was reminiscent of its earlier days.

During the early 1990s the company began writing custom software that corporate HR departments could use to offer more tailored "self-serve" options for their employees. In addition, a program called EasyScript was introduced, which allowed customers to make phone system changes on IBM personal computers without the help of programmers. In the wake of this newfound prosperity, Interface Technology changed its name to TALX Corporation, claiming the new title was a better reflection of its business activity in the voice response systems arena.

In order to keep the momentum going, TALX sought $3 million in venture capital, adding to funding it had already secured from Intech Group Inc., a fund headed by President William Canfield, as well as Missouri Venture Partners and Gateway Venture Partners. At the time, TALX held about 2 percent of the $350 million interactive voice response systems market, which included competitors like Dallas, Texas–based Intervoice, Phoenix, Arizona–based Syntellect, as well as AT&T.

In 1991 TALX opened a regional office in Minneapolis to further expansion in the Midwest. The location augmented existing sites in Los Angeles and Boston. New applications continued to emerge for TALX's products. That year, a partnership was formed with time and attendance systems company Kronos Inc. to codevelop a telephone-based reporting system. By 1994, Canada's CP Rail System was using TALX technology to manage 5,000 railroad crew members who were dispersed throughout the country.

It was in 1994 that TALX unveiled an automated employment verification service called The Work Number for Everyone, which would go on to become one of its most popular offerings—and a cash cow. According to the February 26, 1996, issue of the *St. Louis Post-Dispatch,* the system was developed for McDonnell Douglas, when the personnel department at its Huntington Beach, California, plant was overwhelmed with calls from lenders needing to verify information about the site's approximately 28,000 workers.

TALX explained that the rollout of The Work Number for Everyone marked a shift to "outsourced services." The company began collecting and storing payroll data from companies in its own data center, and providing verification services, instead of building

KEY DATES

1973: IBM's H. Richard Grodsky and four Monsanto employees establish Interface Technology Inc. in a basement office.

1983: MiTek Industries Inc. acquires Interface Technology.

1990: Interface Technology changes its name to TALX Corporation.

1994: TALX unveils an automated employment verification service called The Work Number for Everyone.

1996: TALX goes public, offering two million shares on NASDAQ.

2007: Equifax acquires TALX for approximately $1.4 billion in cash and stock.

systems companies used to perform this function on their own.

In 1995 TALX began moving more toward online tools when it introduced an Internet-based software application called MailLink, which was used in conjunction with the company's TalxWare product. Growth continued the following year via the acquisition of Intech Group.

By this time, TALX's sales had increased fourfold over 1987 levels, reaching $25 million in 1996, and the company's employee base had swelled to 225 workers. Recurring revenue, as opposed to onetime sales, had become a key factor in the company's growth, representing about 65 percent of revenue. Of the nation's five leading mortgage lenders, four used The Work Number for Everyone to search approximately 5.7 million employment records from about 69 different companies. In addition to users of The Work Number, TALX had installed some 575 custom systems for 350 corporations.

While TALX had found much success, the company decided to go public in 1996 as a way to reach higher plateaus. TALX offered two million shares of its stock, worth about $20 million, on NASDAQ. From the proceeds of the initial public offering (IPO), about half ($9 million) was earmarked for debt reduction, with the remainder devoted to expansion efforts and licensing agreements.

Several important developments occurred in 1997. Early in the year, TALX sold its document services arm to Sterling Direct Inc. in a $1.5 million deal. Bolstered by two consecutive years of 36 percent growth, the company introduced new offerings like Employee

Central. In the August 22, 1997, issue of the *St. Louis Post-Dispatch,* writer Jerri Stroud explained that the new system allowed a company's employees "to browse through benefits programs, enroll in them, fill out time sheets and sign up for training programs using an Internet browser or touch-screen kiosks. The program gives employees easy access to information and frees personnel departments from many routine chores."

TALX rounded out the 1990s with phenomenal financial performance. In 1997 the company's profits soared to $793,000, up from $123,000 the year before. More than 33 percent of revenues were generated by The Work Number, which had grown to include employment records for some 24 million workers at 400 companies. Customers included the likes of Wal-Mart Stores Inc., The Boeing Company, and Microsoft Corporation.

ACQUISITION AND EXPANSION

TALX used the proceeds from its strong performance to fund a bevy of acquisitions. The company also raised cash by selling two of its business operations in early 2000. After selling its database services operation to WPZ Holdings Inc. for $1.27 million in March, TALX sold its Director Division to WorldPages.com for $1.3 million the following month.

In July 2001, TALX acquired Ti3 Inc. in an $11.8 million cash and stock deal. In March of the following year, TALX's Garcia Acquisition Sub Inc. subsidiary acquired Gates, McDonald's and Company's unemployment cost management business for $44.3 million. At the same time, James E. Frick Inc. was acquired for $79.7 million. TALX rounded out its acquisition activity during this time by acquiring Johnson & Associates LLC in July 2003.

TALX's expansion into unemployment cost management was significant in that this sector would account for roughly 60 percent of the company's revenues by late 2003. TALX benefited from its ability to cross-sell unemployment services to existing customers, and verification services to its unemployment customers.

A setback occurred when an investigation by the Securities and Exchange Commission (SEC) led to charges of accounting fraud. TALX, which admitted to no wrongdoing, settled with the SEC for $2.5 million, while CEO William Canfield agreed to pay $960,000. Craig Cohen, the company's former chief financial officer who resigned in 2004, vowed to fight the SEC, which was pursuing a civil suit against him.

Despite this setback, acquisition activity kicked into high gear. In October 2004 alone, TALX acquired three companies: UI Advantage Inc., TBT Enterprises Inc., and Net Profit Inc. In April of the following year, TALX acquired Jon-Jay Associates Inc. in a $24 million deal, bolstering its capabilities in the areas of employment verification and unemployment cost management services. During the same month, Glick & Glick Consultants LLC, a tax credit and incentive services firm, was acquired for $5 million.

For the 2005 fiscal year, TALX saw its revenues rise 27 percent, to $158 million. Employment verification services still accounted for most of the company's sales at this time, according to a Stifel Nicolaus analyst cited in the June 6, 2005, issue of *Investor's Business Daily*. TALX continued to grow in late 2005 via the $30 million purchase of Employers Unity Inc.'s unemployment tax management arm, as well as Business Incentives Inc.'s (Management Insights) tax credit and incentives operations for $24 million.

TALX continued to find prosperity in 2006, as its sales rose to $207 million, resulting in profits of $30.4 million. Over the past three years, the company's revenue had grown at a compound annual rate of more than 29 percent, with profits increasing nearly 55 percent during the same period. In April, a $75 million deal resulted in the addition of Performance Assessment Network Inc., a talent management and psychometric testing and assessment firm.

The company's acquisition activity did not go unnoticed. Midway through 2006, TALX revealed that the Federal Trade Commission was trying to determine whether or not its many acquisitions had resulted in reduced competition in the employment verification and unemployment tax consulting sectors.

By the year's end, TALX had relocated to a new headquarters facility in St. Louis. In addition, The Work Number had swelled to include 142.8 million employment records, covering nearly 30 percent of U.S. workers.

A major development occurred in early 2007, when TALX agreed to be acquired by Equifax Inc. for $1.4 billion in cash and stock. Completed in May, the deal made TALX a wholly owned subsidiary of Equifax. Chairman and CEO William Canfield, who owned 6.4 percent of TALX stock, remained at the company's helm as president, allowing the company to move forward under new ownership, but familiar leadership.

Paul R. Greenland

PRINCIPAL SUBSIDIARIES

Net Profit Inc.; TALX FasTime Services Inc.; TALX UCM Services Inc.; TALX Employer Services LLC; TBT Enterprises Inc.; UI Advantage Inc.; Johnson & Associates LLC; Jon-Jay Associates Inc.; TALX Tax Incentive Services LLC; Unemployment Services LLC; TALX Tax Credits and Incentives LLC; Management Insight Incentives LLC; Performance Assessment Network Inc.; TALX Ltd. (United Kingdom).

PRINCIPAL COMPETITORS

Automatic Data Processing Inc.; Ceridian Corporation; TeamStaff Inc.

FURTHER READING

Belsky, Gary, "Interface Keeps Its Customers on Its TOES," *St. Louis Business Journal*, April 22, 1985.

Desloge, Rick, "TALX Seeking $3 Million in Capital for Expansion," *St. Louis Business Journal*, April 16, 1990.

Showalter, Monica, "TALX CORP. St. Louis, Missouri; 'Sell or Die' Strategy Gives Way to More Stable Plan," *Investor's Business Daily*, June 6, 2005.

Stroud, Jerri, "Equifax Buys Talx for $1.4 Billion," *St. Louis Post-Dispatch*, February 15, 2007.

———, "For Talx Corp., the Payoff Is in Its Work Number Employment Verification Service. Has Steady Growth, Predictable Revenue," *St. Louis Post-Dispatch*, June 11, 2006.

———, "Talx Expects Its Growth to Continue," *St. Louis Post-Dispatch*, August 22, 1997.

———, "TALX of the Future; Company Keeps the Computer Lines Humming with High-Tech Solutions," *St. Louis Post-Dispatch*, February 26, 1996.

"TALX Corp. Plans Sale of Stock; Seeks to Raise $20 Million," *St. Louis Post-Dispatch*, September 5, 1996.

"TALX Takes Action, Changes with Times," *St. Louis Post-Dispatch*, August 27, 1990.

Thor Industries Inc.

419 West Pike Street
P.O. Box 629
Jackson Center, Ohio 45334-0629
U.S.A.
Telephone: (937) 596-6849
Fax: (937) 596-6539
Web site: http://www.thorindustries.com

Public Company
Incorporated: 1980 as Thor Industries, Inc.
Employees: 7,000
Sales: $2.86 billion (2007)
Stock Exchanges: New York
Ticker Symbol: THO
NAIC: 336214 Travel Trailer and Camper Manufacturing; 336213 Motor Home Manufacturing; 336111 Automobile Manufacturing; 336211 Motor Vehicle Body Manufacturing

∎ ∎ ∎

Thor Industries, Inc., is the largest manufacturer of recreation vehicles in the world. It is also a leading maker of small to midsize buses. Since buying Airstream in 1980, it has accumulated a score of towable trailer brands, including Dutchmen, Komfort, Tahoe, Wanderer, and Skamper. Motorized RV lines include Daymon RV, Four Winds, and Canada's General Coach. Thor sells commercial buses under the El Dorado National name, and produces smaller ones via Goshen Coach and Champion Bus. Built through a stream of acquisitions, Thor typically leaves a great deal of independence to its subsidiaries, motivating management and workers alike with a compensation program heavy on incentives. Most of its production is based in Indiana; a California travel trailer plant was launched from scratch in 1996.

WALLY BYAM INVENTS THE AIRSTREAM

Thor was founded in 1980 with the purchase of Airstream, a legendary maker of aluminum trailers that had set the standard for quality in the recreational vehicle (RV) industry for half a century. These distinctive, silver, bullet-shaped trailers were immensely popular travel vehicles in the late 1940s and throughout the 1950s, becoming famous for their unique design and durability. Airstreams would later be exhibited at both the Smithsonian Institution and the Henry Ford museum, and early models would be highly prized by collectors. More than 60 percent of all Airstreams ever built were still rolling along the nation's highways and back roads in the 21st century.

The Airstream was the creation of one man: Wally Byam. Born in Oregon on the Fourth of July in 1896, Byam was a prototypical American wanderer and inventor. As a boy, he traveled through the Northwest with his grandfather, who led a mule train in Oregon. As a teenager, he worked as a shepherd, living in a small donkey cart, outfitted with only the most basic equipment and tools. After high school, seeking adventure, Byam signed on with the merchant marine, where, in three years, he graduated from cabin boy to ship's mate.

He then worked his way through Stanford University, graduating in 1923 with a law degree.

Opting not to practice law, Byam entered the booming advertising business of the late 1920s. He first worked as a copywriter for the *Los Angeles Times* and then became owner of his own ad agency. Later, he started a number of magazines, one of which published an article on how to build a travel trailer. When readers wrote to complain that their homemade trailer projects had failed, Byam tested the directions himself and found that they were, indeed, defective. So, he decided to build a trailer according to his own plans.

His first attempts were primitive. One was a plywood platform built on top of a Ford Model T chassis. Another was a cramped plywood box that was, Byam wrote in his book *Trailer Travel Here and Abroad,* "little more than a bed you could crawl into, a shelf to hold a water bottle, a flashlight and some camping equipment." Nonetheless, the trailer attracted attention, and Byam began to receive requests to build similar models for others.

When Byam wrote an article in *Popular Mechanics* describing how to build his new, improved plywood trailer for less than $100, many readers responded with orders for the $5 plans he offered. Meanwhile, he had turned over his Los Angeles backyard to building made-to-order trailers for customers who often arrived to lend a hand in the construction process. Byam's tiny home-based business survived the stock market crash of 1929, and by 1930 he had abandoned magazine publishing to build travel trailers full time.

Continuing to modify the basic design, Byam began to introduce a more aerodynamic look to his trailers and to adopt aircraft construction methods in order to lessen wind resistance. In 1934, he christened his ovoid-shaped trailers "Airstream," because "that's the way they travel, like a stream of air." According to Bryan Burkhardt and David Hunt in *Airstream: The History of the Land Yacht,* "the single most important designer in determining the final shape of what would become the classic Airstream Clipper" was William Hawley Bowlus, whose vehicle designs and travel trailer company Byam took over in a 1935 bankruptcy auction. In 1936, the Airstream Trailer Company introduced the famous Clipper model, named after the Pan Am Clipper, the first transatlantic plane to carry people in numbers. With the capacity to sleep four, the bullet-shaped Clipper had a shiny, riveted aluminum body, carried its own water supply, featured an enclosed galley, and was fitted with electric lights. Even with a $1,200 price tag—very expensive during the Depression—the meticulously constructed Airstream was a winner. Of more than 300 travel trailer companies in operation in 1936, Byam's company was the only one to survive.

The company closed its doors during World War II since aluminum was critical to the war, and tires and gasoline were strictly rationed. Byam spent the war working in the engineering departments of aircraft companies, and he put that experience to good use at war's end. By 1948, he had built a new manufacturing facility in Van Nuys, California, to meet the surging demand for Airstreams by returning servicemen and their young families. In 1952, the company leased a facility in Jackson Center, Ohio, to build Airstreams for the Midwest and Eastern markets, and soon thereafter, the California factory was moved to larger quarters in Santa Fe Springs.

Over the next decade, until his death in 1962, Byam continued to refine the Airstream design, and his company prospered. Putting into practice his mission "to refine and perfect our product by continuous travel-testing of the highways and byways of the world," he led a group of Airstream drivers through remote areas of Central America in 1951. This was the first of many such caravans that he and other Airstream enthusiasts made to Africa, Europe, the Soviet Union, China, Australia, New Zealand, and more. Intrepid travelers, organized as the Wally Byam Caravan Club International, would continue to explore the world in their Airstreams through the 1990s.

CONGLOMERATE OWNERSHIP: 1967–80

Airstream's reputation for quality solidified the company's existence, and the company continued to thrive following the death of its founder in 1962. Its design excellence placed it at the forefront anywhere trailers were required, and the vehicle proved easily

KEY DATES

1931: Wally Byam begins to manufacture travel trailers.

1934: The Airstream name is adopted.

1936: Byam's Airstream Co. introduces the "Clipper."

1967: Beatrice Foods acquires Airstream.

1980: Thor Industries, Inc., is founded with acquisition of Airstream.

1988: Thor enters bus industry with purchase of several companies.

2000: Thor named to the *Forbes* Platinum 400 list.

2002: Total revenues exceed $1 billion following purchase of fast-growing Keystone RV Company.

2003: Class A specialist Damon Motor Corporation is acquired for $46 million.

2004: Revenues exceed $2 billion; CrossRoads RV is acquired.

2005: Midsize bus manufacturer Goshen Coach acquired.

adaptable to government and military needs. Specially equipped Airstream trailers, for example, were set up around the vast White Sands missile range to provide a temporary office for President John F. Kennedy when he visited the site. When astronauts Neil Armstrong, Mike Collins, and Ed Aldrin returned from the first lunar landing in 1969, they were quarantined in a specially designed Airstream Mobile Quarantine Facility aboard the U.S.S. *Hornet*. An Airstream carried the crew of the space shuttle *Discovery* to their launch vehicle for their historic nine-day mission; in fact, every shuttle astronaut since has ridden in an Airstream.

In 1967, Airstream was acquired by Beatrice Foods, as part of that company's aggressive acquisition strategy into a bevy of nonfood interests. Beatrice made Airstream a division, allowing it, however, to operate autonomously. Airstream continued to produce high-quality vehicles, and in 1979, introduced its first motor home. Featuring riveted aluminum construction, like its trailer counterpart, and pioneering a new level of aerodynamic efficiency, the motor home soon became a popular addition to the Airstream line.

However, the gasoline crisis of the 1970s and the resulting economic downturn hit Airstream hard. The company reportedly lost $12 million on sales of $22 million in 1979, and similar losses continued in 1980.

Moreover, parent Beatrice was struggling to manage its vast holdings and remain profitable. A new CEO in 1980, James Dutt, began selling noncore companies, and those that could not provide Beatrice with at least a 20 percent return on net assets. Airstream was among those to go.

1980: THOR TAKES OVER

When Wade F. B. Thompson and Peter B. Orthwein purchased Airstream in 1980, they had been involved in the recreational vehicle business for only three years. In 1977, the two entrepreneurs had combined their marketing and financial expertise to purchase HI-LO Trailer, a small player in the industry. Under their leadership, HI-LO prospered, and the two looked around for a bigger opportunity. Airstream was an obvious target.

Combining the first two letters of their last names, Thompson and Orthwein formed Thor Industries, Inc., in order to acquire Airstream. The acquisition of the legendary recreational vehicle and motor home manufacturer and the formation of the new company occurred simultaneously on August 29, 1980. The two new owners acted immediately to reverse the downward trend of Airstream's fortunes. They moved to improve quality, reduce costs, strengthen dealer relationships, and enhance their famous product. Within a year, sales had increased to $26 million, and they had achieved net income before taxes of $1 million, a $13 million turnaround.

With Airstream again a profitable enterprise, Thompson and Orthwein searched for another likely acquisition. In 1982, they purchased the recreational vehicle operations of Commodore Corporation. Known in Canada as General Coach, this new addition to the Thor line manufactured travel trailers and motor homes in British Columbia and Ontario. Under Thor, General Coach would build Citation and Corsair travel trailers, fifth wheels, motor homes, and truck campers, and maintain one of the highest customer satisfaction indexes and lowest warranty costs of any North American recreational vehicle manufacturer.

In 1984, Thor went public, and in 1986 it gained listing on the New York Stock Exchange. That year, *Forbes* magazine ranked Thor sixth out of 200 best small companies in America. In 1987, *Money* magazine named Airstream travel trailers one of 99 "best-made products" in the United States.

GROWTH AND EXPANSION

On September 8, 1988, Thor entered the small- and midsize bus industry with the acquisition of El Dorado, a company based in Salina, Kansas. Under Thor, El Dorado would more than quadruple its sales, all from internal growth, to become the largest manufacturer of small buses in the United States. The Thor acquisition of National Coach, a bankrupt builder of midsize buses, followed in 1991. Under Thor, National would become its parent's most profitable bus operation. Finally, in 1998, Thor added Champion to its bus-manufacturing group.

Meanwhile, Thompson and Orthwein continued to make strategic acquisitions on the recreational vehicle side. Dutchmen, purchased in 1991, became Thor's largest towable company and a major profit center. Motor home manufacturer Four Winds International, acquired in 1992, became Thor's largest company by the start of the 21st century. Four Winds was a major supplier to most of the large recreational vehicle rental operations throughout the United States and Canada. CruiseAmerica, the largest of these operators, agreed to make Four Winds its primary supplier after Thor provided financing so that CruiseAmerica's former owners could repurchase their company. As a result of that transaction, Thor expected sales of some $30 million to CruiseAmerica in 2001.

In 1995, Thor introduced the lightweight Aerolite, a laminated, aerodynamic European-style travel trailer. Sold at an affordable price, the Aerolite proved ideal for towing behind smaller cars as well as minivans and sport-utility vehicles. Sales of this model in 2000 hit all-time records. Thor California started up in 1995 with the introduction of two new lines of travel trailers and fifth wheel vehicles, called Tahoe and Wanderer. In less than five years, Tahoe or Wanderer had become the best-selling vehicle of its kind in Colorado, Arizona, Nevada, New Mexico, and Alberta, Canada.

If Thor executives had succeeded, another major addition would have taken place in 2000. That year, the company made two strong attempts to purchase Coachmen Industries Inc., a major motor home and modular home manufacturer. Had the deal gone through, it would have made Thor the second largest motor home builder in the United States. In April 2000, however, Coachmen's board rejected Thor's April 17 bid of $289.6 million in a cash and stock transaction. According to Thor's 2000 annual report, "Although this offer was a substantial premium above Coachmen's price and we made it clear we wished to complete a friendly transaction, our proposal was rejected by Coachmen's board of directors and withdrawn by us."

Acquisitions aside, Thor was also cultivating a sense of civic responsibility as part of its corporate culture. Specifically, Thor took the lead in raising the awareness level of prostate cancer and in encouraging its early detection. Its "Drive against Prostate Cancer," inspired by the company's chairman, president, and CEO, Wade Thompson, a cancer survivor, offered free screening to more than 8,000 men and raised significant funds for cancer research. The New York Stock Exchange recognized Thor's public service initiative by offering company executives the opportunity to ring the stock market's closing bell on June 16, 2000.

CONSOLIDATION AFTER 2001

As it entered 2001, Thor believed that the $8 billion recreational vehicle industry, which included about 75 manufacturers, would continue to consolidate. Thompson and Orthwein, who retained control of the company, planned to continue to seek acquisition opportunities in recreational vehicles, buses, and related industries.

Some industry observers agreed with Thor executives that, as baby boomers moved into their 50s and 60s (the target recreational vehicle demographic), sales would enjoy significant growth. They pointed out that, between 2000 and 2005, four million people, or 11,000 potential new buyers each day, would turn 50. Other analysts, however, observed an industry-wide decrease in demand for recreational vehicles in 2000, due to higher interest rates, lower consumer confidence levels, and rising gasoline prices, as a cause for concern, at least in the short run.

Meanwhile, the company's bus business was on track to continued success. In the growing $700 million midsize bus industry, Thor had an estimated 35 percent market share and was larger than its next three competitors combined. Major bus customers included rental car companies, who used the buses to ferry customers around airports; New Jersey Transit; the Los Angeles Department of Transportation; Cal Trans; and Marriott Hotels. Believing that fuel cells were the power of the future, Thor announced in 2000 that the company would build the world's first commercially viable fuel-cell-powered, zero-emissions transit buses, in an exclusive alliance with International Fuel Cells (IFC), Inc., a United Technologies company, and ISE Research. (IFC's fuel cells had powered every NASA space shuttle mission.) The first fuel-cell-powered bus was scheduled to be built in California in 2001. Thor had exclusive rights for the use of IFC's fuel cells in the complete drive system, called ThunderPower, for all North American midsized buses.

Thor typically left the management of acquired companies in place after acquisitions. In 2001, however, it merged Aero Coach Inc. with its Dutchmen Manufacturing Inc. subsidiary. Thor made its largest acquisition to date in November of the year: its total revenues jumped 50 percent with the addition of Keystone, making Thor a $1 billion enterprise for the first time.

Keystone had been formed in 1995 by former Coachmen Industries Inc. executives. It soon grew to prominence in the fifth wheel/travel trailer segment of the RV market. Revenues were nearly $250 million in 2000 and growth showed no signs of abating. Keystone had many brands (Outback, Springdale, Montana, Sprinter, Mountaineer, Bobcat, Cougar, Challenger, Everest, and Laredo) and 14 factories. Construction started on two more plants the year after the acquisition. Keystone's acceleration continued after the takeover: it became a $1 billion company in its own right by 2004, CEO Wade Thompson told the *Wall Street Transcript.*

The terrorist attacks of September 11, 2001, on the United States affected the industry in a couple of ways, Thompson explained to *RV Business.* Since more Americans felt reluctant to travel overseas, many turned to RVs for their vacations. Slack in the tourism industry led to the first drop in Thor's sales of transit buses in ten years.

Thor extended its involvement in the Class A part of the RV industry by buying Damon Motor Corp. for $46 million in September 2003. Class A motor homes were the largest type, making up a small but relatively lucrative segment of the industry. However, since they were the most expensive RVs, their sales tended to react first to bad economic news. Damon was the seventh largest Class A manufacturer and was growing at a double-digit clip, grabbing a 5 percent market share before it was bought out by Thor.

Before the Damon acquisition, Thor had about a 3 percent share of the Class A market, according to *RV Business.* Since these vehicles accounted for a small share of its business, Thor had relatively little exposure to the category's big drop in sales that accompanied the rise in gas prices to historic highs after the war in Iraq. In 2004 CEO Wade Thompson told the *Wall Street Transcript* that he was more concerned about the possibility of a recession or a hike in interest rates. He noted that unlike many other industries, RVs had not yet seen a threat from offshore imports.

Thor's revenues exceeded $2 billion in the fiscal year ended July 31, 2004. RVs accounted for 90 percent of the total; three-quarters of the RV sales came from towables. The company continued to act as an industry consolidator. Thor bought DS Corporation (doing business as CrossRoads RV), an Indiana manufacturer of travel trailers and fifth wheels, in 2004. Thor expanded its involvement outside of its core RV business through the 2005 acquisition of Goshen Coach, a leading

manufacturer of small to midsize buses. Thor paid about $10 million for the company.

Those bullish on the company's future prospects continued to cite the aging of the baby boomers, as retirees made up the bulk of RV purchasers. The age 35- to 55-year-old demographic was also growing and Thor was trying to develop products to appeal to younger generations, such as trailers light enough to be towed by passenger cars and versatile enough to be used for storage or hauling gear when they were not out camping.

Margery M. Heffron
Updated, Frederick C. Ingram

PRINCIPAL SUBSIDIARIES

Airstream, Inc.; Citair, Inc.; Citair, Inc.; DS Corporation dba CrossRoads RV; Damon Corporation; Dutchmen Manufacturing, Inc.; Four Winds International, Inc.; Thor California, Inc.; Komfort Corp.; Keystone RV Company; ElDorado National California, Inc.; ElDorado National Kansas, Inc.; Champion Bus, Inc.; General Coach America, Inc.; Goshen Coach, Inc.; Thor Tech, Inc.; T.H.O.R. Insurance Company Ltd. (Bermuda).

PRINCIPAL DIVISIONS

Airstream; Four Winds; Dutchmen; CrossRoads; Citair; Keystone; Komfort; Thor California; Damon Motor Coach; Breckenridge; General Coach America; El Dorado National; Champion Bus; Goshen Coach.

PRINCIPAL OPERATING UNITS

Recreation Vehicles; Buses.

PRINCIPAL COMPETITORS

Coachmen Industries, Inc.; Fleetwood Enterprises, Inc.; Winnebago Industries Inc.; Monaco Coach Corporation.

FURTHER READING

Ashley, Bob, "Thor California Taps Hot Western Market," *RV Business,* October 2004, pp. 47–48.

Burkhardt, Bryan, and David Hunt, *Airstream: The History of the Land Yacht,* San Francisco: Chronicle Books, 2000.

Byam, Wally, *Trailer Travel Here and Abroad: The New Way to Adventurous Living,* New York: McKay, 1960.

"Company Interview: Wade F.B. Thompson; Thor Industries, Inc.," *Wall Street Transcript,* November 15, 2004.

Fahey, Jonathan, "Lord of the Rigs," *Forbes Global,* March 29, 2004, p. 40.

Goldenberg, Sherman, "Thompson: Taking the Consolidation Track," *RV Business,* November 2003, pp. 39–46.

Innis, Jack, "A Legend in Its Own Time," *Trailer Life,* February 1998, pp. 52–60.

Kachadourian, Gail, "Coachmen Rejects Thor's Takeover Bid," *Automotive News,* May 8, 2000, p. 24.

Kelleher, James B., "RV Shares Face an Uphill Climb," *National Post's Financial Post & FP Investing* (Canada), November 29, 2006, p. FP12.

Kurowski, Jeff, "Consolidation: Thor Buys Damon in $46 Million Deal," *RV Business,* October 2003, pp. 7, 38.

———, "Dutchmen Eyes Opportunities, Returns to Entrepreneurial Roots," *RV Business,* October 2002, pp. 22, 23, 44.

———, "Thor Aims to Be Industry 'Consolidator'; Industry 'Ripe' for Mergers," *RV Business,* July 2002, pp. 7, 47.

———, "Thor Assumes No. 1 Towable Slot with Keystone Buy," *RV Business,* December 2001, pp. 9, 115.

———, "Thor Combines Towable Firms Aero and Dutchmen," *RV Business,* December 2001, pp. 38, 113.

Lazo, Shirley A., "Hit the Road—RVs Are So Hot, They're Cool; And Market Leader Thor Industries, Which Just Doubled Its Quarterly Payout, Has the Numbers to Prove It," *Barron's,* June 9, 2003, p. 36.

Robson, Toby, "King of the Road: Tenacity Buys a Fortune," *Dominion Post* (Wellington, New Zealand), April 17, 2004, Bus. Sec., p. 1.

Santiago, Chiori, "House Trailers Have Come a Long Way, Baby," *Smithsonian,* June 1998, pp. 76–85.

Setton, Dolly, "Demographic Play," *Forbes,* August 9, 1999, p. 136.

Thomas, Martha, "Updating the Airstream; Nissan and Thor Industries Partner to Produce the BaseCamp," *Architectural Digest,* June 2006, p. 252.

White, Roger B., *Home on the Road: The Motor Home in America,* Washington, D.C.: Smithsonian Institution Press, 2000.

THQ, Inc.

29903 Agoura Road
Agoura Hills, California 91301
U.S.A.
Telephone: (818) 871-5000
Fax: (818) 871-7400
Web site: http://www.thq.com

Public Company
Incorporated: 1989 as Trinity Acquisition Corporation
Employees: 2,000
Sales: $1.02 billion (2007)
Stock Exchanges: NASDAQ
Ticker Symbol: THQI
NAIC: 511210 Software Publishers

■ ■ ■

THQ, Inc., is one of the largest developers and publishers of gaming software for use on dedicated play stations, portable game players, personal computers, and wireless devices. The company produces a combination of licensed and self-developed titles, and is a major publisher of games for children. It has had long-term license agreements with major media companies Disney/Pixar, MGA, Nickelodeon, and World Wrestling Entertainment. Its licensed games include *WWE Smackdown vs. Raw*, *SpongeBob SquarePants*, *Bratz*, *Ratatouille*, *American Girl*, and *Scooby-Doo*. Its internally developed franchises include *Saints Row*, *Red Faction*, *Juiced*, and *Stuntman*. THQ games are sold in North America, Europe, and the Asia Pacific region.

BEGINNINGS: 1990–94

THQ was founded by Jack Friedman, a toy-industry veteran. Friedman had entered the business with LJN Toys in the mid-1960s and had risen to the position of company president 20 years later. After entertainment conglomerate MCA, Inc., purchased LJN, Friedman grew disenchanted with working for a giant corporation and left to start his own company. In April 1990 he formed THQ, Inc., investing $1 million of his own money. The name was short for Toy Headquarters, and the company, based in Calabasas, California, planned to produce a full line of toys including dolls, board games, and electronic games.

Soon after its formation, the company purchased Broderbund Software's video-games division, and the first products came to market in October. Some early offerings were Peter Pan and the Pirates board games and action figures and Videomation and Wayne Gretzky Hockey games. THQ staffers came up with ideas for the products, but contracted out the actual design and manufacturing to other firms.

Needing cash to develop new product licenses, in the summer of 1991 Friedman merged THQ with Trinity Acquisition Corporation. The publicly traded Trinity had been formed some time earlier to raise capital for as yet unrealized ventures. The new entity retained the name of THQ, Inc., and continued to trade on the NASDAQ. By the end of its first full year THQ, with 16 employees, had achieved annual sales of $33 million. The company could boast of two genuine hits: a video game based on the popular movie *Home Alone* and another drawn from the successful *Where's Waldo* book

COMPANY PERSPECTIVES

THQ and its subsidiaries worldwide are committed to growing our position as a leading global developer and publisher of interactive entertainment software, in a manner that promotes the long-term success of THQ, its employees, and its stakeholders. In pursuit of our goal, we strive to achieve the highest business and personal standards of ethics and honesty as well as compliance with all applicable government laws, rules and regulations.

series. THQ video games were licensed to run on Nintendo game stations, and the company had extended its contract with Nintendo to allow it to market the games beyond North America to Europe, Australia, and parts of Asia. Nintendo manufactured the games, which were designed by THQ and programmed by an outside software company. Each of these parties took a cut of the profits, as did the licensor of the game's subject matter.

In the spring of 1992, THQ began working with Nintendo rival Sega to produce games for that company's home play system. THQ was also developing games for Nintendo's portable Game Boy units. Again needing more working capital, the company issued a secondary stock offering, selling 1.5 million shares at $4 each. THQ was actively seeking more licenses from popular entertainment or sports commodities on which to base products. Although its sales were rapidly climbing, its net profits were flat, due in part to problems with the dollar in overseas markets and higher product development and promotion costs. In 1993 Jack Friedman agreed to take an 11 percent pay cut and give up his options on 2.2 million shares of stock. Nevertheless, the company's founder was still earning a handsome $850,000 per year and held options on one million shares. During that same year, THQ purchased a Chicago-based home and arcade software company, Black Pearl Software.

Struggling to come up with new hits in an increasingly competitive and costly marketplace, the company saw its net profits begin to shrink, then turn into losses, which mounted quickly. Sales for 1993 reached $37.5 million, but losses totaled $16.2 million. The next year was even bleaker, with revenues of only $13.3 million and losses of $17.5 million. The company attempted to stop the hemorrhaging of money by cutting costs and

even selling 3.5 million shares of stock for 50 cents apiece, but this had little impact.

PRODUCING VIDEO-GAME CONTENT EXCLUSIVELY: 1995–98

In 1995, founder Jack Friedman departed, turning over the reins to the chief financial officer, Brian J. Farrell. In the months preceding Friedman's departure, THQ had focused on developing games for the new Nintendo Super NES platform, but this platform wound up being less popular than Sega's Genesis system. Sitting on a huge backlog of unsold Super NES games, Farrell immediately instituted strict inventory control procedures. He also eliminated half of THQ's staff of 60, and moved the company's product lineup exclusively to video games.

Using a new marketing tactic, Farrell decided to focus on supplying the needs of consumers who were still using older game platforms and avoid gambling on which new system would be most popular. Meeting with creditors, many of whom also happened to be product licensors such as Walt Disney Interactive, LucasArts, MTV, and Nickelodeon, Farrell was able to convince them to cut better deals on licenses to produce software for the older 16-bit systems. THQ developed new games that would cost only $9.99 to $14.99, compared with $40 to $60 for games for the most recent platforms. The company also increased its offerings, debuting 24 new games in 1995, more than twice the number it had introduced in 1994. The results were swift and gratifying. Sales in 1995 rebounded to more than $33 million, with a net profit of $600,000. The company was also able to establish a distribution office in the United Kingdom during the year.

Results for 1996 were even better, with sales reaching $50.2 million and profits hitting $1.9 million. The company released more than 30 titles and also invested in a software maker, Inland Productions, Inc., and acquired a design company, Heliotrope Studios, Inc. Deciding that the time was right to reenter the big leagues, THQ began to design games for the newly released 64-bit systems. It struck a major new licensing agreement with World Championship Wrestling (WCW) to produce games based on its players, who included Hulk Hogan and Macho Man Randy Savage. The company was making games for Nintendo's portable Game Boy, Sony's PlayStation, and for personal computers, in addition to Nintendo's other platforms. The Christmas shopping season of 1997 saw copies of *WCW versus NWO: World Tour* flying off the shelves, with nearly 40 percent of the company's $90 million in sales for the year coming from the wrestling game.

KEY DATES

1990: Jack Friedman founds THQ and acquires Broderbund Software's video-game division.

1991: THQ goes public after a merger with Trinity Acquisition Corporation.

1993: The company acquires Black Pearl Software.

1994: Sales stall, and losses reach $17.5 million for the year.

1995: Friedman exits, and Brian Farrell is named CEO; company's focus shifts to low-priced games for older 16-bit systems.

1996: The company invests in Inland Productions, Inc., and acquires Heliotrope Studios, Inc.

1999: THQ signs a deal with the World Wrestling Federation and moves to new headquarters.

2000: THQ is named a key publisher of games for forthcoming Microsoft Xbox system.

2007: Company acquires Paradigm Entertainment and Mass Media, Inc.

The bubble appeared to burst the following spring, when THQ lost the WCW license to its archrival, Electronic Arts, in a bidding war. Within two days, THQ's stock value dropped by 40 percent. Quickly bouncing back, the ever-resilient Farrell obtained a license from Nickelodeon to make games based on the hit cartoon *Rugrats* and within a year had replaced the wrestling deal with a license from WCW's chief competitor, the World Wrestling Federation (WWF).

ACQUISITIONS AND MORE SPORTS-BASED GAMES: 1998–2000

During 1998 the company added two new subsidiaries. It purchased 3D graphics developer GameFX, Inc., for 246,000 shares of stock and $790,000 in cash. The Massachusetts-based firm was soon joined by German software distributor Rushware Microhandelsgesellschaft mbH, acquired for $6 million. Despite the loss of the WCW contract, THQ was allowed to produce its licensed games into 1999, and the company had successful offerings in *WCW/NWO Revenge*, *WCW Nitro*, and *WCW/NWO Thunder*. It conducted major advertising campaigns for the launch of these games, as well as for the company's Rugrats: *Search for Reptar*, targeted at children 7 to 12 years old. THQ was realizing 55 percent of its revenues from 64-bit Nintendo games, 30 percent from Sony PlayStation, and 8 percent from Nintendo Game Boy. Only 2 percent came from sales of

PC-based games. The majority of revenue, 85 percent, was earned in the United States.

THQ was also developing games that targeted fans of real sports, offering *Brunswick Bowling*, *Championship Motocross*, and several *Bass Masters Classic* fishing simulation games in 1999. It also signed licensing deals with motocross star Ricky Carmichael, MTV Sports, and the makers of TV's *Power Rangers* series. That same year, THQ made another acquisition in the spring when it purchased Pacific Coast Power & Light Co., a developer of game consoles. That company later changed its name to Locomotive Games, becoming part of THQ's studio system.

At the end of the year the company also acquired Genetic Anomalies, Inc., bringing THQ a developer of online gaming products. This area was heating up, as the possibilities of making games interactive via the Internet seemed to be the next major step for the industry. As the year ended THQ had its best Christmas sales season ever. The company had also moved to a new, larger headquarters site during the year.

The spring of 2000 saw the release of THQ's first online wrestling game, *WWF with Authority*, developed by Genetic Anomalies. The game could be played online in real time against another player anywhere in the world. Other features included chat capabilities and a world ranking system.

The volatile nature of the gaming marketplace was affecting THQ again, however, and the company announced in May that it would lose significantly more money than it had expected during the year. A transition in game console technology was pegged as the cause.

THQ still had new ventures in the works, including an investment in Japanese game developer Yuke's Co. Ltd., a joint venture to market games with the Communication Devices division of Siemens AG of Germany, and the opening of an Australian office. In September, THQ announced it would begin developing games for the newly announced Microsoft Xbox game system, due out in the fall of 2001. New releases included several more WWF titles and games based on television quiz show *Who Wants to Be a Millionaire*, the *Star Wars* and *Evil Dead* movie series, and cartoon dog Scooby-Doo.

EXPANDING INTERNAL PRODUCT DEVELOPMENT: 2001–07

THQ raised $140 million in a secondary stock offering in 2001. It also completed its largest acquisition to date, purchasing Volition, Inc., of Illinois for approximately $20 million. Volition was an established designer of original game concepts such as Descent and Freespace, and THQ had earlier teamed with the company to create Summoner and Red Faction. That year, the company had revenues of $379 million.

THQ continued its buying spree, increasing its capabilities to develop original games while also gaining access to new market segments. In 2002, it purchased Rainbow Studios for $48.5 million and ValuSoft for an undisclosed amount. ValuSoft provided access to the value-priced segment of the gaming software market. Acquisitions in 2004 included Blue Tongue Entertainment Pty. Ltd. of Melbourne, Australia, and Canadian-based Relic Entertainment. In 2006, Vigil Games of Texas and Juice Games, in the United Kingdom, were added. In 2007, Paradigm Entertainment and Mass Media joined the system.

THQ was not depending solely on acquisitions to expand. Beginning with the founding of Heavy Iron Studios in 1999, THQ also established its own development studios. These included Helixe Games in 2000; Cranky Pants Games in 2002; THQ Studio Australia in 2003; Concrete Games in 2004; Incinerator Studios and Kaos Studios in 2005; and Vigil Games in 2006. By 2007, there were 16 studios within THQ's internal system, developing original content and contributing to licensed products.

MOBILE GAMING AND NEW LICENSES: 2001–06

In 2001, THQ set up its mobile gaming division, THQ Wireless, from what was originally its joint venture with Seimens. In 2003, the wireless subsidiary acquired controlling interest in the European-based Minick, adding to the 25 percent it already owned. This vendor of mobile applications brought to THQ Wireless the ability to add more to its games, including mobile voting and information and alert services. However, at the end of 2006, THQ sold its interest in Minick to Swisscom and reexamined its wireless strategies.

Meanwhile, THQ was having few problems with its traditional game efforts. It continued its licensing agreements with Nickelodeon and World Wrestling Entertainment and began creating games under license with Games Workshop and Ultimate Fighting Championship. THQ also reached a licensing agreement with Disney and Pixar Animation Studios to produce three games based on Pixar movies: *Finding Nemo* in 2003, *The Incredibles* in 2004, and *Cars* in 2005. By 2003, THQ was the world's largest publisher of children's video games. By 2005, THQ was also moving into war and fighting games and preparing for the next generation of game consoles.

2007 AND BEYOND

THQ's game based on the Pixar movie *Cars,* was the top-selling family game for 2006 on a number of platforms. The company hoped its games based on the movie *Ratatouille,* released in 2007, would repeat that success. Under its latest agreement with Pixar, THQ had exclusive rights to publish up to two game concepts based on each of the next four Pixar animated films, beginning with *Ratatouille.* Also in 2007, THQ signed an agreement with Ultimate Fighting Championship and brought out "El Tigre: The Adventures of Manny Rivera" for Nickelodeon. Along with its licensed franchises, THQ produced internally created products, including *Saints Row, Stuntman, Red Faction, Juiced,* and *Company of Heroes.*

Although sales of video games overall had fallen in the United States, analysts expected worldwide sales to expand, along with sales of gaming platforms. A major challenge facing game publishers was the move by the companies that owned the content, such as Disney, to establish their own game studios rather than rely on licenses. THQ's ability to develop strong original franchises would have to play a major role in its future as it attempted to move from mass market games for families and children to games that would attract the core gamer segment of the market.

The company had more than 70 products in development. Its 16-studio system employed over 1,500 people. Its global distribution network delivered its games to more than 77 countries. It was developing games for every demographic group of the gaming audience, and gamers could play THQ's games whether they used Sony's PlayStation 2 or 3 computer entertainment system or PlayStation game console; Microsoft's Xbox video-game system; Nintendo's GameCube, Game Boy Advance, or Wii; a personal computer; or a mobile phone or other wireless device.

Frank Uhle
Updated, Ellen Wernick

PRINCIPAL SUBSIDIARIES

THQ Wireless, THQ XDG; Locomotive Games; Volition, Inc.; Juice Games; Mass Media; Blue Tongue Entertainment; THQ Asia Pacific Pty. Ltd.; THQ Deutschland GmbH; THQ France; THQ International Ltd.

PRINCIPAL COMPETITORS

Activision, Inc.; Electronic Arts, Inc.; Take-Two Interactive Software, Inc.; Ubisoft Entertainment.

FURTHER READING

Ali, Rafat, "THQ Sells Its Stake in Mobile Content Apps Firm Minick to Swisscom," *MocoNews.net*, December 4, 2006.

Armstrong, David, "Gaming the System," *Forbes*, March 12, 2007, p. 104.

Beirne, Mike, "THQ Tries Out New Stunts with an Old Franchise," *Brandweek*, August 20, 2007, p. 10.

Bond, Paul, "Play Is the Thing: Video Flame Stocks Looking Bullish," *Hollywood Reporter*, May 8, 2007, p. 75.

Dano, Mike, "Mforma, THQ Wireless Make Acquisitions," *RCR Wireless News*, May 10, 2004, p. 16.

Dunphy, Laura, "Spate of Recent Deals Boosts Video-Game Maker THQ," *Los Angeles Business Journal*, September 11, 2000, p. 21.

"Gamer THQ Scores Big with Nic, Dis Pacts," *Hollywood Reporter*, February 19, 2003, p. 10.

Gaudiosi, John, "'El Tigre' Leads Next Wave of Nick Games from THQ," *Hollywood Reporter*, May 8, 2007, p. 8.

Gaudiosi, John, and Jesse Heistand, "Gaming Players Rise from Consolidation," *Hollywood Reporter*, May 23, 2002, p. 12.

"Heavy Losses Continue for Game Maker THQ Inc.," *Los Angeles Times*, April 4, 1995, p. 2.

Huffstutter, P. J., "THQ Shares Take a Hit from Video Games Console Wars," *Los Angeles Times*, May 26, 2000, p. C3.

"Loss of License to Wrestling Hurts THQ," *Consumer Multimedia Report*, March 23, 1998.

MacCallum, Martha, "Power Lunch—THQ Chairman & CEO Interview," *CNBC/Dow Jones Business Video*, August 25, 1999.

O'Steen, Kathleen, "CEO's Sense of Integrity, Ethics Cited Reputation: People Have Faith in THQ Leader Because of His Honest and Straightforward Manner, Supporters Say," *Los Angeles Times*, October 26, 1999, p. B6.

Pearse, Justin, "Playing for Keeps: Mobile Gaming Will Go Mass Market (Probably), but Only if the Mainstream Games Companies Get Behind It," *New Media Age*, September 25, 2003, p. 18.

Peltz, James F., "THQ Inc. to Develop Software for Sega Videos," *Los Angeles Times*, May 26, 1992, p. 4.

———, "THQ's Video-Game Success Comes with Betting on Winners," *Los Angeles Times*, December 24, 1991, p. 9A.

Szalai, Georg, "H'wood Fare Powers THQ Vid Games," *Hollywood Reporter*, March 15, 2004, p. 10.

"THQ and the Art of Bass Fishing: CEO Farrell Takes 'Platform-Agnostic' Stance in Boom Market," *Hollywood Reporter*, December 7, 2001, p. 16.

"THQ Bags Developer, Inks MTV, Bodacious Rodeo and Motocross Deals," *mmWire*, May 18, 1999.

"THQ Chief Executive to Take 11% Pay Cut," *Los Angeles Times*, March 16, 1993, p. 2.

"THQ Hopes for Strike with 'Brunswick Circuit Pro Bowling,'" *Multimedia Publisher*, November 1, 1998.

"THQ Playing with Future at Incinerator," *Hollywood Reporter*, July 19, 2006, p. 17.

"THQ Shares Slide After Loss of Wrestling License to Electronic Arts," *Dow Jones Online News*, March 11, 1998.

"The Ultimate Game Gear," *Economist*, September 8, 2007, p. 12.

Ward, David, "'Ratatouille' Game Has Right Ingredients, Too," *Hollywood Reporter*, July 2, 2007, p. 15.

———, "Wanted: Game of Their Own," *Hollywood Reporter—International Edition*, August 17, 2007, p. 5.

Young, D. B., "Taking Stock of the 3rd Quarter: THQ Among Valley's Top Gainers," *Los Angeles Times*, October 12, 1999, p. B2.

TIC Holdings Inc.

———— ■ ————

2211 Elk River Road
Steamboat Springs, Colorado 80487-5076
U.S.A.
Telephone: (970) 879-2561
Fax: (970) 879-5052
Web site: http://www.tic-inc.com

Private Company
Incorporated: 1974
Employees: 9,000
Sales: $1.2 billion (2006 est.)
NAIC: 237990 Other Heavy and Civil Engineering
   Construction

■ ■ ■

TIC Holdings Inc. is one of the country's largest direct-hire, heavy industrial contractors, providing construction services in several areas, including power; mining and minerals processing; oil, gas, and chemicals; renewable energy; water and wastewater; marine; food and beverage; and pulp and paper. Its three principal subsidiaries are: TIC-The Industrial Company Wyoming Inc., in Casper, Wyoming; TIC International, Inc.; and TIC Maintenance in Steamboat Springs, Colorado.

As a highly diversified corporation, the company operates throughout North America, including also Canada and Mexico. The company functions according to nine major regional operations: Northwest, Western, Southwest, Rocky Mountain, North Central, Great Lakes, Gulf Coast, Northeast, and Southeast. TIC—The Industrial Company Wyoming, Inc., operates one

subsidiary, T.E. Ibberson Company of Hopkins, Minnesota, a provider of agricultural, food, and heavy industrial design and build construction services. TIC International operates two subsidiaries: TIC Canada, Inc., in Edmonton, Alberta, and MexTICa in Mexico City, Mexico. Both of these subsidiary units enable TIC to pursue interests in all of TIC's traditional markets. TIC Maintenance operates one subsidiary, Gulf States, Inc., located in Freeport, Texas, which focuses on the oil, gas, and chemical markets.

ORIGINS

TIC was founded in 1974 by Ron McKensie and a group of construction professionals in Steamboat Springs, Colorado. McKensie grew up in Grand Junction, Colorado, and lived in Steamboat where he worked for his father's construction company during the early 1970s. He liked the small isolated town and the surrounding natural beauty of the region. He began the firm by building condominiums, water systems, and ski lifts in Steamboat. The company then expanded into the coal and mineral markets in 1977 by forming TIC-The Industrial Company Wyoming, Inc., which focused on plant construction and repair of heavy mining equipment. As the company grew, its construction projects included processing facilities of gold, silver, copper, and other minerals. As a result of the oil crises of the 1970s, TIC also chased soaring energy profits by entering into construction of petroleum and refinery projects, as well as projects for the oil shale industry.

In 1980, TIC boosted its electrical construction capabilities through Canyon Valley Electric, a division

COMPANY PERSPECTIVES

Can Do Attitude: aggressively pursue challenges with a sense of urgency, a desire to succeed, and a commitment to hard work and having fun. We take pride in our achievements in the face of challenges and difficult projects, and use our "Can Do Attitude" to facilitate our clients' goals. We work hard and play hard knowing that a balance between the two makes for productive, engaged, superior employees, which in turn makes for satisfied clients and exceptional project results.

that provided services to the light industrial, commercial, and public sectors. The company, which had 17 original investors, remained closely held until 1982 when construction firm Raymond International acquired it. Company managers bought it back several years later, however, after growing dissatisfied with the ownership. Unlike its mostly union competitors in the early years, TIC ran a largely nonunion shop and could keep its labor costs comparatively low. In subsequent years, it took on larger projects, becoming a major presence in heavy construction first in the western United States and then nationally.

In 1986, TIC Holdings Inc. was formed as a holding company for the company's two main operating companies: TIC The Industrial Company and Western Summit Constructors, a leading builder of water and wastewater treatment facilities. In that same year, TIC entered the industrial and marine construction business in the Southeast, establishing regional operations there, including the TIC marine group. TIC followed these developments by forming its Western Region operations in 1988 to serve refining, power, and other heavy industries in California and other West Coast states. In succeeding years, the Western Region won some of the firm's largest and most profitable contracts in building co-generating, geothermal, and gas-fired turbine power plants.

EXPANSION AS A HOLDING COMPANY

During the 1990s, TIC continued to expand its business in constructing fossil-fuel related power facilities as well as simple and gas-fired plants throughout the United States. The company also began entering international markets, mostly Canada and Mexico. In 1992, TIC won contracts to build the Brady geothermal and Steamboat

geothermal power plants in Nevada, signaling the firm's entry into providing combined engineering, procurement, and construction operations, or EPC services. With the establishment of these operations, the firm's EPC services soon expanded to serve a number of industrial markets and clients with the development of highly sophisticated projects.

Further, in 1993, the company bought Denver-based Western Summit Constructors, a $200 million dollar enterprise that built water and wastewater treatment plants. The acquisition comprised one of TIC Holdings' two companies. In 1994, the company formed TIC International to pursue global markets. It completed its first project in 1996 in one of the Philippine Islands where it built a geothermal power plant. Since its beginning, the international operating unit has completed projects in Latin America, South Pacific, Southeast Asia, West Africa, Great Britain, and other international locations.

The company's considerable expansion during the mid-1990s also came from an unprecedented boom in construction of natural gas-fired power plants. In Colorado, the company assisted in converting the Fort St. Vrain nuclear power plant to natural-gas power and built a new gas-fired plant south of Colorado Springs. In 1997, TIC sought to pursue increasing demand for these power plants by forming the Gulf Coast Region. The company already had operations established in the Baton Rouge area before 1997, but it moved the regional offices to Houston to better focus on the vast refining and chemical industry along the Gulf Coast.

In 1997, *Forbes* magazine ranked TIC Holdings as one of the largest privately held companies in the United States. In 1998, TIC also formed ERS Constructors as its pipeline division, which increased its capacity to serve developers and municipalities in a multistate area. In that same year, the company completed construction of a synthetic fuel production facility located in Clearfield County, Pennsylvania. The new plant was anticipated to employ 25 people and create additional jobs in transportation, equipment, operating supplies and maintenance. Utilizing patented technology by Covol Technologies, Inc., the synthetic fuel plant would convert small particles of coal into a solid synthetic fuel, providing an efficient high-value product.

Among many of its projects, in 2000 TIC also won a contract to build the Lisbon Valley Copper Project located in San Juan County, Utah, an open pit heap-leach operation designed to yield 40 million pounds of cathode copper annually over an 8½ year period. By 2002, TIC was the nation's eighth largest builder of ing export terminals, oil extraction, animal feed processing plants, oilseed processing plants, chimneys and other specialty slipform, and biofuel processing plants. It had built grain and feed facilities for corporate giants like Purina and Cargill, as well as worked on ethanol projects for such companies as Adkins Energy, Badger State, and Midwest Grain. One of the Ibberson's most significant projects involved designing a major portion of the world's largest grain elevator in China.

Before acquiring T.E. Ibberson, TIC had entered into a major joint venture with both the firm and Williamsburg, Virginia–based Delta-T Corporation to design and build ethanol plants throughout North America. TIC's entry into the dry mill plant building business signaled a trend of larger players entering the alternative energy field as oil prices began to soar. Under the partnership, Delta-T would design the process technology and procure the equipment, while TIC would build most of the plant. The T.E. Ibberson Company would provide the detail engineering and construct the grain handling and load out systems. As a powerhouse in the American construction business, TIC brought considerable heft to the joint venture. With annual revenues exceeding $1 billion, it ranked 38th among all U.S. industrial construction companies. In connection with the ethanol industry, TIC ranked 13th in refinery and petrochemical plant construction, sixth in power plant construction, and sixth in wastewater treatment plants. The firm's ethanol projects included construction of the wet mill facility and two fuel-ethanol plants for Minnesota Corn Processors. Moreover, TIC was operating in Mexico, Canada, and all 50 U.S. states, as well internationally.

Although TIC had broad experience handling large projects, it routinely built $300 million to $400 million plants. A large number of the firm's projects were done on a small scale with comparatively few workers. When TIC's 2001 revenues topped a billion dollars, 82 percent of its contracts were for projects $2 million or less. The company remained competitive by exerting as much control over a project as possible and thereby limiting costs. Whenever possible, TIC performed 70 to 80 percent of the work itself, subcontracting the rest locally. It also paid attention to the details of scheduling, cost control, documentation, procurement, warehousing, and productivity. Moreover, TIC had organized the company by region, enabling its workers to be within four to six hours of any job site in North America. The regional organization, together with TIC's size and financial strength, enabled it to work on several major projects simultaneously in any part of North America.

power plants and sixth in construction of mining and wastewater treatment facilities. Reputed for its training program in Steamboat, it also stood as the 32nd largest contractor in the country. Despite its success, two Colorado construction firms were bigger: PLC Construction Enterprises, a Denver-based subsidiary of the Canadian construction conglomerate, and Hensel Phelps Construction of Greeley. Bolstering its North American presence, in 2002 the company also formed TIC Canada from certain assets of a Canadian company. The new venture allowed the company to be involved in construction, module construction, and pipe fabrication for Canadian oil sands, one of the world's most promising oil and gas regions at a time of increasing global demand for energy. In 2002, the company also opened a Denver office to house the operations of its Rocky Mountain region, Canyon Valley Electric, the electrical division, and ERS Constructors, the pipeline division.

THE IBBERSON ACQUISITION

With these various business ventures in play, TIC's revenues more than doubled to $1.3 billion in 2003. In that same year, TIC acquired Hopkins, Minnesota–based T.E. Ibberson Company, a leader in engineering and construction for the food, pet and livestock food, and beverage industries. The Ibberson Company had been in the engineering and construction business since 1881 when founder Thomas E. Ibberson started building grain elevators in small farming communities across the Midwest. By the time of its acquisition, Ibberson had diversified to include wide-ranging projects involv-

In 2003, TIC also acquired Gulf States Inc. of Freeport, Texas, adding capabilities in plant maintenance and general services for the oil, gas, and chemical industries throughout the Gulf Coast. By 2004, TIC had quietly become a global construction giant that was content to keep a low profile. While founding investor McKensie and his brother Gary, president of TIC—The Industrial Company, may have been publicity averse, a $2.5 million settlement with the U.S. Equal Employment Opportunity Commission in 2003 cast the firm in the spotlight. The company agreed to pay the fine to settle allegations originating out of its Louisiana operations that over eight years it had rejected 130 black job applicants on the basis of race. TIC denied the allegations, and it settled the case out of court while also initiating programs to recruit African Americans to the firm.

The company's position among the top contractors in the United States was secured through its efforts to expand geographically. During this time, TIC's Mexican subsidiary, MexTICa, signed an agreement with Metallica Resources Inc. to provide engineering, procurement, and construction management services for the development of a recovery plant regarding a heap-leach gold and silver project in Central Mexico. The company also attributed its success to its expertise in a wide variety of fields as well as what it regarded as a unique corporate culture that demanded excellence in its workforce, which, in turn, fostered long-term relationships with clients.

Bruce P. Montgomery

PRINCIPAL SUBSIDIARIES

TIC International, Inc.; Gulf States, Inc.; TIC—The Industrial Company Wyoming Inc.; MexTICa S. de R.L. de CV; TIC-Canada Inc.

PRINCIPAL OPERATING UNITS

TIC Industrial; TIC Infrastructure; TIC Diversified.

PRINCIPAL COMPETITORS

Black & Veatch Holding Company; Foster Wheeler Ltd.; Zachry Construction Corporation.

FURTHER READING

"Central States Enterprises to Build Ethanol Production Plant in Blackford County, Indiana," *PR Newswire,* May 2, 2006.

"Constellation Power Source Building Illinois Power Plant in Holland Township," *PR Newswire,* August 17, 2000.

"Covol Technologies, Inc. Today Announced the Completion of Three Synthetic Fuel Manufacturing Facilities Located in Pennsylvania and Ohio," *PR Newswire,* June 26, 1998.

"Heavy Industrial Contractor," *Power Engineering,* November 2005, p. 215.

"Metallica Resources Announces Commencement of Construction of Cerro San Pedro Project, Mexico," *Business Wire,* February 20, 2004.

Southerland, Randy, "TIC Beat Technical, Time Challenges to Win Award," *Atlanta Business Chronicle,* December 1, 2000, p. 41C.

"Summo Minerals Corporation: Lisbon Valley Copper SX-EW Project Final Bankable Feasibility Study Completed," *Business Wire,* September 6, 2000.

Touton S.A.

BP 13, 1 rue Rene Magne
Bordeaux, F-30083 Cedex
France
Telephone: (33 05 56) 69 33 69
Fax: (33 05 56) 69 33 66
Web site: http://www.touton.fr

Private Company
Incorporated: 1848
Employees: 400
Sales: EUR 225 million ($297 million) (2006)
NAIC: 311320 Chocolate and Confectionery Manufacturing from Cacao Beans

■ ■ ■

Touton S.A. is a leading trading house focused on the African continent. The Bordeaux, France–based company, in existence since 1848, has long been one of the world's leading conditioners and traders of high-quality cocoa beans. The company's cocoa imports come primarily from the Ivory Coast, the world's largest single cocoa bean producer, responsible for some 37 percent of the global supply.

The company operates its own cocoa conditioning and production facilities in the Ivory Coast, with facilities in both Abidjan and San Pedro capable of processing more than 80,000 metric tons of cocoa each year. The company also operates a coffee grading plant, adding another 40,000 metric tons of capacity, and three plantations producing cacao, coffee, and palm oil on nearly 1,200 hectares. Touton also sources green coffee from other markets, including Madagascar, Vietnam, and Indonesia, trading more than 50,000 metric tons yearly.

Since the early 1990s, Touton has sought other sources of cocoa outside of perennially strife-ridden Ivory Coast. As such the company has developed subsidiaries in Singapore, Malaysia, and Indonesia, as well as in Nigeria. The company's Nigerian subsidiary operates drying and processing facilities with a capacity of more than 10,000 metric tons, giving it control of about 15 percent of the Nigerian cocoa trade.

Touton has also long held a leading position in the spice trade, particularly vanilla, through subsidiary Sivanil. That company, focusing on the main vanilla-producing region in the Indian Ocean, Papua New Guinea and Tahiti, trades more than 100 metric tons of the highly sought after spice each year. Other spices handled by Sivanil include cloves, cinnamon, and pepper. Privately held Touton is led by Chairman Patrick de Boussac. The company's revenues topped EUR 235 million ($297 million) in 2006.

THE TOUTONS: BORDEAUX TRADING FAMILY IN THE 19TH CENTURY

The city of Bordeaux played a major role in the development of France's international trade industry. Long focused on the sugar market, especially cane sugar brought in from the country's colonial possessions, the Bordeaux traders were also prominent traders in cocoa, brought to Europe in small quantities from the New World, as well as prominent participants in the slave trade. However, the banning of private companies from the slave trade in the late 18th century, coupled with the French Revolution, resulted in the loss of much of the momentum at the great Bordeaux trading houses. Into the next century, the development of methods of extracting sugar from beets deepened the city's trading crisis. Toward the middle of the century, the fortunes of the city's prominent trading families were hurt again with the abolition of slavery in the French colonies, and by legislation removing protectionist pricing policies in favor of the cane sugar market.

These events forced the city's trading families to look beyond the sugar trade, and many of the prominent Bordeaux families succeeded in developing new operations as importers and traders of a variety of new goods from Africa, the Indies, Nova Scotia, and elsewhere. As such, in the second half of the 19th century, the Bordeaux trading houses introduced such goods and commodities as nickel, codfish, wood, and peanuts. However, the new vigor of the Bordeaux trading houses was mostly due to the city's development as one of the western world's most prominent spice, coffee, and cocoa ports. Much of the subsequent growth of the city's trading industry occurred in partnership with the region's long-standing tradition as a center of France's wine and drinks industries. The arrival of new varieties of spices, fruits, and other ingredients played an important role in the creation of many of France's most popular liqueurs during the 19th century and into the 20th century.

Among the families that were to help raise Bordeaux to international prominence as a major spice port was the Touton family, who developed a specialty in the importation and processing of cocoa starting from 1848. Bordeaux had long played a central role in the growth of the cocoa and chocolate market in France. While the country had been introduced to cocoa in the early 17th century, it was the development of chocolate making in Bayonne and other cities along France's southern coast that heralded the true beginning of the French chocolate industry in the middle of the 18th century. The position

of Bordeaux as the region's major port, and one of the largest points of entry of cocoa into Europe, encouraged the growth of a local industry devoted to the production of cocoa-based products. By the beginning of the 20th century, the Toutons counted among the notables of Bordeaux's newly illustrious trading families.

The dawn of the 20th century witnessed a new development in the global cocoa industry, as production was introduced into the European-controlled African continent. France emerged as an important proponent in this development. In 1912, for example, France's demands that its colony in the Ivory Coast develop a cash crop in order to provide both a source of revenues and a source of supply for France itself led to the creation of a cocoa industry there, and the creation of the country's first cocoa plantations.

Over the next decades, much of the cocoa industry remained controlled by the French colonial government, which, through its own trade organizations, such as Compagnie Française d'Afrique Occidentale, developed its own network of plantations. Into the 1950s, however, a growing number of local farmers had begun to plant their own cocoa plantations. The latter were typically on a small scale. Nevertheless, by 1960, when the Ivory Coast gained independence, the country had developed a strong technological foundation for the launch of cocoa cultivation on a massive scale. By 1970, the country claimed the position as the world's number one producer, with a global market share of 27 percent.

EVOLUTION OF THE COCOA INDUSTRY

The impact on Ivory Coast's economy was significant, and by the end of the 1970s, cocoa exports accounted for nearly one-third of the country's total exports. By the late 20th century, Ivory Coast counted more than 600,000 cocoa farmers, and more than 620,000 plantations, with an average size of just six hectares. This enthusiastic embrace of cocoa allowed Ivory Coast to solidify its position as the world's leading supplier of the crop. By the beginning of the 21st century, Ivory Coast claimed a 37 percent share of the global market.

The country's economic conversion to cocoa, and related commodities, including coffee, rubber, and palm oil, had a dramatic impact on its environment. The country's rain forest suffered especially, dropping from a total surface of 12 million hectares to just nine million in the mid-1960s. By the 1990s, fewer than three million hectares of rain forest remained. At the same time, the intensive use of pesticides, herbicides, and fertilizers by cocoa growers brought further distress to the environment.

The cocoa industry's influence in Ivory Coast had important political implications as well. The vast majority of the country's cocoa growers belonged to the Baoulé ethnic group, which represented 40 percent of Ivory Coast's population. Transport of the beans from the country's remote rural regions to its principal ports was controlled by its "foreign" population, largely ethnic Lebanese and Malinese. However, the country's cocoa storage, processing, and export operations were dominated by foreign companies, especially French companies, such as Bolloré (transportation) and Delmas (port operations and freight handling), and traders, including Maison Touton. At the same time, the country's political power was controlled by another ethnic group, the Bété, representing 12 percent of the country's population. Under this leadership, which included future strongman Laurent Gbagbo, government-imposed taxes on cocoa farmers often reached extortionist levels.

These factors combined to expose the country's vulnerability to the crisis in the global cocoa market in the 1980s, when over-capacity slashed cocoa prices and left the Ivory Coast, and other cocoa producers, reeling from the loss of export income. In response, producers set out to make up for the lost revenues by a massive increase in volume. Starting from 1984, cocoa planting expanded by some 400 percent, reaching its peak in 1990.

By the early 1990s, the Ivory Coast had gained another 10 percent share in the worldwide cocoa industry. Yet this dominance of the supply side had little impact on the actual control of the market, which had shifted firmly into the hands of a few major multinational companies, such as Cargill, Archer Daniels Midland, EDF&Man, Cacao Barry, and Continat. French traders, who had long controlled the cocoa trade, had seen their influences dramatically reduced, particularly as the market shifted toward a more vertically integrated structure.

VERTICAL INTEGRATION MODEL INTO THE 21ST CENTURY

Touton, which remained highly focused on cocoa trading, was forced to adapt to the new global market conditions. For this, the company developed a multifaceted strategy. One part of the company's new focus into the beginning of the 21st century was to develop a more diversified geographical focus. This process began in the 1980s, when Touton began developing trading networks in new emerging cocoa markets, such as Malaysia and Indonesia. This led the company to create a dedicated subsidiary for the region, Touton Far East Ltd., based in Singapore. Touton's presence in this major trading center enabled it to position itself as an important supplier of both West African and Asian cocoas to the fast-growing Chinese and Southeast Asian cocoa markets. The company's efforts to diversify its geographic focus came in part due to the worsening political situation in the Ivory Coast.

At the same time, Touton expanded its African trading operations as well, reinforcing its presence in Ghana. Cocoa from that country was generally considered to be inferior in quality to the Ivory Coast's production, however. As Touton positioned itself as a high-quality cocoa supplier, it turned to the promising Nigerian market, which was considered to be a viable substitute for the increasingly strife-torn Ivory Coast. Touton's efforts to diversify its cocoa sourcing helped the company maintain its position among the top five cocoa traders in the world, handling some 250,000 metric tons per year by about 2005. More than 100,000 metric tons of that total came from outside of the Ivory Coast.

Another fast-growing part of Touton's operations in the 21st century was its move into the processing field. This too came as a result of changes in the cocoa market, in which producing nations, especially the Ivory Coast, became more insistent on gaining control over their primary commodities. The multinationals responded by converging their own operations with the growing numbers of domestic processors, developing an increasingly vertically integrated model.

Touton joined in this trend, starting with the creation of a new subsidiary, Touton Côte d'Ivoire, in 1995. That business grew into a major local processor, operating two facilities in the major ports of Abidjan and San Pedro with a total processing capacity of 80,000 metric tons. In 1997, the company founded its Nigerian subsidiary, Touton Nigeria Ltd., which developed its own conditioning facilities, including a cocoa-drying unit capable of processing 10,000 metric tons per year. In 2004, the company founded a new subsidiary, PT Coklat Murni, in Indonesia's Makassar peninsula, where it began conditioning and exporting cocoa from that region.

Touton deepened its integrated operations two years later when it acquired its own cocoa plantation, Abengourou, established in the 1950s north of Abidjan. That plantation, with a total of 300 hectares, was supplemented by two others, Soubré, created in 1953 some 120 kilometers north of San Pedro, and Ganoa, founded in the 1930s. These purchases gave the company control of more than 1,200 hectares. Following its acquisitions, the company invested heavily in revitalizing and replanting its plantations. By about 2005, the company's industrial and agricultural operations employed some 300 people, becoming the largest part of Touton's total employee base of 400.

While cocoa remained Touton's primary focus, the company was also developing its non-cocoa trade. The company had long been a major player in the global trade of vanilla and other spices, such as cloves, cinnamon, and pepper. In 1995, the company created a dedicated subsidiary for these activities, Sivanil, with subsidiaries in Madagascar (the largest producer of vanilla in the world) and Papua New Guinea. By the middle of the first decade of the 21st century, Sivanil's vanilla exports topped 100,000 metric tons.

In the 21st century, Touton also targeted the coffee market for growth. In the Ivory Coast, the company's plantations began planting coffee as well. The company created a dedicated coffee-trading subsidiary in the early years of the century, called Gepro S.A. That company specialized in trading green coffees, sourced from such regions as the Ivory Coast, Vietnam, Madagascar, and Indonesia. By displaying its ability to adapt to changes in the global market, Maison Touton appeared certain to remain a major trading house in the new century.

M. L. Cohen

PRINCIPAL SUBSIDIARIES

Gepro S.A.; Proci—Sucproci; Pt Cocklat Murni; SIO; Sivanil SAS; Touton Far East Pte Ltd.; Touton Moscou; Touton Nigeria Ltd.; Touton S.A.

PRINCIPAL COMPETITORS

Nestlé S.A.; Cargill Inc.; ADM Cocoa B.V.; EDF&Man Ltd.; Barry Callebaut AG; Continat BV; Olam; Cemoi-Cantalou S.A.; Noble AG; Armajoro Ltd.

FURTHER READING

"Le Cacao Ivoirien Est Soluble dans le Chocolat Basque," *Le Journal Idatzia*, April 18, 2004.

"Le Chocolat à ses Racines," *Les Echos*, March 30, 2007.

"L'Exemple de la Filière Cacaoyere: le Role Declinant des Interêts Français," *Le Patriote*, January 7, 2005.

TŘINECKÉ ŽELEZÁRNY

Třinecké Železárny A.S.

Prumyslova 1000
Třinec–Staré Mesto, 739 70
Czech Republic
Telephone: (420 558) 531 111
Fax: (420 558) 533 760
Web site: http://www.trz.cz

Public Company
Incorporated: 1839
Employees: 5,417
Sales: CZK 35.09 billion ($1.67 billion) (2006)
Stock Exchanges: Prague
Ticker Symbol: TZ
NAIC: 331111 Iron and Steel Mills

■ ■ ■

Třinecké Železárny (TZ), or Třinec Iron and Steel Works, is one of the largest steel producers in the Czech Republic. The company is also the largest privately held steel group in the Czech Republic. TZ operates four rolling mills in Třinec, a mill in Bohumín, and, in partnership with Moravia Steel, two mills in Kladno and Vítkovice. The company produces more than two million tons of pig iron, and more than 2.5 million tons of crude steel each year. The company also sold nearly 2.4 million tons of rolled steel products in 2006. Wire rod accounted for approximately one-third of this production, while semifinished steel added 26 percent. Sections and bars, rebars,and rails accounted for 14.5 percent, 8 percent,and 9.5 percent of the group's rolled steel

output, respectively. TZ also produces wide steel products.

Other parts of the TZ group include VUHZ, which produces components for the automotive industry; pipe producer VVT—Vítkovice Válcovna Trub; Energetika Třinec, which produces electricity and other power supplies (including process steam, compressed air, and blast air) for TZ and neighboring industries; machinery engineering specialist Strojírny Třinec, producing machinery and other steel structures as well as railway components; the Slévárny Třinec foundry; and Refrasil, which produces refractory materials. In partnership with Moravia Steel, TZ also operates the Sochorová válcovna TŽ billet mill; the Ferromoravia drawing mill; and the Retezárna chain mill. TZ is led by chairman and CEO Jirí Cienciala, and is listed on the Prague Stock Exchange. Moravia Steel, led by Tomáš Chrenek, controls nearly 70 percent of TZ's stock. In 2006, the company posted revenues of CZK 35.09 billion.

ORIGINS IN 1839

Třinecké Železárny, the Třinec iron and steel works, was established by Archduke Karl von Habsburg in order to exploit the natural resources of the Moravian-Silesian Region of what later became the Czech Republic. With plentiful supplies of iron ore, as well as rich limestone and clay deposits, and the Olza River providing both a water resource and a main transportation route, the region along the Czech-Slovak border emerged as an important industrial center. Construction of a pig iron foundry began in 1836, under direction of the Chamber of Tešín, and was completed in 1839. Through the middle of the century, the works continued to expand, adding a number of new facilities along the river. The vast forests in the area provided much of the early fuel source for the foundry operations before they were converted to coal. Transport of both timber and the work's iron production was facilitated by the proximity to the Olza River. During this period, the group also constructed its own canals to provide better access to the river.

The construction of the Košice-Bohumín railway into the 1870s introduced a new era of industrialization for the region. By 1871, the railway had reached Třinec, and access to this new transportation network led the Chamber of Těšín to relocate all of their foundry operations to a single, central facility in Třinec itself. The new works, completed in 1877, then became known as Třinecké Železárny (TZ). The newly integrated and modernized works, coupled with access to the national and international railway network, enabled TZ to grow rapidly into one of the Czechoslovakian region's largest steel producers.

The company became a major producer of steel and steel products for the railway industry. By 1885, the company had also launched production of engineering machinery and equipment. In 1894, the company also began manufacturing steel chain products, later brought under subsidiary Retezárna a.s. By 1906, TZ had become the centerpiece of the state-controlled Mining and Metallurgical Company. In that year, also, the company became the first in the world to add an electric drive to its reversing rolling mill.

With this powerful backing, TZ underwent a new modernization phase in the post–World War I period. Into the 1920s, the company had become one of the most modern and fully integrated steel mills in the Central European region. TZ had also become a dominant steel producer in Czechoslovakia itself and by the end of the 1920s controlled nearly one-fourth of the country's crude steel output and nearly one-third of its rolled products production.

This strategic position made TZ a primary target for takeover following Czechoslovakia's annexation by Germany in 1938. The steelworks' production was turned to supporting the Nazi war effort. Nonetheless, the works managed to escape destruction during the war. After Czechoslovakia came under Soviet control in 1946, the Třinec played a central role in carrying out the new government's industrialization policies. The Communist government invested heavily in TZ, greatly expanding its capacity.

In 1960, TZ installed its continuous light section mill, as part of the expansion of its rolled steel products operations. This mill was complemented by the addition of a continuous wire rod rolling mill, added in 1973.

A significant milestone in the company's history came in 1983, when TZ installed its first BOF (basic oxygen furnace) converter, providing a new boost in output. Other technology advancements carried out at the site included the addition of bloom and billet continuous-casting machinery. By the end of the 1980s, TZ's total output had soared to more than 3.2 million tons per year, making it the largest steel producer in the country.

PRIVATIZED IN 1996

The collapse of the Soviet regime and the subsequent breakup of Czechoslovakia set the stage for the privatization program carried out by the Czech government in the 1990s. The country's steel industry became an important feature of its privatization drive. However, decades under Soviet control had transformed the steel sector, like much of the region's industrial sectors, into a sprawling and highly inefficient industry, dogged by antiquated equipment and technology. Into the early 1990s, the Czech industry still employed as many as 100,000 workers, placing the country's per-employee output among the lowest in Europe. As the largest of the Czech steel operations, TZ had emerged from the Soviet era as its most modern as well. This led the company to become the government's first privatization target for the steel industry.

TZ's stature was converted to that of joint stock company in 1991, with the Czech government retaining full control of its stock. Movement toward privatization lasted into the middle of the decade, as the government slowly sold its stake in the company. By 1996, the Czech government announced that it had completed TZ's privatization, with a newly established investment group, Moravia Steel, controlling more than 60 percent of TZ. However, Moravia Steel quickly became caught up in scandal, however, when it was revealed that it had been providing gifts to government officials.

The original investment group, which included Czech tennis star Milan Šrejber, was forced to give up their shareholding. This gave Tomáš Chrenek, then serv-

KEY DATES

1839: Construction of a pig iron foundry near Tři-nec, in the Moravia-Silesia region, is completed.

1878: Třinec steelworks (TZ) is centralized in Třinec.

1906: Company becomes centerpiece of Metal and Metallurgical Corporation.

1946: Company is nationalized by Soviet-backed government.

1991: Company is restructured as joint stock company as part of privatization process.

1996: Privatization is completed, with Moravia Steel becoming majority shareholder.

2005: Company acquires steel tube products group Vítkovice Válcovna Trub (VVT).

2007: VUHZ automotive machine tools and components operations are acquired.

ing as Moravia Steel's general director, the opportunity to lead a new shareholder group, which reportedly $100 million to acquire 100 percent control of Moravia Steel in 1997. This gave Chrenek, then 34, control of more than 60 percent of the Czech Republic's largest and only privatized steel group.

Both TZ and Moravia Steel were subsequently restructured, with Moravia Steel taking over as the company's purchasing and sales arm. In this respect, Moravia steel became responsible for TZ's raw materials supply, while also handled marketing of the company's finished products. Moravia Steel also became responsible for TZ's logistics operations.

TZ's own restructuring took place over most of the 1990s and into the 2000s. In 1993, the company established a separate subsidiary for its chain steel production, Retezárna a.s. This was followed by the spinoff of the group's power generation operations into Energetika Třinec, A.S. in 1994. That company then began supplying the power needs of neighboring industries, in addition to TZ. Also in 1994, TZ set up REFRASIL, Ltd., which took over the company's refractory materials production. The company's engineering products division came next, in 1997, taking on the name of Strojírny Třinec, a.s. in 2005. By 1999, the company's foundry division had been regroup into Slévárny Třinec, a.s.

TZ had also launched an expansion of its product range during this period. The company carried out a major refurbishment and expansion of its wire rod rolling mill capacity in 1997, with a second phase completed in 2000.

CZECH STEEL LEADER IN THE 21ST CENTURY

TZ also expanded through acquisitions into the 2000s, amid the ongoing privatization of the Czech steel sector. In 1998, the company became joint owner of Sochorová válcovna TŽ, operator of a billet mill that produced steel semi products using TZ's rolled steel. In 2002, TZ took full control of that company. The following year, the company bought the wire drawing mill operated by Uherské Hradiště in Staré Mesto, renaming the operation as Ferromoravia. Another major acquisition came in 2005, with the purchase of Vítkovice Válcovna Trub (VVT), owned by part of the Shiran Group since its privatization. VVT added its production of tube steel to TZ's increasingly complete steel products range.

This range grew again in 2007 when the company completed its acquisition of the VUHZ (the company's original name translated to Research Institute of Ferrous Metallurgy), which had grown into a group of companies specialized in the production of machine tools and components for the automotive industry. Also in that year, the company bought Vítkovice–Vyzkum a vyvoj, a move that expanded TZ's research and development operations. These acquisitions came amid a CZK 1.6 billion investment program designed to upgrade the company's production, while also investing in environmental protection initiatives, launched in 2006. With sales topping CZK 35 billion that year, TZ remained the Czech Republic's leading privately controlled steel group, accounting for one-third of the country's total steel output.

M. L. Cohen

PRINCIPAL SUBSIDIARIES

Energetika Třinec, A.S.; REFRASIL, s.r.o.; Retezárna a.s.; Slévárny Třinec, a.s.; Steel Consortium Partners, a.s.; Strojírny Třinec, a.s.; TRIALFA, s.r.o.; Třinecké gastroslužby, s.r.o.; TRISIA, a.s.; VVT—Vítkovice Válcovna Trub a.s.

PRINCIPAL COMPETITORS

Mittal Steel Ostrava A.S.; BONAVIA servis A.S.; OKD OKK A.S.; ZDB GROUP A.S.; Ferromet Group S.R.O.; VALCOVNY PLECHU A.S.; JAeKL Karvina A.S.; Hayes Lemmerz Autokola A.S.; OSRAM Bruntal spol S.R.O.; NIKOM A.S.

FURTHER READING

Anderson, Robert, "Czech Steel Companies Seek Partners to Improve Sector," *Financial Times,* November 9, 1999.

Burgert, Philip, "CMC Purchasing 11% Portion of Czech Steel Firm," *American Metal Market,* March 30, 2004, p. 4.

————, "Czech Privatization Sweeps Steel Mills," *American Metal Market,* September 24, 1996, p. 2.

"Commission Gives Go Ahead for Takeover of Czech Steel Group, VVT," *European Report,* September 24, 2005, p. 211.

"Czech Steelworks Trinecke Zelezarny Buys Car Parts Supplier VUHZ, Metallurgical Research Groups," *Czech Business News,* June 26, 2007.

"Czech Steelworks Trinecke Zelezarny to Invest CZK 6 bln into Production Upgrade by End 2011," *Czech Business News,* July 30, 2007.

"Gov't Approves State Aid to Trinecke Steelworks Despite EC Opposition," *Czech Business News,* November 13, 2003.

"South Korean Carmaker Hyundai's Czech Unit Mulls Deal with Czech Steelworks Trinecke Zelezarny," *Czech Business News,* April 12, 2007.

"TZ Steelworks Owner Moravia Steel Changes Ownership Structure," *Czech Business News,* May 31, 2002.

Underberg AG

Industriestrasse 31
Dietlikon, CH-8305
Switzerland
Telephone: (41 44) 805-1846
Fax: (41 44) 805-1800
Web site: http://www.underberg.com

Private Company
Incorporated: 1846 as H. Underberg-Albrecht
Employees: 1,000 (est.)
Sales: EUR 500 million ($630 million) (2006 est.)
NAIC: 312130 Wineries; 422820 Wine and Distilled Alcoholic Beverage Wholesalers; 312111 Soft Drink Manufacturing

■ ■ ■

Underberg AG is the holding company for the Underberg group of companies, a Swiss-based manufacturer and wholesaler of alcoholic and nonalcoholic beverages, including premium spirits and liqueurs, wines and sparkling wines, fruit juices, and syrups. About half of the group's sales are generated by Semper Idem Underberg AG, Germany's fourth largest spirits manufacturer and distributor. Underberg herbal digestive, the company's traditional flagship product, which is exported to over 100 countries, accounts for roughly one-fifth of total sales.

The Underberg group's production subsidiaries are located in Germany, Austria, Switzerland, France, Brazil, and Hungary. Besides Underberg, the company manufactures and distributes a variety of well-known branded products, including Asbach fine brandy, Schlumberger sparkling wine, Pitú sugarcane brandy, Grasovka Premium-Zubrowka Wódka, and Riemerschmid fruit and bar syrups. Underberg is owned and managed by Emil Underberg II (a great-grandson of the company founder Hubert Underberg), his wife Christiane, and his daughter Hubertine Underberg-Ruder.

CREATION OF AN INTERNATIONAL BRAND IN 1846

When Hubert Underberg was a teenager, years before he created the now-famous *digestif* of the same name and established his own enterprise, he helped his mother run the family business, which today would be called a drugstore, after his father's sudden death. Underberg later traveled to the Netherlands and Belgium to get commerce experience and hands-on training at trading firms and banks. It was there that Underberg discovered a special digestive drink. Made from herbal elixirs and mixed with genever, a special kind of gin, it was said to aid digestion after a heavy meal. The bitter concoction (each innkeeper had his own house recipe) piqued Underberg's curiosity, and he took advantage of every opportunity he could to learn about the beverage.

After he had returned to his hometown of Rheinberg, a small town about ten miles north of Duisburg, Underberg began a systematic study of the herbs used in the digestive bitter. Utilizing the traditional recipes he had found, Underberg began to experiment, searching for the right combination of herbs as well as for methods to extract their essence. Underberg also looked for methods of manufacture that yielded a product of consistent composition and quality. The dark brown elixir that finally resulted from this process tasted rather bitter and consisted of extracts from herbs stemming from 43 different countries. The elixir was diluted in highly concentrated alcohol, mixed with fresh spring water, and then put into large oak barrels where it ripened for many months.

Underberg called his new product "Boonekamp or Maagbitter." On June 17, 1846, 29-year-old Hubert Underberg married Catharina Albrecht, the daughter of a wealthy upper-class family, and on their wedding day the couple founded the firm H. Underberg-Albrecht. Catharina not only lent her maiden name to the new enterprise, she also helped purchase the ingredients, make and mix the herbal extracts, and acted as authorized representative in the management of the business.

Hubert Underberg was convinced that, in addition to consistently high product quality, his brand had to possess a distinctive look to set it apart from competing and imitators' products on the market. He designed a bottle with a distinctive shape and acquired a glassworks where the bottles could be manufactured. The bottle was wrapped in yellowish straw paper with a label attached. The label was also Underberg's distinctive design; the product name, Boonekamp or Maagbitter, was framed left and right by two official-looking stamps with the Underberg seal and a Latin phrase underneath: *Occidit qui non servat* ("what does not serve, will go down"). Another characteristic element was Hubert Underberg's artfully handwritten signature at the bottom right corner of the label.

MASSIVE MARKETING BOOSTS SUCCESS AND BREEDS COMPETITION

Convinced of the exceptional quality of his product, Underberg took every effort to gather testimonials, soliciting them anyone, from doctors to travelers who were served a sample of his product as soon as they exited the coach upon arrival in Rheinberg. Over time he was able to persuade even kings to drink his herbal digestive after the heavy meals (more often than not difficult to digest) consumed regularly at their courts. Among his most famous testimonials were Napoleon III, the emperor of Prussia, the Russian czar, and the emperor of Japan, all of whom made Underberg one of their selected suppliers. To educate the masses about his product, the entrepreneur ran regular advertisements in the German press and distributed pamphlets and brochures to retailers and customers. Beginning in 1851 he presented his product at World and Industrial Exhibitions where the product received numerous awards.

Due to its purported stomach-soothing properties and Underberg's massive marketing campaigns, Boonekamp or Maagbitter quickly gained in popularity. Within a few years the company, which was located in Rheinberg's city center, employed 30 workers. Underberg's digestive bitters were sold all across Germany and shipped to countries around the world, such as the United States, Australia, and even to countries in Africa. The commercial success of Underberg's Boonekamp or Maagbitter also stirred the imagination of competitors who tried to reproduce his product. In order to protect the identity of his branded product, Underberg took a bottle to the Commercial Court of Krefeld in 1851, where it was deposited and registered, long before the first brand protection legislation was enacted in Germany. After this visionary act, the words "officially deposited" were printed in bright red letters across the very official-looking label of the bottle. This did not, however, prevent imitators from attempting to get a piece of Underberg's action.

Using similar-sounding company names, such as Unkerberg or Unterbrecht, imitating the bottle shape, or printing labels similar in appearance, competitors attempted to replicate Underberg's success. When a con man appeared who claimed to know the formula for making the popular drink, Underberg took an even more serious step to prevent his product idea from being stolen. On January 24, 1857, the company founder gathered his family and employees along with 21 Rheinsberg dignitaries and declared publicly that he had disclosed the secret recipe for his Boonekamp only to his wife and to no other third party. Underberg added that he would never give or sell this secret to anyone. His declaration was officially documented and deposited at 15 embassies of foreign countries. These measures, along with additional newspaper campaigns that educated customers about the "product pirates" trying to trick them by selling them a product of lower quality under a

KEY DATES

1846: Hubert Underberg and Catharina Albrecht found the firm H. Underberg-Albrecht; Underberg's new digestive beverage debuts.

1851: A sample bottle of Boonekamp or Maagbitter is officially deposited at the Commercial Court of Krefeld.

1857: Public announcement is made that the manufacturing process for Underberg's *digestif* is kept a family secret.

1896: The product name Underberg is registered at the Imperial Patent Office.

1924: Underberg herbal digestive is approved as a medicinal preparation by the U.S. Food and Drug Administration.

1941: Production ceases during World War II.

1949: Emil Underberg I invents the single-portion bottle as a sole packaging unit.

1956: Management holding company Underberg Handels AG is established in Switzerland.

1962: The company's new production subsidiary in West Berlin begins operations.

1973: Underberg acquires the oldest Austrian sparkling wine manufacturer, Schlumberger.

1981: Emil Underberg II takes over the family enterprise.

1990: The company buys a stake in Swiss specialty distiller Arnold Dettling AG.

1996: Brandy and liqueur manufacturer Anton Riemerschmid Weinbrennerei und Likörfabrik is acquired.

2002: Underberg takes over a German manufacturer of fine brandy, Asbach GmbH.

similar label, consequently helped a great deal in defending his brand in numerous legal battles, most of which were decided in Underberg's favor.

FIGHTING PRODUCT PIRACY BECOMES ONGOING TASK

In 1886 Hubert Underberg made his 25-year-old son a business partner and transformed the company from a sole proprietorship into a general partnership. When his wife Catharina died in 1880, the company founder passed his most-guarded secret, the ingredients and manufacturing process for his product, on to his son Hubert. After Underberg's death in 1891, Hubert Un-

derberg II became the sole owner of the family enterprise. Aware of the fact that the uniqueness of his father's invention was the foundation for the success of his business, Hubert Underberg II fought as fiercely as his father to protect the unique identity of his brand.

In 1894, a new law granted extensive legal protection to the creators of commercial brands, including symbols and forms. Shortly afterward, the Underbergs brought one of the first lawsuits under the new law against a merchant of the name van Res who had manufactured and sold a Boonekamp imitator under the company name H. Underborg Alberth. Van Res eventually lost the case. However, the registration of the Boonekamp or Maagbitter brand at the newly established Imperial Patent Office as an Underberg trademark prompted resistance from Germany's distillers who argued that the name Boonekamp had existed before Underberg launched its branded product. The German Patent Office ultimately ruled that the name Boonekamp had become a descriptive word for the category of herb-based bitters and hence could be used by any distiller. Consequently the patent office deleted Underberg's registrations for Boonekamp or Maagbitter in 1896.

Although this was likely an even more bitter medicine to swallow than his own, Hubert Underberg II came up with an even better solution. He changed the name of his product to Underberg-Boonekamp and registered it, and the word "Underberg," with the Imperial Patent Office. In addition, the new slogan *Semper idem* ("always the same") replaced the old slogan *Occidit qui non servat* and was registered as well. Over time the word "Boonekamp" was printed in ever smaller letters until it disappeared completely from the label in 1916. From then on the product was simply called Underberg.

The legal protection of the Underberg brand name and slogan was an important step but by far not the last legal battle against imitators. In addition to copying the product and bottle shape, imitators created their own versions of the Underberg straw paper wrapping. Finally, two courts ruled in 1909 and 1913 that the wrapping was part of Underberg's brand identity and therefore legally protected.

MODERNIZATION, GENERATION CHANGE AND WORLD WARS

At the beginning of the 20th century Underberg took major steps to prepare his enterprise, which by then employed 55 workers, for the dawning age of industrialization. In 1905 a new factory was built to expand production capacity. The new facility was equipped with the most modern technologies available;

it even had its own power station to generate electricity. Two years later the first automated bottling station was set up there.

The outbreak of World War I in 1914 abruptly cut the company off from the rest of the world. The herbs needed to make Underberg could no longer be imported nor could the herbal bitter be exported. As a result, the manufacturing of the popular beverage was stopped. At the end of the war, after the Belgian soldiers had vacated the production halls they had occupied, production of Underberg resumed in 1924 and sales soon climbed to their previous high levels.

From his 12 children, Underberg chose his three sons Josef, the oldest of the three, who had a doctorate in law; Carl, who had studied economics and political science and also graduated with a Ph.D.; and Emil, with his commercial education and practice, to become business partners. In 1924, Underberg sent Carl, who had just finished his dissertation on the international registration of commercial trademarks and their economic significance, to the United States. As president and CEO of the New York City–based Underberg Sales Corporation, the 28-year-old managed to get approval from the U.S. Food and Drug Administration to sell his product as a medicinal preparation. This was not surprising; during Prohibition, between 1920 until 1933, when beverages containing 0.5 percent alcohol or more were declared "intoxicants," Americans gladly stocked their medicine chests with one-liter-bottles of the high-percentage digestive aid.

After Hubert Underberg II died in 1935, Josef, Carl, and Emil managed the company jointly for the next decade, not without friction but in the end successfully. The beginning of World War II four years later again made it impossible to continue the production of Underberg, due to the lack of a supply of the necessary ingredients and the company's isolation from its export markets. During the war, production facilities were closed down completely and sustained no damage. American troops occupied the Underberg factory in the final months before Nazi Germany's defeat.

POSTWAR PRODUCTION

A century after its foundation the Underberg family had to rebuild the enterprise almost from scratch. Luckily, their residence in Rheinberg's city center as well as the company's production halls had survived the war with little damage. Most importantly, the secret recipe for Underberg had been kept within the family. Still, scarcity prevailed in the first years after the war while Underberg began to rebuild its network of distributors. The raw materials and new equipment had to be

acquired at a time when almost everything was in short supply. Most Germans were happy just to have food to eat; herbal bitter was a luxury the masses were not able to afford.

Just a few months before the company's 100th anniversary, Josef Underberg died. According to his will, his brother Emil inherited his shares in the company. Emil and Carl Underberg, who jointly managed the business after Josef's death, made the decision to sell Underberg only in single-portion bottles beginning in 1949; this was possibly the single most influential business decision since 1896. It was based on several reasons. First, because of the lack of purchasing power and the enormous tax on alcohol, few could afford to buy a one-liter bottle of Underberg. If, however, the bitter was sold one serving at a time (the company founder had recommended 20 milliliters for one serving) it became much more affordable. Second, it was not unusual in bars and restaurants, where Underberg was most often consumed, for owners to fill up empty Underberg bottles with a less expensive Boonekamp and charge their customers for an Underberg. The introduction of the single-portion bottle, which was supposed to be brought to the customer's table, gave the company more control, and, not surprisingly, prompted bar and restaurant keepers to boycott the novelty at first. Retailers, on the other hand, were pleased about the quickly rising popularity of the new "three-packs" with no recommended price printed on them. Finally, the much smaller unit enabled the company to raise the profit generated from the same amount of product.

At the center of the company's massive postwar marketing campaigns was the new slogan "An Underberg a day will keep you feeling fine." In 1953 a helicopter, which was "dressed up" as a flying Underberg bottle, flew endless loops over large German cities at mass events such as a carnival in Cologne. Later the helicopter was replaced by an airship. In 1956 the company launched a promotional campaign the scope of which was unheard of at the time. Over a period of five years, Underberg distributed coupons for one single-portion bottle of the *digestif* to roughly six million German households that could be redeemed at retail stores as well as in bars or restaurants. As a result of these efforts, Underberg's sales skyrocketed, reaching nearly 300 million single-portion bottles a year. The company's renewed financial success became visible with the so-called Underberg-Turm, a gigantic warehouse tower in Rheinberg's city center. It was 11 stories tall with enough space to store six million liters of the company's popular beverage.

AN INTERNATIONAL BEVERAGE GROUP

After Emil Underberg's death in 1958, his wife Margarete took his place in the company management as a partner. Three years later the company built an eight-story apartment, office, bottling, and warehouse complex in West Berlin. Starting out in 1962 with 78 employees, the new subsidiary put out 200,000 single-portion bottles a day. Part of that output was exported to East Germany and other Eastern European countries via a Hamburg-based wholesaler. In 1972 Underberg was the first West German enterprise to get a permit from the government of East Germany to deliver Underberg bitter to the state-owned distiller Bärensiegel in East Berlin, where it was bottled and then sold to the countries behind the iron curtain.

Carl Underberg's death in 1972 marked the beginning of a new era for the company. Carl Hubertus and Emil Underberg II, who had become personally liable business partners in 1964, followed in the footsteps of their fathers. The business environment they found themselves in, however, presented them with a great challenge. Sales of Underberg bitter soared in the 1960s but began to stagnate in the 1970s, partly due to changing consumer habits and tastes and partly because the tax on alcoholic beverages was raised significantly in 1973. At the same time, more and more distillers from abroad successfully launched their brand products in the shrinking German market. To stay competitive in such an environment, Underberg ventured into new markets and away from being a one-product manufacturer.

This process had begun in 1967, when Underberg established several new subsidiaries for producing other spirits in addition to their *digestif.* Four years later the company set up a distribution subsidiary that marketed well-known spirit brands by other manufacturers. In 1981 Carl Hubertus left the company, and Emil Underberg II took over the reins. Over the following two decades, Underberg made numerous acquisitions and distribution deals with other distillers, broadening the scope of his enterprise.

While not all of Emil Underberg's deals came through (a planned merger in the late 1980s with a German sparkling wine manufacturer failed and a few distribution joint ventures were later discontinued), he successfully managed the company's transition from a German one-product manufacturer to a diversified international beverage group. By 1989 the Underberg group included 24 subsidiaries, minority holdings, and joint ventures, from distillers to wineries to fruit juice and cocktail syrup manufacturers. At the end of the decade the company was reorganized under the new management holding Underberg AG based in Dietlikon

near Zürich in Switzerland. Underberg's activities in Germany were run by Semper idem Underberg AG.

In 1991 (the year when the company reached the DEM 1 billion sales mark) Hubertine Underberg-Ruder, Emil Underberg's oldest daughter and designated successor, became president of Underberg AG's board of directors at age 29. Her husband Franz Ruder became director of finances and holdings. Throughout the 1990s and beyond the company continued to acquire other beverage manufacturers or to set up joint ventures with them. The extended list of Underberg alcoholic beverage brands included Schlumberger sparkling wine from Austria; Blanc Foussy sparkling wine from France; Grasovka Bison-Wódka from Poland; Unicum herbal bitter from Hungary; Pitú sugarcane spirit from Brazil; Riemerschmid fruit and bar syrups; XUXU strawberry-and-vodka cocktails; and Asbach fine brandy from Rüdesheim on the Rhine. In addition, the company manufactured and distributed nonalcoholic beverages such as Sangrita. One of Underberg's latest start-ups was Biodyn-AG, an research and development subsidiary that worked on food products free of histamine, an agent in fish, meat, cheese, or wine that might be responsible for food allergies.

After more than 160 years, Underberg herbal digestive still generated roughly 20 percent of the company's revenues. Its alcohol content was reduced somewhat from 49 to 44 percent, and the recipe for the herb elixir as well as the technology to make it underwent only a few changes within five generations when they were updated according to the most current knowledge available. The circle of insiders who knew how to make it was extended to include two Catholic priests, just in case. The latest slogan, "Underberg worldwide after a good meal," reflected the fact that the herbal bitter was exported to over 100 countries around the world. Hubertine Underberg-Ruder told *menstyle international* in 2006 that she was convinced that keeping the recipe for Underberg bitter a secret was a necessary measure to secure the foundation of the family business, because patents are made public and after a while they expire. The Underberg family also kept the balance sheet of their enterprise secret.

Evelyn Hauser

PRINCIPAL SUBSIDIARIES

Semper idem Underberg AG (Germany); Schlumberger AG (Austria); Arnold Dettling AG; Underberg Sales Corporation (United States); Underberg do Brasil Indústria de Bebidas Ltda. (Brazil); Asbach GmbH (Germany); Diversa Spezialitäten GmbH (Germany).

PRINCIPAL COMPETITORS

Fratelli Branca Distillerie S.r.l.; Pernod Ricard S.A.; Belvedere; Henkell & Söhnlein Sektkellereien KG.

FURTHER READING

Barbier, Hans D., *Die Person hinter dem Produkt*, edited by Fides Krause-Brewer, Bonn, Germany: Norman Rentrop, 1987, pp. 144–51.

Covell, Pauline, "Paper Soothes Liqueur Case Consumption," *Packaging Digest*, October 1995, p. 68.

"Germany: Seagram, Underberg Split Marketing," *Frankfurter Allgemeine Zeitung*, January 21, 2000, p. 42.

"Germany: Underberg Takes Stake in Asbach," *Frankfurter Allgemeine Zeitung*, December 2, 1999, p. 18.

"Jan Becher-Karlovarska Becherovka Buys a Competitor," *Hospodarske Noviny*, July 12, 1999, p. 11.

Magyar, Kasimir M., and Patrick K. Magyar, *Marketingpioniere*, Zollikon, Switzerland: Verlag moderne industrie, 1987, pp. 66–75.

"Paterno Imports 'Digestif,'" *Modern Brewery Age*, May 16, 1994, p. 2.

Pizmoht, Rudolf, "Dem Posthalter beim Brauen zugeschaut," *Neue Ruhr Zeitung*, July 13, 1996.

———, "Emil II., König des Kräuterbitterlikörs," *Neue Ruhr Zeitung*, December 31, 1996.

———, "… noch einen Koffer in Berlin," *Neue Ruhr Zeitung*, January 3, 1998.

———, "Triumvirat im Hause Underberg," *Neue Ruhr Zeitung*, July 27, 1996.

———, "Wirte-Boykott bremste Underberg nicht," *Neue Ruhr Zeitung*, August 3, 1996.

Rus, Katerina, "Bottling Up the Czech Spirit for Privatization," *Prague Post*, March 5, 1997.

"Underberg—ein Magenbitter vom Niederrhein erobert die Welt," *menstyle international*, Spring/Summer 2006, p. 18.

"Underberg in US Distribution Deal with Haleybrooke International," *Duty-Free News International*, March 15, 2006, p. 35.

"Underberg-Chef kauft die Marke Valensina," *Frankfurter Allgemeine Zeitung*, November 20, 2001, p. 24.

Zentek, Sabine, *ProduktProzesse*, Ludwigsburg, Germany: Avedition, 1999, pp. 159–79.

Unión de Cervecerias Peruanas Backus y Johnston S.A.A.

———— ■ ————

Jirón Chiclayo 594
Lima,
Peru
Telephone: (51 1) 311-3000
Fax: (51 1) 311-3059
Web site: http://www.backus.com.pe

Wholly Owned Subsidiary of SABMiller plc
Incorporated: 1888 as Backus y Johnston Sociedad
   Industrial
Employees: 1,560
Sales: 1.61 billion nuevo soles ($491.75 million) (2006)
Stock Exchanges: Lima
Ticker Symbol: BACKUSI1
NAIC: 312111 Soft Drink Manufacturing; 312112
   Bottled Water Manufacturing; 312120 Breweries

■ ■ ■

Unión de Cervecerias Peruanas Backus y Johnston
S.A.A. dominates the market for beer in Peru through
the brands that it manufactures, bottles, and sells,
especially Cristal and Pilsen. The company also
produces, bottles, and distributes bottled water and soft
drinks. The company is a subsidiary of SABMiller plc,
the world's second largest brewery.

A CENTURY OF BEER
PRODUCTION IN PERU

The enterprise was founded by J. Howard Johnston and
Jacob Backus, U.S. engineers who came to Peru to build

a railway. In 1876 they purchased riverside property,
including a mill, for an ice factory in Lima. They began
making beer in 1880 and incorporated their company in
1888 in Peru and the following year in Great Britain.
Backus and Johnston soon sold out to English investors,
who appointed a succession of British executives to
manage the company. Germans played an important
part in the more technical aspects.

Beer was still a luxury product in Peru at this time.
The water needed came from wells as deep as 500 feet
below the surface, and sugar was easily obtainable, but
all other ingredients, including malt and hops, had to be
imported. Oak barrels were replaced by steel tanks in
1913. Returned bottles were washed and reused. The
last British managing director was Alexander Laurie
Dunlop, a Scot who has working for an Argentine
brewery when he was appointed in 1922. Backus y
Johnston had produced 347,164 cases of beer the previous year; when Dunlop yielded his post in 1954, it was
turning out 5.35 million cases a year.

A group of Peruvian investors headed by Ricardo
Bentín Mujíca bought Backus y Johnston in 1954 and
also acquired Maltería Lima S.A. and Compañia Manu-
facturera de Vidrio del Perú Ltda. S.A., a glassmaker.
The following year these investors renamed the
company Cervecería Backus y Johnston S.A. and
installed a modern laboratory. The new owners were
sportsmen as well as businessmen. In 1955 they founded
Club Sporting Cristal on property purchased near the
brewery. Backus y Johnston fielded and subsidized a soccer team and also baseball, boxing, and men's and
women's basketball teams. Club Sporting Cristal won its

first professional soccer championship in 1956 and 15 national championships through 2005.

Beer production tripled over the first decade and a half under Peruvian ownership, reaching 17.63 million cases in 1970, or about half of all beer produced in Peru. In 1973 Backus y Johnston founded Cervecería San Juan S.A. and Cervecería del Norte S.A. to extend its scope to the Amazonian parts of the country and northern Peru, respectively, and it also founded Industrial Cacer S.A., a manufacturer of plastic bottles that changed its name to Industrias del Envase S.A. in 1994. By 1976, when Backus y Johnston was the third largest brewery in South America, its share of the nation's beer output had declined somewhat, to 42 percent, but its stock was one of the three most traded on Lima's stock exchange. The company established Transporte 77 S.A. in 1977 for its delivery vehicles and acquired Editorial Imprenta Amaru S.A. in 1978 to print its labels. The latter was later absorbed by Industrial Cacer. A new brewery plant opened on the outskirts of Lima in 1981.

Cristal, a pale lager, was the most popular Backus y Johnston beer. Others included Elefante, Victoria, Pilsen, Rey de Oro, Llave de Oro, El Aguila, Aguila Verde, El Voluntario, Cristal Tropicalizada, and Bock Bier. There were also a large number of dark beers, including Aguila Negra, Negra Llama, Negra Bulldog, Crown Stout, Africana, Export Cerveza Negra, Malta Backus, and Maltina. The company's only export market was the United States. A joint venture had been established with another brewery in 1956 to make malt in Peru, but it could meet only part of the demand, and imports continued. Jugos del Norte was founded in 1981 to produce fruit juices.

During the 1980s, Backus y Johnston's share of the national market for beer grew from 41 percent to 53 percent as a consequence of such actions as improved marketing and distribution. There was an internal struggle within the company, however. In 1986 its vice-president sold his shares to the Brescia group, which, with support from the Romero and Raffo groups and the Banco de Lima, attempted to take it over. However, the Bentíns, with backing from the Picasso and other family groups, Backus y Johnston distributors, and shareholders of another brewery, Compañia Cervecera del Sur, rebuffed the attempt.

MOVING TOWARD MONOPOLY: 1990–2000

During the 1980s, Backus y Johnston's share of the national market for beer grew from 41 percent to 53 percent as a consequence of such actions as improved marketing and distribution. In 1992 the company established Agro Inversiones S.A. in Chile to provide malt and hops. By 1993 Backus' share of the Peruvian beer market had reached 60 percent.

By the end of 1993 the Backus y Johnston group had estimated annual sales of $330 million. The group included two brewery companies, Backus y Johnston and Cervecería San Juan; the glassmaker Compañia Manufacturera de Vidreo; Backus & Johnston Trading S.A., founded in 1989 or 1990 to obtain foreign currency for the group; Jugos del Norte; Industrias Cacer, and Editorial Imprenta Amaru. In 1994 Backus y Johnston acquired Esmeralda Holding Ltd., which held a 43 percent stake (and 62 percent voting stake) in the brewery Compañia Nacional de Cerveza S.A. (CNC). This company, its now-struggling archrival, had been producing Pilsen Callao. The funds for the $134 million purchase came in large part from the Banco de Crédito del Perú, which was controlled by the Romero group, also a principal shareholder in Backus y Johnston. After the acquisition, Backus fired half of CNC's workers.

CNC also was the majority shareholder of Sociedad Cervecera de Trujillo S.A., producer of Pilsen Trujillo, the leading beer in that region of northern Peru; the mineral water company Agua Mineral Litinada San Mateo S.A.; Transportes Centauro S.A., owner of delivery vehicles; and a half-share in Maltería Lima. All these enterprises, plus Cervecería del Norte, were, on the last day of 1996, incorporated into what became Unión de Cervecerías Peruanas Backus y Johnston S.A. The following year Jugos del Norte and Alitec, a processor of asparagus and other vegetable products, were merged into a new subsidiary, Agro Industrias Backus S.A. In 1998 Backus y Johnston closed its original Lima plant. Agro Industrias Backus, apparently chronically unprofitable, was sold in 2004.

By 2000 Backus y Johnston controlled about 80 percent of the beer market in Peru with its Cristal, Pilsen, and San Juan brands. Almost all the rest was in the hands of Compañia Cervecera del Sur del Perú S.A.A. (Cervesur). Based in Peru's second city, Arequipa, Cervesur had been gaining market share since introducing its Cusqueña brand in 1995. It was also producing

```
┌─────────────────────────────────────────────┐
│                                             │
│              KEY DATES                      │
│                   ■                         │
│  ─────────────────────────────────────────  │
│                                             │
│  1880:  Two Americans, J. Howard Johnston   │
│         and Jacob Backus, open a brewery in │
│         Lima.                               │
│  1954:  The brewery, long owned by British  │
│         investors, is sold to Peruvian      │
│         buyers.                             │
│  1955:  The company is renamed Cervecería   │
│         Backus y Johnston S.A. and a modern │
│         laboratory is installed.            │
│  1976:  Backus y Johnston is the third      │
│         largest brewery in South America.   │
│  2000:  Purchase of Cervesur gives Backus a │
│         virtual monopoly on beer production │
│         in Peru.                            │
│  2002:  The Colombian brewery Bavaria S.A.  │
│         buys 44 percent of Backus y         │
│         Johnston.                           │
│  2005:  Bavaria, which holds a majority     │
│         stake in Backus, is bought by       │
│         SABMiller.                          │
│                                             │
└─────────────────────────────────────────────┘
```

and marketing Arequipeña, another popular brand. No foreign brewer had bought into a Peruvian beer maker or established a manufacturing presence in Peru, and imports of beer were virtually nonexistent. Thus, when Backus purchased Cervesur in 2000 for $124 million, it eliminated virtually all competition. Also in 2000, Backus acquired Embotelladora Frontera S.A., a soft drink bottler in southern Peru and Bolivia with licenses from PepsiCo., Inc. This company was sold in 2004.

THE STRUGGLE FOR CONTROL: 2000–05

Backus y Johnston seemed to be in an ideal position. Its stock was still the third most traded in Peru, trailing only giant Southern Peru Copper Corp. and the Peruvian telephone monopoly. For years, net earnings had averaged 20 percent of sales and generous dividends kept the investors happy. Nevertheless, Backus y Johnston was seen as having greatly overpaid to purchase CNC. The juice business was foundering. South American breweries outside Peru were believed to be preparing to enter the national market. The Bentín family, which had presided over Backus y Johnston for over 40 years, had internal problems: some members wanted to sell out. The Romero group, hard hit by a banking crisis, also wanted to sell, while the Brescia group, another large shareholder and one flush with mining profits, wanted to hold out longer for the best possible terms.

Over the next few years Backus y Johnston shrugged off its detractors, introducing a new beer, Cri-

stal Light, cutting costs, and raising its profits by one-third. Two big foreign breweries, Venezuela's Empresas Polar SA and Chile's Compañia de Cervecerías Unidas S.A. (CCU), had purchased 8 percent and 6.5 percent, respectively, of the company's shares in 1999. Backus y Johnston was maintaining its market share in a country in which beer consumption remained low and the company had enough capacity to satisfy growth in demand. As one of the few remaining independent brewers in South America, it was an attractive candidate for takeover by even bigger beer makers. In 2001 Polar purchased another 13 percent of Backus from the Romero family, raising its stake to about 25 percent.

The next suitor turned out to be Bavaria S.A., a brewery with a monopoly position in its own country of Colombia. The company, in 2002, paid $420 million for a 24.5 percent stake in Backus y Johnston sold by the Bentín family. This sum was more than twice the market value of the shares. The fallout was immediate. Venezuela's Cisneros group, a bitter rival of Polar, secured an option—soon exercised—to purchase the Bentíns' remaining 15 percent stake in Backus for $165 million and another 7 percent on the stock exchange for an additional $77 million. By the end of the year, Bavaria had raised its share of Backus to 44 percent. Polar's angry managers charged that Bavaria and Cisneros had illegally colluded to freeze Polar out, but to no avail. The company conceded defeat in 2003, selling its stake to Bavaria.

The endgame in the struggle for UCP Backus y Johnston came in the spring of 2005, when London-based SABMiller plc, one of the world's largest brewers, acquired Bavaria. A few months later, SABMiller purchased Cisneros' 20 percent stake for $469 million. SABMiller owned 93 percent of Backus y Johnston's stock. Cervecería San Juan, Cervesur, and Industrias del Envase were made separate subsidiaries of SABMiller, which in 2006 announced a tender offer to acquire all the shares of these companies still remaining in public hands.

Backus y Johnston claimed an approximate 92 percent share of the Peruvian beer market in 2005, with Cristal, its principal brand, holding more than 40 percent and Pilsen Callao, 20 percent. The company claimed to maintain its market share in 2006. According to another account, Cristal alone had more than half of the Peruvian beer market, followed by about 30 percent for Pilsen Callao. The company introduced a regional brand, Barena, in October 2006, and a premium beer, Peroni Nastro Azzuro, in February 2007. Other Backus lagers were Arequipeña, Cusqueña, Dorada, Del Altiplano, Pilsen Trujillo, and San Juan. Malta Ariquipeña, Malta Cusqueña, and Malta Polar were dark beers. The company was also producing Saboré soft drinks in four flavors, Guaraná orange soda, and Cristallina and San Mateo mineral water. Nevertheless, beer accounted for 92 percent of Backus' sales volume in 2006. The only significant competition came from Brazil's Companhia de Bebidas das Américas (AmBev), a company whose Brahma brand, introduced to Peru in 2005, had about 8 percent of national beer consumption.

The war between the beer companies was being waged on the soccer field as well as supermarkets, other retailers, and bars. AmBev Perú scored a coup by luring away from Club Sporting Cristal sponsorship of two noted teams, Alianza Lima and Sport Boys. Backus y Johnston countered by taking on sponsorship of Universitario de Deportes.

Robert Halasz

PRINCIPAL SUBSIDIARIES

Agro Inversiones S.A. (Chile); Agua Mineral Litinada San Mateo S.A.; Backus & Johnston Trading S.A.; Cor-poración Backus y Johnston S.A.; Naviera Oriente S.A.C.; Transportes 77 S.A.

PRINCIPAL COMPETITOR

Compañía Cervecera AmBev Perú S.A.C.

FURTHER READING

Galloway, Jennifer, "Quenching Corporate Thirst," *LatinFinance,* December 2002, pp. 22–24, 26.

Hudson, Peter, "Cuidado, Mr. Backus!" *AméricaEconomía,* January 1996, pp. 24–26.

Lifsher, Marc, "Venezuelan Beer Moguls Fight to Control Peruvian Monopoly," *Wall Street Journal,* September 10, 2002, p. A11.

Sanchez, Luis Alberto, *Historia de una industria peruana: Cervecería Backus y Johnston S. A.* Lima: Cervecería Backus y Johnston, 1978.

Vera, Héctor, "Backus en la mira," *AméricaEconomía,* February 24, 2000, pp. 24–25, 27.

Vera Ramírez, Natalia, "Backus lidera guerra de las cervezas con el 91.3% del mercado nacional," *El Comercio del Perú,* April 5, 2007.

Specialty Contracting & Waste Management

Veit Companies

∎

14000 Veit Place
Rogers, Minnesota 55374
U.S.A.
Telephone: (763) 428-2242
Toll Free: (866) 428-2242
Fax: (763) 428-1334
Web site: http://www.veitcompanies.com

Private Company
Incorporated: 1928 as Veit & Company, Inc.
Employees: 500
Sales: $60 million (2007 est.)
NAIC: 235940 Wrecking and Demolition Contractors; 235930 Excavation Contractors; 562212 Solid Waste Landfills; 562219 Other Nonhazardous Waste Treatment and Disposal; 562211 Hazardous Waste Treatment and Disposal

∎ ∎ ∎

Veit Companies is the name applied to a set of privately owned businesses specializing in large scale earthwork, demolition, waste disposal, environmental abatement, and sewer reparation projects throughout the upper Midwest. Considered an industry leader in large-scale demolition and removal, Veit has completed contracts for numerous prominent projects, including the dismantling of civic arenas and sports stadiums and the destruction of some 150 Minuteman III missile silos in North Dakota under contract with the Army Corps of Engineers. In addition, Veit Disposal Systems boasts one of the largest roll-off container operations in the United States and provides sanitation services and recycling in key metropolitan areas of Minnesota. Veit offers unique capabilities, and typically is involved in projects from excavation, to driving piles, to final cleanup. The company prides itself on working in challenging conditions while maintaining an impressive safety and environmental record.

FROM FAMILY FARM TO FAMILY-RUN COMPANY

Few would have thought that in 1928, when Frank Veit began leasing his produce farm trucks to Hennepin County for their road construction projects, that this would mark the beginning of one of the largest excavating and demolition companies in the upper Midwest.

Frank Veit began Veit & Company, Inc., as a sideline to his produce farm. During the Great Depression of the 1930s the Veit family would supplement their income through lease agreements with Hennepin County, which encompassed Minneapolis and the western half of the Twin Cities metro area, for use of the family's equipment. Veit's corporate history, like the Veit family farm, was very much a family history as well.

In 1928, having purchased one Chevy dump truck specifically for construction work, Frank Veit founded the company. His son Arthur joined the operation in 1931. Arthur made Veit his life's work and began to acquire more equipment throughout the 1930s. These were primarily trucks, but in 1941 Arthur purchased the company's first excavating equipment and used it primarily for small residential and commercial development projects. The projects were local initially but as the

COMPANY PERSPECTIVES

Veit is one of the Midwest's leading specialty contracting and waste management companies. Got a tough project? Bring it on! Veit is a company of innovators and problem solvers. As customer advocates and project catalysts, we take pride in driving your project forward and helping you succeed. Through our two businesses, Specialty Contracting and Waste Management, we offer comprehensive services to general contractors and customers in private industry, municipalities, and local governments.

company grew so did the area that it served. Construction was at a peak in the following decade and Veit Companies (as it was eventually named), in addition to its new role in excavation, served the region by hauling construction equipment to job sites.

The expansion of the company led to a more permanent shop in Brooklyn Park, Minnesota, in 1946. In keeping with the conservative family ethic, many of the materials used in that construction were recycled from a demolition project with which the company was involved.

Coinciding with the rapid growth of the 1940s Veit made its focus the earthwork contracting needed to build subdivisions and the many municipal streets that line the northern suburbs of Minneapolis, Minnesota. With the Depression of the 1930s well out of the way and the economic expansion that followed World War II, Veit Companies grew steadily. The demand for new housing was spurred by a growing population and an overall sense of economic well-being.

In the mid-1950s Vaughn Veit, Arthur's only son, began to work for the company in the field. From general laborer, he moved up the ranks, experiencing most aspects of the company's operations. It was at this time that the company began to purchase equipment that had not been previously used in the area. The first was a Caterpillar rubber-tired loader that proved more efficient than the track loaders then commonly in use. In 1960 Veit purchased its first lowboy tractor and, in 1969, its first Caterpillar articulated loader, steps that would help position Veit as a company of choice for large excavating and demolition jobs in Minnesota.

In the 1950s and 1960s many of the downtown buildings in the Minneapolis and St. Paul area had begun to fall into disrepair. This was an era when new

construction, rather than restoration, appealed to city planners, and Veit was hired to demolish significant numbers of older buildings and warehouses dotting the cityscape.

Seven years after he had begun working in the family company, Vaughn Veit was given a management role, and then promoted to president of the company in 1966. In 1975 Arthur retired from his role as chairman and CEO and Vaughn bought the company. Vaughn's strategy was and continued to be one of expansion.

The growth of the Twin Cities metro area led many businesses to evaluate the placement of their company operation centers and Veit was no exception. In 1958 Veit had moved its shop to the northwest suburb of Osseo, building its first landfill operation there; then, in 1981, the company moved its headquarters further west to Rogers, Minnesota. Strategically located between the Twin Cities metro area and the city of St. Cloud, Veit was thus positioned to play a more significant role in the future of greater Minnesota and surrounding areas.

RAPID DIVERSIFICATION

In 1990 Don Rachel was appointed president of Veit Companies. Vaughn Veit remained as chairman and CEO, leaving many of the day-to-day operations to Rachel. Under the leadership of Vaughn Veit and Don Rachel, the company branched out into new areas related to its earthwork and demolition operations, creating a family of companies under the Veit logo.

In 1990 Vaughn Veit saw an opportunity for expansion and launched Veit Disposal Systems (VDS). VDS began with one truck and 30 container boxes and soon expanded to more than 45 trucks and 1,500 containers. In 1996 Veit grew its Twin Cities sanitation services with the addition of Disposal Systems, Inc.

In 1998, Veit continued the expansion of VDS with the acquisition of Adams Roll-Off Container in Rochester, Minnesota. This allowed Veit to enlarge its service area into the Rochester/Austin market, where Adams already had a large customer base.

Veit's disposal division grew substantially and was operating in the St. Paul/Minneapolis, St. Cloud, and Rochester/Austin sales areas. A new start-up operation in the Duluth/Superior area in 1999 began with two trucks and 60 boxes.

The increase in customers led the company to develop two new landfills. To keep up with demand, VDS opened landfills in Big Lake, Minnesota, in 1993, and Austin, Minnesota, in 1998. In addition to its waste disposal, VDS concentrated its efforts in recycling as well. At Veit's Rochester facility, recyclables were sorted

KEY DATES

1928: Frank Veit founds Veit & Company, Inc.

1931: Arthur Veit, Frank's son, joins the company.

1941: Arthur Veit purchases first excavating equipment.

1955: Vaughn Veit, Arthur's son, begins working at Veit Companies.

1966: Vaughn Veit takes over as president; Arthur remains as chairman and CEO.

1975: Arthur retires; Vaughn Veit purchases the company and becomes chairman and CEO.

1981: Company establishes new headquarters in Rogers, Minnesota.

1990: Company launches Veit Disposal Systems (VDS); Don Rachel is appointed president.

1999: Veit Environmental is created to provide asbestos, lead, and mold abatement services.

2002: Veit Foundation Division formed.

and compacted and then temporarily stored at the building. Veit took pride in its recycling record: "70% of construction/demolition debris," was, according to the company, "recycled or reduced with the remainder going to Veit's demolition debris landfill near Austin, Minnesota."

Veit, through its work on a series of demolition projects, gained a regional reputation for demolishing and clearing away antiquated sports stadiums. The Memorial Stadium at the University of Minnesota was the first notable sports facility that Veit tore down and disposed of. Then, in 1995, Veit razed the Metropolitan Stadium in Bloomington, which became home to the internationally known Mall of America. In 1999 the demolition of the St. Paul Civic Center with its River Centre Arena was also tackled by Veit. For this project, Veit was awarded contracts to tear down the Center, and to do the earthwork for the new Excel Energy Center, which would be home to the National Hockey League expansion team, the Minnesota Wild.

In 1998 Veit Companies began a $3.9 million earthwork project for the city of Minneapolis. The Minneapolis Water Works needed to expand its water reserves and called upon Veit to excavate a 40-million-gallon, 450-foot-by-432-foot reservoir on a hilltop site in New Brighton. The hilltop site was at the highest elevation in the Twin Cities metropolitan area, which in case of a water emergency would allow gravity to take the water to the city's customers. The completion of the

new water storage facility increased water supplies by 30 percent for well over half a million water works customers.

LARGER PROJECTS, GREATER CAPABILITIES

Although best known for its work with sports arenas, Veit in the late 1990s oversaw a broad spectrum of demolition jobs. On October 6, 1999, Veit began to fulfill a $12.1 million contract for the implosion of 150 Minuteman III missile silos just outside Langdon, North Dakota. This historic three-year project included the permanent destruction of the launch facilities and the standby power facilities connected to the silos. These underground control centers were imploded and the debris was buried and sealed with concrete slabs. Operating under the Strategic Arms Reduction Treaty (START), the Air Force had begun compliance with the treaty in 1994, moving the missiles from the silos near Langdon in 1995.

The completion of the Minuteman silo demolition was scheduled for the end of 2001, in compliance with the terms of the treaty. As with all of Veit's projects, large amounts of salvageable materials were hauled away to be recycled at Veit's demolition disposal site in Austin, Minnesota.

Veit Environmental first appeared under the Veit umbrella of companies in 1999. Due to a growing area of public health concern, Veit created its environmental agency to provide abatement services for problem materials such as asbestos, lead, and mold. Many public and private buildings still harbored such hazardous materials and the demand for services appeared to be expanding with what some epidemiologists interpreted as an increased environmental sensitivity in the population. Legislative enactments were leading to mandated removal of hazardous materials in public spaces and Veit predicted a lucrative future in the abatement industry.

Another growing field related to Veit's earthwork business was in the geotechnical arena, specifically in the construction and repair of storm sewers and water mains. Veit acquired Solidification, Inc., in the fall of 1999. Solidification, a specialty grouting and concrete plumbing company, had been operating in the Minneapolis/St. Paul area for over three decades. Making use of sophisticated developments in the area of robotics, Solidification used video components and robotic technology to repair damaged sewers and pipelines. These aging water systems were leaking and causing contamination to city water supplies and, in the case of sewer systems, contaminated ground water. Veit believed its acquisition of Solidification would capture a large market share of this growing industry.

In 2000 Veit began working on concurrent projects in downtown Minneapolis at the Conservatory, the old Minnegasco building, the Federal Reserve building, and the Old Milwaukee depot. Entering a new century, Veit continued as a well-recognized name in the construction and demolition industries. It was well diversified, having adapted to meet new opportunities for growth within its areas of expertise. Veit seemed well placed to be a strong competitor in its region, providing both equipment and services that would meet the challenges of some of the largest jobs the area had to offer. While there were many smaller contractors capable of providing services on a lesser scale, Veit stood out among its peers as a leader in both the range of services it could deliver and the magnitude of the jobs it was able to complete.

CONTINUED GROWTH IN 2001 AND BEYOND

The Veit Companies continued to grow in the first few years of the new millennium. Acquisitions extended Veit's geographic reach and increased market share. New, unique equipment helped differentiate the firm from its regional competitors.

Veit acquired W.G. Jaques, Inc., in 2000. This was a geotechnical construction business based in Des Moines. Two years later Jaques and Solidification were folded into the new Veit Foundation Division. Veit bought Minnesota's Viking Pipe Services in 2001.

While many of Veit's demolitions involved the recycling of materials, one job in February 2004 was perhaps more environmentally friendly than most. This involved the tearing down of an ice castle constructed for St. Paul's Winter Carnival. Veit carted away more than 300 truckloads of icy rubble. One of more than two-dozen contractors involved, Veit had also been responsible for excavating and grading the site.

In 2006 Veit was given an opportunity to demonstrate its environmental sensitivity. The firm was chosen to build a 5,120-foot boardwalk through northwestern Minnesota's Big Bog State Recreation Area. The spongy peat prevented the use of heavy equipment; the boardwalk was installed section by section to reduce ground damage.

The Veit Companies were involved in a number of urban renewal projects in the Twin Cities area. These included leveling factories such as Brockway Glass Company and Graco, Inc. Veit also removed several buildings at Minneapolis–St. Paul International Airport, and cleared away a 1960s vintage shopping mall called Apache Plaza. Among the biggest projects was demolition of a onetime Sears facility in south Minneapolis that covered three city blocks. In another major downtown project, demolition of the St. Paul Civic Center, Veit reported recycling 98 percent of the materials, noted *Construction Bulletin*.

Around the time of Veit's 75th anniversary in 2003, its disposal fleet included 2,000 containers—more than anyone else in Minnesota—and 45 roll-off trucks. Veit had signed up to distribute construction disposal containers built by Rebuild Resources, a local jobs program for people in recovery, whose motto was, "Let's build lives, not prisons." One of the more unique vehicles in the Veit fleet was a dump truck, acquired at an auction, that had been used to clear debris from the World Trade Center after the September 11, 2001, terrorist attacks.

Veit continued its tradition of introducing novel equipment to its home state by introducing Minnesota's first downhole hammer drill in 2005. This was used to install piles in solid rock. A few years later, Veit added the state's first high-reach backhoe, a unique piece of machinery that had been used more in Europe. Reaching more than 125 feet high, it could tear down tall structures in a more controlled way than a wrecking ball.

Other technical advances, such as GPS, made their way into Veit's construction operations. Wireless devices including mobile phones and two-way radios simplified life at sites lacking telecommunications infrastructure.

Veit introduced a new corporate logo in June 2006. Three months later, a tornado ravaged Rogers, Minnesota, including Veit's property. Naturally, the community in the wake of the destructive storm needed the firm's waste management capabilities.

Susan B. Culligan
Updated, Frederick C. Ingram

PRINCIPAL SUBSIDIARIES

Veit & Company, Inc.; Veit Companies, LLC; Veit Container Corporation; Veit Disposal Systems of Wisconsin, LLC; Veit Environmental, Inc.; Vcit Group, LLC; Veit Management, Inc.; Veit USA, Inc.

PRINCIPAL DIVISIONS

Veit Disposal Systems; Veit Foundation Group.

PRINCIPAL OPERATING UNITS

Rogers, Minnesota; Duluth, Minnesota; Rochester, Minnesota.

PRINCIPAL COMPETITORS

Carl Bolander & Sons Co.; Onyx Waste Services; Braun Intertec Corporation.

FURTHER READING

Bartemio, Nicholas, "The Wild Arrival; New Arena for the Minnesota Wild Hockey Team," *Demolition,* January/ February 1999.

Chang, Ivy, "Communications Increases Construction Productivity," *Construction Bulletin,* January 22, 2007, p. 6.

"End of an Era: Minuteman III Missile Silos Go Out with a Bang in North Dakota," *Construction Bulletin Magazine,* November 5, 1999.

"Growing from the Ground Up," *Veit Vibes,* Spring 2000.

Johnson, Brian, "Veit Cos. Fleet Include a Piece of Sept. 11 History," *Finance and Commerce Daily Newspaper* (Minn.), September 12, 2002.

"Masters of Demolition," *Construction Bulletin,* April 15, 2005, p. 14.

Parish, Richard, "Storming the Palace," *C&D Recycler,* May/ June 2004, pp. 40, 42.

Sanem, Jane, "Focus On: Veit Companies," *Associated General Contractors (AGC) of Minnesota Constructive Comment Newsletter Online,* Vol. 78, iss. 6, June 30, 2003, http:// www.agcmn.org/Documents/6-30-03.asp.

"Series III, Conquers Downtown Demolition," *Attachment Briefings,* Summer 1998.

"Site Preparation: The Campaign for Rebuild Academy Project Celebrates Actual Start of Construction at Blaine, Minn., Site," *Construction Bulletin Magazine,* January 16, 1998.

Thornley, Stew, "New Reservoir; Construction Actively Kicks into High Gear at the City of Minneapolis' Hilltop Reservoir Site," *Construction Bulletin Magazine,* May 15, 1998.

"Walkin' the (Board) Walk; Veit Companies Used Environmentally Conscious Construction Practices to Build a Mile-Long Boardwalk in the Big Bog State Recreation Area," *Construction Bulletin,* April 7, 2006, p. 4.

Volcan Compañia Minera S.A.A.

Avenida Gregorio Escobedo 710
Lima,
Peru
Telephone: (51 1) 219-4000
Fax: (51 1) 261-9716
Web site: http://www.volcan.co.pe

Public Company
Incorporated: 1943 as Volcan Mines Company
Employees: 2,657
Sales: PEN 2.35 billion ($738.5 million) (2006)
Stock Exchanges: Lima
Ticker Symbol: VCAN F
NAIC: 212222 Silver Ore Mining; 212231 Lead Ore and Zinc Ore Mining; 212234 Copper Ore and Nickel Ore Mining

■ ■ ■

Volcan Compañia Minera S.A.A., in terms of annual revenue, is one of the two largest Peruvian-owned mining companies in a country whose plentiful metal ores are chiefly exploited by enterprises based abroad and financed by foreign capital. The mining and processing of metal ores is Peru's largest industry, and the nation ranks among the top four world producers of the metals that Volcan extracts—copper, lead, silver and zinc—from its high altitude mines in the Andes Mountains of central Peru. Volcan is the largest producer in Peru of concentrates of zinc, lead, and silver. These are sent for refining in smelters owned by other companies.

CERRO DE PASCO: PERU'S RICHEST MINING AREA

The main mining area in Peru has historically been Cerro de Pasco, where metal deposits were discovered in 1630. A major expansion in production began in the 1780s. It was the main Peruvian mine throughout the 19th century, but the ore deposits containing silver had been largely depleted by 1900. Some of the largest and richest deposits of copper-bearing ore in the world remained, but to extract and reduce the ore would require a great deal of capital and technology, which was not available until the late 19th century, when centuries-old restrictions on foreign owned mining enterprises were lifted. In 1902 James Ben Ali Hoggin, who had struck it rich with the Homestake gold mine in South Dakota and the Anaconda copper mine of Butte, Montana, formed a syndicate that included financier J. P. Morgan and mining and industrial tycoon Henry Clay Frick. The syndicate, in turn, established the Cerro de Pasco Mining Company, which, by the end of 1904, had paid $2.65 million for 730 mining claims covering 5,900 acres in the Cerro de Pasco area. A railway was completed in that year, and a smelter was opened in 1906. Cerro de Pasco later bought more mining claims, built hydroelectric plants for needed power, and erected another railway and a cableway. The La Oroya smelter, Peru's largest, was completed in 1922.

Between 1906 and 1945 Cerro de Pasco accounted for 83 percent of all copper, 56 percent of all silver, and 29 percent of all gold produced in Peru. It had a controlling interest in almost every company engaged in mining and processing metals. By the late 1930s, however, the richest copper-yielding ores had been

KEY DATES

1942: Founding of Volcan Mines Company (later Volcan Compañia Minera).
1968: Volcan is earning a small profit on metal ores extracted from two mines.
1997: Volcan purchases the Mahr Túnel mining complex for $127.8 million.
1999: Purchase of another mine makes Volcan Peru's second largest zinc producer.
2000: Volcan acquires two more mines.
2001: The company acquires a group of hydroelectric power stations.
2003: Cash flow problems cause Volcan's production to drop 20 percent.
2006: Higher zinc prices and record production have restored Volcan to financial health.

depleted, and production consisted largely of cheaper lead and zinc. Because of the immense size of the remaining low-grade deposits and the high cost of exploiting them, the company began open pit mining on a massive scale in 1957. It had spun off the most important mining operations as the Southern Peru Copper Corporation, which became Peru's most important mining company, but Volcan would later gain title to some of the bounty that remained.

LOW-PROFILE VOLCAN: 1942–96

Leon James Rosenshine, a North American, founded Volcan Mines Leasing Company in Panama in 1935 and immediately created a subsidiary in Peru with $1,000 capital. The object was to explore and exploit various mines in the district and province of Yauli, department of Junín. The entry of the United States in World War II made possible long-term credits for this purpose and guaranteed high commodity prices for a number of years. Volcan Mines Company was founded in 1942 and began operations in the Ticlio mine, nearly 16,000 feet above sea level in the valley of Anticona, where the highest passenger railway in the world is located. Its mining activities expanded from there to the Carahuacra mine, southeast of Ticlio. Silver, lead, copper, and gold ores were extracted, but the company's main product was zinc. Volcan was one of several locally owned middle-level enterprises that were prospering by supplying Cerro de Pasco's giant La Oroya smelter with its concentrates—that is, the metal compounds that remain after they have been separated from waste rock. The

company also leased claims from Cerro de Pasco and depended on it for its power supplies.

Rosenshine began to sell his shares in Volcan during the 1950s, and his heirs continued to do the same, with control passing to Peruvian shareholders between 1965 and 1968. Among these was the Picasso group, which had owned small mines for a long time. The group's controlling interest was held by the Picasso Peralta family. Others involved in Volcan included the Rizo Patrón and Beltrán families. Volcan, in 1968, treated 219,000 metric tons of ore, converting it into 36,000 metric tons of zinc concentrate as well as lead concentrate and small yields of silver. The firm's net profit of 7.7 million soles that year (about $200,000) represented 5 percent of its total assets and about 7 percent of its sales. Analyzing these figures in his book *Metal-Mining in Peru*, W. F. C. Purser wrote, "In short, zinc mining, except on the large scale, is a risky business, and a dollar per ton pre-tax profit is rather light."

Volcan Hispanicized its name in 1975. Its gross sales came to $11 million in 1979, and its net sales to $14.3 million in 1986. It was publicly traded on the Lima stock exchange, but much of the stock remained in the hands of wealthy family groups. The Beltrán, Moreyra, and Letts families were represented by two directors each on the company's board.

Peru's mining sector underwent great change after an intensely nationalistic military government seized power in 1968. Cerro de Pasco's remaining properties were of lesser importance and declining profitability, so in 1972 it offered to sell out to Peru's government, which on the first day of 1974 nationalized the corporation for a payment of $58 million. It was turned over to a state body, Empresa Minera del Centro del Perú S.A. (Centromín Perú). However, this organization lacked the funds to modernize the facilities in order to improve productivity and compete with other suppliers in the world market. As Centromín Perú's debts and operating deficits piled up in the early 1990s, the government decided to privatize its facilities. Most of them were sold to foreign companies, but in 1997 Volcan purchased Empresa Minera Mahr Túnel S.A. for $127.8 million.

A MAJOR MINING PLAYER: 1997–2006

The Mahr Túnel purchase included two mines—San Cristóbal and Andaychagua to the south and southeast, respectively, of Carahuacra. They were opened in 1935 by Cerro de Pasco, which developed them as an integrated unit and constructed a tramway to carry the ore to a railway about seven miles away. The ore was then transported to a concentrator plant adjoining the

Mahr Túnel, a drainage tunnel built in 1937. The operation was closed as unprofitable in 1948 but reopened in 1955. The purchased Centromín complex also consisted of some 31,000 hectares (about 76,000 acres) of mining concessions. Volcan, despite having significantly increased its capacity to treat its ores in the early 1980s, was at the time of this purchase a "rundown and undercapitalized mining operation," according to Sally Bowen of the *Financial Times*. The company raised $22 million of the purchase price by issuing nonvoting shares of stock

In 1999 Volcan purchased Empresa Minera Paragsha S.A., another Centromín Perú property, for $61.8 million. It was the only bidder. Located to the north of the Mahr Túnel area on barren tundra in the district of Yanacancha, province and department of Cerro de Pasco, at about 4,300 meters (about 14,100 feet) above sea level, Paragsha—also called Cerro de Pasco for the city around it—was an open pit operation and Peru's most important source of zinc and lead. The property included a concentration plant built in 1941. Paragsha's sales came to about $105 million in 1998. The acquisition almost tripled Volcan's zinc production, making it the world's fifth largest zinc producer and the second largest in Peru. However, it brought with it environmental issues that required a commitment to invest $70 million in the enterprise over five years, and it was not clear how the company could finance it in the face of declining world zinc prices. Volcan's sales had totaled only $20 million in 1997 and $67 million in 1998, following the Mahr Túnel purchase.

These limitations did not dissuade Volcan from continuing to pursue a $300 million expansion that would double its production of metal concentrates to 600,000 metric tons a year. Despite low zinc prices at the time, the company remained focused on this metal. "Our goal is to be a world class zinc producer, and we are achieving that goal," Volcan's general manager told Lucien O. Chauvin for an article that appeared in *Latin Trade*. A British mining consultant told Chauvin, "The reserves are open-ended. We are drilling deep and wide and we have yet to find any indication of the end. There's great potential here to vastly increase profit."

During 2000 Volcan added two more mines by purchasing Empresa Administradora Chungar S.A.C. for $24.6 million and Empresa Explotadora de Vinchos Ltda. S.A.C., both of which became subsidiaries of Volcan. These acquisitions added the Aminón and Vinchos mines, located to the south and north of Paragsha, respectively. Chungar also had a 300-ton-per day plant and zinc concentrator, while the Vinchos property, whose mine had been worked since at least the 18th century, included a concentrator producing lead, copper,

and silver concentrates. Volcan ended the year with sales of $197 million. In 2001 Volcan acquired a group of hydroelectric power stations owned by Centromín and Banco Minero del Perú in order to improve Chungar's operations. Volcan's chief shareholders in that year were the Moreyra and Picasso groups and the Letts family. Roberto Letts Colmenares was chairman of the board in 2006.

The ambitious acquisition program raised Volcan's debt from $34 million at the end of 1997 to $141 million at the end of 2000. Besides the stock issue, it also issued bonds and lent money from Peruvian banks. In 2000 a syndicate headed by a German bank extended a $110 million credit over five years, including a two-year grace period, so that the company could restructure its short-term debts. As a result of the continuing decline of world zinc prices, Volcan lost nearly $22 million during 2000–01. In 2003 it signed a long-term agreement with Glencore International AG, a Swiss trading house that was operating two zinc mines farther to the west in Peru. In return for a $40 million, seven-year loan with a two-year grace period, Volcan agreed to sell part of its metal concentrate production to Glencore between 2004 and 2010. The infusion of cash enabled the company to make repairs and buy supplies after its output had fallen about 20 percent in 2003 because of its cash flow problems.

The subsequent increase in zinc prices restored Volcan to financial health. The bulk of its production continued to come from its zinc-producing mines, formerly owned by Centromín, in the Mahr Túnel area in the department of Junín, and the Cerro de Pasco, or Paragsha, mine in the department of the same name. The former area also yielded a significant amount of lead concentrates and smaller amounts of copper and silver concentrates. The Animón mine owned by Volcan's Chungar subsidiary was also a significant producer of zinc concentrates.

The year 2006 was the best in Volcan's history, yielding a net profit of about 30 percent of revenues. Production of zinc concentrates reached a record 551,139 metric tons. A new $120 million, five-year loan extended by a syndicate of banks in 2006 allowed the company to pay off the previous one. Volcan paid a dividend to its shareholders for the first time in four years. The following year promised to be even better. Volcan's annual revenue seemed certain to surpass $1 billion, and its net profit seemed likely to reach 30 percent of that amount. The company, which was trading on the Lima stock exchange (Bolsa de Lima) and Latibex, the Madrid stock exchange for Latin American companies, announced that it would also list its shares on the London and Santiago (Chile) stock exchanges.

Mining operations, as of 2006, were principally being realized in the subterranean mines of San Cristóbal, Andaychagua, and Chungar, and the subterranean and open cut mine of Carahuacra Paragsha, or Cerro de Pasco. Volcan's six treatment plants were Animón, Andaychagua, Mahr Túnel, Paragsha, San Expedito, and Victoria. By far the most important was Paragsha, followed, in amount of minerals treated, by Animón, Victoria, and Andaychagua. In 2007 Volcan owned 609 mining concessions totaling 156,593 hectares (about 387,000 acres) and six concentrator plants.

Robert Halasz

PRINCIPAL SUBSIDIARIES

Compañia Industria Ltda. De Huacho S.A. (93%); Empresa Administradora Chungar S.A.C.; Empresa Explotadora de Vinchos Ltda. S.A.C.; Empresa Minera Paragsha S.A.C.

PRINCIPAL OPERATING UNITS

Cerro de Pasco; Yauli.

PRINCIPAL COMPETITORS

Compañia de Minas Buenaventura S.A.A.; Compañia Minera Antamina S.A.; Compañia Minera Milpo S.A.; Empresa Minera Los Quenuales S.A.; Sociedad Minera El Brocal S.A.

FURTHER READING

Becker, David G., *The New Bourgeoisie and the Limits of Dependency: Mining, Class and Power in "Revolutionary" Peru,* Princeton, N.J.: Princeton University Press, 1983.

Bowen, Sally, "Only One Bid for Peruvian Zinc Mine," *Financial Times,* May 25, 1999, p. 32.

————, "Volcan Makes the Peruvian Zinc Big League," *Financial Times,* May 26, 1999, p. 36.

Chauvin, Lucien O., "Volcan Erupts in Peru," *Latin Trade,* February 2001, p. 41.

"Deal Expands Glencore Zinc Presence in Peru," *American Metal Market,* September 3, 2003, p. 5.

DeWind, Josh, *Peasants Become Miners,* New York: Garland, 1987.

Ferro, Raúl, "Asunto de tamaño," *AméricaEconomía,* October 7, 1999, pp. 26–27.

————, "El brillo del zinc," *AméricaEconomía,* June 14, 2001, pp. 30–31.

Malpica, Carlos Silva Santiestaban, *El poder económico en el Perú,* Lima: Ediciones Mosca Azul, 1989, Vol. 2, pp. 704–06.

Purser, W. F. C., *Metal-Mining in Peru, Past and Present,* New York: Praeger, 1971.

"Volcan Considers Diversifying into Other Metals," *Metal Bulletin,* November 27, 2000, p. 4.

"Volcan Looks for Partner with Know-How After Rapid Growth," *Metal Bulletin,* November 8, 2001, p. 5.

"Volcan Marks Gains After Deal with Glencore," *American Metal Market,* February 27, 2004.

Wagon plc

3500 Parkside
Birmingham Business Park
Birmingham, B37 7YG
United Kingdom
Telephone: (44 0121) 770 4030
Fax: (44 0121) 3295150
Web site: http://www.wagonplc.com

Public Company
Incorporated: 1918 as Wagon Repairs Company Ltd.
Employees: 6,649
Sales: £710 million ($1.44 billion) (2007)
Stock Exchanges: London
Ticker Symbol: WAGN
NAIC: 336399 All Other Motor Vehicle Parts Manufacturing; 336370 Motor Vehicle Metal Stamping

■ ■ ■

Birmingham, England–based Wagon plc is one of the leading European manufacturers of automotive body systems. The company operates through two primary divisions. The Structures and Closures division makes auto bodies and doors, among other mechanisms, and accounted for nearly 95 percent of the group's annual revenues of £710 million ($1.44 billion) in 2007. The Innovative Solutions division is engaged in engineering shading and glazing systems. The company maintains factories in the United Kingdom, France, Italy, Belgium, Germany, the United States, and the Czech Republic. The bulk of its annual revenues come from the European automotive market, with customers including most of the region's major automotive companies, especially PSA Peugeot-Citroën, Mercedes Benz, Fiat, Renault, and Ford. Wagon is listed on the London Stock Exchange and is led by Chairman Christopher Clark, who oversaw a restructuring plan in 2007 in order to successfully integrate the newly acquired Oxford Automotive, a major European producer of stampings and assemblies, as well as to respond to challenges in the fluctuating European auto market.

CONSOLIDATING THE BRITISH WAGON INDUSTRY IN 1918

Wagon plc was created following World War I when nine of the United Kingdom's leading railway wagon and rolling stock constructors and owners merged their repair operations. The nine groups (Birmingham Railway Carriage & Wagon Co.; British Wagon Co.; S.J. Claye; Harrison & Camm Ltd.; Gloucester Railway Carriage & Wagon Co.; Hurst, Nelson & Co.; Metropolitan-Cammell Carriage & Wagon Co.; Midland Railway-Carriage & Wagon; and North Central Wagon) had all grown strongly from the mid-19th century, as the Industrial Revolution spawned one of the world's most developed railroad systems.

Many of these companies were created in the 1840s and 1850s, as construction of the country's railroad system grew in tandem with the development of its coal mining industry. In the 1850s alone, the British railway system doubled in mileage. By the mid-1870s, the railway network had doubled again.

As England grew into the world's industrial powerhouse, the need to supply rolling stock for the railway network kept pace. By the turn of the century, a number of manufacturers had grown into national and even international prominence; at the same time, demand for rolling stock also stimulated the creation of companies focused on the ownership of wagons. The existence of such large numbers of railway wagons and rolling stock also prompted the growth of a wagon repair industry, with manufacturers and wagon owners developing their own repair works.

Wagon Repairs Company, as the new entity was called, took over the mandate of repairing, rebuilding, reconstructing, converting, equipping, and adapting the railway wagons and other vehicles manufactured and/or owned by its shareholder companies. As part of the creation of Wagon Repairs, the wagon companies transferred their repair works into the new company.

Wagon Repairs became something of a consolidator for the country's wagon repair sector. In 1925, Wagon Repairs added the repair business from two more wagon owners, R.Y. Pickering & Company, based in Scotland, and The Hamilton Wagon Company, based in Lanarkshire, in England. By 1930, the company added the repair business of Charles Roberts & Co., based in Wakefield, which also became one of its shareholders. Over the next three years, Wagon Repairs added the repair operations of C. Clough & Co., Lincoln Wagon & Engine Co., Yorkshire Railway Waggon Co., and W.R. Davies & Co. In 1933, Wagon Repairs also bought another wagon group, Wigan Wagon Company.

In the meantime, the British wagon industry had also been undergoing a consolidation. This process had begun as early as the turn of the century, with the creation of Metropolitan Amalgamated Railway Carriage and Wagon Company in 1902, formed through the merger of several Birmingham and Lancaster-based companies. Metropolitan, which was acquired by industrial giant Vickers in 1919, grew again in 1927,

with the purchase of Blake Boiler Wagon and Engineering Company in 1927. In the meantime, another company, Cammell Laird & Company, which launched its own rail wagon operations in 1919, took over the Midland Railway company and the Leeds Forge Company in the next decade. When Vickers took over Cammell Laird in 1929, it merged all of its wagon operations into Metropolitan, creating one of the world's largest wagon operation at the time.

As a result of the merger and acquisition activities of its parent companies, Wagon Repairs continued to expand its range of operations. By the mid-1930s, Wagon Repairs had built up a national network of 35 factories, where it produced replacement parts and components, along with 350 repair depots. The company's extension operations enabled it to offer its services beyond its founding shareholders. By 1936, when Wagon Repairs went public, the company was repairing more than 400,000 wagons each year. Only 25 percent of these were owned by its major shareholders.

CHANGE OF FOCUS IN THE POSTWAR ERA

By the start of World War II, Wagon Repairs could claim to be the single largest company of its kind anywhere in the world. Its vast resources played an important, if unsung, role in the British war effort, as the company's operations proved vital to ensuring the continued operations of the country's rail system. By the end of the war, the company had carried out repairs on more than 2.7 million wagons, including fully overhauling more than 300,000 of them. Still, the aftermath of the war was to have a dramatic impact on the company's operations.

The creation of British Railways and the subsequent nationalization of the British railroad system marked the beginning of the end of the Wagon Repairs core business. Over the next decades, British Railways gradually took over responsibility for its wagon repairs. As a result, Wagon Repairs was forced to seek new areas of operations in order to maintain itself as a going concern.

The need to diversify led Wagon into two new areas through the 1950s. The company first began acquiring operations producing office furniture. By 1951, the company had added a second line of business, the production of storage systems including pallets and related products, through its purchase of the Handy Angle Company. This business was subsequently complemented by a move into the retail storage market, as well as the creation of a materials handling wing. In 1969, Wagon added another business line, manufacturing railroad buffers, through the purchase of Oleo Pneumatics Ltd.

KEY DATES

1918: Wagon Repairs Company is created from several major British railway rolling stock manufacturers.

1936: Wagon Repairs goes public on London Stock Exchange.

1951: Company acquires office furniture group Handy Angle Company as part of diversification following nationalization of British railway system.

1974: Now known as Wagon Industries, company sells remaining repairs business in 1979.

1988: Company acquires Banro Industries and launches new focus on automotive components industry.

1998: Name is changed to Wagon plc.

2006: Company acquires Oxford Automotive operations in France, doubling in size.

The company's diversification efforts enabled it to achieve consistent growth in its profit levels into the 1970s. By then, the company's net profits had topped the £1 million mark. The company in the meantime had nearly achieved its full exit from its original business, transferring its remaining repairs business into a small subsidiary. In 1974, the company restructured its operations, placing them under a new holding company, Wagon Industrial Holdings Ltd. The wagon repairs business was finally sold in 1979. Once the world's largest railway wagon repair company, the remnants of Wagon Repairs sold for just £4.4 million.

ENTERING THE AUTOMOTIVE MARKET IN 1979

That year marked the beginnings of the group's activity in what was to become its core business by the turn of the 21st century, as Wagon turned its years of engineering expertise toward the automotive market for the first time. Specifically, Wagon sought to position itself as an innovative partner for the automotive industry, and the company became a pioneer in the production of aluminum-based automotive components in the early 1980s.

Nonetheless, throughout the 1980s Wagon's growth continued to be driven by its office equipment operations, as well as its materials handling business, which formed the bulk of the group's sales of £50 million in 1980 and the majority of its profits as well. The office

equipment division in particular enabled Wagon to gain experience on an international level, particularly in France, following the company's acquisition of French office furniture maker Vinco at the beginning of the decade.

By the end of the decade, Wagon's focus had turned more firmly toward the automotive market. This effort took a big leap forward with the 1988 acquisition of Banro Industries plc and its two main subsidiaries, Edward Rose Ltd. and Farnier Penin. That purchase provided Wagon with major automotive components manufacturing facilities in England and in France.

Following the Banro acquisition, Wagon sought to achieve critical mass for its automotive division and in 1989 completed a series of acquisitions including Polypal Europe, based in Belgium, and Permar, based in Spain. The company also added expertise in precision engineering through the acquisition of Paul Forkardt Group in Germany.

With its automotive division growing strongly, Wagon began the process of streamlining its operations through the 1990s, starting with the sell-off of its office furniture division in 1990. The group then launched a new series of small acquisitions, including Salter Springs and Pressings in 1993 for £2.4 million from Stavely Industries. By the end of 1994, Wagon had spent nearly £25 million in order to add nine more acquisitions.

Not all of the group's acquisitions came through its automotive division. The company also developed its retail systems, precision engineering, and storage divisions. Following a strategic review in 1997, however, the company opted to exit the retail systems sector and sold those operations.

AUTOMOTIVE FOCUS IN THE 21ST CENTURY

The company shortened its name to Wagon plc in 1998 and then targeted still more growth through acquisitions. The company added new factories in Germany and Belgium through its purchase of Ymos AG that year. At the same time, Wagon entered the Czech Republic, buying the former Skoda Pressworks in Bela.

Wagon continued to chip away at its increasingly noncore holdings. The company sold its precision engineering division in 1999. Despite continued growth in its storage systems operations, including the purchase of Netherlands-based Magista in 1998, the company finally shed that division as well in 2002.

In the meantime, the company had restructured its various automotive subsidiaries into a single company:

Wagon Automotive. That company continued to grow, adding France's Aries Industries Emboutissage and its seven French factories and one Italian factory in 1999. In 2000, Wagon purchased Hawtal Whiting Engineering Ltd., which including operations in the United States.

By 2004, Wagon had finalized its new strategy, refocusing the company entirely around its core automotive components and systems business. At the same time, the company confirmed its primary interest in working with the European automotive industry. The company had by then become a major partner for many of the continent's largest automakers. In 2003, for example, the company was awarded the contract to supply the body to the new Peugeot 307 CC. In this way, the company placed itself at the heart of a growing trend among European automakers to outsource production for many of their models' components. Other major customers for Wagon's components and systems included Honda, Ford, Range Rover, Jaguar, Fiat, Citroën, and Mercedes Benz, among many others.

Despite its focus on Europe, Wagon also began to develop outposts in the United States and in China, where it opened a factory in Shanghai. Meanwhile, in Europe the company expanded its range of expertise with the purchase of FKT GmbH, based in Germany, adding that company's operations in the development of automobile cargo systems, as well in developing sunblinds.

Wagon took a new step toward the top ranks of Europe's automotive components suppliers when it merged with Oxford Automotive, a producer of structural assemblies, parts and other metals-based automotive components, largely based in France. Initially a U.S. company, Oxford had gone into bankruptcy protection in 1995, before its European operations were bought by the Wilbur Ross investment group. The merger with Wagon was in the form of a reverse takeover, by which Wagon agreed to acquire Oxford in a deal worth £128 million ($250 million). Ross then took control of more than 53 percent of Wagon's shares. Following the merger, Wagon shed five of its pressings plants, including two plants in the United Kingdom, and three in France, which it sold to Sonas Automotive Ltd.

Following the integration of the Oxford operations, Wagon had doubled in size, with sales topping £700 million and a network of 23 factories in ten countries. The company had proved itself a remarkable survivor, having evolved from being a leading railway wagon repair specialist to one of Europe's top automotive components producers in the new century.

M. L. Cohen

PRINCIPAL SUBSIDIARIES

Endustri Ticaret Anonim Sirketi (Turkey); Oleo Buffers Shanghai Co., Ltd (China); Oxford Automotive France Douai S.A.; Oxford Automotive France Industries S.A.; Oxford Automotive France Paris S.A.; Oxford Automotive Mecanismes Champigny S.A. (France); Oxford Automotive Mecanismes Essomes SAS (France); Oxford Automotive Mecanismes SAS (France); Oxford Automotive Mecanismes St Pierre SAS (France); Oxford Mekanizma Metal Isleri Ve Montaj (Turkey); Wagon Automotive FKT GmbH (Germany); Wagon Automotive GmbH (Germany); Wagon Automotive Iberica SL (Spain); Wagon Automotive Inc. (United States); Wagon Automotive Innovative Solutions Shanghai Co., Ltd. (China); Wagon Automotive Nagold GmbH (Germany); Wagon Automotive S.A. (Belgium); Wagon Automotive SAS (France); Wagon Automotive Spol. Sro. (Czech Republic); Wagon Automotive srl (Italy); Wagon Industrial Ltd.; Wagon SAS (France).

PRINCIPAL DIVISIONS

Structures and Closures; Innovative Solutions.

PRINCIPAL COMPETITORS

Johnson Matthey plc; GKN plc; Smiths Group plc; Tomkins plc; McLaren Group Ltd.; TI Automotive Ltd.; UGC Ltd.; Johnson Controls Automotive (UK) Ltd.; IBC Vehicles Ltd.; ITT Industries Ltd.; Senior plc; Titan Europe plc; Alvis Ltd.

FURTHER READING

Chew, Edmund, "Lightweight Auto Bodies Drive Growth at Wagon," *Automotive News,* December 30, 2002, p. 16F.

Graham, Alex, "Wagon Uses New Plant to Attract More Niche Deals," *Automotive News Europe,* November 3, 2003, p. 7.

Griffin, Jon, "Pressing Deal Brings in Pounds 10m," *Birmingham Mail,* November 17, 2006, p. 81.

Saint-Seine, Sylviane de, "Wagon Gains on Oxford Tie Up," *Automotive News Europe,* April 17, 2006, p. 28.

"Wagon Industrial: Hit the Growth Trail," *Investors Chronicle,* August 25, 1995, p. 34.

"Wagon's Role," *Manufacturer,* January 2003.

Wingett, Steven, "Wagon Gives Citroen C4 Picasso an Open Feel," *Automotive News Europe,* January 22, 2007, p. 20.

Western Digital Corporation

8105 Irvine Center Drive
Irvine, California 92618
U.S.A.
Telephone: (714) 932-5000
Fax: (714) 932-6629
Web site: http://www.wdc.com

Public Company
Incorporated: 1971
Employees: 29,572
Sales: $5.47 billion (2007)
Stock Exchanges: New York
Ticker Symbol: WDC
NAIC: 334290 Other Communication Equipment
Manufacturing

■■■

Western Digital Corporation is one of the world's leading developers and manufacturers of data storage solutions for the computer and other industries. The company has been a pioneering force in the development of internal and external hard drives for desktops, laptops, and other computer applications, in both the original equipment manufacturers (OEM) and retail sectors. While the desktop hard-drive market remains the company's largest source of revenues, accounting for more than 55 percent of its 2007 revenues of $5.47 billion, the company has successfully expanded its data storage technologies to a number of nontraditional markets, such as the launch of a range of branded products, including the My Book line of external data

storage appliances, hard drives for the Xbox game consoles, and digital video storage drives.

The company's branded sales have grown strongly, accounting for more than 16 percent of its sales in 2007. Western Digital remains at the forefront of hard-drive technologies—in 2007, the company debuted a line of GreenPower low-energy consuming hard drives, as well as a hard-drive system capable of storing up to two terabytes of data. Western Digital operates manufacturing facilities in California, Malaysia, and Thailand, and sales and distribution subsidiaries throughout much of the world. The company is listed on the New York Stock Exchange, and is led by President and CEO John F. Coyne.

THE EARLY YEARS

The invention of the computer microprocessor and all that followed is surely matchless in the history of U.S. manufacturing. The computer industry is loaded with sweeping epics like that of the rise and tumble of Steven Jobs and Apple Computer, but the Western Digital saga is reasonably serene. While Western Digital miscalculated the evolutionary direction of the computer industry on several occasions, it has always managed to recover and to maintain a significant presence.

In 1970, Western Digital began producing special semiconductors in its incarnation as Emerson Electric Company of St. Louis. Based in Santa Ana, California, the company was financially backed by the Emerson Electric Company of St. Louis and various other independent investors. A year later, the Western Digital appellation was born and headquarters were shifted to

COMPANY PERSPECTIVES

Our business strategy to efficiently produce reliable, high-quality hard drives for a growing, worldwide market continues. This approach distinguishes us in a competitive industry. It also provides value to our customers and allows us to achieve consistent financial performance. With this proven approach, we aim to hold and build our leadership position in traditional markets and grow our presence in newer markets.

Newport Beach, California. Alvin B. Phillips was the founder and president of Western Digital from its inception until 1976. His technical experience in semiconductors was a critical element of the early formation of the company. The most important company event of the 1970s was the manufacture of a 4K RAM chip. Technological breakthroughs multiplied exponentially in this period.

The 1980s proved to be the least predictable period of growth in the electronics/computer industry. The company underestimated the importance of IBM's PC/XT and its related floppy drives and interfaces. However, in 1983, Western Digital engineers produced a wire-wrapped prototype of a hard-drive controller for IBM's PC/AT in only 14 days. Western Digital then elected to concentrate its attention on supplying components for the newly developed personal computer (PC) market.

Of the innovations that President and Chief of Operations Roger W. Johnson brought to Western Digital in the early 1980s, nurturing a stable of engineering innovators was one of the most important. Within four years of Johnson's start, sales doubled and earnings grew to $21 million. Among the achievements at Western Digital in the early 1980s was the first Winchester disk drive controller in 1982. Almost 90 percent of Western Digital's income was coming from storage controller products by 1985. The company was one of the first to choose to provide controllers to the preeminent PC manufacturers, such as IBM, Compaq, Hewlett-Packard, and Tandy, thus positioning it for later successes and perhaps foreshadowing Western Digital's later partnership with IBM.

EXPANSION AND NEW DIRECTIONS

By the mid-1980s, Western Digital was in the position to acquire new business and start off in new directions.

The Massachusetts Institute of Technology worked in concert with Western Digital to develop the "Nu machine," an artificial intelligence computer later sold to Texas Instruments. Another result of this hybrid team was the "Nu bus," designed to open Macintosh buses to peripherals. Macintosh had developed several of their own versions of this product, but the "Nu bus" was chosen over all of them.

The late 1980s brought Kathryn Braun into the administrative spotlight in the Personal Storage Division, and the decisions she made would affect the future success of the company profoundly. In a time of fiscal strength for Western Digital, Braun recommended that the company focus on supplying hard disk storage to OEMs—such as IBM and its compatibles. By acquiring Tandon drive manufacturers at this time, Western Digital gained a foothold in this growing sector. In Singapore, the Western Digital team labored to convert Tandon's production line into a smoother and more profitably run facility. Braun succeeded in increasing her division's annual income from $15 million to more than $2 billion.

Western Digital went on to buy several other smaller peripheral manufacturers, such as Adaptive Data Systems, Paradise, and Verticom. These companies provided Western Digital with key components to diversify and expand. In 1988, Western Digital became a *Fortune* 500 company. Two years later, the silicon wafer fabrication facility was opened in Irvine, California, and corporate headquarters, Irvine Spectrum, also transferred to Irvine.

CHALLENGES IN THE NEXT DECADE

The early 1990s saw many changes for the worse at Western Digital, reflecting the woes of the computer industry at large. The company reported that large-scale layoffs, financial write-offs, and debt restructure were necessary to keep Western Digital afloat. A recession similarly affected many other U.S. markets. Charles A. Haggarty was hired at Western Digital in 1992, having come from IBM. At Western Digital, he filled a variety of executive management needs. In 1993, he was first elected director, then chairman, and then chief executive officer of the company. At IBM, his Rochester, Minnesota, storage products team had won the Malcolm Baldrige National Quality Award in 1990. His years of OEM storage expertise were put to good use at Western Digital.

Under Haggarty's leadership, Western Digital was weaned from stand-alone memory storage to integrated disk drive storage. Western Digital fabricated the first

KEY DATES

1970: Semiconductor production division of Emerson Electric Company in California is founded.

1971: Semiconductor division of Emerson Electric becomes Western Digital.

1982: Launch of first Winchester disk drive controller.

1988: Data storage division is formed, and Tandon is acquired.

2003: Company acquires one of its primary parts suppliers, buying bankrupt Read-Rite Corporation.

2007: My Book data storage appliance line is launched.

two-platter, 3.5-inch, 340-megabyte drive in 1993. A year later, the first 3.5-inch, 1-gigabyte, 3-platter Enhanced Integrated Drive Electronic (IDE) drive was produced, otherwise known as a hard-drive interface. An Enhanced IDE drive was faster, had more expansion options, and handled more material. By 1995, Western Digital's IDE storage capacity was increased by another half gigabyte. These products were members of the well-received Caviar family of hard drives, which were found in Apples, Bull-Zeniths, Compaqs, Gateway 2000s, NECs, IBMs, and many other PCs.

In 1994, Western Digital was proud to announce that it had become the first U.S.-headquartered, multinational company to be awarded ISO 9001 status by the International Standards Organization. The ISO 9001 status linked all of Western Digital's operations with a global standard for high-quality processes.

While Western Digital's revenues increased steadily in the late 1990s, it was still experiencing an industry-wide slump based on increased competition, overproduction of drives that moldered in warehouses while inventory values declined, and a struggle to keep up with rapidly advancing technology.

One of Western Digital's sources of technological weakness was the lack of giant magnetoresistive (GMR) research advancement. The GMR technology was based on the property of certain magnetic materials that increase electrical resistance when exposed to a magnetic field. The resulting sensors are extraordinarily sensitive, making it possible to store enormous amounts of data in the disk. It was speculated that this technology could

eventually make chip memory storage obsolete. IBM's research scientists announced that they had fit "more than 11.6 billion bits of data in one square inch on the surface of a rotating magnetic disk," according to a February 1998 issue of the *New York Times.*

The disastrous declines in Asian markets near the end of the 1990s hurt U.S. technology revenues in general, and compounded Western Digital's woes. Not only did Western Digital manufacture drives in the East, but it also sold 10 to 15 percent of those drives there, before selling the remainder in the United States. The declining values of Asian currency had at least one benefit—however temporary—for Western Digital: "Sales in Asia have fallen, but profits are rising," the *New York Times* reported in late 1997. "The disk drives are sold in dollars, while the manufacturing costs are incurred in the weakening Asian currencies." It was predicted that inflation would eventually correct this phenomenon, but Western Digital enjoyed it while it lasted.

Western Digital's struggle to keep up, technology-wise, led industry experts to speculate that the company was perfect for purchase in 1998. The *Orange County Business Journal* quoted David Takata, an analyst with Gruntal & Co., in February 1998: "One of the reasons people are speculating about IBM buying a desktop drive company like Western Digital [is that] IBM would gain manufacturing expertise and Western Digital would gain R&D talent." Takata speculated that Haggarty's previous relationship with IBM might smooth the way for a takeover. As the situation developed, however, market researcher Jim Porter of Disk/Trend, Inc., had a different outlook: "My take on the management out there is they would rather do it themselves. I can't imagine Chuck [Haggarty] going back to work for IBM."

Instead of a takeover, IBM and Western Digital entered into an agreement to work together for the very reasons Porter cited. Haggarty told his board of directors that the move was a "major step in changing the game," according to a Western Digital press release. "Last fall we rolled up our sleeves, did a lot of soul searching and seriously examined our business model. We concluded that pursuing a significantly expanded relationship with IBM ... was in the best interests of our company, our employees and shareholders." Haggarty went on to detail the advantages of the agreement, and to emphasize the enthusiasm of company officers in both companies.

Concern had been raised in late 1997 among Western Digital shareholders that the company had misrepresented its assets, and that losses were not taken in a timely fashion. A class-action suit was announced against Western Digital on February 2, 1998, alleging that some key insiders had manipulated financial numbers to their benefit, while the average stockholder took a loss. The New York law firm of Stull, Stull & Brody represented what one source called a "handful" of plaintiffs, while Western Digital denied all charges against it.

Western Digital had indeed sustained hard financial blows late in 1997; the company went from debt-free to $513.1 million in debt between December 27, 1997, and March 28, 1998. While Western Digital stock went as high as 54.75 and split at 44 in 1997, it had yet to regain its original value a year later, going as low as 14.5. Funding was tight, and Western Digital raised money the old-fashioned way: they sold $400 million of zero coupon convertible subordinated debentures. The *Dow Jones Newswires* reported on February 12, 1998, that Western Digital "intends to use the net proceeds of the offering for general corporate purposes." A month before, the company had broken ground on a new manufacturing facility in San Jose, California. Meanwhile in Rochester, Minnesota, the new Enterprise Storage Group's headquarters were in the process of being built. The new research and development facility was planned to include a clean room, administrative and engineering offices, and design laboratories.

Western Digital took special measures to recover its financial equilibrium. In mid-1998, the company entered into a special partnership agreement whereby IBM would share its areal-density GMR heads with Western Digital, and IBM in turn would have a foothold in the PC peripherals market.

SURVIVOR IN THE NEW CENTURY

Western Digital continued to suffer from the massive oversupply of the hard-drive market into the end of the decade. Worse for the company, the oversupply of the market was forcing prices down. The company attempted to offset its reliance in that sector with a thrust into new product areas, including software development, launching a high-end drive unit, and developing video image storage systems, investing over $100 million in order to diversify its operations. In the meantime, the company continued to suffer from major revenue losses, as hard-drive prices dropped by some 45 percent by the end of the decade.

In 1999, the already fragile Western Digital faced a new problem after it discovered that it had shipped out more than 400,000 hard drives—to Dell and other major computer makers—with defective chips. The company was forced to recall and replace the drives. The losses involved in the recall were exacerbated by the damage done to the company's reputation. Over the

next two years, the company's sales continued to fall, dropping by more than $1.2 billion.

In response, Western Digital named Matt Massengill, then serving as co-COO, to take up the chief executive officer's job. Massengill launched the company on a restructuring, selling its diversified operations, and shutting down two factories in Singapore to refocus its manufacturing base on its Malaysian factory.

Refocused on its core hard-drive operations, Western Digital recognized the potential of adapting its existing technology and formats for a newly emerging market of hard disk–based home entertainment products. This effort paid off when the company was picked to supply the new Xbox game console system developed by Microsoft as a rival to the Sony PlayStation. From this success, the company also emerged as a major supplier of hard drives for the new generation of digital video recording systems, such as TIVO. At the same time, the company, which had remained focused on the larger desktop sector, also developed the technology to enter the fast-growing laptop market. Western Digital also made strives in its core hard-drive technology, launching a 10,000 rpm drive in 2003.

By then, while the rest of the high technology industry continued to struggle through the effects of a collapse in the global market, Western Digital had shed its years of losses. The company acquired one of its primary parts suppliers in 2003, buying bankrupt Read-Rite Corp. for $95.4 million. The purchase gave the company production facilities in Thailand. The acquisition of Read-Rite also gave the company control over the production of the read-write heads needed for its hard drives.

Western Digital profited from the surge in the sales in laptops at mid-decade, selling more than one million of its 2.5 mobile drives in the first quarter of 2005 alone. The company's early positioning in the non-PC hard-drive market also enabled it to become a major supplier to this market, selling more than 2.5 million hard drives for the personal and digital video recorder segment. At the same time, the company prepared to expand its range of products, developing drives for such uses as cell phones, portable music devices, digital cameras, and the like. By 2007, the company had also debuted its innovative line of My Book data storage appliances.

Western Digital had not only survived the high-technology shakeup of the early years of the new century, it had successfully reduced its reliance on its core computer hard disk operations by repositioning itself as a diversified manufacturer of data storage solutions for a variety of applications. With revenues of nearly $5.5 billion in its 2007 fiscal year, Western Digital claimed a market share of more than 16 percent.

Christine L. Ferran
Updated, M. L. Cohen

PRINCIPAL SUBSIDIARIES

Read-Rite (Malaysia) Sdn. Bhd; Read-Rite International (Cayman Islands); Read-Rite Philippines, Inc.; Western Digital (Deutschland) GmbH; Western Digital (France) SARL; Western Digital (Fremont) LLC; Western Digital (Malaysia) Sdn. Bhd.; Western Digital (S.E. Asia) Pte Ltd.; Western Digital (Thailand) Company Ltd.; Western Digital (U.K.) Ltd.; Western Digital Canada Corporation; Western Digital Hong Kong Ltd.; Western Digital Ireland, Ltd.; Western Digital Japan Ltd.; Western Digital Korea, Ltd.; Western Digital Latin America, Inc.; Western Digital Netherlands B.V.; Western Digital Taiwan Co., Ltd.; Western Digital Technologies, Inc.; Western Digital Ventures, Inc.

PRINCIPAL COMPETITORS

Seagate Technology, Inc.; Fujitsu Corporation; Samsung Corporation.

FURTHER READING

"Applied Magnetics Down; IBM-Western Dig Deal Hurts Outlook," *Dow Jones Newswires*, May 5, 1998.

Grimes, Christopher, "Disk Drives' Woes Continues in 1Q; Slow Recovery Seen," *Dow Jones Newswires*, April 13, 1998.

Markoff, John, "Crowding Even More Data into Even Smaller Spaces," *New York Times*, February 23, 1998.

"Rumors Rife of Western Digital Takeover by IBM," *Orange County Business Journal*, February 23–March 1, 1998, p. 1.

"Technology Brief—Western Digital Corp.: Quarterly Loss Is Posted as Charges Are Recorded," *Wall Street Journal*, January 30, 1998.

Twenty-Five Years of Innovation: The History of Western Digital, Irvine, Calif.: Western Digital Corp., 1995, 10 p.

Uchitelle, Louis, "Dimming Economies of Asia Cast Shadows on U.S. Firms," *New York Times*, December 14, 1997.

"Western Digital Begins Construction on R&D Center," *Dow Jones Newswires*, May 22, 1998.

"Western Digital Boosts Conv Sub Deb Offering to $400M," *Dow Jones Newswires*, February 12, 1998.

"Western Digital Breaks New Ground," *Business Journal Serving San Jose & Silicon Valley*, January 26, 1998, p. 58.

Writers Guild of America, West, Inc.

———————— ■ ————————

7000 West Third Street
Los Angeles, California 90048
U.S.A.
Telephone: (323) 951-4000
Toll Free: (800) 548-4532
Fax: (323) 782-4800
Web site: http://www.wga.org

Union
Founded: 1920 as The Writers Club
Employees: 160
Sales: $22.3 million (2006)
NAIC: 813930 Labor Unions and Similar Labor Organizations

■ ■ ■

Based in Los Angeles, California, Writers Guild of America, West, Inc. (WGAW), is a labor union representing more than 9,500 members, who write for movies, television shows, animation, documentaries, news programs, CD-ROMS, and new-media content. WGAW represents members in contract negotiations and enforcement and determines credits on WGA-covered projects. The guild also provides members with health insurance and a pension plan.

To gain membership in WGAW, writers must accumulate 24 "units" within a three-year period from companies that have signed the Guild's collective bargaining agreement. Sale of a feature-length screenplay, for example, earns a writer 24 units and immediate eligibility to WGAW. Applicants must then pay a $2,500 initial fee, and ongoing dues of 1.5 percent of gross earnings. WGAW also maintains a registry to protect writers from plagiarism, receiving more than 50,000 written works each year. WGAW is affiliated with Writers Guild of America, East. The sister organizations administer the Writers Guild of America Awards. Unlike WGAE, WGAW is not part of the AFL-CIO but is a member of the International Affiliation of Writers Guilds. It is run by a 16-member board of directors.

WRITERS BAND TOGETHER IN THE EARLY 20TH CENTURY

The roots of WGAW reach back to the early 20th century when in 1912 the Authors League of America was formed, its membership mostly comprised of book and magazine writers as well as a few playwrights. In 1921 the playwrights, with their own unique needs, branched off to form the Dramatists Guild within the Authors League, and in turn the Authors Guild was formed to represent book and magazine writers, leaving the Leagues as the parent body of both guilds. During this period writers, many of them League members, had also begun to migrate to the West Coast to work in the fledgling motion picture industry, which at the time was a silent medium but still required the services of writers to develop scenarios and on-screen dialogue.

In 1920 they also formed an organization, the Writers Club, which became part of the Authors League as a screenwriters subsidiary of the Dramatists Guild. As the name suggested, the Club was little more than a social organization in a town very much opposed to unions.

Hollywood moguls were not interested in sharing power and sought to head off unionization in 1927 by forming the Academy of Motion Picture Arts and Sciences to cover writers, actors, directors, producers, and technicians. Although better known today for administering the Academy Awards, this organization was little more than a studio-controlled company union. For - years the Academy succeeded in scuttling any attempts at labor organizing in the motion picture industry. That would change in 1933, however, when Franklin Roosevelt was sworn in as president and began implementing his promised "New Deal," which included improved conditions for unionization.

In February 1933 ten film writers met at the Hollywood Knickerbocker Hotel to discuss how they could improve conditions for writers. They included John Howard Lawson and Lester Cole, politically radical members of New York's New Playwrights Theater; former advertising executive turned playwright Samson Raphaelson, whose play *The Jazz Singer* was filmed as the first "talkie"; former Chicago newspaperman John Bright and his writing partner Kubec Glasmon, the two men responsible for writing *The Public Enemy;* Edwin Justus Mayer, a friend of F. Scott Fitzgerald; and Louis Weitzenkorn, former editor of the *Socialist Call* and writer of the play *Five Star Final*. The other participants were writers Brian Marlow, Bertram Block, and Courtenay Terrett. They decided to revamp the Writers Club by seeking control of the charter from the Dramatists Guild. A month later the studios implemented a wage cut that provided incentive to the writers and the Writers Club was reorganized as the Screen Writers Guild of the Authors League of America with 173 charter members, most of them under 30 years of age, many under 25. John Howard Lawson was named the Guild's first president, and the organization was incorporated as a nonprofit corporation and the constitution and bylaws rewritten.

RIVAL UNION VANQUISHED: 1938

The studios were not about to accept the Guild without a fight, of course, and attempted to revive the writers'

branch of the Academy. The Guild responded by drawing up an amalgamation plan with the Authors League and Dramatists Guild to in effect control virtually all material available for the screen. Many writers, a large number of whom were studio friendly, then split off from the Guild in May 1936 to form Screen Playwrights, Inc. It was led by Rupert Hughes, uncle of Howard Hughes. The two organizations became bitter enemies, and following the 1937 U.S. Supreme Court ruling that Roosevelt's National Labor Relations Act, which established the right for unions to collectively bargain was constitutional, they battled to gain the right to negotiate for Hollywood writers. In June 1938 the Screen Writers Guild triumphed in Labor Relations Board elections at 13 Hollywood studios, putting an end to the Screen Playwrights, which had enjoyed the tacit support of the studios (having reached a five-year basic agreement with eight major studios) and, according to the *New York Times,* "charged the Guild with being an agent of Moscow and dedicated to spreading communism."

With no choice, the studios began negotiations with the Guild in 1939. A year later the producers formally recognized the Guild as the collective bargaining agent for writers, and in June 1941 a contract was accepted in principle, although not finalized until 1942. The deal called for minimum pay of $125 per week for all writers (the Guild had asked for $150), and the Guild gained control of screen credits.

Following World War II and the rise of the Cold War between the Western powers and the Soviet Union and its satellites, concerns that communism had infiltrated Hollywood turned into hysteria. The House Un-American Activities Committee summoned a number of writers, actors, directors, and others who were suspected of having been members of the American Communist Party to Washington, D.C., to give testimony in the fall of 1947. Nineteen of them were deemed unfriendly witnesses because they indicated they would refuse to give testimony. Of these, eleven were called, and one, playwright Bertolt Brecht, ultimately testified and promptly fled the country. Ten others, the infamous "Hollywood Ten," refused to admit whether they had ever been members of the party and some attempted to read statements condemning the unconstitutionality of the proceedings. They were ultimately accused of contempt of Congress, convicted, and served one-year prison sentences. The ten included WGA members Alvah Bessie, Lester Cole, Ring Lardner, Jr., John Howard Lawson, Albert Maltz, Samuel Ornitz, Adrian Scott, and Dalton Trumbo. After their release from prison they were blacklisted by the studios, as were others who were named by cooperating witnesses or whose anticommunist bona fides were considered insuf-

---

KEY DATES

1920: The Writers Club formed in Hollywood.

1933: Writers Club is reorganized as Screen Writers Guild.

1938: Guild wins right to collectively bargain for screenwriters.

1942: First studio contract ratified.

1954: Reorganizations of writing unions leads to creation of Writers Guild of America, West, and Writers Guild of America, East.

1960: Guild strike lasts five months.

1988: Strike costs entertainment industry $500 million.

2007: WGA launches first industry-wide strike in nearly 20 years.

---

ficient during the 1950s. Others who refused to cooperate were fired by the studios. WGA was one of several Hollywood unions that failed to support blacklisted members during this dark period of the 1950s. Many of the blacklisted continued to write through "fronts," and it was not until a half-century later that the WGA attempted to make amends by giving credits for projects written by blacklisted writers.

While Hollywood dealt with the implications of life during a Cold War, it also had to contend with the postwar rise of television, much of which at first was broadcast live from New York. The Authors League formed the Television Writers Group, and a group of New York writers formed their own group, Television Writers of America, which was quick to file with the National Labor Relations Board to bargain on behalf of writers. With television shows also being filmed in Hollywood, it was natural that the Screen Writers Guild should also form a television wing. The situation was clearly too unwieldy, and the heads of the various groups began meeting, resulting in a reorganization of the various writers' organizations in 1954. Two new groups emerged, WGAW based in Los Angeles and WGAE based in New York, the Mississippi River serving as a geographic boundary for the affiliated groups. The Authors League retained the Authors Guild and Dramatists Guild, whose members owned their copyrights and leased their material, making them not eligible for protection by the National Labor Relations Act. The Guilds then filed for a new election to represent television writers and after they won certification the Television Writers of America disbanded. At

first WGAW maintained two branches, the Screen Branch and TV-Radio Branch. In 1973 they were merged into a single branch.

The increasing popularity of television created a number of new issues for WGAW to negotiate. A strike against the television networks was averted in 1956 when a contract was signed that ran until 1960. The sticking points were separation of rights for writers and nonexclusivity of services. As a result, there was no distinction drawn between writers working on a single television series and those assigned to multiple series, and writers hired on an exclusive basis were guaranteed a minimum amount of work. The deal was in line with what had already been negotiated with the television production units of the major studios and included rerun payments. However, reruns were just the beginning of the ancillary payments from television the Guild would begin to seek for its members. The studios were already leasing or selling movies to satisfy television's appetite for programming but writers were denied a share of these new revenues. Moreover, in the late 1950s WGAW began lobbying for payments for future "pay-TV" profits, whether they came from subscription television or closed-circuit television. The worry at the time was that writers would not share in the revenues of movies shown to paying video audiences, not just on advertised-support television.

The question of movies shown on television was at the heart of a strike that began in January 1960 after WGAW and the studios failed to reach agreement on a new contract. The strike was not settled until June when the studios agreed to pay $600,000 into the Guild's health, pension, and welfare funds as well as 5 percent of income received on pre-1960 films. For post-1960 films writers were to receive 2 percent of television income but no additional payments if the films were shown on pay-television. The Guild was also successful in shifting writer compensation from a residual formula to a royalty system.

Although Guild members were ready to walk out when contract negotiations stalled in both 1963 and 1966, strikes were averted at the last minute in both cases. The 1963 contract merely postponed the question of salary until the next round of negotiations. The television writers received some pay increases in 1966 and the studios agreed to let them return to a residual formula, because, according to the *New York Times*, "the world market for TV reruns had been 'glutted' and that the increasing use of motion pictures on television had reduced the rerun market in this country." Thus, 4 percent television royalties were traded for fixed residuals.

In 1973 the Guild sought greater wage increases from the major television and movie producers and this time the writers did go on strike in March of that year. The walkout lasted 16½ weeks and led to significant increases in payments but far from the amount the Guild had been seeking. For example, a one-hour prime-time television script increased from $4,500 to $6,000, but the Guild had wanted $12,000. Also growing out of the 1973 strike were supplemental market payments and the creation of the WGAW Health Fund. Later in the 1970s the Guild won TV residuals in perpetuity, eliminating the ten-run cap on residual payments to writers.

LONGEST STRIKE SETTLED: 1988

Guild members walked the picket lines once again in April 1981. Areas of contention involved the growing home television market that included cable television as well as video disks and cassettes. A settlement was quickly reached with independent producers, but negotiations with the major studios continued until July when the 13-week strike came to an end after a revenue formula was found for the home video market. The Guild voted to strike again in 1985, but the ranks were not especially committed and the strike ended after just two weeks with the Guild essentially caving in. The 9,000-member WGAW was far more militant three years later, however. A strike lasted one day longer than the 1960 stoppage, stretching from March 7 to August 7, 1988, delaying the start of the next television season and costing the entertainment industry an estimated $500 million. The main point of contention were foreign residual television payments. The new contract provided writers with a chance to earn 1.2 percent of a program's gross foreign earnings after a revenues threshold was met. The writers also won concessions from producers that increased their access to film sets, the right to comment on casting, and a chance to review the director's cut, provisions that did not sit well with the Directors Guild. According to the *New York Times,* however, the "strike was generally seen as a defeat for the guild, with no major issues resolved."

The 1980s also saw the Guild finding common cause with similar organizations in other English-speaking countries: the United Kingdom, Canada, Australia, and New Zealand. In 1985 they formed the International Affiliation of Writers Guilds to serve the needs of their members who were operating in a world of media consolidation and globalization. Under the terms of the affiliation, a member of one guild who traveled to work in the jurisdiction of another would be automatically transferred to the local guild, which could better protect that member's rights.

The 1990s were a time of relative peace for the WGAW. At the start of the decade WGAW and the Directors Guild tried to mend strained relationships between their memberships, drawing up a "creative rights understanding." The suggested practices included the two unions refraining "from making collective bargaining proposals in the creative rights area that contravene the other's agreements or interfere with the authority of the writer or director in the creative process." In addition, the Guilds agreed to share collective bargaining proposals before presenting them to the producers. The 1990s also saw the WGAW taking steps to exorcize the ghost of the 1950s' communist witch hunt era, awarding writing credits to members of the Hollywood Ten and other blacklisted writers. The decade also brought satellite television and expanding cable television systems as well as the emergence of the Internet, which opened up new ways to distribute and profit from film entertainment content.

Hollywood was poised for a WGAW strike in 2001, residuals serving again as the bone of contention, this time related to reruns on cable TV or works sold in video and overseas markets. The old contract expired but a strike was averted when an agreement was reached three days later. When that contract expired three years later in 2004 the Guild again avoided a walkout, but it did not win increases in residual payments, setting the stage for a showdown in 2007 when the latest contract expired on October 31. Most of the 26 demands of WGAW and WGAE centered on increased residuals for writers on content that was distributed digitally, via computers and mobile devices. A federal mediator was brought into the talks, but the two sides were unable to reach an agreement and in the early morning hours of November 5, 2007, the members of WGAW and WGAE launched the first industry-wide strike in nearly 20 years.

Ed Dinger

PRINCIPAL SUBSIDIARIES

The Writers Guild Foundation.

FURTHER READING

Albiniak, Paige, "Silver Lining in WGA Strike?" *Broadcasting & Cable,* October 29, 2007, p. 11.

Bart, Peter, "Accord on Coast Averts TV Strike," *New York Times,* June 16, 1966.

Cieply, Michael, "Screenwriters Begin Strike As Negotiations Continue," *New York Times,* November 5, 2007, p. A20.

Harmetz, Aljean, "Movie and TV Writers, Rejecting 'Final' Offer, Take to Picket Lines," *New York Times,* March 8, 1988, p. C13.

————, "Writers Ratify Contract, Ending Longest Strike," *New York Times,* August 8, 1988, p. C15.

Kahn, Gordon, *Hollywood on Trial,* New York: Boni & Gaer, Inc., 1948, 229 p.

Lippman, John, "Writer's Tentative Accord with Studios Sets Tone for Negotiations of Performers," *Wall Street Journal,* May 7, 2001, p. A2.

"Pact Ratified, Writers Return," *New York Times,* July 16, 1981, p. C20.

Pryor, Thomas M., "Screen Writers Back New Union," *New York Times,* May 21, 1954.

Reinhold, Robert, "Screen Writers and Directors Reach Pact," *New York Times,* January 25, 1990.

Schumach, Murray, "Screen Writers and 7 Studios Settle Strike Begun on Jan. 16," *New York Times,* June 11, 1960.

Schwartz, Nancy Lynn, *The Hollywood Writers' Wars,* New York: Alfred A. Knopf, Inc., 1981, 334 p.

"Screen Guild Wins Labor Board Vote," *New York Times,* August 10, 1938.

Weinraub, Bernard, "The Blacklist Era Won't Fade to Black," *New York Times,* October 5, 1997, p. 4.

"Writers Guild Strikes Major Producers on Coast," *New York Times,* March 7, 1973.

Yarnell Ice Cream Company, Inc.

205 South Spring Street
Searcy, Arkansas 72143
U.S.A.
Telephone: (501) 268-2414
Web site: http://www.yarnells.com

Private Company
Incorporated: 1932
Employees: 175
Sales: $51.8 million (2006 est.)
NAIC: 311520 Ice Cream and Frozen Dessert Manufacturing

∎ ∎ ∎

Yarnell Ice Cream Company, Inc., is a private company based in Searcy, Arkansas, the manufacturer of Yarnell's Premium Ice Cream and other frozen desserts. About 20 flavors of ice cream are available in half-gallon containers, including the standard vanilla, chocolate, and strawberry, as well as such flavors as Ozark Black Walnut, Peanut Butter Trax, Rocky Road, Sonic Cherry Limeade, and other seasonal and specialty flavors. The "super regional" company also sells a dozen flavors in pint containers. Other products include four flavors of sherbet, five flavors of frozen yogurt, and a dozen flavors of Yarnell's Guilt Free, no-fat, no-sugar frozen treat. Novelties include ice cream sandwiches, ice cream bars, fudge bars, and Strawberry Cheesecake Cups. Yarnell also offers a custom-manufacturing program, providing clients with research and development and packaging development capabilities.

As the only ice cream company in Arkansas, Yarnell dominates its home market and also serves Mississippi and parts of other neighboring states: the eastern corner of Tennessee, the southwest tip of Kentucky, bands of southern Missouri, western Oklahoma, and northern Louisiana, and a small incursion into northeast Texas. Yarnell also manufactures and distributes ice cream under the Angel Food brand and has distribution relationships with Häagen-Dazs, Nestlé, and Dreyer's/Edy's. In addition, the company exports ice cream to Russia through a relationship with an Arkansas food distributor. To ensure quality, the company delivers directly to supermarket freezer cases through its staff of route salespeople. All production is done at the Searcy plant, its seven production lines capable of producing 16 million gallons of ice cream and other treats each year.

PREDECESSOR COMPANY FOUNDED 1923

Yarnell grew out of the Grisham Ice Cream Company, founded in Searcy in 1923 by Ben Grisham. With additional plants in McGehee and Morrilton, Arkansas, it sold the Angel Food Ice Cream brand, which was different from the softer ice cream product of the day because of a hardening room that relied on an ammonia freezing system rather than the usual ice and salt. In 1927 Grisham merged with Terry Dairy Co., adding four more Arkansas plants located in El Dorado, Hot Springs, Little Rock, and Newport. Ben Grisham served as general manager of the enlarged enterprise and to help him as assistant manager he hired Ray Albert Yarnell, who had been working at a Searcy hardware store. The

Yarnell family had first come to the area from Tennessee in 1858 when 24-year-old William Andrew Harrison Yarnell arrived by steamboat in hopes of teaching school but instead became a merchant.

Two years after the Grisham and Terry merger, the business was sold to Southwest Dairy Products. Yarnell stayed on, becoming manager of the Hot Springs and Camden plants. Due to the Great Depression, Southwest Dairy soon went bankrupt and Yarnell took advantage of the situation in 1932 to acquire the company's Searcy ice cream plant. He scraped together the purchase price, borrowing money on his life insurance policy as well as from his wife's family who owned some real estate, but about a year would pass before a final purchase price was set. In the meantime, Yarnell operated the plant as the Yarnell Ice Cream Company, ending the year with an inventory of 333 gallons of ice cream worth less than $1,000. He barely managed to survive the winter months when sales were negligible. Yarnell drew no salary and went deeper in debt to keep the company running. His wife Hallie kept the books, and his son Albert helped out by serving as a bagger and delivering ice cream on his bicycle.

Yarnell managed to hang on and slowly built up the business, reinvesting whatever profits he made into the company, such as with the purchase of the company's first electrically refrigerated truck in the late 1930s, which replaced trucks with sides that had to be filled with ice and salt. There was no shortage of challenges in the early years. Defense spending resulting from World War II brought an end to the Depression but it also led to the rationing of commodities that Yarnell Ice Cream needed, such as sugar to make ice cream, and gas and tires the trucks required to deliver the product. Moreover, in 1943 much of the Searcy plant was damaged when faulty wiring led to an attic fire.

The end of the war brought an end to rationing, allowing Yarnell Ice Cream to begin a growth spurt. The postwar years would also see Albert Yarnell joining the company on a full-time basis. After graduating from high school in 1941 he attended the Kemper Military Academy before serving a three-year stint in the Army Signal Corp, half of which was spent fighting the Japanese in the China-Burma-India theater. Upon his discharge he returned home to study dairy technology at the University of Missouri. He then went to work at the family business in 1948 as a sales manager, and two years later was named vice-president of operations. In this capacity he oversaw the company's first major plant expansion in 1951, including a new mix-making facility. With increased production capacity, Yarnell Ice Cream was able to expand its sales territory, spreading throughout central and south Arkansas.

FOUNDER DIES: 1974

Albert Yarnell became general manager of the company in 1960 and in March 1974 became president and chief executive officer after his father died at the age of 77. By this time Yarnell Ice Cream was doing more than $1 million in business each year, having topped that mark for the first time in 1970. A year after Ray Yarnell's death, a third generation of the family became involved in running the business. Albert's son, Rogers Yarnell, after graduating from the University of Arkansas, had considered a career in the military, serving in Europe in the Army before deciding to return home to work with his father. In 1985 he would become president and CEO while his father stayed on as chairman of the board.

When Albert Yarnell had gone to work for his own father, there were nearly 50 Arkansas ice cream manufacturers. A commitment to quality gave Yarnell Ice Cream an edge, and steadily the competition fell by the wayside, eventually leaving Yarnell as the only ice cream manufacturer in the state. The company continued to add to its production capacity, allowing it to increase its sales territory to include all of Arkansas and spread into adjacent states. Part of the company's success was also due to innovation. In 1978 it introduced the United States' first all-natural ice milk product in response to the increasing health consciousness of consumers.

Eleven years later the ice milk product was replaced with a 95 percent fat-free Premium Lite ice cream. A year after that, 1990, the company added a 98 percent fat-free Low Fat Frozen Yogurt line of products, as well as a nonfat cholesterol-free frozen yogurt. Then, in 1991, Yarnell introduced the industry's first fat-free ice cream using NutraSweet, sold under the Guilt Free label. Two years later the Guilt Free line was expanded to include a frozen yogurt product. In the meantime, Yarnell's sherbet was upgraded and reintroduced as Yarnell's FrostiFruit, a 99 percent fat-free product supplemented by fruit chunks. Also during this period, Yarnell added to its novelty ice cream products lines. In 1990 it introduced a nonfat fudge bar sweetened with NutraSweet and a no-sugar version of the chocolate-

To meet increasing demand for its branded products and contract manufacturing, Yarnell launched the largest expansion program to date in its history. Completed in 1995, the project doubled the Searcy plant's production and cold storage facilities. Extra hardening capacity was especially in need, a problem solved by the installation of a multilevel hardening system. Because it employed multiple levels that allowed three different types of products to be carried through the blast freezer at different speeds simultaneously, it replaced three hardening units.

With added capacity, Yarnell was able to supplement its Guilt Free product line, and add low-fat ice cream sandwiches and Guilt Free Sorbet in 1996. The following year the company debuted its Yarnell's Homemade line of premium ice cream. At the same time, the company revamped the premium ice cream line with new package graphics. In 1998 Yarnell's Premium Light ice cream, offering half the fat of the premium product, was introduced. The company closed out the 1990s by beefing up its advertising budget to launch four new premium flavors: Blackberry Cobbler, Cotton Candy, Hog Heaven, and Homemade Apple Pie.

coated ice cream Pal Bar. In 1993 the Guilt Free label was also applied to ice cream bars and fudge bars. The brand provided industry-wide recognition for Yarnell, which looked to license the Guilt Free name to other manufacturers in other territories. A major step in this direction came in early 1994 when Yarnell awarded an exclusive license to manufacture and market nonfat and low-fat dairy and other foods products under the Guilt Free name to Dean Foods Company.

While Yarnell was building up the Guilt Free name, it did not neglect its premium ice cream, frozen yogurt, or frozen novelty lines. Its delivery trucks also distributed Häagen-Dazs, Healthy Choice, FrozFruit, and partner brands such as Snickers. Moreover, Yarnell pursued other opportunities, perhaps none more unlikely than the idea posed to Rogers Yarnell by a Little Rock attorney, S. Graham Catlett. The founder of Quality Products International, distributor of U.S. food products into Russia, Catlett suggested that Yarnell consider selling ice cream in the heart of the former Soviet Union through his company. Yarnell agreed and soon his company was doing a tidy, if not surprising, business in Russia, a country that previously had little more to offer than a bland rendition of vanilla ice cream. Russian consumers were delighted with the exotic Yarnell flavors and willingly paid $6 per half-gallon, and the company was pleased with the condition of the product that made its way to Russian freezer cases.

NEW CENTURY BRINGS PLANT EXPANSION

Enjoying steady growth, Yarnell expanded its plant once again at the start of the new century, adding 56,000 square feet to accommodate a pair of new frozen treat lines, able to turn out nearly 500,000 items a day. The additional novelty capacity would be put to use in 2002 when the company introduced three new Guilt Free novelty items: Fruit Bars, Chocolate Decadence Sundae cups, and Strawberry Cheesecake Sundae cups. To meet the rising interest in low-carbohydrate diets, Yarnell in 2003 reformulated its Guilt Free line to lower its carbohydrate content, resulting in the Guilt Free CarbAware label.

The new century also brought the fourth generation of the Yarnell family to the leadership ranks. After graduating from Vanderbilt University in 2000, Christina Yarnell, daughter of Rogers Yarnell, joined the company full time, serving formally as treasurer of the corporation but also heavily involved in product development. She also played a key role in the company's "Pink Promise" campaign in 2007, which dedicated Yarnell's 75th anniversary to the fight against breast cancer, which had personally touched the family: her mother was a breast cancer survivor. The company teamed up with the Arkansas chapter of the Susan G. Komen Foundation, pledging five cents for every carton sold of three limited-edition ice cream flavors: Chocolate Caramel Celebration, a combination of chocolate ice cream, caramel ribbon, caramel-filled chocolate stars, and chocolate chunks; Anniversary Cake, white cake flavored ice cream with cake pieces and a black raspberry ribbon; and the campaign's signature flavor, Pink Promise, a mix of strawberry and raspberry ice cream accented by a lemon flavoring.

In 2006 Yarnell acquired the Angel Food ice cream brand from Memphis, Tennessee–based Klinke Brothers Ice Cream Company, which elected to concentrate on its chain of Baskin-Robbins stores. Yarnell assumed all manufacturing, distribution, and promotion of Angel Food ice cream, a popular brand in Tennessee, Mississippi, and southwest Kentucky. The Yarnell family appeared well positioned for continued prosperity, but remained cautiously optimistic. "There are no guarantees for any of us," Rogers Yarnell told *Arkansas Times.* "We're in a mature business that's consolidating, but I feel strongly that we'll make 100 years. I feel comfortable that our management team and the customer base is one that will allow us to survive when others haven't."

Ed Dinger

PRINCIPAL BRANDS

Angel Food Ice Cream; Yarnell's Premium Ice Cream; Guilt Free.

PRINCIPAL COMPETITORS

Blue Bell Creameries, L.P.; Unilever.

FURTHER READING

"Albert R. Yarnell: Chairman Yarnell Ice Cream Co., Searcy, Arkansas," *Arkansas Business,* January 29, 2007, p. S18.

"Beat the Odds," *Food and Drink,* March–April 2005, p. 108.

Cottingham, Jan, "Yarnell's: 75 Years and Going Strong," Arkansasbusiness.com, July 30, 2007.

"Dean Foods Gets License for 'Guilt Free' Products," *Frozen Food Age,* March 1994, p. 56.

Hendricks, Nancy, "Yarnell Ice Cream Company," *The Encyclopedia of Arkansas History & Culture,* http://www.encyclopediaofarkansas.net.

Reiter, Jeff, "Sweet Times in Searcy: With Guilt Free, Yarnell Ice Cream Co. Is Finding Success Where Others Have Not," *Dairy Foods,* September 1993, p. 33.

"The Scoop: Arkansas Beats Texas," *Arkansas Times,* July 26, 2007.

Zanett, Inc.

———■———

635 Madison Avenue, 15th Floor
New York, New York 10022
U.S.A.
Telephone: (646) 502-1800
Fax: (646) 502-1808
Web site: http://www.zanett.com

Public Company
Incorporated: 1992 as BAB Holdings, Inc.
Employees: 194
Sales: $45.3 million
Stock Exchanges: NASDAQ
Ticker Symbol: ZANE
NAIC: 541990 All Other Professional, Scientific, and
    Technical Services

■ ■ ■

Zanett, Inc., is a New York City–based information technology company operating in two business segments: Commercial Solutions and Government Solutions. The company refers to their combined efforts as "The IT Commonwealth," a term it has chosen to trademark. On the commercial side, Zanett serves *Fortune* 500 corporations as well as mid-market companies, providing such services as network design, systems integration, e-business systems implementation, supply chain management, and consulting. The company's government unit focuses on homeland defense and homeland security agencies, primarily offering software and satellite engineering services. While Zanett is a public company listed on the NASDAQ, it

is majority-owned by Cofounder, Chairman, and Chief Executive Officer Claudio M. Guazzoni, who holds a 56 percent stake. His uncle, Bruno Guazzoni, owns a 29 percent interest, leaving very little of Zanett not in the hands of the Guazzoni family.

CORPORATION HISTORY DATES TO 1992

The history of Zanett, Inc., is the tale of two companies. It was originally formed in Illinois in November 1992 as BAB Holdings, Inc., to house the assets of the Big Apple Bagels chain of shops. BAB Holdings, Inc., was founded by partners Michael Evans and Paul Stolzer, the latter a native New Yorker who gave up a career in risk management in the mid-1980s to open a bagel shop. In the 1990s he and Evans launched Chicago-based Big Apple Bagels to become a consolidator in the bagel field, which was highly fragmented and considered to possess a great deal of untapped potential as many Americans were just becoming familiar with an item that had traditionally been limited to major East Coast cities. They would not be alone in drawing this conclusion, and several other companies pursued a similar strategy.

In November 1995 BAB, Inc., was taken public in an initial offering of stock that raised less than $7 million. By early 1996 the Big Apple Bagels chain grew to 80 units in 14 states, a large percentage of them located in Illinois and most of them franchised operations. The company grew through acquisition, adding other smaller bagel chains and branching out by acquiring the My Favorite Muffin chain of bakery shops and Brewster's Coffee Company to provide gourmet

COMPANY PERSPECTIVES

We strive to attract entrepreneur-led profitable IT Service shops that currently are not for sale. These are the "best of the best," with an enviable reputation amongst their peers in their particular segments of industry.

coffees for both the bagel and muffin operations. While the Big Apple chain grew to more than 260 units by the end of the 1990s, the American appetite for bagels was not as great as many had hoped, the bagel sector was overpopulated, and BAB, Inc., lost about $3.5 million in fiscal 1999. The stores began offering eggs and regular sandwiches on regular bread in hopes of luring in customers through the day and evening instead of early mornings. Management also looked for opportunities to bring in some money in another, more unusual manner, by essentially selling its NASDAQ listing to a company called Planet Zanett Corporate Incubator, Inc.

The men behind the Planet Zanett name were Claudio Guazzoni and David M. McCarthy, who in 1993 founded Zanett Securities Corporation in New York City. The son of nuclear physicists who immigrated to the United States from Italy at the age of 16, Guazzoni started out as a photographer after completing his studies in economics and comparative literature. Disillusioned with the field he decided to pursue a career in investment banking, acting on a suggestion by a friend who recognized that Guazzoni's ability to speak six languages made him a valuable asset to a financial institution. He became a trainee at Salomon Brothers in the bond department in the mid-1980s, and worked in London for the government bond department. He then went to work for a leveraged buyout firm and then struck out on his own. His cofounder of Zanett Securities, McCarthy, graduated from the University of Massachusetts, became a derivatives trader and then a risk arbitrage professional at European American Corporation. Zanett Securities focused on privately placed equity investments in public companies involved in emerging new technologies: Internet, wireless, optical, and telecom. Some of the firm's notable success stories included Robotic Visions Systems, Inc.; SmartServe Online; YouthStream Media, Inc.; and FiberNet Telecom Group, Inc.

Guazzoni and McCarthy formed Planet Zanett Corporate Incubator, Inc., to provide financial, managerial, and other support services to affiliate companies,

which were early-stage Internet-related companies in which Zanett Securities had made investments. This corporate shell was originally incorporated in Nevada as Willow Bay Associates, LLC, and took the Planet Zanett name in June 2000. The company prepared to merge with BAB Holdings in a deal that would give Planet Zanett a NASDAQ listing and the parent company for Big Apple Bagels a 10 percent stake in Planet Zanett. After the transaction was completed, BAB, Inc., was spun off and its shares were traded on the Over-the-Counter Bulletin Board.

PLANET ZANETT BEGINS OPERATIONS: 2000

BAB Holdings began doing business under the Planet Zanett, Inc., name in October 2000, setting up shop in 1,000 square feet of space leased from Zanett Securities with McCarthy serving as CEO and Guazzoni as president. It was not long, however, before Planet Zanett experienced a change in strategy. Because of a downturn in the market, in early 2001 a number of information technology (IT) companies became available at attractive prices. Guazzoni and McCarthy decided that rather than use Planet Zanett as a service provider to start-ups it would become a consolidator of established IT companies. A review of affiliate companies was conducted to determine which ones were viable enough to become part of Planet Zanett's new IT Commonwealth strategy. Not making the cut were such ventures as World Wide Web Institute, Inc.; Failsafe.com, Inc.; IJE, Inc.; and RecruitmentBox.com. The four companies that were kept to become part of the Commonwealth were: GlobeDrive.Com, a software company involved in the field of secure virtual private networks operating over the Internet; Fanlink Networks, Inc., a software company that was developing a wireless in-seat ordering system for food and souvenirs at stadiums, arenas, and concert venues; InfoDream Corporation, a software company devoted to bringing web browser capabilities to corporate intranets; and Applied Discovery, Inc., an electronic document discovery service for lawyers.

Planet Zanett's first acquisition after its shift in strategy came in December 2001 when it acquired Needham, Massachusetts–based Back Bay Technologies, Inc., a four-year-old technology consulting firm that served blue-chip corporate clients in the New England market by providing strategic planning, analysis, vendor selection, systems architecture, systems integration, and support services. The next addition to the Commonwealth was made in May 2001 with the acquisition of Brandywine Computer Group, Inc., a Cincinnati, Ohio–area technology consulting company founded in 1997 to help corporate clients with the implementation

KEY DATES

1992: BAB Holdings, Inc., formed for Big Apple Bagels chain.
1995: Company taken public.
2000: Planet Zanett Corporate Incubator assumes BAB's NASDAQ listing through merger.
2002: Company named changed to Zanett, Inc.
2005: Zanett Commercial Solutions formed.

of enterprise resource planning (ERP), supply chain management, and customer relationship management systems. In October 2002 the Planet Zanett Corporate Incubator name was formally dropped in favor of Zanett, Inc. Revenues for the year totaled $10.5 million and the company posted a net loss of about $1 million.

Two more acquisitions were completed in 2003. In January Zanett paid $4.8 million for Paragon Dynamics, an Englewood, Colorado–based contractor that provided software and satellite engineering services to the U.S. military and *Fortune* 500 aerospace companies. Near the end of 2003 Zanett acquired Delta Communications Group, an Aliso Viejo, California–based voice and data communications network integrator serving government agencies as well as major corporations.

Zanett turned a profit of more than $1.2 million on revenues of $17 million in 2003. To grow the business further one acquisition was made in 2004, completed in April. Brandywine added the ERP consulting group of INRANGE Global Consulting, based in Indianapolis with an office in Mason, Ohio. The ERP offerings of Brandywine and INRANGE were combined under the INRANGE Consulting banner. To fund further acquisitions, Zanett also arranged for new sources of financing in 2004. In September a $5 million loan was obtained from Fifth Third Bank. This was followed in December by a filing for a public offering of Renewable Unsecured Subordinated Notes, which became effective in February 2005 and raised nearly $2.5 million over the course of the year.

Although Zanett increased revenues to more than $25 million in 2004, the company recorded a net loss of about $250,000. While the government side of the business was doing well at this juncture, the same could not be said for the commercial, due in large part to consolidation within the IT industry. PeopleSoft had become a consolidator in its field, acquiring JD Edwards and Siebel Systems before adding Oracle, Inc. Many of Zanett's customers took a wait-and-see attitude,

postponing IT projects or canceling them altogether while they waited to see what direction Oracle would take with its collection of three disparate platforms. In late 2004 Zanett tried to anticipate a shift in strategy on Oracle's part, and in March 2005 acquired Whitbread Technology Partners, Inc., a Stoneham, Massachusetts–based consulting firm whose field of expertise was Oracle ERP systems. Once Oracle announced its plans to combine the software code of its platforms, Zanett responded by merging its Back Bay, INRANGE, and Whitbread operations to create a new wholly owned subsidiary, Zanett Commercial Solutions, Inc., the goal being to achieve economies of scale and position the company better to exploit the evolving commercial ERP segment.

MCCARTHY STEPS DOWN: 2006

Uncertainty in the market hurt Zanett, which increased sales to $34.9 million in 2005 but suffered a net loss of $13.2 million in 2005. Zanett took several steps to bring improvements in 2006. A number of strategic initiatives were developed, including an effort to trim corporate overhead expenses by at least 30 percent. The company also looked to target government sector acquisitions, especially in the growing homeland defense area. On the commercial side, Zanett sought acquisitions that could bring greater depth to its Oracle business, both in terms of service offerings and geography. This refocusing effort also brought a change at the top ranks of the company. Guazzoni was elected chairman of the board and then replaced David McCarthy as the company's chief executive. The presidency was then awarded to Jack Rapport, the company's former chief financial officer. Zanett's controller, Ken DeRobertis, was then promoted to CFO.

Three months after the shakeup, Zanett completed the acquisition of Data Road, Inc., in a cash and stock transaction. Based in Jacksonville, Florida, Data Road was an Oracle services consulting firm doing about $5 million in business each year, specializing in managed services. The deal not only broadened Zanett's service offerings and brought additional blue chip customers into the fold; it helped the company increase its national reach.

The consolidation of the commercial business quickly paid dividends in 2006, as synergies between the different units resulted in a significant increase in business. The government sector, on the other hand, experienced a dip in sales. All told, revenues grew to more than $45.2 million and Zanett cut its net loss for the year to less than $1.8 million.

The company's government sector received a major boost in early 2007 when it received a portion of a $45 billion contract from the U.S. Department of Homeland Security. As a result, the price of Zanett stock more than doubled. On the commercial side, Zanett in March 2007 acquired DBA Group, LLC, an Alpharetta, Georgia–based provider of database management services, a move that bolstered Zanett's database service offerings. In operation for just five years, Zanett appeared to be poised to enjoy strong growth in the years to come.

Ed Dinger

PRINCIPAL SUBSIDIARIES

Back Bay Technologies, Inc.; INRANGE Consulting Corporation; Paragon Dynamics, Inc.; Delta Communications Group, Inc.

PRINCIPAL COMPETITORS

Accenture Ltd; Akamai Technologies, Inc.; Electronic Data Systems Corporation.

FURTHER READING

"Big Apple Bagels," *Restaurants & Institutions,* February 15, 1996, p. 58.

Murphy, H. Lee, "Eggs Part of BAB's Plan to Rouse Sales," *Crain's Chicago Business,* October 2, 2000, p. 69.

Schwager, Jack D., *Stock Wizards,* New York: HarperCollins, 2001.

Walkup, Carolyn, "Big Bagel Seeks 'New Life,'" *Nation's Restaurant News,* September 18, 2000, p. 4.

Zipcar, Inc.

25 1st Street, Floor 4
Cambridge, Massachusetts 02141
U.S.A.
Telephone: (617) 995-4231
Fax: (617) 995-4300
Web site: http://www.zipcar.com

Private Company
Incorporated: 2000
Sales: $30 million (2006 est.)
NAIC: 423110 Automobile and Other Mobile Vehicle
Merchant Wholesalers

■ ■ ■

Maintaining its headquarters in Cambridge, Massachusetts, Zipcar, Inc., is the United States' leading car-sharing company, serving about 180,000 consumer and business drivers. The privately held company maintains a fleet of more than 5,000 cars, which members can rent by the hour or the day, the price including insurance and gas. Zipcar operates in 50 cities in North America, including Atlanta, Boston, Chicago, New York, Philadelphia, San Francisco, Seattle, Toronto, Vancouver, and Washington, D.C. Zipcar also maintains a hub in London, England. Cars are parked throughout a city, and members reserve them online or by phone, gaining access to the vehicles with "Zipcards" that use radio-frequency identification (RFID) technology that allows data to be transmitted from the vehicles to the company's reservation system via a Cingular Wireless connection.

Zipcar's fleet is comprised of 25 different makes and models, including SUVs, pickup trucks, high-end cars, and gas/electric hybrids such as the Toyota Prius. In addition to major cities, Zipcar provides car-sharing services to more than 50 universities, and has partnered with apartment property owners to provide residents with Zipcar memberships and in some cases to make parking spaces available for Zipcar vehicles, creating on-site car sharing. The company also serves businesses through its Zipcar for Business program, which has allowed many companies, such as PricewaterhouseCoopers, to save money by eliminating fleets of underutilized vehicles. In the same vein, many consumer Zipcar members have also sold their vehicles because Zipcar serves their needs in a more cost effective manner. According to the company, each Zipcar replaces 20 privately owned vehicles, thus easing urban congestion while lessening the harmful impact of vehicle emissions on the environment.

CAR SHARING: POSTWAR ROOTS

The idea of car sharing began to take shape in Europe in the late 1940s following World War II as a way for people to contend with high gas prices, a scarcity of vehicles, and difficult economic conditions as the continent began to rebuild. The idea of car sharing regained interest in the late 1980s when a number of crowded European communities began forming car-sharing organizations as a way to cut back on individual ownership. Most notable were Mobility Car Sharing Switzerland and StattAuto in Germany, which both began their operations in 1987. Although for the most part these groups were unable to achieve profitability, it

```
╔══════════════════════════════════════╗
║  COMPANY PERSPECTIVES                ║
║             ■                        ║
╟──────────────────────────────────────╢
║  Our mission at Zipcar is to offer a  ║
║  new model for automobile transport-  ║
║  ation.                              ║
╚══════════════════════════════════════╝
```

was inevitable that the concept would cross the ocean to North America. In 1994 Benoit Robert established a car-sharing cooperative called Auto-Com in Quebec City. A year later CommunAuto, Inc., was formed in Montreal, and in 1997 the two organizations were merged under CommunAuto, Inc. During this time interest in car sharing was developing in Portland, Oregon, the flames fanned by several public talks that were given in the area by Mobility CarSharing founder Conrad Wagner. The City of Portland and the Air Quality Division of the Oregon Department of Environmental Quality created a discussion group and out of it grew CarSharing Portland, which began operations in March 1998 with a pair of vehicles. By the end of the first year there were nine vehicles parked at seven sites serving 110 active members. Further north, in Seattle, Washington, a public-private partnership was forged between King County, the city of Seattle, and Mobility, Inc., to create a car-sharing service called Flexcar, which began operations in January 2000.

Unaware of what was transpiring in Canada and in the Pacific Northwest involving car sharing were a pair of Cambridge, Massachusetts, friends, Robin Chase and Antje Danielson. While having coffee in a neighborhood café in September 1999 Danielson told Chase of a car-sharing service she noticed during a trip to her native Germany. "Antje discovered this cool idea and asked what I thought," Chase told the *New York Times*. "The concept was brilliant; the technology was there. I also realized that I had the background to make it happen." In addition to holding an MBA from the Sloan School of Management at the Massachusetts Institute of Technology (MIT), Chase was herself the target market for car sharing: she was 39, lived in the crowded Boston area with her husband and three children, and had need for a second car to run occasional errands while her husband used the family car to commute to work, but was hesitant to make the investment in another car and was concerned about polluting the atmosphere with more greenhouse gases. She was also looking for a business venture, eager to strike out on her own after working for several companies since earning her MBA.

Because of her background, Chase immediately realized that the Internet was the perfect tool to make a resource like a car available to a large pool of people.

After researching other car-sharing attempts, she used her financial training, according to *Inc.*, to complete "a business plan that calculated to the penny how Zipcar would make money. She concluded, for example, that a Zipcar location could break even if it had 70 cars averaging six hours of daily use." To raise capital she turned to Investor's Circle, an organization that brought together investors and entrepreneurs at biannual meetings in Boston and San Francisco. At the Boston meeting in 1999 she shared her business plan for Zipcar, which led to a $250,000 investment from Boston Community Capital, a fund of Community Development Venture Capital that sought to make investments in start-up companies which offered both commercial potential and community improvement. Zipcar fit the bill on both points.

ZIPCAR OPERATIONS LAUNCHED: 2000

In January 2000 Chase and Danielson incorporated Zipcar, and Chase became the company's chief executive officer. The company began operations in late June 2000 with ten vehicles at sites in Cambridge and Boston: Volkswagen Beetles, four-door Golfs, and Passat station wagons, each equipped with a magnetic ID card reader and a minicomputer. Zipcar's handful of initial members paid a $75 annual fee and a onetime $300 deposit to serve as an accident deductible. Hourly rates, depending on the time of day, ranged from $4.50 to $6.50, and members also paid $0.40 per mile. Reservations could be made through the Zipcar web site or on the car's minicomputer. The company employed four full-time people and several part-timers. By the fall of 2001 Zipcar's fleet had increased to 54 cars and its membership ballooned to 1,100. After 18 months, Boston-area membership reached 1,700

Chase capitalized on the early success of Zipcar to raise more funds in order to invest in Internet technology that would help the company grow and provide an edge over emerging competition in the field. By early 2001 she raised an additional $1 million, a large portion of which was invested in the Internet-based reservation and tracking system. She raised more money in 2001 to help take Zipcar to new markets. The service was introduced in Washington, D.C., in October 2001 and made its debut in New York City in February 2002 with ten Volkswagens, which were leased for $10 to $14 an hour due to higher garage costs. Also in 2002 Zipcar began exploring a new source of potential customers, college students, whom the company also hoped to keep as long-term customers once they graduated. A test service launched on the campus of MIT proved successful, which would lead Zipcar to set up operations at other schools.

KEY DATES

1999: Robin Chase and Antje Danielson conceive of Zipcar.
2000: Zipcar incorporates and begins Boston service.
2001: Washington, D.C., service added.
2002: New York City operation launched.
2003: Scott Griffith named CEO.
2006: Service brought to Toronto and London.
2007: Zipcar and Flexcar merge.

Rather than continue to expand, Zipcar took a step back to focus on building up its Boston, New York, and Washington business to achieve profitability and convince investors that the business plan truly worked. Taking charge at this stage was new CEO Scott Griffith, who joined Zipcar in February 2003. Chase remained as a Zipcar director and then went on to spend a year at the Harvard Graduate School of Design as a Loeb Fellow. Her next endeavor would build upon her Zipcar experience. Called GoLoco.org, the online service was part social network and part ride board, connecting drivers with passengers in an effort to further reduce the number of cars on the road.

Griffith held an engineering degree from Carnegie Mellon University and an MBA from the University of Chicago. He was also a well-traveled executive with varied business experience, having held senior-level posts at Parthenon Group, a business strategy and investment firm; Information America, a public record information provider; Digital Goods, a software and services firm; and the Boeing Company. One of the first changes he made after taking the wheel at Zipcar was to add more attractive cars to the mix of the fleet, which had been focused purely on mileage. The new Mini Coopers and SUVs helped to attract new members. Because many of the cars were not used during daylight hours when members were at work, he also established a sales force to market Zipcar to businesses, creating a "Z2B" revenue stream. He also abandoned the previous marketing approach that invested in advertising, which resulted in increased brand awareness but did little to drive up membership numbers. The company adopted what it called "zone marketing," an effort to promote Zipcar in the neighborhoods where the vehicles were actually parked. Thus, posters and brochures were made available in local businesses, informational cards were distributed, and in some cases the cars were parked in front of

Whole Foods Markets and Zipcar employees gave shoppers a lift home.

Griffith's strategy worked, as Zipcar increased revenues from $4 million in 2003 to $7 million in 2004, when the company was able to break even. Although the company would return to red ink as it resumed expansion, existing operations remained profitable, convincing investors that Zipcar was a viable enterprise. It 2005 the company was able to raise $10 million from the venture capital firm Benchmark Capital, the money earmarked to expand the business to the West Coast. For the year 2005, Zipcar increased revenues to about $15 million.

Zipcar received further financial backing in 2006. In May the company was able to arrange $20 million in vehicle leasing financing from GE Commercial Finance Fleet Services, allowing Zipcar to double its fleet, which at this stage totaled 1,500 cars. Many of those cars would be made available to the new Toronto operations, Zipcar's first foray outside of the United States. Others would be dispatched to Chicago where in the summer of 2006 Zipcar established a Midwest hub. Later in the year Zipcar raised more money to back additional expansion. Another equity round raised $25 million from Benchmark Capital, Greylock Partners, and Globespan Capital Partners. Some of the new capital was used to take Zipcar overseas to London, establishing a beachhead in the European market. In November 2006, 25 cars were placed in the borough of Kensington and Chelsea, and more than 100 additional cars were waiting in the wings to serve other London neighborhoods. Zipcar members from North America would also be able to lease these vehicles when in the United Kingdom.

MERGER WITH FLEXCAR COMPLETED: 2007

Zipcar's strong growth continued in 2007. The Chicago location was doing especially well. In the fall the company announced plans to double the hub's fleet to 500 cars and add another 50 to 60 area locations where the cars could be found. Zipcar had 120,000 members, a fleet of 3,500 cars, and was on pace to top $65 million in annual revenues. Both of those tallies were soon to increase significantly, however. In late October Zipcar merged with its largest competitor, Flexcar. The combined operation would take the Zipcar name, Griffith would remain as CEO, and the headquarters stayed in Cambridge. Flexcar's CEO, Mark Norman, became president and chief operating officer.

Since its launch in 1999, Flexcar had grown at a slower pace than Zipcar but it attracted the attention of

Stephen Case, America Online founder, who began using the service in Washington, D.C. In 2005 he decided to acquire the company through an entity he controlled, Revolution LLC. By the time of the merger, Flexcar had grown its business to 1,500 cars in 15 markets serving about 60,000 members. What made the combination of the two companies especially attractive was that there was little overlap in markets. Only in San Francisco and Washington did they compete directly. Flexcar added such desirable markets as Los Angeles and Philadelphia, providing Zipcar members with several new markets where they could lease vehicles. Zipcar also planned to expand further into college markets and make it even easier for members to reserve vehicles through a new mobile device version of its web-reservation site. Through partner uLocate Communications members would be able to use GPS technology to locate and view on their mobile screen Zipcar vehicles located in their vicinity and to quickly place a reservation. While Griffith admitted to the press that Zipcar might be interested in making an initial public offering of stock, in the short-term the company would focus on integrating the Flexcar operations and implementing the new mobile system.

Ed Dinger

PRINCIPAL COMPETITORS

CityCarShare; I-go; OZOcar.

FURTHER READING

Bajaj, Vikas, "A Few Keyboard Clicks Put Car Sharers on Wheels," *New York Times,* November 30, 2005, p. C1.

Beirne, Mike, "Temporary Plates," *Brandweek,* July 9, 2007, p. 30.

Breskin, Ira, "Renting Wheels by the Hour," *New York Times,* June 22, 2003, p. 3.

Everson, Darren, "Car-Sharing Firms to Merge," *Wall Street Journal,* November 1, 2007, p. D3.

——, "Zipcar Goes to College," *Wall Street Journal,* August 22, 2007, p. D1.

Gates, Dominic, "Seattle's Flexcar Merges with Rival Zipcar," *Seattle Times,* October 31, 2007.

Gewertz, Ken, "Zipcar Creator Looks Toward Bigger Challenges," *Harvard Gazette,* October 21, 2004.

Johnson, Caroline Y., "Zipcar Is Expected to Join with Rival Flexcar," *Boston Globe,* October 31, 2007.

Kirsner, Scott, "4 Leaders You Need to Know," *Fast Company,* February 2005, p. 68.

Mochari, Ilan, "Deals on Wheels," *Inc.,* February 1, 2001, p. 25.

Retsinas, Joan, "Investors with a Mission," *In Business,* September/October 2001, p. 10.

Index to Companies

Listings in this index are arranged in alphabetical order under the company name. Company names beginning with a letter or proper name such as Eli Lilly & Co. will be found under the first letter of the company name. Definite articles (The, Le, La) are ignored for alphabetical purposes as are forms of incorporation that precede the company name (AB, NV). Company names printed in **bold** type have full, historical essays on the page numbers appearing in bold. Updates to entries that appeared in earlier volumes are signified by the notation (**upd.**). Company names in light type are references within an essay to that company, not full historical essays. This index is cumulative with volume numbers printed in bold type.

A

A and A Limousine Renting, Inc., **26** 62
A & A Medical Supply, **61** 206
A&E Plastics, **12** 377
A&E Television Networks, 32 3–7
A&K Petroleum Company *see* Kerr-McGee Corp.
A&M Records, **23** 389
A&N Foods Co., *see* Nippon Suisan Kaisha, Ltd.
A&P *see* The Great Atlantic & Pacific Tea Company, Inc.
A & W Brands, Inc., 25 3–5 *see also* Cadbury Schweppes PLC.
A-dec, Inc., 53 3–5
á la Zing, **62** 259
A-Mark Financial Corporation, 71 3–6

A-1 Supply *see* International Game Technology.
A-R Technologies, **48** 275
A.A. Mathews *see* CRSS Inc.
A. Ahlström Oy *see* Ahlstrom Corp.
A.B. Chance Industries Co., Inc. *see* Hubbell Inc.
A.B.Dick Company, 28 6–8
A.B. Leasing Corp., *see* Bozzuto's, Inc.
A.B. Watley Group Inc., 45 3–5
A-BEC Mobility, **11** 487
A.C. Delco, **26** 347, 349
A.C. Moore Arts & Crafts, Inc., 30 3–5
A.C. Nielsen Company, 13 3–5 *see also* ACNielsen Corp.
A. Duda & Sons, Inc., 88 1–4
A/E/C/ Systems International, *see* Penton Media, Inc.
A.E. Fitkin & Company, **6** 592–93; **50** 37
A.E. Lottes, **29** 86
A. F. Blakemore & Son Ltd., 90 1–4
A.G. Becker, **20** 260
A.G. Edwards, Inc., 8 3–5; 32 17–21 (upd.)
A.G. Industries, Inc., *see* American Greetings Corp.
A.G. Stanley Ltd. *see* The Boots Company PLC.
A.H. Belo Corporation, 10 3–5; 30 13–17 (upd.)
A.H. Robins Co., *see* Wyeth.
A. Hirsh & Son, **30** 408
A. Hölscher GmbH, **53** 195
A. Johnson & Co. *see* Axel Johnson Group.
A.L. Pharma Inc., 12 3–5 *see also* Alpharma Inc.
A.L. Van Houtte Inc. *see* Van Houtte Inc.

A. Leon Capel and Sons, Inc. *see* Capel Inc.
A.M. Castle & Co., 25 6–8
A. Michel et Cie., **49** 84
A. Moksel AG, 59 3–6
A. Nelson & Co. Ltd., 75 3–6
A.O. Smith Corporation, 11 3–6; 40 3–8 (upd.)
A.P. Møller - Maersk A/S, 57 3–6
A.P. Orleans, Inc., *see* Orleans Homebuilders, Inc.
A.S. Abell Co., **IV** 678
A.S. Watson & Company Ltd., 84 1–4
A.S. Yakovlev Design Bureau, 15 3–6
A. Schilling & Company *see* McCormick & Company, Inc.
A. Schulman, Inc., 8 6–8; 49 3–7 (upd.)
A. Sulka & Co., **29** 457
A.T. Cross Company, 17 3–5; 49 8–12 (upd.)
A.T. Massey Coal Company, Inc., **34** 164; **57** 236
A.T. Mays, **55** 90
A-T-O Inc. *see* Figgie International, Inc.
A.W. Baulderstone Holdings Pty. Ltd., **55** 62
A.W. Faber-Castell Unternehmensverwaltung GmbH & Co., 51 3–6
A. Wilhelmsen A/S, **74** 278
AA Energy Corp., *see* AMR Corp.
AADC Holding Company, Inc., **62** 347
AAF-McQuay Incorporated, 26 3–5
AAI Corporation, **37** 399
Aai.FosterGrant, Inc., **60** 131, 133
Aalborg Industries A/S, 90 5–8
AAON, Inc., 22 3–6
AAPT, **54** 355–57
AAR Corp., 28 3–5

Allsport plc., **31** 216, 218

The Allstate Corporation, 10 50–52; **27** 30–33 (upd.)

ALLTEL Corporation, 6 299–301; **46** 15–19 (upd.)

Alltrista Corporation, 30 38–41

Allwaste, Inc., 18 10–13

Allweiler, **58** 67

Alma Media Group, **52** 51

Almac Electronics Corporation, *see* Arrow Electronics, Inc.

Almacenes de Baja y Media, **39** 201, 204

Almacenes Exito S.A., 89 47–50

Almaden Vineyards, *see* Canandaigua Brands, Inc.

Almanacksförlaget AB, **51** 328

Almanij NV, 44 15–18 *see also* Algemeene Maatschappij voor Nijverheidskrediet.

Almay, Inc. *see* Revlon Inc.

Almeida Banking House *see* Banco Bradesco S.A.

ALNM *see* Ayres, Lewis, Norris & May.

Aloha Airlines, Incorporated, 24 20–22

ALP *see* Associated London Properties.

Alp Sport Sandals, **22** 173

Alpargatas S.A.I.C., 87 13–17

Alpex, S.A. de C.V., **19** 12

Alpha Airports Group PLC, 77 32–35

Alpha Beta Co., *see* American Stores Co.

Alpha Engineering Group, Inc., **16** 259–60

Alpha Healthcare Ltd., *see* Sun Healthcare Group Inc.

Alpha Networks Inc. *see* D-Link Corp.

Alpha Processor Inc., **41** 349

Alpha Technical Systems, **19** 279

Alphaform, **40** 214–15

AlphaGraphics Inc. *see* G A Pindar & Son Ltd.

Alphanumeric Publication Systems, Inc., **26** 518

Alpharma Inc., 35 22–26 (upd.)

Alphonse Allard Inc., *see* Provigo Inc.

Alpine Confections, Inc., 71 22–24

Alpine Electronics, Inc., 13 30–31

Alpine Gaming *see* Century Casinos, Inc.

Alpine Lace Brands, Inc., 18 14–16 *see also* Land O'Lakes, Inc.

Alpine Securities Corporation, **22** 5

Alpnet Inc. *see* SDL PLC.

Alpre, **19** 192

Alps Electric Co., Ltd., II 5–6; **44** 19–21 (upd.)

Alric Packing, *see* Associated British Foods plc.

Alrosa Company Ltd., 62 7–11

Alsco *see* Steiner Corp.

ALSO Holding AG, **29** 419, 422

Alsthom, *see* Alcatel S.A.

ALTA Health Strategies, Inc., **11** 113

Alta Vista Company, **50** 228

Altadis S.A., 72 6–13 (upd.)

ALTANA AG, 87 18–22

AltaSteel Ltd., **51** 352

AltaVista Company, 43 11–13

ALTEC International, **21** 107–09

Altera Corporation, 18 17–20; **43** 14–18 (upd.)

Alternative Living Services *see* Alterra Healthcare Corp.

Alternative Tentacles Records, 66 3–6

Alternative Youth Services, Inc., *see* Res-Care, Inc.

Alterra Healthcare Corporation, 42 3–5

Altex, **19** 192–93

Alticor Inc., 71 25–30 (upd.)

Altiris, Inc., 65 34–36

Altman Weil Pensa, **29** 237

Alton Towers, **55** 378

Altos Hornos de México, S.A. de C.V., 42 6–8

Altra Broadband Inc., **63** 34

Altran Technologies, 51 15–18

Altron Incorporated, 20 8–10

Altura Energy Ltd. *see* Occidental Petroleum Corp.

Aluar Aluminio Argentino S.A.I.C., 74 10–12

Aluma Systems Corp., *see* Tridel Enterprises Inc.

Alumalsa *see* Aluminoy y Aleaciones S.A.

Alumax Inc., **I** 508; **22** 286; **56** 11

Aluminoy y Aleaciones S.A., **63** 303

Aluminum and Stainless, Inc. *see* Reliance Steel & Aluminum Co.

Aluminum Company of America, IV 14–16; **20** 11–14 (upd.) *see also* Alcoa Inc.

Aluminum Forge Co., *see* Marmon Group, Inc.

Alupak, A.G., **12** 377

Alusuisse, **73** 212–13

Alvic Group, **20** 363

Alvin Ailey Dance Foundation, Inc., 52 14–17

Alvis Plc, 47 7–9

ALZA Corporation, 10 53–55; **36** 36–39 (upd.)

Alzouman Aviation, **56** 148

AM Cosmetics, Inc., **31** 89

Am-Safe, Inc., *see* The Marmon Group, Inc.

AM-TEX Corp., Inc., **12** 443

Amagasaki Spinners Ltd. *see* Unitika Ltd.

Amalgamated Bank, 60 20–22

Amalgamated Sugar Co., **14** 18; **19** 467–68

Amana Refrigeration Company, **38** 374; **42** 159

Amaray International Corporation, **12** 264

Amarillo Gas Company *see* Atmos Energy Corp.

Amarillo Railcar Services, **6** 580

Amati Communications Corporation, **57** 409

Amax Gold, **36** 316

AMAX Inc., IV 17–19 *see also* Cyprus Amex.

Amazon.com, Inc., 25 17–19; **56** 12–15 (upd.)

AMB Generali Holding AG, 51 19–23

AMB Property Corporation, 57 25–27

Ambac Financial Group, Inc., 65 37–39

Ambassadors International, Inc., 68 16–18 (upd.)

Amberg Hospach AG, **49** 436

AmBev *see* Companhia de Bebidas das Américas.

Amblin Entertainment, 21 23–27

AMBRA, Inc., **48** 209

AMC Entertainment Inc., 12 12–14; **35** 27–29 (upd.)

AMCA International Corporation, *see* United Dominion Industries Ltd.

AMCC *see* Applied Micro Circuits Corp.

Amcell *see* American Cellular Network.

AMCOL International Corporation, 59 29–33 (upd.)

Amcor Ltd., IV 248–50; **19** 13–16 (upd.); **78** 1–6 (upd.)

AMCORE Financial Inc., 44 22–26

Amcraft Building Products Co., Inc., **22** 15

AMD *see* Advanced Micro Devices, Inc.

Amdahl Corporation, III 109–11; **14** 13–16 (upd.); **40** 20–25 (upd.) *see also* Fujitsu Ltd.

Amdocs Ltd., 47 10–12

AME Finanziaria, **IV** 587; **19** 19; **54** 20

Amec Spie S.A., 57 28–31

Amedysis, Inc., 53 33–36

Amer Group plc, 41 14–16

Amer Sport, **68** 245

Amerace Corporation, **54** 373

Amerada Hess Corporation, IV 365–67; **21** 28–31 (upd.); **55** 16–20 (upd.)

Amerchol Corporation *see* Union Carbide Corp.

AMERCO, 6 351–52; **67** 11–14 (upd.)

Ameren Corporation, 60 23–27 (upd.)

AmerGen Energy LLC, **49** 65, 67

Ameri-Kart Corp., *see* Myers Industries, Inc.

America Online, Inc., 10 56–58; **26** 16–20 (upd.) *see also* CompuServe Interactive Services, Inc.; AOL Time Warner Inc.

America Today, *see* Koninklijke Vendex KBB N.V. (Royal Vendex KBB N.V.)

America West Holdings Corporation, 6 72–74; **34** 22–26 (upd.)

America's Car-Mart, Inc., 64 19–21

America's Favorite Chicken Company, Inc., 7 26–28 *see also* AFC Enterprises, Inc.

American & Efird, Inc., 82 5–9

American Acquisitions, Inc., **49** 279

American Air Filter, **26** 3–4

American Airlines, I 89–91; **6** 75–77 (upd.) *see also* AMR Corp.

American Apparel, Inc., 90 21–24

American Association of Retired Persons *see* AARP.

American Austin Quality Foods Inc., **44** 40

American Aviation Manufacturing Corp., **15** 246

American Axle & Manufacturing Holdings, Inc., 67 15–17

American Bancshares, Inc., **11** 457

American Medical Association, 39
15–18
American Medical Disposal, Inc. *see*
Stericycle, Inc.
American Medical Holdings, **55** 370
American Medical International, Inc.,
III 73–75
American Medical Response, Inc., 39
19–22
American Medical Services, *see* TW
Services, Inc.
American Metal Climax, Inc. *see* AMAX.
American Metals and Alloys, Inc., **19** 432
American Metals Corporation *see* Reliance
Steel & Aluminum Co.
American Modern Insurance Group *see*
The Midland Co.
American Motors Corp., I 135–37 *see*
also DaimlerChrysler AG.
América Móvil, S.A. de C.V., 80 5–8
American MSI Corporation *see* Moldflow
Corp.
American Multi-Cinema *see* AMC
Entertainment Inc.
American National Can Co., *see* Pechiney
SA.
American National Insurance Company,
8 27–29; 27 45–48 (upd.)
American Natural Snacks Inc., **29** 480
American Olean Tile Company, *see*
Armstrong Holdings, Inc.
American Optical Co., **38** 363–64
American Pad & Paper Company, 20
18–21
American Paging, *see* Telephone and Data
Systems, Inc.
American Patriot Insurance, **22** 15
American Payment Systems, Inc., **21** 514
American Petrofina, Inc., *see* FINA, Inc.
American Pfauter, *see* Gleason Corp.
American Pharmaceutical Partners, Inc.,
69 20–22
American Phone Centers, Inc., **21** 135
American Pop Corn Company, 59
40–43
American Port Services (Amports), **45** 29
American Power & Light Co., **6** 545,
596–97; **49** 143
American Power Conversion
Corporation, 24 29–31; 67 18–20
(upd.)
American Premier Underwriters, Inc.,
10 71–74
American Prepaid Professional Services,
Inc. *see* CompDent Corp.
American President Companies Ltd., 6
353–55 *see also* APL Ltd.
American Printing House for the Blind,
26 13–15
American Prospecting Equipment Co., **49**
174
American Public Automotive Group, **37**
115
American Publishing Co., *see* Hollinger
International Inc.
American Re Corporation, 10 75–77; 35
34–37 (upd.)

American Recreation Company Holdings,
Inc., **16** 53; **44** 53–54
American Red Cross, 40 26–29
American Reprographics Company, 75
24–26
American Residential Mortgage
Corporation, 8 30–31
American Residential Services, **33** 141
American Retirement Corporation, 42
9–12 *see also* Brookdale Senior Living.
American Rice, Inc., 33 30–33
American Rug Craftsmen, *see* Mohawk
Industries, Inc.
American Safety Razor Company, 20
22–24
American Salt Co., **12** 199
American Satellite Co., **15** 195
American Savings Bank, *see* Hawaiian
Electric Industries, Inc.
American Science & Engineering, Inc.,
81 22–25
American Sealants Company *see* Loctite
Corp.
American Seating Company, 78 7–11
American Seaway Foods, Inc, *see* Riser
Foods, Inc.
American Securities Capital Partners, L.P.,
59 13; **69** 138–39
American Service Corporation, **19** 223
American Ships Ltd., **50** 209
American Skiing Company, 28 18–21
American Sky Broadcasting, **27** 305; **35**
156
American Smelting and Refining Co. *see*
ASARCO.
American Society for the Prevention of
Cruelty to Animals (ASPCA), 68
19–22
The American Society of Composers,
Authors and Publishers (ASCAP), 29
21–24
American Software Inc., 22 214; 25
20–22
American Standard Companies Inc., III
663–65; 30 46–50 (upd.)
American States Water Company, 46
27–30
American Steamship Company *see* GATX.
American Steel & Wire Co., *see*
Birmingham Steel Corp.
American Steel Foundries, **7** 29–30
American Stores Company, II 604–06;
22 37–40 (upd.) *see also* Albertson's,
Inc.
American Sugar Refining Company *see*
Domino Sugar Corp.
American Sumatra Tobacco Corp., **15** 138
American Superconductor Corporation,
41 141
American Surety Co., **26** 486
American Teaching Aids Inc., **19** 405
American Technical Ceramics Corp., 67
21–23
American Technical Services Company *see*
American Building Maintenance
Industries, Inc.; ABM Industries Inc.
American Telephone and Telegraph
Company *see* AT&T.

American Television and Communications
Corp., **IV** 675
American Thermos Bottle Company *see*
Thermos Co.
American Threshold, **50** 123
American Tile Supply Company, **19** 233
American Tissue Company, **29** 136
American Tobacco Co. *see* American
Brands Inc.; B.A.T. Industries PLC.;
Fortune Brands, Inc.
American Tool Companies, Inc., **52** 270
American Tourister, Inc., 16 19–21 *see*
also Samsonite Corp.
American Tower Corporation, 33 34–38
American Trans Air, **34** 31
American Transitional Hospitals, Ltd., **65**
307
American Transport Lines, **6** 384
American Twist Drill Co., **23** 82
American Vanguard Corporation, 47
20–22
American VIP Limousine, Inc., **26** 62
American Water Works Company, Inc.,
6 443–45; 38 49–52 (upd.)
American Woodmark Corporation, 31
13–16
American Yard Products, **22** 26, 28
American Yearbook Company, *see* Jostens,
Inc.
Americana Entertainment Group, Inc., **19**
435
Americana Foods, LP, *see* TCBY
Enterprises Inc.
Americana Healthcare Corp., **15** 522
Americana Ships Ltd., **50** 210
AmeriCares Foundation, Inc., 87 23–28
Americom, **61** 272
Americrown Service Corporation *see*
International Speedway Corp.
Ameridrive, **58** 67
AmeriGas Partners, L.P., **56** 36
AMERIGROUP Corporation, 69 23–26
Amerihost Properties, Inc., 30 51–53
AmeriKing Corp., **36** 309
Amerin Corporation *see* Radian Group
Inc.
AmeriServe Food Distribution *see* Holberg
Industries, Inc.
Amerisex, **64** 198
AmeriSource Health Corporation, 37
9–11 (upd.)
AmerisourceBergen Corporation, 64
22–28 (upd.)
Ameristar Casinos, Inc., 33 39–42; 69
27–31 (upd.)
AmeriSteel Corp., **59** 202
AmeriSuites, **52** 281
Ameritech Corporation, V 265–68; 18
30–34 (upd.)
Ameritech Illinois *see* Illinois Bell
Telephone Co.
Ameritrade Holding Corporation, 34
27–30
Ameritrust Corporation, **9** 476
Ameriwood Industries International
Corp., 17 15–17 *see also* Dorel
Industries Inc.
Amerock Corporation, 53 37–40

Arvin Industries, Inc., 8 37–40 *see also*
ArvinMeritor, Inc.
ArvinMeritor, Inc., 54 24–28 (upd.)
A/S Air Baltic Corporation, 71 35–37
AS Estonian Air, 71 38–40
ASA Holdings, 47 30
Asahi Breweries, Ltd., I 220–21; 20
28–30 (upd.); 52 31–34 (upd.)
Asahi Corporation, *see* Casio Computer
Co., Ltd.
Asahi Denka Kogyo KK, 64 33–35
Asahi Glass Company, Ltd., III 666–68;
48 39–42 (upd.)
Asahi Komag Co., Ltd., *see* Komag, Inc.
Asahi Kyoei Co., *see* Asahi Breweries, Ltd.
Asahi Medix Co., Ltd., 36 420
Asahi National Broadcasting Company,
Ltd., 9 29–31
Asahi Real Estate Facilities Co., Ltd. *see*
Seino Transportation Company, Ltd.
Asahi Shimbun, 9 29–30
Asanté Technologies, Inc., 20 31–33
ASARCO Incorporated, IV 31–34; 40
220–22, 411
Asatsu-DK Inc, 82 16–20
ASB Air, 47 286–87
Asbury Associates Inc., 22 354–55
Asbury Automotive Group Inc., 60
42–44
Asbury Carbons, Inc., 68 35–37
ASC, Inc., 55 31–34
ASCAP *see* The American Society of
Composers, Authors and Publishers.
Ascend Communications, Inc., 24
47–51 *see also* Lucent Technologies Inc.
Ascension Health, 61 206
Ascential Software Corporation, 59
54–57
ASCO Healthcare, Inc., *see* NeighborCare,
Inc.
Asco Products, Inc., 22 413
Ascom AG, 9 32–34
ASCP *see* American Securities Capital
Partners.
ASD Specialty Healthcare, Inc., 64 27
ASDA Group Ltd., II 611–12; 28 34–36
(upd.); 64 36–38 (upd.)
ASEA AB *see* ABB Ltd.
Aseam Credit Sdn Bhd, 72 217
ASF *see* American Steel Foundries.
ASG *see* Allen Systems Group, Inc.
Asgrow Seed Co., 29 435; 41 306
Ash Resources Ltd., 31 398–99
Ashanti Goldfields Company Limited,
43 37–40
Ashbourne PLC, *see* Sun Healthcare
Group Inc.
Ashdown *see* Repco Corporation Ltd.
Ashland Inc., 19 22–25; 50 45–50
(upd.)
Ashland Oil, Inc., IV 372–74 *see also*
Marathon.
Ashley Furniture Industries, Inc., 35
49–51
Ashtead Group plc, 34 41–43
Ashworth, Inc., 26 25–28
ASIA & PACIFIC Business Description
Paid-in Capital Voting Rights, 68 30

Asia Oil Co., Ltd., IV 404, 476; 53 115
Asia Pacific Breweries Limited, 59
58–60
Asia Pulp & Paper, 38 227
Asia Shuang He Sheng Five Star Beer Co.,
Ltd., 49 418
Asia Television, IV 718; 38 320
Asia Terminals Ltd., IV 718; 38 319
AsiaInfo Holdings, Inc., 43 41–44
Asiamerica Equities Ltd. *see* Mercer
International.
Asiana Airlines, Inc., 46 39–42
ASIX Inc. *see* Manatron, Inc.
ASICS Corporation, 57 52–55
ASK Group, Inc., 9 35–37
Ask Jeeves, Inc., 65 50–52
Ask Mr. Foster Agency, *see* Carlson
Companies, Inc.
ASMI *see* Acer Semiconductor
Manufacturing Inc.
ASML Holding N.V., 50 51–54
ASPCA *see* American Society for the
Prevention of Cruelty to Animals
(ASPCA).
Aspect Telecommunications
Corporation, 22 51–53
ASPECTA Global Group AG, 53 162
Aspen Imaging International, Inc., *see*
Pubco Corp.
Aspen Mountain Gas Co., 6 568
Aspen Publishers, *see* Wolters Kluwer NV.
Aspen Skiing Company, 15 23–26
Asplundh Tree Expert Co., 20 34–36;
59 61–65 (upd.)
Asprofos S.A., 64 177
Asset Marketing Inc. *see* Commercial
Financial Services, Inc.
Assicurazioni Generali SpA, III 206–09;
15 27–31 (upd.)
Assisted Living Concepts, Inc., 43
45–47
Associated British Foods plc, II 465–66;
13 51–53 (upd.); 41 30–33 (upd.)
Associated British Ports Holdings Plc,
45 29–32
Associated Bulk Carriers Ltd., 38 345
Associated Container Transportation, 23
161
Associated Cooperative Investment Trust
Ltd. *see* Hammerson plc.
Associated Dry Goods Corp., V 134; 12
54–55; 63 259
Associated Estates Realty Corporation,
25 23–25
Associated Fire Marine Insurance Co., 26
486
Associated Fresh Foods, 48 37
Associated Gas & Electric Company *see*
General Public Utilities Corp.
Associated Gas Services, Inc., 11 28
Associated Grocers, Incorporated, 9
38–40; 31 22–26 (upd.)
The Associated Group, 10 45
Associated Hospital Service of New York
see Empire Blue Cross and Blue Shield.
Associated Inns and Restaurants Company
of America, 26 459

Associated International Insurance Co. *see*
Gryphon Holdings, Inc.
Associated Lead Manufacturers Ltd. *see*
Cookson Group plc.
Associated London Properties *see* Land
Securities PLC.
Associated Madison Companies, *see*
Primerica Corp.
Associated Milk Producers, Inc., 11
24–26; 48 43–46 (upd.)
Associated Natural Gas Corporation, 11
27–28
Associated Newspapers Holdings P.L.C.,
see Daily Mail and General Trust plc.
The Associated Press, 13 54–56; 31
27–30 (upd.); 73 37–41 (upd.)
Associates First Capital Corporation, 22
207; 59 126
Association des Centres Distributeurs E.
Leclerc, 37 19–21
Association of Junior Leagues
International Inc., 60 45–47
Assurances Générales de France, 63
45–48
AST Holding Corp. *see* American
Standard Companies, Inc.
AST Research, Inc., 9 41–43
Astakos Terminal S.A., 64 8
Astec Industries, Inc., 79 34–37
Astech, 18 370
AstenJohnson Inc., 90 31–34
Asteroid, IV 97
Aston Brooke Software, 14 392
Aston Villa plc, 41 34–36
Astor Holdings Inc., 22 32
Astoria Financial Corporation, 44
31–34
Astra *see* PT Astra International Tbk.
Astra Resources, 12 543
AstraZeneca PLC, I 625–26; 20 37–40
(upd.); 50 55–60 (upd.)
Astrium N.V., 52 113
Astrolink International LLC, 54 406–07
Astronics Corporation, 35 52–54
Astrotech Space Operations, L.P., 37 365
Astrum International Corp., 12 88; 16
20–21; 43 355
Asur *see* Grupo Aeropuerto del Sureste,
S.A. de C.V.
Asurion Corporation, 83 29–32
ASV, Inc., 34 44–47; 66 13–15 (upd.)
ASW *see* American Steel & Wire Corp.
Asylum Records, 23 33; 26 150
AT&T Bell Laboratories, Inc., 13 57–59
see also Lucent Technologies Inc.
AT&T Corporation, V 259–64; 29
39–45 (upd.); 61 68 38–45 (upd.)
AT&T Istel Ltd., 14 35–36
AT&T Microelectronics, 63 397
AT&T Wireless Services, Inc., 54 29–32
(upd.)
At Home Corporation, 43 48–51
AT TOKYO Corp., 74 348
ATA Holdings Corporation, 82 21–25
Atanor S.A., 62 19–22
Atari Corporation, 9 44–47; 23 23–26
(upd.); 66 16–20 (upd.)
ATAS International, 26 527, 530

Beazer Plc, *see* Hanson PLC.
bebe stores, inc., 31 50–52
BEC Group Inc., **22** 35; **60** 133
BEC Ventures, **57** 124–25
Bechstein, **56** 299
Bechtel Group, Inc., I 558–59; **24**
    64–67 (upd.)
Beck's North America, Inc. *see* Brauerei
    Beck & Co.
Becker Drill, Inc., **19** 247
Becker Group of Germany, **26** 231
Beckett Papers, 23 48–50
Beckley-Cardy Group *see* School Specialty,
    Inc.
Beckman Coulter, Inc., 22 74–77
Beckman Instruments, Inc., 14 52–54
BECOL *see* Belize Electric Company Ltd.
Becton, Dickinson & Company, I
    630–31; **11** 34–36 (upd.); **36** 84–89
    (upd.)
Bed Bath & Beyond Inc., 13 81–83; **41**
    49–52 (upd.)
Bedcovers, Inc., **19** 304
Bee Chemicals, *see* Morton International.
Bee Discount, **26** 476
Beech Aircraft Corporation, 8 49–52 *see*
    also Raytheon Aircraft Holdings Inc.
Beech Holdings Corp., **9** 94
Beech-Nut Nutrition Corporation, 21
    53–56; **51** 47–51 (upd.)
Beecham Group PLC, *see*
    GlaxoSmithKline plc.
Beechcroft Developments Ltd., **51** 173
Beeck-Feinkost GmbH, **26** 59
ZAO BeeOnLine-Portal, **48** 419
Beer Nuts, Inc., 86 30–33
Beerman Stores, Inc., *see* Elder-Beerman
    Stores Corp.
Beers Construction Company, **38** 437
Befesa *see* Abengoa S.A.
Behr GmbH & Co. KG, 72 22–25
Behring Diagnostics *see* Dade Behring
    Holdings Inc.
Behringwerke AG, **14** 255; **50** 249
BEI Technologies, Inc., 65 74–76
Beiersdorf AG, 29 49–53
Beijing Contact Lens Ltd., **25** 56
Beijing Dentsu, **16** 168
Beijing-Landauer, Ltd., **51** 210
Beijing ZF North Drive Systems Technical
    Co. Ltd., **48** 450
Beirao, Pinto, Silva and Co. *see* Banco
    Espírito Santo e Comercial de Lisboa
    S.A.
Bejam Group PLC *see* The Big Food
    Group plc.
Bekaert S.A./N.V., 90 53–57
Bekins Company, 15 48–50
Bel *see* Fromageries Bel.
Bel Air Markets, *see* Raley's Inc.
Bel Fuse, Inc., 53 59–62
Bel/Kaukauna USA, 76 46–48
Belco Oil & Gas Corp., 40 63–65
Belcom Holding AG, **53** 323, 325
Belden CDT Inc., 19 43–45; **76** 49–52
    (upd.)
Beldis, **23** 219

Beldoch Industries Corp., *see* Donnkenny,
    Inc.
Belgacom, 6 302–04
Belgian Rapid Access to Information
    Network Services, **6** 304
Belgo Group plc, **31** 41
Belize Electric Company Limited, **47** 137
Belk, Inc., V 12–13; **19** 46–48 (upd.);
    72 26–29 (upd.)
Bell and Howell Company, 9 61–64; **29**
    54–58 (upd.)
Bell Atlantic Corporation, V 272–74; **25**
    58–62 (upd.) *see also* Verizon
    Communications.
Bell Canada Enterprises Inc. *see* BCE, Inc.
Bell Canada International, Inc., 6
    305–08
Bell Communications Research *see*
    Telcordia Technologies, Inc.
Bell Fibre Products, **12** 377
Bell Helicopter Textron Inc., 46 64–67
Bell Helmets Inc., **22** 458
Bell Industries, Inc., 47 40–43
Bell Laboratories *see* AT&T Bell
    Laboratories, Inc.
Bell Microproducts Inc., 69 63–65
Bell Mountain Partnership, Ltd., **15** 26
Bell-Northern Research, Ltd. *see* BCE Inc.
Bell Resources, *see* TPG NV.
Bell Sports Corporation, 16 51–53; **44**
    51–54 (upd.)
Bellcore *see* Telcordia Technologies, Inc.
Belleek Pottery Ltd., 71 50–53
**Belleville Shoe Manufacturing
    Company, 92** 17–20
BellSouth Corporation, V 276–78; **29**
    59–62 (upd.) *see also* AT&T Corp.
Bellway Plc, 45 37–39
Belmin Systems, *see* AT&T Istel Ltd.
Belo Corporation *see* A.H. Belo
    Corporation
Beloit Corporation, 14 55–57 *see also*
    Metso Corp.
Beloit Tool Company *see* Regal-Beloit
    Corp.
Belron International Ltd., 76 53–56
Bemis Company, Inc., 8 53–55; **91**
    53–60 (upd.)
Ben & Jerry's Homemade, Inc., 10
    146–48; **35** 58–62 (upd.); **80** 22–28
    (upd.)
Ben Bridge Jeweler, Inc., 60 52–54
Ben E. Keith Company, 76 57–59
Ben Franklin Retail Stores, Inc. *see*
    FoxMeyer Health Corp.
Ben Myerson Candy Co., Inc., **26** 468
Benair Freight International Limited *see*
    Gulf Agency Company
Benchmark Capital, 49 50–52
Benchmark Electronics, Inc., 40 66–69
Benchmark Tape Systems Ltd, **62** 293
Benckiser Group, **37** 269
Benckiser N.V. *see* Reckitt Benckiser plc.
Benderson Development Company, **69**
    120
Bendick's of Mayfair *see* August Storck
    KG.
Bendix Corporation, I 141–43

Beneficial Corporation, 8 56–58
Benefits Technologies, Inc., **52** 382
Benelli Arms S.p.A., **39** 151
Benesse Corporation, 76 60–62
Bénéteau SA, 55 54–56
Benetton Group S.p.A., 10 149–52; **67**
    47–51 (upd.)
Benfield Greig Group plc, 53 63–65
Benguet Corporation, 58 21–24
Benihana, Inc., 18 56–59; **76** 63–66
    (upd.)
Benjamin Moore and Co., 13 84–87; **38**
    95–99 (upd.)
Benjamin Sheridan Corporation, **62** 82
Benlee, Inc., **51** 237
Benn Bros. plc, IV 687
Bennett's Smokehouse and Saloon, **29**
    201
Bennigan's, *see* Metromedia Co.
Benpres Holdings, **56** 214
BenQ Corporation, 67 52–54
Bensdorp, **29** 47
Benson & Hedges, Ltd. *see* Gallaher Ltd.
Bentalls, **37** 6, 8
Bentex Holding S.A., **48** 209
Bentley Laboratories, **22** 360
Bentley Mills, Inc., *see* Interface, Inc.
Bentley Motor Ltd., **21** 435
Bentley's Luggage Corp., **58** 370
Bentoel, PT, **62** 97
Benton International, Inc., **29** 376
Benton Oil and Gas Company, 47
    44–46
Bentwood Ltd., **62** 342
Bercy Management *see* Elior SA.
Beresford International plc, **27** 159
Beretta *see* Fabbrica D' Armi Pietro
    Beretta S.p.A.
Bergdorf Goodman Inc., 52 45–48
Bergen Brunswig Corporation, V
    14–16; **13** 88–90 (upd.) *see also*
    AmerisourceBergen Corp.
Berger Associates, Inc., **26** 233
Berger Bros Company, 62 31–33
Berger Manufacturing Company, **26** 405
Bergerat Monnoyeur *see* Groupe
    Monnoyeur.
Berges electronic GmbH, **56** 357
Beringer Blass Wine Estates Ltd., 22
    78–81; **66** 34–37 (upd.)
Berisford International plc *see* Enodis plc.
Berjaya Group Bhd., 67 55–57
Berk Corp., **52** 193
Berkeley Farms, Inc., 46 68–70
Berkey Photo Inc., *see* Fuqua Industries,
    Inc.
Berkley Dean & Co., **15** 525
Berkley Petroleum Corporation, **52** 30
Berkline Corp., **17** 183; **20** 363; **39** 267
Berkshire Hathaway Inc., III 213–15;
    18 60–63 (upd.); **42** 31–36 (upd.);
    89 92–99 (upd.)
Berkshire Realty Holdings, L.P., 49
    53–55
Berlex Laboratories, Inc., 66 38–40
BerlinDat Gesellschaft für
    Informationsverarbeitung und
    Systemtechnik GmbH, **39** 57

General DataComm Industries, Inc., **14** 200–02

General Dynamics Corporation, I 57–60; **10** 315–18 (upd.); **40** 204–10 (upd.); **88** 105–13 (upd.)

General Electric Capital Aviation Services, **48** 218–19

General Electric Capital Corporation, **15** 257, 282; **19** 190; **20** 42; **59** 265, 268; **71** 306

General Electric Company, II 27–31; **12** 193–97 (upd.); **34** 183–90 (upd.); **63** 159–68 (upd.)

General Electric Company, PLC, II 24–26 *see also* Marconi plc.

General Electric International Mexico, S.A. de C.V., **51** 116

General Electric Mortgage Insurance Company, **52** 244

General Employment Enterprises, Inc., **87** 172–175

General Export Iron and Metals Company, **15** 116

General Felt Industries Inc., **I** 202; **17** 182–83

General Finance Service Corp., **11** 447

General Fire Extinguisher Co. *see* Grinnell Corp.

General Foods Corp., **I** 608, 712; **V** 407; **26** 251; **44** 341 *see also* Kraft Foods Inc.

General Frozen Foods S.A. *see* Vivartia S.A.

General Furniture Leasing *see* CORT Business Services Corp.

General Growth Properties, Inc., 57 155–57

General Host Corporation, 12 198–200

General Housewares Corporation, 16 234–36

General Injectables and Vaccines Inc., **54** 188

General Instrument Corporation, 10 319–21 *see also* Motorola, Inc.

General Insurance Co. of America *see* SAFECO Corp.

General Maritime Corporation, 59 197–99

General Merchandise Services, Inc., **15** 480

General Mills, Inc., II 501–03; **10** 322–24 (upd.); **36** 234–39 (upd.); **85** 141–49 (upd.)

General Motors Acceptance Corporation, **21** 146

General Motors Corporation, I 171–73; **10** 325–27 (upd.); **36** 240–44 (upd.); **64** 148–53 (upd.)

General Nutrition Companies, Inc., 11 155–57; **29** 210–14 (upd.)

General Office Products Co., *see* U.S. Office Products Co.

General Packing Service, Inc., **19** 78

General Parts Inc., **29** 86

General Petroleum Authority *see* Egyptian General Petroleum Corp.

General Physics Corporation, *see* National Patient Development Corp.

General Portland Inc., **28** 229

General Printing Ink Corp. *see* Sequa Corp.

General Public Utilities Corporation, V 629–31 *see also* GPU, Inc.

General Radio Company *see* GenRad, Inc.

General Railway Signal Company *see* General Signal Corp.

General Re Corporation, III 258–59; **24** 176–78 (upd.)

General Sekiyu K.K., IV 431–33 *see also* TonenGeneral Sekiyu K.K.

General Shale Building Materials Inc. *see* Wienerberger AG.

General Signal Corporation, 9 250–52 *see also* SPX Corp.

General Telephone and Electronics Corp. *see* GTE Corp.

General Telephone Corporation *see* GTE Corp.

General Tire, Inc., 8 212–14

General Turbine Systems, **58** 75

General Utilities Company, **6** 555

General Waterworks Corporation, **40** 449

Generale Bank, II 294–95 *see also* Fortis, Inc.

Generale Biscuit Glico France S.A. *see* Ezaki Glico Company Ltd.

Générale Biscuit S.A., **II** 475

Générale de Banque, **36** 458

Générale de Mécanique Aéronautique, *see* Avions Marcel Dassault-Breguet Aviation

Générale de Restauration, **49** 126

Générale des Eaux Group, V 632–34 *see* Vivendi Universal S.A.

Générale Occidentale, **II** 475; **IV** 614–16

Générale Restauration S.A., **34** 123

Generali *see* Assicurazioni Generali.

Génération Y2K, **35** 204, 207

Genesco Inc., 17 202–06; **84** 143–149 (upd.)

Genesee & Wyoming Inc., 27 179–81

Genesee Iron Works *see* Wickes Inc.

Genesis Health Ventures, Inc., 18 195–97 *see also* NeighborCare,Inc.

Genesis Microchip Inc., 82 133–37

Genesse Hispania, **60** 246

Genetic Anomalies, Inc., **39** 395

Genetics Institute, Inc., 8 215–18

Geneva Metal Wheel Company, **20** 261

Geneva Rubber Co., *see* Park-Ohio Industries Inc.

Geneva Steel, 7 193–95

Geneve Corporation, **62** 16

GENEX Services, Inc., **52** 379

Genix Group *see* MCN Corp.

Genmar Holdings, Inc., 45 172–75

Genoc Chartering Ltd, **60** 96

Genosys Biotechnologies, Inc., **36** 431

Genovese Drug Stores, Inc., 18 198–200

Genpack Corporation, **21** 58

GenRad, Inc., 24 179–83

Gensec Bank, **68** 333

GenSet, *see* Thermadyne Holding Corp.

Genstar, **22** 14; **23** 327

Genstar Rental Electronics, Inc., **58** 110

Genstar Stone Products Co., **15** 154; **40** 176

GenSys Power Ltd., **64** 404

GenTek Inc., **37** 157; **41** 236

Gentex Corporation, 26 153–57

Genting Bhd., 65 152–55

Gentiva Health Services, Inc., 79 189–92

GenTrac, **24** 257

Gentry Associates, Inc., **14** 378

Gentry International, **47** 234

Genty-Cathiard, **39** 183–84; **54** 306

Genuardi's Family Markets, Inc., 35 190–92

Genuin Golf & Dress of America, Inc., **32** 447

Genuine Parts Company, 9 253–55; **45** 176–79 (upd.)

Genzyme Corporation, 13 239–42; **38** 203–07 (upd.); **77** 164–70 (upd.)

Genzyme Transgenics Corp., **37** 44

Geo. H. McFadden & Bro., **54** 89

GEO SA, **58** 218

GEO Specialty Chemicals, Inc., **27** 117

geobra Brandstätter GmbH & Co. KG, **48** 183–86

Geodis S.A., 67 187–90

Geofizikai Szolgáltató Kft., **70** 195

Geographics, Inc., **25** 183

GEOINFORM Mélyfúrási Információ Szolgáltató Kft., **70** 195

Geomarine Systems, **11** 202

The Geon Company, 11 158–61

Geon Industries, Inc. *see* Johnston Industries, Inc.

GeoQuest Systems Inc., **17** 419

Georesources, Inc., **19** 247

Georg Fischer AG Schaffhausen, 61 106–09

Georg Neumann GmbH, **66** 288

George A. Hormel and Company, II 504–06 *see also* Hormel Foods Corp.

George Buckton & Sons Limited, **40** 129

The George F. Cram Company, Inc., 55 158–60

The George Hyman Construction Company, *see* The Clark Construction Group, Inc.

George K. Baum & Company, **25** 433

George Kerasotes Corporation *see* Carmike Cinemas, Inc.

George P. Johnson Company, 60 142–44

George R. Rich Manufacturing Company *see* Clark Equipment Co.

George S. May International Company, **55** 161–63

George Smith Financial Corporation, **21** 257

George Weston Ltd., II 631–32; **36** 245–48 (upd.); **88** 114–19 (upd.)

George Wimpey plc, 12 201–03; **51** 135–38 (upd.)

Georgetown Group, Inc., **26** 187

Georgia Carpet Outlets, *see* The Maxim Group.

Georgia Cotton Producers Association *see* Gold Kist Inc.

Hungarian Telephone and Cable Corp., 75 193–95

Hungry Howie's Pizza and Subs, Inc., 25 226–28

Hungry Minds, Inc. *see* John Wiley & Sons, Inc.

Hunt Consolidated, Inc., 7 228–30; 27 215–18 (upd.)

Hunt Manufacturing Company, 12 262–64

Hunt-Wesson, Inc., 17 240–42 *see also* ConAgra Foods, Inc.

Hunter Fan Company, 13 273–75

Hunting plc, 78 163–16

Huntingdon Life Sciences Group plc, 42 182–85

Huntington Bancshares Incorporated, 11 180–82; 87 232–238 (upd.)

Huntington Learning Centers, Inc., 55 212–14

Huntleigh Technology PLC, 77 199–202

Hunton & Williams, 35 223–26

Huntsman Chemical Corporation, 8 261–63

Huntstown Power Company Ltd., 64 404

Hurd & Houghton, *see* Houghton Mifflin Co.

Huron Consulting Group Inc., 87 239–243

Huron Steel Company, Inc., *see* The Marmon Group, Inc.

Hurricane Hydrocarbons Ltd., 54 174–77

Husky Energy Inc., 47 179–82

Husky Oil Ltd., IV 695

Husqvarna AB, 53 126–27

Husqvarna Forest & Garden Company, *see* White Consolidated Industries Inc.

Hussmann Corporation, 67 299

Hussmann Distributing Co., Inc. *see* IC Industries Inc.

Hutcheson & Grundy, 29 286

Hutchinson-Mapa, IV 560

Hutchinson Technology Incorporated, 18 248–51; 63 190–94 (upd.)

Hutchison Microtel, 11 548

Hutchison Whampoa Limited, 18 252–55; 49 199–204 (upd.)

Huth Inc., 56 230

Hüttenwerke Kayser AG, 62 253

Huttepain, 61 155

Huttig Building Products, Inc., 73 180–83

HVB Group, 59 237–44 (upd.)

Hvide Marine Incorporated, 22 274–76

HWI *see* Hardware Wholesalers, Inc.

Hy-Form Products, Inc., *see* Defiance, Inc.

Hy-Vee, Inc., 36 275–78

Hyatt-Clark Industries Inc., 45 170

Hyatt Corporation, III 96–97; 16 273–75 (upd.) *see* Global Hyatt Corp.

Hyatt Legal Services, 20 435; 29 226

Hyco-Cascade Pty. Ltd. *see* Cascade Corp.

Hycor Biomedical Inc. *see* Stratagene Corp.

Hyde Athletic Industries, Inc., 17 243–45 *see also* Saucony Inc.

Hyde Company, A.L., *see* Danaher Corp.

Hyder plc, 34 219–21

Hydrac GmbH, 38 300

Hydril Company, 46 237–39

Hydro-Carbon Light Company, *see* The Coleman Company, Inc.

Hydro Electric, 49 363–64

Hydro-Electric Power Commission of Ontario, 6 541

Hydro-Québec, 6 501–03; 32 266–69 (upd.)

Hydrocarbon Technologies, Inc., 56 161

Hydrodynamic Cutting Services, 56 134

Hygrade Operators Inc., 55 20

Hylsa *see* Hojalata y Laminas S.A.

Hylsamex, S.A. de C.V., 39 225–27

Hynix Semiconductor Inc., 56 173

Hyper Shoppes, Inc., *see* Supervalu Inc.

Hypercom Corporation, 27 219–21

Hyperion Software Corporation, 22 277–79

Hyperion Solutions Corporation, 76 187–91

HyperRoll Israel Ltd., 76 190

Hyplains Beef, L.C., *see* Farmland Foods, Inc.

Hypo-Bank *see* Bayerische Hypotheken-und Wechsel-Bank AG.

Hyponex Corp., *see* Scotts Co.

Hyster Company, 17 246–48

Hyundai Group, III 515–17; 7 231–34 (upd.); 56 169–73 (upd.)

I

I Can't Believe It's Yogurt, Inc., 35 121

I Pellettieri d'Italia S.p.A., 45 342

I. Appel, 30 23

I.B. Kleinert Rubber Company, 37 399

I.C. Isaacs & Company, 31 260–62

I.D. Systems, Inc., 11 444

I-DIKA Milan SRL, 12 182

I. Feldman Co., 31 359

I.G. Farbenindustrie AG, *see* BASF A.G.; Bayer A.G.; Hoechst A.G.

I.M. Pei & Associates *see* Pei Cobb Freed & Partners Architects LLP.

I. Magnin Inc., *see* R. H. Macy & Co., Inc.

I.N. Kote, *see* Inland Steel Industries, Inc.

I.N. Tek, *see* Inland Steel Industries, Inc.

I-X Corp., 22 416

IAC/InterActive Corporation *see* Ticketmaster

Iacon, Inc., 49 299, 301

IAL *see* International Aeradio Ltd.

Iams Company, 26 205–07

IAN S.A. *see* Viscofan S.A.

IAWS Group plc, 49 205–08

IBANCO, 26 515

Ibanez *see* Hoshino Gakki Co. Ltd.

IBC Group plc, 58 189, 191

IBC Holdings Corporation, 12 276

IBCA *see* International Banking and Credit Analysis.

Iberdrola, S.A., 49 209–12

Iberia Líneas Aéreas De España S.A., 6 95–97; 36 279–83 (upd.); 91 247–54 (upd.)

IBERIABANK Corporation, 37 200–02

Iberpistas *see* Abertis Infraestructuras, S.A.

Iberswiss Catering *see* Iberia.

IBJ *see* The Industrial Bank of Japan Ltd.

IBM *see* International Business Machines Corp.

IBM Foods, Inc., 51 280

IBP, Inc., II 515–17; 21 287–90 (upd.)

Ibstock Brick Ltd., 37 203–06 (upd.)

Ibstock plc, 14 248–50

IC Designs, Inc., 48 127

IC Industries Inc., I 456–58 *see also* Whitman Corp.

ICA AB, II 639–40

ICA Fluor Daniel, S. de R.L. de C.V., 41 148

Icahn Capital Corp., 35 143

Icarus Consulting AG, 29 376

ICEE-USA, *see* J & J Snack Foods Corp.

Iceland Group plc, 33 205–07 *see also* The Big Food Group plc.

Icelandair, 52 166–69

Icelandic Group hf, 81 182–85

ICF Kaiser International, Inc., 28 200–04

ICH Corporation, 19 468

Ichikoh Industries Ltd., 26 154

ICI *see* Imperial Chemical Industries plc.

ICL plc, 6 240–42

ICN Pharmaceuticals, Inc., 52 170–73

Icon Health & Fitness, Inc., 38 236–39

Icon International, 24 445

iConcepts, Inc., 39 95

Icreo Co., Ltd., 72 125

ICS *see* International Care Services.

ICS, 26 119

id Software, 31 237–38; 32 9

Idaho Candy Co. *see* Wagers Inc.

Idaho Power Company, 12 265–67

IDB Communications Group, Inc., 11 183–85

Idé *see* GiFi S.A.

Ideal Basic Industries, *see* Holnam Inc.

Ideal Corp., 23 335

Ideal Loisirs Group, 23 388

Idearc Inc., 90 241–44

Ideas Publishing Group, 59 134

IDEC Pharmaceuticals Corporation *see* Biogen Idec Inc.

Idemitsu Kosan Co., Ltd., IV 434–36; 49 213–16 (upd.)

Identification Business, Inc., 18 140

Identix Inc., 44 237–40

IDEO Inc., 65 171–73

IDEXX Laboratories, Inc., 23 282–84

IDG Books Worldwide, Inc., 27 222–24 *see also* International Data Group, Inc.

IDG Communications, Inc, *see* International Data Group, Inc.

IDI, 22 365

IDI Temps, 34 372

iDine Rewards Network *see* Rewards Network Inc.

IDO *see* Nippon Idou Tsushin.

Ido Bathroom Ltd, 51 324

IdraPrince, Inc., 76 192–94

IDS Ltd., *see* American Express Co.

IDT Corporation, 34 222–24

MBE *see* Mail Boxes Etc.

MBG Marketing, **62** 154

MBIA Inc., **73 223–26**

MBNA Corporation, **12 328–30; 33 291–94 (upd.)**

MBRD *see* Moscow Bank for Reconstruction & Development.

MC Distribution Services, Inc., **35** 298

MC Sporting Goods *see* Michigan Sporting Goods Distributors Inc.

MCA Inc., **II 143–45** *see also* Universal Studios.

McAfee Associates *see* Network Associates, Inc.

McAlister's Corporation, **66 217–19**

McBride plc, **82 226–30**

MCall, **64** 57

The McAlpin Company, *see* Mercantile Stores Company, Inc.

McAndrew & Forbes Holdings Inc., **23** 407; **26** 119

MCC *see* Maxwell Communications Corporation; Morris Communications Corp.

McCain Foods Limited, **77 253–56**

McCall Pattern Company, **23** 99

McCall's Corp., **23** 393

McCann-Erickson Worldwide, *see* Interpublic Group of Companies, Inc.

McCann-Erickson Hakuhodo, Ltd., **42** 174

McCarthy Building Companies, Inc., **48 280–82**

McCathren Vending Corporation, **74** 14

McCaw Cellular Communications, Inc., **6 322–24** *see also* AT&T Wireless Services, Inc.

McClain Industries, Inc., **51 236–38**

The McClatchy Company, **23 342–44; 92 231–35 (upd.)**

McColl-Frontenac Petroleum Inc., **IV** 439; **25** 232

McCormick & Company, Incorporated, **7 314–16; 27 297–300 (upd.)**

McCormick & Schmick's Seafood Restaurants, Inc., **71 219–21**

McCown De Leeuw & Co., **71** 363–64

McCoy Corporation, **58 223–25**

McCracken Brooks, **23** 479; **25** 91

McCrory Stores, *see* Riklis Family Corp.

McCullough Environmental Services, **12** 443

McDATA Corporation, **75 254–56**

McDermott International, Inc., **III 558–60; 37 242–46 (upd.)**

McDonald's Corporation, **II 646–48; 7 317–19 (upd.); 26 281–85 (upd.); 63 280–86 (upd.)**

McDonnell Douglas Corporation, **I 70–72; 11 277–80 (upd.)** *see also* Boeing Co.

McDowell Energy Center, **6** 543

MCG PCS Inc., **69** 233

McGrath RentCorp, **91 326–29**

McGaw Inc., **11** 208

McGraw-Edison Co., **II** 17, 87

McGraw Electric Company *see* Centel Corp.

The McGraw-Hill Companies, Inc., **IV 634–37; 18 325–30 (upd.); 51 239–44 (upd.)**

McGregor Corporation, **26** 102

McHugh Software International Inc. *see* RedPrairie Corp.

MCI *see* Manitou Costruzioni Industriali SRL; Melamine Chemicals, Inc.

MCI WorldCom, Inc., **V 302–04; 27 301–08 (upd.)** *see also* Verizon Communications Inc.

McIlhenny Company, **20 364–67**

McJunkin Corporation, **63 287–89**

McKechnie plc, **34 270–72**

McKee Foods Corporation, **7 320–21; 27 309–11 (upd.)**

McKesson Corporation, **I 496–98; 12 331–33 (upd.); 47 233–37 (upd.)**

McKesson General Medical, **29** 299

McKinsey & Company, Inc., **9 343–45**

MCL Land *see* Jardine Cycle & Carriage Ltd.

McLane America, Inc., **29** 481

McLane Company, Inc., **13 332–34**

McLean Clinic, **11** 379

McLeod's Accessories *see* Repco Corporation Ltd.

McLeodUSA Incorporated, **32 327–30**

MCM Electronics, *see* Premier Industrial Corp.

MCMC *see* Minneapolis Children's Medical Center.

McMenamins Pubs and Breweries, **65 224–26**

McMoRan, *see* Freeport-McMoRan Copper & Gold, Inc.

McMullen & Yee Publishing, **22** 442

MCN Corporation, **6 519–22**

McNaughton Apparel Group, Inc., **92 236–41 (upd.)**

McNeil Corporation, **26** 363

McNeil Laboratories *see* Johnson & Johnson

MCO Properties Inc., *see* MAXXAM Inc.

McPaper AG, **29** 152

McPherson's Ltd., **66 220–22**

McQuay International *see* AAF-McQuay Inc.

McRae's, Inc., **19** 324–25; **41** 343–44

MCS, Inc., *see* Mestek, In.

MCSi, Inc., **41 258–60**

MCT Dairies, Inc., **18** 14–16

MCTC *see* Medical Center Trading Corp.

McWane Corporation, **55 264–66**

MD Distribution Inc., **15** 139

MD Foods (Mejeriselskabet Danmark Foods), **48** 35

MDC *see* Mead Data Central, Inc.

MDC Partners Inc., **63 290–92**

MDI Entertainment, LLC, **64** 346

MDP *see* Madison Dearborn Partners LLC.

MDU Resources Group, Inc., **7 322–25; 42 249–53 (upd.)**

Mead & Mount Construction Company, **51** 41

The Mead Corporation, **IV 310–13; 19 265–69 (upd.)** *see also* MeadWestvaco Corp.

Mead Data Central, Inc., **10 406–08** *see also* LEXIS-NEXIS Group.

Mead Johnson & Company, **84 257–262**

Meade Instruments Corporation, **41 261–64**

Meadowcraft, Inc., **29 313–15**

MeadWestvaco Corporation, **76 262–71 (upd.)**

Measurement Specialties, Inc., **71 222–25**

Measurex Corporation, **14** 56; **38** 227

MEC *see* Mitsubishi Estate Company, Ltd.

Mecair, S.p.A., *see* Duriron Co. Inc.

Mecalux S.A., **74 183–85**

MECAR S.A. *see* The Allied Defense Group.

Mecca Bingo Ltd., **64** 320

Mecca Bookmakers, **49** 450

Mecca Leisure PLC, **12** 229; **32** 243

Meccano S.A., **52** 207

Mecklermedia Corporation, **24 328–30** *see also* Jupitermedia Corp.

Meconic, **49** 230, 235

Medarex, Inc., **85 256–59**

Medco Containment Services Inc., **9 346–48** *see also* Merck & Co., Inc.

Médecins sans Frontières, **85 260–63**

Medeco Security Locks, Inc., *see* Hillenbrand Industries, Inc.

Medford, Inc., **19** 467–68

Medi Mart Drug Store Company *see* The Stop & Shop Companies, Inc.

Media Arts Group, Inc., **42 254–57**

Media Exchange International, **25** 509

Media General, Inc., **7 326–28; 38 306–09 (upd.)**

Media Groep West B.V., **23** 271

Media Play *see* Musicland Stores Corp.

MediaBay, **41** 61

Mediacom Communications Corporation, **69 250–52**

Mediamark Research, **28** 501, 504

Mediamatics, Inc., **26** 329

MediaNews Group, Inc., **70 177–80**

MediaOne Group Inc. *see* U S West, Inc.

Mediaplex, Inc., **49** 433

Mediaset SpA, **50 332–34**

Media24 *see* Naspers Ltd.

Medic Computer Systems LLC, **16** 94; **45** 279–80

Medical Arts Press, Inc., **55** 353, 355

Medical Care America, Inc., **15** 112, 114; **35** 215–17

Medical China Publishing Limited, **51** 244

Medical Development Corp. *see* Cordis Corp.

Medical Device Alliance Inc., **73** 33

Medical Economics Data, **23** 211

Medical Equipment Finance Corporation, **51** 108

Medical Information Technology Inc., **64 266–69**

Medical Innovations Corporation, **21** 46

Merrill Lynch Capital Partners, **47** 363

Merrill Lynch Investment Managers *see* BlackRock, Inc.

Merrill, Pickard, Anderson & Eyre IV, **11** 490

Merrill Publishing, **29** 57

Merrimack Services Corp., **37** 303

Merry-Go-Round Enterprises, Inc., 8 362–64

Merry Group *see* Boral Ltd.

Merry Maids *see* ServiceMaster Inc.

Merryhill Schools, Inc., **37** 279

The Mersey Docks and Harbour Company, 30 318–20

Mervyn's California, 10 409–10; 39 269–71 (upd.) *see also* Target Corp.

Merz Group, 81 253–56

Mesa Air Group, Inc., 11 298–300; 32 334–37 (upd.); 77 265–70 (upd.)

Mesaba Holdings, Inc., 28 265–67

Messerschmitt-Bölkow-Blohm GmbH., I 73–75 *see also* European Aeronautic Defence and Space Company EADS N.V.

Mestek, Inc., 10 411–13

Met Food Corp. *see* White Rose Food Corp.

Met-Mex Penoles *see* Industrias Penoles, S.A. de C.V.

META Group, Inc., **37** 147

Metal Box plc, I 604–06 *see also* Novar plc.

Metal-Cal *see* Avery Dennison Corp.

Metal Casting Technology, Inc., **23** 267, 269

Metal Management, Inc., 92 247–50

AB Metal Pty Ltd, **62** 331

Metalcorp Ltd, **62** 331

Metales y Contactos, **29** 461–62

Metaleurop S.A., 21 368–71

MetalExchange, **26** 530

Metallgesellschaft AG, IV 139–42; 16 361–66 (upd.)

MetalOptics Inc., **19** 212

Metalúrgica Gerdau *see* Gerdau S.A.

Metalurgica Mexicana Penoles, S.A. *see* Industrias Penoles, S.A. de C.V.

Metaphase Technology, Inc., *see* Control Data Systems, Inc.

Metatec International, Inc., 47 245–48

Metcalf & Eddy Companies, Inc., **6** 441; **32** 52

Metcash Trading Ltd., 58 226–28

Meteor Film Productions, **23** 391

Meteor Industries Inc., 33 295–97

Methane Development Corporation, **6** 457

Methanex Corporation, 40 316–19

Methode Electronics, Inc., 13 344–46

MetLife *see* Metropolitan Life Insurance Co.

MetPath, Inc., *see* Corning Inc.

Metra Corporation *see* Wärtsilä Corp.

Metra Steel, **19** 381

Metragaz, **69** 191

Metrastock Ltd., **34** 5

Metric Constructors, Inc., **16** 286

Metric Systems Corporation, *see* Tech-Sym Corp.

Metris Companies Inc., 56 224–27

Metro AG, 50 335–39

Metro Distributors Inc., **14** 545

Metro-Goldwyn-Mayer Inc., 25 326–30 (upd.); 84 263–270 (upd.)

Metro Holding AG, **38** 266

Métro Inc., 77 271–75

Metro Information Services, Inc., 36 332–34

Metro International SA, **36** 335

Metro-Mark Integrated Systems Inc., **11** 469

Metro-North Commuter Railroad Company, **35** 292

Metro Pacific, *see* First Pacific Co. Ltd.

Metro Southwest Construction *see* CRSS Inc.

Metro Support Services, Inc., **48** 171

Metrocall, Inc., 41 265–68

Metrol Security Services, Inc., **32** 373

Metroland Printing, Publishing and Distributing Ltd., **29** 471

Metromail Corp., **IV** 661; **18** 170; **38** 370

Metromedia Company, 7 335–37; 14 298–300 (upd.); 61 210–14 (upd.)

Metronic AG, **64** 226

Metroplex, LLC, **51** 206

Métropole Télévision S.A., 76 272–74 (upd.)

Metropolis Intercom, **67** 137–38

Metropolitan Baseball Club Inc., 39 272–75

Metropolitan Clothing Co., **19** 362

Metropolitan Edison Company, *see* GPU, Inc.

Metropolitan Financial Corporation, 13 347–49

Metropolitan Life Insurance Company, III 290–94; 52 235–41 (upd.)

The Metropolitan Museum of Art, 55 267–70

Metropolitan Opera Association, Inc., 40 320–23

Metropolitan Reference Laboratories Inc., **26** 391

Metropolitan Tobacco Co., **15** 138

Metropolitan Transportation Authority, 35 290–92

MetroRed, **57** 67, 69

Metrostar Management, **59** 199

METSA, Inc., **15** 363

Metsä-Serla Oy, IV 314–16 *see also* M-real Oyj.

Metsec plc, **57** 402

Metso Corporation, 30 321–25 (upd.); 85 269–77 (upd.)

Mettler-Toledo International Inc., 30 326–28

Metwest, **26** 391

Metz Baking Company, **36** 164

Metzdorf Advertising Agency, **30** 80

Metzeler Kautschuk, **15** 354

Mexican Metal Co. *see* Industrias Penoles, S.A. de C.V.

Mexican Restaurants, Inc., 41 269–71

Meyer International Holdings, Ltd., 87 312–315

Meyerland Company, **19** 366

Meyers Motor Supply, **26** 347

Meyers Parking, *see* Central Parking Corp.

The Meyne Company, **55** 74

Meyr Melnhof Karton AG, **41** 325–27

M4 Data (Holdings) Ltd., **62** 293

M40 Trains Ltd., **51** 173

MFS Communications Company, Inc., 11 301–03 *see also* MCI WorldCom, Inc.

MG&E *see* Madison Gas & Electric.

MG Holdings *see* Mayflower Group Inc.

MGD Graphics Systems *see* Goss Holdings, Inc.

MGIC Investment Corp., 52 242–44

MGM *see* McKesson General Medical.

MGM Grand Inc., 17 316–19

MGM Mirage *see* Mirage Resorts, Inc.

MGM Studios, **50** 125

MGM/UA Communications Company, II 146–50 *see also* Metro-Goldwyn-Mayer Inc.

MGN *see* Mirror Group Newspapers Ltd.

MGT Services Inc. *see* The Midland Co.

MH Alshaya Group, **28** 96

MH Media Monitoring Limited, **26** 270

MHI Group, Inc., **16** 344

MHS Holding Corp., **26** 101

MHT *see* Manufacturers Hanover Trust Co.

MI *see* Masco Corp.

MI S.A., **66** 244

Mi-Tech Steel Inc., **63** 359–60

Miami Computer Supply Corporation *see* MCSi, Inc.

Miami Herald Media Company, 92 251–55

Miami Power Corporation *see* Cincinnati Gas & Electric Co.

Miami Subs Corp., **29** 342, 344

Mich-Wis *see* Michigan Wisconsin Pipe Line.

Michael Anthony Jewelers, Inc., 24 334–36

Michael Baker Corporation, 14 333–35; 51 245–48 (upd.)

MICHAEL Business Systems Plc, *see* Control Data Systems, Inc.

Michael C. Fina Co., Inc., 52 245–47

Michael Foods, Inc., 25 331–34

Michael Joseph, **IV** 659

Michael Page International plc, 45 272–74

Michaels Stores, Inc., 17 320–22; 71 226–30 (upd.)

MichCon *see* MCN Corp.

Michelin *see* Compagnie Générale des Établissements Michelin.

Michie Co., **33** 264–65

Michigan Automotive Compressor, Inc., *see* Toyoda Automatic Loom Works, Ltd.

Michigan Automotive Research Corporation, **23** 183

Michigan Bell Telephone Co., 14 336–38

Mindpearl, **48** 381

Mindport, **31** 329

Mindset Corp., **42** 424–25

Mindspring Enterprises, Inc., **36** 168

Mine Safety Appliances Company, **31** 333–35

Minebea Co., Ltd., **90** 298–302

The Miner Group International, **22** 356–58

Minera Loma Blanca S.A., **56** 127

Mineral Point Public Service Company, **6** 604

Minerales y Metales, S.A. *see* Industrias Penoles, S.A. de C.V.

Minerals & Metals Trading Corporation of India Ltd., **IV** 143–44

Minerals and Resources Corporation Limited *see* Minorco.

Minerals Technologies Inc., **11** 310–12; **52** 248–51 (upd.)

Minerva SA, **72** 289

Minerve, **6** 208

Minitel, **21** 233

Minneapolis Children's Medical Center, **54** 65

Minneapolis Steel and Machinery Company, **21** 502

Minnehoma Insurance Company, **58** 260

Minnesota Brewing Company *see* MBC Holding Co.

Minnesota Mining & Manufacturing Company, **I** 499–501; **8** 369–71 (upd.); **26** 296–99 (upd.) *see also* 3M Co.

Minnesota Power, Inc., **11** 313–16; **34** 286–91 (upd.)

Minntech Corporation, **22** 359–61

Minn-Dak Farmers Cooperative, **32** 29

Minolta Co., Ltd., **III** 574–76; **18** 339–42 (upd.); **43** 281–85 (upd.)

Minorco, **IV** 97; **16** 28, 293

Minstar Inc., **15** 49; **45** 174

Minton China, **38** 401

The Minute Maid Company, **28** 271–74

Minuteman International Inc., **46** 292–95

Minyard Food Stores, Inc., **33** 304–07; **86** 272–77 (upd.)

Mippon Paper, **21** 546; **50** 58

Miquel y Costas Miquel S.A., **68** 256–58

Miracle Food Mart, *see* The Great Atlantic & Pacific Tea Co., Inc.

Miracle-Gro Products, Inc., *see* Scotts Co.

Mirage Resorts, Incorporated, **6** 209–12; **28** 275–79 (upd.)

Miraglia Inc., **57** 139

Miramax Film Corporation, **64** 282–85

Mirant, **39** 54, 57

MIRAX Corporation *see* JSP Corp.

Mircor Inc., **12** 413

Miroglio SpA, **86** 278–81

Mirror Group Newspapers plc, **7** 341–43; **23** 348–51 (upd.)

Misonix, Inc., **80** 248–51

Misr Airwork *see* EgyptAir.

Misrair *see* AirEgypt.

Miss Erika, Inc., *see* Norton McNaughton, Inc.

Miss Selfridge *see* Sears plc.

Misset Publishers, **IV** 611

Mission Group *see* SCEcorp.

Mission Jewelers, **30** 408

Mission Valley Fabrics, **57** 285

Mississippi Chemical Corporation, **39** 280–83

Mississippi Gas Company, **6** 577

Mississippi Power Company, **38** 446–47

Mississippi River Recycling, **31** 47, 49

Mississippi Valley Title Insurance Company, **58** 259–60

Missoula Bancshares, Inc., **35** 198–99

Missouri Gaming Company, **21** 39

Missouri Gas & Electric Service Company, **6** 593

Missouri Public Service Company *see* UtiliCorp United Inc.

Missouri Utilities Company, **6** 580

Mist Assist, Inc. *see* Ballard Medical Products.

Misys PLC, **45** 279–81; **46** 296–99

Mitchell Energy and Development Corporation, **7** 344–46 *see also* Devon Energy Corp.

Mitchells & Butlers PLC, **59** 296–99

MiTek Industries Inc., *see* Rexam PLC.

Mitel Corporation, **18** 343–46

MITRE Corporation, **26** 300–02

MITROPA AG, **37** 250–53

Mitsubishi Bank, Ltd., **II** 321–22 *see also* Bank of Tokyo-Mitsubishi Ltd.

Mitsubishi Chemical Corporation, **I** 363–64; **56** 236–38 (upd.)

Mitsubishi Corporation, **I** 502–04; **12** 340–43 (upd.)

Mitsubishi Electric Corporation, **II** 57–59; **44** 283–87 (upd.)

Mitsubishi Estate Company, Limited, **IV** 713–14; **61** 215–18 (upd.)

Mitsubishi Group, **21** 390

Mitsubishi Heavy Industries, Ltd., **III** 577–79; **7** 347–50 (upd.); **40** 324–28 (upd.)

Mitsubishi Kasei Corp., **14** 535

Mitsubishi Kasei Vinyl Company, **49** 5

Mitsubishi Materials Corporation, **III** 712–13

Mitsubishi Motors Corporation, **9** 349–51; **23** 352–55 (upd.); **57** 245–49 (upd.)

Mitsubishi Oil Co., Ltd., **IV** 460–62

Mitsubishi Rayon Co. Ltd., **V** 369–71

Mitsubishi Trust & Banking Corporation, **II** 323–24

Mitsui & Co., Ltd., **I** 505–08; **28** 280–85 (upd.)

Mitsui Bank, Ltd., **II** 325–27 *see also* Sumitomo Mitsui Banking Corp.

Mitsui Group, **20** 310; **21** 72

Mitsui Marine and Fire Insurance Company, Limited, **III** 295–96

Mitsui Mining & Smelting Co., Ltd., **IV** 145–46

Mitsui Mining Company, Limited, **IV** 147–49

Mitsui Mutual Life Insurance Company, **III** 297–98; **39** 284–86 (upd.)

Mitsui-no-Mori Co., Ltd., **IV** 716

Mitsui O.S.K. Lines, Ltd., **V** 473–76

Mitsui Petrochemical Industries, Ltd., **9** 352–54

Mitsui Real Estate Development Co., Ltd., **IV** 715–16

Mitsui Trust & Banking Company, Ltd., **II** 328

Mitsukoshi Ltd., **V** 142–44; **56** 239–42 (upd.)

Mity Enterprises, Inc., **38** 310–12

MIVA, Inc., **83** 271-275

Mizuho Financial Group Inc., **25** 344–46; **58** 229–36 (upd.)

MJ Pharmaceuticals Ltd., **57** 346

MK-Ferguson Company, *see* Morrison Knudsen Corp.

MLC *see* Medical Learning Co.

MLC Ltd., **IV** 709; **52** 221–22

MLH&P *see* Montreal Light, Heat & Power Co.

MLT Vacations Inc., **30** 446

MM Merchandising Munich, **54** 296–97

MMAR Group Inc., **19** 131

MMC Networks Inc., **38** 53, 55

MML Investors Services, *see* Massachusetts Mutual Life Insurance Co.

MMS America Corp., **26** 317

MNC Financial *see* MBNA Corp.

MNC Financial Corp., **11** 447

MND Drilling, *see* Mitchell Energy and Development Corp.

MNet, *see* First USA, Inc.

MNS, Ltd., **65** 236–38

Mo och Domsjö AB, **IV** 317–19 *see also* Holmen AB

MOB, **56** 335

Mobil Corporation, **IV** 463–65; **7** 351–54 (upd.); **21** 376–80 (upd.) *see also* Exxon Mobil Corp.

Mobil Oil Indonesia, **56** 273

Mobile America Housing Corporation *see* American Homestar Corp.

Mobile Corporation, **25** 232

Mobile Mini, Inc., **58** 237–39

Mobile Telecommunications Technologies Corp., **18** 347–49

Mobile TeleSystems OJSC, **59** 300–03

Mobilefone, Inc., **25** 108

MobileMedia Corp., **39** 23, 24

MobileStar Network Corp., **26** 429

Mochida Pharaceutical Co. Ltd., **II** 553

Mocon, Inc., **76** 275–77

Modar, *see* Knape & Vogt Manufacturing Co.

Mode 1 Communications, Inc., **48** 305

Modell's Sporting Goods *see* Henry Modell & Company Inc.

Modeluxe Linge Services SA, **45** 139–40

Modem Media, **23** 479

Modern Controls, Inc. *see* Mocon, Inc.

Modern Food Industries Limited *see* Hindustan Lever Limited

Modern Furniture Rentals Inc., **14** 4

Modern Handling Methods Ltd., **21** 499

Modern Times Group AB, **36** 335–38

Nippon Light Metal Company, Ltd., IV
153–55

Nippon Meat Packers, Inc., II 550–51;
78 255–57 (upd.)

Nippon Mining Co., Ltd., IV 475–77

Nippon Mitsubishi Oil Corporation, **49**
216

Nippon Oil Corporation, IV 478–79;
63 308–13 (upd.)

Nippon Paper Industries Co., Ltd., **57**
101

Nippon Phonogram, **23** 390

Nippon Reizo Co. *see* Nichirei Corp.

Nippon Seiko K.K., III 589–90

Nippon Sekiyu Co *see* Nippon Oil
Company, Ltd.

Nippon Sheet Glass Company, Limited,
III 714–16

Nippon Shinpan Co., Ltd., II 436–37;
61 248–50 (upd.)

Nippon Soda Co., Ltd., 85 303–06

Nippon Steel Corporation, IV 156–58;
17 348–51 (upd.)

Nippon Suisan Kaisha, Limited, II
552–53; **92** 269–72 (upd.)

Nippon Telegraph and Telephone
Corporation, V 305–07; **51** 271–75
(upd.)

Nippon Tire Co., Ltd. *see* Bridgestone
Corp.

Nippon Unipac Holding, **57** 101

Nippon Yusen Kabushiki Kaisha (NYK),
V 481–83; **72** 244–48 (upd.)

Nippondenso Co., Ltd., III 591–94 *see*
also DENSO Corp.

NIPSCO Industries, Inc., 6 532–33

NiSource, Inc., **38** 81

Nissan Motor Company Ltd., I 183–84;
11 350–52 (upd.); **34** 303–07 (upd.);
92 273–79 (upd.)

Nissay Dowa General Insurance Company
Ltd., **60** 220

Nisshin Seifun Group Inc., II 554; **66**
246–48 (upd.)

Nisshin Steel Co., Ltd., IV 159–60

Nissho Iwai K.K., I 509–11

Nissin Food Products Company Ltd.,
75 286–88

Nisso *see* Nippon Soda Co., Ltd.

Nissui *see* Nippon Suisan Kaisha.

Nitches, Inc., 53 245–47

Nittsu *see* Nippon Express Co., Ltd.

Niugini Mining Ltd., **23** 42

Nixdorf Computer AG, III 154–55 *see*
also Wincor Nixdorf Holding GmbH.

Nixdorf-Krein Industries Inc. *see* Laclede
Steel Co.

Nizhny Novgorod Dairy, **48** 438

NKI B.V., **71** 178–79

NKK Corporation, IV 161–63; **28**
322–26 (upd.)

NL Industries, Inc., 10 434–36

NLG *see* National Leisure Group.

NLI Insurance Agency Inc., **60** 220

NLM City-Hopper, *see* Koninklijke
Luchtvaart Maatschappij N.V.

NM Acquisition Corp., **27** 346

NMC Laboratories Inc., *see* Alpharma Inc.

NMT *see* Nordic Mobile Telephone.

NNG *see* Northern Natural Gas Co.

Noah's New York Bagels *see*
Einstein/Noah Bagel Corp.

Nob Hill Foods, **58** 291

Nobel Drilling Corporation, **26** 243

Nobel Industries AB, 9 380–82 *see also*
Akzo Nobel N.V.

Nobel Learning Communities, Inc., 37
276–79; **76** 281–85 (upd.)

Noble Affiliates, Inc., 11 353–55

Noble Broadcast Group, Inc., **23** 293

Noble Roman's Inc., 14 351–53

Nobleza Piccardo SAICF, 64 291–93

Noboa *see also* Exportadora Bananera
Noboa, S.A.

Nobody Beats the Wiz *see* Cablevision
Electronic Instruments, Inc.

Nocibé SA, 54 265–68

Nocona Belt Company, **31** 435–36

Nocona Boot Co. *see* Justin Industries,
Inc.

Noel Group, Inc., *see* Lincoln Snacks Co.

NOF Corporation, 72 249–51

NOK Corporation, **41** 170–72

Nokia Corporation, II 69–71; **17**
352–54 (upd.); **38** 328–31 (upd.); **77**
308–13 (upd.)

Nokian Tyres PLC, **59** 91

NOL Group *see* Neptune Orient Lines
Ltd.

Noland Company, 35 311–14

Nolo.com, Inc., 49 288–91

Nolte Mastenfabriek B.V., *see* Valmont
Industries, Inc.

Nomura Securities Company, Limited,
II 438–41; **9** 383–86 (upd.)

Nomura Toys Ltd., *see* Hasbro, Inc.

Non-Stop Fashions, Inc., *see* The Leslie
Fay Companies, Inc.

Noodle Kidoodle, 16 388–91

Noodles & Company, Inc., 55 277–79

Nooter Corporation, 61 251–53

NOP Research Group, **28** 501, 504

Nopri *see* GIB Group.

Norampac Inc., **71** 95

Norand Corporation, **72** 189

Noranda Inc., IV 164–66; **7** 397–99
(upd.); **64** 294–98 (upd.)

Norandex, *see* Fibreboard Corp.

Norbro Corporation *see* Stuart
Entertainment Inc.

Norcal Pottery Products, Inc., **58** 60

Norcal Waste Systems, Inc., 60 222–24

Norcon, Inc., *see* VECO International,
Inc.

Norcore Plastics, Inc., **33** 361

Nordbanken, **9** 382

Norddeutsche Affinerie AG, 62 249–53

Norddeutscher-Lloyd *see* Hapag-Lloyd
AG.

Nordea AB, 40 336–39

Nordic Baltic Holding *see* Nordea AB.

Nordica S.r.l., **15** 396–97; **53** 24

NordicTrack, 22 382–84 *see also* Icon
Health & Fitness, Inc.

Nordisk Film A/S, 80 269–73

Nordson Corporation, 11 356–58; **48**
296–99 (upd.)

Nordstrom, Inc., V 156–58; **18** 371–74
(upd.); 67 277–81 (upd.)

Nordwestdeutsche Kraftwerke AG *see*
PreussenElektra AG.

Norelco Consumer Products Co., 26
334–36

Norelec, *see* Eiffage.

Norex Leasing, Inc., **16** 397

Norfolk Shipbuilding & Drydock
Corporation, **73** 47

Norfolk Southern Corporation, V
484–86; **29** 358–61 (upd.); **75**
289–93 (upd.)

Norge Co., *see* Fedders Corp.

Noric Corporation, **39** 332

Norinchukin Bank, II 340–41

Norlin Industries, **16** 238–39; **75** 262

Norm Thompson Outfitters, Inc., 47
275–77

Norma AS *see* Autoliv, Inc.

Norman BV, **9** 93; **33** 78

Normandy Mining Ltd., **23** 42

Normark Corporation *see* Rapala-Normark
Group, Ltd.

Norment Security Group, Inc., **51** 81

Normond/CMS, *see* Danaher Corp.

Norrell Corporation, 25 356–59

Norris Cylinder Company, *see* TriMas
Corp.

Norris Oil Company, **47** 52

Norshield Corp., **51** 81

Norsk Aller A/S, **72** 62

Norsk Helikopter AS *see* Bristow
Helicopters Ltd.

Norsk Hydro ASA, 10 437–40; **35**
315–19 (upd.)

Norsk Rengjorings Selskap a.s., **49** 221

Norske Skog do Brasil Ltda., **73** 205

Norske Skogindustrier ASA, 63 314–16

Norstan, Inc., 16 392–94

Nortek, Inc., 34 308–12

Nortel Inversora S.A., **63** 375–77

Nortel Networks Corporation, 36
349–54 (upd.)

Nortex International, **19** 338

North African Petroleum Ltd., **IV** 455

North American Aviation, *see* Rockwell
Automation.

North American Carbon, **19** 499

North American Coal Corporation, *see*
NACCO Industries, Inc.

North American Company, **6** 552–53,
601–02

North American Energy Conservation,
Inc., **35** 480

North American InTeleCom, Inc., **IV** 411

North American Medical Management
Company, Inc., **36** 366

North American Mogul Products Co. *see*
Mogul Corp.

North American Nutrition Companies
Inc. (NANCO) *see* Provimi

North American Philips Corporation, *see*
Philips Electronics North America
Corp.

North American Plastics, Inc., **61** 112

North American Site Developers, Inc., **69** 197

North American Training Corporation *see* Rollerblade, Inc.

North American Van Lines *see* Allied Worldwide, Inc.

North American Watch Company *see* Movado Group, Inc.

North Atlantic Energy Corporation, **21** 411

North Atlantic Laboratories, Inc., **62** 391

North Atlantic Trading Company Inc., 65 266–68

North British Rubber Company, **20** 258

North Broken Hill Peko, **IV** 61

North Carolina Motor Speedway, Inc., **19** 294

North Carolina National Bank Corporation *see* NCNB Corp.

North Carolina Natural Gas Corporation, **6** 578

North Central Utilities, Inc., *see* Otter Tail Power Co.

North East Insurance Company, **44** 356

The North Face, Inc., 18 375–77; **78** 258–61 **(upd.)**

North Fork Bancorporation, Inc., 46 314–17

North Pacific Group, Inc., 61 254–57

North Ridge Securities Corporation, **72** 149–50

North Sea Ferries, **26** 241, 243

North Shore Gas Company, **6** 543–44

North Star Communications Group Inc., **73** 59

North Star Container, Inc., **59** 290

North Star Steel Company, 18 378–81

North Star Transport Inc., **49** 402

North Star Tubes, **54** 391, 393

North Star Universal, Inc., *see* Michael Foods, Inc.

North State Supply Company, **57** 9

The North West Company, Inc., 12 361–63

North-West Telecommunications *see* Pacific Telecom, Inc.

North West Water Group plc, 11 359–62 *see also* United Utilities PLC.

Northbridge Financial Corp., **57** 137

Northbrook Holdings, Inc., **22** 495

Northcliffe Newspapers, *see* Daily Mail and General Trust plc.

Northeast Utilities, V 668–69; **48** 303–06 **(upd.)**

Northern and Shell Network plc, 87 341–344

Northern Animal Hospital Inc., **58** 355

Northern Arizona Light & Power Co., **6** 545

Northern Dairies, *see* Northern Foods PLC.

Northern Drug Company, **14** 147

Northern Electric Company *see* Northern Telecom Ltd.

Northern Energy Resources Company *see* NERCO, Inc.

Northern Engineering Industries Plc *see* Rolls-Royce Group PLC.

Northern Fibre Products Co., **I** 202

Northern Foods plc, 10 441–43; **61** 258–62 **(upd.)**

Northern Illinois Gas Co., *see* Nicor Inc.

Northern Indiana Power Company, **6** 556

Northern Indiana Public Service Company, **6** 532–33

Northern Infrastructure Maintenance Company, **39** 238

Northern Leisure, **40** 296–98

Northern Natural Gas Co. *see* Enron Corp.

Northern Pacific Corp., **15** 274

Northern Pacific Railroad, **26** 451

Northern Rock plc, 33 318–21

Northern Star Co., *see* Michael Foods, Inc.

Northern States Power Company, V 670–72; **20** 391–95 **(upd.)** *see also* Xcel Energy Inc.

Northern Telecom Limited, V 308–10 *see also* Nortel Networks Corp.

Northern Trust Company, 9 387–89

Northfield Metal Products, **11** 256

Northland *see* Scott Fetzer Co.

Northland Cranberries, Inc., 38 332–34

Northland Publishing, *see* Justin Industries, Inc.

NorthPrint International, *see* Miner Group Int.

Northrop Grumman Corporation, I 76–77; **11** 363–65 **(upd.); 45** 304–12 **(upd.)**

Northwest Airlines Corporation, I 112–14; **6** 103–05 **(upd.); 26** 337–40 **(upd.); 74** 204–08 **(upd.)**

Northwest Engineering Co. *see* Terex Corp.

Northwest Express *see* Bear Creek Corp.

Northwest Industries *see* Chicago and North Western Holdings Corp.

Northwest Natural Gas Company, 45 313–15

Northwest Telecommunications Inc., **6** 598

NorthWestern Corporation, 37 280–83

Northwestern Flavors LLC, **58** 379

Northwestern Manufacturing Company, *see* Crane Co.

Northwestern Mutual Life Insurance Company, III 321–24; **45** 316–21 **(upd.)**

Northwestern Public Service Company, **6** 524

Northwestern Telephone Systems *see* Pacific Telecom, Inc.

Norton Company, 8 395–97

Norton Healthcare Ltd., **11** 208

Norton McNaughton, Inc., 27 346–49 *see also* Jones Apparel Group, Inc.

Norton Opax PLC, **34** 140

Norton Professional Books *see* W.W. Norton & Company, Inc.

NORWEB plc, **24** 270

Norwegian Cruise Lines *see* NCL Corporation

Norweld Holding A.A., **13** 316

Norwest Bank, **19** 412

Norwest Corp., **16** 135

Norwest Mortgage Inc., **11** 29; **54** 124

Norwich & Peterborough Building Society, 55 280–82

Norwich-Eaton Pharmaceuticals, Inc. *see* The Procter & Gamble Co.

Norwood Promotional Products, Inc., 26 341–43

Nouveaux Loisirs *see* Éditions Gallimard.

Nouvelle Elastelle, **52** 100–01

Nova Corporation, *see* Dynegy Inc.

Nova Corporation of Alberta, V 673–75

Nova Mechanical Contractors, **48** 238

NovaCare, Inc., 11 366–68

Novacor Chemicals Ltd., 12 364–66

Novaction Argentina SA, **48** 224

Novagas Clearinghouse Ltd., *see* Dynegy Inc.

Novalta Resources Inc., **11** 441

Novamax Technologies Inc., **34** 209

Novanet Semiconductor, **36** 124

Novapak Corporation *see* PVC Container Corp.

Novar plc, 49 292–96 **(upd.)**

Novara plc, **60** 123

Novartis AG, 39 304–10 **(upd.)**

NovaStar Financial, Inc., 91 354–58

Novatec Plastics Corporation *see* PVC Container Corp.

Novation, **53** 346–47

Novell, Inc., 6 269–71; **23** 359–62 **(upd.)**

Novellus Systems, Inc., 18 382–85

Noven Pharmaceuticals, Inc., 55 283–85

Noveon International, Inc. *see* The Lubrizol Corp.

Novgorodnefteprodukt, **48** 378

Novo Nordisk A/S, I 658–60; **61** 263–66 **(upd.)**

Novobord, **49** 353

Novotel *see* Accor SA.

NOVUM *see* Industrie Natuzzi S.p.A.

NOVUS Financial Corporation, **33** 314

NOW *see* National Organization for Women, Inc.

NPBI International B.V., **56** 141

NPC International, Inc., 40 340–42

The NPD Group, Inc., 68 275–77

NPI-Omnipoint Wireless LLC, **63** 132

NPM (Nationale Portefeuille Maatschappij) *see* Compagnie Nationale à Portefeuille.

NPR *see* National Public Radio, Inc.

NRC Handelsblad BV, **53** 273

NRF B.V., **56** 247

NRG Energy, Inc., 79 290–93

NRT Incorporated, 61 267–69

NS *see* Norfolk Southern Corp.

NS Group, **31** 287

NS Petites Inc., *see* The Leslie Fay Companies, Inc.

NSF International, 72 252–55

NSK *see* Nippon Seiko K.K.

NSK Ltd., **42** 384

NSMO *see* Nederlandsche Stoomvart Maatschappij Oceaan.

NSN Network Services, **23** 292, 294

NSP *see* Northern States Power Co.

PCI Services, Inc. *see* Cardinal Health, Inc.

PCL Construction Group Inc., 50 347–49

PCM Uitgevers NV, 53 270–73

PCO *see* Corning Inc.

PCS *see* Potash Corp. of Saskatchewan Inc.

PCS Health Systems Inc., **12** 333; **47** 115, 235–36

PCX *see* Pacific Stock Exchange.

PDA Engineering, **25** 305

PDA Inc., **19** 290

PDI, Inc., 52 272–75

PDL BioPharma, Inc., 90 322–25

PDO *see* Petroleum Development Oman.

PDQ Food Stores Inc., 79 310–13

PDQ Machine, **58** 75

PDS Gaming Corporation, 44 334–37

PDV America, Inc., **31** 113

PDVSA *see* Petróleos de Venezuela S.A.

Peabody Energy Corporation, 10 447–49; **45** 330–33 (upd.)

Peabody Holding Company, Inc., IV 169–72

Peace Arch Entertainment Group Inc., 51 286–88

Peachtree Doors, **10** 95

Peak Audio Inc., **48** 92

Peak Oilfield Service Company, *see* Nabors Industries, Inc.

The Peak Technologies Group, Inc., 14 377–80

Peapod, Inc., 30 346–48

Pearl Health Services, **I** 249

Pearl Musical Instrument Company, 78 297–300

Pearle Vision, Inc., 13 390–92

Pearson plc, IV 657–59; **46** 337–41 (upd.)

Peasant Restaurants Inc., **30** 330

Pease Industries, **39** 322, 324

Peat Marwick *see* KPMG Peat Marwick.

Peavey Electronics Corporation, 16 408–10

Peavey Paper Mills, Inc., **26** 362

Pechenganickel MMC, **48** 300

Pechiney S.A., IV 173–75; **45** 334–37 (upd.)

PECO Energy Company, 11 387–90 *see also* Exelon Corp.

Pecom Nec S.A., **72** 279–80

Pediatric Services of America, Inc., 31 356–58

Pediatrix Medical Group, Inc., 61 282–85

Pedigree Petfoods, *see* Kal Kan Foods, Inc.

Peebles Inc., 16 411–13; **43** 296–99 (upd.)

Peek & Cloppenburg KG, 46 342–45

Peekskill Chemical Works *see* Binney & Smith Inc.

Peet's Coffee & Tea, Inc., 38 338–40

Peg Perego SpA, 88 300–03

Pegasus Solutions, Inc., 75 315–18

PEI *see* Process Engineering Inc.

Pei Cobb Freed & Partners Architects LLP, 57 280–82

Pei Wei Asian Diner, Inc. *see* P.F. Chang's China Bistro, Inc.

Pelican Homestead and Savings, **11** 107

Pelican Products, Inc., 86 331–34

Pelikan Holding AG, 92 296–300

Pella Corporation, 12 384–86; **39** 322–25 (upd.); **89** 349–53 (upd.)

Pelmorex, Inc., **52** 402

Pelto Oil Corporation, **44** 362

PEM International Ltd., **28** 350

Pemco Aviation Group Inc., 54 283–86

Pemex *see* Petróleos Mexicanos.

Pen Computing Group, **49** 10

Penaflor S.A., 66 252–54

Penauille Polyservices SA, 49 318–21

Penda Corp., **19** 415

Pendaflex *see* Esselte.

Pendaries Petroleum Ltd. *see* Ultra Petroleum Corp.

Pendle Travel Services Ltd. *see* Airtours Plc.

Pendleton Grain Growers Inc., 64 305–08

Pendleton Woolen Mills, Inc., 42 275–78

Penford Corporation, 55 296–99

Pengrowth Gas Corp., **25** 232

The Penguin Group, **46** 337

Penguin Publishing Co. Ltd., **IV** 659

Penhaligon's Ltd, *see* Intimate Brands, Inc.

Peninsula Stores, Ltd. *see* Lucky Stores, Inc.

The Peninsular and Oriental Steam Navigation Company, V 490–93; **38** 341–46 (upd.)

Peninsular and Oriental Steam Navigation Company (Bovis Division), I 588–89 *see also* DP World.

Peninsular Power, **6** 602

Penn Central Corp., **10** 71, 73, 547; **70** 34

Penn Champ Co., *see* BISSELL, Inc.

Penn Corp., *see* Western Publishing Group, Inc.

Penn Engineering & Manufacturing Corp., 28 349–51

Penn National Gaming, Inc., 33 327–29

Penn Traffic Company, 13 393–95

Penn Virginia Corporation, 85 324–27

Penn-Western Gas and Electric, **6** 524

PennEnergy, **55** 302

Penney's *see* J.C. Penney Company, Inc.

Pennington Seed, Inc. of Delaware, **58** 60

Pennon Group Plc, 45 338–41

Pennsy Supply, Inc., **64** 98

Pennsylvania Blue Shield, III 325–27 *see also* Highmark Inc.

Pennsylvania Dutch Candies Company *see* Warrell Corp.

Pennsylvania Electric Company, *see* GPU, Inc.

Pennsylvania Farm Bureau Cooperative Association, **7** 17–18

Pennsylvania Gas and Water Company, **38** 51

Pennsylvania General Insurance Company, **48** 431

Pennsylvania House, Inc., **12** 301

Pennsylvania International Raceway *see* Penske Corp.

Pennsylvania Power & Light Company, V 693–94

Pennsylvania Railroad, **10** 71–73; **26** 295

Pennsylvania Steel Foundry and Machine Co., **39** 32

Pennwalt Corporation, I 382–84

PennWell Corporation, 55 300–03

Penny Curtiss Baking Co., Inc., *see* Penn Traffic Co.

Pennzoil-Quaker State Company, IV 488–90; **20** 418–22 (upd.); **50** 350–55 (upd.)

Penobscot Shoe Company, **70** 221

Penske Corporation, V 494–95; **19** 292–94 (upd.); **84** 305–309 (upd.)

Pentair, Inc., 7 419–21; **26** 361–64 (upd.); **81** 281–87 (upd.)

Pental Insurance Company, Ltd., **11** 523

Pentastar Transportation Group, Inc. *see* Dollar Thrifty Automotive Group, Inc.

Pentax Corporation, 78 301–05

Pentech International, Inc., 29 372–74

Pentes Play, Inc., *see* PlayCore, Inc.

Pentland Group plc, 20 423–25

Penton Media, Inc., 27 360–62

Pentzer Corporation *see* Avista Corp.

Penzeys Spices, Inc., 79 314–16

People Express Airlines Inc., I 117–18

People That Love (PTL) Television, *see* International Family Entertainment Inc.

People's Radio Network, **25** 508

People's Trust Company, **49** 412

Peoples Bank & Trust Co., **31** 207

Peoples Energy Corporation, 6 543–44

Peoples Gas Light & Coke Co., **6** 529, 543–44

Peoples Heritage Financial Group, Inc. *see* Banknorth Group, Inc.

Peoples National Bank, **41** 178–79

Peoples Natural Gas Company of South Carolina, **6** 576

Peoples Security Life Insurance Co., *see* Capital Holding Corp.

Peoples Trust of Canada, **49** 411

PeopleServe, Inc., **29** 401

PeopleSoft Inc., 14 381–83; **33** 330–33 (upd.) *see also* Oracle Corp.

The Pep Boys—Manny, Moe & Jack, 11 391–93; **36** 361–64 (upd.); **81** 288–94 (upd.)

PEPCO *see* Portland Electric Power Company; Potomac Electric Power Co.

Pepper *see* J. W. Pepper and Son Inc.

Pepper Hamilton LLP, 43 300–03

Pepperidge Farm, Incorporated, 81 295–300

The Pepsi Bottling Group, Inc., 40 350–53

PepsiAmericas, Inc., 67 297–300 (upd.)

PepsiCo, Inc., I 276–79; **10** 450–54 (upd.); **38** 347–54 (upd.)

Pequiven *see* Petroquímica de Venezuela S.A.

Perdigao SA, 52 276–79

PHH Arval, V 496–97; 53 274–76 (upd.)
PHH Monomers, L.L.C., 61 113
PHI see Pizza Hut, Inc.
PHI, Inc., 80 282–86 (upd.)
Phibro Corporation, IV 80; 21 67
Philadelphia Company, 6 484, 493
Philadelphia Eagles, 37 305–08
Philadelphia Electric Company, V 695–97 see also Exelon Corp.
Philadelphia Gas Works Company, 92 301–05
Philadelphia Media Holdings LLC, 92 306–10
Philadelphia Sports Clubs see Town Sports International, Inc.
Philadelphia Suburban Corporation, 39 326–29
Phildar, 37 22
Phildrew Ventures, 44 147
PhileoAviation Sdn Bhd, 65 350
Philharmonic-Symphony Society of New York, Inc. (New York Philharmonic), 69 293–97
Philip Environmental Inc., 16 414–16
Philip Morris Companies Inc., V 405–07; 18 416–19 (upd.); 44 338–43 (upd.) see also Kraft Foods Inc.
Philip Services Corp., 73 257–60
Philip Smith Theatrical Enterprises see GC Companies, Inc.
Philipp Brothers Chemicals, Inc., 25 82
Philipp Holzmann AG, 17 374–77
Philippine Airlines, Inc., 6 106–08; 23 379–82 (upd.)
Philippine National Oil Company, 58 270
Philips, V 339; 22 194
Philips Electronics N.V., 13 400–03 (upd.) see also Koninklijke Philips Electronics N.V.
Philips Electronics North America Corp., 13 396–99
N.V. Philips Gloeilampenfabriken, II 78–80 see also Philips Electronics N.V.
Philips Medical Systems, 29 299
Phillip Securities, 16 14; 43 8
Phillippe of California, 36 24
Phillips Colleges Inc., 22 442; 39 102
Phillips, de Pury & Luxembourg, 49 325–27
Phillips Foods, Inc., 63 320–22; 90 330–33 (upd.)
Phillips International, Inc., 78 311–14
Phillips Petroleum Company, IV 521–23; 40 354–59 (upd.) see also ConocoPhillips.
Phillips-Van Heusen Corporation, 24 382–85
Philmay Holding Inc., 72 217
Phitech, Inc., 56 112
PHLCorp., see Leucadia National Corp.
Phoenix AG, 68 286–89
Phoenix Assurance Co., see Royal & Sun Alliance Insurance Group plc.
Phoenix Footwear Group, Inc., 70 220–22
Phoenix Mecano AG, 61 286–88

The Phoenix Media/Communications Group, 91 383–87
Phoenix Microsystems Inc., 13 8
PhoneCharge Inc. see CheckFree Corporation
Phones 4u Ltd., 85 328–31
Phonogram, 23 389
Photo Corporation of America see PCA International, Inc.
Photo-Me International Plc, 83 302-306
Photo Research Inc. see Excel Technology, Inc.
PhotoChannel Networks, Inc., 45 283
PhotoDisc Inc., 31 216, 218
PHP Healthcare Corporation, 22 423–25
Phuket Air Catering Company Ltd. see Thai Airways International.
PhyCor, Inc., 36 365–69
Physical Measurements Information, 31 357
Physician Corporation of America, 24 231
Physician Sales & Service, Inc., 14 387–89
Physio-Control International Corp., 18 420–23
Physiotherapy Associates Inc., 29 453
Piaget see Vendôme Luxury Group plc.
Piaggio & C. S.p.A., 20 426–29
Piam Pty. Ltd., 48 364
PIC International Group PLC, 24 386–88 (upd.)
Pic 'N' Save, 16 298–99
Picard Surgeles, 76 305–07
Piccadilly Cafeterias, Inc., 19 299–302
Pick 'n Pay Stores Ltd., 82 280–83
Pick Pay, 48 63
Pick Up Stix see Carlson Restaurants Worldwide.
Pickfords Ltd. see Exel plc.
Pickfords Removals, 49 22
Pico Ski Area Management Company, 28 21
Picture Classified Network, IV 597
PictureTel Corp., 10 455–57; 27 363–66 (upd.)
Piece Goods Shops, 16 198
Piedmont Natural Gas Company, Inc., 27 367–69
Piedmont Pulp and Paper Co. see Westvaco Corp.
Pier 1 Imports, Inc., 12 393–95; 34 337–41 (upd.)
Pierburg GmbH, see Rheinmetall Berlin AG.
Pierce Leahy Corporation, 24 389–92 see also Iron Mountain Inc.
Pierce National Life, see Liberty Corp.
Piercing Pagoda, Inc., 29 382–84
Pierre & Vacances SA, 48 314–16
Pierre Fabre see bioMérieux S.A.
Pietrafesa Corporation, 29 208
Piezo Electric Product, Inc., 16 239
Piggly Wiggly Southern, Inc., 13 404–06
Pike Street Industries Inc. see Marchex, Inc.
Pilgrim House Group, 50 134

Pilgrim's Pride Corporation, 7 432–33; 23 383–85 (upd.); 90 334–38 (upd.)
Pilkington Group Limited, II 724–27; 34 342–47 (upd.); 87 375–383 (upd.)
Pillar Corp., 52 185
Pilliod Furniture, Inc., see LADD Furniture, Inc.
Pillowtex Corporation, 19 303–05; 41 299–302 (upd.)
Pillsbury Company, II 555–57; 13 407–09 (upd.); 62 269–73 (upd.)
Pillsbury Madison & Sutro LLP, 29 385–88
Pilot Air Freight Corp., 67 301–03
Pilot Corporation, 49 328–30
Pilot Pen Corporation of America, 82 284–87
Pilsa, 55 189
PIMCO Advisors, 57 20
Pin 'n' Save, 50 98
Pinault-Printemps-Redoute S.A., 19 306–09 (upd.) see also PPR S.A.
Pindar see G A Pindar & Son Ltd.
Pine Tree Casting see Sturm, Ruger & Company, Inc.
Pinelands, Inc., 26 33
Pinelands Water Company, 45 275, 277
Ping An Insurance Company Ltd., 65 104
Pinguely-Haulotte SA, 51 293–95
Pinkerton's Inc., 9 406–09 see also Securitas AB.
Pinnacle Airlines Corp., 73 261–63
Pinnacle Art and Frame, 31 436
Pinnacle Distribution, 52 429
Pinnacle Fitness, 25 42
Pinnacle Global Group Inc. see Sanders Morris Harris Group Inc.
Pinnacle Stix, 70 325
Pinnacle West Capital Corporation, 6 545–47; 54 290–94 (upd.)
Pinole Point Steel, 63 272
Pinto Island Metals Company, 15 116
Pioneer Asphalt Co., 36 146–47
Pioneer Bank, 41 312
Pioneer Concrete Services Ltd. see Pioneer International Limited
Pioneer Corporations, 62 374
Pioneer Cotton Mill, 12 503
Pioneer Electronic Corporation, III 604–06; 28 358–61 (upd.) see also Agilysys Inc.
Pioneer Engineering and Manufacturing Co., 55 32
Pioneer Federal Savings Bank, see First Hawaiian, Inc.
Pioneer Financial Corp., 11 447
Pioneer Hi-Bred International, Inc., 9 410–12; 41 303–06 (upd.)
Pioneer Hotel Inc. see Archon Corp.
Pioneer International Limited, III 728–30
Pioneer Natural Resources Company, 59 335–39
Pioneer Plastics Corporation, 31 399–400
Pioneer-Standard Electronics Inc., 19 310–14 see also Agilysys Inc.
Pipasa, 41 329
Pipe Line Service Company see Plexco.

Poof-Slinky, Inc., **61** 298–300
Poore Brothers, Inc., **44** 348–50
Pop Warner Little Scholars, Inc., **86** 335–38
Pop.com, **43** 144
Pope & Talbot, Inc., **12** 406–08; **61** 301–05 (upd.)
Pope Cable and Wire B.V. *see* Belden CDT Inc.
Pope Resources LP, **74** 240–43
Popeyes Chicken & Biscuits *see* AFC Enterprises, Inc.
Pophitt Cereals, Inc., **22** 337
Poppe Tyson Inc., **23** 479; **25** 91
Popsicle, *see* Unilever PLC.
Popular Club Plan, *see* J. Crew Group Inc.
Popular, Inc., **41** 311–13
Popular Merchandise, Inc., *see* J. Crew Group Inc.
The Porcelain and Fine China Companies Ltd., **69** 301–03
Poron, S.A., **42** 268–69
Porsche AG, **13** 413–15; **31** 363–66 (upd.)
Port Arthur Finance Corp., **37** 309
The Port Authority of New York and New Jersey, **48** 317–20
Port Dickson Power Sdn. Bhd., **36** 435–36
Port Imperial Ferry Corporation, **70** 226–29
Port of London Authority, **48** 317
Port Stockton Food Distributors, Inc., *see* Smart & Final, Inc.
Portage Industries Corp. *see* Spartech Corp.
El Portal Group, Inc., **58** 371
Portal Software, Inc., **47** 300–03
Porter-Cable Corporation, **26** 361–63
Porter Chadburn plc, **28** 252
Portex, **25** 431
Portia Management Services Ltd., **30** 318
Portillo's Restaurant Group, Inc., **71** 284–86
Portland General Corporation, **6** 548–51
Portland General Electric, **45** 313; **50** 103
Portland Plastics, **25** 430–31
Portland Shipyard LLC *see* Cascade General Inc.
Portland Trail Blazers, **50** 356–60
Portland-Zementwerke Heidelberg A.G., **23** 326
Portmeirion Group plc, **88** 308–11
Portnet, **6** 435
Portsmouth & Sunderland, **35** 242, 244
Portucel *see* Grupo Portucel Soporcel.
Portugal Telecom SGPS S.A., **69** 304–07
Portugalia, **46** 398
Posadas *see* Grupo Posadas, S.A. de C.V.
POSCO, **57** 287–91 (upd.)
Posful Corporation, **68** 9
Positive Response Television, Inc., *see* National Media Corp.
Post Office Group, **V** 498–501
Post Properties, Inc., **26** 377–79
Postabank és Takarékpénztár Rt., **69** 155, 157

La Poste, **V** 470–72
Posterscope Worldwide, **70** 230–32
Posti- Ja Telelaitos, **6** 329–31
PostScript, *see* Fay's Inc.
Potain SAS, **59** 274, 278
Potash Corporation of Saskatchewan Inc., **18** 431–33
Potbelly Sandwich Works, Inc., **83** 307–310
Potelco, Inc. *see* Quanta Services, Inc.
Potlatch Corporation, **8** 428–30; **34** 355–59 (upd.); **87** 396–403 (upd.)
Potomac Edison Company, **38** 39–40
Potomac Electric Power Company, **6** 552–54
Potter & Brumfield Inc., **11** 396–98
Pottery Barn, *see* Williams-Sonoma, Inc.
Pottsville Behavioral Counseling Group, **64** 311
Pou Chen Corporation, **81** 309–12
Poul Due Jensen Foundation *see* Grundfos Group
Poulan/Weed Eater *see* White Consolidated Industries Inc.
Powell Duffryn plc, **31** 367–70
Powell Group, **33** 32
Powell's Books, Inc., **40** 360–63
Power Applications & Manufacturing Company, Inc., **6** 441
Power Corporation of Canada, **36** 370–74 (upd.); **85** 332–39 (upd.)
Power-One, Inc., **79** 334–37
Power Parts Co., **7** 358
Power Team, *see* SPX Corp.
PowerBar Inc., **44** 351–53
Powercor *see* PacifiCorp.
POWEREDCOM Inc., **74** 348
Powergen PLC, **11** 399–401; **50** 361–64 (upd.)
Powerhouse Technologies, Inc., **27** 379–81
PowerSoft Corp., **15** 374
Powerteam Electrical Services Ltd., **64** 404
Powertel Inc., **48** 130
Powerware Corporation *see* Eaton Corp.
POZEN Inc., **81** 313–16
PP&L *see* Pennsylvania Power & Light Co.
PPB Group Berhad, **57** 292–95
PPG Industries, Inc., **III** 731–33; **22** 434–37 (upd.); **81** 317–23 (upd.)
PPI *see* Precision Pattern Inc.
PPI Two Corporation, **64** 334
PPL Corporation, **41** 314–17 (upd.)
PPR S.A., **74** 244–48 (upd.)
PR Holdings, **23** 382
PR Newswire, **35** 354–56
PRS *see* Paul Reed Smith Guitar Co.
Practical Business Solutions, Inc., **18** 112
PracticeWorks.com, **69** 33–34
Prada Holding B.V., **45** 342–45
Prairie Farms Dairy, Inc., **47** 304–07
Prairielands Energy Marketing, Inc., *see* MDU Resources Group, Inc.
Prakla Seismos, **17** 419
Pranda Jewelry plc, **70** 233–35
Prandium Inc., **51** 70
Pratt & Whitney, **9** 416–18

Pratt Hotel Corporation, **21** 275
Pratta Electronic Materials, Inc., **26** 425
Praxair, Inc., **11** 402–04; **48** 321–24 (upd.)
Praxis Bookstore Group LLC, **90** 339–42
Praxis Corporation, **30** 499
Pre Finish Metals Incorporated, **63** 270–71
Pre-Paid Legal Services, Inc., **20** 434–37
PreAnalytiX, **39** 335
Precept Foods, LLC, **54** 168
Precise Fabrication Corporation, **33** 257
Precise Imports Corp., **21** 516
Precision Castparts Corp., **15** 365–67
Precision Engineered Products, Inc., **70** 142
Precision Husky Corporation, **26** 494
Precision IBC, Inc., **64** 20–21
Precision Interconnect Corporation, *see* AMP Inc.
Precision Moulds, Ltd., *see* Mattel, Inc.
Precision Optical Industry Company, Ltd. *see* Canon Inc.
Precision Pattern Inc., **36** 159
Precision Power, Inc., **21** 514
Precision Response Corporation, **47** 420
Precision Software Corp., **14** 319
Precision Spring of Canada, Ltd., **55** 305
Precision Stainless Inc., **65** 289
Precision Standard Inc. *see* Pemco Aviation Group Inc.
Precision Tool, Die & Machine Company Inc., **51** 116–17
Precisionaire *see* Flanders Corp.
Precoat Metals, **54** 331
Predica, **II** 266
Prefco Corporation, **57** 56–57
Preferred Medical Products *see* Ballard Medical Products.
Preferred Products, Inc., *see* Supervalu Inc.
PREINCO Holdings, Inc., *see* Transatlantic Holdings, Inc.
PREL&P *see* Portland Railway Electric Light & Power Co.
Premark International, Inc., **III** 610–12 *see also* Illinois Tool Works Inc.
Premcor Inc., **37** 309–11
Premier Cement Ltd., **64** 98
Premier Industrial Corporation, **9** 419–21
Premier Insurance Co., **26** 487
Premier Medical Services, **31** 357
Premier Milk Pte Ltd., **54** 117
Premier One Products, Inc., **37** 285
Premier Parks, Inc., **27** 382–84 *see also* Six Flags, Inc.
Premier Radio Networks, Inc., **23** 292, 294
Premier Rehabilitation Centers, **29** 400
Premier Sport Group Inc., **23** 66
Premiere Labels Inc., **53** 236
Premium Standard Farms, Inc., **30** 353–55
PremiumWear, Inc., **30** 356–59
Premix-Marbletite Manufacturing Co. Inc. *see* Imperial Industries, Inc.

Proffitt's, Inc., 19 323–25 *see also* Belk, Inc.
Profile Extrusion Company, *see* Malt-O-Meal Co.
Profimatics, Inc., 11 66
PROFITCo., *see* Bankers Trust New York Corp.
Progenx, Inc., 47 221
Programmer's Paradise, Inc., 81 324–27
Progress Energy, Inc., 74 249–52
Progress Software Corporation, 15 371–74
Progressive Bagel Concepts, Inc. *see* Einstein/Noah Bagel Corp.
Progressive Corporation, 11 405–07; 29 395–98 (upd.)
Progressive Distributions Systems, 44 334
Progressive Distributors, *see* Hannaford Bros. Co.
Progressive Networks, Inc. *see* RealNetworks, Inc.
Project Carriers *see* Hansa Linie.
Projexions Video Supply, Inc., 24 96
Projiis, *see* Société Générale.
ProLab Nutrition, Inc., 49 275, 277
Proland, *see* ECS S.A.
Proler International Corp., *see* Schnitzer Steel Industries, Inc.
ProLogis, 57 300–02
Promarkt Holding GmbH, *see* Kingfisher plc.
Promeca S.A. de C.V., 72 262
Promodès SA, 26 158, 161; 37 21; 64 66, 69
Promonte *see* Telenor ASA.
Promotional Graphics, 15 474
Promus Companies, Inc., 9 425–27 *see also* Hilton Hotels Corp.
Propaganda Films, Inc., 23 389, 391
Property Automation Software Corporation, 49 290
Property Intelligence PLC, 73 97
Prophecy Ltd., 55 24
ProSiebenSat.1 Media AG, 54 295–98
Proskauer Rose LLP, 47 308–10
ProSource Distribution Services, Inc. *see* Onex Corp.
The Prospect Group, Inc., 11 188
Prospect Provisions, Inc. *see* King Kullen Grocery Co., Inc.
Protan & Fagertun, 25 464
Protection One, Inc., 32 372–75
Protective Insurance Company, 51 37, 39
Protiviti, 70 284
Proton *see* Perusahaan Otomobil Nasional Bhd.
Protravel S.A., 69 7
Proveedora de Seguridad del Golfo, S.A. de C.V., 45 425–26
Provell Inc., 58 276–79 (upd.)
Proventus Handels AB, 35 362
Providence Health System, 90 343–47
The Providence Journal Company, 28 367–69; 30 15
The Providence Service Corporation, 64 309–12
Providence Steam and Gas Pipe Co. *see* Grinnell Corp.

Provident Bankshares Corporation, 85 340–43
Provident Life and Accident Insurance Company of America, III 331–33 *see also* UnumProvident Corp.
Provident National Corporation *see* PNC Financial Corp.
Providian Financial Corporation, 52 284–90 (upd.)
Provigo Inc., II 651–53; 51 301–04 (upd.)
Provimi S.A., 80 292–95
Province Healthcare Company, 69 236
Les Provinces Réunies, *see* Commercial Union PLC.
Provincial Gas Company, 6 526
Provincial Newspapers Ltd., 28 502
PROWA, 22 89
Proximity Technology, 23 210
Prudential-Bache Trade Corporation, II 51; 21 331
Prudential Financial Inc., III 337–41; 30 360–64 (upd.); 82 292–98 (upd.)
Prudential Oil & Gas, Inc. *see* Gulf States Utilities Co.
Prudential plc, III 334–36; 48 325–29 (upd.)
Prudential Steel Ltd., 59 280, 282
Prymetall GmbH & Co. KG, 62 253
PS Business Parks, Inc., 52 291
PSA *see* Pacific Southwest Airlines.
PSA Peugeot Citroen S.A., 28 370–74 (upd.); 54 126
PSB Company, 36 517
PSCCo. *see* Public Service Company of Colorado.
PSE, Inc., *see* Destec Energy, Inc.
PSF *see* Premium Standard Farms, Inc.
PSI *see* Process Systems International.
PSI Resources, 6 555–57
Psion PLC, 45 346–49
Psychemedics Corporation, 89 358–61
Psychiatric Solutions, Inc., 68 297–300
Psychological Corp., *see* Harcourt Brace and Co.
PT Abacus Distribution System Indonesia, 58 140
PT Aerowisata, 58 140
PT Astra International Tbk, 56 283–86
PT Bank Buana Indonesia Tbk, 60 240–42
PT Bank MayBank Indocorp, 72 217
PT Capura Angkasa, 58 140
Ptarmigan Airways Ltd., 56 39
PTI Communications, Inc. *see* Pacific Telecom, Inc.
PTN Publishing, Inc., 56 73
PTT Nederland N.V., 30 393–94
PTT Public Company Ltd., 56 287–90
PTT Telecom BV, V 299–301
PTV *see* Österreichische Post- und Telegraphenverwaltung.
Pubco Corporation, 17 383–85
Publi-Graphics, 16 168
Public Broadcasting Stations, 29 426; 51 309

Public/Hacienda Resorts, Inc. *see* Santa Fe Gaming Corp.
Public Savings Insurance Co., *see* Capital Holding Corp.
Public Service Company of Colorado, 6 558–60
Public Service Company of Indiana *see* PSI Energy.
Public Service Company of New Hampshire, 21 408–12; 55 313–18 (upd.)
Public Service Company of New Mexico, 6 561–64 *see also* PNM Resources Inc.
Public Service Corporation of New Jersey, 44 360
Public Service Enterprise Group Inc., V 701–03; 44 360–63 (upd.)
Public Service Market *see* The Golub Corp.
Public Storage, Inc., 21 52 291–93
Publicaciones Citem, S.A. de C.V., 39 188
Publicis Groupe, 19 329–32; 77 346–50 (upd.)
PubliGroupe, 49 424
Publishers Clearing House, 23 393–95; 64 313–16 (upd.)
Publishers Group, Inc., 35 357–59
Publishers Paper Co., IV 677–78
Publishing and Broadcasting Limited, 54 299–302
Publix Super Markets Inc., 7 440–42; 31 371–74 (upd.)
Pubmaster Finance Ltd, 70 242
Puck Holdings, 35 474, 476
Puck Lazaroff Inc. *see* The Wolfgang Puck Food Company, Inc.
Pueblo Xtra International, Inc., 47 311–13
Puerto Rican Aqueduct and Sewer Authority, 6 441
Puerto Rico Electric Power Authority, 47 314–16
Puget Mill Company, *see* Pope and Talbot, Inc.
Puget Sound Alaska Van Lines *see* Alaska Hydro-Train.
Puget Sound Energy Inc., 6 565–67; 50 365–68 (upd.)
Puig Beauty and Fashion Group S.L., 60 243–46
Pulaski Furniture Corporation, 33 349–52; 80 296–99 (upd.)
Pulitzer Inc., 15 375–77; 58 280–83 (upd.)
Pulsar Internacional S.A., 21 413–15
Pulse Engineering, Inc., 29 461
Pulte Homes, Inc., 8 436–38; 42 291–94 (upd.)
Puma AG Rudolf Dassler Sport, 35 360–63
Pumpkin Masters, Inc., 48 330–32
Punch International N.V., 66 258–60
Punch Taverns plc, 70 240–42
Punter Southall *see* Sanlam Ltd.
Puratos S.A./NV, 92 315–18
Pure-Gar, Inc., 49 276

Rhodia SA, **38** 378–80
Rhône Moulage Industrie, **39** 152, 154
Rhône-Poulenc S.A., **I** 388–90; **10**
470–72 (upd.)
RhoxalPharma Inc., **69** 209
Rhymney Iron Company, **31** 369
Rica Foods, Inc., **41** 328–30
Ricardo Gallo *see* Vidrala S.A.
Ricardo plc, **90** 352–56
Rich Products Corporation, **7** 448–49;
38 381–84 (upd.)
Rich's Inc., *see* Federated Department
Stores Inc.
Richard A. Shaw, Inc., *see* Dean Foods
Co.
Richard D. Irwin Inc. *see* Dow Jones &
Company, Inc.
Richard Ginori 1735 S.p.A., **73** 248–49
Richard R. Dostie, Inc. *see* Toll Brothers
Inc.
Richards & O'Neil LLP, **43** 70
The Richards Group, Inc., **58** 300–02
Richardson Company, **36** 147
Richardson Electronics, Ltd., **17** 405–07
Richardson Industries, Inc., **62** 298–301
Richardson-Vicks Company *see* The
Procter & Gamble Company
Richardson's, **21** 246
Richfood Holdings, Inc., **7** 450–51; *see
also* Supervalu Inc.
Richman Gordman Half Price Stores, Inc.
see Gordmans, Inc.
Richmond Cedar Works Manufacturing
Co., **19** 360
Richmond Corp., **15** 129
Richmond Paperboard Corp., **19** 78
Richton International Corporation, **39**
344–46
Richtree Inc., **63** 328–30
Richwood Building Products, Inc., *see* Ply
Gem Industries Inc.
Rickel Home Centers, *see* Supermarkets
General Holdings Corp.
Rickenbacker International Corp., **91**
408–12
Ricoh Company, Ltd., **III** 159–61; **36**
389–93 (upd.)
Ricola Ltd., **62** 302–04
Ricolino, **19** 192
Riddarhyttan Resources AB *see*
Agnico-Eagle Mines Ltd.
Riddell Inc., **33** 467
Riddell Sports Inc., **22** 457–59; **23** 449
Ridder Publications *see* Knight-Ridder,
Inc.
Ride, Inc., **22** 460–63
Ridge Tool Co., *see* Emerson.
Ridgewell's Inc., **15** 87
Ridgway Co., **23** 98
Ridley Corporation Ltd., **62** 305–07
Riedel-de Haën AG, **22** 32; **36** 431
The Riese Organization, **38** 385–88
Rieter Holding AG, **42** 315–17
Riggs National Corporation, **13** 438–40
Right Associates, **27** 21; **44** 156
Right Management Consultants, Inc.,
42 318–21
Right Source, Inc., **24** 96

RightPoint, Inc., **49** 124
RightSide Up, Inc., *see* AHL Services,
Inc..
Rijnhaave Information Systems, **25** 21
Riken Kagaku Co. Ltd., **48** 250
Riklis Family Corp., **9** 447–50
Rimage Corp., **89** 369–72
Rinascente S.p.A., **71** 308–10
Ring King Visibles, Inc., *see* HNI Corp.
Ring Ltd., **43** 99
Ringnes Bryggeri, *see* Orkla ASA.
Rinker Group Ltd., **65** 298–301
Rio de Janeiro Refrescos S.A., **71** 140
Rio Grande Industries, Inc., **12** 18–19
Rio Grande Servaas, S.A. de C.V., **23** 145
Rio Sportswear Inc., **42** 269
Rio Sul Airlines *see* Varig, SA.
Rio Tinto plc, **19** 349–53 (upd.) **50**
380–85 (upd.)
Riocell S.A. *see* Klabin S.A.
Ripley Entertainment, Inc., **74** 273–76
Ripotot, **68** 143
Riser Foods, Inc., **9** 451–54 *see also*
Giant Eagle, Inc.
Risk Management Partners Ltd., **35** 36
Risk Planners, *see* Supervalu Inc.
Ritchie Bros. Auctioneers Inc., **41**
331–34
Rite Aid Corporation, **V** 174–76; **19**
354–57 (upd.); **63** 331–37 (upd.)
Riteway Distributor, **26** 183
Rittenhouse Financial Services, **22** 495
Ritter Co. *see* Sybron Corp.
Ritter Sport *see* Alfred Ritter GmbH &
Co. KG.
Ritter's Frozen Custard *see* RFC
Franchising LLC.
Ritz Camera Centers, **34** 375–77
**The Ritz-Carlton Hotel Company,
L.L.C.**, **9** 455–57; **29** 403–06 (upd.);
71 311–16 (upd.)
Riunione Adriatica di Sicurtà SpA, **III**
345–48
Riva Group Plc, **53** 46
Riva Fire *see* Gruppo Riva Fire SpA.
The Rival Company, **19** 358–60
Rivaud Group, **29** 370
River City Broadcasting, **25** 418
River Metals Recycling LLC, **76** 130
River North Studios *see* Platinum
Entertainment, Inc.
River Oaks Furniture, Inc., **43** 314–16
River Ranch Fresh Foods LLC, **88**
322–25
River Thames Insurance Co., Ltd., **26** 487
Riverdeep Group plc, **41** 137
Riverside Insurance Co. of America, **26**
487
Riverside Press, *see* Houghton Mifflin Co.
Riverside Publishing Company, **36** 272
Riverwood International Corporation,
11 420–23; **48** 340–44 (upd.)
Riviana Foods, **27** 388–91
Riviera Holdings Corporation, **75**
340–43
Riviera Tool Company, **89** 373–76
Riyadh Armed Forces Hospital, **16** 94
Rizzoli Publishing, **23** 88

RJMJ, Inc., **16** 37
RJR Nabisco Holdings Corp., **V** 408–10
see also R.J Reynolds Tobacco Holdings
Inc., Nabisco Brands, Inc.; R.J.
Reynolds Industries, Inc.
RK Rose + Krieger GmbH & Co. KG,
61 286–87
RKO *see* Radio-Keith-Orpheum.
RM Auctions, Inc., **88** 326–29
RMC Group p.l.c., **III** 737–40; **34**
378–83 (upd.)
RMH Teleservices, Inc., **42** 322–24
Roadhouse Grill, Inc., **22** 464–66
Roadmaster Industries, Inc., **16** 430–33
Roadmaster Transport Company, **18** 27;
41 18
RoadOne *see* Miller Industries, Inc.
Roadstone-Wood Group, **64** 98
Roadway Express, Inc., **V** 502–03; **25**
395–98 (upd.)
Roanoke Capital Ltd., **27** 113–14
Roanoke Electric Steel Corporation, **45**
368–70
Robbins & Myers Inc., **15** 388–90
Robeco Group, **26** 419–20
Roberds Inc., **19** 361–63
Robert Allen Companies, *see* Masco Corp.
Robert Benson, Lonsdale & Co. Ltd. *see*
Dresdner Kleinwort Wasserstein.
Robert Bosch GmbH, **I** 392–93; **16**
434–37 (upd.); **43** 317–21 (upd.)
Robert E. McKee Corporation, **6** 150
Robert Gair Co., **15** 128
Robert Half International Inc., **18**
461–63; **70** 281–84 (upd.)
Robert Hansen Trucking Inc., **49** 402
Robert McLane Company *see* McLane
Company, Inc.
Robert Mondavi Corporation, **15**
391–94; **50** 386–90 (upd.)
Robert Skeels & Company, **33** 467
Robert Stigwood Organization Ltd., **23**
390
Robert Talbott Inc., **88** 330–33
Robert W. Baird & Co. Incorporated,
67 328–30
Robert Wood Johnson Foundation, **35**
375–78
Robertet SA, **39** 347–49
Roberts Express, **V** 503
Roberts Pharmaceutical Corporation, **16**
438–40
Roberts Trading Corporation, **68** 99
Robertson Animal Hospital, Inc., **58** 355
Robertson Building Products, *see* United
Dominion Industries Ltd.
Robertson-Ceco Corporation, **19**
364–66
Robin Hood Flour Mills, Ltd., *see*
International Multifoods Corp.
Robin International Inc., *see* Algo Group
Inc.
Robinair, *see* SPX Corp.
Robins, Kaplan, Miller & Ciresi L.L.P.,
89 377–81
Robinson & Clark Hardware *see* Clarcor
Inc.

Socal *see* Standard Oil Company (California).
Socamel-Rescaset, **40** 214, 216
Socar, Incorporated, **45** 370
Socata *see* EADS SOCATA.
Sociade Intercontinental de Compressores Hermeticos SICOM, S.A., *see* Tecumseh Products Co.
La Sociale di A. Mondadori & C. *see* Arnoldo Mondadori Editore S.P.A.
Sociedad Aeronáutica de Medellín, S.A., **36** 53
Sociedad Andina de Grandes Almeneces, **69** 312
Sociedad Anonima de Instalaciones de Control, **73** 4
Sociedad Anónima Viña Santa Rita, **67** 136–37
Sociedad Anonimo de Electricidad, **72** 278
Sociedad de Inversiones Internacionales Parque Arauco S.A., **72** 269
Sociedad Española Zig Zag, S.A., **68** 258
Sociedad Estatal de Participaciones Industriales, **69** 11
Sociedad Macri S.A., **67** 346
Sociedade Anónima Concessionária de Refinacao em Portugal *see* SACOR.
Sociedade de Vinhos da Herdade de Espirra-Produçao e Comercializaçao de Vinhos, S.A., **60** 156
Società Anonima Lombarda Fabbrica Automobili, *see* Alfa Romeo
Società Finanziaria Idrocarburi, **69** 148
Società Finanziaria Telefonica per Azioni, **V** 325–27
Societa Industria Meccanica Stampaggio S.p.A., **24** 500
Societa Italiana Gestione Sistemi Multi Accesso *see* Alitalia—Linee Aeree Italiana, S.P.A.
Società Italiana per L'Esercizio delle Telecommunicazioni p.A., **V** 325–27
Società Meridionale Finanziaria, **49** 31
Società Sportiva Lazio SpA, **44** 386–88
Société Africaine de Déroulage des Ets Rougier, **21** 439
Société Air France, **27** 417–20 (**upd.**) *see also* Groupe Air France.
Société Anonyme Automobiles Citroën *see* PSA Peugeot Citroen S.A.
Société Anonyme Belge des Magasins Prisunic-Uniprix, **26** 159
Société Anonyme des Assurances Générales *see* Assurances Générales de France.
Société Anonyme des Fermiers Reúnis, **23** 219
Société Anonyme Française du Ferodo *see* Valeo.
La Societe Anonyme Francaise Holophane, *see* Holophane Corp.
Société, Auxiliaire d'Entrepreses SA, **13** 206
Société BIC S.A., **73** 312–15
Société Centrale d'Investissement, **29** 48
Société Civil des Mousquetaires *see* ITM Entreprises SA.

Société Civile Valoptec, **21** 222
Société Commercial d'Affrètements et de Combustibles, **67** 198
Société Commerciale Citroën, *see* Automobiles Citroën
Société Congolaise des Grands Magasins Au Bon Marché, **26** 159
Société d'Emboutissage de Bourgogne *see* Groupe SEB.
Société d'Exploitation AOM Air Liberté SA (AirLib), **53** 305–07
Société d'Investissement de Travaux Publics, **31** 128
Société de Développements et d'Innovations des Marchés Agricoles et Alimentaires *see* SODIMA.
Société de Diffusion de Marques *see* SODIMA.
Société de Diffusion Internationale Agro-Alimentaire *see* SODIAAL.
Société de Fiducie du Québec, **48** 289
Société de Caves et des Producteurs Reunis de Roquefort, *see* Besnier SA.
Société des Ciments Français, **33** 339
Société des Etablissements Gaumont *see* Gaumont SA.
Société des Fibres de Carbone S.A., **51** 379
Société des Grandes Entreprises de Distribution, Inno-France, **V** 58
Société des Immeubles de France, **37** 357, 359
Société des Magasins du Casino, **59** 109
Société des Moteurs Gnôme, **46** 369
Societe des Produits Marnier-Lapostolle S.A., **88** 373–76
Société du Figaro S.A., **60** 281–84
Société du Louvre, **27** 421–23
Société Economique de Rennes, **19** 98
Société Européenne de Production de L'avion E.C.A.T. *see* SEPECAT.
Société Française de Casinos, **48** 198
Société Générale, **II** 354–56; **42** 347–51 (**upd.**)
Société Générale de Banque *see* Generale Bank.
Société Générale de Belgique S.A. *see* Generale Bank.
Société Générale des Entreprises *see* Vinci.
Société Générale du Telephones, **21** 231
Société Industrielle Belge des Pétroles, **IV** 498–99
Société Industrielle Lesaffre, **84** 356–359
Société Internationale Pirelli S.A., **V** 250
Société Laitière Vendômoise, **23** 219
Société Luxembourgeoise de Navigation Aérienne S.A., **64** 357–59
Societe Mecanique Automobile de l'Est/du Nord, *see* PSA Peugeot Citroen S.A.
Société Nationale de Programmes de Télévision Française 1 *see* Télévision Française 1.
Société Nationale des Chemins de Fer Français, **V** 512–15; **57** 328–32 (**upd.**)
Société Nationale des Pétroles d'Aquitaine, **21** 203–05

Société Nationale Elf Aquitaine, **IV** 544–47; **7** 481–85 (**upd.**)
Société Norbert Dentressangle S.A., **67** 352–54
Société Nouvelle d'Achat de Bijouterie, *see* Finlay Enterprises, Inc.
Société Nouvelle des Etablissements Gaumont *see* Gaumont SA.
Société Parisienne Raveau-Cartier, **31** 128
Société pour l'Étude et la Realisation d'Engins Balistiques *see* SEREB.
Société pour le Financement de l'Industrie Laitière, **19** 51
Société Samos, **23** 219
Société Succursaliste S.A. d'Approvisonnements Guyenne et Gascogne *see* Guyenne et Gascogne.
Société Suisse de Microelectronique & d'Horlogerie *see* The Swatch Group SA.
Société Tefal *see* Groupe SEB.
Société Tunisienne de l'Air-Tunisair, **49** 371–73
Society Corporation, **9** 474–77
Socma *see* Sociedad Macri S.A.
Socony *see* Standard Oil Co. (New York).
Socony-Vacuum Oil Company *see* Mobil Corp.
Socpresse, **60** 281
Sodak Gaming, Inc., **41** 216
Sodexho SA, **29** 442–44; **91** 433–36 (**upd.**)
Sodiaal S.A., **19** 50; **36** 437–39 (**upd.**)
SODIMA, **II** 576–77 *see also* Sodiaal S.A.
Sodimac S.A., **69** 312
La Sodis *see* Éditions Gallimard.
Sodiso, **23** 247
Soeker Exploration & Production Pty, Ltd., **59** 336–37
Soekor, **IV** 93
Sofamor Danek Group, Inc. *see* Medtronic, Inc.
Soffo, **22** 365
Soficom, *see* Eiffage.
SOFIL *see* Société pour le Financement de l'Industrie Laitière.
Sofimex *see* Sociedad Financiera Mexicana.
Sofitam, S.A., **21** 493, 495
Sofitels *see* Accor SA.
Sofora Telecomunicaciones S.A., **63** 377
Soft Sheen Products, Inc., **31** 416–18
Soft*Switch, **25** 301
Softbank Corporation, **13** 481–83; **38** 439–44 (**upd.**); **77** 387–95 (**upd.**)
Softimage Inc., **38** 71–72
SoftKat *see* Baker & Taylor, Inc.
Softsel Computer Products, *see* Merisel, Inc.
Software Architects Inc., **74** 258
Software Development Pty., Ltd., **15** 107
Software Dimensions, Inc. *see* ASK Group, Inc.
The Software Group Inc., **23** 489, 491
Software Plus, Inc., **10** 514
Software Publishing Corp., **14** 262
Softwood Holdings Ltd., *see* CSR Ltd.
Sogara S.A., **23** 246–48
Sogedis, **23** 219
Sogo Co., **42** 342

Southern New England
  Telecommunications Corporation, 6
  338–40
Southern Oregon Broadcasting Co., *see*
  Affiliated Publications, Inc.
Southern Pacific Transportation
  Company, V 516–18 *see also* Union
  Pacific Corp.
Southern Peru Copper Corp.,
Southern Peru Copper Corporation, 40
  411–13
Southern Phenix Textiles Inc., 15 247–48
Southern Poverty Law Center, Inc., 74
  312–15
Southern Power Company *see* Duke
  Energy Corp.
Southern Recycling Inc., 51 170
Southern States Cooperative
  Incorporated, 36 440–42
Southern Sun Hotel Corporation *see*
  South African Breweries Ltd.; Sun
  International Hotels Ltd.
Southern Union Company, 27 424–26
Southern Water plc, *see* Scottish Power
  plc.
Southern Wine and Spirits of America,
  Inc., 84 371–375
Southgate Medical Laboratory System, 26
  391
Southington Savings Bank, 55 52
The Southland Corporation, II 660–61;
  7 490–92 (upd.) *see also* 7-Eleven, Inc.
Southland Mobilcom Inc., 15 196
Southland Royalty Co., 10 190
Southmark Corp., 11 483; 33 398
Southport, Inc., 44 203
Southtrust Corporation, 11 455–57 *see
  also* Wachovia Corp.
Southwest Airlines Co., 6 119–21; 24
  452–55 (upd.); 71 343–47 (upd.)
Southwest Convenience Stores, LLC, 26
  368
Southwest Gas Corporation, 19 410–12
Southwest Property Trust Inc., 52 370
Southwest Sports Group, 51 371, 374
Southwest Water Company, 47 370–73
Southwestern Bell Corporation, V
  328–30 *see also* SBC Communications
  Inc.
Southwestern Bell Publications, 26 520
Southwestern Electric Power Co., 21
  468–70
Southwestern Explosives, Inc., 76 34
Southwestern Gas Pipeline, *see* Mitchell
  Energy and Development Corp.
Southwestern Public Service Company,
  6 579–81
Southwire Company, Inc., 8 478–80; 23
  444–47 (upd.)
Souza Cruz S.A., 65 322–24
Souza Pinto Industria e Comercio de
  Artefatos de Borracha Ltda., 71 393
Soviba, 70 322
Sovintel, 59 209, 211
Sovion NV *see* Vion Food Group NV.
Sovran Financial, 10 425–26
Sovran Self Storage, Inc., 66 299–301
SovTransavto, 6 410

Soyco Foods, Inc., 58 137
SP Alpargatas *see* Sao Paulo Alpargatas
  S.A.
SP Pharmaceuticals, LLC, 50 123
SP Reifenwerke, V 253
SP Tyres, V 253
Space Control GmbH, 28 243–44
Space Craft Inc., *see* SCI Systems, Inc.
Space Systems Corporation *see* Orbital
  Sciences Corp.
Space Systems/Loral, *see* Loral Corp.
Spacehab, Inc., 37 364–66
Spacelabs Medical, Inc., 71 348–50
Spacesaver Corporation, 57 208–09
Spaghetti Warehouse, Inc., 25 436–38
Spago *see* The Wolfgang Puck Food
  Company, Inc.
Spalding, Inc., 23 449; 54 73
Spanco Yarns, 62 375
Spangler Candy Company, 44 392–95
Spanish Broadcasting System, Inc., 41
  383–86
Spanish International Communications
  Corp. *see* Univision Communications
  Inc.
Spansion Inc., 80 352–55
Spanx, Inc., 89 423–27
SPAO, 39 184
Spar Aerospace Limited, 32 435–37
SPAR Handels AG, 35 398–401
SpareBank 1 Gruppen, 69 177, 179
Spark Networks, Inc., 91 437–40
Sparkassen-Finanzgruppe *see* Deutscher
  Sparkassen- und Giroverband (DSGV).
Sparks-Withington Company *see* Sparton
  Corp.
Sparrow Records, 22 194
Sparta Surgical Corporation, 33 456
Spartan Communications, 38 308–09
Spartan Industries, Inc., 45 15
Spartan Insurance Co., 26 486
Spartan Motors Inc., 14 457–59
Spartan Stores Inc., 8 481–82; 66
  302–05 (upd.)
Spartech Corporation, 19 413–15; 76
  329–32 (upd.)
Sparton Corporation, 18 492–95
Spear & Jackson, Inc., 73 320–23
Spear, Leeds & Kellogg, 66 306–09
Spec's Music, Inc., 19 416–18 *see also*
  Camelot Music, Inc.
Special Project Films, Inc., 58 124
Special Zone Limited, 26 491
Specialist Computer Holdings Ltd., 80
  356–59
Specialized Bicycle Components Inc., 50
  445–48
Specialty Brands Inc., 25 518
Specialty Coatings Inc., 8 483–84
Specialty Equipment Companies, Inc.,
  25 439–42
Specialty Foods Inc., 29 29, 31; 74 202
Specialty Products & Insulation Co., 59
  381–83
Specialty Products Co., *see* NCH Corp.
Specialty Restaurant Group, LLC, 71 319
Specialty Retailers, Inc., *see* Stage Stores,
  Inc.

Spector Photo Group N.V., 82 344–47
Spectra-Physics, Inc. *see* Newport Corp.
Spectradyne, 28 241
Spectral Dynamics Corporation *see*
  Scientific- Atlanta, Inc.
Spectron MicroSystems, *see* Dialogic Corp.
Spectrum Brands *see* United Industries
  Corp.
Spectrum Club, *see* The Sports Club
  Company.
Spectrum Concepts, *see* Legent Corp.
Spectrum Control, Inc., 67 355–57
Spectrum Data Systems, Inc., 24 96
Spectrum Health Care Services, *see*
  Aramark Corp.
Spectrum Medical Technologies, Inc., *see*
  Palomar Medical Technologies, Inc.
Spectrum Numismatics International, Inc.,
  60 146
Spectrum Organic Products, Inc., 68
  346–49
Spectrum Technology Group, Inc., 18 112
Spectrumedia, 21 361
Speech Design GmbH, 62 38–39
SpeeDee Oil Change and Tune-Up, 25
  443–47
Speedway Motorsports, Inc., 32 438–41
Speedway SuperAmerica LLC, 49 330
Speedy Auto Glass, 30 501
Speedy Europe, 54 207
Speedy Hire plc, 84 376–379
Speedy Muffler King, 10 415
Speizman Industries, Inc., 44 396–98
Spelling Entertainment, 14 460–62; 35
  402–04 (upd.)
Spenard Builders Supply *see* Lanoga Corp.
Spencer & Spencer Systems, Inc., *see*
  Ciber, Inc.
Spencer Gifts, Inc., 15 464
Spencer Stuart and Associates, Inc., 14
  463–65
Sperry & Hutchinson Co., 23 243–44
Sperry Aerospace Group, 6 283
Sperry Corporation, *see* Unisys Corp.
Sperry New Holland *see* New Holland
  N.V.
Sperry Top-Sider, Inc., 37 377, 379
Spezialpapierfabrik Blankenstein GmbH,
  64 275
Sphere Drake Holdings Ltd., 57 136
Spherion Corporation, 52 316–18
Spicecraft Co. *see* Newly Weds Foods, Inc.
Spider Software, Inc., 46 38
Spie *see* Amec Spie S.A.
Spie Batignolles SA, 13 206
Spiegel, Inc., 10 489–91; 27 427–31
  (upd.)
SPIEGEL-Verlag Rudolf Augstein
  GmbH & Co. KG, 44 399–402
Spike's Holding, Inc. *see* The Finish Line,
  Inc.
Spin Master, Ltd., 61 335–38
SpinCircuit Inc., 38 188
Spinelli Coffee Co., 51 385
Spinnaker Exploration Company, 72
  334–36
Spinnaker Industries, Inc., 43 276

Sumitomo Corporation, I 518–20; 11 477–80 (upd.)

Sumitomo Electric Industries, II 104–05

Sumitomo Heavy Industries, Ltd., III 634–35; 42 360–62 (upd.)

Sumitomo Life Insurance Company, III 365–66; 60 292–94 (upd.)

Sumitomo Metal Industries Ltd., IV 211–13; 82 361–66 (upd.)

Sumitomo Metal Mining Co., Ltd., IV 214–16

Sumitomo Mitsui Banking Corporation, 51 356–62 (upd.)

Sumitomo Realty & Development Co., Ltd., IV 726–27

Sumitomo Rubber Industries, Ltd., V 252–53

Sumitomo Trading, 45 8

The Sumitomo Trust & Banking Company, Ltd., II 363–64; 53 320–22 (upd.)

Summa International, 56 284

Summer Paper Tube, 19 78

SummerGate Inc., 48 148

Summers Group Inc., 15 386

The Summit Bancorporation, 14 472–74 *see also* FleetBoston Financial Corp.

Summit Constructors *see* CRSS Inc.

Summit Family Restaurants Inc., 19 433–36

Summit Systems Inc., 45 280

Summit Technology Inc., 30 485

Sumolis, 54 315, 317

Sun Alliance Group PLC, III 369–74 *see also* Royal & Sun Alliance Insurance Group plc.

Sun Apparel Inc., 39 247

Sun Capital Partners Inc., 63 79

Sun Chemical Corp. *see* Sequa Corp.

Sun Communities Inc., 46 377–79

Sun Company, Inc., IV 548–50 *see also* Sunoco, Inc.

Sun Country Airlines, I 30 446–49

Sun-Diamond Growers of California, 7 496–97 *see also* Diamond of California.

Sun Distributors L.P., 12 459–461

Sun Electric, 15 288

Sun Equities Corporation, 15 449

Sun Financial Group, Inc., 25 171

Sun Gro Horticulture Inc., 49 196, 198

Sun Healthcare Group Inc., 25 455–58

Sun Hydraulics Corporation, 74 319–22

Sun International Hotels Limited, 26 462–65 *see also* Kerzner International Ltd.

Sun Life Financial Inc., 85 409–12

Sun Life Group of America, *see* SunAmerica Inc.

Sun Live Co., 56 201

Sun-Maid Growers of California, 82 367–71

Sun Mark, Inc., 21 483

Sun Media, 29 471–72; 47 327

Sun Men's Shop Co., Ltd. *see* Nagasakiya Co., Ltd.

Sun Microsystems, Inc., 7 498–501; 30 450–54 (upd.); 91 455–62 (upd.)

Sun Oil Co., IV 424, 548–50; 11 35; 36 86–87 *see also* Oryx Energy Co; Sunoco, Inc.

Sun Optical Co., Ltd. *see* Nagasakiya Co., Ltd.

Sun Pac Foods, 45 161

Sun Pharmaceutical Industries Ltd., 57 345–47

Sun-Rype Products Ltd., 76 336–38

Sun Shades 501 Ltd., 21 483

Sun Ship, IV 549

Sun Sportswear, Inc., 17 460–63

Sun State Marine Services, Inc. *see* Hvide Marine Inc.

Sun Techno Services Co., Ltd. *see* Nagasakiya Co., Ltd.

Sun Technology Enterprises, *see* Sun Microsystems, Inc.

Sun Television & Appliances Inc., 10 502–03

Sun Valley Equipment Corp., 33 363

SunAir, 11 300

SunAmerica Inc., 11 481–83 *see also* American International Group, Inc.

Sunbeam-Oster Co., Inc., 9 484–86

Sunbelt Beverage Corporation, 32 520

Sunbelt Coca-Cola Bottling Co., *see* Coca-Cola Bottling Co. Consolidated.

Sunbelt Nursery Group, Inc., 12 179, 200, 394

Sunbelt Rentals Inc., 34 42

Sunbird *see* Nagasakiya Co., Ltd.

Sunburst Hospitality Corporation, 26 458–61

Sunburst Shutters Corporation, 78 370–72

Sunburst Technology Corporation, 36 273

Sunco N.V., 22 515

Suncoast Motion Picture Company, 63 65

Suncoast Toys, Inc., 74 14

SunCor Development Company, 6 546–47

Suncor Energy Inc., 54 352–54

Suncorp-Metway Ltd., 91 463–66

Sundance Publishing, IV 609; 12 559

Sundor Group, 54 213

Sundstrand Corporation, 7 502–04; 21 478–81 (upd.)

Sundt Corp., 24 466–69

Sundwig Eisenhütte Maschinenfabrik GmbH & Co., 51 25

SunGard Data Systems Inc., 11 484–85

Sunglass Hut International, Inc., 21 482–84; 74 323–26 (upd.)

Sunkiss Thermoreactors, 21 65

Sunkist Growers, Inc., 26 466–69

Sunkus & Associates, 49 427

Sunkus Co. Ltd. *see* Nagasakiya Co., Ltd.

Sunlight Services Group Limited, 45 139

Sunlit Industries, 44 132

Sunnyside Feedmill, 60 316

Sunoco, Inc., 28 438–42 (upd.); 83 373–380 (upd.)

SunOpta Inc., 79 406–10

SunPower Corporation, 91 467–70

SunQuest HealthCare Corp. *see* Unison HealthCare Corp.

Sunquest Information Systems Inc., 45 279, 281

The Sunrider Corporation, 26 470–74

Sunrise Greetings, 88 385–88

SunRise Imaging, 44 358

Sunrise Inc., 55 48

Sunrise Medical Inc., 11 486–88

Sunrise Senior Living, Inc., 81 380–83

Sunrise Test Systems, 11 491

Sunsations Sunglass Company, 21 483

Sunshine Biscuit Co., 35 181; 36 313

Sunshine Bullion Co., 25 542

Sunshine Mining Company, 20 149

SunSoft Inc., *see* Sun Microsystems, Inc.

Sunstate Airlines Pty Ltd. *see* Qantas Airways Ltd.

Sunsweet Growers, *see* Diamond of California.

Suntech Power Holdings Company Ltd., 89 432–35

Sunterra Corporation, 75 354–56

Suntory Ltd., 65 328–31

SunTrust Banks Inc., 23 455–58

Sunward Technologies, Inc., 10 464

Supasnaps, V 50

Supelco, Inc., 36 431

Super Bazars, 26 159

Super Dart *see* Dart Group Corp.

Super 8 Motels, Inc., 83 381-385

Super Food Services, Inc., 15 479–81

Super 1 Stores *see* Brookshire Grocery Co.

Super Sagless Spring Corp., 15 103

Super Sol Ltd., 41 56–57

Superb Manufacturing, 60 56

La Supercalor S.P.A. *see* De'Longhi S.p.A.

Supercuts Inc., 26 475–78

Superdrug plc *see* Rite Aid Corp.

Superfast Ferries SA, 64 45

Superior Bearings Company *see* Federal-Mogul Corp.

Superior Coach Co. *see* Accubuilt, Inc.

Superior Energy Services, Inc., 65 332–34

Superior Essex Inc., 80 364–68

Superior Foam and Polymers, Inc., 44 261

Superior Healthcare Group, Inc., 11 221

Superior Industries International, Inc., 8 505–07

Superior Oil Co., 49 137

Superior Recycled Fiber Industries, 26 363

Superior Uniform Group, Inc., 30 455–57

SuperMac Technology Inc., 16 419

Supermarchés GB, 26 159

Supermarkets General Holdings Corporation, II 672–74 *see also* Pathmark Stores, Inc.

Supersaver Wholesale Club, Inc. *see* Wal-Mart Stores, Inc.

Supersnaps, 19 124

SuperStation WTBS *see* Turner Broadcasting System, Inc.

SUPERVALU INC., II 668–71; 18 503–08 (upd.); 50 453–59 (upd.)

Supplyon AG, 48 450

Suprema Specialties, Inc., 27 440–42

Trans World Airlines, Inc., I 125–27; 12 487–90 (upd.); 35 424–29 (upd.)

Trans-World Corp., **19** 456; **47** 231

Trans World Entertainment Corporation, 24 501–03; 68 374–77 (upd.)

Trans World International, *see* International Management Group.

Trans World Life Insurance Company, **27** 46–47

Transaction Systems Architects, Inc., 29 477–79; 82 397–402 (upd.)

TransAlta Utilities Corporation, 6 585–87

Transamerica—An AEGON Company, I 536–38; 13 528–30 (upd.); 41 400–03 (upd.)

Transamerica Pawn Holdings *see* EZCORP Inc.

Transamerica Retirement Services, **63** 176

TransAmerican Waste Industries Inc., **41** 414

Transat *see* Compagnie Générale Transatlantique (Transat).

Transatlantic Holdings, Inc., 11 532–33

Transatlantische Gruppe, *see* Winterthur Group.

Transax, **63** 102

TransBrasil S/A Linhas Aéreas, 31 443–45

TransCanada PipeLines Limited, V 737–38

Transco Energy Company, V 739–40 *see also* The Williams Companies.

Transcontinental Air Transport, *see* Trans World Airlines, Inc.

Transcontinental Gas Pipe Line Corporation *see* Transco Energy Co.

TransCor America, Inc., **23** 154

Transfer Drivers, Inc., **46** 301

Transfracht, **6** 426

Transiciel SA, 48 400–02

Transit Homes of America, Inc., **46** 301

Transitions Optical, Inc., 83 411-415

Transkaryotic Therapies Inc., **54** 111

Transking Inc. *see* King Kullen Grocery Co., Inc.

Transkrit Corp., **IV** 640; **26** 273

Translittoral, **67** 353

Transmanche-Link, *see* Eurotunnel PLC.

Transmedia Network Inc., 20 494–97 *see also* Rewards Network Inc.

Transmedica International, Inc., **41** 225

Transmisiones y Equipos Mecanicos, S.A. de C.V., **23** 171

TransMontaigne Inc., 28 470–72

Transmontane Rod and Gun Club, **43** 435–36

Transnation Title Insurance Company *see* LandAmerica Financial Group, Inc.

Transnet Ltd., 6 433–35

Transocean Sedco Forex Inc., 45 417–19

Transport Corporation of America, Inc., 49 400–03

Transport International Pool, **58** 239

TransPoint L.L.C. *see* CheckFree Corporation

Transportacion Ferroviaria Mexicana, **50** 209

Transportacion Maritima Mexicana S.A. de C.V., **12** 279; **26** 236; **47** 162; **50** 208

Transportation Technologies Industries Inc., **51** 155

Transportation.com, **45** 451

Transportes Aéreas Centro-Americanos *see* Grupo TACA.

Transportes Aereos Portugueses, S.A., 6 125–27 *see also* TAP—Air Portugal Transportes Aéreos Portugueses S.A.

Transportes Aeromar, **39** 188

TransPro, Inc., 71 356–59

Transrack S.A., **26** 363

TransWestern Holdings L.P. *see* Yell Group PLC

Transworld Communications, **35** 165

Transworld Drilling Company Limited *see* Kerr-McGee Corp.

The Tranzonic Companies, 15 500–02; 37 392–95 (upd.)

Trasgo, S.A. de C.V., **14** 516; **50** 493

Travel Inc., **26** 309

Travel Ports of America, Inc., 17 493–95

Travelers/Aetna Property Casualty Corp., **63** 14

Travelers Book Club, *see* Book-of-the-Month Club.

Travelers Corporation, III 387–90 *see also* Citigroup Inc.

Travelers Property Casualty Corp. *see* The St. Paul Travelers Companies, Inc.

Travelocity.com, Inc., 46 434–37

Travelzoo Inc., 79 419–22

Travers Morgan Ltd., **42** 183

Travis Boats & Motors, Inc., 37 396–98

Travis Perkins plc, 34 450–52

TRC *see* Tennessee Restaurant Co.

TRC Companies, Inc., 32 461–64

TRE Corp., **23** 225

Treadco, Inc., 19 454–56

Treasure Chest Advertising Company, Inc., 32 465–67

Treatment Centers of America, **11** 379

Tredegar Corporation, 52 349–51

Tree of Life, Inc., 29 480–82

Tree Sweet Products Corp., **26** 325

Tree Top, Inc., 76 357–59

TreeHouse Foods, Inc., 79 423–26

Trego Systems Inc., **64** 190

Trek Bicycle Corporation, 16 493–95; 78 406–10 (upd.)

Tremec *see* Transmisiones y Equipos Mecanicos, S.A. de C.V.

Tremont Corporation, **21** 490

Trencherwood Plc, **45** 443

Trend-Lines, Inc., 22 516–18

Trends Magazine NV, **48** 347

Trendwest Resorts, Inc., 33 409–11 *see also* Jeld-Wen, Inc.

TrentonWorks Limited *see* The Greenbrier Companies.

Trevor Sorbie of America, Inc., **60** 287

Trex Company, Inc., 71 360–62

Tri-City Utilities Company, **6** 514

Tri-Miller Packing Company, *see* Thorn Apple Valley, Inc.

Tri-State Baking, **53** 21

Tri-State Improvement Company *see* Cincinnati Gal & Electric Co.

Tri-State Publishing & Communications, Inc., **22** 442

Tri-State Recycling Corporation, **15** 117

Tri-Union Seafoods LLC, *see* Chicken of the Sea International.

Tri Valley Growers, 32 468–71

Tri-Village Developments BV, **58** 359

Triad Artists Inc., **23** 514

Triad Systems Corp., **38** 96

The Triangle Group, *see* The Marmon Group, Inc.

Triangle Pharmaceuticals, Inc., **54** 131

Triangle Sheet Metal Works, Inc., **45** 327

Triarc Companies, Inc., 8 535–37; 34 453–57 (upd.)

Triax Midwest Associates L.P. *see* Mediacom Communications Corp.

Tribe Computer Works *see* Zoom Technologies, Inc.

Tribeca Grill *see* Myriad Restaurant Group, Inc.

Tribune Company, IV 682–84; 22 519–23 (upd.); 63 389–95 (upd.)

Tricap Restructuring Fund, **59** 162

Trick & Murray, **22** 153

Trico Marine Services, Inc., 89 450–53

Trico Products Corporation, 15 503–05

Tricon Global Restaurants, Inc. *see* Yum! Brands Inc.

Tricor Direct Inc. *see* Brady Corporation

Tridel Enterprises Inc., 9 512–13

Trident Data Systems, **54** 396

Trident II, Inc., **64** 253

Trident NGL Holdings Inc., *see* Dynegy Inc.

Trident Seafoods Corporation, 56 359–61

Tridon Ltd., **69** 206

Trigen Energy Corporation, 42 386–89

Trigon Industries, *see* Dynatech Corp.

Trilan Developments Ltd., *see* Tridel Enterprises Inc.

Trilogy Fabrics, Inc., **16** 125

Trilogy Retail Enterprises L.P., **58** 186

Trilon Financial Corporation, II 456–57

TriMas Corp., 11 534–36

Trimble Navigation Limited, 40 441–43

Trimel Corp., **47** 54

Trinc Company, **59** 320

Třinecké Železárny A.S., 92 384–87

TriNet Corporate Realty Trust, Inc., **65** 146

Trinity Beverage Corporation, **11** 451

Trinity Broadcasting, *see* International Family Entertainment Inc.

Trinity Distributors, **15** 139

Trinity Industries, Incorporated, 7 540–41

Trinity Mirror plc, 49 404–10 (upd.)

TRINOVA Corporation, III 640–42

TriPath Imaging, Inc., 77 446–49

Triple Five Group Ltd., 49 411–15

Triple P N.V., 26 496–99

Whiting Petroleum Corporation, 81 424–27

Whitman Corporation, 10 553–55 (upd.) *see also* PepsiAmericas, Inc.

Whitman Education Group, Inc., 41 419–21

Whitmire Distribution *see* Cardinal Health, Inc.

Whitney Group, 40 236–38

Whitney Holding Corporation, 21 522–24

Whitney Partners, L.L.C., 40 237

Whittaker Corporation, I 544–46; 48 432–35 (upd.)

Whittard of Chelsea Plc, 61 394–97

Whittman-Hart Inc. *see* marchFIRST, Inc.

Whole Foods Market, Inc., 20 523–27; 50 530–34 (upd.)

Wholesale Cellular USA *see* Brightpoint, Inc.

The Wholesale Club, Inc., *see* Wal-Mart Stores, Inc.

Wholesome Foods, L.L.C., 32 274, 277

Wholly Harvest, 19 502

WHSC Direct, Inc., 53 359

WHX Corporation, 58 360

Whyte & Mackay Distillers Ltd., *see* Gallaher Group Plc.

Wicanders Group, 48 119

Wicell Research Institute, 65 367

Wickes Inc., V 221–23; 25 533–36 (upd.)

Wicor, Inc., 54 419

Widmer Brothers Brewing Company, 76 379–82

Wiener Städtische, 58 169

Wiesner, Inc., 22 442

Wight Nurseries *see* Monrovia Nursery Co.

Wikimedia Foundation, Inc., 91 523–26

Wilbert, Inc., 56 377–80

Wilbur Chocolate Company, 66 369–71

Wild by Nature *see* King Cullen Grocery Co., Inc.

Wild Harvest, 56 317

Wild Leitz G.m.b.H., 23 83

Wild Oats Markets, Inc., 19 500–02; 41 422–25 (upd.)

WildBlue Communications Inc., 54 406

Wilderness Systems *see* Confluence Holdings Corp.

Wildlife Conservation Society, 31 462–64

Wildlife Land Trust, 54 172

Wildwater Kingdom, *see* Cedar Fair, L.P.

Wiles Group Ltd. *see* Hanson PLC.

Oy Wilh. Schauman AB *see* UPM-Kymmene

Wilhelm Weber GmbH, 22 95

Wilhelm Wilhelmsen Ltd., 7 40; 41 42

Wilkinson Hardware Stores Ltd., 80 416–18

Wilkinson Sword Ltd., 60 349–52

Willamette Falls Electric Company *see* Portland General Corp.

Willamette Industries, Inc., IV 357–59; 31 465–68 (upd.) *see also* Weyerhaeuser Co.

Willamette Valley Vineyards, Inc., 85 465–69

Willbros Group, Inc., 56 381–83

Willcox & Gibbs Sewing Machine Co., 15 384

Willey Brothers, Inc. *see* BrandPartners Group, Inc.

William Benton Foundation, *see* Encyclopaedia Britannica, Inc.

The William Brooks Shoe Company *see* Rocky Shoes & Boots, Inc.

William Byrd Press Inc., 23 100

William Cory & Son Ltd., 6 417

William Esty Company, 16 72

William George Company, 32 519

William Grant & Sons Ltd., 60 353–55

William Hewlett, 41 117

William Hill Organization Limited, 49 449–52

William Hodges & Company, 33 150

William Hollins & Company Ltd., 44 105

William L. Bonnell Company, Inc., 66 372–74

William Lyon Homes, 59 420–22

William Morris Agency, Inc., 23 512–14

William P. Young Contruction, 43 400

William Penn Life Insurance Company of New York, *see* Legal & General Group plc.

William Reed Publishing Ltd., 78 467–70

William Zinsser & Company, Inc., 58 365–67

Williams & Connolly LLP, 47 445–48

Williams & Wilkins *see* Waverly, Inc.

Williams Advanced Materials Inc., *see* Brush Wellman Inc.

Williams Communications Group, Inc., 34 507–10

The Williams Companies, Inc., IV 575–76; 31 469–72 (upd.)

Williams Electronics Games, Inc., 15 539

The Williams Manufacturing Company, *see* Escalade, Inc.

Williams/Nintendo Inc., 15 537

Williams Oil-O-Matic Heating Corporation, 21 42

Williams plc, 44 255

Williams Printing Company *see* Graphic Industries Inc.

Williams Scotsman, Inc., 65 361–64

Williams-Sonoma, Inc., 17 548–50; 44 447–50 (upd.)

Williamsburg Restoration, Incorporated, 53 106

Williamson-Dickie Manufacturing Company, 14 549–50; 45 438–41 (upd.)

Williamsport Barber and Beauty Corp., 60 287

Willie G's, 15 279

Willis Corroon Group plc, 25 537–39

Willis Group Holdings Ltd., 73 36

Willis Stein & Partners, 21 404; 58 318, 321; 73 397

Williston Basin Interstate Pipeline Company, *see* MDU Resources Group, Inc.; WBI Holdings, Inc.

Wilmington Trust Corporation, 25 540–43

Wilsdorf & Davis, *see* Montres Rolex S.A.

Wilshire Real Estate Investment Trust Inc., 30 223

Wilshire Restaurant Group Inc., 28 258

Wilson Bowden Plc, 45 442–44

Wilson Brothers, *see* Triarc Companies, Inc.

Wilson Foods Corp., *see* Doskocil Companies, Inc.

Wilson Greatbatch Technologies Ltd *see* Greatbatch Inc.

Wilson Jones Company, 7 4–5

Wilson Sonsini Goodrich & Rosati, 34 511–13

Wilson Sporting Goods Company, 24 530–32; 84 431–436 (upd.)

Wilson's Supermarkets, *see* Hannaford Bros. Co.

Wilsons The Leather Experts Inc., 21 525–27; 58 368–71 (upd.)

Wimbledon Tennis Championships *see* The All England Lawn Tennis & Croquet Club.

Win-Chance Foods, *see* H.J. Heinz Co.

Winbond Electronics Corporation, 74 389–91

Wincanton plc, 52 418–20

Winchell's Donut Houses Operating Company, L.P., 60 356–59

WinCo Foods Inc., 60 360–63

Wincor Nixdorf Holding GmbH, 69 370–73 (upd.)

Wind River Systems, Inc., 37 419–22

Windmere Corporation, 16 537–39 *see also* Applica Inc.

Windmere-Durable Holdings, Inc., 30 404

WindowVisions, Inc., 29 288

Windsong Exports, 52 429

Windsor Forestry Tools, Inc., 48 59

Windstar Sail Cruises *see* Carnival Corp.

Windstream Corporation, 83 462-465

Windsurfing International, 23 55

Windswept Environmental Group, Inc., 62 389–92

Windward Capital Partners, 28 152, 154

The Wine Group, Inc., 39 419–21

Winegard Company, 56 384–87

Winfire, Inc., 37 194

Wingate Partners, *see* United Stationers Inc.

Winget Ltd. *see* Seddon Group Ltd.

Wings & Wheels Express, Inc., *see* Air Express International Corp.

WingspanBank.com, 38 270

Winkelman Stores, Inc., *see* Petrie Stores Corp.

Winlet Fashions, 22 223

Winmark Corporation, 74 392–95

Winn-Dixie Stores, Inc., II 683–84; 21 528–30 (upd.); 59 423–27 (upd.)

Winnebago Industries Inc., 7 589–91; 27 509–12 (upd.)

Index to Industries

Accounting

American Institute of Certified Public
    Accountants (AICPA), 44
Andersen, 29 (upd.); 68 (upd.)
Automatic Data Processing, Inc., III; 9
    (upd.); 47 (upd.)
CROSSMARK, 79
Deloitte Touche Tohmatsu International,
    9; 29 (upd.)
Ernst & Young, 9; 29 (upd.)
FTI Consulting, Inc., 77
Grant Thornton International, 57
Huron Consulting Group Inc., 87
KPMG International, 33 (upd.)
L.S. Starrett Co., 13
McLane Company, Inc., 13
NCO Group, Inc., 42
Paychex, Inc., 15; 46 (upd.)
PKF International 78
Plante & Moran, LLP, 71
PRG-Schultz International, Inc., 73
PricewaterhouseCoopers, 9; 29 (upd.)
Resources Connection, Inc., 81
Robert Wood Johnson Foundation, 35
Saffery Champness, 80
Schenck Business Solutions, 88
StarTek, Inc., 79
Travelzoo Inc., 79
Univision Communications Inc., 24; 83
    (upd.)

Advertising & Other Business Services

ABM Industries Incorporated, 25 (upd.)
AchieveGlobal Inc., 90
Ackerley Communications, Inc., 9
ACNielsen Corporation, 13; 38 (upd.)

Acosta Sales and Marketing Company,
    Inc., 77
Acsys, Inc., 44
Adecco S.A., 36 (upd.)
Adia S.A., 6
Administaff, Inc., 52
The Advertising Council, Inc., 76
The Advisory Board Company, 80
Advo, Inc., 6; 53 (upd.)
Aegis Group plc, 6
Affiliated Computer Services, Inc., 61
AHL Services, Inc., 27
Alloy, Inc., 55
Amdocs Ltd., 47
American Building Maintenance
    Industries, Inc., 6
American Library Association, 86
The American Society of Composers,
    Authors and Publishers (ASCAP), 29
Amey Plc, 47
Analysts International Corporation, 36
aQuantive, Inc., 81
The Arbitron Company, 38
Ariba, Inc., 57
Armor Holdings, Inc., 27
Asatsu-DK Inc., 82
Ashtead Group plc, 34
The Associated Press, 13
Avalon Correctional Services, Inc., 75
Bain & Company, 55
Barrett Business Services, Inc., 16
Barton Protective Services Inc., 53
Bates Worldwide, Inc., 14; 33 (upd.)
Bearings, Inc., 13
Berlitz International, Inc., 13
Bernard Hodes Group Inc., 86
Bernstein-Rein, 92
Big Flower Press Holdings, Inc., 21
Billing Concepts, Inc., 26; 72 (upd.)

The BISYS Group, Inc., 73
Boron, LePore & Associates, Inc., 45
The Boston Consulting Group, 58
Bozell Worldwide Inc., 25
BrandPartners Group, Inc., 58
Bright Horizons Family Solutions, Inc., 31
Broadcast Music Inc., 23; 90 (upd.)
Buck Consultants, Inc., 55
Bureau Veritas SA, 55
Burke, Inc., 88
Burns International Services Corporation,
    13; 41 (upd.)
Cambridge Technology Partners, Inc., 36
Campbell-Ewald Advertising, 86
Campbell-Mithun-Esty, Inc., 16
Cannon Design, 63
Capita Group PLC, 69
Career Education Corporation, 45
Carmichael Lynch Inc., 28
Cazenove Group plc, 72
CCC Information Services Group Inc., 74
CDI Corporation, 6; 54 (upd.)
Central Parking Corporation, 18
Century Business Services, Inc., 52
Chancellor Beacon Academies, Inc., 53
ChartHouse International Learning
    Corporation, 49
Chiat/Day Inc. Advertising, 11
Chicago Board of Trade, 41
Chisholm-Mingo Group, Inc., 41
Christie's International plc, 15; 39 (upd.)
Cintas Corporation, 21
CMG Worldwide, Inc., 89
COMFORCE Corporation, 40
Command Security Corporation, 57
Computer Learning Centers, Inc., 26
Concentra Inc., 71
Corporate Express, Inc., 47 (upd.)
CoolSavings, Inc., 77

Airlines

Beverages

Moët-Hennessy, I
Molson Coors Brewing Company, I; 26 (upd.); 77 (upd.)
Montana Coffee Traders, Inc., 60
Mott's Inc., 57
National Beverage Corporation, 26; 88 (upd.)
National Grape Cooperative Association, Inc., 20
National Wine & Spirits, Inc., 49
Nestlé Waters, 73
New Belgium Brewing Company, Inc., 68
Nichols plc, 44
Ocean Spray Cranberries, Inc., 7; 25 (upd.); 83 (upd.)
Odwalla, Inc., 31
OENEO S.A., 74 (upd.)
Old Orchard Brands, LLC, 73
Oregon Chai, Inc., 49
Panamerican Beverages, Inc., 47
Parmalat Finanziaria SpA, 50
Paulaner Brauerei GmbH & Co. KG, 35
Peet's Coffee & Tea, Inc., 38
Penaflor S.A., 66
The Pepsi Bottling Group, Inc., 40
PepsiAmericas, Inc., 67 (upd.)
PepsiCo, Inc., I; 10 (upd.); 38 (upd.)
Pernod Ricard S.A., I; 21 (upd.); 72 (upd.)
Pete's Brewing Company, 22
Philip Morris Companies Inc., 18 (upd.)
Pittsburgh Brewing Company, 76
Pyramid Breweries Inc., 33
Quilmes Industrial (QUINSA) S.A., 67
R.C. Bigelow, Inc., 49
Radeberger Gruppe AG, 75
Rainier Brewing Company, 23
Red Bull GmbH, 60
Redhook Ale Brewery, Inc., 31; 88 (upd.)
Rémy Cointreau Group, 20; 80 (upd.)
Robert Mondavi Corporation, 15; 50 (upd.)
Royal Crown Company, Inc., 23
Royal Grolsch NV, 54
S&D Coffee, Inc., 84
SABMiller plc, 59 (upd.)
San Miguel Corporation, 57 (upd.)
Sapporo Breweries Limited, I; 13 (upd.); 36 (upd.)
Scheid Vineyards Inc., 66
Schieffelin & Somerset Co., 61
Scottish & Newcastle plc, 15; 35 (upd.)
The Seagram Company Ltd., I; 25 (upd.)
Sebastiani Vineyards, Inc., 28
Shepherd Neame Limited, 30
Sidney Frank Importing Co., Inc., 69
Sierra Nevada Brewing Company, 70
Skalli Group, 67
Skyy Spirits LLC 78
Sleeman Breweries Ltd., 74
Snapple Beverage Corporation, 11
Societe des Produits Marnier-Lapostolle S.A., 88
The South African Breweries Limited, I; 24 (upd.)
South Beach Beverage Company, Inc., 73
Southcorp Limited, 54

Southern Wine and Spirits of America, Inc., 84
Starbucks Corporation, 13; 34 (upd.); 77 (upd.)
The Stash Tea Company, 50
Stewart's Beverages, 39
The Stroh Brewery Company, I; 18 (upd.)
Suntory Ltd., 65
Sutter Home Winery Inc., 16
Taittinger S.A., 43
Taiwan Tobacco & Liquor Corporation, 75
Takara Holdings Inc., 62
Tata Tea Ltd., 76
The Terlato Wine Group, 48
Tetley USA Inc., 88
Todhunter International, Inc., 27
Triarc Companies, Inc., 34 (upd.)
Tropicana Products, Inc., 73 (upd.)
Tsingtao Brewery Group, 49
Tully's Coffee Corporation, 51
Underberg AG, 92
Unilever, II; 7 (upd.); 32 (upd.); 89 (upd.)
Unión de Cervecerias Peruanas Backus y Johnston S.A.A., 92
V&S Vin & Sprit AB, 91 (upd.)
Van Houtte Inc., 39
Vermont Pure Holdings, Ltd., 51
Vin & Spirit AB, 31
Viña Concha y Toro S.A., 45
Vincor International Inc., 50
Whitbread and Company PLC, I
Widmer Brothers Brewing Company, 76
Willamette Valley Vineyards, Inc., 85
William Grant & Sons Ltd., 60
The Wine Group, Inc., 39
The Wolverhampton & Dudley Breweries, PLC, 57
Young & Co.'s Brewery, P.L.C., 38

Bio-Technology

Actelion Ltd., 83
Amersham PLC, 50
Amgen, Inc., 10; 30 (upd.)
ArQule, Inc., 68
Biogen Idec Inc., 71 (upd.)
Biogen Inc., 14; 36 (upd.)
bioMérieux S.A., 75
BTG Plc, 87
Caliper Life Sciences, Inc., 70
Cambrex Corporation, 44 (upd.)
Celera Genomics, 74
Centocor Inc., 14
Charles River Laboratories International, Inc., 42
Chiron Corporation, 10; 36 (upd.)
Covance Inc., 30
CryoLife, Inc., 46
Cytyc Corporation, 69
Delta and Pine Land Company, 33
Dionex Corporation, 46
Dyax Corp., 89
Embrex, Inc., 72
Enzo Biochem, Inc., 41
Eurofins Scientific S.A., 70
Gen-Probe Incorporated, 79
Genentech, Inc., 32 (upd.)

Genzyme Corporation, 38 (upd.)
Gilead Sciences, Inc., 54
Howard Hughes Medical Institute, 39
Huntingdon Life Sciences Group plc, 42
IDEXX Laboratories, Inc., 23
ImClone Systems Inc., 58
Immunex Corporation, 14; 50 (upd.)
IMPATH Inc., 45
Incyte Genomics, Inc., 52
Inverness Medical Innovations, Inc., 63
Invitrogen Corporation, 52
The Judge Group, Inc., 51
Kendle International Inc., 87
Life Technologies, Inc., 17
LifeCell Corporation, 77
Lonza Group Ltd., 73
Martek Biosciences Corporation, 65
Medarex, Inc., 85
Medtronic, Inc., 30 (upd.)
Millipore Corporation, 25; 84 (upd.)
Minntech Corporation, 22
Mycogen Corporation, 21
Nektar Therapeutics, 91
New Brunswick Scientific Co., Inc., 45
Pacific Ethanol, Inc., 81
Pharmion Corporation, 91
Qiagen N.V., 39
Quintiles Transnational Corporation, 21
Seminis, Inc., 29
Senomyx, Inc., 83
Serologicals Corporation, 63
Sigma-Aldrich Corporation, 36 (upd.)
Starkey Laboratories, Inc., 52
STERIS Corporation, 29
Stratagene Corporation, 70
Tanox, Inc., 77
TECHNE Corporation, 52
TriPath Imaging, Inc., 77
Waters Corporation, 43
Whatman plc, 46
Wisconsin Alumni Research Foundation, 65
Wyeth, 50 (upd.)

Chemicals

A. Schulman, Inc., 8
Aceto Corp., 38
Air Products and Chemicals, Inc., I; 10 (upd.); 74 (upd.)
Airgas, Inc., 54
Akzo Nobel N.V., 13; 41 (upd.)
Albemarle Corporation, 59
AlliedSignal Inc., 22 (upd.)
ALTANA AG, 87
American Cyanamid, I; 8 (upd.)
American Vanguard Corporation, 47
Arab Potash Company, 85
Arch Chemicals Inc. 78
ARCO Chemical Company, 10
Asahi Denka Kogyo KK, 64
Atanor S.A., 62
Atochem S.A., I
Avantium Technologies BV, 79
Avecia Group PLC, 63
Baker Hughes Incorporated, 22 (upd.); 57 (upd.)
Balchem Corporation, 42

Conglomerates

Construction

Jarvis plc, 39
JE Dunn Construction Group, Inc., 85
JLG Industries, Inc., 52
John Brown PLC, I
John Laing plc, I; 51 (upd.)
John W. Danforth Company, 48
Kajima Corporation, I; 51 (upd.)
Kaufman and Broad Home Corporation, 8
KB Home, 45 (upd.)
Kellogg Brown & Root, Inc., 62 (upd.)
Kitchell Corporation, 14
The Koll Company, 8
Komatsu Ltd., 16 (upd.)
Kraus-Anderson Companies, Inc., 36; 83 (upd.)
Kumagai Gumi Company, Ltd., I
L'Entreprise Jean Lefebvre, 23
Ledcor Industries Limited, 46
Lennar Corporation, 11
Lincoln Property Company, 8
Lindal Cedar Homes, Inc., 29
Linde A.G., I
MasTec, Inc., 55
Matrix Service Company, 65
McCarthy Building Companies, Inc., 48
Mellon-Stuart Company, I
Michael Baker Corp., 14
Modtech Holdings, Inc., 77
Morrison Knudsen Corporation, 7; 28 (upd.)
Morrow Equipment Co. L.L.C., 87
New Holland N.V., 22
Newpark Resources, Inc., 63
NVR Inc., 70 (upd.)
NVR L.P., 8
Obayashi Corporation 78
Obrascon Huarte Lain S.A., 76
Ohbayashi Corporation, I
Opus Group, 34
Orascom Construction Industries S.A.E., 87
Orleans Homebuilders, Inc., 62
The Parsons Corporation, 56 (upd.)
PCL Construction Group Inc., 50
The Peninsular & Oriental Steam Navigation Company (Bovis Division), I
Perini Corporation, 8; 82 (upd.)
Peter Kiewit Sons' Inc., 8
Philipp Holzmann AG, 17
Post Properties, Inc., 26
Pulte Homes, Inc., 8; 42 (upd.)
Pyramid Companies, 54
Redrow Group plc, 31
Rinker Group Ltd., 65
RMC Group p.l.c., 34 (upd.)
Rooney Brothers Co., 25
The Rottlund Company, Inc., 28
Roy Anderson Corporation, 75
The Ryland Group, Inc., 8; 37 (upd.)
Sandvik AB, 32 (upd.)
Schuff Steel Company, 26
Seddon Group Ltd., 67
Shorewood Packaging Corporation, 28
Simon Property Group Inc., 27; 84 (upd.)
Skanska AB, 38

Skidmore, Owings & Merrill LLP, 69 (upd.)
SNC-Lavalin Group Inc., 72
Speedy Hire plc, 84
Stabler Companies Inc. 78
Standard Pacific Corporation, 52
Stone & Webster, Inc., 64 (upd.)
Sundt Corp., 24
Swinerton Inc., 43
Taylor Woodrow plc, I; 38 (upd.)
Technical Olympic USA, Inc., 75
Terex Corporation, 7; 40 (upd.); 91 (upd.)
ThyssenKrupp AG, IV; 28 (upd.); 87 (upd.)
TIC Holdings Inc., 92
Toll Brothers Inc., 15; 70 (upd.)
Trammell Crow Company, 8
Tridel Enterprises Inc., 9
Turner Construction Company, 66
The Turner Corporation, 8; 23 (upd.)
U.S. Aggregates, Inc., 42
U.S. Home Corporation, 8; 78 (upd.)
Urbi Desarrollos Urbanos, S.A. de C.V., 81
VA TECH ELIN EBG GmbH, 49
Veit Companies, 43; 92 (upd.)
Walbridge Aldinger Co., 38
Walter Industries, Inc., 22 (upd.)
The Weitz Company, Inc., 42
Willbros Group, Inc., 56
William Lyon Homes, 59
Wilson Bowden Plc, 45
Wood Hall Trust PLC, I
The Yates Companies, Inc., 62

Containers

Ball Corporation, I; 10 (upd.); 78 (upd.)
BWAY Corporation, 24
Clarcor Inc., 17
Continental Can Co., Inc., 15
Continental Group Company, I
Crown Cork & Seal Company, Inc., I; 13 (upd.); 32 (upd.)
Crown Holdings, Inc., 83 (upd.)
Gaylord Container Corporation, 8
Golden Belt Manufacturing Co., 16
Graham Packaging Holdings Company, 87
Greif Inc., 15; 66 (upd.)
Grupo Industrial Durango, S.A. de C.V., 37
Hanjin Shipping Co., Ltd., 50
Inland Container Corporation, 8
Interpool, Inc., 92
Kerr Group Inc., 24
Keyes Fibre Company, 9
Libbey Inc., 49
Liqui-Box Corporation, 16
The Longaberger Company, 12
Longview Fibre Company, 8
The Mead Corporation, 19 (upd.)
Metal Box PLC, I
Molins plc, 51
National Can Corporation, I
Owens-Illinois, Inc., I; 26 (upd.); 85 (upd.)

Packaging Corporation of America, 51 (upd.)
Primerica Corporation, I
PVC Container Corporation, 67
Rexam PLC, 32 (upd.); 85 (upd.)
Reynolds Metals Company, 19 (upd.)
Royal Packaging Industries Van Leer N.V., 30
RPC Group PLC, 81
Sealright Co., Inc., 17
Shurgard Storage Centers, Inc., 52
Smurfit-Stone Container Corporation, 26 (upd.); 83 (upd.)
Sonoco Products Company, 8; 89 (upd.)
Thermos Company, 16
Toyo Seikan Kaisha, Ltd., I
U.S. Can Corporation, 30
Ultra Pac, Inc., 24
Viatech Continental Can Company, Inc., 25 (upd.)
Vidrala S.A., 67
Vitro Corporativo S.A. de C.V., 34

Drugs & Pharmaceuticals

A. Nelson & Co. Ltd., 75
A.L. Pharma Inc., 12
Abbott Laboratories, I; 11 (upd.); 40 (upd.)
Actelion Ltd., 83
Akorn, Inc., 32
Albany Molecular Research, Inc., 77
Allergan, Inc., 77 (upd.)
Alpharma Inc., 35 (upd.)
ALZA Corporation, 10; 36 (upd.)
American Home Products, I; 10 (upd.)
American Pharmaceutical Partners, Inc., 69
AmerisourceBergen Corporation, 64 (upd.)
Amersham PLC, 50
Amgen, Inc., 10; 89 (upd.)
Amylin Pharmaceuticals, Inc., 67
Andrx Corporation, 55
AstraZeneca PLC, I; 20 (upd.); 50 (upd.)
Axcan Pharma Inc., 85
Barr Pharmaceuticals, Inc., 26; 68 (upd.)
Bayer A.G., I; 13 (upd.)
Berlex Laboratories, Inc., 66
Biovail Corporation, 47
Block Drug Company, Inc., 8
Boiron S.A., 73
Bristol-Myers Squibb Company, III; 9 (upd.); 37 (upd.)
BTG Plc, 87
C.H. Boehringer Sohn, 39
Caremark Rx, Inc., 10; 54 (upd.)
Carter-Wallace, Inc., 8; 38 (upd.)
Celgene Corporation, 67
Cephalon, Inc., 45
Chiron Corporation, 10
Chugai Pharmaceutical Co., Ltd., 50
Ciba-Geigy Ltd., I; 8 (upd.)
D&K Wholesale Drug, Inc., 14
Discovery Partners International, Inc., 58
Dr. Reddy's Laboratories Ltd., 59
Elan Corporation PLC, 63
Eli Lilly and Company, I; 11 (upd.); 47 (upd.)

Electrical & Electronics

Engineering & Management Services

Day & Zimmermann Inc., 9; 31 (upd.)
Donaldson Co. Inc., 16
Dycom Industries, Inc., 57
Edwards and Kelcey, 70
EG&G Incorporated, 8; 29 (upd.)
Eiffage, 27
Essef Corporation, 18
FKI Plc, 57
Fluor Corporation, 34 (upd.)
Forest City Enterprises, Inc., 52 (upd.)
Foster Wheeler Corporation, 6; 23 (upd.)
Foster Wheeler Ltd., 76 (upd.)
Framatome SA, 19
Fraport AG Frankfurt Airport Services
    Worldwide, 90
Georg Fischer AG Schaffhausen, 61
Gilbane, Inc., 34
Great Lakes Dredge & Dock Company,
    69
Grupo Dragados SA, 55
Halliburton Company, 25 (upd.)
Harding Lawson Associates Group, Inc.,
    16
Harza Engineering Company, 14
HDR Inc., 48
HOK Group, Inc., 59
ICF Kaiser International, Inc., 28
IHC Caland N.V., 71
Jacobs Engineering Group Inc., 6; 26
    (upd.)
Jacques Whitford, 92
The Judge Group, Inc., 51
JWP Inc., 9
The Keith Companies Inc., 54
Klöckner-Werke AG, 58 (upd.)
Kvaerner ASA, 36
Layne Christensen Company, 19
The MacNeal-Schwendler Corporation, 25
Malcolm Pirnie, Inc., 42
McDermott International, Inc., 37 (upd.)
McKinsey & Company, Inc., 9
Michael Baker Corporation, 51 (upd.)
Nooter Corporation, 61
Oceaneering International, Inc., 63
Odebrecht S.A., 73
Ogden Corporation, 6
Opus Group, 34
PAREXEL International Corporation, 84
Parsons Brinckerhoff, Inc., 34
The Parsons Corporation, 8; 56 (upd.)
The PBSJ Corporation, 82
Quanta Services, Inc., 79
RCM Technologies, Inc., 34
Renishaw plc, 46
Ricardo plc, 90
Rosemount Inc., 15
Roy F. Weston, Inc., 33
Royal Vopak NV, 41
Rust International Inc., 11
Sandia National Laboratories, 49
Sandvik AB, 32 (upd.)
Sarnoff Corporation, 57
Science Applications International
    Corporation, 15
Serco Group plc, 47
Siegel & Gale, 64
Siemens AG, 57 (upd.)
SRI International, Inc., 57

SSOE Inc., 76
Stone & Webster, Inc., 13; 64 (upd.)
Sulzer Ltd., 68 (upd.)
Susquehanna Pfaltzgraff Company, 8
Sverdrup Corporation, 14
Tech-Sym Corporation, 44 (upd.)
Technip 78
Tetra Tech, Inc., 29
ThyssenKrupp AG, IV; 28 (upd.); 87
    (upd.)
Towers Perrin, 32
Tracor Inc., 17
TRC Companies, Inc., 32
Underwriters Laboratories, Inc., 30
United Dominion Industries Limited, 8;
    16 (upd.)
URS Corporation, 45; 80 (upd.)
U.S. Army Corps of Engineers, 91
VA TECH ELIN EBG GmbH, 49
VECO International, Inc., 7
Vinci, 43
The Weir Group PLC, 85
Willbros Group, Inc., 56
WS Atkins Plc, 45

Entertainment & Leisure

A&E Television Networks, 32
Aardman Animations Ltd., 61
ABC Family Worldwide, Inc., 52
Academy of Television Arts & Sciences,
    Inc., 55
Acclaim Entertainment Inc., 24
Activision, Inc., 32; 89 (upd.)
AEI Music Network Inc., 35
Affinity Group Holding Inc., 56
Airtours Plc, 27
Alaska Railroad Corporation, 60
All American Communications Inc., 20
The All England Lawn Tennis & Croquet
    Club, 54
Alliance Entertainment Corp., 17
Alternative Tentacles Records, 66
Alvin Ailey Dance Foundation, Inc., 52
Amblin Entertainment, 21
AMC Entertainment Inc., 12; 35 (upd.)
American Golf Corporation, 45
American Gramaphone LLC, 52
American Kennel Club, Inc., 74
American Skiing Company, 28
Ameristar Casinos, Inc., 33; 69 (upd.)
AMF Bowling, Inc., 40
Anaheim Angels Baseball Club, Inc., 53
Anchor Gaming, 24
AOL Time Warner Inc., 57 (upd.)
Applause Inc., 24
Apple Corps Ltd., 87
Aprilia SpA, 17
Argosy Gaming Company, 21
Aristocrat Leisure Limited, 54
Arsenal Holdings PLC, 79
The Art Institute of Chicago, 29
The Arthur C. Clarke Foundation, 92
Artisan Entertainment Inc., 32 (upd.)
Asahi National Broadcasting Company,
    Ltd., 9
Aspen Skiing Company, 15
Aston Villa plc, 41
The Athletics Investment Group, 62

Atlanta National League Baseball Club,
    Inc., 43
The Atlantic Group, 23
Autotote Corporation, 20
Aztar Corporation, 13
Bad Boy Worldwide Entertainment
    Group, 58
Baker & Taylor Corporation, 16; 43
    (upd.)
Bally Total Fitness Holding Corp., 25
Baltimore Orioles L.P., 66
Barden Companies, Inc., 76
The Baseball Club of Seattle, LP, 50
The Basketball Club of Seattle, LLC, 50
Bertelsmann A.G., IV; 15 (upd.); 43
    (upd.); 91 (upd.)
Bertucci's Inc., 16
Big Idea Productions, Inc., 49
BigBen Interactive S.A., 72
BioWare Corporation, 81
Blockbuster Inc., 9; 31 (upd.); 76 (upd.)
Boca Resorts, Inc., 37
Bonneville International Corporation, 29
Booth Creek Ski Holdings, Inc., 31
Boston Celtics Limited Partnership, 14
Boston Professional Hockey Association
    Inc., 39
The Boy Scouts of America, 34
Boyne USA Resorts, 71
Brillstein-Grey Entertainment, 80
British Broadcasting Corporation Ltd., 7;
    21 (upd.); 89 (upd.)
The British Film Institute, 80
The British Museum, 71
British Sky Broadcasting Group plc, 20;
    60 (upd.)
Brunswick Corporation, III; 22 (upd.); 77
    (upd.)
Busch Entertainment Corporation, 73
Cablevision Systems Corporation, 7
California Sports, Inc., 56
Callaway Golf Company, 45 (upd.)
Canterbury Park Holding Corporation, 42
Capcom Company Ltd., 83
Capital Cities/ABC Inc., II
Capitol Records, Inc., 90
Carlson Companies, Inc., 6; 22 (upd.); 87
    (upd.)
Carlson Wagonlit Travel, 55
Carmike Cinemas, Inc., 14; 37 (upd.); 74
    (upd.)
Carnival Corporation, 6; 27 (upd.); 78
    (upd.)
The Carsey-Werner Company, L.L.C., 37
CBS Inc., II; 6 (upd.)
Cedar Fair, L.P., 22
Central European Media Enterprises Ltd.,
    61
Central Independent Television, 7; 23
    (upd.)
Century Casinos, Inc., 53
Century Theatres, Inc., 31
Championship Auto Racing Teams, Inc.,
    37
Chelsea Piers Management Inc., 86
Chicago Bears Football Club, Inc., 33
Chicago National League Ball Club, Inc.,
    66

Financial Services: Banks

Financial Services: Excluding Banks

Resource America, Inc., 42
Robert W. Baird & Co. Incorporated, 67
Ryan Beck & Co., Inc., 66
Safeguard Scientifics, Inc., 10
St. James's Place Capital, plc, 71
Salomon Inc., II; 13 (upd.)
Sanders Morris Harris Group Inc., 70
Sanlam Ltd., 68
SBC Warburg, 14
Schroders plc, 42
Scottrade, Inc., 85
Shearson Lehman Brothers Holdings Inc.,
    II; 9 (upd.)
Siebert Financial Corp., 32
Skipton Building Society, 80
SLM Holding Corp., 25 (upd.)
Smith Barney Inc., 15
Soros Fund Management LLC, 28
Spear, Leeds & Kellogg, 66
State Street Boston Corporation, 8
Stephens Inc., 92
Student Loan Marketing Association, II
Sun Life Financial Inc., 85
T. Rowe Price Associates, Inc., 11; 34
    (upd.)
Teachers Insurance and Annuity
    Association-College Retirement Equities
    Fund, 45 (upd.)
Texas Pacific Group Inc., 36
3i Group PLC, 73
Total System Services, Inc., 18
TradeStation Group, Inc., 83
Trilon Financial Corporation, II
United Jewish Communities, 33
The Vanguard Group, Inc., 14; 34 (upd.)
VeriFone Holdings, Inc., 18; 76 (upd.)
Viel & Cie, 76
Visa International, 9; 26 (upd.)
Wachovia Corporation, 12; 46 (upd.)
Waddell & Reed, Inc., 22
Washington Federal, Inc., 17
Waterhouse Investor Services, Inc., 18
Watson Wyatt Worldwide, 42
Western Union Financial Services, Inc., 54
WFS Financial Inc., 70
Working Assets Funding Service, 43
World Acceptance Corporation, 57
Yamaichi Securities Company, Limited, II
The Ziegler Companies, Inc., 24; 63
    (upd.)
Zurich Financial Services, 42 (upd.)

Food Products

A. Duda & Sons, Inc., 88
A. Moksel AG, 59
Agri Beef Company, 81
Agway, Inc., 7
Ajinomoto Co., Inc., II; 28 (upd.)
Alabama Farmers Cooperative, Inc., 63
The Albert Fisher Group plc, 41
Alberto-Culver Company, 8; 36 (upd.); 91
    (upd.)
Alfred Ritter GmbH & Co. KG, 58
Alfesca hf, 82
Allen Canning Company, 76
Alpine Confections, Inc., 71
Alpine Lace Brands, Inc., 18

American Crystal Sugar Company, 11; 32
    (upd.)
American Foods Group, 43
American Italian Pasta Company, 27; 76
    (upd.)
American Licorice Company, 86
American Maize-Products Co., 14
American Pop Corn Company, 59
American Rice, Inc., 33
Amfac/JMB Hawaii L.L.C., 24 (upd.)
Amy's Kitchen Inc., 76
Annie's Homegrown, Inc., 59
Archer-Daniels-Midland Company, 32
    (upd.)
Archway Cookies, Inc., 29
Arcor S.A.I.C., 66
Arla Foods amba, 48
Arnott's Ltd., 66
Associated British Foods plc, II; 13 (upd.);
    41 (upd.)
Associated Milk Producers, Inc., 11; 48
    (upd.)
Atkinson Candy Company, 87
Atlantic Premium Brands, Ltd., 57
August Storck KG, 66
Aurora Foods Inc., 32
Awrey Bakeries, Inc., 56
B&G Foods, Inc., 40
The B. Manischewitz Company, LLC, 31
Bahlsen GmbH & Co. KG, 44
Bakkavör Group hf., 91
Balance Bar Company, 32
Baltek Corporation, 34
The Bama Companies, Inc., 80
Bar-S Foods Company, 76
Barbara's Bakery Inc., 88
Barilla G. e R. Fratelli S.p.A., 17; 50
    (upd.)
Barry Callebaut AG, 71 (upd.)
Bear Creek Corporation, 38
Beatrice Company, II
Beech-Nut Nutrition Corporation, 21; 51
    (upd.)
Beer Nuts, Inc., 86
Bel/Kaukauna USA, 76
Ben & Jerry's Homemade, Inc., 10; 35
    (upd.); 80 (upd.)
Berkeley Farms, Inc., 46
Bernard Matthews Ltd., 89
Besnier SA, 19
Best Kosher Foods Corporation, 82
Bestfoods, 22 (upd.)
Better Made Snack Foods, Inc., 90
Bettys & Taylors of Harrogate Ltd., 72
Birds Eye Foods, Inc., 69 (upd.)
Blue Bell Creameries L.P., 30
Blue Diamond Growers, 28
Bob's Red Mill Natural Foods, Inc., 63
Bobs Candies, Inc., 70
Bolton Group B.V., 86
Bonduelle SA, 51
Bongrain SA, 25
Booker PLC, 13; 31 (upd.)
Borden, Inc., II; 22 (upd.)
Boyd Coffee Company, 53
Brach and Brock Confections, Inc., 15
Brake Bros plc, 45
Bridgford Foods Corporation, 27

Brigham's Inc., 72
Brioche Pasquier S.A., 58
British Sugar plc, 84
Brothers Gourmet Coffees, Inc., 20
Broughton Foods Co., 17
Brown & Haley, 23
Bruce Foods Corporation, 39
Bruegger's Corporation, 63
Bruster's Real Ice Cream, Inc., 80
BSN Groupe S.A., II
Bumble Bee Seafoods L.L.C., 64
Bunge Brasil S.A. 78
Bunge Ltd., 62
Bourbon Corporation, 82
Burns, Philp & Company Ltd., 63
Bush Boake Allen Inc., 30
Bush Brothers & Company, 45
The C.F. Sauer Company, 90
C.H. Robinson Worldwide, Inc., 40
    (upd.)
C.H. Guenther & Son, Inc., 84
Cactus Feeders, Inc., 91
Cadbury Schweppes PLC, II; 49 (upd.)
Cagle's, Inc., 20
Cal-Maine Foods, Inc., 69
Calavo Growers, Inc., 47
Calcot Ltd., 33
Callard and Bowser-Suchard Inc., 84
Campbell Soup Company, II; 7 (upd.); 26
    (upd.); 71 (upd.)
The Campina Group, 78
Campofrío Alimentación S.A, 59
Canada Packers Inc., II
Cape Cod Potato Chip Company, 90
Cargill, Incorporated, II; 13 (upd.); 40
    (upd.); 89 (upd.)
Carnation Company, II
The Carriage House Companies, Inc., 55
Carroll's Foods, Inc., 46
Carvel Corporation, 35
Castle & Cooke, Inc., II; 20 (upd.)
Cattleman's, Inc., 20
Celestial Seasonings, Inc., 16
Cemoi S.A., 86
Central Soya Company, Inc., 7
Chaoda Modern Agriculture (Holdings)
    Ltd., 87
Charal S.A., 90
Chase General Corporation, 91
Chattanooga Bakery, Inc., 86
Chef Solutions, Inc., 89
Chelsea Milling Company, 29
Chicken of the Sea International, 24
    (upd.)
China National Cereals, Oils and
    Foodstuffs Import and Export
    Corporation (COFCO), 76
Chiquita Brands International, Inc., 7; 21
    (upd.); 83 (upd.)
Chock Full o'Nuts Corp., 17
Chocoladefabriken Lindt & Sprüngli AG,
    27
Chr. Hansen Group A/S, 70
CHS Inc., 60
Chupa Chups S.A., 38
Clif Bar Inc., 50
Cloetta Fazer AB, 70

Food Services & Retailers

United Natural Foods, Inc., 32; 76 (upd.)
Uno Restaurant Holdings Corporation, 18; 70 (upd.)
Uwajimaya, Inc., 60
Vail Resorts, Inc., 43 (upd.)
VICORP Restaurants, Inc., 12; 48 (upd.)
Victory Refrigeration, Inc., 82
Village Super Market, Inc., 7
The Vons Companies, Incorporated, 7; 28 (upd.)
W. H. Braum, Inc., 80
Waffle House Inc., 14; 60 (upd.)
Wakefern Food Corporation, 33
Waldbaum, Inc., 19
Wall Street Deli, Inc., 33
Wawa Inc., 17; 78 (upd.)
Wegmans Food Markets, Inc., 9; 41 (upd.)
Weis Markets, Inc., 15
Wendy's International, Inc., 8; 23 (upd.); 47 (upd.)
The WesterN SizzliN Corporation, 60
Wetterau Incorporated, II
White Castle Management Company, 12; 36 (upd.); 85 (upd.)
White Rose, Inc., 24
Whittard of Chelsea Plc, 61
Whole Foods Market, Inc., 50 (upd.)
Wild Oats Markets, Inc., 19; 41 (upd.)
Winchell's Donut Houses Operating Company, L.P., 60
WinCo Foods Inc., 60
Winn-Dixie Stores, Inc., II; 21 (upd.); 59 (upd.)
Wm. Morrison Supermarkets PLC, 38
Wolfgang Puck Worldwide, Inc., 26, 70 (upd.)
Worldwide Restaurant Concepts, Inc., 47
Yoshinoya D & C Company Ltd., 88
Young & Co.'s Brewery, P.L.C., 38
Yucaipa Cos., 17
Yum! Brands Inc., 58
Zingerman's Community of Businesses, 68

Health & Personal Care Products

Abaxis, Inc., 83
Advanced Medical Optics, Inc., 79
Advanced Neuromodulation Systems, Inc., 73
Akorn, Inc., 32
ALARIS Medical Systems, Inc., 65
Alberto-Culver Company, 8; 36 (upd.); 91 (upd.)
Alco Health Services Corporation, III
Alès Groupe, 81
Allergan, Inc., 10; 30 (upd.); 77 (upd.)
American Safety Razor Company, 20
American Stores Company, 22 (upd.)
Amway Corporation, III; 13 (upd.)
AngioDynamics, Inc., 81
ArthroCare Corporation, 73
Artsana SpA, 92
Atkins Nutritionals, Inc., 58
Aveda Corporation, 24
Avon Products, Inc., III; 19 (upd.); 46 (upd.)

Bally Total Fitness Holding Corp., 25
Bare Escentuals, Inc., 91
Bausch & Lomb Inc., 7; 25 (upd.)
Baxter International Inc., I; 10 (upd.)
BeautiControl Cosmetics, Inc., 21
Becton, Dickinson & Company, I; 11 (upd.)
Beiersdorf AG, 29
Big B, Inc., 17
Bindley Western Industries, Inc., 9
Biolase Technology, Inc., 87
Biosite Incorporated, 73
Block Drug Company, Inc., 8; 27 (upd.)
The Body Shop International plc, 53 (upd.)
Boiron S.A., 73
Bolton Group B.V., 86
The Boots Company PLC, 24 (upd.)
Boston Scientific Corporation, 77 (upd.)
Bristol-Myers Squibb Company, III; 9 (upd.)
Bronner Brothers Inc., 92
C.R. Bard Inc., 9
Candela Corporation, 48
Cantel Medical Corporation, 80
Cardinal Health, Inc., 18; 50 (upd.)
Carl Zeiss AG, III; 34 (upd.); 91 (upd.)
Carson, Inc., 31
Carter-Wallace, Inc., 8
Caswell-Massey Co. Ltd., 51
CCA Industries, Inc., 53
Chattem, Inc., 17; 88 (upd.)
Chesebrough-Pond's USA, Inc., 8
Chronimed Inc., 26
Church & Dwight Co., Inc., 68 (upd.)
Cintas Corporation, 51 (upd.)
The Clorox Company, III; 22 (upd.); 81 (upd.)
CNS, Inc., 20
Colgate-Palmolive Company, III; 14 (upd.); 35 (upd.)
Combe Inc., 72
Conair Corp., 17
CONMED Corporation, 87
Connetics Corporation, 70
Cordis Corp., 19
Cosmair, Inc., 8
Coty, Inc., 36
Covidien Ltd., 91
Cybex International, Inc., 49
Cytyc Corporation, 69
Dade Behring Holdings Inc., 71
Dalli-Werke GmbH & Co. KG, 86
Datascope Corporation, 39
Del Laboratories, Inc., 28
Deltec, Inc., 56
Dentsply International Inc., 10
DEP Corporation, 20
DePuy, Inc., 30
DHB Industries Inc., 85
Diagnostic Products Corporation, 73
The Dial Corp., 23 (upd.)
Direct Focus, Inc., 47
Drackett Professional Products, 12
Drägerwerk AG, 83
E-Z-EM Inc., 89
Elizabeth Arden, Inc., 8; 40 (upd.)
Empi, Inc., 26

Enrich International, Inc., 33
The Estée Lauder Companies Inc., 9; 30 (upd.)
Ethicon, Inc., 23
Farouk Systems Inc. 78
Forest Laboratories, Inc., 11
Forever Living Products International Inc., 17
FoxHollow Technologies, Inc., 85
French Fragrances, Inc., 22
Gambro AB, 49
General Nutrition Companies, Inc., 11; 29 (upd.)
Genzyme Corporation, 13; 77 (upd.)
GF Health Products, Inc., 82
The Gillette Company, III; 20 (upd.)
Given Imaging Ltd., 83
Groupe Yves Saint Laurent, 23
Grupo Omnilife S.A. de C.V., 88
Guerlain, 23
Guest Supply, Inc., 18
Guidant Corporation, 58
Guinot Paris S.A., 82
Hanger Orthopedic Group, Inc., 41
Helen of Troy Corporation, 18
Helene Curtis Industries, Inc., 8; 28 (upd.)
Henkel KGaA, III
Henry Schein, Inc., 31; 70 (upd.)
Herbalife Ltd., 17; 41 (upd.); 92 (upd.)
Huntleigh Technology PLC, 77
Immucor, Inc., 81
Inamed Corporation, 79
Integra LifeSciences Holdings Corporation, 87
Integrated BioPharma, Inc., 83
Inter Parfums Inc., 35; 86 (upd.)
Intuitive Surgical, Inc., 79
Invacare Corporation, 11
IVAX Corporation, 11
IVC Industries, Inc., 45
The Jean Coutu Group (PJC) Inc., 46
John Paul Mitchell Systems, 24
Johnson & Johnson, III; 8 (upd.); 36 (upd.); 75 (upd.)
Kanebo, Ltd., 53
Kao Corporation, III; 79 (upd.)
Kendall International, Inc., 11
Kensey Nash Corporation, 71
Keys Fitness Products, LP, 83
Kimberly-Clark Corporation, III; 16 (upd.); 43 (upd.)
Kyowa Hakko Kogyo Co., Ltd., III
Kyphon Inc., 87
L'Oréal SA, III; 8 (upd.); 46 (upd.)
Laboratoires de Biologie Végétale Yves Rocher, 35
The Lamaur Corporation, 41
Lever Brothers Company, 9
Lion Corporation, III; 51 (upd.)
Luxottica SpA, 17; 52 (upd.)
Mandom Corporation, 82
Mannatech Inc., 33
Mary Kay Inc., 9; 30 (upd.); 84 (upd.)
Matrix Essentials Inc., 90
Maxxim Medical Inc., 12
Medco Containment Services Inc., 9
Medline Industries, Inc., 61

Health Care Services

NewYork-Presbyterian Hospital, 59
NovaCare, Inc., 11
NSF International, 72
Operation Smile, Inc., 75
Option Care Inc., 48
Orthodontic Centers of America, Inc., 35
Oxford Health Plans, Inc., 16
PacifiCare Health Systems, Inc., 11
Palomar Medical Technologies, Inc., 22
Pediatric Services of America, Inc., 31
Pediatrix Medical Group, Inc., 61
PHP Healthcare Corporation, 22
PhyCor, Inc., 36
PolyMedica Corporation, 77
Primedex Health Systems, Inc., 25
Providence Health System, 90
The Providence Service Corporation, 64
Psychemedics Corporation, 89
Psychiatric Solutions, Inc., 68
Quest Diagnostics Inc., 26
Radiation Therapy Services, Inc., 85
Ramsay Youth Services, Inc., 41
Renal Care Group, Inc., 72
Res-Care, Inc., 29
Response Oncology, Inc., 27
Rural/Metro Corporation, 28
Sabratek Corporation, 29
St. Jude Medical, Inc., 11; 43 (upd.)
Salick Health Care, Inc., 53
The Scripps Research Institute, 76
Select Medical Corporation, 65
Shriners Hospitals for Children, 69
Sierra Health Services, Inc., 15
Smith & Nephew plc, 41 (upd.)
The Sports Club Company, 25
SSL International plc, 49
Stericycle Inc., 33
Sun Healthcare Group Inc., 25
Sunrise Senior Living, Inc., 81
Susan G. Komen Breast Cancer
    Foundation 78
SwedishAmerican Health System, 51
Tenet Healthcare Corporation, 55 (upd.)
Twinlab Corporation, 34
U.S. Healthcare, Inc., 6
U.S. Physical Therapy, Inc., 65
Unison HealthCare Corporation, 25
United HealthCare Corporation, 6
United Nations International Children's
    Emergency Fund (UNICEF), 58
United Way of America, 36
Universal Health Services, Inc., 6
Vanguard Health Systems Inc., 70
VCA Antech, Inc., 58
Vencor, Inc., 16
VISX, Incorporated, 30
Vivra, Inc., 18
Volunteers of America, Inc., 66
WellPoint Health Networks Inc., 25
YWCA of the U.S.A., 45

Hotels

Accor S.A., 69 (upd.)
Amerihost Properties, Inc., 30
Ameristar Casinos, Inc., 69 (upd.)
Archon Corporation, 74 (upd.)
Aztar Corporation, 13; 71 (upd.)
Bass PLC, 38 (upd.)

Boca Resorts, Inc., 37
Boyd Gaming Corporation, 43
Boyne USA Resorts, 71
Bristol Hotel Company, 23
The Broadmoor Hotel, 30
Caesars World, Inc., 6
Candlewood Hotel Company, Inc., 41
Carlson Companies, Inc., 6; 22 (upd.); 87
    (upd.)
Castle & Cooke, Inc., 20 (upd.)
Cedar Fair, L.P., 22
Cendant Corporation, 44 (upd.)
Choice Hotels International, Inc., 14; 83
    (upd.)
Circus Circus Enterprises, Inc., 6
City Developments Limited, 89
Club Méditerranée S.A., 6; 21 (upd.); 91
    (upd.)
Compagnia Italiana dei Jolly Hotels
    S.p.A., 71
Doubletree Corporation, 21
Extended Stay America, Inc., 41
Fairmont Hotels & Resorts Inc., 69
Fibreboard Corporation, 16
Four Seasons Hotels Inc., 9; 29 (upd.)
Fuller Smith & Turner P.L.C., 38
Gables Residential Trust, 49
Gaylord Entertainment Company, 11; 36
    (upd.)
Global Hyatt Corporation, 75 (upd.)
Granada Group PLC, 24 (upd.)
Grand Casinos, Inc., 20
Grand Hotel Krasnapolsky N.V., 23
Great Wolf Resorts, Inc., 91
Grupo Posadas, S.A. de C.V., 57
Helmsley Enterprises, Inc., 9
Hilton Hotels Corporation, III; 19 (upd.);
    49 (upd.); 62 (upd.)
Holiday Inns, Inc., III
Hospitality Franchise Systems, Inc., 11
Hotel Properties Ltd., 71
Howard Johnson International, Inc., 17;
    72 (upd.)
Hyatt Corporation, III; 16 (upd.)
ILX Resorts Incorporated, 65
Interstate Hotels & Resorts Inc., 58
ITT Sheraton Corporation, III
JD Wetherspoon plc, 30
John Q. Hammons Hotels, Inc., 24
Jumeirah Group, 83
Kerzner International Limited, 69 (upd.)
The La Quinta Companies, 11; 42 (upd.)
Ladbroke Group PLC, 21 (upd.)
Landry's Restaurants, Inc., 65 (upd.)
Las Vegas Sands, Inc., 50
Madden's on Gull Lake, 52
Mandalay Resort Group, 32 (upd.)
Manor Care, Inc., 25 (upd.)
The Marcus Corporation, 21
Marriott International, Inc., III; 21
    (upd.); 83 (upd.)
McMenamins Pubs and Breweries, 65
Millennium & Copthorne Hotels plc, 71
Mirage Resorts, Incorporated, 6; 28 (upd.)
Monarch Casino & Resort, Inc., 65
Morgans Hotel Group Company, 80
Motel 6, 13; 56 (upd.)
MTR Gaming Group, Inc., 75

MWH Preservation Limited Partnership,
    65
NH Hoteles S.A., 79
Omni Hotels Corp., 12
Paradores de Turismo de Espana S.A., 73
Park Corp., 22
Players International, Inc., 22
Preussag AG, 42 (upd.)
Prime Hospitality Corporation, 52
Promus Companies, Inc., 9
Real Turismo, S.A. de C.V., 50
Red Roof Inns, Inc., 18
Resorts International, Inc., 12
The Ritz-Carlton Hotel Company, L.L.C.,
    9; 29 (upd.); 71 (upd.)
Riviera Holdings Corporation, 75
Sandals Resorts International, 65
Santa Fe Gaming Corporation, 19
The SAS Group, 34 (upd.)
SFI Group plc, 51
Shangri-La Asia Ltd., 71
Showboat, Inc., 19
Sol Meliá S.A., 71
Sonesta International Hotels Corporation,
    44
Starwood Hotels & Resorts Worldwide,
    Inc., 54
Sun International Hotels Limited, 26
Sunburst Hospitality Corporation, 26
Super 8 Motels, Inc., 83
Thistle Hotels PLC, 54
Trusthouse Forte PLC, III
Vail Resorts, Inc., 43 (upd.)
WestCoast Hospitality Corporation, 59
Westin Hotels and Resorts Worldwide, 9;
    29 (upd.)
Whitbread PLC, 52 (upd.)
Young & Co.'s Brewery, P.L.C., 38

Information Technology

A.B. Watley Group Inc., 45
AccuWeather, Inc., 73
Acxiom Corporation, 35
Adaptec, Inc., 31
Adobe Systems Incorporated, 10; 33
    (upd.)
Advanced Micro Devices, Inc., 6
Agence France-Presse, 34
Agilent Technologies Inc., 38
Akamai Technologies, Inc., 71
Aldus Corporation, 10
Allen Systems Group, Inc., 59
AltaVista Company, 43
Altiris, Inc., 65
Amdahl Corporation, III; 14 (upd.); 40
    (upd.)
Amdocs Ltd., 47
America Online, Inc., 10; 26 (upd.)
American Business Information, Inc., 18
American Management Systems, Inc., 11
American Software Inc., 25
AMICAS, Inc., 69
Amstrad PLC, III
Analex Corporation, 74
Analytic Sciences Corporation, 10
Analytical Surveys, Inc., 33
Anker BV, 53
Ansoft Corporation, 63

Insurance

Legal Services

Manufacturing

The Middleton Doll Company, 53
Midwest Grain Products, Inc., 49
Miele & Cie. KG, 56
Mikasa, Inc., 28
Mikohn Gaming Corporation, 39
Milacron, Inc., 53 (upd.)
Miller Industries, Inc., 26
Millipore Corporation, 25; 84 (upd.)
Milton Bradley Company, 21
Mine Safety Appliances Company, 31
Minebea Co., Ltd., 90
Minolta Co., Ltd., III; 18 (upd.); 43
   (upd.)
Minuteman International Inc., 46
Misonix, Inc., 80
Mitsubishi Heavy Industries, Ltd., III; 7
   (upd.)
Mity Enterprises, Inc., 38
Mobile Mini, Inc., 58
Mocon, Inc., 76
Modine Manufacturing Company, 8; 56
   (upd.)
Modtech Holdings, Inc., 77
Moen Incorporated, 12
Mohawk Industries, Inc., 19; 63 (upd.)
Molex Incorporated, 11
The Monarch Cement Company, 72
Monnaie de Paris, 62
Monster Cable Products, Inc., 69
Montblanc International GmbH, 82
Montres Rolex S.A., 13; 34 (upd.)
Montupet S.A., 63
Moog Music, Inc., 75
The Morgan Crucible Company plc, 82
Morrow Equipment Co. L.L.C., 87
Motorcar Parts & Accessories, Inc., 47
Moulinex S.A., 22
Movado Group, Inc., 28
Mr. Coffee, Inc., 15
Mr. Gasket Inc., 15
Mueller Industries, Inc., 7; 52 (upd.)
Multi-Color Corporation, 53
Musco Lighting, 83
Nashua Corporation, 8
National Envelope Corporation, 32
National Gypsum Company, 10
National Oilwell, Inc., 54
National Picture & Frame Company, 24
National Semiconductor Corporation, 69
   (upd.)
National Standard Co., 13
National Starch and Chemical Company,
   49
Natrol, Inc., 49
Natural Alternatives International, Inc., 49
NCI Building Systems, Inc., 88
NCR Corporation, III; 6 (upd.); 30
   (upd.); 90 (upd.)
Neenah Foundry Company, 68
Neopost S.A., 53
NETGEAR, Inc., 81
New Balance Athletic Shoe, Inc., 25
New Holland N.V., 22
Newcor, Inc., 40
Newell Rubbermaid Inc., 9; 52 (upd.)
Newport Corporation, 71
Newport News Shipbuilding Inc., 13; 38
   (upd.)

Nexans SA, 54
NGK Insulators Ltd., 67
NHK Spring Co., Ltd., III
Nidec Corporation, 59
NIKE, Inc., 36 (upd.)
Nikon Corporation, III; 48 (upd.)
Nintendo Company, Ltd., III; 7 (upd.);
   67 (upd.)
Nippon Seiko K.K., III
Nippondenso Co., Ltd., III
NKK Corporation, 28 (upd.)
NOF Corporation, 72
NordicTrack, 22
Nordson Corporation, 11; 48 (upd.)
Nortek, Inc., 34
Norton Company, 8
Norton McNaughton, Inc., 27
Novellus Systems, Inc., 18
NSS Enterprises Inc. 78
NTN Corporation, III; 47 (upd.)
Nu-kote Holding, Inc., 18
O'Sullivan Industries Holdings, Inc., 34
Oak Industries Inc., 21
Oakley, Inc., 49 (upd.)
Oakwood Homes Corporation, 15
ODL, Inc., 55
The Ohio Art Company,14; 59 (upd.)
Oil-Dri Corporation of America, 20; 89
   (upd.)
The Oilgear Company, 74
Okuma Holdings Inc., 74
Old Town Canoe Company, 74
180s, L.L.C., 64
Oneida Ltd., 7; 31 (upd.); 88 (upd.)
Optische Werke G. Rodenstock, 44
Orange Glo International, 53
Orbotech Ltd., 75
Orthofix International NV, 72
Osmonics, Inc., 18
Osram GmbH, 86
Otis Elevator Company, Inc., 13; 39
   (upd.)
Otor S.A., 77
Outboard Marine Corporation, III; 20
   (upd.)
Outdoor Research, Incorporated, 67
Overhead Door Corporation, 70
Owens Corning Corporation, 20 (upd.)
Owosso Corporation, 29
P & F Industries, Inc., 45
Pacer Technology, 40
Pacific Coast Feather Company, 67
Pacific Dunlop Limited, 10
Pagnossin S.p.A., 73
Pall Corporation, 9; 72 (upd.)
Palm Harbor Homes, Inc., 39
Paloma Industries Ltd., 71
Panavision Inc., 24
Park Corp., 22
Park-Ohio Holdings Corp., 17; 85 (upd.)
Parker-Hannifin Corporation, III; 24
   (upd.)
Parlex Corporation, 61
Patrick Industries, Inc., 30
Paul Mueller Company, 65
Pearl Corporation 78
Pechiney SA, IV; 45 (upd.)
Peg Perego SpA, 88

Pelican Products, Inc., 86
Pelikan Holding AG, 92
Pella Corporation, 12; 39 (upd.); 89
   (upd.)
Penn Engineering & Manufacturing
   Corp., 28
Pentair, Inc., 7; 26 (upd.); 81 (upd.)
Pentax Corporation 78
Pentech International, Inc., 29
PerkinElmer Inc. 7; 78 (upd.)
Peterson American Corporation, 55
Phillips-Van Heusen Corporation, 24
Phoenix AG, 68
Phoenix Mecano AG, 61
Photo-Me International Plc, 83
Physio-Control International Corp., 18
Pilkington Group Limited, III; 34 (upd.);
   87 (upd.)
Pilot Pen Corporation of America, 82
Pinguely-Haulotte SA, 51
Pioneer Electronic Corporation, III
Pirelli & C. S.p.A., 75 (upd.)
Piscines Desjoyaux S.A., 84
Pitney Bowes, Inc., 19
Pittway Corporation, 33 (upd.)
Planar Systems, Inc., 61
PlayCore, Inc., 27
Playmates Toys, 23
Playskool, Inc., 25
Pleasant Company, 27
Ply Gem Industries Inc., 12
Pochet SA, 55
Polaris Industries Inc., 12; 35 (upd.); 77
   (upd.)
Polaroid Corporation, III; 7 (upd.); 28
   (upd.)
The Porcelain and Fine China Companies
   Ltd., 69
Portmeirion Group plc, 88
Pou Chen Corporation, 81
PPG Industries, Inc., III; 22 (upd.); 81
   (upd.)
Prada Holding B.V., 45
Pranda Jewelry plc, 70
Praxair, Inc., 48 (upd.)
Precision Castparts Corp., 15
Premark International, Inc., III
Pressman Toy Corporation, 56
Presstek, Inc., 33
Price Pfister, Inc., 70
Prince Sports Group, Inc., 15
Printpack, Inc., 68
Printronix, Inc., 18
Puig Beauty and Fashion Group S.L., 60
Pulaski Furniture Corporation, 33; 80
   (upd.)
Pumpkin Masters, Inc., 48
Punch International N.V., 66
Pure World, Inc., 72
Puritan-Bennett Corporation, 13
Purolator Products Company, 21; 74
   (upd.)
PVC Container Corporation, 67
PW Eagle, Inc., 48
Q.E.P. Co., Inc., 65
QSC Audio Products, Inc., 56
Quixote Corporation, 15
R. Griggs Group Limited, 23

Materials

Publishing & Printing

Tridel Enterprises Inc., 9
Trizec Corporation Ltd., 10
The Trump Organization, 23; 64 (upd.)
Unibail SA, 40
United Dominion Realty Trust, Inc., 52
Vistana, Inc., 22
Vornado Realty Trust, 20
W.P. Carey & Co. LLC, 49
William Lyon Homes, 59

Retail & Wholesale

A-Mark Financial Corporation, 71
A.C. Moore Arts & Crafts, Inc., 30
A.S. Watson & Company Ltd., 84
A.T. Cross Company, 49 (upd.)
Aaron Rents, Inc., 14; 35 (upd.)
Abatix Corp., 57
ABC Appliance, Inc., 10
ABC Carpet & Home Co. Inc., 26
Abercrombie & Fitch Company, 15; 75 (upd.)
Academy Sports & Outdoors, 27
Ace Hardware Corporation, 12; 35 (upd.)
Action Performance Companies, Inc., 27
ADESA, Inc., 71
Adolfo Dominguez S.A., 72
AEON Co., Ltd., 68 (upd.)
Aéropostale, Inc., 89
After Hours Formalwear Inc., 60
Alabama Farmers Cooperative, Inc., 63
Alain Afflelou SA, 53
Alba-Waldensian, Inc., 30
Alberto-Culver Company, 8; 36 (upd.); 91 (upd.)
Albertson's, Inc., 65 (upd.)
Alimentation Couche-Tard Inc., 77
Alldays plc, 49
Allders plc, 37
Alliance Boots plc (updates Boots Group PLC), 83 (upd.)
Allou Health & Beauty Care, Inc., 28
Almacenes Exito S.A., 89
Alpha Airports Group PLC, 77
Alrosa Company Ltd., 62
Alticor Inc., 71 (upd.)
Amazon.com, Inc., 25; 56 (upd.)
AMERCO, 67 (upd.)
American Coin Merchandising, Inc., 28; 74 (upd.)
American Eagle Outfitters, Inc., 24; 55 (upd.)
American Furniture Company, Inc., 21
American Girl, Inc., 69 (upd.)
American Stores Company, 22 (upd.)
AmeriSource Health Corporation, 37 (upd.)
Ames Department Stores, Inc., 9; 30 (upd.)
Amscan Holdings, Inc., 61
Amway Corporation, 13; 30 (upd.)
The Anderson-DuBose Company, 60
The Andersons, Inc., 31
AnnTaylor Stores Corporation, 13; 37 (upd.); 67 (upd.)
Appliance Recycling Centers of America, Inc., 42
Arbor Drugs Inc., 12
Arcadia Group plc, 28 (upd.)

Army and Air Force Exchange Service, 39
Art Van Furniture, Inc., 28
ASDA Group plc, 28 (upd.)
Ashworth, Inc., 26
Au Printemps S.A., V
Audio King Corporation, 24
Authentic Fitness Corporation, 20; 51 (upd.)
Auto Value Associates, Inc., 25
Autobytel Inc., 47
AutoNation, Inc., 50
AutoTrader.com, L.L.C., 91
AutoZone, Inc., 9; 31 (upd.)
AVA AG (Allgemeine Handelsgesellschaft der Verbraucher AG), 33
Aveda Corporation, 24
Aviall, Inc., 73
Aviation Sales Company, 41
AWB Ltd., 56
B. Dalton Bookseller Inc., 25
Babbage's, Inc., 10
Baby Superstore, Inc., 15
Baccarat, 24
Bachman's Inc., 22
Bailey Nurseries, Inc., 57
Ball Horticultural Company 78
Banana Republic Inc., 25
Bare Escentuals, Inc., 91
Barnes & Noble, Inc., 10; 30 (upd.); 75 (upd.)
Barnett Inc., 28
Barney's, Inc., 28
Barrett-Jackson Auction Company L.L.C., 88
Bass Pro Shops, Inc., 42
Baumax AG, 75
Beacon Roofing Supply, Inc., 75
Bear Creek Corporation, 38
Bearings, Inc., 13
bebe stores, inc., 31
Bed Bath & Beyond Inc., 13; 41 (upd.)
Belk Stores Services, Inc., V; 19 (upd.)
Belk, Inc., 72 (upd.)
Ben Bridge Jeweler, Inc., 60
Benetton Group S.p.A., 67 (upd.)
Bergdorf Goodman Inc., 52
Bergen Brunswig Corporation, V; 13 (upd.)
Bernard Chaus, Inc., 27
Best Buy Co., Inc., 9; 23 (upd.); 63 (upd.)
Bestseller A/S, 90
Bhs plc, 17
Big A Drug Stores Inc., 79
Big Dog Holdings, Inc., 45
Big 5 Sporting Goods Corporation, 55
The Big Food Group plc, 68 (upd.)
Big Lots, Inc., 50
Big O Tires, Inc., 20
Birkenstock Footprint Sandals, Inc., 42 (upd.)
Birthdays Ltd., 70
Black Box Corporation, 20
Blacks Leisure Group plc, 39
Blair Corporation, 25; 31 (upd.)
Blokker Holding B.V., 84
Bloomingdale's Inc., 12
Blue Nile Inc., 61

Blue Square Israel Ltd., 41
Bluefly, Inc., 60
Blyth Industries, Inc., 18
The Body Shop International PLC, 11
The Bombay Company, Inc., 10; 71 (upd.)
The Bon Marché, Inc., 23
The Bon-Ton Stores, Inc., 16; 50 (upd.)
Booker Cash & Carry Ltd., 68 (upd.)
Books-A-Million, Inc., 14; 41 (upd.)
Bookspan, 86
The Boots Company PLC, V; 24 (upd.)
Borders Group, Inc., 15; 43 (upd.)
Boscov's Department Store, Inc., 31
Bozzuto's, Inc., 13
Bradlees Discount Department Store Company, 12
Brambles Industries Limited, 42
Bricorama S.A., 68
Brioni Roman Style S.p.A., 67
Brodart Company, 84
Broder Bros. Co., 38
Bronner Display & Sign Advertising, Inc., 82
Brooks Brothers Inc., 22
Brookstone, Inc., 18
Brown Shoe Company, Inc., 68 (upd.)
Brunswick Corporation, 77 (upd.)
The Buckle, Inc., 18
Buhrmann NV, 41
Build-A-Bear Workshop Inc., 62
Building Materials Holding Corporation, 52
Burdines, Inc., 60
Burlington Coat Factory Warehouse Corporation, 10; 60 (upd.)
Burt's Bees, Inc., 58
The Burton Group plc, V
Buttrey Food & Drug Stores Co., 18
buy.com, Inc., 46
C&A, V; 40 (upd.)
C&J Clark International Ltd., 52
Cabela's Inc., 26; 68 (upd.)
Cablevision Electronic Instruments, Inc., 32
Cache Incorporated, 30
Cactus S.A., 90
Caldor Inc., 12
Calloway's Nursery, Inc., 51
Camaïeu S.A., 72
Camelot Music, Inc., 26
Campeau Corporation, V
Campo Electronics, Appliances & Computers, Inc., 16
Car Toys, Inc., 67
The Carphone Warehouse Group PLC, 83
Carrefour SA, 10; 27 (upd.); 64 (upd.)
Carson Pirie Scott & Company, 15
Carter Hawley Hale Stores, Inc., V
Carter Lumber Company, 45
Cartier Monde, 29
Casas Bahia Comercial Ltda., 75
Casey's General Stores, Inc., 19; 83 (upd.)
Castro Model Ltd., 86
Casual Corner Group, Inc., 43
Casual Male Retail Group, Inc., 52
Catherines Stores Corporation, 15
Cato Corporation, 14

Rubber & Tires

Telecommunications

Textiles & Apparel

British American Tobacco PLC, 50 (upd.)
Brooke Group Ltd., 15
Brown & Williamson Tobacco
  Corporation, 14; 33 (upd.)
Culbro Corporation, 15
Dibrell Brothers, Incorporated, 12
DIMON Inc., 27
800-JR Cigar, Inc., 27
Gallaher Group Plc, V; 19 (upd.); 49
  (upd.)
General Cigar Holdings, Inc., 66 (upd.)
Holt's Cigar Holdings, Inc., 42
House of Prince A/S, 80
Imasco Limited, V
Imperial Tobacco Group PLC, 50
Japan Tobacco Incorporated, V
KT&G Corporation, 62
Nobleza Piccardo SAICF, 64
North Atlantic Trading Company Inc., 65
Philip Morris Companies Inc., V; 18
  (upd.)
R.J. Reynolds Tobacco Holdings, Inc., 30
  (upd.)
RJR Nabisco Holdings Corp., V
Rothmans UK Holdings Limited, V; 19
  (upd.)
Seita, 23
Souza Cruz S.A., 65
Standard Commercial Corporation, 13; 62
  (upd.)
Swedish Match AB, 12; 39 (upd.); 92
  (upd.)
Swisher International Group Inc., 23
Tabacalera, S.A., V; 17 (upd.)
Taiwan Tobacco & Liquor Corporation,
  75
Universal Corporation, V; 48 (upd.)
UST Inc., 9; 50 (upd.)
Vector Group Ltd., 35 (upd.)

Transport Services

Abertis Infraestructuras, S.A., 65
The Adams Express Company, 86
Aegean Marine Petroleum Network Inc.,
  89
Aéroports de Paris, 33
Air Express International Corporation, 13
Air T, Inc., 86
Airborne Freight Corporation, 6; 34
  (upd.)
Alamo Rent A Car, Inc., 6; 24 (upd.); 84
  (upd.)
Alaska Railroad Corporation, 60
Alexander & Baldwin, Inc., 10, 40 (upd.)
Allied Worldwide, Inc., 49
AMCOL International Corporation, 59
  (upd.)
Amerco, 6
AMERCO, 67 (upd.)
American Classic Voyages Company, 27
American President Companies Ltd., 6
Anderson Trucking Service, Inc., 75
Anschutz Corp., 12
APL Limited, 61 (upd.)
Aqua Alliance Inc., 32 (upd.)
Arriva PLC, 69
Atlas Van Lines, Inc., 14
Attica Enterprises S.A., 64

Avis Group Holdings, Inc., 75 (upd.)
Avis Rent A Car, Inc., 6; 22 (upd.)
BAA plc, 10
Bekins Company, 15
Berliner Verkehrsbetriebe (BVG), 58
Bollinger Shipyards, Inc., 61
Boyd Bros. Transportation Inc., 39
Brambles Industries Limited, 42
The Brink's Company, 58 (upd.)
British Railways Board, V
Broken Hill Proprietary Company Ltd.,
  22 (upd.)
Buckeye Partners, L.P., 70
Budget Group, Inc., 25
Budget Rent a Car Corporation, 9
Burlington Northern Santa Fe
  Corporation, V; 27 (upd.)
C.H. Robinson Worldwide, Inc., 40
  (upd.)
Canadian National Railway Company, 71
  (upd.)
Canadian National Railway System, 6
Canadian Pacific Railway Limited, V; 45
  (upd.)
Cannon Express, Inc., 53
Carey International, Inc., 26
Carlson Companies, Inc., 6; 22 (upd.); 87
  (upd.)
Carolina Freight Corporation, 6
Celadon Group Inc., 30
Central Japan Railway Company, 43
Chargeurs International, 6; 21 (upd.)
CHC Helicopter Corporation, 67
CHEP Pty. Ltd., 80
Chicago and North Western Holdings
  Corporation, 6
Christian Salvesen Plc, 45
Coach USA, Inc., 24; 55 (upd.)
Coles Express Inc., 15
Compagnie Générale Maritime et
  Financière, 6
Consolidated Delivery & Logistics, Inc.,
  24
Consolidated Freightways Corporation, V;
  21 (upd.); 48 (upd.)
Consolidated Rail Corporation, V
CR England, Inc., 63
Crowley Maritime Corporation, 6; 28
  (upd.)
CSX Corporation, V; 22 (upd.); 79 (upd.)
Dachser GmbH & Co. KG, 88
Danaos Corporation, 91
Danzas Group, V; 40 (upd.)
Dart Group PLC, 77
Deutsche Bahn AG, V; 46 (upd.)
DHL Worldwide Network S.A./N.V., 6;
  24 (upd.); 69 (upd.)
Dollar Thrifty Automotive Group, Inc.,
  25
Dot Foods, Inc., 69
DP World, 81
East Japan Railway Company, V; 66
  (upd.)
EGL, Inc., 59
Emery Air Freight Corporation, 6
Emery Worldwide Airlines, Inc., 25 (upd.)
Enterprise Rent-A-Car Company, 6
Estes Express Lines, Inc., 86

Eurotunnel Group, 37 (upd.)
EVA Airways Corporation, 51
Evergreen International Aviation, Inc., 53
Evergreen Marine Corporation (Taiwan)
  Ltd., 13; 50 (upd.)
Executive Jet, Inc., 36
Exel plc, 51 (upd.)
Expeditors International of Washington
  Inc., 17; 78 (upd.)
Federal Express Corporation, V
FedEx Corporation, 18 (upd.); 42 (upd.)
FirstGroup plc, 89
Forward Air Corporation, 75
Fritz Companies, Inc., 12
Frontline Ltd., 45
Frozen Food Express Industries, Inc., 20
Garuda Indonesia, 58 (upd.)
GATX Corporation, 6; 25 (upd.)
GE Capital Aviation Services, 36
Gefco SA, 54
General Maritime Corporation, 59
Genesee & Wyoming Inc., 27
Geodis S.A., 67
The Go-Ahead Group Plc, 28
The Greenbrier Companies, 19
Greyhound Lines, Inc., 32 (upd.)
Groupe Bourbon S.A., 60
Grupo Aeroportuario del Pacífico, S.A. de
  C.V., 85
Grupo TMM, S.A. de C.V., 50
Grupo Transportación Ferroviaria
  Mexicana, S.A. de C.V., 47
Gulf Agency Company Ltd. 78
GulfMark Offshore, Inc., 49
Hanjin Shipping Co., Ltd., 50
Hankyu Corporation, V; 23 (upd.)
Hapag-Lloyd AG, 6
Harland and Wolff Holdings plc, 19
Harper Group Inc., 17
Heartland Express, Inc., 18
The Hertz Corporation, 9
Holberg Industries, Inc., 36
Hospitality Worldwide Services, Inc., 26
Hub Group, Inc., 38
Hvide Marine Incorporated, 22
Illinois Central Corporation, 11
International Shipholding Corporation,
  Inc., 27
J.B. Hunt Transport Services Inc., 12
J Lauritzen A/S, 90
John Menzies plc, 39
Kansas City Southern Industries, Inc., 6;
  26 (upd.)
The Kansas City Southern Railway
  Company, 92
Kawasaki Kisen Kaisha, Ltd., V; 56 (upd.)
Keio Teito Electric Railway Company, V
Keolis SA, 51
Kinki Nippon Railway Company Ltd., V
Kirby Corporation, 18; 66 (upd.)
Knight Transportation, Inc., 64
Koninklijke Nedlloyd Groep N.V., 6
Kuehne & Nagel International AG, V; 53
  (upd.)
La Poste, V; 47 (upd.)
Laidlaw International, Inc., 80
Landstar System, Inc., 63
Leaseway Transportation Corp., 12

Utilities

Waste Services

Geographic Index

Algeria

Sonatrach, IV; 65 (upd.)

Argentina

Acindar Industria Argentina de Aceros
   S.A., 87
Aerolíneas Argentinas S.A., 33; 69 (upd.)
Alpargatas S.A.I.C., 87
Aluar Aluminio Argentino S.A.I.C., 74
Arcor S.A.I.C., 66
Atanor S.A., 62
Coto Centro Integral de Comercializacion
   S.A., 66
Cresud S.A.C.I.F. y A., 63
Grupo Clarín S.A., 67
Grupo Financiero Galicia S.A., 63
IRSA Inversiones y Representaciones S.A.,
   63
Ledesma Sociedad Anónima Agrícola
   Industrial, 62
Molinos Río de la Plata S.A., 61
Nobleza Piccardo SAICF, 64
Penaflor S.A., 66
Petrobras Energia Participaciones S.A., 72
Quilmes Industrial (QUINSA) S.A., 67
Renault Argentina S.A., 67
Sideco Americana S.A., 67
Siderar S.A.I.C., 66
Telecom Argentina S.A., 63
Telefónica de Argentina S.A., 61
YPF Sociedad Anonima, IV

Australia

Amcor Limited, IV; 19 (upd.), 78 (upd.)
Ansell Ltd., 60 (upd.)
Aquarius Platinum Ltd., 63
Aristocrat Leisure Limited, 54
Arnott's Ltd., 66

Austal Limited, 75
Australia and New Zealand Banking
   Group Limited, II; 52 (upd.)
AWB Ltd., 56
BHP Billiton, 67 (upd.)
Billabong International Ltd., 44
Blundstone Pty Ltd., 76
Bond Corporation Holdings Limited, 10
Boral Limited, III; 43 (upd.)
Brambles Industries Limited, 42
Broken Hill Proprietary Company Ltd.,
   IV; 22 (upd.)
Burns, Philp & Company Ltd., 63
Carlton and United Breweries Ltd., I
Coles Group Limited, V; 20 (upd.); 85
   (upd.)
Cochlear Ltd., 77
CRA Limited, IV; 85 (upd.)
CSR Limited, III; 28 (upd.)
David Jones Ltd., 60
Elders IXL Ltd., I
Foster's Group Limited, 7; 21 (upd.); 50
   (upd.)
Goodman Fielder Ltd., 52
Harvey Norman Holdings Ltd., 56
Holden Ltd., 62
James Hardie Industries N.V., 56
John Fairfax Holdings Limited, 7
Lend Lease Corporation Limited, IV; 17
   (upd.); 52 (upd.)
Lion Nathan Limited, 54
Lonely Planet Publications Pty Ltd., 55
Macquarie Bank Ltd., 69
McPherson's Ltd., 66
Metcash Trading Ltd., 58
MYOB Ltd., 86
News Corporation Limited, IV; 7 (upd.);
   46 (upd.)
Nufarm Ltd., 87

Pacific Dunlop Limited, 10
Pioneer International Limited, III
PMP Ltd., 72
Publishing and Broadcasting Limited, 54
Qantas Airways Ltd., 6; 24 (upd.); 68
   (upd.)
Repco Corporation Ltd., 74
Ridley Corporation Ltd., 62
Rinker Group Ltd., 65
Rural Press Ltd., 74
Santos Ltd., 81
Smorgon Steel Group Ltd., 62
Southcorp Limited, 54
Suncorp-Metway Ltd., 91
TABCORP Holdings Limited, 44
Telecom Australia, 6
Telstra Corporation Limited, 50
Village Roadshow Ltd., 58
Westpac Banking Corporation, II; 48
   (upd.)
WMC, Limited, 43
Zinifex Ltd., 85

Austria

AKG Acoustics GmbH, 62
Andritz AG, 51
Austrian Airlines AG (Österreichische
   Luftverkehrs AG), 33
Bank Austria AG, 23
Baumax AG, 75
BBAG Osterreichische
   Brau-Beteiligungs-AG, 38
BÖHLER-UDDEHOLM AG, 73
Erste Bank der Osterreichischen
   Sparkassen AG, 69
Gericom AG, 47
Glock Ges.m.b.H., 42
Julius Meinl International AG, 53
Lauda Air Luftfahrt AG, 48

Germany

United States

Meade Instruments Corporation, 41
Meadowcraft, Inc., 29
MeadWestvaco Corporation, 76 (upd.)
Measurement Specialties, Inc., 71
Mecklermedia Corporation, 24
Medarex, Inc., 85
Medco Containment Services Inc., 9
Media Arts Group, Inc., 42
Media General, Inc., 7; 38 (upd.)
Mediacom Communications Corporation, 69
MediaNews Group, Inc., 70
Medical Information Technology Inc., 64
Medical Management International, Inc., 65
Medical Staffing Network Holdings, Inc., 89
Medicis Pharmaceutical Corporation, 59
MedImmune, Inc., 35
Medis Technologies Ltd., 77
Meditrust, 11
Medline Industries, Inc., 61
Medtronic, Inc., 8; 30 (upd.); 67 (upd.)
Medusa Corporation, 24
Megafoods Stores Inc., 13
Meier & Frank Co., 23
Meijer Incorporated, 7; 27 (upd.)
Mel Farr Automotive Group, 20
Melaleuca Inc., 31
Melamine Chemicals, Inc., 27
Mellon Bank Corporation, II
Mellon Financial Corporation, 44 (upd.)
Mellon-Stuart Company, I
The Melting Pot Restaurants, Inc., 74
Melville Corporation, V
Melvin Simon and Associates, Inc., 8
MEMC Electronic Materials, Inc., 81
Memorial Sloan-Kettering Cancer Center, 57
Memry Corporation, 72
The Men's Wearhouse, Inc., 17; 48 (upd.)
Menard, Inc., 34
Menasha Corporation, 8; 59 (upd.)
Mendocino Brewing Company, Inc., 60
The Mentholatum Company Inc., 32
Mentor Corporation, 26
Mentor Graphics Corporation, 11
Mercantile Bankshares Corp., 11
Mercantile Stores Company, Inc., V; 19 (upd.)
Mercer International Inc., 64
Merck & Co., Inc., I; 11 (upd.); 34 (upd.)
Mercury Air Group, Inc., 20
Mercury General Corporation, 25
Mercury Interactive Corporation, 59
Mercury Marine Group, 68
Meredith Corporation, 11; 29 (upd.); 74 (upd.)
Merge Healthcare, 85
Meridian Bancorp, Inc., 11
Meridian Gold, Incorporated, 47
Merillat Industries Inc., 13
Merillat Industries, LLC, 69 (upd.)
Merisant Worldwide, Inc., 70
Merisel, Inc., 12
Merit Medical Systems, Inc., 29
MeritCare Health System, 88

Meritage Corporation, 26
Merix Corporation, 36; 75 (upd.)
Merrell Dow, Inc., I; 9 (upd.)
Merriam-Webster Inc., 70
Merrill Corporation, 18; 47 (upd.)
Merrill Lynch & Co., Inc., II; 13 (upd.); 40 (upd.)
Merry-Go-Round Enterprises, Inc., 8
Mervyn's California, 10; 39 (upd.)
Mesa Air Group, Inc., 11; 32 (upd.); 77 (upd.)
Mesaba Holdings, Inc., 28
Mestek Inc., 10
Metal Management, Inc., 92
Metatec International, Inc., 47
Meteor Industries Inc., 33
Methode Electronics, Inc., 13
Metris Companies Inc., 56
Metro Information Services, Inc., 36
Metro-Goldwyn-Mayer Inc., 25 (upd.); 84 (upd.)
Metrocall, Inc., 41
Metromedia Company, 7; 14; 61 (upd.)
Metropolitan Baseball Club Inc., 39
Metropolitan Financial Corporation, 13
Metropolitan Life Insurance Company, III; 52 (upd.)
The Metropolitan Museum of Art, 55
Metropolitan Opera Association, Inc., 40
Metropolitan Transportation Authority, 35
Mexican Restaurants, Inc., 41
MFS Communications Company, Inc., 11
MGIC Investment Corp., 52
MGM Grand Inc., 17
MGM/UA Communications Company, II
Miami Herald Media Company, 92
Michael Anthony Jewelers, Inc., 24
Michael Baker Corporation, 14; 51 (upd.)
Michael C. Fina Co., Inc., 52
Michael Foods, Inc., 25
Michaels Stores, Inc., 17; 71 (upd.)
Michigan Bell Telephone Co., 14
Michigan National Corporation, 11
Michigan Sporting Goods Distributors, Inc., 72
Micrel, Incorporated, 77
Micro Warehouse, Inc., 16
MicroAge, Inc., 16
Microdot Inc., 8
Micron Technology, Inc., 11; 29 (upd.)
Micros Systems, Inc., 18
Microsoft Corporation, 6; 27 (upd.); 63 (upd.)
MicroStrategy Incorporated, 87
Mid-America Apartment Communities, Inc., 85
Mid-America Dairymen, Inc., 7
Midas Inc., 10; 56 (upd.)
The Middleby Corporation, 22
Middlesex Water Company, 45
The Middleton Doll Company, 53
The Midland Company, 65
Midway Airlines Corporation, 33
Midway Games, Inc., 25
Midwest Air Group, Inc., 35; 85 (upd.)
Midwest Grain Products, Inc., 49
Midwest Resources Inc., 6
Mikasa, Inc., 28

Mike-Sell's Inc., 15
Mikohn Gaming Corporation, 39
Milacron, Inc., 53 (upd.)
Milbank, Tweed, Hadley & McCloy, 27
Miles Laboratories, I
Millennium Pharmaceuticals, Inc., 47
Miller Brewing Company, I; 12 (upd.)
Miller Industries, Inc., 26
Miller Publishing Group, LLC, 57
Milliken & Co., V; 17 (upd.); 82 (upd.)
Milliman USA, 66
Millipore Corporation, 25; 84 (upd.)
The Mills Corporation, 77
Milnot Company, 46
Milton Bradley Company, 21
Milton CAT, Inc., 86
Milwaukee Brewers Baseball Club, 37
Mine Safety Appliances Company, 31
The Miner Group International, 22
Minerals Technologies Inc., 11; 52 (upd.)
Minnesota Mining & Manufacturing Company (3M), I; 8 (upd.); 26 (upd.)
Minnesota Power, Inc., 11; 34 (upd.)
Minntech Corporation, 22
The Minute Maid Company, 28
Minuteman International Inc., 46
Minyard Food Stores, Inc., 33; 86 (upd.)
Mirage Resorts, Incorporated, 6; 28 (upd.)
Miramax Film Corporation, 64
Misonix, Inc., 80
Mississippi Chemical Corporation, 39
Mitchell Energy and Development Corporation, 7
MITRE Corporation, 26
Mity Enterprises, Inc., 38
MIVA, Inc., 83
MNS, Ltd., 65
Mobil Corporation, IV; 7 (upd.); 21 (upd.)
Mobile Mini, Inc., 58
Mobile Telecommunications Technologies Corp., 18
Mocon, Inc., 76
Modern Woodmen of America, 66
Modine Manufacturing Company, 8; 56 (upd.)
Modtech Holdings, Inc., 77
Moen Incorporated, 12
Mohawk Industries, Inc., 19; 63 (upd.)
Mohegan Tribal Gaming Authority, 37
Moldflow Corporation, 73
Molex Incorporated, 11; 54 (upd.)
Molson Coors Brewing Company, 77 (upd.)
Monaco Coach Corporation, 31
Monadnock Paper Mills, Inc., 21
Monarch Casino & Resort, Inc., 65
The Monarch Cement Company, 72
Monfort, Inc., 13
Monro Muffler Brake, Inc., 24
Monrovia Nursery Company, 70
The Mosaic Company, 91
Monsanto Company, I; 9 (upd.); 29 (upd.); 77 (upd.)
Monster Cable Products, Inc., 69
Monster Worldwide Inc., 74 (upd.)
Montana Coffee Traders, Inc., 60